University Casebook Series

March, 1991

ACCOUNTING AND THE LAW, Fourth Edition (1978), with Problems Pamphlet (Successor to Dohr, Phillips, Thompson & Warren)

  George C. Thompson, Professor, Columbia University Graduate School of Business.
  Robert Whitman, Professor of Law, University of Connecticut.
  Ellis L. Phillips, Jr., Member of the New York Bar.
  William C. Warren, Professor of Law Emeritus, Columbia University.

ACCOUNTING FOR LAWYERS, MATERIALS ON (1980)

  David R. Herwitz, Professor of Law, Harvard University.

ADMINISTRATIVE LAW, Eighth Edition (1987), with 1989 Case Supplement and 1983 Problems Supplement (Supplement edited in association with Paul R. Verkuil, Dean and Professor of Law, Tulane University)

  Walter Gellhorn, University Professor Emeritus, Columbia University.
  Clark Byse, Professor of Law, Harvard University.
  Peter L. Strauss, Professor of Law, Columbia University.
  Todd D. Rakoff, Professor of Law, Harvard University.
  Roy A. Schotland, Professor of Law, Georgetown University.

ADMIRALTY, Third Edition (1987), with Statute and Rule Supplement

  Jo Desha Lucas, Professor of Law, University of Chicago.

ADVOCACY, see also Lawyering Process

AGENCY, see also Enterprise Organization

AGENCY—PARTNERSHIPS, Fourth Edition (1987)

  Abridgement from Conard, Knauss & Siegel's Enterprise Organization, Fourth Edition.

AGENCY AND PARTNERSHIPS (1987)

  Melvin A. Eisenberg, Professor of Law, University of California, Berkeley.

ANTITRUST: FREE ENTERPRISE AND ECONOMIC ORGANIZATION, Sixth Edition (1983), with 1983 Problems in Antitrust Supplement and 1990 Case Supplement

  Louis B. Schwartz, Professor of Law, University of Pennsylvania.
  John J. Flynn, Professor of Law, University of Utah.
  Harry First, Professor of Law, New York University.

BANKRUPTCY, Second Edition (1989), with 1990 Case Supplement

  Robert L. Jordan, Professor of Law, University of California, Los Angeles.
  William D. Warren, Professor of Law, University of California, Los Angeles.

BANKRUPTCY AND DEBTOR–CREDITOR LAW, Second Edition (1988)

  Theodore Eisenberg, Professor of Law, Cornell University.

UNIVERSITY CASEBOOK SERIES—Continued

BUSINESS CRIME (1990)
Harry First, Professor of Law, New York University.

BUSINESS ORGANIZATION, see also Enterprise Organization

BUSINESS PLANNING, Temporary Second Edition (1984)
David R. Herwitz, Professor of Law, Harvard University.

BUSINESS TORTS (1972)
Milton Handler, Professor of Law Emeritus, Columbia University.

CHILDREN IN THE LEGAL SYSTEM (1983) with 1990 Supplement (Supplement edited in association with Elizabeth S. Scott, Professor of Law, University of Virginia)
Walter Wadlington, Professor of Law, University of Virginia.
Charles H. Whitebread, Professor of Law, University of Southern California.
Samuel Davis, Professor of Law, University of Georgia.

CIVIL PROCEDURE, see Procedure

CIVIL RIGHTS ACTIONS (1988), with 1990 Supplement
Peter W. Low, Professor of Law, University of Virginia.
John C. Jeffries, Jr., Professor of Law, University of Virginia.

CLINIC, see also Lawyering Process

COMMERCIAL AND DEBTOR–CREDITOR LAW: SELECTED STATUTES, 1990 EDITION

COMMERCIAL LAW, Second Edition (1987)
Robert L. Jordan, Professor of Law, University of California, Los Angeles.
William D. Warren, Professor of Law, University of California, Los Angeles.

COMMERCIAL LAW, Fourth Edition (1985), with 1990 Case Supplement
E. Allan Farnsworth, Professor of Law, Columbia University.
John Honnold, Professor of Law, University of Pennsylvania.

COMMERCIAL PAPER, Third Edition (1984), with 1990 Case Supplement
E. Allan Farnsworth, Professor of Law, Columbia University.

COMMERCIAL PAPER, Second Edition (1987) (Reprinted from COMMERCIAL LAW, Second Edition (1987))
Robert L. Jordan, Professor of Law, University of California, Los Angeles.
William D. Warren, Professor of Law, University of California, Los Angeles.

COMMERCIAL PAPER AND BANK DEPOSITS AND COLLECTIONS (1967), with Statutory Supplement
William D. Hawkland, Professor of Law, University of Illinois.

COMMERCIAL TRANSACTIONS—Principles and Policies, Second Edition (1991)
Alan Schwartz, Professor of Law, Yale University.
Robert E. Scott, Professor of Law, University of Virginia.

COMPARATIVE LAW, Fifth Edition (1988)
Rudolf B. Schlesinger, Professor of Law, Hastings College of the Law.
Hans W. Baade, Professor of Law, University of Texas.
Mirjan P. Damaska, Professor of Law, Yale Law School.
Peter E. Herzog, Professor of Law, Syracuse University.

UNIVERSITY CASEBOOK SERIES—Continued

COMPETITIVE PROCESS, LEGAL REGULATION OF THE, Fourth Edition (1990), with 1989 Selected Statutes Supplement

Edmund W. Kitch, Professor of Law, University of Virginia.
Harvey S. Perlman, Dean of the Law School, University of Nebraska.

CONFLICT OF LAWS, Ninth Edition (1990)

Willis L. M. Reese, Professor of Law, Columbia University.
Maurice Rosenberg, Professor of Law, Columbia University.
Peter Hay, Professor of Law, University of Illinois.

CONSTITUTIONAL LAW, Eighth Edition (1989), with 1990 Case Supplement

Edward L. Barrett, Jr., Professor of Law, University of California, Davis.
William Cohen, Professor of Law, Stanford University.
Jonathan D. Varat, Professor of Law, University of California, Los Angeles.

CONSTITUTIONAL LAW, CIVIL LIBERTY AND INDIVIDUAL RIGHTS, Second Edition (1982), with 1989 Supplement

William Cohen, Professor of Law, Stanford University.
John Kaplan, Professor of Law, Stanford University.

CONSTITUTIONAL LAW, Eleventh Edition (1985), with 1990 Supplement (Supplement edited in association with Frederick F. Schauer, Professor, Harvard University)

Gerald Gunther, Professor of Law, Stanford University.

CONSTITUTIONAL LAW, INDIVIDUAL RIGHTS IN, Fourth Edition (1986), (Reprinted from CONSTITUTIONAL LAW, Eleventh Edition), with 1990 Supplement (Supplement edited in association with Frederick F. Schauer, Professor, Harvard University)

Gerald Gunther, Professor of Law, Stanford University.

CONSUMER TRANSACTIONS, Second Edition (1991), with Selected Statutes and Regulations Supplement

Michael M. Greenfield, Professor of Law, Washington University.

CONTRACT LAW AND ITS APPLICATION, Fourth Edition (1988)

Arthur Rosett, Professor of Law, University of California, Los Angeles.

CONTRACT LAW, STUDIES IN, Third Edition (1984)

Edward J. Murphy, Professor of Law, University of Notre Dame.
Richard E. Speidel, Professor of Law, Northwestern University.

CONTRACTS, Fifth Edition (1987)

John P. Dawson, late Professor of Law, Harvard University.
William Burnett Harvey, Professor of Law and Political Science, Boston University.
Stanley D. Henderson, Professor of Law, University of Virginia.

CONTRACTS, Fourth Edition (1988)

E. Allan Farnsworth, Professor of Law, Columbia University.
William F. Young, Professor of Law, Columbia University.

CONTRACTS, Selections on (statutory materials) (1988)

CONTRACTS, Second Edition (1978), with Statutory and Administrative Law Supplement (1978)

Ian R. Macneil, Professor of Law, Cornell University.

UNIVERSITY CASEBOOK SERIES—Continued

COPYRIGHT, PATENTS AND TRADEMARKS, see also Competitive Process; see also Selected Statutes and International Agreements

COPYRIGHT, PATENT, TRADEMARK AND RELATED STATE DOCTRINES, Third Edition (1990), with 1989 Selected Statutes Supplement and 1981 Problem Supplement

Paul Goldstein, Professor of Law, Stanford University.

COPYRIGHT, Unfair Competition, and Other Topics Bearing on the Protection of Literary, Musical, and Artistic Works, Fifth Edition (1990), with 1990 Statutory Supplement

Ralph S. Brown, Jr., Professor of Law, Yale University.
Robert C. Denicola, Professor of Law, University of Nebraska.

CORPORATE ACQUISITIONS, The Law and Finance of (1986), with 1990 Supplement

Ronald J. Gilson, Professor of Law, Stanford University.

CORPORATE FINANCE, Third Edition (1987)

Victor Brudney, Professor of Law, Harvard University.
Marvin A. Chirelstein, Professor of Law, Columbia University.

CORPORATION LAW, BASIC, Third Edition (1989), with Documentary Supplement

Detlev F. Vagts, Professor of Law, Harvard University.

CORPORATIONS, see also Enterprise Organization

CORPORATIONS, Sixth Edition—Concise (1988), with 1990 Case Supplement and 1990 Statutory Supplement

William L. Cary, late Professor of Law, Columbia University.
Melvin Aron Eisenberg, Professor of Law, University of California, Berkeley.

CORPORATIONS, Sixth Edition—Unabridged (1988), with 1990 Case Supplement and 1990 Statutory Supplement

William L. Cary, late Professor of Law, Columbia University.
Melvin Aron Eisenberg, Professor of Law, University of California, Berkeley.

CORPORATIONS AND BUSINESS ASSOCIATIONS—STATUTES, RULES, AND FORMS (1990)

CORRECTIONS, SEE SENTENCING

CREDITORS' RIGHTS, see also Debtor-Creditor Law

CRIMINAL JUSTICE ADMINISTRATION, Fourth Edition (1991)

Frank W. Miller, Professor of Law, Washington University.
Robert O. Dawson, Professor of Law, University of Texas.
George E. Dix, Professor of Law, University of Texas.
Raymond I. Parnas, Professor of Law, University of California, Davis.

CRIMINAL LAW, Fourth Edition (1987)

Fred E. Inbau, Professor of Law Emeritus, Northwestern University.
Andre A. Moenssens, Professor of Law, University of Richmond.
James R. Thompson, Professor of Law Emeritus, Northwestern University.

CRIMINAL LAW AND APPROACHES TO THE STUDY OF LAW, Second Edition (1991)

John M. Brumbaugh, Professor of Law, University of Maryland.

UNIVERSITY CASEBOOK SERIES—Continued

CRIMINAL LAW, Second Edition (1986)
Peter W. Low, Professor of Law, University of Virginia.
John C. Jeffries, Jr., Professor of Law, University of Virginia.
Richard C. Bonnie, Professor of Law, University of Virginia.

CRIMINAL LAW, Fourth Edition (1986)
Lloyd L. Weinreb, Professor of Law, Harvard University.

CRIMINAL LAW AND PROCEDURE, Seventh Edition (1989)
Ronald N. Boyce, Professor of Law, University of Utah.
Rollin M. Perkins, Professor of Law Emeritus, University of California, Hastings College of the Law.

CRIMINAL PROCEDURE, Third Edition (1987), with 1990 Supplement
James B. Haddad, Professor of Law, Northwestern University.
James B. Zagel, Chief, Criminal Justice Division, Office of Attorney General of Illinois.
Gary L. Starkman, Assistant U. S. Attorney, Northern District of Illinois.
William J. Bauer, Chief Judge of the U.S. Court of Appeals, Seventh Circuit.

CRIMINAL PROCESS, Fourth Edition (1987), with 1990 Supplement
Lloyd L. Weinreb, Professor of Law, Harvard University.

DAMAGES, Second Edition (1952)
Charles T. McCormick, late Professor of Law, University of Texas.
William F. Fritz, late Professor of Law, University of Texas.

DECEDENTS' ESTATES AND TRUSTS, Seventh Edition (1988)
John Ritchie, late Professor of Law, University of Virginia.
Neill H. Alford, Jr., Professor of Law, University of Virginia.
Richard W. Effland, late Professor of Law, Arizona State University.

DISPUTE RESOLUTION, Processes of (1989)
John S. Murray, President and Executive Director of The Conflict Clinic, Inc., George Mason University.
Alan Scott Rau, Professor of Law, University of Texas.
Edward F. Sherman, Professor of Law, University of Texas.

DOMESTIC RELATIONS, see also Family Law

DOMESTIC RELATIONS, Second Edition (1990)
Walter Wadlington, Professor of Law, University of Virginia.

EMPLOYMENT DISCRIMINATION, Second Edition (1987), with 1990 Supplement
Joel W. Friedman, Professor of Law, Tulane University.
George M. Strickler, Professor of Law, Tulane University.

EMPLOYMENT LAW, Second Edition (1991), with Statutory Supplement
Mark A. Rothstein, Professor of Law, University of Houston.
Andria S. Knapp, Visiting Professor of Law, Golden Gate University.
Lance Liebman, Professor of Law, Harvard University.

ENERGY LAW (1983) with 1986 Case Supplement
Donald N. Zillman, Professor of Law, University of Utah.
Laurence Lattman, Dean of Mines and Engineering, University of Utah.

UNIVERSITY CASEBOOK SERIES—Continued

ENTERPRISE ORGANIZATION, Fourth Edition (1987), with 1987 Corporation and Partnership Statutes, Rules and Forms Supplement

Alfred F. Conard, Professor of Law, University of Michigan.
Robert L. Knauss, Dean of the Law School, University of Houston.
Stanley Siegel, Professor of Law, University of California, Los Angeles.

ENVIRONMENTAL POLICY LAW 1985 Edition, with 1985 Problems Supplement (Supplement in association with Ronald H. Rosenberg, Professor of Law, College of William and Mary)

Thomas J. Schoenbaum, Professor of Law, University of Georgia.

EQUITY, see also Remedies

EQUITY, RESTITUTION AND DAMAGES, Second Edition (1974)

Robert Childres, late Professor of Law, Northwestern University.
William F. Johnson, Jr., Professor of Law, New York University.

ESTATE PLANNING, Second Edition (1982), with 1985 Case, Text and Documentary Supplement

David Westfall, Professor of Law, Harvard University.

ETHICS, see Legal Profession, Professional Responsibility, and Social Responsibilities

ETHICS OF LAWYERING, THE LAW AND (1990)

Geoffrey C. Hazard, Jr., Professor of Law, Yale University.
Susan P. Koniak, Professor of Law, University of Pittsburgh.

ETHICS AND PROFESSIONAL RESPONSIBILITY (1981) (Reprinted from THE LAWYERING PROCESS)

Gary Bellow, Professor of Law, Harvard University.
Bea Moulton, Legal Services Corporation.

EVIDENCE, Sixth Edition (1988 Reprint), with 1990 Case Supplement (Supplement edited in association with Roger C. Park, Professor of Law, University of Minnesota)

John Kaplan, Professor of Law, Stanford University.
Jon R. Waltz, Professor of Law, Northwestern University.

EVIDENCE, Eighth Edition (1988), with Rules, Statute and Case Supplement (1990)

Jack B. Weinstein, Chief Judge, United States District Court.
John H. Mansfield, Professor of Law, Harvard University.
Norman Abrams, Professor of Law, University of California, Los Angeles.
Margaret Berger, Professor of Law, Brooklyn Law School.

FAMILY LAW, see also Domestic Relations

FAMILY LAW Second Edition (1985), with 1991 Supplement

Judith C. Areen, Professor of Law, Georgetown University.

FAMILY LAW AND CHILDREN IN THE LEGAL SYSTEM, STATUTORY MATERIALS (1981)

Walter Wadlington, Professor of Law, University of Virginia.

FEDERAL COURTS, Eighth Edition (1988), with 1990 Supplement

Charles T. McCormick, late Professor of Law, University of Texas.
James H. Chadbourn, late Professor of Law, Harvard University.
Charles Alan Wright, Professor of Law, University of Texas, Austin.

UNIVERSITY CASEBOOK SERIES—Continued

FEDERAL COURTS AND THE FEDERAL SYSTEM, Hart and Wechsler's Third Edition (1988), with 1989 Case Supplement, and the Judicial Code and Rules of Procedure in the Federal Courts (1989)

Paul M. Bator, Professor of Law, University of Chicago.
Daniel J. Meltzer, Professor of Law, Harvard University.
Paul J. Mishkin, Professor of Law, University of California, Berkeley.
David L. Shapiro, Professor of Law, Harvard University.

FEDERAL COURTS AND THE LAW OF FEDERAL–STATE RELATIONS, Second Edition (1989), with 1990 Supplement

Peter W. Low, Professor of Law, University of Virginia.
John C. Jeffries, Jr., Professor of Law, University of Virginia.

FEDERAL PUBLIC LAND AND RESOURCES LAW, Second Edition (1987), with 1990 Case Supplement and 1990 Statutory Supplement

George C. Coggins, Professor of Law, University of Kansas.
Charles F. Wilkinson, Professor of Law, University of Oregon.

FEDERAL RULES OF CIVIL PROCEDURE and Selected Other Procedural Provisions, 1990 Edition

FEDERAL TAXATION, see Taxation

FOOD AND DRUG LAW (1980), with Statutory Supplement

Richard A. Merrill, Dean of the School of Law, University of Virginia.
Peter Barton Hutt, Esq.

FUTURE INTERESTS (1970)

Howard R. Williams, Professor of Law, Stanford University.

FUTURE INTERESTS AND ESTATE PLANNING (1961), with 1962 Supplement

W. Barton Leach, late Professor of Law, Harvard University.
James K. Logan, formerly Dean of the Law School, University of Kansas.

GOVERNMENT CONTRACTS, FEDERAL, Successor Edition (1985), with 1989 Supplement

John W. Whelan, Professor of Law, Hastings College of the Law.

GOVERNMENT REGULATION: FREE ENTERPRISE AND ECONOMIC ORGANIZATION, Sixth Edition (1985)

Louis B. Schwartz, Professor of Law, Hastings College of the Law.
John J. Flynn, Professor of Law, University of Utah.
Harry First, Professor of Law, New York University.

HEALTH CARE LAW AND POLICY (1988)

Clark C. Havighurst, Professor of Law, Duke University.

HINCKLEY, JOHN W., JR., TRIAL OF: A Case Study of the Insanity Defense (1986)

Peter W. Low, Professor of Law, University of Virginia.
John C. Jeffries, Jr., Professor of Law, University of Virginia.
Richard C. Bonnie, Professor of Law, University of Virginia.

INJUNCTIONS, Second Edition (1984)

Owen M. Fiss, Professor of Law, Yale University.
Doug Rendleman, Professor of Law, College of William and Mary.

INSTITUTIONAL INVESTORS, (1978)

David L. Ratner, Professor of Law, Cornell University.

UNIVERSITY CASEBOOK SERIES—Continued

INSURANCE, Second Edition (1985)
William F. Young, Professor of Law, Columbia University.
Eric M. Holmes, Professor of Law, University of Georgia.

INSURANCE LAW AND REGULATION (1990)
Kenneth S. Abraham, University of Virginia.

INTERNATIONAL LAW, see also Transnational Legal Problems, Transnational Business Problems, and United Nations Law

INTERNATIONAL LAW IN CONTEMPORARY PERSPECTIVE (1981), with Essay Supplement
Myres S. McDougal, Professor of Law, Yale University.
W. Michael Reisman, Professor of Law, Yale University.

INTERNATIONAL LEGAL SYSTEM, Third Edition (1988), with Documentary Supplement
Joseph Modeste Sweeney, Professor of Law, University of California, Hastings.
Covey T. Oliver, Professor of Law, University of Pennsylvania.
Noyes E. Leech, Professor of Law Emeritus, University of Pennsylvania.

INTRODUCTION TO LAW, see also Legal Method, On Law in Courts, and Dynamics of American Law

INTRODUCTION TO THE STUDY OF LAW (1970)
E. Wayne Thode, late Professor of Law, University of Utah.
Leon Lebowitz, Professor of Law, University of Texas.
Lester J. Mazor, Professor of Law, University of Utah.

JUDICIAL CODE and Rules of Procedure in the Federal Courts, Students' Edition, 1989 Revision
Daniel J. Meltzer, Professor of Law, Harvard University.
David L. Shapiro, Professor of Law, Harvard University.

JURISPRUDENCE (Temporary Edition Hardbound) (1949)
Lon L. Fuller, late Professor of Law, Harvard University.

JUVENILE, see also Children

JUVENILE JUSTICE PROCESS, Third Edition (1985)
Frank W. Miller, Professor of Law, Washington University.
Robert O. Dawson, Professor of Law, University of Texas.
George E. Dix, Professor of Law, University of Texas.
Raymond I. Parnas, Professor of Law, University of California, Davis.

LABOR LAW, Eleventh Edition (1991), with 1991 Statutory Supplement
Archibald Cox, Professor of Law, Harvard University.
Derek C. Bok, President, Harvard University.
Robert A. Gorman, Professor of Law, University of Pennsylvania.
Matthew W. Finkin, Professor of Law, University of Illinois.

LABOR LAW, Second Edition (1982), with Statutory Supplement
Clyde W. Summers, Professor of Law, University of Pennsylvania.
Harry H. Wellington, Dean of the Law School, Yale University.
Alan Hyde, Professor of Law, Rutgers University.

UNIVERSITY CASEBOOK SERIES—Continued

LAND FINANCING, Third Edition (1985)
    The late Norman Penney, Professor of Law, Cornell University.
    Richard F. Broude, Member of the California Bar.
    Roger Cunningham, Professor of Law, University of Michigan.

LAW AND MEDICINE (1980)
    Walter Wadlington, Professor of Law and Professor of Legal Medicine, University of Virginia.
    Jon R. Waltz, Professor of Law, Northwestern University.
    Roger B. Dworkin, Professor of Law, Indiana University, and Professor of Biomedical History, University of Washington.

LAW, LANGUAGE AND ETHICS (1972)
    William R. Bishin, Professor of Law, University of Southern California.
    Christopher D. Stone, Professor of Law, University of Southern California.

LAW, SCIENCE AND MEDICINE (1984), with 1989 Supplement
    Judith C. Areen, Professor of Law, Georgetown University.
    Patricia A. King, Professor of Law, Georgetown University.
    Steven P. Goldberg, Professor of Law, Georgetown University.
    Alexander M. Capron, Professor of Law, University of Southern California.

LAWYERING PROCESS (1978), with Civil Problem Supplement and Criminal Problem Supplement
    Gary Bellow, Professor of Law, Harvard University.
    Bea Moulton, Professor of Law, Arizona State University.

LEGAL METHOD (1980)
    Harry W. Jones, Professor of Law Emeritus, Columbia University.
    John M. Kernochan, Professor of Law, Columbia University.
    Arthur W. Murphy, Professor of Law, Columbia University.

LEGAL METHODS (1969)
    Robert N. Covington, Professor of Law, Vanderbilt University.
    E. Blythe Stason, late Professor of Law, Vanderbilt University.
    John W. Wade, Professor of Law, Vanderbilt University.
    Elliott E. Cheatham, late Professor of Law, Vanderbilt University.
    Theodore A. Smedley, Professor of Law, Vanderbilt University.

LEGAL PROFESSION, THE, Responsibility and Regulation, Second Edition (1988)
    Geoffrey C. Hazard, Jr., Professor of Law, Yale University.
    Deborah L. Rhode, Professor of Law, Stanford University.

LEGISLATION, Fourth Edition (1982) (by Fordham)
    Horace E. Read, late Vice President, Dalhousie University.
    John W. MacDonald, Professor of Law Emeritus, Cornell Law School.
    Jefferson B. Fordham, Professor of Law, University of Utah.
    William J. Pierce, Professor of Law, University of Michigan.

LEGISLATIVE AND ADMINISTRATIVE PROCESSES, Second Edition (1981)
    Hans A. Linde, Judge, Supreme Court of Oregon.
    George Bunn, Professor of Law, University of Wisconsin.
    Fredericka Paff, Professor of Law, University of Wisconsin.
    W. Lawrence Church, Professor of Law, University of Wisconsin.

LOCAL GOVERNMENT LAW, Second Revised Edition (1986)
    Jefferson B. Fordham, Professor of Law, University of Utah.

UNIVERSITY CASEBOOK SERIES—Continued

MASS MEDIA LAW, Fourth Edition (1990)

Marc A. Franklin, Professor of Law, Stanford University.
David A. Anderson, Professor of Law, University of Texas.

MUNICIPAL CORPORATIONS, see Local Government Law

NEGOTIABLE INSTRUMENTS, see Commercial Paper

NEGOTIATION (1981) (Reprinted from THE LAWYERING PROCESS)

Gary Bellow, Professor of Law, Harvard Law School.
Bea Moulton, Legal Services Corporation.

NEW YORK PRACTICE, Fourth Edition (1978)

Herbert Peterfreund, Professor of Law, New York University.
Joseph M. McLaughlin, Dean of the Law School, Fordham University.

OIL AND GAS, Fifth Edition (1987)

Howard R. Williams, Professor of Law, Stanford University.
Richard C. Maxwell, Professor of Law, University of California, Los Angeles.
Charles J. Meyers, late Dean of the Law School, Stanford University.
Stephen F. Williams, Judge of the United States Court of Appeals.

ON LAW IN COURTS (1965)

Paul J. Mishkin, Professor of Law, University of California, Berkeley.
Clarence Morris, Professor of Law Emeritus, University of Pennsylvania.

PENSION AND EMPLOYEE BENEFIT LAW (1990)

John H. Langbein, Professor of Law, University of Chicago.
Bruce A. Wolk, Professor of Law, University of California, Davis.

PLEADING AND PROCEDURE, see Procedure, Civil

POLICE FUNCTION, Fifth Edition (1991)

Reprint of Chapters 1–10 of Miller, Dawson, Dix and Parnas's CRIMINAL JUSTICE ADMINISTRATION, Fourth Edition.

PREPARING AND PRESENTING THE CASE (1981) (Reprinted from THE LAWYERING PROCESS)

Gary Bellow, Professor of Law, Harvard Law School.
Bea Moulton, Legal Services Corporation.

PROCEDURE (1988), with Procedure Supplement (1989)

Robert M. Cover, late Professor of Law, Yale Law School.
Owen M. Fiss, Professor of Law, Yale Law School.
Judith Resnik, Professor of Law, University of Southern California Law Center.

PROCEDURE—CIVIL PROCEDURE, Second Edition (1974), with 1979 Supplement

The late James H. Chadbourn, Professor of Law, Harvard University.
A. Leo Levin, Professor of Law, University of Pennsylvania.
Philip Shuchman, Professor of Law, Cornell University.

PROCEDURE—CIVIL PROCEDURE, Sixth Edition (1990)

Richard H. Field, late Professor of Law, Harvard University.
Benjamin Kaplan, Professor of Law Emeritus, Harvard University.
Kevin M. Clermont, Professor of Law, Cornell University.

UNIVERSITY CASEBOOK SERIES—Continued

PROCEDURE—CIVIL PROCEDURE, Fifth Edition (1990)

Maurice Rosenberg, Professor of Law, Columbia University.
Hans Smit, Professor of Law, Columbia University.
Rochelle C. Dreyfuss, Professor of Law, New York University.

PROCEDURE—PLEADING AND PROCEDURE: State and Federal, Sixth Edition (1989), with 1990 Case Supplement

David W. Louisell, late Professor of Law, University of California, Berkeley.
Geoffrey C. Hazard, Jr., Professor of Law, Yale University.
Colin C. Tait, Professor of Law, University of Connecticut.

PROCEDURE—FEDERAL RULES OF CIVIL PROCEDURE, 1990 Edition

PRODUCTS LIABILITY AND SAFETY, Second Edition, (1989), with 1989 Statutory Supplement

W. Page Keeton, Professor of Law, University of Texas.
David G. Owen, Professor of Law, University of South Carolina.
John E. Montgomery, Professor of Law, University of South Carolina.
Michael D. Green, Professor of Law, University of Iowa

PROFESSIONAL RESPONSIBILITY, Fifth Edition (1991), with 1991 Selected Standards on Professional Responsibility Supplement

Thomas D. Morgan, Professor of Law, George Washington University.
Ronald D. Rotunda, Professor of Law, University of Illinois.

PROPERTY, Sixth Edition (1990)

John E. Cribbet, Professor of Law, University of Illinois.
Corwin W. Johnson, Professor of Law, University of Texas.
Roger W. Findley, Professor of Law, University of Illinois.
Ernest E. Smith, Professor of Law, University of Texas.

PROPERTY—PERSONAL (1953)

S. Kenneth Skolfield, late Professor of Law Emeritus, Boston University.

PROPERTY—PERSONAL, Third Edition (1954)

Everett Fraser, late Dean of the Law School Emeritus, University of Minnesota. Third Edition by Charles W. Taintor, late Professor of Law, University of Pittsburgh.

PROPERTY—INTRODUCTION, TO REAL PROPERTY, Third Edition (1954)

Everett Fraser, late Dean of the Law School Emeritus, University of Minnesota.

PROPERTY—FUNDAMENTALS OF MODERN REAL PROPERTY, Second Edition (1982), with 1985 Supplement

Edward H. Rabin, Professor of Law, University of California, Davis.

PROPERTY, REAL (1984), with 1988 Supplement

Paul Goldstein, Professor of Law, Stanford University.

PROSECUTION AND ADJUDICATION, Fourth Edition (1991)

Reprint of Chapters 11–26 of Miller, Dawson, Dix and Parnas's CRIMINAL JUSTICE ADMINISTRATION, Fourth Edition.

PSYCHIATRY AND LAW, see Mental Health, see also Hinckley, Trial of

PUBLIC UTILITY LAW, see Free Enterprise, also Regulated Industries

UNIVERSITY CASEBOOK SERIES—Continued

REAL ESTATE PLANNING, Third Edition (1989), with Revised Problem and Statutory Supplement (1991)

Norton L. Steuben, Professor of Law, University of Colorado.

REAL ESTATE TRANSACTIONS, Revised Second Edition (1988), with Statute, Form and Problem Supplement (1988)

Paul Goldstein, Professor of Law, Stanford University.

RECEIVERSHIP AND CORPORATE REORGANIZATION, see Creditors' Rights

REGULATED INDUSTRIES, Second Edition, (1976)

William K. Jones, Professor of Law, Columbia University.

REMEDIES, Second Edition (1987)

Edward D. Re, Chief Judge, U. S. Court of International Trade.

REMEDIES, (1989)

Elaine W. Shoben, Professor of Law, University of Illinois.
Wm. Murray Tabb, Professor of Law, Baylor University.

SALES, Second Edition (1986)

Marion W. Benfield, Jr., Professor of Law, University of Illinois.
William D. Hawkland, Chancellor, Louisiana State Law Center.

SALES AND SALES FINANCING, Fifth Edition (1984)

John Honnold, Professor of Law, University of Pennsylvania.

SALES LAW AND THE CONTRACTING PROCESS, Second Edition (1991)

(Reprinted from Commercial Transactions, Second Edition (1991)
Alan Schwartz, Professor of Law, Yale University.
Robert E. Scott, Professor of Law, University of Virginia.

SECURED TRANSACTIONS IN PERSONAL PROPERTY, Second Edition (1987) (Reprinted from COMMERCIAL LAW, Second Edition (1987))

Robert L. Jordan, Professor of Law, University of California, Los Angeles.
William D. Warren, Professor of Law, University of California, Los Angeles.

SECURITIES REGULATION, Sixth Edition (1987), with 1990 Selected Statutes, Rules and Forms Supplement and 1990 Cases and Releases Supplement

Richard W. Jennings, Professor of Law, University of California, Berkeley.
Harold Marsh, Jr., Member of California Bar.

SECURITIES REGULATION, Second Edition (1988), with Statute, Rule and Form Supplement (1988)

Larry D. Soderquist, Professor of Law, Vanderbilt University.

SECURITY INTERESTS IN PERSONAL PROPERTY, Second Edition (1987)

Douglas G. Baird, Professor of Law, University of Chicago.
Thomas H. Jackson, Dean of the Law School, University of Virginia.

SECURITY INTERESTS IN PERSONAL PROPERTY (1985) (Reprinted from Sales and Sales Financing, Fifth Edition)

John Honnold, Professor of Law, University of Pennsylvania.

SELECTED STANDARDS ON PROFESSIONAL RESPONSIBILITY, 1991 Edition

UNIVERSITY CASEBOOK SERIES—Continued

SELECTED STATUTES AND INTERNATIONAL AGREEMENTS ON UNFAIR COMPETITION, TRADEMARK, COPYRIGHT AND PATENT, 1989 Edition

SELECTED STATUTES ON TRUSTS AND ESTATES, 1991 Edition

SOCIAL RESPONSIBILITIES OF LAWYERS, Case Studies (1988)
> Philip B. Heymann, Professor of Law, Harvard University.
> Lance Liebman, Professor of Law, Harvard University.

SOCIAL SCIENCE IN LAW, Second Edition (1990)
> John Monahan, Professor of Law, University of Virginia.
> Laurens Walker, Professor of Law, University of Virginia.

TAXATION, FEDERAL INCOME (1989)
> Stephen B. Cohen, Professor of Law, Georgetown University

TAXATION, FEDERAL INCOME, Second Edition (1988), with 1990 Supplement (Supplement edited in association with Deborah H. Schenk, Professor of Law, New York University)
> Michael J. Graetz, Professor of Law, Yale University.

TAXATION, FEDERAL INCOME, Sixth Edition (1987)
> James J. Freeland, Professor of Law, University of Florida.
> Stephen A. Lind, Professor of Law, University of Florida and University of California, Hastings.
> Richard B. Stephens, late Professor of Law Emeritus, University of Florida.

TAXATION, FEDERAL INCOME, Successor Edition (1986), with 1990 Legislative Supplement
> Stanley S. Surrey, late Professor of Law, Harvard University.
> Paul R. McDaniel, Professor of Law, Boston College.
> Hugh J. Ault, Professor of Law, Boston College.
> Stanley A. Koppelman, Professor of Law, Boston University.

TAXATION, FEDERAL INCOME, OF BUSINESS ORGANIZATIONS (1991)
> Paul R. McDaniel, Professor of Law, Boston College.
> Hugh J. Ault, Professor of Law, Boston College.
> Martin J. McMahon, Jr., Professor of Law, University of Kentucky.
> Daniel L. Simmons, Professor of Law, University of California, Davis.

TAXATION, FEDERAL INCOME, OF PARTNERSHIPS AND S CORPORATIONS (1991)
> Paul R. McDaniel, Professor of Law, Boston College.
> Hugh J. Ault, Professor of Law, Boston College.
> Martin J. McMahon, Jr., Professor of Law, University of Kentucky.
> Daniel L. Simmons, Professor of Law, University of California, Davis.

TAXATION, FEDERAL INCOME, OIL AND GAS, NATURAL RESOURCES TRANSACTIONS (1990)
> Peter C. Maxfield, Professor of Law, University of Wyoming.
> James L. Houghton, CPA, Partner, Ernst and Young.
> James R. Gaar, CPA, Partner, Ernst and Young.

TAXATION, FEDERAL WEALTH TRANSFER, Successor Edition (1987)
> Stanley S. Surrey, late Professor of Law, Harvard University.
> Paul R. McDaniel, Professor of Law, Boston College.
> Harry L. Gutman, Professor of Law, University of Pennsylvania.

UNIVERSITY CASEBOOK SERIES—Continued

TAXATION, FUNDAMENTALS OF CORPORATE, Second Edition (1987), with 1989 Supplement

Stephen A. Lind, Professor of Law, University of Florida and University of California, Hastings.
Stephen Schwarz, Professor of Law, University of California, Hastings.
Daniel J. Lathrope, Professor of Law, University of California, Hastings.
Joshua Rosenberg, Professor of Law, University of San Francisco.

TAXATION, FUNDAMENTALS OF PARTNERSHIP, Second Edition (1988)

Stephen A. Lind, Professor of Law, University of Florida and University of California, Hastings.
Stephen Schwarz, Professor of Law, University of California, Hastings.
Daniel J. Lathrope, Professor of Law, University of California, Hastings.
Joshua Rosenberg, Professor of Law, University of San Francisco.

TAXATION, PROBLEMS IN THE FEDERAL INCOME TAXATION OF PARTNERSHIPS AND CORPORATIONS, Second Edition (1986)

Norton L. Steuben, Professor of Law, University of Colorado.
William J. Turnier, Professor of Law, University of North Carolina.

TAXATION, PROBLEMS IN THE FUNDAMENTALS OF FEDERAL INCOME, Second Edition (1985)

Norton L. Steuben, Professor of Law, University of Colorado.
William J. Turnier, Professor of Law, University of North Carolina.

TORT LAW AND ALTERNATIVES, Fourth Edition (1987)

Marc A. Franklin, Professor of Law, Stanford University.
Robert L. Rabin, Professor of Law, Stanford University.

TORTS, Eighth Edition (1988)

William L. Prosser, late Professor of Law, University of California, Hastings.
John W. Wade, Professor of Law, Vanderbilt University.
Victor E. Schwartz, Adjunct Professor of Law, Georgetown University.

TORTS, Third Edition (1976)

Harry Shulman, late Dean of the Law School, Yale University.
Fleming James, Jr., Professor of Law Emeritus, Yale University.
Oscar S. Gray, Professor of Law, University of Maryland.

TRADE REGULATION, Third Edition (1990)

Milton Handler, Professor of Law Emeritus, Columbia University.
Harlan M. Blake, Professor of Law, Columbia University.
Robert Pitofsky, Professor of Law, Georgetown University.
Harvey J. Goldschmid, Professor of Law, Columbia University.

TRADE REGULATION, see Antitrust

TRANSNATIONAL BUSINESS PROBLEMS (1986)

Detlev F. Vagts, Professor of Law, Harvard University.

TRANSNATIONAL LEGAL PROBLEMS, Third Edition (1986) with 1991 Revised Edition of Documentary Supplement

Henry J. Steiner, Professor of Law, Harvard University.
Detlev F. Vagts, Professor of Law, Harvard University.

TRIAL, see also Evidence, Making the Record, Lawyering Process and Preparing and Presenting the Case

UNIVERSITY CASEBOOK SERIES—Continued

TRUSTS, Fifth Edition (1978)
    George G. Bogert, late Professor of Law Emeritus, University of Chicago.
    Dallin H. Oaks, President, Brigham Young University.

TRUSTS AND ESTATES, SELECTED STATUTES ON, 1991 Edition

TRUSTS AND SUCCESSION (Palmer's), Fourth Edition (1983)
    Richard V. Wellman, Professor of Law, University of Georgia.
    Lawrence W. Waggoner, Professor of Law, University of Michigan.
    Olin L. Browder, Jr., Professor of Law, University of Michigan.

UNFAIR COMPETITION, see Competitive Process and Business Torts

WATER RESOURCE MANAGEMENT, Third Edition (1988)
    The late Charles J. Meyers, formerly Dean, Stanford University Law School.
    A. Dan Tarlock, Professor of Law, IIT Chicago-Kent College of Law.
    James N. Corbridge, Jr., Chancellor, University of Colorado at Boulder, and Professor of Law, University of Colorado.
    David H. Getches, Professor of Law, University of Colorado.

WILLS AND ADMINISTRATION, Fifth Edition (1961)
    Philip Mechem, late Professor of Law, University of Pennsylvania.
    Thomas E. Atkinson, late Professor of Law, New York University.

WRITING AND ANALYSIS IN THE LAW, Second Edition (1991)
    Helene S. Shapo, Professor of Law, Northwestern University
    Marilyn R. Walter, Professor of Law, Brooklyn Law School
    Elizabeth Fajans, Writing Specialist, Brooklyn Law School

University Casebook Series

EDITORIAL BOARD

DAVID L. SHAPIRO
DIRECTING EDITOR
Professor of Law, Harvard University

EDWARD L. BARRETT, Jr.
Professor of Law, University of California, Davis

ROBERT C. CLARK
Dean of the School of Law, Harvard University

OWEN M. FISS
Professor of Law, Yale Law School

GERALD GUNTHER
Professor of Law, Stanford University

THOMAS H. JACKSON
Dean of the School of Law, University of Virginia

HARRY W. JONES
Professor of Law, Columbia University

HERMA HILL KAY
Professor of Law, University of California, Berkeley

PAGE KEETON
Professor of Law, University of Texas

ROBERT L. RABIN
Professor of Law, Stanford University

CAROL M. ROSE
Professor of Law, Yale University

CASS R. SUNSTEIN
Professor of Law, University of Chicago

SAMUEL D. THURMAN
Professor of Law, Hastings College of the Law

LEGAL METHOD
CASES AND TEXT MATERIALS

By

HARRY W. JONES
Cardozo Professor Emeritus of Jurisprudence
Columbia University

JOHN M. KERNOCHAN
Nash Professor of Law
Columbia University

ARTHUR W. MURPHY
Vice-Dean and Joseph L. Solomon Professor in
Wills, Trusts and Estates
Columbia University

SUCCESSOR TO DOWLING, PATTERSON AND POWELL,
MATERIALS FOR LEGAL METHOD
(SECOND EDITION By HARRY W. JONES, 1952)

Mineola, New York
THE FOUNDATION PRESS, INC.
1980

COPYRIGHT © 1980 By THE FOUNDATION PRESS, INC.
All rights reserved
Printed in the United States of America

Library of Congress Cataloging in Publication Data

Jones, Harry Willmer.
   Cases and text materials on legal method.

   (University casebook series)
   Edition for 1978 published under title: Legal method.
   Includes index.
   1. Law—United States—Cases. 2. Law—Study and teaching—United States. 3. Law—United States—Interpretation and construction. I. Kernochan, John M., joint author. II. Murphy, Arthur W., joint author. III. Title. IV. Series.
KF379.J66   1980   349.73   80-13230
ISBN 0-88277-004-7

J., K. & M.Ca.Legal Method—UCB
9th Reprint—1991

PREFACE

This casebook is the successor to Dowling, Patterson and Powell, Materials for Legal Method (Second Edition by Jones 1952), which at one time or another has been used as the basis of instruction at more than sixty law schools in first semester-first year courses variously entitled Legal Method, Introduction to Law, Legal Processes, and the like. Twenty-eight years is a long life for an unrevised casebook, even for one concerned with fundamental insights and basic professional skills. Although these fundamentals of analysis do not change very much as compared with the pace of change in the substance of American law, years of classroom experience have convinced us that the intellectual goals sought by a Legal Method course are best achieved when the cases and other materials of study are reasonably up to date and the general casebook approach fully in line with present-day ideas concerning the aims, ways and means of university legal education. Law teachers familiar with the 1946 or 1952 editions of Materials for Legal Method will meet a good many old acquaintances in this successor volume, e.g. the center-stage appearance of *Macpherson v. Buick* in the section on *Synthesis*, but the volume, although in the tradition of its predecessor and resembling it in chapter headings, is not a revision but a new book.

In putting this coursebook together, we have profited from and gratefully acknowledge the comments, criticisms and suggestions we have received from more than thirty law teachers who have used the 1952 book in Legal Method and similar first semester-first year courses at other American law schools. One recurring suggestion, for example, was that far greater attention be given than formerly to legislative institutions and processes to assist the first-year student in the understanding of legislative law, and an extensive text note on the legislative process appears as the first section of Chapter V (The Interpretation of Statutes) in this casebook. The present book has been developed in successive mimeographed editions over a period of several years, and the three of us are also grateful to the energetic and imaginative first-year students at the Columbia Law School, and to the generations of Associates in Law, who have been, in a real sense, our partners in the enterprise.

We are particularly grateful to our colleague, Peter L. Strauss, many of whose invaluable suggestions are incorporated into the materials and to Mrs. Adria G. Kaplan LL.B., Harvard, without whose wise counsel and heroic labors there would be no new book.

We are convinced that our predecessors, Professors Dowling, Patterson and Powell, were entirely right when they said, in their preface

PREFACE

to the original (1946) Legal Method casebook that "the job of introducing the student to the study of law can be more efficiently done by concentrating upon it at the outset." Indeed, the case for a separate Legal Method course seems even stronger today than it was in 1946. Few advocates of the old "sink or swim" approach to the first law school year are found in the present generation of law teachers, and the pressures on the law school curriculum are far greater today than they were thirty or even twenty years ago. Although every first year law offering is and has to be a course in legal reasoning as well as an examination of the specific doctrines of Torts, Contracts, Civil Procedure or whatever, it is surely wasteful of precious classroom time to have the fundamentals of case and statutory analysis taught four or five times in as many first semester courses. And such dispersion often results in a disorganized, hit-or-miss approach to some of the most profoundly important aspects of law and the legal process. A well managed course on the fundamentals of professional method can, we believe, liberate the other first-year teachers from a most exacting and time-consuming task and enable them to focus their class discussions more on the analysis of specific subjects—Contracts, Torts, etc.—which they are primarily concerned to explore. More than that we think it will provide the students with a sound needed, initial foundation of coherent knowledge about the legal system, its institutions, source materials and processes, and with a disciplined understanding of basic theory and skills, that will be invaluable to them not only in law school work but for the rest of their professional lives.

Chapter I of the casebook consists of materials, in text form, intended to introduce beginning law students to the authoritative forms —case law and legislation—of American law, to the tasks and modes of thought of the lawyer, and to the assumptions and objectives of the case method of law study. Chapters II, III and IV—what we think of as primarily the "case law part" of the book and the course—are designed to provide the basis for intensive study and classroom discussion of, respectively, the analysis and synthesis of judicial decisions, the problem of retroactivity in the application of overruling decisions, and the status of state decisions in the federal courts. Chapter V, the book's "legislation part," is devoted to the insights and skills required in the interpretation of statutes and Chapter VI brings case law and legislation together in the study of the coordination of judge-made and statute law. In these two chapters, a number of problems have been included in addition to the cases so that instructor may choose between emphasis on a traditional case method approach or emphasis on a problem method or varying combinations of both. The concluding Chapter (VII), entitled "Historical and Jurisprudential Perspectives on Law and its Study," is intended to give students a better basis for understanding and appraisal of the sources and techniques they have studied in Legal Method and consists of brief readings on the purposes

PREFACE

of law in society, the common law origin of the American legal system, and the problem of justice in judicial dispute settlement.

HARRY W. JONES
JOHN M. KERNOCHAN
ARTHUR W. MURPHY

April, 1980

*

SUMMARY OF CONTENTS

	Page
PREFACE	xix
TABLE OF CASES	xxxi

CHAPTER I. THE MATERIALS AND METHODS OF LAW STUDY — 1
Section
1. Introductory Note to the Beginning Law Student — 1
2. Case Law: Origins, Nature and Authority — 3
3. Legislation: Attributes and Types — 12
4. The Tasks of the Lawyer — 21
5. The Case Method of Studying Law — 25

CHAPTER II. CASE LAW: THE ANALYSIS AND SYNTHESIS OF JUDICIAL DECISIONS — 37
Section
1. The State and Federal Courts — 37
2. The Structure of a Lawsuit — 54
3. The Technique of Case Law Development — 73

CHAPTER III. THE PROBLEM OF RETROACTIVITY — 220

CHAPTER IV. THE AUTHORITATIVE STATUS OF JUDICIAL DECISIONS — 240
Section
1. Introduction — 240
2. Status of State Decisions in Federal Courts — 241

CHAPTER V. THE INTERPRETATION OF STATUTES — 255
Section
1. The Legislative Process — 255
2. Finding and Stating Issues of Statute Law — 318
3. Resolving Statutory Issues—A General View — 327
4. Interpretation According to "The Intention of the Legislature" — 344
5. Interpretation According to the Letter of the Statute—The Plain Meaning Rule — 388
6. The Development of Current Doctrine — 402
7. The Weight of Prior Interpretations — 469
8. Maxims — 543
9. Some Statutory Problems — 566

CHAPTER VI. COORDINATION OF JUDGE-MADE AND STATUTE LAW — 594

SUMMARY OF CONTENTS

CHAPTER VII. HISTORICAL AND JURISPRUDENTIAL PERSPECTIVES ON LAW AND ITS STUDY 737

Section

1. The Social Ends to Which Law Is Means 738
2. The Common Law and Its Reception in the United States ... 744
3. Dispute-Settlement and the Problem of Justice 759

Appendix 771

Index 781

TABLE OF CONTENTS

	Page
PREFACE	xix
TABLE OF CASES	xxxi

CHAPTER I. THE MATERIALS AND METHODS OF LAW STUDY — 1

Section

1. Introductory Note to the Beginning Law Student — 1
2. Case Law: Origins, Nature and Authority — 3
   - A. How Cases Make Law — 3
   - B. The Common Law Doctrine of Precedent — 5
   - C. "Res Judicata" and "Stare Decisis"; "Reversal" and "Overruling" — 7
   - D. Decisions From Other Jurisdictions — 8
   - E. Administrative Adjudication — 10
3. Legislation: Attributes and Types — 12
   - A. The Generality of Legislation and the Problem of Determining Its Application in Concrete Cases — 12
   - B. Types of Legislation — 13
     - *The Constitution of the United States* — 14
     - *Federal Statutes* — 15
     - *Treaties* — 15
     - *Federal Administrative Regulations* — 16
     - *State Constitutions* — 17
     - *State Statutes* — 18
     - *State Administrative Regulations* — 18
     - *Municipal Ordinances* — 19
     - *Rules of Court* — 20
4. The Tasks of the Lawyer — 21
   - *Introduction* — 21
   - A. The Lawyer as Advocate — 22
   - B. The Lawyer as Counselor — 22
   - C. The Lawyer as Judge — 23
5. The Case Method of Studying Law — 25
   - *Another Note to the Beginning Law Student* — 25
   - *Edwin W. Patterson, The Case Method in American Legal Education: Its Origins and Objectives* — 25

CHAPTER II. CASE LAW: THE ANALYSIS AND SYNTHESIS OF JUDICIAL DECISIONS — 37

Section

1. The State and Federal Courts — 37
   - A. The State Court Systems — 37
     - *Trial Courts of "Inferior" Jurisdiction* — 37
     - *Trial Courts of General Jurisdiction* — 38
     - *Appellate Courts* — 39

TABLE OF CONTENTS

Section

1. The State and Federal Courts—Continued **Page**
   - B. The Federal Courts — 41
     - *The District Courts of the United States* — 42
     - *Courts of Appeals of the United States* — 45
     - *The Supreme Court of the United States* — 47
   - C. Note on Administrative Agencies — 50
2. The Structure of a Lawsuit — 54
   - A. Introduction — 54
   - B. Note on Procedure — 55
     - *The Pleading Stage* — 55
     - *The Trial Stage* — 59
     - *Motions in the Trial Court After Verdict* — 61
     - *Execution of the Judgment* — 63
     - *The Appeal Stage* — 63
     - Gumperz v. Hofmann — 64
     - Grand Lodge of the Independent Order of Good Templars of the State of California v. Farnham — 66
     - Warshauer v. Lloyd Sabaudo S.A. — 68
     - Barholt v. Wright — 71
3. The Technique of Case Law Development — 73
   - A. Introduction — 73
   - B. Judicial Decisions on "New Questions" — 75
     - Priestly v. Fowler — 75
     - Albro v. The Agawam Canal Co. — 77
     - Baker v. Libbie — 80
     - Estate of Hemingway v. Random House, Inc. — 87
     - Watkins v. Clark — 93
     - King v. Smythe — 94
     - J'Aire Corp. v. Gregory — 100
     - Hynes v. New York Cent. R. Co. — 107
   - C. The Effect of a Precedent on a Subsequent Case — 112
     - *A More or Less Definition* — 113
     - Humphrey's Executor v. United States — 114
     - *Stare Decisis in Operation* — 118
     - Cullings v. Goetz — 119
     - *The Scope of a Precedent* — 122
     - Problem Case — 124
     - *The Option to Overrule* — 125
     - Silver v. Great American Ins. Co. — 126
     - *The Uses of Dictum* — 131
     - *The Positive Aspects of the Doctrine* — 132
   - D. Synthesis — 132
     - Seixas v. Woods — 134
     - Thomas and Wife v. Winchester — 136
     - Loop v. Litchfield — 144
     - Losee v. Clute — 147

TABLE OF CONTENTS

Section

3. The Technique of Case Law Development—Continued   Page

    Devlin v. Smith 149
    Kellogg Bridge Co. v. Hamilton 154
    Burkett v. Studebaker Bros. Mfg. Co. 158
    Boyd v. Coca Cola Bottling Works 161
    MacPherson v. Buick Motor Co. 163
    Friend v. Childs Dining Hall Co. 175
    Ash v. Childs Dining Hall Co. 178
    Windram Mfg. Co. v. Boston Blacking Co. 180
    Chysky v. Drake Bros. Co. 183
    Pine Grove Poultry Farm, Inc. v. Newton By-Products Mfg. Co., Inc. 186
    Baxter v. Ford Motor Co. 188
    Greenberg v. Lorenz 191
    Randy Knitwear, Inc. v. American Cyanamid Co. 194
    Goldberg v. Kollsman Instrument Corp. 202
    Codling v. Paglia 209
    Problem Case 217

CHAPTER III. THE PROBLEM OF RETROACTIVITY 220

    Great Northern Ry. Co. v. Sunburst Oil & Refining Co. .. 221
    Molitor v. Kaneland Comm. Unit Dist. No. 302 225

CHAPTER IV. THE AUTHORITATIVE STATUS OF JUDICIAL DECISIONS 240

Section

1. Introduction 240
2. Status of State Decisions in Federal Courts 241
    Erie Railroad Co. v. Tompkins 241
    King v. Order of United Commercial Travelers of America 248

CHAPTER V. THE INTERPRETATION OF STATUTES 255

Section

1. The Legislative Process 255
    A. Introduction 255
    B. Structure, Powers, Functions 257
    C. Source and Development of Legislative Proposals 261
    D. Introduction and Reference 267
    E. The Committee Stage 273
        Committee Machinery 273
        Committee Operation 277
        Fiscal Control and the New Budget Act 281
    F. Getting to the Floor 285
        Legislative Leadership 286
        Getting a Bill Out of Committee 287

TABLE OF CONTENTS

Section

1. The Legislative Process—Continued   **Page**
    - *Securing Floor Consideration for Reported Bills in the House* 289
    - *Securing Floor Consideration of Reported Bills in the Senate* 292
    - G. Floor Consideration 293
        - *On the House Floor* 293
        - *On the Senate Floor* 297
        - *The Congressional Record* 300
    - H. Inter-house Coordination 301
    - I. Executive Action 304
    - J. Some Aspects of State Legislative Processes 309
        - *Standing Committees* 309
        - *Scheduling and Floor Consideration* 313
        - *Inter-house Coordination* 314
        - *Executive-Legislative Relations* 315

2. Finding and Stating Issues of Statute Law 318
    - A. Introductory Note 318
    - B. Some Problem Cases 319
        - *Problem Case No. 1* 319
        - *Problem Case No. 2* 320
        - *Problem Case No. 3* 321
        - *Problem Case No. 4* 323

3. Resolving Statutory Issues—A General View 327
    - Johnson v. Southern Pacific Co. 327
    - Johnson v. Southern Pacific Co. 337

4. Interpretation According to "The Intention of the Legislature" 344
    - *Introductory Note* 344
    - *Some Causes of Uncertainty in Statutes* 346
    - *An Addendum on the Problem of Drafting Unambiguous Rules* 348
    - Holy Trinity Church v. United States 349
    - *Francis Lieber, Some Remarks on Interpretation* 355
    - Gossnell v. Spang 357
    - Mitchell v. Kentucky Finance Co. 360
    - Securities and Exchange Commission v. Robert Collier & Co. 364
    - Johnson v. Southern Pacific Co. 367
    - Woollcott v. Shubert 368
    - O'Hara v. Luckenbach Steamship Co. 373
    - The People ex rel. Fyfe v. Barnett 378
    - Commonwealth v. Maxwell 381
    - *Problems Under the Act of 1885 on Foreign Contract Labor* 383

TABLE OF CONTENTS

Section	Page
5. Interpretation According to the Letter of the Statute—The Plain Meaning Rule	388
Introductory Note	388
Temple v. City of Petersburg	390
Caminetti v. United States	393
Chung Fook v. White	398
A Note on Certainty in Statutes	400
6. The Development of Current Doctrine	402
United States v. American Trucking Ass'ns	402
Schwegmann Bros. v. Calvert Distillers Corp.	413
United States v. McKesson & Robbins, Inc.	437
Post Adoption Material: Some Queries	451
Commissioner v. Acker	458
Current Status of the Plain Meaning Rule	464
Some Exercises in Finding, Stating and Resolving Issues Under the President's Executive Order of August 15, 1971	466
7. The Weight of Prior Interpretations	469
Woollcott v. Shubert	469
Alaska Steamship Co. v. United States	474
United States v. American Trucking Ass'ns	477
Cammarano v. United States	478
Fishgold v. Sullivan Drydock & Repair Corporation	488
Girouard v. United States	496
Cleveland v. United States	506
Windust v. Department of Labor and Industries	513
Federal Housing Administration v. The Darlington, Inc.	528
Flora v. United States	539
8. Maxims	543
Introductory Note	543
Weiler v. Dry Dock Savings Institution	544
McBoyle v. United States	548
United States v. Alpers	551
Noscitur A Sociis	555
Last Antecedent	557
Taylor v. Michigan Public Utilities Commission	558
Gooch v. United States	562
9. Some Statutory Problems	566
A. A Problem on the Use of Maxims	566
B. A Problem Under the Rivers and Harbors Act	574
C. Problems Under the Comprehensive Drug Abuse Prevention and Control Act of 1970	577
Problem 1	586
Problem 2	587
Problem 3	592
Problem 4	593

TABLE OF CONTENTS

	Page
CHAPTER VI. COORDINATION OF JUDGE-MADE AND STATUTE LAW	594
Introductory Note	594
Roscoe Pound, Common Law and Legislation	595
James M. Landis, Statutes and the Sources of Law	595
Harlan Fiske Stone, The Common Law in the United States	597
Johnson v. Southern Pacific Company	600
Johnson v. Southern Pacific Company	600
King v. City of Owensboro	600
Panama Railroad Co. v. Rock	604
Funk v. United States	608
Hawkins v. United States	614
Moragne v. States Marine Lines, Inc.	623
Osborne v. McMasters	644
Martin v. Herzog	645
Problems	649
Sirkin v. Fourteenth St. Store	650
Marx v. Jaffe	657
Modern Industrial Bank v. Taub	660
Problems	663
United States v. Acme Process Equipment Co.	664
Note on Implying Private Civil Remedies in Relation to Federal Statutes	670
Cannon v. University of Chicago	671
Schuster v. City of New York	697
Problem	710
Morton v. Mancari	715
Some Final Problems	725
Problem 1	725
Problem 2	726
Problem 3	731
CHAPTER VII. HISTORICAL AND JURISPRUDENTIAL PERSPECTIVES ON LAW AND ITS STUDY	737

Section

1. The Social Ends to Which Law Is Means ... 738
2. The Common Law and Its Reception in the United States ... 744
    Harry W. Jones, The Reception of the Common Law in the United States ... 746
3. Dispute-Settlement and the Problem of Justice ... 759

Appendix ... 771

Index ... 781

TABLE OF CASES

The principal cases are in italic type. Cases cited or discussed are in roman type. References are to Pages.

Acker, Commissioner v., 130, 437, *458*
Acme Process Equipment Co., United States v., 664, 670, 697
Addiss v. Selig, 547
Alaska Steamship Co. v. United States, 474
Albro v. The Agawam Canal Co., 77, 79, 80
Alpers, United States v., 551
American Chicle Co. v. United States, 487
American Metal Climax, Inc. v. Claimant of Butler, 466
American Newspaper Publishers Ass'n v. National Labor Relations Bd., 452, 455
American Timber & Trading Co. v. First Nat. Bank of Oregon, 253
American Trucking Ass'ns, United States v., 402, 433, 464, 466, 477
Ash v. Childs Dining Hall Co., 178

Baker v. Libbie, 80, 87
Ballard v. Anderson, 455
Banco Nacional de Cuba v. Sabbatino, 131
Barholt v. Wright, 71
Barnett, People ex rel. Fyfe, 378
Barnette v. West Virginia State Bd. of Educ., 241
Baxter v. Ford Motor Co., 188, 190
Bell v. Lawrence, 66
Bernstein v. Hakim, 66
Bingler v. Johnson, 477
Blanchette v. Connecticut General Ins. Corps., 452
Bole v. Horton, 112
Bolton v. Travelers Ins. Co., 247
Boyd v. Coca Cola Bottling Works, 161
Boys Markets, Inc. v. Retail Clerks' Union, 528
Buchanan & Co., Ltd., James v. Babco Forwarding & Shipping (U.K.), Ltd., 436
Burkett v. Studebaker Bros. Mfg. Co., 158, 160
Bush v. Steinman, 77
Bushell's Case, 764

Calamaro, United States v., 487
Caminetti v. United States, 393
Cammarano v. United States, 478, 488
Camp, State v., 466
Cannon v. University of Chicago, 671, 693, 694, 696
Carroll v. Carroll's Lessee, 114
Carter v. Yardley & Co., 183
Cartwright v. Sharpe, 455
Cass v. United States, 464, 466
Chicago, Milwaukee, St. Paul & Pacific Railroad Co. v. Acme Fast Freight, Inc., 448
Chrysler Corp. v. Brown, 447
Chung Fook v. White, 398
Chysky v. Drake Bros. Co., 183
City of (see name of city)
Cleveland v. United States, 506, 513
Coates v. Cincinnati, 550
Coca Cola Bottling Works v. Lyons, 186
Codling v. Paglia, 209, 216, 217
Cohen v. Franchard Corp., 73
Cohens v. Virginia, 131
Commissioner v. _____ (see opposing party)
Commonwealth v. _____ (see opposing party)
Conger v. Strutt, 735
Connally v. General Construction Co., 549
Constance v. Harvey, 455, 456
Correll, United States v., 488
Cort v. Ash, 671, 695, 696, 697
Coulter v. Superior Court of San Mateo County, 734
Cramp v. Board of Public Instruction, 550
Cullings v. Goetz, 119, 122, 130, 220

Dege, United States v., 620, 711
Demko, United States v., 528
Department of Air Force v. Rose, 367
Devlin v. Smith, 149, 154, 160
Dr. Bonham's Case, 763

TABLE OF CASES

Dole v. Dow Chemical Co., 219
Doney v. Northern Pacific Railway Co., 225
Dreisonstok v. Volkswagenwerk, A. G., 217

Erie Railroad Co. v. Tompkins, 220, *241*, 247, 670
Estate of (see name of party)
Esterly v. Broadway Garage Co., 473

Farwell v. Boston & Worcester R. Corp., 79, 80
Federal Housing Administration v. The Darlington, Inc., 457, *528*, 539
Federal Power Comm. v. Panhandle Eastern Pipeline Co., 527
Federal Trade Comm. v. Anheuser-Busch, Inc., 448
Federal Trade Comm. v. Mandel Brothers, Inc., 557
Federal Trade Comm. v. Raladam Co., 360
Federal Trade Comm. v. Sun Oil Co., 452
Filmore v. Metropolitan Life Ins. Co., 59
Fishgold v. Sullivan Drydock & Repair Corp., 488
Fitzgerald v. Meissner & Hicks, Inc., 239
Flora v. United States, 539
Ford Motor Co. v. New Jersey Dept. of Labor & Industry, 555
Foti v. Immigration & Naturalization Service, 450
Friend v. Childs Dining Hall Co., 175, 209
Funk v. United States, 608
Fyfe, People ex rel. v. Barnett, 378

Galvan v. Press, 538, 539
Genesee Cty. P. F. R. A. v. L. Sonneborn Sons, 182
Girouard v. United States, 496, 506
Glus v. Brooklyn Eastern Dist. Terminal, 355
Goldberg v. Kollsman Instrument Corp., 202, 209
Goldstein, Estate of v. C. I. R., 254
Gooch v. United States, 562
Gossnell v. Spang, 272, *357*
Grand Lodge of the Independent Order of Good Templars of the State of California v. Farnham, 66, 114
Grayned v. Rockford, 551
Great Northern Ry. Co. v. Sunburst Oil & Refining Co., 221, 225
Greenberg v. Lorenz, 186, 190, *191*

Greenman v. Yuba Power Products Inc., 201
Griswold v. Connecticut, 763
Gumperz v. Hofmann, 56, *64*, 66

Hadley v. Baxendale, 756
Hassett v. Welch, 547
Hawkins v. United States, *614*, 621
Hayes v. Western R. Corp., 80
Haynes v. United States, 539
Healy, United States v., 565
Helvering v. _____ (see opposing party)
Hemingway, Estate of v. Random House, Inc., 87, 92
Henningsen v. Bloomfield Motors, Inc., 201
Hewitt v. Hewitt, 107
Heydon's Case, 367
Holy Trinity Church v. United States, 349, 383, 388
Holytz v. City of Milwaukee, 238, 239
Houghton v. Payne, 477
Howell Electric Motors Co., United States v., 455
Humphrey's Executor v. United States, 114, 117
Hynes v. New York Central Railroad Co., 107

Illinois Brick Co. v. Illinois, 527
In re (see name of party)
Iowa State University Research Foundation, Inc. v. Sperry Rand Corp., 455
Iselin v. United States, 400

J'Aire Corp. v. Gregory, 100, 105
James v. United States, 221
Jarecki v. G. D. Searle & Co., 556
Johnson v. Southern Pacific Co., 256, 263, *327, 337, 367, 528, 600,* 670
Jones v. State Highway Comm., 239
Juhnke v. EIG Corp., 62

Kellogg Bridge Co. v. Hamilton, 154, 158, 178
King v. City of Owensboro, 600
King v. Order of United Commercial Travelers of America, 248, 253
King v. Smythe, *94*, 99
King v. United States, 555
Kirby, United States v., 354

Lawrence Chrysler Plymouth Inc. v. Chrysler Corp., 62
Lewis v. Benedict Coal Corp., 619
Lewis v. Manufacturers Nat. Bank of Detroit, 455

TABLE OF CASES

Linn v. Rand, 733
Longmeid v. Holliday, 143
Loop v. Litchfield, **144,** 147, 160
Los Angeles Department of Water and Power, City of v. Manhart, 449
Losee v. Buchanan, 149
Losee v. Clute, **147,** 149
Lumley v. Gye, 756

MacPherson v. Buick Motor Co., **163,** 174, 175, 182
McBoyle v. United States, **548**
McKesson & Robbins, Inc., United States v., 437, 446, 449
Marbury v. Madison, 756
Marqueze v. Caldwell, 473
Marshall v. Industrial Comm., 614
Martin v. Herzog, **645**
Marvin v. Marvin, 107
Marx v. Jaffe, **657**
Mason v. Libbey, 66
Massachusetts Bonding & Ins. Co. v. United States, 446
Mattz v. Arnett, 539
Maxwell, Commonwealth v., 256, **381**
Meads v. United States, 131
Mitchell v. Kentucky Finance Co., **360**
Mitchell v. W. T. Grant Co., 123, 130
Modern Industrial Bank v. TAUB, **660**
Molitor v. Kaneland Comm. Unit Dist. No. 302, pp. 130, **225,** 239
Moragne v. States Marine Lines, Inc., **623,** 697
Mortensen v. United States, 513
Morton v. Mancari, **715**
Morton, People v., 711
Mount Sinai Hospital of Greater Miami, Inc. v. Jordan, 68
Murray v. Wilson Oak Flooring Co., 247
Myers v. United States, 117, 118

Nashville Milk Co. v. Carnation Co., 451
National Labor Relations Bd. v. Lion Oil Co., 452
National Muffler Dealers Ass'n, Inc. v. United States, 487, 557
New York State Department of Social Services v. Dublino, 453

O'Hara v. Luckenbach Steamship Co., **373**
Olson v. McConihe, 66
Oregon, United States v., 464
Osborne v. McMasters, **644,** 670

Panama Railroad Co. v. Rock, **604**
Paragon Jewel Coal Co. v. C. I. R., 539
Park, State v., 466
Parker & Edgarton v. Foote, 755
Pellet v. Industrial Comm., 354
People v. ——— (see opposing party)
People ex rel. (see name of party)
Philadelphia Nat. Bank, United States v., 452
Pine Grove Poultry Farm, Inc. v. Newton By-Products Mfg. Co., **186**
Polaroid Corp. v. Commissioner, 556
Powell, United States v., 555
Price, United States v., 539
Priestly v. Fowler, 62, 75, 77, 80, 87, 756
Public Utilities Comm. of California, United States v., 432, 433, 434

Rabon v. South Carolina State Highway Dept., 466
Race v. Krum, 178
Racine, State v., 466
Rainwater v. United States, 539
Ramspeck v. Federal Trial Examiners Conference, 452
Randy Knitwear, Inc. v. American Cyanamid Co., **194**
Red Lion Broadcasting Co. v. F. C. C., 539
Reid, United States v., 465
Reynolds Tobacco Co., R. J., Helvering v., 486, 487
Rice v. Alcoholic Beverages Control Appeals Bd. of California, 446
Riggs v. Palmer, 354
Rinaldi v. Mohican Co., 185
Roberson v. Rochester Folding Box Co., 106
Robinson v. International Harvester Co., 219
Roginsky v. Richardson-Merrell, Inc., 253
Rylands v. Fletcher, 756

Sales v. Stewart, 354
Schuster v. City of New York, **697,** 708
Schwegmann Bros. v. Calvert Distillers Corp., 255, **413,** 429
Secretary of Labor v. O'Toole, 731
Securities & Exchange Comm. v. Capital Gains Research Bureau, Inc., 539
Securities & Exchange Comm. v. Robert Collier & Co., **364**
Seixas v. Woods, **134,** 136
Seymour v. Superintendent of Washington State Penitentiary, 539

TABLE OF CASES

Shaugnessy, United States v., 130
Shumway v. The Walworth & Neville Mfg. Co., 80
Silver v. Great American Ins. Co., 126
Simpson v. United States, 447
Sinclair Refining Co. v. Atkinson, 528
Sioux Tribe v. United States, 539
Sirkin v. Fourteenth St. Store, 650
Slate v. Zitomer, 466
Sorrells v. United States, 355
Southwestern Cable Co., United States v., 452
Spanel v. Mounds View School Dist. No. 621, p. 239
Standard Oil Co., United States v., 575
State v. _____ (see opposing party)
State Wholesale Grocers v. Great Atlantic & Pacific Tea Co., 454
Stewart v. Hansen, 474
Swift v. Tyson, 220, 247

Tarlo's Estate, In re, 354
Taylor v. Michigan Public Utilities Comm., 558
Temple v. City of Petersburg, 390
Tennessee Valley Authority v. Hill, 466
Texas & Pacific Railway Co. v. Rigsby, 670, 671, 697
Thomas and Wife v. Winchester, 136, 143, 147, 149, 154, 175
Touche Ross & Co. v. Redington, 671, 693, 694, 695, 696, 697
Train v. Colorado Public Interest Research Group, Inc., 465
Transamerica Mortgage Advisers, Inc. v. Lewis, 671, 695, 697
Trans-Missouri Freight Ass'n, United States v., 360
Tulk v. Moxhay, 756

United Gas Improvement Co. v. Continental Oil Co., 527
United Mine Workers, United States v., 539
United States v. _____ (see opposing party)

Van Beeck v. Sabine Towing Co., 608
Vermilya-Brown Co. v. Connell, 458

Warshauer v. Lloyd Sabaudo S. A., 68, 71
Waterman Steamship Corp. v. United States, 456
Watkins v. Clark, 93, 99
Wecker v. Kilmer, 253
Weiler v. Dry Dock Savings Institution, 544
Wilshire Oil Co., Helvering v., 486
Wiltberger, United States v., 549
Windram Mfg. Co. v. Boston Blacking Co., 180, 182
Windust v. Department of Labor & Industries, 513
Winterbottom v. Wright, 217
Wise, United States v., 452
Wohl v. Keene, 253
Woollcott v. Shubert, 314, 360, *368, 469*
Wright v. Vinton Branch of the Mountain Trust Bank of Roanoke, 360
Wyatt v. United States, 619, 620

Zuber v. Allen, 447, 477

LEGAL METHOD
CASES AND TEXT MATERIAL

Chapter I

THE MATERIALS AND METHODS OF LAW STUDY

SECTION 1. INTRODUCTORY NOTE TO THE BEGINNING LAW STUDENT

A Legal Method course is, among other things, a bridge from college to law school. The first intellectual challenges that confront you as an entering law student are tasks of understanding, of arriving at an informed and genuinely perceptive comprehension of the nature of legal sources and the norms of legal reasoning. The development of this understanding is not only the indispensable first step in law study; it is, for many excellent students, the hardest step of all. It is not to be expected, then, that Legal Method will be or can be an easy course. Lawyers are neither born nor made by their teachers; law students make themselves lawyers. Many members of the legal profession, and most of the great ones, remain students of (lower case) legal method as long as they live.

This casebook is designed to introduce you to the basic materials —case law and legislation—of our legal system and to help you develop a working grasp of the methods by which lawyers make use of these materials for the accomplishment of practical professional tasks. A few words may be helpful at the outset to make clear the reasons underlying the inclusion of Legal Method in the first semester of the law school curriculum. Modern legal education is not a process of turning a class of law students into so many walking encyclopedias of legal rules and principles. A person can buy a pretty good legal encyclopedia for a thousand dollars or so, and it would be pointless to spend three years of hard work trying to become one. In all your first year courses, and particularly and explicitly in Legal Method, your instructors are not so much concerned with your *knowledge* of legal rules as with your development of the fundamental *skills* of the lawyer. Law students who learn to read as a lawyer reads, to think as a lawyer and, as the old saying has it, to "make a noise like a lawyer" gain something that endures, a professional training that will equip them to discharge their duties to their clients, to the courts, and to the profession, long after they have forgotten most of the specific rules they learned in law school.

A course in Legal Method or some equivalent has been established at many law schools in recognition of the experienced fact that almost all beginning law students have to go through a period of groping frustration in the first year, and especially in the first semester of the first year, before they acquire even a moderate understanding of what to look for in the body of material presented to them for study and how to go about organizing what they find there for their own future use. This course is designed to lessen the duration of that fumbling period and to reduce its tensions as much as possible. In this significant sense, the course in Legal Method is not so much an end in itself as an instrument for better student performance in other courses. We were told long ago that the law is a "seamless web." Law, like other disciplines, has its special fields of study and practice, but the kinds of authoritative materials and the modes of thought do not differ essentially from field to field.

Present-day American law is a mixture composed partly of rules[1] derived from past judicial decisions and partly, at least equally, of rules prescribed by legislative enactments. Our law thus exists in two authoritative forms: case law and legislation. A hundred years ago, case law was—or seemed—the dominant ingredient of American law, and legislation of only secondary importance in the work of lawyers and judges. In certain areas of the law's operation, criminal justice for example, the governing precepts were cast in legislative form, but such "private law" fields as contracts, property and torts were still governed almost entirely by case law rules. The practicing lawyer of a hundred years ago probably had far more frequent occasion to refer to the reports in which judicial decisions are published than to statute books and statutory compilations.

The quantitative relation between case law and legislation is far different today. In the 20th century, and particularly since the 1930's, the national government has vastly expanded and intensified its regulatory activities, to an extent that makes it necessary for any American lawyer to take federal law, as well as local state law, into his professional calculations. And federal law is wholly legislative in

---

1. In this chapter, the word "rules" is used in a broad sense, as the equivalent of "norms," and so includes not only narrowly stated legal precepts but also the more broadly stated precepts that are often referred to in legal discourse as "principles" or "standards." American law is not to be thought of as a body of precise and narrowly worded propositions; in most areas of the law, the most important "rules" are likely to be expressed in terms of wide connotation like "reasonable care," "consideration," and "due process of law."

Throughout the casebook, footnotes are numbered consecutively from the beginning of each Chapter. Many footnotes to opinions and other quoted materials are omitted; those that are retained have been renumbered. Editors' footnotes to opinions and other quoted materials are identified as such. All others are from the quoted material.

origin, or virtually so. Over the same span of years, legislation has become an increasingly important ingredient of state law. Even in the private law areas, state legislatures have replaced many old case law rules with new statutory norms deemed more appropriate for the handling of contemporary problems, and there is a marked tendency towards comprehensive law codification, as in the Uniform Commercial Code. In short, legislation has fully come of age as a form of American law. In the work of today's lawyer, the interpretation of legislation is fully as important as the analysis and synthesis of case law sources. In this first, essentially survey, chapter of the casebook, we consider case law at the start and then move on to legislation, not because case law is the more important form but because case law and its processes are farther from the past experience of most beginning law students and because the "case method" of American legal education assumes and requires from the very outset some introductory understanding of case law institutions.

SECTION 2. CASE LAW: ORIGINS, NATURE AND AUTHORITY

A. HOW CASES MAKE LAW

Case law originates in the decisions of judges or other officials who have been empowered by the constitution or laws of a political entity to hear and decide particular controversies. How, one may ask, can particular decisions make general law? From the point of view of the parties to a lawsuit or other contested controversy, what matters is the immediate outcome, the result decreed by the tribunal in their particular case. A has sued B for damages for asserted breach of contract, and the court has reached a decision in their case. The significance of this decision to A and to B is simple and plain: does B have to pay damages to A and, if so, how much? The practicing lawyer, and so the law student, approaches judicial and other decisions from a different perspective, one in which the decision of the court in A $v.$ B is seen chiefly as a source, or possible source, of generally applicable case law.

Let us imagine the existence of a society in which every disputed claim is heard and decided on its own individual merits and with no regard whatever for consistency of the results from case to case. Dispute-settlement machinery exists in that society, but it is without "case law." Case law arises only when today's decision in the case of A $v.$ B becomes in some way and to some extent relevant to the decision of tomorrow's similar controversies between C and D or X and Y. Case law, however primitive or sophisticated and whatever its precise status as authority in a particular legal system, is in a very real sense a by-product of the ongoing process of settling particular controveries.

How are we to account for this widespread inclination to make general law from particular decisions? Karl N. Llewellyn, the leading spokesman for the group of legal philosophers known as the American Legal Realists, offered the following explanation:

> "Case law in some form and to some extent is found wherever there is law. A mere series of decisions of individual cases does not of course in itself constitute a system of law. But in any judicial system rules of law arise sooner or later out of such decisions of cases, as rules of action arise out of the solution of practical problems, whether or not such formulations are desired, intended or consciously recognized. These generalizations contained in, or built upon, past decisions, when taken as normative for future disputes, create a legal system of precedent. Precedent, however, is operative before it is recognized. Toward its operation drive all those phases of human make-up which build habit in the individual and institutions in the group: laziness as to the reworking of a problem once solved; the time and energy saved by routine, especially under any pressure of business; the values of routine as a curb on arbitrariness and as a prop of weakness, inexperience and instability; the social values of predictability; the power of whatever exists to produce expectations and the power of expectations to become normative. The force of precedent in the law is heightened by an additional factor: that curious, almost universal, sense of justice which urges that all men are properly to be treated alike in like circumstances. As the social system varies we meet infinite variations as to what men or treatments or circumstances are to be classed as 'like'; but the pressure to accept the views of the time and place remains."[2]

Students will become aware, as their study of law proceeds, that adherence to precedent has its other side. A court that follows precedents mechanically or too strictly will at times perpetuate legal rules and concepts that have outworn their usefulness. The continuing problem in a legal system that recognizes past decisions as authoritative sources of law for future cases is how to maintain an acceptable accommodation of the competing values of stability in the law, served by adherence to precedent, and responsiveness to social change, which may call for the abandonment of an outworn legal doctrine. This problem of stability *versus* change will be a recurring theme in this casebook.

2. "Case Law," 3 Encyclopedia of the Social Sciences 249 (1930).

B. THE COMMON LAW DOCTRINE OF PRECEDENT

Professor Llewellyn was undoubtedly right in his contention that case law can be found "in some form and to some extent" in every legal system. But case law is uniquely authoritative and influential in a "common law country," which the United States is by inheritance from England. The Anglo-American legal system, unlike the "civil law" system which prevails with variations in most of the countries of the western world, explicitly recognizes the doctrine of precedent, known also as the principle of *stare decisis*. It is the distinctive policy of a "common law" legal system that past judicial decisions are "generally binding"[3] for the disposition of factually similar present controversies. This basic principle, firmly established centuries ago in the royal courts of England, was naturalized as American by the "reception" of the common law in the United States.[4]

When, and for what future cases, will a judicial decision or group of decisions operate as precedent? The term "precedent" is a crucially important word of art in the vocabulary of our law and must be used cautiously and with intellectual discrimination. Let us note, first, a kind of territorial limitation: a judicial decision is a precedent in the full sense of the word only within the same judicial system or "jurisdiction." Thus a decision of the Supreme Court of California is a precedent and so generally binding in future "like" cases in that court and, *a fortiori*, in "lower" California courts, but it is not a full-fledged precedent for future cases arising in the courts of Ohio or Vermont or some other state. Even a decision of the Supreme Court of the United States is not a binding precedent in a state court, say the Court of Appeals of New York, unless the legal issue decided by the Supreme Court decision was a federal question, that is, one involving the interpretation or effect of a federal statute or regulation or of the Constitution of the United States. The possible influence of a judicial decision on future cases arising in other jurisdictions will be considered later in this chapter (pages 8–10); it is sufficient to note now that a decision has the full status and effect of precedent only on the deciding court's home grounds.

A second restriction on what is and is not "precedent" in the full and technical sense has already been suggested, perhaps, by our discussion so far. Even within the same jurisdiction, a decision is

---

3. "Generally" binding is an imprecise but unavoidable way of saying that a court will follow precedent almost all the time, and except when it is persuaded, in unusual and quite undefinable circumstances, that the precedent is too unsound or socially unjust to be adhered to. For a long time in England, precedents were taken to be absolutely binding, but that rigid notion never caught on in American courts and, since 1966, has been on the way out in England.

4. Historically inclined students, or students unsure about what "common law" is or means, may want at this point to look at the text material in Chapter VII of the casebook (pages 744–759) on the common law and its "reception" in the United States.

precedent only for "like," that is, factually similar, future cases. To put the matter more precisely, a judicial decision is a precedent, and so generally binding, only in future cases involving the *same material facts*. As the first-year law student will soon discover, this limitation is far easier to state in general terms than to apply in concrete situations. No two disputes will ever be identical in every factual particular. How is one to determine, or argue, that a factual difference between a past decided case and a case now presented for decision is, or is not, a difference in *material* facts? Case law processes call for great subtlety in the analysis, matching and distinguishing of the facts of cases. This is one of the distinctive arts of the common or case lawyer and will be explored in depth in Chapter II of this casebook. By the end of the first semester, the beginning law student will find that case matching and comparison has become a matter of his or her second nature.

Even when the jurisdiction is the same and the pending new case is found to possess the same material facts, some judicial decisions will have greater weight as precedent than others. Thus, for example, the weight or influence of a precedent is greatly affected by the place of the court that decided it in the judicial hierarchy of its jurisdiction, that is, by whether it was a "higher court" decision or a "lower court" decision. Three tiers of courts exist in the federal judicial structure and in the more populous states: (1) trial courts, (2) intermediate appellate courts, and (3) a highest appellate court or "court of last resort," called in most jurisdictions the Supreme Court. Less populous states are likely to have only two tiers in their judicial structures: trial courts and an appellate court of last resort. The American state court systems and federal court system are described in some detail at pages 37–48 of this casebook. Our present point, an obvious but important one, is that the prudent lawyer or law student will not assign the same force as precedent to the decision of a state intermediate appellate court as to a decision of that state's court of last resort and will not expect a decision of a United States Court of Appeals to have the same precedent force as a decision of the Supreme Court of the United States. As to the decisions of the trial courts, where most of law's day-to-day business is done, these are rarely published and, even when published, are not likely to have much force as precedent except in future cases in the same trial court. It is for this reason chiefly that the overwhelming majority of the cases included in this and most other law school casebooks are decisions of appellate courts.

The decision of cases by reference to precedent is a complex operation. This introductory section of the casebook is but a sketch or suggestion of the whole cluster of norms that together make up the doctrine of precedent, and so govern the influence past decisions are to exert on the determination of new controversies. Analysis of a single case to assess its potential as a precedent can be difficult enough, but often, even usually, not just one case but an entire series of cases must be taken into account and the authoritative rule of case law arrived at by a process of *synthesis*, (see pages 132–219, infra.) Approximately the first half of this Legal Method course will be devoted to case law and is designed in large part to give first-year law students a professional understanding of the realities of *stare decisis* in action. One fundamental point, to be recalled now and remembered, is that it is because of the existence of our institution of precedent that case law enjoys the authoritative status it has in American law and other common law legal systems. The norms that constitute the doctrine of precedent largely determine the way our case law is made and the way it develops to meet the new problems and needs of an endlessly changing society.

C. "RES JUDICATA" AND "STARE DECISIS"; "REVERSAL" AND "OVERRULING"

Every final decision of an appellate court has a twofold impact or effect: (1) as an authoritative settlement of the particular controversy then before the court; and (2) as a precedent, or potential precedent, for future cases. A Latin tag has been attached by lawyers to each of these effects, *stare decisis*, as we have seen, to the impact of the decision as precedent, *res judicata* to its effect as a settlement of the immediate controversy. It is essential in legal analysis that these Latin terms and the concepts they symbolize not be confused. By way of illustration, let us suppose a simple case. *P*, a former surgical patient, sues the *D Hospital* to recover damages for injuries caused, according to *P*'s allegations, by *D Hospital*'s negligence in the maintenance of its operating room. The trial court judgment is in favor of the defendant, and this judgment is affirmed by the supreme court of the state, the court of last resort in the jurisdiction, on the ground, clearly stated in the opinion of the court, that a hospital is a "charitable corporation" and, as such, enjoys immunity from suits for negligence. This decision is a final and conclusive settlement of the controversy between *P* and *D Hospital*; the case, as lawyers say, is now *res judicata*, and the losing party, *P*, cannot have it tried, or bring his claim, again.

Now, to make plain the difference between *res judicata* and *stare decisis* as legal terms of art, let us suppose further that the same state supreme court, two years later and in another hospital case, is persuaded that the principle of charitable immunity from suit for negligence is not a sound legal doctrine for present-day conditions and so "overrules" *P v. D Hospital* and finds in favor of the injured plaintiff in the new case. This overruling decision is a deviation from the norm of *stare decisis*, of course, but American courts of last resort have never regarded precedents as absolutely binding—only as "generally" binding—and have reserved to themselves a largely undefined authority to overrule even clear precedents when considerations of public policy require a change in the case law.

What, however, of the particular claim of P against the D Hospital? Now that the supreme court of the jurisdiction has changed the law and flatly "overruled" the decision that was reached in P's case two years ago, it might seem that P should be able to bring his suit again and prevail in his claim. The answer is clear, and adverse to P. His particular claim has been finally and conclusively settled against him; P is barred by the doctrine of *res judicata* from ever suing on that claim again. The final decision of a court of last resort is, we observe, more conclusive and permanent in its aspect (*res judicata*) as a settlement of a particular case than it is in its aspect (*stare decisis*) as general law for the future.

One other nicety in legal terminology should be noted at this point. We have just said that the state supreme court, in the later hospital case, "overruled" its decision in P v. D Hospital. It would have been seriously inaccurate usage if we had said that the state supreme court had "reversed" P v. D Hospital. And this error in usage might have led to a substantial error in problem-analysis, because "reverse," as a legal word of art, carries with it the idea that a court judgment has been set aside, and is no longer effective, as between the parties to a controversy. In short, "reversal" and "overruling" are not to be used interchangeably, as beginning law students and analytically careless lawyers often do. "Reversal" has reference to the action of an appellate court on a lower court's judgment in the same particular controversy. When an appellate court reviews the judgment of a lower court in a case and concludes that the lower court reached an erroneous result in the case, the appellate court will "reverse," that is, set aside, the lower court's judgment. When a court of last resort "overrules" one of its past decisions, the conclusiveness of that earlier decision as a settlement of its particular controversy is not affected, but the overruled decision is no longer an authoritative precedent.

D. DECISIONS FROM OTHER JURISDICTIONS

A judicial decision, as we have seen, is a "precedent" in the full sense only within the same jurisdiction. In their opinions, however, American appellate courts frequently—indeed, more often than not—cite and draw upon decisions from other jurisdictions. Thus, for example, the Supreme Court of Tennessee, in support of the result it has reached in a case, may quote from or cite decisions from the courts of last resort of Massachusetts, Oregon, Virginia and a half-dozen other states—even perhaps decisions from England and other "common law" jurisdictions. Such outstate decisions are not full-fledged precedents, but they are accorded the status and weight of *persuasive authority*, which means that they are not "binding" in any sense but may have influence, often very great influence, in cases where there is no local precedent or the local precedents are conflicting or unclear.

The case law process in American courts thus has a considerable comparative-law ingredient: a court of last resort in one state does not consider itself bound to follow another state's case law rules, but it will carefully consider the outstate decisions and, if it finds their reasoning persuasive, make use of them as sources of guidance and justification. This disposition to give persuasive weight to outstate case authority is in no way surprising. A court faced with a difficult and locally new problem needs all the help it can get, and where is better guidance to be found than in the recorded past solutions of the same problem arrived at by the courts in states where more or less the same social and economic conditions prevail? Even beyond this, the "reception" of the common law in the United States means that all the states (except Louisiana) share a common legal tradition, so that the case law decisions of each state are, at least presumably, accurate reflections of common law principle.

It is largely because of the important influence of outstate decisions as persuasive authority in American law that law school casebooks, other than those on Constitutional Law and other federal law subjects, are usually composed of cases drawn from many jurisdictions. The law student, as he or she reads cases from different jurisdictions, will find that American appellate courts exhibit a marked degree of comity, mutual respect, for each other's decisions. Some decisions, of course, will have greater influence than others on the thinking of judges in other states. An outstate decision's persuasiveness may be affected, for example, by the prestige of the court that handed it down or by the prestige of the particular judge (e. g., Cardozo) who wrote the opinion of the court. The factors that have to be taken into account in determining just how persuasive a given outstate decision will prove to be cannot be set out fully in this introductory chapter and must be left to the intensive study of cases that will be carried on later in Legal Method and in the student's other law school courses.

However hospitable a court of last resort may be to persuasive authority from other jurisdictions, an outstate case, it must not be forgotten, is not as authoritative and should not be assigned the same force as a true local "precedent." The difference in degree of influence is much like the difference to be considered later in this casebook (pages 112–132) between the *holding* of a case and a *dictum* in a judicial opinion, the "holding" being fully authoritative and generally binding and the "dictum" only, again, persuasive authority. The student-user of this casebook will find that the section entitled *"Synthesis"* at pages 132–219 consists very largely of cases from a single jurisdiction, New York. This is not to be taken as an indication that the authors of this casebook are typically parochial New Yorkers and so chiefly concerned with New York law. The explanation is that the realities of *stare decisis* in action can be grasped only if the student concentrates for a time on the development of case law in a single jurisdiction, and so witnesses a court struggling with *its own* "generally binding" past decisions, striving to make general sense of its precedents and restricting or extending their reach as the court believes fair and just for new problems and changed social conditions. A sequence of decisions, if all from the same jurisdiction, might equally well have been taken from Iowa, Missouri, Texas or any other state. The New York cases on product liability were chosen for emphasis in the *Synthesis* section because they happen to present fact-situations and examples of opinion-styles that lend themselves exceptionally well to the teaching and learning of case law legal method.

E. ADMINISTRATIVE ADJUDICATION

The courts are our society's traditional instrumentalities for the authoritative disposition of controversies and, at the start of this century, seemed to have a virtual monopoly of the public business of dispute-settlement. But just as legislation has made great inroads into what were once the largely exclusive preserves of the case law, administrative agencies like the National Labor Relations Board and the Federal Trade Commission have come to exercise powers of adjudication—sometimes called "quasi-judicial" to differentiate them from the powers of the "regular" courts—in many areas of American social and economic life. [The exercise by administrative agencies of delegated legislative authority—usually called "rule-making" to differentiate it from the legislative work of Congress and the state legislatures—is of equal importance in present-day law and government and will be treated in a later section (pages 16–17) of this chapter.] If a person has a disputed claim for federal retirement benefits, he or she does not begin by going to court to sue on it; the claim will be judged and authoritatively determined, at least as a matter of first instance, by an adjudicatory official in the Social Security Administration of the Department of Health and Human Services. A power company that wishes to construct a nuclear reactor applies for the required license not to a court but to the Nuclear Regulatory Commission, which, after proper hearing and deliberation by its atomic safety and licensing board, will grant or deny the application. Administrative agencies entrusted with power to hear and pass upon claims, applications and charges of law violation are found everywhere in the federal governmental structure, sometimes as divisions within cabinet departments, sometimes as independent regulatory establishments. Quantitatively, far more controversies are decided by federal administrative agencies than by all the federal courts. (See p. 50, infra).

Administrative adjudication has similarly been a growth industry in the state and local governments. Administrative bodies are empowered to issue or refuse, and to revoke or suspend, the licenses required to engage in a wide variety of professions and businesses. Workmen's compensation commissions hear and decide claims arising from industrial accidents, and public utility commissions pass on applications for rate increases submitted by gas, light and water companies. Every municipal government has its administrative complex of local tax boards, licensing officials, zoning appeals boards and the like, all performing in one way or another the essentially judicial function—or quasi-judicial function—of hearing and deciding particular claims, charges and disputes. To be sure, the decisions reached by federal, state and local administrative agencies are, to one or another extent, subject to judicial review in the (regular) courts, but the scope of this review is usually limited and constitutes not a retrial of the case or claim but an inquiry into whether the administrative adjudicative agency has acted illegally, arbitrarily or without sufficient evidence to support its findings.

For many decades, well into the 1940's, most lawyers looked with distrust and hostility on the proliferation of administrative agencies and the extension of their decision-making powers. The ultimate consensus, it would appear, was that administrative adjudication is inevitable, given the vastly increased range of government's regulatory and public welfare programs, and, being here to stay, should be ordered and regularized. The great step in this direction, insofar as the federal agencies are concerned, was the enactment in 1946 of the Administrative Procedure Act. By this Act, which was passed by the unanimous vote of both houses of Congress, the adjudicative processes of the federal agencies were largely "judicialized," that is, subjected to uniform procedural standards designed to secure fairness in the hearing, determination and review of particular cases. Similar legislation to regularize the processes of administrative adjudication in the state and local governments is well on its way. The Revised Model State Administrative Procedure Act, proposed by the National Conference of Commissioners on Uniform State Laws, has been adopted in twenty-six states, and more than twenty other states have enacted legislation substantially influenced in content by the model act. If administrative adjudication was ever "a mad dog at loose in our legal order," as an enraged critic declaimed in 1936, it has at the very least been taken in, house-broken, and accepted as an integral part of the American system of case-settlement.

In this chapter, and indeed elsewhere in this Legal Method casebook, administrative decisions have not been given equal time with the decisions of courts. This is not because administrative decisions are not of comparable significance in the work of present-day lawyers—for manifestly they are—but because administrative case law, if it may be called that, differs from the case law of the courts in significant respects, and particularly as concerns the status of an administrative decision as a possible precedent in like cases coming before the same administrative agency in the future. Very generally speaking, the adjudicative officials of administrative agencies share and respond to the feelings and aspirations that are reflected in the principle of *stare decisis*: the urge for intellectual consistency in decision-making and the wish to demonstrate that equality of treatment is being given to all claimants and respondents. There are situations, too, when a "regular" court to which an administrative decision has been appealed may point to the agency's inconsistent past decisions as an indication that it has acted unfairly or arbitrarily in the case on appeal. But it would be grossly misleading to suggest that the common law doctrine of precedent is, as in the courts, the pervasive and governing norm of administrative adjudication. Many considerations apply in administrative adjudication; the needs of efficiency, flexibility and basic regulatory effectiveness can have greater weight than decisional consistency in the thinking of agency officials and reviewing judges. Intensive examination of administrative decision-making procedures and of administrative decisions as a special type of case law must be left to the course in Administrative Law and to other courses like Taxation, Labor Law and Corporations in which administrative adjudication is of central and dominant importance.

SECTION 3. LEGISLATION: ATTRIBUTES AND TYPES

A. THE GENERALITY OF LEGISLATION AND THE PROBLEM OF DETERMINING ITS APPLICATION IN CONCRETE CASES

Legislation, as a form of law, has been likened to a proverb, case law to a parable. There is something to these old characterizations. Case law, as we have seen, is made up of rules inferred from decisions in past cases. The movement, in other words, is from the particular to the general. By contrast, legislation is general from its inception and in its original statement. A legislative precept is, in short, a prescribed general rule, one expressed as such in authoritative verbal form by the law-making body or agency. As the late Edwin W. Patterson wrote in the first Legal Method casebook:

> "A proposition of case law may be correctly stated in several different ways, each of which is equally 'official.' A statute (proposition of legislation) is stated as an exclusive official wording of the rule. Case law is flexible; legislation is (textually) rigid."

There may be great uncertainty as to how the general proposition expressed in a legislative precept is to be applied in a concrete case, but there is no room for argument as to what the words of the legislative text actually are. The authoritative text is to be interpreted, not rewritten or paraphrased. Courts inevitably have great latitude in determining the meaning and effect of statutory language in concrete situations, but only the legislature is authorized to change a statute's wording by the process of amendment.

Since legislation differs from case law in political origin and verbal form, legal method in the use of legislation for guidance in particular controversies and counseling situations involves insights and skills that differ significantly from those involved in the analysis and use of case law precedents. There is, to be sure, some intersection or overlapping of the case law and legislative skills when the legislation concerned has been in effect for many or at least several years. The principle of *stare decisis* applies, of course, to judicial decisions arrived at by the application of legislative precepts, and, when a statute has been long on the books, the judicial decisions that have interpreted and applied its provisions in past cases are precedents for future factually similar cases within, or asserted to be within, the reach of the statute. Because of this, lawyers of an older cast of thought liked to say that statutes, even Acts of Congress, are not really law but only "sources" from which law is made by the courts. This is an interesting theoretical speculation but, among other things, takes insufficient account of the practical impact a statute has on behavior in society during the period, which may be a very long one, before any court or judge has had occasion to pass on it. The sounder view, both theoretically and practically, is that a statute is an authoritative norm of the legal system not from the time of its first interpretation by the courts, perhaps years later, but from the time of its enactment by the legislature.

In advising their clients or representing them in particular litigated controversies, lawyers, more often than not, must work with "unconstrued" legislation, that is, with statutes or statutory provisions that have never before been subjected to judicial scrutiny and interpretation. In the interpretation of legislation, the leading cases—and those most instructive to law students—are what might be called cases of first impression, fact-situations in which the arguments of opposed counsel and the ultimate decision of the court must proceed, without the help of prior judicial interpretations, from the text of the statute and from its underlying purposes and legislative history. Most of the cases in Chapter V (pages 255–593) of this casebook are, in this sense, cases of first impression. The student who has worked through the materials in Chapter V should not be at a loss, as many lawyers of an earlier generation seem to have been, when required to work with a statute itself rather than with a statute's later judicial exegesis.

B. TYPES OF LEGISLATION

Legislative precepts, we have said, are prescribed general rules expressed in authoritative verbal form. The statutes enacted by Congress and the legislatures of the states are legislation of the classic and most familiar kind; indeed "statute law" is frequently used as a synonym or equivalent for "legislation" and will be so used from time to time in this casebook. In the present section, however, we are using the term "legislation" in a sense broad enough to include not only federal and state statutes but also the other types of general legal rules that are prescribed in administrative regulations, municipal ordinances and the like. Even the Constitution of the United States or a state constitution is "legislation" in this broad sense, although of higher political and legal obligation than "ordinary" legislation, because a constitution, too, is a rule-prescribing instrument, one which expresses in authoritative form the general rules, or principles, that govern the exercise of political power in an organized society and safeguard individual interests from unwarranted governmental intrusion.

Because of the wide dispersion of law-making power in the United States—the constitutional division of legislative authority between the national government and the states and the delegation of subordinate legislative power to administrative agencies and, in the states, to city councils and other municipal bodies—American legislation is an aggregate of precepts from many sources. Conflicting directions are frequently encountered in this mix; a state statute, for example, may be or seem in conflict with existing federal legislation or a state administrative regulation with a municipal ordinance on the same subject. Individuals and corporations, and so the lawyers advising them, are often faced with the problem of what to do when one law-maker has commanded certain behavior and another law-maker has ordered a quite different course of action. In determining which of two competing legislative commands is the one to be obeyed, or to be given controlling force by a court in a litigated case, the manifest first step is to consider the degree of authority with which each of the two law-makers spoke to the subject at hand. The types of legislation briefly sketched in the following paragraphs are listed, for the most part, in the order of their *authoritativeness* as norms of our legal system.

The Constitution of the United States

The Constitution sets out the norms that govern the distribution of political powers in our society and the ways in which—and purposes for which—these powers are to be exercised. In our legal order the Constitution is "law," and law of the highest authoritativeness and obligation. Even a deliberately enacted federal statute can be challenged in the courts as beyond the legislative power delegated to the Congress by the Constitution or as violative of some provision of the Bill of Rights or other constitutional guarantee of individual interests against impairment by government action. Similarly, the Constitution of the United States, as "supreme Law of the Land," is the ultimate authority to which reference must be made to determine the validity of state and municipal legislation. The Constitution, in its inception, related almost entirely to the structure and operations of the national (or "federal") government, but since the adoption of the 13th, 14th and 15th Amendments in the years following the Civil War, the prohibitions of the Constitution have been of equal importance in relation to state legislation and to action taken by state and local officials.

Federal Statutes

Article I, Section 1 of the Constitution of the United States provides that "all legislative Powers herein granted shall be vested in a Congress of the United States." The powers so granted to Congress are enumerated in considerable detail in Article I, Section 8, which concludes with a broadly worded grant of authority to "make all Laws which shall be necessary and proper for carrying into Execution the foregoing Powers." What are the constitutional and legal consequences when Congress, as it has done quite often in recent years, enacts a statute which, although clearly within the scope of its lawmaking authority under Article I, Section 8, conflicts directly with existing state legislation or state constitutional provisions? We turn for our answer to what is known as the "supremacy clause" (Article VI, paragraph 2) of the Constitution.

The supremacy clause, one of the key provisions of the Constitution, provides in full as follows:

> "This Constitution, and the Laws of the United States which shall be made in Pursuance thereof; and all Treaties made, or which shall be made, under the Authority of the United States, shall be the supreme Law of the Land; and the Judges in every state shall be bound thereby, any Thing in the Constitution or Laws of any State to the Contrary notwithstanding."

The words are carefully chosen and their meaning and effect perfectly clear. A federal statute "made in pursuance" of the Constitution is a part of "the supreme Law of the Land" and so of superior authoritativeness to any state constitutional provision, state statute or other type of state legislation.

Treaties

Article II, Section 2 of the Constitution provides that the President

> "shall have power, by and with the Advice and Consent of the Senate, to make Treaties, provided two-thirds of the Senators present concur * * *."

A treaty in its essence is a diplomatic instrument, a compact between nations, and it may seem strange to see treaties included in an inventory of the types of legislation. We include them because there are a few circumstances in which a treaty made by the President with the advice and consent of the Senate has much the same legal effect as a federal statute. Suppose, for example, that a treaty between the United States and some other nation provides that the citizens of each country shall be fully entitled to inherit property or to engage in all kinds of business in the other country. By the explicit terms of the supremacy clause of the Constitution of the United States, just considered in its relation to federal statutes, the treaty we have supposed is a part of the "supreme law of the land" and so superior in legal authoritativeness to any type of state legislation. The citizens of the nation with whom our supposed treaty was made are thus entitled to inherit property or to engage in any kind of business in State *X*, even if State *X* has a statute or state constitutional provision restricting the inheritance of property or the carrying on of designated kinds of business to American citizens. The place of treaties and the treaty power in our constitutional system raises many complex questions, some of them of lively contemporary importance, but these questions must be left to later courses in International Law and Constitutional Law. It is sufficient now to note the possibility that a treaty may, if only on very rare occasions, have an incidental side-effect as federal legislation.

Federal Administrative Regulations

Earlier in this chapter (pages 10–12), account was taken of administrative adjudication as an important element in the contemporary American pattern of controversy-settlement. But administrative agencies are not only appliers of law in particular cases; they are also law-makers, and the general rules formulated and prescribed by the agencies constitute a major ingredient of American legislation. More than ninety federal agencies, some of them established as independent commissions and others as more or less separate branches within cabinet departments, are now involved in the regulation of business and other private activities. Many, perhaps most of the ninety have been entrusted by Acts of Congress with subordinate legislative power, subordinate in the sense that the regulations made and issued by an administrative agency must be within the scope of the authority delegated to the agency by Congress.

Regulations prescribed by a federal agency within the scope of its delegated rule-making power are authoritative norms of the legal order and, assuming the constitutional validity of the underlying federal statute, superior in authoritativeness to state law. Thus a properly issued regulation of the Securities and Exchange Commission, the National Labor Relations Board, or the Food and Drug Administration has legal effect everywhere in the United States, and any conflicting rule on the same subject in a state's case law or statutes, or even in its constitution, must yield to the superior authority of the federal regulation. The rule-making processes of the federal administrative agencies, like their adjudicatory processes, are governed by the Administrative Procedure Act (page 11, supra), which, in its application to administrative rule-making has been characterized by an eminent scholar as "one of the most significant jurisprudential inventions of the century." Similar developments in the direction of regularization have taken place with respect to the more adequate publication of the products of administrative rule-making. Acts of Congress now require publication of administrative regulations in a daily and official gazette called the Federal Register, and it is further required that regulations be systematically arranged and codified, by a continuing process, in the Code of Federal Regulations. The rule-making functions of administrative agencies, as well as their adjudicatory and executive (largely enforcement) functions, are examined intensively in law school courses on Administrative Law.

State Constitutions

State constitutions existed before the drafting of the Constitution of the United States. Almost all of the thirteen original states (recently colonies) adopted constitutions in 1776 or 1777. These first state constitutions and those adopted early in the 19th century were much like the Constitution of the United States in content and style, that is, they were largely confined to essential matters like basic governmental structure and the definition and distribution of political powers and, except in their bills of individual rights, expressed in terms of broad principles or standards as distinguished from narrowly stated rules.

Every state has its constitution, and the typical state constitution of today is a far bulkier document and is likely to deal at length and in very specific terms with subjects like school and police administration, lotteries, state and municipal budgeting, the tenure of civil service employees, and the powers to be exercised by irrigation and sewer districts. Such explicit and detailed provisions are written into a state constitution for the manifest purpose of making it impossible for a subsequent state legislature to change the law on the subject by simple statutory enactment. It is far harder politically to amend a state constitution than to repeal or amend a statute; a two-thirds majority in each house of the state legislature is commonly required to propose a state constitutional amendment, and an amendment so proposed must typically be approved by popular referendum which may, in its turn, require more than a simple-majority vote of the electorate.

State statutes are, of course, subject to challenge in the courts on federal constitutional grounds, but, because of the great specificity of most state constitutions, the state constitutional barrier may be the more difficult one to get over. A state statute that would unquestionably pass Supreme Court scrutiny as consistent with the Constitution of the United States can nonetheless be held invalid by a state court of last resort as a violation of some provision of the local state constitution. And that will be a final and conclusive determination because the Supreme Court of the United States is not superior in authority to state courts on questions of local state law.

State Statutes

It is sometimes said that state statutes are less important in the day-to-day work of lawyers than they were fifty or so years ago, because of the vast extension of federal regulatory activity that has come about since the 1930's. To say this is to overlook two other developments during approximately the same time: (1) the extension and intensification of state controls, imposed by or based on statutes, in such areas as consumer protection, environmental management and equal employment opportunity; and (2) the increasing tendency of state legislatures to intervene in traditional private law fields by replacing old case law rules with new and presumably more up-to-date legislative norms. The past decades have made it far more likely than it was that a lawyer advising private clients will have to take account of federal statutes and regulations, but it by no means follows that he or she will be consulting state statute books less often than lawyers used to do. For most lawyers and state court judges, state statutes still constitute one of the most important forms or types of law.

The effectiveness of a state statutory provision as an authoritative rule may be challenged in court, as we have seen, on one or more of several grounds: that it violates some more or less explicit prohibition in the Constitution of the United States, that it contravenes some provision of the local state constitution or that it conflicts with some more authoritative federal statute, treaty or administrative regulation. But it is misleading to concentrate too much on the possible vulnerability of state statutes to constitutional challenge. 90% or more of the statutes enacted by a busy state legislature at one of its sessions will raise no serious question of federal or state constitutional law. The lawyer's work in dealing with state statutes is chiefly a work of interpretation, of determining the meaning and effect of enacted statutory language for specific cases and counseling situations. Chapter V of this casebook (pages 255–593) is designed to develop the insights and skills that are necessary in the interpretation of state, as of federal, statutes.

State Administrative Regulations

State governments have committed many businesses and pursuits to administrative supervision, much of which calls for rule-making by state agencies. The list of regulated activities differs from state to state, reflecting differences in economic conditions and in prevailing political attitudes, but it is everywhere a long list. Regulations are prescribed by state and local agencies and officials on a bewildering variety of subjects: agriculture, civil service, fishing, horse racing, water resources and zoning, to mention just a few. State administrative regulations, in their vast aggregate, loom large in the picture of American legislation.

Administrative rule-making, by and large, is far less professionalized in the states than in the federal agencies and departments, and state and local rule-making processes are often unstructured and informal, informal at times to the point of disorderliness. Until a few years ago, persons who might be seriously affected by the issuance of this or that set of state regulations often had no effective way to present relevant information or make their views known to the administrative law-maker or even to find out that regulations were under consideration. And state regulations, once drafted and officially prescribed, were sometimes left unpublished, or so obscurely published that affected persons or interests were left in the dark as to their requirements. Great improvements in the regularity of state administrative rule-making seem to be taking place, particularly in the many states that have adopted the Revised Model State Administrative Procedure Act (page 11, supra), which sets standards of fair procedure not only for state administrative adjudication but also (in different sections of the Act) for state administrative rule-making. A section of the Model Act deals specifically with the problem of access to administrative regulations by requiring that rules prescribed by the agencies be promptly published in an official state bulletin and regularly compiled.

Municipal Ordinances

The rules enacted by the legislative branch of a local or "municipal" unit of government are authoritative precepts of legislation within the unit's territorial limits. These prescribed rules of local legislative origin are commonly called "ordinances" (to distinguish them from the "statutes" enacted by Congress and the state legislatures), and that is what we shall call them here, even though they sometimes bear another name (e. g., "by-law".) A municipal ordinance is, of course, legally ineffective if inconsistent with a higher norm of federal law or with a provision of the state constitution and is usually, but not always, inferior in authoritativeness to a conflicting state statute. We have said "not always" because many state constitutions contain so-called "home rule" provisions which, to one or another extent, may empower cities and other municipal units to enact ordinances, on a few designated subjects, that are not vulnerable to disapproval or modification by the state legislature. Insofar as the law-making power of the municipal unit comes to it by statutory delegation from the state legislature, however, the rule prescribed by a municipal ordinance must yield to the conflicting direction of a state statute and may, like an administrative regulation, be repealed or modified by subsequent action of the legislature.

Local governments have been entrusted, increasingly in recent years, with substantial legislative powers. Many of the ordinances passed by municipal law-making bodies are essentially internal measures relating to government organization, administration and finance or to the furnishing of city services. Other ordinances govern and affect the behavior of private persons within the city's boundaries: for example, parking and other traffic regulations or ordinances prescribing health and safety rules for restaurants, hotels and theaters. Ordinances that apply directly to private persons or companies are usually supported by the sanction of a fine or other penalty; the enforcement of ordinances against persons charged with violating them is a mass-production operation in municipal courts.

The importance of municipal ordinances as a type of legislation is often underestimated, partly because of the low esteem in which municipal legislative bodies are commonly held and partly because municipal ordinances are hardly ever relevant in ordinary business transactions or in litigation between private parties. Even in ardently "home rule" states, city law-makers, for manifest reasons, have not been empowered to pass ordinances that would make tort law, contract law or general property law different within the territory of the city than elsewhere in the state. But municipal ordinances, by their immediacy, influence the welfare and day-to-day behavior of the many millions of people now clustered in the great cities of the United States. They are low in the hierarchy of authoritative legal norms but not in most people's apprehension of what "the law" requires.

Rules of Court

A few words by way of historical background are necessary here to make plain the nature and function of rules of court. Until the second half of the 19th century, pleading (the formal statement of claims and defenses by the litigants) and other aspects of procedure in court litigation were governed chiefly by case law rules that had evolved in the long history of common law judicial institutions. Widespread dissatisfaction with the super-technical quality of these old rules, and particularly with the occult mysteries of "common law pleading," caused even the earliest American state legislatures to intervene from time to time by passing statutes simplifying particular steps in court procedure. More drastic reform came when a Benthamite lawyer, David Dudley Field, drafted a comprehensive procedural code, designed to make court proceedings more rational and expeditious. Field's code was enacted by the New York legislature in 1848 and, with minor variations, by the California legislature in 1849. By the end of the 19th century, statutes replacing common law pleading and practice with "code" pleading and practice had been enacted in more than half the states. The first basic reforms of American procedure were thus brought about by statutory enactments.

The tendency in more recent years has been to accomplish needed improvements in the law of procedure not through the enactment of procedural statutes but by empowering the courts themselves to formulate and prescribe "rules of court" governing the procedures to be followed by litigants and judges in contested cases. Rules of court are legislation, analytically, because they are general in statement and prospective in operation. They are placed last in this inventory of the types of legislation not because they are lower in authoritativeness than some of the types listed above, but because they are somewhat anomalous, being judicial in governmental origin but legislative in form and operation.

The best known of American rules of court are the Federal Rules of Civil Procedure which, although applicable only to procedure in federal courts, have also had great influence on the reform of procedure in the state courts. An enabling act empowering the Supreme Court "to prescribe by general rules" the course of procedure in the district courts of the United States was passed by Congress in 1934. An extremely well qualified advisory committee was appointed by the Court to assist it in the task and, after much hard work, the Rules were approved by the Court, with minor changes in the advisory committee's final draft, and went into effect in 1938. A similar process was followed in the preparation and adoption of the Federal Rules of Criminal Procedure, which became effective in 1946.

SECTION 4. THE TASKS OF THE LAWYER

INTRODUCTION

Like other kinds of professional education—for medicine, for engineering, and for the ministry—university law training is profession-oriented. In three years of law study, a student will acquire a great deal of enlightening knowledge about legal institutions and should, if he or she is a thoughtful person, develop a certain critical judgment concerning the social adequacy, or inadequacy, of our law's case law and legislative norms. But most of the men and women who come to law school do it not because they want to learn *about* law but because they have chosen law as their vocation. Whatever its other goals, American legal education is education for work as a lawyer. This introductory chapter on the materials and methods of law study would be woefully incomplete, therefore, without some discussion of the variety and range of the lawyer's professional tasks.

In American society, perhaps more than anywhere else in the world, lawyers play many parts. They are, on occasion or by specialty, negotiators, mediators, draftsmen, business advisors and, in a true sense, social engineers. The American lawyer, one might say, is the nearest thing to a generalist that exists in our increasingly specialized society. The lawyer's three traditional and distinctive roles, however, are as advocate, as counselor, and as judge, roles which have been characterized as involving, respectively, tasks of *persuasion, prediction*, and *justification*. We consider now, briefly and in necessarily general terms, the way case law and legislative precepts are approached and used by members of the legal profession for each of these three purposes.

A. THE LAWYER AS ADVOCATE

The advocate's role is a work of persuasion. Our legal order is an "adversary" system, and, subject to the standards of ethical conduct set out in the Code of Professional Responsibility, it is the advocate's function to persuade the court or other tribunal to reach a decision in favor of his or her client. In a great many litigated cases, the crucial issue disputed by the parties will be a question of fact, and the advocate's work then is to persuade the court, or a jury, that his or her client's version of the facts is the true one. But instead, or additionally, the advocate may be called on to argue a disputed question of law, that is to present arguments, based on the case law or legislation of the jurisdiction, which, if accepted, lead to a decision favorable to the advocate's client. When the relevant precedents are unclear or conflicting or the relevant statute ambiguous or of doubtful constitutionality, the advocate for each side will present a statement of "what the law is" that resolves the doubts in a way favorable to his or her client's claim or defense. The advocate, in short, reads case law and legislative sources in a professionally responsible but partisan way, construing them strictly or broadly as best serves his or her client's interest in the litigation, and advances the strongest possible valid arguments to persuade the court to accept this reading of what the law is.

B. THE LAWYER AS COUNSELOR

Advocates are retained when people are already in legal trouble, that is, involved in disputes that have hardened or are about to harden into contested lawsuits. Counselors are consulted earlier, when people need legal advice as to their future, out-of-court, action. In his law office, the counselor is engaged in what we may call the engineering of expectations, the working out of contemplated transactions so that they will not be frustrated by future legal difficulties. Thus the work of the counselor has its aspect of prediction. How, the counselor must ask himself or herself, would a court rule if there is some future litigated controversy concerning the legality or legal effect of the client's contemplated will or contract or plan of business organization? Since the counselor's predictions must above all be reliable, the counselor approaches the relevant case law and legislative sources with a certain conservatism that contrasts sharply with the advocate's tendency to resolve all doubts in favor of the client's side. Thus the counselor will often reject, as risky and unreliable, interpretations of the applicable case law or legislation that he or she, functioning as an advocate in litigation, would urge the court to accept.

Perhaps a simple illustration will be helpful to make plain this difference between the advocate's and the counselor's perspective. Suppose that it is honestly debatable, under the law existing in a certain jurisdiction, whether a will written out and signed by the testator but not subscribed to by witnesses is legally effective. Litigation arises concerning an unwitnessed will of this nature, and Lawyer X is retained to represent the claimants under the will. Resolving the doubt in his clients' favor, as advocates properly do, Lawyer X will forcefully argue that the unwitnessed will is legally effective. But if the problem had come to Lawyer X in his role as counselor, as it would have if a living client had asked Lawyer X whether the client should have his will witnessed, Lawyer X would unhesitatingly have urged the client to take the safe course and insure the effectiveness of his will by having it witnessed. In the discharge of his or her professional responsibilities, the counselor, of course, must be far more than a nay-sayer. The resourceful counselor uses case law and legislation not just to tell clients what they cannot do but to show them how to do what manifestly has to be done to secure their objectives, and with the least possible risk of adverse legal consequences. Where the state of the law is doubtful, the advocate may properly rush in where any sensible counselor would fear to tread.

C. THE LAWYER AS JUDGE

In a society governed by the rule of law, as virtually all contemporary societies are or purport to be, judges are under obligation to decide controversies not according to their own personal preferences but according to law. American judges thus use the precepts of case law and legislation as guides for decision-making. If a clear and unequivocal rule can be found in the jurisdiction's case law or legislation, the judge, generally speaking, is bound to apply that rule to the facts of the particular case at hand. The decisional task is far more complex when, as often happens, the existing precedents and statutes provide no single and unambiguous rule for disposition of the controversy before the court. As the first-year law student will soon discover, the judicial process often compels judges to exercise discriminating and responsible judgment in choosing, from the competing versions presented by opposing advocates, the rule of law to be applied in a close case. However close the case, the court is under obligation to decide it, and to decide it "according to law."

The work of the lawyer as judge has its aspect as justification because a court not only reaches decisions but must also justify them, that is, explain its decisions as products of reason and authority rather than as acts of arbitrary power. In the appellate courts, this statement of justification takes the form of a written and published "opinion" in which the applicable case law or legislation is cited and discussed and the result reached in the present case accounted for, principally, in most instances, by reference to what the court believes to be the controlling precedents or statutory provision. There are, of course, certain variations from this simple opinion-writing model. Often the opinion of the court will go beyond the task of justifying a present decision and will endeavor to clarify the general law and so provide guidance for the future. Sometimes one or more members of an appellate court will file a "concurring" opinion, agreeing with the result arrived at in a case but arguing that the result should have been reached on different legal grounds, or a "dissenting" opinion, contending that the prevailing majority of the court is wrong both in its reasoning and in its result. And there are times, most notably when a court has arrived at a decision that modifies or flatly overrules some doctrine established by its past decisions, when the justification embodied in the opinion of the court must go beyond the formal legal sources and state the considerations of public policy that have convinced the court that the old rule must be abandoned. Whatever the variation in opinion-style, when a majority of an appellate court have manifested their agreement with an opinion written by one if its judges, it is the "opinion of the court" (not, as the barbarism has it, the mere "majority" opinion.) This opinion of the court, although originally written as a statement of the reasons justifying a particular decision, becomes an authoritative source of law for future controversies.

Law students, in their three years of study, will have occasion to consider case law and legislation from all three of the perspectives just considered. In case method discussions and on law school examinations, students are called on to assume at different times the role of advocate, of counselor, and of judge. The student may be asked, for example, to state the best legal argument for one side or the other in a stated case, and so to function as an advocate. Or the student may be thrust into the role of office counselor by being asked to draft a contract clause for a hypothetical client in terms that will avoid the pitfalls pointed to by a past series of contracts cases. Most often perhaps, and particularly at examination time, the student may find himself or herself in the position of judge, that is, presented with a set of facts and asked to decide the case and state the reasons for the decision. These variations in assigned perspective can be disquieting at times to one who comes to law school with the notion that law is a perfect logical system and its processes mere deductive operations, but most students in time get used to the idea and find it easy enough —even exhilarating on occasion—to shift from perspective to perspective and from role to role. This is as it should be. After all, every law graduate who moves into the practicing profession will at one time or another function both as an advocate and as a counselor, and a few, some day, will be playing the judicial role for real.

SECTION 5. THE CASE METHOD OF STUDYING LAW

ANOTHER NOTE TO THE BEGINNING LAW STUDENT

One or another version of the "case method" (or its fraternal twin, the "problem method") is used in practically all first-year law courses and in most of the courses offered in the second and third law school years. Every experienced law teacher has found that much of the confusion of the first law school semester is traceable to student uncertainty concerning the assumptions and the objectives of case method law instruction. Why should law study proceed by way of the laborious fashioning of legal rules from the raw materials of past judicial decisions rather than by the law faculty's systematic exposition of legal principles? Unless you can see why your law teachers are using the case method, what insights and skills they want you to develop in the course of this slow and sometimes tedious process, you will remain in doubt as to what is expected of you and will miss the point and purpose of class discussion in Legal Method and all other courses. You will find, as generations of beginning law students have found before you, that a clear grasp of the assumptions and aims of case method law study is indispensable to put you on the right track in your study and discussion of law.

You may be one of the many law students who respond to the case method and find its demands and its more or less free-form classroom procedures a stimulating change of pace from the lecturer-to-listeners model that prevails in most undergraduate instruction. Or you may be one of those, also numerous, who do not like the case method at all, or who tire of it in the second or third year of law school as too much of an originally good thing. Either way, the case method is a fact of life for your law school years. Willingly or unwillingly, you will find yourself called on to be an active participant in case method class discussions, and you will want to profit from your participation, and from the participation of your classmates, to the fullest possible extent. Set out immediately following this note is an abridgement of an article which, although written twenty-nine years ago, is still regarded as a classic exposition of the case method's origins and sought educational objectives, and you are urged to give it a close and careful reading.

EDWIN W. PATTERSON, THE CASE METHOD IN AMERICAN LEGAL EDUCATION: ITS ORIGINS AND OBJECTIVES [5]

4 Journal of Legal Education 1 (1951).

* * *

The case method of instruction was introduced into American legal education at the Harvard Law School in the fall of 1870 by Pro-

---

5. Edwin W. Patterson, until his retirement in 1957, was Cardozo Professor of Jurisprudence at Columbia University.

fessor Christopher Columbus Langdell. At that time Langdell used in his class on contracts the advance sheets of his Cases on Contracts which was published in a completed volume in 1871. In its Preface (to be quoted below) Langdell gave his reasons for adopting this startling departure in legal education, and in later years he added very little to his original statement. His followers at Harvard and elsewhere gave other arguments in favor of the Langdell method. Most of these arguments were referred to in Professor Josef Redlich's report to the Carnegie Foundation in 1914. Professor Redlich was brought in to investigate the case method and report on its merits because he was a disinterested outsider, a distinguished Austrian jurist who had acquired considerable understanding of English law. His arguments in favor of the case method were widely read by American law teachers and lawyers, and had a very great influence in ending the controversy over casebook *vs.* textbook as the primary basis of law teaching. After 1914, as I see it, the debates about legal education accepted the case method as an essential device of instruction and proposed to modify or supplement it.

The presuppositions of the case method, as I gather them from the words and deeds of the case method protagonists, were fourfold: Scientific, pedagogical, pragmatic and historical.

1. *Scientific.* The case method is a "scientific" method of teaching law. When Langdell became a member of the Harvard law faculty in 1869, on the invitation of President Charles W. Eliot, American law schools had been for nearly a century conducted as practitioner-training schools, that is, they sought chiefly to do for law students, more efficiently and thoroughly, what the practitioner did for the training of his law-clerk apprentices. This historical development throws light on what Langdell meant when he said in 1886:

> First, that law is a science; secondly, that all the available materials of that science are contained in printed books. If law be not a science, a university will best consult its own dignity in declining to teach it. If it be not a science, it is a species of handicraft, and may best be learned by serving an apprenticeship to one who practices it.

At about the same time when the case method was introduced, Eliot was "reforming" the Harvard College curriculum by introducing laboratory work in the natural sciences. This contemporary development seems to have influenced Langdell's argument that the law, to be worthy of inclusion in a university curriculum, must be taught and studied as a "science." Nearly all of the later protagonists of the case method argued that it was a "scientific" method.

What did they mean by "scientific"? Most of them invoked analogies from the natural sciences, though they did not consistently use the same analogies. Thus Langdell in 1886 said the law library was the proper workshop of both professors and students:

> * * * it is to us all that the laboratories of the university are to the chemists and physicists, the museum of natural history to the zoologists, the botanical garden to the botanists.

Keener, who introduced the case method at Columbia, regarded the case method as scientific in this sense:

> Under this system the student is taught to look upon law as a science consisting of a body of principles to be found in the adjudged cases, the cases being to him what the specimen is to the mineralogist.

Further on he quoted A. V. Dicey as saying that "judicial decisions are legal experiments." Wambaugh in 1906 regarded the case method as "an extremely early attempt to apply the inductive method of the laboratory to matters foreign to the natural sciences." One finds allusions only to the natural sciences, not to the budding "social sciences" nor "cultural sciences," and never to philosophy.

How seriously should one take this argument that the case method is "scientific" in the sense of natural science? In the first place, the difference between experimental sciences, such as physics and chemistry, and those which are not experimental (except in so far as they depend on physics and chemistry) was not observed. A judicial decision is not a controlled experiment of the kind that one can make in physics or chemistry, because one cannot repeat the judicial "experiment" with the same or varying conditions. At best one can say that reported cases are the reports of "experiments" made by others. Yet reports of other experiments are obtained by the scientific student in the library rather than in the laboratory. Secondly, the analogy of mineralogy or geology seems closer; yet even there the specimen is not found, in its natural surroundings, with a label or a memorandum stating its significance. The reported cases used in casebooks have, or at least had in the early books, opinions of courts which explained their significance. As Professor Hans Kelsen has pointed out, a basic difference between law and the natural sciences is that the "data" of positive law, the acts of officials, ordinarily carry with them a statement of their significance. Keener seems to have been aware of this when he said, in 1894, that the student in geology would not study a mineral specimen alone, without a "memoir" of one who had developed a theory about it, and that the case is, to the law student, "both a laboratory and a library," that is, both a specimen of litigated facts and an opinion providing a theoretical explanation of it. This is a better analogy. Yet in none of these discussions was it recognized that a rule or principle of law is primarily normative or prescriptive in meaning, whereas scientific propositions are either true or false upon the basis of empirical observations. The tendency to regard legal propositions as descriptive continues to be manifested.

The argument that the case method is "scientific" must, then, be taken as chiefly rhetorical. The word "science" was a potent and persuasive word in the late nineteenth century, and it still is. The core of truth behind the rhetoric is that, as it was said many times by the protagonists of the case method, in studying cases the student is going to the "original sources" of the law, as opposed to studying the secondary sources, the textbooks. The students in a case-method course are learning to construct their own textbooks. In a legal system, such as that of England and the United States, which gives no independent authoritative status to text writers as legal experts, legal treatises are "secondary" sources, and the law student learns how generalizations are derived from cases in a way loosely analogous to that in which the chemistry student, for instance, learns how generalizations are constructed from experiments.

* * *

2. *Pedagogical.* The chief pedagogical presupposition of the case method was that students learn better when they participate in the teaching process through problem-solving than when they are merely passive recipients of the teacher's solutions. When Charles W. Eliot in his declining years was called upon to discuss the introduction of the case method by Langdell, he said nothing about the natural science analogy and characterized Langdell's innovation as the application in the law school of some of the teaching methods invented by Froebel, Montessori, Pestalozzi, and others for children and mental defectives. However unflattering this comparison may be to the able and alert students who come, and then came, to our law schools, it states a thesis which recurs again and again in the early arguments for the case method. Keener said: "We understand most thoroughly and remember longest that which we have acquired by labor on our own part." Gray gave as one of the reasons for the superiority of the case method that the exact analysis and statement of a case and of its bearing upon the law as previously laid down was a task worthy of the faculties of the cleverest man; and he added that the case method "counteracts the laziness of the prior education of the student," a statement with which most law teachers will heartily agree. Oliver Wendell Holmes, Jr., who had a brief experience in teaching by the case method at Harvard shortly before he was appointed to the Supreme Judicial Court of Massachusetts, speaking of the case method in 1886, said:

> It seems to me that nearly all the education which men can get from others is moral, not intellectual. * * * The mark of a master is that facts, which before lay scattered in an inorganic mass, when he shoots through them the magnetic current of his thought, leap into an organic order and

live and bear fruit. But you cannot make a master by teaching. He makes himself [one] by aid of his natural gifts.

Under the case method, said Mr. (now Dean) Young B. Smith in 1913, the student studies the things to be defined, rather than ready-made definitions, and when he understands those things, he does not need any definitions. The case method was designed to produce independent and creative thinking.

Several conclusions were drawn from this pedagogical principle. First, the student's participation in the class discussion is an essential feature of the case method. Secondly, the cases studied were not to be used merely as "illustrative" cases, that is, merely as examples of the application of definitions and principles laid down by the teacher, but as original sources from which the student was to derive his own generalizations. The "illustrative" casebook was always a heresy to the orthodox assumptions of the case method. Thirdly, the casebook should, according to Keener and most protagonists of the case method, contain "bad" cases as well as "good" ones, in order that the student might be stirred to independent thinking. While Langdell did not state either of these conclusions in his initial explanation of the case method, his casebook on contracts was consistent with them. Fourthly, it was the conclusion of many case-method teachers that the teacher should merely put questions and hypothetical cases to the student, but should not give him a summary of the legal rules or principles to be derived from the cases and the class discussion. On this conclusion there was not complete agreement. * * *

Two other pedagogical aspects of the case method were also emphasized: (1) The reported cases have a dramatic interest for the student, they are far more exciting than the dry generalizations of textbook or lecture. (2) The case method trains students to solve practical problems, to do the work that they will later have to do as practicing lawyers. The latter argument, peculiar to teaching law, merits a separate discussion.

3. *Pragmatic.* The argument that the case method trains law students to make judgments on concrete facts in a way similar to that of the practicing lawyer was frequently made by the early defenders of the case method. Thus J. C. Gray said: "To extract law from fact is *the* thing that a lawyer has to do all his life. * * *" Keener, quoting A. V. Dicey, urged that the student, by the study of cases, "sees what is the true meaning of legal doctrines as applied to facts"; he "becomes familiar with the tone of thought, the attitude of mind which prevails in our courts." That is, by the study of cases the student learns about the judicial process. Holmes stated a slightly different pragmatic aspect of the case method when he said:

> And is not a principle more exactly and intimately grasped as the unexpressed major premise of the half-dozen

examples which mark its extent and its limits than it can be in any abstract form of words?

While Langdell and Keener thought that cases should be used to extract principles of law, which were relatively few, Holmes emphasized reasoning by analogy without an explicit major premise.

The pragmatic argument for the case method was made in response to the criticisms of practicing lawyers that it was "academic" and "impractical." Having had the good fortune to begin the practice of law in an office where one partner was a Harvard case-method man and the other was trained by the textbook and lecture method, I can testify that the former was much better at dealing with the legal problems of a law office (especially counseling) than the latter. Probably this was generally true. However, the pragmatic assumption was somewhat inconsistent with the lofty assumption that law was a "science," with the ideal of the "university law school." The conflict between these two conceptions of legal education has continued down to the present time. * * *

4. *Historical.* Running like a *leitmotif* through many of the early discussions of the case method was the argument that by the study of cases the student can best grasp the historical development of the law. Langdell stated the historical assumption thus:

> Each of these doctrines [of the law] has arrived at its present state by slow degrees; in other words, it is a growth, extending in many cases through centuries. This growth is to be traced in the main through a series of cases; and much the shortest and best, if not the only way of mastering the doctrine effectually is by studying the cases in which it is embodied. But the cases which are useful and necessary for this purpose at the present day bear an exceedingly small proportion to all that have been reported. The vast majority are useless and worse than useless for any purpose of systematic study.

The last sentence of this quotation seems hard to reconcile with the view that law is a science of principles extracted from its data, the reported cases; for surely no scientist would throw away geological specimens merely because they did not fit into his system. Would he not try to interpret or modify his system so as to include them?
* * *

J. C. Gray, a great teacher of real property and an able jurisprudent, stated the historical argument somewhat more plausibly when he contended that the casebook "accustoms the student to consider the law not merely as a series of propositions * * * having only a logical interdependence, but as a living thing, with a continuous history, sloughing off the old, taking on the new." Holmes, in his oration at the quarter-millenial celebration of Harvard University in

1886, urged that a principle of law, "expressed or unexpressed," is better known "when you have studied its embryology and the lines of its growth than when you merely see it lying dead before you on a printed page"; and he added that the Harvard teachers were "entirely right" in believing that if the students mastered the common law and equity systems they would have "no trouble with the improvements of the last half century." Gray and Holmes invoked the conception of legal history as an organic evolution.

The historical approach dominated the making of casebooks for more than a generation after Langdell's innovation. The story is told that Langdell began his course on mortgages with the study of the rights of the mortgagor and mortgagee at common law, and when the Christmas vacation came he had not yet revealed to the students that the mortgagor had acquired that modern innovation, an equity of redemption. The historical approach came to its best fruition in the casebooks of James Barr Ames, which are still valuable source books for the historical development of English case law. In the United States, as earlier in Germany, the influence of the historical school led to much careful and patient labor in tracing each river to its rivulet. One who did not have the training and ability to carry on this type of investigation could scarcely be regarded as a legal scholar.

The historical presupposition no longer dominates the case method as it once did. What values does it still have for American legal education? First, in a sense every casebook is at least a source book of "recent legal history," even one that is "kept up to date" with pocket supplements. Secondly, in our uncodified system of law, there is no authoritative univocal body of definitions or statements of the meaning of basic legal concepts, and many of them can be understood best by reference to their history. * * * Thirdly, it often happens that the reasons for the adoption of a legal rule or principle are more thoroughly explored in some old crucial case than they have been in later cases, which merely accepted the rule or principle as established. Such cases may well be included in a casebook intended to show the reasons for legal rules and concepts.

* * *

II

Essential Devices of the Case Method

While the case method of instruction has varied considerably in different courses, under different teachers and in different law schools, three devices have generally been deemed essential: (1) The casebook. (2) The participation of students in the class discussion. (3) The problem type of examination. Each of these has its variations.

1. *The casebook.* Langdell was driven to the preparation of his first casebook by the physical impossibility of providing for all the

students in the class ready and convenient access to the original reports in the library. The casebook saves wear and tear on the library, and on the student, too. The casebook still fulfills this minimum function.

But if one asks, what cases shall be included in the casebook, what excisions shall be made from the original report, how shall they be arranged, and what other material shall be included with them?—one finds considerable diversity in theory and in practice.

The casebook ordinarily includes some English cases and selections from the case law of different American states. The underlying assumption was that the student was to learn the common law (or equity) as a systematic, rational body of doctrine rather than the law currently prevailing in any particular jurisdiction. Langdell implied this when he said:

> It seemed to me * * * to be possible to take such a branch of the law as Contracts, for example, and, without exceeding comparatively moderate limits, to select, classify, and arrange all the cases which had contributed in any important degree to the growth, development or establishment of any of its essential doctrines; and that such a work could not fail to be of material service to all who desire to study that branch of law systematically and in its original sources.

The assumption that there were "essential doctrines" of the law of contracts which were common to all Anglo-American jurisdictions was justified by the historic continuity of the law of all of those jurisdictions with English law and by the practice of American courts of citing and relying upon judicial precedents from England and from other states as persuasive authorities, in the absence of contrary local precedents. The assumption was further justified by the cultural similarities of the peoples of those various jurisdictions. Moreover, the assumption, even if we deem it partly fictitious, was justified by its consequences. It tended to make the study of law more a process of analysis and deduction than a precise study of authority. * * * The widespread use of "national" casebooks and the migratory habits of American law students have tended in some measure to counteract the isolated provincialism of forty-nine separate jurisdictions and thus to bring about the uniformity which the casebook presupposed.

* * *

* * * Langdell sought to include only influential cases, those which had "contributed" to essential doctrines. More recently casebook makers have chosen cases which now serve to exemplify problematic situations, or which have dramatic interest, even though they did not initiate nor establish a novel doctrine. Moreover, a choice must often be made by the casebook editor between one case which has interesting and problematic facts with a poorly written opinion, and another which has obscure or atypical facts with a well-written

opinion. The former may be preferred not only on pedagogical grounds but also because a systematic development may call for a case presenting a certain type of factual situation. Thus the present trend in casebook making, as I see it, minimizes the importance of historical development and of "influential" cases as well as the assumption that the student is to study law in the "original sources," and emphasizes the pedagogical, pragmatic and rational aspects of law teaching. If only influential cases are to be included it is hard to see how any case less than twenty-five years old could qualify as having established its influence, nor how any case from a lower or intermediate appellate court could be chosen. Yet very recent cases often give a sense of immediacy to the problem involved, and lower court cases are often necessary to round out a line of legal synthesis.
* * *

2. *The class discussion.* Student participation in the class discussion is still, I believe, an essential feature of the case method, and one which ought to be preserved at the sacrifice of some other values, such as additional information or a more orderly and explicit presentation of the teacher's ideas about the subject matter. The "Socratic dialogue" was the early ideal of class discussion. A student was asked to summarize orally a case in the book, the teacher asked him questions about it or put to him a hypothetical case; the student was called upon to defend his decision in relation to the case in the book or other cases. The hypothetical case, skillfully chosen by the teacher, thus became one of the chief instruments for pulling out the significance of the main case and for extending or limiting its doctrine or principle. The teacher, like Socrates, should ask more questions than either he or the student can answer. This process can be intellectually stimulating to the entire class and can give the students clues to what they should investigate further. The creation of doubt followed by its resolution is one of the important steps in the process of learning. Yet the Socratic method calls for great skill on the part of the teacher and considerable quick-wittedness on the part of the student. When protracted to the point where interest lags, it becomes tiresome and wasteful of time. * * *

One corollary of the basic principles of the case method was that the teacher ought never to lecture, or to summarize the conclusions to be derived from the cases and the class discussion. The student was supposed to work out the conclusions from the questions of the teacher. I doubt if it is strictly applied by most law teachers today. It does not seem to be necessary to the attainment of the aims of the case method. One can lead students to "think for themselves" by bringing out the arguments for and against a particular legal doctrine, and yet give them some conclusions as to which arguments seem preferable to the teacher, and which ones are more likely to prevail with the courts. The teacher should at least help the student acquire a consistent terminology, to replace the inconsistent terminologies used by courts in different cases. Moreover, after the student's doubts have been raised, he should eventually have the benefit of the teacher's mature conclusions.

Another variation in class discussion is the student's "statement of the case." The orthodox tradition is that the student called upon is asked to summarize the facts, legal issues, rulings or orders of the court, and the reasons given in the opinion, as a preliminary to further discussion. I find this still a useful technique for beginning students. I can often detect in the student's omission of some material fact that he has not correctly understood the legal issue in the reported case. A perception of how the legal issue was raised, procedurally, is often necessary in order to understand the difference between holding and dictum. Yet too much time can easily be spent on these details, and once the routine analysis is learned, many students become bored with the formal statement of cases. Hence the tendency is to dispense with it in the third year, or even in the second year. The chief difficulty here is to make the student read the cases carefully and be *prepared* to state them, without going through that formality. Unless he is so prepared, he is likely to have only a fumbling notion of the significance of the case. The casebook is a rather wasteful method of merely imparting the information contained in the opinion. Its value depends upon the student's doing some hard work on his own before he comes to the class.

The use of the case method in large classes is another paradox of legal education. The Socratic discourse of the case method would seem to require a small group of hearers and questioners. To place a legal Socrates in a room with 200 or even 250 questioners and victims seems like a travesty on Socratic dialogue. Yet the victim of the moment suffers vicariously for the others, who can perceive his errors and confusions better than he can. Besides, the ordeal of hypothetical questioning by a skillful teacher is good preparation for similar ordeals in the courtroom.

Three features of a good casebook can contribute to the interest and the orderliness of class discussion. One is the inclusion of cases whose facts provide some dramatic interest. Another is the choice and arrangement of cases so as to raise the question of conflicts between decisions. Economy of time may require that some topics be relegated to a note in order to permit the presentation of a series of divergent or conflicting cases on others. Conflict sharpens the edge of casuistry. A third feature is the editorial matter which enables the student to discover in advance of the class discussion the general significance of the case, and thus saves some of the victim's impromptu groping for answers to hypothetical questions.

3. *The examination.* The case method course calls for a hypothetical-case type of examination. The student has to give not only the decisions of a limited number of controversies, but also the rea-

sons for his decision, in terms of analysis of the facts and statements of legal propositions. Beyond this the better student may give more basic reasons of social ethics or political principle, or may criticize the present legal rules because of the absence of such reasons. However, the examination period is not a very good time to do a careful job of constructive legal criticism. The best skill required for the hypothetical-case-essay examination is the ability to analyze the facts and to see all of the "points" or legal issues involved. The examinations with which I am familiar accomplish this by making the statements of facts rather complicated, so that a half hour per question is allowed for answering. In grading this type of question the mere decision (e. g., for the plaintiff) is usually unimportant and the grade depends on the quality of the essay.

Although the hypothetical-case-essay examination was much superior to the older type which called for definitions or explanations of legal terms, the grading of it called for a considerable latitude of discretion (since the answers could and did properly vary in analysis) and required the judgment of the man in charge of the course. In most, if not all, law schools it is a settled tradition that examination grading is not to be delegated to assistants. In large classes the delay in grading not only leaves the students in suspense but also creates some risks that the professor's standard of grading may change between the first papers he reads and the last. These and other arguments led to the introduction of the objective-type of examination in larger classes—75 or more. As far as I know this type of examination was first used, in law classes at Columbia in 1923. When carefully prepared and expertly tested such an examination can test most of the qualities or skills that the case method is intended to develop; that is, the analysis of a hypothetical case and the recognition of accurate or inaccurate use of terms. It measures diligence in preparation (a virtue not to be overlooked) more thoroughly because of the much larger number of questions than on the essay examination, and the corresponding lessening of the influence of Lady Luck.

However, one of the skills that it does not test is the ability to construct a reasoned argument about a set of facts. Hence, a part of the final examination should always be of the essay type. Without digressing further, one should mention that the true-false type of examination is not as well adapted to call for subtle discriminations as is the multiple-choice variety. At any rate, one of the incidental advantages of the case method is that it calls for the skill and judgment of the professor in charge of the course both in the preparation and in the grading of the final examination.

* * *

The Future?

In theory, at least three of the four basic presuppositions of the case-method founders are still sound, and even the fourth (the "scientific" one) provides a suggestive analogy. These major objectives should not be overlooked in any revision of teaching methods. In practice the case method has never stood still; it was not the same with Ames as with Langdell, and today, with all due admiration for these men, it need not be the same as either. It will be squeezed more and more by the pressure for kinds of training (e. g., accounting, legislative drafting, collective-bargaining negotiation) which law students need because of the increasing demands upon the versatility of lawyers. That law-trained men are called upon to do these peripheral jobs is a tribute to their basic training in "legal reasoning" by the case method.

* * *

NOTE

Langdell, as we have just seen, thought of legal education as the communication to students of scientific knowledge of essential legal principles. The innovations of the case method approach—the study of casebooks and the use of a Socratic method in classroom discussions—were both thought of by Langdell and his associates as necessary to the "scientific" examination of law's presumably basic doctrines and concepts.

Few case method law teachers of today would attempt to justify the method on Langdell's grounds. The present-day defense of the case method, against the attacks mounted from time to time against it, is a profession-related justification, that the case method forces the law student to use legal materials in a manner resembling as closely as manageable the use which practicing lawyers make of the same sources in advocacy and counseling, and judges in decision-making. The great intellectual virtue now claimed for the case method is that it is the study and teaching procedure best suited for development of the "legal mind"—respect for facts, abilities at case analysis and synthesis, and habitual distrust of the undocumented assertion and the easy generalization.

Not everyone is persuaded that the case method actually accomplishes its sought intellectual objectives. By those who dislike it, it is criticized variously as unduly time-consuming, as intimidating and oppressive to students (e. g., The Paper Chase), and as putting too much emphasis on precision of analysis and not enough on sensitizing law students to urgent social needs. A movement has been under way for several years to augment the "clinical" ingredient in legal education, that is, to bring law students into touch with living clients (e. g., in legal aid offices) and with court proceedings that are actually going on. It may be, in the law school of the future, that the effort and time now given to case method instruction will be appreciably reduced and correspondingly greater use made of lectures, seminars, assigned essays, clinical work and other educational approaches. It is most unlikely, however, that such educational innovations will displace the case method as the norm of law school instruction, particularly in the first and second years. The case method, in one or another form or version, is still the prevailing and distinctive method by which law is studied and taught in the law schools of the United States, and it seems destined to occupy that position for a long time.

Chapter II

CASE LAW: THE ANALYSIS AND SYNTHESIS OF JUDICIAL DECISIONS

SECTION 1. THE STATE AND FEDERAL COURTS

A. THE STATE COURT SYSTEMS

Each of the fifty states of the United States has its own system of courts. Court structures and court nomenclature differ greatly from state to state, but all the state court systems exhibit what may be called a hierarchical structure, that is, a pattern of organization in which the decisions of "lower" courts may be taken for review to a higher ranking tribunal. 90% or more of the state "cases" a law student reads in his casebooks are appellate decisions, but all these appellate cases will have passed through a "trial" stage and perhaps an intermediate appellate stage before reaching the state's "court of last resort."

The following sketch of the tiers in a typical state court hierarchy is unavoidably very much generalized—for example, some states with relatively small populations do not have an intermediate appellate court—but should be sufficient for present purposes. A first year law student will find it interesting and worthwhile to familiarize himself with the pattern of court organization that exists in the state in which he expects to practice and with the names by which the various courts in his state are known.

Trial Courts of "Inferior" Jurisdiction

Every state has its "inferior" or "petty" trial courts with jurisdiction limited to civil suits involving relatively small amounts of money and to minor violations of the criminal law. In many, perhaps most, rural areas, these courts still go by the ancient name, Justice of the Peace (or "J.P.") Courts; in the cities, they are more often called Municipal Courts or City Courts. The civil jurisdiction of an "inferior" or "petty" trial court is usually defined in terms of the amount of money in dispute; thus the jurisdiction of the Justice of the Peace Court may be limited to claims not exceeding $100, while a metropolitan Municipal Court may be empowered to decide claims up to $1,000. Similarly, the jurisdiction of an "inferior" criminal court is likely to be defined in terms of the maximum jail sentence, commonly six months, or maximum fine that may be imposed if the defendant is found guilty of the particular offense charged.

"Inferior" and "petty" are unfortunate terms for these first-tier trial courts, because these are the tribunals in which most of the controversies that occur in a community are heard and, at least provisionally, decided. Disputes involving a $100 grocery bill or a $350 conditional sales contract or the possible sentence of an accused person to a 60-day jail term may be triable only in a court of "inferior" jurisdiction, but they are not "petty" to the human beings caught up in them. The courts of inferior jurisdiction may be at the bottom of the judicial totem pole, but they are the courts closest to the people. It is as important to society that justice be administered fairly and with dignity in the "inferior" or "petty" courts as that justice be done in the highest and most prestigous of judicial tribunals. But our legal order is only beginning to recognize this social fact.

Trial Courts of General Jurisdiction

If a civil claim or criminal prosecution involves an amount of money, or a potential criminal sentence, beyond the jurisdiction of an "inferior" trial court, it must be filed and heard in what lawyers call a "trial court of general jurisdiction," that is, a court empowered to try all kinds of cases, without monetary or subject matter limitation. Practically all the appellate cases in law school casebooks will have been tried originally (or *re*-tried, on appeal by the losing party, after earlier judgment in an "inferior" court) in a trial court of general jurisdiction.

Every state has a set of trial courts of general jurisdiction, but there are differences in nomenclature from state to state. In some states, the trial court of general jurisdiction is known as the Superior Court ("superior," presumably, to the "petty" courts described above), in other states as the District Court or Circuit Court, names reflecting the typical division of the states into judicial districts or circuits. A few states retain old common law names, e. g., Court of Common Pleas. New York, to the great confusion of out-of-state lawyers and frequent bewilderment of its own electorate, calls its trial court of general jurisdiction the Supreme Court, with the incidental consequence that New York trial judges of general jurisdiction are "justices," whereas the members of the State's distinguished court of last resort are mere "judges."

In every state, trial courts of general jurisdiction are distributed geographically throughout the state, so that litigants can have access to them without journeying to the state capital. Thus each state is divided into a number of judicial districts or circuits and a court established for each district or circuit, with at least one district or circuit judge for each of these geographical units. In metropolitan districts and other areas of large population, there will be many judges for each district; the Superior Court of Los Angeles, for example, has more than one hundred judges. Although their principal function is the trial and initial (final, if unappealed) determination of important civil and criminal controversies, state trial courts of general jurisdiction typically act also as appellate tribunals to decide appeals from the judgments of "inferior" trial courts and to review the actions of certain state administrative agencies, such as workmen's compensation boards, licensing authorities, and public utility commissions.

A complete inventory of any state's trial courts will have to take account, also, of the specialized trial courts that are found in almost every state: Family Courts, Probate Courts, and the like. Some states have separate courts, with specially appointed or elected judges, for probate, divorce or criminal matters. In other states, only the one multi-judge trial court of general jurisdiction exists in each district but specialization is achieved by assigning one or more judges of that court to a particular task (e. g., the Family Court) at the beginning of each judicial term. As recently as fifty years ago, a number of states still had a set of courts for "common law" actions and another set for "equity" cases,[1] but procedural reforms, specifically the so-called "merger of law and equity," have brought about a virtual disappearance of this terminological survival of days past.

Appellate Courts

Every state has its "court of last resort," the appellate court at the top of the judicial hierarchy and the one which determines with finality (subject to occasional review on "federal questions" by the Supreme Court of the United States) what the particular state's law is and should be. In most states, this highest court in the hierarchy is called the Supreme Court of the state, but other names are in use here and there: Supreme Judicial Court, Supreme Court of Appeals and, as in New York, Court of Appeals. "Whatever the name," writes a well known Civil Procedure scholar, "its function is the same: to review the action of the lower judicial tribunals of the state. This is the exercise of appellate jurisdiction. The scope of judicial review which the court exercises in such cases is relatively narrow; it does not retry the case on the merits, and it does not substitute its ideas of justice for those of the trial court; what it does is to review the record of the proceedings to determine whether or not the lower court committed error in its procedure or in applying the substantive law to the facts of the case." Green, "The Business of the Trial Courts," in Jones (ed.), The Courts, the Public and the Law Explosion 7, 16 (1965).

---

1. In the vocabulary of Anglo-American law, certain claims and certain remedies (e. g., the injunction) are characterized, even today, as "equitable" in character. This uniquely Anglo-American distinction between "common law" and "equity" has its historical origins in the division of jurisdiction that once existed in England between the three royal courts of "common law" (King's Bench, Common Pleas, and Court of Exchequer) and the Court of Chancery, originally the judicial arm of the King's Lord Chancellor. The emergence of "equity", the case-law of the Court of Chancery, is one of the great chapters in English (and so American) legal history.

The contemporary idea that one's "day in court" includes the right to appellate review of every adverse trial court judgment is a quite recent development. Appeal was a "matter of grace," not a "matter of right," at English common law and even during the first century or so of American legal history. Appeals were allowed only by leave of the trial court or at the discretion of the appellate court, and appeals in civil and criminal cases were, accordingly, far less common than they are today. This older notion that litigants have no "right" to more than a day in a *trial* court strikes present-day lawyers as grudging and ungenerous. Under existing statutes in every state, the party who loses at the trial court stage of a litigated controversy has a right to have the trial court judgment reviewed at least once by a court other than the one that originally entered it. One inevitable result of this recognition of appeal as a matter of right was, of course, a vast increase in appellate litigation which, particularly in the more populous states, soon led to hopeless congestion of the dockets of the state courts of last resort. Some states have attempted, with varying degrees of success, to meet this problem by dividing the court of last resort into coordinate parts or divisions, with each division empowered to decide appeals that formerly would have been heard and decided by the full court, and with occasional hearings of the full court (*en banc*) to iron out the inconsistencies in theory and result which inevitably attend the splitting of a court into two or more coordinate panels.

In other states, and this has been the prevailing tendency in state court reorganization since World War II, the decision has been to create an *intermediate appellate court*, empowered to strain out and finally dispose of the bulk of appellate litigation—cases, for example, that raise no new or difficult issue of law—so that the court of last resort can give its full attention to novel and socially important controversies. There are again great variations from state to state with respect to the jurisdiction of the intermediate appellate courts, but their jurisdiction is typically broad and includes all appeals except those in a few specified classes of important cases, e. g., criminal cases where the death penalty has been imposed or cases involving the constitutionality of a statute. These excepted cases are the only ones in which a litigant who has lost in the trial court can bypass the intermediate appellate court and go directly to the state's court of last resort. In some of the states which have intermediate appellate courts, appeals (or some appeals) go first to the intermediate appellate court with further appeal possible to the court of last resort, but the prevailing contemporary policy is to give the court of last resort very wide discretion over the granting or denial of applications for this second appellate review. If appeals from a state's intermediate appellate court to its court of last resort were granted too freely, the intermediate appellate court would not be performing the vital "screening out" function for which it was created. As the volume of litigation continues to grow in almost every state, the intermediate appellate courts become increasingly the final tribunal for authoritative disposition of far more cases than will ever reach the state's court of last resort.

B. THE FEDERAL COURTS

There was no regular federal judiciary under the Articles of Confederation. In the 22nd Federalist, Alexander Hamilton described this "want of a judiciary power" as "a circumstance which crowns the defects of the confederation," for, he continued, "Laws are a dead letter without courts to expound them and define their true meaning and operation."

Hamilton's views on this issue are an accurate report of the consensus arrived at, with surprisingly little debate or discussion, when the delegates to the Constitutional Convention had assembled in Philadelphia in May, 1785. Max Farrand, author of the classic study of the Convention, concluded simply: "That there should be a national judiciary was readily accepted by all." As the Convention proceeded, there were lively disagreements over methods for the selection of federal judges and over the categories of cases to which the federal judicial power was to extend, but the necessity of a federal judiciary—at least of a national Supreme Court as ultimate arbiter of foreseen disputes between states or between a state and the new national government—was universally recognized.

Article III of the Constitution reflects this consensus:

> "Article III. Section 1. The judicial Power of the United States shall be vested in one supreme Court and in such inferior Courts as the Congress may from time to time ordain and establish."

Note that the Supreme Court is the only federal court directly created by the Constitution itself. The other courts in the federal judicial system are created by Acts of Congress enacted pursuant to Article III. The landmark statute in the evolution of the federal judicial system was passed by the first Congress as one of its early orders of business and became law on September 24, 1789. This statute, entitled "An Act to establish the Judicial Courts of the United States," embodied the first Congress's decision on the issue that the Constitution itself had not resolved: whether there should be federal *trial* courts as well as a Supreme Court or whether the interpretation and enforcement of federal law should be left entirely to the existing state trial and appellate courts, subject to review by the Supreme Court of the United States. The organization of the federal judiciary has greatly changed over the years since 1789, but the decision of the first Congress to establish a federal judicial system, of trial as well as appellate courts, set the course for the national judicial future.

The basic federal court system as it now exists is a simple three-tier hierarchy: (1) trial courts of general jurisdiction,[2] known as the *District Courts*; (2) intermediate appellate courts, called the *Courts of Appeals*; and (3) the *Supreme Court*, specifically provided for by Article III of the Constitution and operating as the court of last resort for the federal judicial system and, in matters of federal law, for the state judicial systems as well. There are a few specialized federal courts (e. g., the Court of Claims or the Tax Court), which operate more or less like District Courts in their specialized jurisdiction, but there is no federal trial court of inferior jurisdiction.

The District Courts of the United States

By existing Congressional legislation, the United States is divided into 91 federal judicial districts,[3] each with its District Court. Every state has at least one District Court; about half the states have only one; e. g., the United States District Court for Nevada. There is a District Court for the District of Columbia and one for Puerto Rico.

The more populous states have been divided into two, three or four districts. In New York, for example, there are four United States District Courts, one each for the Southern, the Northern, the Eastern and the Western District. There are now about 500 federal district judges, distributed more or less according to the differing volume of judicial business in the 91 districts. Thus, there are now 27 judges for the Southern District of New York and 17 for the Central District of California, as against 3 for the Western District of Wisconsin and only 1 for the District of Wyoming. Trials in a District Court are normally presided over by a single judge, although there are a few situations, chiefly cases in which injunctions are sought on federal constitutional grounds against the enforcement of state or federal statutes, in which a three-judge court must be convened.

---

2. Scholarly specialists in federal jurisdiction and procedure might take exception to this characterization of the United States District Courts as "trial courts of general jurisdiction," since, as will be explained in a closely following paragraph, there is a special sense in which the jurisdiction of the District Courts is "limited." But there are two related reasons for use of the "trial court of general jurisdiction" characterization in these Legal Method materials: (1) the essential function of the District Courts is more closely analogous to that of the state trial courts of general jurisdiction than to that of any other tier in a state court hierarchy; and (2) the word "limited" is often used, in this context, as synonymous with "inferior" or "petty," which might convey the seriously misleading impression that the United States District Courts occupy a place in the federal judicial system corresponding to that of the state Justice of the Peace or other "petty" courts.

3. Not including the District Court of the Virgin Islands and the District Court of Guam, which for some purposes are treated as District Courts of the United States.

Although they correspond in essential function to the state trial courts of general jurisdiction, there is a sense in which the jurisdiction of the District Courts of the United States is a limited one: they, like other federal courts, cannot entertain cases that fall outside the "judicial power of the United States" as defined in the Constitution. Article III, Section 2 of the Constitution is the controlling text and sets the outer bounds beyond which the federal courts cannot exercise, or be vested by Congress with, jurisdiction. Article III, Section 2 provides, in pertinent part, as follows:

> "The judicial power [of the United States] shall extend to all cases, in law and equity, arising under this Constitution, the laws of the United States, and treaties made, or which shall be made, under their authority;—to all cases affecting ambassadors, other public ministers and consuls;—to all cases of admiralty and maritime jurisdiction;—to controversies to which the United States shall be a party;—to controversies between two or more States;—between a State and citizens of another State;—between citizens of different States,—between citizens of the same State claiming lands under grants of different States, and between a State, or the citizens thereof, and foreign States, citizens or subjects."

Manifestly, then, the jurisdiction of a District Court of the United States must be based either on the *character of the controversy* (for example, that it is a case "arising under this Constitution [or] the laws of the United States") or on the *character of the parties* to the controversy (for example, that it is a controversy "to which the United States shall be a party" or one "between citizens of different States").

Most of the cases which make up the workload of the District Courts are within one or another of three categories: (1) cases to which the United States is a party, which includes both civil cases in which the United States is plaintiff or defendant and all prosecutions for violation of federal criminal statutes; (2) cases involving a "federal question," which means essentially a question involving the interpretation or effect of a provision of the Constitution or of some federal statute or regulation; and (3) cases involving "diversity of citizenship," that is, suits between citizens of different states of the United States. For the purposes of this "diversity" jurisdiction, a corporation is deemed to be a "citizen" both of the state in which it is incorporated and of the state in which it has its principal place of business.

Existing federal legislation imposes a further limitation on District Court jurisdiction in some "federal question" and all "diversity of citizenship" cases: the "matter in controversy must exceed $10,-

000." A case within federal jurisdiction—for example, a controversy between citizens of different states and involving more than $10,000—may, as a matter of "venue," be brought in a district in which either the plaintiff or the defendant resides. If the plaintiff in such a case chooses, as he may, to file his suit not in a federal District Court but in a state trial court, the defendant may in certain circumstances have the case "removed" to the federal court for the same district, where it will then be heard and decided. A case cannot be removed by the defendant, however, if brought in a state court of the state in which the defendant himself resides. The historical origins of "diversity of citizenship" jurisdiction are in a concern of former times that a citizen of one state might not be fairly treated in the courts of the state of his adversary's residence, and even this old concern is inapplicable when the defendant is, so to speak, sued on his own home grounds.

The foregoing sketch of federal jurisdiction can be made more meaningful, the editors believe, by a simple exercise, which we strongly recommend. Whenever you encounter a federal court decision in this Legal Method casebook, ask yourself two (additional) questions: (1) *Why* is this case within federal court jurisdiction; i. e., is it a "diversity of citizenship" case, a "federal question" case, an "admiralty" case, or what? and (2) *How* did this case actually get into the federal courts; i. e., was it originally filed there or, if not, what was the basis for its removal from the state to the federal court? Faithful performance of this little exercise will provide useful background and perspective when the Legal Method course gets to Erie Railroad Co. v. Tompkins and the other cases on the authority of state court precedents in the federal courts.

Procedure in the District Courts is uniform throughout the United States and takes no account of the differences in court procedures that exist from state to state. This has always been true in "equity" and admiralty cases, but was not true in former times as concerns what were, historically, "actions at common law," in which a federal trial court was obliged to "conform as near as may be" to the procedures of the state courts of the state in which the federal court was situated. In 1934, however, Congress empowered the Supreme Court to prescribe uniform Rules of Civil Procedure applicable both to "actions at law" and "cases in equity" in District Courts throughout the country. The new uniform rules, commonly referred to as the "Federal Rules" were promulgated by the Supreme Court and have been in effect since September 1, 1938.

Courts of Appeals of the United States

Existing federal legislation further divides the United States into eleven judicial *circuits*,[4] each with its own Court of Appeals.[5] Appeals lie as a matter of right to each Court of Appeals from the District Courts located within the geographical area comprised by its circuit. Since the circuits are plotted, or were originally plotted, to correspond to differences in the volume of federal litigation, the circuits vary greatly in area from the Court of Appeals for the District of Columbia, the smallest, to the vast Ninth Circuit, which extends over virtually the entire Far West and includes Alaska and Hawaii as well. The number of circuit judges for each Court of Appeals varies similarly—and, in fact, corresponds considerably more closely than existing circuit boundaries do to contemporary Court of Appeals workloads. Thus there are presently 26 circuit judges for the heavily burdened Fifth Circuit, 23 for the vast Ninth Circuit, and only 4 for the First Circuit.

Federal appeals in both civil and criminal cases are heard by panels of three judges, although, on very rare occasions, the full complement of circuit judges may sit to hear and decide a case of particular difficulty or importance. Normally the three judges who participate in a federal appeal are all circuit judges, but Congressional legislation authorizes the summoning of district judges to sit temporarily in the Courts of Appeals when pressure of appellate business requires. In recent years, as the volume of federal appellate litigation continues to mount, it has become quite common to have federal appeals heard and decided by a Court of Appeals consisting of two circuit judges and one district judge.

---

4. Legislation has recently been proposed to create another circuit. The District of Columbia counts as one of these eleven federal judicial circuits. A Court of Appeals is provided for this small area because the Court of Appeals for the District of Columbia has special and heavy adjudicative burdens as the principal tribunal for judicial review of the decisions of the federal regulatory agencies.

5. In older case reports, the student will find the federal intermediate appellate courts referred to as the "*Circuit* Courts of Appeals." The accurate usage now is simply "Courts of Appeals"; e. g., United States Court of Appeals, Second Circuit.

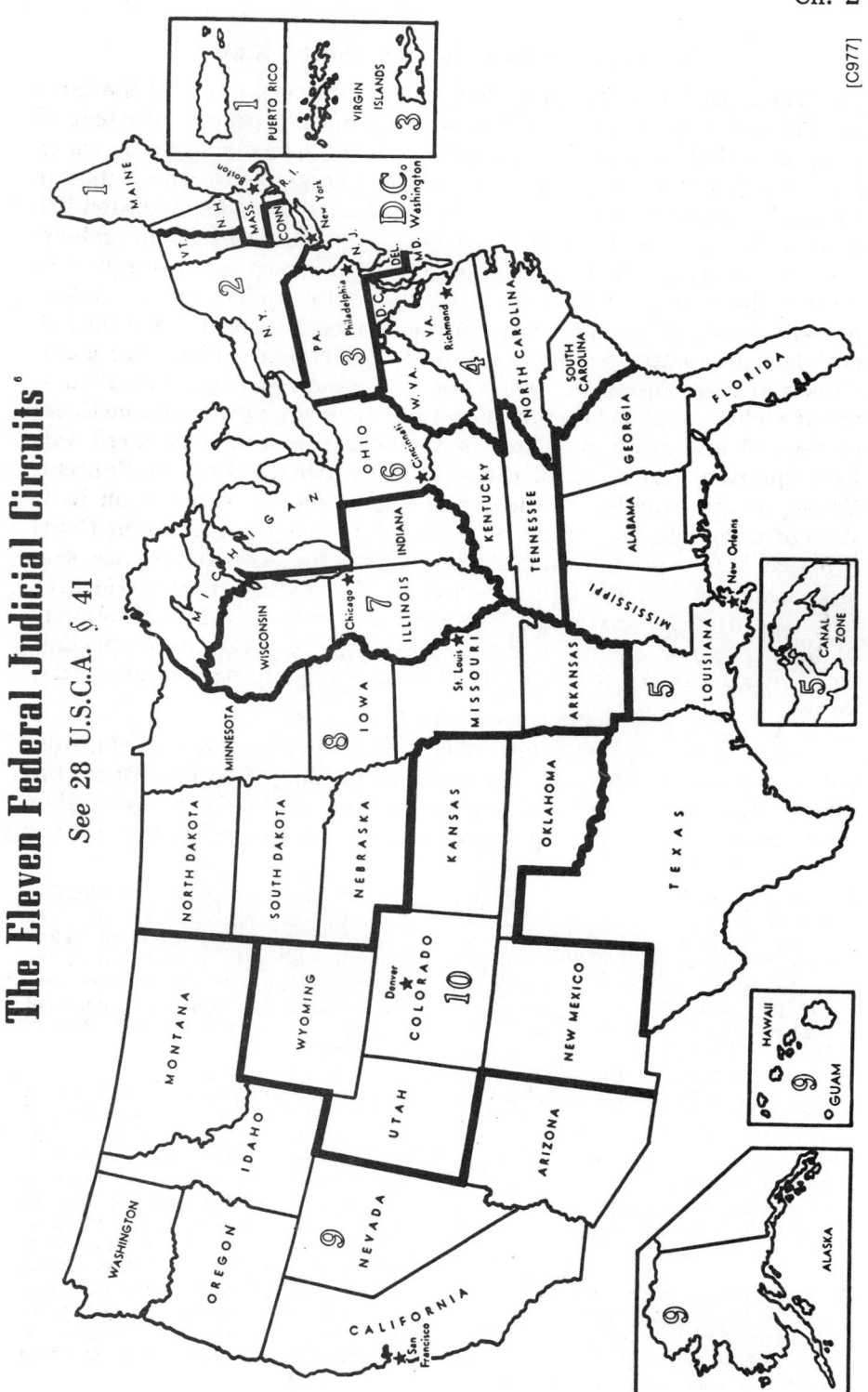

The Eleven Federal Judicial Circuits
See 28 U.S.C.A. § 41

6. See Note 6 on Page 47.

The Supreme Court of the United States

The most important point to grasp and remember about the functioning of the Supreme Court as the court of last resort of the federal system is that only a small fraction of the controversies in which Supreme Court review is sought is ever accepted by the Supreme Court for hearing and decision "on the merits." A disappointed litigant cannot secure Supreme Court review merely by contending, however persuasively, that the decision handed down against him was wrong; he must first persuade the Supreme Court that the issues presented by his case are important enough, as issues of general federal law, to justify Supreme Court consideration. There are a few classes of cases in which appeal lies to the Supreme Court as a "matter of right,"[7] but in all other situations review by the Supreme Court of federal and state appellate court judgments can be secured only by a "petition for a writ of certiorari,"[8] which petition the Supreme Court, in the exercise of the broad discretion conferred upon it by Acts of Congress, may grant or deny. As a matter of Supreme Court practice, if four or more of the nine justices vote to take the case, that is, to hear and decide it on its merits, the Court will "grant certiorari." If the petition for certiorari is denied, as the overwhelming majority of them are, the judgment of the Court of Appeals or state appellate court stands as the authoritative last word in the particular controversy.

It is to be kept in mind, then, that Supreme Court denial of a petition for certiorari does not necessarily imply Supreme Court approval of the theory or result reached by the Court of Appeals or other court from which the review was sought. Denial of certiorari may

---

6. As may not be entirely clear on this map, the District of Columbia constitutes an eleventh, and separate, federal judicial circuit. The District of Columbia is federally administered, and its court system consists of (1) trial courts of specialized and of "inferior" jurisdiction; (2) a United States District Court, over which Judge Sirica has recently and prominently presided; and (3) a Court of Appeals, which ranks equally with the other ten United States Courts of Appeals and has traditionally included among its members some of the country's most distinguished appellate judges.

7. One example, very important in recent years, is that appeal lies to the Supreme Court in any case in which the highest court of a state has upheld the validity of a state statute against a challenge based on federal constitutional grounds. 28 U.S.C.A. 1254(2). But such an appeal, even though it lies "as a matter of right," may be summarily disposed of by the Supreme Court if the justices conclude that the appellant has not presented a "substantial" federal question.

8. Certiorari, historically, was one of the "extraordinary legal remedies," a common law writ by which a court ordered an inferior tribunal or a public officer to "certify" and send up the record of a proceeding for the issuing court's examination and possible correction. Certiorari practice in the Supreme Court of the United States is something quite different; the student is warned not to confuse certiorari as a means of appellate review with certiorari as a common law remedy.

mean no more than that the justices do not believe the issues involved in the case important enough, in terms of the sound development of federal law, for full-dress Supreme Court attention. A sound policy basis underlies the discretionary nature of Supreme Court appellate jurisdiction: if appeal to the Supreme Court were available in all cases, the Court would be swamped with ordinary mine-run appeals and unable to give full and deliberate consideration to the great cases it must decide with finality as umpire of the federal system, authoritative guardian of constitutional liberties and final overseer of the consistency and substantial justice of the general law administered in the courts of the United States. The records for a recent and not untypical year demonstrate the extent to which the Supreme Court exercises its discretion under the certiorari procedure to keep its adjudicative workload within manageable bounds: during the October Term, 1976, 1669 petitions for certiorari were acted on by the Supreme Court, of which only 178 (10.7%) were granted.[9]

9. Petitions for certiorari *in forma pauperis* (chiefly petitions by indigent persons convicted of crime) are excluded from this calculation as unrepresentative of the ordinary operation of the certiorari procedure. 50 petitions for certiorari *in forma pauperis* were granted by the Supreme Court during the October Term, 1969 (2.5% of those acted upon).

Sec. 1   THE STATE AND FEDERAL COURTS   49

NEW YORK COURTS OF CIVIL JURISDICTION

Court of Appeals

Appellate Division — Third and Fourth Departments

- Surrogate's Court
- Family Court
- County Courts Original Cases
- County Courts Appellate Cases
  - Village Police Justices
  - Courts of Justices of the Peace
  - City Courts
- Supreme Court Special and Trial Terms
- Court of Claims

Appellate Division — Second Department

- Supreme Court Appellate Term Second Department[10]
- Supreme Court Special and Trial Terms
- Surrogate's Court
- Family Court
- N.Y. City Civil Court
- City Courts (outside N.Y.City)
- County Courts (outside N.Y.City) Original Cases
- County Courts (outside N.Y.City) Appellate Cases
  - Village Police Justices
  - Courts of Justices of the Peace
- District Courts

Appellate Division — First Department

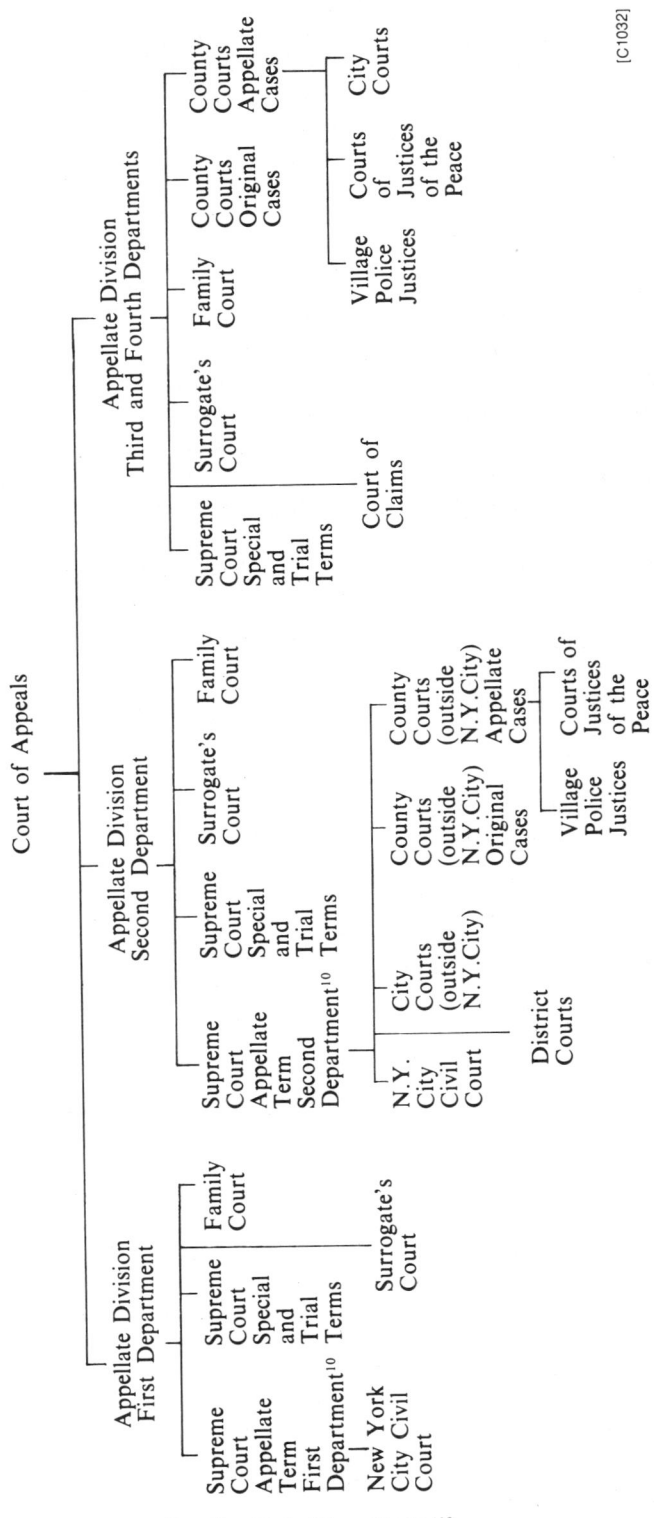

- Supreme Court Appellate Term First Department[10]
- Supreme Court Special and Trial Terms
- Family Court
- New York City Civil Court
- Surrogate's Court

10. See Note 10 on Page 50.

C. NOTE ON ADMINISTRATIVE AGENCIES

As noted in chapter I, in most first year courses little is said about the work of administrative agencies. In the second half of this course there will be some discussion of the significance of administrative agency interpretation of statutes, but our primary focus is on the courts and the legislature. There are sound pedagogical and other reasons for this preoccupation but it should not blind you to the central importance of administrative agencies in our system. As one noted administrative law scholar has observed: "The average person is much more directly and much more frequently affected by the administrative process than by the judicial process. * * * [A] large portion of all people go through life without ever being a party to a lawsuit. But the administrative process affects nearly every one in many ways nearly every day." K. C. Davis, Administrative Law Text 3 (1972). Professor Davis goes on to point out that in terms of number of cases and volume of output, federal agencies far exceed the courts and the legislature. The state and municipal agencies are even more numerous and productive.

The following observation on the reasons for establishing administrative agencies (instead of relying on the courts and the legislature) is from Gellhorn and Byse, Administrative Law Cases and Comments 3–7 (6th Ed. 1974):

"In the Federal realm, as is well known, the administrative process may be traced in an unbroken line from 1789, the first year of government under the Constitution of the United States. Commencing in that year with the administration of customs laws, the regulation of ocean-going vessels and the coasting trade, and the payment of veterans' pensions, Congress provided the statutory foundation for the considerable body of agencies which now administer the public laws. The circumstance that the national legislature has through so many generations seen wisdom in the administrative process suggests that bureaucracy may after all have its admissible virtues.

"The striking fact is that new agencies have been created or old ones expanded not to satisfy an abstract governmental theory, but to cope with problems of recognized public concern. The growth of steam navigation, rather than a predisposition toward administrative agencies, gave rise in 1838 to 'An Act to provide for the better security of the lives of passengers on board of vessels propelled in

---

10. Each appellate division is authorized by Article 6, § 8 of the New York State Constitution to create (and discontinue) an appellate term for the department. The appellate term may not hear appeals from the supreme court, surrogate's court, family court, or appeals in certain criminal cases.

whole or in part by steam', and so commenced the process of steamboat inspection which continues until the present day in the United States Coast Guard. No different in essence were the considerations that exactly a century later led to the creation of the Civil Aeronautics Authority to coordinate regulation of the air transportation industry. If human relationships within society had remained unchanged, if the Nation's territorial limitations had been unexpanded, if the arts and sciences had not progressed with the years, the machinery of government might similarly have remained undeveloped. Instead, in the span of a century and a half, new rights and duties among men have emerged, and the Government has responded to demands for their adjustment, their execution, and their protection.

"Of course, precisely similar considerations did not lead to the utilization of the administrative device in all the various situations in which it is to be found today. True, in each instance prescriptions by the legislature or decisions in individual cases by the judiciary were deemed to be comparatively inadequate mechanisms for dealing with governmental problems. But the reasons for the inadequacy were not always the same, nor did they by any means reflect discredit on Congress or the courts. In some cases decision to create an agency outside the courts was influenced by desire to avoid referring to the judiciary myriad controversies which would interfere with existing duties. In some instances, decision to transfer subordinate legislative authority to administrative agencies was influenced by the need of relieving Congress from details so that its essential policy-making work might go forward. In yet other cases, the choice of the administrative agency was essential to the effectuation of a preventive program, necessitating constant supervision and inspection for which neither judicial nor legislative organization is adapted.

"Illustration may be found in the possible choices of methods for the granting of a privilege or license or the fixing of prices or wages. The granting of licenses is an individual and private act and, at the same time, a step in the effectuation of a general policy. To fix a price or wage is to prescribe future conduct. The legislature may formulate policy and, indeed, this is its traditional function; but its attention to the specific is necessarily spasmodic because it does not remain constantly in session, nor is its machinery most suitable for the finding of facts which are necessary to the issuance of licenses or the fixing of prices or wages. Hence, though these functions might, without disregard of constitutional divisions of power, be performed by the legislature itself, practical considerations argue that they be undertaken elsewhere. Nor are these functions readily susceptible of initial judicial treatment; the judicial function is traditionally to weigh the merits of particular controversies, but not to engage in a consistent determination of policy or to maintain steady contact with a general and continuing problem. Accordingly, a body which could combine both functions—ascertainment of facts and the establishment of a continuous and uniform policy the development of which is not dependent upon the largely accidental emergence of litigated cases—would be logically chosen to perform functions of this nature. So administrative agencies have been devised to concentrate their attention upon phases of work somewhat alien to the basic functions of courts and legislatures, and from their concentration have developed the special knowledge and special skills which characterize the administrative process at its best.

* * *

"The choice of administrative machinery has been influenced by another factor that may be identified in some instances, of which the adjudication of workmen's compensation disputes is a notable example. Suits growing out of industrial accidents were originally tried and determined in the courts; they presented problems of legal rights between individuals which were traditionally of the stuff making up private litigation for the judiciary. When workmen's compensation laws were enacted, they constituted something of a revolt against the rules of law which the courts had created and applied in this field. The legislature, having chosen to adopt an entirely original approach to a problem that had not been successfully solved by the courts, rather naturally thought a new and sympathetic agency would be more likely than the courts to further the policies declared.

"One may perceive a similar element, too, in the creation of the Federal Trade Commission and, more particularly, the National Labor Relations Board. The policy declared in the Federal Trade Commission Act and the National Labor Relations Act departed from what had previously been the law on the subject. Indeed, judicial hostility to, or at least lack of sympathy with, the efforts of labor to organize and bargain collectively was in no small part responsible for the Labor Act. Over a substantial period prior to 1935, the courts had, through judicial legislation, emphasized labor's wrongs at the expense of labor's rights. Congressional skepticism concerning the cordial treatment of labor by the judiciary crystallized in the Norris-LaGuardia Act, divesting the federal courts of jurisdiction over a considerable area of labor relations. The selection of an independent agency to administer the Wagner Act was a logical development of the policy reflected in the Norris-LaGuardia Act; the proponents of the new law felt that the courts might have difficulty in sloughing off their former attitudes, and that those attitudes were not consonant with present policies. Since the Labor Act was intended to reverse an existing legal and judicial trend, the task of carrying out the Congressional mandate was assigned to an official instrumentality other than that which had developed, if not created, the rejected policy.

"To these several factors which have made for the choice of the administrative over the judicial or legislative—(1) the need for expertness, (2) the need for specialization and continuity, (3) the desirability of sympathetic administration—may be added a fourth consideration, the tremendous volume of cases to be decided.

"This often imperatively calls for the substitution of the administrative for the judicial tribunal, lest the courts be so overborne by the mass of business that they find themselves unable to perform their important and traditional tasks. One agency alone—the Social Security Administration—must dispose annually of claims more than twenty times greater in number than all the criminal and civil (other than bankruptcy) cases that are determined in the Federal district courts. Of course the cases committed to the Social Security Administration infrequently approach the complexity often encountered in the matters considered by the judiciary. But if Congress had chosen, as it might conceivably have done, to require claimants against the United States to proceed by a conventional form of court action, the judges would soon be frantically preoccupied by tasks that might better be assigned to others. Even if the burden on the judges would not have been intolerable, moreover, a cogent argument would remain against placing matters of this type in the courts: characteristics arising from the so-called rigidity and formality of the judicial process are commonly stated to be factors leading to the rejection of the judicial for the administrative method.

"The administrative agency is at least hypothetically capable of shaping itself in such a way as to avoid technicalities which are popularly associated with 'the law's delays'. A cheap and speedy forum is intended to be made available through administrative agencies to those whose circumstances and immediate needs might be ill-served by extensive litigation of a traditional type. Alas, the expectation that the administrative process would provide quick and inexpensive justice has—to put the matter charitably—not always been fully realized."

SECTION 2. THE STRUCTURE OF A LAWSUIT

A. INTRODUCTION

Professor Karl Llewellyn described substantive law as follows:[11]

> "[C]ertain bodies of law, which we call substantive—the substance of the law—deal with what ought to be, with whether contracts ought to be enforced at law, and when; with what formalities are necessary to make a last will stick; with how to form a corporation and how to issue its stock, and how to keep investors from having any say in it; with what words are necessary to make an effective lease or deed of land; and so on."

Procedure (or if you wish procedural law),[12] constitutes the mechanism through which rules of substantive law have effect. It is meaningless to speak of a rule of substantive law existing unless there exists some device whereby the rule can be made significant with respect to the people affected by it.

Procedure controls all aspects of the manner in which rules of substantive law are made significant: whether a particular person has standing to bring a particular suit; the forum in which the suit may be brought; the manner in which his claim must be asserted;

---

11. Llewellyn, The Bramble Bush 16 (1930). [Hereafter cited as The Bramble Bush.]

12. Professor Llewellyn had the following to say concerning the distinction between substantive law and procedure:
    "But from another angle this distinction tends to disappear. For if you whistle your soup you may be looked at queerly, you may be laughed at; you may even fail to be invited out again, another time. But if you slip in your legal etiquette it is not a question of queer looks or laughter or of what may happen later; it is likely to cost you your case right here and now; your case, and your client's case. The lawyer's slip in etiquette is the client's ruin. From this angle I say procedural regulations are the door, and the only door, to making real what is laid down by substantive law. Procedural regulations enter into and condition all substantive law's becoming actual when there is a dispute. Again this is no reason for not marking off procedure and evidence and trial practice as fields for special and peculiar study apart from substantive law. They should be so marked off. They should be marked off for the most intensive study. But they should be so marked off not because they are really separate, but because they are of such transcendent importance as to need special emphasis. They should be marked off not to be kept apart and distinct but solely in order that they may be more firmly learned, more firmly ingrained into the student *as conditioning the existence of any substantive law at all.* Everything that you know of procedure you must carry into *every* substantive course. You must read each substantive course, so to speak, through the spectacles of that procedure. For what substantive law says should be means nothing except in terms of what procedure says that you can make real."

    The Bramble Bush 17–18.

the ground rules of proof of his claim; the remedy which is afforded; the manner in which the judgment is enforced. In the words of one scholar, "the road to court-made justice is paved with good procedures."[13]

You will learn about various aspects of procedure in other courses, such as Civil Procedure, Evidence, Administrative Law, Federal Courts and Conflicts of Law. But even at this stage you need to know something about procedure. The first half of the course is devoted to a study of case law. In reading cases we are seeking to determine what the case decides as to the substantive law, or, to phrase it somewhat differently, what proposition of substantive law a case may be said to stand for. This depends upon the exact question the court had before it for decision, which in turn depends on the procedure to date in the case.

What follows is a brief outline of the steps in a lawsuit specifically designed for the purposes of this course. We have attempted to cover the major steps in the law suit but have focused on those procedural devices which typically raise questions of substantive law.

B. NOTE ON PROCEDURE

At first, the profusion of procedural steps encountered in a lawsuit may prove bewildering, a bewilderment not a little deepened by the wide variety of names given (especially under older practice) in different jurisdictions to the same procedural devices.

To clarify the subject and put it in perspective let us take a look at a typical lawsuit.

The Pleading Stage

The "client" when he first comes to the lawyer does not have a case; he has a problem. The lawyer's first task is to ascertain "the facts"—a task frequently not so easy as it sounds, even in the uncomplicated situation. Clients are no less—sometimes they may be more—prone to misunderstanding, misimpression and faulty recollection than the next man. Sometimes clients lie and even when they aim at the truth they miss—for all of the reasons encountered in non-legal contexts.

Let us assume that you are the lawyer and that your client (X) tells you the following: he bought a new Toyota automobile from a

---

13. Rosenberg, Devising Procedures that are Civil to Promote Justice that is Civilized, 69 Mich.L.Rev. 797 (1971). Professor Rosenberg also observed (at 797):

"In a democracy, process is king to a very large extent, and this is especially so in the judicial branch. Even though substantive laws command attention, procedural rules ensure respect. Why is this true? One powerful reason is that when people end up in court, their case typically is not a matter of right against wrong, but of right against right. Decent process makes the painful task of deciding which party will prevail bearable and helps make the decision itself acceptable."

Toyota dealer and as he was driving the car home from the showroom, the brakes failed and he suffered a broken leg (personal injury) and extensive damage to the car (property damage). Under principles which will soon be familiar to you, X would certainly seem to have a cause of action against the dealer (D) but let us suppose that the dealer is bankrupt and that you conclude it would be unproductive to sue him. You might (you probably would) sue the manufacturer (M).

Assume further that you are satisfied that the facts are as claimed by your client, and that they can be proved in court.[14]

The first question is in what court will you "bring your action." This will depend on what courts "have jurisdiction" of the type of action, which may turn on such factors as the amount of money involved and the states of residence of the parties. Assuming that the court has "subject matter jurisdiction," it will ordinarily be necessary to subject the person sued (the "defendant") to the jurisdiction of the court. Without personal jurisdiction no valid judgment can be rendered against the defendant.[15]

Ordinarily personal jurisdiction is acquired by the service of process on the defendant. The forms vary in different jurisdictions but in most you will initiate the lawsuit by "serving" a "summons" and "complaint" on the defendant. Service of process is a story in itself which we will leave for the course in Civil Procedure. Some of the difficulties which may be encountered are illustrated by Gumperz v. Hoffman, infra p. 64.

The complaint (it is also called a declaration and a petition) is the "pleading" in which the person suing (the "plaintiff") states the facts which in his view entitle him to a judgment against the "defendant," M in our case. The drafting of a complaint—about which you will learn in other courses—is a much less technical operation than it once was. Today all that is required is a statement of the al-

---

14. The rules governing what can be proved in court are covered in the course in Evidence.

15. "Although a court cannot render a valid judgment against the defendant personally unless it has jurisdiction over him, it may render a judgment affecting interests in property if it has jurisdiction over the property. In other words, although it has no jurisdiction to render a judgment *in personam*, it may have jurisdiction to render a judgment *in rem* or *quasi in rem*. For example, a proceeding may be brought against a defendant by an attachment of his property within the state, and even though the court has no jurisdiction over the person of the defendant, it may order that the property be sold and the proceeds applied to the discharge of the plaintiff's claim against the defendant. Similarly, although the defendant is not personally subject to the jurisdiction of the court, yet if it has jurisdiction over a person who is indebted to the defendant, that person may be compelled to pay to the plaintiff what he owes to the defendant and the defendant owes to the plaintiff. In other words, by the process called garnishment, a credit of the defendant can be reached by a creditor of the defendant even though the defendant himself cannot be reached."

Scott and Simpson, Cases and Other Materials on Civil Procedure 41–42 (1950).

legations clear enough to enable the defendant to prepare his defense. Of course, the plaintiff must, as we will see, allege facts sufficient to "constitute a cause of action," that is, he must allege facts which under the controlling law entitle him to judgment.

Once the complaint has been served, the next move is up to the defendant and his lawyer. There are four courses of action open to you (now as defendant's lawyer):

1. *Do nothing,* in which event, the court, after a proper interval, will enter a *"default"* judgment against your client, which the plaintiff will be able to collect against your client's property. For obvious reasons this is not often the recommended response.

2. *Serve (and/or file in court) a motion to dismiss for failure to state a cause of action.* (Formerly called and still frequently referred to as a "demurrer.") By this pleading you would say, in effect, "even if the alleged facts are true, there is no rule of law that permits X to recover against M on those facts. The demurrer is the pleading involved in the *Grand Lodge* and *Warshauer* cases, infra pp. 66 and 68. Since the demurrer admits, temporarily, the truth of the facts alleged by the plaintiff it raises a pure issue of substantive law.

3. *Serve (and/or file) an answer.* (Plea by way of traverse.) An *answer* denies all (or some) of the facts alleged in the complaint. It thus raises an issue of *fact* between the parties, not an issue of *law*. (Usually, in our pleading theory, all facts stated in the complaint and not denied by the defendant are taken as true.)

4. *Serve (and/or file) an affirmative defense.* (What the old cases call a plea by way of confession and avoidance.) By this pleading, you admit (again, as in the case of the demurrer, temporarily) the truth of the facts alleged and (unlike the demurrer) that those facts standing alone would win for plaintiff, but allege new facts which require a different result. In our supposed case, the pleading might be in effect, "yes, the car was defective when X received it but he discovered the defect immediately and instead of calling the dealer he continued on until his accident" or, alternatively, "your statement of facts is true but it happened five years ago and your claim is barred by the statute of limitations." [16]

16. At one time, the assertion of new facts by way of an affirmative defense would have necessitated a further pleading by the plaintiff called a "replication," which might be followed in due course by a "rejoinder," a "sur-rejoinder," a "rebutter" and a "sur-rebutter." Today the general practice is to permit only a complaint and an answer; any facts pleaded by way of an affirmative defense are deemed to be denied.

As noted above, the motion to dismiss for failure to state a cause of action raises a pure question of substantive law. It is as though the defendant said: I concede (for the sake of argument) that the facts alleged are true, but the law does not provide for a recovery against me on the basis of those facts. In our case the automobile manufacturer might say, in effect, I concede that you bought the car from the dealer, that the brakes were defective at the moment of delivery, that the accident was caused by the brake failure, and that you suffered the injuries claimed; nevertheless, the law in this jurisdiction does not permit you to sue the manufacturer in such a case, although you may have a remedy against the dealer. The decision by the court on a demurrer decides a question of substantive law, i. e., whether an automobile manufacturer is liable to a purchaser in such a case.[17]

Under ancient practice, the demurrer was a final concession of the truth of the facts alleged, not simply for the purpose of the motion. The defendant had to choose between challenging the complaint as legally insufficient or controverting it on the facts. If he chose wrong, e. g., demurred, but the demurrer was "overruled," he would lose his case even though he could have won by challenging the facts. Today's practice is much less technical and the defendant can challenge the complaint's legal sufficiency, and, if he loses, challenge the facts. Indeed both challenges may be made in the same pleading. While mistakes in pleading are less apt to be lethal than once was the case, poor practice technique is still somewhat worse than poor etiquette. At best it will be expensive, and litigation is already extremely costly; and at worst, it still may be fatal in some cases.

Assuming that the defendant moves to dismiss for failure to state a cause of action, the motion will be argued before the court and either granted or denied. If it is granted, usually the plaintiff will be given an opportunity to "replead," i. e., to allege additional facts, if they exist, sufficient to state a cause of action. If he is unable to do so, he may appeal. If the motion to dismiss is denied, and the defendant has, in addition to demurring, controverted the plaintiffs' allegations of fact, the case will go to trial (or in some jurisdictions he may appeal immediately).[18] If he does not dispute the facts, there is no need for a trial. The case proceeds directly to judgment, on the law, which may be reviewed on appeal.

---

17. Those comfortable with formal logic may find it helpful to view the complaint as a syllogism, the *implicit* (because the complaint states facts, not law) major premise of which is the rule of law relied upon by the plaintiff; the minor premise is the statement of facts, and the conclusion is the prayer for relief. The demurrer is said to attack the major premise of the complaint. For more on the subject, see Dowling et al., Materials for Legal Method, Chapter 8 (Jones ed. 1950).

18. In those jurisdictions where an appeal does not "lie" immediately, the denial may be appealed at the end of the trial.

Up to now we have been talking about the defendant's demurrer to the complaint. Precisely the same kind of issue (i. e., an issue of substantive law) can be raised where the defendant pleads by way of "confession and avoidance" and the plaintiff demurs to his pleading.[19] For example, suppose that in our case M had admitted the allegations of the complaint but alleged that X had continued to operate the car after discovering the defect. X could challenge the legal sufficiency of the new facts, i. e., admit that he drove after discovering the defect but contend that his doing so was not a legal bar to recovery. X could also, of course, challenge the new facts alleged, i. e., deny that he drove after discovery.

The Trial Stage

Although it may not appear so from case books, the overwhelming majority of cases do not raise issues of substantive law. The parties do not dispute the law, but only the facts.

Let us assume that an issue of fact has been raised by the pleadings, that is, that your client, at the pleading stage, filed an answer denying some or all of the facts stated in the plaintiff's complaint.[20] Thus an issue of fact is raised between the parties, which will require trial,[21] before a jury or (if a jury is waived by the parties) trial before a judge sitting as a jury—"bench trial."

What are the principal procedural events that occur, or can occur, at the trial stage?[22] We begin with the presentation of the plaintiff's case:

    1. Plaintiff's opening statement to the jury "I expect to prove * * *." In some states (e. g., New York) this is followed immediately by defendant's opening statement as to what defendant expects to prove. In other states, defendant's opening statement comes later, at the start of the defendant's case.

    2. Next comes the direct and cross-examination of plaintiff's witnesses—the witnesses called by plaintiff's counsel testify and are cross-examined by defendant's coun-

---

19. An example of such a plea is contained in Filmore v. Metropolitan Life Ins. Co., 82 Ohio St. 208, 92 N.E. 26 (1910).

20. As noted earlier, an issue of fact could also be raised if defendant entered a plea of confession and avoidance, and plaintiff denied the truth of the new facts alleged by defendant.

21. It is, of course, possible that although the pleadings may raise an issue, there may be "no *genuine* issue of fact" between the parties, i. e., that there is no evidence to support the claim or demand in the pleadings. Such cases may be disposed of without trial by "summary judgment."

22. We have skipped over the very important procedural devices by which the parties obtain information in advance of trial, such as examinations before trial, requests for admission, document discovery and interrogatories. We also do not discuss the important and interesting process of jury selection.

sel. Here you may have "objections" to the introduction of evidence, for example, on the ground that the evidence is inadmissible as hearsay. If the court, after defendant's objection, lets the evidence in, defendant will "except" to the ruling and so preserve his right to challenge the ruling on appeal if the jury verdict goes against him.

3. At the end of plaintiff's evidence, defendant may ask the trial court for a "directed verdict" or a "nonsuit." By making one of these motions, defendant is saying, in effect, that plaintiff has not proved enough—i. e., has not offered adequate evidence in support of his allegations of fact —to enable any reasonable jury to bring in a verdict for him. You will note that these motions—for a directed verdict or for a nonsuit (a nonsuit is also called a "motion to dismiss" in some modern jurisdictions)—attack the sufficiency of plaintiff's proof of facts and, ordinarily, do not raise a question of substantive law.

4. Assuming that defendant's motions have been made but denied by the court, defendant presents his evidence, i. e., calls witnesses to prove his version of the facts. Thus again, we will have the direct testimony and cross-examination of witnesses and may have objections to evidence (this time from counsel for plaintiff) and exceptions to the court's rulings thereon.

5. At the end of the defendant's evidence, plaintiff may move for a directed verdict (rarely granted, however, to the party with the "burden of proof") or the defendant may again move for a directed verdict on the ground he has now shown so clearly that plaintiff's asserted version of the facts is not true that no reasonable jury could do otherwise than find for the defendant.

6. If all these motions are denied, plaintiff and defendant sum up before the jury, plaintiff having the right, usually, to make the closing argument.

7. The next, and crucial, stage of the trial is the "charge to the jury." The judge gives his instructions to the jury as to the applicable law of the case. Thus, for example, in our hypothetical case, the judge might advise the jury about as follows: "If you the jury find that the brakes were defective when the car was turned over to plaintiff, and that plaintiff did not operate the car after discovering the defect, you will bring in a verdict for plaintiff in the amount of his medical expenses, loss of work and personal suffering and property damage." The instruction stage is one of the most important for our immediate purposes (see

Barholt v. Wright, infra p. 71) and you should know something about its realities:

A. In actual practice, few instructions are ever drawn up by the trial judge as a matter of his own literary initiative. What usually happens is that each side draws up draft instructions and submits them to the judge. The judge then looks at the draft instructions submitted by both sides and decides which ones to give to the jury (he will probably revise the words). Either side in the litigation may:

(i) except, i. e., record objections, to any instruction or part thereof, which he believes is an erroneous statement of the law; or

(ii) except to the refusal of the judge to give *his* instruction.

B. Since the instruction is, in substance, a statement to the jury of the substantive law applicable to the facts of the case, it is at the instruction stage that you are quite likely to have a sharp issue of law between the parties, decided by the trial judge and specified by the losing party as the ground for his appeal. This is particularly true in tort actions, where a very large percentage of appeals in modern cases come up on, or involve, an appeal from the instructions given to the jury.

8. After the judge delivers his instructions, the jury retires for deliberation and, ultimately, brings in its "verdict." Most jury verdicts are general, a statement of result in some such form as "We, the jury, find for the plaintiff in the sum of $1,000." So-called "special" verdicts, by which the jury answers specific questions of fact submitted to it by the judge, are now rare.

Motions in the Trial Court After Verdict

After the jury has returned its verdict, but before the trial court has entered "judgment" [23] in the action, the party who lost before the jury can make one or more of several motions. Many appeals come up to the appellate courts from the action of trial courts granting or denying one of these motions, so you should get a general idea now as to the kind of question each motion raises. Terminology and practice will differ considerably from state to state, but it should be possible to get a general understanding without too much difficulty.

Most sweeping of the motions after verdict is the motion for judgment notwithstanding the verdict which is also referred to by the

23. Note and remember the difference between "verdict" and "judgment."

"law-Latin" name "judgment non obstante veredicto" (or, familiarly, judgment n.o.v.), in which the party against whom the verdict is pronounced goes so far as to ask that judgment be given for him in spite of the jury findings.

More common is the motion to set aside the verdict as against the weight of the evidence and grant a new trial. Both this motion and the modern motion for judgment n.o.v. are attacks on the sufficiency of the evidence to support the verdict. You may well ask at this point what gives the judge (to whom all motions are addressed) the right to disregard a verdict of a jury which in our system is the cherished and time-honored instrument for finding the facts. The answer is that we require *as a matter of law* a minimum amount of evidence to support the jury verdict.[24] This amount, variously phrased as "more than a scintilla," or such that "reasonable men may not differ," is obviously an imprecise standard and susceptible to abuse. In practice, however, most judges will only rarely displace a jury verdict, and when they do, will ordinarily not grant judgment n.o.v., but instead set aside the verdict and grant a new trial.

The losing party may also move for a new trial on a number of other grounds such as an error by the judge in ruling on evidence, an error in the instructions, misconduct by the jurors, or excessive damages. The usual rule is that a losing party cannot appeal any errors of the trial court which he did not call to the trial court's attention by filing a motion for a new trial.

Mention should be made here of certain other motions after verdict found in older cases—such as the motion in arrest of judgment (see, e. g., Priestly v. Fowler, infra p. 75) or an earlier version of the motion for judgment n.o.v.—which are, in effect, delayed demurrers attacking the legal sufficiency of a pleading.

---

24. The following definition of the test for the correctness of the grant of a motion for a directed verdict is from Lawrence Chrysler Plymouth Inc. v. Chrysler Corp., 461 F.2d 608, 609 (7th Cir. 1972):

"The test of the legal correctness of the direction of a verdict for the defendant at the close of the plaintiff's evidence is whether the court is justified in concluding that as measured by the applicable and controlling principles of law the plaintiff's evidence together with all reasonable inferences to be drawn therefrom, when viewed in the light most favorable to the plaintiff, is such that reasonable men in a fair and impartial exercise of judgment could reach no conclusion other than that liability of the defendant had not been established. In other words, the primary issue in this appeal is whether under the statute which plaintiff invoked in Count I of its complaint the plaintiff's evidence was such that the jury could have reasonably concluded that the defendants, or any of them, were liable. If such was not the case, the District Court did not err in withdrawing Count I from consideration by the jury, and entering judgment for the defendants thereon, Pinkowski v. Sherman Hotel, 7 Cir., 313 F.2d 190; Woods v. Geifman Food Stores, 7 Cir., 311 F.2d 711; Lambie v. Tibbits, 7 Cir., 267 F.2d 902."

The test for the granting of a judgment notwithstanding the verdict is substantially the same. Juhnke v. EIG Corp., 444 F.2d 1323 (9th Cir. 1971).

If all motions after verdict are denied, the trial court formally enters judgment for the party to whom the jury awarded the verdict. This judgment is *res judicata* of the controversy between the parties unless notice of appeal is given by the losing party within a required number of days.

Execution of the Judgment

If the plaintiff has obtained a judgment against the defendant and the defendant does not pay or otherwise satisfy the judgment, the plaintiff is entitled to execution. In the case of a judgment for money, (the usual case in our system) the plaintiff obtains a writ from the court directing the sheriff (or similar official) to seize property of the defendant, sell it, and with the proceeds pay to the plaintiff the amount of his judgment.

At common law, the plaintiff was also entitled to have the defendant arrested and kept in custody until the judgment should be satisfied. The writ directed the sheriff to seize the defendant in order to satisfy the judgment, and the writ was called a *capias ad satisfaciendum*. Today, the right of the plaintiff to have the defendant arrested is very much restricted, and even in cases in which the defendant is arrested he will be released on showing that he is unable to pay the judgment. Neither in England nor in the United States today do we have the kind of imprisonment for debt so graphically described by Dickens in his story of Little Dorritt.

Execution, like service of process, is a story by itself. Just as it can be very difficult to serve a reluctant defendant, it can be very difficult to collect from a determined, unscrupulous, judgment debtor. The securing of a judgment can be only the beginning of a long trail to compensation. Execution is of great importance to the client. Inability to enforce a judgment because of the insolvency or intransigence of the defendant may make meaningless all that has gone before, but the possibility that execution cannot be had does not affect the reading of a case—in which we are immediately interested.

The Appeal Stage

Most cases you will read in law school are appeal cases and you need to have some background on the appellate process if you are fully to understand them.

First of all, the appellate court does not retry the case on its merits or take additional evidence. The focus of the appellate court's scrutiny is on the correctness of the rulings of the trial court. The documents at which the appellate court will look in its review include the record—the pleadings, the transcript of the testimony at the trial or an edited portion, the trial court's rulings—and the "briefs" of counsel, i. e., statements (usually printed) of the arguments supporting each side's position in the litigation. No additional testimony is taken. The library has many copies of briefs and records and you should look at a few.

After the briefs and the record are filed, the case is set up for oral argument and argued before the appellate court. Fifteen minutes, thirty minutes, or sometimes as much as an hour on each side is allowed, but in modern times usually about fifteen minutes. Remember that the written briefs have been presented and probably have been read by the court beforehand. After oral argument and study of the briefs, the judges of the appellate court meet in conference, discuss the case, and assign the writing of the opinion of the court to one of its members. The opinions are more than individual essays of the judge. When written by the assigned judge, the draft opinion will be circulated for initialing, and when approved by all the members of the court, or a majority, the opinion is filed as the opinion of the court.

There may also be concurring opinions (the concurring judges agreeing with the result but differing in some way from the majority opinion) and dissenting opinions.

One last point should be emphasized. A lawsuit is a complicated and long drawn out proceeding. Many points of dispute will come up. A trial judge would have to be a superman to avoid error in all his rulings in a complicated case. This is particularly true of rulings from the bench during the course of trial. Unlike the appellate judges who have, ordinarily, no time limit except conscience on their deliberation, the trial court frequently must shoot from the hip; not surprisingly his snap decisions are sometimes wrong. Should all such errors warrant reversal by the appellate court? Many times, the errors are "cured" by subsequent events, or the questions on which erroneous rulings are made turn out to be unimportant. Although it was not always the case, today an error in the trial court will not result in reversal unless it is "prejudicial," i. e., unless it did—or might have—prejudicially influenced the outcome of the case.

GUMPERZ v. HOFMANN

Supreme Court of New York, Appellate Div., First Dept. 1935.
245 App.Div. 622, 283 N.Y.S. 823, affirmed without opinion
271 N.Y. 544, 2 N.E.2d 687.

Appeal from Supreme Court, New York County. Action by Julian Gumperz against Dr. Herbert Hofmann. From an order of the Supreme Court, granting defendant's motion to vacate service of summons, plaintiff appeals.

UNTERMYER, J. The defendant, a physician who resides in Buenos Aires, was sojourning at a hotel in the city of New York when served with the summons in this action. According to the defendant's affidavit, the process server called several times at the defendant's rooms while the defendant was absent and on each occasion left a message that Dr. Goldman had called. Eventually the process server, still representing himself to be Dr. Goldman with a letter from the president of the New York County Medical Society to be personally delivered to the defendant, arranged with the defendant to meet him in the lobby of the hotel. When the defendant arrived, he was served with the summons in this action. The process server, in fact, was not a doctor, though his name was Goldman; he was not sent by the president of the New York County Medical Society, and he had no letter for delivery to the defendant. The Special Term vacated the service upon the ground that "the alleged service of the summons was effected through fraud and deceit." Even though we agree with the Special Term in its determination of the facts, we are of opinion that service of the summons ought not to have been set aside.

Whether such a deception as was practiced here will vitiate service of process is a question which does not appear ever to have been decided by this court or by the Court of Appeals. It has indeed frequently been held that service of process will be set aside where the defendant has been enticed into the jurisdiction for that purpose. Olean St. Ry. Co. v. Fairmount Const. Co., 55 App.Div. 292, 67 N.Y.S. 165; Garabettian v. Garabettian, 206 App.Div. 502, 201 N.Y.S. 548; Snelling v. Watrous, 2 Paige, 314; Beacom v. Rogers, 79 Hun, 220, 29 N.Y.S. 507; Metcalf v. Clark, 41 Barb. 45. These and like cases are distinguishable because in each of them the party was induced to come here from another state to which our jurisdiction did not extend. Atlantic & Pacific Telegraph Co. v. Baltimore & Ohio R. Co. et al., 46 N.Y.Super.Ct. 377, affirmed 87 N.Y. 355. There are, however, some decisions of courts of first instance (Mason v. Libbey, 1 Abb.N. C. 354; Bell v. Lawrence [City Ct.N.Y.] 140 N.Y.S. 1106; Olson v. McConihe, 54 Misc. 48, 105 N.Y.S. 386), and one decision of the Appellate Term (Bernstein et al. v. Hakim, 126 Misc. 582, 214 N.Y.S. 82), which hold that even where the defendant is within the jurisdiction, service of process will be set aside if made under conditions similar to those which existed here. It is necessary to decide now whether we will follow these decisions.

We think that legal as well as practical considerations preponderate in favor of the rule that service is not to be invalidated merely because secured by a deception practiced on the defendant, which, in no true sense, was injurious to him. It may fairly be said that there is a duty upon persons within the jurisdiction to submit to the service of process. Although that duty is not legally enforceable, it is, broadly speaking, none the less an obligation which ought not to be evaded by a defendant whom it is attempted to serve. The deception here was, therefore, practiced for the purpose, and had only the effect, of inducing the defendant to do that which in any event he should voluntarily have done.

We cannot fail to be aware of the difficulties which beset the server of process on a defendant who is unwilling to be served, for it is evident that if he discloses his intentions, such a defendant is likely to be even more inaccessible than before. For that reason alone, we should hesitate to surround the service of process with unnecessary limitations. Needless to say, we do not approve of misstatements made to procure service of process, but, except where the defendant has been lured into the jurisdiction, we think the service is separable from these. Where real injury ensues, the person who is responsible may be held liable for damages in a civil suit. In a proper case, he may even be prosecuted criminally. We do not need to go further by holding that service otherwise valid is vitiated on account of a misstatement by which it was procured. The situation in this respect is quite analogous to cases which hold that the court will not reject evidence merely because it has been illegally secured. People v. Adams, 176 N.Y. 351, 68 N.E. 636, 63 L.R.A. 406, 98 Am.St.Rep. 675; People v. Defore, 242 N.Y. 13, 150 N.E. 585.

The order should be reversed with $20 costs and disbursements, and the motion denied.

Order reversed with $20 costs and disbursements and motion denied. Order filed. All concur.

NOTES

1. What was the procedural device employed by the defendant in this case?

2. What does this case *decide*?

3. To what extent, if at all, did this decision settle the dispute between Mr. Gumperz and Dr. Hofmann? Is the case now *res judicata*?

4. What is the effect of the decision in Gumperz v. Hofmann on the cases of Mason v. Libbey, Bell v. Lawrence, Olson v. McConihe and Bernstein et al. v. Hakim, cited therein?

GRAND LODGE OF THE INDEPENDENT ORDER OF GOOD TEMPLARS OF THE STATE OF CALIFORNIA v. FARNHAM

Supreme Court Commission and Supreme Court of California, 1886.
70 Cal. 158, 11 P. 592.

Appeal from a judgment of the Superior Court of Solano County.

The facts are stated in the opinion.

BELCHER, C. C. The court below sustained a demurrer to the complaint, and whether it erred in so doing or not, is the only question presented for decision.

The facts as stated in the complaint are substantially as follows:

The plaintiff was the owner of certain real property in Solano County, on which was erected the Good Templar's Home for Orphans.

At the time of filing the complaint, and for a long time prior thereto, the home was conducted and managed by the plaintiff. In 1883 it was deemed important to erect an addition to the home, so that a greater number of orphans could be taken care of thereat; and to raise money for that purpose, subscription papers were circulated and subscriptions solicited by an agent employed by the plaintiff.

In September, 1883, S. C. Farnham, the defendant's testator, subscribed one of these papers and placed opposite his name as the amount of his subscription one thousand dollars.

On the first day of December, 1883, Farnham died, leaving a will. The will was admitted to probate, and notice to creditors published; and then plaintiff presented to the executrix its claim for the one thousand dollar subscription, and the claim was rejected. In October, 1883, the agent employed to get subscriptions reported to the plaintiff the amount of money collected and then on hand, and the money subscribed and unpaid, of which the larger part was the one thousand dollars subscribed by Farnham. The plaintiff afterwards, but it does not appear when, commenced to erect an addition to the home, and was still prosecuting the work when this action was commenced.

The demurrer was upon the ground that the complaint did not state facts sufficient to constitute a cause of action.

The general rule is, that a promise to pay a subscription like that declared on here is a mere offer, which may be revoked at any time before it is accepted by the promisee. And an acceptance can only be shown by some act on the part of the promisee whereby some legal liability is incurred or money is expended on the faith of the promise.

If the promisor dies before his offer is accepted, it is thereby revoked, and cannot afterwards, by any act showing acceptance, be made good as against his estate. Pratt v. Trustees, 93 Ill. 475; Beach v. First M. E. Church, 96 Ill. 177, 179; Phipps v. Jones, 20 Pa.St. 260; Helfenstein's Estate, 77 Pa.St. 328, 331; Cottage Street Church v. Kendall, 121 Mass. 528.

The rule is otherwise where subscribers agree together to make up a specified sum, and where the withdrawal of one increases the amount to be paid by the others. In such case, as between the subscribers, there is a mutual liability, and the co-subscribers may maintain an action against one who refuses to pay. George v. Harris, 4 N.H. 533; Curry v. Rogers, 21 N.H. 247; 1 Wharton on Contracts, p. 719.

Here it is not alleged in the complaint that the plaintiff entered into any contract, incurred any liability, or expended any money for the erection of an addition to the home for orphans before the death of Farnham. His subscription was therefore withdrawn by his death, and was not a valid claim against his estate. * * *

We think the demurrer was properly sustained, and the judgment should be affirmed.

SEARLES, C., and FOOTE, C., concurred.

THE COURT. For the reasons given in the foregoing opinion, the judgment is affirmed.

NOTES

1. What can you conclude concerning the type of question which is before an appellate court for decision on an appeal from a judgment which

    a. sustains a demurrer to a complaint?

    b. overrules a demurrer to a complaint?

2. Does this decision put an end to any hope of the plaintiff to recover the amount of the $1,000 pledge from the estate of Mr. Farnham?

3. The same result was reached by the Florida Supreme Court in Mount Sinai Hospital of Greater Miami, Inc. v. Jordan, 290 So.2d 484 (Fla. 1974.).

WARSHAUER v. LLOYD SABAUDO S.A.

United States Circuit Court of Appeals, Second Cir. 1934.
71 F.2d 146, cert. denied 293 U.S. 610, 55 S.Ct. 140, 79 L.Ed. 700.

Appeal from the District Court of the United States for the Southern District of New York.

Action by David Warshauer against Lloyd Sabaudo S. A., a foreign corporation, for personal injuries. From a judgment dismissing, on motion, plaintiff's complaint on ground that facts therein alleged did not state a cause of action (6 F.Supp. 433), plaintiff appeals.

SWAN, Circuit Judge. This is an action at law by the plaintiff Warshauer, a citizen of the United States and a resident of New York City, against an Italian corporation which owned and operated the steamship Conte Biancamano.[25] In substance the complaint alleges that on the afternoon of October 31, 1931, the plaintiff and a companion were adrift on the high seas in a disabled motorboat, without gasoline and without food, when the defendant's steamer passed within hailing distance; that he exhibited a recognized signal of distress and requested the steamer to come to his assistance, and the defendant's servants on said steamer particularly its operating personnel, clearly observed his signals of distress, but refused to heed them or to stop and take the plaintiff aboard, although they could have done so without peril to themselves or their vessel; that two days later the plaintiff was rescued by a Coastguard cutter. In the

---

25. [Be careful in this case, as in all others, to keep your consideration of this plaintiff's right to what he asks from this defendant, free from your feeling that somebody ought to get something from somebody!—Ed.]

meantime and in consequence of the exposure and deprivations to which he was subjected by the failure of the defendant's steamship to render the requested aid, the plaintiff suffered permanent physical injuries for which, together with the attendant pain and subsequently incurred medical expenses, he demands damages. On motion to dismiss, equivalent to a demurrer, the District Court held the complaint insufficient, and the correctness of this ruling is the issue presented by this appeal.

Argument of counsel has taken a wider range than the precise issue presented by the pleadings requires. The question chiefly debated was whether the common law or the law of the sea recognizes the existence of a legal duty coextensive with the universally admitted moral duty to rescue a stranger from peril, when this can be done without risk to the one called upon for help. This interesting problem we pass by as unnecessary to the decision, as did the District Court.

The precise issue is whether a shipowner is liable for damages to a stranger in peril on the high seas to whom the ship's master has failed to give aid. This situation, it may be noted, involves no personal dereliction of a moral duty by the person sought to be held to respond in damages. Such dereliction was that of the master, and only by applying the doctrine of respondeat superior can it be imputed to the ship's owner; moral obliquity is not imputed to one personally innocent. It is conceded that no authority can be found which has imposed legal liability on the owner in such circumstances. Dicta adverse to liability are contained in Saunders v. The Hanover, Fed. Cas.No.12,374, and United States v. Knowles, Fed.Cas.No.15,540. Cf. Harris v. Pennsylvania R. Co., 50 F.2d 866, (C.C.A.4); Cortes v. Baltimore Insular Line, 287 U.S. 367, 377, 53 S.Ct. 173, 77 L.Ed. 368. The absence of specific precedent, however, is no insuperable barrier, for the law of the sea can grow by judicial decision no less than the common law. See Cain v. Alpha S. S. Corp., 35 F.2d 717, 722 (C.C. A.2). But a court should be slow to establish a new legal principle not in harmony with the generally accepted views of the great maritime nations.

Their views on this subject are disclosed in the International Salvage Treaty, which was drafted by representatives of more than twenty nations, meeting at Brussels in 1910, and to which both Italy and the United States are parties. 37 Stat. 1658, 1672. Articles 11 and 12 of the treaty relate to the matter under consideration and read as follows:

"Article 11.

"Every master is bound, so far as he can do so without serious danger to his vessel, her crew and passengers, to render assistance to everybody, even though an enemy, found at sea in danger of being lost.

"The owner of the vessel incurs no liability by reason of contravention of the foregoing provision.

"Article 12.

"The High Contracting Parties whose legislation does not forbid infringements of the preceding article bind themselves to take or to propose to their respective legislatures the measures necessary for the prevention of such infringements. * * *"

The treaty was ratified by the United States in 1912, to become effective on March 1, 1913. In the meantime Congress passed legislation in fulfillment of the obligation imposed by Article 12 of the treaty. Section 2 of the Act of Aug. 1, 1912, provides as follows (37 Stat. 242, 46 U.S.C.A. § 728):

"Sec. 2. That the master or person in charge of a vessel shall, so far as he can do so without serious danger to his own vessel, crew, or passengers, render assistance to every person who is found at sea in danger of being lost; and if he fails to do so, he shall, upon conviction, be liable to a penalty of not exceeding $1,000 or imprisonment for a term not exceeding two years, or both."

The appellant contends that the declaration in Article 11 that the shipowner "incurs no liability by reason of contravention" of the master's obligation to render assistance refers only to criminal liability of the owner. Such an interpretation would seem a most unlikely meaning. Unless it was intended to cover civil liability, no reason is apparent for mentioning the shipowner's exemption from liability. It is almost inconceivable that criminal responsibility should be imputed to an owner who had not directed the dereliction of his agent. In the United States, at least, imputed crime is substantially unknown. A penal statute is construed to apply only to the class of persons to whom it specifically refers. Field v. United States, 137 F. 6, 8 (C.C.A.8). The same principle should be equally applicable to the construction of a treaty. Hence if the first sentence of Article 11 refers only to the master's public duty, breach of which is to be enforced by the criminal law, there was no need to express the owner's exemption from responsibility. If, however, the master's liability may be civil as well as criminal, then the provision referring to the owner serves a purpose and clearly relieves him from civil liability.

It is further urged that the treaty is not self-executing, that Article 11 is no more than an expression of policy and by the very terms of Article 12 requires legislation to carry it into effect (cf. Foster v.

Neilson, 2 Pet. 253, 314, 7 L.Ed. 415), and that Congress in enacting such legislation dealt only with the criminal liability of the master, leaving untouched the civil liability of both master and owner, so that no implication can be drawn, either from the treaty or the statute, that civil liability does not exist. On the contrary, the argument proceeds, the enactment of a criminal statute for the protection of a class creates a right of civil action in a member of the class who is caused harm by an infraction of the statute. Texas & P. Ry. Co. v. Rigsby, 241 U.S. 33, 39, 36 S.Ct. 482, 60 L.Ed. 874. Granting all this, the appellant advances no further than to establish a cause of action against the violator of the criminal statute; that is, the master. He must still prove that the master's breach of duty is imputable to his employer. It is at this point that the absence of precedent and the declaration of the treaty against liability on the part of the owner stands in his way. As a declaration of the views of the great maritime nations, the treaty needs no "implementation" by legislation. We are not at liberty to make new law in the face of that declaration. See Article 15 of the Treaty (37 Stat. 1672).

Judgment affirmed.

NOTES

1. To what extent did this decision end the plaintiff's chances of recovering damages from the defendant?

2. To what extent, if at all, did this decision have a finality greater or less than in the preceding case?

3. Article 15 of the International Salvage Treaty, referred to by the court in the *Warshauer* case provides in part (37 Stat. 1673):

> "2. Where all the persons interested belong to the same State as the court trying the case, the provisions of the national law and not of the convention are applicable."

BARHOLT v. WRIGHT

Supreme Court of Ohio, 1887.
45 Ohio St. 177, 12 N.E. 185.

Error to the Circuit Court of Portage County.

The plaintiff below brought suit against the defendant to recover damages for an assault and battery committed upon his person. The answer was a general denial. Upon the trial of the issue, the jury, under the charge of the court, rendered a verdict for the defendant. A motion for a new trial, assigning error in the charge, was overruled by the court, and a bill of exceptions taken. Upon error the judgment was reversed in the Circuit Court, and the cause remanded for a new trial; and the defendant below now prosecutes error in this court to reverse the judgment of the Circuit Court.

The evidence is not set out in the bill of exceptions; but it appears from the bill, that, upon the trial, the plaintiff offered evidence tending to show that he and the defendant went out to fight by agreement, and did fight, and was severely injured by the defendant; among other injuries inflicted upon him, one of his fingers was so bitten by the defendant that it had to be amputated. By reason of the injuries so received, he became ill, was disabled for work for a long time, and was put to considerable expense in being cured. The court, however, charged the jury that if the parties went out to fight by agreement, and the plaintiff received the injuries complained of from the defendant while the fight was going on and in the course of it, he could not recover. The accuracy of this charge is the question presented by the record.

MINSHALL, J. It would seem at first blush contrary to general legal principles of remedial justice to allow a plaintiff to recover damages for an injury inflicted on him by a defendant in a combat of his own seeking; or where, as in this case, the fight occurred by an agreement between the parties to fight. Thus in cases for damages resulting from the clearest negligence on the part of the defendant, a recovery is denied the plaintiff, if it appear that his own fault in any way contributed to the injury of which he complains. And a maxim, as old as the law, *volenti non fit injuria*, forbids a recovery by a plaintiff where it appears that the ground of his complaint had been induced by that to which he had assented; for, in judgment of law, that to which a party assents is not deemed an injury. Broom's Leg. Max. 268.

But as often as the question has been presented, it has been decided that a recovery may be had by a plaintiff for injuries inflicted by the defendant in a mutual combat, as well as in a combat where the plaintiff was the first assailant, and the injuries resulted from the use of excessive and unnecessary force by the defendant in repelling the assault. These apparent anomalies rest upon the importance which the law attaches to the public peace as well as to the life and person of the citizen. From considerations of this kind it no more regards an agreement by which one man may have assented to be beaten, than it does an agreement to part with his liberty and become the slave of another. But the fact that the injuries were received in a combat in which the parties had engaged by mutual agreement may be shown in mitigation of damages. 2 Greenleaf Ev. § 85; Logan v. Austin, 1 Stewart, 476. This, however, is the full extent to which the cases have gone. * * *

* * *

It is upon the same principle of public policy that one, who is the first assailant in a fight, may recover of his antagonist for injuries inflicted by the latter, where he oversteps what is reasonably necessary to his defence, and unnecessarily injures the plaintiff; or that, with apparent want of consistency, permits each to bring an action in such case, the assaulted party for the assault first committed upon him, and the assailant, for the excess of force used beyond what was necessary for self-defence. * * *

* * *

* * * We think the court erred in its charge to the jury. The injury inflicted, the loss of a finger, was a severe one; it amounted, in fact, to a mayhem. "Where the injury" (a mayhem), says the author of a recent and quite valuable work on criminal procedure, "takes place during a conflict, it is not necessary to a conviction that the accused should have formed the intent before engaging in the conflict. It is sufficient if he does the act voluntarily, unlawfully, and on purpose." Maxwell's Crim.Proc. 260. It was permissible to the defendant to show the agreement to fight in mitigation of damages, but not as a bar to the action.

Judgment affirmed.

NOTES

1. What was the exact question presented to the Supreme Court of Ohio by the appeal in this case? Was it a question of the sufficiency of a pleading, a question of the sufficiency of the proof of facts, or a question of the propriety of a ruling made by the trial judge?

2. What does this case *decide*? That is, how broad or how narrow is the proposition of law for which this case can be taken as authority in later cases?

3. What was the fault found by the Supreme Court in the instruction given by the trial court in this case? What would have been a proper instruction in the case?

4. Ordinarily, an appellate court will not consider questions which were not raised in the trial court. For a discussion of the circumstances in which a federal appellate court will review errors not objected to in the trial court, see Cohen v. Franchard Corp., 478 F.2d 115 (2d. Cir. 1973.).

SECTION 3. THE TECHNIQUE OF CASE LAW DEVELOPMENT

A. INTRODUCTION

The primary objective of the study of law—at least in the first year—is the acquisition of basic skills necessary to function as a lawyer, a process sometimes overbroadly described as "learning to think like a lawyer." No one has ever adequately described what that means but certainly it would include an ability to analyze cases and statutes, a sense of relevance, a habit of approaching problems through facts, and an ability to reason cogently. Of course, one cannot learn such skills in a vacuum; it is necessary to have as a context some knowledge of substantive law. The materials which follow— particularly the cases on product liability—will provide that context.

But while you should be absorbing the substantive rules of these cases, learning "what the law is" is only a secondary objective of this course in Legal Method, and indeed of most law school courses. For now, learning the technique comes first.

So far in Legal Method you have become generally acquainted with the forms of case law and legislation, have acquired some understanding of the assumptions and objectives of the case method of law study, and have learned at least a little about courts and their reporters. The readings and cases in Section 2 have alerted you to the importance of procedure in the analysis of case law precedents. What are the other irreducible minimum insights which must be developed before you are equipped to start the effective study of case law? First you must understand the vital importance of the facts of the case. After mastering the facts—and only then—you can focus on the considerations which caused the court to arrive at the decision handed down in the case. But, unlike some other fields of study, the understanding of past events is not your only objective. You must also try to assess the influence that this case is likely to have on the thinking of judges before whom somewhat similar cases will come for decision in the future.

This Section is organized in a manner designed to introduce you to case law processes by way of three more or less separate stages of emphasis. In your preparation of the cases in Subsection B, the emphasis should be on painstaking analysis of the factors which led the court in each case to decide the controversy as it did. In short, the emphasis is on what might be described as clinical dissection. After you have developed at least a fair idea of what is involved in taking a case apart, the materials and discussion will move on to a second stage. In connection with the cases and other materials in Subsection C, the emphasis will shift to a consideration of the weight of a case as a precedent in later cases involving somewhat different out-of-court facts. Here you will meet for the first time the ever-present professional problem of determining the *ratio decidendi* of a decision.

The third and most advanced stage of your introduction to the study of case law is provided by the cases in Subsection D, where you will have your first try at the challenging intellectual operation of studying a long line of cases and working out an accurate and useful synthesis of their holdings. Do not fall into the error of thinking that the synthesis of decisions is a problem unique to the course in Legal Method. The function of Legal Method, here, as on so many other points, is essentially that of setting the stage for the continuing practice in case synthesis which you will receive in your other courses throughout law school.

B. JUDICIAL DECISIONS ON "NEW QUESTIONS"

PRIESTLY v. FOWLER

Exchequer of Pleas, 1837.
3 Mees. & Wels. 1, 150 Eng.Rep. 1030.

Case. The declaration stated that the plaintiff was a servant of the defendant in his trade of a butcher; that the defendant had desired and directed the plaintiff, so being his servant, to go with him and take certain goods of the defendant, in a certain van of the defendant then used by him, and conducted by another of his servants, in carrying goods for hire upon a certain journey; that the plaintiff, in pursuance of such desire and direction, accordingly commenced and was proceeding and being carried and conveyed by the said van with the said goods; and it became the duty of the defendant on that occasion, to use due and proper care that the said van should be in a proper state of repair, that it should not be overloaded, and that the plaintiff should be safely and securely carried thereby; nevertheless, the defendant did not use proper care that the van should be in a sufficient state of repair, or that it should not be overloaded, or that the plaintiff should be safely and securely carried thereby, in consequence of the neglect of all and each of which duties the van gave way and broke down, and the plaintiff was thrown with violence to the ground, and his thigh was fractured.

At the trial before Parke, J., at the Lincolnshire Summer Assizes, 1836, the plaintiff, having given evidence to shew that the injury arose from the overloading of the van, and that it was so loaded with the defendant's knowledge, had a verdict for 100 pounds. In the following Michaelmas Term, Adams, Serjt., obtained a rule to shew cause why the judgment should not be arrested, on the ground that the defendant was not liable in law, under the circumstances stated in the declaration.

The judgment of the Court was now delivered by

LORD ABINGER, C. B. This was a motion in arrest of judgment, after verdict for the plaintiff, upon the insufficiency of the declaration. (His Lordship stated the declaration). It has been objected to this declaration, that it contains no premises from which the duty of the defendant, as therein alleged, can be inferred in law; or, in other words, that from the mere relation of master and servant no contract, and therefore no duty, can be implied on the part of the master to cause the servant to be safely and securely carried, or to make the master liable for damage to the servant, arising from any vice or imperfection, unknown to the master, in the carriage, or in the mode of handling and conducting it. For, as the declaration contains no charge that the defendant knew of the defects mentioned, the

Court is not called upon to decide how far such knowledge on his part of a defect unknown to the servant, would make him liable.

It is admitted that there is no precedent for the present action by a servant against a master. We are therefore to decide the question upon general principles, and in doing so we are at liberty to look at the consequences of a decision the one way or the other.

If the master be liable to the servant in this action, the principle of that liability will be found to carry us to an alarming extent. He who is responsible by his general duty, or by the terms of his contract, for all the consequences of negligence in a matter in which he is the principal, is responsible for the negligence of all his inferior agents. If the owner of the carriage is therefore responsible for the sufficiency of his carriage to his servant, he is responsible for the negligence of his coach-maker, or his harness-maker, or his coachman. The footman, therefore, who rides behind the carriage, may have an action against his master for a defect in the carriage owing to the negligence of the coach-maker, or for a defect in the harness arising from the negligence of the harness-maker, or for drunkenness, neglect, or want of skill in the coachman; nor is there any reason why the principle should not, if applicable in this class of cases, extend to many others. The master, for example, would be liable to the servant for the negligence of the chambermaid, for putting him into a damp bed; for that of the upholsterer, for sending in a crazy bedstead, whereby he was made to fall down while asleep and injure himself; for the negligence of the cook, in not properly cleaning the copper vessels used in the kitchen; of the butcher, in supplying the family with meat of a quality injurious to the health; of the builder, for a defect in the foundation of the house, whereby it fell, and injured both the master and the servant by the ruins.

The inconvenience, not to say the absurdity of these consequences, afford a sufficient argument against the application of this principle to the present case. But, in truth, the mere relation of the master and the servant can never imply an obligation on the part of the master to take more care of the servant than he may reasonably be expected to do of himself. He is, no doubt, bound to provide for the safety of his servant in the course of his employment, to the best of the judgment, information and belief. The servant is not bound to risk his safety in the service of his master, and may, if he thinks fit, decline any service in which he reasonably apprehends injury to himself: in most of the cases in which danger may be incurred, if not in all, he is just as likely to be acquainted with the probability and extent of it as the master. In that sort of employment, especially, which is described in the declaration in this case, the plaintiff must have known as well as his master, and probably better, whether the van was sufficient, whether it was overloaded, and whether it was likely to carry him safely. In fact, to allow this sort of action to prevail would be an encouragement to the servant to omit that diligence and caution which he is in duty bound to exercise on behalf of his master, to protect him against the misconduct or negligence of others who serve him, and which diligence and caution, while they protect the master, are a much better security against any injury the servant may sustain by the negligence of others engaged under the same master, than any recourse against his master for damages could possibly afford.

We are therefore of opinion that the judgment ought to be arrested.

Rule absolute.

NOTES

1. What, precisely, was the *new question* presented to the court in Priestly v. Fowler? In this connection it should be observed that the doctrine of *respondeat superior*, imposing liability on a master or principal for injuries caused by the fault of his servant or agent, had been recognized in English law long before the decision in Priestly v. Fowler. See, for example, Bush v. Steinman, 1 Bos. & Pul. 404, 126 Eng.Rep. 978 (1799).

2. "In 1837, the steam railway had supplanted the horse-drawn vehicle as a means of long distance travel; factories in textile and other industries were flourishing; intricate and high-powered machinery was coming more and more into use and its products were displacing those of individual craftsmen. It is noteworthy that all the analogies set forth in Lord Abinger's opinion were drawn from domestic service, or from trades essentially of the cottage type, carried on by local artisans; and that not a single example was taken from the large units of industry, such as the factory, the steam railway, or the shipbuilding or mining industries, all of which were being carried on in England at that time. Therefore, the law which was to be applied by the courts to those employees injured through complicated or dangerous industrial processes was based on instances taken from an already dying industrial age." Dodd, Administration of Workmen's Compensation 5–6 (1936).

ALBRO v. THE AGAWAM CANAL CO.

Supreme Judicial Court of Massachusetts, 1850.
60 Mass. (6 Cushing) 75.

This was an action on the case, to recover damages for an injury sustained by the plaintiff, while in the employment of the defendants, in consequence of the gross negligence of their superintendent. The case was tried before Fletcher, J., who, being of opinion, upon the facts stated and the evidence offered, that the action could not be maintained, reserved and reported the case for the consideration of the whole court.

It appeared in evidence that the defendants were the proprietors of a large manufacturing establishment in West Springfield, and engaged in the manufacture of cotton goods; that in November, 1849, when the injury complained of occurred, the plaintiff was in the employment of the defendants as a spinner; that one Jaquith was then and ever since had been the defendants' superintendent, having a general supervision and charge of their establishment, and of the manufacture there carried on * * *.

The plaintiff offered to introduce evidence to prove, that she received the injury for which this action was brought through the gross negligence and want of skill of the superintendent, on the occasion in question, in directing the person employed in the manufacture of the gas, with which the mill was lighted, to throw off all the weights from the gasometer, by means of which the gas was forced into the mill, where the plaintiff worked, in great quantities, extinguishing the lights, and so filling the room, where the plaintiff was, as to throw her into spasmodic fits, and occasion her a very serious and lasting injury. And it was admitted that the management of lighting the mill, and manufacturing gas for the purpose, was a matter under the control of the superintendent.

FLETCHER, J. This case cannot be distinguished in principle from the case of Farwell v. Boston and Worcester Railroad, 4 Met. [Mass.] 49; and the same point has been since adjudged in the case of Hayes v. Western Railroad, 3 Cush. 270.

The principle of these decisions is, that when one person engages in the service of another, he undertakes, as between him and his employer, to run all the ordinary risks of the service, and this includes the risk of negligence on the part of others in the service of the same employer, whenever he, such servant, is acting in the discharge of his duty to his employer, who is the common employer of both. In the present case, the injury of which the plaintiff complains appears to have happened while she was acting in the discharge of her duty to the defendants, as her employers, in their factory, and to have been occasioned by the negligence of another person, who was also engaged in the defendants' service, in the same factory.

It cannot affect the principle, that the duties of the superintendent may be different, and perhaps may be considered as of a somewhat higher character than those of the plaintiff; inasmuch as they are both the servants of the same master, have the same employer, are engaged in the accomplishment of the same general object, are acting in one common service, and derive their compensation from the same source.

The plaintiff and the superintendent must be considered as fellow-servants, within the principle and meaning of the cases above referred to, and the other adjudged cases on this subject. There is no allegation, that the superintendent was not a fit and proper person to be employed by the defendants to perform the duties assigned to him, but only that he was chargeable with negligence and unskilfulness, on the particular occasion when the plaintiff was injured in the manner described. It would have presented a very different case, if the defendants had employed an unfit and improper person, and in that way the plaintiff had been exposed to and had suffered injury.

In the decision of the case of Farwell v. Boston and Worcester Railroad, the case of Priestly v. Fowler, 3 N. & W. 1, was referred to as an authority in point. There have recently been two other English cases (Hutchinson v. York, Newcastle, and Berwick Railway, 5 W. H. & G. 343; Wigmore v. Jay, Ib. 354) which fully sustain the doctrine and decision of Priestly v. Fowler. It is very clear, therefore, upon the adjudged cases, that this action cannot be maintained, and that judgment must be entered for the defendants.

NOTES

1. In Farwell v. Boston & Worcester R. Corp., 45 Mass. (4 Met.) 49 (1842), cited in the *Albro* case, the plaintiff was an engineer employed by the defendant railroad. He was injured when the engine on which he was riding was derailed as the result of the negligence of a switchman, also employed by the defendant, who left a switch in a wrong position. The opinion of Judge Shaw reads in part (45 Mass. at 55–56):

> "This is an action of new impression in our courts, and involves a principle of great importance. It presents a case, where two persons are in the service and employment of one company, whose business it is to construct and maintain a rail road, and to employ their trains of cars to carry persons and merchandise for hire. They are appointed and employed by the same company to perform separate duties and services, all tending to the accomplishment of one and the same purpose—that of the safe and rapid transmission of the trains; and they are paid for their respective services according to the nature of their respective duties, and the labor and skill required for their proper performance. The question is, whether, for damages sustained by one of the persons so employed, by means of the carelessness and negligence of another, the party injured has a remedy against the common employer. It is an argument against such an action, though certainly not a decisive one, that no such action has before been maintained.

> "It is laid down by Blackstone, that if a servant, by his negligence, does any damage to a stranger, the master shall be answerable for his neglect. But the damage must be done while he is actually employed in the master's service; otherwise, the servant shall answer for his own misbehavior. 1 Bl.Com. 431. McManus v. Crickett, 1 East, 106. This rule is obviously founded on the great principle of social duty, that every man, in the management of his own affairs, whether by himself or by his agents or servants, shall so conduct them as not to injure another; and if he does not, and another thereby sustains damage, he shall answer for it. If done by a servant, in the course of his employment, and acting within the scope of his authority, it is considered, in contemplation of law, so far the act of the master, that the latter shall be answerable civiliter. But this presupposes that the parties stand to each other in the relation of strangers, between whom there is no privity; and the action, in such case, is an action sounding in

tort. The form is trespass on the case, for the consequential damage. The maxim respondeat superior is adopted in that case, from general considerations of policy and security.

"But this does not apply to the case of a servant bringing his action against his own employer to recover damages for an injury arising in the course of that employment, where all such risks and perils as the employer and the servant respectively intend to assume and bear may be regulated by the express or implied contract between them, and which, in contemplation of law, must be presumed to be thus regulated."

In Hayes v. Western R. Corp., 57 Mass. (3 Cush.) 270 (1849), also cited in *Albro*, plaintiff was a brakeman employed by the defendant railroad. He was injured when six cars of a train broke loose on a grade and rolled back into a following train on which plaintiff was riding. The accident would not have occurred but for the negligence of the acting conductor of the first train (also a brakeman in the employ of the defendant) in failing to station a brakeman on the last car of that train.

2. To what extent, if at all, was this case decided upon the basis of precedent? Was the court "bound" in this case by the decision in Priestly v. Fowler? By the decision in Farwell v. Boston & Worcester Railroad? Do you agree with the court that the *Albro* case "cannot be distinguished in principle" from the *Farwell* and *Hayes* cases?

3. What would have been the best line of argument for counsel for the plaintiff in the principal case? What considerations should have been (perhaps were) urged upon the court by counsel for the plaintiff as calling for a resolution of the "new problem" in plaintiff's favor? See, for a decision the other way, Shumway v. The Walworth & Neville Mfg. Co., 98 Mich. 411 (1894).

4. The problem of compensation for the victims of industrial accidents was never satisfactorily solved by the common law. Widespread dissatisfaction with such common law defenses as the fellow servant doctrine led to the enactment of workmen's (now frequently called workers') compensation legislation throughout the country. Under workmen's compensation, liability is imposed on the employer irrespective of his or the employee's fault, and an informal administrative system is established to make recoveries possible without expensive and protracted court action. However, the amount recovered is usually substantially less than could be recovered in a tort action.

BAKER v. LIBBIE

Supreme Judicial Court of Massachusetts, 1912.
210 Mass. 599, 97 N.E. 109.

Bill in Equity, filed in the Superior Court on February 17, 1911, by the executor of the will of Mary Baker G. Eddy, late of Concord in the State of New Hampshire, against the members of a firm engaged in business in Boston as auctioneers of books and manuscripts, alleging that a number of private unpublished letters written by the plaintiff's testatrix had come into the possession of the defendants in the course of their business, that the defendants had advertised such letters for public sale in their auction rooms in Boston and already had printed and published material and substantial parts of the letters in their sale catalogue, that the catalogue was being distributed by the defendants, and would be further distributed to the persons in attendance at such auction and that portions of the letters also had been published in the newspapers of Boston, New York and other cities of the country; and praying that the defendants might be enjoined and restrained "from further printing, publishing, selling, circulating, or in any manner making public or showing said letters, or any of them, or any copy or copies, extract or extracts therefrom, or any of them, to any person or persons," and "from further circulating or distributing or making public in any manner copies of said catalogue containing extracts from any of said letters."

The case came on to be heard before Richardson, J., who by agreement of the parties reserved and reported it, upon the bill and answer, and all questions of law therein, for determination by this court.

RUGG, C. J. The plaintiff as executor of the will of Mary Baker G. Eddy, the founder of "Christian Science" so called, seeks to restrain an auctioneer of manuscripts from publishing for advertising purposes and from selling certain autographed letters of his testatrix. These letters were written in her own hand by Mrs. Eddy, as is said, "during one of the most interesting periods of her career, that is, just after the first publication of her 'Science and Health with Key to the Scriptures,'" in 1875. It is averred in the answer that the letters have no attribute of literature, but are merely friendly letters written to a cousin about domestic and business affairs. Extracts from the letters show that they refer to household matters, to health and to the work she was doing. The questions raised relate to the existence, extent and character of the proprietary right of the writer of private letters upon indifferent subjects not possessing the qualities of literature and to the degree of protection to be given in equity to such rights as are found to exist. These points have never been presented before for decision in this Commonwealth. The nearest approach was in Tomkins v. Halleck, 133 Mass. 32, 43 Am.Rep. 480, where the rights of an author of a dramatic composition put upon the stage but not printed were protected against a rival presentation made possible by human memory (overruling upon this point the earlier case of Keene v. Kimball, 16 Gray, 545, 77 Am.Dec. 426) and Dodge Co. v. Construction Information Co., 183 Mass. 62, 66 N.E. 204, 60 L.R.A. 810, 97 Am.St.Rep. 412, where property rights in valuable commercial information distributed to subscribers in writing, in print, by telegraph or orally, were recognized and protected against use by a rival concern. Neither of these decisions touches at all closely the points involved in the case at bar.

The rights of the authors of letters of a private or business nature have been the subject of judicial determination in courts in England and this country for a period of at least one hundred and seventy years. The first English case was Pope v. Curl, 2 Atk. 341, which was in 1741. It was a suit by Alexander Pope to restrain the publication of letters written by him to Swift and others. In continuing an injunction Lord Chancellor Hardwicke, after remarking that no distinction could be drawn between letters and books or other learned works, said, "Another objection has been made * * * that where a man writes a letter, it is in the nature of a gift to the receiver. But I am of opinion that it is only a special property in the receiver, possibly the property of the paper may belong to him; but this does not give a license to any person whatsoever to publish them to the world, for at most the receiver has only a joint property with the writer. * * * It has been insisted * * * that this is a sort of work which does not come within the meaning of the act of Parliament [as to copyright], because it contains only letters on familiar subjects, and inquiries after the health of friends, and cannot properly be called a learned work. It is certain that no works have done more service to mankind, than those which have appeared in this shape, upon familiar subjects, and which perhaps were never intended to be published; and it is this makes them so valuable."

Thompson v. Stanhope, 2 Ambl. 737 (1774) was a suit by the executors of Lord Chesterfield to restrain the publication of his now famous letters to his son, which the widow of the latter proposed to print and sell. Some of these possessed literary merit of a high order. Lord Chancellor Apsley was "very clear" that an injunction should be granted, upon the authority of the foregoing decision and the somewhat kindred cases of Forrester v. Waller, cited 4 Burr. 2331, and Webb v. Rose, cited 4 Burr. 2330, where notes and conveyancer's draughts were held to be the literary property of the writer or his representatives, and Duke of Queensbury v. Shebbeare, 2 Eden, 329, where the publication of a part of Lord Clarendon's History by a possessor of the manuscript was restrained.

Gee v. Pritchard, 2 Swanst. 402, 426, was decided by Lord Eldon in 1818. Letters apparently without literary or other special interest by the plaintiff to the son of her husband were the subject of the suit, and publication was restrained on the ground of the property right of the writer. In Lytton v. Devey, 54 L.J. (N.S.) Ch. 293, 295, it was said: "The property in the letters remains in the person to whom they are sent. The right to retain them remains in the person to whom the letters are sent; but the sender of the letters has still that kind of interest, if not property, in the letters that he has a right to restrain any use being made of the communication which he has made in the letters so sent by him." See also Prince Albert v. Strange, 2 DeG. & Sm. 652; S.C. 1 MacN. & G. 25, 43. This same principle was followed expressly in the Irish case of Earl of Granard v. Dunkin, 1 Ball & Beatty, 207, and in Labouchere v. Hess, 77 L.T. (N.S.) Ch. 559. There are several dicta to the same effect by great English judges. For example, Lord Campbell said in Boosey v. Jefferys, 6 Exch. 580, at 583, "A court of equity will grant an injunction to prevent the publication of a letter by a correspondent against the will of the writer. That is a recognition of property in the writer, although he has parted with the manuscript; since he wrote to enable his correspondent to know his sentiments, not to give them to the world." Lord Cairns said, respecting correspondence in Hopkinson v. Burghley, L.R. 2 Ch. 447, at 448: "The writer is supposed to intend that the receiver may use it for any lawful purpose, and it has been held that publication is not such a lawful purpose." See also Jefferys v. Boosey, 4 H.L.Cas. 815, 867, 962. The latest English case on the subject recognizes this as the well settled rule. Philip v. Pennell, [1907] 2 Ch. 577. In 1804 the Scottish court on the suit of his children interdicted the publication of manuscript letters of Robert Burns. Cadell & Davies v. Stewart, 1 Bell's Com. 116 n.

The earliest case in this country, Denis v. Leclerc, 1 Martin O.S., La., 297, arose in 1811. A single letter of no literary pretension was there in question and its publication was enjoined, and the writer's property interest in the letter was distinctly upheld.

The question was elaborately discussed by Mr. Justice Story in Folsom v. Marsh, Fed.Cas.No.4901, 2 Story 100, 110, who held that "The author of any letter or letters, (and his representatives), whether they are literary compositions, or familiar letters, or letters of business, possess the sole and exclusive copyright therein; and that no persons, neither those to whom they are addressed, nor other persons, have any right or authority, to publish the same upon their own account, or for their own benefit."

In Bartlett v. Crittenden, Fed.Cas.No.1076, 5 McLean, 32, at 42, Mr. Justice McLean said: "Even the publication of private letters by the person to whom they were addressed, may be enjoined. This is done upon the ground that the writer has a right of property in the purpose for which they were written."

In Woolsey v. Judd, 11 How.Prac. 49, 4 Duer, 379, the question was considered exhaustively, and all the earlier cases were reviewed. The conclusion was reached that the writer of even private letters of no literary value has such a proprietary interest as required a court of equity at his instance to prohibit their publication by the receiver.

Grigsby v. Breckinridge, 2 Bush, Ky., 480, decided that "the recipient of a private letter, sent without any reservation, express or implied, 'held' the general property, qualified only by the incidental right in the author to publish and prevent publication by the recipient, or any other person."

In Barrett v. Fish, 72 Vt. 18, at 20, 47 A. 174, 51 L.R.A. 754, 82 Am.St.Rep. 914, it was said "that a court of equity will protect the right of property in such [private] letters, by enjoining their unauthorized publication." The same doctrine has been held, either expressly or by way of dictum, in Dock v. Dock, 180 Pa. 14, 22, 36 A.

411, 57 Am.St.Rep. 617; Rice v. Williams, 32 F. 437; Eyre v. Higbee, 22 How.Pr. 198, 35 Barb. 502; Palmer v. DeWitt, 47 N.Y. 532, 536, 7 Am.Rep. 480.

Against these opinions are Wetmore v. Scovell, 3 Edw.Ch. 515, and Hoyt v. Mackenzie, 3 Barb.Ch. 320, 49 Am.Dec. 178; decided respectively by Vice-Chancellor McCoun and Chancellor Walworth while sitting alone. They were criticised and overruled in Woolsey v. Judd, 11 How.Prac. 49, 4 Duer, 379, by a court of six judges. There are also certain doubtful dicta by a vice-chancellor in Percival v. Phipps, 2 V. & B. 19, 28, which are relied upon as asserting a somewhat similar view. But it is not necessary to discuss them in detail, for this review of cases demonstrates that the weight of decisions by courts of great authority, speaking often through judges of high distinction for learning and ability, supports the conclusion that equity will afford injunctive relief to the author against the publication of his private letters upon commonplace subjects without regard to their literary merit or the popular attention or special curiosity aroused by them.

The same conclusion is reached on principle and apart from authority. It is generally recognized that one has a right to the fruits of his labor. This is equally true, whether the work be muscular or mental or both combined. Property in literary productions, before publication and while they rest in manuscript, is as plain as property in the game of the hunter or in the grain of the husbandman. The labor of composing letters for private and familar correspondence may be trifling, or it may be severe, but it is none the less the result of an expenditure of thought and time. The market value of such an effort may be measured by the opinions of others, but the fact of property is not created thereby. A canvas upon which an obscure or unskilful painter has toiled does not cease to be property merely because by conventional standards it is valueless as a work of art. Few products of the intellect reveal individual characteristics more surely than familiar correspondence, entries in diaries or other unambitious writings. No sound distinction in this regard can be made between that which has literary merit and that which is without it. Such a distinction could not be drawn with any certainty. While extremes might be discovered, compositions near the dividing line would be subject to no fixed criterion at any given moment, and scarcely anything is more fluctuating than the literary taste of the general public. Even those counted as experts in literature differ widely in opinion both in the same and in successive generations as to the relative merits of different authors. The basic principle on which the right of the author is sustained even as to writings confessedly literature is not their literary quality, but the fact that they are the product of labor.

The existence of a right in the author over his letters, even though private and without worth as literature, is established on

Sec. 3   TECHNIQUE OF CASE LAW DEVELOPMENT   85

principle and authority. The right is property in its essential features. It is, therefore, entitled to all the protection which the Constitution and laws give to property. From this general statement are to be excepted special instances, such as letters by an agent to or for his principal and others where the conditions indicate that the property in the form or expression is in another than the writer. The absolute right of the author to prevent publication by the receiver may also be subject to limitations arising from the nature of the letter or the circumstances under which it is written or received. Some of these are pointed out in Folsom v. Marsh, Fed.Cas.No.4901, 2 Story, 100. But these exceptions are narrow and rare, and do not affect materially the general rule.

The extent of this proprietary right, as between the writer and the recipient of letters, requires a closer analysis. It depends upon implications raised by law from the circumstances. This test is a general one, and has been applied to the public delivery of lectures, the presentation of dramas, and other analogous cases. Abernethy v. Hutchinson, 3 L.J.Ch. 209; S.C. 1 Hall & Tw. 28. Tompkins v. Halleck, 133 Mass. 32, 43 Am.Rep. 480. Nicols v. Pitman, 26 Ch.D. 374, 380. The relative rights of the writer and receiver may vary with different conditions. If there be a request for return or if the correspondence is marked in definite terms, as personal or confidential, such special considerations would need to be regarded. The case at bar presents the ordinary example of friendly correspondence between kinswomen upon topics of mutual private interest. Under such circumstances, what does the writer retain and what does he give to the person to whom the letter is sent? The property right of the author has been described as "an incorporeal right to print [and it should be added to prevent the printing of, if he desires] a set of intellectual ideas or modes of thinking, communicated in a set of words and sentences and modes of expression. It is equally detached from the manuscript, or any other physical existence whatsoever." Millar v. Taylor, 4 Burr. 2303, at 2396. It has been called also "the order of words in the * * * composition." Jefferys v. Boosey, 4 H.L.Cas. 815, 867. Holmes v. Hurst, 174 U.S. 82, 86, 19 S.Ct. 606, 43 L.Ed. 904. Kalem Co. v. Harper Bros., 222 U.S. 55, 63, 32 S.Ct. 20, 56 L.Ed. 92, Ann.Cas.1913A, 1285. The right of the author to publish or suppress publication of his correspondence is absolute in the absence of special considerations, and is independent of any desire or intent at the time of writing. It is an interest in the intangible and impalpable thought and the particular verbal garments in which it has been clothed. Although independent of the manuscript, this right involves a right to copy or secure copies. Otherwise, the author's right of publication might be lost. The author parts with the physical and material elements which are conveyed by and in the envelope. These are given to the receiver. The paper upon which the letter is written belongs to the receiver. Oliver v. Oliver, 11 C.B.

(N.S.) 139. Grigsby v. Breckinridge, 2 Bush, Ky., 480, 486, 92 Am. Dec. 509. Pope v. Curl, 2 Atk. 341. Werckmeister v. American Lithographic Co., 142 F. 827, 830. A duty of preservation would impose an unreasonable burden in most instances. It is obvious that no such obligation rests upon the receiver, and he may destroy or keep at pleasure. Commonly there must be inferred a right of reading or showing to a more or less limited circle of friends and relatives. But in other instances the very nature of the correspondence may be such as to set the seal of secrecy upon its contents. See Kenrick v. Danube Collieries & Minerals Co., 39 W.R. 473. Letters of extreme affection and other fiduciary communications may come within this class. There may be also a confidential relation existing between the parties, out of which would arise an implied prohibition against any use of the letters, and a breach of such trust might be restrained in equity. On the other hand, the conventional autograph letters by famous persons signify on their face a license to transfer. Equitable rights may exist in the author against one who by fraud, theft or other illegality obtains possession of letters. The precise inquiry is whether indifferent letters written by one at the time perhaps little known or quite unknown which subsequently acquire value as holographic manuscripts, may be marketed as such. This case does not involve personal feelings or what has been termed the right to privacy. 4 Harvard Law Review, 193. The author has deceased. Moreover, there appears to be nothing about these letters, knowledge of which by strangers would violate even delicate feelings. Although the particular form of the expression of the thought remains the property of the writer, the substance and material on which this thought has been expressed have passed to the recipient of the letter. The paper has received the impression of the pen, and the two in combination have been given away. The thing which has value as an autograph is not the intactable thought, but the material substance upon which a particular human hand has been placed, and has traced the intelligible symbols. Perhaps the autographic value of letters may fluctuate in accordance with their length or the nature of their subject matter. But whatever such value may be, in its essence it does not attach to the intellectual but material part of the letter.

This exact question has never been presented for adjudication, so far as we are aware. There are some expressions in opinions, which dissociated from their connection may be laid hold of to support the plaintiff's contention. See Dock v. Dock, 180 Pa. 14, 22, 36 A. 411, 57 Am.St.Rep. 617; Eyre v. Higbee, 22 How.Pr. 198, 35 Barb. 502; Palin v. Gathercole, 1 Collyer, 565. It may well be that title such as appears to exist in the recipient may not go to the extent of being assets in the hands of a decedent, a bankrupt or an insolvent. Eyre v. Higbee, 22 How.Pr. 198, 35 Barb. 502; Sibley v. Nason, 196 Mass. 125, 81 N.E. 887, 12 L.R.A.,N.S. 1173, 124 Am.St.Rep. 520, 12 Ann.Cas. 938. But on principle it seems to flow from the nature of the right transferred by the author to the receiver and of that retained by the writer in ordinary correspondence, that the extent of the latter's proprietary power is to make or to restrain a publication, but not to prevent a transfer. The rule applicable to the facts of this case, as we conceive it to be, is that in the absence of some special limitation imposed either by the subject matter of the letter or the circumstances under which it is sent, the right in the receiver of an ordinary letter is one of unqualified title in the material on which it is written. He can deal with it as absolute owner subject only to the proprietary right retained by the author for himself and his representatives to the publication or non-publication of idea in its particular verbal expression. In this opinion publication has been used in the sense of making public through printing or multiplication of copies.

The result is that an injunction may issue against publication or multiplication in any way, in whole or in part, for advertising or other purposes, of any of the letters described in the bill, and allowing the plaintiff, if he desires, to make copies thereof within a reasonable time, but going no further.

NOTES

1. What were the "new questions" before the court in Baker v. Libbie?

2. To what sources does the court look for assistance in "finding" the law which it applies here? Are they the same sources to which Lord Abinger looked in Priestly v. Fowler? Are they the same sources to which a legislature would look in deciding whether to give statutory protection to authors of letters?

ESTATE OF HEMINGWAY v. RANDOM HOUSE, INC.

Court of Appeals of New York, 1968.
23 N.Y.2d 341, 296 N.Y.S.2d 771, 244 N.E.2d 250.

Chief Judge FULD. On this appeal—involving an action brought by the estate of the late Ernest Hemingway and his widow against the publisher and author of a book, entitled "Papa Hemingway"—we are called upon to decide, primarily, whether conversations of a gifted and highly regarded writer may become the subject of common-law copyright, even though the speaker himself has not reduced his words to writing.

Hemingway died in 1961. During the last 13 years of his life, a close friendship existed between him and A. E. Hotchner, a younger and far less well-known writer. Hotchner, who met Hemingway in the course of writing articles about him became a favored drinking and traveling companion of the famous author, a frequent visitor to his home and the adapter of some of his works for motion pictures and television. During these years, Hemingway's conversation with Hotchner, in which others sometimes took part, was filled with anecdote, reminiscence, literary opinion and revealing comment about actual persons on whom some of Hemingway's fictional characters were based. Hotchner made careful notes of these conversations soon after they occurred, occasionally recording them on a portable tape recorder.

During Hemingway's lifetime, Hotchner wrote and published several articles about his friend in which he quoted some of this talk at length. Hemingway, far from objecting to this practice, approved of it. Indeed, the record reveals that other writers also quoted Hemingway's conversation without any objection from him, even when he was displeased with the articles themselves.

After Hemingway's death, Hotchner wrote "Papa Hemingway," drawing upon his notes and his recollections, and in 1966 it was published by the defendant Random House. Subtitled "a personal memoir", it is a serious and revealing biographical portrait of the world-renowned writer. Woven through the narrative, and giving the book much of its interest and character, are lengthy quotations from Hemingway's talks as noted or remembered by Hotchner. Included also are two chapters on Hemingway's final illness and suicide in which Hotchner writing of his friend with obvious feeling and sympathy, refers to events, and even to medical information, to which he was privy as an intimate of the family. Hemingway's widow, Mary, is mentioned frequently in the book, and is sometimes quoted, but only incidentally.

The complaint, which seeks an injunction and damages, alleges four causes of action. The first three, in which the Estate of Hemingway and his widow join as plaintiffs, are, briefly stated, (1) that "Papa Hemingway" consists, in the main, of literary matter composed by Hemingway in which he had a common-law copyright; (2) that publication would constitute an unauthorized appropriation of Hemingway's work and would compete unfairly with his other literary creations; and (3) that Hotchner wrongfully used material which was imparted to him in the course of a confidential and fiduciary relationship with Hemingway. In the fourth cause of action, Mary Hemingway asserts that the book invades the right to privacy to which she herself is entitled under section 51 of the Civil Rights Law.

The plaintiffs moved for a preliminary injunction. The motion was denied (49 Misc.2d 726, affd. 25 A.D.2d 719), and the book was thereafter published. After its publication, the defendants sought and were granted summary judgment dismissing all four causes of action. The Appellate Division unanimously affirmed the resulting orders and granted the plaintiffs leave to appeal to this court.

Turning to the first cause of action, we agree with the disposition made below but on a ground more narrow than that articulated by the court at Special Term. It is the position of the plaintiffs (under this count) that Hemingway was entitled to a common-law copyright on the theory that his directly quoted comment, anecdote and opinion were his "literary creations", his "literary property", and that the defendant Hotchner's note-taking only performed the mechanics of recordation. And, in a somewhat different vein, the plaintiffs argue that "[w]hat for Hemingway was oral one day would be or could become his written manuscript the next day", that his speech, constituting not just a statement of his ideas but the very form in which he conceived and expressed them, was as much the subject of common-law copyright as what he might himself have committed to paper.

Common-law copyright is the term applied to an author's proprietary interest in his literary or artistic creations before they have been made generally available to the public. It enables the author to exercise control over the first publication of his work or to prevent publication entirely—hence, its other name, the "right of first publication". (Chamberlain v. Feldman, 300 N.Y. 135, 139).[26] No cases deal directly with the question whether it extends to conversational speech and we begin, therefore, with a brief review of some relevant concepts in this area of law.

It must be acknowledged—as the defendants point out—that nearly a century ago our court stated that common-law copyright extended to "'[e]very new and innocent product of mental labor which has been *embodied in writing, or some other material form*'". (Palmer v. De Witt, 47 N.Y. 532, 537; emphasis supplied.) And, more recently, it has been said that "an author has no property right in his ideas unless * * * given embodiment in a tangible form." (O'Brien v. RKO Radio Pictures, 68 F.Supp. 13, 14.) However, as a noted scholar in the field has observed, "the underlying rationale for common law copyright (i. e., the recognition that a property status should attach to the fruits of intellectual labor) is applicable regardless of whether such labor assumes tangible form" (Nimmer, Copyright, § 11.1, p. 40). The principle that it is not the tangible embodiment of the author's work but the creation of the work itself which is protected finds recognition in a number of ways in copyright law.

One example, with some relevance to the problem before us, is the treatment which the law has accorded to personal letters—a

---

26. Although common-law copyright in an unpublished work lasts indefinitely, it is extinguished immediately upon publication of the work by the author. He must then rely, for his protection, upon Federal statutory copyright. (See Nimmer, Copyright, § 11, pp. 38, 42 and ch. 4, p. 183 et seq.) Section 2 of the Copyright Act (U.S.Code, tit. 17) expressly preserves common-law rights in *unpublished* works against any implication that the field is pre-empted by the Federal statute. [While the court's statements with respect to common law copyright in unpublished works were accurate when this opinion was written, the Copyright Act of 1976 made most unpublished, as well as published, works of authorship exclusively subject to Federal statutory protection. See Act of Oct. 19, 1976, Pub.L. No. 94–553, 90 Stat. 2541.— Ed.]

kind of half-conversation in written form. Although the paper upon which the letter is written belongs to the recipient, it is the author who has the right to publish them or to prevent their publication. (See Baker v. Libbie, 210 Mass. 599, 605, 606.) In the words of the Massachusetts court in the *Baker* case (210 Mass., at pp. 605–606), the author's right "is an interest in the intangible and impalpable thought and the particular verbal garments in which it has been clothed." Nor has speech itself been entirely without protection against reproduction for publication. The public delivery of an address or a lecture or the performance of a play is not deemed a "publication," and, accordingly, it does not deprive the author of his common-law copyright in its contents. (See Ferris v. Frohman, 223 U.S. 424; King v. Mister Maestro, Inc., 224 F.Supp. 101, 106; Palmer v. De Witt, 47 N.Y. 532, 543, supra; see, also, Nimmer, Copyright, § 53, p. 208.)

Letters, however—like plays and public addresses, written or not—have distinct, identifiable boundaries and they are, in most cases, only occasional products. Whatever difficulties attend the formulation of suitable rules for the enforcement of rights in such works (see, e. g., Note, Personal Letters: In Need of a Law of Their Own, 44 Iowa L.Rev. 705), they are relatively manageable. However, conversational speech, the distinctive behavior of man, is quite another matter, and subjecting any part of it to the restraints of common-law copyright presents unique problems.

One such problem—and it was stressed by the court at Special Term (SCHWEITZER, J.) [27]—is that of avoiding undue restraints on the freedoms of speech and press and, in particular, on the writers of history and of biographical works of the genre of Boswell's "Life of Johnson". The safeguarding of essential freedoms in this area is, though, not without its complications. The indispensable right of the press to report on what people have *done*, or on what has *happened* to them or on what they have *said in public* (see Time, Inc. v. Hill, 385 U.S. 374; Curtis Pub. Co. v. Butts, 388 U.S. 130; Associated Press v. Walker, 388 U.S. 130) does not necessarily imply an unbounded freedom to publish whatever they may have *said in private conversation*, any more than it implies a freedom to copy and publish what people may have put down in *private writings*.

Copyright, both common-law and statutory, rests on the assumption that there are forms of expression, limited in kind, to be sure, which should not be divulged to the public without the consent of their author. The purpose, far from being restrictive, is to encour-

---

27. Another problem—also remarked by the court—is the difficulty of measuring the relative self-sufficiency of any one party's contributions to a conversation, although it may be, in the case of some kinds of dialogue or interview, that the difficulty would not be greater than in deciding other questions of degree, such as plagiarism. (See, e. g., Nichols v. Universal Pictures Corp., 45 F.2d 119.)

age and protect intellectual labor. (See Note, Copyright: Right to Common Law Copyright in Conversation of a Decedent, 67 Col.L. Rev. 366, 367, commenting on the decision denying the plaintiffs before us a preliminary injunction, 49 Misc.2d 726.) The essential thrust of the First Amendment is to prohibit improper restraints on the *voluntary* public expression of ideas; it shields the man who wants to speak or publish when others wish him to be quiet. There is necessarily, and within suitably defined areas, a concomitant freedom *not* to speak publicly, one which serves the same ultimate end as freedom of speech in its affirmative aspect.

The rules of common-law copyright assure this freedom in the case of written material. However, speech is now easily captured by electronic devices and, consequently, we should be wary about excluding all possibility of protecting a speaker's right to decide when his words, uttered in private dialogue, may or may not be published at large. Conceivably, there may be limited and special situations in which an interlocutor brings forth oral statements from another party which both understand to be the unique intellectual product of the principal speaker, a product which would qualify for common-law copyright if such statements were in writing. Concerning such problems, we express no opinion; we do no more than raise the questions, leaving them open for future consideration in cases which may present them more sharply than this one does.

On the appeal before us, the plaintiffs' claim to common-law copyright may be disposed of more simply and on a more narrow ground.

The defendant Hotchner asserts—without contradiction in the papers before us—that Hemingway never suggested to him or to anyone else that he regarded his conversational remarks to be "literary creations" or that he was of a mind to restrict Hotchner's use of the notes and recordings which Hemingway knew him to be accumulating. On the contrary, as we have already observed, it had become a continuing practice, during Hemingway's lifetime, for Hotchner to write articles about Hemingway, consisting largely of quotations from the latter's conversation—and of all of this Hemingway approved. In these circumstances, authority to publish must be implied, thus negativing the reservation of any common-law copyright.

Assuming, without deciding, that in a proper case a common-law copyright in certain limited kinds of spoken dialogue might be recognized, it would, at the very least, be required that the speaker indicate that he intended to mark off the utterance in question from the ordinary stream of speech, that he meant to adopt it as a unique statement and that he wished to exercise control over its publication. In the conventional common-law copyright situation, this indication is afforded by the creation of the manuscript itself. It would have to be evidenced in some other way if protection were ever to be accorded to some forms of conversational dialogue.

Such an indication is, of course, possible in the case of speech. It might, for example, be found in prefatory words or inferred from the circumstances in which the dialogue takes place.[28] Another way of formulating such a rule might be to say that, although, in the case of most intellectual products, the courts are reluctant to find that an author has "published," so as to lose his common-law copyright (see Nimmer, Copyright, § 58.2, pp. 226–228), in the case of conversational speech,—because of its unique nature—there should be a presumption that the speaker has not reserved any common-law rights unless the contrary strongly appears. However, we need not carry such speculation further in the present case since the requisite conditions are plainly absent here.

For present purposes, it is enough to observe that Hemingway's words and conduct, far from making any such reservation, left no doubt of his willingness to permit Hotchner to draw freely on their conversation in writing about him and to publish such material. What we have said disposes of the plaintiffs' claim both to exclusive and to joint copyright and we need not consider this aspect of the case any further. It follows, therefore, that the courts below were eminently correct in dismissing the first cause of action.

[The court's discussion of the second, third and fourth causes of action is omitted]

In brief, then, it is our conclusion that, since no triable issues have been raised, the courts below very properly dismissed the complaint.

The orders appealed from should be affirmed, with costs.

Judges BURKE, SCILEPPI, BERGAN, KEATING, BREITEL and JASEN concur.

Orders affirmed.

NOTES

1. What was the "new question" before the court in *Estate of Hemingway?* What answer does the court give to that question?

2. To what extent does the difficulty of protecting speech—as opposed to written communication—influence the court here?

---

28. This was the situation in Jenkins v. News Syndicate Co. (128 Misc. 284). The plaintiff alleged that she had had a conference with a newspaper editor in which she described in detail the proposed content of some articles she was requested to write. Later, she decided not to write them and the newspaper thereupon published an "interview" with her, precisely quoting much of her conversation with the editor. The court held that she had stated a cause of action for damages on the theory of common-law copyright.

WATKINS v. CLARK

Supreme Court of Kansas, 1918.
103 Kan. 629, 176 P. 131.

BURCH, J. The action was one for damages for personal injuries which the plaintiff suffered in an automobile accident. A demurrer to the plaintiff's evidence was sustained, and he appeals.

The fact of the accident was not disputed. The automobile belonged to the defendant, but was operated by his daughter, a minor. The defendant purchased the automobile for the use of his family. His daughter had general permission, implied at least, to use the car whenever she desired, and she used it, with her father's assent, whenever it suited her pleasure. Other members of the family used it as they pleased. On the occasion in question the daughter was out on a pleasure trip of her own, and was accompanied by another young lady.

The foregoing facts were embraced in the opening statement of the defendant's attorney to the jury, and the plaintiff's evidence added nothing to the admitted relationship of the defendant to the car and its use.

The demurrer to the evidence was properly sustained. There was neither admission nor evidence to submit to the jury proving, prima facie or otherwise, or tending to prove, that the defendant's daughter was acting for him as agent, or servant, or in any other representative capacity, or under his direction or control, or in any joint enterprise from which agency might be implied. Halverson v. Blosser, 101 Kan. 683, 168 P. 863, L.R.A.1918B, 498.

The automobile was not a dangerous instrumentality which the defendant let loose in the community. The automobile was not a guilty agent in the accident, bringing punishment on the owner like the deodands of English law. Mismanagement by the driver was the cause of the accident. The purchase of the automobile by the defendant for the use of his family, including his daughter, operated as a gift to them of the right to use it. When using it to accomplish his purposes, whether business or pleasure, they represent him, but when they exercise their privilege and use it to accomplish their own distinct purposes, whether business or pleasure, they act for themselves, and are alone responsible for their negligent conduct. The fact that the automobile was purchased for use by the owner's family did not make him generally responsible for its subsequent operation, and because the car was subject to appropriation by the members of his family for their own use, there is no presumption that any particular trip was made in his behalf. The use made of the car on any particular occasion is a question of fact, to be determined by evidence showing the fact, and in this instance there was no evidence that anybody was concerned except the daughter.

The development of the law on this subject has been attended by a rather slow process of clarification. When the automobile was new and strange, and was regarded with some wonder and considerable fear, there was a tendency to look upon it as a dangerous thing, fraught with such possibility for harm that the owner should always be held responsible for its use. When it commenced to take the place of the family horse, this view had to be abandoned. The notion, however, of general liability on the part of the owner for use of his car having been planted in the mind, it lingered there like a superstition. Courts were reluctant to ignore it, and as a result, an adaptation of the law of master and servant, and principal and agent, was resorted to, to explain the liability. If a man purchased an automobile and allowed his wife and his son and his daughter to use it, the use was his by virtue of representation, whether representation existed in fact or not. The deduction was facilitated by employment of the fine art of definition—putting into the definition of the term "business" the attributes necessary to bolster up liability. So, if daughter took her friend riding, she might think she was out purely for the pleasure of herself and her friend, but she was mistaken; she was conducting father's "business" as his "agent." As this incongruity became more and more apparent, a further concession was sometimes made. If the owner allowed a member of his family to use the automobile, he might not be liable, but it was "presumed" the use was his by representation. If son took his best girl riding, prima facie it was father's little outing by proxy, and if an accident happened, prima facie father was liable. Some courts were inclined to get rid of the difficulty of resting liability on the one existing fact—ownership of the car—by declaring that the question of "agency" was one for the jury—a process known in some quarters as "passing the buck." The sooner the courts settle down and deal on the basis of fact and actuality with a vehicle which has revolutionized the business and the pleasure of the civilized world, the better it will be, not only for society, but for the courts.

The judgment of the district court is affirmed.

KING v. SMYTHE

Supreme Court of Tennessee, 1918.
140 Tenn. 217, 204 S.W. 296.

Action by Sherman G. King against F. D. Smythe. A judgment for plaintiff was reversed by the Court of Civil Appeals, and plaintiff appeals.

LANSDEN, J. King brought this suit in the circuit court of Shelby county to recover damages for injuries to an automobile occasioned by a collision between it and an automobile owned by the defendant being driven by his son. The defendant is a physician and surgeon in the city of Memphis, and his practice is confined to sur-

Sec. 3   *TECHNIQUE OF CASE LAW DEVELOPMENT*   95

gery and teaching surgery. His statement of the relationship of the son to himself and the automobile was accepted by plaintiff below, and is as follows:

"I was not in my car at the time of this accident, and no member of my family was in the car at the time, except my son, Frank W. Smythe. At the time this accident occurred, Frank, my son, was not on any of my business nor engaged in the performance of any service for me. Frank is now in his twenty-fifth year, and at that time was a year younger than he is now. My son is in the senior class at the Tennessee University Medical College, and at the time of the accident he was a medical student, and residing at my home, where he is still living. He is not employed by me—I am just simply taking care of him and trying to educate him. I do not know how he happened to have the car out on that night or that particular occasion. He frequently drives out in the evenings alone or with his friends when I am not using the car. He is at liberty to use my car, and he don't have to ask me for permission on a specific occasion. If he had any duty to perform for me, I would direct him to do it, but, generally speaking, my chauffeur drives me and my family when we are using the car. When he (Frank) is using the car he is using it on his own business, his own pleasure, and not mine. My son lives with me as a part of my family, has always done so, and has never had any home except my home. At the time of this accident he was, and has always been a member of my family, and has been a student at the university. I have supported him and maintained him, as he had no chance to make a living himself. I own and maintain this car for my professional purposes and for the pleasure of any members of my family; if I am not using the car, of course it is at their disposal. Generally speaking, my son has my permission to use my car if it is not likely to be summoned, and he understands when he is out visiting I have to keep in touch with him so as to be able to get my car. I would not deny him the use of the car if he wanted to go out to the park, or some place, if I was not using it, and it was the same with any other member of my family—if I was not using the car they didn't have to have my consent for a specific occasion, for they understand it is subject to their use, if I am not using it. He was not using my car wrongfully on the occasion this accident happened; that is, he had a right to use it, and I would not object to his using it."

The statement of Dr. Smythe contains some conclusions of law made by him, but it fairly establishes that his son was a member of his family, was provided for in every particular as other members of the family, and that the son had the permission of the father to use the automobile upon the occasion of the accident. It can make no difference that the permission given the son by the father was general and not particular. He expressly says that the son did not need to ask him for the car if he was not using it himself, and admittedly he was not using it, or wanting to use it, at this particular time. He also states that the son was not upon his business or on any service for him, but was on his own business. This is a conclusion of law. The son was on his own pleasure. We also think that it can make no difference, so far as liability is concerned, that the son was the only member of the family in the car at the time of the collision. The car was bought and maintained for the professional purposes of the defendant, and for the pleasure of his family. This can only mean that when the car was not in use by the defendant for his professional purposes, and is in use by any member of his family for pleasure, it is being used for one of the purposes for which it was bought and maintained.

Hence the question for decision is whether defendant is liable for accidents occurring by reason of the admitted negligence of his son while driving defendant's automobile bought for the purposes stated, by defendant's permission, and for the son's pleasure.

Under well-settled principles, the defendant's liability must depend upon whether the son operating the automobile was his servant and engaged upon his business at the time the negligence occurred. Goodman v. Wilson, 129 Tenn. 464, 166 S.W. 752, 51 L.R.A.(N.S.) 1116; Kayser v. Van Nest, 125 Minn. 277, 146 N.W. 1091, 51 L.R.A. (N.S.) 970; Hartley v. Miller, 165 Mich. 115, 130 N.W. 336, 33 L.R. A.(N.S.) 81; McNeal v. McKain, 33 Okl. 449, 126 Pac. 742, 41 L.R. A.(N.S.) 775; Birch v. Abercrombie, 74 Wash. 486, 133 Pac. 1020, 50 L.R.A.(N.S) 59; Griffin v. Russell, 144 Ga. 275, 87 S.E. 10, L.R. A.1916F, 216, Ann.Cas.1917D, 994; Van Blaricom v. Dodgson, 220 N.Y. 111, 115 N.E. 443, L.R.A.1917F, 363. The selected cases cited are elaborated, annotated, and show that all the courts apply this rule.

The rule as stated excludes the idea that defendant could be liable for the torts of his son because of the relationship existing between them. Mirick v. Suchy, 74 Kan. 715, 87 Pac. 1141, 11 Ann.Cas. 366; Chastain v. Johns, 120 Ga. 977, 48 S.E. 343, 66 L.R.A. 958.

It is also well established that an automobile is not a dangerous agency so that its owner is liable for injuries to travelers on the highways inflicted while being driven by another, irrespective of the relationship of master and servant, or principal and agent. Jones v. Hoge, 47 Wash. 663, 92 Pac. 433, 14 L.R.A.(N.S.) 216, 125 Am.St. Rep. 915; Goodman v. Wilson, supra.

The Court of Appeals was of opinion that the facts stated did not create a prima facie case of liability which would authorize a submission of the question of defendant's liability to a jury, and for that reason alone dismissed the suit. The question of the parent's liability for damages occasioned by his automobile when driven by a member of his family, with his permission, and which he bought for the use and pleasure of his family, has not so far been decided in this state.

Sec. 3　TECHNIQUE OF CASE LAW DEVELOPMENT

The authorities cited above all discuss the question, and the annotator's notes to the cases, as well as the cases themselves, show that the numerical weight of authority is in favor of the parent's liability. In a recent case by the Court of Appeals of New York, the theory of liability is vigorously combated in an opinion prepared by Chief Justice Hiscock. The courts of last resort in many states sustain liability upon the theory that the member of the family is upon the defendant's business, and is his agent for the purpose when driving for pleasure in a car furnished by the father for the pleasure and entertainment of his family. It is said substantially that the father has made it his business to entertain the members of his family when he purchases an automobile for that purpose and delivers it to them for such use. In many cases it is said that no difference can be perceived between such a case and a case where a man buys a business truck and employs a chauffeur to drive it in the prosecution of his business. This idea is combated by the Court of Appeals of New York in Van Blaricom v. Dodgson, 220 N.Y. 111, 115 N.E. 443, L.R.A.1917F, 363. This case admits that the numerical weight of authority is perhaps against the opinion, but says the views therein expressed find support directly and indirectly in several cases cited. We have not examined all of those cases, but we have examined some of them, and they do not directly support the opinion. They do support the idea expressed in the opinion concerning the rule of agency, but they do not discuss or apply the rule in the case of an automobile driven by the son of defendant under conditions stated in the cases which the opinion combats. The gist of the reasoning of this authority is contained in the following excerpt:

"The proposition of liability urged in this case, however, goes further. It asserts that the father is liable for negligence in the management of his automobile by an adult son when the latter is pursuing his own exclusive ends, absolutely detached from accommodation of the family or any other member thereof. On its face a proposition seems to be self-contradictory which asserts that a person who is wholly and exclusively engaged in the prosecution of his own concerns is nevertheless engaged as agent in doing something for some one else. It has always been supposed that a person who was permitted to use a car for his own accommodation was not acting as agent for the accommodation of the owner of the car. Reilly v. Connable, 214 N.Y. 586, L.R.A.1916A, 954, 108 N.E. 853, Ann.Cas. 1916A, 656. The attempt is made, however, to reconcile these apparently contradictory features of this proposition by the assertion that the father had made it his business to furnish entertainment for the members of his family, and that, therefore, when he permitted one of them to use the car, even for the latter's personal and sole pleasure, such one was really carrying out the business of the parent, and the latter thus became a principal, and liable for misconduct. This is an advanced proposition in the law of principal and agent, and the question which it presents really resolves itself into the one whether, as a matter of common sense and practical experience, we ought to say that a parent who maintains some article for family use, and occasionally permits a capable son to use it for his individual convenience, ought to be regarded as having undertaken the occupation of entertaining the latter, and to have made him his agent in this business, although the act being done is solely for the benefit of the son. That really is about all there is to the question."

It seems to us that the foregoing reasoning is more concerned with what the learned court considered pure logic than with the practical administration of the law. If a father purchases an automobile for the pleasure and entertainment of his family, and as Dr. Smythe did, gives his adult son, who is a member of his family, permission to use it for pleasure, except when needed by the father, it would seem perfectly clear that the son is in the furtherance of this purpose of the father while driving the car for his own pleasure. It is immaterial whether this purpose of the father be called his business or not. The law of agency is not confined to business transactions. It is true that an automobile is not a dangerous instrumentality so as to make the owner liable, as in the case of a wild animal loose on the streets; but, as a matter of practical justice to those who are injured, we cannot close our eyes to the fact that an automobile possesses excessive weight, that it is capable of running at a rapid rate of speed, and when moving rapidly upon the streets of a populous city, it is dangerous to life and limb and must be operated with care. If an instrumentality of this kind is placed in the hands of his family by a father, for the family's pleasure, comfort, and entertainment, the dictates of natural justice should require that the owner should be responsible for its negligent operation, because only by doing so, as a general rule, can substantial justice be attained. A judgment for damages against an infant daughter or an infant son, or a son without support and without property, who is living as a member of the family, would be an empty form. The father, as owner of the automobile and as head of the family, can prescribe the conditions upon which it may be run upon the roads and streets, or he can forbid its use altogether. He must know the nature of the instrument and the probability that its negligent operation will produce injury and damage to others. We think the practical administration of justice between the parties is more the duty of the court than the preservation of some esoteric theory concerning the law of principal and agent. If owners of automobiles are made to understand that they will be held liable for injury to person and property occasioned by their negligent operation by infants or others who are financially irresponsible, they will doubtless exercise a greater degree of care in selecting those who are permitted to go upon the public streets with such dangerous instrumentalities. An automobile cannot be compared with golf sticks and other small articles bought for the pleasure of the family. They are not used on public highways, and are not of the same nature as automobiles.

The Court of Appeals held that there was no evidence to support the verdict. We think this was error. The ownership of the automobile by defendant Smythe, and the fact that it was being driven by a member of his family with his permission, coupled with the further fact that the automobile was purchased and maintained for this purpose, among others, made a prima facie case of liability. Many cases hold that the ownership of the automobile merely makes a prima facie case that it was then in the possession of the owner, and whoever was driving it was doing so for the owner. Birch v. Abercrombie, supra. But this case is not left to such presumption. It is further proven that the automobile was being driven by defendant's son with defendant's permission, for the son's pleasure, and that defendant bought the automobile partly for such purpose.

The negligence of defendant's son and the amount of damages inflicted are not in dispute. The only question made here is the liability of defendant for the injuries sustained. Accordingly, the judgment of the Court of Civil Appeals is reversed, and that of the circuit court is affirmed.

NOTES

1. By this time it should be apparent that however the courts may couch the result, they are in reality "making law" in the same sense as, if in somewhat different manner than, would a legislature if it addressed itself to the problems. To what do the courts look as sources of policy on which to base their "legislative judgments"? To the extent that their judgments are rooted in facts, where and how do they acquire those facts? Are the sources and manner of acquisition the same as for a legislative body?

2. The problem addressed in Watkins v. Clark and King v. Smythe was that of accidents caused by presumably judgment proof drivers of cars owned by others. But what of accidents caused by the owners themselves? The rule adopted by the courts for Tennessee and other jurisdictions, or by statutes such as that in New York (McKinney's N.Y. Vehicle and Traffic Law § 388) imposing liability on the owner for damages caused by the negligence of persons driving with the owner's permission did not help when the owner was judgment proof, as was often the case. Several measures have been adopted to deal with the problem of judgment proof owners of which the most drastic is compulsory insurance required first in Massachusetts in 1925. But even with compulsory insurance there are many problems posed for the tort system by automobile accidents, not the least of which is the burden of automobile litigation on the courts. Recently some states have adopted "no fault" insurance laws about which you will surely hear in your Torts course.

J'AIRE CORP. v. GREGORY

Supreme Court of California, 1979.
24 Cal.3d 779, 157 Cal.Rptr. 407, 598 P.2d 60.

BIRD, Chief Justice.

Appellant, a lessee, sued respondent, a general contractor, for damages resulting from the delay in completion of a construction project at the premises where appellant operated a restaurant. Respondent demurred successfully and the complaint was dismissed. This court must decide whether a contractor who undertakes construction work pursuant to a contract with the owner of premises may be held liable in tort for business losses suffered by a lessee when the contractor negligently fails to complete the project with due diligence.

I

The facts as pleaded are as follows. Appellant, J'Aire Corporation, operates a restaurant at the Sonoma County Airport in premises leased from the County of Sonoma. Under the terms of the lease the county was to provide heat and air conditioning. In 1975 the county entered into a contract with respondent for improvements to the restaurant premises, including renovation of the heating and air conditioning systems and installation of insulation.

As the contract did not specify any date for completion of the work, appellant alleged the work was to have been completed within a reasonable time as defined by custom and usage. (Civ.Code, § 1657.) Despite requests that respondent complete the construction promptly, the work was not completed within a reasonable time. Because the restaurant could not operate during part of the construction and was without heat and air conditioning for a longer period, appellant suffered loss of business and resulting loss of profits.

Appellant alleged two causes of action in its third amended complaint. The first cause of action was based upon the theory that it was a third party beneficiary of the contract between the county and respondent. The second cause of action sounded in tort and was based upon negligence in completing the work within a reasonable time. Damages of $50,000 were claimed.

Respondent demurred on the ground that the complaint did not state facts sufficient to constitute a cause of action. (Code Civ.Proc., § 430.10 subd. (e).) The trial court sustained the demurrer without leave to amend and the complaint was dismissed. On appeal only the sustaining of the demurrer to the second cause of action is challenged.

II

In testing the sufficiency of a complaint, a reviewing court must assume the truth of all material allegations in the complaint (Serrano

v. Priest (1971) 5 Cal.3d 584, 591, 96 Cal.Rptr. 601, 487 P.2d 1241), including the allegations of negligence and cause in fact. The only question before this court is whether a cause of action for negligent loss of expected economic advantage may be maintained under these facts.

Liability for negligent conduct may only be imposed where there is a duty of care owed by the defendant to the plaintiff or to a class of which the plaintiff is a member. (Richards v. Stanley (1954) 43 Cal.2d 60, 63, 271 P.2d 23.) A duty of care may arise through statute or by contract. Alternatively, a duty may be premised upon the general character of the activity in which the defendant engaged, the relationship between the parties or even the interdependent nature of human society. (See Valdez v. J. D. Diffenbaugh Co. (1975) 51 Cal. App.3d 494, 505, 124 Cal.Rptr. 467.) Whether a duty is owed is simply a shorthand way of phrasing what is " 'the essential question—whether the plaintiff's interests are entitled to legal protection against the defendant's conduct.' " (Dillon v. Legg (1968) 68 Cal.2d 728, 734, 69 Cal.Rptr. 72, 76, 441 P.2d 912, 916, quoting from Prosser, Law of Torts (3d ed. 1964) pp. 332–333. See also Prosser, Law of Torts (4th ed. 1971) pp. 324–327; Fleming, An Introduction to the Law of Torts (1967) pp. 43–50.)

This court has held that a plaintiff's interest in prospective economic advantage may be protected against injury occasioned by negligent as well as intentional conduct. For example, economic losses such as lost earnings or profits are recoverable as part of general damages in a suit for personal injury based on negligence. (Connolly v. Pre-Mixed Concrete Co. (1957) 49 Cal.2d 483, 489, 319 P.2d 343; Neumann v. Bishop (1976) 59 Cal.App.3d 451, 462, 130 Cal.Rptr. 786.) Where negligent conduct causes injury to real or personal property, the plaintiff may recover damages for profits lost during the time necessary to repair or replace the property. (Reynolds v. Bank of America (1959) 53 Cal.2d 49, 50–51, 345 P.2d 926.)

Even when only injury to prospective economic advantage is claimed, recovery is not foreclosed. Where a special relationship exists between the parties, a plaintiff may recover for loss of expected economic advantage through the negligent performance of a contract although the parties were not in contractual privity. Biakanja v. Irving (1958) 49 Cal.2d 647, 320 P.2d 16; Lucas v. Hamm (1961) 56 Cal.2d 583, 15 Cal.Rptr. 821, 364 P.2d 685 and Heyer v. Flaig (1969) 70 Cal.2d 223, 74 Cal.Rptr. 225, 449 P.2d 161 held that intended beneficiaries of wills could sue to recover legacies lost through the negligent preparation of the will. (See also Prosser, Law of Torts (4th ed. 1971) p. 952.)

In each of the above cases, the court determined that defendants owed plaintiffs a duty of care by applying criteria set forth in Biakanja v. Irving, supra, 49 Cal.2d at page 650, 320 P.2d 16. Those criteria are (1) the extent to which the transaction was intended to affect the plaintiff, (2) the foreseeability of harm to the plaintiff, (3) the degree of certainty that the plaintiff suffered injury, (4) the closeness of the connection between the defendant's conduct and the injury suffered, (5) the moral blame attached to the defendant's conduct and (6) the policy of preventing future harm. (See also Connor v. Great Western Sav. & Loan Assn. (1968) 69 Cal.2d 850, 865, 73 Cal. Rptr. 369, 447 P.2d 609.) [29]

Applying these criteria to the facts as pleaded, it is evident that a duty was owed by respondent to appellant in the present case. (1) The contract entered into between respondent and the county was for the renovation of the premises in which appellant maintained its business. The contract could not have been performed without impinging on that business. Thus respondent's performance was intended to, and did, directly affect appellant. (2) Accordingly, it was clearly foreseeable that any significant delay in completing the construction would adversely affect appellant's business beyond the normal disruption associated with such construction. Appellant alleges this fact was repeatedly drawn to respondent's attention. (3) Further, appellant's complaint leaves no doubt that appellant suffered harm since it was unable to operate its business for one month and suffered additional loss of business while the premises were without heat and air conditioning. (4) Appellant has also alleged that delays occasioned by the respondent's conduct were closely connected to, indeed directly caused its injury. (5) In addition, respondent's lack of diligence in the present case was particularly blameworthy since it continued after the probability of damage was drawn directly to respondent's attention. (6) Finally, public policy supports finding a duty of care in the present case. The wilful failure or refusal of a contractor to prosecute a construction project with diligence, where another is injured as a result, has been made grounds for disciplining a licensed contractor. (Bus. & Prof. Code, § 7119.) [30] Although this section does not provide a basis for imposing liability where the delay in completing construction is due merely to negligence, it does indicate the seriousness with which the Legislature views unnecessary delays in the completion of construction.

---

29. Countervailing public policies may preclude recovery for injury to prospective economic advantage in some cases, such as the strong public policy favoring organized activity by workers. Accordingly, interference with the prospective economic advantage of an employer or business has traditionally not been considered tortious when it results from union activity, including picketing, striking, primary and secondary boycotts or similar activity, that is otherwise lawful and reasonably related to labor conditions. (See, e. g., C. S. Smith Met. Market Co. v. Lyons (1940) 16 Cal.2d 389, 397–400, 106 P. 2d 414; Fortenbury v. Superior Court (1940) 16 Cal.2d 405, 409–410, 106 P. 2d 411.) The present case does not alter this principle.

30. Business and Professions Code section 7119, provides:
"Wilful failure or refusal without legal excuse on the part of a licensee as a contractor to prosecute a construction project or operation with reasonable diligence causing material injury to another constitutes a cause for disciplinary action."

In light of these factors, this court finds that respondent had a duty to complete construction in a manner that would have avoided unnecessary injury to appellant's business, even though the construction contract was with the owner of a building rather than with appellant, the tenant. It is settled that a contractor owes a duty to avoid injury to the person or property of third parties. (See Stewart v. Cox (1961) 55 Cal.2d 857, 862–863, 13 Cal.Rptr. 521, 362 P.2d 345.) As appellant points out, injury to a tenant's business can often result in greater hardship than damage to a tenant's person or property. Where the risk of harm is foreseeable, as it was in the present case, an injury to the plaintiff's economic interests should not go uncompensated merely because it was unaccompanied by any injury to his person or property.

To hold under these facts that a cause of action has been stated for negligent interference with prospective economic advantage is consistent with the recent trend in tort cases. This court has repeatedly eschewed overly rigid common law formulations of duty in favor of allowing compensation for foreseeable injuries caused by a defendant's want of ordinary care. (See, e. g., Dillon v. Legg, supra, 68 Cal.2d at p. 746, 69 Cal.Rptr. 72, 441 P.2d 912 [liability for mother's emotional distress when child killed by defendant's negligence]; Rowland v. Christian (1968) 69 Cal.2d 108, 119, 70 Cal.Rptr. 97, 443 P.2d 561 [liability of host for injury to social guest on premises]; cf. Brown v. Merlo (1973) 8 Cal.3d 855, 106 Cal.Rptr. 388, 506 P.2d 212 [liability of automobile driver for injury to nonpaying passenger]; Rodriguez v. Bethlehem Steel Corp. (1974) 12 Cal.3d 382, 115 Cal. Rptr. 765, 525 P.2d 669 [liability for loss of consortium].) Rather than traditional notions of duty, this court has focused on foreseeability as the key component necessary to establish liability: "While the question whether one owes a duty to another must be decided on a case-by-case basis, every case is governed by the rule of general application that all persons are required to use ordinary care to prevent others from being injured as a result of their conduct. * * * [F]oreseeability of the risk is a primary consideration in establishing the element of duty." (Weirum v. RKO General, Inc. (1975) 15 Cal. 3d 40, 46, 123 Cal.Rptr. 468, 471, 539 P.2d 36, 39, fn. omitted.) Similarly, respondent is liable if his lack of ordinary care caused foreseeable injury to the economic interests of appellant.

In addition, this holding is consistent with the Legislature's declaration of the basic principle of tort liability, embodied in Civil Code section 1714, that every person is responsible for injuries caused by his or her lack of ordinary care.[31] (See Rowland v. Christian, supra,

---

31. Civil Code section 1714 provides in pertinent part:

"(a) Every one is responsible, not only for the result of his willful acts, but also for any injury occasioned to another by his want of ordinary care or skill in the management of his property or person, except so far as the latter has, willfully or by want of ordinary care brought the injury upon himself."

69 Cal.2d at p. 119, 70 Cal.Rptr. 97, 443 P.2d 561.) That section does not distinguish among injuries to one's person, one's property or one's financial interests. Damages for loss of profits or earnings are recoverable where they result from an injury to one's person or property caused by another's negligence. Recovery for injury to one's economic interests, where it is the foreseeable result of another's want of ordinary care, should not be foreclosed simply because it is the only injury that occurs.

Respondent cites Fifield Manor v. Finston (1960) 54 Cal.2d 632, 7 Cal.Rptr. 377, 354 P.2d 1073 for the proposition that recovery may not be had for negligent loss of prospective economic advantage. *Fifield* concerned the parallel tort of interference with contractual relations. (See Prosser, supra, Law of Torts (4th ed.) at p. 952.) There a nonprofit retirement home that had contracted with Ross to provide him with lifetime medical care sued a driver who negligently struck and killed Ross. The plaintiff argued it had become liable under the contract for Ross' medical bills and sought recovery from the driver, on both a theory of direct liability and one of subrogation. Recovery was denied.

The critical factor of foreseeability distinguishes *Fifield* from the present case. Although it was reasonably foreseeable that defendant's negligence might cause injury to Ross, it was less foreseeable that it would injure the retirement home's economic interest. Defendant had not entered into any relationship or undertaken any activity where negligence on his part was reasonably likely to affect plaintiff adversely. Thus, the nexus between the defendant's conduct and the risk of the injury that occurred to the plaintiff was too tenuous to support the imposition of a duty owing to the retirement home. (Id., at p. 637, 7 Cal.Rptr. 377, 354 P.2d 1073.) In contrast, the nexus in the present case between the injury that occurred and respondent's conduct is extremely close. *Fifield* does not entirely foreclose recovery for negligent interference with prospective economic advantage.

Respondent also relies on Adams v. Southern Pac. Transportation Co. (1975) 50 Cal.App.3d 37, 123 Cal.Rptr. 216. In *Adams* plaintiff employees were held unable to sue the railroad whose cargo of bombs exploded, destroying the factory where they worked. It should be noted that the Court of Appeal in *Adams* clearly believed that plaintiffs should be permitted to maintain an action for negligent interference with prospective economic interests. It reluctantly held they could not only under the belief that *Fifield* precluded such recovery.[32] Adhering to the *Fifield* rule, the Court of Appeal in *Adams* did not

---

32. The *Fifield* case has been the subject of some criticism. In addition to Adams v. Southern Pac. Transportation Co., supra, 50 Cal.App.3d 37, 123 Cal.Rptr. 216, see, e. g., Note (1964) 16 Stan.L.Rev. 664, 671; Comment (1961) 34 So.Cal.L.Rev. 467; Comment (1961) 46 Iowa L.Rev. 876; Prosser, supra, Law of Torts (4th ed.) at page 940.

determine whether the railroad owed plaintiffs a duty of care. (50 Cal.App.3d at p. 47, 123 Cal.Rptr. 216.) In the present case, plaintiff's injury stemmed directly from conduct intended to affect plaintiff and was more readily foreseeable than the damage to the employer's property in *Adams*. To the extent that *Adams* holds that there can be no recovery for negligent interference with prospective economic advantage, it is disapproved.

The chief dangers which have been cited in allowing recovery for negligent interference with prospective economic advantage are the possibility of excessive liability, the creation of an undue burden on freedom of action, the possibility of fraudulent or collusive claims and the often speculative nature of damages. (See, e. g., Prosser, supra, Law of Torts (4th ed.) at p. 940 and Note. Negligent Interference with Economic Expectancy: The Case for Recovery (1964) 16 Stan. L.Rev. 664, 679–693, neither of which considers these fears to justify denial of recovery in all cases.) Central to these fears is the possibility that liability will be imposed for remote consequences, out of proportion to the magnitude of the defendant's wrongful conduct.

However, the factors enumerated in *Biakanja* and applied in subsequent cases place a limit on recovery by focusing judicial attention on the foreseeability of the injury and the nexus between the defendant's conduct and the plaintiff's injury. These factors and ordinary principles of tort law such as proximate cause are fully adequate to limit recovery without the drastic consequence of an absolute rule which bars recovery in all such cases. (See Dillon v. Legg, supra, 68 Cal.2d at p. 746, 69 Cal.Rptr. 72, 441 P.2d 912.) Following these principles, recovery for negligent interference with prospective economic advantage will be limited to instances where the risk of harm is foreseeable and is closely connected with the defendant's conduct, where damages are not wholly speculative and the injury is not part of the plaintiff's ordinary business risk.

III

Accordingly, this court holds that a contractor owes a duty of care to the tenant of a building undergoing construction work to prosecute that work in a manner which does not cause undue injury to the tenant's business, where such injury is reasonably foreseeable. The demurrer to appellant's second cause of action should not have been sustained. The judgment of dismissal is reversed.

TOBRINER, MOSK, MANUEL and NEWMAN, JJ., concur.

CLARK and RICHARDSON, JJ., concur in the judgment.

NOTES

1. The use of statutes as "premises for reasoning" is the major focus of Chapter VI.

2. Plaintiff in J'Aire Corp v. Gregory relied on "custom and usage" to define a reasonable time for performing the contract. To what extent

should courts look to custom as a source of policy on which to base judge-made law. On this point see Cardozo, The Nature of the Judicial Process 58–61 (1921):

"If history and philosophy do not serve to fix the direction of a principle, custom may step in. When we speak of custom, we may mean more things than one. 'Consuetudo,' says Coke, 'is one of the maine triangles of the lawes of England; these lawes being divided into common law, statute law and customs.' Here common law and custom are thought of as distinct. Not so, however, Blackstone: 'This unwritten or Common Law is properly distinguishable into three kinds: (1) General customs, which are the universal rule of the whole Kingdom, and form the Common Law, in its stricter and more usual signification. (2) Particular customs, which for the most part affect only the inhabitants of particular districts. (3) Certain particular laws, which by custom are adopted and used by some particular courts of pretty general and extensive jurisdiction'.

"Undoubtedly the creative energy of custom in the development of common law is less today than it was in bygone times. Even in bygone times, its energy was very likely exaggerated by Blackstone and his followers. 'Today we recognize,' in the words of Pound, 'that the custom is a custom of judicial decision, not of popular action.' It is 'doubtful,' says Gray, 'whether at all stages of legal history, rules laid down by judges have not generated custom, rather than custom generated the rules.' In these days, at all events, we look to custom, not so much for the creation of new rules, but for the tests and standards that are to determine how established rules shall be applied. When custom seeks to do more than this, there is a growing tendency in the law to leave development to legislation. Judges do not feel the same need of putting the *imprimatur* of law upon customs of recent growth, knocking for entrance into the legal system, and viewed askance because of some novel aspect of form or feature, as they would if legislatures were not in frequent session, capable of establishing a title that will be unimpeached and unimpeachable. But the power is not lost because it is exercised with caution."

3. How much importance should the court attach to the general understanding of the community as to what constitutes appropriate conduct? In Roberson v. Rochester Folding Box Co., 171 N.Y. 538, 64 N.E. 442 (1902) defendant without plaintiff's knowledge or consent, obtained a photograph of her, had 25,000 prints made and used them as part of an advertising campaign for its product throughout the United States and other countries. Although one judge thought it "inconceivable" that the law would not afford redress against such conduct—a feeling with which most people would probably agree—plaintiff was denied relief on the ground that "the so-called 'right of privacy' has not as yet found an abiding place in our jurisprudence, and, as we view it, the doctrine cannot now be incorporated without doing violence to settled principles of law by which the profession and the public have long been guided." 171 N.Y. at 556.

Sec. 3   TECHNIQUE OF CASE LAW DEVELOPMENT   107

In Marvin v. Marvin, 18 Cal.3d 660, 134 Cal.Rptr. 815, 557 P.2d 106 (1976) (the well-known "palimony" case) the California Supreme Court said:

> "In summary, we believe that the prevalence of non-marital relationships in modern society and the social acceptance of them, marks this as a time when our courts should by no means apply the doctrine of the unlawfulness of the so-called meretricious relationship to the instant case. * * *
>
> * * *
>
> The mores of the society have indeed changed so radically in regard to cohabitation that we cannot impose a standard based on alleged moral considerations that have apparently been so widely abandoned by so many." 18 Cal.3d 660, 683–84, 557 P.2d 106, 122, 134 Cal.Rptr. 815, 831.

But see Hewitt v. Hewitt, 62 Ill.App.3d 861, 20 Ill.Dec. 476, 380 N.E.2d 454 (1979):

> "The question whether change is needed in the law governing the rights of parties in this delicate area of marriage-like relationships involves evaluations of sociological data and alternatives we believe best suited to the superior investigative and fact-finding facilities of the legislative branch in the exercise of its traditional authority to declare public policy in the domestic relations field."

HYNES v. NEW YORK CENT. R. CO.

Court of Appeals of New York, 1921.
231 N.Y. 229, 131 N.E. 898.

Appeal from a judgment of the Appellate Division of the Supreme Court in the second judicial department, entered January 12, 1920, affirming a judgment in favor of defendant entered upon a dismissal of the complaint by the court at a Trial Term.[33]

CARDOZO, J. On July 8, 1916, Harvey Hynes, a lad of sixteen, swam with two companions from the Manhattan to the Bronx side of the Harlem river or United States Ship Canal, a navigable stream. Along the Bronx side of the river was the right of way of the defendant, the New York Central Railroad, which operated its trains at that point by high tension wires, strung on poles and crossarms. Project-

---

33. [After the defendant had interposed an answer to the plaintiff's complaint the case was tried and the plaintiff was given a verdict for $8,000. The defendant moved to set this verdict aside and, on this motion, persuaded the trial court that the boy was a trespasser. The trial judge, therefore, set the first verdict aside on June 11, 1917 and granted a new trial. The plaintiff appealed and the Appellate Division (by a vote of 3–2) affirmed the result below thus holding that the boy was a trespasser (188 App.Div. 178, 176 N.Y.S. 795 (1919)). Thereupon the new trial occurred. At the close of the plaintiff's evidence the defendant moved for a directed verdict and the dismissal of the complaint. The Trial Court granted this motion and it is an appeal therefrom that is now before the court.—Ed.]

ing from the defendant's bulkhead above the waters of the river was a plank or springboard from which boys of the neighborhood used to dive. One end of the board had been placed under a rock on the defendant's land, and nails had been driven at its point of contact with the bulkhead. Measured from this point of contact the length behind was five feet; the length in front eleven. The bulkhead itself was about three and a half feet back of the pier line as located by the government. From this it follows that for seven and a half feet the springboard was beyond the line of the defendant's property, and above the public waterway. Its height measured from the stream was three feet at the bulkhead, and five feet at its outermost extremity. For more than five years swimmers had used it as a diving board without protest or obstruction.

On this day Hynes and his companions climbed on top of the bulkhead intending to leap into the water. One of them made the plunge in safety. Hynes followed to the front of the springboard, and stood poised for his dive. At that moment a cross-arm with electric wires fell from the defendant's pole. The wires struck the diver, flung him from the shattered board, and plunged him to his death below. His mother, suing as administratrix, brings this action for her damages. Thus far the courts have held that Hynes at the end of the springboard above the public waters was a trespasser on the defendant's land. They have thought it immaterial that the board itself was a trespass, an encroachment on the public ways. They have thought it of no significance that Hynes would have met the same fate if he had been below the board and not above it. The board, they have said, was annexed to the defendant's bulkhead. By force of such annexation, it was to be reckoned as a fixture, and thus constructively, if not actually, an extension of the land. The defendant was under a duty to use reasonable care that bathers swimming or standing in the water should not be electrocuted by wires falling from its right of way. But to bathers diving from the springboard, there was no duty, we are told, unless the injury was the product of mere willfulness or wantonness, no duty of active vigilance to safeguard the impending structure. Without wrong to them, cross-arms might be left to rot; wires highly charged with electricity might sweep them from their stand, and bury them in the subjacent waters. In climbing on the board, they became trespassers and outlaws. The conclusion is defended with much subtlety of reasoning, with much insistence upon its inevitableness as a merely logical deduction. A majority of the court are unable to accept it as the conclusion of the law.

We assume, without deciding, that the springboard was a fixture, a permanent improvement of the defendant's right of way. Much might be said in favor of another view. We do not press the inquiry, for we are persuaded that the rights of bathers do not depend upon these nice distinctions. Liability would not be doubtful, we are told, had the boy been diving from a pole, if the pole had been

Sec. 3 TECHNIQUE OF CASE LAW DEVELOPMENT 109

vertical. The diver in such a situation would have been separated from the defendant's freehold. Liability, it is said, has been escaped because the pole was horizontal. The plank when projected lengthwise was an extension of the soil. We are to concentrate our gaze on the private ownership of the board. We are to ignore the public ownership of the circumambient spaces of water and of air. Jumping from a boat or a barrel, the boy would have been a bather in the river. Jumping from the end of a springboard, he was no longer, it is said, a bather, but a trespasser on a right of way.

Rights and duties in systems of living law are not built upon such quicksands.

Bathers in the Harlem river on the day of this disaster were in the enjoyment of a public highway, entitled to reasonable protection against destruction by the defendant's wires. They did not cease to be bathers entitled to the same protection while they were diving from encroaching objects or engaging in the sports that are common among swimmers. Such acts were not equivalent to an abandonment of the highway, a departure from its proper uses, a withdrawal from the waters, and an entry upon land. A plane of private right had been interposed between the river and the air, but public ownership was unchanged in the space below it and above. The defendant does not deny that it would have owed a duty to this boy if he had been leaning against the springboard with his feet upon the ground. He is said to have forfeited protection as he put his feet upon the plank. Presumably the same result would follow if the plank had been a few inches above the surface of the water instead of a few feet. Duties are thus supposed to arise and to be extinguished in alternate zones or strata. Two boys walking in the country or swimming in a river stop to rest for a moment along the side of the road or the margin of the stream. One of them throws himself beneath the overhanging branches of a tree. The other perches himself on a bough a foot or so above the ground. Hoffman v. Armstrong, 48 N.Y. 201, 8 Am. Rep. 537. Both are killed by falling wires. The defendant would have us say that there is a remedy for the representatives of one, and none for the representatives of the other. We may be permitted to distrust the logic that leads to such conclusions.

The truth is that every act of Hynes, from his first plunge into the river until the moment of his death, was in the enjoyment of the public waters, and under cover of the protection which his presence in those waters gave him. The use of the springboard was not an abandonment of his rights as bather. It was a mere by-play, an incident, subordinate and ancillary to the execution of his primary purpose, the enjoyment of the highway. The by-play, the incident, was not the cause of the disaster. Hynes would have gone to his death if he had been below the springboard or beside it. Laidlaw v. Sage, 158 N.Y. 73, 97, 52 N.E. 679, 44 L.R.A. 216. The wires were not stayed by the presence of the plank. They followed the boy in his fall, and overwhelmed him in the waters. The defendant assumes that the identification of ownership of a fixture with ownership of land is complete in every incident. But there are important elements of difference. Title to the fixture, unlike title to the land, does not carry with it rights of ownership *usque ad coelum*. There will hardly be denial that a cause of action would have arisen if the wires had fallen on an aeroplane proceeding above the river, though the location of the impact could be identified as the space above the springboard. The most that the defendant can fairly ask is exemption from liability where the use of the fixture is itself the efficient peril. That would be the situation, for example, if the weight of the boy upon the board had caused it to break and thereby throw him into the river. There is no such causal connection here between his position and his injuries. We think there was no moment when he was beyond the pale of the defendant's duty—the duty of care and vigilance in the storage of destructive forces.

This case is a striking instance of the dangers of "a jurisprudence of conceptions" (Pound, Mechanical Jurisprudence, 8 Columbia Law Review, 605, 608, 610), the extension of a maxim or a definition with relentless disregard of consequences to a "dryly logical extreme." The approximate and relative become the definite and absolute. Landowners are not bound to regulate their conduct in contemplation of the presence of trespassers intruding upon private structures. Landowners *are* bound to regulate their conduct in contemplation of the presence of travelers upon the adjacent public ways. There are times when there is little trouble in marking off the field of exemption and immunity from that of liability and duty. Here structures and ways are so united and commingled, super-imposed upon each other, that the fields are brought together. In such circumstances, there is little help in pursuing general maxims to ultimate conclusions. They have been framed *alio intuitu*. They must be reformulated and readapted to meet exceptional conditions. Rules appropriate to spheres which are conceived of as separate and distinct cannot, both, be enforced when the spheres become concentric. There must then be readjustment or collision. In one sense, and that a highly technical and artificial one, the diver at the end of the springboard is an intruder on the adjoining lands. In another sense, and one that realists will accept more readily, he is still on public waters in the exercise of public rights. The law must say whether it will subject him to the rule of the one field or of the other, of this sphere or of that. We think that considerations of analogy, of convenience, of policy, and of justice, exclude him from the field of the defendant's immunity and exemption, and place him in the field of liability and duty. Beck v. Carter, 68 N.Y. 283, 23 Am.Rep. 175; Jewhurst v. City of Syracuse, 108 N.Y. 303, 15 N.E. 409; McCloskey v. Buckley, 223 N.Y. 187, 192, 119 N.E. 395.

Sec. 3   TECHNIQUE OF CASE LAW DEVELOPMENT   111

The judgment of the Appellate Division and that of the Trial Term should be reversed, and a new trial granted, with costs to abide the event.

HOGAN, POUND and CRANE, JJ., concur; HISCOCK, Ch. J., CHASE and McLAUGHLIN, JJ., dissent.

Judgments reversed, etc.

NOTES

1. What caused the four judges who concurred in this opinion to choose that one of the two conflicting analogies which was used to justify this reversal? Do you agree with these four, or with the three judges who dissented?

Judge Cardozo in Growth of the Law 99–103 (1924) thus comments on the above decision:

> "We had in my court a year or more ago a case that points my meaning. A boy was bathing in a river. He climbed upon a springboard which projected from a bank. As he stood there, at the end of the board, poised for his dive into the stream, electric wires fell upon him, and swept him to his death below. In the suit for damages that followed, competitive analogies were invoked by counsel for the administratrix and counsel for the railroad company, the owner of the upland. The administratrix found the analogy that suited her in the position of travelers on a highway. The boy was a bather in navigable waters; his rights were not lessened because his feet were on the board. The owner found the analogy to its liking in the position of a trespasser on land. The springboard, though it projected into the water, was, none the less, a fixture, and as a fixture it was constructively a part of the land to which it was annexed. The boy was thus a trespasser upon land in private ownership; the only duty of the owner was to refrain from wanton and malicious injury; if these elements were lacking, the death must go without requital. Now, the truth is that, as a mere bit of dialectics, these analogies would bring a judge to an impasse. No process of merely logical deduction could determine the choice between them. Neither analogy is precise, though each is apposite. There had arisen a new situation which could not force itself without mutilation into any of the existing moulds. When we find a situation of this kind, the choice that will approve itself to this judge or to that, will be determined largely by his conception of the end of the law, the function of legal liability; and this question of ends and functions is a question of philosophy.
>
> "In the case that I have instanced, a majority of the court believed that liability should be adjudged. The deductions that might have been made from preestablished definitions were subordinated and adapted to the fundamental principles that determine, or ought to determine, liability for conduct in a system of law wherein liability is adjusted to the ends which law should serve. Hynes v. The New York Central Railroad Co., was decided in May, 1921. Dean Pound's Introduction to the Philosophy of Law had

not yet been published. It appeared in 1922. In these lectures, he advances a theory of liability which it may be interesting to compare with the theory of liability reflected in our decision. 'The law,' he says, 'enforces the reasonable expectations arising out of conduct, relations and situations.' I shall leave it to others to say whether the cause of the boy diving from the springboard would be helped or hindered by resort to such a test. This much I cannot doubt. *Some* theory of liability, some philosophy of the end to be served by tightening or enlarging the circle of rights and remedies, is at the root of any decision in novel situations when analogies are equivocal and precedents are silent. As it stands today, the judge is often left to improvise such a theory, such a philosophy, when confronted overnight by the exigencies of the case before him. Often he fumbles about, feeling in a vague way that some such problem is involved, but missing the universal element which would have quickened his decision with the inspiration of a principle. If he lacks an adequate philosophy, he either goes astray altogether, or at least does not rise above the empiricism that pronounces judgment upon particulars. We must learn that all methods are to be viewed not as idols but as tools. We must test one of them by the others, supplementing and reenforcing where there is weakness, so that what is strong and best in each will be at our service in the hour of need. Thus viewing them we shall often find that they are not antagonists but allies."

2. How frequently, do you suppose, litigated cases present "new questions" to Courts? Would more cases be likely to come clearly within accepted and well established rules, or to constitute "new questions"?

C. THE EFFECT OF A PRECEDENT ON A SUBSEQUENT CASE

In this and other courses during your first year in law school, you will begin to develop a "feel" for certain of the basic skills and arts of the case lawyer: e. g., the distinguishing of cases on their facts, the narrowing of an asserted precedent in terms of its procedural issue, the following of the distinguishable case. But the role of precedents in the common law judicial process cannot be grasped unless you know what a judge or a lawyer means when he speaks of the "holding" or *ratio decidendi* of a case and what he means when he says that a statement in a judicial opinion is "dictum" or "obiter dictum." The distinction between "holding" and "dictum" runs through Anglo-American legal literature and is a recurring theme in case method law classes.[34]

34. Although the holding-dictum distinction is an unquestioned assumption in the thinking of British and American lawyers, legal historians have demonstrated that the distinction was not made in the use of case precedents in early English law.

Prior to Bole v. Horton, Vaughan 360 (Mich. 25 Car. II in C.B.), reported cases were used largely as if they were textbooks, with no distinction drawn between those judicial observations that were in any way "necessary" to the decision of the case and

If you have ever heard an oral argument in an appellate court, you undoubtedly have heard counsel for one side or the other quote a statement from some past judicial opinion in support of his legal argument in the case then before the court. And, it is almost equally certain, you have heard some member of the court interrupt the quoting counsel and ask: "Yes, but what were the *facts* of that case?" Why do judges—and law professors, for that matter—insist on asking that question? If the statement being quoted was, in truth, made in the earlier judicial opinion, what difference does it make what the *facts* of that case were? After you have read and thought through the cases and other materials in this Section, you should be able to see that the question, "What were the facts of that [earlier] case?" is, essentially, another way of asking, "Was the statement in the past judicial opinion 'holding' or 'dictum' in that case?"

By then, too, you will have realized that the question is deceptively simple. Central as it is to our system of precedent the concept of holding and dictum is elusive.

A More or Less Definition

Let us start our analysis by accepting at face value the importance of the distinction. The holding of a case, under our system, must be followed in similar cases, until overruled. Dicta are pronouncements which may be persuasive, but are not binding. You will soon realize that this is a somewhat oversimplified view of case law but let us start there.

How does one tell the difference? The conventional definition is that dictum is any statement in a judicial opinion not necessary to the decision of the case actually before the court. The following is a typical statement of the matter:

> "* * * if it [the point of law commented on in the opinion] might have been decided either way without affecting any right brought into question, then, according to the principles of the common law, an opinion on such a question is not a decision. To make it so, there must have been an application of the judicial mind to the precise question necessary to be determined, to fix the rights of the parties, and to decide to whom the property in contestation belongs. And, therefore, this court, and other courts organized under the common law, has never held itself bound by any part of an opinion, in any case, which was not needful to the ascertainment of the right or title in question between the parties."

those observations that went beyond the facts and the procedural issue of the case. The historical development is documented in the series of cases reprinted in Goebel, Cases and Materials on the Development of Legal Institutions 679 et seq. (6th Ed., 1937).

Curtis, J. in Carroll v. Carroll's Lessee, 57 U.S. (16 How.) 275, 286–287, 14 L.Ed. 936 (1853). A good example of dictum in this sense is the statement in Grand Lodge v. Farnham (supra p. 66.): "The rule is otherwise where subscribers agree together to make up a specified sum. * * * In such case, as between the subscribers, there is mutual liability, and the co-subscribers may maintain an action against one who refuses to pay." Since the *Farnham* case did not involve a suit by co-subscribers, the statement is clearly dictum.

You may well ask why any distinction should be made between holding and dictum. We have designated certain officials judges and made them, subject to legislative overruling, the final law makers in certain spheres. Why should we not give binding effect to all their official pronouncements? Is the following a sufficient answer?

> "No *dictum* is authority of the highest sort. To give it such weight would be to give judges power to decide in advance a case not before them for adjudication, a merely hypothetical case, and to bind by their opinion the court before which that hypothetical case may eventually become a practical problem. This would be a legislative power, and, still worse, a power exercised in the absence of full argument of the hypothetical case." Wambaugh, The Study of Cases 19 (2d Ed. 1894).

The last clause deserves reemphasis. It is a cardinal tenet of the Anglo-American judicial system that the best result will be produced through "the fire of controversy." Given adequate legal representation on both sides, the theory runs, the court will have presented to it the best possible arguments for alternative decisions on a disputed point; the defects of either position will be shown up and the best course to pursue be made apparent. The critical word is "disputed" and therein lies the reason for the distinction between holding and dictum: Dicta are pronouncements on points which need not be considered in order to reach a decision and are, therefore, in most cases, pronouncements on points on which the court has not had the benefit of argument.

HUMPHREY'S EXECUTOR v. UNITED STATES

Supreme Court of the United States, 1935.
295 U.S. 602, 55 S.Ct. 869, 79 L.Ed. 1611.

[Plaintiff brought suit in the Court of Claims to recover a sum of money alleged to be due to the deceased, William E. Humphrey, for salary as a Federal Trade Commissioner from October 8, 1933, when President Roosevelt undertook to remove him from office, to the time of his death, on February 14, 1934. At the time of the attempted removal, Humphrey had almost five years left to serve of the seven year term to which he had been appointed by President Hoover in

Sec. 3   TECHNIQUE OF CASE LAW DEVELOPMENT   115

1931. The Court of Claims certified the following two questions to the Supreme Court:

"1. Do the provisions of Section 1 of the Federal Trade Commission Act, stating that 'any commissioner may be removed by the President for inefficiency, neglect of duty, or malfeasance in office' restrict or limit the power of the President to remove a commissioner except upon one or more of the causes named?

"If the foregoing question is answered in the affirmative, then—

"2. If the power of the President to remove a commissioner is restricted or limited as shown by the foregoing interrogatory and the answer made thereto, is such a restriction or limitation valid under the Constitution of the United States?"]

Mr. Justice SUTHERLAND delivered the opinion of the Court.

* * *

* * * the language of the act, the legislative reports, and the general purposes of the legislation as reflected by the debates, all combine to demonstrate the Congressional intent to create a body of experts who shall gain experience by length of service—a body which shall be independent of executive authority, except in its selection, and free to exercise its judgment without the leave or hindrance of any other official or any department of the government. To the accomplishment of these purposes, it is clear that Congress was of opinion that length and certainty of tenure would vitally contribute. And to hold that, nevertheless, the members of the commission continue in office only at the mere will of the President, might be to thwart, in large measure, the very ends which Congress sought to realize by definitely fixing the term of office.

We conclude that the intent of the act is to limit the executive power of removal to the causes enumerated, the existence of none of which is claimed here; and we pass to the second question.

Second. To support its contention that the removal provision of section 1, as we have just construed it, is an unconstitutional interference with the executive power of the President, the government's chief reliance is Myers v. United States, 272 U.S. 52, 47 S.Ct. 21, 71 L.Ed. 160. That case has been so recently decided, and the prevailing and dissenting opinions so fully review the general subject of the power of executive removal, that further discussion would add little of value to the wealth of material there collected. These opinions examine at length the historical, legislative, and judicial data bearing upon the question, beginning with what is called "the decision of 1789" in the first Congress and coming down almost to the day when the opinions were delivered. They occupy 243 pages of the volume in which they are printed. Nevertheless, the narrow point actually decided was only that the President had power to remove a postmaster of the first class, without the advice and consent of the Senate as required by act of Congress. In the course of the opinion of the court, expressions occur which tend to sustain the government's contention, but these are beyond the point involved and, therefore, do not come within the rule of stare decisis. In so far as they are out of harmony with the views here set forth, these expressions are disapproved. A like situation was presented in the case of Cohens v. Virginia, 6 Wheat. 264, 399, 5 L.Ed. 257, in respect of certain general expressions in the opinion in Marbury v. Madison, 1 Cranch, 137, 2 L.Ed. 60. Chief Justice Marshall, who delivered the opinion in the Marbury Case, speaking again for the court in the Cohens Case, said: "It is a maxim, not to be disregarded, that general expressions, in every opinion, are to be taken in connection with the case in which those expressions are used. If they go beyond the case, they may be respected, but ought not to control the judgment in a subsequent suit, when the very point is presented for decision. The reason of this maxim is obvious. The question actually before the court is investigated with care, and considered in its full extent. Other principles which may serve to illustrate it, are considered in their relation to the case decided, but their possible bearing on all other cases is seldom completely investigated."

And he added that these general expressions in the case of Marbury v. Madison were to be understood with the limitations put upon them by the opinion in the Cohens Case. See, also, Carroll v. Lessee of Carroll et al., 16 How. 275, 286–287, 14 L.Ed. 936; O'Donoghue v. United States, 289 U.S. 516, 550, 53 S.Ct. 740, 77 L.Ed. 1356.

The office of a postmaster is so essentially unlike the office now involved that the decision in the Myers Case cannot be accepted as controlling our decision here. A postmaster is an executive officer restricted to the performance of executive functions. He is charged with no duty at all related to either the legislative or judicial power. The actual decision in the Myers Case finds support in the theory that such an officer is merely one of the units in the executive department and, hence, inherently subject to the exclusive and illimitable power of removal by the Chief Executive, whose subordinate and aid he is. Putting aside dicta, which may be followed if sufficiently persuasive but which are not controlling, the necessary reach of the decision goes far enough to include all purely executive officers. It goes no farther; much less does it include an officer who occupies no place in the executive department and who exercises no part of the executive power vested by the Constitution in the President.

* * *

The result of what we now have said is this: Whether the power of the President to remove an officer shall prevail over the authority of Congress to condition the power by fixing a definite term and pre-

Sec. 3　　TECHNIQUE OF CASE LAW DEVELOPMENT　　117

cluding a removal except for cause will depend upon the character of the office; the Myers decision affirming the power of the President alone to make the removal, is confined to purely executive officers; and as to officers of the kind here under consideration, we hold that no removal can be made during the prescribed term for which the officer is appointed, except for one or more of the causes named in the applicable statute.

To the extent, that between the decision in the Myers Case, which sustains the unrestrictable power of the President to remove purely executive officers, and our present decision that such power does not extend to an office such as that here involved, there shall remain a field of doubt, we leave such cases as may fall within it for future consideration and determination as they may arise.

In accordance with the foregoing, the questions submitted are answered:

Question No. 1, Yes.

Question No. 2, Yes.

Mr. Justice McREYNOLDS agrees that both questions should be answered in the affirmative. A separate opinion in Myers v. United States, 272 U.S. 52, at page 178, 47 S.Ct. 21, at page 46, 71 L.Ed. 160, states his views concerning the power of the President to remove appointees.

NOTES

1. The opinion in the *Myers* case occupies about 70 pages of Volume 272 of the United States Reports. To what language in that case does the court in *Humphrey's Executor* point as embodying the "holding"?

Would it have changed the situation if the Court in *Myers* had said, on one of those 70 pages: "We hold that the President may at his discretion, remove from office any person appointed by him or a predecessor."?

The point of these questions is to focus your attention on the fact that when we speak of the holding of a case we refer not to anything which was *said*, but to what was decided. It is true that we may conclude that a particular formulation of words in a decision is an accurate statement of the holding of the case but, as we shall see, the fact that the court states its "holding" in a particular way does not control in subsequent cases.

2. Is the following statement on page 116, supra, holding or dictum? "In so far as they are out of harmony with the views here set forth, these expressions are disapproved."

3. Suppose that after the decision in the *Myers* case, but before the *Humphrey's Executor* case, you had been writing a law review article and had stated that in *Myers* the Supreme Court held that Congress may not constitutionally limit the President's power to remove a presidential appointee from office. Would you have been wrong?

Suppose that during that same period you were working in the Justice Department and the President had asked you whether he could fire Humphrey. If you had told him that *Myers* held he could, would you have been wrong?

Suppose, instead, you had been Humphrey's lawyer, and he asked you if he should take another job. If you had said, "Yes, under *Myers* you don't have a claim for your salary," would you have been wrong?

4. In recent years the burden of increasing caseloads and the cost to the profession of purchasing, storing and retrieving larger and larger volumes of opinions have led many courts to refrain from writing or publishing opinions in some cases where the court feels no purpose would be served by an opinion. "Our test * * * is whether the district courts, future litigants, or we ourselves would be likely to benefit from the opportunity to read or cite the opinion * * *" Plan for the Publication of Opinions, United States Court of Appeals for the First Circuit, 1st Cir. Rules Appendix B. Frequently, the courts forbid the citation of these unpublished opinions in other cases. Given that, as you have just learned, the precedential importance of a decision lies not in what the court says but in what it decides, why should courts forbid citation of any decisions? What are the implications of the practice for the doctrine of stare decisis? For a discussion of the practice in federal courts, and the problems created, see Reynolds & Richman, The Non-Precedential Precedent—Limited Publication and No-Citation Rules in the United States Courts of Appeals, 78 Colum.L.Rev. 1167 (1178). See also Seligson & Warnlof, The Use of Unreported Cases in California, 24 Hastings L.J. 37 (1972) for a more favorable view of the practice.

Stare Decisis in Operation

It should be apparent by now that to ask the question, "What is the holding of a case?" is really to ask, "What fact situations can the rule of law of that case be said to govern?", i. e., "As to what future cases does the decision of the case constitute binding authority?" Since the decision as to whether or not a precedent governs a particular case rests, in the last analysis, with the court deciding the later case, the answer to the question "What is the holding?" is a prediction that as to certain future fact situations the court will consider the decision governing. Whether the prediction is accurate will not be known until the question is finally adjudicated.

Perhaps the best definition of a holding for you as an advocate is that the holding of a case is what you can persuade the court in a later case the court in the first case held. Such a definition is misleading, however, and, especially to the neophyte, is too atomistic to be of much value. It leads to the too quick conclusion that *stare decisis* is a myth, that judges are not really governed by precedent and that there is no minimum or maximum to what can be called the holding of a case. This is not true. The very fact that judges believe in *stare decisis* and are trying to make it work gives the doctrine validity and gives us a standard by means of which we can usually predict that as to certain fact situations a decision must be considered a holding and as to others it cannot be so considered.

CULLINGS v. GOETZ

Court of Appeals of New York, 1931.
256 N.Y. 287, 176 N.E. 397.

Action by Joseph Cullings against Edward Goetz and others. From a judgment (231 App.Div. 266, 247 N.Y.S. 109), reversing a judgment of the Trial Term in favor of the plaintiff, and dismissing the complaint, the plaintiff appeals.

CARDOZO, C. J. Plaintiff brought his automobile to a garage, intending to drive in. There were two sliding doors at the entrance, one open, the other closed. He tried to push the closed one open, but it did not move upon its track. When he shook it with some force, it fell upon his back, causing injuries for which he sues. His action is against Goetz, lessee of the garage, and the Nickleys, the owners, who were also the lessors. The lease was an oral one, and ran from month to month. The trial judge left the question to the jury whether as one of its provisions the owners had agreed to make the necessary repairs. In the event of that agreement and of failure to repair after notice of the need, owners as well as lessee were to be held for any negligence in the unsafe condition of the doors. The jury found a verdict against all the parties sued. On an appeal by the owners, the Appellate Division reversed, and dismissed the complaint, upon the ground that the failure of the owners to keep the promise to repair was unavailing to charge them with liability in tort.

The evidence of the supposed promise is at best confused and uncertain, if there be evidence at all. For the purpose of this appeal we assume without deciding that it permits conflicting inferences. We assume also that there was freedom from contributory negligence, though another entrance was available, and there is evidence of notice that the one chosen was out of use. Giving the plaintiff's case the aid of these assumptions, we concur with the Appellate Division in its ruling that liability in tort must be confined to the lessee, whose possession and dominion were exclusive and complete.

The subject has divided juridical opinion. Generally, however, in this country as in England, a covenant to repair does not impose upon the lessor a liability in tort at the suit of the lessee or of others lawfully on the land in the right of the lessee. See, e. g., Tuttle v. Gilbert Mfg. Co., 145 Mass. 169, 13 N.E. 465; Miles v. Janvrin, 196 Mass. 431, 82 N.E. 708, 13 L.R.A.(N.S.) 378, 124 Am.St.Rep. 575; Fiorntino v. Mason, 233 Mass. 451, 454, 124 N.E. 283; Carroll v. Intercolonial Club of Boston, 243 Mass. 380, 383, 137 N.E. 656; Dustin v. Curtis, 74 N.H. 266, 67 A. 220, 11 L.R.A.(N.S.) 504, 13 Ann.Cas. 169; Davis v. Smith, 26 R.I. 129, 58 A. 630, 66 L.R.A. 478, 106 Am. St.Rep. 691, 3 Ann.Cas. 832; Brady v. Klein, 133 Mich. 422, 95 N.W. 557, 62 L.R.A. 909, 103 Am.St.Rep. 455, 2 Ann.Cas. 464; Cavalier v. Pope, [1905] 2 K.B. 757, 762, 764; Cavalier v. Pope, [1906] A.C. 428, 433; Cameron v. Young, [1908] A.C. 176; and see, also, 8 A.L.R.

766, collating the decisions. There are decisions to the contrary (Flood v. Pabst Brewing Co., 158 Wis. 626, 149 N.W. 489, L.R.A. 1916F, 1101; Merchants' Cotton Press & Storage Co. v. Miller, 135 Tenn. 187, 186 S.W. 87, L.R.A.1916F, 1137; Barron v. Liedloff, 95 Minn. 474, 104 N.W. 289), but they speak the voice of a minority. Liability in tort is an incident to occupation or control. American Law Inst., Restatement of the Law of Torts, § 227. By preponderant opinion, occupation and control are not reserved through an agreement that the landlord will repair. Cavalier v. Pope, [1906] A.C. 428, at page 433; Pollock, Torts (13th Ed.) 532; Salmond, Torts (7th Ed.) 477. The tenant and no one else may keep visitors away till the danger is abated, or adapt the warning to the need. The landlord has at most a privilege to enter for the doing of the work, and at times not even that if the occupant protests. "The power of control necessary to raise the duty * * * implies something more than the right or liability to repair the premises. It implies the power and the right to admit people to the premises and to exclude people from them." Cavalier v. Pope, supra. In saying this we assume the possibility of so phrasing and enlarging the rights of the lessor that occupation and control will be shared with the lessee. There are decisions in Massachusetts that draw a distinction between a covenant merely to repair and one to maintain in safe condition with supervision adequate to the end to be achieved. Miles v. Janvrin, supra; Fiorntino v. Mason, supra; Carroll v. Intercolonial Club, supra; see, also, Robinson v. Heil, 128 Md. 645, 98 A. 195; Collison v. Curtner, 141 Ark. 122, 216 S.W. 1059, 8 A.L.R. 760. In the case now at hand, the promise, if there was any, was to act at the request of the lessee. What resulted was not a reservation by an owner of one of the privileges of ownership. It was the assumption of a burden for the benefit of the occupant with consequences the same as if there had been a promise to repair by a plumber or a carpenter. Cf. Zurich General Accident & Liability Ins. Co. v. Watson Elevator Co., 253 N.Y. 404, 409, 171 N.E. 688; Mollino v. Ogden & Clarkson Corporation, 243 N.Y. 450, 154 N.E. 307, 49 A.L.R. 518.

The rule in this state is settled in accord with the prevailing doctrine. Dicta, supposed to be inconsistent, are summoned to the support of a contrary position. They will be considered later on. Whatever their significance, they cannot overcome decisions directly to the point. As often as the question has been squarely up, the answer has been consistent that there is no liability in tort. Some of the decisions rejecting liability are judgments of this court. Kushes v. Ginsberg, 188 N.Y. 630, 81 N.E. 1168, affirming 99 App.Div. 417, 91 N. Y.S. 216; Sterger v. Van Sicklen, 132 N.Y. 499, 30 N.E. 987, 16 L.R. A. 640, 28 Am.St.Rep. 594; cf. Reynolds v. Van Beuren, 155 N.Y. 120, 125, 49 N.E. 763, 42 L.R.A. 129; Wolf v. American Tract Soc., 164 N.Y. 30, 35, 58 N.E. 31, 51 L.R.A. 241; Golob v. Pasinsky, 178 N.Y. 458, 461, 70 N.E. 973. Others, too many to be fully numbered,

Sec. 3   TECHNIQUE OF CASE LAW DEVELOPMENT   121

are in courts of intermediate appeal. Schick v. Fleischhauer, 26 App.Div. 210, 49 N.Y.S. 962; Frank v. Mandel, 76 App.Div. 413, 417, 78 N.Y.S. 855; Stelz v. Van Dusen, 93 App.Div. 358, 87 N.Y.S. 716; Boden v. Scholtz, 101 App.Div. 1, 2, 91 N.Y.S. 437; Pernick v. Central Union Gas Co., 183 App.Div. 543, 170 N.Y.S. 245. The doctrine, wise or unwise in its origin, has worked itself by common acquiescence into the tissues of our law. It is too deeply imbedded to be superseded or ignored. Hardly a day goes by in our great centers of population but it is applied by judges and juries in cases great and small. Countless tenants, suing for personal injuries and proving nothing more than the breach of an agreement, have been dismissed without a remedy in adherence to the authority of Schick v. Fleischhauer and Kushes v. Ginsberg. Countless visitors of tenants and members of a tenant's family have encountered a like fate. If there is no remedy for the tenant, there is none for visitors or relatives present in the tenant's right. Miles v. Janvrin, supra, 196 Mass. at page 440, 82 N.E. 708, 13 L.R.A.(N.S.) 378, 124 Am.St.Rep. 575; Elefante v. Pizitz, 182 App.Div. 819, 821, 169 N.Y.S. 910. Liability has been enlarged by statute where an apartment in a tenement house in a city of the first class is the subject of the lease. Altz v. Leiberson, 233 N.Y. 16, 134 N.E. 703. The duty in such instances is independent of the contract. It is one imposed by law, with liability in tort where the duty is ignored. Here the plaintiff was injured in the use of a garage. His remedy is against the tenant at whose invitation he was there.

We have spoken of dicta that are cited to the contrary. They do not touch the liability of the landlord for conditions within the premises affecting only the lessee or those who enter upon the premises in the right of the lessee. They have to do with nuisances threatening danger to the public beyond the land demised. Cf. Sterger v. Van Sicklen, supra, 132 N.Y. at page 501, 30 N.E. 987, 16 L.R.A. 640, 28 Am.St.Rep. 594; Ahern v. Steele, 115 N.Y. 203, 209, 22 N.E. 193, 5 L.R.A. 449, 12 Am.St.Rep. 778; City of Brooklyn v. Brooklyn City R. Co., 47 N.Y. 475, 483, 7 Am.Rep. 469; Clancy v. Byrne, 56 N.Y. 129, 15 Am.Rep. 391; Jaffe v. Harteau, 56 N.Y. 398, 15 Am.Rep. 438; Brady v. Klein, supra; 18 Halsbury, Laws of England, § 989; 21 Id. §§ 651, 955. Even when thus confined, they are dicta, and nothing more, at least in this state, though reiteration may have given them an authority not otherwise belonging to them. Be that as it may, the fact remains that the decision in every instance exonerated the lessor. One case, it is true, there is (Kilmer v. White, 254 N.Y. 64, 69, 171 N.E. 908), which had to do with conditions within the premises, and not with those outside, but it cites Jaffe v. Harteau, supra, and does not suggest even remotely a purpose to establish a new rule. There is merely a cautious reservation of the doctrine to be applied in situations different from any before us at the time.

* * *

Other grounds of liability suggested in the plaintiff's argument have been considered and are found to be untenable.

We state for greater caution, though the caution should be needless, that nothing said in this opinion has relation to a case where a part only of the building is in the possession of the lessee, and the dangerous condition is in the ways or other parts retained by the lessor. Dollard v. Roberts, 130 N.Y. 269, 29 N.E. 104, 14 L.R.A. 238; Kilmer v. White, supra; American Law Inst., Restatement of the Law of Torts, § 230.

The judgment should be affirmed with costs.

POUND, CRANE, LEHMAN, KELLOGG, O'BRIEN, and HUBBS, JJ., concur.

Judgment affirmed.

NOTES

1. It is manifest from the opinion of the court in the principal case that counsel for the plaintiff-appellant Cullings had cited past decisions of the Court of Appeals in which the opinions had contained statements generally supporting the plaintiff-appellant's position in the principal case. What is the theory on which Judge Cardozo, in his opinion for the court in the principal case, characterizes these past judicial utterances as *dicta*?

2. Note the care with which Judge Cardozo, in the final paragraph of his opinion, attempts to make it certain that Cullings v. Goetz will not, in its turn, be cited out of context by counsel for the defendant in some future suit against a lessor in part possession of a building.

The Scope of a Precedent

The principle of *stare decisis*, simply stated, is that the decision in a case should govern the decision in all like cases—but only in like cases. The best guide in the determination of what are "like cases" is a constant awareness of the underlying assumption of the Anglo-American system of case-by-case progress: that the court in every case will have before it all the facts necessary to a decision and that it will make its decision cognizant of all factors that should be considered. Here we have a standard by which to judge what are "like cases"—they are those whose fact situations present to the court the same factors to be considered in reaching a decision.

There are in any case a number of facts which obviously play no part in the determination, i. e., facts whose absence will not change the factors which must be considered by the court in reaching its decision. In formulating our statement of the rule of law established by that case, we can safely exclude these obviously nonsignificant (immaterial) facts from our consideration. So stated the rule of law derived from that case will cover only fact situations so similar to that case that no court can distinguish it without resorting to pain-

Sec. 3   *TECHNIQUE OF CASE LAW DEVELOPMENT*   123

fully obvious sophistry, a course which courts are usually reluctant to pursue. Here we have the minimum of what can be called the holding.

As we continue to abstract from the facts of our case we eventually reach a level of generalization which clearly includes fact situations materially different from that of the case, i. e., fact situations containing facts which present different considerations for the court to take account of in reaching its decision. When we reach this level of generalization we have gone beyond the maximum of what can be called the holding. An example of such a generalization is that of Baker v. Libbie that all men are entitled to the fruits of their labors.

These limits, however, guide us only in the easy cases. Between these limits lies a large area in which no one can be sure that his statement of the holding is not too general or too specific—that his view of what the material facts were is the right one—until the court has decided his case. This is the area in which most litigated cases fall. The best that can be done in this area is to state a reasonable rule of law abstracted from the precedent case. Your job as a counselor will be to make a reasonable prediction as to the extent to which a precedent will control. Your initial job as an advocate will be to state the holding of the precedent case in sufficiently general terms so that it covers the facts of your case. Your opponent will be stating the holding in much narrower terms—sufficiently narrow so that it does not cover the facts of your case (he will be "distinguishing the case on its facts"). Until the new case is decided no one can say with certainty that either statement of the holding is right or wrong. Each statement may be eminently reasonable and until the court has been persuaded to adopt one or the other no flat answer can be given to the question of which statement more nearly approximated the holding of the precedent case. It may (or may not) be some consolation that judges often disagree as to what the prior case held. See, for example, Mitchell v. W. T. Grant Co., 416 U.S. 600, 94 S.Ct. 1895, 40 L.Ed.2d 406 (1974) where the majority and minority differed as to whether the Court was overruling an earlier decision.

The job of stating a reasonable rule of law—of predicting the decision of the court on the new facts—is not easy; it is an art rather than a science and as such is primarily a matter of feel—the feel which will be developed as you read and use more cases, know your courts better and know better the circumstances out of which the first decision came and the different circumstances, if any, of your own case.

The key to the determination is policy. What was the policy (or policies) underlying the earlier decision? Are there facts in the new case which raise different policy considerations? Of course, if the court believes the policy of the original decision was wrong, it may overrule it or, as we shall see, "confine it to its special facts," but usually one stands a better chance to win by arguing that the facts are "materially different." How do we know what the policies underlying the first decision were?

The best guide that can be used is the language of the court deciding the case; while not absolutely controlling it often shows you which facts the court thought significant and makes the job of distinguishing a subsequent case much more difficult where that job involves emphasizing facts other than those the court thought significant. It is not, as you will see in the cases on product liability, an insurmountable handicap, but no good lawyer fails to take the language of the court into account.

But useful as the language may be, the most important element of any case is its facts; the first job you must do is to compare the facts of your case with the facts of those cases upon which you intend to rely as precedent and you must be prepared to reconcile factual differences if any exist.

PROBLEM CASE

The following is the opinion of the court in the recent case of Abbott v. Owner, decided by the Supreme Court of the [hypothetical] State of Minnewaska in January, 1952:

"JARNDYCE, J. The facts in this case can be simply stated. Early in 1950, the defendant Otto Owner purchased a new Packard automobile for the use of himself and the members of his immediate family. On March 6, 1950, the defendant Owner gave his 16-year-old daughter, Alice, permission to drive the Packard to a beauty shop. As is well known, the law of this State forbids the issuance of a driver's license to any person under 18 years of age. While Alice was driving through the streets of Terryville on the way to the beauty shop, she lost control of the car, which ran up on the curb and seriously injured the plaintiff Abbott.

"The facts stated in the foregoing paragraph are alleged in the plaintiff Abbott's complaint in this action. A demurrer filed by the defendant Owner in the court below was overruled, and the case proceeded to trial. The jury brought in a verdict for $5,000 damages in plaintiff Abbott's favor, and the defendant Owner moved for a new trial. The motion for a new trial was overruled by the trial court, and the defendant appeals to this Court.

"The development of the law on this subject has been attended by a slow process of clarification. When the automobile was new and regarded as no more dangerous than the horse and buggy, courts were disposed to hold that no strict liability attached to a registered car owner. Today, mounting traffic accident statistics have brought home to us that the modern, 100-mile-an-hour automobile is, indeed, fraught with such possibility for harm that the owner must bear strict responsibility for its use. *When a man purchases a high-powered automobile and allows his wife or his son or his daughter to use it, he is responsible for all injuries to pedestrians which may result from the wife's or the son's or the daughter's negligence in the operation of the automobile.* The question of law is one of first impression in this jurisdiction, but we have no doubt at all about it.

"Defendant's counsel contend that there are other reasons why the verdict below should have been for the defendant. We must decline to enter upon a consideration of these questions. It follows from what has already been said that the court below was right in refusing to grant the defendant Owner's motion for a new trial. The judgment of the trial court is affirmed."

Since, as stated in Judge Jarndyce's opinion, the decision in Abbott v. Owner is the first decision in Minnewaska on the subject of the liability of a car owner for injuries resulting from another's negligence in the operation of the car, it is important to determine the scope of the principle of law for which Abbott v. Owner can be taken as authority. Is the italicized sentence in the opinion "holding" or "dictum?"

The Option to Overrule

In England, prior to 1966, the House of Lords (in its judicial capacity) took the position that it could not overrule prior decisions. Whether this position was as rigid as it purported to be is a matter for some argument. However, it is true that the doctrine of *stare decisis* was more strictly applied in England than in the United States where it has always been accepted that a court could overrule its prior decisions.

The fact that a court can, in the last analysis overrule a prior decision makes the concept of "holding" even more elusive than it might otherwise be. What, you may ask, is all of the fuss about "binding" decisions if they aren't really binding. But don't conclude too quickly that *stare decisis* is a paper tiger. It probably is true that courts overrule more easily than they once did but overruling is still rare. If you cannot distinguish a case you must take on the additional battle of persuading the court that *stare decisis* should not be applied. But the option to overrule—or distinguish on meaningless differences—should underscore that the process is not often mechanistic. Courts do not simply match up facts; the lawyers must persuade them that there is good reason in justice, fairness or the needs of the legal system to follow the earlier decision.

SILVER v. GREAT AMERICAN INS. CO.

Court of Appeals of New York, 1972.
29 N.Y.2d 356, 328 N.Y.S.2d 398, 278 N.E.2d 619.

FULD, Chief Judge.

We have previously held that "[o]ur courts are bound to try an action for a foreign tort when either the plaintiff or the defendant is a resident of this State" and that it is only when such an action is brought by one nonresident against another that "our courts may refuse to take cognizance of the controversy" on the ground of *forum non conveniens*. (de la Bouillerie v. de Vienne, 300 N.Y. 60, 62, 89 N.E.2d 15; see Crashley v. Press Pub. Co., 179 N.Y. 27, 71 N.E. 258; Gregonis v. Philadelphia & Reading Coal & Iron Co., 235 N.Y. 152, 139 N.E. 223.) The defendant in the case before us asks us to reconsider and overrule those decisions.

The plaintiff is a neurosurgeon residing and practicing in Hawaii, the defendant, a New York corporation, authorized to do business in Hawaii and the other 48 States. In 1969, the plaintiff filed the present complaint in the Supreme Court, New York County, consisting of three causes of action, one for an injunction and the other two for damages, compensatory and punitive, totaling four million dollars. It charges the defendant with defamation and with a conspiracy to injure the plaintiff in his profession—not only, he asserts, because he "has testified as a physician in malpractice cases" in Hawaii against doctors and hospitals insured by the defendant but also because he is "of the Jewish faith." More specifically, he alleges that the defendant, in New York, Hawaii and elsewhere, conspired to injure and defame him and that, as part of the conspiracy, the defendant provided insurance protection, by means of a special "libel and slander rider", for persons who "spoke" of the plaintiff as being "a rough technician", "intellectually dishonest" and "mentally sick." He claims that, as a result of the defendant's conduct, his patients have been "subjected to inhuman treatment" and he has been seriously damaged, his applications to publicly supported hospitals "arbitrarily rejected" and his staff privileges in such hospitals "arbitrarily" taken from him.[35]

Although the complaint, in several of its paragraphs (6, 8, 10, 12), recites that the defendant committed certain acts in New York, which purportedly advanced the conspiracy, the defendant moved to dismiss the complaint on the ground of *forum non conveniens*. It is its position that, despite such recitals, the import and thrust of the plaintiff's allegations in this action, as well as the allegations in the

---

[35]. The plaintiff has brought four somewhat similar actions against the defendant and local Hawaiian doctors and hospital administrators charging them with conspiring to prevent him from practicing in Hawaii, and those suits are currently pending in that jurisdiction. In those actions, the plaintiff seeks damages totaling some 20 million dollars.

Sec. 3   TECHNIQUE OF CASE LAW DEVELOPMENT   127

other similar actions brought by the plaintiff in Hawaii [see n. 35], "refer to and deal with matters originating in * * * Hawaii, where plaintiff resides and practices medicine" and that "none of [his] contentions in any way whatsoever relate to incidents or events in * * * New York." Moreover, in order to assure the plaintiff a forum in which to bring suit if its motion is granted, the defendant asserted its willingness to accept service of process in Hawaii and waive any defense of the Statute of Limitations.[36]

The court at Special Term denied the motion, relying upon the *de la Bouillerie* case, 300 N.Y. 60, 89 N.E.2d 15, supra. The Appellate Division, 316 N.Y.S.2d 186, 35 A.D.2d 317, also considering itself bound by *stare decisis*, affirmed Special Term's order but, in so doing, declared that the existing decisional law should be reconsidered. Indeed, the court stated that Hawaii was the most appropriate forum and indicated that, were it not for our earlier decisions, it would have granted the defendant's motion and dismissed the complaint (35 A.D.2d 317–318, 316 N.Y.S.2d 186–187). The appeal is in this court by leave of the Appellate Division on a certified question.

As a general rule, a plaintiff with a transitory cause of action has a wide choice of forums in which to sue. Such forums often bear little relation either to the cause of action or to the parties and are selected by the plaintiff with the purpose of unduly burdening or harassing a defendant. (See, e. g., Gulf Oil Corp. v. Gilbert, 330 U.S. 501, 507–508, 67 S.Ct. 839, 91 L.Ed. 1055; Restatement, Second, Conflict of Laws, § 84, p. 251; Note, 73 Harv.L.Rev. 909, 1013.) The doctrine of *forum non conveniens* was developed by the courts to counter such a step, "to justify", it has been noted (Smit, Report on Uniform Interstate and International Procedure Act, Thirteenth Annual Report of N.Y. Judicial Conference, 1968, p. 136), "stay or dismissal in situations in which it was found that, on balancing the interests and conveniences of the parties and the court, the action could better be adjudicated in another forum." (See, also, Varkonyi v. Varig, 22 N.Y.2d 333, 337–338, 292 N.Y.S.2d 670, 673, 239 N.E.2d 542, 544; Bata v. Bata, 304 N.Y. 51, 56–57, 105 N.E.2d 623, 626; Gulf Oil Corp. v. Gilbert, 330 U.S. 501, 507–509, 67 S.Ct. 839, 91 L. Ed. 1055, supra; Restatement, Second, Conflict of Laws, § 84, pp. 251–252.)

The doctrine rests, in large part, on considerations of "public policy" (see Bata v. Bata, 304 N.Y. 51, 56, 105 N.E.2d 623, 626, supra) and, even though there be no prohibition, statutory or otherwise, against maintaining a particular action in this State, our courts should not be under any compulsion to add to their heavy burdens by

---

36. In our court, the defendant repeats its consent to accept service in Hawaii and to waive any limitations defense that it may acquire from the date of the service of the complaint in this suit—September 17, 1969—if the plaintiff institutes action in Hawaii within a reasonable time after entry of an order dismissing the complaint.

accepting jurisdiction of a cause of action having no substantial nexus with New York. The question whether the principle of *forum non conveniens* should or should not be applied in such a case "is one" we declared in Varkonyi v. Varig, 22 N.Y.2d 333, 337, 292 N.Y.S.2d 670, 673, 239 N.E.2d 542, 544, supra, "which is in general committed to the discretion of the courts below, to be exercised by reviewing and evaluating all the pertinent competing considerations."

Further thought persuades us that our current rule—which prohibits the doctrine of *forum non conveniens* from being invoked if one of the parties is a New York resident—should be relaxed. Its application should turn on considerations of justice, fairness and convenience and not solely on the residence of one of the parties. Although such residence is, of course, an important factor to be considered, *forum non conveniens* relief should be granted when it plainly appears that New York is an inconvenient forum and that another is available which will best serve the ends of justice and the convenience of the parties. The great advantage of the doctrine—its flexibility based on the facts and circumstances of a particular case—is severely, if not completely, undercut when our courts are prevented from applying it solely because one of the parties is a New York resident or corporation.

It has become increasingly apparent that a greater flexibility in applying the doctrine is not only wise but, perhaps, necessary. (See, e. g. Rosenberg, One Procedural Genie Too Many or Putting *Seider* Back Into Its Bottle, 71 Col.L.Rev. 660, 672; 1 Weinstein-Korn-Miller, N.Y.Civ.Prac., ¶ 301.07; Smit, Report on Uniform Interstate and International Procedure Act, Thirteenth Annual Report of N. Y. Judicial Conference, 1968, p. 138.) The fact that litigants may more easily gain access to our courts—with the consequent increase in litigation—stemming from enactment of the long-arm statute (CPLR 302), changing choice of law rules (see, e. g., Babcock v. Jackson, 12 N.Y.2d 473, 240 N.Y.S.2d 743, 191 N.E.2d 279) and decisions such as Seider v. Roth, 17 N.Y.2d 111, 269 N.Y.S.2d 99, 216 N.E.2d 312, requires a greater degree of forbearance in accepting suits which have but minimal contact with New York. (See 1 Weinstein-Korn-Miller, N.Y. Civ.Prac., ¶ 301.07.) With that in mind, it was suggested in Simpson v. Loehmann, 21 N.Y.2d 305, 312, 287 N.Y.S.2d 633, 638, 234 N.E.2d 669, 672; mot. for rearg. den. 21 N.Y.2d 990, 290 N.Y.S.2d 914, 238 N.E.2d 319 that further study be given to the subject of *forum non conveniens*. And, a short time later, the State's Judicial Conference recommended a bill reciting, in part, that "[t]he domicile or residence in this state of any party to the action shall not preclude the court from staying or dismissing the action."

Indeed, such has been the conclusion reached by judicial decision in at least two States. (See Winsor v. United Air Lines, 2 Storey 161, 52 Del. 161, 167–168, 154 A.2d 561; Gore v. United States Steel Corp., 15 N.J. 301, 311, 104 A.2d 670, cert. den. 348 U.S. 861, 75 S.Ct.

84, 99 L.Ed. 678; see, also Blair, The Doctrine of Forum Non Conveniens in Anglo-American Law, 29 Col.L.Rev. 1, 20 et seq.) In the *Gore* case, 15 N.J. 301, 104 A.2d 670, supra, for example, the New Jersey high court dismissed an action brought by nonresidents against a New Jersey corporation based on an alleged tort committed in Alabama. Rejecting the plaintiffs' argument that the defendant's residence compelled acceptance of the case the court wrote (p. 311, 104 A.2d p. 676) that the doctrine turns "on considerations of convenience and justice * * *. It is only in those exceptional cases where a weighing of all of the many relevant factors, *of which residence is but part*, decisively establishes that there is available another forum where trial will best serve the convenience of the parties and the ends of justice, that the doctrine is ever invoked." (Emphasis supplied.)[37]

Having concluded that reason and substantial justice call for modifying our prior decisions and relaxing our inflexible rule, there is nothing to deter this court from so doing. Certainly, we need not wait on legislative action. (See, e. g., Gelbman v. Gelbman, 23 N.Y. 2d 434, 437, 297 N.Y.S.2d 529, 530, 245 N.E.2d 192, 193; Greenberg v. Lorenz, 9 N.Y.2d 195, 199–200, 213 N.Y.S.2d 39, 41, 173 N.E.2d 773, 775; Bing v. Thunig, 2 N.Y.2d 656, 667, 163 N.Y.S.2d 3, 11, 143 N.E.2d 3, 9; Woods v. Lancet, 303 N.Y. 349, 355, 102 N.E.2d 691, 694.) As the cited decisions establish, *stare decisis* does not compel us to follow blindly a court-created rule—particularly one, as here, relating to a procedural matter—once we are persuaded that reason and a right sense of justice recommend its change.

The present appeal is before us, by leave of the Appellate Division, on a certified question and, accordingly, we remit the proceeding to that court so that it may decide—taking all pertinent factors into account, including the complaint's references to acts assertedly committed by the defendant in this State—whether, in the exercise of its sound discretion, it should deny or grant the defendant's motion to dismiss the complaint on the ground of *forum non conveniens*.

The order appealed from should be reversed, without costs, the certified question answered in the negative and the matter remitted to the Appellate Division for further proceedings in accordance with this opinion.

BURKE, SCILEPPI, BERGAN, BREITEL, JASEN and GIBSON, JJ., concur.

Order reversed, etc.

NOTES

1. What conclusions do you draw from this case as to the factors which a court will consider in deciding whether to overrule a prior

---

37. As bearing on the availability of another forum, we note the defendant's consent to accept service of process in Hawaii and to waive the Statute of Limitations defense.

decision? How often, do you suppose, do people "rely on precedents"? See Cardozo, Growth of the Law 122 (1924):

> "The picture of the bewildered litigant lured into a course of action by the false light of a decision, only to meet ruin when the light is extinguished and the decision is overruled, is for the most part a figment of excited brains. The only rules there is ever any thought of changing are those that are invoked by injustice after the event to shelter and intrench itself. In the rarest instances, if ever, would conduct have been different if the rule had been known and the change foreseen. At times the change means the imposition of a bill of costs that might otherwise have been saved. That is a cheap price to pay for the uprooting of an ancient wrong."

See also Gray, The Nature and Sources of Law 100 (1921):

> "Practically, in its application to actual affairs, for most of the laity, the law, except for a few crude notions of the equity involved in some of its general principles, is all ex post facto. When a man marries, or enters into a partnership, or buys a piece of land, or engages in any other transaction, he has the vaguest possible idea of the law governing the situation, and with our complicated system of jurisprudence, it is impossible it should be otherwise. If he delayed to make a contract or do an act until he understood exactly all the legal consequences it involved, the contract would never be made or the act done. Now the law of which a man has no knowledge is the same to him as if it did not exist."

On the other hand, see Cullings v. Goetz, supra, p. 119, Molitor v. Kaneland Community Unit District No. 302, infra, p. 225, and Commissioner v. Acker, infra, p. 458.

2. In the area of constitutional law, *stare decisis* is not so strong as in non-constitutional areas. Can you think of an explanation for why that should be so? See, e. g., the concurring opinion of Powell, J. in Mitchell v. W. T. Grant Co., 416 U.S. 600, 626–7, 94 S.Ct. 1895, 1909, 40 L.Ed.2d 406 (1974).

3. Should *stare decisis* ever be relied on by the government? Consider the statement from United States v. Shaughnessy, 234 F.2d 715, 719 (2d Cir. 1955) (a deportation proceeding):

> "In such a case, since *stare decisis* then rests on a sort of estoppel, it should not lead to the perpetuation of injustice when the party who urges the court to abide by the precedent has actually not, before the suit began, changed his position in reliance on it. Even, therefore, in civil cases, courts should heed Lord Wright's comment: 'Great judges have said that the function of the common law was the perpetual quest for justice. I should be sorry if quest for certitude were substituted for quest for justice.' Especially should that comment guide a court in a case like this when the government cites a precedent embodying an unjust ruling adverse to the appellant. For the government is not in the position of a businessman who has purchased property, or incurred a business risk, in reliance on a judicial precedent. Rather is the gov-

ernment like one who objects to a change in a substantive rule relative to negligence or a procedural rule of evidence or practice; as to such rules, *stare decisis* has relatively little vigor."

But see, Meads v. United States, 156 F.Supp. 938 (Ct.Cl.1957) applying the doctrine in a contract action against the United States.

The Uses of Dictum

As a matter of practical legal method, should a competent advocate cite dicta supporting his position, particularly when there is no past case squarely in point? As you read these cases, is a dictum merely to be discounted—or to be disregarded altogether? Note Justice Sutherland's reference, (*Humphrey's Executor*, supra) to "* * * dicta, which may be followed if sufficiently persuasive, but which are not controlling." And compare Chief Justice Marshall's statement in Cohens v. Virginia, 19 U.S. 264, 399, 5 L.Ed. 257 (1821) that "they [i. e., dicta] may be respected, but ought not to control the judgment in a subsequent suit when the very point is presented for decision." Another formulation often seen is the following:

> "* * * Nevertheless some weight is very properly given to a *dictum*, a weight similar to that assigned to the sayings of learned text-writers; and in this sense a *dictum* is authority, its weight varying with the learning of the court and with the amount of thought bestowed by the court upon the point covered by the *dictum*." Wambaugh, The Study of Cases 19 (2d Ed. 1894).

But these formulations tend to stress the mechanistic aspects. Of course, courts are not required to follow dictum but if one is looking for guidance as to what courts will do, a well-considered recent dictum may be a better guide than an old holding. Consider in this respect the decision of the United States Supreme Court in Banco Nacional de Cuba v. Sabbatino, 376 U.S. 398, 84 S.Ct. 923, 11 L.Ed.2d 804 (1964). One of the unsettled questions involved in the controversy was whether state or federal law controlled. In *Sabbatino* it did not matter since New York law (which would have been applicable if state law controlled) and federal law were the same. Nevertheless the Court said:

> "We could perhaps in this diversity action avoid the question whether federal or state law is applicable * * *. However, we are constrained to make it clear that an issue concerned with a basic choice regarding the competence and function of the Judiciary * * * must be treated exclusively as an aspect of federal law." [376 U.S. at 424–5].

Who would be brave enough in a subsequent case as to tell the Court that its statement should be ignored as mere dictum—or so foolish as to advise a client that the dictum did not represent "the law"?

The Positive Aspects of the Doctrine

Do you agree with the following statement of Judge Jerome Frank?

> "Stare decisis has no bite when it means merely that a court adheres to a precedent it considers correct. It is significant only when a court feels constrained to stick to a former ruling although the Court has come to regard it as unwise or unjust." United States v. Shaughnessy, 234 F.2d 715, 719 (2d Cir. 1955).

Most discussions of holding and dictum focus exclusively on the negative aspects of the concept: the extent to which the holding of a case is "binding" on subsequent cases. But the concept has another, very important aspect. As noted above it is possible to phrase the holding of a case at many levels of generality. By restricting the prior "holding" to its narrowest formulation, judges can avoid the binding effect; but they also can, by using the broadest formulation, move the law significantly without seeming to do violence to the doctrine of precedent. When you study the cases on product liability, observe how much flexibility there is in the system and how much courts move the law while they purport to be following binding precedent.

D. SYNTHESIS

It should be clear by now that one case standing by itself does not tell us much about the law in a particular field.[38] To know "what the law is" we need to put together all the related cases—to "synthesize" them. The process of synthesis is the most important element in working with case law; one synthesizes decisions for a number of purposes: to write scholarly articles, to write opinion letters, to write briefs—indeed, just about every time one makes a statement about what the law is. In real life, before you synthesize you will need to find the cases; here, in the rest of this chapter, we give you a ready-made, albeit not complete, group of cases for you to synthesize.

Our primary objective is to show you how over one hundred and fifty years the law relating to a manufacturer's liability for damages caused by its products has changed—as new fact situations have

---

38. "For the truth of the matter is a truth so obvious and trite that it is somewhat regularly overlooked by students. *That no case can have a meaning by itself!* Standing alone it gives you no guidance. It can give you no guidance as to how far it carries, as to how much of its language will hold water later. What counts, what gives you leads, what gives you sureness, *that is the background of the other cases* in relation to which you must read the one. They color the language, the technical terms, used in the opinion. But above all they give you the wherewithal to find which of the facts are significant, and in what aspect they are significant, and how far the rules laid down are to be trusted." The Bramble Bush 48–9.

Sec. 3   TECHNIQUE OF CASE LAW DEVELOPMENT   133

been presented for decision or, more fundamentally, as the social, political and economic environment has evolved—and how this change has taken place within our doctrine of precedent, largely without benefit of statute. Your emphasis should be on learning *how* the law has changed, although you should gather as much as time permits as to *why*.

In order to get the most out of this exercise, you should put yourself in the position of the lawyers who had to deal with the law during its development. It is easy to find others' descriptions of what happened, and why, but resort to such sources will be self-defeating. When you are faced with the task of making your own predictions, it will not be possible to peek ahead; all you will have to go on are the cases decided to date and your own understanding of the process by which law is made and unmade in our system. After each case, then, you should try to synthesize that case and the earlier cases as though they were all the information that was available, and to formulate a "rule of law" which will accommodate these cases.[39] This process is described with respect to the required simultaneous existence of "offer" and "acceptance" in the law of contracts by Professor Llewellyn, (The Bramble Bush 49–50):

> "The first case involves a man who makes an offer and gets in his revocation before his offer is accepted. The court decides that he cannot be sued upon his promise, and says that no contract can be made unless the minds of both parties are at one at once. The second case involves a man who has made a similar offer and has mailed a revocation, but to whom a letter of acceptance has been sent before his revocation was received. The court holds that he can be sued upon his promise, and says that his offer was being repeated every moment from the time that it arrived until the letter of acceptance was duly mailed. Here are two rules which are a little difficult to put together, and to square with sense, and which are, too, a little hard to square with the two holdings in the cases. We set to work to seek a way out which will do justice to the holdings. We arrive perhaps at this, that it is not necessary for the two minds to be at one at once, if the person who has received an offer thinks, and thinks reasonably, as he takes the last step of acceptance, that the offeror is standing by the offer."

---

39. Moreover, you should do it *before* you discuss the cases in class. In the words of Professor Llewellyn (The Bramble Bush 53):

"* * * it is vital, it is the very basic element of case law study, for you to have done your matching of the cases before you meet with his [the instructor's]. For it is not by watching him juggle the balls that you will learn. It is by matching his results against your own, by criticizing the process you have gone through in the light of the process he is going through. Indeed if you have not tried the game yourself, *you will not follow him*."

You will probably find the process of putting cases together difficult at first. Some of you will acquire the skill quickly; most of you will have mastered it by the end of the first year. All of you will learn it eventually, but *only* if you work at it on your own.

SEIXAS v. WOODS

Supreme Court of New York, 1804.
2 Caines 48.

This was an action on the case for selling peachum wood for brazilletto. The former worth hardly anything, the latter of considerable value. The defendant had received the wood in question from a house in New Providence, to whom he was agent, and in the invoice it was mentioned as brazilletto. He had also advertised it as brazilletto, had shown the invoice to the plaintiffs, and had made out the bill of parcels for brazilletto. But it was not pretended that he knew that it was peachum, nor did the plaintiffs suspect it to be so, as it was delivered from the vessel, and picked out from other wood by a person on their behalf. In short, neither side knew it to be other than brazilletto, nor was any fraud imputed. On discovery, however, of the real quality of the wood it was offered to the defendant, and the purchase money demanded. On his refusal to accept the one or return the other, as he had remitted the proceeds, the present action was brought, in which a verdict was taken for the plaintiffs, subject to the opinion of the court.

KENT, J. This is a clear case for the defendant. If upon a sale, there be neither a warranty nor deceit, the purchaser purchases at his peril. This seems to have been the ancient, and the uniform language of the English law, and the only writer of authority, that calls this doctrine in question is Professor Woodeson, in his Vinerian Lectures, and he does not cite any judicial decision as the basis of his opinion. In the case of Chandelor v. Lopus, (Cro. Jac. 4) it was determined in the exchequer, by all the judges except one, that for selling a jewel, which was affirmed to be a bezoar stone, when it was not, no action lay, unless the defendant knew it was not a bezoar stone, or had warranted it to be one. This appears to me to be a case in point and decisive. And in the case of Parkinson v. Lee, 2 East 315, it was decided, that a fair merchantable price, did not raise an implied warranty, and that if there was no warranty, and the seller, sell the thing, such as he believes it to be, without fraud, he will not be liable for a latent defect. These decisions are two centuries apart, and the intermediate cases, are to the same effect. Co.Litt. 102 a. Cro.J. 197, 1 Sid. 146 Yelv. 21.1 L.Raym. 1121. Per Holt, C. J. Doug. 20. Alleyn. 91, cited 2 East 498, notis. By the civil law, says L. Coke, every man is bound to warrant the thing that he selleth, albeit there be no express warranty; but the common law bindeth him not, unless there be a warranty in deed, or law. So Fitzherbert, (N.B. 94

C.) says, that if a man sell wine that is corrupted, or a horse that is diseased, and there be no warranty, it is at the buyer's peril, and his eyes and his taste ought to be his judges in that case. In the case cited from 2 East. the judges were unanimous that the rule applied to sales of all kinds of commodities. That without a warranty by the seller, or fraud on his part, the buyer must stand to all losses arising from latent defects, and that there is no instance in the English law of a contrary rule being laid down. The civil law, and the law of those countries, which have adopted the civil as their common law, is more rigorous towards the seller, and make him responsible in every case for a latent defect, (see the Dig. lib. 1. tit. 2, ch. 13. n. 1. which gives the very case of selling vitiated wood) and, if the question was *res integra* in our law, I confess I should be overcome by the reasoning of the civilians. And yet the rule of the common law has been well and elegantly vindicated by Fonblanque, as most happily reconciling the claims of convenience, with the duties of good faith. It requires the purchaser to apply his attention to those particulars, which may be supposed, within the reach of his observation and judgment, and the vendor to communicate, those particulars, and defects, which cannot be supposed to be immediately within the reach of such attention. And even against his want of vigilance, the purchaser may provide, by requiring the vendor expressly to warrant the article. The mentioning the wood, as brazilletto wood, in the bill of parcels, and in the advertisement some days previous to the sale, did not amount to a warranty to the plaintiffs. To make an affirmation at the time of the sale, a warranty, it must appear by evidence to be so intended, and not to have been a mere matter of judgment and opinion, and of which the defendant had no particular knowledge. Here it is admitted, the defendant was equally ignorant with the plaintiffs, and could have had no such intention.

The cases in which the ship, in a policy of insurance has been described as *neutral* or *American*, and that description held to be a warranty, are not at all analogous to the present case. The policy is a special contract, in which the whole agreement is precisely stated, and no question was ever made in those cases, but that the assured knew, and intended to be understood to mean that the vessel was of the character described. I am therefore for the defendant.

LEWIS, C. J. contra.

NOTES

1. In a separate opinion, Thompson, J. makes the following observation about the application of the maxim *caveat emptor* (literally, let the buyer beware) to this transaction:

"* * * Fonblanque, in his valuable *Treatise of Equity*, * * * speaking of the justice and propriety of this principle, says, 'To excite that diligence which is necessary to guard against imposition, and to secure that good faith which is necessary to justify a certain degree of confidence, is essential to the intercourse of society. These objects are attained by those rules of law which require the purchaser to apply his attention to those particulars, which may be supposed to be within the reach of his observation and judgment; and the vendor to communicate those particulars and defects, which cannot be supposed to be immediately within the reach of such attention. If the purchaser be wanting of attention to those points, where attention would have been sufficient to protect him from surprise or imposition, the maxim *caveat emptor* ought to apply. But even against this maxim he may provide, by requiring the vendor expressly to warrant that which the law would not imply to be warranted. If the vendor be wanting in good faith, *fides servanda* is the rule of law, and may be enforced, both in equity and at law.' These observations, I think, apply with peculiar force in the case before us. The agent of the plaintiffs, who made the purchase, was present at the delivery of the wood; and the defect now complained of was within the reach of his observation and judgment, had he bestowed proper attention. * * * I see no injustice or inconvenience resulting from this doctrine, but, on the contrary, think it is best calculated to excite that caution and attention which all prudent men ought to observe in making their contracts."

2. What facts not present in this case would be necessary to make out a case of warranty or deceit?

3. If a client, as incapable of distinguishing between peachum and brazilletto as the plaintiff in Seixas v. Woods, wanted to purchase brazilletto, what precautions would you advise?

THOMAS and WIFE v. WINCHESTER

Court of Appeals of New York, 1852.
6 N.Y. 397.

Action in the supreme court, commenced in August, 1849, against Winchester and Gilbert, for injuries sustained by Mrs. Thomas, from the effects of a quantity of extract of belladonna, administered to her by mistake as extract of dandelion.

In the complaint it was alleged, that the defendants from the year 1843, to the first of January, 1849, were engaged in putting up and vending certain vegetable extracts, at a store in the city of New York, designated as "108 John-street," and that the defendant Gilbert had for a long time previous thereto been so engaged, at the same place. That among the extracts so prepared and sold by them, were those respectively known as the "extract of dandelion," and the "extract of belladonna"; the former a mild and harmless medicine, and the latter a vegetable poison, which, if taken as a medicine in such quantity as might be safely administered of the former, would destroy the life, or seriously impair the health of the person to whom the same might be administered. That at some time between the peri-

Sec. 3   TECHNIQUE OF CASE LAW DEVELOPMENT   137

ods above mentioned, the defendants put up and sold to James S. Aspinwall, a druggist in the city of New York, a jar of the extract of belladonna, which had been labeled by them as the extract of dandelion, and was purchased of them as such by said Aspinwall. That said Aspinwall afterwards, and on the 10th day of May, 1845, relying upon the label so affixed by the defendants, sold the said jar of belladonna to Alvin Foord, a druggist of Cazenovia, in the county of Madison, as the extract of dandelion. That afterwards, and on the 27th of March, 1849, the plaintiff Mrs. Thomas, being sick, a portion of the extract of dandelion was prescribed for her by her physician, and the said Alvin Foord, relying upon the label affixed by the defendants to said jar of belladonna, and believing the same to be the extract of dandelion, did on the application of the plaintiff, Samuel Thomas, sell and deliver to him from the said jar of belladonna, a portion of its contents, which was administered to the plaintiff, Mrs. Thomas, under the belief that it was the extract of dandelion; by which she was greatly injured, so that her life was despaired of, etc. The plaintiffs also alleged that the whole injury was occasioned by the negligence and unskillfulness of the defendants in putting up and falsely labeling the jar of belladonna as the extract of dandelion, whereby the plaintiffs, as well as the druggists, and all other persons through whose hands it passed before being administered as aforesaid, were induced to believe, and did believe that it contained the extract of dandelion. Wherefore, etc.

The defendants in their answers, severally denied the allegations of the complaint, and insisted that they were not liable for the medicines sold by Aspinwall and Foord.

The cause was tried at the Madison circuit, in December 1849, before Mason, J. The defendant Gilbert was acquitted by the jury under the direction of the court, and a verdict was rendered against Winchester, for eight hundred dollars. A motion for a new trial made upon a bill of exceptions taken at the trial, having been denied at a general term in the sixth district, the defendant Winchester, brought this appeal. The facts which appeared on the trial are sufficiently stated in the opinion of RUGGLES, Ch. J.

RUGGLES, Ch. J., delivered the opinion of the court. This is an action brought to recover damages from the defendant for negligently putting up, labeling and selling as and for the extract of *dandelion*, which is a simple and harmless medicine, a jar of the extract of *belladonna*, which is a deadly poison; by means of which the plaintiff Mary Ann Thomas, to whom, being sick, a dose of dandelion was prescribed by a physician, and a portion of the contents of the jar, was administered as and for the extract of dandelion, was greatly injured, etc.

The facts proved were briefly these: Mrs. Thomas being in ill health, her physician prescribed for her a dose of dandelion. Her husband purchased what was believed to be the medicine prescribed, at the store of Dr. Foord, a physician and druggist in Cazenovia, Madison County, where the plaintiffs reside.

A small quantity of the medicine thus purchased was administered to Mrs. Thomas on whom it produced very alarming effects; such as coldness of the surface and extremities, feebleness of circulation, spasms of the muscles, giddiness of the head, dilation of the pupils of the eyes, and derangement of mind. She recovered however, after some time, from its effects, although for a short time her life was thought to be in great danger. The medicine administered was *belladonna, and not dandelion.* The jar from which it was taken was labeled "½ lb. *dandelion, prepared by A. Gilbert, No. 108 John-street, N. Y. Jar 8 oz.*" It was sold for and believed by Dr. Foord to be the extract of dandelion as labeled. Dr. Foord purchased the article as the extract of dandelion from Jas. S. Aspinwall, a druggist at New York. Aspinwall bought it of the defendant as extract of dandelion, believing it to be such. The defendant was engaged at No. 108 John-street, New York, in the manufacture and sale of certain vegetable extracts for medicinal purposes, and in the purchase and sale of others. The extracts manufactured by him were put up in jars for sale, and those which he purchased were put up by him in like manner. The jars containing extracts manufactured by himself and those containing extracts purchased by him from others, were labeled alike. Both were labeled like the jar in question, as "prepared by A. Gilbert." Gilbert was a person employed by the defendant at a salary, as an assistant in his business. The jars were labeled in Gilbert's name because he had been previously engaged in the same business on his own account at No. 108 John-street, and probably because Gilbert's labels rendered the articles more salable. The extract contained in the jar sold to Aspinwall, and by him to Foord, was not manufactured by the defendant, but was purchased by him from another manufacturer or dealer.

The extract of dandelion and the extract of belladonna resemble each other in color, consistence, smell and taste; but may on careful examination be distinguished the one from the other by those who are well acquainted with these articles. Gilbert's labels were paid for by Winchester and used in his business with his knowledge and assent.

The defendant's counsel moved for a nonsuit on the following grounds:

1. That the action could not be sustained, as the defendant was the remote vendor of the article in question: and there was no connection, transaction or privity between him and the plaintiffs, or either of them.

2. That this action sought to charge the defendant with the consequences of the negligence of Aspinwall and Foord.

Sec. 3   TECHNIQUE OF CASE LAW DEVELOPMENT   139

3. That the plaintiffs were liable to, and chargeable with the negligence of Aspinwall and Foord, and therefore could not maintain this action.

4. That according to the testimony Foord was chargeable with negligence, and that the plaintiffs therefore could not sustain this suit against the defendant: if they could sustain a suit at all it would be against Foord only.

5. That this suit being brought for the benefit of the wife, and alleging her as the meritorious cause of action, cannot be sustained.

6. That there was not sufficient evidence of negligence in the defendant to go to the jury.

The judge overruled the motion for a nonsuit, and the defendant's counsel excepted.

The judge among other things charged the jury, that if they should find from the evidence that either Aspinwall or Foord was guilty of negligence in vending as and for dandelion, the extract taken by Mrs. Thomas, or that the plaintiff Thomas, or those who administered it to Mrs. Thomas were chargeable with negligence in administering it, the plaintiffs were not entitled to recover; but if they were free from negligence, and if the defendant Winchester was guilty of negligence in putting up and vending the extracts in question, the plaintiffs were entitled to recover, provided the extract administered to Mrs. Thomas was the same which was put up by the defendant and sold by him to Aspinwall and by Aspinwall to Foord. That if they should find the defendant liable, the plaintiffs in this action were entitled to recover damages only for the personal injury and suffering of the wife, and not for loss of service, medical treatment or expense to the husband, and that the recovery should be confined to the actual damages suffered by the wife.

The action was properly brought in the name of the husband and wife for the personal injury and suffering of the wife; and the case was left to the jury with the proper directions on that point. 1 Chitty on Pleadings, 62, ed. of 1828.

The case depends on the first point taken by the defendant on his motion for a nonsuit; and the question is, whether the defendant, being a remote vendor of the medicine, and there being no privity or connection between him and the plaintiffs, the action can be maintained.

If, in the labeling a poisonous drug with the name of a harmless medicine, for public market, no duty was violated by the defendant, excepting that which he owed to Aspinwall, his immediate vendee, in virtue of his contract of sale, this action cannot be maintained. If A build a wagon and sell it to B, who sells it to C, and C hires it to D, who in consequence of the gross negligence of A in building the wagon is overturned and injured, D cannot recover damages against A, the builder. A's obligation to build the wagon faithfully, arises solely out of his contract with B. The public have nothing to do with it. Misfortune to third persons, not parties to the contract, would not be a natural and necessary consequence of the builder's negligence; and such negligence is not an act imminently dangerous to human life.

So, for the same reason, if a horse be defectively shod by a smith, and a person hiring the horse from the owner is thrown and injured in consequence of the smith's negligence in shoeing; the smith is not liable for the injury. The smith's duty in such case grows exclusively out of his contract with the owner of the horse; it was a duty which the smith owed to him alone, and to no one else. And although the injury to the rider may have happened in consequence of the negligence of the smith, the latter was not bound, either by his contract or by any considerations of public policy or safety, to respond for his breach of duty to any one except the person he contracted with.

This was the ground on which the case of Winterbottom v. Wright, 10 Mees. & Welsb. 109, was decided. A contracted with the postmaster general to provide a coach to convey the mail bags along a certain line of road, and B and others also contracted to horse the coach along the same line. B and his co-contractors hired C, who was the plaintiff, to drive the coach. The coach, in consequence of some latent defect, broke down; the plaintiff was thrown from his seat and lamed. It was held that C could not maintain an action against A for the injury thus sustained. The reason of the decision is best stated by Baron Rolfe. A's duty to keep the coach in good condition, was a duty to the postmaster general, with whom he made his contract, and not a duty to the driver employed by the owners of the horses.

But the case in hand stands on a different ground. The defendant was a dealer in poisonous drugs. Gilbert was his agent in preparing them for market. The death or great bodily harm of some person was the natural and almost inevitable consequence of the sale of belladonna by means of the false label.

Gilbert, the defendant's agent, would have been punishable for manslaughter if Mrs. Thomas had died in consequence of taking the falsely labeled medicine. Every man who, by his culpable negligence, causes the death of another, although without intent to kill, is guilty of manslaughter. 2 R.S. 662, § 19. A chemist who negligently sells laudanum in a phial labeled as paregoric, and thereby causes the death of a person to whom it is administered, is guilty of manslaughter. Tessymond's case, 1 Lewin's Crown Cases, 169. "So highly does the law value human life that it admits of no justification wherever life has been lost and the carelessness or negligence of one person has contributed to the death of another." Regina v. Swindall, 2 Car. &

Sec. 3   TECHNIQUE OF CASE LAW DEVELOPMENT   141

Kir. 232–3. And this rule applies not only where the death of one is occasioned by the negligent act of another, but where it is caused by the negligent omission of a duty of that other. 2 Car. & Kir. 368, 371. Although the defendant Winchester may not be answerable criminally for the negligence of his agent, there can be no doubt of his liability in a civil action, in which the act of the agent is to be regarded as the act of the principal.

In respect to the wrongful and criminal character of the negligence complained of, this case differs widely from those put by the defendant's counsel. No such imminent danger existed in those cases. In the present case the sale of the poisonous article was made to a dealer in drugs, and not to a consumer. The injury therefore was not likely to fall on him, or on his vendee who was also a dealer; but much more likely to be visited on a remote purchaser as actually happened. The defendant's negligence put human life in imminent danger. Can it be said that there was no duty on the part of the defendant, to avoid the creation of that danger by the exercise of greater caution? or that the exercise of that caution was a duty only to his immediate vendee, whose life was not endangered? The defendant's duty arose out of the nature of his business and the danger to others incident to its mismanagement. Nothing but mischief like that which actually happened could have been expected from sending the poison falsely labeled into the market; and the defendant is justly responsible for the probable consequences of the act. The duty of exercising caution in this respect did not arise out of the defendant's contract of sale to Aspinwall. The wrong done by the defendant was in putting the poison, mislabeled, into the hands of Aspinwall as an article of merchandise to be sold and afterwards used as the extract of dandelion, by some person then unknown. The owner of a horse and cart who leaves them unattended in the street is liable for any damage which may result from his negligence. Lynch v. Nurdin, 1 Ad. & Ellis, N.S. 29; Illidge v. Goodwin, 5 Car. & Payne, 190. The owner of a loaded gun who puts it into the hands of a child by whose indiscretion it is discharged, is liable for the damage occasioned by the discharge. 5 Maule & Sel. 198. The defendant's contract of sale to Aspinwall does not excuse the wrong done to the plaintiffs. It was a part of the means by which the wrong was effected. The plaintiffs' injury and their remedy would have stood on the same principle, if the defendant had given the belladonna to Dr. Foord without price, or if he had put it in his shop without his knowledge, under circumstances which would probably have led to its sale on the faith of the label.

In Longmeid v. Holliday, 6 Law and Eq.Rep. 562, the distinction is recognized between an act of negligence imminently dangerous to the lives of others, and one that is not so. In the former case, the party guilty of the negligence is liable to the party injured, whether there be a contract between them or not; in the latter, the negligent party is liable only to the party with whom he contracted, and on the ground that negligence is a breach of the contract.

The defendant, on the trial, insisted that Aspinwall and Foord were guilty of negligence in selling the article in question for what it was represented to be in the label; and that the suit, if it could be sustained at all, should have been brought against Foord. The judge charged the jury that if they, or either of them, were guilty of negligence in selling the belladonna for dandelion, the verdict must be for the defendant; and left the question of their negligence to the jury, who found on that point for the plaintiff. If the case really depended on the point thus raised, the question was properly left to the jury. But I think it did not. The defendant, by affixing the label to the jar, represented its contents to be dandelion; and to have been "prepared" by his agent Gilbert. The word "prepared" on the label, must be understood to mean that the article was manufactured by him, or that it had passed through some process under his hands, which would give him personal knowledge of its true name and quality. Whether Foord was justified in selling the article upon the faith of the defendant's label, would have been an open question in an action by the plaintiffs against him, and I wish to be understood as giving no opinion on that point. But it seems to me to be clear that the defendant cannot, in this case, set up as a defense, that Foord sold the contents of the jar as and for what the defendant represented it to be. The label conveyed the idea distinctly to Foord that the contents of the jar was the extract of dandelion; and that the defendant knew it to be such. So far as the defendant is concerned, Foord was under no obligation to test the truth of the representation. The charge of the judge in submitting to the jury the question in relation to the negligence of Foord and Aspinwall, cannot be complained of by the defendant.

GARDINER, J. concurred in affirming the judgment, on the ground that selling the belladonna without a label indicating that it was a *poison*, was declared a misdemeanor by statute; (2 R.S. 694, § 23;) but expressed no opinion upon the question whether, independent of the statute, the defendant would have been liable to these plaintiffs.

* * *

Judgment affirmed.

NOTES

1. According to the Report (6 N.Y. 397, at 404) counsel for plaintiffs made the following argument:

> "The rule contended for by the defendant, that each vendor is liable only to his immediate vendee, has no application to the present case. 1. This rule is founded on the principle that a right or duty *wholly created by contract*, can only be enforced between the contracting parties. * * * The case of Wright v.

Winterbottom was decided on this principle, the declaration being expressly on a duty created *by contract*, and not *by law*. * * * The duty violated by [this] defendant was not created *by contract*, but *by law*; every one being under an obligation to abstain from acts tending naturally and probably to endanger human life."

Does the opinion of the Court of Appeals sustain that argument?

2. Why, do you suppose, did the plaintiffs not sue their immediate vendee, Foord?

3. After Thomas v. Winchester how would you expect the following cases to come out?

   a. A buys a can of tunafish from her local grocer Z. Because of negligence in the canning process the tunafish is contaminated and both A and her guest B suffer serious food poisoning. They sue M the canner of the tunafish.

   b. A buys a chair from Z the owner of the local furniture store. The chair legs are made of poor quality wood (possibly peachum) which M the manufacturer should have known would not support the weight of a normal-size person. A suffers a broken leg when the chair collapses under him and sues M, the manufacturer.

4. In Longmeid v. Holliday, 155 E.R. 752 (1851), cited in Thomas v. Winchester, a man bought a lamp from the manufacturer for use in his store. When the lamp was used it exploded and the purchaser's wife was injured. She (and her husband) sued to recover for her injuries. In affirming the grant of a motion for a nonsuit, the court said:

"There are other cases, no doubt, besides those of fraud, in which a third person, though not a party to the contract, may sue for the damage sustained, if it be broken. These cases occur where there has been a wrong done to that person, for which he would have had a right of action, though no such contract had been made. As for example, if an apothecary administered improper medicines to his patient, or a surgeon unskilfully treated him, and thereby injured his health, he would be liable to the patient, even where the father or friend of the patient may have been the contracting party with the apothecary or surgeon; for though no such contract had been made, the apothecary, if he gave improper medicines, or the surgeon, if he took him as a patient and unskilfully treated him, would be liable to an action for a misfeasance * * *. And it may be the same when any one delivers to another without notice an instrument in its nature dangerous, or under particular circumstances, as a loaded gun which he himself loaded, and that other person to whom it is delivered is injured thereby, or if he places it in a situation easily accessible to a third person, who sustains damage from it. A very strong case to that effect is Dixon v. Bell (5 M. & Selw. 198). But it would be going much too far to say, that so much care is required in the ordinary intercourse of life between one individual and another, that, if a machine not in its nature dangerous,—a carriage for instance, but which might become so by a latent defect entirely unknown, although discoverable by the exercise of ordinary care, should be lent or given by one person, even by the person who manufactured it, to another, the former should be answerable to the latter for a subsequent damage accruing by the use of it. Could it be contended with justice in the present case, that if the lamp had been lent or given by the defendant to the plaintiff's wife, and used by her, he would have been answerable for the personal damage which she sustained, the defendant not knowing or having any reason to believe it was not perfectly safe, although liable to the party to whom he contracted to sell it, upon an implied warranty that it was fit for use, so far as reasonable care could make it for the breach of that contract as to all damage sustained by him.

"We are of opinion, therefore, that if there had been in this case a breach of contract with the plaintiffs, the husband might have sued for it; but there being no misfeasance towards the wife independently of the contract, she cannot sue and join herself with her husband. Therefore a nonsuit must be entered.

"Rule absolute."

LOOP v. LITCHFIELD

Court of Appeals of New York, 1870.
42 N.Y. 351.

Appeal from a judgment of the General Term in the fourth district, reversing a judgment entered upon a verdict in favor of the plaintiffs, and ordering a new trial. [As the law then required, plaintiffs stipulated that if the Court of Appeals agreed with the General Term, judgment absolute should be entered for the defendants.—Ed.]

* * *

The complaint alleged that in 1861 the defendants were partners in manufacturing iron castings and machinery, and made a cast-iron balance wheel to be used with a circular saw. That the balance wheel had a large hole in its rim, occasioned by negligence in casting it, by which its thickness and strength were diminished, and by defendants' wrongful act this hole was concealed by filling it with lead and finishing the surface of the rim so as to resemble a sound wheel. The strength of the rim was further diminished by boring through it, so as to insert a rivet to hold the lead in the hole, and by the wrongful act of defendants they sold this wheel to Leverett Collister as a sound wheel and fit for use. That in 1864 Collister leased to Jeremiah Loop a frame for a circular wood saw, to be used with a circular saw for the purpose of sawing wood, to the arbor shaft on which frame said balance wheel was attached. That Loop put a saw on the arbor, and used the saw, balance wheel and frame in sawing wood for himself and Collister and for others, without knowledge of the hole in the rim of the balance wheel, and in the belief that it was a sound balance wheel and fit for use. That in October, 1866, Loop was so using the saw and balance wheel attached in sawing wood for one Van Rensse-

Sec. 3   TECHNIQUE OF CASE LAW DEVELOPMENT   145

laer Loop, in a careful and prudent manner, when the balance wheel burst in the hole in its rim and directly through the hole made to insert the rivet to hold the lead in its place. That such bursting was caused by said hole and boring in the rim, and that a fragment of the wheel when it burst hit Jeremiah Loop in his side and inflicted a mortal wound, of which he died on the 29th of October, 1866. That such death was occasioned by said wrongful act and negligence of defendants, and plaintiffs bring this action as his legal representatives, for the benefit of his widow and next of kin. There was a motion for a nonsuit at the close of the plaintiffs' evidence and also at the close of all the evidence in the case, on the ground, amongst others, that the plaintiffs had failed to make out a case entitling them to recover; and to the refusal of the court denying this motion, the defendants excepted. There was evidence tending to show that when the defendants sold the wheel to Collister they pointed out to him the defect in the rim of the wheel, and that lead was fastened in the hole by means of a rivet, and that Collister selected and purchased it with full knowledge of such defect, because it was lighter and cheaper than heavier balance wheels which the defendants were accustomed to put upon horse-power for sawing wood, and after he was informed of that fact. The judge stated that the only question upon which counsel could go to the jury would be, whether, in the manufacture and sale of the balance wheel, the defendants were guilty of negligence, which negligence produced the injury complained of.

* * *

HUNT, J. A piece of machinery already made and on hand, having defects which weaken it, is sold by the manufacturer to one who buys it for his own use. The defects are pointed out to the purchaser and are fully understood by him. This piece of machinery is used by the buyer for five years, and is then taken into the possession of a neighbor, who uses it for his own purposes. While so in use, it flies apart by reason of its original defects, and the person using it is killed. Is the seller, upon this state of facts, liable to the representatives of the deceased party? I omit at this stage of the inquiry the elements, that the deceased had no authority to use the machine; that he knew of the defects and that he did not exercise proper care in the management of the machine. Under the circumstances I have stated, does a liability exist, supposing that the use was careful, and that it was by permission of the owner of the machine?

To maintain this liability, the appellants rely upon the case of Thomas v. Winchester (6 N.Y., 2 Seld., 397). * * *

The appellants recognize the principle of this decision, and seek to bring their case within it, by asserting that the fly wheel in question was a dangerous instrument. Poison is a dangerous subject. Gunpowder is the same. A torpedo is a dangerous instrument, as is a spring gun, a loaded rifle or the like. They are instruments and articles in their nature calculated to do injury to mankind, and generally intended to accomplish that purpose. They are essentially, and in their elements, instruments of danger. Not so, however, an iron wheel, a few feet in diameter and a few inches in thickness although one part may be weaker than another. If the article is abused by too long use, or by applying too much weight or speed, an injury may occur, as it may from an ordinary carriage wheel, a wagon axle, or the common chair in which we sit. There is scarcely an object in art or nature, from which an injury may not occur under such circumstances. Yet they are not in their nature sources of danger, nor can they, with any regard to the accurate use of language, be called dangerous instruments. That an injury actually occurred by the breaking of a carriage axle, the failure of the carriage body, the falling to pieces of a chair or sofa, or the bursting of a fly wheel, does not in the least alter its character.

It is suggested that it is no more dangerous or illegal to label a deadly poison as a harmless medicine than to conceal a defect in a machine and paint it over so that it will appear sound. Waiving the point that there was no concealment, but the defect was fully explained to the purchaser, I answer, that the decision in Thomas v. Winchester was based upon the idea that the negligent sale of poisons is both at common law and by statute an indictable offence. If the act in that case had been done by the defendant instead of his agent, and the death of Mrs. Thomas had ensued, the defendant would have been guilty of manslaughter, as held by the court. The injury in that case was a natural result of the act. It was just what was to have been expected from putting falsely labeled poisons in the market, to be used by whoever should need the true articles. It was in its nature an act imminently dangerous to the lives of others. Not so here. The bursting of the wheel and the injury to human life was not the natural result or the expected consequence of the manufacture and sale of the wheel. Every use of the counterfeit medicines would be necessarily injurious, while this wheel was in fact used with safety for five years.

It is said that the verdict of the jury established the fact that this wheel was a dangerous instrument. I do not see how this can be, when there is no such allegation in the complaint, and no such question was submitted to the jury. "The court stated to the counsel that the only question on which they would go to the jury would be that of negligence. Whether in the manufacture and sale of this article, the defendants are guilty of negligence, which negligence produced the injury complained of." If the action had been for negligence in constructing a carriage, sold by the defendants to Collister, by him lent to the deceased, which had broken down, through the negligence of its construction, it might have been contended with the same propriety, that the finding of those facts by the jury established that a carriage was a dangerous instrument, and thereby the liability of the defendants became fixed. The jury found simply that there was negligence in the construction of the wheel, and that the injury resulted therefrom. It is quite illogical to deduce from this, the conclusion that the wheel was itself a dangerous instrument.

Upon the facts as stated, assuming that the deceased had no knowledge of the defects complained of, and assuming that he was in the rightful and lawful use of the machine, I am of the opinion that the verdict cannot be sustained. The facts constitute no cause of action.

NOTES

1. Who decides whether the product causing the injury is a "dangerous instrument"—the court or the jury?

2. Of what significance was the fact (apparently proved at the trial) that Collister bought the wheel knowing of the defect? Would that fact be material in a suit brought by Collister? By an employee of Collister? In the actual case it appears that the wheel was not manufactured in accordance with its design. Suppose that the actual design had been for a wheel of the kind manufactured in order to save expense and weight and had been deliberately chosen by the purchaser in preference to a stronger heavier wheel. Would—should—that fact be significant?

3. After Loop v. Litchfield, how would you answer question 3 following Thomas v. Winchester?

LOSEE v. CLUTE

Commission of Appeals of New York, 1873.
51 N.Y. 494.

Appeal from judgment of the General Term of the Supreme Court in the fourth judicial district, affirming a judgment entered upon an order dismissing plaintiff's complaint on the trial.

The action was brought to recover damages caused to the property of the plaintiff by the explosion of a steam boiler while the same was owned and being used by the Saratoga Paper Company at their mill situated in the village of Schuylerville, Saratoga county and State of New York, on the thirteenth day of February, 1864, by means whereof the boiler was thrown on to the plaintiff's premises and through several of his buildings, thereby injuring and damaging the same.

The defendants, Clute, were made parties defendants to the action with the Saratoga Paper Company and Coe S. Buchanan and Daniel A. Bullard, trustees and agents of said company, on the ground that they were the manufacturers of the boiler, and made the same out of poor and brittle iron and in a negligent and defective manner, in consequence of which negligence said explosion occurred.

At the close of the evidence the complaint was dismissed as to the defendants Clute.

* * *

LOTT, Ch. C. It appears by the case that the defendants Clute manufactured the boiler in question for the Saratoga Paper Company, in which they were stockholders, for the purposes and uses to which it was subsequently applied by it; and the testimony tended to show that it was constructed improperly and of poor iron, that the said defendants knew at the time that it was to be used in the immediate vicinity of and adjacent to dwelling-houses and stores in a village, so that, in case of an explosion while in use, it would be likely to be destructive to human life and adjacent property, and that, in consequence of the negligence of the said defendants in the improper construction of the boiler, the explosion that took place occurred and damaged the plaintiff's property. The evidence also tended to show that the boiler was tested by the company to its satisfaction, and then accepted, and was thereafter used by it for about three months prior to the explosion, and that after such test and acceptance the said defendants had nothing whatever to do with the boiler, and had no care or management of it at the time of the explosion, but that the company had the sole and exclusive ownership, management and conduct of it.

In determining whether the complaint was properly dismissed, we must assume all the facts which the evidence tended to show as established, and the question is thereby presented whether the defendants have incurred any liability to the plaintiff. They contracted with the company, and did what was done by them for it and to its satisfaction, and when the boiler was accepted they ceased to have any further control over it or its management, and all responsibility for what was subsequently done with it devolved upon the company and those having charge of it, and the case falls within the principle decided by the Court of Appeals in The Mayor, etc., of Albany v. Cunliff, 2 Comst., N. Y., 165, which is, that the mere architect or builder of a work is answerable only to his employes [40] for any want of care or skill in the execution thereof, and he is not liable for accidents or injuries which may occur after the execution of the work; and the opinions published in that case clearly show that there is no ground of liability by the defendants to the plaintiff in this action. They owed *him* no *duty* whatever at the time of the explosion either growing out of contract or imposed by law.

It may be proper to refer to the case of Thomas v. Winchester, 2 Selden 397, 57 Am.Dec. 455, cited by the appellant's counsel, and I deem it sufficient to say that the opinion of Hunt, J., in Loop v. Litchfield, 42 N.Y. 351, 1 Am.Rep. 513, clearly shows that the principle decided in that case has no application to this.

It appears from these considerations that the complaint was properly dismissed, and it follows that there was no case made for

---

40. [So in original. Probably should read employer.—Ed.]

the consideration of the jury, and, consequently, there was no error in the refusal to submit it to them.

There was an exception taken to the exclusion of evidence to show that two persons were killed by this boiler in passing through a dwelling-house in its course, but as it is not urged on this appeal, it is, I presume, abandoned; but if not, it was matter, as the judge held at the trial, wholly immaterial to the issue between the parties in this action.

There is, for the reasons stated, no ground for the reversal of the judgment. It must, therefore, be affirmed, with costs.

All concur.

NOTES

1. The decision reported above involved the appeal of plaintiff Losee from the affirmance of the trial court's dismissal of his complaint (based on negligence) against the Clutes, the manufacturers of the boiler. In the trial court plaintiffs had judgment against Saratoga Paper Co. and its trustees, Buchanan and Bullard on a theory of trespass to land (no negligence on their part was proved). That judgment was reversed and a new trial held. On the new trial, the jury returned a verdict against Saratoga Paper Co. (based on negligence) but in favor of Buchanan and Bullard (presumably on a finding that no negligence on their part had been proved). In Losee v. Buchanan, 51 N.Y. 476, the Commission of Appeals held that knowledge of the defect in manufacture or negligence in failing to discover the defect was a prerequisite to liability of Bullard and Buchanan.

2. In 1869 the New York State Constitution was amended to provide for a new Court of Appeals. As part of the reorganization it was provided that cases pending in the Court of Appeals on January 1, 1869 should be heard and determined by a Commission to consist of the members (four in number) of the old Court of Appeals and a fifth commissioner to be appointed by the governor. The decisions of the Commission of Appeals are treated as equal in authority to decisions of the Court of Appeals.

3. What would be the effect of the decision in Losee v. Clute in a suit brought against the Clutes by the next of kin of the "two persons * * * killed by this boiler in passing through a dwelling-house * * *"?

4. After Losee v. Clute how would you answer question 3 following Thomas v. Winchester?

DEVLIN v. SMITH

Court of Appeals of New York, 1882.
89 N.Y. 470.

This is an appeal from a judgment of the General Term, second department, affirming a judgment entered upon an order dismissing plaintiff's complaint, at the trial. Reported below, 25 Hun 206.

This action was commenced to recover damages for the benefit of the next of kin of Hugh Devlin, deceased, who was killed through the alleged negligence of the defendants.

The deceased, at the time he was killed, was upon a scaffold erected in the rotunda of the court-house, in Brooklyn, washing off the panels of the dome preparatory to its being painted; while thus engaged the portion of the scaffold upon which the deceased was at work broke and fell, precipitating him to the ground, a distance of ninety feet, thereby causing his death.

The defendant Smith entered into a contract with the board of supervisors, of the county of Kings, whereby he agreed to paint and fresco the inside of the county court-house, and furnish all the material and labor necessary therefor. In the performance of his contract it became necessary to have a scaffold erected in the rotunda of the court-house, and he made a contract with the defendant Stevenson to erect the scaffold in question, and to furnish the material therefor.

The scaffold erected consisted of six sections, one built on top of the other, and known as a rope and pole scaffold. Plank being laid across the ledgers, or horizontal poles and forming a flooring to enable the men to work upon the dome.

The portion of the scaffold that broke at the time of accident was not constructed like the other portions; the end of one of the top ledgers was not supported by an upright, but instead thereof, a piece of plank was used as a brace by resting the lower end upon the ledger below, the upper end being nailed to the end of the ledger in question.

The deceased, together with a fellow workman, was upon a plank resting on this ledger at the time it broke. The defendant Stevenson knew that the brace in question was nailed to the ledger as above described, he having examined it before the accident. The defendant Smith in whose employ the deceased was, had many contracts going on at the same time, and would go about each day from one job to another, remaining at each place about half an hour. The scaffold was not examined by the defendant Smith nor his superintendent until after the accident.

RAPALLO, J. Upon a careful review of all the testimony in this case, we are of opinion that there was sufficient evidence to require the submission to the jury of the question, whether the breaking down of the scaffold was attributable to negligence in its construction. It appears that the ledger which supported the plank upon which the deceased was sitting broke down without any excessive weight being put upon it, and without any apparent cause sufficient to break a well-constructed scaffold. One witness on the part of the plaintiff, accustomed to work on scaffolds and to see them built, testified that the upright which supported the end of the ledger should have been fastened to it by lashing with ropes, instead of by nailing, and that lashing would have made it stronger, giving as reasons for this opinion, that the springing of the planks when walked upon was liable to break nails or push them out, whereas lashings would only become tighter, and the witness testified that the kind of scaffold in

Sec. 3   TECHNIQUE OF CASE LAW DEVELOPMENT   151

question was generally fastened by lashing and that it was not the proper way to support the end of the ledger which broke with an upright nailed to the ledger, and that the ledger in question was fastened by nailing.

Another, a carpenter and builder, testified, that when, on account of the curving of a dome, it became necessary to put in a cripple, the cripple as well as the main uprights should be tied to the ledgers with rope; that the springing of the scaffold will break nails.

The appearances after the breakage were described to the jury, and a model of the scaffold was exhibited to them. Testimony touching the same points was submitted on the part of the defendants, and we think that on the whole evidence it was a question of fact for the jury, and not of law for the court, whether or not the injury was the result of the negligent construction of the scaffold.

The question of contributory negligence on the part of the deceased was also one for the jury. They had before them the circumstances of the accident. It appeared that the deceased was sitting on a plank, performing the work for which the scaffold had been erected. He was washing the interior wall of the dome, preparatory to its being painted. There was nothing to indicate that he was in an improper place, or that he unnecessarily exposed himself to danger, or did any act to contribute to the accident. It is suggested that he, or some of his fellow-servants, may have kicked against the upright or brace which supported the end of the ledger, and thus thrown it out of place, but there was no evidence which would entitle the court to assume that the accident occurred from any such cause. The case was, therefore, one in which the jury might have found from the evidence that the death was caused by the improper or negligent construction of the scaffold, and without any fault on the part of the deceased, and the remaining question is, whether, if those facts should be found, the defendants, or either of them, should be held liable in this action.

The defendant Smith claims that no negligence on his part was shown.

[The part of the opinion in which the Court decided to affirm the dismissal of the complaint as to the defendant Smith, is omitted.]

If any person was at fault in the matter it was the defendant Stevenson. It is contended, however, that even if through his negligence the scaffold was defective, he is not liable in this action, because there was no privity between him and the deceased, and he owed no duty to the deceased, his obligation and duty being only to Smith, with whom he contracted.

As a general rule the builder of a structure for another party, under a contract with him or one who sells an article of his own manufacture, is not liable to an action by a third party who uses the same with the consent of the owner or purchaser, for injuries resulting from a defect therein, caused by negligence. The liability of the builder or manufacturer for such defects is, in general, only to the person with whom he contracted. But, notwithstanding this rule, liability to third parties has been held to exist when the defect is such as to render the article in itself imminently dangerous, and serious injury to any person using it is a natural and probable consequence of its use. As where a dealer in drugs carelessly labeled a deadly poison as a harmless medicine, it was held that he was liable not merely to the person to whom he sold it, but to the person who ultimately used it, though it had passed through many hands. This liability was held to rest, not upon any contract or direct privity between him and the party injured, but upon the duty which the law imposes on every one to avoid acts in their nature dangerous to the lives of others. Thomas v. Winchester, 6 N.Y. 397, 57 Am.Dec. 455. In that case Mayor, etc., v. Cunliff, 2 N.Y. 165, was cited as an authority for the position that a builder is liable only to the party for whom he builds. Some of the examples there put by way of illustration were commented upon, and among others the case of one who builds a carriage carelessly and of defective materials, and sells it, and the purchaser lends it to a friend, and the carriage, by reason of its original defect, breaks down and the friend is injured, and the question is put, can he recover against the maker? The comments of Ruggles, Ch. J., upon this suppositious case, in Thomas v. Winchester, and the ground upon which he answers the question in the negative, show clearly the distinction between the two classes of cases. He says that in the case supposed, the obligation of the maker to build faithfully arises only out of his contract with the purchaser. The public have nothing to do with it. Misfortunes to third persons, not parties to the contract, would not be a natural and necessary consequence of the builder's negligence, and such negligence is not an act imminently dangerous to human life.

Applying these tests to the question now before us, the solution is not difficult. Stevenson undertook to build a scaffold ninety feet in height, for the express purpose of enabling the workmen of Smith to stand upon it to paint the interior of the dome. Any defect or negligence in its construction, which should cause it to give way, would naturally result in these men being precipitated from that great height. A stronger case where misfortune to third persons not parties to the contract would be a natural and necessary consequence to the builder's negligence, can hardly be supposed, nor is it easy to imagine a more apt illustration of a case where such negligence would be an act imminently dangerous to human life. These circumstances seem to us to bring the case fairly within the principle of Thomas v. Winchester.

The same principle was recognized in Coughtry v. The Globe Woolen Co. (56 N.Y. 124), and applied to the case of a scaffold. It is true there was in that case the additional fact that the scaffold was erected by the defendant upon its own premises, but the case did not depend wholly upon that point. The scaffold was erected under a contract between the defendant and the employers of the person killed. The deceased was not a party to that contract, and the same argument was made as is urged here on the part of the defendant, that the latter owed no duty to the deceased; but this court held that in view of the facts that the scaffold was upwards of fifty feet from the ground, and unless properly constructed was a most dangerous trap, imperiling the life of any person who might go upon it, and that it was erected for the very purpose of accommodating the workmen, of whom the person killed was one, there was a duty toward them resting upon the defendant, independent of the contract under which the structure was built, to use proper diligence in its construction. The additional fact that the structure was on the premises of the defendant was relied upon, but we think that, even in the absence of that feature, the liability can rest upon the principle of Thomas v. Winchester.

Loop v. Litchfield (42 N.Y. 351, 1 Am.Rep. 543) was decided upon the ground that the wheel which caused the injury was not in itself a dangerous instrument, and that the injury was not a natural consequence of the defect or one reasonably to be anticipated. Losee v. Clute (51 N.Y. 494, 10 Am.Rep. 638) was distinguished from Thomas v. Winchester, upon the authority of Loop v. Litchfield.

We think there should be a new trial as to the defendant Stevenson, and that it will be for the jury to determine whether the death of the plaintiff's intestate was caused by negligence on the part of Stevenson in the construction of the scaffold.

The judgment should be affirmed, with costs, as to the defendant Smith, and reversed as to the defendant Stevenson, and a new trial ordered as to him, costs to abide the event.

NOTES

1. In affirming the dismissal of the complaint as to Smith the court said:

> "An employer does not undertake absolutely with his employes for the sufficiency or safety of the implements and facilities furnished for their work, but only for the exercise of reasonable care in that respect, and where injury to an employe results from a defect in the implements furnished, knowledge of the defect must be brought home to the employer, or proof given that he omitted the exercise of proper care to discover it. Personal negligence is the gist of the action."

Under modern workers compensation laws, Smith would be liable regardless of negligence. Under some laws the remedy against the employer is exclusive. Under others the employee retains his right to sue third parties (e. g., Stephenson in the instant case) and such claims make up a substantial segment of today's flood of product liability claims.

2. After Devlin v. Smith how would you answer question 3 following Thomas v. Winchester?

KELLOGG BRIDGE CO. v. HAMILTON

Supreme Court of the United States, 1884.
110 U.S. 108, 3 S.Ct. 537, 28 L.Ed. 86.

The Kellogg Bridge Company, * * * the defendant below, undertook to construct, for the Lake Shore and Michigan Southern Railroad Company, an iron bridge across Maumee River at Toledo, Ohio. After doing a portion of the work it entered into a written contract with [Hamilton] for completion of the bridge * * *.

* * *

The bridge which Hamilton undertook to erect consisted of three independent fixed spans, each to be one hundred and seventy-five feet six inches in length, suspended between and resting at each end of the span upon stone piers, which had been prepared to receive the same, and one draw span of one hundred and eighty-five feet in length, resting upon a pier in the centre, also then prepared. In erecting the several spans it was necessary to build and use what the contract described as 'false work,' which consisted of piles driven in the river between the piers upon which the spans were to rest, and upon which was placed a platform.

As indicated in the written contract, the Bridge Company had previously constructed a part of this false work between the first and second spans, the cost of which Hamilton paid, as by the contract he agreed to do. Assuming this work to be sufficient for the purposes for which it was designed, Hamilton proceeded to complete the erection of the bridge according to the plans furnished him.

There was evidence before the jury tending to establish the following facts:

A part of the false work or scaffolding put up by the company sank under the weight of the first span, and was replaced by Hamilton. When the second fixed span was about two-thirds completed, the ice, which before that had formed in the river, broke up in consequence of a flood, carrying away the false work under that span, and causing the whole of the iron material then in place on the span, or on the span ready to be put in place, to fall in the river, which at that place was about sixteen feet deep. If the piles driven by the Bridge Company had been driven more firmly into the bed of the river, they would have withstood the force of the ice and flood. In consequence of the insufficiency of the false work done by that company, Hamilton was delayed in the completion of the bridge and subjected to increased expense.

The bridge being completed, Hamilton brought suit in the State court to recover the contract price of the bridge, extra work claimed to have been done on it, and damages sustained by reason of the insufficiency of the false work constructed by the Bridge Company: in all $3,693.78. The cause was removed to the Circuit Court of the United States, where the Bridge Company answered, setting up a counterclaim for $6,619.70. Trial was had with verdict and judgment for plaintiff for $3,039.89. The defendant below brought a writ of error to reverse that judgment.

Mr. Justice HARLAN delivered the opinion of the court.

* * *

It was not claimed on the trial, nor is it contended here, that the company made any statement or representation as to the nature or character of the false work it did, and which, by the contract, Hamilton agreed to assume and pay for. But there was evidence tending to show that the insufficiency of that false work was unknown to Hamilton at the time the contract was made; was not apparent upon any examination he then made, or could have made; and was not discovered, indeed, could not have been discovered, until, during the progress of the erection of the bridge, the false work was practically tested.

The court, among other things, instructed the jury, at the request of plaintiff and over the objections of the defendant, that by the contract—looking at all the circumstances attending its execution and giving to its terms a fair and reasonable interpretation—there was an implied warranty upon the part of the company that the false work it did, and which plaintiff agreed to assume and pay for, was suitable and proper for the purposes for which the Bridge Company knew it was to be used. This instruction was accompanied by the observation that if the evidence showed "that the particular work which was said to be defective was such that the plaintiff could not by examination ascertain its defects—for if they were apparent by mere examination of the false work it was the duty of the plaintiff to make that good—he had the right to rely upon the implied warranty; that is, if the defects were such that they could not be, by ordinary observation and care on behalf of the plaintiff, ascertained and found out." That instruction presents the only question we deem it necessary to determine. Although there are several assignments of error, they depend, as counsel for plaintiff in error properly concede, upon the inquiry whether the court erred in ruling that by the terms of the contract there was an implied warranty that the false work constructed by the Bridge Company was suitable and proper for the purposes for which it was to be used by Hamilton.

The argument in behalf of plaintiff in error proceeds upon the ground that there was a simple transfer by the company of its ownership of the work and materials as they existed at the time of the contract; that Hamilton took the false work for what it was, and just as it stood; consequently, that the rule of *caveat emptor* applies with full force. The position of counsel for Hamilton is that, as in cases of sales of articles by those manufacturing or making them, there was an implied warranty by the Bridge Company that the work sold or transferred to Hamilton was reasonably fit for the purposes for which it was purchased. * * *

* * *

* * * According to the principles of decided cases, and upon clear grounds of justice, the fundamental inquiry must always be whether, under the circumstances of the particular case, the buyer had the right to rely and necessarily relied on the judgment of the seller and not upon his own. In ordinary sales the buyer has an opportunity of inspecting the article sold; and the seller not being the maker, and therefore having no special or technical knowledge of the mode in which it was made, the parties stand upon grounds of substantial equality. If there be, in fact, in the particular case, any inequality, it is such that the law cannot or ought not to attempt to provide against; consequently, the buyer in such cases—the seller giving no express warranty and making no representations tending to mislead—is holden to have purchased entirely on his own judgment. But when the seller is the maker or manufacturer of the thing sold, the fair presumption is that he understood the process of its manufacture, and was cognizant of any latent defect caused by such process and against which reasonable diligence might have guarded. This presumption is justified, in part, by the fact that the manufacturer or maker by his occupation holds himself out as competent to make articles reasonably adapted to the purposes for which such or similar articles are designed. When, therefore, the buyer has no opportunity to inspect the article, or when, from the situation, inspection is impracticable or useless, it is unreasonable to suppose that he bought on his own judgment, or that he did not rely on the judgment of the seller as to latent defects of which the latter, if he used due care, must have been informed during the process of manufacture. If the buyer relied, and under the circumstances had reason to rely, on the judgment of the seller, who was the manufacturer or maker of the article, the law implies a warranty that it is reasonably fit for the use for which it was designed, the seller at the time being informed of the purpose to devote it to that use.

Whether these principles control, or to what extent they are applicable, in the present case, we proceed to inquire. Although the plaintiff in error is not a manufacturer in the common acceptation of that word, it made or constructed the false work which it sold to Hamilton. The transaction, if not technically a sale, created between the parties the relation of vendor and vendee. The business of the company was the construction of bridges. By its occupation, apart from its contract with the railroad company, it held itself out as reasonably competent to do work of that character. * * * It is suggested that, as Hamilton undertook to erect the bridge in a thorough and workmanlike manner, he was not bound to use the false work put up by the company, and that if he used it in execution of his contract, he did so at his own risk. This is only one mode of saying that, in the absence of an express warranty or fraud upon the part of the company, the law will not, under any circumstances, imply a warranty as to the quality or sufficiency of this false work. But the answer to this argument is that no question was raised as to its sufficiency; that, while Hamilton must be charged with knowledge of all defects apparent or discernible upon inspection, he could not justly be charged with knowledge of latent defects which no inspection or examination, at or before the sale, could possibly have disclosed. * * * That he did not exact an express warranty against latent defects not discoverable by inspection, constitutes, under the circumstances, no reason why a warranty may not be implied against such defects as were caused by the mode in which this false work was constructed. In the cases of sales by manufacturers of their own articles for particular purposes, communicated to them at the time, the argument was uniformly pressed that, as the buyer could have required an express warranty, none should be implied. But, plainly, such an argument impeaches the whole doctrine of implied warranty, for there can be no case of a sale of personal property in which the buyer may not, if he chooses, insist on an express warranty against latent defects.

All the facts are present which, upon any view of the adjudged cases, must be held essential in an implied warranty. The transaction was, in effect, a sale of this false work, constructed by a company whose business it was to do such work, to be used in the same way the maker intended to use it, and the latent defects in which, as the maker knew, the buyer could not, by any inspection or examination at the time, discover; the buyer did not, because in the nature of things he could not, rely on his own judgment; and, in view of the circumstances of the case, and the relations of the parties, he must be deemed to have relied on the judgment of the company, which alone of the parties to the contract had or could have knowledge of the manner in which the work had been done. The law, therefore, implies a warranty that this false work was reasonably suitable for such use as was contemplated by both parties. It was constructed for a particular purpose, and was sold to accomplish that purpose; and it is intrinsically just that the company, which held itself out as possessing the requisite skill to do work of that kind, and therefore as having special knowledge of its own workmanship, should be held to indemnify its vendee against latent defects, arising from the mode of construction, and which the latter, as the company well knew, could not, by any inspection, discover for himself.

For the reasons stated, we are of opinion that the court did not err in the law of the case, and the judgment must be

Affirmed.

158 CASE LAW Ch. 2

NOTES

1. A warranty may be *express*, i. e., explicitly stated by the seller, *implied in fact*, i. e., not explicitly stated but inferable from the conduct of the parties as an intended term of the transaction, or *implied in law*, i. e., neither explicitly stated or understood from the conduct of the parties but, given certain circumstances, added by *law* as a term of the transaction. Which type of warranty was involved in the *Kellogg Bridge* case?

2. Treating, for our purposes, the *Kellogg Bridge* case as a decision of the New York Court of Appeals, does it represent a change in prior New York law?

BURKETT v. STUDEBAKER BROS. MFG. CO.

Supreme Court of Tennessee, 1912.
126 Tenn. 467, 150 S.W. 421.

NEIL, J. This is an action for damages, brought against the defendant to recover for injuries alleged to have been inflicted upon the person of the plaintiff, resulting from a defect in a carriage made by the defendant, by reason of which one of the rear wheels gave way, and caused the carriage to partly overturn and throw the plaintiff out in such manner as to inflict serious injury upon her. The trial judge directed a verdict in favor of the defendant. From the judgment rendered thereon the plaintiff appealed to the Court of Civil Appeals, and there the judgment was reversed. The case was then brought to this court by certiorari on the part of the defendant.

The undisputed facts disclosed by the record are as follows:

A short time prior to September 30, 1908, the plaintiff and her then husband, Col. T. M. Burkett, were desirous of purchasing a carriage for the use of Mrs. Burkett. They applied to Reed Hardware Company, a business firm in Athens, Tenn., where they resided. That firm wrote to several manufacturers of carriages, among others the defendants. Thereupon, on the 30th of September, the defendant wrote a letter to plaintiff, in which it recommended two of their carriages of the kind known as a "station wagon." This letter, after describing the carriages in detail, stated: "We use the best material throughout in the construction of these carriages, and every attention is given to detail of finish, to make them complete in every respect. We would like very much to have you ride in a Studebaker carriage, and we trust that you will conclude to favor the Reed Hardware Company with your order." Shortly after this an agent of the defendant called upon Burkett and wife, in Athens, and exhibited cuts of the vehicle desired, in the presence of Mr. Sherman, a member of the firm of Reed Hardware Company, but no purchase was at that time made. A month or two after this Col. Burkett took up the matter with Gillespie-Ford Company, a business concern of Chattanooga. * * *
[On receipt of an order from Col. Burkett] Gillespie-Ford Company

Sec. 3   TECHNIQUE OF CASE LAW DEVELOPMENT   159

sent the order to defendant, with orders to ship the goods direct to Col. Burkett at Athens. This was done, and the bill was charged by defendant to Gillespie-Ford Company. The vehicle reached the Burketts in the early days of January, and was presentd by Col. Burkett to the plaintiff. A few days thereafter, the first time it was used, one of the wheels broke down. There were only three persons in the conveyance besides the driver, and it was standing still, except that the horses were moving backward slowly, because crowded in front by another vehicle. There was no violent movement at all. One of the rear wheels slipped down a slight declivity, a few inches in length, and all the spokes broke off at the hub, causing the carriage to overturn, and plaintiff to be thrown to the ground, and injured. The testimony shows that the wood of which these spokes were made was, as an expert witness says, "brash"; that is brittle, and hence very inferior as spoke timber. The declaration, in its several counts, presents the case in two aspects: First, as an article purchased from the defendant; second, as an article purchased from a dealer who had bought from the defendant—the liability being placed on negligent construction by defendant.

It is perceived from the stated facts that the purchase was not made from the defendant, but from Gillespie-Ford Company. There can be no doubt, however, that the letter which defendant wrote to plaintiff on September 30th, and the subsequent representations of its agent, had a direct influence upon plaintiff and her husband in inducing them to finally buy the vehicle, although they did not purchase it through Reed Hardware Company, whom the defendant was assisting in its effort to sell the vehicle to the Burketts. It does not appear that defendant knew anything of the negotiations with Gillespie-Ford Company until it received the order from that firm. Likewise it does not appear that defendant had any knowledge of the defect in the wheel which caused it to crush in the manner already stated.

Col. Burkett died before the accident happened.

The general rule is that a manufacturer is not liable to a third person, who buys his goods from an intermediate dealer, because of the want of any privity between the parties. The rule is different, however, if the manufacturer had knowledge of the defect, and put it upon the market in that condition. In such case he is guilty of fraud and is liable to any one into whose hands the article falls, and who is injured while using it properly. He is also liable to such third person, where the article sold is of such kind as to be imminently dangerous to human life or health; also, when the article, although not apparently dangerous, is known by him to be such, and he gives no notice of its qualities when he puts it upon the market. * * *

Under the principles stated, it is clear the trial judge acted correctly in directing a verdict, unless the plaintiff had a cause of action arising out of the fact that the defendant wrote the letter of September 30th, recommending the special make or kind of vehicle as being fashioned from the best materials, and thereby aided in the sale. It is possible that, if the sale had been made by Reed & Co., the defendant would have been properly treated as jointly liable with that firm, on the ground that it aided these persons in making the sale. But Reed & Co. did not make the sale. Their services were rejected, and they were passed over. Negotiations for a carriage were begun, and then concluded, with Gillespie-Ford Company, and the carriage that inflicted the injury was purchased of them. Defendant had nothing to do with that transaction, except to honor the order of Gillespie-Ford Company and ship the goods at their request to plaintiff and her husband. In this transaction there was no privity of contract between plaintiff and defendant. The distinction may seem technical between this transaction and the dealing with Reed & Co.; but it is not. It is substantial. It is clear, under the great weight of authority, that the manufacturer, when the article is not imminently dangerous, can be held liable to a third party only when he knew of the defect, and with this knowledge put the article upon the market. Some of the cases cited supra show that the manufacturer's knowledge may be proven by circumstances; but no effort of the kind was made in the present case. In the absence of knowledge of the defect, his liability is only to those with whom he has contractual relations. The main reasons assigned for the rule are that any injury that might occur to a third party could not be within the contemplation of the parties to the contract, and that if suits of the kind were sanctioned against manufacturers there would be no end to litigation, and practically no means, in the great majority of the cases, for the manufacturer to protect himself, and therefore that useful class of producers would be so loaded with litigation that their labor, skill, and enterprise would be greatly discouraged, if not destroyed, to the great detriment of the public welfare. Hence it is said that such suits are against public policy, and not to be entertained.

It follows that the judgment of the Court of Civil Appeals must be reversed, and that of the trial court affirmed.

NOTES

1. Is the decision in the *Burkett* case consistent with Devlin v. Smith? With Loop v. Litchfield?

2. What, do you suppose, is the basis of the court's statement as to the consequences of a rule permitting suit in cases such as this? If you had been counsel for the plaintiff how would you have gone about convincing the court that the "reasons assigned for the [existing] rule" are unsound?

3. Liability insurance, which came to be an all-important factor in the development of tort law, was not written before 1880 and in the early years was confined to employers' liability. Mowbray & Blanchard, Insurance 159–160 (4th ed. 1955). At the time of the *Burkett* case it was still a matter of doubt whether insurance against one's own negligence was contrary to public policy. See Prosser, Torts 543 (4th ed. 1971).

Sec. 3   TECHNIQUE OF CASE LAW DEVELOPMENT   161

BOYD v. COCA COLA BOTTLING WORKS

Supreme Court of Tennessee, 1914.
132 Tenn. 23, 177 S.W. 80.

Mr. Justice GREEN delivered the opinion of the Court.

This damage suit was instituted by W. C. Boyd, and wife, Lou J. Boyd, and pending the suit Mrs. Boyd died. W. D. Boyd was appointed her administrator, and the case was revived.

A motion for a directed verdict in favor of defendant below was sustained by the trial court. Upon appeal this judgment was reversed by the court of civil appeals, and the case is before us on petition for certiorari, which has been granted.

Mrs. Lou Boyd was a lady in delicate health who was in the habit of occasionally drinking coca cola as a tonic and for its invigorating effects. Her husband bought for her a sealed bottle of this beverage from a retail dealer in Nashville. He carried the bottle home and poured a portion of its contents into a glass. His wife drank the liquid poured out, and immediately became intensely nauseated and suffered seriously from its effects.

Mrs. Boyd examined the bottle and found therein a cigar stub about two inches long which had apparently been in the liquid for some time. It was shown on the trial that complaint was made by Mr. Boyd to an agent of the Coca Cola Bottling Works about the incident referred to, and this agent expressed regret and indignation and said that the company had employed some workers who were careless about washing bottles into which coca cola was poured. The proof shows that it was the custom of defendant company to buy empty bottles around town and refill them. A physician testified for plaintiff below as to the poisonous effect of a fluid impregnated with nicotine from a cigar stub.

Defendant below introduced no proof, but made a motion for peremptory instructions, which was sustained on the ground that there was no privity of contract between the Boyds and the Coca Cola Bottling Works, inasmuch as the purchase was made from an intermediate dealer.

* * *

The trial judge doubtless based his action on the case of Burkett v. Mfg. Company, 126 Tenn. 467, 150 S.W. 421, and this case is pressed upon the court by counsel for defendant company as being conclusive of this controversy. [After discussing the Burkett case, the Court continued.]

We do not think the foregoing case sustains the action of the court below. The present case falls within the second exception stated in Burkett v. Mfg. Co. All medicines, foods, and beverages are articles of such kind as to be imminently dangerous to human life or health unless care is exercised in their preparation.

Upon a person who undertakes the performance of an act, which if not done with care and skill will imperil the lives of others, the law imposes the duty of exercising the requisite care and skill. In such matters such a person is liable to others suffering from his negligence.

This liability does not depend on contract or privity, but arises from a breach of the legal duty, to which we have just referred. A tort is committed, a legal right invaded, by practices which prejudice another's health. * * *

Upon the principles stated, a negligent manufacturer has been held liable for injuries to consumers, purchasing from intermediate dealers, for the careless labeling of poisons and patent medicines. Thomas v. Winchester, 6 N.Y. 397, 57 Am.Dec. 455; Blood Balm Co. v. Cooper, 83 Ga. 457, 10 S.E. 118, 5 L.R.A. 612, 20 Am.St.Rep. 324. For negligently bottling beer with broken glass in the bottle. Watson v. Augusta Brewing Co., 124 Ga. 121, 52 S.E. 152, 1 L.R.A.,N.S., 1178, 110 Am.St.Rep. 157. For negligent preparation of mincemeat put up in a package. Salmon v. Libby, 219 Ill. 421, 76 N.E. 573. For the careless and negligent canning of spoiled meat. Tomlinson v. Armour & Co., 75 N.J.L. 748, 70 A. 314, 19 L.R.A.,N.S., 923. See, also, Bishop v. Weber, 139 Mass. 411, 1 N.E. 154, 52 Am.Rep. 715.

So when the manufacturer of this beverage undertook to place it on the market in sealed bottles, intending it to be purchased and taken into the human stomach, under such circumstances that neither the dealer nor the consumer had opportunity for knowledge of its contents, he likewise assumed the duty of exercising care to see that there was nothing unwholesome or injurious contained in said bottles. For a negligent breach of this duty, the manufacturer became liable to the person damaged thereby.

Practically all the modern cases are to the effect that the ultimate consumer of foods, medicines, or beverages may bring his action against the manufacturer for injuries caused by the negligent preparation of such articles. This is certainly true where the articles are sold in sealed packages and are not subject to inspection. Some of the cases place the liability on the grounds heretofore stated. Others place it on pure food statutes. Others say there is an implied warranty when goods are dispensed in original packages, which is available to all damaged by their use, and another case says that the liability rests upon the demands of social justice. See the cases collected in a note to Mazetti v. Armour & Co., 48 L.R.A.,N.S., 213, 219, and in a note to Tomlinson v. Armour & Co., 19 L.R.A.,N.S., 923.

Upon whatever ground the liability of such a manufacturer to the ultimate consumer is placed, the result is eminently satisfactory, conducive to the public welfare, and one which we approve.

The judgment of the court of civil appeals is affirmed.

Sec. 3   *TECHNIQUE OF CASE LAW DEVELOPMENT*   163

MacPHERSON v. BUICK MOTOR CO.

Court of Appeals of New York, 1916.
217 N.Y. 382, 111 N.E. 1050.

Appeal, by permission, from a judgment of the Appellate Division of the Supreme Court in the third judicial department, entered January 8, 1914, affirming a judgment in favor of plaintiff entered upon a verdict.

* * *

CARDOZO, J. The defendant is a manufacturer of automobiles. It sold an automobile to a retail dealer. The retail dealer resold to the plaintiff. While the plaintiff was in the car, it suddenly collapsed. He was thrown out and injured. One of the wheels was made of defective wood, and its spokes crumbled into fragments. The wheel was not made by the defendant; it was bought from another manufacturer. There is evidence, however, that its defects could have been discovered by reasonable inspection, and that inspection was omitted. There is no claim that the defendant knew of the defect and wilfully concealed it. The case, in other words, is not brought within the rule of Kuelling v. Lean Mfg. Co., 183 N.Y. 78, 75 N.E. 1098, 2 L.R.A.,N.S., 303, 111 Am.St.Rep. 691, 5 Ann.Cas. 124. The charge is one not of fraud, but of negligence. The question to be determined is whether the defendant owed a duty of care and vigilance to any one but the immediate purchaser.

The foundations of this branch of the law, at least in this state, were laid in Thomas v. Winchester, 6 N.Y. 397, 57 Am.Dec. 455. A poison was falsely labeled. The sale was made to a druggist, who in turn sold to a customer. The customer recovered damages from the seller who affixed the label. "The defendant's negligence," it was said, "put human life in imminent danger." A poison falsely labeled is likely to injure any one who gets it. Because the danger is to be foreseen, there is a duty to avoid the injury. Cases were cited by way of illustration in which manufacturers were not subject to any duty irrespective of contract. The distinction was said to be that their conduct, though negligent, was not likely to result in injury to any one except the purchaser. We are not required to say whether the chance of injury was always as remote as the distinction assumes. Some of the illustrations might be rejected today. The principle of the distinction is for present purposes the important thing.

Thomas v. Winchester became quickly a landmark of the law. In the application of its principle there may at times have been uncertainty or even error. There has never in this state been doubt or disavowal of the principle itself. The chief cases are well known, yet to recall some of them will be helpful. Loop v. Litchfield, 42 N.Y. 351, 1 Am.Rep. 513, is the earliest. It was the case of a defect in a small balance wheel used on a circular saw. The manufacturer pointed out the defect to the buyer, who wished a cheap article and was ready to assume the risk. The risk can hardly have been an imminent one, for the wheel lasted five years before it broke. In the meanwhile the buyer had made a lease of the machinery. It was held that the manufacturer was not answerable to the lessee. Loop v. Litchfield was followed in Losee v. Clute, 51 N.Y. 494, 10 Am.Rep. 638, the case of the explosion of a steam boiler. That decision has been criticised (Thompson on Negligence, 233; Shearman & Redfield on Negligence [6th ed.], § 117); but it must be confined to its special facts. It was put upon the ground that the risk of injury was too remote. The buyer in that case had not only accepted the boiler, but had tested it. The manufacturer knew that his own test was not the final one. The finality of the test has a bearing on the measure of diligence owing to persons other than the purchaser. Beven, Negligence (3d ed.), pp. 50, 51, 54; Wharton, Negligence (2d ed.) § 134.

These early cases suggest a narrow construction of the rule. Later cases, however, evince a more liberal spirit. First in importance is Devlin v. Smith, 89 N.Y. 470, 42 Am.Rep. 311. The defendant, a contractor, built a scaffold for a painter. The painter's servants were injured. The contractor was held liable. He knew that the scaffold, if improperly constructed, was a most dangerous trap. He knew that it was to be used by the workmen. He was building it for that very purpose. Building it for their use, he owed them a duty, irrespective of his contract with their master, to build it with care.

From Devlin v. Smith we pass over intermediate cases and turn to the latest case in this court in which Thomas v. Winchester was followed. That case is Statler v. Ray Mfg. Co., 195 N.Y. 478, 480, 88 N.E. 1063. The defendant manufactured a large coffee urn. It was installed in a restaurant. When heated, the urn exploded and injured the plaintiff. We held that the manufacturer was liable. We said that the urn "was of such a character inherently that, when applied to the purposes for which it was designed, it was liable to become a source of great danger to many people if not carefully and properly constructed."

It may be that Devlin v. Smith and Statler v. Ray Mfg. Co. have extended the rule of Thomas v. Winchester. If so, this court is committed to the extension. The defendant argues that things imminently dangerous to life are poisons, explosives, deadly weapons—things whose normal function it is to injure or destroy. But whatever the rule in Thomas v. Winchester may once have been, it has no longer that restricted meaning. A scaffold (Devlin v. Smith, supra) is not inherently a destructive instrument. It becomes destructive only if imperfectly constructed. A large coffee urn (Statler v. Ray Mfg. Co., supra) may have within itself, if negligently made, the potency of danger, yet no one thinks of it as an implement whose normal function is destruction. What is true of the coffee urn is equally true of bottles of aerated water, Torgeson v. Schultz, 192 N.Y. 156, 84 N.

Sec. 3   TECHNIQUE OF CASE LAW DEVELOPMENT   165

E. 956, 18 L.R.A.,N.S., 726, 127 Am.St.Rep. 894. We have mentioned only cases in this court. But the rule has received a like extension in our courts of intermediate appeal. In Burke v. Ireland, 26 App.Div. 487, 50 N.Y.S. 369, in an opinion by Cullen, J., it was applied to a builder who constructed a defective building; in Kahner v. Otis Elevator Co., 96 App.Div. 169, 89 N.Y.S. 185, to the manufacturer of an elevator; in Davies v. Pelham Hod Elevating Co., 65 Hun 573, 20 N. Y.S. 523, affirmed in this court without opinion, 146 N.Y. 363, 41 N. E. 88, to a contractor who furnished a defective rope with knowledge of the purpose for which the rope was to be used. We are not required at this time either to approve or to disapprove the application of the rule that was made in these cases. It is enough that they help to characterize the trend of judicial thought.

Devlin v. Smith was decided in 1882. A year later a very similar case came before the Court of Appeal in England (Heaven v. Pender, L. R. [11 Q.B.D.] 503). We find in the opinion of Brett, M. R., afterwards Lord Esher (p. 510), the same conception of a duty, irrespective of contract, imposed upon the manufacturer by the law itself: "Whenever one person supplies goods, or machinery or the like, for the purpose of their being used by another person under such circumstances that every one of ordinary sense would, if he thought, recognize at once that unless he used ordinary care and skill with regard to the condition of the thing supplied or the mode of supplying it, there will be danger of injury to the person or property of him for whose use the thing is supplied, and who is to use it, a duty arises to use ordinary care and skill as to the condition or manner of supplying such thing." He then points out that for a neglect of such ordinary care or skill whereby injury happens, the appropriate remedy is an action for negligence. The right to enforce this liability is not to be confined to the immediate buyer. The right, he says, extends to the persons or class of persons for whose use the thing is supplied. It is enough that the goods "would in all probability be used at once * * * before a reasonable opportunity for discovering any defect which might exist," and that the thing supplied is of such a nature "that a neglect of ordinary care or skill as to its condition or the manner of supplying it would probably cause danger to the person or property of the person for whose use it was supplied, and who was about to use it." On the other hand, he would exclude a case "in which the goods are supplied under circumstances in which it would be a chance by whom they would be used or whether they would be used or not, or whether they would be used before there would probably be means of observing any defect," or where the goods are of such a nature that "a want of care or skill as to their condition or the manner of supplying them would not probably produce danger of injury to person or property." What was said by Lord Esher in that case did not command the full assent of his associates. His opinion has been criticised "as requiring every man to take affirmative precautions to protect his neighbors as well as to refrain from injuring them". Bohlen, Affirmative Obligations in the Law of Torts, 44 Am.Law Reg., N.S., 341. It may not be an accurate exposition of the law of England. Perhaps it may need some qualification even in our own state. Like most attempts at comprehensive definition, it may involve errors of inclusion and of exclusion. But its tests and standards, at least in their underlying principles, with whatever qualification may be called for as they are applied to varying conditions, are the tests and standards of our law.

We hold, then, that the principle of Thomas v. Winchester is not limited to poisons, explosives, and things of like nature, to things which in their normal operation are implements of destruction. If the nature of a thing is such that it is reasonably certain to place life and limb in peril when negligently made, it is then a thing of danger. Its nature gives warning of the consequences to be expected. If to the element of danger there is added knowledge that the thing will be used by persons other than the purchaser, and used without new tests, then, irrespective of contract, the manufacturer of this thing of danger is under a duty to make it carefully. That is as far as we are required to go for the decision of this case. There must be knowledge of a danger, not merely possible, but probable. It is possible to use almost anything in a way that will make it dangerous if defective. That is not enough to charge the manufacturer with a duty independent of his contract. Whether a given thing is dangerous may be sometimes a question for the court and sometimes a question for the jury. There must also be knowledge that in the usual course of events the danger will be shared by others than the buyer. Such knowledge may often be inferred from the nature of the transaction. But it is possible that even knowledge of the danger and of the use will not always be enough. The proximity or remoteness of the relation is a factor to be considered. We are dealing now with the liability of the manufacturer of the finished product, who puts it on the market to be used without inspection by his customers. If he is negligent, where danger is to be foreseen, a liability will follow. We are not required at this time to say that it is legitimate to go back to the manufacturer of the finished product and hold the manufacturers of the component parts. To make their negligence a cause of imminent danger, an independent cause must often intervene; the manufacturer of the finished product must also fail in his duty of inspection. It may be that in those circumstances the negligence of the earlier members of the series is too remote to constitute, as to the ultimate user, an actionable wrong. Beven on Negligence (3d ed.) 50, 51, 54; Wharton on Negligence (2d ed.) § 134; Leeds v. N. Y. Tel. Co., 178 N.Y. 118, 70 N.E. 219; Sweet v. Perkins, 196 N.Y. 482, 90 N.E. 50; Hayes v. Hyde Park, 153 Mass. 514, 516, 27 N.E. 522, 12 L.R.A. 249. We leave that question open. We shall have to deal with it when it arises. The difficulty which it suggests is not present in this case. There is

Sec. 3   TECHNIQUE OF CASE LAW DEVELOPMENT   167

here no break in the chain of cause and effect. In such circumstances, the presence of a known danger, attendant upon a known use, makes vigilance a duty. We have put aside the notion that the duty to safeguard life and limb, when the consequences of negligence may be foreseen, grows out of contract and nothing else. We have put the source of the obligation where it ought to be. We have put its source in the law.

From this survey of the decisions, there thus emerges a definition of the duty of a manufacturer which enables us to measure this defendant's liability. Beyond all question, the nature of an automobile gives warning of probable danger if its construction is defective. This automobile was designed to go fifty miles an hour. Unless its wheels were sound and strong, injury was almost certain. It was as much a thing of danger as a defective engine for a railroad. The defendant knew the danger. It knew also that the car would be used by persons other than the buyer. This was apparent from its size; there were seats for three persons. It was apparent also from the fact that the buyer was a dealer in cars, who bought to resell. The maker of this car supplied it for the use of purchasers from the dealer just as plainly as the contractor in Devlin v. Smith supplied the scaffold for use by the servants of the owner. The dealer was indeed the one person of whom it might be said with some approach to certainty that by him the car would not be used. Yet the defendant would have us say that he was the one person whom it was under a legal duty to protect. The law does not lead us to so inconsequent a conclusion. Precedents drawn from the days of travel by stage coach do not fit the conditions of travel today. The principle that the danger must be imminent does not change, but the things subject to the principle do change. They are whatever the needs of life in a developing civilization require them to be.

In reaching this conclusion, we do not ignore the decisions to the contrary in other jurisdictions. It was held in Cadillac M. C. Co. v. Johnson, 221 F. 801, 137 C.C.A. 279, L.R.A.1915E, 287, that an automobile is not within the rule of Thomas v. Winchester. There was, however, a vigorous dissent. Opposed to that decision is one of the Court of Appeals of Kentucky. Olds Motor Works v. Shaffer, 145 Ky. 616, 140 S.W. 1047, 37 L.R.A.,N.S., 560, Ann.Cas.1913B, 689. The earlier cases are summarized by Judge Sanborn in Huset v. J. I. Case Threshing Machine Co., 120 F. 865, 57 C.C.A. 237, 61 L.R.A. 303. Some of them, at first sight inconsistent with our conclusion, may be reconciled upon the ground that the negligence was too remote, and that another cause had intervened. But even when they cannot be reconciled, the difference is rather in the application of the principle than in the principle itself. Judge Sanborn says, for example, that the contractor who builds a bridge, or the manufacturer who builds a car, cannot ordinarily foresee injury to other persons than the owner as the probable result. 120 F. 865, at p. 867, 57 C.C.A.

237, at page 239, 61 L.R.A. 303. We take a different view. We think that injury to others is to be foreseen not merely as a possible, but as an almost inevitable result. See the trenchant criticism in Bohlen, supra, at p. 351. Indeed, Judge Sanborn concedes that his view is not to be reconciled with our decision in Devlin v. Smith, supra. The doctrine of that decision has now become the settled law of this state, and we have no desire to depart from it.

In England the limits of the rule are still unsettled. Winterbottom v. Wright, 10 M. & W. 109, is often cited. The defendant undertook to provide a mail coach to carry the mail bags. The coach broke down from latent defects in its construction. The defendant, however, was not the manufacturer. The court held that he was not liable for injuries to a passenger. The case was decided on a demurrer to the declaration. Lord Esher points out in Heaven v. Pender, supra, at p. 513, that the form of the declaration was subject to criticism. It did not fairly suggest the existence of a duty aside from the special contract which was the plaintiff's main reliance. See the criticism of Winterbottom v. Wright, in Bohlen, supra, at pp. 281, 283. At all events, in Heaven v. Pender, supra, the defendant, a dock owner, who put up a staging outside a ship, was held liable to the servants of the shipowner. In Elliott v. Hall, 15 Q.B.D. 315, the defendant sent out a defective truck laden with goods which he had sold. The buyer's servants unloaded it, and were injured because of the defects. It was held that the defendant was under a duty "not to be guilty of negligence with regard to the state and condition of the truck." There seems to have been a return to the doctrine of Winterbottom v. Wright in Earl v. Lubbock, L. R. [1905] 1 K.B. 253. In that case, however, as in the earlier one, the defendant was not the manufacturer. He had merely made a contract to keep the van in repair. A later case, White v. Steadman, L. R. [1913], 3 K.B. 340, 348, emphasizes that element. A livery stable keeper who sent out a vicious horse was held liable not merely to his customer but also to another occupant of the carriage, and Thomas v. Winchester was cited and followed. White v. Steadman, supra, at pp. 348, 349. It was again cited and followed in Dominion Natural Gas Co. v. Collins, L. R. [1909] A.C. 640, 646. From these cases a consistent principle is with difficulty extracted. The English courts, however, agree with ours in holding that one who invites another to make use of an appliance is bound to the exercise of reasonable care. Caledonian Ry. Co. v. Mulholland, L. R. [1898] A.C. 216, 227; Indermaur v. Dames, L. R. [1 C.P.] 274. That at bottom is the underlying principle of Devlin v. Smith. The contractor who builds the scaffold invites the owner's workmen to use it. The manufacturer who sells the automobile to the retail dealer invites the dealer's customers to use it. The invitation is addressed in the one case to determinate persons and in the other to an indeterminate class, but in each case it is equally plain, and in each its consequences must be the same.

Sec. 3   TECHNIQUE OF CASE LAW DEVELOPMENT   169

There is nothing anomalous in a rule which imposes upon A, who has contracted with B, a duty to C and D and others according as he knows or does not know that the subject-matter of the contract is intended for their use. We may find an analogy in the law which measures the liability of landlords. If A leases to B a tumble-down house he is not liable, in the absence of fraud, to B's guests who enter it and are injured. This is because B is then under the duty to repair it, the lessor has the right to suppose that he will fulfill that duty, and, if he omits to do so, his guests must look to him. Bohlen, supra, at p. 276. But if A leases a building to be used by the lessee at once as a place of public entertainment, the rule is different. There injury to persons other than the lessee is to be foreseen, and foresight of the consequences involves the creation of a duty. Junkermann v. Tilyou R. Co., 213 N.Y. 404, 108 N.E. 190, L.R.A.1915F, 700, and cases there cited.

In this view of the defendant's liability there is nothing inconsistent with the theory of liability on which the case was tried. It is true that the court told the jury that "an automobile is not an inherently dangerous vehicle." The meaning, however, is made plain by the context. The meaning is that danger is not to be expected when the vehicle is well constructed. The court left it to the jury to say whether the defendant ought to have foreseen that the car, if negligently constructed, would become "imminently dangerous." Subtle distinctions are drawn by the defendant between things inherently dangerous and things imminently dangerous, but the case does not turn upon these verbal niceties. If danger was to be expected as reasonably certain, there was a duty of vigilance, and this whether you call the danger inherent or imminent. In varying forms that thought was put before the jury. We do not say that the court would not have been justified in ruling as a matter of law that the car was a dangerous thing. If there was any error, it was none of which the defendant can complain.

We think the defendant was not absolved from a duty of inspection because it bought the wheels from a reputable manufacturer. It was not merely a dealer in automobiles. It was a manufacturer of automobiles. It was responsible for the finished product. It was not at liberty to put the finished product on the market without subjecting the component parts to ordinary and simple tests. Richmond & Danville R. R. Co. v. Elliott, 149 U.S. 266, 272, 13 S.Ct. 837, 37 L.Ed. 728. Under the charge of the trial judge nothing more was required of it. The obligation to inspect must vary with the nature of the thing to be inspected. The more probable the danger, the greater the need of caution. There is little analogy between this case and Carlson v. Phoenix Bridge Co., 132 N.Y. 273, 30 N.E. 750, where the defendant bought a tool for a servant's use. The making of tools was not the business in which the master was engaged. Reliance on the skill of the manufacturer was proper and almost inevitable. But that is not the defendant's situation. Both by its relation to the work and by the nature of its business, it is charged with a stricter duty.

Other rulings complained of have been considered, but no error has been found in them.

The judgment should be affirmed with costs.

WILLARD BARTLETT, C. J. (dissenting). The plaintiff was injured in consequence of the collapse of a wheel of an automobile manufactured by the defendant corporation which sold it to a firm of automobile dealers in Schenectady, who in turn sold the car to the plaintiff. The wheel was purchased by the Buick Motor Company, ready made, from the Imperial Wheel Company of Flint, Mich., a reputable manufacturer of automobile wheels which had furnished the defendant with 80,000 wheels, none of which had proved to be made of defective wood prior to the accident in the present case. The defendant relied upon the wheel manufacturer to make all necessary tests as to the strength of the material therein, and made no such test itself. The present suit is an action for negligence, brought by the subvendee of the motor car against the manufacturer as the original vendor. The evidence warranted a finding by the jury that the wheel which collapsed was defective when it left the hands of the defendant. The automobile was being prudently operated at the time of the accident, and was moving at a speed of only eight miles an hour. There was no allegation or proof of any actual knowledge of the defect on the part of the defendant, or any suggestion that any element of fraud or deceit or misrepresentation entered into the sale.

The theory upon which the case was submitted to the jury by the learned judge who presided at the trial was that, although an automobile is not an inherently dangerous vehicle, it may become such if equipped with a weak wheel; and that if the motor car in question, when it was put upon the market was in itself inherently dangerous by reason of its being equipped with a weak wheel, the defendant was chargeable with a knowledge of the defect so far as it might be discovered by a reasonable inspection and the application of reasonable tests. This liability, it was further held, was not limited to the original vendee, but extended to a subvendee like the plaintiff, who was not a party to the original contract of sale.

I think that these rulings, which have been approved by the Appellate Division, extend the liability of the vendor of a manufactured article further than any case which has yet received the sanction of this court. It has heretofore been held in this state that the liability of the vendor of a manufactured article for negligence arising out of the existence of defects therein does not extend to strangers injured in consequence of such defects, but is confined to the immediate vendee. The exceptions to this general rule which have thus far been recognized in New York are cases in which the article sold was of such a character that danger to life or limb was involved in the ordinary use thereof; in other words, where the article sold was inherently dangerous. As has already been pointed out, the learned trial judge instructed the jury that an automobile is not an inherently dangerous vehicle.

The late Chief Justice Cooley of Michigan, one of the most learned and accurate of American law writers, states the general rule thus:

"The general rule is that a contractor, manufacturer, vendor or furnisher of an article is not liable to third parties who have no contractual relations with him, for negligence in the construction, manufacture, or sale of such article." 2 Cooley on Torts (3d Ed.) 1486.

The leading English authority in support of this rule, to which all the later cases on the same subject refer, is Winterbottom v. Wright, 10 Meeson & Welsby, 109, which was an action by the driver of a stagecoach against a contractor who had agreed with the postmaster general to provide and keep the vehicle in repair for the purpose of conveying the royal mail over a prescribed route. The coach broke down and upset, injuring the driver, who sought to recover against the contractor on account of its defective construction. The Court of Exchequer denied him any right of recovery on the ground that there was no privity of contract between the parties, the agreement having been made with the postmaster general alone.

"If the plaintiff can sue," said Lord Abinger, the Chief Baron, "every passenger or even any person passing along the road who was injured by the upsetting of the coach might bring a similar action. Unless we confine the operation of such contracts as this to the parties who enter into them the most absurd and outrageous consequences, to which I can see no limit, would ensue."

The doctrine of that decision was recognized as the law of this state by the leading New York case of Thomas v. Winchester, 6 N.Y. 397, 408, 57 Am.Dec. 455, which, however, involved an exception to the general rule. There the defendant, who was a dealer in medicines, sold to a druggist a quantity of belladonna, which is a deadly poison, negligently labeled as extract of dandelion. The druggist in good faith used the poison in filling a prescription calling for the harmless dandelion extract, and the plaintiff for whom the prescription was put up was poisoned by the belladonna. This court held that the original vendor was liable for the injuries suffered by the patient. Chief Judge Ruggles, who delivered the opinion of the court, distinguished between an act of negligence imminently dangerous to the lives of others and one that is not so, saying:

"If A. build a wagon and sell it to B., who sells it to C., and C. hires it to D., who in consequence of the gross negligence of A. in building the wagon is overturned and injured, D. cannot recover damages against A., the builder. A.'s obligation to build the wagon faithfully arises solely out of his contract with B. The public have nothing to do with it. * * * So, for the same reason, if a horse be defectively shod by a smith, and a person hiring the horse from the owner is thrown and injured in consequence of the smith's negligence in shoeing, the smith is not liable for the injury."

In Torgesen v. Schultz, 192 N.Y. 156, 159, 84 N.E. 956, 18 L.R. A.(N.S.) 726, 127 Am.St.Rep. 894, the defendant was the vendor of bottles of aerated water which were charged under high pressure and likely to explode unless used with precaution when exposed to sudden changes of temperature. The plaintiff, who was a servant of the purchaser, was injured by the explosion of one of these bottles. There was evidence tending to show that it had not been properly tested in order to insure users against such accidents. We held that the defendant corporation was liable notwithstanding the absence of any contract relation between it and the plaintiff—

"under the doctrine of Thomas v. Winchester, supra, and similar cases based upon the duty of the vendor of an article dangerous in its nature, or likely to become so in the course of the ordinary usage to be contemplated by the vendor, either to exercise due care to warn users of the danger or to take reasonable care to prevent the article sold from proving dangerous when subjected only to customary usage."

The character of the exception to the general rule limiting liability for negligence to the original parties to the contract of sale, was still more clearly stated by Judge Hiscock, writing for the court in Statler v. Ray Manufacturing Co., 195 N.Y. 478, 482, 88 N.E. 1063, where he said that:

"In the case of an article of an inherently dangerous nature, a manufacturer may become liable for a negligent construction which, when added to the inherent character of the appliance, makes it imminently dangerous, and causes or contributes to a resulting injury not necessarily incident to the use of such an article if properly constructed, but naturally following from a defective construction."

In that case the injuries were inflicted by the explosion of a battery of steam-driven coffee urns, constituting an appliance liable to become dangerous in the course of ordinary usage.

The case of Devlin v. Smith, 89 N.Y. 470, 42 Am.Rep. 311, is cited as an authority in conflict with the view that the liability of the manufacturer and vendor extends to third parties only when the article manufactured and sold is inherently dangerous. In that case the builder of a scaffold 90 feet high, which was erected for the purpose of enabling painters to stand upon it, was held to be liable to the administratrix of a painter who fell therefrom and was killed, being at the time in the employ of the person for whom the scaffold was built. It is said that the scaffold, if properly constructed, was not inherently dangerous, and hence that this decision affirms the existence of liability in the case of an article not dangerous in itself, but made so only in consequence of negligent construction. Whatever logical force there may be in this view it seems to me clear from the language of Judge Rapallo, who wrote the opinion of the court that the scaffold was deemed to be an inherently dangerous structure, and that the case was decided as it was because the court entertained that view. Otherwise he would hardly have said, as he did, that the circumstances seemed to bring the case fairly within the principle of Thomas v. Winchester.

I do not see how we can uphold the judgment in the present case without overruling what has been so often said by this court and other courts of like authority in reference to the absence of any liability for negligence on the part of the original vendor of an ordinary carriage to any one except his immediate vendee. The absence of such liability was the very point actually decided in the English case of Winterbottom v. Wright, supra, and the illustration quoted from the opinion of Chief Judge Ruggles in Thomas v. Winchester, supra, assumes that the law on the subject was so plain that the statement would be accepted almost as a matter of course. In the case at bar the defective wheel on an automobile, moving only eight miles an hour, was not any more dangerous to the occupants of the car than a similarly defective wheel would be to the occupants of a carriage drawn by a horse at the same speed, and yet, unless the courts have been all wrong on this question up to the present time, there would be no liability to strangers to the original sale in the case of the horse-drawn carriage.

The rule upon which, in my judgment, the determination of this case depends, and the recognized exceptions thereto, were discussed by Circuit Judge Sanborn, of the United States Circuit Court of Appeals in the Eighth Circuit, in Huset v. J. I. Case Threshing Machine Co., 120 Fed. 865, 57 C.C.A. 237, 61 L.R.A. 303, in an opinion which reviews all the leading American and English decisions on the subject up to the time when it was rendered (1903). I have already discussed the leading New York cases, but as to the rest I feel that I can add nothing to the learning of that opinion or the cogency of its reasoning. I have examined the cases to which Judge Sanborn refers, but if I were to discuss them at length, I should be forced merely to paraphrase his language, as a study of the authorities he cites has led me to the same conclusion; and the repetition of what has already been so well said would contribute nothing to the advantage of the bench, the bar, or the individual litigants whose case is before us.

A few cases decided since his opinion was written, however, may be noticed. In Earl v. Lubbock, [1905] L.R. 1 K.B.Div. 253, the Court of Appeal in 1904 considered and approved the propositions of law laid down by the Court of Exchequer in Winterbottom v. Wright, supra, declaring that the decision in that case, since the year 1842, had stood the test of repeated discussion. The Master of the Rolls approved the principles laid down by Lord Abinger as based upon sound reasoning; and all the members of the court agreed that his decision was a controlling authority which must be followed. That the federal courts still adhere to the general rule, as I have stated it, appears by the decision of the Circuit Court of Appeal in the Second Circuit, in March, 1915, in the case of Cadillac Motor Car Co. v. Johnson, 221 Fed. 801, 137 C.C.A. 279, L.R.A.1915E, 287. That case, like this, was an action by a subvendee against a manufacturer of automobiles for negligence in failing to discover that one of its wheels was defective, the court holding that such an action could not be maintained. It is true there was a dissenting opinion in that case, but it was based chiefly upon the proposition that rules applicable to stagecoaches are archaic when applied to automobiles, and that if the law did not afford a remedy to strangers to the contract, the law should be changed. If this be true, the change should be effected by the Legislature and not by the courts. A perusal of the opinion in that case and in the Huset case will disclose how uniformly the courts throughout this country have adhered to the rule and how consistently they have refused to broaden the scope of the exceptions. I think we should adhere to it in the case at bar, and therefore I vote for a reversal of this judgment.

HISCOCK, CHASE, and CUDDEBACK, JJ., concur with CARDOZO, J., and HOGAN, J., concurs in result. WILLARD BARTLETT, C. J., reads dissenting opinion. POUND, J., not voting.

Judgment affirmed.

NOTES

1. The *MacPherson* case is one of the most famous, oft-cited, nonconstitutional, decisions you will encounter. To what extent does the decision represent an "advance" from prior law?

2. In The Ages of American Law (1977) at p. 75, Professor Grant Gilmore says about Cardozo:

> Before his appointment to the Supreme Court of the United States in succession to Holmes, Cardozo served for nearly twenty years on the New York Court of Appeals and evidently dominated that great court, intellectually, throughout his tenure. Cardozo was a truly innovative judge of a type which had long since gone out of fashion. In his opinions, however, he was accustomed to hide his light under a bushel. The more innovative the decision to which he had persuaded his brethren on the court, the more his opinion strained to prove that no novelty—not the slightest depar-

Sec. 3   TECHNIQUE OF CASE LAW DEVELOPMENT   175

ture from prior law—was involved. Since Cardozo was one of the best case lawyers who ever lived, the proof was invariably marshalled with a masterly elegance. It is not until the reader gets to the occasional angry dissent that he realizes that Cardozo had been turning the law of New York upside down. During his twenty years Cardozo succeeded to an extraordinary degree in freeing up —and, of course, unsettling—the law of New York. It is true that he went about doing this in such an elliptical, convoluted, at times incomprehensible, fashion that the less gifted lower court New York judges were frequently at a loss to understand what they were being told.

3. After the decision in *MacPherson*, how would you answer question 3 following Thomas v. Winchester?

4. What is left of the requirement of privity in cases involving negligent manufacture? Would the absence of privity be a good defense for the manufacturer of a negligently manufactured product in the following cases:

A suit by a passenger in an automobile, not the purchaser, for personal injuries.

A suit by a "bystander," e. g., a pedestrian injured by the automobile when it collapsed, for personal injuries.

A suit for personal injuries by the purchaser against the manufacturer of a component part.

5. After *MacPherson* does the nature of the article matter any more?

FRIEND v. CHILDS DINING HALL CO.

Supreme Judicial Court of Massachusetts, 1918.
231 Mass. 65, 120 N.E. 407.

[Plaintiff began the action by a declaration which sought, first, recovery in tort, and second, recovery in contract. She abandoned the first basis of claim and this report deals exclusively with the second.—Ed.]

In the Superior Court the case was tried before Bell, J. The plaintiff's evidence is described in the opinion. At the close of the plaintiff's evidence, the defendant asked the judge to order a verdict for it. Whereupon the judge with the consent of the parties reported the case for determination by this court and, the parties agreeing upon $150 as the amount of the damages, the judge ordered the jury to return a verdict for the defendant, with leave reserved, with the consent of the jury, to enter a verdict for the plaintiff for $150 if this court should decide that the ordering of the verdict was wrong and that the plaintiff was entitled to recover; otherwise, the verdict for the defendant was to stand.

St.1908, c. 237, § 15 [Uniform Sales Act § 15], begins as follows:

"Section 15. Subject to the provisions of this act and of any other statute in that behalf, there is no implied warranty or condition as to the quality or fitness for any particular purpose of goods supplied under a contract to sell or a sale, except as follows:

"(1) Where the buyer, expressly or by implication, makes known to the seller the particular purpose for which the goods are required, and it appears that the buyer relies on the seller's skill or judgment, whether he be the grower or manufacturer or not, there is an implied warranty that the goods shall be reasonably fit for such purpose.

"(2) Where the goods are bought by description from a seller who deals in goods of that description, whether he be the grower or manufacturer or not, there is an implied warranty that the goods shall be of merchantable quality.

"(3) If the buyer has examined the goods, there is no implied warranty as regards defects which such examination ought to have revealed."

RUGG, C. J. The plaintiff introduced evidence tending to show that the defendant kept a restaurant in Boston, which she entered and ordered from a waitress of the defendant from its menu, "New York baked beans and corned beef." This food was served to her and she sat at a table to eat it. She further testified, "I started to eat the food and there were two or three dark pieces which I thought were hard beans, that is, baked more than the others, and I put two in my mouth and bit down hard on them, and * * * I was hurt. * * * I took those things out of my mouth and found they were stones." There was no further evidence that the plaintiff had anything to do with the selection of the beans. She gave no instructions respecting the food other than to order it. There was no evidence of express warranty or that the defendant knew of the presence of the stones in the food. There was evidence of injury to the plaintiff. [The court first addresses the question whether the service of food by the defendant was a "sale," and, after discussing several cases continues—Ed.]

In view of these decisions it would be difficult for this court to hold that the transaction arising from a contract to serve to a guest food to be eaten by him upon the premises of the keeper of an eating house, is not a sale. If it is a sale, then plainly it is governed by the sales act, St.1908, c. 237, § 15(1), which is in these words: "Where the buyer, expressly or by implication, makes known to the seller the particular purpose for which the goods are required, and it appears that the buyer relies on the seller's skill or judgment, whether he be the grower or manufacturer or not, there is an implied warranty that the goods shall be reasonably fit for such purpose." It is manifest that at least it might be inferred from the relations of the parties, that the guest who asks to be served food upon the premises of one who is the keeper of a restaurant makes known as the particular pur-

Sec. 3   TECHNIQUE OF CASE LAW DEVELOPMENT   177

pose for which the food is required that it is then and there to be eaten, and that he relies upon the latter's skill or judgment in the selection and preparation of the food. Hence there would be an implied warranty that it was reasonably fit for such purpose.

If the transaction is a sale, the rule is the same apart from the sales act. That was settled after great consideration in Farrell v. Manhattan Market Co., 198 Mass. 271, 84 N.E. 481, 15 L.R.A.,N.S., 884, 126 Am.St.Rep. 436, 15 Ann.Cas. 1076, a case decided before the sales act took effect. * * *

But there is authority to the effect that, when food is furnished to a guest by the keeper of a restaurant or inn, the transaction does not constitute a sale, that the title to the food does not pass, that the customer may consume so much as he pleases, but that he cannot carry away of the portion ordered that which he does not eat, or give or sell it to another; and that the charge made is not for the food alone, but includes the service rendered and the providing of a place in which to eat. It is stated in Beale on Innkeepers, § 169, "The title to food never passes as a result of an ordinary transaction of supplying food to a guest; or, as it was quaintly put in an old case, 'he does not sell but utters his provision.'" Parker v. Flint, 12 Mod. 254.

* * *

* * * It would be an incongruity in the law amounting at least to an inconsistency to hold with reference to many keepers of restaurants who conduct the business both of supplying food to guests and of putting up lunches to be carried elsewhere and not eaten on the premises, that, in case of want of wholesomeness, there is liability to the purchaser of a lunch to be carried away founded on an implied condition of the contract, but that liability to the guest who eats a lunch at a table on the premises rests solely on negligence. The guest of a keeper of an eating house or of an innkeeper is quite as helpless to protect himself against deleterious food or drink as is the purchaser of a fowl from a provision dealer. The opportunity for the innkeeper or restaurant keeper, who prepares and serves food to his guest, to discover and provide against deleterious food is at least as ample as is that of the retail dealer in foodstuffs. The evil consequences in the one case are of the same general character as in the other. Both concern the health and physical comfort and safety of human beings.

On principle and on authority it seems to us that the liability of the proprietor of an eating house to his guest for serving bad food rests on an implied term of the contract and does not sound exclusively in tort, although of course he may be held for negligence if that is proved. * * *

* * *

It has been argued that it should have been ruled as matter of law that the plaintiff was not in the exercise of due care, and on that ground could not prevail. Due care is not a term of the law of contract, but of torts. This is an action of contract. The obligation resting upon the defendant and accruing to the plaintiff arose out of the contract.

The defendant has urged that, if liability be treated as arising either out of a sale or a breach of contract, the plaintiff fails to show requisite examination on her own part, and that reasonable inspection would have revealed the existing defect in the food, and that under such circumstances as matter of law there can be no recovery. Whatever may be the merit of these contentions under appropriate conditions, they are not pertinent to the facts disclosed on this record. If these contentions in favor of the plaintiff are assumed to be sound, and if further it be assumed that § 15(3) of the sales act is applicable, to the effect that there is "no implied warranty as regards defects which such examination ought to have revealed," nevertheless it was a question of fact whether rational investigation was made by the plaintiff respecting the character of the food set before her and whether the noxious nature of the thing which caused the harm reasonably ought to have been discovered.

Our conclusion is that, whether the transaction established on the evidence between the plaintiff and the defendant be treated as a sale of food, or as a contract for entertainment where the defendant simply "utters his provision" (to use the neat phrase of Parker v. Flint, 12 Mod. 254, employed more than two centuries ago) for the benefit of the plaintiff, there was a case to be submitted to the jury.

[The dissenting opinion of Crosby, J. is omitted.]

NOTES

1. Does this case represent an "advance" in the law over the *Kellogg Bridge Co.* case, supra p. 154.

2. Would this case have been decided differently if Massachusetts had not adopted the Uniform Sales Act? In Race v. Krum, 222 N.Y. 410, 118 N.E. 853 (1918), decided before New York adopted the Uniform Sales Act, the court said (222 N.Y. at 414):

"The general rule established by the weight of authority in the United States and England is that accompanying all sales by a retail dealer of articles of food for immediate use there is an implied warranty that the same is fit for human consumption."

3. Why, do you suppose, did plaintiff abandon her cause of action in tort?

ASH v. CHILDS DINING HALL CO.

Supreme Judicial Court of Massachusetts, 1918.
231 Mass. 86, 120 N.E. 396.

RUGG, C. J. This is an action of tort. It rests solely upon allegations of negligence. The burden of proving that the proximate cause of the plaintiff's injury was the negligence of the defendant or its servants or agents rested on the plaintiff. It is well settled that the duty rests upon the keeper of an inn, restaurant or other eating place to use due care to furnish wholesome food, fit to eat. Failure in this respect resulting in injury is foundation for an action for negligence. Bishop v. Weber, 139 Mass. 411, 417. Crocker v. Baltimore Dairy Lunch Co., 214 Mass. 177. Wilson v. J. G. & B. S. Ferguson Co., 214 Mass. 265. Tomlinson v. Armour & Co., 46 Vroom, 748, 762.

The testimony of the plaintiff tended to show that she received injuries from the presence of a tack in a piece of blueberry pie which she was eating while a guest of the defendant in its restaurant. Her description was that "there lodged in her throat, in her right tonsil, a very thin small-headed tack, the head a little mite larger than a pin head. * * * it was a little longer than a carpet tack." It was not the same shape as a carpet tack. "It was thin, long and a very small head." The head was flat. "It was a black tack."

The pie was made by the defendant on its premises and served as food by its waitress to the plaintiff. The manager of the defendant testified that at that time its blueberries came in ordinary quart berry baskets, made of wood in which were tacks "hardly an eighth of an inch long, with a flat head, and that this was the first time in the eighteen years that he had been in the business that he had seen a tack in blueberries." There was other testimony to the effect that a high degree of care was exercised in the preparation of the blueberries for the pies. That is laid on one side, as it may not have been credited by the jury. But disbelief of the defendant's testimony as to the precautions used by it cannot take the place of evidence of negligence.

There is nothing in the record from which it can be inferred that the harm to the plaintiff resulted directly from any failure of duty on the part of the defendant. The precise cause of her injury is left to conjecture. It may as reasonably be attributed to a condition for which no liability attaches to the defendant as to one for which it is responsible. Under such circumstances the plaintiff does not sustain the burden of fastening tortious conduct on the defendant by a fair preponderance of all the evidence, and a verdict ought to be directed accordingly. Leavitt v. Fiberloid Co., 196 Mass. 440, 444.

The tack was very small. It was so tiny that it readily might have become embedded in a blueberry. If so, its color and shape were such that it would naturally escape the most careful scrutiny. It might as readily have stuck into a blueberry before it came to the possession of the defendant as afterwards. The carelessness of some person for whom the defendant in no way was responsible might have caused its presence in the pie. The maker of the basket, some previous owner of the berry, or some other third person, is as likely to have been the direct cause of the tack being in the pie as the defendant or those for whose conduct it is liable. The facts are quite different from those disclosed in Hunt v. Rhodes Brothers Co., 207 Mass. 30.

These suggestions make it plain that this is not a case for the application of *res ipsa loquitur*. That doctrine may be invoked in the case of an unexplained accident which, according to the common experience of mankind, would not have happened without fault on the part of the defendant. St. Louis v. Bay State Street Railway, 216 Mass. 255, 257. It does not avail where the cause of the injury is just as likely to have been the fault of another. The mere fact of injury does not show negligence. The burden of proof resting upon the plaintiff to establish that fact must be sustained by evidence either direct or inferential. Waters-Pierce Oil Co. v. Deselms, 212 U.S. 159, 176. The case falls within the class of which Crocker v. Baltimore Dairy Lunch Co., 211 Mass. 177, Kusick v. Thorndike & Hix, Inc., 224 Mass. 413, and Burnham v. Lincoln, 225 Mass. 408, are examples. See in this connection Hasbrouck v. Armour & Co., 139 Wis. 357.

No question arises as to the contractual relations between the parties.

In the opinion of a majority of the court, the entry must be Exceptions sustained.

WINDRAM MFG. CO. v. BOSTON BLACKING CO.

Supreme Judicial Court of Massachusetts, 1921.
239 Mass. 123, 131 N.E. 454.

DE COURCY, J. The first count in the amended declaration alleges in substance that the plaintiff was engaged in the business of pasting linings to fabrics by means of machinery, using in the process a paste or cement, which it purchased from one Ellis; that the defendant manufactured the cement for Ellis, and was aware that it was to be so used by the plaintiff; and that said blacking company negligently manufactured and mixed the paste, so that it injured the fabrics on which it was used, to the pecuniary loss of the plaintiff.

The allegation that the defendant "carelessly and negligently" manufactured and mixed the cement is equivalent legally to a statement that the defendant owed to the plaintiff a duty to exercise reasonable care in making the cement, and failed to perform that duty. Bergeron v. Forest, 233 Mass. 392, 399, 124 N.E. 74. The long established general rule is that the manufacturer of an article is not liable for negligence in its manufacture to a third person with whom he has no contractual relations. Winterbottom v. Wright, 10 M. & W. 109; Huset v. J. I. Case Threshing Machine Co., 120 F. 865, 61 L.R.A. 303; Davidson v. Nichols, 11 Allen, 514. Lebourdais v. Vitrified Wheel Co., 194 Mass. 341, 80 N.E. 482; Tompkins v. Quaker Oats Co., 239 Mass. 147, 131 N.E. 456. See cases collected in 1 Ann.Cas. 755 note;

Sec. 3 TECHNIQUE OF CASE LAW DEVELOPMENT 181

24 R.C.L. 512; 48 L.R.A.,N.S., 213 note. Whatever legal obligation the defendant may be under to its customer, Ellis, does not extend to sub-vendees. See Leavitt v. Fiberloid Co., 196 Mass. 440, 444, 82 N.E. 682, 15 L.R.A.,N.S., 855; Farrell v. Manhattan Market Co., 198 Mass. 271, 84 N.E. 481, 15 L.R.A.,N.S., 884, 126 Am.St.Rep. 436, 15 Ann.Cas. 1076; Gearing v. Berkson, 223 Mass. 257, 260, 111 N.E. 785, L.R.A.1916D, 1006. The plaintiff has not stated a cause of action in the first count.

The second count contains an allegation that "the defendant in such a way manufactured and mixed and put such materials into the cement * * * that said cement was, as the defendant was well aware, of a deleterious and dangerous character and certain to injure the fabrics and linings to which it should be applied by the plaintiff." Apparently it is sought thereby to bring the case within a recognized exception to the above general rule. As that exception ordinarily is stated, "an act of negligence of a manufacturer or seller which is imminently dangerous to the life or health of mankind, and which is committed in the preparation or sale of an article intended to preserve, destroy, or affect human life, is actionable by third persons who suffer from the negligence regardless of privity of contract." 24 R.C.L. 512. Carter v. Towne, 98 Mass. 567, 96 Am.Dec. 682; Wellington v. Downer Kerosene Oil Co., 104 Mass. 64; Wilson v. J. G. & B. S. Ferguson Co., 214 Mass. 265, 101 N.E. 381; Thornhill v. Carpenter-Morton Co., 220 Mass. 593, 108 N.E. 474; 1 Ann.Cas. 755 note. A tendency appears in some recent cases to extend the class of "inherently dangerous" articles, so as to include not only those that in their ordinary state are dangerous to health and safety, such as poisons and explosives, but also those that are reasonably certain to place life and limb in peril because of negligent preparation. MacPherson v. Buick Motor Co., 217 N.Y. 382, 111 N.E. 1050, L.R.A. 1916F, 696, Ann.Cas.1916C, 440; Johnson v. Cadillac Motor Car Co., 261 F. 878, 8 A.L.R. 1023; Krahn v. J. L. Owens Co., 125 Minn. 33, 145 N.W. 626, 51 L.R.A.,N.S., 650; Ann.Cas.1917E, 584 note. No authority has been called to our attention which imposes a common law duty of care toward strangers to the contract, upon the maker of an article which is not inherently dangerous, but is likely to cause a loss to property because of careless preparation. See Lukens v. Freiund, 27 Kan. 664, 51 Am.Rep. 429.

The second count also includes an element distinct from negligence, and quite apart from the contract of sale,—namely, that of scienter. For the purposes of the demurrer we must assume that the defendant knew that this product was made for the sole use of the plaintiff, and was aware that by reason of its (the defendant's) carelessness in the process of manufacture the cement was certain to injure the fabrics of the plaintiff. This has some of the characteristics of an intentional tort, for which a wrongdoer is liable unless he has a legal justification; but the declaration falls short of that charge.

There is present no allegation of a representation made by the defendant, either by word or conduct, which might mislead; no averment of any artifice employed, or of active concealment of defects; no alleged utterance of a half truth which is in effect a lie, or the use of other means to throw the plaintiff off its guard; any of which might be sufficient to prevent the application of the general rule as to non-disclosure, and render the defendant guilty of fraud. Langridge v. Levy, 2 M. & W. 519; George v. Skivington, L.R. 5 Ex. 1; Burns v. Dockray, 156 Mass. 135, 30 N.E. 551; Roberts v. Anheuser Busch Brewing Ass'n, 211 Mass. 449, 98 N.E. 95; Thornhill v. Carpenter-Morton Co., supra; Kuelling v. Roderick Lean Manuf. Co., 183 N.Y. 78, 75 N.E. 1098, 2 L.R.A.,N.S., 303, 111 Am.St.Rep. 691, 5 Ann.Cas. 124, and cases cited; Woodward v. Miller, 119 Ga. 618, 46 S.E. 847, 64 L.R.A. 932, 100 Am.St.Rep. 188; Skinn v. Reutter, 135 Mich. 57, 97 N.W. 152, 63 L.R.A. 743, 106 Am.St.Rep. 384; Lewis v. Terry, 111 Cal. 39, 43 P. 398, 31 L.R.A. 220, 52 Am.St.Rep. 146; Huset v. J. I. Case Threshing Machine Co., 120 F. 865, 871, 57 C.C.A. 237, 61 L.R. A. 303. Mere silence on the part of the defendant is all that is charged. But failure to disclose known facts does not amount to fraud, and is not the basis of an action for deceit, unless the parties stand in such relation to one another that one is under legal or equitable obligation to communicate the facts to the other. "It may now be said to be firmly established that silence as to matters which there is no duty, original or supervening, to divulge, however actionable a positive misrepresentation of such matters may be, and however censurable in foro conscientiae even the withholding of them may be, subjects the party observing silence to no legal liability whatever." Bower on Actionable Non-Disclosure, 135. Potts v. Chapin, 133 Mass. 276; Van Houten v. Morse, 162 Mass. 414, 417, 38 N.E. 705, 26 L.R.A. 430, 44 Am.St.Rep. 373; Phinney v. Friedman, 224 Mass. 531, 533, 113 N.E. 285.

The demurrer was sustained rightly; and the judgment for the defendant must be affirmed.

So ordered.

NOTES

1. Is it significant in the *Windram* case that the negligently made product, although "dangerous" to property, does not appear likely to cause bodily injury? Where the defective article is dangerous to the person, it is well established that a tort action lies for property damage only. (E. g., Genesee Cty. P.F.R.A. v. L. Sonneborn Sons, 263 N.Y. 463, 189 N.E. 551 (1934). It is less well established, in the cases at least, that a product dangerous only to property will be treated the same—although it seems likely that it will be.

2. Although, after *MacPherson*, persons suffering personal injuries because of negligently manufactured products were usually able to recover damages from the manufacturer in tort actions, courts continued to debate the issue in terms of the requirement of privity. See, e. g., 1943 Reports

of the New York Law Revision Commission 417, 432 et seq. One of the few cases to flatly reject the privity doctrine as inappropriate to tort actions was Carter v. Yardley & Co., 319 Mass. 92, 64 N.E.2d 693 (1946), a case involving perfume.

CHYSKY v. DRAKE BROS. CO.
Court of Appeals of New York, 1923.
235 N.Y. 468, 139 N.E. 576.

McLAUGHLIN, J. The plaintiff was employed as a waitress in a lunchroom run by one Abraham, for which she was paid thirty dollars a week and furnished board and lodging. On the 4th of May, 1918, she received from her employer, as part of her lunch, a piece of cake which had been made and sold to him by defendant. While she was eating it a nail, baked into the cake in such a way that it could not be discovered by inspection, stuck in her gum, which became so infected as to necessitate the removal of three of her teeth. She brought this action against the maker of the cake to recover the damages alleged to have been sustained, upon the theory it was liable to her, since it had impliedly warranted, when the cake was sold, that it was fit for human consumption and that such implied warranty inured to her benefit. This was the cause of action alleged in the complaint, as amplified by the bill of particulars, and this was the theory upon which the action was tried and submitted to the jury. She had a verdict and the judgment entered thereon was unanimously affirmed by the Appellate Division. Appeal to this court followed.

In Race v. Krum, 222 N.Y. 410, 118 N.E. 853, L.R.A.1918F, 1172, we held that accompanying all sales by a retail dealer of articles of food for immediate use there is an implied warranty that the same is fit for human consumption. We did not consider or pass upon, as will appear from the opinion, whether such a warranty existed in the case of hotel proprietors or those engaged in a similar business. The cause of action arose before section 96 of the Personal Property Law took effect. Cons.Laws, chap. 41. In the present case the cause of action arose after the section took effect. This section [Uniform Sales Act § 15] provides that "there is no implied warranty or condition as to the quality or fitness for any particular purpose of goods supplied under a contract to sell or a sale, except as follows: 1. Where the buyer, expressly or by implication, makes known to the seller the particular purpose for which the goods are required, and it appears that the buyer relies on the seller's skill or judgment (whether he be the grower or manufacturer or not), there is an implied warranty that the goods shall be reasonably fit for such purpose."

If there be any liability, therefore, it must be under this section and the jury was so instructed.

In Rinaldi v. Mohican Co., 225 N.Y. 70, 121 N.E. 471, where the cause of action arose after the section of the Personal Property Law quoted took effect, we held "that the mere purchase by a customer from a retail dealer in foods of an article ordinarily used for human consumption does by implication make known to the vendor the purpose for which the article is required. Such a transaction standing by itself permits no contrary inferences."

Under the section of the Personal Property Law referred to and the Rinaldi case, an action may be maintained to recover damages caused by the breach of an implied warranty in the sale of food to a consumer for immediate consumption. Whether this warranty extends to a wholesaler was expressly reserved in the Rinaldi case, but is now squarely presented.

The plaintiff received the cake from her employer. By reason of its condition it was not fit for human consumption. Her employer bought the cake from the defendant. Is it liable to the plaintiff for the injury sustained? We do not think so. If there were an implied warranty which inured to the benefit of the plaintiff it must be because there was some contractual relation between her and the defendant and there was no such contract. She never saw the defendant, and so far as appears, did not know from whom her employer purchased the cake. The general rule is that a manufacturer or seller of food, or other articles of personal property, is not liable to third persons, under an implied warranty, who have no contractual relations with him. The reason for this rule is that privity of contract does not exist between the seller and such third persons, and unless there be privity of contract there can be no implied warranty. The benefit of a warranty, either express or implied, does not run with a chattel on its resale, and in this respect is unlike a covenant running with the land so as to give a subsequent purchaser a right of action against the original seller on a warranty.

It may be assumed that under certain facts and conditions the manufacturer of an article would be liable to a third person, even though no contractual relation existed between them, if the article sold were negligently prepared or manufactured. MacPherson v. Buick Motor Co., 217 N.Y. 382, 111 N.E. 1050, L.R.A.1916F, 696, Ann.Cas.1916C, 440, and authorities there cited; Williston on Sales, § 244; Tompkins v. Quaker Oats Co., 239 Mass. 147, 131 N.E. 456; Gearing v. Berkson, 223 Mass. 257, 111 N.E. 785, L.R.A.1916D, 1006; Tomlinson v. Armour & Co., 75 N.J.L. 748, 70 A. 314, 19 L.R.A.,N.S., 923; Johnson v. Cadillac Motor Car Co., 261 F. 878, 8 A.L.R. 1023; Haley v. Swift & Co., 152 Wis. 570, 140 N.W. 292. But the recovery in the present case was not based upon the negligence of the defendant. Plaintiff limited her right to recover to a breach of warranty. She specifically stated in her bill of particulars "such breach of warranty by defendant she makes the issue in this action." I have not been able to find any authority, in this state at least, which would permit a recovery upon that ground and the great weight of authority in this country and England is directly to the contrary. See Ket-

Sec. 3   TECHNIQUE OF CASE LAW DEVELOPMENT   185

terer v. Armour & Co., 247 F. 921, L.R.A.1918D, 798, and authorities there cited.

The judgments appealed from, therefore, should be reversed and the complaint dismissed, with costs in all courts.

NOTES

1. The Uniform Sales Act was initially promulgated in 1906 and ultimately adopted in thirty-seven states; it was (insofar as we are concerned with it here) largely copied from the English Sale of Goods Act of 1894 "which was itself a restatement and codification of the common law of England as it existed at that date." Prosser, Implied Warranty of Merchantable Quality, 27 Minn.L.Rev. 117 (1943). The Act was treated in a very different fashion than the statutes you will encounter in the next Chapter. Indeed, Professor Grant Gilmore has said:

> "Statutes like the Uniform Sales Act were not statutes at all. That is, they were not designed to provide rules for decision. Drafted in terms of loose and vague generality, they were designed to provide access to the prevailing academic wisdom. The rules for decision in sales cases were to be found, not in the Uniform Sales Act which had been drafted by Samuel Williston of the Harvard Law School, but in Professor Williston's treatise on the law of sales. This aspect of codification was, apparently, generally understood. The courts—and counsel—paid no attention at all to the Sales Act; they paid enormous attention to Professor Williston's treatise. What we had was not so much a codification as a non-codification —a method of preserving the common law purged of all impurities. Gilmore, The Ages of American Law 71–2 (1977)."

Cf. A. Hill, Damages for Innocent Misrepresentation, 73 Colum.L.Rev. 679, 743, n. 273 (1973), where the author, says of the Uniform Commercial Code, which supplanted the Uniform Sales Act: "[T]he courts have generally treated the Code as inapplicable, at least in cases of personal injury or property damage * * * typically the Code is simply ignored."

While the statements of Professors Gilmore and Hill seem substantially true as to the question of immediate concern in this course—the effect of lack of privity on a cause of action for breach of implied warranty—the Act was not always without impact. See, e. g., Rinaldi v. Mohican Co., 225 N.Y. 70, 121 N.E. 471 (1919):

> "Article 5 of the Personal Property Law is not merely a codification of the existing rules regarding sales in this state. It was the design as far as possible to make our law uniform with the legislation and laws on this subject existing throughout the country. To this end changes were made in what had previously been here the law. In section 96 itself, for instance, the distinction between the liability of sellers who were growers and manufacturers and others was ended. A warranty may now be established by proof of the usage of trade. Although an express warranty of quality is given, one not inconsistent with it may also be implied. Having in view the purpose of the article and the fact that in some states no implied warranty based on grounds other than those

186   CASE LAW   Ch. 2

which affect every sale of a chattel was enforced, we have no doubt that section 96, expressed as it is in general terms, applies to all sales, including sales of food, and that any rules hitherto applied inconsistent with this section are abolished."

2. In the series of cases in this section we are primarily concerned with the liability of manufacturers for products causing injury, and more narrowly, with the requirement of privity. The "no privity" defense was of great importance to manufacturers, who ordinarily did not sell directly to the public. Lack of privity also could be a problem in suits against retailers or others selling directly to the public where the person injured was not the actual purchaser. A and B enter a drugstore and order bottled soft drinks; A pays for both. B's drink contains ground glass and she suffers bodily injury. Had A been the lucky one she could clearly have recovered against the seller, but can B? Cf. Coca Cola Bottling Works v. Lyons, 145 Miss. 876, 111 So. 305 (1927). For other variations on this theme, see Greenberg v. Lorenz, infra p. 191.

PINE GROVE POULTRY FARM, INC. v. NEWTON BY-PRODUCTS MFG. CO., INC.

Court of Appeals of New York, 1928.
248 N.Y. 293, 162 N.E. 84.

O'BRIEN, J. Plaintiff operated an extensive duck farm on the south shore of Long Island. Defendant manufactures a brand of poultry feed known as meat scrap. It consists of scraps of meat procured from butcher shops, seasoned and ground and sifted through a screen, then packed in bags and sold to retail dealers. From such a dealer plaintiff purchased large quantities and upon it fed its ducks. Several thousand died. This high mortality was traced to the presence in the feed of fine particles of steel wire which had been fastened by butchers to the meat, and, still attached to the scraps, was ground with them. The question is presented whether in the absence of privity between the manufacturer and the ultimate purchaser, plaintiff can recover.

Theories based upon common-law rules of negligence need not now be considered. An answer to the question whether the doctrine of common-law negligence founded upon the principles applied in such decisions as Thomas v. Winchester, 6 N.Y. 397, 57 Am.Dec. 455, and MacPherson v. Buick Motor Company, 217 N.Y. 382, 111 N.E. 1050, L.R.A.1916F, 696, Ann.Cas.1916C, 440, shall be further extended to include damage to property rights as distinguished from personal injuries, may prudently be reserved for the future. Before us now is a set of facts which requires disposition according to statutory enactment. The action is based upon negligence. The complaint alleges it. The jury found it. The verdict rests upon evidence, so clear that its truth cannot be and is not assailed, proving that the feed contained ground wire and that the loss of the poultry resulted from that cause. The court adopting the theory of negligence pleaded by plain-

Sec. 3   TECHNIQUE OF CASE LAW DEVELOPMENT   187

tiff, charged the rule relating to reasonable care. In view of the statute he might have correctly charged negligence as matter of law.

The Farms and Markets Law (Cons.Laws, ch. 69) controls this case. Section 130 prohibits the sale of any concentrated commercial feeding stuffs containing any substances injurious to the health of animals, and section 128 defines "concentrated commercial feeding stuffs" as including ground "beef" or fish scraps and "all other materials of a similar nature." The meat scraps sold by defendant and fed to plaintiff's poultry are alleged in the complaint to be "Red X Brand Meat Scraps." Throughout the trial reference was usually made to them as such, yet on several occasions, without objection by defendant, they were described as "beef" scraps. The scraps of meat of which the feed was composed were gathered indiscriminately from a thousand shops. A proportion of this meat must have been beef. Even if the proportion of beef to the other meats were low, the material in the finished product, being meat, was of a similar nature to ground beef scrap. The feed falls within the type of food defined by sections 128 and 130. It was proved to be injurious to the health of animals and, therefore, its sale was prohibited. Violation of the duty to refrain from the sale of this feed as imposed by section 130 constitutes negligence as matter of law and anyone having a special interest in the performance of that duty may sue for a breach. Willy v. Mulledy, 78 N.Y. 310; Marino v. Lehmaier, 173 N.Y. 530, 535, 66 N. E. 572, 61 L.R.A. 811; Amberg v. Kinley, 214 N.Y. 531, 108 N.E. 830, L.R.A.1915E, 519. The right to maintain an action for the breach of a statutory duty is not restricted to one suffering an injury to the person. Property rights also come within the protection of a statute imposing a duty for the benefit of the general public. Such a rule has been applied by us to a violation of the Farms and Markets Law in a case where no privity of contract existed between the party guilty of the violation and the one incurring the damage. No element of ordinary negligence is essential. Violation of the statute becomes actionable default. Abounader v. Strohmeyer & Arpe Co., 243 N.Y. 458, 154 N.E. 309. A public statute, such as the Farms and Markets Law, need not be pleaded. Neither is there any requirement that during the trial it shall be brought to the attention of the court or opposing counsel. The facts found by the jury upon abundant evidence constitute as matter of law a violation of the statute. The court may have charged more favorably to defendant than the statute contemplates. Defendant cannot complain.

The judgment of the Appellate Division should be reversed and that of the Trial Term affirmed, with costs in the Appellate Division and in this court.

CASE LAW

BAXTER v. FORD MOTOR CO.

Supreme Court of Washington, 1932.
168 Wash. 456, 12 P.2d 409.

HERMAN, J.—During the month of May, 1930, plaintiff purchased a Model A Ford town sedan from defendant St. John Motors, a Ford dealer, who had acquired the automobile in question by purchase from defendant Ford Motor Company. Plaintiff claims that representations were made to him by both defendants that the windshield of the automobile was made of non-shatterable glass which would not break, fly or shatter.

October 12, 1930, while plaintiff was driving the automobile through Snoqualmie pass, a pebble from a passing car struck the windshield of the car in question, causing small pieces of glass to fly into plaintiff's left eye, resulting in the loss thereof. Plaintiff brought this action for damages for the loss of his left eye, and for injuries to the sight of his right eye. The case came on for trial, and, at the conclusion of plaintiff's testimony, the court took the case from the jury and entered judgment for both defendants. From that judgment, plaintiff appeals.

* * *

The second assignment of error is that the court refused to admit in evidence certain catalogues and printed matter furnished by respondent Ford Motor Company to respondent St. John Motors for distribution and assistance in sales. * * *

So far as that respondent, St. John Motors, is concerned, the written contract limits its responsibility to appellant. The purchase order stated that it contained the entire contract, and there was contained therein the following agreement:

> "It is further agreed that no warranty either express or implied is made by the dealer under this order or otherwise covering said car."

To have permitted the introduction of the testimony in question as against respondent St. John Motors, would have been to have countenanced an attempt to vary the terms of the written instrument by parol testimony. Such evidence was not competent against respondent St. John Motors, and there was not sufficient evidence against that respondent to justify submission of the cause to the jury. Judgment was properly entered for respondent St. John Motors.

The principal question in this case is whether the trial court erred in refusing to admit in evidence, as against respondent Ford Motor Company, the catalogues and printed matter furnished by that respondent to respondent St. John Motors to be distributed for sales assistance. Contained in such printed matter were statements which appellant maintains constituted representations or warranties with

Sec. 3   TECHNIQUE OF CASE LAW DEVELOPMENT   189

reference to the nature of the glass used in the windshield of the car purchased by appellant. A typical statement, as it appears in appellant's exhibit for identification No. 1, is here set forth:

> "Triplex Shatter-Proof Glass Windshield. All of the new Ford cars have a Triplex shatter-proof glass windshield —so made that it will not fly or shatter under the hardest impact. This is an important safety factor because it eliminates the dangers of flying glass—the cause of most of the injuries in automobile accidents. In these days of crowded, heavy traffic, the use of this Triplex glass is an absolute necessity. Its extra margin of safety is something that every motorist should look for in the purchase of a car—especially where there are women and children."

Respondent Ford Motor Company contends that there can be no implied or express warranty without privity of contract, and warranties as to personal property do not attach themselves to, and run with, the article sold.

* * *

In the case at bar, the automobile was represented by the manufacturer as having a windshield of non-shatterable glass "so made that it will not fly or shatter under the hardest impact." An ordinary person would be unable to discover by the usual and customary examination of the automobile whether glass which would not fly or shatter was used in the windshield. In that respect, the purchaser was in a position similar to that of the consumer of a wrongly labeled drug, who has bought the same from a retailer, and who has relied upon the manufacturer's representation that the label correctly set forth the contents of the container. For many years, it has been held that, under such circumstances, the manufacturer is liable to the consumer, even though the consumer purchased from a third person the commodity causing the damage. Thomas v. Winchester, 6 N.Y. 397, 57 Am.Dec. 455.

The rule in such cases does not rest upon contractual obligations, but rather on the principle that the original act of delivering an article is wrong, when, because of the lack of those qualities which the manufacturer represented it as having, the absence of which could not be readily detected by the consumer, the article is not safe for the purposes for which the consumer would ordinarily use it.

Since the rule of *caveat emptor* was first formulated, vast changes have taken place in the economic structures of the English speaking peoples. Methods of doing business have undergone a great transition. Radio, bill boards and the products of the printing press have become the means of creating a large part of the demand that causes goods to depart from factories to the ultimate consumer. It would be unjust to recognize a rule that would permit manufacturers

J.K. & M.Cs.Leg.Method 3rd Ed. U.C.B.—8

of goods to create a demand for their products by representing that they possess qualities which they, in fact, do not possess; and then, because there is no privity of contract existing between the consumer and the manufacturer, deny the consumer the right to recover if damages result from the absence of those qualities, when such absence is not readily noticeable.

"An exception to a rule will be declared by courts when the case is not an isolated instance, but general in its character and the existing rule does not square with justice. Under such circumstances, a court will, if free from the restraint of some statute, declare a rule that will meet the full intendment of the law." Mazetti v. Armour & Co., 75 Wash. 622, 135 Pac. 633.

We hold that the catalogues and printed matter furnished by respondent Ford Motor Company for distribution and assistance in sales (appellant's exhibits for identification Nos. 1, 2, 3, 4 and 5) were improperly excluded from evidence, because they set forth representations by the manufacturer that the windshield of the car which appellant bought contained Triplex non-shatterable glass which would not fly or shatter. The nature of non-shatterable glass is such that the falsity of the representations with reference to the glass would not be readily detected by a person of ordinary experience and reasonable prudence. Appellant, under the circumstances shown in this case, had the right to rely upon the representations made by respondent Ford Motor Company relative to qualities possessed by its products, even though there was no privity of contract between appellant and respondent Ford Motor Company.

NOTES

1. Would this case have come out the same if Ford's advertising had not mentioned the "shatterproof" glass? Why?

2. In a portion of the opinion not included here, the court holds that since there was no privity of contract between Ford and Baxter, Ford could not (as the dealer could) rely on the disclaimer in the sales contract to restrict the extent of its warranty.

3. Before reading the next three cases try (1) to synthesize the decisions in this section to date; and (2) list the policy factors which you feel should be taken into account by the New York Court of Appeals in deciding whether to change the law in that state.

4. Over the twenty-nine years between the decision in Baxter v. Ford Motor Co. and the decision of the New York Court of Appeals in Greenberg v. Lorenz, infra, p. 191, the law in many states moved strongly in the direction of imposing liability on the basis of implied warranty without privity of contract. By 1960 some thirteen states had followed the lead of the *Baxter* case and imposed liability based on express language (in labels, advertising or other literature) which turned out to be untrue even though there was no intention to deceive. And, at least in cases of food or other products intended for bodily use, many more states had imposed liability

Sec. 3   TECHNIQUE OF CASE LAW DEVELOPMENT   191

based on implied warranty to users not in privity with the manufacturer. See, Prosser, The Assault Upon the Citadel (Strict Liability to the Consumer), 69 Yale L.J. 1099 (1960). The article contains among other valuable materials, an extensive citation of the literature on the subject. On the other hand, New York State, which had taken the lead in the "assault on the citadel of privity" with the MacPherson decision, lagged behind other states and, by 1960, was something of a backwater in the law of product liability.

5. Negligence and breach of warranty were not the only theories on which liability was imposed. As pointed out by Professor Prosser in the article cited in note 4, "there was an extended period during which courts proceeded to invent a remarkable variety of highly ingenious, and equally unconvincing theories of fictitious agency, third-party beneficiary contract, and the like, to get around the lack of privity between the plaintiff and the defendant." 69 Yale L.J. at 1124. See, in this connection, Jeanblanc, Manufacturers' Liability, 24 Va.L.Rev. 134 (1937).

GREENBERG v. LORENZ

Court of Appeals of New York, 1961.
9 N.Y.2d 195, 213 N.Y.S.2d 39, 173 N.E.2d 773.

DESMOND, Chief Judge.

The infant plaintiff and her father sue a retail food dealer for damages for breach of alleged warranties of fitness and wholesomeness (Personal Property Law, Consol.Laws, c. 41, § 96, subds. 1, 2). Defendant they say, sold the father a can of salmon for consumption in the family home. The tinned fish, so it is alleged, was unfit for use as food because it contained some pieces of sharp metal which injured the child's teeth and mouth. The trial at City Court produced a judgment for both plaintiffs on the warranty theory. The Trial Justice commented on the trend away from such decisions as Chysky v. Drake Bros. Co., 235 N.Y. 468, 139 N.E. 576, 27 A.L.R. 1533 and Redmond v. Borden's Farm Products Co., 245 N.Y. 512, 157 N.E. 838 and held that although the father had bought the can of salmon the implied warranty extended to his 15-year-old daughter as a member of his household. The Appellate Term affirmed by a vote of 2 to 1. The majority in that court held that the old cases were no longer controlling. The Appellate Division, however, decided (nonunanimously) that the Chysky case is still law and that it forbids a recovery on warranty breach to anyone except the purchaser. As the case comes to us, the father has a judgment for his expenses but the child's own suit has been dismissed for lack of privity.

Our difficulty is not in finding the applicable rule but in deciding whether or not to change it. The decisions are clear enough. There can be no warranty, express or implied, without privity of contract (Turner v. Edison Storage Battery Co., 248 N.Y. 73, 74, 161 N. E. 423, 424; Pearlman v. Garrod Shoe Co., 276 N.Y. 172, 11 N.E.2d

- Warranty is part of contract
- Husbands and wives (or sisters) can act as agents → extend warranty to enable recovery
- But – a dependent child is not a contracting party and ∴ cannot be a warrantee so no damages are due him (w/o warranty – nothing to breach)

718) since a warranty is an incident of a contract of sale (Fairbank Canning Co. v. Metzger, 118 N.Y. 260, 265, 23 N.E. 372, 373). The warranty does not run with the chattel (Nichols v. Clark, MacMullen & Riley, 261 N.Y. 118, 184 N.E. 729). Therefore, as to food or other merchandise, there are no implied warranties of merchantability or fitness except as to the buyer (Chysky v. Drake Bros. Co., 235 N.Y. 468, 139 N.E. 576, supra; Ryan v. Progressive Grocery Stores, 255 N. Y. 388, 175 N.E. 105, 74 A.L.R. 339). A wife buying food for her husband may be considered his agent so as to allow a recovery by him (Ryan v. Progressive Grocery Stores, supra) and she can bring an action of her own if she makes the purchase and suffers from the breach of warranty (Gimenez v. Great A. & P. Tea Co., 264 N.Y. 390, 191 N.E. 27). When two sisters lived in a common household, the one who bought the food was deemed an agent of the other (Bowman v. Great A. & P. Tea Co., 308 N.Y. 780, 125 N.E.2d 165). The same (Bowman) theory was expanded to let both husband and wife recover (Mouren v. Great A. & P. Tea Co., 1 N.Y.2d 884, 154 N.Y.S.2d 642, 136 N.E.2d 715). But a dependent child is not a contracting party and cannot be a warrantee so no damages are due him (Redmond v. Borden's Farm Products Co., 245 N.Y. 512, 157 N.E. 838, supra).

The unfairness of the restriction has been argued in writings so numerous as to make a lengthy bibliography (see, as examples: Starke, Implied Warranties of Quality and Wholesomeness in the Sale of Food, N.Y.L.J., April 8, 9, 10, 1957, p. 4, col. 1 [Vol. 137, Nos. 67–69]; 1943 Report of N.Y.Law Rev.Comm., p. 413; 1945 Report of N. Y.Law Rev.Comm., p. 23; 1959 Report of N.Y.Law Rev.Comm., p. 57; Miller, N.Y. State Bar Bulletin, Oct., 1952, p. 313; Melick, Sale of Food and Drink, p. 94; Prosser, Torts [2d ed.], p. 493; 29 Fordham L.Rev. 183 [Oct., 1960]; 44 Cornell L.Q. 608; 34 N.Y.U.L.Rev. 1442; 35 St. John's L.Rev. 178 [Dec., 1960]). About 20 States have abolished such requirements of privity, the latest being Virginia and New Jersey (Swift & Co. v. Wells, 1959, 201 Va. 213, 110 S.E.2d 203; Henningsen v. Bloomfield Motor, 1960, 32 N.J. 358, 161 A.2d 69). The Uniform Commercial Code (§ 2–318) provides that: "A seller's warranty whether express or implied extends to any natural person who is in the family or household of his buyer or who is a guest in his home if it is reasonable to expect that such person may use, consume or be affected by the goods and who is injured in person by breach of the warranty." In 1943, 1945 and 1959 the New York State Law Revision Commission, each time after careful study, recommended that the implied warranty of fitness for use should extend to the buyer's household, members, employees and guests. The Legislature did not act on any of the commission's proposals.

The injustice of denying damages to a child because of nonprivity seems too plain for argument. The only real doubt is as to the propriety of changing the rule. Of course, objection will be made (as it has been made before in other such situations, see Woods v. Lancet,

Sec. 3 TECHNIQUE OF CASE LAW DEVELOPMENT   193

303 N.Y. 349, 102 N.E.2d 691, 27 A.L.R.2d 1250; Bing v. Thunig, 2 N.Y.2d 656, 163 N.Y.S.2d 3, 143 N.E.2d 3). But the present rule which we are being asked to modify is itself of judicial making since our statutes say nothing at all about privity and in early times such liabilities were thought to be in tort (Prosser, Torts [2d ed.], p. 507; 1 Williston on Sales [Rev. ed.], p. 502). Alteration of the law in such matters has been the business of the New York courts for many years (MacPherson v. Buick Motor Co., 217 N.Y. 382, 111 N.E. 1050, L.R.A. 1916F, 696; Ultramares Corp. v. Touche, 255 N.Y. 170, 174 N.E. 441, 74 A.L.R. 1139).

The Ryan Gimenez and Bowman cases, supra, in our court show an increasing tendency to lessen the rigors of the rule. In Blessington v. McCrory Stores Corp., 305 N.Y. 140, 111 N.E.2d 421, 37 A.L.R.2d 698 we passed on a Statute of Limitations point only but we did not (as we could have under the old cases) dismiss for insufficiency a complaint which demanded damages for an infant's death when the dangerous article had been purchased by the infant's mother. There are a great many well-considered lower court decisions in this State which attest to the prevalent feeling that at least as to injured members of a buyer's family the strict privity rule is unfair and should be revised.

So convincing a showing of injustice and impracticality calls upon us to move but we should be cautious and take one step at a time. To decide the case before us, we should hold that the infant's cause of action should not have been dismissed solely on the ground that the food was purchased not by the child but by the child's father. Today when so much of our food is bought in packages it is not just or sensible to confine the warranty's protection to the individual buyer. At least as to food and household goods, the presumption should be that the purchase was made for all the members of the household.

Sections 199–a and 200 of the Agriculture and Markets Law, Consol.Laws, c. 69, have no relevance here since those laws refer to food which has become unfit because of adulteration, decomposition, etc.

The judgment should be modified by reinstating the infant's recovery and, as so modified, affirmed, with costs to the plaintiffs in this court and in the Appellate Division.

FROESSEL, J. (concurring).

I concur for modification here, but limited to the facts of this case. The infant plaintiff asked for the food purchased, and it was but normal that the father, who was in any event liable for her necessaries, should make the purchase on behalf of both (see Bowman v. Great A. & P. Tea Co., 308 N.Y. 780, 125 N.E.2d 165).

The Chief Judge has clearly and succinctly stated the problem before us, and has reviewed the applicable authorities. This is an action in contract based on a statute (Personal Property Law, § 96), not for negligence, and it is basic law that unless privity exists there can be no warranty, and where there is no warranty there can be no breach. We may not convert an action in contract into what really amounts to an action in tort.

However much one may think liability should be broadened, that must be left to the Legislature. There are two sides to the problem before us—and one of them is the plight of the seller. It is just as unfair to hold liable a retail groceryman, as here, who is innocent of any negligence or wrong, on the theory of breach of warranty, for some defect in a canned product which he could not inspect and with the production of which he had nothing to do, as it is to deny relief to one who has no relationship to the contract of purchase and sale, though eating at the purchaser's table. As Justice Steuer aptly observed at the Appellate Term, "it may be odd that the purchaser can recover while others cannot, but it is odder still that one without fault has to pay at all". [12 Misc.2d 883, 178 N.Y.S.2d 414]. This distinguishes these cases from situations such as presented in Woods v. Lancet, 303 N.Y. 349, 102 N.E.2d 691, 27 A.L.R.2d 1250 and Bing v. Thunig, 2 N.Y.2d 656, 163 N.Y.S.2d 3, 143 N.E.2d 3, where the defendant has clearly committed a wrong.

It is for the Legislature to determine the policy of accommodating those conflicting interests after affording all concerned an opportunity to be heard. Indeed, the Legislature has not been unaware of the problem for, in three separate years—1943, 1945, 1959—as noted by the Chief Judge, the New York State Law Revision Commission recommended that the benefits of implied warranties be extended to the buyer's employees and to the members of his household, but the Legislature has declined to act, despite the introduction of legislation. I do not think we should now assume their powers and change the rules, which will undoubtedly affect many cases in which lawyers and litigants understood the law to be otherwise, and governed themselves accordingly.

DYE, FULD, VAN VOORHIS, BURKE and FOSTER, JJ., concur with DESMOND, C. J.

FROESSEL, J., concurs in result in a separate opinion.

Judgment accordingly.

RANDY KNITWEAR, INC. v. AMERICAN CYANAMID CO.

Court of Appeals of New York, 1962.
11 N.Y.2d 5, 226 N.Y.S.2d 363, 181 N.E.2d 399.

FULD, Judge.

"The assault upon the citadel of privity", Chief Judge Cardozo wrote in 1931, "is proceeding in these days apace." (Ultramares

Sec. 3   TECHNIQUE OF CASE LAW DEVELOPMENT   195

Corp. v. Touche, 255 N.Y. 170, 180, 174 N.E. 441, 445, 74 A.L.R. 1139.) In these days, too, for the present appeal, here by leave of the Appellate Division on a certified question, calls upon us to decide whether, under the facts disclosed, privity of contract is essential to maintenance of an action against a manufacturer for breach of express warranty.

American Cyanamid Company is the manufacturer of chemical resins, marketed under the registered trade-mark "Cyana", which are used by textile manufacturers and finishers to process fabrics in order to prevent them from shrinking. Apex Knitted Fabrics and Fairtex Mills are manufacturers of fabrics who were licensed or otherwise authorized by Cyanamid to treat their goods with "Cyana" and to sell such goods under the "Cyana" label and, with the guaranty that they were "Cyana" finished. Randy Knitwear, a manufacturer of children's knitted sportswear and play clothes, purchased large quantities of these "Cyana" treated fabrics from Apex and Fairtex. After most of such fabrics had been made up into garments and sold by Randy to customers, it was claimed that ordinary washing caused them to shrink and to lose their shape. This action for breach of express warranty followed, each of the 3 parties being made the subject of a separate count. After serving its answer, Cyanamid, urging lack of privity of contract, moved for summary judgment dismissing the cause of action asserted against it, and it is solely with this cause of action that we are concerned.[41]

Insofar as relevant, the complaint alleges that Cyanamid "represented" and "warranted" that the "Cyana" finished fabrics sold by Fairtex and Apex to the plaintiff would not shrink or lose their shape when washed and that the plaintiff purchased the fabrics and agreed to pay the additional charge for the cost involved in rendering them shrink-proof "in reliance upon" Cyanamid's representations. However, the complaint continues, the fabrics were not as represented since, when manufactured into garments and subjected to ordinary washing, they shrank and failed to hold their shape. The damages suffered are alleged to be over $208,000.

According to the complaint and the affidavits submitted in opposition to Cyanamid's motion, the representations relied upon by the plaintiff took the form of written statements expressed not only in numerous advertisements appearing in trade journals and in direct

---

41. We previously had before us an appeal involving the defendant Fairtex's motion for summary judgment in which it attacked the cause of action directed against it. The Appellate Division agreed with Fairtex's contention that it had, in its contract with the plaintiff, effectively disclaimed any and all warranties and representations and granted summary judgment dismissing the cause of action (7 A.D.2d 116, 180 N.Y.S.2d 471). We reversed that judgment on the ground that issues of fact were raised which required a trial (7 N.Y.2d 791, 194 N.Y.S.2d 530, 163 N.E.2d 349).

mail pieces to clothing manufacturers, but also in labels or garment tags furnished by Cyanamid. These labels bore the legend,

"A
CYANA
FINISH
This Fabric Treated for
SHRINKAGE
CONTROL
Will Not Shrink or
Stretch Out of Fit
CYANAMID",

and were issued to fabric manufacturers using the "Cyana Finish" only after Cyanamid had tested samples of the fabrics and approved them. Cyanamid delivered a large number of these labels to Fairtex and Apex and they, with Cyanamid's knowledge and approval, passed them on to garment manufacturers, including the plaintiff, so that they might attach them to the clothing which they manufactured from the fabrics purchased.

As noted, Cyanamid moved for summary judgment dismissing the complaint against it on the ground that there was no privity of contract to support the plaintiff's action. The court at Special Term denied the motion and the Appellate Division unanimously affirmed the resulting order.

Thirty-nine years ago, in Chysky v. Drake Bros. Co., 235 N.Y. 468, 139 N.E. 576, 27 A.L.R. 1533, this court decided that an action for breach of implied warranty could not succeed, absent privity between plaintiff and defendant and, some time later, in Turner v. Edison Storage Battery Co., 248 N.Y. 73, 161 N.E. 423, we reached a similar conclusion with respect to express warranties, writing, "There can be no warranty where there is no privity of contract" (p. 74, 161 N.E. p. 424).[42] This traditional privity limitation on a sell-

---

42. These decisions proceed, manifestly, from a characterization of the breach of warranty action as one essentially *contractual* in nature. The soundness of this characterization becomes highly questionable, however, when the problem is seen against the backdrop of legal history. The action for breach of warranty "was, in its origin, a pure action of tort". (Ames, Lectures on Legal History [1913], p. 136, reprinted, with revisions, from 2 Harv.L.Rev. 1, 8; see, also, 1 Williston, Sales [rev. ed., 1948], § 195, pp. 501–502; Prosser, Torts [2d ed., 1955], § 83, p. 493.) Indeed, the earliest reported case upon a warranty arose in 1383 (Fitz. Abr. Monst. de Faits, pl. 160; see Ames, Lectures on Legal History [1913], p. 136), a century before special assumpsit found its place among the forms of action. And it was not until 1778 that the first decision was reported in which an action on a warranty was brought in assumpsit. (Stuart v. Wilkins, 1 Dougl. 18; see Ames, Lectures on Legal History [1913], p. 137.) Accordingly, for some 400 years the action rested not on an enforceable promise but on a wrong or tort. In the historical development of the law of warranty, however, as so often happens in law and life in general, accident was evidently confused with essence: from the fact that the cases which arose involved contractual relationships and represented enforceable promises, the courts seem to have concluded that

Sec. 3   TECHNIQUE OF CASE LAW DEVELOPMENT   197

er's liability for damage resulting from breach of warranty has not, however, been adhered to with perfect logical consistency (see e. g., Ryan v. Progressive Grocery Stores, 255 N.Y. 388, 175 N.E. 105, 74 A.L.R. 339; Bowman v. Great A. & P. Tea Co., 308 N.Y. 780, 125 N. E.2d 165; Mouren v. Great A. & P. Tea Co., 1 N.Y.2d 884, 154 N.Y. S.2d 642, 136 N.E.2d 715) and, just a year ago, in Greenberg v. Lorenz, 9 N.Y.2d 195, 213 N.Y.S.2d 39, 173 N.E.2d 773, we noted the definite shift away from the technical privity requirement and recognized that it should be dispensed with in a proper case in the interest of justice and reason. More specifically, we held in Greenberg that, in cases involving foodstuffs and other household goods, the implied warranties of fitness and merchantability run from the retailer to the members of the purchaser's household, regardless of privity of contract. We are now confronted with the further but related question whether the traditional privity limitation shall also be dispensed with in an action for breach of express warranty by a remote purchaser against a manufacturer who induced the purchase by representing the quality of the goods in public advertising and on labels which accompanied the goods.

It was in this precise type of case, where express representations were made by a manufacturer to induce reliance by remote purchasers, that "the citadel of privity" was successfully breached in the State of Washington in 1932. (See Baxter v. Ford Motor Co., 168 Wash. 456, 12 P.2d 409, 15 P.2d 1118, 88 A.L.R. 521; same case after new trial, 179 Wash. 123, 35 P.2d 1090.) It was the holding in the Baxter case that the manufacturer was liable for breach of express warranty to one who purchased an automobile from a retailer since such purchaser had a right to rely on representations made by the manufacturer in its sales literature, even though there was no privity of contract between them. And in the 30 years which have passed since that decision, not only have the courts throughout the country shown a marked, and almost uniform, tendency to discard the privity limitation and hold the manufacturer strictly accountable for the truthfulness of representations made to the public and relied upon by the plaintiff in making his purchase, but the vast majority of the authoritative commentators have applauded the trend and approved the result.

The rationale underlying the decisions rejecting the privity requirement is easily understood in the light of present-day commercial practices. It may once have been true that the warranty which really induced the sale was normally an actual term of the contract of sale. Today, however, the significant warranty, the one which effectively induces the purchase, is frequently that given by the manufac-

the contract was of the essence of the action. (See Prosser, Torts [2d ed., 1955], § 84, p. 507.) The occa-   sion for the warranty was constituted a necessary condition of it.

turer through mass advertising and labeling to ultimate business users or to consumers with whom he has no direct contractual relationship.

The world of merchandising is, in brief, no longer a world of direct contract; it is, rather, a world of advertising and, when representations expressed and disseminated in the mass communications media and on labels (attached to the goods themselves) prove false and the user or consumer is damaged by reason of his reliance on those representations, it is difficult to justify the manufacturer's denial of liability on the sole ground of the absence of technical privity. Manufacturers make extensive use of newspapers, periodicals and other media to call attention, in glowing terms, to the qualities and virtues of their products, and this advertising is directed at the ultimate consumer or at some manufacturer or supplier who is not in privity with them. Equally sanguine representations on packages and labels frequently accompany the article throughout its journey to the ultimate consumer and, as intended, are relied upon by remote purchasers. Under these circumstances, it is highly unrealistic to limit a purchaser's protection to warranties made directly to him by his immediate seller. The protection he really needs is against the manufacturer whose published representations caused him to make the purchase.

The policy of protecting the public from injury, physical or pecuniary, resulting from misrepresentations outweighs allegiance to an old and out-moded technical rule of law which, if observed, might be productive of great injustice. The manufacturer places his product upon the market and, by advertising and labeling it, represents its quality to the public in such a way as to induce reliance upon his representations. He unquestionably intends and expects that the product will be purchased and used in reliance upon his express assurance of its quality and, in fact, it is so purchased and used. Having invited and solicited the use, the manufacturer should not be permitted to avoid responsibility, when the expected use leads to injury and loss, by claiming that he made no contract directly with the user.

It is true that in many cases the manufacturer will ultimately be held accountable for the falsity of his representations, but only after an unduly wasteful process of litigation. Thus, if the consumer or ultimate business user sues and recovers, for breach of warranty, from his immediate seller and if the latter in turn, sues and recovers against his supplier in recoupment of his damages and costs, eventually, after several separate actions by those in the chain of distribution, the manufacturer may finally be obliged "to shoulder the responsibility which should have been his in the first instance." (Hamon v. Digliani, 148 Conn. 710, 717, 174 A.2d 294, 297; see Kasler & Cohen v. Slavouski [1928], 1 K.B. 78, where there was a series of 5 recoveries, the manufacturer ultimately paying the consumer's damages, plus a much larger sum covering the costs of the entire

Sec. 3   TECHNIQUE OF CASE LAW DEVELOPMENT   199

litigation.) As is manifest, and as Dean Prosser observes, this circuity of action is "an expensive, time-consuming and wasteful process, and it may be interrupted by insolvency, lack of jurisdiction, disclaimers, or the statute of limitations". (Prosser, The Assault upon the Citadel [Strict Liability to the Consumer], 69 Yale L.J. 1099, 1124.)

Indeed, and it points up the injustice of the rule, insistence upon the privity requirement may well leave the aggrieved party, whether he be ultimate business user or consumer, without a remedy in a number of situations. For instance, he would be remediless either where his immediate seller's representations as to quality were less extravagant or enthusiastic than those of the manufacturer [43] or where—as is asserted by Fairtex in this very case (7 N.Y.2d 791, 194 N.Y.S.2d 530, 163 N.E.2d 349; see, also, supra, 11 N.Y.2d p. 9, n. 1, 226 N.Y.S.2d 365, 181 N.E.2d 400)—there has been an effective disclaimer of any and all warranties by the plaintiff's immediate seller. Turning to the case before us, even if the representations respecting "Cyana" treated fabric were false, the plaintiff would be foreclosed of all remedy against Fairtex, if it were to succeed on its defense of disclaimer, and against Cyanamid because of a lack of privity. (Cf. Baxter v. Ford Motor Co., 168 Wash. 456, 12 P.2d 409, 15 P.2d 1118, 88 A.L.R. 521; same case, 179 Wash. 123, 35 P.2d 1090, supra.)

Although we believe that it has already been made clear, it is to be particularly remarked that in the present case the plaintiff's reliance is not on newspaper advertisements alone. It places heavy emphasis on the fact that the defendant not only made representations (as to the nonshrinkable character of "Cyana Finish" fabrics) in newspapers and periodicals, but also repeated them on its own labels and tags which accompanied the fabrics purchased by the plaintiff from Fairtex and Apex. There is little in reason or logic to support Cyanamid's submission that it should not be held liable to the plaintiff even though the representations prove false in fact and it is ultimately found that the plaintiff relied to its harm upon such representations in making its purchases.

We perceive no warrant for holding—as the appellant urges—that strict liability should not here be imposed because the defect involved, fabric shrinkage, is not likely to cause personal harm or injury. Although there is language in some of the opinions which ap-

---

[43]. Typical of this would be a case where the consumer, relying on representations contained on labels or in advertisements for which the manufacturer is responsible, purchases a brand-name article from the shelves of the retailer. In such a case, the retailer ordinarily makes no express warranty and the purchaser may not even invoke an implied warranty of fitness. (Personal Property Law, Consol.Laws c. 41, § 96, subd. 4). Consequently, if privity were prerequisite to an action by the consumer against the manufacturer, whose representations induced his purchase, he would (absent proof of negligence) be denied all redress except, perhaps, for breach of the implied warranty of merchantability (Personal Property Law, § 96, subd. 2).

> liability turns not upon character of pdt. but upon the representation

pears to support Cyanamid's contention (see Worley v. Procter & Gamble Mfg. Co., 241 Mo.App. 1114, 1121, 253 S.W.2d 532; Dimoff v. Ernie Majer, Inc., 55 Wash.2d 385, 347 P.2d 1056; see, also, Laclede Steel Co. v. Silas Mason Co., D.C., 67 F.Supp. 751), most of the courts which have dispensed with the requirement of privity in this sort of case have not limited their decisions in this manner. (See, e. g., Burr v. Sherwin Williams Co., 42 Cal.2d 682, 696–697, 268 P.2d 1041 [insecticide; damage to crops]; State Farm Mut. Auto Ins. Co. v. Anderson-Weber, Inc., 110 N.W.2d 449 [Iowa], [automobile; property damage]; Graham v. John R. Watts & Son, 238 Ky. 96, 36 S.W.2d 859 [mislabeled seed; wrong crop]; Silberman v. Samuel Mallinger Co., 375 Pa. 422, 428–429, 100 A.2d 715 [glass jars; commercial loss]; United States Pipe & Foundry Co. v. City of Waco, 130 Tex. 126, 108 S.W.2d 432, cert. den. 302 U.S. 749, 58 S.Ct. 266, 82 L.Ed. 579 [cast iron pipes; property damage].) And this makes sense. Since the basis of liability turns not upon the character of the product but upon the representation, there is no justification for a distinction on the basis of the type of injury suffered or the type of article or goods involved.

We are also agreed that the present case may not be distinguished, and liability denied, on the ground that the article sold by the appellant, *resin*, is different from that purchased by the plaintiff, *fabric*. To be sure, as Cyanamid urges, the failure to render the fabric shrink-proof may rest with Fairtex and Apex, but the short and simple answer is that Cyanamid actually and expressly represented that fabrics accompanied by the labels which it supplied were "Cyana Finish" and would not shrink or lose their shape. Since it made such representations, Cyanamid may not disclaim responsibility for them. If the ultimate fault for the plaintiff's loss is actually that of Fairtex and Apex, Cyanamid's appropriate recourse is against them.

Nor may it be urged that section 93 of the Personal Property Law renders privity of contract necessary. The Legislature has there defined a warranty as an "affirmation" (or "promise") made by a seller, but the section nowhere states that liability for breach of express warranty extends only to the warranting seller's immediate buyer and cannot extend to a later buyer who made the purchase from an intermediate seller but in foreseeable and natural reliance on the original seller's affirmations. Indeed, we made the matter clear in Greenberg v. Lorenz when, after observing that the rule requiring a direct contractual relationship between the plaintiff and the defendant is of "judicial making", we went on to say, "our statutes say nothing at all about privity" (9 N.Y.2d 195, 200, 213 N.Y.S.2d 39, 42, 173 N.E.2d 773, 775).

In concluding that the old court-made rule should be modified to dispense with the requirement of privity, we are doing nothing more or less than carrying out an historic and necessary function of the court to bring the law into harmony "with modern-day needs and with concepts of justice and fair dealing." (Bing v. Thunig, 2 N.Y. 2d 656, 667, 163 N.Y.S.2d 3, 11, 143 N.E.2d 3, 9; see Greenberg v. Lorenz, 9 N.Y.2d 195, 200, 213 N.Y.S.2d 39, 42, 173 N.E.2d 773, 775, supra; Woods v. Lancet, 303 N.Y. 349, 355, 102 N.E.2d 691, 694, 27 A.L.R.2d 1250.)

The order appealed from should be affirmed, with costs, and the question certified answered in the negative.

FROESSEL, Judge (concurring).

We concur in result only. We agree with Judge FULD that defendant, American Cyanamid Company, may be held liable for its express representations (as to the nonshrinkable character of "Cyana Finish" fabrics) in newspapers and periodicals where they have been repeated on its own labels and tags delivered by Cyanamid to fabric manufacturers such as Fairtex and Apex, to be passed on to garment manufacturers such as plaintiff, so that they might attach them to the clothing cut from the fabrics purchased, all allegedly with Cyanamid's knowledge and authorization.

We do not agree that the so-called "old court-made rule" should be modified to dispense with the requirement of privity without limitation. We decide cases as they arise, and would affirm in this case under the facts here disclosed.

DESMOND, C. J., and BURKE and FOSTER, JJ., concur with FULD, J.

FROESSEL, J., concurs in result only in a separate opinion in which DYE and VAN VOORHIS, JJ., concur.

Order affirmed, etc.

NOTES

1. The early 1960's were a period of rapid development in the law of product liability. Implied warranties were held to run to persons not in privity with the manufacturer of many products other than food or items intended for bodily use. E. g., Henningsen v. Bloomfield Motors, Inc., 32 N.J. 358, 161 A.2d 69 (1960). And, in Greenman v. Yuba Power Products Inc., 59 Cal.2d 57, 27 Cal.Rptr. 697, 377 P.2d 897 (1962) the California Supreme Court discarded the warranty theory and imposed "strict liability in tort" on the manufacturer of a combination power tool used in a home workshop by the husband of the purchaser.

2. Under a breach of warranty, or strict liability theory, it does not matter whether a product was negligently manufactured; the question is whether it is "defective." What constitutes a defect? In the Greenman v. Yuba Power case cited in Note 1, liability is said to attach in cases of defective manufacture or design. What constitutes a defective design?

3. Consider whether the rule announced in these cases applies to persons not using the product who are injured as a result of the defect; or to non-consumer products.

GOLDBERG v. KOLLSMAN INSTRUMENT CORP.

Court of Appeals of New York, 1963.

12 N.Y.2d 432, 240 N.Y.S. 592, 191 N.E.2d 81.

DESMOND, Chief Judge.

We granted leave to appeal in order to take another step toward a complete solution of the problem partially cleared up in Greenberg v. Lorenz, 9 N.Y.2d 195, 213 N.Y.S.2d 39, 173 N.E.2d 773 and Randy Knitwear, Inc. v. American Cyanamid Co., 11 N.Y.2d 5, 226 N.Y.S.2d 363, 181 N.E.2d 399 (both decided after the making of the Special Term and Appellate Division orders here appealed from). The question now to be answered is: does a manufacturer's implied warranty of fitness of his product for its contemplated use run in favor of all its intended users, despite lack of privity of contract?

The suit is by an administratrix for damages for the death of her daughter-intestate as the result of injuries suffered in the crash near La Guardia Airport, New York City, of an airplane in which the daughter was a fare-paying passenger on a flight from Chicago to New York. American Airlines, Inc., owner and operator of the plane, is sued here for negligence (with present respondents Lockheed and Kollsman) but that cause of action is not the subject of this appeal. The two causes of action, from the dismissal of which for insufficiency plaintiff appeals to us, run against Kollsman Instrument Corporation, manufacturer or supplier of the plane's altimeter, and Lockheed Aircraft Corporation, maker of the plane itself. Kollsman and Lockheed are charged with breaching their respective implied warranties of merchantability and fitness. Those breaches, it is alleged, caused the fatal crash.

There is nothing in the complaint that says where the plane or its altimeter were manufactured or sold nor does the pleading inform us as to decedent's place of residence, although it is alleged that plaintiff's appointment as administratrix was by a New York court. Plaintiff argues that California law should apply on the "grouping of contracts" theory and it is clear (indeed in effect conceded by respondents) that California law allows recovery for a proven breach of implied warranties as to dangerous instrumentalities (see Peterson v. Lamb Rubber Co., 54 Cal.2d 339, 347, 5 Cal.Rptr. 863, 353 P.2d 575; Greenman v. Yuba Power Prods., Inc., 59 Cal.2d 67, 27 Cal. Rptr. 697, 377 P.2d 897). Special Term, however, said in its opinion in the present case that the governing law is that of New York State where the accident took place, citing Poplar v. Bourjois, Inc., 298 N. Y. 62, 80 N.E.2d 334 and that under New York law no claim for breach of implied warranty may be enforced by one not in privity with the warrantor. The Appellate Division, affirming, wrote no opinion. The Special Term opinion, as we have said above, was filed before our Greenberg and Randy Knitwear decisions (supra) and

Sec. 3 TECHNIQUE OF CASE LAW DEVELOPMENT 203

Greenberg and Randy Knitwear declared that in New York privity of contract is not always a requisite for breach of warranty recoveries. The Randy Knitwear opinion (11 N.Y.2d p. 16, 226 N.Y.S.2d p. 370, 181 N.E.2d p. 404) at least suggested that all requirements of privity have been dispensed with in our State. That is the immediate, or at least the logical and necessary result of our decisions and, accordingly, it really makes no difference whether New York or California law be applied, since in this respect both States use the same rules.

The enormous literature on this subject and the historical development of the law of warranties to its present state need not be reviewed beyond the references in our Greenberg and Randy Knitwear opinions (supra). A breach of warranty, it is now clear, is not only a violation of the sales contract out of which the warranty arises but is a tortious wrong suable by a noncontracting party whose use of the warranted article is within the reasonable contemplation of the vendor or manufacturer. As to foodstuffs we definitively ruled in Greenberg v. Lorenz, 9 N.Y.2d 195, supra, 213 N.Y.S.2d 39, 173 N.E.2d 773, that the persons thus protected and eligible to sue include the purchaser's family. We went no further in that case because the facts required no farther reach of the rule.

The concept that as to "things of danger" the manufacturer must answer to intended users for faulty design or manufacture is an old one in this State. The most famous decision is MacPherson v. Buick Motor Co., 217 N.Y. 382, 111 N.E. 1050, L.R.A.1916F, 696, holding the manufacturer liable in negligence to one who purchased a faulty Buick automobile from a dealer (see the recent and similar case of Markel v. Spencer, 5 A.D.2d 400, 171 N.Y.S.2d 770, affd. 5 N.Y.2d 958, 184 N.Y.S.2d 835, 157 N.E.2d 713). But the MacPherson opinion cites much older cases such as Devlin v. Smith, 89 N.Y. 470 [1882], where one who negligently built a scaffold for a contractor was adjudged liable to the contractor's injured employee. MacPherson and its successors dispelled the idea that a manufacturer was immune from liability in tort for violation of his duty to make his manufactures fit and safe. In MacPherson's day enforcement required a suit in negligence. Today, we know from Greenberg v. Lorenz; Randy Knitwear, Inc. v. American Cyanamid Co. (supra) and many another decision in this and other States (see, for instance, Henningsen v. Bloomfield Motors, Inc., 32 N.J. 358, 161 A.2d 69, 75 A.L.R.2d 1, and Thomas v. Leary, 15 A.D.2d 438, 225 N.Y.S.2d 137) that, at least where an article is of such a character that when used for the purpose for which it is made it is likely to be a source of danger to several or many people if not properly designed and fashioned, the manufacturer as well as the vendor is liable, for breach of law-implied warranties, to the persons whose use is contemplated. The MacPherson holding was an "extension" of existing court-made liability law. In a sense, Greenberg v. Lorenz and Randy Knitwear, Inc. v. American Cyanamid Co. (supra) were extensions in favor of noncontracting consumers. But it is no extension at all to include airplanes and the passengers for whose use they are built—and, indeed, decisions are at hand which have upheld complaints, sounding in breach of warranty, against manufacturers of aircraft where passengers lost their lives when the planes crashed (see, e. g., Conlon v. Republic Aviation Corp., D.C., 204 F.Supp. 865; Middleton v. United Aircraft Corp., D.C., 204 F.Supp. 856; Ewing v. Lockheed Aircraft Corp., D.C., 202 F.Supp. 216; Hinton v. Republic Aviation Corp., D. C., 180 F.Supp. 31).

As we all know, a number of courts outside New York State have for the best of reasons dispensed with the privity requirement (see Jaeger, Privity of Warranty: Has the Tocsin Sounded?, 1 Duquesne U.L.Rev. 1). Very recently the Supreme Court of California (Greenman v. Yuba Power Prods., Inc., 59 Cal.2d 67, 27 Cal.Rptr. 697, 377 P.2d 897 [1963], supra) in a unanimous opinion imposed "strict tort liability" (surely a more accurate phrase) regardless of privity on a manufacturer in a case where a power tool threw a piece of wood at a user who was not the purchaser. The California court said that the purpose of such a holding is to see to it that the costs of injuries resulting from defective products are borne by the manufacturers who put the products on the market rather than by injured persons who are powerless to protect themselves and that implicit in putting such articles on the market are representations that they will safely do the job for which they were built. However, for the present at least we do not think it necessary so to extend this rule as to hold liable the manufacturer (defendant Kollsman) of a component part. Adequate protection is provided for the passengers by casting in liability the airplane manufacturer which put into the market the completed aircraft.

The judgment appealed from should be modified, without costs, so as to provide for the dismissal of the third (Kollsman) cause of action only and, as so modified, affirmed.

BURKE, Judge (dissenting). We dissent.

If this were a case in which a manufacturer made express representations concerning the quality of its product calculated to promote its sale or use by persons in the plaintiff's position, our decision in Randy Knitwear, Inc. v. American Cyanamid Co., 11 N.Y.2d 5, 226 N.Y.S.2d 363, 181 N.E.2d 399, would allow a recovery. If it were a case where a defendant sold a food or other household product to a member of a family, the warranty incident thereto would extend to all for whose consumption or use the product was obviously purchased. (Greenberg v. Lorenz, 9 N.Y.2d 195, 213 N.Y.S.2d 39, 173 N.E.2d 773; Greenman v. Yuba Power Prods., Inc., 59 Cal.2d 67, 27 Cal.Rptr. 697, 377 P.2d 897). The conclusion reached by the majority might be correct even if the defective product were sold to an employer for the use of his employees. (Thomas v. Leary, 15 A.D.2d

Sec. 3   TECHNIQUE OF CASE LAW DEVELOPMENT   205

438, 225 N.Y.S.2d 137; Peterson v. Lamb Rubber Co., 54 Cal.2d 339, 5 Cal.Rptr. 863, 353 P.2d 575.) This, however, is none of those cases. The conditions present in those cases are entirely different. There the manufacturer knew that the article he made was not to be inspected thereafter. Here Federal regulations provide for rigorous inspection and certification from the Federal Aviation Agency. There the risk of loss was a trap for the unwary. Here all are aware of the hazards attending air travel and accident and special insurance is readily available at moderate rates. Plaintiff [44] is a purchaser of a service from an airline seeking to assert a warranty cause of action against Lockheed, the assembler of an airplane, and Kollsman, the manufacturer of an allegedly defective component part thereof. In such a situation we see no satisfactory basis on which to uphold against Lockheed a cause of action not grounded in negligence, while disallowing it against the manufacturer of an alleged defective part.

First, we do not find a cause of action stated under the implied warranty provisions of section 96 of the Personal Property Law, Consol.Laws, c. 41. Plaintiff purchased no goods; she entered into a contract of carriage with American Airlines. By a long line of cases in this court, the most recent being Kilberg v. Northeast Airlines, Inc., 9 N.Y.2d 34, 211 N.Y.S.2d 133, 172 N.E.2d 526, it is settled that the measure of American Airlines' duty towards plaintiff was an undertaking of reasonably safe carriage. This duty is, of course, discharged by the use of due care. Crucial is the fact that this duty would be unaffected if American assembled its own planes, even if they contained a latent defect. Why, then, should plaintiff's rights be any greater simply because American chose to contract this work out instead of doing it itself? Absent some equity of direct reliance on the advertised representations of one of the manufacturers, which might invoke the reasoning of Randy Knitwear, Inc. v. American Cyanamid Co., 11 N.Y.2d 5, 226 N.Y.S.2d 363, 181 N.E.2d 399, supra, it is no concern of plaintiff how the person with whom she dealt, American, subdivided its responsibility of furnishing the machines and services in discharge of its undertaking of safe carriage.

Of course, plaintiff's right to due care cannot be diminished by American's delegating certain tasks to others. What would be actionable negligence if done by American is not less so because done by another; such a person may be sued by plaintiff, and so may American if the negligence was discoverable by it. By the same token, however, plaintiff's primary right to care from American (and, indeed, all whose actions foreseeably affect her) should not be enlarged to insurance protection simply because American chose to have a certain task performed by another. We note that the argument made in some cases based on the avoidance of a multiplicity of actions is inap-

   44. Edith Feis, for whose death this action is brought, will be referred to herein as plaintiff.

plicable here. In such cases, the plaintiff himself is the recipient of a warranty incident to the sale of goods and if the defect is in the manufacture it is at least reasonable to suggest a procedure by which liability may be imposed by the person entitled to the recovery directly against the one who, through a chain of warranties, is ultimately liable. Here, however, plaintiff (or her family, etc.) was not sold the chattel which caused her injury and hence there is no warranty.

It is true we have extended the benefit of an implied warranty beyond the immediate purchaser to those who could be fairly called indirect vendees of the product. (Greenberg v. Lorenz, 9 N.Y.2d 195, 213 N.Y.S.2d 39, 173 N.E.2d 773, supra.) Without stressing the weakness of the analogy that plaintiff here is the indirect vendee of the airplane and its parts, or the effect of the interposition between plaintiff and defendants of a federally regulated service industry of dominant economic and legal significance, it must be recognized that the true grounds of decision in a case of this sort lie outside the purpose and policy of the Sales Act and must be evaluated accordingly. Most scholars who have considered this question acknowledge that the warranty rationale is at best a useful fiction. (See, e. g., Prosser, The Assault upon the Citadel [Strict Liability to the Consumer], 69 Yale L.J. 1099; James, Products Liability, 34 Tex.L.Rev. 192.) If a strict products or enterprise liability is to be imposed here, this court cannot escape the responsibility of justifying it. We cannot accept the implication of the majority that the difference between warranty and strict products liability is merely one of phrasing.

Inherent in the question of strict products or enterprise liability is the question of the proper enterprise on which to fasten it. Here the majority have imposed this burden on the assembler of the finished product, Lockheed. The principle of selection stated is that the injured passenger needs no more protection. We suggest that this approach to the identification of an appropriate defendant does not answer the question: Which enterprise should be selected if the selection is to be in accord with the rationale upon which the doctrine of strict products liability rests?

The purpose of such liability is not to regulate conduct with a view to eliminating accidents,[45] but rather to remove the economic consequences of accidents from the victim who is unprepared to bear them and place the risk on the enterprise in the course of whose business they arise. The risk, it is said, becomes part of the cost of doing business and can be effectively distributed among the public through

---

45. In view of the ease with which lack of care can be brought to light through devices such as *res ipsa loquitur*, any marginal increase in the stimulus to care would be clearly outweighed by the harshness of the means used to achieve it—the removal of due care as a defense. Prosser, The Assault upon the Citadel (Strict Liability to the Consumer). 69 Yale L.J. 1099, 1119. Apparently the majority agree since Kollsman, the actual manufacturer of the chattel that allegedly caused the accident, is not held liable.

insurance or by a direct reflection in the price of the goods or service. As applied to this case we think the enterprise to which accidents such as the present are incident is the carriage of passengers by air— American Airlines. The fact that this accident was due to a defective altimeter should be of no legal significance to plaintiff absent some fault (negligence) on the part of Kollsman or Lockheed. Here, the dominant enterprise and the one with which plaintiff did business and relied upon was the airline.

If the carrier which immediately profited from plaintiff's custom is the proper party on which to fasten whatever enterprise liability the social conscience demands, enterprises which supply the devices with which the carrier conducts its business should not be subject to an action based on this theory. This seems most persuasive where the business that deals directly with the public is not merely a conduit for the distribution of the manufacturer's consumer goods but assumes the responsibility of selecting and using those goods itself as a capital asset in the conduct of a service enterprise such as common carriage. In such a case the relationship between the assembler of these goods and the air traveller is minimal as compared to that obtaining between the traveller and the carrier. In a theory of liability based, not on the regulation of conduct, but on economic considerations of distributing the risk of accidents that occur through no one's neglect, the enterprise most strategically placed to perform this function—the carrier, rather than the enterprise that supplies an assembled chattel thereto, is the logical subject of the liability, if liability there is to be.

Whatever conclusions may flow from the fact that the accident was caused by a defective altimeter should be merged in whatever responsibility the law may place on the airline with which plaintiff did business. To extend warranty law to allow plaintiff to select a defendant from a multiplicity of enterprises in a case such as this would not comport with the rationale of enterprise liability and would only have the effect of destroying whatever rights that exist among the potential defendants by virtue of agreement among themselves. If, on the other hand, plaintiff's maximum rights lie against the carrier, the rules of warranty can perform their real function of adjusting the rights of the parties to the agreements through which the airline acquired the chattel that caused the accident. If, as we maintain in this case, the true theory relied on by plaintiff is enterprise liability, then the rights of those from whom compensation is sought, no less than of those who seek it, "ought not to be made to depend upon the intricacies of the law of sales." (Ketterer v. Armour & Co., 2 Cir., 200 F. 322, 323.)

We are therefore of the opinion that any claim in respect of an airplane accident that is grounded in strict enterprise liability should be fixed on the airline or none at all. Only in this way do we meet and resolve, one way or another, the anomaly presented by the reasoning of the majority, which, through reliance on warranty incident to sales, grants a recovery to a passenger injured through a nonnegligent failure of equipment but denies it to one injured through a nonnegligent failure of maintenance or operation.

Although no such claim is raised by the pleadings, as we stated earlier, it is clear that our cases limit the airline's duty to that of due care. (McPadden v. New York Cent. R. R. Co., 44 N.Y. 478; Stierle v. Union Ry. Co., 156 N.Y. 70, 50 N.E. 419; Williams v. Long Island R. R. Co., 294 N.Y. 318, 62 N.E.2d 212; Kilberg v. Northeast Airlines, Inc., 9 N.Y.2d 34, 211 N.Y.S.2d 133, 172 N.E.2d 526, supra.) It is this rule, avowedly formed to deal with the problem of accidents, that must be reevaluated by those who would support the theory of strict enterprise liability. A stricter rule is not without precedent in this court (Alden v. New York Cent. R. R. Co., 26 N.Y. 102, holding that the carrier "must be held accountable, in every event, to furnish a road-worthy coach; and that, if the event proved it not to have been so, he must suffer the consequences" [26 N.Y. p. 104]; see, also, cases collected in McLean v. Triboro Coach Corp., 302 N.Y. 49, 96 N. E.2d 83). However, as long as our law holds a carrier chargeable only with negligence, what part of reason is it to hold to a greater duty an enterprise which supplied an assembled aircraft which was certified for commercial service by the Federal Aviation Agency?

Our reluctance to hold an air carrier to strict liability for the inevitable toll of injury incident to its enterprise is only the counsel of prudence. Aside from the responsibility imposed on us to be slow to cast aside well-established law in deference to a theory of social planning that is still much in dispute (Prosser, Torts, [2d ed.] § 84; Patterson, The Apportionment of Business Risks through Legal Devices, 24 Colum.L.Rev. 335, 358; Pound, Introduction to the Philosophy of Law 100–104 [1954]), there remains the inquiry whether the facts fit the theory. It is easy, in a completely free economy, to envision the unimpeded distribution of risk by an enterprise on which it is imposed; but how well will such a scheme work in an industry which is closely regulated by Federal agencies? In consideration of international competition and other factors weighed by those responsible for rate regulation, how likely is it that rate scales will rise in reflection of increased liability? (See Pound, supra, pp. 102–103.) In turn, how likely is it that the additional risk will be effectively distributed as a cost of doing business? Such questions can be intelligently resolved only by analysis of facts and figures compiled after hearings in which all interested groups have an opportunity to present economic arguments. These matters, which are the factual cornerstones supporting the theory adopted by the majority, aside from our view that they apply it to the wrong enterprise, are classically within the special competence of the Legislature to ascertain. For a court to assume them in order to support a theory that displaces much of the law of negligence from its ancestral environment involves an omniscience not shared by us. For a court to apply them, not to the enterprise with which plaintiff dealt and relied upon, or to the enterprise which manufactured the alleged defective part, but to the assembler of the aircraft used by the carrier, involves a principle of selection which is purely arbitrary.

DYE, FULD and FOSTER, JJ., concur with DESMOND, C. J.

BURKE, J., dissents in an opinion in which VAN VOORHIS and SCILEPPI, JJ., concur.

Judgment modified in accordance with the opinion herein and, as so modified, affirmed, without costs.

NOTES

1. Is anything left of the privity requirement in New York after the *Goldberg* decision? Does the case apply only to a product which is "likely to be a source of danger to several or many people if not properly designed and fashioned?"

2. In Friend v. Childs Dining Hall, supra p. 175, the court rejected defendant's argument that plaintiff had not exercised due care in the following words: "Due care is not a term of the law of contract, but of torts. This is an action of contract." After *Goldberg*, would assumption of risk or contributory negligence by the plaintiff be a good defense to an action against a manufacturer?

3. In what circumstances would the manufacturer of a component part be liable?

CODLING v. PAGLIA

Court of Appeals of New York, 1973.
32 N.Y.2d 330, 345 N.Y.S.2d 461, 298 N.E.2d 622.

JONES, Judge.

We hold that today the manufacturer of a defective product may be held liable to an innocent bystander, without proof of negligence, for damages sustained in consequence of the defect.

On August 2, 1967, a clear, dry day, Christino Paglia was driving his Chrysler automobile southerly on Route 144 just south of Albany, when suddenly the vehicle crossed the solid double line into the northbound lane of traffic and collided head on with an automobile owned by Marcia Codling and being driven by her husband, Frank, in the opposite or northerly direction.

Paglia had purchased his 1967 Chrysler Newport Custom sedan about four months before the accident and had driven it just over 4,000 miles. At no time prior to the accident had he experienced any difficulty with its steering mechanism. At the time of the accident he was traveling at a speed of 45 to 50 miles per hour, when suddenly and unexplainably his vehicle started to drift over the double solid line into the northbound lane. There was evidence that Paglia neither blew his horn nor applied his brakes, although short skid marks were observed. The Codling vehicle, on the other hand, had slowed down and nearly stopped just before the collision.

In Action No. 1 Marcia Codling, owner and passenger, and Frank Codling, her husband and driver of the Codling vehicle, sued Paglia in negligence and Chrysler in negligence and breach of warranty, seeking recovery for personal injuries and medical expenses and loss of services; Paglia cross-claimed against Chrysler to recover over any judgment returned against him in favor of the Codlings. After the jury was drawn the Codlings settled their claims against Paglia on his payment of $50,000 to each of them, and Paglia's cross claim against Chrysler was severed and reserved for adjudication by the court after trial.

In Action No. 2 Paglia sued Chrysler in negligence and warranty for his own personal injuries and for property damage to his automobile.

The two cases proceeded to trial together. Over objections of Chrysler the trial court submitted two specific written questions to the jury, the first related to the negligence theory, and the second concerning the breach of warranty count:

"Did the defendant Chrysler Corporation negligently manufacture and assemble the Paglia automobile with a defective power assist steering system?"

"Did the defendant Chrysler Corporation breach its implied warranty of merchantability and fitness of the Paglia automobile?"

The court further charged the jury: "If the product is in fact defective * * * the manufacturer is liable to any person properly using the product and to persons not using the defective product who are innocent bystanders, for injury resulting from its defective and unfit condition." Chrysler also took exception to a charge that in Action No. 2 contributory negligence was not a defense to Paglia's action for personal injuries and property damage against Chrysler for breach of warranty.

By a vote of 10 to 2, the jury answered the first specific question submitted in the negative (i. e., made a finding of no negligence on the part of Chrysler) and the second question in the affirmative (i. e., made a finding of breach of warranty by Chrysler). In Action No. 1 the jury returned verdicts in favor of Frank Codling against Chrysler in the amount of $150,000, which after deduction of the $50,000 paid by Paglia resulted in a net verdict of $100,000; and in favor of Marcia Codling against Chrysler, in the amount of $200,000, which after deduction of the corresponding $50,000 paid by Paglia resulted in a net verdict of $150,000. Both verdicts were, of course, based on breach of warranty and not negligence. Following

Sec. 3   TECHNIQUE OF CASE LAW DEVELOPMENT   211

the trial, in Action No. 1 Paglia was granted summary judgment against Chrysler on his cross claim to recoup the $100,000 he had paid the Codlings.

In Action No. 2 the jury returned a verdict for Paglia, as plaintiff, in the amount of $15,000 to which was added, pursuant to stipulation, $2,760 for property damage suffered by him. Recovery here, too, was on the theory of breach of warranty. Again, we note that the jury found no negligence on Chrysler's part.

On cross appeals, the Appellate Division, Third Department, in Action No. 1, affirmed the jury verdicts in favor of the Codlings against Chrysler, but reversed the judgment for Paglia on his cross claim against Chrysler and dismissed that cross claim. In Action No. 2 the Appellate Division affirmed the jury verdict against Chrysler in favor of Paglia for his own injuries and property damage.

In Action No. 1 Paglia has appealed as of right to our court from the Appellate Division's reversal of his judgment over against Chrysler and the dismissal of his cross claim. Chrysler appeals by permission in both Actions No. 1 and No. 2.

In our view there was ample evidence in the record to support the factual determinations made by the jury—that Chrysler breached its implied warranty of merchantability and fitness, and that such breach was a proximate cause of the accident.

The uncontradicted proof was that Paglia's automobile "went to the left" and that he "tried to steer to the right" but that "she locked on me or something." "I couldn't steer right. It went to the left and I tried to steer to the right and she wouldn't budge, she wouldn't give." Counsel for Chrysler lay great stress on the alleged failure of proof of any specific defect in the power steering system and the inadequacy of plaintiffs' tests to prove the defect. Claim is also made that even if a defect at the time of the accident be assumed, there was no proof that the defect existed at the time the automobile left the Chrysler plant. These issues were fairly put to the jury by the trial court on the instructions (to which no exceptions were taken):

> "While the burden is upon the plaintiff to prove that the product was defective and that the defect existed while the product was in the manufacturer's possession, plaintiff is not required to prove the specific defect, especially where the product is complicated in nature. Proof of necessary facts may be circumstantial. Though the happening of the accident is not proof of a defective condition, a defect may be inferred from proof that the product did not perform as intended by the manufacturer."
>
> "* * * that for the defendant Chrysler Corporation to be held liable, the defect need not be apparent at the time the product left the factory, but may be merely a latent defect or hidden defect which later arises and causes damage."

We are bound under the circumstances to respect the findings of fact made by the jury, there being evidence in the record for their support. With the jury's conclusion that the steering mechanism of the automobile was not fit for the purpose for which it was intended and that Chrysler, therefore, breached its implied warranty, we reach the question whether Chrysler's liability for such breach extends to the Codlings, nonuser innocent bystanders with respect to the vehicle.

We start with a thumbnail historical catalogue of products liability cases in our court. For many years the law was clear that "[t]here can be no warranty where there is no privity of contract." (Turner v. Edison Stor. Battery Co., 248 N.Y. 73, 74, 161 N.E. 423, 424). The crumbling of the citadel began with Greenberg v. Lorenz, 9 N.Y.2d 195, 213 N.Y.S.2d 39, 173 N.E.2d 773 in which recovery was allowed an infant plaintiff for injuries caused by pieces of sharp metal found in a can of salmon, notwithstanding that the canned food had been purchased by her father. Next came Randy Knitwear v. American Cyanamid Co., 11 N.Y.2d 5, 226 N.Y.S.2d 363, 181 N.E.2d 399 in which the manufacturer of a chemical used for treating fabrics to prevent shrinkage was held liable to a remote purchaser. Then in Goldberg v. Kollsman Instrument Corp., 12 N.Y.2d 432, 240 N.Y.S.2d 592, 191 N.E.2d 81 an airplane manufacturer, though not the manufacturer of the defective component part, was cast in liability for wrongful death of a passenger. And in Guarino v. Mine Safety Appliance Co., 25 N.Y.2d 460, 306 N.Y.S.2d 942, 255 N.E.2d 173 the manufacturer of a defective oxygen-type protective mask was held liable for injuries sustained by persons who attempted to rescue users of the mask, under the doctrine of "danger invites rescue".

As we are aware, the erosion of the citadel of privity has been proceeding apace and even more rapidly in other jurisdictions, all with the enthusiastic support of text writers and the authors of law review articles as evidenced by an extensive literature. Once one exception has been made, others have followed as appealing fact situations presented instances in which, in language of result, liability has been imposed to avoid injustice and for the protection of the public. Fact situations where recovery was allowed have shifted from those in which the touchstone was said to be the character of the product manufactured (e. g., dangerous instrumentalities, or household products) to those in which the result turned on the classification of the injured person (e. g., member of the family, employee, user, rescuer).

The dynamic growth of the law in this area has been a testimonial to the adaptability of our judicial system and its resilient capacity to respond to new developments, both of economics and of manufacturing and marketing techniques. A developing and more analytical sense of justice, as regards both the economics and the operational aspects of production and distribution has imposed a heavier and heavier burden of responsibility on the manufacturer. It is significant that the Appellate Divisions in three of our four Judicial De-

Sec. 3   TECHNIQUE OF CASE LAW DEVELOPMENT   213

partments, the First, Third and Fourth, have now found sufficient encouragement in the decisions and opinions of our court, and elsewhere, to extend the liability of the manufacturer of a defective product to a nonuser bystander. (Singer v. Walker, 39 A.D.2d 90, 331 N.Y.S.2d 823; Codling v. Paglia, 38 A.D.2d 154, 327 N.Y.S.2d 978; and Ciampichini v. Ring Bros., 40 A.D.2d 289, 339 N.Y.S.2d 716.)

We think that the time has now come when our court, instead of rationalizing broken field running, should lay down a broad principle, eschewing the temptation to devise more proliferating exceptions. (Cf. B. R. DeWitt, Inc. v. Hall, 19 N.Y.2d 141, 278 N.Y.S.2d 596, 225 N.E.2d 195, with reference to the doctrine of mutuality of estoppel as an absolute test for *res judicata*.)

Much of what we have written in extending the liability of the manufacturer to the noncontracting user is equally applicable to the bystander. "The policy of protecting the public from injury, physical or pecuniary, resulting from misrepresentations outweighs allegiance to old and out-moded technical rules of law which, if observed, might be productive of great injustice. The manufacturer * * * unquestionably intends and expects that the product will be purchased and used in reliance upon his express assurance of its quality and, in fact, it is so purchased and used. Having invited and solicited the use, the manufacturer should not be permitted to avoid responsibility, when the expected use leads to injury and loss, by claiming that he made no contract directly with the user." (Randy Knitwear v. American Cyanamid Co., 11 N.Y.2d 5, 13, 226 N.Y.S.2d 363, 368, 181 N.E.2d 399, 402, supra.)

The Appellate Divisions, confronting this issue and concluding that protection should now be extended to the innocent bystander, have spoken firmly. "[T]he ultimate purpose in widening the scope of the warranty is to cast the burden on the manufacturer who put his product in the marketplace." (Singer v. Walker, 39 A.D.2d 90, 97, 331 N.Y.S.2d 823, 831, supra.) "[T]here would appear to be no logic or reason in denying a right to relief to persons injured by a defective dangerous instrumentality solely on the ground that they were not themselves a user of the instrument. * * * Manufacturers of articles which may be a source of danger to several people if not properly manufactured should not be immune from liability for breach of implied warranty, a tortious wrong, to persons injured by a defectively manufactured article, where the manufacturer could reasonably contemplate injury to such persons by reason of the defect." (Codling v. Paglia, 38 A.D.2d 154, 158, 327 N.Y.S.2d 978, 983, supra.) "To restrict recovery to those who are users is unrealistic in view of the fact that bystanders have less opportunity to detect any defect than either purchasers or users. Our decision is one of policy but is mandated by both justice and common sense." (Ciampichini v. Ring Bros., 40 A.D.2d 289, 293, 339 N.Y.S.2d 716, 720, supra.)

214   CASE LAW   Ch. 2

Today as never before the product in the hands of the consumer is often a most sophisticated and even mysterious article. Not only does it usually emerge as a sealed unit with an alluring exterior rather than as a visible assembly of component parts, but its functional validity and usefulness often depend on the application of electronic, chemical or hydraulic principles far beyond the ken of the average consumer. Advances in the technologies of materials, of processes, of operational means have put it almost entirely out of the reach of the consumer to comprehend why or how the article operates, and thus even farther out of his reach to detect when there may be a defect or a danger present in its design or manufacture. In today's world, it is often only the manufacturer who can fairly be said to know and to understand when an article is suitably designed and safely made for its intended purpose. Once floated on the market, many articles in a very real practical sense defy detection of defect, except possibly in the hands of an expert after laborious and perhaps even destructive disassembly. By way of direct illustration, how many automobile purchasers or users have any idea how a power steering mechanism operates or is intended to operate, with its "circulating worm and piston assembly and its cross shaft splined to the Pitman arm"? Further, as has been noted, in all this the bystander, the nonuser, is even worse off than the user—to the point of total exclusion from any opportunity either to choose manufacturers or retailers or to detect defects. We are accordingly persuaded that from the standpoint of justice as regards the operating aspect of today's products, responsibility should be laid on the manufacturer, subject to the limitations we set forth.

Consideration of the economics of production and distribution point in the same direction. We take as a highly desirable objective the widest feasible availability of useful, nondefective products. We know that in many, if not most instances, today this calls for mass production, mass advertising, mass distribution. It is this mass system which makes possible the development and availability of the benefits which may flow from new inventions and new discoveries. Justice and equity would dictate the apportionment across the system of all related costs—of production, of distribution, of postdistribution liability. Obviously, if manufacturers are to be held for financial losses of nonusers, the economic burden will ultimately be passed on in part, if not in whole, to the purchasing users. But considerations of competitive disadvantage will delay or dilute automatic transferral of such added costs. Whatever the total cost, it will then be borne by those in the system, the producer, the distributor and the consumer. Pressures will converge on the manufacturer, however, who alone has the practical opportunity, as well as a considerable incentive, to turn out useful, attractive, but safe products. To impose this economic burden on the manufacturer should encourage safety in design and production; and the diffusion of this cost in the purchase price of in-

Sec. 3   TECHNIQUE OF CASE LAW DEVELOPMENT   215

dividual units should be acceptable to the user if thereby he is given added assurance of his own protection.

Finally, we invite attention to the number of other States which have preceded us in imposing strict products liability in favor of non-users.

* * *

We accordingly hold that, under a doctrine of strict products liability, the manufacturer of a defective product is liable to any person injured or damaged if the defect was a substantial factor in bringing about his injury or damages; provided: (1) that at the time of the occurrence the product is being used (whether by the person injured or damaged or by a third person) for the purpose and in the manner normally intended, (2) that if the person injured or damaged is himself the user of the product he would not by the exercise of reasonable care have both discovered the defect and perceived its danger, and (3) that by the exercise of reasonable care the person injured or damaged would not otherwise have averted his injury or damages.

In the present case, we conclude that the jury properly found that Chrysler had produced an automobile with a defective steering mechanism; that that defect was a substantial factor in bringing about the accident and thus the injuries to the Codlings; that at the time of the accident Paglia was using the automobile for the purpose and in the manner normally intended; that by the exercise of reasonable care, Paglia would neither have discovered the defective steering mechanism nor perceived its danger; and that, as to the Codlings, the exercise of reasonable care on their part would otherwise not have averted the accident.

Thus, we affirm the judgments in favor of the Codlings against Chrysler.

As to Paglia's claims against Chrysler, one for his own injuries and property damages and the other for possible recoupment of the payments he made to the Codlings, two aspects call for further consideration and disposition.

The judgment in favor of Paglia against Chrysler in Action No. 2 for his personal injuries and property damage must be reversed, and the action remanded for a new trial. Paglia's claims were submitted to the jury on theories both of negligence and breach of warranty. The jury found no negligence but returned a verdict in Paglia's favor for breach of warranty. As to this latter theory, however, the trial court charged that contributory negligence was not a defense, to which charge counsel for Chrysler took exception.

As indicated, contributory fault of the plaintiff is a defense to an action for strict products liability, and the charge that it was not, even when taken in combination with the other, more specific charges given here, constituted reversible error. (See Eisenbach v. Gimbel Bros., 281 N.Y. 474, 24 N.E.2d 131; Maiorino v. Weco Prods. Co., 45

N.J. 570, 214 A.2d 18; 47 N.Y.Jur., Products Liability, § 72, p. 208; cf. Fredendall v. Abraham & Strauss, Inc., 279 N.Y. 146, 18 N.E.2d 11; and Razey v. Colt Co., 106 App.Div. 103, 94 N.Y.S. 59.)

The contributory fault of a plaintiff could be found in use of the product for other than its normally intended purpose or other than in the manner normally intended. This jury was properly charged on this aspect of the case, and its finding in favor of Paglia as plaintiff cannot be disturbed. Or, contributory fault could be found in the failure to exercise such reasonable care as would have disclosed the defect and the danger attributable thereto. Here again there is no basis for a finding of error in the record in this case. There remains, however, the question whether Paglia independently exercised that degree of care for his own safety that a reasonably prudent person would have exercised under the same circumstances, quite apart from the defective steering mechanism. Thus, in this case, the issue whether Paglia as plaintiff had exercised reasonable care in the operation of his automobile, quite separate and distinct from the defective steering mechanism, and if he did not whether such lack of care was a substantial factor in producing his damages, was never submitted to the jury. Our examination of this record discloses that it cannot fairly be said to be entirely barren of evidence which might have supported a jury verdict against Paglia on this combined issue. Accordingly there must be a new trial in Action No. 2.

[The court's discussion of the appropriateness of adopting a rule of comparative negligence and the concurring opinion of Judge Jason are omitted].

The orders of the Appellate Division in Action No. 1 affirming the Codling judgments against Chrysler and reversing the judgment of Paglia on his cross claim against Chrysler and dismissing the cross claim are affirmed. The order of the Appellate Division in Action No. 2 affirming Paglia's judgment against Chrysler is reversed and the action remanded for a new trial.

NOTES

1. Two years after Codling v. Paglia the New York legislature enacted the following statute (McKinney's N.Y. CPLR 1411):

§ 1411. Damages recoverable when contributory negligence or assumption of risk is established

In any action to recover damages for personal injury, injury to property, or wrongful death, the culpable conduct attributable to the claimant or to the decedent, including contributory negligence or assumption of risk, shall not bar recovery, but the amount of damages otherwise recoverable shall be diminished in the proportion which the culpable conduct attributable to the claimant or decedent bears to the culpable conduct which caused the damages.

2. Starting with Winterbottom v. Wright and ending (for this course) with Codling v. Paglia, the law has changed markedly. Where once a manufacturer was liable only to his contracting party even for negligence, today he is liable, regardless of the care he may take, to all persons foreseeably injured (in person or property) as a result of his defective product, and the change has taken place largely without statutory intervention. One thing seems clear; the law will continue to change as the law adapts to new or newly perceived problems. One area which seems ripe for further refinement is liability for "defective" design. Where a product is, for whatever reason, not manufactured properly and causes damage, a rule of strict liability makes generally good sense. But suppose the manufacturer does exactly what he planned! In some cases, of course, he will simply have adopted a bad design; but in other cases he will have been forced to trade off one value against a competing value. Is he to be *strictly* liable in all cases? The Restatement, Second, Torts, § 402A imposes strict liability only where the defective condition is "unreasonably dangerous." Is that a different standard than negligence? See Note, Products Liability: Is § 402A Strict Liability Really Strict in Kentucky? 62 Ky.L.J. 866 (1976). Cf. Dreisonstok v. Volkswagenwerk, A.G., 489 F.2d 1066 (4th Cir. 1974).

3. For a further discussion of the curious role of the Uniform Commercial Code in the development of the law in this field, see M. Franklin, When Worlds Collide: Liability Theories and Disclaimers in Defective-Product Cases, 18 Stan.L.Rev. 974 (1966); H. Titus, Restatement, Second, Torts, § 402A and the Uniform Commercial Code, 22 Stan.L.Rev. 713 (1970).

4. If fault is not to be the touchstone of liability, what should be the law's objective? To what extent do you feel the current law promotes those objectives? For the views of some economists on these questions, see Symposium, Products Liability: Economic Analysis and the Law, 38 U. of Chi.L.Rev. 1 (1970).

PROBLEM CASE

The Bowie Machine Tool Company (Bowie) is a small family-owned company incorporated and with its principal place of business in the state of Kent, a mythical jurisdiction to be treated as any other state. It has been in business for approximately fifty years. Over the last ten or fifteen years its gross sales have been approximately $1.5 million per year and its net profit approximately $50,000 per year. Its principal business is the manufacture of various tools and small machines used in a number of small appliance manufacturing operations. Virtually all of its sales are to manufacturing companies and almost none are to the consuming public.

Prior to World War II, Bowie carried no product liability insurance. However, in 1948 it took out a modest product liability policy covering liability up to $500,000 on account of any one accident. From approximately 1948 to 1970 the premium on that insurance was $1,000 per year. In 1971 the cost of insurance doubled; in 1972 it doubled again; and in 1975 Bowie was notified by its insurer that the maximum insurance available would be reduced to $300,000 and that the annual premium for the reduced coverage would be $35,000. Upon investigation, Bowie learned that no better offer of insurance was available in the market; Bowie, therefore, decided to "go bare," i. e., to let its product liability insurance lapse. Bowie's experience in this respect is typical of the experience of other companies as related in testimony to the United States Senate Select Committee on Small Business at hearings held in 1975 and 1976.

Prior to 1976, Bowie had never suffered a claim for product liability. However, in 1976 an employee of one of Bowie's customers sued to recover for bodily injury incurred while using one of Bowie's products. The particular machine in question had been sold in 1963 by Bowie (at a sale price of $2,500) to the Home Appliance Corp., a Kent corporation. So far as is known, it had been used until 1976 without any injuries being caused. The injured employee, N. O. Fear, also a resident of the state of Kent, was injured when she attempted to clear a stoppage in the machine. Such stoppages occur from time to time and Fear, an experienced employee, had performed the clearing operation often without injury (as had other employees). However, on this occasion a shield designed to protect the person performing the operation gave way and Fear was injured. Any danger from the clearing operation could be avoided by shutting down the machine, but the process of restarting was long, and the employees—who were paid on a piece rate—were reluctant to shut it down, and only inexperienced operators did so—usually to the annoyance of their crew mates.

Fear's injuries are covered by the Kent Workers' Compensation Law. However, the maximum amount recoverable under the Workers' Compensation Law would be approximately $15,000. Under Kent law the workers' compensation remedy is the exclusive remedy of the employee against the employer. An employee is permitted to sue third parties. However, the law does not permit such a third party to sue the employer to recover damages paid to the worker.

The particular machine in question is of a type standard in the industry. For a few years before and after 1963, it was offered by Bowie at the same price, in a slightly different version incorporating a safety feature which would make impossible the type of accident which actually occurred in this case (by automatic shutdown in case of a stoppage). However, there was considerable sales resistance by customers and their employees; there were a number of instances in which employees refused to use that model (or indeed disconnected the safety feature). After a few years the alternative model was discontinued because of customer resistance and is not now generally offered in the market.

Fear brought suit against Bowie in the District Court of Kent, seeking damages of $100,000. The trial judge charged the jury that if it found that Fear's injuries were caused by the failure of the shield, they should bring in a verdict for Fear, unless they found that

Sec. 3 TECHNIQUE OF CASE LAW DEVELOPMENT 219

negligence on her part contributed to the accident. The jury brought in a verdict of $75,000 for Ms. Fear.

The law of Kent is substantially identical to the law of the State of New York as it existed after the decision of the New York Court of Appeals in Codling v. Paglia. Both sides agree that if Codling v. Paglia controls this case, the decision below must be affirmed. Bowie argues, however, that there are material differences between this case and earlier cases which make a rule of strict liability inapplicable here.

You are the law clerk to a judge in the Kent Supreme Court. He asks you to draft an opinion on the appeal. Your opinion should

    A.   State the issue or issues raised.

    B.   Indicate and justify your solution to such issue or issues, and identify, and deal with, the arguments that would probably have been made thereon by counsel for Bowie and counsel for Fear.

NOTE

Workplace injuries attributable to "defective" machinery have become a major source of product liability litigation. Such injuries pose a special problem because of the general rule which prohibits recovery against the employer (frequently the person primarily at fault) in excess of that paid by workers' compensation laws. Thus, even in a jurisdiction which permits contribution among joint tortfeasors, a product manufacturer may be unable to collect from the employer. But cf. Dole v. Dow Chemical Co., 30 N.Y.2d 143, 331 N.Y.S.2d 382, 282 N.E.2d 288 (1972) and Robinson v. International Harvester Co., 70 Ill.2d 47, 15 Ill.Dec. 850, 374 N.E.2d 458 (1977). On the general subject, see Weisgall, Product Liability in the Workplace: The Effect of Workers' Compensation on the Right and Liability of Third Parties, 1977 Wis.L.Rev. 1035.

Chapter III

THE PROBLEM OF RETROACTIVITY

When a judicial decision announces a new rule of law, or overrules an old one, it almost always operates retroactively—i. e., it applies to events that occurred before the new or changed rule was declared. This is most obvious with respect to the parties to the particular litigation. Take for example, the famous decision in Erie Railroad Co. v. Tompkins (to be studied in the next chapter) in which the United States Supreme Court broke the news on April 25, 1938, that its earlier decision in Swift v. Tyson was no longer "the law." Whatever its jurisprudential virtues, the change was an unhappy one for plaintiff Tompkins, who had suffered his injuries on the dark night of July 24, 1934, while Swift v. Tyson still held sway. None the less, the new rule deprived him of his judgment.

And Tompkins was by no means the only one so affected. Countless other actual or potential litigants suffered (or enjoyed) similar retroactive consequences. The new rule now applied to all pending or prospective suits (final judgments being in general protected, of course, by the doctrine of *res judicata*) no matter how long before April 25, 1938, the events giving rise to them had occurred.

Why do judicial decisions operate in this retroactive way? Should they? Could it, or should it, be otherwise? The materials in this section are intended to introduce some of the considerations involved in these and related questions. Preliminarily, it may be noted that matters already treated in Legal Method have an obvious bearing on the present topic. We have considered the basic proposition that courts in our system, unlike legislatures, are not constituted deliberately for the purpose of "lawmaking." Rather, at least in strict theory, judge-made law is created "merely" as an incident, and necessary corollary, of the dispute-settling process. It has been thought to follow from this that a court, unlike a legislature, ought not to pronounce new rules apart from particular disputes before it, but only as by-products of concrete adjudications. On this view, the new judge-made rule inevitably "happens" to apply retroactively. Indeed, as we shall see, it was strongly urged not long ago that there were constitutional barriers to prospective law-changes by the courts.

You will have observed by now that the problem of retroactivity is one of the forces promoting stability and conservatism in the judicial process. Where people have acted—or are thought or claimed to have acted—in reliance on existing rules, this may in itself be a substantial argument for adherence to those rules. See, e. g., Cullings v. Goetz, supra p. 119. Turning this proposition around, it has been argued that courts should not undertake to limit the retroactive impact of their decisions because this would tempt them to usurp the legislature's functions. This is to say that retroactivity is good precisely because of its inhibiting effects upon innovative judicial impulses. As the point was put by Mr. Justice Black, "one of the great inherent restraints upon this [the Supreme] Court's departure from the field of interpretation to enter that of lawmaking has been the fact that its judgments could not be limited to prospective application." James v. United States, 366 U.S. 213, 225, 81 S.Ct. 1052, 1058, 6 L.Ed.2d 246 (1961).

But the law, including judge-made law and judicial interpretations of constitutions and statutes, must not be frozen. And so we deal here again, in a still hotly debated aspect, with the pervasive and perennial tension between stability and change.

GREAT NORTHERN RY. CO. v. SUNBURST OIL & REFINING CO.

Supreme Court of the United States, 1932.
287 U.S. 358, 53 S.Ct. 145, 77 L.Ed. 360.

Mr. Justice CARDOZO delivered the opinion of the Court.

Sunburst Oil & Refining Company, the respondent, brought suit against petitioner, Great Northern Railway Company, to recover payments claimed to be overcharges for freight. The charges were in conformity with a tariff schedule approved by the Railroad Commission of Montana for intrastate traffic. After payment had been made, the same commission which had approved the schedule held, upon a complaint by the shipper, that the rates so approved were excessive and unreasonable. In this action to recover the excess so paid, the shipper recovered a judgment which was affirmed upon appeal. 7 P.(2d) 927. The question, broadly stated, is whether the annulment by retroaction of rates valid when exacted is an unlawful taking of property within the Fourteenth Amendment. A writ of certiorari brings the case here.

By a statute of Montana the Board of Railroad Commissioners is empowered to fix rates of carriage for intrastate shipments. The rates thereby established are not beyond recall. They may be changed by the board itself on the complaint either of shipper or of carrier, if found to be unreasonable. Revised Codes of Montana, § 3796. In an action against the board, they may be set aside upon a like showing by a judgment of the court. Sections 3809, 3810. Until changed or set aside, they "shall prima facie be deemed to be just, reasonable, and proper." Section 3810.

The meaning of the statute was considered by the Supreme Court of Montana in a cause determined in May, 1921. Doney v. Northern Pacific Railway Co., 60 Mont. 209, 199 P. 432. A shipper of lumber brought suit against a carrier to recover transportation charges which were alleged to be unreasonable, though they were in accordance with the published tariff. He did this without a preliminary application to the board to modify the schedule. He did it without a preliminary suit in which the board, being brought into court as a defendant, would have opportunity to sustain the schedule and resist the change. The court held that, until one of these preliminary conditions had been satisfied, no action for restitution could be maintained against the carrier. It coupled that decision with the statement that, upon compliance with one or other of the conditions, the excess, thus ascertained, might be the subject of recovery.

The procedure there outlined was followed by this respondent. It filed a complaint with the board to the effect that the existing tariff for the carriage of crude petroleum distillate was excessive and unreasonable, in that the rate of 20½ cents was based upon an estimated weight of 7.4 pounds per gallon, whereas the actual weight is not more than 6.6 pounds per gallon. The board sustained the complaint. In doing so it ruled, in conformity with the decision in the Doney case, that the published schedule prescribed the minimum and the maximum to which carrier and shipper were required to adhere while the schedule was in force, but that by the true construction of the statute the duty of adherence was subject to a condition or proviso whereby annulment or modification would give a right of reparation for the excess or the deficiency. The revision of the tariff was followed by this suit against the carrier, and later by a judgment for the shipper which is now before us for review.

The appeal to the Supreme Court of Montana was heard at the same time as an appeal in another cause involving a like question, and the two were decided together, though with separate opinions. Montana Horse Products Co. v. Great Northern Railway Co., 7 P. (2d) 919; Sunburst Oil & Refining Co. v. Great Northern Railway Co., 7 P.(2d) 927. The court held that the ruling in the Doney case was erroneous and would not be followed in the future; that a rate established by the Commission had the same effect as one established by the Legislature; that the statute giving power to the Commission or the court to declare a rate unreasonable was not to be read as meaning that a declaration of invalidity should apply to intermediate transactions; but none the less that the ruling in the Doney case was law until reversed and would constitute the governing principle for shippers and carriers who, during the period of its reign, had acted on the faith of it. An opinion handed down upon a motion for rehearing restates the rationale of the decision, and perhaps with greater clearness. 7 P.(2d) 927, 929. We are thus brought to the inquiry whether the judgment thus rendered does violence to any right secured to the petitioner by the Federal Constitution.

The subject is likely to be clarified if we divide it into two branches. Was a federal right infringed by the action of the trial court in adhering to the rule imposed upon it in the Doney case by the highest court of the state? If there was no infringement then, did one come about later when the Supreme Court of Montana disavowed the rule of the Doney case for the future, but applied it to the past?

1. The trial court did not impair a federal right by giving to a statute of the state the meaning that had been ascribed to it by the highest court of the state, unless such impairment would have resulted if the meaning had been written into the statute by the Legislature itself. But plainly no such consequence would have followed if that course had been pursued. The Doney case was decided, as we have seen, in 1921. The transactions complained of occurred between August, 1926, and August, 1928. Carrier and shipper understood at that time that the rates established by the Commission as the delegate of the Legislature were provisional and tentative. Valid for the time being the rates indubitably were, a prop for conduct while they stood, but the prop might be removed, and charges, past as well as present, would go down at the same time. By implication of law there had been written into the statute a notice to all concerned that payments exacted by a carrier in conformity with a published tariff were subject to be refunded if found thereafter, upon sufficient evidence, to be excessive and unreasonable. The Constitution of the United States would have nothing to say about the validity of a notice of that tenor written in so many words into the body of the act. Carrier and shipper would be presumed to bargain with each other on the basis of existing law. Coombes v. Getz, 285 U.S. 434, 52 S.Ct. 435, 76 L.Ed. 866. The validity of the notice is no less because it was written into the act by a process of construction. Supreme Lodge, Knights of Pythias v. Meyer, 265 U.S. 30, 32, 44 S.Ct. 432, 68 L.Ed. 885. The inquiry is irrelevant whether we would construe the statute in the same way if the duty of construction were ours and not another's. Supreme Lodge, Knights of Pythias v. Meyer, supra, page 33 of 265 U.S., 44 S.Ct. 432, 433. Enough for us that the construction, whether we view it as wise or unwise, does not expose the court that made it to the reproach of withholding from the carrier the privileges and immunities established by the Constitution of the nation.

* * *

2. If the carrier did not suffer a denial of due process through the action of the trial court in subjecting the published tariff to the doctrine of the Doney case then standing unimpeached, the petitioner, to prevail, must be able to show that a change was brought about through something done or omitted by the Supreme Court of Montana in deciding the appeal.

We think the posture of the case from the viewpoint of constitutional law was the same after the decision of the appeal as it was after the trial. There would certainly have been no denial of due process if the court in affirming the judgment had rendered no opinion or had stated in its opinion that the Doney case was approved. The petitioner is thus driven to the position that the Constitution of the United States has been infringed because the Doney case was disapproved, and yet, while disapproved, was followed. Adherence to precedent as establishing a governing rule for the past in respect of the meaning of a statute is said to be a denial of due process when coupled with the declaration of an intention to refuse to adhere to it in adjudicating any controversies growing out of the transactions of the future.

We have no occasion to consider whether this division in time of the effects of a decision is a sound or an unsound application of the doctrine of *stare decisis* as known to the common law. Sound or unsound, there is involved in it no denial of a right protected by the Federal Constitution. This is not a case where a court, in overruling an earlier decision, has given to the new ruling a retroactive bearing, and thereby has made invalid what was valid in the doing. Even that may often be done, though litigants not infrequently have argued to the contrary. Tidal Oil Co. v. Flanagan, 263 U.S. 444, 450, 44 S. Ct. 197, 68 L.Ed. 382; Fleming v. Fleming, 264 U.S. 29, 44 S.Ct. 246, 68 L.Ed. 547; Brinkerhoff-Faris Co. v. Hill, 281 U.S. 673, 680, 50 S. Ct. 451, 74 L.Ed. 1107; cf. Montana Bank v. Yellowstone County, 276 U.S. 499, 503, 48 S.Ct. 331, 72 L.Ed. 673. This is a case where a court has refused to make its ruling retroactive, and the novel stand is taken that the Constitution of the United States is infringed by the refusal.

We think the Federal Constitution has no voice upon the subject. A state in defining the limits of adherence to precedent may make a choice for itself between the principle of forward operation and that of relation backward. It may say that decisions of its highest court, though later overruled, are law none the less for intermediate transactions. Indeed, there are cases intimating, too broadly (cf. Tidal Oil Co. v. Flanagan, supra), that it *must* give them that effect; but never has doubt been expressed that it *may* so treat them if it pleases, whenever injustice or hardship will thereby be averted. Gelpeke v. Dubuque, 1 Wall. 175, 17 L.Ed. 520; Douglass v. County of Pike, 101 U.S. 677, 687. * * * On the other hand, it may hold to the ancient dogma that the law declared by its courts had a Platonic or ideal existence before the act of declaration, in which event the discredited declaration will be viewed as if it had never been, and the reconsidered declaration as law from the beginning. * * * The alternative is the same whether the subject of the new decision is common law (Tidal Oil Co. v. Flanagan, supra) or statute. Gelpcke v. Dubuque, supra; Fleming v. Fleming, supra. The choice for any state may be determined by the juristic philosophy of the judges of her courts, their conceptions of law, its origin and nature. We review, not the wisdom of their philosophies, but the legality of their acts. The state of Montana has told us by the voice of her highest court that, with these alternative methods open to her, her preference is for the first. In making this choice, she is declaring common law for those within her borders. The common law as administered by her judges ascribes to the decisions of her highest court a power to bind and loose that is unextinguished, for intermediate transactions, by a decision overruling them. As applied to such transactions, we may say of the earlier decision that it has not been overruled at all. It has been translated into a judgment of affirmance and recognized as law anew. Accompanying the recognition is a prophecy, which may or may not be realized in conduct, that transactions arising in the future will be governed by a different rule. If this is the common-law doctrine of adherence to precedent as understood and enforced by the courts of Montana, we are not at liberty, for anything contained in the Constitution of the United States, to thrust upon those courts a different conception either of the binding force of precedent or of the meaning of the judicial process.

* * *

The judgment of the Supreme Court of Montana is accordingly Affirmed.

NOTES

1. What had the Montana Supreme Court *held* in the *Doney* case? Why, or how, did it conclude that the *Doney* decision required affirmance of the judgment for the shipper in the instant case? Could it responsibly have reached some different conclusion in the instant case?

2. What was the holding or holdings of the Montana Supreme Court in the instant case? Consider who won and who would win in a case involving events later in time than this Montana decision.

3. Following this decision of the United States Supreme Court, State X enacts a statute forbidding its courts to announce decisional rules having only prospective application. Is the statute constitutional?

4. This *Sunburst* decision sustains a *state* court in giving only prospective effect to an overruling decision. Would it follow that federal courts have similar power? Consider in this connection that Article III, Section 2, of the Federal Constitution, conferring jurisdiction upon the federal courts to decide "cases" or "controversies," has been held to preclude the rendering by these courts of "advisory opinions"—i. e., of abstract answers to questions not posed by "real" or "actual" disputes.

MOLITOR v. KANELAND COMM. UNIT DIST. NO. 302

Supreme Court of Illinois, 1959.
18 Ill.2d 11, 163 N.E.2d 89.

KLINGBIEL, Justice.

Plaintiff, Thomas Molitor, a minor, by Peter his father and next friend, brought this action against Kaneland Community Unit School District for personal injuries sustained by plaintiff when the school bus in which he was riding left the road, allegedly as a result of the driver's negligence, hit a culvert, exploded and burned.

The complaint alleged, in substance, the negligence of the School District, through its agent and servant, the driver of the school bus; that plaintiff was in the exercise of such ordinary care for his own safety as could be reasonably expected of a boy of his age, intelligence, mental capacity and experience; that plaintiff sustained permanent and severe burns and injuries as a proximate result of defendant's negligence, and prayed for judgment in the amount of $56,000. Plaintiff further alleged that defendant is a voluntary unit school district organized and existing under the provisions of sections 8–9 to 8–13 of the School Code and operates school buses within the district pursuant to section 29–5. Ill.Rev.Stat.1957, chap. 122, pars. 8–9 to 8–13 and par. 29–5.

The complaint contained no allegation of the existence of insurance or other nonpublic funds out of which a judgment against defendant could be satisfied. Although plaintiff's abstract of the record shows that defendant school district did carry public liability insurance with limits of $20,000 for each person injured and $100,000 for each occurrence, plaintiff states that he purposely omitted such an allegation from his complaint.

Defendant's motion to dismiss the complaint on the ground that a school district is immune from liability for tort was sustained by the trial court, and a judgment was entered in favor of defendant. Plaintiff elected to stand on his complaint and sought a direct appeal to this court on the ground that the dismissal of his action would violate his constitutional rights. At that time we held that no fairly debatable constitutional question was presented so as to give this court jurisdiction on direct appeal, and accordingly the cause was transferred to the Appellate Court for the Second District. The Appellate Court affirmed the decision of the trial court and the case is now before us again on a certificate of importance.

In his brief, plaintiff recognizes the rule, established by this court in 1898, that a school district is immune from tort liability, and frankly asks this court either to abolish the rule *in toto*, or to find it inapplicable to a school district such as Kaneland which was organized through the voluntary acts of petition and election by the voters of the district, as contrasted with a school district created *nolens volens* by the State.

With regard to plaintiff's alternative contention, we do not believe that a logical distinction can be drawn between a community unit school district organized by petition and election of the voters of the district pursuant to article 8 of the School Code (Ill.Rev.Stat. 1957, chap. 122, pars. 8–9 to 8–13), and any other type of school district, insofar as the question of tort liability is concerned. All are "quasi-municipal corporations" created for the purpose of performing certain duties necessary for the maintenance of a system of free schools. The reasons for allowing or denying immunity apply equally to all school districts without regard to the manner of their creation. We are unwilling to further complicate the law relating to governmental torts by now drawing highly technical distinctions between the various types of Illinois school districts and making tort liability depend thereon.

Thus we are squarely faced with the highly important question —in the light of modern developments, should a school district be immune from liability for tortiously inflicted personal injury to a pupil thereof arising out of the operation of a school bus owned and operated by said district?

It appears that while adhering to the old immunity rule, this court has not reconsidered and re-evaluated the doctrine of immunity of school districts for over fifty years. During these years, however, this subject has received exhaustive consideration by legal writers and scholars in articles and texts, almost unanimously condemning the immunity doctrine. See, Borchard, Governmental Liability in Tort, 34 Yale L.J. 1; Green, Freedom of Litigation, 38 Ill.L.Rev. 355; Harno, Tort Immunity of Municipal Corporation, 4 Ill.L.Q. 28; Prosser on Torts, chap. 21, sec. 108, p. 1063; Pugh, Historical Approach to the Doctrine of Sovereign Immunity, 13 La.L.Rev. 476; Repko, American Legal Commentary on the Doctrines of Municipal Tort Liability, 9 Law and Contemporary Problems 214; Rosenfield, Governmental Immunity from Liability for Tort in School Accidents, 5 Legal Notes on Local Government 380; Approaches to Governmental Liability in Tort, 9 Law and Contemporary Problems 182; Note: Limitations on the Doctrine of Governmental Immunity from Suit, 41 Col. L.Rev. 1236; Note: The Sovereign Immunity of the States, The Doctrine and Some of Its Recent Developments, 40 Minn.L.Rev. 234; Tort Claims Against the State of Illinois and Its Subdivisions, 47 N.W.L.Rev. 914.

Historically we find that the doctrine of the sovereign immunity of the state, the theory that "the King can do no wrong," was first extended to a subdivision of the state in 1788 in Russell v. Men of Devon, 2 Term Rep. 671, 100 Eng.Rep. 359. As pointed out by Dean Prosser (Prosser on Torts, p. 1066), the idea of the municipal corporate entity was still in a nebulous state at that time. The action was brought against the entire population of the county and the decision that the county was immune was based chiefly on the fact that there were no corporate funds in Devonshire out of which satisfaction could be obtained, plus a fear of multiplicity of suits and resulting inconvenience to the public.

It should be noted that the Russell case was later overruled by the English courts, and that in 1890 it was definitely established that in England a school board or school district is subject to suit in tort for personal injuries on the same basis as a private individual or corporation. (Crisp v. Thomas, 63 L.T.N.S. 756 (1890).) Non-immunity has continued to be the law of England to the present day. See: Annotation, 160 A.L.R. 7, 84.

The immunity doctrine of Russell v. Men of Devon was adopted in Illinois with reference to towns and counties in 1870 in Town of Waltham v. Kemper, 55 Ill. 346. Then, in 1898, eight years after the English courts had refused to apply the Russell doctrine to schools, the Illinois court extended the immunity rule to school districts in the leading case of Kinnare v. City of Chicago, 171 Ill. 332, 49 N.E. 536, where it was held that the Chicago Board of Education was immune from liability for the death of a laborer resulting from a fall from the roof of a school building, allegedly due to the negligence of the Board in failing to provide scaffolding and safeguards. That opinion reasoned that since the State is not subject to suit nor liable for the torts or negligence of its agents, likewise a school district, as a governmental agency of the State, is also "exempted from the obligation to respond in damages, as master, for negligent acts of its servants to the same extent as is the State itself." Later decisions following the Kinnare doctrine have sought to advance additional explanations such as the protection of public funds and public property, and to prevent the diversion of tax moneys to the payment of damage claims. Leviton v. Board of Education, 374 Ill. 594, 30 N.E.2d 497; Thomas v. Broadlands Community Consolidated School Dist., 348 Ill. App. 567, 109 N.E.2d 636.

Surveying the whole picture of governmental tort law as it stands in Illinois today, the following broad outlines may be observed. The General Assembly has frequently indicated its dissatisfaction with the doctrine of sovereign immunity upon which the Kinnare case was based. Governmental units, including school districts, are now subject to liability under the Workmen's Compensation and Occupational Disease Acts. Ill.Rev.Stat.1957, chap. 48, pars. 138.1, 172.36; McLaughlin v. Industrial Board, 281 Ill. 100, 117 N.E. 819; Board of Education, etc. v. Industrial Com., 301 Ill. 611, 134 N.E. 70. The State itself is liable, under the 1945 Court of Claims Act, for damages in tort up to $7,500 for the negligence of its officers, agents or employees. (Ill.Rev.Stat.1957, chap. 37, pars. 439.1–439.24.) Cities and villages have been made directly liable for injuries caused by the negligent operation of fire department vehicles, and for actionable wrong in the removal or destruction of unsafe or unsanitary buildings. (Ill.Rev.Stat.1957, chap. 24, pars. 1–13, 1–16.) Cities and villages, and the Chicago Park District, have also been made responsible, by way of indemnification, for the nonwilful misconduct of policemen. (Ill.Rev.Stat.1957, chap. 24, par. 1–15.1; chap. 105, par. 333.23k.) In addition to the tort liability thus legislatively imposed upon governmental units, the courts have classified local units of government as "quasi-municipal corporations" and "municipal corporations." And the activities of the latter class have been categorized as "governmental" and "proprietary," with full liability in tort imposed if the function is classified as "proprietary." The incongruities that have resulted from attempts to fit particular conduct into one or the other of these categories have been the subject of frequent comment. Rhyne, Municipal Law, p. 732; Phillips, "Active Wrongdoing" and the Sovereign-Immunity Principle in Municipal Tort Liability, 38 Ore.L.Rev. 122, 124; Davis, Tort Liability of Governmental Units, 40 Minn.L.Rev. 751, 774; Note, Tort Claims Against the State of Illinois and Its Subdivisions, 47 N.W.L.Rev. 914, 921; Green, Freedom of Litigation (III): Municipal Liability for Torts, 38 Ill.L.Rev. 355. See also Roumbos v. City of Chicago, 332 Ill. 70, 163 N.E. 361, 60 A.L.R. 87.

Of all the anomalies that have resulted from legislative and judicial efforts to alleviate the injustice of the results that have flowed from the doctrine of sovereign immunity, the one most immediately pertinent to this case is the following provision of the Illinois School Code: "Any school district, including any non-high school district, which provides transportation for pupils may insure against any loss or liability of such district, its agents or employees, resulting from or incident to the ownership, maintenance or use of any school bus. Such insurance shall be carried only in companies duly licensed and authorized to write such coverage in this state. Every policy for such insurance coverage issued to a school district shall provide, or be endorsed to provide, that the company issuing such policy waives any right to refuse payment or to deny liability thereunder within the limits of said policy, by reason of the non-liability of the insured school district for the wrongful or negligent acts of its agents and employees, and, its immunity from suit, as an agency of the state performing governmental functions." Ill.Rev.Stat.1957, c. 122, § 29–11a.

Thus, under this statute, a person injured by an insured school district bus may recover to the extent of such insurance, whereas, under the Kinnare doctrine, a person injured by an uninsured school district bus can recover nothing at all.

Defendant contends that the quoted provision of the School Code constitutes a legislative determination that the public policy of this State requires that school districts be immune from tort liability. We can read no such legislative intent into the statute. Rather, we interpret that section as expressing dissatisfaction with the court-created doctrine of governmental immunity and an attempt to cut down that immunity where insurance is involved. The difficulty with this legislative effort to curtail the judicial doctrine is that it allows each school district to determine for itself whether, and to what extent, it will be financially responsible for the wrongs inflicted by it.

Coming down to the precise issue at hand, it is clear that if the above rules and precedents are strictly applied to the instant case, plaintiff's complaint, containing no allegation as to the existence of insurance, was properly dismissed. On the other hand, the complaint may be held to state a good cause of action on either one of two theories, (1) application of the doctrine of Moore v. Moyle, 405 Ill. 555, 92 N.E.2d 81, or (2) abolition of the rule that a school district is immune from tort liability.

As to the doctrine of Moore v. Moyle, that case involved an action for personal injuries against Bradley University, a charitable education institution. Traditionally, charitable and educational institutions have enjoyed the same immunity from tort liability as have governmental agencies in Illinois. Parks v. Northwestern University, 218 Ill. 381, 75 N.E. 991, 2 L.R.A.,N.S., 556. The trial court dismissed the complaint on the ground that Bradley was immune to tort liability. The Supreme Court reversed, holding that the complaint should not have been dismissed since it alleged that Bradley was fully insured. Unfortunately, we must admit that the opinion in that case does not make the basis of the result entirely clear. (See Note, 45 Ill.L.Rev. 776.) However, the court there said, 405 Ill. at page 564, 92 N.E.2d at page 86: " * * * the question of insurance in no way affects the liability of the institution, but would only go to the question of the manner of collecting any judgment which might be obtained, without interfering with, or subjecting the trust funds or trust-held property to, the judgment. The question as to whether or not the institution is insured in no way affects its liability any more than whether a charitable institution holding private nontrust property or funds would affect its liability. These questions would only be of importance at the proper time, when the question arose as to the collection of any judgment out of nontrust property or assets. * * * Judgments may be obtained, but the question of collection of the judgment is a different matter." If we were to literally apply this reasoning to the present school district case, we would conclude that it was unnecessary that the complaint contain an allegation of the existence of insurance or other nonpublic funds. Plaintiff's complaint was sufficient as it stood without any reference to insurance, and plaintiff would be entitled to prosecute his action to judgment. Only at that time, in case of a judgment for plaintiff, would the question of insurance arise, the possession of nonpublic funds being an execution rather than a liability question. It cannot be overlooked, however, that some doubt is cast on this approach by the last paragraph of the Moore opinion, where the court said: "It appears that the trust funds of Bradley will not be impaired or depleted by the prosecution of the complaint, and therefore it was error to dismiss it." These words imply that if from the complaint it did not appear that the trust funds would not be impaired, the complaint should have been dismissed. If that is the true holding in the case, then liability itself, not merely the collectability of the judgment, depends on the presence of nontrust assets, as was pointed out by Justice Crampton in his dissenting opinion. The doctrine of Moore v. Moyle does not, in our opinion, offer a satisfactory solution. Like the provision of the

School Code above quoted, it would allow the wrongdoer to determine its own liability.

It is a basic concept underlying the whole law of torts today that liability follows negligence, and that individuals and corporations are responsible for the negligence of their agents and employees acting in the course of their employment. The doctrine of governmental immunity runs directly counter to that basic concept. What reasons, then, are so impelling as to allow a school district, as a quasi-municipal corporation, to commit wrongdoing without any responsibility to its victims, while any individual or private corporation would be called to task in court for such tortious conduct?

The original basis of the immunity rule has been called a "survival of the medieval idea that the sovereign can do no wrong," or that "the King can do no wrong." (38 Am.Jur., Mun.Corps., sec. 573, p. 266.) In Kinnare v. City of Chicago, 171 Ill. 332, 49 N.E. 536, 537, the first Illinois case announcing the tort immunity of school districts, the court said: "The state acts in its sovereign capacity, and does not submit its action to the judgment of courts, and is not liable for the torts or negligence of its agents, and a corporation created by the state as a mere agency for the more efficient exercise of governmental functions is likewise exempted from the obligation to respond in damages, as master, for negligent acts of its servants to the same extent as is the state itself, unless such liability is expressly provided by the statute creating such agency." This was nothing more nor less than an extension of the theory of sovereign immunity. Professor Borchard has said that how immunity ever came to be applied in the United States of America is one of the mysteries of legal evolution. (Borchard, Governmental Liability in Tort, 34 Yale L.J. 1, 6.) And how it was then infiltrated into the law controlling the liability of local governmental units has been described as one of the amazing chapters of American common-law jurisprudence. (Green, Freedom of Litigation, 38 Ill.L.Rev. 355, 356.) "It seems, however, a prostitution of the concept of sovereign immunity to extend its scope in this way, for no one could seriously contend that local governmental units possess sovereign powers themselves." 54 Harv.L.Rev. 438, 439.

We are of the opinion that school district immunity cannot be justified on this theory. As was stated by one court, "The whole doctrine of governmental immunity from liability for tort rests upon a rotten foundation. It is almost incredible that in this modern age of comparative sociological enlightenment, and in a republic, the medieval absolutism supposed to be implicit in the maxim, 'the King can do no wrong,' should exempt the various branches of the government from liability for their torts, and that the entire burden of damage resulting from the wrongful acts of the government should be imposed upon the single individual who suffers the injury, rather than distributed among the entire community constituting the government, where it could be borne without hardship upon any individual, and where it justly belongs." Barker v. City of Santa Fe, 47 N.M. 85, 136 P.2d 480, 482. Likewise, we agree with the Supreme Court of Florida that in preserving the sovereign immunity theory, courts have overlooked the fact that the Revolutionary War was fought to abolish that "divine right of kings" on which the theory is based.

The other chief reason advanced in support of the immunity rule in the more recent cases is the protection of public funds and public property. This corresponds to the "no fund" or "trust fund" theory upon which charitable immunity is based. This rationale was relied on in Thomas v. Broadlands Community Consolidated School Dist., 348 Ill.App. 567, 109 N.E.2d 636, 640, where the court stated that the reason for the immunity rule is "that it is the public policy to protect public funds and public property, to prevent the diversion of tax moneys, in this case school funds, to the payment of damage claims." This reasoning seems to follow the line that it is better for the individual to suffer than for the public to be inconvenienced. From it proceeds defendant's argument that school districts would be bankrupted and education impeded if said districts were called upon to compensate children tortiously injured by the negligence of those districts' agents and employees.

We do not believe that in this present day and age, when public education constitutes one of the biggest businesses in the country, that school immunity can be justified on the protection-of-public-funds theory.

* * *

We are of the opinion that none of the reasons advanced in support of school district immunity have any true validity today. Further we believe that abolition of such immunity may tend to decrease the frequency of school bus accidents by coupling the power to transport pupils with the responsibility of exercising care in the selection and supervision of the drivers. As Dean Harno said: "A municipal corporation today is an active and virile creature capable of inflicting much harm. Its civil responsibility should be co-extensive. The municipal corporation looms up definitely and emphatically in our law, and what is more, it can and does commit wrongs. This being so, it must assume the responsibilities of the position it occupies in society." (Harno, Tort Immunity of Municipal Corporations, 4 Ill.L.Q. 28, 42.) School districts will be encouraged to exercise greater care in the matter of transporting pupils and also to carry adequate insurance covering that transportation, thus spreading the risk of accident, just as the other costs of education are spread over the entire district. At least some school authorities themselves have recognized the need for the vital change which we are making. * * *

* * *

We conclude that the rule of school district tort immunity is unjust, unsupported by any valid reason, and has no rightful place in modern day society.

Defendant strongly urges that if said immunity is to be abolished, it should be done by the legislature, not by this court. With this contention we must disagree. The doctrine of school district immunity was created by this court alone. Having found that doctrine to be unsound and unjust under present conditions, we consider that we have not only the power, but the duty, to abolish that immunity. "We closed our courtroom doors without legislative help, and we can likewise open them." Pierce v. Yakima Valley Memorial Hospital Ass'n, 43 Wash.2d 162, 260 P.2d 765, 774.

We have repeatedly held that the doctrine of *stare decisis* is not an inflexible rule requiring this court to blindly follow precedents and adhere to prior decisions, and that when it appears that public policy and social needs require a departure from prior decisions, it is our duty as a court of last resort to overrule those decisions and establish a rule consonant with our present day concepts of right and justice. Bradley v. Fox, 7 Ill.2d 106, 111, 129 N.E.2d 699; Nudd v. Matsoukas, 7 Ill.2d 608, 615, 131 N.E.2d 525; Amann v. Faidy, 415 Ill. 422, 114 N.E.2d 412. As was stated by the New Jersey Supreme Court in overruling the doctrine of charitable immunity: "The unmistakable fact remains that judges of an earlier generation declared the immunity simply because they believed it to be a sound instrument of judicial policy which would further the moral, social and economic welfare of the people of the State. When judges of a later generation firmly reach a contrary conclusion they must be ready to discharge their own judicial responsibilities in conformance with modern concepts and needs. It should be borne in mind that we are not dealing with property law or other fields of the law where stability and predictability may be of the utmost concern. We are dealing with the law of torts where there can be little, if any, justifiable reliance and where the rule of *stare decisis* is admittedly limited. See Pound, supra, 13 N.A.C.C.A.L.J. at 22; Seavey, Cogitations on Torts, 68 (1954); Cowan, 'Torts,' 10 Rutgers L.Rev. 115, 119 (1955)." Collopy v. Newark Eye and Ear Infirmary, 27 N.J. 29, 141 A.2d 276, 283.

In here departing from *stare decisis* because we believe justice and policy require such departure, we are nonetheless cognizant of the fact that retrospective application of our decision may result in great hardship to school districts which have relied on prior decisions upholding the doctrine of tort immunity of school districts. For this reason we feel justice will best be served by holding that, except as to the plaintiff in the instant case, the rule herein established shall apply only to cases arising out of future occurrences. This result is in accord with a substantial line of authority embodying the theory that an overruling decision should be given only prospective operation whenever injustice or hardship due to reliance on the overruled decisions would thereby be averted. Gelpcke v. City of Dubuque, 1 Wall. 175, 68 U.S. 175, 17 L.Ed. 520; Harmon v. Auditor of Public Accounts, 123 Ill. 122, 13 N.E. 161 (where decision sustaining validity of statute authorizing bond issue is, subsequent to the issue, overruled, overruling decision operates prospectively); Davies Warehouse Co. v. Bowles, 321 U.S. 144, 64 S.Ct. 474, 88 L.Ed. 635; People ex rel. Attorney General v. Salomon, 54 Ill. 39 (where public officers have relied on statutes subsequently held unconstitutional, decision given only prospective operation); State v. Jones, 44 N.M. 623, 107 P.2d 324 (prospective operation given decision overruling precedent as to what constitutes a lottery); Continental Supply Co. v. Abell, 95 Mont. 148, 24 P.2d 133 (prospective operation given decision overruling prior cases as to corporate directors' liability to stockholders); Hare v. General Con. Purchase Corp., 220 Ark. 601, 249 S.W.2d 973 (prospective operation given decision changing prior rule as to what constitutes usury.) See also: Snyder, Retrospective Operation of Overruling Decisions, 35 Ill.L.Rev. 121; Kocourek, Retrospective Decisions and Stare Decisis, 17 A.B.A.J. 180; Freeman, The Protection Afforded Against the Retroactive Operation of an Overruling Decision, 18 Col.L.Rev. 230; Carpenter, Court Decisions and the Common Law, 17 Col.L.Rev. 593; Note, Prospective Operation of Decisions Holding Statutes Unconstitutional or Overruling Prior Decisions, 60 Harv.L.Rev. 437.

Likewise there is substantial authority in support of our position that the new rule shall apply to the instant case. (Citing cases) At least two compelling reasons exist for applying the new rule to the instant case while otherwise limiting its application to cases arising in the future. First, if we were to merely announce the new rule without applying it here, such announcement would amount to mere *dictum*. Second, and more important, to refuse to apply the new rule here would deprive appellant of any benefit from his effort and expense in challenging the old rule which we now declare erroneous. Thus there would be no incentive to appeal the upholding of precedent since appellant could not in any event benefit from a reversal invalidating it.

It is within our inherent power as the highest court of this State to give a decision prospective or retrospective application without offending constitutional principles. Great Northern Railway Co. v. Sunburst Oil & Refining Co., 287 U.S. 358, 53 S.Ct. 145, 77 L.Ed. 360.

Although ordinarily the cases which have invoked the doctrine of prospective operation have involved contract or property rights or criminal responsibility, the basis of the doctrine is reliance upon an overruled precedent. Despite the fact that the instant case is one sounding in tort, it appears that the "reliance test" has been met here. We do not suggest that the tort itself was committed in reliance on the substantive law of torts, i. e., the bus driver did not drive negligently in reliance on the doctrine of governmental immunity, but rather that school districts and other municipal corporations have relied upon immunity and that they will suffer undue hardship if abolition of the immunity doctrine is applied retroactively. In reliance on the immunity doctrine, school districts have failed to adequately insure themselves against liability. In reliance on the immunity doctrine, they have probably failed to investigate past accidents which they would have investigated had they known they might later be held responsible therefor. Our present decision will eliminate much of the hardship which might be incurred by school districts as a result of their reliance on the overruled doctrine, and at the same time reward appellant for having afforded us the opportunity of changing an outmoded and unjust rule of law.

For the reasons herein expressed, we accordingly hold that in this case the school district is liable in tort for the negligence of its employee, and all prior decisions to the contrary are hereby overruled.

The judgment of the Appellate Court sustaining the dismissal of plaintiff's complaint is reversed and the cause is remanded to the circuit court of Kane County with instructions to set aside the order dismissing the complaint, and to proceed in conformity with the views expressed in this opinion.

Reversed and remanded, with directions.

DAVIS, Justice.

I dissent from the decision of the court which, in one fell swoop, severs from the body of our Illinois law the ancient and established doctrine of governmental immunity from tort liability. The rule of immunity of the people collectively charged with a governmental function was well established by 1607, the fourth year of James I. (Russell v. Men of Devon, 2 Term Rep. 671, 100 Eng.Rep. 359.) The rule of decision was adopted prior to the constitution of 1870 and was incorporated in the Revised Statutes of 1874 in its present form. It appears today as section 1 of the act adopting the common law (Ill.Rev.Stat.1959, chap. 28, par. 1), and provides: "That the common law of England, so far as the same is applicable and of a general nature, and all statutes or acts of the British parliament made in aid of, and to supply the defects of the common law, prior to the fourth year of James the First, excepting the second section of the sixth chapter of 43d Elizabeth, the eighth chapter of 13th Elizabeth, and ninth chapter of 37th Henry Eighth, and which are of a general nature and not local to that kingdom, shall be the rule of decision, and shall be considered as of full force *until repealed by legislative authority*." (Italics mine.)

* * *

This opinion was adopted May 21, 1959, and we allowed petition for rehearing at the September, 1959, term. In the original opinion, the court made no reference to whether it would operate retroactively or prospectively. In Braxon v. Bressler, 64 Ill. 488, at page 493, we stated: "Legislation can only affect the future, but when courts vacillate and overturn their own decisions, the evils may be incalculable. They operate retrospectively, and may often disturb rights which should be regarded as certain and fixed." Consequently, such opinion operated retroactively. Also see: Grasse v. Dealer's Transport Co., 412 Ill. 179, 106 N.E.2d 124; Duke v. Olson, 240 Ill.App. 198.

Upon rehearing, the court modified its opinion by holding that, except as to the plaintiff in the instant case, the rule of liability should apply only to cases arising out of future occurrences. The inability of the judiciary to practically cope with this problem is demonstrated by the labored efforts of the court to resolve it and the unusual doctrine which the court announced as the solution of the enigma in which it was entangled.

The other jurisdictions, which have given prospective operation to decisions overruling cases long recognized as the law, have largely predicated such result upon the opinion of Mr. Justice Cardozo in Great Northern Railway Co. v. Sunburst Oil & Refining Co., 287 U.S. 358, 53 S.Ct. 145, 77 L.Ed. 360.

It was there held that the choice of whether decisions should be given prospective or retrospective application rested with the judges of the State court and that there was nothing in the United States constitution to preclude the Montana court from providing that its decisions overruling prior cases should be given prospective application only, "whenever injustice or hardship will thereby be averted." The basis of the Sunburst doctrine was reliance upon an overruled precedent and ensuing hardship therefrom.

In this case the court recognized that "In reliance on the immunity doctrine, school districts have failed to adequately insure themselves against liability" and "have probably failed to investigate past accidents which they would have investigated had they known they might later be held responsible therefor," and conceded that the reliance test had been met. Yet, the court included within the ambit of its opinion the action of the plaintiff, while the element of reliance and ensuing hardship were as real and present with this defendant as with other potential defendant school districts which escaped liability by virtue of the prospective application of the court's opinion.

The principle announced by the court is an aborted offspring of the Sunburst theory. It is without legal justification other than that the plaintiff should be rewarded for bringing the action, and it has thwarted the reasonable expectations of the well-intentioned governing body of defendant school district. While the court stated that its decision is in accord with a substantial line of authority, the cases cited, other than Dooling v. Overholser, 100 U.S.App.D.C. 247, 243 F.2d 825, and Barker v. St. Louis County, 340 Mo. 986, 104 S.W.2d 371, offer no support for the result obtained.

Eighteen pupils of defendant school district were riding on its bus on March 10, 1958, when the bus crashed into a culvert which resulted in an explosion of the gasoline tank whereby most of them were burned and injured. Molitor v. Kaneland Community Unit Dist. 302, 20 Ill.App.2d 555, 155 N.E.2d 841. When we consider that under the court's decision only Thomas Molitor can recover even though the other pupils were similarly injured in the same accident, the position of the court becomes even less tenable.

After this opinion was announced on May 21, 1959, and in response to it, the legislature, by an overwhelming vote, adopted five bills granting tort immunity to park districts (Ill.Rev.Stat.1959, chap. 105, par. 12.1–1 and par. 491), counties (Ill.Rev.Stat.1959, chap. 34, par. 301.1), forest preserve districts (Ill.Rev.Stat.1959, chap. 57½, par. 3a), and the Chicago Park District (Ill.Rev.Stat.1959, chap. 105, par. 333.2a). It also passed a bill granting limited tort immunity to school districts and nonprofit private schools. (Ill.Rev. Stat.1959, chap. 122, pars. 821–831, incl.) These enactments became effective on divers dates in July, 1959.

In view of this legislation, the decision of the court may be of limited significance relative to the liability of school districts in tort actions. Cf.: O'Callaghan v. Waller & Beckwith Realty Co., 15 Ill.2d 436, 155 N.E.2d 545, and Ill.Rev.Stat.1959, chap. 80, par. 15a; In re Estate of Day, 7 Ill.2d 348, 131 N.E.2d 50, and Ill.Rev.Stat.1957, chap. 3, par. 197, wherein the decisions of this court were annulled by legislative enactment; and Jencks v. United States, 353 U.S. 657, 77 S.Ct. 1007, 1 L.Ed.2d 1103, and 18 U.S.C.A. § 3500, wherein a decision of the United States Supreme Court was nullified by an act of Congress. See: Palermo v. United States, 360 U.S. 343, 79 S.Ct. 1217, 3 L.Ed.2d 1287.

The opinion of the court fails to make any reference to the action of the General Assembly concerning the question of tort immunity. This is significant in that we have frequently held that where the legislature has changed the law pending an appeal, the case must be disposed of by the reviewing court under the law as it then exists. Fallon v. Illinois Commerce Com., 402 Ill. 516, 84 N.E.2d 641; People ex rel. Hanks v. Benton, 301 Ill. 32, 133 N.E. 700; People ex rel. Askew v. Ryan, 281 Ill. 231, 117 N.E. 992; People ex rel. Law v. Dix, 280 Ill. 158, 117 N.E. 496. Thus, I believe the court erred in not reviewing this judgment in the light of the foregoing 1959 amendment to the School Code.

However, this epochal decision will be the source of much confusion and litigation. The statutes passed after the adoption of the opinion and within the last 40 days of the sesssion, restoring the doctrine of immunity to certain municipal agencies, indicate to me that it is, and by future legislation will be, the policy of the legisature to restore governmental immunity in Illinois, subject to such modification as hearings, study and research under the legislative process may indicate desirable.

While this opinion determines the issues before the court, the problems which it has created remain and will continue to plague us until they are justly resolved.

I would affirm the trial and Appellate courts.

HERSHEY, J., joins in this dissent.

BRISTOW, Justice, concurring in part and dissenting in part:

I concur with the reasoning and the results reached by this court in the case of the instant plaintiff. But the dissenting opinion of Mr. Justice DAVIS reads the court's opinion as abolishing the immunity of school districts only as to the instant plaintiff but as retaining that immunity as to the other children who were injured with the plaintiff in the same accident. To the extent that the majority opinion is subject to the construction imparted to it by the dissenting opinion, I must withhold assent.

This is a test case brought by a father on behalf of one of his four children, all of whom were injured at the same time and under identical circumstances. It is clear that all of the children, having the same father and next friend and being represented by the same counsel, have identical interests in this appeal, which has been an important test case. There was a common question of law in the cases of all of the children and it serves the interests of justice to encourage and entertain a test case respecting all of the children.

I would reject any intimation that the court's holding in this case is limited to the named plaintiff and would repel any inference that the court's opinion pretermits the rights of the other children. I also dissent from the court's order denying the leave of the instant plaintiff's brothers and sisters to intervene in this case and request a clarification of the court's present opinion.

With these reservations, prompted by the dissent, I join the majority of the court in its opinion and judgment in this case.

NOTES

1. In Holytz v. City of Milwaukee, 17 Wis.2d 26, 115 N.W.2d 618 (1962), another case abolishing the defense of sovereign immunity, the court ruled as follows:

"To enable the various public bodies to make financial arrangements to meet the new liability implicit in this holding, the effective date of the abolition of the rule of governmental immunity for torts shall be July 15, 1962. * * * The new rule shall not apply to torts occurring before July 15, 1962. However, for the reasons set forth in the supplemental opinion in Kojis v. Doctors Hospital (1961), 12 Wis.2d 367, 374, 107 N.W.2d 131, 107 N.W.2d 292, this decision shall apply to the case at bar."

July 15, 1962, the date designated as the "effective date" of the new rule was forty days after the date of decision. Compare Jones v. State Highway Comm., 557 S.W.2d 225 (Mo. banc 1977) where the Missouri Supreme Court (in still another sovereign immunity case) adopted an "effective date" almost a year later than its original decision. Does the practice of choosing an effective date other than the date of decision seem more "legislative"? Does that trouble you?

2. In Spanel v. Mounds View School Dist. No. 621, 264 Minn. 279, 118 N.W.2d 795 (1962) the court affirmed the dismissal of a tort suit against a school district " * * * with the caveat, however, that subject to the limitations we now discuss, the defense of sovereign immunity will no longer be available to school districts, municipal corporations, and other subdivisions of government on whom immunity has been conferred by judicial decision *with respect to torts which are committed after the adjournment of the next regular session of the Minnesota Legislature.*" (Emphasis added.)

3. What, in your view, are the relative merits and demerits of (a) making the overruling wholly prospective as in *Spanel*; (b) making the overruling prospective except as to the plaintiff in the immediate case, as in *Holytz*; or (c) making the overruling prospective except as to those involved in the same accident, as advocated by Mr. Justice Bristow in *Molitor*?

4. Widespread use of prospective overruling seemed imminent in the 1960's. See, e. g., Schaefer, The Control of "Sunbursts": Techniques of Prospective Overruling, 42 N.Y.U.L.J. 631 (1967); Rogers, Perspectives on Prospective Overruling, 36 U.M.K.C. L.Rev. 35 (1968); Annotation: Prospective or Retroactive Operation of Overruling Decisions, 10 A.L.R.3d 1371 (1967). The impression of the editors (not based on empirical research) is that courts have not used the technique as widely as was then predicted. See, in this connection, Fitzgerald v. Meissner & Hicks, Inc., 38 Wis.2d 571, 157 N.W.2d 595 (1968) where the court stated that overrulings were ordinarily to be given retrospective effect unless there were "compelling judicial reasons for not doing so." 157 N.W.2d at 599. What would be such reasons?

Chapter IV

THE AUTHORITATIVE STATUS OF JUDICIAL DECISIONS

SECTION 1. INTRODUCTION

The last section of Chapter 2 and all of Chapter 3 are primarily concerned with the courts' response to *their own* precedents [1]—of divining the extent to which they are bound to follow earlier decisions; and the circumstances in which, as well as the manner of overruling. This chapter will focus on a different problem, the authoritative status of a judicial decision in *other* courts.

When the courts are in the same system, answers to questions of authoritative status are fairly easy. As a general rule a court must follow the decision of any court which, in the event of an appeal, can reverse the decision of the lower court. When decisions are rendered by the highest court in the system, ordinarily they must be followed by all lower courts. Thus, a decision by the New York Court of Appeals must be followed by all lower New York courts and a decision by the United States Supreme Court must be followed by all lower federal courts and, with respect to questions of federal law, by state courts as well.

For decisions rendered by courts other than the highest court problems can arise. A decision of the Appellate Division, First Department in New York, for example, is binding on the Supreme Court, New York County, or any other court within the First Department. It is not binding on a lower court within the Second, Third or Fourth Department. So too, a decision by the Court of Appeals for the Second Circuit is binding on all United States district courts within the Second Circuit but has only persuasive effect on district courts in other circuits.[2]

By and large courts do follow precedents which are decided by courts superior to them in the hierarchy. Occasionally, however, there may be decisions which are obsolete or of doubtful validity (i. e., decisions as to which it is doubtful that the court when faced with

---

1. A special problem exists in the case of courts which sit in panels (as do all United States Courts of Appeals today). Is a panel consisting of judges A, B and C required to follow a decision on point by judges D, E and F? And what can be done, if it does not? 28 U.S.C.A. §46C and Rule 35 of the Federal Rules of Appellate Procedure for the United States Courts of Appeals provide for hearings by the full court "en banc" when consideration by the full court is necessary to secure or maintain uniformity of its decision.

2. Where courts occupy the same level in the hierarchy, of course, as has been seen earlier, their decisions are at most persuasive to each other.

the same problem again will follow its own precedent) and there have been instances over the years in which courts have refused to follow higher court precedent. See for example the decision by Judge Parker in Barnette v. West Virginia State Bd. of Educ., 47 F.Supp. 251 (C.D.W.Va.1942) in which he refused to follow a 1940 decision of the United States Supreme Court requiring Jehovah's Witnesses to obey a local requirement to salute the flag. In that case Judge Parker's temerity was justified a year later when the Supreme Court overruled its earlier decision.[3] The Jehovah's Witnesses case represents a special situation however, because between the first and second Supreme Court decision three of the justices on the five-four majority in 1940 announced that they felt the earlier decision had been incorrect. For recent manifestations of refusal to follow precedent, see Note: Lower Court Disavowal of Supreme Court Precedent, 60 Va.L.Rev. 494 (1974).

As a general rule where decisions are from different systems they have no authoritative status although, as seen above, they may very well be persuasive. In the United States however, there are several circumstances in which our two systems—the federal court system and the state court system—have concurrent jurisdiction and a question can arise as to which law is applicable. Although the question can arise in a number of contexts, by far the most important context is that of the status of state decisions in cases in which federal jurisdiction is based upon diversity of citizenship.

SECTION 2. STATUS OF STATE DECISIONS IN FEDERAL COURTS

ERIE RAILROAD CO. v. TOMPKINS

Supreme Court of the United States, 1938.
304 U.S. 64, 58 S.Ct. 817, 82 L.Ed. 1188.

Certiorari, 302 U.S. 671, 58 S.Ct. 50, 82 L.Ed. 518, to review the affirmance of a judgment recovered against the railroad company in an action for personal injuries. The accident was in Pennsylvania. The action was in New York jurisdiction being based on diversity of citizenship.

Mr. Justice BRANDEIS delivered the opinion of the Court.

The question for decision is whether the oft-challenged doctrine of Swift v. Tyson [16 Pet. 1, 10 L.Ed. 865 (1842)] shall now be disapproved.

Tompkins, a citizen of Pennsylvania, was injured on a dark night by a passing freight train of the Erie Railroad Company while walk-

---

3. Jones v. City of Opelika, 316 U.S. 584, 62 S.Ct. 1231, 86 L.Ed. 1691 (1942). The earlier decision was Minersville School District v. Gobitis, 310 U.S. 586, 60 S.Ct. 1010, 84 L.Ed. 1375 (1940) (Mr. Justice Stone dissented).

ing along its right of way at Hughestown in that State. He claimed that the accident occurred through negligence in the operation, or maintenance of the train; that he was rightfully on the premises as licensee because of a commonly used beaten footpath which ran for a short distance alongside the tracks; and that he was struck by something which looked like a door projecting from one of the moving cars. To enforce that claim he brought an action in the federal court for southern New York, which had jurisdiction because the company is a corporation of that State. It denied liability; and the case was tried by a jury.

The Erie insisted that its duty to Tompkins was no greater than that owed to a trespasser. It contended, among other things, that its duty to Tompkins, and hence its liability, should be determined in accordance with the Pennsylvania law; that under the law of Pennsylvania, as declared by its highest court, persons who use pathways along the railroad right of way—that is a longitudinal pathway as distinguished from a crossing—are to be deemed trespassers; and that the railroad is not liable for injuries to undiscovered trespassers resulting from its negligence, unless it be wanton or wilful. Tompkins denied that any such rule had been established by the decisions of the Pennsylvania courts; and contended that, since there was no statute of the State on the subject, the railroad's duty and liability is to be determined in federal courts as a matter of general law.

The trial judge refused to rule that the applicable law precluded recovery. The jury brought in a verdict of $30,000; and the judgment entered thereon was affirmed by the Circuit Court of Appeals, which held, 90 F.2d 603, 604, that it was unnecessary to consider whether the law of Pennsylvania was as contended, because the question was one not of local, but of general, law and that "upon questions of general law the federal courts are free, in the absence of a local statute, to exercise their independent judgment as to what the law is; and it is well settled that the question of the responsibility of a railroad for injuries caused by its servants is one of general law. * * * Where the public has made open and notorious use of a railroad right of way for a long period of time and without objection, the company owes to persons on such permissive pathway a duty of care in the operation of its trains. * * * It is likewise generally recognized law that a jury may find that negligence exists toward a pedestrian using a permissive path on the railroad right of way if he is hit by some object projecting from the side of the train."

The Erie had contended that application of the Pennsylvania rule was required, among other things, by § 34 of the Federal Judiciary Act of September 24, 1789, c. 20, 28 U.S.C.A. § 725, which provides:

"The laws of the several States, except where the Constitution, treaties, or statutes of the United States otherwise require or provide, shall be regarded as rules of decision in trials at common law, in the courts of the United States, in cases where they apply."

Because of the importance of the question whether the federal court was free to disregard the alleged rule of the Pennsylvania common law, we granted certiorari.

First. Swift v. Tyson, 16 Pet. 1, 18, 10 L.Ed. 865, held that federal courts exercising jurisdiction on the ground of diversity of citizenship need not, in matters of general jurisprudence, apply the unwritten law of the State as declared by its highest court; that they are free to exercise an independent judgment as to what the common law of the State is—or should be; and that, as there stated by Mr. Justice Story:

> "the true interpretation of the thirty-fourth section limited its application to state laws strictly local, that is to say, to the positive statutes of the state, and the construction thereof adopted by the local tribunals, and to rights and titles to things having a permanent locality, such as the rights and titles to real estate, and other matters immovable and intraterritorial in their nature and character. It never has been supposed by us, that the section did apply, or was intended to apply, to questions of a more general nature, not at all dependent upon local statutes or local usages of a fixed and permanent operation, as, for example to the construction of ordinary contracts or other written instruments, and especially to questions of general commercial law, where the state tribunals are called upon to perform the like functions as ourselves, that is, to ascertain upon general reasoning and legal analogies, what is the true exposition of the contract or instrument, or what is the just rule furnished by the principles of commercial law to govern the case."

The Court in applying the rule of § 34 to equity cases, in Mason v. United States, 260 U.S. 545, 559, 43 S.Ct. 200, 67 L.Ed. 396, said: "The statute, however, is merely declarative of the rule which would exist in the absence of the statute." The federal courts assumed, in the broad field of "general law," the power to declare rules of decision which Congress was confessedly without power to enact as statutes. Doubt was repeatedly expressed as to the correctness of the construction given § 34, and as to the soundness of the rule which it introduced. But it was the more recent research of a competent scholar, who examined the original document, which established that the construction given to it by the Court was erroneous; and that the purpose of the section was merely to make certain that, in all matters except those in which some federal law is controlling, the federal courts exercising jurisdiction in diversity of citizenship cases would apply as their rules of decision the law of the State, unwritten as well as written.[4]

Criticism of the doctrine became widespread after the decision of Black & White Taxicab Co. v. Brown & Yellow Taxicab Co., 276 U.S. 518. There, Brown and Yellow, a Kentucky corporation owned by Kentuckians, and the Louisville and Nashville Railroad, also a Kentucky corporation, wished that the former should have the exclusive privilege of soliciting passenger and baggage transportation at the Bowling Green, Kentucky, railroad station; and that the Black and White, a competing Kentucky corporation, should be prevented from interfering with that privilege. Knowing that such a contract would be void under the common law of Kentucky, it was arranged that the Brown and Yellow reincorporate under the law of Tennessee, and that the contract with the railroad should be executed there. The suit was then brought by the Tennessee corporation in the federal court for western Kentucky to enjoin competition by the Black and White; an injunction issued by the District Court was sustained by the Court of Appeals; and this Court, citing many decisions in which the doctrine of Swift v. Tyson had been applied, affirmed the decree.

Second. Experience in applying the doctrine of Swift v. Tyson, had revealed its defects, political and social; and the benefits expected to flow from the rule did not accrue. Persistence of state courts in their own opinions on questions of common law prevented uniformity; and the impossibility of discovering a satisfactory line of demarcation between the province of general law and that of local law developed a new well of uncertainties.

On the other hand, the mischievous results of the doctrine had become apparent. Diversity of citizenship jurisdiction was conferred in order to prevent apprehended discrimination in state courts against those not citizens of the State. Swift v. Tyson introduced grave discrimination by non-citizens against citizens. It made rights enjoyed under the unwritten "general law" vary according to whether enforcement was sought in the state or in the federal court; and the privilege of selecting the court in which the right should be determined was conferred upon the non-citizen. Thus, the doctrine rendered impossible equal protection of the law. In attempting to promote uniformity of law throughout the United States, the doctrine had prevented uniformity in the administration of the law of the State.

The discrimination resulting became in practice far-reaching. This resulted in part from the broad province accorded to the so-called "general law" as to which federal courts exercised an independent judgment. In addition to questions of purely commercial law, "general law" was held to include the obligations under contracts

---

4. Charles Warren, New Light on the History of the Federal Judiciary Act of 1789 (1923) 37 Harv.L.Rev. 49, 51–52, 81–88, 108.

entered into and to be performed within the State, the extent to which a carrier operating within a State may stipulate for exemption from liability for his own negligence or that of his employee; the liability for torts committed within the State upon persons resident or property located there, even where the question of liability depended upon the scope of a property right conferred by the State; and the right to exemplary or punitive damages. Furthermore, state decisions construing local deeds, mineral conveyances, and even devises of real estate were disregarded.

In part the discrimination resulted from the wide range of persons held entitled to avail themselves of the federal rule by resort to the diversity of citizenship jurisdiction. Through this jurisdiction individual citizens willing to remove from their own State and become citizens of another might avail themselves of the federal rule. And, without even change of residence, a corporate citizen of the State could avail itself of the federal rule by re-incorporating under the laws of another State, as was done in the Taxicab Case. 276 U.S. 518, 48 S.Ct. 404, 72 L.Ed. 681, 57 A.L.R. 426.

The injustice and confusion incident to the doctrine of Swift v. Tyson have been repeatedly urged as reasons for abolishing or limiting diversity of citizenship jurisdiction. Other legislative relief has been proposed. If only a question of statutory construction were involved, we should not be prepared to abandon a doctrine so widely applied throughout nearly a century. But the unconstitutionality of the course pursued has now been made clear and compels us to do so.

Third. Except in matters governed by the Federal Constitution or by Acts of Congress, the law to be applied in any case is the law of the State. And whether the law of the State shall be declared by its Legislature in a statute or by its highest court in a decision is not a matter of federal concern. There is no federal general common law.[5] Congress has no power to declare substantive rules of common law applicable in a State whether they be local in their nature or "general," be they commercial law or a part of the law of torts. And no clause in the Constitution purports to confer such a power upon the federal courts. As stated by Mr. Justice Field when protesting in Baltimore & Ohio R. Co. v. Baugh, 149 U.S. 368, 401, 13 S.Ct. 914, 37 L.Ed. 772; against ignoring the Ohio common law of fellow servant liability: "I am aware that what has been termed the general law of the country—which is often little less than what the judge advancing the doctrine thinks at the time should be the general law on a particular subject—has been often advanced in judicial opinions of this

---

5. [Note carefully the word "general" in this sentence. See United States v. Kearns, 595 F.2d 729, 732 (D.C. Cir. 1978): "Despite misreadings of Justice Brandeis's position in *Erie*, it is by now accepted that federal common law provides remedies in many situations." See generally Friendly, In Praise of Erie—and of the New Federal Common Law, 39 N.Y.U.L. Rev. 383 (1964).—Ed.]

court to control a conflicting law of a State. I admit that learned judges have fallen into the habit of repeating this doctrine as a convenient mode of brushing aside the law of a State in conflict with their views. And I confess that, moved and governed by the authority of the great names of those judges, I have, myself, in many instances, unhesitatingly and confidently, but I think now erroneously, repeated the same doctrine. But, notwithstanding the great names which may be cited in favor of the doctrine, and notwithstanding the frequency with which the doctrine has been reiterated, there stands, as a perpetual protest against its repetition, the Constitution of the United States, which recognizes and preserves the autonomy and independence of the States—independence in their judicial departments. Supervision over either the legislative or the judicial action of the States is in no case permissible except as to matters by the Constitution specifically authorized or delegated to the United States. Any interference with either, except as thus permitted, is an invasion of the authority of the State, and, to that extent, a denial of its independence."

The fallacy underlying the rule declared in Swift v. Tyson is made clear by Mr. Justice Holmes. Kuhn v. Fairmont Coal Co., 215 U.S. 349, 370–372, 30 S.Ct. 140, 54 L.Ed. 228; Black & White Taxicab Co. v. Brown & Yellow Taxicab Co., 276 U.S. 518, 532–36, 48 S. Ct. 404, 72 L.Ed. 681, 57 A.L.R. 426. The doctrine rests upon the assumption that there is a "transcendental body of law outside of any particular State but obligatory within it unless and until changed by statute," that federal courts have the power to use their judgment as to what the rules of common law are; and that in the federal courts "the parties are entitled to an independent judgment on matters of general law": * * * "but law in the sense in which courts speak of it today does not exist without some definite authority behind it. The common law so far as it is enforced in a State, whether called common law or not, is not the common law generally but the law of that State existing by the authority of that State without regard to what it may have been in England or anywhere else. * * * "the authority and only authority is the State, and if that be so, the voice adopted by the State as its own [whether it be of its Legislature or of its Supreme Court] should utter the last word."

Thus the doctrine of Swift v. Tyson is, as Mr. Justice Holmes said, "an unconstitutional assumption of powers by courts of the United States which no lapse of time or respectable array of opinion should make us hesitate to correct." In disapproving that doctrine we do not hold unconstitutional § 34 of the Federal Judiciary Act of 1789 or any other Act of Congress. We merely declare that in applying the doctrine this Court and the lower courts have invaded rights which in our opinion are reserved by the Constitution to the several States.

Fourth. The defendant contended that by the common law of Pennsylvania as declared by its highest court in Falchetti v. Pennsylvania R. Co., 307 Pa. 203, 160 A. 859, the only duty owed to the plaintiff was to refrain from wilful or wanton injury. The plaintiff denied that such is the Pennsylvania law. In support of their respective contentions the parties discussed and cited many decisions of the Supreme Court of the State. The Circuit Court of Appeals ruled that the question of liability is one of general law; and on that ground declined to decide the issue of state law. As we hold this was error, the judgment is reversed and the case remanded to it for further proceedings in conformity with our opinion.

Reversed.

Mr. Justice CARDOZO took no part in the consideration or decision of this case. [The concurring opinion of Mr. Justice REED and the dissenting opinion of Mr. Justice BUTLER, in which Mr. Justice McREYNOLDS concurred, are omitted.]

NOTES

1. Prior to 1938, the Federal Courts were required to follow the procedural law of the state in which they sat, but (within the limits noted in *Erie*) free under Swift v. Tyson, to find their own substantive law. With the adoption of the Federal Rules of Civil Procedure in 1938, and the overruling of Swift v. Tyson by *Erie*, the situation was reversed. You should be warned, however, that it is not always easy to distinguish substance from procedure. See e. g., Bolton v. Travelers Ins. Co., 475 F.2d 176 (5th Cir. 1973) (statute of limitations held to be substantive but time for answer and appearance held to be procedural); and see Murray v. Wilson Oak Flooring Co., Inc., 475 F.2d 129 (7th Cir. 1973) in which both sides agreed, and the court did not discuss, that the law of Illinois controlled the question whether it was appropriate to grant judgment n. o. v.

2. If the law to be applied is the same, what factors would lead a party to choose a federal court over a state court?

3. As federal court dockets grow larger, calls for the abolition or sharp restriction of diversity jurisdiction grow louder. See e. g., Friendly, Federal Jurisdiction: A General Review, Part VII (1973). A major objection is that the federal court is not free to decide the case as it feels it should be decided but must either, where the state decision is clear, act as a "ventriloquist's dummy" to the state court or, where the law is not clear, speculate about how the state court would decide it if the case were before it. Id. at 142–43.

KING v. ORDER OF UNITED COMMERCIAL TRAVELERS OF AMERICA

Supreme Court of the United States, 1948.
333 U.S. 153, 68 S.Ct. 488, 92 L.Ed. 608.

On Writ of Certiorari to the United States Circuit Court of Appeals for the Fourth Circuit.

* * *

Mr. Chief Justice VINSON delivered the opinion of the Court.

This is a suit to obtain payment of the proceeds of a $5,000 insurance policy. Federal jurisdiction is founded on diversity of citizenship, and, for present purposes, South Carolina law is controlling. We granted certiorari in order to determine whether the Circuit Court of Appeals' refusal (161 F.2d 108) to follow the only South Carolina decision directly in point, the decision of a Court of Common Pleas, was consistent with the Rules of Decision Act as applied in Erie R. Co. v. Tompkins, 1938, 304 U.S. 64, 58 S.Ct. 817, 82 L.Ed. 1188, 114 A.L.R. 1487, and subsequent cases.

The petitioner, Mrs. King, is the beneficiary of the policy; her husband, Lieutenant King, was the insured; and the respondent Order of United Travelers of America is the insurer. The policy insured against King's accidental death, but contained a clause exempting the respondent from liability for "death resulting from participation * * * in aviation." It is this aviation exclusion clause which gave rise to the litigation now before us.

King lost his life one day in the winter of 1943 when a land-based Civil Air Patrol plane in which he was flight observer made an emergency landing thirty miles off the coast of North Carolina. The plane sank, but King was not seriously hurt and managed to get out of the plane and don his life jacket. He was still alive two and a half hours later, when an accompanying plane was forced to leave the scene. When picked up about four and a half hours after the landing, however, he was dead. The medical diagnosis was "drowning as a result of exposure in the water."

The respondent took the position that death, while "accidental," resulted from "participation * * * in aviation." Accordingly, it refused to pay Mrs. King the proceeds of the policy. A resident of South Carolina, she then sued the respondent in a court of that State, contending that drowning rather than the airplane flight was the cause of death within the meaning of the policy. The respondent, an Ohio corporation, exercised its statutory right to remove the cause to the federal District Court for the Western District of South Carolina.

The parties agreed that South Carolina law was controlling, but up to the time of the District Court's decision neither of them had located any decision on aviation exclusion clauses by any South Carolina court. The District Court therefore fell back on what it deemed to be general principles of South Carolina insurance law, as enunciated by the State supreme court: that ambiguities in an insurance contract are to be resolved in favor of the beneficiary, and that the cause of death, within the meaning of accident insurance policies, is the immediate, not the remote cause. Applying these principles, the court held that King's death resulted from drowning, not from participation in aviation, and that Mrs. King was entitled to recover.

Two months later, a South Carolina court, the Court of Common Pleas for Spartanburg County, likewise ruled in favor of Mrs. King in a suit against a different insurer on a $2,500 policy which contained an almost identical aviation exclusion clause. The judge followed the same reasoning as the District Court had and relied, at least in part, on that court's decision. Under South Carolina statutes the insurer in this second case had the right to appeal to the State Supreme Court, but did not do so.

On appeal of the present case, the Circuit Court of Appeals reversed the District Court's judgment for Mrs. King. The court acknowledged that under South Carolina law ambiguities in insurance policies are to be construed against the insurer, but it found no ambiguity in the aviation exclusion clause insofar as its application to the facts of this case was concerned. On the contrary, King's death was thought clearly to have resulted from "participation * * * in aviation." Nothing in South Carolina Supreme Court decisions, it was said, was inconsistent with this view, whereas that court's accepted theories of proximate cause in tort cases supported it. Under these circumstances, the Circuit Court of Appeals expressed its disbelief that the Supreme Court of South Carolina would have ruled for Mrs. King, had her case been before it, "in the face of reason and the very considerable authority" from other jurisdictions. The Common Pleas decision in Mrs. King's favor, it was thought, was not binding on the Circuit Court of Appeals as a final expression of South Carolina law since it was not binding on other South Carolina courts and since the court rendering it had relied on the District Court's ruling in the present case.

After we granted certiorari, a new factor was interjected in the case. Another South Carolina Court of Common Pleas, the one for Greenville County, handed down an opinion which, so far as relevant here, expressly rejected the reasoning of the Spartanburg Court of Common Pleas and espoused that of the Circuit Court of Appeals.

What effect, if any, we should give to this second Common Pleas decision becomes an appropriate subject for inquiry only if it is first determined that the Circuit Court of Appeals erred in not following the Spartanburg decision, which was the only one outstanding at the time of its action.[6] We therefore address ourselves first to that question.

The Rules of Decision Act commands federal courts to regard as "rules of decision" the substantive "laws" of the appropriate state, except only where the Constitution, treaties or statutes of the United States provide otherwise. And the Erie R. Co. case decided that "laws," in this context, include not only state statutes, but also the unwritten law of a state as pronounced by its courts.

The ideal aimed at by the Act is, of course, uniformity of decision within each state. So long as it does not impinge on federal interests, a state may shape its own law in any direction it sees fit, and it is inadmissible that cases dependent on that law should be decided differently according to whether they are before federal or state courts. This is particularly true where accidental factors such as diversity of citizenship and the amount in controversy enable one of the parties to choose whether the case is tried in a federal or a state court.

Effectuation of that policy is comparatively easy when the issue confronting a federal court has previously been decided by the highest court in the appropriate state; the Erie R. Co. case decided that decisions and opinions of that court are binding on federal courts. The Erie R. Co. case left open, however, the more difficult question of the effect to be given to decisions by lower state courts on points never passed on by the highest state court.

Two years later, a series of four cases presented some aspects of that question. In three of the cases this Court held that federal courts are bound by decisions of a state's intermediate appellate courts unless there is persuasive evidence that the highest state court would rule otherwise. Six Companies of California v. Joint Highway District No. 13 of California, 1940, 311 U.S. 180, 61 S.Ct. 186, 85 L. Ed. 114; West v. American Telephone & Telegraph Co., 1940, 311 U. S. 223, 61 S.Ct. 179, 85 L.Ed. 139, 132 A.L.R. 956; and Stoner v. New York Life Ins. Co., 1940, 311 U.S. 464, 61 S.Ct 336, 85 L.Ed. 284.[7] In the fourth case, Fidelity Union Trust Co. v. Field, 1940, 311 U.S. 169, 61 S.Ct. 176, 85 L.Ed. 109, the Court went farther and held that a federal court had to follow two decisions announced four years ear-

---

6. Although the decision by the Spartanburg Court of Common Pleas was rendered after the District Court decision, it was proper for the Circuit Court of Appeals to consider it. See Vandenbark v. Owens-Illinois Glass Co., 1941, 311 U.S. 538, 61 S.Ct. 347, 85 L.Ed. 327.

7. In all three cases the state supreme court had refused to review the intermediate appellate court decision; in the West and Stoner cases, the intermediate appellate court's decision had involved the same parties engaged in the subsequent case before the federal courts; and in the Six Companies case, the intermediate appellate court's decision had remained on the books for over twenty years without disapproval. These factors were mentioned in our opinions, but were not necessarily determinative. See Fidelity Union Trust Co. v. Field, 1940, 311 U.S. 169, 178, 61 S.Ct. 176, 178, 85 L.Ed. 109.

Sec. 2   STATE DECISIONS IN FEDERAL COURTS   251

lier by the New Jersey Court of Chancery, a court of original jurisdiction.

The Fidelity Union Trust Co. case did not, however, lay down any general rule as to the respect to be accorded state trial court decisions. This Court took pains to point out that the status of the New Jersey Court of Chancery was not that of the usual *nisi prius* court. It had state-wide jurisdiction. Its standing on the equity side was comparable to that of New Jersey's intermediate appellate courts on the law side. A uniform ruling by the Court of Chancery over a course of years was seldom set aside by the state's highest court. And chancery decrees were ordinarily treated as binding in later cases in chancery.

The present case involves no attack on the policy of the Rules of Decision Act, the principle of the Erie R. Co. case, or the soundness of the other cases referred to above. It involves the practical administration of the Act; and the question it raises is whether, in the long run, it would promote uniformity in the application of South Carolina law if federal courts confronted with questions under that law were obliged to follow the ruling of a Court of Common Pleas.

The Courts of Common Pleas make up South Carolina's basic system of trial courts for civil actions.[8] There are fourteen judges for these courts, one for each of the judicial circuits into which the state's forty-six counties are grouped. A circuit judge hears civil cases at specified times in each county comprising the circuit to which he is then assigned, and at such times his court is called the Court of Common Pleas for that particular county. In addition, he presides over a parallel set of criminal courts, the Courts of General Sessions. South Carolina has no tier of intermediate appellate courts, and appeal from Common Pleas decisions is directly, and as a matter of right, to the State supreme court.

While the Courts of Common Pleas are denominated courts of record, their decisions are not published or digested in any form whatsoever. They are filed only in the counties in which the cases are tried, and even there the sole index is by the parties' names. Perhaps because these facts preclude ready availability to bench and bar, the Common Pleas decisions seem to be accorded little weight as precedents in South Carolina's own courts. In this connection, respondent has submitted a certificate from the Chief Justice of the Su-

---

8. S.C.Const. Art. 5, § 15. These courts also have limited appellate jurisdiction, varying somewhat from county to county. The Court of Common Pleas for Spartanburg County handles appeals from the county's probate court, 1 S.C.Code Ann. § 228, its court of domestic relations, 1 id. §§ 256–24 and 256–44, and its magistrates courts. The latter have civil jurisdiction concurrent with the courts of Common Pleas only in suits involving less than $100, 1 id. § 257.

The county court for Spartanburg County has concurrent jurisdiction in civil suits involving less than $3,000, but appeal from its decisions is directly to the Supreme Court of South Carolina, 1 id. §§ 184 and 190.

preme Court of South Carolina to the effect that "under the practice in this State an unappealed decision of the Court of Common Pleas is binding solely upon the parties who are before the Court in that particular case and would not constitute a precedent in any other case in that Court or in any other court in the State of South Carolina."

Consideration of these facts leads us to the conclusion that the Circuit Court of Appeals did not commit error. While that court properly attributed some weight to the Spartanburg Common Pleas decision, we believe that it was justified in holding the decision not controlling and in proceeding to make its own determination of what the Supreme Court of South Carolina would probably rule in a similar case.

In the first place, a Court of Common Pleas does not appear to have such importance and competence within South Carolina's own judicial system that its decisions should be taken as authoritative expositions of that State's "law." In future cases between different parties, as indicated above, a Common Pleas decision does not exact conformity from either the same court or lesser courts [9] within its territorial jurisdiction; and it may apparently be ignored by other Courts of Common Pleas without the compunctions which courts often experience in reaching results divergent from those reached by another court of coordinate jurisdiction. Thus a Common Pleas decision does not, so far as we have been informed, of itself evidence one of the "rules of decision commonly accepted and acted upon by the bar and inferior courts." Furthermore, as we have but recently had occasion to remark, a federal court adjudicating a matter of state law in a diversity suit is, "in effect, only another court of the State"; it would be incongruous indeed to hold the federal court bound by a decision which would not be binding on any state court.

Secondly, the difficulty of locating Common Pleas decisions is a matter of great practical significance. Litigants could find all the decisions on any given subject only by laboriously searching the judgment rolls in all of South Carolina's forty-six counties. To hold that federal courts must abide by Common Pleas decisions might well put a premium on the financial ability required for exhaustive screening of the judgment rolls or for the maintenance of private records. In cases where the parties could not afford such practices, the result would often be to make their rights dependent on chance; for every decision cited by counsel there might be a dozen adverse decisions outstanding but undiscovered.[10]

In affirming the decision below, we are deciding only that the Circuit Court of Appeals did not have to follow the decision of the

---

9. I.e., county courts, magistrates courts, probate courts, and courts of domestic relations.

10. In the present case, the Spartanburg decision came to light because petitioner had been a party to it, the Greenville decision because respondent's counsel had been a party to it.

Court of Common Pleas for Spartanburg County. We do not purport to determine the correctness of its ruling on the merits. Nor is our decision to be taken as promulgating a general rule that federal courts need never abide by determinations of state law by state trial courts. As indicated by the Fidelity Union Trust Co. case, other situations in other states may well call for a different result.

It may also be well to add that even if the Circuit Court of Appeals had been in error at the time of its decision, reversal of its judgment would not necessarily be appropriate in view of the second Common Pleas decision. But we prefer to regard that second decision as an illustration of the perils of interpreting a Common Pleas decision as a definitive expression of "South Carolina law," not as a controlling factor in our decision.

Affirmed.

NOTES

1. In Roginsky v. Richardson-Merrell, Inc., 378 F.2d 832, 851 (2d Cir. 1967) the court said: "We do not regard ourselves as bound by the rulings of a state *nisi prius* judge although we treat these with respect."

2. As illustrated by King v. Commercial Travelers, the ascertainment of state law is not always a simple matter: sometimes there are no decisions on, or near, point; sometimes the only decisions on point are old, and the federal court must guess whether they would be followed today; sometimes the cases are muddled. What should the court do? With rare exceptions, the federal court must *decide* the case before it. It cannot wait for clarification or refer the matter back to the states. In some states, there is a procedure available by which some questions can be certified to the highest court of the state for resolution. Wecker v. Kilmer, 471 F.2d 782 (7th Cir. 1972). There are also some special circumstances in which it may be proper for the federal court to abstain from exercising jurisdiction. The special circumstances do not include difficulty in deciding questions of state law. Wohl v. Keene, 476 F.2d 171 (4th Cir. 1973).

3. If there is no controlling state court decision, should the views of a federal district court sitting in the state be given weight? In American Timber & Trad. Co. v. First Nat. Bank of Oregon, 511 F.2d 980 (9th Cir. 1973) the court said:

> "We attach great weight to the district court's determination as to the law of the particular state in which it sits, especially where, as here, there has been no clear exposition of the controlling principle by the highest court of Oregon. Insurance Co. of North America v. Thompson, 381 F.2d 677, 681 (9th Cir. 1967). The district court's determination will be accepted on review unless shown to be clearly wrong. Owens v. White, 380 F.2d 310, 315 (9th Cir. 1967). The bank has not convinced us that the decision of the district court (Judge Goodwin, a former Justice of the Oregon Supreme Court) is a clearly incorrect statement of Oregon law."

4. Federal court decisions on state law questions are not, of course, binding on the state courts—although they may be persuasive.

5. Diversity cases are not the only occasions in which federal courts must divine state laws. Frequently in federal tax cases the nature of a property transfer is determined by state law. See, e. g., Estate of Goldstein v. C.I.R., 479 F.2d 813 (10th Cir. 1973). For other situations, see Moore's Federal Practice, Para. 0.319 et seq., (2d ed. 1977).

6. There are many situations in which state courts have jurisdiction over *federal* questions. In applying federal law, the state courts must follow United States Supreme Court decisions. How about lower federal courts?

Chapter V

THE INTERPRETATION OF STATUTES

We turn now to the subject of legislation. At the beginning of our study, substantial attention was devoted to the organization and operation of courts in order to provide a basis for a better understanding of the case law the courts produce. In the same way, initial consideration is given here to legislative institutions and processes to assist in the understanding of legislative law. With this as a foundation, we then take up, in the balance of Chapter V, the finding, stating and resolution of statutory issues.

SECTION 1. THE LEGISLATIVE PROCESS

A. INTRODUCTION

A working knowledge of legislative institutions and processes is indispensable for many aspects of a lawyer's work.

Lawyers may, for example, be directly involved in the legislative process itself. They may represent clients seeking to promote or defeat legislation or clients appearing before legislative committees. They may serve as legislators themselves, lawyers being generally one of the most numerous occupational group among legislators. In all such cases the need for knowledge of the legislature's functioning seems clear beyond any need for discussion.

Lawyers may also undertake the labor of legislative drafting. Virtually all, be it observed, of the professional draftsmen now serving our legislatures and administrative agencies are lawyers, and lawyers who are not professional draftsmen may well be called upon to do such work too. In any event the task of bill drafting demands an understanding of the process of enactment. Bills are made to pass, said Lord Thring, as razors are made to sell. They must be framed in such a way as to maximize their chances of survival in the legislature, in addition to complying with any formal requirements laid down by that body. For an example of the strategies that may be necessary, consider the McGuire Act passed in response to Schwegmann Bros. v. Calvert Distillers Corp. (infra p. 413). Why is it drawn to amend the Federal Trade Commission Act rather than the Miller-Tydings Amendment?

Of all the professional tasks a lawyer is called on to perform, one of the most frequent is that of interpreting legislation. He may be called on for interpretation, for example, as counsel advising clients of their rights under statutes, or as advocate urging, or defending against, a statutory claim, or as a judge or administrator ruling on the application of legislative language, or as a scholar explaining or appraising its significance. That a knowledge of the legislative process is needed in interpretation should become apparent from the cases. For example, in the sequence of cases from Johnson v. Southern Pacific Co. through Commonwealth v. Maxwell (infra pp. 327 through 381) one sees dramatic illustrations of the American judicial practice of resort to legislative history in aid of interpretation. It plainly requires an acquaintance with institutions and processes to find such material readily and reliably and to weigh it discriminatingly once found.

But the need for such knowledge is not restricted to the foregoing explicitly legislative aspects of a lawyer's work. In his general role of problem-solver, a lawyer needs to know what his resources are —including legislative resources—and when and how they can be best applied. Does a particular problem before him call for resolution by non-official means, or by courts or legislatures or administrative agencies or by some combination of these? Such questions demand, in the day to day work of lawyers, a sure sense of the capabilities and limitations of legislative institutions and processes, among others, and of their role in the development of law.

Bearing such needs in mind we have set out in the ensuing pages some basic information on the legislature and its operation, with emphasis on the Congress of the United States but with some comparative comments regarding the states. Those to whom this subject is familiar from political science courses or the like may find it useful as a refresher. Those to whom it is new or nearly so should use these pages as a starting point only and supplement them by reference to some of the more detailed works listed in the Bibliographical Note appearing at the end of this Section.

In going through the material that follows, especially as the stages of the legislative process are reviewed, it may be helpful to keep in view some general and specific questions. As a general question, a reader might well ask himself at each stage—what does this aspect of the legislature or its procedures disclose about the nature of the legislative institution, about the special advantages and disadvantages of legislative lawmaking and its part in the American legal system? More specifically, and with an eye to the practical use of the process, he should also ask himself the legislative advocate's (lobbyist's) question—what can be done at this stage to speed a bill on its way or obstruct its advance? The effort to answer this last question will surely shed light on the more general question first suggested. Finally, with an eye to interpretive considerations, it is instructive to ask—what does this phase of the process yield in the way of records of legislative deliberations and where are they to be found? What is or should be the weight of these particular records in the search for "legislative intent"?

B. STRUCTURE, POWERS, FUNCTIONS

Before the lawmaking process is examined it will be well to review briefly some general elements of legislative structure, powers and functioning at both the federal and state levels. The Constitution provides a starting point.

The foundations of the national legislature are laid in Article I, Section 1 of the Constitution of the United States of 1789. That section creates the Congress of the United States, composed of a Senate and House of Representatives, and gives it all of the national legislative power. Other sections sketch the organization and procedures, and enumerate the specific powers, of Congress and establish it as a force distinct from the executive. From such provisions, fortified by interpretation and practice, Congress emerges as one of the most redoubtable legislative bodies in today's world. Its power is especially remarkable at a time when the position of legislatures has generally been declining vis-a-vis the executive.

Congress stands apart not only for its power but also as a truly bicameral body. That is, it is a body in which the two houses have comparable power or, to look at it from the legislative advocate's viewpoint, one in which the sponsor of legislation must persuade not one but two houses to his view. Why bicameral? The Founding Fathers perhaps took their cue from Parliament or from contemporary colonial legislatures. But the decision to have two houses was certainly cemented by the so-called Connecticut Compromise devised to reconcile the self-protective view of some small states that all states should be equally represented with the view of other states that state representation should be based on population. Under the Compromise, one house, the Senate, was organized according to the view of the small states; the other, the House of Representatives, according to the opposing view. Even without the historical justification of this compromise, forty-nine of fifty states have also clung to the bicameral form with its dispersion of power. They have done this despite the urgings of political scientists that a single chamber is more efficient and conducive to more responsible lawmaking. Only Nebraska has a unicameral legislature.

The strength of the United States Senate stands at 100 members, a figure reached following the admission of Alaska and Hawaii to statehood in the late 1950's. Each state has two Senators. The term of office of each Senator is six years and the terms of all Senators are staggered so that approximately one-third of the membership comes up for election every two years and so that the terms of the two Senators representing a particular state do not coincide. Such staggering provides continuity but also tends to insulate the Senate in some measure from the immediate reflection of shifts of popular feeling.

258   THE INTERPRETATION OF STATUTES   Ch. 5

More than four times as large, the number of House members has been stabilized since the 1960 census at a total of 435. Within this total, the number of Representatives elected from each state is adjusted after each decennial census so as to reflect the state's current proportion of the total United States population, but each state is entitled to at least one Representative. The term of office of a Representative is two years and, since the terms are not staggered, all members of the House come up for election every two years. While the effect of this short term is, to a degree, to make the House more responsive to shifts of popular sentiment, it affords members very little respite from the pressures of campaigning for reelection.

Obedient to Article I, Section 4 of the Constitution which requires it to "assemble at least once in every year," Congress regularly convenes each January. Although the Senate holds over, a new "Congress" is reckoned to begin in each odd-numbered year, following the election of a new House of Representatives, and lasts for a cycle of two "sessions." The first session of a Congress commences in January of the odd-numbered year; the second session in January of the even-numbered year. Under the Twentieth Amendment each session begins at noon on January 3 unless otherwise provided. There may of course be special sessions but these are not apt to occur when, as has been the case in recent years, regular sessions continue throughout most of every year.

The state legislatures vary widely in size. New Hampshire's lower house is largest with 400 members and Alaska's and Nevada's are the smallest with 40 each; New York's has 150. Minnesota's senate is the largest upper house with 67 members and Alaska's and Nevada's are the smallest with 20 each; New York's has 60. Most state senators serve 4-year terms (often staggered), the rest 2-year terms. The members of all but a few lower houses have terms of 2 years. Specially to be noted, however, is the matter of sessions in the state legislatures. In the past, because of hobbling constitutional provisions adopted in a 19th century wave of reaction against state legislative corruption, a significant number of state legislatures met only biennially and in many states only short sessions were allowed. The trend in recent years is toward annual sessions and more flexibility in the length of sessions.

As for the membership of legislatures, studies show that the nation's legislators are mainly drawn from three groups of citizens—lawyers, businessmen and farmers—and that a large number come from middle and upper class backgrounds and have attended college. Although there is some evidence that the situation may be changing, lawyers predominate both in Congress and the state legislatures. In part this is because the demands of law practice can be better reconciled with legislative service than those of many other occupations. In part, also, the problem-solving abilities and proclivities of lawyers, their skills of analysis, of negotiation and compromise, of debate, and the like, are specific advantages in relation to legislative activity. Lawyers have been so widely preferred in America as spokesmen for economic and other interests and powers that it is not surprising to find them representing the citizenry in the legislature.

It is not proposed to discuss here the large subject of nominations and elections for legislative office. With respect to the members of the Congress suffice it to note that the nature of the processes by which they are nominated and elected has a decided bearing on their behavior in office. In practice, nomination and election are frequently dominated by local coalitions or circumstances, the role of central parties being often weak. Such weakness contributes in turn to a result of considerable significance for the legislative process: general weakness of the national parties as forces to control attitudes in the Congress. With respect to state legislators, a similar decentralization in nominations and elections is frequently observable.

A vast and varied business is carried on by the Congress we have been describing. The primary function of Congress is of course that of lawmaking. All the legislative power entrusted by the Constitution to the national government is conferred upon the Congress in Article I, Section 1. In our American scheme, it is to the Congress that the citizenry looks for the major declarations and shifts of public policy. Among others, the most difficult and substantial problems of society commonly come to this forum for negotiation, compromise and authoritative settlement. And the extent of Congress's lawmaking concerns in the present era is little short of staggering. The enumeration of Congress's legislative powers in Article I, Section 8 of the Constitution—including familiar powers to tax, borrow, and spend, to regulate commerce, to provide for defense and for the general welfare, etc.—merely sketches the underpinning. On this constitutional foundation of granted powers, generously construed by the courts, Congress legislates today for the ongoing needs of a huge government establishment and for substantive concerns as diverse as tariffs, public lands, currency, transportation, highways, aviation, atomic energy, space exploration, urban renewal, communications, environmental protection, social security, welfare, housing, education, industrial safety, wages and hours, labor-management relations, agriculture, foreign aid, defense, sale of securities, armed services, and so forth. Its responsibilities for public finance, for taxes and other revenue, for borrowing and for appropriations inevitably require it to scrutinize and deal with an enormous range of activities embracing all those just mentioned by way of illustration and others too numerous to itemize. Lawyers, in particular, should be mindful too that Congressional responsibilities include the revision and updating of the substantial body of federal statute law, to say nothing of "back-up" work in dealing with unsatisfactory lawmaking by judicial and administrative agencies. Beyond all these aspects of general legislation, there is a continuing and not negligible concern with private legislation in settlement, for example, of individual claims against the government or individual immigration or naturalization cases.

Lawmaking is not the only function of Congress or Congressmen. There is too, for example, the conduct of investigations—commonly in aid of lawmaking and often in pursuit of another major Congressional concern, that of checking on the administration of the laws. The Legislative Reorganization Act of 1946 focused a spotlight on this last concern and called for "continuous oversight" by Congressional committees of the administrative arms of government. Such checking seemed to the sponsors and has seemed to many since to be particularly necessary at a time when the speed and complexity of modern industrial society have required Congress to delegate much power to administrators. "Oversight" permits Congress to appraise administrative performance and to revise the machinery and rules and to provide funds for administrative activity as appropriate.

Other functions are performed by Congress as well, for example in the exercise of its constitutional powers regarding impeachment of executive and judicial officers, regarding the election and qualification of Senators and Representatives, and regarding, in certain cases, the election of the President and Vice President. The importance of the seldom-used impeachment power was dramatically demonstrated by the Congressional proceedings regarding President Nixon. The Senate participates to a degree—i. e. by "advice and consent"—in the making of appointments and in the treaty-making process. Both houses devote some time to internal housekeeping.

No sketch of Congressional business and functions can be adequate which fails to indicate two other areas of activity which account for a substantial part of the workload and time of all legislators: the rendering of services to constituents and campaigning for reelection. Reelection is a virtually constant preoccupation of Representatives whose brief two-year term leaves, as we noted, little breathing space between campaigns. The six-year term of Senators gives them a relatively substantial period of relief from reelection politics. But for both Senators and Representatives, so-called "errand-running" for constituents, responding to constituents' letters and telephone calls, seeing them when they come to Washington, and contacting administrative agencies on their behalf consume a major share of the legislators' energy and scarce time. This activity is felt by almost all legislators to be important, and the proximity of campaigns reinforces this attitude. Insofar as it provides a humanizing link between many citizens and their government it may indeed be vital, notwithstanding that it cuts so heavily into the time available for lawmaking and other functions.

Allowances for staff assistance—perhaps the most important contribution of the Legislative Reorganization Act of 1946 was its strengthening of Congressional staffing—provide the legislators with crucial aid in performing constituent services and other tasks, but a heavy burden remains for the individual legislator. It is sometimes instructive to recall the range of Congressional functions and business, and the extensive pressures steadily brought to bear on Congress and its members, in appraising the validity of the various calls upon the legislature found from time to time in judicial opinions.

The functions of the state legislatures resemble those of Congress—e. g., lawmaking, investigations, oversight of administration, service to constituents. The all-important lawmaking function builds, however, on different premises in the States. In our constitutional system, the state legislature possesses residual power. That is, except as the state constitution otherwise provides, it has all lawmaking power not granted exclusively to the national government, or denied to the states, in the national constitution. The limitations on state legislative power are thus crucial in defining that power.

Some of the powers granted (not all are exclusive) to the national government by the Constitution were suggested earlier. As for powers denied the states, Article I, Section 10 of the Constitution, for example, bars the states from such activities as making treaties, coining money, or passing bills of attainder, ex post facto laws or laws impairing the obligation of contracts. It forbids also the levying of import duties and, unless there be Congressional consent, the making of compacts between states. Beyond this, recall too that the Fourteenth Amendment as interpreted by the Supreme Court has served to set limits upon state legislatures.

The state constitutions themselves contain many and serious limitations on state legislative power. Such limitations are to an important degree monuments to 19th century distrust of the state legislatures. They include express prohibitions of various kinds and, on occasion, have been read to imply other limitations. They include restrictions on special, local or private legislation, on the power to tax, on the power to incur debt, on spending (as by earmarking of revenues), on legislative procedures and so on. Shackled as they are by such constitutional restrictions, the state legislatures have nevertheless a wide field in which they may act to tax, spend and regulate. Their reach embraces legislation on—to name but a few important areas out of many—education, highways, welfare, public health, local government, utilities, banking, business organization, agriculture, insurance, motor vehicles, domestic relations, trades and professions, elections and criminal law. Many more subjects within the broad ambit of state legislation will occur to almost any reader. They include the revision and updating of state statute law and the correction of unsatisfactory judicial and administrative lawmaking.

C. SOURCE AND DEVELOPMENT OF LEGISLATIVE PROPOSALS

From this point on, perhaps the best way to pursue our examination of legislative institutions and processes is to consider—in roughly the order which they occur—the various stages in the development and enactment of a legislative proposal. Discussion will focus on the legislative machinery and procedures at each stage to the extent that seems appropriate to our present concerns, leaving fuller exploration of the subject to independent study and to courses in Legislation. Attention will be concentrated on the Congress of the United States. Comments comparing state legislative organization and processes with those of Congress are reserved to a concluding section.

Where and how do the legislative proposals that come to Congress originate? Not infrequently the origins of such proposals are impossible to trace. As with folk songs, so many different persons and forces may have been involved over time with a particular proposal that its authorship is lost in the mazes. Ideas can and do spring from private interest groups or constituents or from Congressmen themselves or from the studies, investigations or hearings of Congressional committees. But it is important to note that the source for a substantial share of major legislation is in the executive, including the bureaus and departments and other agencies of the national government which are in day to day contact with the practical operation of laws within their charge. The administrative agencies have technical staffs equipped to draft needed proposals and very commonly present their proposals to the Congress in the form of draft bills ready for legislative consideration. Also important are proposals which have their immediate source in the private sector—in labor or civic groups, in professional associations or in industrial or agricultural organizations. Here too, the proposals may be tendered in the form of bills. As for the role of Congress, George Galloway some years ago observed that "today less than half of all legislation originates in Congress." But, he added, "that body is still responsible for sifting, testing, and debating the final shape of public policy." In such circumstances, it is apparent that to a significant degree and for much legislation, Congress is not an initiator but is engaged in review and revision of proposals originating elsewhere. Wherever a bill originates, however, it must, as we shall later see, be introduced by some member or members of Congress before Congress will act upon it.

If as many commentators claim there is an increasing trend in Congress to look for executive initiative in the formulation and submission of legislative proposals, it is appropriate to consider more closely the involvement of the executive, especially the President. It is a familiar fact that the President plays a part of great importance —as initiator, advocate and wielder of the veto—in the development of federal legislation. His role as initiator concerns us here, a role crystallized in the annual flow of general and special messages from the White House to Capitol Hill.

The President today transmits to Congress three general messages at the beginning of each year. One is expressly mentioned in Article II, Section 3 of the Constitution which provides that the Presi-

Sec. 1 *THE LEGISLATIVE PROCESS* 263

dent shall "from time to time give to the Congress Information of the State of the Union, and recommended to their Consideration such Measures as he shall judge necessary and expedient." The State of the Union message prepared pursuant to this provision typically sets out the President's program, including recommendations for legislative action. The second general message, required by the Budget and Accounting Act of 1921, is the President's Budget Message, which embraces proposals for appropriations legislation. His third general message is the Economic Report, which is required by the Employment Act of 1946 and also, when deemed appropriate, includes legislative proposals. In addition to these three major "executive communications" the President every year sends a multitude of special messages to Congress dealing with particular legislative subjects, sometimes on his own initiative, sometimes in accordance with statutory requirements; and he makes many proposals for legislation through letters and through contacts with the leaders of Congress, with standing committee chairmen and with rank-and-file members. Note that the formal executive communications here referred to may be of value as extrinsic aid materials to assist in the interpretation of enactments to which they relate. At the least such documents may serve to illuminate the circumstances leading to a measure's enactment and so clarify the purpose of Congress in adopting it. This is the case in Johnson v. Southern Pacific Co., infra p. 337, where Mr. Chief Justice Fuller in his opinion for the Supreme Court refers to annual messages of President Harrison for light on the background of the Act of 1893.

The President of course does not operate without assistance in these matters and his role in the federal legislative process and as executive head of a vast administrative establishment cannot be understood without some awareness of the Office of Management and Budget (OMB)—formerly the Bureau of the Budget—in the Executive Office of the President. The Office is a major, and many-sided, presidential instrument. While originating, and anchored, in budgetary matters, as its original title implies, its operations have grown to embrace staff assistance in matters of substantive policy, fiscal or otherwise, on a very broad basis. In addition to shaping and overseeing the executive budget under the President's direction (Congressional budget activities are discussed later), OMB has a large role in the development of the overall "presidential program." No less important and wide-ranging is the so-called central legislative clearance function of the OMB's Legislative Reference unit. The diverse activities of the Office in aid of these or other functions include, for example, participation in the devising of various "administration bills" and other proposed legislation, the preparation of executive orders, proclamations, messages and statements, and the rendering of information services to both the Executive and Congress, as well as many other staff chores aimed in the main at assisting the President to discharge effectively his manifold responsibilities. The significance of the Office in relation to the President's role as initiator of legislation should be plain enough.

An added word should be said here about the Office's legislative clearance function, just mentioned, which may shed further light on executive involvement in the legislative process. As a basis for understanding this work of the Office, it is useful to recall that relations between Congress and the executive branch are not confined to relations between Congress and the President. They include relations between Congress and, within the executive branch, a host of federal agencies whose respective interests may be mutually conflicting or may be at odds with the policies of the President. Some machinery of coordination is needed. Professor Richard E. Neustadt, in an excellent article (which deserves to be read in its entirety) entitled Presidency and Legislation: The Growth of Central Clearance, 48 Am.Pol.Sci.Rev. 641 (1954) succinctly summarizes the operation of legislative clearance as follows:

" * * * Essentially [legislative clearance operations] amount to central coordination and review of stands taken by the various federal agencies at three successive stages of the legislative process.

"Large numbers of the public measures introduced in Congress are formally proposed by agencies of the executive branch; departmental drafts officially en route to Congress first have to clear the Bureau of the Budget for interagency coordination and approval on the President's behalf. Once bills are introduced, regardless of their source, congressional committees ordinarily solicit views from interested agencies; official agency responses—in whatever form, to whomever addressed—first channel through the Budget Bureau for coordination and advice on each bill's relation to the President's program. When enrolled enactments come from Congress to the President for signature or veto, the Budget Bureau, as his agent, obtains, coordinates, and summarizes agency opinion on the merits, preparing in each case a presidential dossier complete with covering recommendation.

"These are the components of 'legislative clearance' as the term is normally employed. In practice, these operations are much more complex and a good deal less absolute than this simple recital would indicate. But generally speaking, central clearance has proceeded along these lines for many years.

"Last year [1953], despite the change of Administration, 380 agency drafts, 3,571 agency reports on pending bills, and 525 enrolled enactments were processed by the Budget Bureau. * * * "

In any consideration of the executive as source of legislative proposals, the points mainly to be stressed are first, that a great many of the proposals introduced in Congress emanate from the various agencies of the executive branch—not just the Office of the President—and, second, that agency bills and other recommendations before presentation to Congress are subject to a vital coordination process to minimize interagency conflict and to assure consonance with the President's program.

Our discussion of the genesis of legislation has so far passed over one essential phase in the development of a proposal and that is the drafting of it in the form of a bill. There is so much misunderstanding among laymen, and even among lawyers and judges (as judicial opinions sometimes demonstrate), of the problems and processes of drafting that a word to the uninitiated seems wise. The art of drafting bills, and it is an art, is a demanding one and it is not merely a branch of English composition for which pad, pencil, imagination, and a facility with the mother tongue are sufficient equipment. Some notion of what is involved in this art can measurably enhance one's skills and understanding in the use of legislation.

Whether the drafting be done in a private interest group, or an executive agency, or in the Congress, the problems of transforming an inchoate idea (virtually all ideas for legislation are more or less inchoate at the outset) into a sound well-thought-out statutory provision are generally the same. A draftsman should be thoroughly familiar at the start with the subject-matter of the legislative proposal before him (for example, with mining operations and conditions if it is a mine safety bill, or with pertinent insurance practices if an insurance bill) and should try to clarify, both at the start and as the job proceeds, the tenor and reach of the policies he is expected to embody in the bill. As to the latter, Bertram M. Gross in his book, The Legislative Struggle (1953) made the following trenchant observation (at p. 188) on a phase of drafting that is poorly understood: "The preparation of a bill * * * is not merely a method of recording policy or general principles that have been previously formulated. It is part and parcel of the process of policy formulation. It is a job of formulating general principles in a precise form and of making a long series of choices between alternative methods of building upon them." Early in the proceedings, the draftsman should master the existing law and experience of the jurisdiction which are pertinent to his proposal, just as an architect should study the site on which he must build. This is essential so that what he drafts can fit smoothly and workably with related laws. As far as he can he needs to search the laws and experience of other jurisdictions against the possibility that others have dealt successfully or unsuccessfully with the same problem. In this way he can profit from practical lessons learned elsewhere. At some point in his work he must come to grips with often difficult basic questions such as these: Is legislation the best route to resolution of the problem at hand? Or is resort to the judicial or administrative process more appropriate? Or should the matter be left to private arrangements? Would better enforcement of existing law solve the issue? If legislation seems the best course, how much territory should the bill cover? The answer may vary, for example, with the state of existing law, with the opposition or support anticipated, with judicial attitudes toward the subject involved. And how detailed should the draft be? Greater generality will increase flexibility, leave more to the courts or other interpreters; detail may assure stricter compliance but can lead to rigidity in the face of change or unforeseen circumstance. Among the sanctions available, which should be chosen to make the legislation most effective to solve the problem posed? Should the choice be the establishment of an administrative agency, licensing, civil penalties, criminal penalties, damage suits, punitive damages, injunctions or some other of the many weapons in the legislative arsenal? And throughout his work the draftsman should constantly keep in view the need to square his work with the commands of the Constitution and other law of higher authority than the one he is preparing. With all this in mind, one must recognize, of course, that time pressures or needs for political accommodation or both may—more often than one would wish—prevent a draftsman from doing his job with the thoroughness and precision it deserves.

Bertram Gross, at p. 191 of the work just quoted above, had this to say about the demands of bill drafting which we have just been sketching:

> " * * * [B]ill drafting calls for more talents than can be obtained through abstract legal training, no matter how excellent it may be or become. It calls for an intensive knowledge of administrative regulations, judicial decisions, existing law and other proposed laws in the fields where the work is being done. It requires an understanding of the realities behind the legal forms; above all, it requires an ability to appraise the line-up of interests and the relative strength of conflicting pressures and to assist in the formulation of basically political decisions. It calls for flexibility and dexterity in the use of language to convey meaning, and where necessary, to avoid meaning; both to avoid emotional connotations, and where necessary, to arouse emotion. In short it calls for a wide range of talents and skills in law, administration, economics, politics and public relations."

When the development of legislation, including bill drafting or the revision of bills submitted by others, is undertaken by committees of Congress or by individual Congressmen, specialized help is obviously needed for such an exacting task. For this purpose committees and members may and do call upon various staff services of the

Sec. 1 *THE LEGISLATIVE PROCESS* 267

Congress itself. First of these is the Congressional Research Service, formerly the Legislative Reference Service, established in 1915 in the Library of Congress as the research arm of the Congress, to which Congressmen and their personal and committee staffs turn extensively in gathering information for legislative and other purposes. Second, there is the Office of Legislative Counsel (two such offices exist, one serving the Senate and one the House) which performs bill-drafting services of high quality for the committees and for individual legislators. It is interesting to note that the Offices of Legislative Counsel were established in 1918 after the nature and value of such services had been successfully demonstrated to the Congress for two years by personnel of Columbia University's Legislative Drafting Research Fund.[1] Professional and clerical staffs of committees, and even personal staffs, are also used as aids in research and drafting work for the Congress. Of course, Congress and its staffs draw heavily for fact-finding and other help on the bureaus and departments of the executive and a not inconsiderable amount of such help is provided by private interest groups.

With the foregoing background on the sources of legislation, on the initiating role played by the executive, and on the tasks and resources involved in converting proposals into draft bills, we can turn more knowledgeably to a consideration of the stages through which a drafted bill must pass on its way to enactment as law by the Congress.

D. INTRODUCTION AND REFERENCE

Once the drafting of our legislative proposal has been completed and the bill is ready for Congressional consideration, it is necessary to take the appropriate formal steps to lay it before the Congress—i. e., to introduce the bill in one or both chambers. In contrast to the British Parliament where cabinet members may introduce bills, only a Representative can introduce legislation in the House of Representatives, only a Senator in the Senate. Thus the supporters of our proposal must find one or more sponsors in one or both chambers to assume responsibility for the bill and accomplish its introduction.

The choice of a sponsor or sponsors can be important. Sponsorship may represent a burdensome commitment and sponsors not infrequently have a degree of power over the fate of a measure. The sponsor identified with a bill is assumed to have taken a position in its favor (to avoid this, members sometimes insist on adding the phrase "on request" to the notice of their sponsorship) and frequently must defend this position in correspondence, in the Congress and in public discussion and in meeting proposals for amendment. From

---

1. Middleton Beaman, Esq., of the Legislative Drafting Research Fund, was appointed as first Legislative Counsel to the House of Representatives, a post he held for more than thirty years. Thomas I. Parkinson, Esq., also of the Fund, served as the Senate's first Legislative Counsel.

the proponents' point of view it is vital to know whether a potential sponsor is truly in favor of the proposal. If he is, will he take his commitment seriously? Is he strategically placed—say as a member of the Congressional leadership or as chairman of a standing committee (or, at least, as an influential member of it) and as a member of the majority party—so as to make his support most telling? Is he a tenacious and effective fighter if there are storms in the offing, as, for example, New York's Senator Wagner was in sponsoring the National Labor Relations Act and the Social Security Act? Significant Administration bills, which account for much of Congressional time and effort, are commonly introduced by the chairmen of the committees or subcommittees concerned with the subject-matter or, especially if the committee's support is in question, by a leader of the President's party in Congress. As to multiple sponsorship of bills, this has long been frequent in the Senate. It is possible now in the House, though the House formerly forbade cosponsorship and members were driven to introduce identical separately numbered bills to achieve their sponsorship objectives. Whether cosponsorship is desirable or not in a given case may depend on the circumstances. Dilution of responsibility and prestige must be weighed against a possible broadening of the base of support.

Once the issue of sponsorship has been settled, the sponsor or one of them introduces our legislative proposal. We shall assume that our proposal is to begin its legislative career in the House. In this case introduction involves nothing more than dropping the proposed bill, with the sponsor's name endorsed upon it, into the hopper at the clerk's desk in the chamber of the House of Representatives. Although there is no opportunity for sponsors to make statements as they introduce legislation in the House, most sponsors will manage to make an explanatory statement about their bills, or have such a statement inserted in the Congressional Record, at some time on the day of introduction. If the decision were made to introduce the bill in the Senate, instead of or in addition to the House, a different procedure would usually be followed there. Senate introduction commonly requires that the sponsor be present on the floor of the Senate, be recognized, rise and say that he is offering the bill for introduction, and send the bill by a page to the Secretary's desk. If the bill is ultimately enacted, the statement made about it by the Senate sponsor at the time of Senate introduction, and the explanatory remarks of the House sponsor some time after House introduction, may have definite utility as one of the aspects of the bill's legislative history which the courts will weigh in ascertaining legislative intent. Lawyers need to be aware that such materials will generally be found in the Congressional Record.

The first action on our bill after introduction is an important one: the referring of the bill to the appropriate House standing committee for consideration. The committees and their operation will be discussed in some detail below. For the moment it is enough to point out that bills are normally referred to whichever of the numerous House standing committees has jurisdiction, under House rules, of the bill's subject-matter. See the Table in Figure B, infra p. 275. A sponsor may request a desired reference. The decision on reference, usually a routine one, is made by the Speaker with the assistance of the Parliamentarian and is recorded in the Congressional Record. From time to time difficult problems of choice arise where bills arguably fall within the jurisdiction of more than one committee. Occasionally, a disputed reference, when the Speaker's ruling is not accepted, has eventuated in a floor fight and a decision by the House itself.

A new rule adopted in 1974 by the House calls on the Speaker to refer bills in such a way that as far as may be each committee that has jurisdiction over any provision of a bill will have responsibility for considering and reporting on that provision. This may be accomplished, it is suggested, by having committees consider legislation concurrently or successively, or by dividing up the bill, or by creating a special ad hoc committee with members drawn from the various standing committees interested in the measure.

In the Senate, the reference process is much the same as in the House, with the decision on reference being made by the presiding officer at the time. Under the Senate rules as amended in 1977 any controversy as to jurisdiction is to be decided by the presiding officer (subject to an appeal) in favor of that committee which has jurisdiction over the subject matter which predominates in the bill. Upon motion by both the Majority and Minority Leaders or their designees, the bill may be referred to two or more committees jointly or sequentially and may be divided up between the committees.

It does not require great perspicacity to see that referral may sometimes be crucial to the fate of a bill. An unsympathetic committee chairman or committee may seal its doom. As a result efforts may be made even at the drafting stage so to shape the bill as to bring it within the jurisdiction of a friendly committee, or pressures may build upon introduction to have any overlap resolved in favor of such a committee. The Civil Rights Bill of 1964 for strategic reasons was referred to the Commerce Committee in the Senate on the basis of its commerce clause underpinning, thus falling under the aegis of Senator Magnuson, a chairman sympathetic to the bill, and thus avoiding the Judiciary Committee whose chairman was Senator Eastland of Mississippi. In the House, the same bill was referred to the Judiciary Committee chaired by Congressman Celler of New York rather than to the Commerce Committee chaired by Congressman

Harris of Arkansas. It remains to be seen how the new Senate and House rules would affect such a situation.

After introduction and reference, the proposed bill is given a number and sent to the Government Printing Office. The next morning printed copies are available in the Senate and House document rooms. The print of the bill following introduction appears as indicated by the example in Figure A following. The designation—e. g. H.R.1868 (note that H.R. means House of Representatives)—will often be used to refer to the bill thereafter. Had it been a Senate bill the designation would have been the letter "S" followed by the bill number.

As you become accustomed to seeing or reading bills or statutes, you will note that their structure commonly contains such elements as these (items 1, 2, 4, and 8 always being present):

1. *Identifying Designation*—"H.R." or "S." and a number for federal bills (See Fig. A), "Chapter" or "Public Law" and a number for federal statutes. State bills have comparable designations.

2. *Title*—This succinctly states the subject or aim of the legislation.

3. *Preamble*—This is found mainly in older legislation. Utilizing one or more "whereas" clauses, a preamble typically has purposes similar to those of the now more widely used Legislative Findings, Purpose or Policy (see below).

4. *Enacting Clause*—This states that the legislature adopts as law what follows.

5. *Short Title*—This gives an easy "handle" or name to the legislation.

6. *Legislative Findings, Purpose or Policy*—This embraces some or all of the following: The reasons or the occasion for the legislation, or the facts found as a basis for it, or arguments for its adoption or constitutionality. Unlike a preamble, it is a part of the Act, since it follows the enacting clause, and, unlike a preamble, it is frequently carried into codifications.

7. *Definitions*—These save repetition and attempt to clarify meaning. Sometimes they are found at the end of a bill or statute.

8. *Purview*—This is the main body of the law containing the administrative, substantive and remedial provisions, etc.

Sec. 1 *THE LEGISLATIVE PROCESS* 271

95TH CONGRESS
1ST SESSION

H. R. 1868

{ Identifying Designation

IN THE HOUSE OF REPRESENTATIVES

JANUARY 13, 1977

Mr. MONTGOMERY (by request) introduced the following bill; which was referred to the Committee on Veterans' Affairs

A BILL

To amend title 38, United States Code, to extend the twenty-year protection to ratings for children permanently incapable of self-support.

{ Title

1 *Be it enacted by the Senate and House of Representa-*
2 *tives of the United States of America in Congress assembled,*

{ Enacting Clause

3 That section 110 of title 38, United States Code, is amended
4 by inserting the following immediately preceding the last
5 sentence: "A determination that a child of a veteran became
6 permanently incapable of self-support before attaining the
7 age of eighteen years which has been made for compensa-
8 tion or pension purposes under laws administered by the
9 Veterans' Administration, and which has been continuously
10 in force for twenty or more years, shall not be terminated
11 thereafter except upon a showing that the rating was based
12 on fraud.".

I

Figure A

[C978]

9. *Standard Clauses*—These may comprehend all or some of the following commonly encountered types of clauses:

    a. Severability Clause

    b. Liberal Interpretation Clause

    c. Saving Clause

    d. Repealer Clause—This may be (1) a general repealer repealing in general terms all laws inconsistent with the legislation in question or (2) a specific schedule explicitly listing laws repealed or (3) both.

    e. Effective Date Clause—This designates the time when the legislation takes effect.

We have spoken only of bills but it is well to note that legislative action by the Congress or its chambers can take other legislative forms. These include joint resolutions, designated as "H. J. Res." or "S. J. Res.," which go through the same legislative process as bills, including signature by the President, and have the same effect, except in the case of joint resolutions proposing constitutional amendments which must be approved by two-thirds of each house and are not signed by the President. There is little, if any, practical difference between bills and those joint resolutions that do not propose constitutional amendments and these forms are sometimes used interchangeably. See Gossnell v. Spang, infra p. 357. The bill form tends to be used routinely for general legislation. The Joint Resolution tends to be used for miscellaneous special cases such as authorizing invitations to foreign governments, or extending statutes due to expire.

There are, in addition, concurrent resolutions, designated as "H. Con. Res." or "S. Con. Res.," which are not submitted to the President and so are not equal in status or legal effect to bills or joint resolutions. They are not used for general legislation but normally deal with matters affecting only the Congress and express principles, opinions and purposes of the two Houses. And there are, finally, simple resolutions, designated "H. Res." and "S. Res.," which are promulgated by one House only and deal with concerns of the enacting House such as the establishment of a committee or the expression of the sense of one House on some public or intra-mural issue.

Joint and Concurrent Resolutions, like enacted bills, are printed in the Statutes at Large after adoption; simple Resolutions are not but may be found in the Congressional Record.

E. THE COMMITTEE STAGE

Once our bill has been introduced and referred to committee, it enters upon what is probably the most important stage of its journey through Congress: committee consideration. It is at this stage that the bill—if it is ever to do so—receives detailed scrutiny. If the bill is a significant or controversial one with some chance of passage, it will probably be the subject of public hearings conducted by the committee. Critical decisions will then be taken regarding its shape and its future. The committees in all this are the work parties of Congress. Years ago, in his classic text on Congressional Government, Woodrow Wilson observed that "[I]t is not far from the truth to say that Congress in session is Congress on public exhibition, whilst Congress in its committee-rooms is Congress at work." The machinery and operation of the committee system strongly deserve closer examination.

Committee Machinery

Each chamber has a set of standing committees. Each standing committee in each chamber is given jurisdiction, as we have noted, over a designated area of subject-matter and every measure is normally referred to the committee within whose jurisdiction its subject falls. In the first session of the 96th Congress, the House of Representatives had 22 such committees and the Senate 15, constituted as shown on the attached Table (Fig. B) based on the committee listings in the Congressional Directory. The House committees range in size from 54 members (Appropriations) down to 12 (Standards of Official Conduct) with many numbering between 36 and 43. The Senate committees range in size from 28 members (Appropriations) down to 10 (Rules and Administration, and Veterans' Affairs), with the rest varying between 14 and 20.

The present committee list reflects several efforts to "streamline" the system, including, notably, the Legislative Reorganization Act of 1946 which established the main outlines of the present pattern, and including House reforms of 1974 and a substantial revision of the Senate Committee structure carried out in 1977. The 1946 Act reduced the number of committee units from 48 to 19 in the House and 33 to 15 in the Senate. But committees tend to proliferate in response to practical pressures and in the ensuing years each chamber added three more standing committees and one Joint Committee (recently abolished) with regular legislative jurisdiction. In 1977, the Senate acted to reduce its standing committees once more to 15. It must be stressed, however, that notwithstanding any decreases in committees, the number of subcommittees (see Table) has grown so large since 1946 that the overall significance of the effort to reduce committee units is debatable.

The 1977 revision of the Senate committee system generally limits each Senator to two major committees and one minor committee and to three subcommittees of each of his major committees and two subcommittees of his minor committees (a total of 11 assignments). As for the House, Representatives typically serve on one or two standing committees, as well as on subcommittees within these committees. In any assessment of the workload thus created for members of Congress, account must of course be taken of conference committees (see the section on Inter-House Coordination, infra p. 314) and of the existence of other types of committees—e. g., select and joint committees—which though not a part of the regular machinery for processing bills nonetheless may make some real and competing demands on the scarce time of legislators.

Assignments to committees are determined ultimately by political party machinery in each chamber. On the Republican side, there is for each chamber a committee on committees which makes the assignments. On the Democratic side in the Senate, the Steering Committee, appointed by the floor leader, performs the task. In the House, Democratic committee assignments were formerly made by a committee consisting of the Democratic members of the Ways and Means Committee, but at the beginning of the 94th Congress this responsibility was transferred and now rests with the Steering and Policy Committee. Senior Senators and Representatives in the past tended to dominate the making of committee assignments and assignments depended on various considerations such as seniority, likelihood of reelection, compatibility, personal interest, special qualifications, geography, and ideology. Seniority was important though not necessarily controlling. The House Democratic Caucus rules now explicitly provide that seniority need not be followed. Moreover, special efforts have been made to assure that non-senior members receive a share of desirable seats and various provisions are in effect restricting members in their holding of places on leading committees and limiting and regulating appointment to subcommittees. In the Senate, the 1977 committee reorganization rules, limiting the number of committees and subcommittees on which Senators can serve, exemplify such efforts. There is some attempt, generally, to see that a number of the committees approximate in their range of membership the diverse geographical, economic and other interests represented in the chamber as a whole. On certain other committees—such as Agriculture—the assignments have been apt to go to legislators with a special interest in the subject-matter. Usually legislators may retain their existing assignments unless they signify a desire for change. The ratio of Republicans to Democrats on committees is a matter for determination by the party organs. On many committees an effort is made to reflect the proportion of Republicans to Democrats in the entire chamber. The ratios for the 96th Congress are shown in Figure B.

Sec. 1   THE LEGISLATIVE PROCESS

TABLE

STANDING HOUSE COMMITTEES, 96th CONGRESS (1979–80)

Committee	Number of Members	Ratio by Party	Number of Sub-Committees
Agriculture	42	D27 – R15	10
Appropriations	54	D36 – R18	13
Armed Services	45	D29 – R16	8
Banking, Finance and Urban Affairs	43	D28 – R15	9
Budget	25	D17 – R8	9
District of Columbia	14	D9 – R5	4
Education and Labor	36	D24 – R12	8
Foreign Affairs	34	D22 – R12	8
Government Operations	39	D25 – R14	7
House Administration	25	D16 – R9	8
Interior and Insular Affairs	43	D28 – R15	7
Interstate and Foreign Commerce	42	D27 – R15	6
Judiciary	31	D20 – R11	7
Merchant Marine and Fisheries	40	D25 – R15	5
Post Office and Civil Service	22	D13 – R9	7
Public Works and Transportation	48	D31 – R17	6
Rules	16	D11 – R5	2
Science and Technology	42	D27 – R15	7
Small Business	39	D25 – R14	6
Standards of Official Conduct	12	D6 – R6	–
Veterans' Affairs	30	D19 – R11	5
Ways and Means	37	D24 – R13	6

STANDING SENATE COMMITTEES, 96th CONGRESS (1979–80)

Committee	Number of Members	Ratio by Party	Number of Sub-Committees
Agriculture, Nutrition, and Forestry	18	D10 – R8	7
Appropriations	28	D17 – R11	13
Armed Services	17	D10 – R7	6
Banking, Housing, and Urban Affairs	15	D9 – R6	8
Budget	20	D12 – R8	–
Commerce, Science, and Transportation	17	D10 – R7	6
Energy and Natural Resources	18	D11 – R7	5
Environment and Public Works	14	D8 – R6	6
Finance	20	D12 – R8	11
Foreign Relations	15	D9 – R6	7
Governmental Affairs	17	D9 – R8	7
Judiciary	17	D10 – R7	7
Labor and Human Resources	15	D9 – R6	7
Rules and Administration	10	D6 – R4	–
Veterans' Affairs	10	D6 – R4	–

Figure B

[C1033]

The chairmanship, and the rank of members, of each committee have for many years and until recently been determined on the basis of seniority. When the seniority system governs, the chairmanship goes to that legislator of the majority party who has had the longest continuous service on the committee; the minority committeeman with the longest continuous service becomes the ranking minority member. A legislator who changes committees starts at the bottom of the ladder in his new committee, however senior he may otherwise be in point of service in the chamber. Awarding chairmanships—with all the power they entail—on the sole basis of seniority gave major advantage to legislators from so-called "one party" districts or states and exalted experience and age over ability, party regularity or other criteria. One result, also, was to decentralize power and further weaken the hold of party discipline as a force in the Congress. In the appointment of subcommittee chairmen, depending on the full committee's chairman, there was often, however, some relaxation of the pervasive seniority principle and, thus, a greater opportunity for the less senior legislators to exercise power.

Lately, the influence of seniority has undergone a substantial reduction. The House Republicans in 1971 agreed to vote by secret ballot on whether to accept nominations made by the committee on committees for the post of chairman or ranking minority member. On the Democratic side, more drastic changes derogating from the seniority system have developed, many of them associated with the preparations for and the opening of the 94th Congress. In the House, the Democratic Caucus rules now make clear that seniority is not necessarily to be controlling in the selection of committee chairmen or ranking members. Caucus votes are taken by secret ballot on nominations for the chairmanship of committees (and of Appropriations subcommittees). And seniority is further eroded by rules prohibiting the holding of multiple chairmanships. The Senate Democrats participated in the recent wave of change by agreeing, for example, that beginning in 1977 any Democratic committee chairman in the Senate would—following nominations by the Steering Committee—be selected by secret ballot of the Caucus if challenged by 20% of Democratic Senators. Limitations on multiple chairmanships, be it noted, exist in the Senate as well and were significantly strengthened by the 1977 Committee Reorganization rules. These various developments, of course, result in a further dispersion of power.

To complete the picture of committee machinery, mention should be made of the committee staffs. While Congress made relatively little use of staff help in the nineteenth century, this century has seen a major change in this respect. One of the principal accomplishments of the Legislative Reorganization Act of 1946 was its authorization of up to four professional staff members and six clerks for each standing committee (except Appropriations, which was allowed to appoint more). The staffs have since been substantially increased, giving Congress a greater capacity to resort to its own expert help in lieu of earlier dependence on the views and expertise of special interests and the executive.

Looking back at the committee apparatus we have described, it is not difficult to see why it has evolved as it has. Indeed, given the guiding premise of Congress, the development of a standing committee system—if not of all its Congressional peculiarities—would seem almost inevitable. The guiding premise was that Congress under the constitutional separation of powers should have an independent policy-formulating and law-developing capacity vis-a-vis the executive. It should be able to frame significant legislation and amendments on its own. It should not follow the model of the English Parliament, with its very different executive-legislative relation, and should not be generally restricted to approval or disapproval of policy formulated by the executive. In its early years Congress experimented with the conducting of its business in the "committee of the whole" and, later, with appointment of ad hoc select committees to give closer study to legislation than was possible before the full chamber or in "committee of the whole." These devices proved too cumbersome and inefficient and the standing committee pattern emerged as the preferred means of securing an appropriate division of labor and fostering a more efficient specialization in the face of a large volume of business of growing complexity. The use of regularized small groups facilitated negotiation and compromise as well as permitting continuity and more effective concentration on detail. The establishment of committee staffs is a further logical step in assuring Congress a coordinate role in policy-making.

Virtually all observers of Congress have been struck by the pervasive importance and power of the standing committees in the legislative process. The reasons for this will hopefully become clearer as we turn from the machinery to its functioning and as we examine the remainder of the process. To be remarked as well, as we proceed, is the fragmentation of power and attention that characterizes the operation of a Congress dominated by the standing committee system. In the latter connection note, for example, that the system of independent and isolated standing committees, each with a predefined area, creates grave difficulties for attempts to deal in a coordinated, large-scale way with great subjects that overlap the defined jurisdictions —e. g., foreign policy. No sure general solutions to this difficulty seem yet to have found acceptance. At this juncture it would not appear that the new House and Senate rules on reference, mentioned in the preceding section, have enhanced the ability of Congress to deal with this problem.

Committee Operation

What happens when our bill has been referred to a standing committee? In most cases, the standing committee chairman will refer the bill to a subcommittee for consideration, if the committee has subcommittees, as most do. Also, copies will often be transmitted to the executive departments or agencies with a request for their views.

One must remark again at this point, the power of the committee as a whole and the power of the standing committee chairman in particular. Only a small percentage of bills referred to committees is reported out. Most gather dust and die there and the mortality is especially heavy among non-Administration bills. The power it possesses to block or to report legislation, with or without amendment—and we shall later see further reasons why its life and death powers are so great—helps to make the committee a crucial factor in any bill's history.

The powers of the committee chairman are especially to be noted at this point where we are discussing reference to a subcommittee. In the past he often had discretion in deciding what subcommittees should be established or maintained, who should be subcommittee chairman, whether to refer the bill to a subcommittee at all, and, if so, to which subcommittee. He could, for example, create ad hoc subcommittees sympathetic or not so sympathetic to the bill. Many chairmen exercised these powers with due regard for their committee's wishes; some used them for "one man rule." But these powers have been appreciably curtailed in the Senate by the Committee System Reorganization Amendments of 1977 and in the House as shown by the recent rules of the Democratic Caucus. Inter alia, the House Democratic Caucus rules (1) regulate subcommittee chairmanships and membership, (2) provide that Democratic committee members, as against chairmen, are to determine the number, jurisdiction, and budgets of subcommittees and to elect subcommittee chairmen by secret ballot, and (3) call for referral of any bill to the appropriate subcommittee as a normal step unless it is voted to keep it at the committee level. Of course the chairman has other practical powers stemming from his other functions—such as calling and presiding over meetings and hearings, setting the agenda, developing and controlling staff, negotiating for floor consideration, designating the floor manager for the bill and participating in conference proceedings. While the Legislative Reorganization Acts of 1946 and 1970 (and, lately, the Senate Committee System Reorganization Amendments and the House Democratic Caucus rules) reduced the chairman's ability to flout the wishes of a committee majority, in any overall view his influence remains significant.

In his turn, the subcommittee chairman will have major power over the fate of the bill and much to say, subject to the power of the full committee and its chairman, over whether the measure is to languish or be pursued with more or less vigor. The subcommittee's decision to table or to endorse or to reshape is often accepted by the full committee and ultimately by the Congress. The Appropriations Committees, for example, regularly endorse the work of their subcommittees. Thus the work of a very few Senators or Representatives and of the chairman may be decisive. Once again the extraordinary fragmentation of Congressional power becomes evident.

Whether the bill is considered by the full committee or a subcommittee, and especially if it is a significant bill and in some degree controversial, the chairman or subcommittee chairman as the case may be will probably decide to hold public hearings on it and he has much discretion as to whether and how such hearings will be conducted. With the staff, who are largely subject to his control, the chairman concerned will schedule the hearings, give notice, plan the pattern of witnesses, and issue requests to testify or, perhaps, subpoenas. On the appointed hearing day, an official reporter will be present to take down testimony. After introductory statements by committee or subcommittee members, the Senators and Representatives who seek to be heard will receive preference as witnesses; officials of the executive departments or agencies may also then be heard, as well as the representatives of interest groups and other private persons. Prepared statements will often be submitted and witnesses will be questioned. Owing to the multiple burdens of committee work that affect legislators, the hearing may only be sparsely attended by members of the sponsoring committee or subcommittee.

The purposes of hearings may vary widely depending on the measure and the aims of the legislators. If well organized by chairman and staff to that end, they can serve as a valuable means for investigating problems*, for gathering information and for testing a proposal's impact on segments of the public. In this aspect it is instructive to compare the modest research and data-gathering capability of the courts to the capabilities of Congressional committees, with their staffs, their access to the Congressional Research Service and the Offices of Legislative Counsel, and their access through hearings and otherwise to the expertise of governmental and private sources. But hearings are not always well managed to serve this informational purpose and may be used to serve, instead or in addition, such other purposes as mobilizing public support or opposition, providing publicity for legislators, stalling the legislative progress of a bill, furnishing a "safety valve" for disturbances, and so forth.

After the hearings, the hard work begins on the bill. A transcript of the hearings is made available. With the help of staff, other data, analyses and drafts are assembled. The legislators then meet, with or without preliminary caucusing and with staff personnel and sometimes representatives of governmental departments (and sometimes representatives of private interests) in attendance. They discuss the bill and any amendments and decide whether and on what terms to report it out. If the vote is to table, that will often be the end of a bill unless pressures in the full committee (in the case of a bill first considered by a subcommittee) or in the chamber as a whole can force a different result. If the bill is not tabled, the next step is to "mark up" the bill and it will often receive its definitive shape in the course of compromises and negotiations on this level at the hands of members and staff and draftsmen. Note must be taken here of

* See concluding bibliographical note.

the ease with which a proposal can be blocked by a strategically placed minority at this stage—unless the pressures against it can be overcome by intense pressures in its behalf.

When a bill is reported out, with or without amendment, by a subcommittee, it must of course run the gauntlet of the full committee, which typically has regular meeting days on which subcommittee reports are taken up. Sometimes the subcommittee's work will be accepted; at other times, the whole process of hearings and "marking up" or revision will be repeated in the full committee which in any event must ultimately vote on its own to table the bill or to report it in some form. Again, there is opportunity for delay and defeat and much may depend on the attitude and practice of the full committee chairman toward the proposal. From the standpoint of the lobbyist, of course, the subcommittee and committee phases of action are key points for the application of favorable or adverse pressures and the same is apt to be true at other points of the process where a small number of persons exercise great power over a measure's progress.

Notice, at the committee stage, three kinds of documents emerging which may be vital elements in the legislative history of the bill when its meaning is later sought by lawyers, administrators or judges or by the public. The first of these is the hearings, if they are printed—as they frequently are—and made generally available to the Congress and the public. These may contain important clues to the impact or sense of legislative provisions, especially, for example, when amendments are made in response to points made at the hearings. The second is the different versions of the bill considered by the committee. Changes in language between the bill as referred to the committee and the bill as reported out may shed significant light on the bill's final meaning. The third and perhaps most important document at this stage is the formal report of the full committee which accompanies the bill when it is transmitted by the committee to the chamber as a whole. This formal report normally discusses the purposes of and reasons for the bill and analyzes its provisions. Committee amendments are indicated and communications from the executive regarding the bill are commonly incorporated in the report. There may be a minority report—i. e., dissenting views—on the same bill. Both the committee report (which will be given a number) and the bill as reported will be printed up and made available promptly after filing. The report has special significance for interpretive purposes, representing, as it does, an expression of views about the bill by the Congressional group charged with detailed knowledge and responsibility. It constitutes a prime source of information about the bill for the Congressmen as well, a source to which they can refer as a basis for their vote. So important is it for this purpose that House and Senate normally require that committee reports be available to the membership for several days before consideration of the measures to which they are addressed.

Fiscal Control and the New Budget Act

It is appropriate at this point to take note of the general problem of fiscal control and planning in the Congress and, especially, of a major recent development in that area—the Congressional Budget and Impoundment Control Act of 1974. This subject has large implications for the work of Congressional standing committees, as well as for other phases of the process and for legislative-executive relations.

Here a bit of background regarding Congressional handling of fiscal affairs is in order. For the first seventy-five years or so of Congressional operation, each chamber had a single committee—Ways and Means in the House, Finance in the Senate—which had jurisdiction over both taxing and spending and so was in a position to weigh and determine budgetary policy and priorities on a comprehensive basis. The Civil War, however, gave rise to such a heavy burden of financial responsibility for these single committees that—following the War—the workload was divided through the creation of an Appropriations Committee in each chamber. Taxation remained the concern of the House Ways and Means Committee and the Senate Finance Committee but control over spending was given to the Appropriations Committees. In later years, the Appropriations Committees in turn lost to other standing committees some of their exclusive jurisdiction over spending. As a result of these changes, taxing and spending were no longer weighed together and there was, in addition, no overall Congressional machinery for choice among competing expenditures. Then, in 1921, the Budget and Accounting Act was passed, establishing the executive budget and the Bureau of the Budget (now the Office of Management and Budget) developed as the central mechanism for management by the executive of its budgetary responsibilities. At this same time, Congress acted to remedy in some measure the splintering of its own fiscal machinery by restoring all authority over appropriations to its Appropriations Committees. Subsequently, in the half century after 1921, however, the control of the Appropriations Committees became seriously diluted once more as a result of the growth of so-called "backdoor" spending arrangements—i. e., spending arrangements that were beyond the Appropriations Committees' control, as in the case of certain "borrowing authority" or "contract authority" or "permanent appropriations" (as for social security, revenue sharing, or interest on the public debt) or various binding obligations (as for public assistance or veterans benefits). The effect of "backdoor" spending was again to divide expenditure control among various committees. It is estimated that by 1973 the Appropriations Committees effectively managed less than 50% of the budget, and even of this remaining fraction an appreciable part was relatively uncontrollable. In sum, then, in the early 1970's, Congress had no effective means for reviewing tax and spending policies together on a comprehensive basis. Its consideration of expenditures was fragmented and in significant aspects the spending process escaped effective Congressional management. The Congressional "power of the purse" seemed to many to have drifted substantially toward the executive with its centralized and relatively efficient budget machinery. Efforts in the 1940's and 1950's to cope with some of these problems had been unsuccessful. Finally, in a bold move to redress the situation, Congress enacted the Congressional Budget and Impoundment Control Act of 1974.

This 1974 Budget Act created new standing Budget Committees in the House and Senate to focus Congressional attention on national fiscal policy and priorities, to establish overall Congressional spending and tax limits and to make spending choices. It set up a nonpartisan Congressional Budget Office (CBO), with a Director appointed by the Speaker and the President Pro Tem, and a supporting staff, to assist the Budget Committees with their work. The Director was empowered to secure information on a broad basis from government agencies.

Section 300 of the 1974 Act established a detailed timetable for the Committees and the Congress in pertinent part as follows:

On or Before * * *	Action to Be Completed * * *
15th day after Congress meets	President submits his budget
March 15	Committees and joint committees submit reports to Budget Committees
April 1	Congressional Budget Office submits report to Budget Committees
April 15	Budget Committees report first concurrent resolution on the Budget to their Houses
May 15	Committees report bills and resolutions authorizing new budget authority
May 15	Congress completes action on first concurrent resolution on the Budget

[Note: This first concurrent resolution sets budget targets for the next fiscal year (each fiscal year is henceforth to begin October 1) including total budget outlays and total new budget authority (with a breakdown for each major functional category), the appropriate budget surplus or deficit, the recommended level of revenues and of public debt. The accompanying report, inter alia, is to provide comparisons with the executive budget. The resolution itself may require that new budget or spending authority not be adopted in final form until after the September 15 or 25 deadline (see below)—Ed.]

7th day after Labor Day — Congress completes action on bills and resolutions providing new budget authority and new spending authority

[Note: As the legislative and Appropriations Committees continue their work up to this deadline, with the stated targets and allocations therefrom before them, the Congressional Budget Office issues periodic reports comparing the actual Congressional decisions with the first resolution—Ed.]

September 15 — Congress completes action on second required concurrent resolution on the budget.

[Note: This second resolution reaffirms or revises the first, and as necessary, it is to (1) specify total amounts by which new budget or spending authority, or budget authority for prior fiscal years, is to be changed by each committee and (2) direct the committees to fix and recommend revisions to achieve such totals—Ed.]

September 25 — Congress completes action on reconciliation bill or resolution, or both, implementing second required concurrent resolution.

[Note: After the adoption of the second concurrent resolution and the subsequent reconciliation measure, if any, measures seeking additional new budget authority or new spending authority are subject to a point of order in the House or Senate—Ed.]

October 1 — Fiscal year begins.

The Act of 1974, in other provisions, lays down requirements designed (with certain exceptions) to bring "backdoor spending" within the budgetary and appropriations processes. In response to controversies over executive impoundment of funds, it provides, also, in Title X (Impoundment Control Act of 1974), for Congressional review of Presidential proposals to delay spending and requires Congressional approval for Presidential cancellation of spending.

Looking at the revolutionary 1974 legislation as a whole, it is obvious that Congress made a sweeping effort to remedy past difficulties. The budget process it established has provided Congress with the means to relate expenditures and revenues, to weigh expenditures as a whole, to accept spending limits and face the problems of priorities and the hard choices they entail. A valiant bid has thus been made by Congress to regain and assert for itself a significant role in the formulation of national fiscal policy, a task previously left in major part to the executive. It remains to be seen how effective and enduring this bid will be in practice. The new budget procedures actually worked quite efficiently in the development of a budget for fiscal 1977. There was more difficulty with the budget for fiscal 1978. Differences over the level of defense expenditures and the relative spending priorities as between defense and social programs were major sources of tension. For the 1979 and 1980 fiscal years, the budget process was under further strain due—on the one hand—to the problem of inflation and—on the other—to the risk of recession. In 1979, for the first time, Congress did not pass a second budget resolution by September 15th, as required under the 1974 Budget Act, or by October 1st, the start of the new fiscal year. The outlook for the future is still uncertain. The success of the new dispensation will depend on, among other things, the willingness of various legislative blocs to accept budgetary priorities and controls that will interfere with their own cherished aims, as well as on the willingness of the Congress as a whole to abide by the stringent timetables for legislative action. Also, the long run viability of the newly redefined executive-legislative relations will need to be assessed in practice over a period of years.

It is apparent that the new regime has major implications for the functioning of the committee system. The Appropriations Committees, for example, are importantly affected. They must deal with the Budget Committees and must concern themselves with budgetary limitations and deadlines. Before reporting its first regular appropriations bill in the period between May 15 and the seventh day after Labor Day, the House Appropriations Committee must "to the extent practicable" complete committee action on all regular appropriation bills for the year concerned and must report to the House a comparison of its recommendations with the targets in the preceding concurrent Budget resolution.

It is still true, of course, that the effectuation of a legislative program that requires funding is basically and generally a two-step process. Such a program emerging from a standing legislative committee must first be enacted by the Congress by bill *authorizing* the necessary expenditures and level of operation. But money does not become available for new programs until a second step is completed, i. e., until it is *appropriated* in appropriations bills. It is a consequence of this pattern that a program authorized and enacted by Congress pursuant to the efforts of its standing legislative committees can be impaired or nullified later at the hands of the Appropriations Committees. The Appropriations Committees thus constitute another power center, among the many such centers in Congress, that must be won over before a legislative program becomes an effectively funded reality. It is interesting to speculate about the extent to which the new Budget Committees may come to represent still another locus of power whose decisions must be reckoned with in relation to a particular program.

Like the Appropriations Committees, the regular legislative standing committees must adopt new ways to conform to the 1974 Act and its iron schedule. They must deal with the Budget Committees and must submit estimates for the fiscal year by March 15. They must report authorization bills by May 15. They must adjust to the other deadlines of the Act and to the discipline of budget limitations.

The committee reports accompanying measures that provide new budget authority or new tax expenditures are now required to contain statements (prepared after consultation with the Director of the CBO) showing, inter alia, how the proposed new authority or expenditure compares with the latest budget resolution and reports and furnishing five-year financial projections. A CBO cost analysis and five-year projection will, to the extent practicable, be prepared for all reported public bills and resolutions and will be included in accompanying reports.

F. GETTING TO THE FLOOR

We have been considering the committee stage in relation to our bill. But if it is to become law, the bill must somehow be laid before the chambers themselves to be voted on and approved by the membership as a whole. How our bill may be gotten to the floor in each chamber is, then, our next concern.

The problem of securing floor consideration has two main aspects. First, by what means, if any, can a bill be brought before the chamber if the committee fails to report it out? The answer to this, and the answer to the related question whether the committee can be bypassed altogether, shed substantial further light on the role and power of the standing committees. Second, by what means can chamber consideration be assured if the committee to which the bill is referred does in fact report it out? The answer to this provides important insight into the relation between the standing committee and other centers of power in the legislature. Whichever aspect is considered, some appreciation of the patterns of leadership in Congress is essential to an understanding of the process. Accordingly, we describe those patterns briefly. Note, incidentally, as we address the topics of leadership and of securing floor consideration that there are differences between the House and Senate in this area and that the differences are significant.

Legislative Leadership

Any effort to describe the patterns of legislative leadership must reckon of course at the outset with the role of the President which we have already discussed. The legislative leadership is organized along party lines and the President as head of his party (which is not necessarily the majority party in the legislature) derives strength from that position. How much may depend of course on the issue and the party's attitude toward it. Constitutionally conceived as a factor in the legislative process, the President has his formal powers of veto, recommendation, and budget submission; and he has informal powers as well that arise out of his ability to bargain over jobs and public works and his ability to rally public support.

Within the Congress, the pattern of leadership varies as between the two chambers. In both chambers, however, the party caucus or conference of each party plays a basic part. It has not for a long time been successfully used as a means of requiring the legislators of a party to adhere to a particular position on legislation. This is no doubt due in large part to the peculiar lack of unity and cohesion which characterizes American political parties and due to the absence of effective means to force reluctant legislators into line. The caucus or conference nonetheless does select the floor leaders in both chambers and the Speaker and, in some cases, other officers as well.

In the House, the most prominent leader of the majority party is the caucus-selected Speaker. Guiding his party in the House is one of his chief concerns. Beyond that he serves as a presiding officer, with multiple and detailed functions—e. g., recognizing members who wish to speak, appointing members to various tasks, maintaining order, participating in scheduling—and in the aggregate these with other, informal, elements can add up to substantial power. Since the 1910 revolt against Speaker Cannon, the office has been shorn of much of the power that made it a virtual dictatorship, but it remains a formidable office. Yet note even here that given the loose and disunited character of the party and the decentralized character of Congressional power distribution (represented especially by the committee system), much of the Speaker's power depends on his own personal qualities, on his ability to persuade. In selecting the Speaker, seniority, a "safe" seat and abilities tested out in other positions are apt to be determinative.

The Senate has no counterpart to the Speaker. The Vice President is President of the Senate but rarely attends. The responsibility for presiding thus falls on the President Pro Tempore, who is generally the member of the Senate with the longest unbroken service. His job is not one of great power or influence. In his absence the task of presiding usually falls to junior Senators for whom it is seen as a kind of apprenticeship.

Sec. 1   *THE LEGISLATIVE PROCESS*   287

The majority floor leader is active in planning the work of the chamber, his party's legislative program and the scheduling and handling of the program and other bills on the floor. Especially is this true in the Senate where the Rules Committee does not perform the traffic-directing functions of its House counterpart and where there is no equivalent to the Speaker. In the Senate, the majority floor leader is the principal agency of traffic control; he is the "man in the middle," a broker in part, between the committees and the chamber and the President; and his miscellaneous functions may if wisely employed provide him with a significant degree of power. But persuasion and negotiation remain his principal tools for achieving his ends. The minority floor leader serves as his party's leader and as the majority leader's "opposite number" in each chamber.

Assisting in both chambers and parties are the majority and minority Whips who keep in touch with the legislators of their party and with their views on pending legislation and who round up their legislators for important votes.

To complete the picture of legislative leadership, mention must be made of the policy committees, which participate in varying degrees in evolving Congressional party strategy but have not generally achieved their hoped-for role in formulating and implementing a defined Congressional party program. Mention should also be made of the "committees on committees" which may be utilized for the task of assigning committee places to the members. And finally, it is essential to reemphasize the all-important leadership role of the standing committees and their chairmen.

What surely emerges from this barebones outline of the leadership pattern, spread over two houses, is its diffuseness and the consequent difficulty, except perhaps under the pressure of unusual personalities or events, of drawing together the diverse elements of power into a working unity. Strong Presidents and times of crisis have sometimes produced a unity and drive but the general state of affairs has been one of fragmentation in which the blocking of action somewhere along the way is much easier than pushing through an affirmative program or proposal.

Getting a Bill Out of Committee

With the patterns described in mind, consider the first question earlier raised in relation to getting bills to the floor. That question was whether and how a bill bottled up in committee might be brought before the chamber. The answer is that it is very difficult, though not impossible; and that fact underlines perhaps better than any other the power of the committees.

What can be done in the House, for example, about a bill pigeonholed in committee? One possible step is for the interested member to file a motion or petition under the rules to discharge the committee from consideration of a bill which has been in its possession for 30 days or more. The petition is placed in the custody of the Clerk and requires the signature of 218 members—a majority of the House membership—before any further action may be taken on it. Without going into the details of the discharge rule, it is enough to note the obvious difficulty of rounding up 218 signatures in favor of a course of action which bypasses the normal methods of the House, which may flout the wishes of a committee and of a committee chairman whose support may be needed at some other time. The pressures thus involved create severe obstacles to successful discharge and history bears witness to their effect. Froman, whose excellent work on Congressional procedures, The Congressional Process (1967), should be consulted by all interested in learning more about such procedures, notes that of 200 discharge petitions filed between 1937 and 1960, only 22 received the required signatures, only 14 were passed by the House, and only 2 eventuated in enacted laws. Of course the threat of a discharge petition, if enough members feel intensely and the signatures mount, may suffice to goad a committee to act. But the rarity of successful use of the motion speaks eloquently of its difficulties.

Another way around the standing committee involves the Rules Committee—to be discussed more fully hereafter—which has the power to report any measure it chooses whether or not previously considered by a committee. But history (only four examples from 1937 to 1964) suggests it is even more unlikely—compared with discharge—that Rules can be persuaded to report out a measure being held in another committee. Rules, a conservative committee, is not geared for affirmative action on new and unreported proposals. As with discharge, there is the reluctance to flout regular standing committees and their chairmen and to bring bills to the floor without the benefit of detailed and expert committee work.

A third possible course of action, so-called suspension of the rules procedure, requires recognition by the Speaker and a two-thirds vote. It seems not to be used to bypass the committee process. Like all the other detours, it is less than promising and serves only to underscore the normal inviolability of the Standing Committee system. Underlying the reluctance to use these devices is surely a recognition that the vital committee system upon which Congress depends would lose its viability if it were circumvented more than very rarely. The life and death importance of the committee phase for any bill becomes even more obvious when this is pondered.

In the Senate, with its smaller size and greater informality, the committees are less likely to bottle up and keep from the floor legislation in which a significant segment is interested and it is easier to bypass the committees than in the House. The Senate's discharge rule is apparently simpler to activate than its House counterpart, though still cumbersome and vulnerable to delays. Interestingly, it too has been rarely used. Froman's The Congressional Process (1967) reports only 16 such motions since 1789, of which only 6 were successful. Suspension of the rules is also easier to achieve in the Senate but, again, rarely used to bypass committees. More feasible, though difficult without the support of the leadership and of a substantial number of Senators, is the tactic of moving the substance of a bill bottled in committee as an amendment to pending legislation (except general appropriation measures). The freedom of floor amendment in the Senate, allowing nongermane modifications to bills, makes this possible. The Rules of the Senate make it practicable also, with leadership cooperation, to keep a House-passed bill from the grasp of the appropriate standing committee. All of the foregoing means of bypassing committees are limited in the Senate by the same general realization by the membership that such bypassing threatens the viability of the committee system and makes potentially dangerous enemies. They are vulnerable too, along the way, to the possibility of a filibuster, a subject to which we will return shortly. Still, one may differentiate the Senate and House by the greater ease of bypassing in the Senate and by the observation that in the Senate, in contrast to the House, bills are very seldom kept from reaching the floor when floor consideration is desired by a majority.

Securing Floor Consideration for Reported Bills in the House

Consider now the second aspect of the problem of getting a bill to the floor—that is, the securing of chamber consideration for a bill that is reported out of committee. Here the more normal route in the progress of a bill is being followed. It is not a question of bypassing the standing committee stage. Once again the House and Senate offer an interesting contrast in the ways in which they handle the difficult problems of traffic control involved in processing the large volume of legislation with which they are faced.

In the House of Representatives, a public bill reported by a committee goes on one of the two House calendars, either on the so-called Union Calendar if it is a "money" bill—i. e., a public bill raising revenue or directly or indirectly appropriating funds or property—or on the House Calendar if it is not a "money" bill. Private bills, that is bills involving individual claims against the United States or individual immigration cases, go on the Private Calendar and follow special procedures thereafter; and while they account for a surprisingly large portion of the annual total of enacted bills, they are not central to our concerns and will not be further dealt with here. In respect of public bills, there is a tremendous press of arduous, complex legislative business which needs to be appreciated in appraising this phase of the process. It is apparent that there is a need for exercise of judgment and of decision-making as to which reported bills on the Calendars will be taken up and in what order. That judgment and decision are supplied for most important controversial public bills by the House Rules Committee which will be discussed shortly but whose role needs to be seen in the context of the various other means of securing floor attention.

If our bill is noncontroversial it may be placed on the so-called Consent Calendar and in due course, if no objection is raised, will be adopted by unanimous consent without debate. If it is sufficiently noncontroversial so that recognition by the Speaker can be secured by the committee chairman or other proponent and a favorable two-thirds vote achieved, it may instead be adopted pursuant to a motion to suspend the rules which is in order at designated times. Recently, use of the suspension procedure has been increasing and there have been complaints that its use has not been restricted to noncontroversial proposals. Guidelines adopted by the Democratic Caucus in 1979 discourage resort to the suspension device for bills with a cost of over $100 million in a single fiscal year. Of course, if the Consent Calendar or suspension of the rules is employed, recourse to the Rules Committee is not needed. Nor is such recourse needed, though it is not infrequently resorted to, in the case of a public bill that falls within any of various types of privileged measures. Privileged bills include, notably, budget resolutions reported by the Budget Committee, revenue bills reported by the Ways and Means Committee, general appropriation bills reported by the Appropriations Committee, and measures reported by the Rules Committee. Also, bills from the District of Columbia Committee have their allotted time for consideration.

Theoretically, an unprivileged public bill on the House or Union Calendar might, without going through the Rules Committee, reach the floor pursuant to a procedure known as Calendar Wednesday. Under this device, unless it is dispensed with, the Speaker calls upon the standing committees in alphabetical order which may then call up any one of their previously reported bills pending on the House or Union Calendar. But this procedure is of very little practical value, as the Wednesday call of committees is usually dispensed with by unanimous consent. The alphabetical requirement and the habitual dispensing mean a long wait between calls of any particular committee, and certain time limitations on floor debate under this procedure make it inappropriate for complex, controversial matters. All in all Calendar Wednesday is a rarely invoked and unattractive alternative to the Rules Committee for controversial public bills.

Except in the case of private or noncontroversial or privileged measures, then, the normal course followed in the House after the reporting of a bill by a committee is for the chairman of the reporting committee to request a hearing before the Rules Committee. If it is granted, the chairman of the reporting committee (or perhaps the appropriate subcommittee chairman) will probably appear, with the sponsor and one or more committee members, before the Rules Committee and plead for the granting of a so-called "special rule" or resolution calling for the bill's consideration forthwith by the House.

Note in this the continuing involvement of the reporting committee and the negotiating role of the chairman as significant elements in the progress of a bill after it is reported out. Other interested members may speak to the proposal; representatives of affected interest groups do not testify but may attend.

The Rules Committee, after the hearing (occasionally hearings are denied), will decide whether to grant a special rule or to deny one with damaging consequences for the fate of the bill. If the decision is to grant a special rule, Rules will set the terms of debate, prescribing by its resolution the time allowed for floor consideration, the pattern of permissible floor amendment and whether or not points of order against the bill are to be waived. A special rule limiting floor amendment and waiving points of order is known as a "closed" or "gag" rule. Most special rules are "open." When a special rule is ordered or promised, the details of order and timing of floor scheduling are determined by the Speaker, majority leader and interested committee chairmen.

The Rules Committee's position athwart the pipeline for significant bills, its ability to delay or turn back legislation, make it a redoubtable center of power in the House legislative process and a natural target of pressure for those seeking to obstruct a particular measure or to promote its passage.

The ability to delay or refuse a special rule gives the Committee leverage not merely over the scheduling of a bill but also over its substance as well. The Committee has been known to insist sometimes on revisions as the price of approval or to barter one bill for another and thus to set itself up in opposition to the standing committee that has basic jurisdiction over the subject-matter. By and large, much of the time, Rules works routinely, in harmony with the majority leadership of the House. When bills are stalled in Rules, it may well be because the leadership desires that result. In recognition of its importance to the majority leadership, the Committee's membership sometimes has had a larger representation of the majority party than some other committees. Moreover, the Democratic Caucus rules were amended in December 1974 to provide that the Democratic members of the Rules Committee are to be nominated by the Speaker subject to approval by the Caucus.

Since the revolt against the dictatorial Speaker Cannon in 1910, Rules has sometimes been a center of power separate in a degree from the Speaker and other elements of party leadership. There have been noted instances in which Rules exercised its power to delay or kill, or to dictate the substantive content of, legislation in a manner to frustrate the leadership and a majority of the House. Such action led in 1961 to a counter-attack by the leadership that increased the size of the Committee by adding two majority members more sympathetic to the President's program and to the leadership. The present practice of appointment of members by the Speaker is intended to bind the Committee more closely to the leadership.

Observe, in this connection, that the several possible modes now in existence for bypassing the Rules Committee are not very effective. Rules is subject to discharge motions; and it may be circumvented for example via Calendar Wednesday or Suspension of the Rules. But these modes of action involve serious difficulties already described. In 1965 and 1966, there was operative in the House a so-called "21-day rule" (a modified version of a rule which had been in effect also in 1949–1950). This allowed the Speaker, in his discretion, to recognize the chairman or authorized member of a standing committee to call up a measure stalled in Rules for more than 21 days. Such a rule gave a clear avenue for the Speaker (who thus regained some of his earlier power) to act on behalf of the majority leadership, and with the interested standing committee, to neutralize anti-leadership action in Rules. This 21-day rule was repealed in January, 1967. All in all, the power of Rules in the House remains very substantial, especially as an instrument of negation or obstruction.

Securing Floor Consideration of Reported Bills in the Senate

Contrast the elaborate House machinery and rules regulating the flow of bills to the floor with the relatively informal and unelaborate modes of getting a reported Senate bill to the floor. There is in the Senate only one Calendar of Business or General Orders to which go all the bills. Nominations and treaties go on the Executive Calendar. Noncontroversial bills, if there is no objection, are brought up at the convenience of the membership several times a month on call of the Calendar and discussed under rules limiting to five minutes each Senator's participation in the debate. In this the Senate approximates the House's Consent Calendar. But in the normal case of a reported bill of a controversial and important character, the interested committee or subcommittee chairman and others will confer with the majority leader to seek an arrangement to bring the bill to the floor. Floor scheduling is handled generally by the majority leader, sometimes in consultation with the majority Policy Committee, but more usually pursuant to agreements, reached by informal negotiation and compromise, between the majority and minority leaders. Note that the role of the leadership in scheduling makes it a logical focus of lobbying pressure in that connection. Note too that there is no Senate institution comparable to the House Rules Committee. The smaller size and simpler rules of the Senate, and the relative equality of power between Senators, result in accentuating the informal processes of consultation between leaders and chairmen, between majority and minority, and even the convenience of rank and file members may be a factor in decision. There is of course the possibility that a motion to take up a bill will be the target of a filibuster. But of that more anon. It suffices for the moment to call attention to the comparative difficulty of securing floor consideration in the House and the comparative ease of securing it in the Senate.

G. FLOOR CONSIDERATION

Once the problems of getting our bill to the floor have been resolved, the bill must undergo the tests of floor consideration. If the House and Senate differ in their approaches to scheduling reported bills, no less do they differ in their approaches to dealing with the bills that come before them. Indeed their roles are in a measure reversed here. On the one hand, in the House, serious risks of delay and obstruction attend the process of getting to the floor but rigid, expeditious procedures speed it to its fate thereafter; on the other hand, in the Senate, getting to the floor is notably less difficult, but serious risks of delay and obstruction arise in connection with floor consideration.

On the House Floor

Let us look first at the patterns of floor action in the House. Assuming our bill is important and controversial, it will in all probability, as we saw, be the subject of a special rule from the Rules Committee. Even bills privileged in their own right, such as revenue bills, not infrequently are brought before the House by preference under a special rule from the Rules Committee limiting the terms of debate. The initial step then in the floor proceedings on our bill—unlike privileged bills or bills coming up on the Private or Consent or Discharge Calendar or Suspension of the Rules or as District of Columbia business—will be the Speaker's recognition of a member of the Rules Committee to call up the rule relating to our bill. Special rules of this kind may be debated for an hour but the debate does not normally consume the allotted time and such rules are often adopted without difficulty by voice vote. Following is an example of a typical special rule, of the "open" kind, for a bill on the Union Calendar:

> *Resolved*, That upon the adoption of this resolution it shall be in order to move that the House resolve itself into the Committee of the Whole House on the State of the Union for the consideration of the bill (H.R. ——) to (here insert the purpose of the bill). After general debate, which shall be confined to the bill and shall continue not to exceed two hours, to be equally divided and controlled by the chairman and ranking minority member of the Committee on ——, the bill shall be read for amendment under the five-minute rule. At the conclusion of the consideration of the bill for amendment, the Committee shall rise and report the bill to the House with such amendments as may have been adopted, and the previous question shall be considered as ordered on

the bill and amendments thereto to final passage without intervening motion except one motion to recommit.

The text of the resolution is of great importance as it sets the pattern for what follows.

Upon adoption of the special rule the House resolves itself into the Committee of the Whole House on the State of the Union. This step, applicable to most significant pieces of legislation, has a number of consequences. In essence it makes less formal, and speeds, the action of the House. In the Committee of the Whole, the House can operate with a quorum of 100 members (as against 218 for the House itself). Time-consuming yea and nay votes are avoided. For the deliberations of the Committee of the Whole, the Speaker steps down from the chair, appointing another chairman in his place.

As the above special rule indicates, the next step in relation to our bill is general debate. The time allowed for this by the rule is equally divided between (a) the bill's floor manager, who is normally the chairman of the responsible standing committee or subcommittee, and, (b) his principal opponent, who is usually a ranking minority member of the same committee or subcommittee. The floor manager speaks first, followed by his opposite number. Both yield time to others for further speeches regarding the bill. Note once again the pervasive role of the standing committee and its leaders in the legislative process.

Following the general debate, the bill is open to amendment, committee amendments having priority. The sponsor of an amendment has five minutes to explain and support his amendment; additional time requires unanimous consent. The floor manager has five minutes to respond. If other members want time to discuss an amendment, they offer fictional or pro forma amendments (motions to "strike the last word") as a basis for receiving five minutes of speaking time. Members of the standing committee are also entitled to preference in recognition. Debate on an amendment can continue for some little time under this system and may be closed by unanimous consent or by motion requiring a majority vote. While there are possibilities for delay in House procedure, as through quorum calls (restricted somewhat by the 1977 rules) and other procedural devices, there is no real opportunity to stop a bill or amendment from being voted on.

Votes on amendments in the Committee of the Whole may be voice votes. If the vote is close or doubtful, a vote by division (proponents and opponents stand in turn to be counted) may be demanded. A teller vote (members pass between appointed tellers to be counted) may be had if enough members request it. And since the Legislative Reorganization Act of 1970, it is possible to have a recorded teller vote if enough members join to require this. A roll call

Sec. 1   *THE LEGISLATIVE PROCESS*   295

vote may be had if the division or teller counting reveals the lack of a quorum.

The amending stage is of course a crucial one in the progress of a bill. The amendments offered may be and often are of such character as to change the bill substantially or weaken it drastically. Their adoption might undermine such support for the bill as already exists. In any case, the skill, dedication and prestige of the floor manager may make the difference between success and failure in warding off crippling revisions. Once again it is appropriate to point to the life and death role of the committee personnel who are proponents for the bill on the floor, as well as having dealt with it in the committee itself and championed it before the Rules Committee. The fact that the standing committee proponents of a measure are for or against a particular amendment has significant weight with many Congressmen in determining how they will vote on the amendment. The notion is that doubts should be resolved in favor of the committee which has done the detailed work on the bill. If the committee represents a cross-section of the House, it may have foreseen and met the need to compromise adequately the divergent interests represented in the full House. Weight may attach, too, to the position of the leadership; and in the case of amendments proposed by minority party spokesmen, party loyalty may play a role. Incidentally, one of the most difficult tasks of those managing bills is to see that needed supporters are available on the floor when critical votes are taken.

Note, for purposes of later comparison with the Senate, that amendments put forward in the Committee of the Whole must be germane to the bill and to that portion of the bill they purport to revise. It may be possible to tack a non-germane amendment to a bill when the Rules Committee's special rule waives points of order against the bill or when the amendment concerned has specifically been made in order.

Not only is the bill open to amendment under the procedures we have been discussing, but it is also possible—though rare—to kill the bill in its entirety if a motion to strike the enacting clause is offered and sustained. If this preferential motion—which must be considered at once and allows ten minutes of debate—is upheld in the Committee of the Whole, the Committee rises and reports back to the full House which then has an opportunity to vote on the same question. If the full House sustains the defeat, the bill is killed; if not, the House resolves itself back into Committee of the Whole and resumes debate.

The process of amending the bill in Committee of the Whole, if not limited by the provisions of the special rule, will normally continue until there are no amendments left to consider, but it may be brought to an end by a unanimous consent agreement or by a motion disposed of by majority vote. Here, too, the inexorable march and expedition of House procedures deserve comparison with the Senate.

When the process of reading the bill for amendment has been concluded, the Committee of the Whole rises, its action is reported to the House itself, the Speaker resumes the chair, the quorum requirement is once again 218 members, and the House itself takes over consideration at this point. Note again the terms of the special rule, supra, governing the remaining steps, and these steps will generally be quite similar as a practical matter even when a privileged measure—such as an appropriation bill—is being considered without a special rule. Under the rule the "previous question" is deemed ordered, a highly privileged procedure which calls for final vote forthwith on the merits.

The House itself now takes up without debate the amendments, if any, reported by the Committee of the Whole and usually, though not necessarily, votes on them en bloc. Amendments rejected in Committee of the Whole are not reported and, in practice, they are lost and may not be voted on again. Once the amendments approved in Committee of the Whole have been voted on by the House—and the House commonly approves the work of the Committee of the Whole —the question before the House is the adoption of the amended bill itself. After vote on engrossment and third reading of the bill, it is in order for a member of the opposition to make a motion to recommit the bill to the original standing committee with or without instructions. If such a motion without instructions carries, the bill is stopped pro tem and goes back to the committee which may however report it back again at some later date for another attempt at passage. If the motion is made and approved with instructions to amend the bill in specified ways—often ways that were defeated in the Committee of the Whole—and to report forthwith, the bill as revised by the standing committee in accordance with the instructions is reported back to the House and put to a vote. When the motion to recommit is defeated, as it normally is, the question before the House becomes the final passage of the bill. The final vote will be a roll-call vote if one fifth of the members so demand. As stated in Riddick, The United States Congress: Organization and Procedure (1949), "if a measure is controversial, one of the members in charge will likely enter a motion to reconsider it, and immediately move to lay that motion on the table, thereby precluding reconsideration." The prerogative of reconsideration is not often put to use.

House floor procedure, taken as a whole, is notable then for the power it gives the majority, the continuing power exercised by the committee, the short shrift (e. g., the 5-minute rule, the "previous question") given to dilatory tactics and to efforts to block a final vote. The amending process can of course be used to delay and perhaps destroy but such action is subject to majority approval and is part and parcel of the ongoing Congressional task of reconciling divergent interests as a basis for social action.

On the Senate Floor

Compare the operation of the Senate when it takes up a bill on the floor, especially its handling of amendments and the limitation of debate. Commonly our bill will come before the Senate pursuant to a unanimous consent arrangement worked out by the majority leader in consultation with the minority leader and other interested Senators. Failing that, a motion may be made to take up the bill. Such a motion is vulnerable to the filibuster tactic which we will discuss more fully at a later point. Pursuant to such a motion, if adopted, or to a unanimous consent agreement, floor consideration of the bill begins —usually with an opening statement by the floor manager who will probably be either the responsible subcommittee chairman or, especially on major bills, the chairman of the standing committee itself. Members of the committee will most likely be on hand on the floor at this point and the opposition will be led by the appropriate ranking minority committee member. There is no reserved time for general debate as in the House and the amendment of the bill is in order at once. Committee amendments are taken up first, then non-committee amendments. And this amendment stage is no less critical, no less dependent on the skill and prestige of the floor managers, than it is in the House. Note, however, that in contrast to the House, where the requirement of germaneness regulates the amending process, in the Senate an amendment to a bill need not be germane to a bill, unless it is a general appropriation bill. Even as to general appropriation bills, for example, a resort to Suspension of the Rules procedure may permit non-germane amendments to be added. Such permissiveness has repercussions not only for the management of the bill on the floor, but also, inter alia, for Senate-House relations and Congressional-executive relations. Although since 1964 there has been a Senate rule requiring that after the morning hour debate must for a prescribed period be germane, readers of Senate proceedings in the Congressional Record will note the episodic character of debate, the frequency with which, by consent, it is broken into by speeches that have nothing to do with the main matter in hand.

The central characteristic of Senate floor procedure which differentiates it from that of the House and, indeed, from that of most other legislative bodies, is the difficulty of limiting debate. At this time, there are only three ways in which debate may close. First, of course, when all Senators have said all they wish to say on a proposal the debate will come to a halt. Second, there is the possibility of a unanimous consent agreement to limit debate on a particular measure. Even on many relatively controversial bills, the discussion is ended pursuant to such agreements. But such a device is not available to close debate against the wishes of even a single Senator. Absent unanimous consent, or the exhaustion of all desires to speak, the only recourse is the so-called cloture rule.

Before 1917, the evolving rules of the Senate allowed it no method of limiting debate. A so-called filibuster regarding the Armed Ship bill during 1917 in President Wilson's administration led to a public hue and cry and to the adoption of an initial cloture rule—Rule XXII—which provided that debate could be ended on petition or motion signed by sixteen Senators (with a two-day waiting period before a vote thereon) followed by a favorable vote of two-thirds of the Senators present and voting. Once such a motion had been approved no Senator could speak over an hour on the measure concerned, dilatory tactics were barred and points of order were to be determined without discussion. The effectiveness of this Rule may be gauged by the fact that from 1917 to 1949 only four of nineteen cloture motions were adopted.

This already weak rule was virtually neutralized in 1948 when the Chair ruled that cloture could not be applied to a motion to take up a measure but could only be applied to debate on the measure itself. From the ensuing struggles emerged the so-called "compromise" rule which was adopted in 1949 and prevailed until 1959. The "compromise" involved one step toward liberalization, in that the cloture rule was extended to cover motions to take up a measure, and two steps designed to make cloture difficult, in that a vote by two-thirds of the entire Senate membership was now necessary and in that cloture could not be applied to motions to change the rules. Throughout the 1950's, struggles continued to strengthen this rule. Much of the discussion turned on the question whether the Senate was a "continuing body" whose rules carried over from Congress to Congress along with two-thirds of the membership or whether the Senate had the right to adopt new rules (including a new cloture rule) by majority vote at the start of each Congress. In 1959 a fresh compromise was adopted, approving the argument that the Senate is a continuing body whose rules carry over, providing that rules changes are subject to cloture and reestablishing the 1917 position that two-thirds of the Senators present and voting (two-thirds of a quorum as against two-thirds of the entire membership) may enforce cloture. Efforts toward further strengthening of the cloture rule continued after 1959. In 1975, Rule XXII was revised once again in response to intense pressure, but the change made was modest. As revised, the Rule permitted the invocation of cloture on the vote of three-fifths of the Senators chosen and sworn, except on measures or motions to amend the rules where cloture still required a vote of two-thirds of the Senators present and voting. While cloture could thus be invoked a little more readily, subsequent experience showed that post-cloture obstructive tactics might still pose a serious problem. For example, in the 1977 debate on natural gas deregulation, two Senators in effect conducted a post-cloture filibuster by successively calling up amendments from a large pool of amendments introduced before cloture. To deal with such tactics, the Senate amended its rules again in 1979 to provide, in substance, that when cloture has once been voted on a bill, a final vote on it must be taken after no more than 100 hours of post-cloture debate.

There has been much argument over the merits of unlimited debate, or filibustering, and the weak cloture rule. On the one hand, the arguments made have cited the importance of unfettered debate in at least one chamber and have stressed the desirability of assuring that legislation with drastic consequences cannot be adopted by ruthless majorities over the intense opposition of a numerous minority. On the other hand there have been arguments based on the desirability of a majority's being ultimately able to prevail in a democratic society. The upshot of the present rule certainly is, in any case, to allow an intense minority to prevail, to block action, unless an extraordinary majority can be mobilized on the other side. And this state of affairs has pervasive implications for Senate procedure and decision-making. A majority cannot act if a large and determined minority opposes. The filibuster and threat of filibuster—even by individuals—offer a tremendous weapon for extracting concessions and compromises in legislative bargaining, especially in the crowded hours before sessions draw to a close. The difficulty of building winning coalitions is greatly increased. The further dispersion of already dispersed Congressional power should be plain enough to any observer.

The device of the filibuster has acquired notoriety as an instrument in the defeat of civil rights legislation and it has been prominently used for that purpose. Perhaps the successful cloture votes on the Civil Rights Act of 1964 and on the Voting Rights Act in 1965, taken together with the erosions of time, are signs that its use for that purpose may be waning as the years pass. The case for and against unlimited debate is complicated however by the fact that filibusters and threats of filibuster have been used more than a few times for other purposes by some of cloture's champions. In the end, the notion that a vote may be indefinitely postponed by a minority seems difficult to defend.

A great deal of business is done by the Senate, nonetheless, without encountering the occasional barrier of an actual filibuster. Assuming our bill is a part of such normal business, it will come in due course to a vote. Unlike the House, the Senate does not deliberate in a Committee of the Whole but, except for the teller vote which is not used in the Senate, it conducts its voting as the House does—by voice, by division and, on the request of one-fifth of a quorum, by roll-call (the yeas and nays). Roll-call votes, due to the chamber's smaller size are easier and more frequent in the Senate.

When the vote has been taken, any Senator on the prevailing side may move to reconsider it within two days. In order to make the result definite and final this motion to reconsider is generally made promptly after the final vote and another Senator moves to table the motion while the supporters of the final vote are still on hand. Tabling the motion has the effect of conclusively nailing down the final vote and usually is approved by voice vote. Once in a while, after a close vote, the result can be upset dramatically due to a change of heart or due to the arrival of new troops. In the House, as we saw, it is common for the opponents of a bill to move to recommit; the same motion is possible in the Senate but infrequent. Generally when the motion to reconsider is tabled, the Senate's deliberations—short of conference—on a bill are finished. Such deliberations it should now be apparent are far more flexible and leisurely than the House's, more prone to delay and liable as well to serious minority obstruction.

The student of votes in the Congressional Record will note references to "pairs." The practice of pairing is followed in both chambers. Pairing permits absent, or otherwise nonvoting, Senators to record their position. Thus, two absent Senators on opposite sides may "pair" with each other and their positions will be noted but will not be counted in the voting tallies.

The Congressional Record

Lawyers investigating the history of bills, and other students of the legislative process will inevitably make extensive use of the Congressional Record, which reports the floor proceedings of Congress and contains other information as well. The Record has been published since 1873. Before that time the proceedings of Congress were published in the Annals of Congress (1789–1824), the Register of Debates (1824–1837) and the Congressional Globe (1833–1873). The modern Record is published daily while Congress is in session. Bound volumes appear later. The bound volumes do not necessarily match the daily edition exactly and, as to both, it must be noted that the Record purports only to be "substantially a verbatim report of proceedings." Unfortunately, the practice of Congressmen and Senators in revising or extending their remarks or inserting undelivered speeches has marred the accuracy of the Record as a transcript of what occurred on the floor. A modest step was taken on March 1, 1978 in both House and Senate toward identifying, in the Record, materials not actually uttered on the floor. But the system adopted falls far short of enabling the reader reliably to know how much of what is printed was said in debate. After all, however, the Record is the best source available and lawyers must learn to make effective use of it. It is necessary to remember that the Record fulfills many purposes for the legislator besides that of providing an accurate record for judicial use. A glance at its pages seasoned with articles, occasional speeches, editorials, etc. and at its swollen Appendix will give some idea of the problem. But it does provide a record of some kind of the floor proceedings, the texts of amendments (which may also be available separately and may be crucial for interpretive purposes), and conference reports, and it contains indices invaluable to the researcher such as the Daily Digest, and, in the permanent edition, the History of Bills and Resolutions. In the Congressional Record and in the headings of bills, one peculiarity appears (particularly in the Senate proceedings) which should be mentioned. That is the phenomenon of the "legislative day." Because the Senate is apt to recess, rather than adjourn, from day to day and because recessing over night does not trigger a new legislative day when the Senate reconvenes in the morning, the Senate may be still operating on a legislative day, begun much earlier, which does not coincide with the calendar day. In the study of the rules this can be important as they may provide for lapses of time in terms of legislative days or calendar days and the difference must be noted.

H. INTER–HOUSE COORDINATION

The House and Senate, acting successively or concurrently in accordance with the procedures already described, may adopt identical measures. When they do, there is nothing to prevent or delay presentation of the legislation to the President for his signature. And the same is true, even when the chambers pass different versions of a bill, if one chamber is willing, without more, to accept the other's version. Much legislation is processed by Congress in these ways without further Congressional steps being required. Froman's The Congressional Process (1967) reports, for example, that in the Eighty-Eighth Congress (1963–64) 1,026 public and private bills were enacted and only 89 of these required resort to special machinery for adjustment of disagreements.

When the differences between the chambers regarding a bill are controversial in character, however, and neither chamber is, or seems, likely to yield its position, special action to compose differences may be needed. Normally a conference will be requested. Then, assuming the request is agreed to, a conference committee will be appointed. Such committees are a useful, important device in the Congressional process. That they work quite effectively may be gauged from Froman's data that 85 of the 89 bills committed to conference in the Eighty-Eighth Congress became law. But it must be stressed that the conference stage when invoked is one of the most critical in the development of a bill. Often it is the point at which, in reality, the law is made.

What happens if a conference committee is to be utilized for our bill? First, conferees or managers from each chamber are appointed by, respectively, the Speaker of the House and the presiding officer of the Senate. At least three conferees—but there may be more—are designated in each chamber. In selecting them, the presiding officer generally follows the recommendations of the appropriate standing committee chairman. Each chamber's team of conferees or managers is very likely to include senior members of the standing committee. Such persons as the standing committee chairman, the ranking majority and minority members, the appropriate subcommittee chairman and the ranking minority subcommittee member will probably be selected. A rule adopted in the House in October, 1974 provides that in appointing conference committee members the Speaker "shall appoint no less than a majority of members who generally supported the House position as determined by the Speaker." A 1977 rule provides that the Speaker, to the extent feasible, is to name as conferees the authors of the principal amendments to the proposed bill. Both political parties are commonly represented on the committee, with the majority party having the larger representation. Because the Senate and House delegations vote separately on all questions arising in the conference committee and because a majority of each delegation must approve every action, it is not essential that the two delegations be of the same size and they frequently are not. Note in regard to the composition of conference committees that the pervasive influence of the standing committee and its chairman which has been remarked in all other phases of the Congressional process is present here also.

The designated conferees meet to discuss the bill, typically under great pressure to reach an accommodation and often under great pressure of time. On rare occasions, conference delegations operate under instructions from the parent chamber but generally there are no instructions. The conferees are generally free to negotiate and resolve all matters in dispute between the chambers, although House rules restrict the power of House conferees to agree to non-germane Senate amendments. The conferees may trade off Senate provisions against House provisions and vice versa; they may seek a middle ground between the Senate and House provisions. They may not add new provisions or change provisions already agreed on by both chambers. Nonetheless they have, in practice, a substantial leeway to compose differences and it is difficult to enforce strict limitations. Sometimes, one chamber will have amended a bill originating in the other by striking out all that follows the enacting clause and inserting its own provisions. When such an amendment "in the nature of a substitute" comes before the conference, the conferees have the entire subject matter before them and are much more free to make changes, to draw a new bill. In such cases, the Legislative Reorganization Act of 1946 forbids them to include in their report matter not committed to them by either house; but they may include matter which is a germane modification of subjects in disagreement. Steiner's well-known study, The Congressional Conference Committee (1951), does not support the charges sometimes heard that conference committees are irresponsible or commonly transgress the limits imposed on them. A conference report that does transgress the limits is vulnerable to a point of order when brought before the chambers.

Conference committee meetings have customarily been held in executive session in the past—that is, in secrecy behind closed doors. Generally, only committee and staff members and expert aides, such as members of the Offices of Legislative Counsel, attended these closed meetings. Now, as a result of rules adopted in 1975 and extended in 1977, conference committee deliberations are to be open to the public unless special action is taken to close them. At the meetings, as suggested earlier, votes upon proposed action are taken by delegation and a majority of each delegation must vote in favor before an action is approved. In rare cases where no agreement can be reached, the impasse must be reported back to the chamber and new conferees may be designated. The House rules provide for the possibility of discharging the conferees if they do not act within 20 days (or within 36 hours during the last 6 days of the session).

The deliberations of a small group of men with a large measure of power over the shape and fate of a controversial bill are a natural target for pressure from special interests for this or that modification of the bill's provisions. By any yardstick, the conference is crucial for a bill, as we have said, and any experienced lobbyist cannot fail to be aware of this. Once more there is a major opportunity for blocking action.

As the figures quoted earlier suggest, conference committees are usually able to arrive at some sort of accommodation of Senate-House differences and to agree on provisions to be recommended to the chambers. Of course, if the chambers cannot be thus brought to agreement, the bill is lost. Assuming, however, that the conferees do concur in recommendations for adjusting the differences, they incorporate these recommendations in a report which must be signed by a majority of each delegation of the conferees and filed with their respective houses. The dissenting managers have no authority to file statements of minority views. The recommendations are accompanied by a statement on the part of the managers explaining the effect of actions recommended. The conference report containing the recommendations and statement is made available in print separately and in the Congressional Record. As a document representing the late and detailed views of representatives of both chambers it is a very important aid to judicial interpretation of the enacted bill.

The engrossed bill and amendments, together with a copy of the report of the conference committee, are transmitted to the chamber which is to act first on the conference report (normally to the house other than the one requesting the conference). Whichever chamber takes up the conference report, it represents a matter of high privilege. In the House of Representatives, for example, the report and bill do not need help from the Rules Committee to reach the floor quickly.

On the floor, a statement will be made on behalf of the managers as a preface to discussion and final vote. The conference measure, however, is not open to amendment in either chamber. It must be accepted or rejected as a whole in each chamber, a point which underscores the great power which is entrusted to a few men in the conference process. If rejected in the first chamber, the report may be recommitted to the conferees. If it is accepted in the first chamber, that chamber's conferees are discharged, and if the second chamber does not pass the bill, the process may have to start over. The pressures that build up for prompt adoption of a conference report can be formidable especially as the session nears an end. The House limits debate on the report to an hour.

The chamber first approving the conference report sends the documents to the other House for final action. When both chambers have approved the conference bill it is sent to the enrolling clerk of the chamber in which the bill had its origin. It is then ready for the last stage of its journey to enactment.

I. EXECUTIVE ACTION

When our bill has weathered the stages of committee review, of getting to the floor, of floor consideration, of inter-house coordination, it faces at least one more critical test—that of Presidential review. In fact, of course, the President's concern with an important bill is not something that merely springs into being at the end of the long process we have described. When discussing the sources of legislation, we noted the President's major role as an initiator of enactments. Through public statements and personal communications, through Cabinet members, staff aides, administrative agency officials and otherwise, the President maintains active contact with the Congress in regard to bills important to him as they make their way forward from stage to stage of the process. His participation in that process comes to a climax or focus, however, when the moment arrives for exercise of the power to approve or veto conferred on him by the Constitution.

Once our bill is approved in identical form by both House and Senate, it is transmitted to the enrolling clerk of the chamber in which it originated, who undertakes the often complex and difficult task of preparing the so-called enrolled bill, incorporating as accurately as may be all amendments adopted along the way. The enrolled bill is printed on parchment and when the proper committee approves the bill as truly enrolled, it is transmitted for signature first to the Speaker of the House, then to the President of the Senate. When both have affixed their signatures to the enrolled bill, it is delivered to the White House and a receipt secured therefor. This delivery is normally regarded as presentation to the President and as triggering the start of the ten day period allowed for Presidential action by the Constitution. Occasionally, in the past, when a President has had to be absent for an extended period—as Wilson was in 1919 and as Franklin D. Roosevelt was some decades later—the step of delivery to the White House has been deferred for a time so as not to trigger the ten day period at an inconvenient moment.

The President has several choices in dealing with a bill presented to him. If he decides to approve the measure, he may do so affirmatively by signing it or passively, if Congress is still in session at the end of ten days following presentation, by leaving it unsigned. In either case the bill becomes a law. In neither of the cases, be it noted, is any message to Congress required by the Constitution. There have, however, been a few special occasions—for example, President Truman's approval of the Hobbs Anti-Racketeering Act of 1946 and the Portal-to-Portal Act of 1947—when the chief executive upon approving a bill has in fact sent a formal message to Congress explaining his approval and discussing the provisions of the legislation concerned. Whether or not there is a formal communication to Congress, the President may in any case issue a more or less detailed public statement on signing the bill.

If the President objects to a bill, the Constitution provides that within ten days after presentation "he shall return it, with his objections to the House in which it shall have originated, who shall enter the objections at large on their Journal and proceed to reconsider it." The veto thus delivered may be overridden, as we shall discuss in a moment, by a two-thirds vote of both Senate and House. In that event the bill becomes a law; without such overriding it does not. There is also the possibility of a "pocket veto." This occurs when the President fails to sign a measure and Congress adjourns before the end of the ten-day period allowed for Presidential action. In this case the bill is lost; Congress has no opportunity to override the veto. When the President vetoes by returning a bill to Congress, there is an obligatory Presidential message that goes with it. Although such a message is not required with a "pocket veto", it has been a Presidential practice in recent years to give the press and the public a full statement of reasons for each "pocket veto."

How is the decision made to veto or approve a bill? Once again, it is necessary to call attention to the Legislative Reference Division of the President's Office of Management and Budget which has a major function to play in the executive consideration of enrolled bills. At the point where an enrolled bill is presented to the President, the Legislative Reference Division of the Office of Management and Budget undertakes a searching review process. Copies of the bill are sent to the executive departments and agencies concerned with its provisions and their recommendations are sought within forty-eight hours as to whether the President should veto or approve. While this may sound like a short period for response, it must be remembered that the departments and agencies in question will generally have been active in the legislative process on the bill—e. g., providing expert views and aid to the Congressional committees in hearings and otherwise—and so will commonly be very familiar with the measure and "primed for a response." When agency responses are received, the Legislative Reference Division has several days to prepare its own "enrolled bill memorandum" for the chief executive. In that memorandum will be the arguments advanced pro and con by the agencies, together with the Division's own analysis and recommendations. In the end of course the President must weigh all this argumentation in relation to his perception of the national interest, his programs and promises, his obligations, his party position, the counsels of staff and other close advisers, and so forth. Note that the lobbying pressures on the President and his advisers may be as intense at this point as they are at earlier critical points in the legislative process. Note also that the President with his national constituency and his own objectives and resources, brings to the decisional process still another perspective from that applied by the Senators and Congressmen who have previously passed on it.

One way or another, a decision must be made at this juncture. Much of the time, the decision is to approve. The number of Presidential vetoes is not in fact very large in comparison to the total number of bills which are presented for signature and become law without exercise of the veto power. But the number of vetoes should not be taken as an index of the veto power's importance. The existence of the veto power and the threat of its possible use extend the President's influence throughout the legislative process. His position must be reckoned with by proponents and opponents at every stage. Here is one more center of power in the panorama of dispersed and divided powers that the legislative processes offer to view. Here is one more opportunity to block action.

If the decision is to approve, and unless the President allows the bill to become law without his signature, there may be more or less elaborate signing ceremonies. Notice of the signing is generally sent by message to the chamber where the bill originated and that chamber informs the other. The action is noted in the Congressional Record.

If the President vetoes a bill, other than by "pocket veto," the bill and his veto message are, as we saw, returned to the chamber of origin. A vetoed bill returned to the Congress in this way is accorded high privilege (there is no need for recourse to the Rules Committee in the House) and will generally be disposed of quickly. Amendments are not in order; in the House, only a limited time is allowed for debate. If there is no real possibility the veto may be overridden, the bill may be tabled or sent back to committee. Otherwise the question is put, "Shall the bill pass, the objections of the President to the contrary notwithstanding?" To override the veto, each chamber must separately vote to do so by a vote of at least two-thirds of those present, a quorum being required to be on hand. A negative vote kills the bill and if it occurs in the first chamber a message is normally sent to the other advising of the decision that the bill is not to pass.

If the President signs our bill or allows it to become law without signature, or if the chambers vote to override a veto, then as the case may be the President or the chamber last voting to override will transmit the bill to the General Services Administration for publication. There a public law number will be given to the bill (the public law number contains the number of the enacting Congress and a number indicating the order in which the bill was adopted as compared with other enactments by the same Congress). The bill is forthwith made available in published form. First, it is made available as a slip law (see Fig. C) in unbound pamphlet form printed by offset process from the enrolled bill. Later, this and other new laws will be published in bound volumes of the Statutes at Large, an official authoritative compilation containing the laws of each Congress in the chronological order of their enactment. Later also, the bill will be incorporated in the United States Code, a compilation consolidating and codifying the general and permanent laws of the United States and arranging them by subject-matter under 50 titles. For the lawyer, the Code is a much more readily usable research tool than the chronologically arranged Statutes at Large. Certain titles of the Code have been enacted into positive law in an ongoing codification effort, and as to these titles the Code is the official and authoritative source of the statute law. The Statutes at Large and the Revised Statutes (an early compilation of the laws in force as of Dec. 1, 1873) remain the official and authoritative source, however, for laws not included in these titles. These versions of the bill—the slip law, the text in the Statutes at Large, the version in the U.S. Code—are of course primary sources for lawyers working with legislation. And other materials, such as veto or approval messages, to which earlier reference was made, may be of high importance as aids to understanding our bill, now a statute, when it comes before lawyers, courts or administrators for interpretation.

As a concluding note on the Congressional processes, observe that the vetoing of a bill and a failure to override the veto may not necessarily signal the irrevocable demise of a legislative proposal. Some kinds of legislation must knock at the gate many times over many years and many sessions of Congress before they are finally admitted. Similarly, even the enactment of a legislative measure (if it requires funding) may not be the end of the struggle. Before money is actually made available to implement it, the appropriation process must be completed.

Public Law 95-172
95th Congress

An Act

To extend for an additional temporary period the existing suspension of duties on certain classifications of yarns of silk, and for other purposes.

Be it enacted by the Senate and House of Representatives of the United States of America in Congress assembled, That (a) items 905.30 and 905.31 of the Appendix to the Tariff Schedules of the United States (19 U.S.C. 1202) are each amended by striking out "11/7/75" and inserting in lieu thereof "6/30/80".

(b) The amendment made by subsection (a) shall apply with respect to articles entered, or withdrawn from warehouse, for consumption on or after the date of the enactment of this Act.

(c) Upon request therefore filed with the customs officer concerned on or before the 90th day after the date of the enactment of this Act, the entry or withdrawal of any article—

(1) which was made after November 7, 1975, and before the date of the enactment of this Act, and

(2) with respect to which there would have been no duty if the amendment made by subsection (a) applied to such entry or withdrawal,

shall, notwithstanding the provisions of section 514 of the Tariff Act of 1930 or any other provision of law, be liquidated or reliquidated as though such entry or withdrawal had been made on the date of the enactment of this Act.

SEC. 2. (a) Section 4254 of the Internal Revenue Code of 1954 (relating to computation of tax) is amended by adding at the end thereof the following new subsection:

"(c) CERTAIN STATE AND LOCAL TAXES NOT INCLUDED.—For purposes of this subchapter, in determining the amounts paid for communications services, there shall not be included the amount of any State or local tax imposed on the furnishing or sale of such services, if the amount of such tax is separately stated in the bill."

(b) The amendment made by this section shall take effect only with respect to amounts paid pursuant to bills first rendered on or after the first day of the first month which begins more than 20 days after the date of the enactment of this Act. For purposes of the preceding sentence, in the case of communications services rendered more than 2 months before the effective date provided in the preceding sentence, no bill shall be treated as having been first rendered on or after such effective date.

Approved November 12, 1977.

LEGISLATIVE HISTORY:

HOUSE REPORT No. 95-426 (Comm. on Ways and Means).
SENATE REPORT No. 95-434 (Comm. on Finance).
CONGRESSIONAL RECORD, Vol. 123 (1977):
    July 18, considered and passed House.
    Sept. 21, considered and passed Senate, amended.
    Oct. 25, House concurred in certain Senate amendments, in others with amendment; disagreed to amendment no. 6.
    Oct. 27, Senate receded and concurred in House amendments.

Figure C

In sum, the legislative process we have described, with all its pitfalls and barriers and other difficulties, is no process for the faint-hearted or the short-winded. The task of compromise and coalition-building needed to secure affirmative final action by the Congress and the President clearly poses a challenge of a high order.

J. SOME ASPECTS OF STATE LEGISLATIVE PROCESSES

No attempt will be made here to deal fully with state legislative processes. In their general outlines these processes bear many resemblances to the Congressional processes we have been considering. For present purposes it will suffice to single out several aspects of the state processes for brief comparison and comment and to note several points which may be of use for those who must work with state legislation.

Standing Committees

Consider first the standing committee system which, we have seen, has central, overriding importance in the federal legislative process. What is the role of standing committees in the states?

In fact, the state legislatures like Congress do use the standing committee system to deal with legislation. An array of different committees, each with its defined area of subject-matter jurisdiction, is provided in each chamber of the legislatures (joint committees are used in some New England states). Every proposal coming before a state legislative chamber is normally referred to committee for initial action and recommendations. Committee memberships and chairmanships are typically assigned (seniority is less vital here than at the federal level) in the lower house by the Speaker, a very powerful officer in many states with authority stemming from such sources as his party office, his position on the rules committee, his power to refer bills, his power to preside at meetings and so on. In the upper house they are often assigned by the presiding officer or a committee on committees. In recent decades, the states have made substantial progress in reducing their formerly swollen lists of standing committees. There remain a few states, however, which still operate with a relatively large number of committees and in some states the committee jurisdictions are still defined in such a way as to overburden important committees and leave others with little to do. State legislators in many cases still have too many committee obligations to be able to attend to them properly.

For a long time, the inadequacy of the standing committee system was a cardinal fact of life in the state legislative process. In many or most states the standing committees, so vital to the quality of legislation, did not exercise initiative in policy-making as did their federal counterparts or contribute comparably to the development of legislation. They did not conduct comparable oversight of administration. They did not carry out a comparably detailed review of proposals submitted to them. And they were simply not equipped to give sustained in-depth attention to problems arising within their areas of concern. Indeed, it can well be argued that the state standing committees very often failed—even for review of legislation—to meet minimum standards for viable legislative participation in policy-making.

For this state of affairs, widespread until recently, there were many reasons and some at least of these may be noted. For example, there was the problem of constitutional limitations on sessions referred to earlier. State constitutions often required that regular sessions be held biennially. Indeed in some states they still do, though a large majority of the states now have annual sessions. Limitations on the length of sessions, we noted, were once common in the constitutions. While special sessions could often be called to fill in the gaps, sometimes the power to call such sessions was given only to the governor and special sessions might also be confined to consideration of subjects designated by the governor. Given these various restrictions, the state standing committees were apt to discharge their work in short, more or less widely separated bursts of activity. Continuity of effort was wanting.

Other factors contributed over the years to the inadequacy of state standing committees. In the short and intermittent sessions, a heavy and concentrated workload had to be dealt with under intense pressure. To cope with this workload there was a membership of part-time legislators, more "amateur" than professional, often inexperienced due to the high turnover of incumbents, often indifferently paid for their efforts and working in poor physical facilities. While some of the deficiency might have been made up by generous provision for staff assistance, the state standing committees lagged far behind their federal counterparts in acquiring and using aid of this kind.

In such circumstances, as one might expect, it was necessary to look to sources outside the legislature—e. g., to the executive, to the administrative agencies and, even, to private interest groups for much of the detailed work on important legislation. And it is not surprising that other activities we associate with federal standing committees were generally curtailed at the state level. For instance, the holding of public hearings tended to be less frequent and effective, though a few states made considerable use of this device.

Notwithstanding all of this, one cannot say that the standing committees have not been important and influential in the context and within the limitations of the state legislative process. On the contrary, though the caucus may have sapped their authority in some states, they have generally been very significant elements in that process. Their recommendations have carried weight and indeed have often been decisive. Though the power to discharge such committees (N.B. that several states require their committees to report all referred bills) is available in the states, as a practical matter it does not seem to have been used to make serious inroads on committee authority. But it bears repeating that the state committees for a long time provided no match for the independence, power, prestige, and effectiveness of their federal counterparts and often fell short, too, of minimum needs for effective lawmaking.

While the longstanding difficulties we have described still hold true for a number of states, it must be stressed that major reforms have been taking place in recent decades and are still continuing. Sustained criticism, sustained efforts to secure improvement, the pressure of increasingly complex problems—among other things—have brought significant change. The barriers to annual sessions have, as we noted, been crumbling; restrictions on the length of sessions are on the wane. There has been a substantial enlargement of the time spent in session, and there is, correspondingly, much more continuity of effort. The pay of legislators, and the physical facilities provided them have been notably bettered. Great strides have been made in providing professional staff and secretarial assistance for standing committees. Hearings are on the increase. Oversight of administration is gaining ground. Such developments as these, together with the extension of standing committee operations into inter-session periods, bid fair to improve markedly the quality of state committee work and thus to reshape the state legislative process as a whole in important ways.

From time to time, in discussing the federal legislative process, mention was made of the various records and documents published along the way for the enlightenment of legislators, the public and the courts. We noted the availability, in particular, of published standing committee reports and, often, of published hearings. Such records and documents, alas, have not been, and still are not, normally available at the state level. In making their recommendations on bills entrusted to them, state standing committees commonly report only their recommendation that the bill "do pass" (or the contrary, where negative reports are made). Few committee reports dealing, as on the federal level, with the substance of legislation are published. Few hearings by standing committees are published. The lack of such documentation penalizes the legislature itself, of course, and the public. In its absence, state courts searching for light on legislation have had to turn mainly to reports and messages of the executive or of administrative agencies, and even to those of private groups.

The difficulties of part-time committees, together with other problems we have described, have given rise over the years to several kinds of remedial devices in the states. Two time-honored devices are the establishment of legislative councils and the use of interim committees.

The legislative council movement began in 1933 in Kansas and has grown apace since then. Today legislative councils are firmly established in a very large number of states. In most cases, such a council amounts essentially to a "super interim committee" which is permanent in character and has a range of action as broad as that of the legislature itself. The council membership consists of legislators, commonly selected from the chambers of the legislature by the presiding officers, with minority representation being normally provided for. All councils conduct research and fact-finding and most prepare proposals, in bill form or otherwise, for legislative action. They are normally equipped with research staffs. As a single organ with general jurisdiction, the council is uniquely situated to provide an overview of legislative problems and priorities. Note that the reports of a council are normally available to the legislature and public; they could well be resorted to by the courts in statutory interpretation.

A second mode of bridging the gap between sessions, of providing continuity and an opportunity for detailed consideration of problems, has been the appointment of interim committees. This device is much older than the legislative council. In essence the interim committee is a special committee created to explore a particular subject between sessions and to report to the legislature thereon. The subject-matter explored by such committees has often depended on the interests of individual members. The staffing of such committees has often been of indifferent quality, though proper staffing may be crucial to the merit of the work done. As used, interim committees have some of the drawbacks associated historically with special committees—a want of coordination, frequent waste and duplication of effort, etc.—but they have done valuable work. Their reports to the legislature can be of help to legislators, courts and public.

In recent years, the problem of discontinuity in state standing committee work has been dealt with more directly and effectively. The Book of the States 1976–1977, published in 1976 by the Council of State Governments, reported (p. 40) that "[o]ver one half of the States now allow standing committees to function virtually year-round either as standing committees or as subcommittees of an umbrella organization such as a legislative council." This would seem a wholly logical and necessary step in the improvement of the committee system, complementing such other reforms as the shift to annual sessions, the loosening of restraints on the length of sessions, the reduction in the number of committees, and the establishment of committee staffs. When there is continuity of standing committees there should be little or no need for resort to the interim committee device.

As a final footnote to this brief consideration of the state standing committee systems, mention should be made of legislative services generally. In this area, too, considerable progress and improvement have characterized the states in recent decades. Thus, many state legislatures, like Congress, have equipped themselves with legislative reference bureaus and bill drafting agencies designed to aid the committees and the members of the legislature in developing legislation. And there are in some states statute revisors, agencies for fiscal analysis, auditors or other services. While legislative services are not substitutes for a sound standing committee system, they can nonetheless make an appreciable contribution to the quality of lawmaking.

Scheduling and Floor Consideration

The states vary among themselves, and differ from the Congress, in their methods of scheduling legislation for floor consideration and in their conduct of floor proceedings. What they do in these matters must be seen in the context of that pervasive phenomenon of the state legislative process—the "end-of-session rush." Sometimes better than half of the legislative measures adopted at a given session will be adopted in the final week. Frantic activity on the floor is common as the date of adjournment nears. Contributing to this phenomenon are the limitations on the length of sessions, the burdens and disabilities of the committees, the heavy volume of business, a felt need to deal with the budget before other matters can be properly attended to, and, most importantly perhaps, the demands of political maneuvering and "logrolling." Whatever the causes, the "end-of-session rush" has resisted cure. It results in hasty action, in the surrender of deliberative functions. It may mean, too, a yielding of power to the governor if opportunities for the legislature to override the gubernatorial veto are abandoned.

As to the means by which legislation is scheduled and brought up for debate in the states, Professors Keefe and Ogul in their American Legislative Process (1973) observe: "Where the party is an effective instrument, party leadership necessarily assumes the function of scheduling. * * * In states in which parties are weak, control over the agenda may rest with calendar committees, rules committees, factions, or a leadership that pays slight attention to partisan considerations." While, as indicated, a rules committee may discharge the sifting function, it may be doubted that any state rules committee duplicates the power of the Rules Committee in the national House of Representatives. In a number of states, however, rules committees do become the traffic control agencies in the hectic closing days of the session and at this juncture, typically under the sway of majority leaders, can wield a life and death power over legislative proposals and a shaping influence on the legislature's accomplishments.

On the floor of the state legislatures, as can be imagined, bills are often passed upon with little floor discussion and the standing committee's recommendation may have great weight. Filibusters are rare, though they occasionally do occur; and debate—such as it is—tends commonly to be conducted under confining rules and time limitations. Of course, any effort to delay or kill a bill by dilatory floor tactics could, except as the rules forbid it, be devastating in the context of a limited session and the final rush to adjournment.

It would surely serve the interests of the public, of scholars, and of the courts, if not of the legislators themselves, to make available a record of the remarks of committee chairmen, sponsors and others, in speeches and colloquies on the floor of the state legislature. At the federal level, the Congressional Record is plainly of major value notwithstanding all its defects. But in the states, such resources are not generally available. The situation is described in Cashman, Availability of Records of Legislative Debates, 24 The Record of the Association of the Bar of the City of New York 153 (1969). All states, with a few exceptions, keep and publish a journal of their proceedings but this journal is only a formal, skeletal record of procedure rather than a complete exposition of floor deliberations. Maine and Pennsylvania alone among the states publish a full verbatim record of their legislative debates. Connecticut, Nebraska and Nevada maintain full verbatim records which, though available to the public, are not published and distributed. A handful of other states keep records but hedge their availability. For example, in Tennessee full tape recordings are made and may be listened to but may not be transcribed without authorization of the presiding officer. New York keeps full records but furnishes transcripts to the public only with the consent of the legislator whose remarks are sought. In Utah records are made but are kept from the public for ten years. For practical purposes verbatim records are not to be had in most other states. For an interesting case in which, in some unexplained way, court and counsel gained access to legislative debates, see Woollcott v. Shubert (infra p. 368).

Inter-house Coordination

The conference committee, so important at the federal level as a device for ironing out differences between chambers, seems to be considerably less important at the state level. Although such committees are used in many states and their recommendations are normally followed when made, they are used with considerably less frequency and may often wield less power. In some of the states where such committees are employed they act merely as a rubber stamp for compromises dictated by the leadership. In a few states, the leadership engineers compromises directly without recourse to the conference committee device.

Whereas Congressional conference committees issue published reports which are a rich source of information on the development of statutes or their interpretation, state conference committees commonly either do not make published reports available or, in such reports as may be available, do not go beyond indicating the text of the recommended compromise.

Executive-Legislative Relations

From modest post-Revolutionary beginnings the office of governor has developed in many states—especially in the wake of changes wrought in the 20th century—into a position of notable power and authority, playing a major role in the processes of legislation.

Typically, the governor possesses powers and sources of power like those of the President in relation to legislation. The governor recommends legislation. Except in North Carolina he has the veto power. In many states, in contrast to the President, he has the power to veto items in appropriation bills. Even the threat of veto gives him leverage. In a handful of states there is a power of executive amendment. The governor also has the power, often exclusive, to call special sessions of the legislature and, frequently, the power to determine the subjects that may be considered at any special session. The executive budget gives him a broad foundation for influence on lawmaking. So does his position as administrative leader with substantial control over technical resources and information, and over personnel and programs, and with consequent awareness of needs for legislation. He has capabilities superior to legislators for mobilizing public opinion, and, often, he has a predominant role in the machinery of party politics and a more or less substantial influence over the legislative leadership. He may be able to dispense patronage.

It is possible to say in general terms that if the President is a major factor in the development of national legislation, the governor tends to be even more important to the state legislative process. This has been due in no small part to the relative weakness of the state legislatures and their committees which was discussed earlier in this section. Ongoing reform of the legislatures and their committee systems may, of course, bring changes. To be sure, there is variation in the governor's practical power from state to state based on local political patterns and other factors. But in any case the governor is likely to be a most significant force.

The governor is, first, a prime source of the legislative proposals considered by the state legislature. In general, of course, the sources of such proposals resemble those described in an earlier section for the Congress. They spring from the executive, from the administrative agencies, from private groups and, occasionally, from the legislature itself. In the states proposals come, too, from legislative councils, from interim committees and from commissions. Of all these sources, however, the governor and his administrative agencies loom largest. They are generators of much of the important legislation dealt with in any session. The gubernatorial budget and program and other initiatives provide the principal items on the legislature's agenda and furnish a focus for deliberation that the legislature seems hardly able to supply for itself.

When legislation has been introduced, on message of the governor or otherwise, he may sometimes play a more directly active role in the legislative consideration of the particular measure than the President would play. At the end of the road there is the possibility of veto, which may often be final in the states because, as noted earlier, the legislature by late action may forego its opportunity to override.

Executive messages and administrative reports may be important sources of light on the legislative process at the state level for legislators, public and courts. The availability of executive materials in New York, for example, is discussed in Dana, Background Materials for Statutory Interpretation, 14 The Record of the Association of the Bar of the City of New York 80 (1959). Mr. Dana writes:

> "The Annual Message of the Governor to the Legislature has contained, in all recent years, many references to bills which are to be introduced as part of the Governor's program. Similarly, in recent years the Governor has issued supplemental Special Messages (in 1958, approximately 25) during the course of the legislative session, urging the adoption of particular bills. Finally, when signing a bill, the Governor will often issue a so-called Approval Message (in 1958, more than 90 such messages were issued).
>
> "These messages of the Governor, usually describing the need for and intended purpose of the bill, and often stating the source or origin of the bill as well, become in later years a helpful aid in legislative background and interpretation.
>
> "The messages are available as part of the Governor's official papers, but as a practical matter it is easier to obtain and read the messages in the New York State Legislative Annual, or in McKinney's bound volume of Session Laws of New York, for the year in question." (pp. 87–88)

* * *

> "Many bills are vetoed with a so-called 'veto message' from the Governor (over 150 in 1958). The veto message's discussion of defective language in the vetoed bill, which defective language is eliminated or altered in a later year when the (corrected) bill is finally enacted, may be of aid in interpreting the bill finally enacted." (pp. 94–95)

It may be of interest to note here an unusual item of special concern in New York. This item is the so-called Governor's bill jacket which may, after a lapse of time, become available for legal research and which broadens the resources for interpretation. It is described by Mr. Dana (pp. 93–94) as follows:

> "Each year, for each and every bill which is before the Governor for action, a separate envelope [i. e., the Governor's bill jacket] is maintained, into which is placed all supporting (and opposing) material which is sent to the Governor or his Counsel on the bill. A jacket will usually contain (a) a memorandum from the sponsoring entity, (b) the * * * required explanatory letter from the legislator who introduced the bill, (c) supporting or opposing memoranda from bar associations, the Citizens Union, and other entities which comment more or less dispassionately on pending legislation, and (d) letters or memoranda from lobby groups or private individuals who may urge or oppose the legislation in not-at-all dispassionate fashion.
>
> "The bill jacket is a kind of 'surprise package,' and you won't know what it contains until you look. * * *"

For a bill which has been vetoed by the Governor, the envelope described above is referred to as the Governor's veto jacket. Copies of the Governor's bill jacket or veto jacket for legislation in 1905 and from 1921 to the present are available, upon request and payment of a fee, from the New York State Library in Albany.

The unavailability of other aids to interpretation and the significant role of the governor in the state legislative process combine to give special importance to the executive aids we have described.

BIBLIOGRAPHICAL NOTE

For material on Congressional organization and processes, see for example: S. Bailey, Congress Makes a Law (1950); S. Bailey and H. Samuel, Congress at Work (2d ed. 1965); S. Bailey, The New Congress (1966); S. Bailey, Congress in the Seventies (1970); D. Berman, In Congress Assembled (1964); G. Blair, American Legislatures: Structure and Process (1967); G. Galloway, The Legislative Process in Congress (1953); B. Gross, The Legislative Struggle (1953); M. Jewell and S. Patterson, The Legislative Process in the United States (3d ed. 1977); W. Keefe and M. Ogul, The American Legislative Process (3d ed. 1973); R. Peabody, J. Berry, W. Frasure and J. Goldman, To Enact a Law: Congress and Campaign Financing (1972); E. Redman, The Dance of Legislation (1973); Woodrow Wilson, Congressional Government (15th ed. 1900); R. Young, This Is Congress (2d ed. 1946); R. Young, The American Congress (1958); and The Congress and America's Future (The American Assembly, 2d ed. D. Truman 1973). Congressional procedure is discussed in L. Froman, The Congressional Process: Strategies, Rules and Procedures (1967) and F. Riddick, The United States Congress: Organization and Procedure (1949). As to Congressional committee investigations, which are not dealt with in the preceding pages, see, for example, J. Hamilton, The Power to Probe: A Study of Congressional Investigations (1976). On state legislatures and legislative processes, see for example—besides some of the general texts listed earlier: American Political Science Association, American State Legislatures (B. Zeller ed. 1954); The Council of State Governments, American State Legislatures: Their Structures and Procedures (1971 and rev. ed. 1977); W. Crane and M. Watts, State Legislative Systems (1968); J. Fordham, The State Legislative Institution (1959); M. Jewell, The State Legislature: Politics and Practice (1962); The Forty-eight States: Their Tasks as Policy Makers and Administrators (The American Assembly, 1955); and State Legislatures in American Politics (The American Assembly, Heard ed. 1966).

SECTION 2. FINDING AND STATING ISSUES OF STATUTE LAW

A. INTRODUCTORY NOTE

Effective legal method in the use of statutes for advocacy and counseling must be based upon a decent respect for statutory language. This truth is obvious enough, but it marks an essential change of emphasis as the beginning law student moves from legal method in the use of case law to legal method in the use of statutes. After even a few weeks of case law analysis and synthesis, the first year law student has discovered that the rule of law derived from a case or from a line of cases can be stated in many different forms of language, each of which may constitute an acceptable statement. But a statutory rule of law is cast in an exclusive textual form. The beginning law student finds it difficult, as, for that matter, do many members of the profession, to work comfortably with a legal principle of which there is only one authorized version. Inevitably the beginner wants to handle statutes with the freedom of paraphrase that he has found permissible in the statement of case law principles.

The Problem Cases in this Section are designed to give you practice in statutory analysis and in the statement of statutory issues. The vital lesson you are to learn in the preparation and discussion of these Problem Cases is this: *The issue in a case of statutory interpretation must be so stated as to include an exact quotation of the precise term of the statute with respect to which the question of statutory applicability arises.* No paraphrase of the statute's terms will be permitted. As to each Problem Case—and, later, as to each judicial opinion in this Chapter—you must be prepared to give an accurate and precise answer to the question: "What does the statute *say*, exactly, with respect to the legal problem at hand?" Accordingly, the following Problem Cases are to be analyzed and discussed solely on the basis of the words of the statutes in point. You are urged not even to look at any judicial decisions interpreting statutes until you have learned that the first indispensable step in the analysis of a statutory problem is the reading and rereading of the text of the statute itself. Unless this simple but fundamental lesson is fully grasped, you will be left unequipped to perform workmanlike statutory analysis and wholly unable to handle the statutory cases of first impression which make up a large part of the work of the contemporary practicing lawyer.

B. SOME PROBLEM CASES

Problem Case No. 1

Humphrey Hume was born in England of English parents in 1940 and came to the United States in 1960. He has never become a naturalized citizen of the United States.

In 1969, Hume was indicted on a charge of wilfully destroying valuable federal property (Selective Service files) earlier in that year in the course of militant anti-war protest activity. He was tried shortly afterward and found guilty by a jury and then sentenced to imprisonment for a year and a day. He served his sentence as required.

Two and a half years ago, Hume drove a motor vehicle on behalf of a labor union engaged in demonstrations against certain West Coast grape growers. In the course of one demonstration his vehicle struck and killed a bystander. Hume was thereafter indicted for manslaughter, based on negligent and reckless operation (without intent to injure the victim) of a motor vehicle in violation of state law. On his plea of guilty he was sentenced to imprisonment by state authorities for a term of two years. He served his sentence and was recently released from the penitentiary. Thereupon deportation proceedings were commenced against him under Section 241(a) of the Immigration and Nationality Act of 1952, 66 Stat. 204, 8 U.S.C.A. Sec. 1251(a).

Section 241(a) of the Immigration and Nationality Act of 1952 (as modified for the purpose of this Problem Case) provides as follows:

> (a) Any alien in the United States shall, upon the order of the Attorney General, be deported who—
>
> * * *
>
> (4) is hereafter convicted of a crime involving moral turpitude committed within five years after entry and either sentenced to confinement or confined therefor in a prison or corrective institution for a year or more, or who hereafter at any time after entry is more than once convicted of a crime involving moral turpitude * * *.

After a procedurally correct deportation hearing, Hume has now been ordered deported and taken into custody for that purpose. He seeks *habeas corpus* in a District Court of the United States on the ground that Section 241(a) does not authorize his deportation.

State the issue or issues of statutory interpretation raised by this case, noting as to each issue the *precise language* of the statute with respect to which the question of statutory applicability arises.

Problem Case No. 2

Prior to 1949, no anti-discrimination legislation had ever been enacted in State X. During its 1949 session, the State Legislature passed the following statute, which was approved by the Governor and became effective June 1, 1949:

> An Act to protect all citizens in the enjoyment of their civil rights.
>
> *Be it enacted by the Legislature of the State of X:*
>
> Section 1: This statute may be cited as "The Anti-Discrimination Act of 1949."
>
> Section 2: All persons within the jurisdiction of this State shall be entitled to the full and equal accommodations, advantages, facilities and privileges of inns, restaurants, hotels, eating-houses, bath-houses, barber shops, theatres, music halls, public conveyances on land and water, and all other places of public accommodation or amusement, subject only to conditions and limitations applicable alike to all citizens.
>
> Section 3: Any person who shall violate any of the provisions of the foregoing section by denying to any citizen, except for reasons applicable alike to all citizens of every race, creed or color, and regardless of race, creed or color, the full enjoyment of any of the accommodations, advantages, facilities or privileges in said section enumerated, or by aiding or inciting such denial, shall for every such offense be subject to a fine of not more than $5,000, or to imprisonment for not more than one year, or to both such fine and such imprisonment.

The facts of this Problem Case are as follows: Dr. Claudius Smythe, a retired physician, is the sole owner of a rest home for persons recovering from major operations or from severe illnesses. The rest home is situated in one of the rural counties of State X, and there are usually about fifteen convalescents in residence there. For some time, all financial and other business details have been handled by Rufus DeLong, who serves as the rest home's resident manager. Recently, DeLong wrote and had printed certain circulars describing the rest home, copies of which circulars were sent to all physicians in State X. At the specific direction of Dr. Smythe, DeLong included in the printed circulars the following statement:

> "*Admission Policy:* It is the policy of the Smythe Rest Home to admit *white* patients only. Applications from Negroes and other non-white persons will not be considered."

Sec. 2   FINDING AND STATING ISSUES   321

No Negro or other non-white person was ever actually turned away by the Smythe Rest Home; in fact, there is no record of any application to the rest home ever having been received from a Negro or other non-white person.

Early this year, copies of the Smythe Rest Home's circular were called to the attention of the prosecuting attorney of the county in which the rest home is situated. Dr. Smythe was promptly indicted for violation of the Anti-Discrimination Act of 1949. After trial before a jury, Dr. Smythe was convicted and fined $1,500. He appeals to the appropriate appellate court of State X.

State the issue or issues of statutory interpretation raised by Dr. Smythe's appeal, noting as to each issue the *precise language* of the statute with respect to which the question of statutory applicability arises.

Problem Case No. 3

The Growers' Irrigation Company (hereinafter called the "Company") owns, maintains and operates within State X an irrigation system consisting of four large storage reservoirs and 400 miles of irrigation canals. More than 100,000 acres of State X farm land, owned by many different farmers, are irrigated with water furnished by the Company. The water distributed by the Company is diverted from streams in State X during the non-irrigation season and runs through canals into the Company's reservoirs. During the irrigation season, this water is released from the reservoirs, carried through the Company's canals, and delivered to the lateral irrigation ditches of the farmers.

Sugar beets, corn, peas and beans are grown on the land irrigated. Virtually all of the sugar beets are processed into refined sugar in plants operated within State X, and large amounts of the corn, peas, and beans are canned in factories within State X. More than 75% of the refined sugar and canned vegetables is shipped in interstate commerce to purchasers outside State X.

There are 1,000 shares of authorized capital stock in the Company, all of which shares are owned by farmers in the irrigation area of State X. Each share of stock entitles the owner thereof to a 1/1,000th share of the property of the Company and of the total supply of water available during the irrigation season. The expenses necessary to the operation of the irrigation system are borne by annual assessments levied on the Company's stockholders, and the proceeds of the assessments constitute the Company's sole source of income. Payment of the assessment on his shares of stock is a condition precedent to the right of a stockholder to receive water for his farm during the irrigation season. The Company does not sell water to persons other than stockholders.

The Company employs 16 reservoir tenders, who take care of the diverting and storage of water during the non-irrigation season and attend the conduct of water through the Company's canals and into the lateral ditches of the farmers during the irrigation season. These reservoir tenders do not look after the lateral ditches of the farmers; in fact, they do not go at all on to the farmers' property. The Company pays its reservoir tenders a flat wage rate of $3 per hour, irrespective of the number of hours worked during any week. During the irrigation season, the 16 reservoir tenders work considerably more than 40 hours a week.

The Administrator of the Wage and Hour Division of the Department of Labor has now filed a complaint in the United States District Court for State X, charging that the Company is violating the federal Fair Labor Standards Act by failing to pay the 16 reservoir tenders time-and-a-half for overtime. The Administrator's complaint asks that the District Court issue an injunction against the Company restraining continued violation of the Act.

The Fair Labor Standards Act (as modified and renumbered for the purposes of this Problem Case) provides, in pertinent part, as follows:

> Section 1: *Declaration of Policy.* The Congress finds that the existence, in industries engaged in commerce, of labor conditions detrimental to the maintenance of minimum standards of living causes commerce and the channels of commerce to be used to spread such detrimental labor conditions among the workers of the several States.
>
> Section 2: No employer shall employ any employee who is engaged in commerce or in the production of goods for commerce for a workweek longer than 40 hours unless such employee receives compensation for his employment in excess of the hours above specified at a rate not less than one and one-half times the regular pay rate at which he is employed.
>
> Section 3: The provisions of Section 2 of this Act shall not apply with respect to: (1) any employee employed in a bona fide executive, administrative, or professional capacity; (2) any employee engaged in any retail or service establishment the greater part of whose selling or servicing is done within the State; (3) any employee employed in agriculture; or (4) any individual employed in handling, packing, storing, or canning agricultural commodities for market.
>
> Section 4: *Definitions.*
>
> (a) "Commerce" means trade, commerce, transportation, transmission, or communication among the several States or from any State to any place outside thereof.

(b) "Employer" includes any person acting directly or indirectly in the interest of an employer in relation to an employee but shall not include the United States or any State or political subdivision of a State.

(c) "Employee" includes any individual employed by an employer.

(d) "Agriculture" includes farming and all its branches and includes any practices performed by a farmer or on a farm as incident to or in conjunction with farming operations, including preparation for market and delivery to storage or to market.

(e) "Goods" means wares, products, commodities, merchandise or articles or subjects of commerce of any character whatsoever.

(f) "Produced" means produced, manufactured, mined, handled, or in any other manner worked on in any State; and for the purposes of this Act an employee shall be deemed to have been engaged in the production of goods if such employee was employed in any process or occupation necessary to the production of goods in any State.

The Growers' Irrigation Company moves to dismiss the Administrator's injunction action on the ground that the Company's activities are not within the area of coverage of the Fair Labor Standards Act.

State the issues of statutory interpretation raised by this case, noting as to each issue the *precise language* of the statute with respect to which the question of statutory applicability arises.

Problem Case No. 4

The Southern Pacific Co. was operating passenger trains between San Francisco and Ogden, Utah. It habitually drew a dining car in these trains. Such a car formed a part of a train leaving San Francisco, and ran through to Ogden, where it was ordinarily turned and put into a train going west to San Francisco. On August 5, 1900, the east-bound train was so late that it was not practicable to get the dining car into Ogden in time to place it in the next west-bound train, and it was therefore left on a side track at Promontory, Utah, to be picked up by the west-bound train when it arrived. While it was standing on this track the conductor of an interstate freight train which arrived there was directed to take this dining car to a turntable, turn it, and place it back upon the side track so that it would be ready to return to San Francisco. The conductor instructed his crew to carry out this direction. The plaintiff, Johnson, the head brakeman, undertook to couple the freight engine to the dining car for the purpose of carrying out the conductor's order. The freight engine and the eight-wheel dining car involved were the property of defendant railroad company. The freight engine, regularly used in interstate hauling of standard eight-wheel freight cars, was equipped with a Janney coupler, which would couple automatically with another Janney coupler, and the dining car was provided with a Miller automatic hook; but the Miller hook would not couple automatically with the Janney coupler, because it was on the same side, and would pass over it. Johnson knew this, and undertook to make the coupling by means of a link and pin. He knew that it was a difficult coupling to make, and that it was necessary to go between the engine and the car to accomplish it, and that it was dangerous to do so. Nevertheless, he went in between the engine and the car without objection or protest and tried three times to make the coupling. He failed twice; the third time his hand was caught and crushed so that it became necessary to amputate his hand above the wrist.

Johnson brought an action for damages for personal injury against the railroad. The case was tried in the Circuit Court of the United States for the District of Utah. At the trial, Southern Pacific, after the plaintiff had rested, moved the court to instruct the jury to find in defendant's favor. The motion was granted and the jury found a verdict accordingly on which judgment was entered. Plaintiff carried the case to the Circuit Court of Appeals for the Eighth Circuit.

Defendant contended in the district and circuit courts that it was not liable for the injury on the ground that plaintiff, under the rules of the common law, had "assumed the risk" involved in coupling the dining car and locomotive. Plaintiff Johnson, on the other hand, contended that at the time of the injury defendant was violating a federal statute (infra) in respect to the dining car and locomotive concerned, and that by reason of such violation plaintiff, under this statute, was not to be deemed to have assumed the risk. It was acknowledged that the locomotive possessed a power driving-wheel brake, that there were train brakes and appliances for operating a train brake system as required and that there was no failure, as to either vehicle, to provide the requisite grab irons or drawbars.

The text of the federal statute relied on by plaintiff, which was in effect at the time of the injury and at all times pertinent to this problem, is set out herewith as it appears in the Statutes at Large (27 Stat. 531):

    Chap. 196.—An act to promote the safety of employees and travelers upon railroads by compelling common carriers engaged in interstate commerce to equip their cars with automatic couplers and continuous brakes and their locomotives with driving-wheel brakes, and for other purposes.

    Be it enacted by the Senate and House of Representatives of the United States of America in Congress assembled, That from and after the first day of January, eighteen hundred and ninety-eight, it shall be unlawful for any common carrier engaged in interstate commerce by railroad to use on its line any locomotive engine in moving interstate traffic not equipped with a power driving-wheel brake and appliances for operating the train-brake system, or to run any train in such traffic after said date that has not a sufficient number of cars in it so equipped with power or train brakes that the engineer on the locomotive drawing such train can control its speed without requiring brakemen to use the common hand brake for that purpose.

Sec. 2. That on and after the first day of January, eighteen hundred and ninety-eight, it shall be unlawful for any such common carrier to haul or permit to be hauled or used on its line any car used in moving interstate traffic not equipped with couplers coupling automatically by impact, and which can be uncoupled without the necessity of men going between the ends of the cars.

Sec. 3. That when any person, firm, company, or corporation engaged in interstate commerce by railroad shall have equipped a sufficient number of its cars so as to comply with the provisions of section one of this act, it may lawfully refuse to receive from connecting lines of road or shippers any cars not equipped sufficiently, in accordance with the first section of this act, with such power or train brakes as will work and readily interchange with the brakes in use on its own cars, as required by this act.

Sec. 4. That from and after the first day of July, eighteen hundred and ninety-five, until otherwise ordered by the Interstate Commerce Commission, it shall be unlawful for any railroad company to use any car in interstate commerce that is not provided with secure grab irons or handholds in the ends and sides of each car for greater security to men in coupling and uncoupling cars.

Sec. 5. That within ninety days from the passage of this act the American Railway Association is authorized hereby to designate to the Interstate Commerce Commission the standard height of drawbars for freight cars, measured perpendicular from the level of the tops of the rails to the centers of the drawbars, for each of the several gauges of railroads in use in the United States, and shall fix a maximum variation from such standard height to be allowed between the drawbars of empty and loaded cars. Upon their determination being certified to the Interstate Commerce Commission, said Commission shall at once give notice of the standard fixed upon to all common carriers, owners, or lessees engaged in interstate commerce in the United States

326 THE INTERPRETATION OF STATUTES Ch. 5

by such means as the Commission may deem proper. But should said association fail to determine a standard as above provided, it shall be the duty of the Interstate Commerce Commission to do so, before July first, eighteen hundred and ninety-four, and immediately to give notice thereof as aforesaid. And after July first, eighteen hundred and ninety-five, no cars, either loaded or unloaded, shall be used in interstate traffic which do not comply with the standard above provided for.

Sec. 6. That any such common carrier using any locomotive engine, running any train, or hauling or permitting to be hauled or used on its line any car in violation of any of the provisions of this act, shall be liable to a penalty of one hundred dollars for each and every such violation, to be recovered in a suit or suits to be brought by the United States district attorney in the district court of the United States having jurisdiction in the locality where such violation shall have been committed, and it shall be the duty of such district attorney to bring such suits upon duly verified information being lodged with him of such violation having occurred. And it shall also be the duty of the Interstate Commerce Commission to lodge with the proper district attorneys information of any such violations as may come to its knowledge: *Provided,* that nothing in this act contained shall apply to trains composed of four-wheel cars or to locomotives used in hauling such trains.

Sec. 7. That the Interstate Commerce Commission may from time to time upon full hearing and for good cause extend the period within which any common carrier shall comply with the provisions of this act.

Sec. 8. That any employee of any such common carrier who may be injured by any locomotive, car, or train in use contrary to the provision of this act shall not be deemed thereby to have assumed the risk thereby occasioned, although continuing in the employment of such carrier after the unlawful use of such locomotive, car, or train had been brought to his knowledge.

Approved, March 2, 1893.

State the issue or issues of statutory interpretation raised by this case, noting as to each issue the *precise language* of the statute with respect to which the question of statutory applicability arises.

NOTE

The importance to lawyers of the disciplines of statutory analysis here proposed, including finding and precise statement of issues, is underlined by the remarks of Erwin N. Griswold[2], then Solicitor General of the United States, in his discussion of "Appellate Advocacy" at 26 The Record of the Association of the Bar of the City of New York 342 (1971). Solicitor General Griswold urged that advocates "orient the court" at the beginning of any oral argument on appeal. As a part of "orienting" the court, he recommended that counsel focus the issue for the judges, commenting as follows:

" * * * [L]et the court see—and I mean 'see'—the exact language with which they have to deal. Tell them, right at the beginning: 'The statutory language involved appears at page 4 of my brief. Though the clause is a somewhat long one, the issue turns, I believe, on the proper construction or effect of words in two lines near the top of the page.' Give the court time to find the two lines, and then read the words to them. At this point, the eye can be as important as the ear in oral argument, and the court will follow all of the rest of your argument much better if you have taken pains to tell them exactly what it is about, and where to find the words if they want to look at them again.

"In the years when I was a law teacher, I suppose that my most famous classroom remark was 'Look at the statute'—or 'What does the statute say?' Over the years, I have had literally hundreds of my former students write me and say that this was the most important thing they learned in law school. There is something about the student, and some oral advocates, too, which leads them to think great thoughts without ever taking the time and care to see just exactly what they are thinking about. Now I would not suggest that the court would make such a mistake. But courts are accustomed to think in terms of concrete, rather specific cases. The oral advocate takes a great step in advancing his cause, I think, if, right at the beginning of his argument, after the procedural setting has been established, he tells the court exactly what the case is about, including specific reference to any statutory language which must be construed or evaluated in bringing the case to a decision. With orientation, the court finds moorings. It is no longer cast adrift on the great sea of all the law. If you can get the court moored to the question as you see it, and so that they see it clearly and distinctly, you may be off to a good start towards leading them to decide the case your way."

SECTION 3. RESOLVING STATUTORY ISSUES— A GENERAL VIEW

JOHNSON v. SOUTHERN PACIFIC CO.
Circuit Court of Appeals, Eighth Circuit, 1902.
117 F. 462.

SANBORN, Circuit Judge, after stating the case * * * [see Problem Case No. 4 supra p. 323 for a statement of the facts], delivered the opinion of the court.

2. Former Dean of the Harvard Law School.

Under the common law the plaintiff assumed the risks and dangers of the coupling which he endeavored to make, and for that reason he is estopped from recovering the damages which resulted from his undertaking. He was an intelligent and experienced brakeman, familiar with the couplers he sought to join, and with their condition, and well aware of the difficulty and danger of his undertaking, so that he falls far within the familiar rules that the servant assumes the ordinary risks and dangers of the employment upon which he enters, so far as they are known to him, and so far as they would have been known to one of his age, experience, and capacity by the use of ordinary care, and that the risks and dangers of coupling cars provided with different kinds of well-known couplers, bumpers, brakeheads and deadwoods are the ordinary risks and dangers of a brakeman's service. [Citations omitted.]

This proposition is not seriously challenged, but counsel base their claim for a reversal of the judgment below upon the position that the plaintiff was relieved of this assumption of risk, and of its consequences, by the provisions of the act of congress of March 2, 1893 (27 Stat. c. 196, p. 531). The title of that act, and the parts of it that are material to the consideration of this contention are these: [See text of Act of 1893, in Problem Case No. 4 supra, for the title and for sections 1, 2, 6 and 8 cited here by the court.]

The first thought that suggests itself to the mind upon a perusal of this law, and a comparison of it with the facts of this case, is that this statute has no application here, because both the dining car and the engine were equipped as this act directs. The car was equipped with Miller couplers which would couple automatically with couplers of the same construction upon cars in the train in which it was used to carry on interstate commerce, and the engine was equipped with a power driving wheel brake such as this statute prescribes. To overcome this difficulty, counsel for the plaintiff persuasively argues that this is a remedial statute; that laws for the prevention of fraud, the suppression of a public wrong, and the bestowal of a public good are remedial in their nature, and should be liberally construed, to prevent the mischief and to advance the remedy, notwithstanding the fact that they may impose a penalty for their violation; and that this statute should be so construed as to forbid the use of a locomotive as well as a car which is not equipped with an automatic coupler. In support of this contention he cites Suth. St. Const. § 360; Wall v. Platt, 169 Mass. 398, 48 N.E. 270; Taylor v. U. S., 3 How. 197, 11 L. Ed. 559; and other cases of like character. The general propositions which counsel quote may be found in the opinions in these cases, and in some of them they were applied to the particular facts which those actions presented. But the interpolation in this act of congress by construction of an ex post facto provision that it is, and ever since January 1, 1898, has been unlawful for any common carrier to use any engine in interstate traffic that is or was not equipped with cou-

Sec. 3   RESOLVING STATUTORY ISSUES   329

plers coupling automatically, and that any carrier that has used or shall use an engine not so equipped has been and shall be liable to a penalty of $100 for every violation of this provision, is too abhorrent to the sense of justice and fairness, too rank and radical a piece of judicial legislation, and in violation of too many established and salutary rules of construction, to commend itself to the judicial reason or conscience. The primary rule for the interpretation of a statute or a contract is to ascertain, if possible, and enforce the intention which the legislative body that enacted the law, or the parties who made the agreement, have expressed therein. But it is the intention expressed in the law or contract, and that only, that the courts may give effect to. They cannot lawfully assume or presume secret purposes that are not indicated or expressed by the statute itself and then enact provisions to accomplish these supposed intentions. While ambiguous terms and doubtful expressions may be interpreted to carry out the intention of a legislative body which a statute fairly evidences, a secret intention cannot be interpreted into a statute which is plain and unambiguous, and which does not express it. The legal presumption is that the legislative body expressed its intention, that it intended what it expressed, and that it intended nothing more. U. S. v. Wiltberger, 5 Wheat. 76, 5 L.Ed. 37 * * *. Construction and interpretation have no place or office where the terms of a statute are clear and certain, and its meaning is plain. In such a case they serve only to create doubt and to confuse the judgment. When the language of a statute is unambiguous, and its meaning evident, it must be held to mean what it plainly expresses, and no room is left for construction. * * *

This statute clearly prohibits the use of any engine in moving interstate commerce not equipped with a power driving wheel brake, and the use of any car not equipped with automatic couplers, under a penalty of $100 for each offense; and it just as plainly omits to forbid, under that or any penalty, the use of any car which is not equipped with a power driving wheel brake, and the use of any engine that is not equipped with automatic couplers. This striking omission to express any intention to prohibit the use of engines unequipped with automatic couplers raises the legal presumption that no such intention existed, and prohibits the courts from importing such a purpose into the act, and enacting provisions to give it effect. The familiar rule that the expression of one thing is the exclusion of others points to the same conclusion. Section 2 of the act does not declare that it shall be unlawful to use any engine or car not equipped with automatic couplers, but that it shall be unlawful only to use any car lacking this equipment. This clear and concise definition of the unlawful act is a cogent and persuasive argument against the contention that the use without couplers of locomotives, hand cars, or other means of conducting interstate traffic, was made a misdemeanor by this act. Where the statute enumerates the persons, things, or acts

330 THE INTERPRETATION OF STATUTES Ch. 5

affected by it, there is an implied exclusion of all others. Suth. St. Const. § 227. And when the title of this statute and its first section are again read; when it is perceived that it was not from inattention, thoughtlessness, or forgetfulness; that it was not because locomotives were overlooked or out of mind, but that it was advisedly and after careful consideration of the equipment which they should have, that congress forbade the use of cars alone without automatic couplers; when it is seen that the title of the act is to compel common carriers to "equip their cars with automatic couplers * * * and their locomotives with driving wheel brakes"; that the first section makes it unlawful to use locomotives not equipped with such brakes, and the second section declares it to be illegal to use cars without automatic couplers,—the argument becomes unanswerable and conclusive.

Again, this act of congress changes the common law. Before its enactment, servants coupling cars used in interstate commerce without automatic couplers assumed the risk and danger of that employment, and carriers were not liable for injuries which the employés suffered in the discharge of this duty. Since its passage the employés no longer assume this risk, and, if they are free from contributory negligence, they may recover for the damages they sustain in this work. A statute which thus changes the common law must be strictly construed. The common or the general law is not further abrogated by such a statute than the clear import of its language necessarily requires. Shaw v. Railroad Co., 101 U.S. 557, 565, 25 L.Ed. 892; Fitzgerald v. Quann, 109 N.Y. 441, 445, 17 N.E. 354; Brown v. Barry, 3 Dall. 365, 367, 1 L.Ed. 638. The language of this statute does not require the abrogation of the common law that the servant assumes the risk of coupling a locomotive without automatic couplers with a car which is provided with them.

Moreover, this is a penal statute, and it may not be so broadened by judicial construction as to make it cover and permit the punishment of an act which is not denounced by the fair import of its terms. The acts which this statute declares to be unlawful, and for the commission of which it imposes a penalty, were lawful before its enactment, and their performance subjected to no penalty or liability. It makes that unlawful which was lawful before its passage, and it imposes a penalty for its performance. Nor is this penalty a mere forfeiture for the benefit of the party aggrieved or injured. It is a penalty prescribed by the statute, and recoverable by the government. It is, therefore, under every definition of the term, a penal statute. The act which lies at the foundation of this suit—the use of a locomotive which was not equipped with a Miller hook to turn a car which was duly equipped with automatic couplers—was therefore unlawful or lawful as it was or was not forbidden by this statute. That act has been done. When it was done it was neither forbidden nor declared to be unlawful by the express terms of this law. There is no language in it which makes it unlawful to use in interstate commerce

Sec. 3   RESOLVING STATUTORY ISSUES   331

a locomotive engine which is not equipped with automatic couplers. The argument of counsel for the plaintiff is, however, that the statute should be construed to make this act unlawful because it falls within the mischief which congress was seeking to remedy, and hence it should be presumed that the legislative body intended to denounce this act as much as that which it forbade by the terms of the law. An ex post facto statute which would make such an innocent act a crime would be violative of the basic principles of Anglo-Saxon jurisprudence. An ex post facto construction which has the same effect is equally abhorrent to the sense of justice and of reason. The mischief at which a statute was leveled, and the fact that other acts which it does not denounce are within the mischief, and of equal atrocity with those which it forbids, do not raise the presumption that the legislative body which enacted it had the intention, which the law does not express, to prohibit the performance of the acts which it does not forbid. Nor will they warrant a construction which imports into the statute such a prohibition. The intention of the legislature and the meaning of a penal statute must be found in the language actually used, interpreted according to its fair and usual meaning, and not in the evils which it was intended to remedy, nor in the assumed secret intention of the lawmakers to accomplish that which they did not express. * * * The decision and opinion of the supreme court in U. S. v. Harris, 177 U.S. 305, 309, 20 Sup.Ct. 609, 44 L.Ed. 780, is persuasive—nay, it is decisive—in the case before us. The question there presented was analogous to that here in issue. It was whether congress intended to include receivers managing a railroad among those who were prohibited from confining cattle, sheep, and other animals in cars more than 28 consecutive hours without unloading them for rest, water, and feeding, under "An act to prevent cruelty to animals while in transit by railroad or other means of transportation," approved March 3, 1873, and published in the Revised Statutes as sections 4386, 4387, 4388, and 4389. This statute forbids the confinement of stock in cars by any railroad company engaged in interstate commerce more than 28 consecutive hours, and prescribes a penalty of $500 for a violation of its provisions. The plain purpose of the act was to prohibit the confinement of stock while in transit for an unreasonable length of time. The confinement of cattle by receivers operating a railroad was as injurious as their confinement by a railroad company, and the argument for the United States was that, as such acts committed by receivers were plainly within the mischief congress was seeking to remedy, the conclusion should be that it intended to prohibit receivers, as well as railroad companies, from the commission of the forbidden acts, and hence that receivers were subject to the provisions of the law. The supreme court conceded that the confinement of stock in transit was within the mischief that congress sought to remedy. But it held that as the act did not, by its terms, forbid such acts when committed by receivers, it could not presume the intention of congress to do so, and import such a provision into the plain terms of the law. Mr. Justice Shiras, who delivered the unanimous opinion of the court, said:

> "Giving all proper force to the contention of the counsel for the government, that there has been some relaxation on the part of the courts in applying the rule of strict construction to such statutes, it still remains that the intention of a penal statute must be found in the language actually used, interpreted according to its fair and obvious meaning. It is not permitted to courts, in this class of cases, to attribute inadvertence or oversight to the legislature when enumerating the classes of persons who are subjected to a penal enactment, nor to depart from the settled meaning of words or phrases in order to bring persons not named or distinctly described within the supposed purpose of the statute."

He cited with approval the decision of the supreme court in Sarlis v. U. S., 152 U.S. 570, 575, 14 Sup.Ct. 720, 38 L.Ed. 556, to the effect that lager beer was not included within the meaning of the term "spirituous liquors" in the penal statute found in section 2139 of the Revised Statutes, and closed the discussion with the following quotation from the opinion of Chief Justice Marshall in U. S. v. Wiltberger, 5 Wheat. 76, 5 L.Ed. 37:

> "The rule that penal statutes are to be construed strictly is perhaps not much less old than construction itself. It is founded on the tenderness of the law for the rights of individuals, and on the plain principle that the power of punishment is vested in the legislative, and not in the judicial, department. It is the legislature, not the court, which is to define a crime and ordain its punishment. It is said that, notwithstanding this rule, the intention of the lawmaker must govern in the construction of penal as well as other statutes. But this is not a new, independent rule, which subverts the old. It is a modification of the ancient maxim, and amounts to this: that, though penal statutes are to be construed strictly, they are not to be construed so strictly as to defeat the obvious intention of the legislature. The maxim is not to be applied so as to narrow the words of the statute, to the exclusion of cases which those words, in their ordinary acceptation, or in that sense in which the legislature ordinarily used them, would comprehend. The intention of the legislature is to be collected from the words they employ. Where there is no ambiguity in the words, there is no room for construction. The case must be a strong one, indeed, which would justify a court in departing from the plain meaning of words,—especially in a penal act,—in search of an intention which the words themselves did not suggest.

Sec. 3   *RESOLVING STATUTORY ISSUES*   333

To determine that a case is within the intention of a statute, its language must authorize us to say so. It would be dangerous, indeed, to carry the principle that a case which is within the reason or mischief of a statute is within its provisions, so far as to punish a crime not enumerated in the statute, because it is of equal atrocity or of a kindred character with those which are enumerated. If this principle has ever been recognized in expounding criminal law, it has been in cases of considerable irritation, which it would be unsafe to consider as precedents forming a general rule in other cases."

The act of March 2, 1893, is a penal statute, and it changes the common law. It makes that unlawful which was innocent before its enactment, and imposes a penalty, recoverable by the government. Its terms are plain and free from doubt, and its meaning is clear. It declares that it is unlawful for a common carrier to use in interstate commerce a car which is not equipped with automatic couplers, and it omits to declare that it is illegal for a common carrier to use a locomotive that is not so equipped. As congress expressed in this statute no intention to forbid the use of locomotives which were not provided with automatic couplers, the legal presumption is that it had no such intention, and provisions to import such an intention into the law and to effectuate it may not be lawfully enacted by judicial construction. The statute does not make it unlawful to use locomotives that are not equipped with automatic couplers in interstate commerce, and it did not modify the rule of the common law under which the plaintiff assumed the known risk of coupling such an engine to the dining car.

There are other considerations which lead to the same result. If we are in error in the conclusion already expressed, and if the word "car," in the second section of this statute, means locomotive, still this case does not fall under the law, (1) because both the locomotive and the dining car were equipped with automatic couplers; and (2) because at the time of the accident they were not "used in moving interstate traffic."

For the reasons which have been stated, this statute may not be lawfully extended by judicial construction beyond the fair meaning of its language. There is nothing in it which requires a common carrier engaged in interstate commerce to have every car on its railroad equipped with the same kind of coupling, or which requires it to have every car equipped with a coupler which will couple automatically with every other coupler with which it may be brought into contact in the usual course of business upon a great transcontinental system of railroads. If the lawmakers had intended to require such an equipment, it would have been easy for them to have said so, and the fact that they made no such requirement raises the legal presumption that they intended to make none. Nor is the reason for their omission to do so far to seek or difficult to perceive. There are several kinds or makes of practical and efficient automatic couplers. Some railroad companies use one kind; others have adopted other kinds. Couplers of each kind will couple automatically with others of the same kind or construction. But some couplers will not couple automatically with couplers of different construction. Railroad companies engaged in interstate commerce are required to haul over their roads cars equipped with all these couplers. They cannot relieve themselves from this obligation or renounce this public duty for the simple reason that their cars or locomotives are not equipped with automatic couplers which will couple with those with which the cars of other roads are provided, and which will couple with equal facility with those of their kind. These facts and this situation were patent to the congress when it enacted this statute. It must have known the impracticability of providing every car with as many different couplers as it might meet upon a great system of railroads, and it made no such requirement. It doubtless knew the monopoly it would create by requiring every railroad company to use the same coupler, and it did not create this monopoly. The prohibition of the statute goes no farther than to bar the handling of a car "not equipped with couplers coupling automatically by impact and which can be uncoupled without the necessity of men going between the ends of the car." It does not bar the handling and use of a car which will couple automatically with couplers of its kind because it will not also couple automatically with couplers of all kinds, and it would be an unwarrantable extension of the terms of this law to import into it a provision to this effect. A car equipped with practical and efficient automatic couplers, such as the Janney couplers or the Miller hooks, which will couple automatically with those of their kind, fully and literally complies with the terms of the law, although these couplers will not couple automatically with automatic couplers of all kinds or constructions. The dining car and the locomotive were both so equipped. Each was provided with an automatic coupler which would couple with those of its kind, as provided by the statute, although they would not couple with each other. Each was accordingly equipped as the statute directs, and the defendant was guilty of no violation of it by their use.

Again, the statute declares it to be unlawful for a carrier "to haul or permit to be hauled or used on its line any car used in moving interstate traffic not equipped," etc. It is not, then, unlawful, under this statute, for a carrier to haul a car not so equipped which is either used in intrastate traffic solely, or which is not used in any traffic at all. It would be no violation of the statute for a carrier to haul an empty car not used to move any interstate traffic from one end of its railroad to the other. It would be no violation of the law for it to haul such a car in its yards, on its side track, to put it into its trains, to move it in any manner it chose. It is only when a car is "used in moving interstate traffic" that it becomes unlawful to haul it unless

Sec. 3   RESOLVING STATUTORY ISSUES   335

it is equipped as the statute prescribes. On the day of this accident the dining car in this case was standing empty on the side track. The defendant drew it to a turntable, turned it, and placed it back upon the side track. The accident occurred during the performance of this act. The car was vacant when it went to the turntable, and vacant when it returned. It moved no traffic on its way. How could it be said to have been "used in moving interstate traffic" either while it was standing on the side track, or while it was going to and returning from the turntable? * * * [In a part of the opinion omitted here, the court argues that its conclusion that the dining car was not "used in moving interstate traffic" is dictated not only by rules of construction earlier referred to, but by limitations on the power of Congress.]

* * * The fact that such cars have been or will be so used does not constitute their use in moving interstate traffic, because the prohibition is not of the hauling of cars that have been or will be used in such traffic, but only of those used in moving that traffic. * * * Neither the empty dining car standing upon the side track, nor the freight engine which was used to turn it at the little station in Utah, was then used in moving interstate traffic, within the meaning of this statute, and this case did not fall within the provisions of this law.

The judgment below must accordingly be affirmed, and it is so ordered.

THAYER, Circuit Judge. I am unable to concur in the conclusion, announced by the majority of the court, that the act of congress of March 2, 1893 (27 Stat. 531, c. 196), does not require locomotive engines to be equipped with automatic couplers; and I am equally unable to concur in the other conclusion announced by my associates that the dining car in question at the time of the accident was not engaged or being used in moving interstate traffic.

In my judgment, it is a very technical interpretation of the provisions of the act in question, and one which is neither in accord with its spirit nor with the obvious purpose of the lawmaker, to say that congress did not intend to require engines to be equipped with automatic couplers. The statute is remedial in its nature; it was passed for the protection of human life; and there was certainly as much, if not greater, need that engines should be equipped to couple automatically, as that ordinary cars should be so equipped, since engines have occasion to make couplings more frequently. In my opinion, the true view is that engines are included by the words "any car," as used in the second section of the act. The word "car" is generic, and may well be held to comprehend a locomotive or any other similar vehicle which moves on wheels; and especially should it be so held in a case like the one now in hand, where no satisfactory reason has been assigned or can be given which would probably have influenced congress to permit locomotives to be used without automatic coupling appliances.

I am also of opinion that, within the fair intent and import of the act, the dining car in question at the time of the accident was being hauled or used in interstate traffic. The reasoning by which a contrary conclusion is reached seems to me to be altogether too refined and unsatisfactory to be of any practical value. It was a car which at the time was employed in no other service than to furnish meals to passengers between Ogden and San Francisco. It had not been taken out of that service, even for repairs or for any other use, when the accident occurred, but was engaged therein to the same extent that it would have been if it had been hauled through to Ogden, and if the accident had there occurred while it was being turned to make the return trip to San Francisco. The cars composing a train which is regularly employed in interstate traffic ought to be regarded as used in that traffic while the train is being made up with a view to an immediate departure on an interstate journey as well as after the journey has actually begun. I accordingly dissent from the conclusion of the majority of the court on this point.

While I dissent on the foregoing propositions, I concur in the other view which is expressed in the opinion of the majority, to the effect that the case discloses no substantial violation of the provisions of the act of congress, because both the engine and the dining car were equipped with automatic coupling appliances. In this respect the case discloses a compliance with the law, and the ordinary rule governing the liability of the defendant company should be applied. The difficulty was that the car and engine were equipped with couplers of a different pattern, which would not couple, for that reason, without a link. Janney couplers and Miller couplers are in common use on the leading railroads of the country, and congress did not see fit to command the use of either style of automatic coupler to the exclusion of the other, while it must have foreseen that, owing to the manner in which cars were ordinarily handled and exchanged, it would sometimes happen, as in the case at bar, that cars having different styles of automatic couplers would necessarily be brought in contact in the same train. It made no express provision for such an emergency, but declared generally that, after a certain date, cars should be provided with couplers coupling automatically. The engine and dining car were so equipped in the present instance, and there was no such violation of the provisions of the statute as should render the defendant company liable to the plaintiff by virtue of the provisions contained in the eighth section of the act. In other words, the plaintiff assumed the risk of making the coupling in the course of which he sustained the injury. On this ground I concur in the order affirming the judgment below.

JOHNSON v. SOUTHERN PACIFIC CO.

Supreme Court of the United States, 1904.
196 U.S. 1, 25 S.Ct. 158, 49 L.Ed. 363.

Certiorari and error to the United States Circuit Court of Appeals for the Eighth Circuit.

Statement by Mr. Chief Justice FULLER:

Johnson brought this action in the district court of the first judicial district of Utah against the Southern Pacific Company to recover damages for injuries received while employed by that company as a brakeman. The case was removed to the circuit court of the United States for the district of Utah by defendant on the ground of diversity of citizenship.

The facts were briefly these: August 5, 1900, Johnson was acting as head brakeman on a freight train of the Southern Pacific Company, which was making its regular trip between San Francisco, California, and Ogden, Utah. On reaching the town of Promontory, Utah, Johnson was directed to uncouple the engine from the train and couple it to a dining car, belonging to the company, which was standing on a side track, for the purpose of turning the car around preparatory to its being picked up and put on the next westbound passenger train. The engine and the dining car were equipped, respectively, with the Janney coupler and the Miller hook, so called, which would not couple together automatically by impact, and it was, therefore, necessary for Johnson, and he was ordered, to go between the engine and the dining car, to accomplish the coupling. In so doing Johnson's hand was caught between the engine bumper and the dining car bumper, and crushed, which necessitated amputation of the hand above the wrist.

On the trial of the case, defendant, after plaintiff had rested, moved the court to instruct the jury to find in its favor, which motion was granted, and the jury found a verdict accordingly, on which judgment was entered. Plaintiff carried the case to the circuit court of appeals for the eighth circuit, and the judgment was affirmed. 54 C.C.A. 508, 117 Fed. 462.

Mr. Chief Justice FULLER delivered the opinion of the court:

This case was brought here on certiorari, and also on writ of error, and will be determined on the merits, without discussing the question of jurisdiction as between the one writ and the other. Pullman's Palace Car Co. v. Central Transp. Co., 171 U.S. 138, 145, 43 L.Ed. 108, 111, 18 Sup.Ct.Rep. 808.

The plaintiff claimed that he was relieved of assumption of risk under common-law rules by the act of Congress of March 2, 1893 (27 Stat. at L. 531, chap. 196, U.S.Comp.Stat.1901, p. 3174), entitled 'An Act to Promote the Safety of Employees and Travelers upon Railroads by Compelling Common Carriers Engaged in Interstate Commerce to Equip their Cars with Automatic Couplers and Continuous Brakes and their Locomotives with Driving-Wheel Brakes, and for Other Purposes."

The issues involved questions deemed of such general importance that the government was permitted to file a brief and be heard at the bar.

The act of 1893 provided:

"That from and after the first day of January, eighteen hundred and ninety-eight, it shall be unlawful for any common carrier engaged in interstate commerce by railroad to use on its line any locomotive engine in moving interstate traffic not equipped with a power driving-wheel brake and appliances for operating the train-brake system. * * *

"Sec. 2. That on and after the first day of January, eighteen hundred and ninety-eight, it shall be unlawful for any such common carrier to haul or permit to be hauled or used on its line any car used in moving interstate traffic not equipped with couplers coupling automatically by impact, and which can be uncoupled without the necessity of men going between the ends of the cars."

"Sec. 6. That any such common carrier using any locomotive engine, running any train, or hauling or permitting to be hauled or used on its line any car in violation of any of the provisions of this act, shall be liable to a penalty of one hundred dollars for each and every such violation, to be recovered in a suit or suits to be brought by the United States District Attorney in the district court of the United States having jurisdiction in the locality where such violation shall have been committed, and it shall be the duty of such district attorney to bring such suits upon duly verified information being lodged with him of such violation having occurred."

"Sec. 8. That any employee of any such common carrier who may be injured by any locomotive, car, or train in use contrary to the provision of this act shall not be deemed thereby to have assumed the risk thereby occasioned, although continuing in the employment of such carrier after the unlawful use of such locomotive, car, or train had been brought to his knowledge."

The circuit court of appeals held, in substance, Sanborn, J., delivering the opinion and Lochren, J., concurring, that the locomotive and car were both equipped as required by the act, as the one had a power driving-wheel brake and the other a coupler; that § 2 did not apply to locomotives; that at the time of the accident the dining car was

Sec. 3   RESOLVING STATUTORY ISSUES   339

not "used in moving interstate traffic;" and, moreover, that the locomotive, as well as the dining car, was furnished with an automatic coupler, so that each was equipped as the statute required if § 2 applied to both. Thayer, J., concurred in the judgment on the latter ground, but was of opinion that locomotives were included by the words "any car" in the 2d section, and that the dining car was being "used in moving interstate traffic."

We are unable to accept these conclusions, notwithstanding the able opinion of the majority, as they appear to us to be inconsistent with the plain intention of Congress, to defeat the object of the legislation, and to be arrived at by an inadmissible narrowness of construction.

The intention of Congress, declared in the preamble and in §§ 1 and 2 of the act, was "to promote the safety of employees and travelers upon railroads by compelling common carriers engaged in interstate commerce to equip their cars with automatic couplers and continuous brakes and their locomotives with driving-wheel brakes," those brakes to be accompanied with "appliances for operating the train-brake system;" and every car to be "equipped with couplers coupling automatically by impact, and which can be uncoupled without the necessity of men going between the ends of the cars," whereby the danger and risk consequent on the existing system was averted as far as possible.

The present case is that of an injured employee, and involves the application of the act in respect of automatic couplers, the preliminary question being whether locomotives are required to be equipped with such couplers. And it is not to be successfully denied that they are so required if the words "any car" of the 2d section were intended to embrace, and do embrace, locomotives. But it is said that this cannot be so because locomotives were elsewhere, in terms, required to be equipped with power driving-wheel brakes, and that the rule that the expression of one thing excludes another applies. That, however, is a question of intention, and as there was special reason for requiring locomotives to be equipped with power driving-wheel brakes, if it were also necessary that locomotives should be equipped with automatic couplers, and the word "car" would cover locomotives, then the intention to limit the equipment of locomotives to power driving-wheel brakes, because they were separately mentioned, could not be imputed. Now it was as necessary for the safety of employees in coupling and uncoupling that locomotives should be equipped with automatic couplers as it was that freight and passenger and dining cars should be; perhaps more so, as Judge Thayer suggests, "since engines have occasion to make couplings more frequently."

And manifestly the word "car" was used in its generic sense. There is nothing to indicate that any particular kind of car was meant. Tested by context, subject-matter, and object, "any car"

340   THE INTERPRETATION OF STATUTES   Ch. 5

meant all kinds of cars running on the rails, including locomotives. And this view is supported by the dictionary definitions and by many judicial decisions, some of them having been rendered in construction of this act. [Citing cases.]

The result is that if the locomotive in question was not equipped with automatic couplers, the company failed to comply with the provisions of the act. It appears, however, that this locomotive was in fact equipped with automatic couplers, as well as the dining car; but that the couplers on each, which were of different types, would not couple with each other automatically, by impact, so as to render it unnecessary for men to go between the cars to couple and uncouple.

Nevertheless, the circuit court of appeals was of opinion that it would be an unwarrantable extension of the terms of the law to hold that where the couplers would couple automatically with couplers of their own kind, the couplers must so couple with couplers of different kinds. But we think that what the act plainly forbade was the use of cars which could not be coupled together automatically by impact, by means of the couplers actually used on the cars to be coupled. The object was to protect the lives and limbs of railroad employees by rendering it unnecessary for a man operating the couplers to go between the ends of the cars; and that object would be defeated, not necessarily by the use of automatic couplers of different kinds, but if those different kinds would not automatically couple with each other. The point was that the railroad companies should be compelled, respectively, to adopt devices, whatever they were, which would act so far uniformly as to eliminate the danger consequent on men going between the cars.

If the language used were open to construction, we are constrained to say that the construction put upon the act by the circuit court of appeals was altogether too narrow.

This strictness was thought to be required because the common-law rule as to the assumption of risk was changed by the act, and because the act was penal.

The dogma as to the strict construction of statutes in derogation of the common law only amounts to the recognition of a presumption against an intention to change existing law; and as there is no doubt of that intention here, the extent of the application of the change demands at least no more rigorous construction than would be applied to penal laws. And, as Chief Justice Parker remarked, conceding that statutes in derogation of the common law are to be construed strictly, "They are also to be construed sensibly, and with a view to the object aimed at by the legislature." Gibson v. Jenney, 15 Mass. 205.

The primary object of the act was to promote the public welfare by securing the safety of employees and travelers; and it was in that aspect remedial; while for violations a penalty of $100, recoverable

Sec. 3   RESOLVING STATUTORY ISSUES   341

in a civil action, was provided for, and in that aspect it was penal. But the design to give relief was more dominant than to inflict punishment, and the act might well be held to fall within the rule applicable to statutes to prevent fraud upon the revenue, and for the collection of customs,—that rule not requiring absolute strictness of construction. Taylor v. United States, 3 How. 197, 11 L.Ed. 559; United States v. Stowell, 133 U.S. 1, 12, 33 L.Ed. 555, 558, 10 Sup. Ct.Rep. 244, and cases cited. And see Farmers' & M. Nat. Bank v. Dearing, 91 U.S. 29, 35, 23 L.Ed. 196, 199; Gray v. Bennett, 3 Met. 529.

Moreover, it is settled that "though penal laws are to be construed strictly, yet the intention of the legislature must govern in the construction of penal as well as other statutes; and they are not to be construed so strictly as to defeat the obvious intention of the legislature." United States v. Lacher, 134 U.S. 624, 33 L.Ed. 1080, 10 Sup. Ct.Rep. 625. * * *

Tested by these principles, we think the view of the circuit court of appeals, which limits the 2d section to merely providing automatic couplers, does not give due effect to the words "coupling automatically by impact, and which can be uncoupled without the necessity of men going between the cars," and cannot be sustained.

We dismiss, as without merit, the suggestion which has been made, that the words "without the necessity of men going between the ends of the cars," which are the test of compliance with § 2, apply only to the act of uncoupling. The phrase literally covers both coupling and uncoupling; and if read, as it should be, with a comma after the word "uncoupled," this becomes entirely clear. Chicago, M. & St. P. R. Co. v. Voelker, 129 Fed. 522; United States v. Lacher, 134 U.S. 624, 33 L.Ed. 1080, 10 Sup.Ct.Rep. 625.

The risk in coupling and uncoupling was the evil sought to be remedied, and that risk was to be obviated by the use of couplers actually coupling automatically. True, no particular design was required, but, whatever the devices used, they were to be effectively interchangeable. Congress was not paltering in a double sense. And its intention is found "in the language actually used, interpreted according to its fair and obvious meaning." United States v. Harris, 177 U.S. 309, 44 L.Ed. 782, 20 Sup.Ct.Rep. 609.

That this was the scope of the statute is confirmed by the circumstances surrounding its enactment, as exhibited in public documents to which we are at liberty to refer. Binns v. United States, 194 U.S. 486, 495, 48 L.Ed. 1087, 1091, 24 Sup.Ct.Rep. 816; Church of Holy Trinity v. United States, 143 U.S. 457, 463, 36 L.Ed. 226, 229, 12 Sup.Ct.Rep. 511.

President Harrison, in his annual messages of 1889, 1890, 1891, and 1892, earnestly urged upon Congress the necessity of legislation to obviate and reduce the loss of life and the injuries due to the pre-

342 THE INTERPRETATION OF STATUTES Ch. 5

vailing method of coupling and braking. In his first message he said: "It is competent, I think, for Congress to require uniformity in the construction of cars used in interstate commerce, and the use of improved safety appliances upon such trains. Time will be necessary to make the needed changes, but an earnest and intelligent beginning should be made at once. It is a reproach to our civilization that any class of American workmen should, in the pursuit of a necessary and useful vocation, be subjected to a peril of life and limb as great as that of a soldier in time of war."

And he reiterated his recommendation in succeeding messages, saying in that for 1892: "Statistics furnished by the Interstate Commerce Commission show that during the year ending June 30, 1891, there were forty-seven different styles of car couplers reported to be in use, and that during the same period there were 2,660 employees killed and 26,140 injured. Nearly 16 per cent of the deaths occurred in the coupling and uncoupling of cars, and over 36 per cent of the injuries had the same origin."

The Senate report of the first session of the Fifty-second Congress (No. 1049) and the House report of the same session (No. 1678) set out the numerous and increasing casualties due to coupling, the demand for protection, and the necessity of automatic couplers, coupling interchangeably. The difficulties in the case were fully expounded and the result reached to require an automatic coupling by impact so as to render it unnecessary for men to go between the cars; while no particular device or type was adopted, the railroad companies being left free to work out the details for themselves, ample time being given for that purpose. The law gave five years, and that was enlarged, by the Interstate Commerce Commission as authorized by law, two years, and subsequently seven months, making seven years and seven months in all.

The diligence of counsel has called our attention to changes made in the bill in the course of its passage, and to the debates in the Senate on the report of its committee. 24 Cong.Rec., pt. 2, pp. 1246, 1273 et seq. These demonstrate that the difficulty as to interchangeability was fully in the mind of Congress, and was assumed to be met by the language which was used. The essential degree of uniformity was secured by providing that the couplings must couple automatically by impact without the necessity of men going between the ends of the cars.

In the present case the couplings would not work together; Johnson was obliged to go between the cars; and the law was not complied with.

March 2, 1903, 32 Stat. 943, c. 976, an act in amendment of the act of 1893 was approved, which provided, among other things, that the provisions and requirements of the former act "shall be held to apply to common carriers by railroads in the Territories and the Dis-

Sec. 3   RESOLVING STATUTORY ISSUES   343

trict of Columbia and shall apply in all cases, whether or not the couplers brought together are of the same kind, make, or type;" and "shall be held to apply to all trains, locomotives, tenders, cars, and similar vehicles used on any railroad engaged in interstate commerce."

This act was to take effect September first, nineteen hundred and three, and nothing in it was to be held or construed to relieve any common carrier "from any of the provisions, powers, duties, liabilities, or requirements" of the act of 1893, all of which should apply except as specifically amended.

As we have no doubt of the meaning of the prior law, the subsequent legislation cannot be regarded as intended to operate to destroy it. Indeed, the latter act is affirmative, and declaratory, and, in effect, only construed and applied the former act. Bailey v. Clark, 21 Wall. 284; United States v. Freeman, 3 How. 556; Cope v. Cope, 137 U.S. 682; Wetmore v. Markoe, post, p. 68. This legislative recognition of the scope of the prior law fortifies and does not weaken the conclusion at which we have arrived.

Another ground on which the decision of the circuit court of appeals was rested remains to be noticed. That court held by a majority that, as the dining car was empty and had not actually entered upon its trip, it was not used in moving interstate traffic, and hence was not within the act. The dining car had been constantly used for several years to furnish meals to passengers between San Francisco and Ogden, and for no other purpose. On the day of the accident the eastbound train was so late that it was found that the car could not reach Ogden in time to return on the next westbound train according to intention, and it was therefore dropped off at Promontory, to be picked up by that train as it came along that evening.

* * *

Confessedly this dining car was under the control of Congress while in the act of making its interstate journey, and in our judgment it was equally so when waiting for the train to be made up for the next trip. It was being regularly used in the movement of interstate traffic, and so within the law.

Finally, it is argued that Johnson was guilty of such contributory negligence as to defeat recovery, and that, therefore, the judgment should be affirmed. But the circuit court of appeals did not consider this question, nor apparently did the circuit court, and we do not feel constrained to inquire whether it could have been open under § 8, or, if so, whether it should have been left to the jury, under proper instructions.

The judgment of the Circuit Court of Appeals is reversed; the judgment of the Circuit Court is also reversed, and the cause remanded to that court with instructions to set aside the verdict, and award a new trial.

SECTION 4. INTERPRETATION ACCORDING TO "THE INTENTION OF THE LEGISLATURE"

INTRODUCTORY NOTE

The orthodox theory that judicial thinking is rarely originative but involves normally only the discovery and application of pre-existing law is implemented by two concepts which, supposedly, enable judges to extract rules of decision for particular cases from existing legal sources. In the decision of controversies by reference to the case law, the formula is that judges are bound to follow the "holdings" or *rationes decidendi* of past cases. In your work during the first part of this course you have become keenly aware of certain inherent difficulties in the use of that formula. In the judicial application of statute law, the basic assumption is that doubts as to the meaning or legal effect of statutory language are to be resolved in accordance with "the intention of the legislature." In your study of the cases in this Chapter, you will find that the establishment of "legislative intention" is, on many occasions at least, quite as difficult and subtle an operation as is the parallel case law job of arriving at the "holding" of a case.

Consider the range of problems involved in the decision of particular cases by reference to the general commands of the statute law. A legislative direction must be expressed in words, and words are notoriously inexact and imperfect symbols for the communication of ideas. In addition, one must reckon with the inexhaustible variety of the facts to which such words must be applied. To determine from the language of an enactment the "legislative intention," in the sense of a pre-existing understanding of the law-makers as to the statute's construction in relation to a particular issue, may involve semantic problems of very great difficulty. If, in Lieber's definition, "Interpretation is the art of finding out the true sense of any form of words, that is the sense which their author intended to convey," it is evident that any serious effort to discover the thought or reference behind the language of a statute must be based upon a painstaking endeavor to reconstruct the setting or context in which the statutory words were employed.

Even more difficult are the cases in which the interpretative issue before the court is one which was not, and perhaps could not have been, foreseen, even in the most general outline, by the legislators responsible for the enactment. In such cases, clearly, the "interpreting" judge must perform the originative function of assigning to the statute a meaning or legal effect which it did not possess before his

Sec. 4   THE INTENTION OF THE LEGISLATURE   345

action. Cardozo saw this with his characteristic clarity when he wrote: [3]

> "Interpretation is often spoken of as if it were nothing but the search and the discovery of a meaning which, however obscure and latent, had none the less a real and ascertainable pre-existence in the legislator's mind. The process is, indeed, that at times, but it is often something more."

Note that the traditional term "legislative intention" may be taken to signify at least two rather different concepts—either the more immediate concept of specific intent or the teleological concept of purpose.[4]

The principle that courts are bound to follow "the intention of the legislature" would normally require in relation to a demonstrated specific intent—i. e., a showing that Congress foresaw the issue presented and meant to resolve it in a particular way—that such a specific intent be given effect by the courts. In the latter or "purpose" signification of legislative intention, it would demand that the interpretive issues unforeseen specifically by the legislators be resolved in such a way as to advance rather than to retard the attainment of the objectives which the legislators sought to achieve by the enactment of the legislation.

As you study the cases in this Section, keep in mind this possible double signification of "legislative intention"—"intention" as specific intent, and "intention" as purpose. You will find it helpful in your analysis to ask yourself, each time you encounter a reference to "legislative intention" in a judicial opinion, "Is this court using 'intention' in the sense of what the legislators specifically thought the statute provided on this issue, or is the court using 'intention' in the sense of the purpose the legislators sought to accomplish by enactment of the statute?"

There are a number of other questions or considerations which should be kept in mind in analyzing the materials to come. What light does this case or other material shed on the nature and application of legislative intent or other basic approach to interpretation? What, if anything, does this case or material reveal as to the types and causes of statutory ambiguity? What, if any, intrinsic and extrinsic aids to interpretation, or interpretative rules or maxims, are employed in this case and what conclusions may be drawn as to their value and use? What lessons emerge from these materials for purposes of advocacy in statutory cases? Note, incidentally, that the materials provide many illustrations of the different types of statutory enactment one may expect to encounter in law practice.

For an understanding of extrinsic aids, as well as for mastery of other aspects of the lawyer's craft, a knowledge of the legislative pro-

---

3. The Nature of the Judicial Process 14 (1921).

4. Landis, A Note on Statutory Interpretation, 43 Harv.L.Rev. 886 (1930).

cess is essential, we have said. After the initial reading of the Note on the Legislative Process, § 1 supra, as a whole, pertinent parts of it should be reviewed in detail as particular aspects of the process and particular types of extrinsic aids are encountered.

An introduction to the subject of statutory ambiguity is provided in Professor Harry W. Jones' article reprinted immediately below and in the brief extract set out thereafter.

SOME CAUSES OF UNCERTAINTY IN STATUTES

Department of Legislation, American Bar Association Journal,
36 A.B.A.J. 321 (1950).

Every lawyer who holds himself out as a legislative draftsman dreams of one perfect job. Let the painter aspire to his one flawlessly balanced composition, the composer to his one consummate harmony, and the big league pitcher to that one crowning game at which no opposing batter will reach first base. The draftsman of bills will be ready to pronounce his *nunc dimittis* the day he sees enacted into law a statute of his devising that leaves no contingency unprovided for and that is clear and unambiguous in its direction as to each and every conceivable fact situation which may take place in the world of affairs.

Unhappily, the gap between aspiration and accomplishment stretches as wide in legislative craftsmanship as in any other professional field. The draftsman can narrow the area of statutory uncertainty by painstaking fact-gathering and intensive study of every facet of existing case and statute law bearing on the matter at hand. He can reduce the incidence of statutory ambiguity by conjuring up hundreds of hypothetical fact-situations which may arise in the future for decision under the statute. But, when the job is done and the bill added to the statute books, there will still be cases for which the statute affords no certain guide. It is the purpose of this sketch to suggest a few of the reasons why any statute, however carefully and imaginatively drawn up, must fall short of the goal of perfect certainty.

Words Are Imperfect Symbols to Communicate Intent

Certain of the draftsman's difficulties are not unique to legislative work but arise in connection with the preparation of all legal documents. The draftsman must express his understanding and purpose in words, and words are notoriously imperfect symbols for the communication of ideas. Justice Cardozo was speaking for our entire word-bound profession when he began his little classic, The Paradoxes of Legal Science, with the mournful exclamation, "They do things better with logarithms." What makes the legislative draftsman's job more trying than the task of the draftsman of a contract or a will is that the words of the statute must communicate the intention to at least three crucial classes of readers; the legislators who are to examine the bill to decide whether it is in accordance with their specifications, the lawyers who must make use of the statute in counseling and litigation, and the judges who will give the statute its final and authoritative interpretation. One does not have to be an expert in semantics to know that words rarely mean the same thing to all men or at all times. An intent that seems "plainly" expressed to the legislative experts on a standing committee may be ambiguous to affected persons and their lawyers and quite unintelligible to judges with no special knowledge or experience in the field of regulation.

Unforeseen Situations Are Inevitable

Unforeseen cases account for the great majority of the instances of statutory uncertainty. The problem here is that the typical drive for legislative action originates not in a desire for an overall codification of the law but in some felt necessity for a better way of dealing with some specific situation or group of situations. The draftsman must make effective provision for the specific needs which are urged upon him, but he must write the statute in the form of a proposition of general applicability. In our legal system we have a longstanding distrust of legislation so narrowly drawn as to affect only designated persons or a few particularized situations. Inequality in the application of legislation is the evil aimed at in such provisions of the Federal Consitution as the Equal Protection and Bill of Attainder Clauses, and the same general idea is reflected in the provision of most state constitutions against local and special legislation. The policy is sound, beyond any question at all, but it leaves to the draftsman of statutes the hard task of formulating a general rule that adequately takes care of the specific situations before the legislature without including in its apparent scope unthought-of cases somewhat similar in fact content but distinguishable on policy grounds.

Case-minded judges and lawyers might be a little less caustic in their comments on the ambiguity of statutes if they were to reflect that the problem of uncertainty in relation to the unthought-of case arises also in the use of case precedents. Every first year law student learns that he must distinguish between the *holding* of a case and the *dicta* which may be set out in the court's opinion. In our common law tradition, we take as binding precedent only the decision of the court on the material facts of the case actually before it. All else we discount as *dictum*—persuasive, perhaps, but not authoritative. This immemorial common law distinction between *holding* and *dictum* is based on a recognition that even the finest judge is at his best only when dealing with the facts of the case at hand, the issues on which he has had the benefit of argument of counsel. The same is true of the statute-law maker and his technical drafting assistants. If the draftsman is respectably skilled and careful, he will make unmistakably clear provision for the specific situations called to his attention at committee hearings and in other ways. If he is at all imaginative, he will anticipate and take care of other situations within the reach of reasonable anticipation. But human foresight is limited and the variety of fact-situations endless. Every generally worded statute, sooner or later, will fail to provide a certain direction as to the handling of those inevitable legislative nuisances, the cases nobody thought of.

Uncertainties May Be Added in Course of Enactment

So far in this sketch, the problems of the legislative draftsman have been considered without reference to the political realities in Congress and the state legislatures. But legislative drafting is not a branch of art for art's sake. After the statute has been drafted it has to be passed, and there are many stages in the process of enactment at which uncertainty may be introduced into the most tightly drafted legislative proposal. The sponsoring legislator or the responsible standing committee is likely to make changes in the bill without having the time to consider the effect of the changes on the articulation of the bill as a whole. An amendment from the floor may add confused or inconsistent provisions which fit awkwardly into the statutory pattern. It sometimes becomes necessary as a matter of political compromise to eliminate some precise key-word in the bill and substitute for it some less exact term, chosen deliberately to leave a controversial issue to the courts for decision. In short, it is wholly unrealistic to read a statute as if it were the product of wholly scientific, detached and uneventful deliberation.

AN ADDENDUM ON THE PROBLEM OF DRAFTING UNAMBIGUOUS RULES

Following is an extract from the Minutes of an English Borough Council Meeting [5]:

> Councillor Trafford took exception to the proposed notice at the entrance of South Park: "No dogs must be brought to this Park except on a lead." He pointed out that this order would not prevent an owner from releasing his pets, or pet, from a lead when once safely inside the Park.
>
> *The Chairman* (Colonel Vine): What alternative wording would you propose, Councillor?
>
> *Councillor Trafford*: "Dogs are not allowed in this Park without leads."
>
> *Councillor Hogg*: Mr. Chairman, I object. The order should be addressed to the owners, not to the dogs.

---

[5]. Reprinted by permission of Random House, Inc. from The Reader Over Your Shoulder by Robert Graves and Alan Hodge. Copyright 1943 by Robert Graves and Alan Hodge.

Sec. 4   *THE INTENTION OF THE LEGISLATURE*   349

Councillor Trafford: That is a nice point. Very well then: "Owners of dogs are not allowed in this Park unless they keep them on leads."

Councillor Hogg: Mr. Chairman, I object. Strictly speaking, this would prevent me as a dog-owner from leaving my dog in the back-garden at home and walking with Mrs. Hogg across the Park.

Councillor Trafford: Mr. Chairman, I suggest that our legalistic friend be asked to redraft the notice himself.

Councillor Hogg: Mr. Chairman, since Councillor Trafford finds it so difficult to improve on my original wording, I accept. "Nobody without his dog on a lead is allowed in this Park."

Councillor Trafford: Mr. Chairman, I object. Strictly speaking, this notice would prevent me, as a citizen who owns no dog, from walking in the Park without first acquiring one.

Councillor Hogg (with some warmth): Very simply, then: "Dogs must be led in this Park."

Councillor Trafford: Mr. Chairman, I object: this reads as if it were a general injunction to the Borough to lead their dogs into the Park.

Councillor Hogg interposed a remark for which he was called to order; upon his withdrawing it, it was directed to be expunged from the Minutes.

The Chairman: Councillor Trafford, Councillor Hogg has had three tries; you have had only two * * *.

Councillor Trafford: "All dogs must be kept on leads in this Park."

The Chairman: I see Councillor Hogg rising quite rightly to raise another objection. May I anticipate him with another amendment: "All dogs in this Park must be kept on the lead."

This draft was put to the vote and carried unanimously, with two abstentions.

HOLY TRINITY CHURCH v. UNITED STATES

Supreme Court of the United States, 1892.
143 U.S. 457, 12 S.Ct. 511, 36 L.Ed. 226.

In error to the circuit court of the United States for the southern district of New York.

Mr. Justice BREWER delivered the opinion of the court.

Plaintiff in error is a corporation duly organized and incorporated as a religious society under the laws of the state of New York. E.

350   THE INTERPRETATION OF STATUTES   Ch. 5

Walpole Warren was, prior to September, 1887, an alien residing in England. In that month the plaintiff in error made a contract with him, by which he was to remove to the city of New York, and enter into its service as rector and pastor; and, in pursuance of such contract, Warren did so remove and enter upon such service. It is claimed by the United States that this contract on the part of the plaintiff in error was forbidden by chapter 164, 23 St. p. 332; and an action was commenced to recover the penalty prescribed by that act. The circuit court held that the contract was within the prohibition of the statute, and rendered judgment accordingly, (36 Fed.Rep. 303,) and the single question presented for our determination is whether it erred in that conclusion.

The first section describes the act forbidden, and is in these words:

> "Be it enacted by the senate and house of representatives of the United States of America, in congress assembled, that from and after the passage of this act it shall be unlawful for any person, company, partnership, or corporation, in any manner whatsoever, to prepay the transportation, or in any way assist or encourage the importation or migration, of any alien or aliens, any foreigner or foreigners, into the United States, its territories, or the District of Columbia, under contract or agreement, parol or special, express or implied, made previous to the importation or migration of such alien or aliens, foreigner or foreigners, to perform labor or service of any kind in the United States, its territories, or the District of Columbia."

It must be conceded that the act of the corporation is within the letter of this section, for the relation of rector to his church is one of service, and implies labor on the one side with compensation on the other. Not only are the general words "labor" and "service" both used, but also, as it were to guard against any narrow interpretation and emphasize a breadth of meaning, to them is added "of any kind;" and, further, as noticed by the circuit judge in his opinion, the fifth section, which makes specific exceptions, among them professional actors, artists, lecturers, singers, and domestic servants, strengthens the idea that every other kind of labor and service was intended to be reached by the first section. While there is great force to this reasoning, we cannot think congress intended to denounce with penalties a transaction like that in the present case. It is a familiar rule that a thing may be within the letter of the statute and yet not within the statute, because not within its spirit nor within the intention of its makers. This has been often asserted, and the Reports are full of cases illustrating its application. This is not the substitution of the will of the judge for that of the legislator; for frequently words of general meaning are used in a statute, words broad enough to include

Sec. 4   THE INTENTION OF THE LEGISLATURE   351

an act in question, and yet a consideration of the whole legislation, or of the circumstances surrounding its enactment, or of the absurd results which follow from giving such broad meaning to the words, makes it unreasonable to believe that the legislator intended to include the particular act. * * *

* * * In U. S. v. Kirby, 7 Wall. 482, 486, the defendants were indicted for the violation of an act of congress providing "that if any person shall knowingly and willfully obstruct or retard the passage of the mail, or of any driver or carrier, or of any horse or carriage carrying the same, he shall, upon conviction, for every such offense, pay a fine not exceeding one hundred dollars." The specific charge was that the defendants knowingly and willfully retarded the passage of one Farris, a carrier of the mail, while engaged in the performance of his duty, and also in like manner retarded the steam-boat Gen. Buell, at that time engaged in carrying the mail. To this indictment the defendants pleaded specially that Farris had been indicted for murder by a court of competent authority in Kentucky; that a bench-warrant had been issued and placed in the hands of the defendant Kirby, the sheriff of the county, commanding him to arrest Farris, and bring him before the court to answer to the indictment; and that, in obedience to this warrant, he and the other defendants, as his posse, entered upon the steam-boat Gen. Buell and arrested Farris, and used only such force as was necessary to accomplish that arrest. The question as to the sufficiency of this plea was certified to this court, and it was held that the arrest of Farris upon the warrant from the state court was not an obstruction of the mail, or the retarding of the passage of a carrier of the mail, within the meaning of the act. In its opinion the court says: "All laws should receive a sensible construction. General terms should be so limited in their application as not to lead to injustice, oppression, or an absurd consequence. It will always, therefore, be presumed that the legislature intended exceptions to its language which would avoid results of this character. The reason of the law in such cases should prevail over its letter. The common sense of man approves the judgment mentioned by Puffendorf, that the Bolognian law which enacted 'that whoever drew blood in the streets should be punished with the utmost severity,' did not extend to the surgeon who opened the vein of a person that fell down in the street in a fit. The same common sense accepts the ruling, cited by Plowden, that the statute of 1 Edw. II., which enacts that a prisoner who breaks prison shall be guilty of felony, does not extend to a prisoner who breaks out when the prison is on fire, 'for he is not to be hanged because he would not stay to be burnt.' And we think that a like common sense will sanction the ruling we make, that the act of congress which punishes the obstruction or retarding of the passage of the mail, or of its carrier, does not apply to a case of temporary detention of the mail caused by the arrest of the carrier upon an indictment for murder." * * *

352   THE INTERPRETATION OF STATUTES   Ch. 5

Among other things which may be considered in determining the intent of the legislature is the title of the act. We do not mean that it may be used to add to or take from the body of the statute, (Hadden v. Collector, 5 Wall. 107,) but it may help to interpret its meaning. In the case of U. S. v. Fisher, 2 Cranch, 358, 386, Chief Justice MARSHALL said: "On the influence which the title ought to have in construing the enacting clauses, much has been said, and yet it is not easy to discern the point of difference between the opposing counsel in this respect. Neither party contends that the title of an act can control plain words in the body of the statute; and neither denies that, taken with other parts, it may assist in removing ambiguities. Where the intent is plain, nothing is left to construction. Where the mind labors to discover the design of the legislature, it seizes everything from which aid can be derived; and in such case the title claims a degree of notice, and will have its due share of consideration." * * *

It will be seen that words as general as those used in the first section of this act were by that decision limited, and the intent of congress with respect to the act was gathered partially, at least, from its title. Now, the title of this act is, "An act to prohibit the importation and migration of foreigners and aliens under contract or agreement to perform labor in the United States, its territories, and the District of Columbia. Obviously the thought expressed in this reaches only to the work of the manual laborer, as distinguished from that of the professional man. No one reading such a title would suppose that congress had in its mind any purpose of staying the coming into this country of ministers of the gospel, or, indeed, of any class whose toil is that of the brain. The common understanding of the terms "labor" and "laborers" does not include preaching and preachers, and it is to be assumed that words and phrases are used in their ordinary meaning. So whatever of light is thrown upon the statute by the language of the title indicates an exclusion from its penal provisions of all contracts for the employment of ministers, rectors, and pastors.

Again, another guide to the meaning of a statute is found in the evil which it is designed to remedy; and for this the court properly looks at contemporaneous events, the situation as it existed, and as it was pressed upon the attention of the legislative body. U. S. v. Railroad Co., 91 U.S. 72, 79. The situation which called for this statute was briefly but fully stated by Mr. Justice Brown when, as district judge, he decided the case of U. S. v. Craig, 28 Fed.Rep. 795, 798: "The motives and history of the act are matters of common knowledge. It had become the practice for large capitalists in this country to contract with their agents abroad for the shipment of great numbers of an ignorant and servile class of foreign laborers, under contracts by which the employer agreed, upon the one hand, to prepay their passage, while, upon the other hand, the laborers agreed to work after their arrival for a certain time at a low rate of wages. The effect of this was to break down the labor market, and to reduce other laborers engaged in like occupations to the level of the assisted immigrant. The evil finally became so flagrant that an appeal was made to congress for relief by the passage of the act in question, the design of which was to raise the standard of foreign immigrants, and to discountenance the migration of those who had not sufficient means in their own hands, or those of their friends, to pay their passage."

It appears, also, from the petitions, and in the testimony presented before the committees of congress, that it was this cheap, unskilled labor which was making the trouble, and the influx of which congress sought to prevent. It was never suggested that we had in this country a surplus of brain toilers, and, least of all, that the market for the services of Christian ministers was depressed by foreign competition. Those were matters to which the attention of congress, or of the people, was not directed. So far, then, as the evil which was sought to be remedied interprets the statute, it also guides to an exclusion of this contract from the penalties of the act.

A singular circumstance, throwing light upon the intent of congress, is found in this extract from the report of the senate committee on education and labor, recommending the passage of the bill: "The general facts and considerations which induce the committee to recommend the passage of this bill are set forth in the report of the committee of the house. The committee report the bill back without amendment, although there are certain features thereof which might well be changed or modified, in the hope that the bill may not fail of passage during the present session. Especially would the committee have otherwise recommended amendments, substituting for the expression, 'labor and service,' whenever it occurs in the body of the bill, the words 'manual labor' or 'manual service,' as sufficiently broad to accomplish the purposes of the bill, and that such amendments would remove objections which a sharp and perhaps unfriendly criticism may urge to the proposed legislation. The committee, however, believing that the bill in its present form will be construed as including only those whose labor or service is manual in character, and being very desirous that the bill become a law before the adjournment, have reported the bill without change." Page 6059, Congressional Record, 48th Cong. And, referring back to the report of the committee of the house, there appears this language: "It seeks to restrain and prohibit the immigration or importation of laborers who would have never seen our shores but for the inducements and allurements of men whose only object is to obtain labor at the lowest possible rate, regardless of the social and material well-being of our own citizens, and regardless of the evil consequences which result to American laborers from such immigration. This class of immigrants care nothing about our institutions, and in many instances never even heard of them. They are men whose passage is paid by the importers. They come here under contract to labor for a certain number of years. They are ignorant of our social condition, and, that they may remain so, they are isolated and prevented from coming into contact with Americans. They are generally from the lowest social stratum, and live upon the coarsest food, and in hovels of a character before unknown to American workmen. They, as a rule, do not become citizens, and are certainly not a desirable acquisition to the body politic. The inevitable tendency of their presence among us is to degrade American labor, and to reduce it to the level of the imported pauper labor." Page 5359, Congressional Record, 48th Cong.

We find, therefore, that the title of the act, the evil which was intended to be remedied, the circumstances surrounding the appeal to congress, the reports of the committee of each house, all concur in affirming that the intent of congress was simply to stay the influx of this cheap, unskilled labor.

* * *

The judgment will be reversed, and the case remanded for further proceedings in accordance with this opinion.

NOTES

1. In the construction of statutes the courts have adopted a favorable attitude toward the use of reports of standing committees, as in the principal case, and of special committees, as in Pellet v. Industrial Comm., 162 Wis. 596, 156 N.W. 956 (1916). See, generally, Chamberlain, The Courts and Committee Reports, 1 U.Chi.L.Rev. 81 (1933); Jones, Extrinsic Aids in the Federal Courts, 25 Iowa L.Rev. 737 (1940).

2. Should reports and materials of law revision commissions, or other commissions, or of other extra-legislative groups be treated differently? If so, how and why? See, e. g., In re Tarlo's Estate, 315 Pa. 321, 172 A. 139 (1934) (law revision commission) and Sales v. Stewart, 134 Cal.App. 661, 20 P.2d 44 (1933). See, also, Note, Non-Legislative Intent as an Aid to Statutory Interpretation, 49 Col.L.Rev. 676 (1949); Sutherland, Statutes and Statutory Construction §§ 48.09, 48.11 and 48.12 (4th ed. Sands 1973, Cumulative Supp. 1979).

3. On interpretation according to the "equity of the statute," see de Sloovère, Equity and Reason of a Statute, 21 Cornell L.Q. 591 (1936); Thorne, The Equity of a Statute and Heydon's Case, 31 Ill.L.Rev. 202 (1936).

4. Contrast the nature of the problem posed for the Court in the principal case with that posed in U. S. v. Kirby (discussed in the Holy Trinity Church case supra) and consider the result reached in the Kirby decision and the quoted justifications therefor. What other reasonable justifications, if any, might have been given? What are the implications of Kirby for the judicial function in interpretation? Compare Riggs v. Palmer, 115 N.Y. 506, 22 N.E. 188 (1889). In that case, the beneficiary under a will had murdered the testator and then claimed the property pursuant to the will's provisions. The question was whether the beneficiary could have the

Sec. 4   *THE INTENTION OF THE LEGISLATURE*   355

property in such circumstances. It was acknowledged that the statutes regulating the making, proof and effect of wills and the devolution of property (which statutes did not in terms deal with "murdering heirs") would if literally construed give the property to the murderer. The Court however ruled that the murderer was not entitled to the property. Inter alia, the Court stated:

> "The purpose of [the statutes concerned] was to enable testators to dispose of their estates to the objects of their bounty at death, and to carry into effect their final wishes legally expressed; and in considering and giving effect to them this purpose must be kept in view. It was the intention of the law-makers that the donees in a will should have the property given to them. But it never could have been their intention that a donee who murdered the testator to make the will operative should have any benefit under it. * * *
>
> * * *
>
> "What could be more unreasonable than to suppose that it was the legislative intention in the general laws passed for the orderly, peaceable, and just devolution of property, that they should have operation in favor of one who murdered his ancestor that he might speedily come into the possession of his estate? Such an intention is inconceivable. We need not, therefore, be much troubled by the general language contained in the laws.
>
> "Besides, all laws as well as all contracts may be controlled in their operation and effect by general, fundamental maxims of the common law. No one shall be permitted to profit by his own fraud, or to take advantage of his own wrong, or to found any claim upon his own iniquity, or to acquire property by his own crime. These maxims are dictated by public policy, have their foundation in universal law administered in all civilized countries, and have nowhere been superseded by statutes. * * * "

Compare, in addition, Glus v. Brooklyn Eastern Dist. Terminal, 359 U.S. 231, 79 S.Ct. 760, 3 L.Ed.2d 770 (1959), where, notwithstanding the existence of an express three-year statute of limitations, the Supreme Court held that an FELA action brought after more than three years was not barred where defendant misled the plaintiff into believing he had more than three years in which to sue. The court relied on the principle that no man may take advantage of his own wrong, noting that it had been shown nothing in the language or history of the Federal Employers' Liability Act to indicate a contrary result. Also illuminating on the issues here raised are No. 4 of the Problems Under the Comprehensive Drug Abuse Prevention and Control Act (infra p. 593) and Sorrells v. United States, 287 U.S. 435, 53 S.Ct. 210, 77 L.Ed. 413 (1932).

FRANCIS LIEBER, SOME REMARKS ON INTERPRETATION [6]

* * * Let us take an instance of the simplest kind, to show in what degree we are continually obliged to resort to interpretation.

---

6. Professor at Columbia's School of Law, 1860–1872. The quoted passage appears in Lieber's Legal and Political Hermeneutics, pp. 17–20 (rev. 3d

By and by we shall find that the same rules which common sense teaches every one to use, in order to understand his neighbor in the most trivial intercourse, are necessary likewise, although not sufficient, for the interpretation of documents or texts of the highest importance, constitutions as well as treaties between the greatest nations.

Suppose a housekeeper says to a domestic: "fetch some soup-meat," accompanying the act with giving some money to the latter; he will be unable to execute the order without interpretation, however easy and, consequently, rapid the performance of the process may be. Common sense and good faith tell the domestic, that the housekeeper's meaning was this: 1. He should go immediately, or as soon as his other occupations are finished; or, if he be directed to do so in the evening, that he should go the next day at the *usual* hour; 2. that the money handed him by the housekeeper is intended to pay for the meat thus ordered, and not as a present to him; 3. that he should buy such meat and of such parts of the animal, as, to his knowledge, has commonly been used in the house he stays at, for making soups; 4. that he buy the best meat he can obtain, for a fair price; 5. that he go to that butcher who usually provides the family, with whom the domestic resides, with meat, or to some convenient stall, and not to any unnecessarily distant place; 6. that he return the rest of the money; 7. that he bring home the meat in good faith, neither adding any thing disagreeable nor injurious; 8. that he fetch the meat for the use of the family and not for himself. Suppose, on the other hand, the housekeeper, afraid of being misunderstood, had mentioned these eight specifications, she would not have obtained her object, if it were to exclude all *possibility* of misunderstanding. For, the various specifications would have required new ones. Where would be the end? We are constrained then, always, to leave a considerable part of our meaning to be found out by interpretation, which, in many cases must necessarily cause greater or less obscurity with regard to the exact meaning, which our words were intended to convey.

Experience is a plant growing as slowly as confidence, which Chatham said increased so tardily. In fact, confidence grows slowly because it depends upon experience. The British spirit of civil liberty induced the English judges to adhere strictly to the law, to its exact expressions. This again induced the law-makers to be, in their phraseology, as explicit and minute as possible, which causes such a tautology and endless repetition in the statutes of that country that even so eminent a statesman as Sir Robert Peel declared, in parliament, that he "contemplates no task with so much distaste as the reading through an ordinary act of parliament." Men have at length

ed. 1880). This work was originally published in The American Jurist, October 1837 and January 1838, and in a revised 2d edition in book form in 1839.

found out that little or nothing is gained by attempting to speak with absolute clearness and endless specifications, but that human speech is the clearer, the less we endeavor to supply by words and specifications that interpretation which common sense must give to human words. However minutely we may define, somewhere we needs must trust at last to common sense and good faith.

GOSSNELL v. SPANG

Circuit Court of Appeals of the United States, Third Circuit, 1936.
84 F.2d 889.

Suit by Benjamin J. Spang, in his own right as a disabled veteran of the World War, and for and on behalf of such other honorably discharged soldiers, sailors, and marines and wives and widows thereof as may become parties plaintiff, against Fred A. Gossnell and others, officials in Philadelphia of the United States Department of Commerce, in charge of the employment and compensation of personnel, required to undertake, carry on, and complete a project of the United States government, known as a business census of the entire United States, and others. Decree for plaintiff (13 F.Supp. 840), and defendants appeal.

Before BUFFINGTON, DAVIS, and THOMPSON, Circuit Judges.

BUFFINGTON, Circuit Judge. In the court below Benjamin J. Spang, a disabled and honorably discharged soldier, who, however, was not a registered relief person, filed a bill in equity against certain employees of the Department of Commerce of the United States alleging that he and his fellows were "being denied the preference to which they were entitled under the law, and personnel for such positions is being recruited from Federal Relief Rolls," and praying they "be enjoined from employing and from compensating any personnel for project of the United States Government known as Business Census of the United States to be taken under and by virtue of provisions contained in the Federal Emergency Relief Act of 1933 and its supplements [15 U.S.C.A. § 721, et seq.] and the Emergency Relief Appropriation Act of 1935 [15 U.S.C.A. § 728 note] in disregard of statutes of the United States, in disregard of opinion of the United States Attorney General and in disregard of civil service rules."

The case was heard on the motion of the defendants to dismiss and the plaintiff's motion for a preliminary injunction and in pursuance to its opinion (13 F.Supp. 840), the court refused to dismiss and granted an injunction forbidding the defendants "from denying * * * to the plaintiff and other honorably discharged soldiers, sailors and marines, who are qualified * * * preference of employment to clerical and other positions incident to the furtherance of said Business Census Project."

Passing by all questions of lack of parties, of equitable jurisdiction of the court below, and of constitutionality, we note that the underlying and decisive question here involved is whether the Act of July 11, 1919, § 1, 41 Stat. 37 (5 U.S.C.A. § 35), giving soldiers a preference, which provides, "In making appointments to clerical and other positions in the executive branch of the Government in the District of Columbia or elsewhere preference shall be given to honorably discharged soldiers, sailors, and marines, and widows of such and to the wives of injured soldiers, sailors, and marines who themselves are not qualified, but whose wives are qualified to hold such positions," applied to the so-called Business Census Act of 1935, under which defendants are acting in refusing a soldier preference.

After due consideration had, we are of opinion it did not. We regard that question as conclusively settled by what took place when the Act of 1935 was being considered by the Congress, viz.:

* * *

"Mr. Metcalf. Mr. President, I offer the amendment which I send to the desk to be inserted at the proper place in the joint resolution.

"The Vice President. The clerk will state the proposed amendment.

"The Chief Clerk. At the proper place, it is proposed to insert the following:

"Provided, That in the employment of all officials and employees paid from funds appropriated by this joint resolution, preference shall be given, where they are qualified, to ex-service men.

"Mr. Hayden. Mr. President, it is with great hesitation that I say a word in opposition to this amendment. The Senator from Rhode Island has offered a proposal to give preference to veterans. The fact is, as I think upon reflection the Senator will recognize, that the amendment is improper. The joint resolution is designed to take care of three and a half million men unemployed. Among them are veterans. The amendment would destroy the purpose of the measure by giving preference to veterans, whether or not they were on relief. The joint resolution limits the benefits of the measure to persons on relief. The Senator from Rhode Island seeks to change that, and, under the amendment, whether a veteran were on relief or not, he would have a preference with respect to obtaining employment.

"Very properly, in the original Public Works Act we gave preference to veterans. That was a measure which took men from the ranks of the unemployed anywhere, and we provided that veterans should have preference, and they

Sec. 4   *THE INTENTION OF THE LEGISLATURE*   359

have been given preference. But here the distinction is whether or not a person is on relief. I think we would destroy the purpose of the joint resolution if we should agree to the amendment.

"Mr. Metcalf. Mr. President, I cannot see how the argument of the learned Senator from Arizona can apply. I see no reason why this amendment should not be agreed to and included in the joint resolution. I ask for a vote.

[Remarks on unrelated amendments are omitted.]

"The Vice President. An amendment is pending, the amendment offered by the Senator from Rhode Island.

"Mr. Metcalf. Mr. President, as my distinguished friend the Senator from Arizona seems to criticize the amendment proposed by me, I shall modify it by adding the words 'on relief' at the end of the proposed amendment, so that it will read 'preference shall be given, where they are qualified, to ex-service men on relief.'

"The Vice President. The question is on agreeing to the amendment offered by the Senator from Rhode Island, as modified. (Putting the question.) The noes seem to have it.

"Mr. McNary. I ask for a division.

"On a division, the amendment was rejected."

From this record it is clear that when the Act of 1935 was on passage, it was sought by the Metcalf amendment to give soldiers a preference in employment, and in opposition thereto it was stated by Mr. Hayden that "we would destroy the purpose of this joint resolution if we should agree to the amendment." Following this, the Metcalf amendment was defeated. Were this court to hold that the soldiers' preference applied to the Business Census Act of 1935, it would fly directly in the face of what the Congress meant and stated when that act was passed. It is for Congress to legislate in that regard and not for courts to nullify what Congress plainly stated and enacted.

In view of these considerations, we are constrained to differ from the court below and to hold the Act of July 11, 1919, gives to the plaintiff no preference. So holding, the decree below is vacated and the record remanded with instructions to dismiss the bill.

NOTES

1. The Emergency Relief Appropriation Act of 1935 (H.J.Res. 117) provides in relevant part: "That in order to provide relief, work relief and to increase employment * * * there is hereby appropriated * * * the sum of $4,000,000,000. * * * Provided, however, that * * *

preference in the employment of labor shall be given * * * to persons receiving relief, where they are qualified * * *." 49 Stat. 115–117.

2. Which legislative enactment is the court interpreting, the Act of 1919 or the Joint Resolution of 1935? On what basis was the court justified in considering the rejection of the proposed amendment as evidence of the Congressional intent?

3. It has been said that statements of individual legislators made in the course of general debate are ordinarily not to be considered relevant on the question of legislative understanding: United States v. Trans-Missouri Freight Ass'n, 166 U.S. 290, 17 S.Ct. 540, 41 L.Ed. 1007 (1897). But exceptions to this have been recognized. For example, explanatory statements by the person in charge of the bill are admissible, Wright v. Vinton Branch of the Mountain Trust Bank of Roanoke, 300 U.S. 440, 57 S.Ct. 556, 81 L. Ed. 736 (1937); and recourse to legislative debates may be permitted in order to show a common agreement among the legislators as to the meaning of an ambiguous provision. Federal Trade Comm. v. Raladam Co., 283 U.S. 643, 51 S.Ct. 587, 75 L.Ed. 1324 (1931). What, if any, further exception is suggested by Woollcott v. Shubert, infra p. 368?

MITCHELL v. KENTUCKY FINANCE CO.

Supreme Court of the United States, 1959.
359 U.S. 290, 79 S.Ct. 756, 3 L.Ed.2d 815.

Mr. Justice HARLAN delivered the opinion of the Court.

Petitioner, the Secretary of Labor, brought suit to enjoin respondents from violating the overtime and record-keeping provisions of the Fair Labor Standards Act, 52 Stat. 1060, as amended, 29 U.S. C. § 201 et seq., 29 U.S.C.A. § 201 et seq. Respondents, two closely affiliated subsidiaries of a common corporate parent, share an office in Louisville, Kentucky. They are engaged in the business of making personal loans, in amounts up to $300, to individuals, and in purchasing conditional sales contracts from dealers in furniture and appliances. Respondents share the services of a common manager and nine full-time and two part-time employees.

By pretrial stipulation and concessions at trial, respondents in effect conceded that an injunction should issue unless their employees are exempted from the overtime and record-keeping provisions of the statute by § 13(a)(2) thereof, which provides that such requirements shall not apply to

"* * * any employee employed by any retail or service establishment, more than 50 per centum of which establishment's annual dollar volume of sales of goods or services is made within the State in which the establishment is located. A 'retail or service establishment' shall mean an establishment 75 per centum of whose annual dollar volume of sales of goods or services (or of both) is not for resale and

Sec. 4   THE INTENTION OF THE LEGISLATURE   361

is recognized as retail sales or services in the particular industry; * * *"

As concededly more than 50 percent of respondents' loan and discount business is with Kentucky residents and none of it involves "resale" transactions, the sole question involved in this litigation is whether respondents should be considered as "retail or service establishment[s]," engaged in the making of "sales of goods or services," within the meaning of § 13(a)(2). The burden is, of course, upon respondents to establish that they are entitled to the benefit of the § 13 exemption, since coverage apart from the exemption is admitted.

After trial the District Court found that respondents had not proved that they are a "retail or service establishment" within the meaning of § 13(a)(2), and issued an injunction restraining respondents from further violating the Act. D.C., 150 F.Supp. 368. The Court of Appeals reversed. 6 Cir., 254 F.2d 8. We granted certiorari, 358 U.S. 811, 79 S.Ct. 39, 3 L.Ed.2d 55, to resolve the conflict between the decision of the court below and that of the Court of Appeals for the First Circuit in Aetna Finance Co. v. Mitchell, 1 Cir., 247 F.2d 190.

Until 1949, § 13(a)(2) exempted from the overtime and recordkeeping provisions of the Fair Labor Standards Act "Any employee engaged in any retail or service establishment the greater part of whose selling or servicing is in intrastate commerce." The Administrator early ruled that personal loan companies and other business entities in what may broadly be called the "financial industry" were not within the scope of that exemption.[7] When Congress amended the Act in 1949 it provided that pre-1949 rulings and interpretations by the Administrator should remain in effect unless inconsistent with the statute as amended. 63 Stat. 920, § 16(c), 29 U.S.C.A. § 208 note. The narrow issue before us, then, is whether Congress in the 1949 amendment of § 13(a)(2) broadened the scope of that section so as to embrace personal loan companies.

The present § 13(a)(2) differs from its predecessor primarily in the addition of a definition of the term "retail or service establishment," such an establishment being one "75 per centum of whose annual dollar volume of sales of goods or services (or of both) is not for resale and is recognized as retail sales or services in the particular industry; * * *" Respondents argue that they plainly come within this definition because (1) more than 75 percent of their loan and discount business is "not for resale," and (2) their activities are recognized in the financial industry as being the "retail end" of that industry. They claim that the intent of Congress in the 1949 amendment was to provide that "local" business was exempt from the over-

---

[7]. Interpretative Bull. No. 6, 1942 WH Manual 326, ¶¶ 29–31. That ruling has been carried over under the amended version of § 13(a)(2), 29 CFR, 1958 Supp., § 779.10.

time requirements of the statute, and that their activities are precisely the kind the § 13 exemption was designed to embrace.

We do not think the issue before us can be disposed of so simply. The Government points out that the concept of "sale" is inherently inapposite to the lending of money at interest, and urges that because respondents cannot properly be said to be engaged in the "sales of goods or services" the exemption cannot as to them come into play even if their activities are recognized as "retail" in the financial industry. Respondents concede that they are not engaged in the sale of "goods," but insist that their activities do constitute a "sale" of a "service" within the intendment of § 13(a)(2), characterizing that "service" as credit or the use of money.[8]

This is not a case where perforce we must attempt to resolve a controversy as to the true meaning of equivocal statutory language unaided by any reliable extrinsic guide to legislative intention. On the contrary, the debates and reports in Congress with reference to this section of the statute are detailed and explicit. To those legislative materials we now turn.

The legislative history of the 1949 amendment to § 13(a)(2) demonstrates beyond doubt that Congress was acting in implementation of a specific and particularized purpose. Before 1949 the Administrator, in interpreting the term "retail or service establishment," then nowhere defined in the statute, had, in addition to excluding from the coverage of the exemption personal loan companies and other financial institutions, ruled that a business enterprise generally would not qualify as such an establishment unless 75 percent of its receipts were derived from the sale of goods or services "to private persons to satisfy their personal wants," on the theory that sales for business use were "nonretail."[9] This administratively announced "business use" test was generally approved by this Court in Roland Electrical Co. v. Walling, 326 U.S. 657, 66 S.Ct. 413, 90 L.Ed. 383.

Congress was dissatisfied with this construction of the statute, and over the objection of the Administrator, who sought to have his "business use" test legislatively confirmed,[10] passed the 1949 amendment to § 13(a)(2) to do away with the rule that sales to other than individual consumers could not qualify as retail in deciding whether a particular business enterprise was a "retail or service establishment," and to substitute a more flexible test, under which selling transactions would qualify as retail if they (1) did not involve "resale," and (2) were recognized in the particular industry as retail. We find nothing in the debates or reports which suggests that Congress in-

---

8. The term "service" is nowhere defined in the Fair Labor Standards Act.

9. See Interpretative Bull. No. 6, 1942 WH Manual 326, ¶¶ 14, 18.

10. The Administrator supported the so-called Lesinski bill, which would have adopted the Administrator's "business use" test in the definition of "retail or service establishment."

Sec. 4 *THE INTENTION OF THE LEGISLATURE* 363

tended by the amendment to broaden the fields of business enterprise to which the exemption would apply. Rather, it was time and again made plain that the amendment was intended to change the prior law only by making it possible for business enterprises otherwise eligible under existing concepts to achieve exemption even though more than 25 percent of their sales were to other than private individuals for personal consumption, provided those sales were not for resale and were recognized in the field or industry involved as retail.[11] Thus enterprises in the financial field, none of which had previously been considered to qualify for the exemption regardless of the class of persons with which they dealt, and regardless of whether they were thought of in the financial industry as engaged in "retail financing," remained unaffected by the amendment of § 13(a)(2).

Any residual doubt on this score is dispelled by the explicit and repeated statements of the sponsors of the amendatory legislation and in the House and Senate Reports to the effect that "The amendment does not exempt banks, insurance companies, building and loan associations, *credit companies*, newspapers, telephone companies, gas and electric utility companies, telegraph companies, etc., because there is no concept of retail selling or servicing in these industries. Where it was intended that such businesses have an exemption one was specifically provided by the law * * *."[12] (Emphasis added.) It is

---

11. See H.R.Conf.Rep., 95 Cong.Rec. 14931, U.S.Code Cong.Service 1949, p. 2263: "[§ 13(a)(2)] * * * clarifies the existing exemption by defining the term 'retail or service establishment' and stating the conditions under which the exemption shall apply. This clarification is needed in order to obviate the sweeping ruling of the Administrator and the courts that no sale of goods or services for business use is retail. See Roland Electrical Co. v. Walling (326 U.S. 657, 66 S.Ct. 413, 90 L.Ed. 383): * * *"; Report of Majority of Senate Conferees, 95 Cong.Rec. 14877: "The conference agreement exempts establishments which are traditionally regarded as retail. * * *" See also the statement of Senator Holland, sponsor of the legislation in the Senate: "The only substantial difference between the Administrator and his recommendation [which would have written the "business use" test into the statute] and the amendment which we propose is that we propose to do away with this artificial distinction between a retail sale on the one hand and a business sale on the other * * *." 95 Cong.Rec. 12498. For other authoritative expressions of the legislative intent in this regard, see 95 Cong. Rec. 11115–11116, 12492–12493, 12496, 12502, 12506, 12508.

12. H.R.Conf.Rep., 95 Cong.Rec. 14932, U.S.Code Cong.Service 1949, p. 2265. See also Report of Majority of Senate Conferees, 95 Cong.Rec. 14877; statement of Senator Holland, 95 Cong. Rec. 12505–12506.

Respondents urge that statements of this kind have no application to them because they are not "credit companies," in that such term properly is to be restricted to commercial credit companies. We agree with the observation of the Court of Appeals in Aetna Finance Co. v. Mitchell, supra, 247 F.2d at page 193, that this contention is "quite unconvincing." There is nothing which indicates that Congress was using the term "credit companies" in any specialized sense, and indeed one of respondents' own expert witnesses testified that personal loan companies are "credit institutions." We think it clear that the House and Senate Conferees used "credit companies" to mean nothing more nor less than companies which deal in credit, as respondents concededly do.

well settled that exemptions from the Fair Labor Standards Act are to be narrowly construed. A. H. Phillips, Inc. v. Walling, 324 U.S. 490, 493, 65 S.Ct. 807, 808, 89 L.Ed. 1095; see also Powell v. United States Cartridge Co., 339 U.S. 497, 517, 70 S.Ct. 755, 766, 94 L.Ed. 1017. In the light of the abundant pointed evidence that Congress did not intend that businesses like those of respondents be exempted from the overtime and record-keeping provisions of the statute by § 13(a)(2), we would not be justified in straining to bring respondents' activities within the literal words of the exemption.

Reversed.

Mr. Justice STEWART took no part in the consideration or decision of this case.

SECURITIES AND EXCHANGE COMMISSION v. ROBERT COLLIER & CO.

Circuit Court of Appeals of the United States, Second Circuit, 1935.
76 F.2d 939.

Appeal from the District Court of the United States for the Southern District of New York.

Suit by the Securities & Exchange Commission against Robert Collier & Co., Inc., and others, to enjoin the defendants under the Securities Act of 1933. From a decree dismissing the bill (10 F.Supp. 95), plaintiff appeals.

Before L. HAND, SWAN, and AUGUSTUS N. HAND, Circuit Judges.

L. HAND, Circuit Judge. The single question presented by this appeal is whether the Securities and Exchange Commission, created under section 4(a) of title 1 of the "Securities Exchange Act of 1934," section 78d, tit. 15, U.S.Code, 15 U.S.C.A. § 78d, may appear in the District Court by its own solicitor and file a bill under section 20(b) [13] of the Securities Act (15 U.S.C.A. § 77t, subd. (b)), or whether it must appear by the Attorney General, or a district attorney. The defendants and the judge thought that the situation fell within our decision in Sutherland v. International Insurance Co., 43

---

13. ["(b) Whenever it shall appear to the Commission that any person is engaged or about to engage in any acts or practices which constitute or will constitute a violation of the provisions of this subchapter, or of any rule or regulation prescribed under the authority thereof, it may in its discretion, bring an action in any district court of the United States, United States court of any Territory, or the Supreme Court of the District of Columbia to enjoin such acts or practices, and upon a proper showing a permanent or temporary injunction or restraining order shall be granted without bond. The Commission may transmit such evidence as may be available concerning such acts or practices to the Attorney General who may, in his discretion, institute the necessary criminal proceedings under this sub-chapter. * * *"— Ed.]

Sec. 4   *THE INTENTION OF THE LEGISLATURE*   365

F.2d 969; the Commission insists that section 20(b) is an exception to the general rule. Though we had before us section 20(b) without any knowledge of its amendments in committee, we might still have held that the contrast between the diction of the two clauses was enough to turn the scale against a tradition of even such long standing as that on which the defendants rely. There would have been strong reasons for supposing that so striking a change in expression could only have proceeded from a deliberate difference of intent, no matter how inveterate the contrary usage. But if that be doubtful, the change in the section on its way through Congress makes the intent entirely plain. When first introduced, the two clauses were in identical language. "Whenever it shall appear to the Commission" (at that time the Federal Trade Commission), "that the practices investigated constitute a fraud * * * it shall transmit such evidence as may be available" to "the Attorney General who may in his discretion bring an action. * * * The Commission may transmit such evidence as may be available concerning such acts and practices to the Attorney General who may, in his discretion institute the necessary criminal proceedings under this sub-chapter." Hearings on H.R. 4314, 73d Congress, 1st Session, p. 6; Hearings on S.R. 875, p. 7. As the bill then stood, its intent was therefore to follow the ancient custom and deny to the Commission control over civil, as well as criminal, prosecutions. During the hearings before the committees, the chief counsel of the Federal Trade Commission, Robert E. Healey, testified; we quote the relevant passages in the margin.[14] It was aft-

---

14. "This bill provides that if the Commission discovers fraud and misrepresentation in connection with the sale of securities, it shall bring that information to the attention of the Attorney General, who shall proceed by injunction to stop that fraud and also to prosecute the guilty person criminally. My suggestion is where there is such a condition existing that Congress by this bill should say to the Attorney General, 'Punish them,' and then say to the Federal Trade Commission, 'Stop them.' I would amend this bill to provide for giving the power to apply for injunctions to the Commission. It is not wise to leave it to us to submit the information to the Attorney General. If we get the information why should we not use it and go after the fellow right then and there and get the injunction against him continuing to sell the stock? Why should we tell the Attorney General about it so he can seek the injunction? We should tell the Attorney General about it so that he can punish them, but why divide the responsibility? Why create such a magnificent buck-passing opportunity as that?

"Now if this Commission is competent to go out and get these facts,—and I will tell you I think that we are,—and if not, there are two vacancies down there, two vacancies that are just yearning to be filled, by some deserving Democrats,—I tell you I believe that we should be allowed to stop the practice. I submit to you gentlemen, first, if this Commission is on to its job and it finds these fellows selling stock by fraud or misrepresentation, we should be given the power to apply to the courts for an injunction and the prosecuting power should be left to the Attorney General where it belongs." [Hearings on H.R. 4312, 73rd Cong., 1st Sess. pp. 240, 241].

"I wish to offer the suggestion that in the section of this bill which provides that the power of injunction shall be given, that provision be made that if the Commission which is charged with the administration of the bill finds people acting contrary to law

er this that the first clause was changed to its present form. We cannot see how any one can doubt what was the purpose of both committees in this amendment, though it is quite true that they said nothing about it in their reports. Healey was not a casual interloper; he was the person chiefly responsible for the prosecution of the new functions about to be conferred, at least so far as they touched legal questions. There cannot be the least question that in fact it was at his suggestion that the change was made and that it was intended to allow the Commission complete autonomy in civil prosecutions. The committees' intent may be irrelevant in construing the section, but the evidence of it as a fact is incontrovertible.

The defendants suggest that the purpose may have been limited to giving power to the Commission to decide when suits should be begun, but yet to require district attorneys to conduct them. Congress has indeed done just that on occasion. Section 12(1) tit. 49, U.S. Code, 49 U.S.C.A. § 12(1); section 413, tit. 33, U.S.Code (33 U.S.C. A. § 413); section 486, tit. 28, U.S.Code (28 U.S.C.A. § 486). But the resulting situation is certainly undesirable administratively, and whenever it has been prescribed, the language has been express. It is extremely unlikely that such a halfway measure should have been here intended. The original bill gave power to the Attorney General not only to decide when to sue, but necessarily to conduct the suit. The amendment was in form at least a transfer of the total power; unless some good reason to the contrary appears, it ought to be construed as total, not as leaving the Commission subject to a public officer whom they could not control. * * *

Finally, it is said that we should not regard the testimony of a witness before the committees; that it is not even as relevant as speeches on the floor of either house, which courts will not consider at all. United States v. Trans-Missouri Freight Association, 166 U.S. 290, 317, 318, 17 S.Ct. 540, 41 L.Ed. 1007; Duplex, etc., Co. v. Deering, 254 U.S. 443, 474, 41 S.Ct. 172, 65 L.Ed. 349, 16 A.L.R. 196; McCaughn v. Hershey Chocolate Co., 283 U.S. 488, 493, 494, 51 S.Ct. 510, 75 L.Ed. 1183. It would indeed be absurd to suppose that the testimony of a witness by itself could be used to interpret an act of Congress; we are not so using it. The bill was changed in a most significant way; we are concerned to learn why this was done; we find that it can most readily be explained, and indeed cannot naturally be explained on any other assumption than by supposing that the committees assented to a request from the very agency to whom the new functions were to be committed. To close our eyes to this patent and compelling argument would be the last measure of arid formal-

or in defiance of the Act, that Commission and not the Attorney General will proceed to ask for an injunction. I would suggest that it is unwise to divide the responsibility and to encounter the delay that would come if we have to send our stuff to the Attorney General. Let him prosecute criminally, let us proceed to stop them." [Hearings on S. 875, 73rd Cong., 1st Sess. p. 226.]

ism. The amendments of a bill in committee are fertile sources of interpretation. Pennsylvania R. Co. v. International Coal Co., 230 U.S. 184, 198, 199, 33 S.Ct. 893, 57 L.Ed. 1446, Ann.Cas.1915A, 315. It is of course true that members who vote upon a bill do not all know, probably very few of them know, what has taken place in committee. On the most rigid theory possibly we ought to assume that they accept the words just as the words read, without any background of amendment or other evidence as to their meaning. But courts have come to treat the facts more really; they recognize that while members deliberately express their personal position upon the general purposes of the legislation, as to the details of its articulation they accept the work of the committees; so much they delegate because legislation could not go on in any other way.

Decree reversed.

NOTES

1. How did the change in the Section in the course of its enactment make the Congressional intent "entirely plain"?

2. In what respect does the contrast in diction of the two clauses indicate a deliberate difference of intent?

3. Under what theory did the court solve the problem of the transference of the committee intent to Congress? See Jones, Extrinsic Aids in the Federal Courts, 25 Iowa L.Rev. 737, 743 et seq. (1940).

4. Based on your reading of the preceding materials, including Section 1, The Legislative Process, would you think it fair to say that the standing committee is the most important element in the Congressional law-making process? Why?

5. An interesting problem is raised when the standing committee reports of the two chambers are inconsistent. How should the Court proceed in such a case? See, e. g., Department of Air Force v. Rose, 425 U.S. 352, 362–370, 96 S.Ct. 1592, 1599–1603, 48 L.Ed.2d 11 (1976).

JOHNSON v. SOUTHERN PACIFIC CO.

Supreme Court of the United States, 1904.
196 U.S. 1, 25 S.Ct. 158, 49 L.Ed. 363.

[Reread opinion, supra p. 337, analyzing particularly the nature of the evidence of legislative intent and the Supreme Court's treatment of it.]

NOTES

1. The technique of "purpose interpretation", of which the Supreme Court opinion in the Johnson case is a good example, is usually traced back to the old classic Heydon's Case, 3 Coke 7a, 76 Eng.Rep. 637 (Court of Exchequer, 1584). The much-quoted "Doctrine of Heydon's Case" was there stated as follows:

> "And it was resolved by them, that for the sure and true interpretation of all statutes in general (be they penal or beneficial,

restrictive or enlarging of the common law) four things are to be discerned and considered:—

"1st. What was the common law before the making of the Act.

"2nd. What was the mischief and defect for which the common law did not provide.

"3rd. What remedy the Parliament hath resolved and appointed to cure the disease of the commonwealth.

"And 4th. The true reason of the remedy; and then the office of all the Judges is always to make such construction as shall suppress the mischief, and advance the remedy, and to suppress subtle inventions and evasions for continuance of the mischief, and *pro privato commodo*, and to add force and life to the cure and remedy, according to the true intent of the makers of the Act, *pro bono publico*."

2. Purpose interpretation is analyzed at some length in Jones, Statutory Doubts and Legislative Intention, 40 Colum.L.Rev. 957, 970–74 (1940).

3. Executive material, such as President Harrison's annual messages in the principal case, is an important extrinsic aid in statutory interpretation. For a discussion of such material see the sections on Source and Development of Legislative Proposals, Executive Action, and Some Aspects of the State Legislative Process in Section 1, The Legislative Process, supra. Gubernatorial messages proposing legislation or approving or vetoing it may be particularly valuable in the states where other aids are hard to come by. On the availability of such messages in New York, for example, see Dana, Background Materials for Statutory Interpretation, 14 The Record of the Association of the Bar of the City of New York 80 (1959), which is quoted supra at p. 316.

WOOLLCOTT v. SHUBERT

Court of Appeals of New York, 1916.
217 N.Y. 212, 111 N.E. 829.

COLLIN, J. The primary question presented by the present appeal is, may the proprietor of a theatre lawfully exclude from it a person upon any ground other than that of race, creed or color? The appellant asserts that the Civil Rights Act of this state, as amended in 1913, answers the question in the negative. The respondents assert that the act forbids the exclusion upon the ground of race, creed or color only.

The complaint alleges in effect: The defendants control and conduct many theatres. The plaintiff gains his livelihood as the dramatic critic on the staff of the New York *Times*. He wrote and the New York *Times* published a legitimate and proper criticism of one of the productions controlled by the defendants. It displeased the defendants and, therefore, they have excluded the plaintiff from one of their theatres and have refused to permit him to enter it upon the same terms as the general public. They have threatened to exclude him

Sec. 4 THE INTENTION OF THE LEGISLATURE 369

from all their theatres. Those acts of the defendants are wrongs against the plaintiff remediable at law only through a multiplicity of actions, in which the penalties recoverable would inadequately compensate him. The complaint demands a judgment permanently restraining the defendants from continuing the acts. The defendants answered the complaint and subsequently applied to the court at Special Term for an order for judgment on the pleadings. The Special Term granted the order. The Appellate Division affirmed it and granted leave to appeal from its order of affirmance to this court.

The acts of the defendants were within their rights at the common law. At the common law a theatre, while affected by a public interest which justified licensing under the police power or for the purpose of revenue, is in no sense public property or a public enterprise. It is not governed by the rules which relate to common carriers or other public utilities. The proprietor does not derive from the state the franchise to initiate and conduct it. His right to and control of it is the same as that of any private citizen in his property and affairs. He has the right to decide who shall be admitted or excluded. His rights at the common law, in the respect of controlling the property, entertainments and audience, have been too recently determined by us to be now questionable. People ex rel. Burnham v. Flynn, 189 N.Y. 180, 82 N.E. 169, 12 Ann.Cas. 420; Collister v. Hayman, 183 N.Y. 250, 76 N.E. 20, 1 L.R.A.,N.S., 1188, 111 Am.St.Rep. 740, 5 Ann.Cas. 344; Aaron v. Ward, 203 N.Y. 351, 38 L.R.A.,N.S., 204. Under the common law the rights of the plaintiff were not violated by the acts of the defendants.

These rights were restricted by the statute of 1895, commonly known as the Civil Rights Act (Laws of 1895, chapter 1042). It was entitled "An Act to protect all citizens in their civil and legal rights." It enacted:

"§ 1. That all persons within the jurisdiction of this State shall be entitled to the full and equal accommodations, advantages, facilities and privileges of inns, restaurants, hotels, eating-houses, bathhouses, barber shops, theatres, music halls, public conveyances on land and water, and all other places of public accommodation or amusement, subject only to the conditions and limitations established by law and applicable alike to all citizens.

"§ 2. That any person who shall violate any of the provisions of the foregoing section by denying to any citizens, except for reasons applicable alike to all citizens of every race, creed or color, and regardless of race, creed and color, the full enjoyment of any of the accommodations, advantages, facilities or privileges in said section enumerated, or by aiding or inciting such denial, shall for every such offense" incur the penalties as prescribed. We held that the purpose of the act was "to declare that no person should be deprived of any of the advantages enumerated, upon the ground of race, creed or color, and that its prohibition was intended to apply to cases of that character, and to none other. It is plain that the legislature did not intend to confer upon every person all the rights, advantages and privileges in places of amusement or accommodation, which might be enjoyed by another. Any discrimination not based upon race, creed or color does not fall within the condemnation of the statute." Grannan v. Westchester Racing Ass'n, 153 N.Y. 449, 465, 47 N.E. 896. The reasons for our decision may be briefly stated: The act in its essential particulars is identical with the Federal act of 1875 which was construed by the Supreme Court of the United States. Civil Rights Cases, 109 U.S. 3, 9, 3 S.Ct. 18, 27 L.Ed. 835. The first section of the Federal act is:

"That all persons within the jurisdiction of the United States shall be entitled to the full and equal enjoyment of the accommodations, advantages, facilities, and privileges of inns, public conveyances on land or water, theatres, and other places of public amusement; subject only to the conditions and limitations established by law, and applicable alike to citizens of every race and color, regardless of any previous condition of servitude." 18 Stat.L. 335.

The Supreme Court said: "The first section, which is the principal one, cannot be fairly understood without attending to the last clause, which qualifies the preceding part. The essence of the law is, not to declare broadly that all persons shall be entitled to the full and equal enjoyment of the accommodations, advantages, facilities, and privileges of inns, public conveyances, and theatres; but that such enjoyment shall not be subject to any conditions applicable only to citizens of a particular race or color, or who had been in a previous condition of servitude." The qualification of the general restrictive language effected by the last clause of the first section of the Federal act inheres in the state act of 1895 by virtue of the last clause of its section 1, namely: "Subject only to the conditions and limitations established by law and applicable alike to all citizens." The qualification is not materially changed or modified by the different wording of the two clauses. The rights conferred by the act of 1895 are expressly made subject to any conditions or limitations established by law which are applicable alike to all citizens. The act forbade that membership of any particular class of citizens should justify or permit exclusion from the enjoyment of the facilities or accommodations designated by it. Except as thus restricted, the rights of the defendants as proprietors of their theatres were those existing at the common law.

The act of 1895 was placed in the Civil Rights Law (Cons. Laws, ch. 6) as sections 40 and 41. In 1913 (L.1913, ch. 265) those sections were amended to read:

"§ 40. All persons within the jurisdiction of this state shall be entitled to the full and equal accommodations, advantages and privileges of any place of public accommodation, resort or amusement, subject only to the conditions and limitations established by law and applicable alike to all persons. No person, being the owner, lessee, proprietor, manager, superintendent, agent or employee of any such place, shall directly or indirectly refuse, withhold from or deny to any person any of the accommodations, advantages or privileges thereof, or directly or indirectly publish, circulate, issue, display, post or mail any written or printed communication, notice or advertisement, to the effect that any of the accommodations, advantages and privileges of any such place shall be refused, withheld from or denied to any person on account of race, creed or color, or that the patronage or custom thereat, of any person belonging to or purporting to be of any particular race, creed or color is unwelcome, objectionable or not acceptable, desired or solicited. The production of any such written or printed communication, notice or advertisement, purporting to relate to any such place and to be made by any person being the owner, lessee, proprietor, superintendent or manager thereof, shall be presumptive evidence in any civil or criminal action that the same was authorized by such person. A place of public accommodation, resort or amusement within the meaning of this article, shall be deemed to include any inn, tavern or hotel, whether conducted for the entertainment of transient guests, or for the accommodation of those seeking health, recreation or rest, any restaurant, eating-house, public conveyance on land or water, bath-house, barber-shop, theater and music hall. Nothing herein contained shall be construed to prohibit the mailing of a private communication in writing sent in response to a specific written inquiry.

"§ 41. Any person who shall violate any of the provisions of the foregoing section, or who shall aid or incite the violation of any of said provisions shall for each and every violation thereof be liable to" the penalties prescribed.

The appellant asserts that the changes in the language of the sections made by the amendment removed those sections from the effect of our decision in the Grannan Case, 153 N.Y. 449, 47 N.E. 896. Therein he errs. Rather is it true that the basis for that decision is broadened by them. The qualification of the comprehensive language of the first part of section 40, as it existed in the first section of the act of 1895, and its effect are retained. While the appellant argued ably and earnestly to the contrary, it seems quite clear to us that the provision, "No person, being the owner, lessee, proprietor, manager, superintendent, agent or employee of any such place, shall directly or indirectly refuse, withhold from or deny to any person any of the accommodations, advantages or privileges thereof," is expressly qualified by the subsequent words "on account of race, creed or color." The qualification referred to is thus made more specific and emphatic.

* * *

The purpose of the act as amended is to give greater efficacy to the policy of the original statute—to forbid the accomplishment of the discrimination barred by the statute, not only by a direct exclusion, but also by the indirect means specified. Such conclusion thoroughly satisfies its language. The purpose and policy of a statute are changed only by language expressly or through unavoidable implication effecting that result.

The respondents assert that the legislative debates during the passage of and relating to the act of 1913 demonstrate that its purpose was that we have just stated. In construing a statute we have a right to consider relevant conditions existing when it was adopted. Bull v. New York City Ry. Co., 192 N.Y. 361, 373; Matter of Jannicky, 209 N.Y. 413, 418. The particular mischief it was designed to remedy and the history of the period and of the statute itself may be considered. Wiley v. Solvay Process Co., 215 N.Y. 584, 588. We are at liberty to study the debates in seeking and determining the evil against which it was aimed as a remedy. In case they clearly and definitely describe an unworthy or mischievous condition necessitating, in the legislative mind, the statute, they furnish the court, laboring to discover the intent of the legislature, with legitimate and trustworthy aid. As Blackstone tersely expressed it, in the interpretation of statutes due regard must be had to the old law, the mischief and the remedy. The mischief may be indicated or made apparent by the debates attending the adoption of the remedy, as well as by contemporaneous events and the relevant situation as it existed. *Tap Line Cases*, 234 U.S. 1, 27; Standard Oil Co. of N. J. v. United States, 221 U.S. 1, 50; Jennison v. Kirk, 98 U.S. 453, 459; American Net & Twine Co. v. Worthington, 141 U.S. 468, 473. A court is at liberty, also, to invoke, as an aid in construction, the history of the passage of a statute, that is, the changes and proposed changes in the original bill, as recorded in the legislative journals. Blake v. National Banks, 23 Wallace, 307; Chesapeake & Potomac Tel. Co. v. Manning, 186 U.S. 238. It is established law, however, that the statements and opinions of legislators uttered in the debates are not competent aids to the court in ascertaining the meaning of statutes. United States v. Trans-Mo. Freight Association, 166 U.S. 290, 318; Dunlap v. United States, 173 U.S. 65, 75; Lapina v. Williams, 232 U.S. 78, 90; Omaha & C. B. Street Ry. Co. v. Interstate Commerce Com., 230 U.S. 324, 333. The Supreme Court of the United States has declared the rule that the formal reports of legislative committees relating to a bill in the course of progress are competent sources from which to discover the meaning of the language employed in a statute McLean v. United States, 226 U.S. 374, 380; Lapina v. Williams, 232 U.S. 78, 90, but cannot be resorted to for the purpose of construing a statute contrary to its plain terms. Penn R. R. Co. v. International Coal Mining Co., 230 U.S. 184, 199.

The debates in the present case conclusively show that the cause which led to the passage of the act of 1913 was the practice of the proprietors of some of the places designated in the act to advertise or notify the public and individuals that the advantages and privileges of those places would be refused to persons on account of race or creed, thereby evading indirectly the effect of the act of 1895; that the practice was deemed disgraceful and mischievous and that the purpose of the act was to prohibit it as well as the denial of those advantages and privileges, on account of race, creed or color, to actual applicants for them—to forbid the proprietors of the enumerated places to preclude, on account of race, creed or color, the attempts contemplated, as well as to defeat for the same reason the attempts actually made for admission.

* * *

WILLARD BARTLETT, Ch. J., HISCOCK, CHASE, HOGAN, CARDOZO and SEABURY, JJ., concur.

Order affirmed.

NOTE

The principal case's reliance on debates is especially to be noted. Such reliance in state cases is unusual. Only a handful of states keep records of the legislative debates and make them publicly available—indeed such records are not readily available in New York State. Cashman, Availability of Records of Legislative Debates, 24 The Record of the Association of the Bar of the City of New York 153 (1969). State legislatures generally do not publish reports of standing or conference committees, or committee hearings, as is done in Congress. In this situation, as we have noted earlier, gubernatorial messages (which are often available) and other executive materials assume greater importance as extrinsic aids and so also do the utterances of special and interim committees, of law revision and other commissions, of judicial councils, and even of extra-legislative groups. The state courts have shown a willingness to make use of relevant aids in interpreting statutes and advocates must be aware of them and be able to employ them effectively. The legislative history problem, as far as the interpretation of state statutes is concerned, has been described as one of "the production, not the use, of extrinsic materials." Horack, Cooperative Action for Improved Statutory Construction, 3 Vand.L.Rev. 383 (1950).

O'HARA v. LUCKENBACH STEAMSHIP CO.

Supreme Court of the United States, 1926.
269 U.S. 364, 46 S.Ct. 157, 70 L.Ed. 313.

On a Writ of Certiorari to the United States Circuit Court of Appeals for the Ninth Circuit.

Mr. Justice SUTHERLAND delivered the opinion of the Court.

Petitioners, libelants below, quit the service of the steamship company and sought to recover their earned wages on the ground of a violation of section 2 of the Seamen's Act of March 4, 1915, c. 153, 38

Stat. 1164 copied in the margin.[15] Omitting the various provisions with which we are not here concerned, the pertinent requirement of that section is that:

> "The sailors shall, while at sea, be divided into at least two, and the firemen, oilers, and water tenders into at least three watches, which shall be kept on duty successively for the performance of ordinary work incident to the sailing and management of the vessel."

For a failure on the part of the master to comply with this, among other provisions of the section, the seamen are entitled to a discharge and to receive the wages earned. The failure complained of was that the sailors were not divided into watches of equal or approximately equal numbers, as, it was insisted, the statute contemplated.

The company was the owner of the steamship Lewis Luckenbach, a vessel of 14,400 tons burden, upon which libelants were hired as sailors for a voyage from New York to Pacific ports and return to some port north of Cape Hatteras on the Atlantic. Altogether, there were 13 sailors on board, 3 of whom, including libelants, were assigned as quartermasters. On the voyage and while at sea, these sailors were not equally divided into watches. Three watches were on duty, each consisting of one quartermaster and one able seaman, the remaining seven sailors being kept at day work only. The District Court dismissed the libel and this was affirmed by the Circuit Court of Appeals. 1 F.(2d) 923. Both courts were of opinion that the primary object of the statutory provision was to fix hours of service so as to

---

15. Sec. 2. That in all merchant vessels of the United States of more than one hundred tons gross, excepting those navigating rivers, harbors, bays, or sounds exclusively, the sailors shall, while at sea be divided into at least two, and the firemen, oilers, and water tenders into at least three watches, which shall be kept on duty successively for the performance of ordinary work incident to the sailing and management of the vessel. The seamen shall not be shipped to work alternately in the fireroom and on deck, nor shall those shipped for deck duty be required to work in the fireroom, or vice versa; but these provisions shall not limit either the authority of the master or other officer or the obedience of the seamen when, in the judgment of the master or other officer, the whole or any part of the crew are needed for the maneuvering of the vessel or the performance of work necessary for the safety of the vessel or her cargo, or for the saving of life aboard other vessels in jeopardy, or when in port or at sea from requiring the whole or any part of the crew to participate in the performance of fire, lifeboat, and other drills. While such vessel is in a safe harbor no seaman shall be required to do any unnecessary work on Sundays or the following named days: New Year's Day, the Fourth of July, Labor Day, Thanksgiving Day, and Christmas Day, but this shall not prevent the dispatch of a vessel on regular schedule or when ready to proceed on her voyage. And at all times while such vessel is in a safe harbor, nine hours, inclusive of the anchor watch, shall constitute a day's work. Whenever the master of any vessel shall fail to comply with this section, the seamen shall be entitled to discharge from such vessel and to receive the wages earned. But this section shall not apply to fishing or whaling vessels or yachts.

prevent overwork, not to prescribe the number of seamen on each watch. The District Court thought that this conception of the law was borne out by the consideration that, if one-half or one-third of the crew must be assigned to duty at night, a majority of them would have little or nothing to do. The Circuit Court of Appeals seemed to think that the purpose of Congress to provide for the safety of the ship was satisfied rather in the selection of qualified quartermasters and men for the lookout than in equality of the watches. With these views we are unable to agree.

The general purpose of the Seamen's Act is not only to safeguard the welfare of the seamen as workmen, but, as set forth in the title, also "to promote safety at sea." The act as a whole shows very clearly that, while hours of work and proper periods of rest were regarded as considerations of primary concern while the vessel is in a safe harbor, these considerations must yield, as they have always yielded, to the paramount necessity of safety while the ship is at sea; and, as indicating that the provision under review was not intended primarily as a regulation of working hours, it is significant that it does not apply to the entire crew, but requires a division into watches only of the sailors and the firemen, oilers, and water tenders. It is natural to suppose that, if the purpose of Congress was chiefly to regulate hours of work, something would have been said about the service, while at sea, of those employed in the steward's department as well. And not only is the division confined to those of the crew engaged in the mechanics of conducting the ship on her voyage, but the imperative requirement is that the watches into which they are divided "shall be kept on duty successively"; that is to say, by turns, so that one watch must come on as another goes off. The evident purpose was to compel a division of the men for duty on deck and in the fireroom, and continuity of service, to the end that in those departments the ship should at all times be actively manned with equal efficiency.

It probably is true, as said below, that to construe the statute as compelling numerical equality of the watches will result, so far as the sailors are concerned, in the performance of less work on deck at night. And it may be noted in that connection that, in the hearings before the House committee having charge of the bill, it was objected on behalf of the shipowners, obviously, as the context shows, upon the theory that such equality was in fact contemplated by the provision that, "on cargo steamers, it would be an injustice to keep a lot of men on watch, all night, and have nothing for them to do." House Hearings on S. 136, Vol. 104, pt. 2, p. 5, Feb. 24, 1914. But the provision, fundamentally, is a measure of precaution against those perilous and often unexpected emergencies of the sea when only immediate and wakeful readiness for action may avert disaster or determine the issue between life and death; its effect as a regulator of working conditions is a matter of subordinate intent. A consideration of other safety provisions of the act will help to make this clear.

Among them, the act (section 13, p. 1169) provides that not less than 75 per centum of the crew in each department shall be able to understand any order given by the officers of such vessel, and that a certain percentage of her deck crew shall be of a rating not less than able seaman—meaning, except on the Great Lakes, a seaman, 19 years of age or upwards, who has had at least 3 years' service on deck at sea or on the Great Lakes. It also contains elaborate provisions (section 14, pp. 1170–1184) for the equipment of ocean-going vessels with life-saving appliances, and, among other things, requires (page 1180) that:

> "At no moment of its voyage may any ocean cargo steam vessel of the United States have on board a total number of persons greater than that for whom accommodation is provided in the lifeboats on board."

None of these provisions is of much, if any, concern, except as a precaution against the unusual crises of the sea.

As a ship pursues her way in security, perhaps for many years, these requirements for safety appliances and for able seamen may seem overexacting, and the language test, as well as a division of the watches into equal numbers, needlessly burdensome. But it is apparent, from the hearings and debates, that Congress looked forward to the possibility of other disasters like those of the Titanic and the Volturno (the facts of which had been subjected to inquiry by its committees), where, in the one, the lack of lifeboats, probably caused the loss of many lives, although in a quiet sea, and where, in the other, lifeboats lowered in a great storm were engulfed, it was thought by some, from the absence of the skill of able seamen in launching them, or like that of the City of Rio de Janeiro (In re Pacific Mail S. S. Co., 130 F. 76) which sank with many of its lifeboats unlaunched because the crew of Chinese sailors were unable to understand the language in which the orders of their officers were given. * * *

* * *

It is not unreasonable to conclude that Congress determined that each of the watches, like the crew as a whole, should be "adequate in number," competent and in a state of readiness "for any exigency that is likely to happen"—such as a collision, the striking of the ship upon a reef of rocks or an iceberg, the sudden breaking out of fire, and other happenings of like disastrous tendency—and to this end meant to provide for successive and continuous watches to be constituted in numbers as nearly equal as the sum of the whole number would permit.

In this conclusion we are fortified by the consideration that the legislation deals with seamen and the merchant marine and, consequently, the phrase "divided into * * * watches" is to be given the meaning which it had acquired in the language and usages of the trade to which the act relates, in accordance with the rule stated in Unwin v. Hanson, [1891] L.R. 2 Q.B. 115, 119:

> "If the act is one passed with reference to a particular trade, business, or transaction, and words are used which everybody conversant with that trade, business or transaction, knows and understands to have a particular meaning in it, then the words are to be construed as having that particular meaning, though it may differ from the common or ordinary meaning of the words."

In the understanding of the sailor, a division into "watches," as applied to the personnel of the ship, connotes a division as nearly equal as possible.

> "At sea a ship's crew is commonly divided into two watches: The master, second mate, fourth mate (if any), with one-half of the seamen and boys, forming the so-called 'starboard watch'; after four hours these are relieved by the chief mate, and the third officer (if any), and the other half of the men, who form the 'port watch.'" Paasch, Marine Encyclopedia, 300, 301.

R. H. Dana, Jr., in his "Dictionary of Sea Terms," p. 129, defines the term "watch" as:

> "Also, a certain portion of a ship's company, appointed to stand a given length of time. In the merchant service all hands are divided into two watches, larboard and starboard, with a mate to command each."

And, at page 133, he says:

> "The men are divided as equally as possible, with reference to their qualities as able seamen, ordinary seamen, or boys (as all green hands are called, whatever their age may be); but, if the number is unequal, the larboard watch has the odd one, since the chief mate does not go aloft and do other duty in his watch, as the second mate does in his."

The point is emphasized by the use of the distinctive terms "anchor watch" and "sea watch"; the former meaning the lookout intrusted to one or two men when the vessel is at anchor, and the latter being used "when one-half of a ship's crew is on duty" at sea. Paasch, 301.

It is true that this meaning had its origin in the customs of the sea before the advent of steam, but there is nothing to show that it has now a different meaning; and, with nothing in the context and no evidential circumstances to suggest the contrary, we fairly may assume that the use of the technical terms of the trade to which the statute relates imports their technical meaning.

Decree reversed.

THE PEOPLE EX REL. FYFE v. BARNETT

Supreme Court of Illinois, 1926.
319 Ill. 403, 150 N.E. 290.

Mr. Justice HEARD delivered the opinion of the court:

Mrs. Hannay Beye Fyfe, the petitioner, filed in the circuit court of Cook county her petition for a writ of *mandamus* against the appellants, who are the jury commissioners for Cook county, to compel them to replace her name upon the jury lists of Cook county. The petition alleged that she is a citizen of the United States, forty-six years of age, a resident of Oak Park, in said county, for more than fifteen years, and for more than four years last past has been an elector and legal voter in the township of Oak Park, in said county; that Cook county has more than 250,000 inhabitants and that appellants are the jury commissioners for said county; that appellants prepared the jury list in 1924, and that the name of the petitioner was included therein and entered in the jury commissioners' books; * * * that * * * the appellants amended and revised the Cook county jury list by eliminating her name therefrom; that she demanded that her name be replaced on the jury list, but that appellants refused to do so, alleging that she did not "possess the necessary legal qualifications for jury duty, in that she was a woman;" that she was willing, able and anxious to perform and discharge the duties of a juror, and that the elimination of her name from the jury list was contrary to law and in violation of her constitutional and statutory rights and privileges. Appellants demurred to the petition. The trial judge overruled the demurrer, and upon appellants electing to stand by the demurrer a final order was entered directing the clerk of the court to issue a peremptory writ of *mandamus* commanding the appellants, as jury commissioners, forthwith to replace upon the jury lists of Cook county the name of the petitioner.

Appellants contend that such order must be reversed for the reason that the existing statutes of the State of Illinois cannot be construed so as to impose upon women electors the obligation to serve on juries, and because by the issuance of the writ in question the court has obligated appellants to perform a duty in conflict with the constitution of this State.

[The general statute relating to jurors applicable in counties of not more than 250,000 population is omitted.]

The Jury Commissioners act in force July 1, 1887, as amended July 1, 1897, and April 24, 1899, (Cahill's Stat.1923, chap. 78, par. 26,) for the appointment of jury commissioners in counties having more than 250,000 inhabitants, provides, in part, as follows: "The said commissioners upon entering upon the duties of their office, and every four years thereafter, shall prepare a list of all electors between the ages of twenty-one and sixty years, possessing the necessary

Sec. 4   *THE INTENTION OF THE LEGISLATURE*   379

legal qualifications for jury duty, to be known as the jury list. The list may be revised and amended annually in the discretion of the commissioners. The name of each person on said list shall be entered in a book or books to be kept for that purpose, and opposite said name shall be entered the age of said person, his occupation, if any, his place of residence, giving street and number, if any, whether or not he is a householder, residing with his family, and whether or not he is a freeholder."

Women were given a limited right of suffrage in Illinois by an act of the legislature in force July 1, 1913. (Laws of 1913, p. 333.) This act gave women the right to vote for presidential electors, certain non-constitutional officers, and on propositions submitted to electors of municipalities and other political divisions of the State. In Scown v. Czarnecki, 264 Ill. 305, 106 N.E. 276, L.R.A.1915B, 247, Ann.Cas.1915A, 772, this act was held constitutional. It remained in force until April 29, 1921, when it was repealed by the Woman's Suffrage act, effective on that date. (Cahill's Stat.1923, chap. 46, pars. 67, 68.)

* * *

The nineteenth amendment to the Constitution of the United States makes no provision whatever with reference to the qualifications of jurors. Since the adoption of the amendment to the Constitution the legislature of the State of Illinois has not enacted any legislation on the subject of the eligibility or liability of women for jury service. While this amendment had the effect of nullifying every expression in the constitution and laws of the State denying or abridging the right of suffrage to women on account of their sex, it did not purport to have any effect whatever on the subject of liability or eligibility of citizens for jury service. Since the adoption of the amendment the legislature of Illinois in 1921 granted to women the full right of suffrage, and they became, equally with men, electors and legal voters.

The question involved in this suit has never been passed upon by this court. Very able briefs and arguments have been filed in the case by both parties and by *amicus curiae,* in which the decisions of other States in which the question has arisen are cited and the construction of the constitution of this State and the right of trial by jury as it existed at common law are discussed. The decisions of the courts of last resort in other States to which we have been cited are based upon constitutions and statutes differing somewhat from ours, and while they contain much forceful argument they cannot be considered as of any binding force in this cause.

It is a primary rule in the interpretation and construction to be placed upon a statute that the intention of the legislature should be ascertained and given effect. People v. Price, 257 Ill. 587, 101 N.E. 196, Ann.Cas.1914A, 1154. If in a statute there is neither ambiguity nor room for construction the intention of the legislature must be held free from doubt. What the framers of the statute would have done had it been in their minds that a case like the one here under consideration would arise is not the point in dispute. The inquiry is what, in fact, they did enact, possibly without anticipating the existence of such facts. This should be determined not by conjecture as to their meaning but by the construction of the language used. Wall v. Pfanschmidt, 265 Ill. 180, 106 N.E. 785, L.R.A.1915C, 328, Ann. Cas.1916A, 674. The only legitimate function of the court is to declare and enforce the law as enacted by the legislature. * * * The true rule is that statutes are to be construed as they were intended to be understood when they were passed. Statutes are to be read in the light of attendant conditions and that state of the law existent at the time of their enactment. The words of a statute must be taken in the sense in which they were understood at the time the statute was enacted. (25 R.C.L. 959.) * * * At the time of the passage by the legislature of the act above mentioned, providing for the appointment of a jury commission and the making of jury lists, the words "voters" and "electors" were not ambiguous terms. They had a well defined and settled meaning. By section 1 of Article 7 of the constitution of 1870 it is provided: "Every person having resided in this State one year, in the county ninety days, and in the election district thirty days next preceding any election therein, who was an elector in this State on the first day of April, in the year of our Lord 1848, or obtained a certificate of naturalization before any court of record in this State prior to the first day of January, in the year of our Lord, 1870, or who shall be a male citizen of the United States, above the age of twenty-one years, shall be entitled to vote at such election." By section 65 of the act on elections in force at that time it was provided: "Every person having resided in this State one year, in the county ninety days, and in the election district thirty days next preceding any election therein, who was an elector in this State on the first day of April, in the year of our Lord 1848, or obtained a certificate of naturalization before any court of record in this State prior to the first day of January, in the year of our Lord 1870, or who shall be a male citizen of the United States, above the age of twenty-one years, shall be entitled to vote at such election." (Rev. Stat.1874, p. 460.)

The legislative intent that controls in the construction of a statute has reference to the legislature which passed the given act. (25 R.C.L. 1029.) Applying the rules of construction herein mentioned, it is evident that when the legislature enacted the law in question, which provided for the appointment of jury commissioners in counties having more than 250,000 inhabitants and imposing upon them the duty of making a jury list, using the words "shall prepare a list of all electors between the ages of twenty-one and sixty years, possessing the necessary legal qualifications for jury duty, to be known as the jury list," it was intended to use the words "electors" and "elector" as the same were then defined by the constitution and laws of the State of Illinois. At that time the legislature did not intend that the name of any woman should be placed on the jury list, and must be held to have intended that the list should be composed of the names of male persons, only. In interpreting a statute the question is what the words used therein meant to those using them. (25 R.C. L. 1029.) The word "electors," in the statute here in question, meant male persons, only, to the legislators who used it. We must therefore hold that the word "electors," as used in the statute, means male persons, only, and that the petitioner was not entitled to have her name replaced upon the jury list of Cook county.

The judgment of the circuit court is therefore reversed.

Judgment reversed.

COMMONWEALTH v. MAXWELL

Supreme Court of Pennsylvania, 1921.
271 Pa. 378, 114 A. 825.

Opinion by Mr. Justice SCHAFFER. In this case, the court below quashed an indictment, charging the defendants with murder, because a woman served on the grand jury which found the bill. The Commonwealth has appealed; and this brings before us the important question whether women are eligible as jurors in Pennsylvania.

It is conceded that, under the 19th Amendment to the Constitution of the United States, women are given the right to vote, and are therefore electors; but the oyer and terminer held that the provision of our Constitution (article I, section 6),—"Trial by jury shall be as heretofore and the right thereof remain inviolate,"—preserves in this State trial by jury as it existed at common law, and that neither the federal amendment nor its effect upon the Act of April 10, 1867, P.L. 62, providing for the selection of jurors, alters the ancient rule that men only may serve.

Let it be noted that what we are called upon to determine is the composition of juries, so far as the qualifications of jurors are concerned, not the conduct of trials before such a body nor the kinds of cases which under the Constitution must be decided by that character of tribunal.

At the time the provision we are considering was placed in Pennsylvania's first Constitution, in 1776, justice had been administered in the Commonwealth according to English forms for about a century. Does the word "heretofore" refer to jury trials as conducted in England or in Pennsylvania? We find the method of selecting juries and the qualifications of jurors, at the time of the promulgation of this Constitution, September 28, 1776, was regulated in Pennsylvania and in England by legislation and not by the common law, in the latter country by the Act of 3 George II, c. 25; 3 Blackstone 361.

* * *

Under the Act of April 10, 1867, P.L. 62, section 2, (2 Purdon 2062, placitum 2), which expressly applies to each of the counties in the Commonwealth, except Philadelphia, the jury commissioners are required to select "from the *whole qualified electors* of the respective county, at large, a number," such as shall be designated by the court of common pleas, "of sober, intelligent and judicious persons, to serve as jurors in the several courts of such county during that year." The seventh section of this act exempts Philadelphia from its provisions. The statutory enactment which covers Philadelphia is section 2 of the Act of April 20, 1858, P.L. 354 (2 Purdon 2077, placitum 94); it sets forth: "That prior to the first day of December in each and every year, the receiver of public taxes of the said city shall lodge with the said sheriff, for the use of the said board [of judges], a duly certified list of *all taxable inhabitants of the said city*, setting out their names, places of residence and occupation; and, prior to the tenth day of December in each and every year, it shall be the duty of the said board, or a quorum thereof, to assemble together and select from the said list of taxables a sufficient number of sober, healthy and discreet citizens, to constitute the several panels of jurors, grand and petit, that may be required for service in the several courts for the next ensuing year, in due proportion from the several wards of the said city and the principal avocations."

It will thus be seen that since 1805, when the Constitution of 1790 was in force, the persons charged with the duty of jury service have been fixed, from time to time, by the legislature and have been "taxable citizens," "white male taxable citizens," "male taxable citizens," "taxable inhabitants" and "qualified electors."

* * *

Without feeling called upon to determine what other matters the word "heretofore" in the Constitution of 1873 refers to, we do say that when that instrument was adopted the uniform method of selecting jurors and determining their qualification was by legislation, both here and in England. This was known to the framers of the first and all succeeding Constitutions, in the first being specifically recognized, and, in guaranteeing the right of trial by jury, it and all the others did not in any way limit the legislature from determining from time to time how juries should be composed.

We have then the Act of 1867, constitutionally providing that the jury commissioners are required to select "from the *whole qualified electors* of the respective county * * * persons to serve as jurors in the several courts of such county," and the 19th Amendment to the federal Constitution putting women in the body of electors. "The term 'elector' is a technical, generic term, descriptive of a citizen having constitutional and statutory qualifications that enable him to vote, and including not only those who vote, but also those who are qualified yet fail to exercise the right of franchise": 20 Corpus Juris 58. If the Act of 1867 is prospective in operation, and takes in new classes of electors as they come to the voting privilege from time to time, then necessarily women being electors are eligible to jury service. That the Act of 1867 does cover those who at any time shall come within the designation of electors there can be no question. "Statutes framed in general terms apply to new cases that arise, and to new subjects that are created from time to time, and which come within their general scope and policy. It is a rule of statutory construction that legislative enactments in general and comprehensive terms, prospective in operation, apply alike to all persons, subjects and business within their general purview and scope coming into existence subsequent to their passage": 25 Ruling Case Law 778.

Summing up, we conclude, (1) there was no absolute and fixed qualification of jurors at common law, and from very ancient times their qualifications were fixed by act of parliament; (2) the qualification of jurors was not the thing spoken of by the section of the Constitution under consideration; (3) the words "as heretofore" in that section refer to the kinds of cases triable before juries and the trial, not the qualifications of the jurors; (4) the designation "qualified elector" embraces all electors at the time jurors are selected from the body of electors; (5) the term "electors" embraces those who may be added to the electorate from time to time.

* * *

The pending case calls for the immediate decision only of the right of women to serve as jurors in those counties which are covered by the Act of 1867. We entertain no doubt, however, that women are eligible to serve as jurors in all the Commonwealth's courts.

The order quashing the indictment is reversed, and the indictment is reinstated with direction to the court below to proceed with the trial of the defendants in due course.

PROBLEMS UNDER THE ACT OF 1885 ON FOREIGN CONTRACT LABOR

The text of the Act of 1885, whose interpretation is in issue in the case of Holy Trinity Church v. United States, supra p. 349, is set out in full below exactly as it appears in the United States Statutes at Large at 23 Stat. 332.

To begin with, read the statute in its entirety with care. Then, considering the text of the statute, and such light as the Holy Trinity opinion provides, try to arrive at a preliminary definition of the problem or "evil" to which the statute is addressed. Then, analyze the manner in which the statute deals with this problem or "evil."

When you have completed this general examination of the statute, tackle the problems which follow it. In connection with each problem, formulate the statutory issue or issues (if any) raised thereby and your answer as to how any such issues should be resolved under the statute and why. If you think there is no substantial issue, be ready to justify your conclusion. Throughout your work on these problems, keep in mind some more general critical questions as to whether Congress did the right thing in seeking to resolve by legislation the "evils" here attacked and as to whether—assuming Congressional legislation was needed—Congress legislated soundly.

February 26, 1885. **CHAP. 164.**—An act to prohibit the importation and migration of foreigners and aliens under contract or agreement to perform labor in the United States, its Territories, and the District of Columbia.

Be it enacted by the Senate and House of Representatives of the United States of America in Congress assembled, That from and after the passage of this act it shall be unlawful for any person, company, partnership, or corporation, in any manner whatsoever, to prepay the transportation, or in any way assist or encourage the importation or migration of any alien or aliens, any foreigner or foreigners, into the United States, its Territories, or the District of Columbia, under contract or agreement, parol or special, express or implied, made previous to the importation or migration of such alien or aliens, foreigner or foreigners, to perform labor or service of any kind in the United States, its Territories, or the District of Columbia.

Prepayment for transportation of, or assisting foreign emigrants under contract for labor or service made previous to emigration, unlawful.

SEC. 2. That all contracts or agreements, express or implied, parol or special, which may hereafter be made by and between any person, company, partnership, or corporation, and any foreigner or foreigners, alien or aliens, to perform labor or service or having reference to the performance of labor or service by any person in the United States, its Territories, or the District of Columbia previous to the migration or importation of the person or persons whose labor or service is contracted for into the United States, shall be utterly void and of no effect.

Such contracts void.

SEC. 3. That for every violation of any of the provisions of section one of this act the person, partnership, company, or corporation violating the same, by knowingly assisting, encouraging or soliciting the migration or importation of any alien or aliens, foreigner or foreigners, into the United States, its Territories, or the District of Columbia, to perform labor or service of any kind under contract or agreement, express or implied, parol or special, with such alien or aliens, foreigner or foreigners, previous to becoming residents or citizens of the United States, shall forfeit and pay for every such offence the sum of one thousand dollars, which may be sued for and recovered by the United States or by any person who shall first bring his action therefor including any such alien or foreigner who may be a party to any such contract or agreement, as debts of like amount are now recovered in the circuit courts of the United States; the proceeds to be paid into the Treasury of the United States; and separate suits may be brought for each alien or foreigner being a party to such contract or agreement aforesaid. And it shall be the duty of the district attorney of the proper district to prosecute every such suit at the expense of the United States.

Penalty for violation of first section, fine; how recovered.

SEC. 4. That the master of any vessel who shall knowingly bring within the United States on any such vessel, and land, or permit to be landed, from any foreign port or place, any alien laborer, mechanic, or artisan who, previous to embarkation on such vessel, had entered into contract or agreement, parol or special, express or implied, to perform labor or service in the United States, shall be deemed guilty of a misdemeanor, and on conviction thereof, shall be punished by a fine of not more than five hundred dollars for each and every such alien laborer, mechanic or artisan so brought as aforesaid, and may also be imprisoned for a term not exceeding six months.

Master of vessel, knowingly bringing such emigrant laborer, guilty of misdemeanor, punishable by fine or imprisonment.

Sec. 4   THE INTENTION OF THE LEGISLATURE   385

Foreigners temporarily residing in the United States may engage other foreigners as private secretaries, servants, etc.
Skilled workman in foreign countries may be engaged to perform labor in any new industry not established in the United States.
Proviso.
Artists, lecturers, servants, etc., excepted.
Proviso, as to assisting relatives and friends.
Laws conflicting herewith, repealed.

SEC. 5. That nothing in this act shall be so construed as to prevent any citizen or subject of any foreign country temporarily residing in the United States, either in private or official capacity, from engaging, under contract or otherwise, persons not residents or citizens of the United States to act as private secretaries, servants, or domestics for such foreigner temporarily residing in the United States as aforesaid; nor shall this act be so construed as to prevent any person, or persons, partnership, or corporation from engaging, under contract or agreement, skilled workman in foreign countries to perform labor in the United States in or upon any new industry not at present established in the United States: *Provided,* That skilled labor for that purpose cannot be otherwise obtained; nor shall the provisions of this act apply to professional actors, artists, lecturers, or singers, nor to persons employed strictly as personal or domestic servants: *Provided,* That nothing in this act shall be construed as prohibiting any individual from assisting any member of his family or any relative or personal friend, to migrate from any foreign country to the United States, for the purpose of settlement here.

SEC. 6. That all laws or parts of laws conflicting herewith be, and the same are hereby, repealed.

Approved, February 26, 1885.   [C980]

1. The Great Atlantic R. R. Co. was building a railroad line along the Atlantic coast at the time of adoption of the Act of 1885. Prior to the passage of the Act, Great Atlantic had been recruiting labor in Europe, specifically for this enterprise. In particular, it had entered, through a European agent, into contracts with numbers of Italian workingmen whereby such workingmen were transported to the U.S.A. at Great Atlantic's expense (the fare to be repaid later out of wages) under agreement that they would do railroad construction work for Great Atlantic for 3 years at 60 cents per day, 10 hours a day, six days a week, with shelter and a stipulated quantity of food to be furnished by the employer. This arrangement was very important to Great Atlantic (which might otherwise have had to pay American workers at least $1.25 per day) in keeping down costs and in assuring eventual profits. Assume you are an attorney practicing law in New York City in March 1885. Great Atlantic seeks your legal advice as to whether further recourse to its past labor-recruiting arrangements, as described, would be illegal under the new 1885 Act.

2. What impact did the Act of 1885 have upon the situation of workmen who as of its effective date were already under contract and in various stages of processing under Great Atlantic's recruiting scheme (see Problem 1, supra), including

   (a) workmen who had not yet left Italy for the U.S.A.

   (b) workmen already aboard ship who had not yet landed in the U.S.A.

   (c) workmen who had landed in the U.S.A. but had not yet begun railroad work.

3. The time is some six months after adoption of the 1885 Act. Your legal advice is sought by Mr. Job Jellicoe, a British subject, who

is a skilled goldbeater (N.B. that goldbeating is a process required for the manufacture of gold leaf or gold foil). Mr. Jellicoe is working at his specialty in New York for the New York firm of Grabber & Co. He brings you for perusal the contract he signed in London in March, 1885, under which he journeyed to the United States in April and commenced work here in May 1885. Since this time, having made the acquaintance of others pursuing the same trade in the U.S.A., he has discovered that his pay is considerably lower than that of his American counterparts for equivalent work. He asks your advice regarding the effect of the new 1885 legislation upon his status and regarding any consequent possibility of his leaving his present employment to work at higher pay for one of Grabber's competitors. Here is the text of the Grabber-Jellicoe contract:

>Messrs. Grabber & Co. of New York City, U.S.A. and Mr. Job Jellicoe of London, England, agree as follows:
>
>Grabber & Co. agrees to employ Job Jellicoe at goldbeating for one year and to pay him the sum of not less than $10.00 for each week's work of sixty hours during that time.
>
>Job Jellicoe agrees to work for Grabber & Co. for the sum and time named and he further agrees not to associate himself with or in any manner assist any society or combination of men to regulate the rate of wages or manner of conducting the said trade of goldbeating.
>
>Grabber & Co. agrees to pay the passage of Job Jellicoe from London to New York and Job Jellicoe agrees to repay it at not less than one dollar per week.
>
>Date: March 15, 1885
>
>   Signed: Grabber & Co.
>   Job Jellicoe

4. The Titanic Coal and Iron Corporation was known to be seeking cheaper labor for its mines and foundries late in 1885. It was approached at that time by Magyar Manpower Co., a firm based in Washington, D.C., which had been importing Hungarian men and women for labor in the United States. Titanic was advised by Magyar that, upon being informed of Titanic's manpower requirements, Magyar for a fee (covering transportation costs and a commission) would import and supply the necessary number of willing and ablebodied Hungarian laborers to fill Titanic's stated need. This was conditioned on Titanic's promising Magyar to employ the said laborers for at least 2 years at specified minimum wages (very low), the employment to be carried out under individual contracts to be executed with the laborers, and to be effective, immediately following their arrival. Magyar planned to recruit the needed laborers in Hungary with promises of free passage and of 2 years' gainful labor at not less than the stated minimum wages in the U.S.A., without any commit-

Sec. 4   THE INTENTION OF THE LEGISLATURE   387

ment as to the identity of the ultimate employer or as to the exact nature of the ultimate employment. Titanic seeks legal advice from you as to whether it would be violating the Act of 1885 if it cooperated with Magyar in the scheme just outlined.

5. Suppose Great Atlantic abandons its original arrangements described in Problem 1, supra, and resorts instead to publishing, in Italian newspapers, promises of 3-year employment (at the indicated low rates) to all able and willing workers who come to the U.S.A. and apply and who meet the company's standards. Suppose further that a number of workers, having borrowed or scraped together just enough funds to cover the trans-Atlantic fare, journey to the U.S. on the strength of such promises and that some are then hired by Great Atlantic and some are not. Does this mode of operation violate the Act of 1885? What legal advice would you give to Great Atlantic?

6. The Society of Happy Hibernians (an association of workingmen of Irish extraction engaged in construction trades) had a program, begun in 1884, whereby each year it prearranged a contract of U.S. employment and prepaid trans-Atlantic transportation for a needy Irish worker (usually the relative or friend of some Society member) and his family. Costs of this program were paid from assessments levied on the membership and from interest on the Society's invested funds. Would you have advised the Society that this program was legally permissible under the Act of 1885?

7. Suppose that Mr. Job Jellicoe of Problem 3, supra, after having been brought to the U.S.A. by Grabber pursuant to their contract, had been fired after 7 months due to a decline in Grabber's business and its consequent need to economize. What recourse would Jellicoe normally have had and what is the impact of the Act's terms on him in this situation?

8. Suppose that Job Jellicoe, after he and Grabber had signed the contract in Problem 3, supra, and his passage had been paid for, fell ill and was unable to travel to the U.S.A. as contemplated. Would Grabber nonetheless be subject to the penalties of § 3 at the suit of the U.S. District Attorney? In resolving this issue what weight should be given, and why, to the following remarks appearing in the Congressional Record at 16 Cong.Rec. 1628–1629 (1885) in the course of Congressional debates on the bill which later became the Act of 1885:

> Senator Blair (who was the Senator in charge of the bill and Chairman of the standing committee which considered it): * * * "It is the bringing to this country of the immigrant that is prohibited in the first section, not merely the making of the contract. The crime is consummated by the actual arrival."

* * *

388   THE INTERPRETATION OF STATUTES   Ch. 5

Senator Hoar: * * * "If the alien is not imported, I agree with the Senator the offense is not complete; * * *."

9. Suppose that Grabber's contract had been drawn to encompass the transportation and services of ten named English goldbeaters (including Job Jellicoe), all of whom had affixed their signatures thereto and had been transported to the U.S.A. If the statute were violated thereby, to what exact penalty, if any, would Grabber have been subject?

10. A plant began operations in Maine in 1884 to meet a rising demand for plush for use on the seats of railroad cars. The work was somewhat specialized and there were a number of well qualified workmen in Belgium and France who had gained experience with the tasks involved. Some of these had been imported for work, and were employed, in the Maine plant before 1885. A Connecticut entrepreneur planned to set up a Connecticut plush-making plant in 1886 to compete with the Maine firm which had hitherto been the only domestic U. S. manufacturer in this field. Advise him as to whether, under the 1885 Act, he could import Belgian and French workers for his projected enterprise.

11. Consider the facts of the *Holy Trinity* case. Under the Act of 1885, was the master of the trans-Atlantic vessel which transported the Reverend Warren from England subject to criminal prosecution for having thus brought Mr. Warren to the U.S.A. to fulfill the latter's contract with the Holy Trinity Church Corporation—assuming the master knew of the Warren-Holy Trinity contract?

SECTION 5. INTERPRETATION ACCORDING TO THE LETTER OF THE STATUTE—THE PLAIN MEANING RULE

INTRODUCTORY NOTE

The traditional judicial formula for the resolution of doubts as to the meaning or legal effect of statutes is that the courts are bound to discover and apply "the intention of the legislature." Analysis of the cases in the preceding Section has made it clear enough that the phrase, "legislative intention," when used in a judicial opinion, may have reference either to a *specific intent* of the members of the lawmaking body or to the *purpose* that the legislature sought to achieve by the statute's enactment. The cases in the preceding Section have also presented a cross-section of the legislative history sources and other "extrinsic aids" on which a lawyer or judge may draw in arriving at "legislative intention" either in the sense of a specific intent or in the sense of purpose.

Sec. 5 THE PLAIN MEANING RULE

But the "legislative intention" approach has not been the only significant interpretative approach in our law. In earlier years, the courts had frequent recourse to another significant doctrine most often referred to as the Plain Meaning Rule. Even now the language of "plain meaning" crops up in the opinions of courts and agencies and in the discourse of lawyers. When cases have been disposed of by the courts on a "plain meaning" basis, the judicial opinions in such cases have sometimes (especially in older cases) been entirely barren of any reference at all to the understanding or purpose of the enacting legislature. The function and effect of the Plain Meaning Rule are suggested by the following two judicial statements, which have been cited innumerable times in later cases as authority for the Plain Meaning Rule:

"The general rule is perfectly well settled that, where a statute is of doubtful meaning and susceptible upon its face of two constructions, the court may look into prior and contemporaneous acts, the reasons which induced the act in question, the mischiefs intended to be remedied, the extraneous circumstances, and the purpose intended to be accomplished by it, to determine its proper construction. But where the act is clear upon its face, and when standing alone it is fairly susceptible of but one construction, that construction must be given to it. * * * The whole doctrine applicable to the subject may be summed up in the single observation that prior acts may be referred to to *solve* but not to *create* an ambiguity." Brown, J. in Hamilton v. Rathbone, 175 U.S. 414, 421, 20 S.Ct. 155, 44 L.Ed. 219 (1899).

"Where words conflict with each other, where the different clauses of an instrument bear upon each other, and would be inconsistent unless the natural and common import of words be varied, construction becomes necessary, and a departure from the obvious meaning of words is justifiable. But if, in any case, the plain meaning of a provision, not contradicted by any other provision in the same instrument, is to be disregarded, because we believe the framers of that instrument could not intend what they say, it must be one in which the absurdity and injustice of applying the provision to the case would be so monstrous that all mankind would, without hesitation, unite in rejecting the application." Marshall, Ch. J., in Sturges v. Crowninshield, 4 Wheat. 122, 202, 4 L.Ed. 529, 550 (1819).

TEMPLE v. CITY OF PETERSBURG

Supreme Court of Appeals of Virginia, 1944.
182 Va. 418, 29 S.E.2d 357.

Appeal from Hustings Court of City of Petersburg.

GREGORY, Justice. The appellants, who were the complainants in the court below, filed their bill in equity against the city of Petersburg, praying that it be restrained and enjoined from using a tract of 1.01 acres of land acquired by it in 1942 for cemetery purposes. This plot of land adjoined Peoples Memorial Cemetery, which had been established and used as a cemetery for more than one hundred years.

The court below temporarily restrained the city from using the 1.01-acre tract as an addition to the cemetery. Later the city filed its answer to the bill and, by consent, the cause was set for hearing upon the bill, the answer, and a stipulation of counsel. The court dissolved the injunction and refused the prayer for relief.

Code, sec. 56 (Michie 1942), provides in part as follows:

"No cemetery shall be hereafter established within the corporate limits of any city or town; nor shall any cemetery be established within two hundred and fifty yards of any residence without the consent of the owner of the legal and equitable title of such residence; * * * ."

We are called upon to ascertain the proper meaning of the statute, and to decide whether or not it has been violated by the city. Specifically the controversy concerns the meaning to be given to the word, "established", used therein. The appellants maintain that under the statute the enlargement of an existing cemetery, such as is sought here, in reality is the establishment of a cemetery, while the appellee contends that to enlarge an existing cemetery is not the establishment of a cemetery and, therefore, constitutes no violation of the statute.

In 1916, John D. Temple, the predecessor in title of the appellants, acquired lot number 169 in the city of Petersburg, and erected a residence thereon. In 1917 he acquired the adjoining lot, number 168. Upon his death, intestate, in 1921, this real estate descended to the appellants, who have maintained a residence thereon since that time. The residence faces St. Andrews street, and is bounded on one side by Talliaferro street.

At the time that John D. Temple erected his residence, Peoples Memorial Cemetery was already established on a tract of eight acres, a portion of which extended to within 80 feet of his residence. Between the residence and the cemetery there is Taliaferro street, which is 30 feet wide, and a vacant strip of land belonging to the city of Petersburg, 50 feet in width. Upon this vacant strip of land there are a number of graves, the nearest of which is 74 feet east of the residence.

The cemetery tract on one side adjoined Crater road. It became necessary for the city to widen and improve Crater road. In order to do so, a strip of the cemetery property was required to be taken by the exercise of eminent domain. Many bodies had been interred upon this strip, and it is necessary to exhume them in order to complete the improvement of the road. The city, desiring to provide a proper place to re-inter these bodies, acquired the tract of 1.01 acres of land on the south side of St. Andrews street adjoining the cemetery tract. The 1.01-acre tract so acquired lies directly across St. Andrews street in front of the appellants' residence, and 70 feet distant therefrom at the nearest point. It is the plan of the city of Petersburg to re-inter the bodies in this proposed addition to the cemetery. Afterwards, the city plans to convey the said tract to trustees to be appointed by the Hustings Court of the city in order that it may be incorporated in the Peoples Memorial Cemetery and be made an integral part thereof.

The principal and determinative issue to be determined in this cause is whether or not the proposed enlargement of Peoples Memorial Cemetery, by the additional 1.01-acre tract, is prohibited by section 56 of the Code.

The appellants most strongly contend that the word, "established", as used in the statute, means "located", and that the evil intended to be inhibited is the location of a cemetery in a city or town upon ground not previously dedicated for cemetery purposes, or the location of a cemetery within 250 yards of a residence, whether by enlargement or otherwise. They contend that the purpose of the statute is to protect residences and lands from the ill effects growing out of close proximity to a cemetery. They further contend that it is unreasonable to say that residences and lands are to be protected against the "establishment" of cemeteries, but are not to be protected against the encroachment or enlargement of existing cemeteries; that the evil created by one is equally as real as that created by the other.

The position of the appellee is that the word "established", has such a clear and precise meaning that no question of statutory construction arises. That the statute provides that no cemetery shall be "hereafter established" in a city or town, and that this language does not mean that a cemetery already established shall not be hereafter enlarged. To hold otherwise would be not to construe the statute, but in effect, to amend it.

It is elementary that the ultimate aim of rules of interpretation is to ascertain the intention of the legislature in the enactment of a statute, and that intention, when discovered, must prevail. If, however, the intention of the legislature is perfectly clear from the language used, rules of construction are not to be applied. We are not allowed to construe that which has no need of construction.

If the language of a statute is plain and unambiguous, and its meaning perfectly clear and definite, effect must be given to it regardless of what courts think of its wisdom or policy. In such cases courts must find the meaning within the statute itself. * * *

In Commonwealth v. Sanderson, 170 Va. 33, 195 S.E. 516, 519, we quoted with approval from Saville v. Virginia Ry. and Power Co., 114 Va. 444, 76 S.E. 954, 957, this statement of the rule:

" 'It is contended that the construction insisted upon by the plaintiff in error is violative of the spirit or reason of the law. The argument would seem to concede that the contention is within the letter of the law. We hear a great deal about the spirit of the law, but the duty of this court is not to make law, but to construe it; not to wrest its letter from its plain meaning in order to conform to what is conceived to be its spirit, in order to subserve, and promote some principle of justice and equality which it is claimed the letter of the law has violated. It is our duty to take the words which the legislature has seen fit to employ and give to them their usual and ordinary signification, and, having thus ascertained the legislative intent, to give effect to it, unless it transcends the legislative power as limited by the Constitution.' "

* * *

The word "established" is defined in Webster's New International Dictionary, 2d Ed., 1936, thus: "To originate and secure the permanent existence of; to found; to institute; to create and regulate;—said of a colony, a State or other institutions."

Just why the Legislature, in its wisdom, saw fit to prohibit the establishment of cemeteries in cities and towns, and did not see fit to prohibit enlargements or additions, is no concern of ours. Certain it is that language could not be plainer than that employed to express the legislative will. From it we can see with certainty that while a cemetery may not be established in a city or town, it may be added to or enlarged without running counter to the inhibition found in section 56. We are not permitted to read into the statute an inhibition which the Legislature, perhaps advisedly, omitted. Our duty is to construe the statute as written.

If construction of the statute were necessary and proper in this case, we would be forced to the same conclusion. Even if it be assumed that there is ambiguity in the language in section 56, the legislative history of its enactment and a consideration of Code, sec. 53, a related statute, would remove all doubt as to what the legislature intended by its language in section 56.

Code, sec. 53, affords a complete answer to the question of legislative intent in the use of the word "established" in section 56, for the former section makes a distinction between "establish" and "enlarge" in these words: "If it be desired at any time to establish a cemetery, for the use of a city, town, county, or magisterial district, or to enlarge any such already established, and the title to land needed cannot be otherwise acquired, land sufficient for the purpose may be condemned. * * *"

The foregoing language, taken from section 53, completely demonstrates that the Legislature did not intend the words "establish" and "enlarge" to be used interchangeably, but that the use of one excluded any idea that it embraced or meant the other. As used, they are mutually exclusive. To enlarge or add to a cemetery is not to establish one within the meaning of section 56.

The language of the statute being so plain and unambiguous, and the intention and meaning of the Legislature so clear, we hold that the city of Petersburg has not violated Code, Sec. 56, and the decree accordingly should be affirmed.

Affirmed.

NOTES

1. Do you agree that "language could not be plainer" than that employed in this statute "to express the legislative will"? Is it plain because the Court is satisfied that it knows the "legislative will"? Or, is the Court satisfied that it knows the legislative will because the language of the statute is "plain"? See Jones, The Plain Meaning Rule and Extrinsic Aids in the Interpretation of Federal Statutes, 25 Wash.U.L.Q. 2 (1939); Nutting, The Ambiguity of Unambiguous Statutes, 24 Minn.L.Rev. 509 (1940).

2. On what ground is the separate section 53 of the Code relevant to the interpretation of the provision in issue in the principal case? Must it be, as the Court said it was, a "related statute"? Assuming that it is relevant, do you agree that it "completely demonstrates" the legislative intention? If so, how?

CAMINETTI v. UNITED STATES

Supreme Court of the United States, 1917.
242 U.S. 470, 37 S.Ct. 192, 61 L.Ed. 442.

Error to the United States Circuit Court of Appeals for the Ninth Circuit.

Mr. Justice DAY delivered the opinion of the court.

These three cases were argued together, and may be disposed of in a single opinion. In each of the cases there was a conviction and sentence for violation of the so-called White Slave Traffic Act of June 25, 1910, 36 Stat. 825, the judgments were affirmed by the Circuit Courts of Appeals, and writs of certiorari bring the cases here.

In the Caminetti case, the petitioner was indicted in the United States District Court for the Northern District of California, upon the sixth day of May, 1913, for alleged violations of the act. The indictment was in four counts, the first of which charged him with transporting and causing to be transported and aiding and assisting in obtaining transportation for a certain woman from Sacramento,

California, to Reno, Nevada, in interstate commerce for the purpose of debauchery, and for an immoral purpose, to wit, that the aforesaid woman should be and become his mistress and concubine. A verdict of not guilty was returned as to the other three counts of this indictment. As to the first count defendant was found guilty and sentenced to imprisonment for eighteen months and to pay a fine of $1,500.00. Upon writ of error to the United States Circuit Court of Appeals for the Ninth Circuit, that judgment was affirmed. 220 F. 545. [The facts of the other two cases are omitted. Section 2 of the Act is printed in the margin.[16]]

It is contended that the act of Congress is intended to reach only "commercialized vice," or the traffic in women for gain, and that the conduct for which the several petitioners were indicted and convicted, however reprehensible in morals, is not within the purview of the statute when properly construed in the light of its history and the purposes intended to be accomplished by its enactment. In none of the cases was it charged or proved that the transportation was for gain or for the purpose of furnishing women for prostitution for hire, and it is insisted that, such being the case, the acts charged and proved, upon which conviction was had, do not come within the statute.

It is elementary that the meaning of a statute must, in the first instance, be sought in the language in which the act is framed, and if that is plain, and if the law is within the constitutional authority of the law-making body which passed it, the sole function of the courts is to enforce it according to its terms. [Citing cases.]

Where the language is plain and admits of no more than one meaning the duty of interpretation does not arise and the rules which are to aid doubtful meanings need no discussion. Hamilton v. Rath-

16. ["Sec. 2. That any person who shall knowingly transport or cause to be transported, or aid or assist in obtaining transportation for, or in transporting, in interstate or foreign commerce, or in any Territory or in the District of Columbia, any woman or girl for the purpose of prostitution or debauchery, or for any other immoral purpose, or with the intent and purpose to induce, entice, or compel such woman or girl to become a prostitute or to give herself up to debauchery, or to engage in any other immoral practice; or who shall knowingly procure or obtain, or cause to be procured or obtained, or aid or assist in procuring or obtaining, any ticket or tickets, or any form of transportation or evidence of the right thereto, to be used by any woman or girl in interstate or foreign commerce, or in any Territory or the District of Columbia, in going to any place for the purpose of prostitution or debauchery, or for any other immoral purpose, or with the intent or purpose on the part of such person to induce, entice, or compel her to give herself up to the practice of prostitution, or to give herself up to debauchery, or any other immoral practice, whereby any such woman or girl shall be transported in interstate or foreign commerce, or in any Territory or the District of Columbia, shall be deemed guilty of a felony, and upon conviction thereof shall be punished by a fine not exceeding five thousand dollars, or by imprisonment of not more than five years, or by both such fine and imprisonment, in the discretion of the court."—Ed.]

bone, 175 U.S. 414, 421, 20 S.Ct. 155, 44 L.Ed. 219. There is no ambiguity in the terms of this act. It is specifically made an offense to knowingly transport or cause to be transported, etc., in interstate commerce, any woman or girl for the purpose of prostitution or debauchery, or for "any other immoral purpose," or with the intent and purpose to induce any such woman or girl to become a prostitute or to give herself up to debauchery, or to engage in any other immoral practice.

Statutory words are uniformly presumed, unless the contrary appears, to be used in their ordinary and usual sense, and with the meaning commonly attributed to them. To cause a woman or girl to be transported for the purposes of debauchery, and for an immoral purpose, to-wit, becoming a concubine or mistress, for which Caminetti and Diggs were convicted; or to transport an unmarried woman, under eighteen years of age, with the intent to induce her to engage in prostitution, debauchery and other immoral practices, for which Hays was convicted, would seem by the very statement of the facts to embrace transportation for purposes denounced by the act, and therefore fairly within its meaning.

While such immoral purpose would be more culpable in morals and attributed to baser motives if accompanied with the expectation of pecuniary gain, such considerations do not prevent the lesser offense against morals of furnishing transportation in order that a woman may be debauched, or become a mistress or a concubine from being the execution of purposes within the meaning of this law. To say the contrary would shock the common understanding of what constitutes an immoral purpose when those terms are applied, as here, to sexual relations.

* * *

But it is contended that though the words are so plain that they cannot be misapprehended when given their usual and ordinary interpretation, and although the sections in which they appear do not in terms limit the offense defined and punished to acts of "commercialized vice," or the furnishing or procuring of transportation of women for debauchery, prostitution or immoral practices for hire, such limited purpose is to be attributed to Congress and engrafted upon the act in view of the language of § 8 and the report which accompanied the law upon its introduction into and subsequent passage by the House of Representatives.

In this connection, it may be observed that while the title of an act cannot overcome the meaning of plain and unambiguous words used in its body [citing cases], the title of this act embraces the regulation of interstate commerce "by prohibiting the transportation therein for immoral purposes of women and girls, and for other purposes." It is true that § 8 of the act provides that it shall be known and referred to as the "White-slave traffic Act," and the report accompanying the introduction of the same into the House of Representatives set forth the fact that a material portion of the legislation suggested was to meet conditions which had arisen in the past few years, and that the legislation was needed to put a stop to a villainous interstate and international traffic in women and girls. Still, the name given to an act by way of designation or description, or the report which accompanies it, cannot change the plain import of its words. If the words are plain, they give meaning to the act, and it is neither the duty nor the privilege of the courts to enter speculative fields in search of a different meaning.

Reports to Congress accompanying the introduction of proposed laws may aid the courts in reaching the true meaning of the legislature in cases of doubtful interpretation [citing cases]. But, as we have already said, and it has been so often affirmed as to become a recognized rule, when words are free from doubt they must be taken as the final expression of the legislative intent, and are not to be added to or subtracted from by considerations drawn from titles or designating names or reports accompanying their introduction, or from any extraneous source. In other words, the language being plain, and not leading to absurd or wholly impracticable consequences, it is the sole evidence of the ultimate legislative intent. See Mackenzie v. Hare, 239 U.S. 299, 308, 36 S.Ct. 106, 60 L.Ed. 297.

* * *

The judgment in each of the cases is

Affirmed.

Mr. Justice McREYNOLDS took no part in the consideration or decision of these cases.

Mr. Justice McKENNA, with whom concurred the Chief Justice [WHITE] and Mr. Justice CLARKE, dissenting.

Undoubtedly in the investigation of the meaning of a statute we resort first to its words, and when clear they are decisive. The principle has attractive and seemingly disposing simplicity, but that it is not easy of application or, at least, encounters other principles, many cases demonstrate. The words of a statute may be uncertain in their signification or in their application. If the words be ambiguous, the problem they present is to be resolved by their definition; the subject-matter and the lexicons become our guides. But here, even, we are not exempt from putting ourselves in the place of the legislators. If the words be clear in meaning but the objects to which they are addressed be uncertain, the problem then is to determine the uncertainty. And for this a realization of conditions that provoked the statute must inform our judgment. Let us apply these observations to the present case.

The transportation which is made unlawful is of a woman or girl "to become a prostitute or to give herself up to debauchery, or to engage in any other immoral practice." Our present concern is with the words "any other immoral practice," which, it is asserted, have a special office. The words are clear enough as general descriptions; they fail in particular designation; they are class words, not specifications. Are they controlled by those which precede them? If not, they are broader in generalization and include those that precede them, making them unnecessary and confusing. To what conclusion would this lead us? "Immoral" is a very comprehensive word. It means a dereliction of morals. In such sense it covers every form of vice, every form of conduct that is contrary to good order. It will hardly be contended that in this sweeping sense it is used in the statute. But if not used in such sense to what is it limited and by what limited? If it be admitted that it is limited at all, that ends the imperative effect assigned to it in the opinion of the court. But not insisting quite on that, we ask again, By what is it limited? By its context, necessarily, and the purpose of the statute.

For the context I must refer to the statute; of the purpose of the statute Congress itself has given us illumination. It devotes a section to the declaration that the "Act shall be known and referred to as the 'White-slave traffic Act.'" And its prominence gives it prevalence in the construction of the statute. It cannot be pushed aside or subordinated by indefinite words in other sentences, limited even there by the context. It is a peremptory rule of construction that all parts of a statute must be taken into account in ascertaining its meaning, and it cannot be said that § 8 has no object. Even if it gives only a title to the act it has especial weight. United States v. Union Pacific R. R. Co., 91 U.S. 72, 82, 23 L.Ed. 224. But it gives more than a title; it makes distinctive the purpose of the statute. The designation "White-slave traffic" has the sufficiency of an axiom. If apprehended, there is no uncertainty as to the conduct it describes. It is commercialized vice, immoralities having a mercenary purpose, and this is confirmed by other circumstances.

The author of the bill was Mr. Mann, and in reporting it from the House Committee on Interstate and Foreign Commerce he declared for the Committee that it was not the purpose of the bill to interfere with or usurp in any way the police power of the States, and further that it was not the intention of the bill to regulate prostitution or the places where prostitution or immorality was practiced, which were said to be matters wholly within the power of the States and over which the federal government had no jurisdiction. And further explaining the bill, it was said that the sections of the act had been "so drawn that they are limited to cases in which there is the act of transportation in interstate commerce of women for purposes of prostitution." And again:

"The White Slave Trade. A material portion of the legislation suggested and proposed is necessary to meet conditions which have arisen within the past few years. The legislation is needed to put a stop to a villainous interstate and international traffic in women and girls. The legislation is not needed or intended as an aid to the States in the exercise of their police powers in the suppression or regulation of immorality in general. It does not attempt to regulate the practice of voluntary prostitution, but aims solely to prevent panderers and procurers from compelling thousands of women and girls against their will and desire to enter and continue in a life of prostitution." House Report No. 47, 61st Cong., 2d sess., pp. 9, 10.

In other words, it is vice as a business at which the law is directed, using interstate commerce as a facility to procure or distribute its victims.

In 1912 the sense of the Department of Justice was taken of the act in a case where a woman of 24 years went from Illinois, where she lived, to Minnesota at the solicitation and expense of a man. She was there met by him and engaged with him in immoral practices like those for which petitioners were convicted. The district attorney forwarded her statement to the Attorney General, with the comment that the element of traffic was absent from the transaction and that therefore, in his opinion, it was not "within the spirit and intent of the Mann Act." Replying, the Attorney General expressed his concurrence in the view of his subordinate.

Of course, neither the declarations of the report of the Committee on Interstate Commerce of the House nor the opinion of the Attorney General are conclusive of the meaning of the law, but they are highly persuasive. * * *

* * *

CHUNG FOOK v. WHITE

Supreme Court of the United States, 1924.
264 U.S. 443, 44 S.Ct. 361, 68 L.Ed. 781.

Certiorari to a judgment of the Circuit Court of Appeals which affirmed a judgment of the District Court denying a petition for a writ of *habeas corpus*.

Mr. Justice SUTHERLAND delivered the opinion of the Court.

Chung Fook is a native-born citizen of the United States. Lee Shee, his wife, is an alien Chinese woman, ineligible for naturalization. In 1922 she sought admission to the United States, but was refused and detained at the immigration station, on the ground that she was an alien, afflicted with a dangerous contagious disease. No question is raised as to her alienage or the effect and character of her disease; but the contention is that nevertheless, she is entitled to admission under the proviso found in § 22 of the Immigration Act of February 5, 1917, c. 29, 39 Stat. 891. The section is copied in the margin.[17] A petition for a writ of *habeas corpus* was denied by the

---

17. "Sec. 22. That whenever an alien shall have been naturalized, or shall have taken up his permanent residence in this country, and thereafter

Federal District Court for the Northern District of California, and upon appeal to the Circuit Court of Appeals, the judgment was affirmed. 287 F. 533.

The pertinent words of the proviso are: "That if the person sending for wife or minor children is naturalized, a wife to whom married or a minor child born subsequent to such husband or father's naturalization shall be admitted without detention for treatment in hospital, * * *" The measure of the exemption is plainly stated and, in terms, extends to the wife of a naturalized citizen only.

But it is argued that it cannot be supposed that Congress intended to accord to a naturalized citizen a right and preference beyond that enjoyed by a native-born citizen. The court below thought that the exemption from detention was meant to relate only to a wife who by marriage had acquired her husband's citizenship, and not to one who, notwithstanding she was married to a citizen, remained an alien under § 1994, Rev.Stats.: "Any woman who is now or may hereafter be married to a citizen of the United States, and who might herself be lawfully naturalized, shall be deemed a citizen." To the same effect, see Ex parte Leong Shee, 275 F. 364. We are inclined to agree with this view; but, in any event, the statute plainly relates only to the wife or children of a naturalized citizen and we cannot interpolate the words "native-born citizen" without usurping the legislative function. Corona Coal Co. v. United States, 263 U.S. 537, 44 S.Ct. 156, 68 L.Ed. 431; United States v. First National Bank, 234 U.S. 245, 259–260, 34 S.Ct. 846, 58 L.Ed. 1298; St. Louis, Iron Mountain & Southern Ry. Co. v. Taylor, 210 U.S. 281, 295, 28 S.Ct. 616, 52 L. Ed. 1061; Amy v. Watertown, 130 U.S. 320, 327, 9 S.Ct. 537, 32 L. Ed. 953. The words of the statute being clear, if it unjustly discriminates against the native-born citizen, or is cruel and inhuman in its results, as forcefully contended, the remedy lies with Congress and

shall send for his wife or minor children to join him, and said wife or any of said minor children shall be found to be affected with any contagious disorder, such wife or minor children shall be held, under such regulations as the Secretary of Labor shall prescribe, until it shall be determined whether the disorder will be easily curable or whether they can be permitted to land without danger to other persons; and they shall not be either admitted or deported until such facts have been ascertained; and if it shall be determined that the disorder is easily curable and the husband or father or other responsible person is willing to bear the expense of the treatment, they may be accorded treatment in hospital until cured and then be admitted, or if it shall be determined that they can be permitted to land without danger to other persons, they may, if otherwise admissible, thereupon be admitted: *Provided*, that if the person sending for wife or minor children is naturalized, a wife to whom married or a minor child born subsequent to such husband or father's naturalization shall be admitted without detention for treatment in hospital, and with respect to a wife to whom married or a minor child born prior to such husband or father's naturalization the provisions of this section shall be observed, even though such person is unable to pay the expense of treatment, in which case the expense shall be paid from the appropriation for the enforcement of this Act."

not with the courts. Their duty is simply to enforce the law as it is written, unless clearly unconstitutional.

Affirmed.

NOTES

1. In Iselin v. United States, 270 U.S. 245, 46 S.Ct. 248, 70 L.Ed. 566 (1926), the question was whether a federal tax should be imposed upon the sale, by a "box owner," of a season's license to use her box at the Metropolitan Opera House in New York. The Government conceded that no provision of the statute provided in terms for taxing a privilege like that in this case. But it argued that Congress clearly intended to tax all sales of theatre and opera tickets; that there was no indication of intent to exempt from the tax any sale of tickets or any resale at a profit; that this general purpose of Congress should be given effect so as to reach any case within the aim of the legislation; and that the Act should consequently be extended by construction to cover this case. The Court rejected the argument, and said:

> "It may be assumed that Congress did not purpose to exempt from taxation this class of tickets. But the Act contains no provision referring to tickets of the character here involved; and there is no general provision in the Act under which classes of tickets not enumerated are subjected to a tax. Congress undertook to accomplish its purpose by dealing specifically, and in some respects differently, with different classes of tickets and with tickets of any one class under different situations. The particularization and detail with which the scope of each provision, the amount of the tax thereby imposed, and the incidence of the tax, were specified, preclude an extension of any provision by implication to any other subject. The statute was evidently drawn with care. Its language is plain and unambiguous. What the Government asks is not a construction of a statute, but, in effect, an enlargement of it by the court, so that what was omitted, presumably by inadvertence, may be included within its scope. To supply omissions transcends the judicial function."

2. Note the suggestion in the principal case that courts are bound to enforce a statute as written, notwithstanding that it may lead to "cruel and inhuman" results. In what cases so far studied in this Chapter is it held, or indicated, that a court has more leeway than this, even though the statute may have a plain meaning as respects the fact situation before the court?

A NOTE ON CERTAINTY IN STATUTES

The cases on statutory interpretation considered in the course on Legal Method deal for the most part with what might be termed the "pathology" of statutes. That is, they deal with serious difficulties and disputes arising out of legislative language.

There is real danger that a reader confronted with such materials will begin to confuse the pathological with the normal. He may conclude that grave interpretive doubts attend every effort to use statutes. But such a conclusion is far from the facts.

Thousands of questions are daily disposed of in lawyers' offices, and in the offices of government, and elsewhere, by recourse to statutory provisions. Only a fraction of the verbiage in our statute books finds its way to the courts for construction. Some of the causes of interpretive problems that do arise have been described earlier. The nature and volume of these problems vary greatly, of course, from statute to statute. But it is essential to an understanding and effective use of legislation to realize that for many, if not most, acts there is normally a substantial body of situations, an "area of no dispute," to which the terms can be applied with assurance and without difficulty.

Consider the bearing of the foregoing upon interpretation in accordance with "plain meaning". In an article entitled An Evaluation of the Rules of Statutory Interpretation, 3 Kan.L.Rev. 1 (1954), Professor Quintin Johnstone states (pp. 12–13):

> "If no statute can be perfectly plain, should the plain meaning rule be abolished? Not necessarily. Although no statute may be absolutely unambiguous, the degree of ambiguity in most statutes is very slight when applied to most situations. The degree of ambiguity is likely to be substantial only in limited peripheral sets of situations. The result is that to a large extent statutes are substantially plain, so plain that except in marginal situations it would be a ridiculous forcing of a statute to put more than one meaning on the statutory language. For purposes of interpretation, a vast area of plain meaning exists. If the term plain in the plain meaning rule is understood as plain beyond reasonable question, then the rule makes sense, although admittedly a problem arises as to what is reasonable doubt or substantial lack of ambiguity.
>
> "To deny that the plain meaning rule has any force or validity opens the door to violation of a fundamental objective in statutory interpretation. This position leads to a denial of legislative supremacy in the statutory field. Under such a view, statutes never are binding on a court as they never are clear. A court can always make whatever rule it wishes and decide cases in any way it wishes, despite statutory meanings because it cannot be restricted by statutory language."

On the basis of cases so far read, would you say that the courts are using the "plain meaning rule" only, or primarily, in cases where "it would be a ridiculous forcing * * * to put more than one meaning on the statutuory language" or where the language is "plain beyond reasonable question"? Would abolition of the "plain meaning rule" necessarily lead to a "denial of legislative supremacy in the statutory field"? If there commonly is, as suggested earlier, a substantial "area of no dispute" in the application of statutes, does the "plain meaning rule" provide a satisfactory theoretical and practical approach to the identification and disposition of cases falling in that area?

SECTION 6. THE DEVELOPMENT OF CURRENT DOCTRINE

UNITED STATES v. AMERICAN TRUCKING ASS'NS

Supreme Court of the United States, 1940.
310 U.S. 534, 60 S.Ct. 1059, 84 L.Ed. 1345.

Appeal from a decree of the District Court of three judges commanding the Interstate Commerce Commission to set aside an order by which it declined, for want of jurisdiction, to determine qualifications and maximum hours of service for all employees of contract and motor carriers subject to the Motor Carrier Act, and commanding it to take jurisdiction and proceed with such determination. The suit was brought against the United States and the Commission, under § 205(h) of the Act, by the above-named Trucking Associations and five common carriers by motor. The Administrator of the Wage and Hour Division of the Department of Labor intervened on the side of the defense.

Mr. Justice REED delivered the opinion of the Court.

This appeal requires determination of the power of the Interstate Commerce Commission under the Motor Carrier Act, 1935, to establish reasonable requirements with respect to the qualifications and maximum hours of service of employees of motor carriers, other than employees whose duties affect safety of operation.

After detailed consideration, the Motor Carrier Act, 1935, was passed. It followed generally the suggestion of form made by the Federal Coordinator of Transportation.[18] The difficulty and wide scope of the problems raised by the growth of the motor carrier industry were obvious. Congress sought to set out its purpose and the range of its action in a declaration of policy which covered the preservation and fostering of motor transportation in the public interest, tariffs, the co-ordination of motor carriage with other forms of transportation and co-operation with the several states in their efforts to systematize the industry.

---

18. S.Doc.No.152, 73rd Cong., 2d Sess., Regulation of Transportation Agencies, p. 350. See p. 25, for discussion of the preliminary steps of motor carrier regulation. Hearings on Regulation of Interstate Motor Carriers, H. R. 5262 and H.R. 6016, before the House Committee on Interstate and Foreign Commerce, 74th Cong., 1st Sess.; Hearings on S.1629, Senate Committee on Interstate Commerce, 74th Cong., 1st Sess.

Sec. 6   *DEVELOPMENT OF CURRENT DOCTRINE*   403

While efficient and economical movement in interstate commerce is obviously a major objective of the Act, there are numerous provisions which make it clear that Congress intended to exercise its powers in the non-transportation phases of motor carrier activity. Safety of operation was constantly before the committees and Congress in their study of the situation.

The pertinent portions of the section of the Act immediately under discussion read as follows:

"Sec. 204(a). It shall be the duty of the Commission—

"(1) To regulate common carriers by motor vehicle as provided in this part, and to that end the Commission may establish reasonable requirements with respect to continuous and adequate service, transportation of baggage and express, uniform systems of accounts, records, and reports, preservation of records, qualifications and maximum hours of service of employees, and safety of operation and equipment.

"(2) To regulate contract carriers by motor vehicle as provided in this part, and to that end the Commission may establish reasonable requirements with respect to uniform systems of accounts, records, and reports, preservation of records, qualifications and maximum hours of service of employees, and safety of operation and equipment.

"(3) To establish for private carriers of property by motor vehicle, if need therefor is found, reasonable requirements to promote safety of operation, and to that end prescribe qualifications and maximum hours of service of employees, and standards of equipment * * *."

Shortly after the approval of the Act, the Commission on its own motion undertook to and did fix maximum hours of service for "employees whose functions in the operation of motor vehicles make such regulations desirable because of safety considerations." A few months after this determination, the Fair Labor Standards Act was enacted. Section 7 of this act limits the work-week at the normal rate of pay of all employees subject to its terms and § 18 makes the maximum hours of the Fair Labor Standards Act subject to further reduction by applicable federal or state law or municipal ordinances. There were certain employees excepted, however, from these regulations by § 13(b). It reads as follows:

"Sec. 13(b). The provisions of section 7 shall not apply with respect to (1) any employee with respect to whom the Interstate Commerce Commission has power to establish qualifications and maximum hours of service pursuant to the provisions of section 204 of the Motor Carrier Act, 1935; * * *."

This exemption brought sharply into focus the coverage of employees by Motor Carrier Act, § 204(a). Clerical, storage and other non-transportation workers are under this or the Fair Labor Standards Act, dependent upon the sweep of the word employee in this act. The Commission again examined the question of its jurisdiction and in Ex parte No. MC–28 again reached the conclusion that its power under "section 204(a)(1) and (2) is limited to prescribing qualifications and maximum hours of service for those employees * * * whose activities affect the safety of operation." It added: "The provisions of section 202 evince a clear intent of Congress to limit our jurisdiction to regulating the motor-carrier industry as a part of the transportation system of the nation. To extend that regulation to features which are not characteristic of transportation or inherent in that industry strikes us as an enlargement of our jurisdiction unwarranted by any express or implied provision in the act, which vests in us all the power we have." The Wage and Hour Division of the Department of Labor arrived at the same result in an interpretation.

Shortly thereafter appellees, an association of truckmen and various common carriers by motor, filed a petition with the Commission in the present case seeking an exercise of the Commission's jurisdiction under § 204(a) to fix reasonable requirements "with respect to qualifications and maximum hours of service of all employees of common and contract carriers, except employees whose duties are related to safety of operation; to disregard its report and order in Ex parte MC–28." The Commission reaffirmed its position and denied the petition. The appellees petitioned a three-judge district court to compel the Commission to take jurisdiction and consider the establishment of qualifications and hours of service of all employees of common and contract carriers by motor vehicle. The Administrator of the Wage and Hour Division was permitted to intervene. The district court reversed the Commission, set aside its order and directed it to take jurisdiction of the appellees' petition. 31 F.Supp. 35. A direct appeal to this Court was granted.

In the broad domain of social legislation few problems are enmeshed with the difficulties that surround a determination of what qualifications an employee shall have and how long his hours of work may be. Upon the proper adjustment of these factors within an industry in relation to competitive activities may well depend the economic success of the enterprises affected as well as the employment and efficiency of the workers. The Motor Carrier Act lays little emphasis upon the clause we are called upon now to construe, "qualifications and maximum hours of service of employees." None of the words are defined by the section 203, devoted to the explanation of the meaning of the words used in the Act. They are a part of an elaborate enactment drawn and passed in an attempt to adjust a new

Sec. 6   DEVELOPMENT OF CURRENT DOCTRINE   405

and growing transportation service to the needs of the public. To find their content, they must be viewed in their setting.

In the interpretation of statutes, the function of the courts is easily stated. It is to construe the language so as to give effect to the intent of Congress. There is no invariable rule for the discovery of that intention. To take a few words from their context and with them thus isolated to attempt to determine their meaning, certainly would not contribute greatly to the discovery of the purpose of the draftsmen of a statute, particularly in a law drawn to meet many needs of a major occupation.[19]

There is, of course, no more persuasive evidence of the purpose of a statute than the words by which the legislature undertook to give expression to its wishes. Often these words are sufficient in and of themselves to determine the purpose of the legislation. In such cases we have followed their plain meaning. When that meaning has led to absurd or futile results, however, this Court has looked beyond the words to the purpose of the act. Frequently, however, even when the plain meaning did not produce absurd results but merely an unreasonable one "plainly at variance with the policy of the legislation as a whole" this Court has followed that purpose, rather than the literal words. When aid to construction of the meaning of words, as used in the statute, is available, there certainly can be no "rule of law" which forbids its use, however clear the words may appear on "superficial examination." The interpretation of the meaning of statutes, as applied to justiciable controversies, is exclusively a judicial function. This duty requires one body of public servants, the judges, to construe the meaning of what another body, the legislators, has said. Obviously there is danger that the courts' conclusion as to legislative purpose will be unconsciously influenced by the judges' own views or by factors not considered by the enacting body. A lively appreciation of the danger is the best assurance of escape from its threat but hardly justifies an acceptance of a literal interpretation dogma which withholds from the courts available information for reaching a correct conclusion. Emphasis should be laid, too, upon the necessity for appraisal of the purposes as a whole of Congress in analyzing the meaning of clauses or sections of general acts. A few words of general connotation appearing in the text of statutes should not be given a wide meaning, contrary to a settled policy, "excepting as a different purpose is plainly shown."

The language here under consideration, if construed as appellees contend, gives to the Commission a power of regulation as to qualifications and hours of employees quite distinct from the settled prac-

19. Cf. Davies, The Interpretation of Statutes in the Light of their Policy by the English Courts, 35 Columbia Law Review 519; Radin, Statutory Interpretation, 43 Harvard Law Review 863; Landis, A Note on "Statutory Interpretation," 43 Harvard Law Review 886; R. Powell, Construction of Written Instruments, 14 Indiana Law Journal 199, 309, 324; Jones, The Plain Meaning Rule, 25 Washington University Law Quarterly 2.

tice of Congress. That policy has been consistent in legislating for such regulation of transportation employees in matters of movement and safety only. The Hours of Service Act imposes restrictions on the hours of labor of employees "actually engaged in or connected with the movement of any train." The Seamen's Act limits employee regulations under it to members of ships' crews. The Civil Aeronautics Authority has authority over hours of service of employees "in the interest of safety."[20] It is stated by appellants in their brief with detailed citations, and the statement is uncontradicted, that at the time of the passage of the Motor Vehicle Act "forty states had regulatory measures relating to the hours of service of employees" and every one "applied exclusively to drivers or helpers on the vehicles." In the face to this course of legislation, coupled with the supporting interpretation of the two administrative agencies concerned with its interpretation, the Interstate Commerce Commission and the Wage and Hour Division, it cannot be said that the word "employee" as used in § 204(a) is so clear as to the workmen it embraces that we would accept its broadest meaning. The word, of course, is not a word of art. It takes color from its surroundings and frequently is carefully defined by the statute where it appears.[21]

We are especially hesitant to conclude that Congress intended to grant the Commission other than the customary power to secure safe-

---

[20]. 52 Stat. 1007, § 601(a)(5). This authority has apparently been exercised only as to pilots and copilots. Dept. of Commerce, Bureau of Air Commerce, Civil Air Regulations, No. 61, Scheduled Airline Rules (Interstate), as amended to May 31, 1938, §§ 61.518–61.5185.

[21]. That the word "employees" is not treated by Congress as a word of art having a definite meaning is apparent from an examination of recent legislation. Thus the Social Security Act specifically provides that "The term 'employee' includes an officer of a corporation," (42 U.S.C.A. § 1301(a)(6) while the Fair Labor Standards Act specifically exempts "any employee employed in a bona fide executive, administrative, professional, or local retailing capacity. * * *" (29 U.S.C.A. § 213(a)(1)). In the Railroad Unemployment Insurance Act, Congress expressly recognized the variable meaning of employee even when defined at length and used only in a single act: " * * * 'employee' (except when used in phrases establishing a different meaning) means * * *" (45 U.S.C.A. § 351(d)). In a statute permitting heads of departments to settle claims up to $1,000 arising from the negligence of "employees of the Government," Congress gives recognition to the fact that the term is not on its face all-inclusive by providing: " 'Employe' shall include enlisted men in the Army, Navy and Marine Corps." (31 U.S.C.A. §§ 215, 216.) See also the varying definitions of "employees" in the following statutes: Railroad Retirement Act, 45 U.S.C.A. § 228a(b) (c); Interstate Commerce Act, 49 U.S.C.A. § 1(7); Emergency Railroad Transportation Act, 49 U.S.C.A. § 251(f); Communications Act, 47 U.S.C.A. § 210; National Labor Relations Act, 29 U.S.C.A. § 152(3); Maritime Labor Relations Act, 46 U.S.C.A. § 1253(c); Classification Act of 1923 (Civil Service), 5 U.S.C.A. § 662; U.S. Employees' Compensation Act, 5 U.S.C.A. § 790; Longshoremen's and Harbor Workers' Compensation Act, 33 U.S.C.A. § 902; Boiler Inspection Act, 45 U.S.C.A. § 22; Railway Labor Act, 45 U.S.C.A. § 151(5). Where the term "employee" has been used in statutes without particularized definition it has not been treated by the courts as a word of definite content. [Cases omitted.]

ty in view of the absence in the legislative history of the Act of any discussion of the desirability of giving the Commission broad and unusual powers over all employees. The Clause in question was not contained in the bill as introduced.[22] Nor was it in the Coordinator's draft.[23] It was presented on the Senate floor as a Committee amendment following a suggestion of the Chairman of the Legislative Committee of the Commission, Mr. McManamy.[24] The committee reports and the debates contain no indication that the regulation of the qualifications and hours of service of all employees was contemplated; in fact the evidence points the other way. The Senate Committee's report explained the provisions of § 204(a)(1), (2) as giving the commission authority over common and contract carriers similar to that given over private carriers by § 204(a)(3).[25] The Chairman of the Senate Committee expressed the same thought while explaining the provisions on the floor of the Senate.[26] When suggesting the addition of the clause, the Chairman of the Commission's Legislative Commit-

---

22. S. 1629, 75th Cong., 1st Sess.

23. S.Doc. 152, 73rd Cong., 2nd Sess., p. 352, § 304(a)(1).

24. See the testimony of Mr. McManamy in Hearings on S. 1629 before the Senate Committee on Interstate Commerce, 74th Cong., 1st Sess., pp. 122, 123:
    "The regulation of the hours of service of bus and truck operators is far more important from a safety standpoint than the regulation of the hours of service of railroad employees because the danger is greater. * * * This could be accomplished by inserting in section 304(a)(1) and (2), lines 9 and 15, page 8, following the word 'records' in both lines, the words which appear in S. 394, as follows: 'Qualifications and maximum hours of service of employees.'"
   The clause in question came from § 2(a)(1) of S. 394, 74th Cong., 1st Sess., a subsection otherwise substantially like the corresponding subsection in S. 1629.
   Senator Wheeler, Chairman of the Committee on Interstate Commerce and sponsor of the bill, explained the provision on the floor of the Senate: "* * * the committee amended paragraphs (1) and (2) [of § 204] to confer power on the Commission to establish reasonable requirements with respect to the qualifications and maximum hours of service of employees of common and contract carriers, * * *. This suggestion came to us, I think from the chairman of the legislative committee of the Interstate Commerce Commission. * * *
   "In order to make the highways more safe, and so that common and contract carriers may not be unduly prejudiced in their competition with peddler trucks and other private operators of motor trucks, a provision was added in subparagraph 3 giving the Commission authority to establish similar requirements with respect to the qualifications and hours of service of the employees of such operators. * * *" 79 Cong.Rec. 5652.

25. S.Rep. 482, 74th Cong., 1st Sess. The report stated: "No regulation is proposed for private carriers except that an amendment adopted in committee authorizes the Commission to regulate the 'qualifications and maximum hours of service of employees and safety of operation and equipment' of private carriers of property by motor vehicle in the event that the Commission determines there is need for such regulation. Other amendments adopted by the committee confer like authority upon the Commission with respect to common and contract carriers." Safety of operation and equipment was in the original bill.

26. See last paragraph of remarks of Senator Wheeler, note 24 supra.

tee said: " * * * it relates to safety." [27] In the House the member in charge of the bill characterized the provisions as tending "greatly to promote careful operation for safety on the highways," and spoke with assurance of the Commission's ability to "formulate a set of reasonable rules * * * including therein maximum labor-hours service on the highway." [28] And in the report of the House Committee a member set out separate views criticizing the delegation of discretion to the Commission and proposing an amendment providing for an eight-hour day for "any employee engaged in the operation of such motor vehicle." [29]

The Commission and the Wage and Hour Division, as we have said, have both interpreted § 204(a) as relating solely to safety of operation. In any case such interpretations are entitled to great weight. This is peculiarly true here where the interpretations involve "contemporaneous construction of a statute by the men charged with the responsibility of setting its machinery in motion, of making the parts work efficiently and smoothly while they are yet untried and new." Furthermore, the Commission's interpretation gains much persuasiveness from the fact that it was the Commission which suggested the provisions' enactment to Congress.

It is important to remember that the Commission has three times concluded that its authority was limited to securing safety of operation. The first interpretation was made on December 29, 1937, when the Commission stated: " * * * until the Congress shall have given us a more particular and definite command in the premises, we shall limit our regulations concerning maximum hours of service to those employees whose functions in the operation of motor vehicles make such regulations desirable because of safety considerations." This expression was half a year old when Congress enacted the Fair Labor Standards Act with the exemption of § 13(b)(1). Seemingly the Senate at least was aware of the Commission's investigation of its powers even before its interpretation was announced. Under the circumstances it is unlikely indeed that Congress would not have explicitly overruled the Commission's interpretation had it intended to exempt others than employees who affected safety from the Labor Standards Act.

It is contended by appellees that the difference in language between subsections (1) and (2) and subsection (3) is indicative of a congressional purpose to restrict the regulation of employees of private carriers to "safety of operation" while inserting broader authority in (1) and (2) for employees of common and contract carriers. Appellants answer that the difference in language is explained by the difference in the powers. As (1) and (2) give powers beyond safety

---

27. Hearings, note 24 supra.

28. 79 Cong.Rec. 12206.

29. H.R.Rep.No.1645, 74th Cong., 1st Sess.

Sec. 6   DEVELOPMENT OF CURRENT DOCTRINE   409

for service, goods, accounts and records, language limiting those subsections to safety would be inapt.

* * *

One amendment made to the then pending Motor Carrier Act has relevance to our inquiry. Section 203(b) reads as set out in the note below.[30] The words, "except the provisions of section 204 relative to qualifications and maximum hours of service of employees and safety of operation or standards of equipment," italicized in the note, were added by amendment in the House after the passage of S. 1629 in the Senate with the addition of the disputed clause to § 204(a)(1) and (2).[31] It is evident that the exempted vehicles and operators include common, contract and private carriers. It seems equally evident that where these vehicles or operators were common or con-

30.   "(b) Nothing in this part, *except the provisions of section 204 relative to qualifications and maximum hours of service of employees and safety of operation or standards of equipment* shall be construed to include (1) motor vehicles employed solely in transporting school children and teachers to or from school; or (2) taxicabs, or other motor vehicles performing a bona fide taxicab service, having a capacity of not more than six passengers and not operated on a regular route or between fixed termini; or (3) motor vehicles owned or operated by or on behalf of hotels and used exclusively for the transportation of hotel patrons between hotels and local railroad or other common carrier stations; or (4) motor vehicles operated, under authorization, regulation, and control of the Secretary of the Interior, principally for the purpose of transporting persons in and about the national parks and national monuments; or (4a) motor vehicles controlled and operated by any farmer, and used in the transportation of his agricultural commodities and products thereof, or in the transportation of supplies to his farm; or (4b) motor vehicles controlled and operated by a cooperative association as defined, in the Agricultural Marketing Act, approved June 15, 1929, as amended; or (5) trolley busses operated by electric power derived from a fixed overhead wire, furnishing local passenger transportation similar to street railway service; or (6) motor vehicles used exclusively in carrying livestock, fish (including shell fish), or agricultural commodities (not including manufactured products thereof); or (7) motor vehicles used exclusively in the distribution of newspapers; nor, unless and to the extent that the Commission shall from time to time find that such application is necessary to carry out the policy of Congress enunciated in section 202, shall the provisions of this part, *except the provisions of section 204 relative to qualifications and maximum hours of service of employees and safety of operation or standards of equipment* apply to: (8) the transportation of passengers or property in interstate or foreign commerce wholly within a municipality or between contiguous municipalities or within a zone adjacent to and commercially a part of any such municipality or municipalities, except when such transportation is under a common control, management, or arrangement for a continuous carriage or shipment to or from a point without such municipality, municipalities, or zone, and provided that the motor carrier engaged in such transportation of passengers over regular or irregular route or routes in interstate commerce is also lawfully engaged in the intrastate transportation of passengers over the entire length of such interstate route or routes in accordance with the laws of each State having jurisdiction; or (9) the casual, occasional, or reciprocal transportation of passengers or property in interstate or foreign commerce for compensation by any person not engaged in transportation by motor vehicle as a regular occupation or business."

31.   H.R.Rep.No.1645, 74th Cong., 1st Sess.

tract carriers, it was not intended by Congress to give the Commission power to regulate the qualifications and hours of service of employees, other than those concerned with the safety of operations.

Our conclusion, in view of the circumstances set out in this opinion, is that the meaning of employees in § 204(a)(1) and (2) is limited to those employees whose activities affect the safety of operation. The Commission has no jurisdiction to regulate the qualifications or hours of service of any others. The decree of the district court is accordingly reversed and it is directed to dismiss the complaint of the appellees.

Reversed.

The Chief Justice, Mr. Justice McREYNOLDS, Mr. Justice STONE, and Mr. Justice ROBERTS, are of opinion that the decree should be affirmed for the reasons stated in the opinion of the district court, 31 F.Supp. 35. [That opinion, in part, is as follows:

"At the hearing counsel stated that, if the Act be construed as plaintiffs insist, the Commission will have to prescribe qualifications and hours for stenographers, clerks, accountants, mechanics, solicitors, and other employees of whose duties and qualifications it has no special knowledge; in this function its determination would not be based upon considerations of transportation—on which it is held to be expert—but upon social and economic considerations, matters on which it is not qualified or equipped, and which would entail the performance of a duty wholly foreign to its normal activities. But even if this be granted, we think there is no doubt that Congress had the power to impose the challenged duty. And the answer to the query cannot be found in the fact of inconvenience to the Commission, but must be first looked for in the language of the statute. If the words are clear, there is no room for construction.

" 'To search elsewhere for a meaning either beyond or short of that which they disclose is to invite the danger, in the one case, of converting what was meant to be open and precise, into a concealed trap for the unsuspecting or, in the other, of relieving from the grasp of the statute some whom the Legislature definitely meant to include.' Van Camp & Sons Co. v. American Can Co., 278 U.S. 245, 253, 49 S.Ct. 112, 73 L.Ed. 311, 60 A.L.R. 1060.

* * *

"Guided by this rule, we find that Congress in the first section of the Act declared the definite policy to regulate motor transportation (1) so as to foster sound economic conditions in the public interest; (2) to promote adequate, economical, and efficient service and reasonable charges; (3) to prevent unjust discriminations, undue preferences or advantages; (4) to avoid destructive competition; (5) to coordinate transportation by motor carriers and other carriers; (6) to develop and preserve a highway transportation system adapted to the needs of commerce and the national defense. The stated objects demonstrate beyond question that Congress has preempted the entire field. To the achievement of the ends sought, Congress provided that it should be the duty of the Commission to regulate carriers by establishing reasonable requirements with respect to (a) service; (b) transportation of baggage and express; (c) uniform systems of accounts, records, and reports; (d) qualifications and maximum hours of service of employees; (e) safety of operation and equipment.

"In (d) the word 'employees' is inclusive. There is nothing in its use or in its relation to other words in the section which, considered in the ordinary sense, can be said to indicate only a particular class of employees. If Congress had intended to distinguish between those employees engaged in the actual operation of motor vehicles and those engaged in other work, it could have done so, as it did in the former statute, by the addition of less than half a dozen words. Hence, to read that limitation into the section would be not only to disregard the letter of the law but to find, without guide or compass in the Act, a legislative intent to that end. To the contrary, such guide as there is—outside the distinct and definite meaning of the words—supports the view that Congress used the language of the section advisedly, and meant precisely what it said. For the third paragraph of Sec. 204, which concerns *private* carriers, expressly limits the power of the Commission over qualifications and hours to those employees whose work relates to safety of operation. This distinction between the two classes of carriers is convincing of a definite purpose, and the reason for it is obvious: private carriers are defined to be persons who transport for themselves—in furtherance of a commercial enterprise—or as bailees, their own or another's property in interstate commerce. As to such carriers, Congress properly concluded that to bring *all* their employees under the Commission's jurisdiction—as well as those engaged in the manufacturing or commercial end of the business, and having in themselves no direct relation to motor transportation—would create an anomalous situation, as it would.

"Unless what has been said is incorrect, nothing remains except to ascertain whether, in giving effect to the words of the statute, we create a situation so 'glaringly absurd' as to impel the conclusion Congress could not have intended such a result. With due deference to the dilemma of the Commission we are unable to say that this is true. At the time of the passage of the statute, the Fair Labor Standards Act had not been passed or even considered by Congress, but there was in effect a law known as the 'National Industrial Recovery Act', under which codes were established to regulate the hours of service of all classes of employees of motor carriers. The Motor Carrier Act expressly provided that it should supersede the provisions of the former codes. There was also in effect in a majority of the states some sort of legislation covering, with diversity of detail and lack of uniformity, hours of service of employees, including drivers of motor vehicles. It is not unreasonable, in these circumstances, to assume that Congress, aware of the problem as it applied to interstate commerce and the advisability of uniformity, chose to place upon the Commission the details of its solution. Certainly, aside from the consumption of the Commission's time, there is nothing glaringly absurd in this, nor reason to suppose a better agency could be found for the purpose. The Commission's fear that it may be called upon to establish qualifications for executive officials, solicitors, and lawyers, is overstrained. None of these classes is within the category of 'employees' as that word is used in public service or labor legislation. The hearings before the committees of Congress developed that the percentage cost of labor was equal to nearly half the total gross revenue of motor carriers, and the special attention of Congress was directed by representatives of the unions to the labor aspect as applied to the problems of uniformity and stabilization, because of widely diversified business organization, absence of labor organization in some regions, and the claimed unreasonable practices of many operators.

"And it is easy to see that stabilization of labor conditions as applied to this industry is an important, and indeed a necessary, part of the establishment of rates and general business regulation, matters as to which the Commission admittedly is expert, and these objectives appear as part and parcel of the purposes of the legislation. In this aspect, it is reasonable to conclude that Congress had them in mind when later, upon the passage of the Fair Labor Standards Act, it provided specifically that Sec. 7 thereof—which establishes maximum hours of service—should not apply 'with respect to (1) any employee with respect to whom the Interstate Commerce Commission has power to establish qualifications and maximum hours of service pursuant to the provisions of section 204 [304 of Title 49] of the Motor Carrier Act, 1935, or (2) any employee of an employer subject to the provisions of Part I of the Interstate Commerce Act.' 29 U.S.C.A. § 213(b). The necessity of separate provisions for the exemption of employees of the two classes of carriers is manifest. There are no private carriers by rail subject to the Commission's jurisdiction. Congress, therefore, used inclusive language as to the employees of railroads. There are, however, many private motor carriers who are subject to a limited regulation by the Commission, and this is true for reasons which we have already explained. Their employees not subject to the jurisdiction of the Commission would, by the use of the language employed in the case of railroads, have been left outside of the provisions of the Fair Labor Standards Act. It was obviously the recognition of this fact alone that induced the use of different language in each instance.

"In the view we take, the language of the disputed section is so plain as to permit only one interpretation, and we find nothing in the

Act as a whole which can with any assurance be said to lead to a different result. The circumstances under which the section was placed in the bill may possibly have created a situation not contemplated by its sponsors, but to say that this is true would be pure speculation, in which we have no right to indulge and upon which we can base no conclusion. We are, therefore, obliged to hold the Commission was mistaken in limiting its powers to the drivers of trucks and buses."]

SCHWEGMANN BROS. v. CALVERT DISTILLERS CORP.

Supreme Court of the United States, 1951.
341 U.S. 384, 71 S.Ct. 745, 95 L.Ed. 1035.

Certiorari to the United States Court of Appeals for the Fifth Circuit.

Mr. Justice DOUGLAS delivered the opinion of the Court.

Respondents, Maryland and Delaware corporations, are distributors of gin and whiskey. They sell their products to wholesalers in Louisiana, who in turn sell to retailers. Respondents have a price-fixing scheme whereby they try to maintain uniform retail prices for their products. They endeavor to make retailers sign price-fixing contracts under which the buyers promise to sell at not less than the prices stated in respondents' schedules. They have indeed succeeded in getting over one hundred Louisiana retailers to sign these agreements. Petitioner, a retailer in New Orleans, refused to agree to the price-fixing scheme and sold respondents' products at a cut-rate price. Respondents thereupon brought this suit in the District Court by reason of diversity of citizenship to enjoin petitioner from selling the products at less than the minimum prices fixed by their schedules.

It is clear from our decisions under the Sherman Act, 26 Stat. 209, 15 U.S.C.A. §§ 1–7, 15 note, that this interstate marketing arrangement would be illegal, that it would be enjoined, that it would draw civil and criminal penalties, and that no court would enforce it. Fixing minimum prices, like other types of price fixing, is illegal *per se*. United States v. Socony-Vacuum Oil Co., 310 U.S. 150, 60 S.Ct. 811, 84 L.Ed. 1129; Kiefer-Stewart Co. v. Joseph E. Seagram & Sons, 340 U.S. 211, 71 S.Ct. 259. Resale price maintenance was indeed struck down in Dr. Miles Medical Co. v. John D. Park & Sons Co., 220 U.S. 373, 31 S.Ct. 376, 55 L.Ed. 502. The fact that a state authorizes the price fixing does not, of course, give immunity to the scheme, absent approval by Congress.

Respondents, however, seek to find legality for this marketing arrangement in the Miller-Tydings Act enacted in 1937 as an amendment to § 1 of the Sherman Act. 50 Stat. 693, 15 U.S.C. § 1, 15 U.S.C.A. § 1. That amendment provides in material part that "nothing herein contained shall render illegal, *contracts or agreements* prescribing minimum prices for the resale" of specified commodities when *"contracts or agreements of that description* are lawful as applied to intrastate transactions" under local law.[32] (Italics added.)

Louisiana has such a law. Act No. 13 of 1936, La.Gen.Stat. §§ 9809.1 et seq., LSA–R.S. 51:391 et seq. It permits a "contract" for the sale or resale of a commodity to provide that the buyer will not resell "except at the price stipulated by the vendor." The Louisiana statute goes further. It not only allows a distributor and retailer to make a "contract" fixing the resale price; but once there is a price-fixing "contract," known to a seller, with any retailer in the state, it also condemns as unfair competition a sale at less than the price stipulated even though the seller is not a party to the "contract."[33] In other words, the Louisiana statute enforces price fixing not only against parties to a "contract" but also against nonsigners. So far as Louisiana law is concerned, price fixing can be enforced against all retailers once any single retailer agrees with a distributor on the resale price. And the argument is that the Miller-Tydings Act permits the same range of price fixing.

The argument is phrased as follows: the present action is outlawed by the Sherman Act—the Miller-Tydings Act apart—only if it is a contract, combination, or conspiracy in restraint of trade. But if a contract or agreement is the vice, then by the terms of the Miller-Tydings Act that contract or agreement is immunized, provided it is immunized by state law. The same is true if the vice is a conspiracy, since a conspiracy presupposes an agreement. That was in essence the view of the Court of Appeals, which affirmed by a divided vote a judgment of a district court enjoining petitioner from price cutting. 184 F.2d 11.

The argument at first blush has appeal. But we think it offends the statutory scheme.

We note to begin with that there are critical differences between Louisiana's law and the Miller-Tydings Act. The latter exempts only "contracts or agreements prescribing minimum prices for the resale". On the other hand, the Louisiana law sanctions the fixing of maxi-

---

32. Resale price maintenance is allowed only as respects commodities which bear, or the label or container of which bear, the trade mark, brand, or name of the producer or distributor and which are in free and open competition with commodities of the same general class produced or distributed by others. Excluded are agreements between manufacturers, between producers, between wholesalers, between brokers, between factors, between retailers or between persons, firms or corporations in competition with each other.

33. The nonsigner clause in the Louisiana Act reads as follows:
"Wilfully and knowingly advertising, offering for sale or selling any commodity at less than the price stipulated in any contract entered into pursuant to the provision of section 1 of this Act [§ 9809.1] *whether the person so advertising, offering for sale or selling is or is not a party to such contract*, is unfair competition and is actionable at the suit of any person damaged thereby."

mum as well as minimum prices, for it exempts any provision that the buyer will not resell "except at the price stipulated by the vendor." We start then with a federal act which does not, as respondents suggest, turn over to the states the handling of the whole problem of resale price maintenance on this type of commodity. What is granted is a limited immunity—a limitation that is further emphasized by the inclusion in the state law and the exclusion from the federal law of the nonsigner provision. The omission of the nonsigner provision from the federal law is fatal to respondents' position unless we are to perform a distinct legislative function by reading into the Act a provision that was meticulously omitted from it.

A refusal to read the nonsigner provision into the Miller-Tydings Act makes sense if we are to take the words of the statute in their normal and customary meaning. The Act sanctions only "contracts or agreements". If a distributor and one or more retailers want to agree, combine, or conspire to fix a minimum price, they can do so if state law permits. Their contract, combination, or conspiracy—hitherto illegal—is made lawful. They can fix minimum prices pursuant to their contract or agreement with impunity. When they seek, however, to impose price fixing on persons who have not contracted or agreed to the scheme, the situation is vastly different. That is not price fixing by contract or agreement; that is price fixing by compulsion. That is not following the path of consensual agreement; that is resort to coercion.

Much argument is made to import into the contracts which respondents make with retailers a provision that the parties may force nonsigners into line. It is said that state law attaches that condition to every such contract and that therefore the Miller-Tydings Act exempts it from the Sherman Act. Such a condition, if implied, creates an agreement respecting not sales made under the contract but other sales. Yet all that are exempted by the Miller-Tydings Act are "contracts or agreements prescribing minimum prices for the resale" of the articles purchased, not "contracts or agreements" respecting the practices of noncontracting competitors of the contracting retailers.

It should be noted in this connection that the Miller-Tydings Act expressly continues the prohibitions of the Sherman Act against "horizontal" price fixing by those in competition with each other at the same functional level.[34] Therefore, when a state compels retailers to follow a parallel price policy, it demands private conduct which the Sherman Act forbids. See Parker v. Brown, 317 U.S. 341, 350, 63 S. Ct. 307, 313, 87 L.Ed. 315. Elimination of price competition at the

34. "Provided further, That the preceding proviso shall not make lawful any contract or agreement, providing for the establishment or maintenance of minimum resale prices on any commodity herein involved, between manufacturers, or between producers, or between wholesalers, * * * or between retailers, or between persons, firms, or corporations in competition with each other." 15 U.S.C.A. § 1.

retail level may, of course, lawfully result if a distributor successfully negotiates individual "vertical" agreements with all his retailers. But when retailers are *forced* to abandon price competition, they are driven into a compact in violation of the spirit of the proviso which forbids "horizontal" price fixing. A real sanction can be given the prohibitions of the proviso only if the price maintenance power granted a distributor is limited to *voluntary* engagements. Otherwise, the exception swallows the proviso and destroys its practical effectiveness.

The contrary conclusion would have a vast and devastating effect on Sherman Act policies. If it were adopted, once a distributor executed a contract with a single retailer setting the minimum resale price for a commodity in the state, all other retailers could be forced into line. Had Congress desired to eliminate the consensual element from the arrangement and to permit blanketing a state with resale price fixing if only one retailer wanted it, we feel that different measures would have been adopted—either a nonsigner provision would have been included or resale price fixing would have been authorized without more. Certainly the words used connote a voluntary scheme. Contracts or agreements convey the idea of a cooperative arrangement, not a program whereby recalcitrants are dragged in by the heels and compelled to submit to price fixing.

The history of the Act supports this construction. The efforts to override the rule of Dr. Miles Medical Co. v. John D. Park & Sons Co., supra, were long and persistent. Many bills had been introduced on this subject before Senator Tydings introduced his. Thus in 1929, in the Seventy-First Congress, the Capper-Kelly fair trade bill was offered. It had no nonsigner provision. It merely permitted resale price maintenance as respects specified classes of commodities by declaring that no such "contract relating to the sale or resale" shall be unlawful. As stated in the House Report that bill merely legalized an agreement "that the vendee will not resell the commodity specified in the contract except at a stipulated price." That bill became the model for the California act passed in 1931—the first state act permitting resale price maintenance. The California act contained no nonsigner clause. Neither did the Capper-Kelly bill that was introduced in the Seventy-Second Congress. So far as material here it was identical with its predecessor.

The Capper-Kelly bill did not pass. And by the time the next bill was introduced—three years later—the California act had been changed by the addition of the nonsigner provision. That was in 1933. Yet when in 1936 Senator Tydings introduced his first bill in the Seventy-Fourth Congress he followed substantially the Capper-Kelly bills and wrote no nonsigner provision into it. His bill merely legalized "contracts or agreements prescribing minimum prices or other conditions for the resale" of a commodity. By this date several additional states had resale price maintenance laws with nonsigner provisions. Even though the state laws were the models for the federal bills, the nonsigner provision was never added. That was true of the bill introduced in the Seventy-Fifth Congress as well as the subsequent one. They all followed in this respect the pattern of the Capper-Kelly bill as it appeared before the first nonsigner provision was written into state law. The "contract" concept utilized by Capper-Kelly before there was a nonsigner provision in state law was thus continued even after the nonsigner provision appeared. The inference, therefore, is strong that there was continuity between the first Tydings bill and the preceding Capper-Kelly bills. The Tydings bills built on the same foundation; they were no more concerned with nonsigner provisions than were their predecessors. In view of this history we can only conclude that, if the draftsman intended that the nonsigning retailer was to be coerced, it was strange indeed that he omitted the one clear provision that would have accomplished that result.

An argument is made from the reports and debates to the effect that "contracts or agreements" nevertheless includes the nonsigner provisions of state law. The Senate Report on the first Tydings bill, after stating that the California law authorized a distributor "to make a contract that the purchaser will not resell" except at the stipulated price, said that the proposed federal law "does no more than to remove Federal obstacles to the enforcement of contracts which the States themselves have declared lawful." The Senate Report on the second Tydings bill, which was introduced in the Seventy-fifth Congress, did little more than reprint the earlier report. The House Report, heavily relied on here, gave a more extended analysis.

The House Report referred to the state fair trade acts as authorizing the maintenance of resale prices by contract and as providing that "third parties with notice are bound by the terms of such a contract regardless of whether they are parties to it"; and the Report also stated that the objective of the Act was to permit the public policy of the states having such acts to operate with respect to interstate contracts for the sale of goods. This Report is the strongest statement for respondents' position which is found in the legislative history. The bill which that Report endorsed, however, did not pass. The bill which became the law was attached by the Senate Committee on the District of Columbia as a rider to the District of Columbia revenue bill. In that form it was debated and passed.

It is true that the House Report quoted above was referred to when the Senate amendment to the revenue measure was before the House. And one Congressman in the debate said that the nonsigner provision of state laws was validated by the federal law.

But we do not take these remarks at face value. In the first place, the House Report, while referring to the nonsigner provision when describing a typical state fair trade act, is so drafted that the voluntary contract is the core of the argument for the bill. Hence, the General Statement in the Report states that the sole objective of the Act was "to permit the public policy of States having 'fair trade acts' to operate with respect to interstate *contracts* for the resale of goods"; and the fair trade acts are referred to as legalizing "the maintenance, *by contract*, of resale prices of branded or trade-marked goods." [Italics added.]

In the second place, the remarks relied on were not only about a bill on which no vote was taken; they were about a bill which sanctioned "contracts or agreements" prescribing not only "minimum prices" but "other conditions" as well. The words "other conditions" were dropped from the amendment that was made to the revenue bill. Why they were deleted does not appear. It is said that they have no relevance to the present problem, since we are dealing here with "minimum prices" not with "other conditions." But that answer does not quite hold. The question is the amount of state law embraced in the words "contracts or agreements". It might well be argued that one of the "conditions" attaching to a contract fixing a minimum price would be the liability of a nonsigner. We do no more than stir the doubt, for the doubt alone is enough to make us skeptical of the full implications of the old report as applied to a new and different bill.

We look for more definite clues; and we find the following statement made on the floor by Senator Tydings: "What does the amendment do? It permits a man who manufactures an article to state the minimum resale price of the article in a contract with the man who buys it for ultimate resale to the public. * * *" Not once did Senator Tydings refer to the nonsigner provisions of state law. Not once did he suggest that the amendment would affect anyone but the retailer who signs the contract. We search the words of the sponsors for a clear indication that coercive as well as voluntary schemes or arrangements are permissible. We find none.[35] What we do find is the expression of fear in the minority report of the Senate Committee that the nonsigner provisions of the state laws would be made effective if the law passed. These fears were presented in the Senate debate by Senator King in opposition to the amendment. But the Senate Report emphasizes the "permissive" nature of the state laws, not once pointing to their coercive features.

The fears and doubts of the opposition are no authoritative guide to the construction of legislation. It is the sponsors that we look to when the meaning of the statutory words is in doubt. And when we read what the sponsors wrote and said about the amendment, we can-

---

35. H.R.Rep.No.1413, 75th Cong., 1st Sess. 10 (the Conference Report of the House) merely stated:
"This amendment provides for an amendment to the antitrust laws under which contracts and agreements stipulating minimum resale prices of certain commodities, and which are similar to contracts and agreements which are lawful as applied to intrastate commerce, are not to be regarded as being illegal under the antitrust laws."

not find that the distributors were to have the right to use not only a *contract* to fix retail prices but a *club* as well. The words they used —"contracts or agreements"—suggest just the contrary.

It should be remembered that it was the state laws that the federal law was designed to accommodate. Federal regulation was to give way to state regulation. When state regulation provided for resale price maintenance by both those who contracted and those who did not, and the federal regulation was relaxed only as respects "contracts or agreements," the inference is strong that Congress left the noncontracting group to be governed by pre-existing law. In other words, since Congress was writing a law to meet the specifications of state law, it would seem that if the nonsigner provision as well as the "contract" provision of state law were to be written into federal law, the pattern of the legislation would have been different.

We could conclude that Congress carved out the vast exception from the Sherman Act now claimed only if we were willing to assume that it took a devious route and yet failed to make its purpose plain.

Reversed.

Mr. Justice JACKSON, whom Mr. Justice MINTON joins, concurring.

I agree with the Court's judgment and with its opinion insofar as it rests upon the language of the Miller-Tydings Act. But it does not appear that there is either necessity or propriety in going back of it into legislative history.

Resort to legislative history is only justified where the face of the Act is inescapably ambiguous, and then I think we should not go beyond Committee reports, which presumably are well considered and carefully prepared. I cannot deny that I have sometimes offended against that rule. But to select casual statements from floor debates, not always distinguished for candor or accuracy, as a basis for making up our minds what law Congress intended to enact is to substitute ourselves for the Congress in one of its important functions. The Rules of the House and Senate, with the sanction of the Constitution, require three readings of an Act in each House before final enactment. That is intended, I take it, to make sure that each House knows what it is passing and passes what it wants, and that what is enacted was formally reduced to writing. It is the business of Congress to sum up its own debates in its legislation. Moreover, it is only the words of the bill that have presidential approval, where that approval is given. It is not to be supposed that, in signing a bill, the President endorses the whole Congressional Record. For us to undertake to reconstruct an enactment from legislative history is merely to involve the Court in political controversies which are quite proper in the enactment of a bill but should have no place in its interpretation.

Moreover, there are practical reasons why we should accept whenever possible the meaning which an enactment reveals on its face. Laws are intended for all of our people to live by; and the people go to law offices to learn what their rights under those laws are. Here is a controversy which affects every little merchant in many States. Aside from a few offices in the larger cities, the materials of legislative history are not available to the lawyer who can afford neither the cost of acquisition, the cost of housing, or the cost of repeatedly examining the whole congressional history. Moreover, if he could, he would not know any way of anticipating what would impress enough members of the Court to be controlling. To accept legislative debates to modify statutory provisions is to make the law inaccessible to a large part of the country.

By and large, I think our function was well stated by Mr. Justice Holmes: "We do not inquire what the legislature meant; we ask only what the statute means." Holmes, Collected Legal Papers, 207. See also Soon Hing v. Crowley, 113 U.S. 703, 710–711, 5 S.Ct. 730, 734, 28 L.Ed. 1145. And I can think of no better example of legislative history that is unedifying and unilluminating than that of the Act before us.

Mr. Justice FRANKFURTER, whom Mr. Justice BLACK and Mr. Justice BURTON join, dissenting.

In 1890, Congress passed the Sherman Law, which declared illegal "[e]very contract, combination in the form of trust or otherwise, or conspiracy, in restraint of trade or commerce among the several States, or with foreign nations". Act of July 2, 1890, § 1, 26 Stat. 209, 15 U.S.C.A. § 1. In 1937, Congress passed the Miller-Tydings Amendment. This excepted from the Sherman Law "contracts or agreements" prescribing minimum prices for the resale of trademarked commodities where such contracts or agreements were valid under State statute or policy. Act of Aug. 17, 1937, Title VIII, 50 Stat. 673, 693, 15 U.S.C.A. § 1. It would appear that, insofar as the Sherman Law made maintenance of minimum resale prices illegal, the Miller-Tydings Amendment made it legal to the extent that State law legalized it. "Contracts or agreements" immunized by the Miller-Tydings Amendment surely cannot have a narrower scope than "contract, combination * * * or conspiracy" in the Sherman Law. The Miller-Tydings Amendment is an amendment to § 1 of the Sherman Law. The category of contract cannot be given different content in the very same section of the same act, and every combination or conspiracy implies an agreement.

The setting of the Miller-Tydings Amendment and its legislative history remove any lingering doubts. The depression following 1929 gave impetus to the movement for legislation which would allow the fixing of minimum resale prices. In 1931, California passed a statute allowing a manufacturer to establish resale prices binding only upon retailers who voluntarily entered into a contract with him. This proved completely ineffective, and in 1933 California amended her statute to provide that such a contract established a minimum price binding upon any person who had notice of the contract. Grether, Experience in California with Fair Trade Legislation Restricting Price Cutting, 24 Calif.L.Rev. 640, 644 (1936). This amendment was the so-called "non-signer" clause which, in effect, allowed a manufacturer or wholesaler to fix a minimum resale price for his product. Every "fair trade" law thereafter passed by any State contained this "non-signer" clause. By the close of 1936, 14 States had passed such laws. In 1937, 28 more States passed them. Today, 45 out of 48 States have "fair trade" laws. See Report of the Federal Trade Commission on Resale Price Maintenance XXVII (Dec. 13, 1945).

A substantial obstacle remained in the path of the "fair trade" movement. In 1911, we had decided Dr. Miles Medical Co. v. John D. Park & Sons Co., 220 U.S. 373, 31 S.Ct. 376, 55 L.Ed. 502. There, in a suit brought against a "non-signer," we held that an agreement to maintain resale prices was a "contract * * * in restraint of trade" which was contrary to the Sherman Law. To remove this block, the Miller-Tydings Amendment was enacted. It is said, however, that thereby Congress meant only to remove the bar of the Sherman Law from agreements between the manufacturer and retailer, that Congress did not mean to make valid the "non-signer" clause which formed an integral part of each of the 42 State statutes in effect when the Amendment was passed.

The Miller-Tydings Amendment was passed as a rider to a Revenue Bill for the District of Columbia. The Senate Committee which attached the rider referred the Senate to S.Rep.No.2053, 74th Cong., 2d Sess. The House Conference Report (H.R.Rep.No.1413, 75th Cong., 1st Sess.), contains only five lines concerning the rider. But the rider was not a new measure. It came as no surprise to the House, which already had before it practically the same language in the Miller Bill, reported favorably by the Committee on the Judiciary. H.R.Rep.No.382, 75th Cong., 1st Sess. Both the House and Senate, therefore, had before them reports dealing with the substance of the Miller-Tydings Amendment. These reports speak for themselves, and I attach them as appendices to this opinion. 341 U.S. 402, 71 S.Ct. 754. Every State act referred to in these reports contained a "non-signer" provision. I cannot see how, in view of these reports, we can conclude that Congress meant the "non-signer" provisions to be invalid under the Sherman Law—unless, that is, we are to depart from the respect we have accorded authoritative legislative history in scores of cases during the last decade. See cases collected in Commissioner of Internal Revenue v. Estate of Church, 335 U.S. 632, 687, Appendix A, 69 S.Ct. 322, 337, 355, 93 L.Ed. 288. In many of these cases the purpose of Congress was far less clearly revealed than here.[36] It has never been questioned in this Court that committee reports, as well as statements by those in charge of a bill or of a report, are authoritative elucidations of the scope of a measure.

It is suggested that we go to the words of the sponsors of the Miller-Tydings Amendment. We have done so. Their words confirm the plain meaning of the words of the statute and of the congressional reports. Senator Tydings made the following statement: "What we have attempted to do is what 42 States have already written on their statute books. It is simply to back up those acts, that is all; to have a code of fair trade practices written not by a national board such as the N.R.A. but by each State, so that the people may go to the State legislature and correct immediately any abuses that may develop." 81 Cong.Rec. 7496.

Representative Dirksen made a statement to the House as a member of its Conference Committee. He referred to the case of Old Dearborn Distributing Co. v. Seagram Distillers Corp., 299 U.S. 183, 57 S.Ct. 139, 81 L.Ed. 109, in which this Court had held that the "non-signer" provision of the Illinois "fair trade" statute did not violate the Due Process Clause. Mr. Dirksen continued: "A question then arose as to whether or not the maintenance of such resale prices under a State fair trade act might not be in violation of the Sherman Anti-Trust Law of 1890 insofar as these transactions sprang from a contract in interstate commerce. This question was presented to the House Judiciary Committee and there determined by the reporting of the Miller bill. It was essentially nothing more than an enabling act

---

36. The intricate verbal arguments used to support the Court's decision do not affect the clarity of the statute and its legislative history. (1) It is said that the proviso to the Miller-Tydings Amendment makes it inapplicable to "non-signer" clauses in State acts. But the proviso only made explicit that the Amendment applied only to vertical agreements and did not make legal horizontal agreements, for example, those between retailers or between manufacturers. See statements of Senator Tydings, 81 Cong.Rec. 7487, 7496. The wording of the proviso, in fact, follows closely a statement of what the Senate Committee thought was implicit in the State acts. See S.Rep.No.2053, 74th Cong., 2d Sess. 2. (2) The fact that the 1931 California statute used wording similar to the Miller-Tydings Amendment and was later amended to refer to nonsigners is beside the mark. The words of the 1933 amendment to the California statute make clear that it was not, like the Miller-Tydings Amendment, designed to remove the bar of an antitrust act. It was enacted to give an affirmative right to recover from nonsigners, something the Miller-Tydings Amendment does not purport to do. In such a statute specific language referring to nonsigners would of course have to be used. (3) It is said that H.R.Rep.No.382, 75th Cong., 1st Sess., refers to a bill containing the phrase "other conditions." The words "other conditions" when used in conjunction with a phrase referring to minimum prices, could scarcely mean anything except "conditions other than minimum prices." We are here concerned with minimum prices. (4) "Permissive" was used in the Senate Report not to refer to retailers but to manufacturers. "[The State acts] merely authorize a manufacturer or producer to enter into contracts for the maintenance of his price, but they do not compel him to do so. In other words, they are merely permissive." S.Rep.No.2053, 74th Cong., 2d Sess. 2.

which placed the stamp of approval upon price maintenance transactions under State acts, notwithstanding the Sherman Act of 1890." 81 Cong.Rec. 8138.

Every one of the 42 State acts which the Miller-Tydings Amendment was to "back up"—the acts on which the Miller-Tydings Amendment was to place a "stamp of approval"—contained a "nonsigner" provision. As demonstrated by experience in California, the State acts would have been futile without the "non-signer" clause. The Court now holds that the Miller-Tydings Amendment does not cover these "non-signer" provisions. Not only is the view of the Court contrary to the words of the statute and to the legislative history. It is also in conflict with the interpretation given the Miller-Tydings Amendment by the Federal Trade Commission,[37] by the Department of Justice,[38] and by practically all persons adversely affected by the "fair trade" laws.[39] The "fair trade" laws may well be unsound as a matter of economics. Perhaps Congress should not pass an important measure dealing with an extraneous subject as a rider to a revenue bill, with the coercive influence it exerts in avoiding a veto; perhaps it should restrict legislation to a single relevant subject, as required by the constitutions of three-fourths of the States. These are matters beyond the Court's concern. Where both the words of a statute and its legislative history clearly indicate the purpose of Congress, it should be respected. We should not substitute our own notion of what Congress should have done.

Appendix to the Opinion of Mr. Justice Frankfurter.

House Report No. 382, 75th Cong., 1st Sess.

The Committee on the Judiciary, to whom was referred the bill (H.R. 1611) to amend the act entitled "An act to protect trade and commerce against unlawful restraints and monopolies", approved July 2, 1890, after consideration, report the same favorably to the House with an amendment with the recommendation that as amended the bill do pass.

37. See letter addressed to the President by the Chairman of the Federal Trade Commission. S.Doc.No.58, 75th Cong., 1st Sess., pp. 2–3. See also Report of the Federal Trade Commission on Resale Price Maintenance LXII (Dec. 13, 1945).

38. The Department of Justice appears to have instituted no prosecutions because of enforcement of "fair trade" acts against nonsigners. The Assistant Attorney General who played an important part in enforcement of the antitrust laws called for repeal of the Miller-Tydings Amendment because it made legal the nonsigner provisions of the State "fair trade" acts. Statement of Mr. Thurman Arnold, T. N. E. C. Hearings, pp. 18162–18165.

39. The contention that the "nonsigner" provisions are not within the Miller-Tydings Amendment appears to have been made in only two reported cases since the Amendment was passed in 1937. Caiamia v. Goldsmith Bros., Inc., 299 N.Y. 636, 87 N.E.2d 50; Id., 299 N.Y. 795, 87 N.E.2d 687; Pepsodent Co. v. Krauss Co., D.C., 56 F.Supp. 922. In both, the argument was rejected.

424   THE INTERPRETATION OF STATUTES   Ch. 5

The committee amendment is as follows: Strike out all after the enacting clause and insert in lieu thereof the following:

"That section 1 of the Act entitled 'An Act to protect trade and commerce against unlawful restraints and monopolies', approved July 2, 1890 (U.S.Code, title 15, sec. 1), be amended to read as follows:

" 'Section 1. Every contract, combination in the form of trust or otherwise, or conspiracy in restraint of trade or commerce among the several States, or with foreign nations, is hereby declared to be illegal. Every person who shall make any such contract or engage in any such combination or conspiracy, shall be deemed guilty of a misdemeanor, and, on conviction thereof, shall be punished by fine not exceeding $5,000, or by imprisonment not exceeding one year, or by both said punishments, in the discretion of the court. Nothing herein contained shall render illegal, contracts or agreements prescribing minimum prices or other conditions for the resale of a commodity which bears, or the label or container of which bears, the trade mark, brand, or name of the producer or distributor of such commodity and which is in free and open competition with commodities of the same general class produced or distributed by others, when such contracts or agreements are lawful as applied to intrastate transactions, under any statute, law, or public policy now or hereafter in effect in any State, Territory, or the District of Columbia in which such resale is made, or to which the commodity is to be transported for such resale, and the making of such contracts or agreements shall not be an unfair method of competition under section 5, as amended and supplemented, of the Act entitled "An Act to create a Federal Trade Commission, to define its powers and duties, and for other purposes", approved September 26, 1914 (U.S.Code, title 15, sec. 45).' "

General Statement

The sole objective of this proposed legislation is to permit the public policy of States having "fair trade acts" to operate with respect to interstate contracts for the resale of goods within those States. The fair-trade acts referred to legalize the maintenance, by contract, of resale prices of branded or trade-marked goods which are in free competition with other goods of the same general class.

To accomplish this end, the reported bill amends section 1 of the Sherman Anti-Trust Act which declares every contract in restraint of trade illegal. The amendment adds a sentence to the section, in the nature of a limitation to the effect, in substance, that nothing therein contained shall render illegal contracts prescribing minimum prices or other conditions for resale of branded or trade-marked goods when such contracts are lawful as to intrastate transactions under the State law of the State in which the resale is to be made; and that the making of such contracts shall not be an unfair method of competition under section 5 of the Federal Trade Commission Act.

In view of the decision of the Supreme Court in Dr. Miles Medical Co. v. John D. Park & Sons Co., 220 U.S. 373, 31 S.Ct. 376, 55 L. Ed. 502, and other cases, it is doubtful, at least, that such contracts are now valid in interstate commerce.

State Fair Trade Acts

State fair trade acts typically provide, first, that contracts may lawfully be made which provide for maintenance by contract of resale prices of branded or trade-marked competitive goods. Second, that third parties with notice are bound by the terms of such a contract regardless of whether they are parties to it.

The pertinent provisions of the Illinois act, recently held constitutional by the Supreme Court in the case of Old Dearborn Distributing Co. v. Seagram-Distillers Corporation, 1936, 299 U.S. 183, 57 S. Ct. 139, 81 L.Ed. 109, read as follows:

"§ 1. No contract relating to the sale or resale of a commodity which bears, or the label or content of which bears, the trade mark, brand, or name of the producer or owner of such commodity and which is in fair and open competition with commodities of the same general class produced by others shall be deemed in violation of any law of the State of Illinois by reason of any of the following provisions which may be contained in such contract:

"(1) That the buyer will not resell such commodity except at the price stipulated by the vendor.

"(2) That the producer or vendee of a commodity require upon the sale of such commodity to another that such purchaser agree that he will not, in turn, resell except at the price stipulated by such producer or vendee.

"Such provisions in any contract shall be deemed to contain or imply conditions that such commodity may be resold without reference to such agreement in the following cases:

"(1) In closing out the owner's stock for the purpose of discontinuing delivery of any such commodity: *Provided, however,* That such stock is first offered to the manufacturer of such stock at the original invoice price, at least ten (10) days before such stock shall be offered for sale to the public.

"(2) When the goods are damaged or deteriorated in quality, and notice is given to the public thereof.

"(3) By any officer acting under the orders of any court.

"§ 2. Wilfully and knowingly advertising, offering for sale, or selling any commodity at less than the price stipulated in any contract entered into pursuant to the provisions of section 1 of this Act, whether the person so advertising, offering for sale, or selling is or is not a party to such contract, is unfair competition and is actionable at the suit of any person damaged thereby."

The following States, the committee is advised, have adopted fair trade acts: California, Washington, Oregon, Montana, Wyoming, Arizona, New Mexico, Utah, North Dakota, South Dakota, Kansas, Louisiana, Arkansas, Iowa, Wisconsin, Illinois, Kentucky, Tennessee, Indiana, Ohio, Georgia, Virginia, West Virginia, Pennsylvania, Maryland, New York, New Jersey, and Rhode Island.

The committee is advised that in addition one house of each of the following States have passed a fair trade bill: South Carolina, North Carolina, Idaho, Colorado, and Oklahoma.

The committee is further advised that bills are pending in the Legislatures of Nevada, Michigan, Minnesota, Texas, Mississippi, Delaware, Missouri, Connecticut, Massachusetts, New Hampshire, and Maine; and that only one State, Vermont, has definitely rejected legislation of this character.

Economic Aspects

The anticipated economic effects of the legislation here proposed were presented both by proponents and opponents of the bill in the hearings held by the subcommittee of the Committee on the Judiciary in charge of the bill. On the one hand it is urged that predatory price cutting is a weapon of monopolistic large distributors to crush small businessmen. On the other hand, it is contended that price-maintenance legislation tends unduly to enhance the price of goods to the consumer. To this argument it is answered that the free play of competition between products of different manufacturers of the same general class will prevent such a result.

However, in the opinion of the committee, those arguments are more properly addressed to the State legislatures considering the enactment of fair trade acts. It is the legislature's responsibility to fix the public policy of the State. This legislation merely seeks to help effectuate a public policy so fixed in a State. It has no application to any State which does not see fit to enact a fair trade act.

In this connection the committee invites attention to the following paragraph of the opinion of the Supreme Court, heretofore referred to, upholding the constitutionality of the Illinois act, the Court speaking through Mr. Justice Sutherland:

"There is a great body of fact and opinion tending to show that price cutting by retail dealers is not only injurious to the good will and business of the producer and distributor of identified goods, but injurious to the general public as well. The evidence to that effect is voluminous; but it would serve no useful purpose to review the evidence or to enlarge further upon the subject. True, there is evidence, opinion, and argument to the contrary; but it does not concern us to determine where the weight lies. We need say no more than that the question may be regarded as fairly open to differences of opinion. The legislation here in question proceeds upon the former and not the latter view; and the legislative determination in that respect, in the circumstances here disclosed, is conclusive so far as this court is concerned. Where the question of what the facts establish is a fairly debatable one we accept and carry into effect the opinion of the legislature. Radice v. [People of State of] New York, 264 U.S. 292, 294, 44 S.Ct. 325, 326, 68 L.Ed. 690; Zahn v. Board of Public Works [of City of Los Angeles], 274 U.S. 325, 328, 47 S.Ct. 594, 595, 71 L.Ed. 1074, and cases cited". [299 U.S. 183, 57 S.Ct. 145.]

Effectuation of State Public Policy

Your committee respectfully submit that sound public policy on the part of the Federal Government lies in the direction of lending assistance to the States to effectuate their own public policy with regard to their internal affairs. It is submitted that this is especially true where such assistance, as in this instance, consists of removing a handicap resulting from the surrender of the power over interstate commerce by the States to the Federal Government.

Senate Report No. 2053, 74th Cong., 2d Sess.

The Committee on the Judiciary, having had under consideration the bill (S. 3822) to amend the act entitled "An Act to protect trade and commerce against unlawful restraints and monopolies", approved July 2, 1890, report the same back with the recommendation that the bill do pass.

In 1933 a law was enacted by the State of California authorizing a manufacturer or producer of a commodity which bears his trade mark, brand, or name, and which is sold in free and open competition with commodities of the same general class produced by others, to make a contract that the purchaser will not resell such commodity except at the price stipulated by the manufacturer or producer.

The purpose of the California act, as expressed in its title, was to protect trade-mark owners, distributors, and the general public against injurious and uneconomic practices in the distribution of articles of standard quality under a trade mark, brand, or name, and the particular practice against which it was directed was the so-called "loss-leader selling."

Since the passage of the California act similar legislation has been enacted in 12 other States, namely, New York, Illinois, Pennsylvania, New Jersey, Oregon, Washington, Wisconsin, Iowa, Maryland, Ohio, Virginia, and Rhode Island (the last three since the introduction of the proposed bill).

In still other States contracts stipulating minimum resale prices are valid at common law.

In the States where such contracts are lawful it has been found that loss-leader selling of identified merchandise sold under competitive conditions operates as a fraud on the consumer, destroys the producer's goodwill in his trade mark, and is used by the large merchant to eliminate his small independent competitor.

In recommending the passage of S. 3822 the committee, while fully recognizing the evils of loss-leader selling, is not required to determine the effectiveness of the device adopted by the States to eliminate the same.

It is sufficient that this type of selling unquestionably has had a disastrous effect upon the small independent retailer, thereby tending to create monopoly, and that a large number of States have found that its evil effects can be mitigated, if not eliminated, by legalizing contracts stipulating minimum resale prices.

The Congress is not called upon to pass upon the effectiveness of the remedy, but it should not put obstacles in the way of efforts of the individual States to make the remedy effective.

Though there is no specific adjudication on the subject, it is believed that contracts stipulating minimum resale prices, even when they are made or are to be performed in a State where such contracts are lawful, may violate the Sherman Act whenever the goods sold under the contract move in interstate commerce.

Consequently, many manufacturers not domiciled in the state of the vendee are unwilling to run the risk of violating the Federal law, and the effectiveness of the State fair-trade laws is thereby seriously impaired.

S. 3822 removes the doubt as to the applicability of the Sherman Act by expressly legalizing such contracts where legal under the laws of the State where made or where they are to be performed.

Moreover, the proposed bill declares such contracts shall not be an unfair method of competition under the Federal Trade Commission law.

The language of the bill, in describing the class of commodities to which it is applicable, follows closely the language of the State acts, and the scope of the bill is therefore carefully limited to com-

Sec. 6   DEVELOPMENT OF CURRENT DOCTRINE   429

modities "in free and open competition with commodities of the same general class produced by others."

The State acts are in no sense general price-fixing acts. They merely authorize a manufacturer or producer to enter into contracts for the maintenance of his price, but they do not compel him to do so. In other words, they are merely permissive.

They do not authorize horizontal contracts, that is to say, contracts or agreements between manufacturers, between producers, or between wholesalers, or between retailers as to the sale or resale price of any commodity.

They apply only to commodities which are in free and open competition with commodities of the same general class produced by others, and they therefore do not in any sense restrain trade or competition. In fact, they legalize a device which is intended to increase competition and prevent monopoly.

But most important, from the standpoint of the Congress, the proposed bill merely permits the individual States to function, without Federal restraint, within their proper sphere, and does not commit the Congress to a national policy on the subject matter of the State laws.

In other words, the bill does no more than to remove Federal obstacles to the enforcement of contracts which the States themselves have declared lawful.

NOTES

1. Some thirteen months after the Supreme Court's decision in Schwegmann Bros. v. Calvert Distillers Corp., Congress adopted and the President signed the McGuire Act which reads:

AN ACT

To amend the Federal Trade Commission Act with respect to certain contracts and agreements which establish minimum or stipulated resale prices and which are extended by State law to persons who are not parties to such contracts and agreements, and for certain other purposes.

Be it enacted by the Senate and House of Representatives of the United States of America in Congress assembled, That it is the purpose of this Act to protect the rights of States under the United States Constitution to regulate their internal affairs and more particularly to enact statutes and laws, and to adopt policies, which authorize contracts and agreements prescribing minimum or stipulated prices for the resale of commodities and to extend the minimum or stipulated prices prescribed by such contracts and agreements to persons who are not parties thereto. It is the further purpose of this Act to permit such statutes, laws, and public policies to apply to commodities, contracts, agreements, and activities in or affecting interstate or foreign commerce.

SEC. 2. Section 5(a) of the Federal Trade Commission Act, as amended, is hereby amended to read as follows: [40]

SEC. 5(a)(1) Unfair methods of competition in commerce, and unfair or deceptive acts or practices in commerce, are hereby declared unlawful.

(2) Nothing contained in this Act or in any of the Antitrust Acts shall render unlawful any contracts or agreements prescribing minimum or stipulated prices, or requiring a vendee to enter into contracts or agreements prescribing minimum or stipulated prices, for the resale of a commodity which bears, or the label or container of which bears, the trade-mark, brand, or name of the producer or distributor of such commodity and which is in free and open competition with commodities of the same general class produced or distributed by others, when contracts or agreements of that description are lawful as applied to intrastate transactions under any statute, law, or public policy now or hereafter in effect in any State, Territory, or the District of Columbia in which such resale is to be made, or to which the commodity is to be transported for such resale.

(3) Nothing contained in this Act or in any of the Antitrust Acts shall render unlawful the exercise or the enforcement of any right or right of action created by any statute, law, or public policy now or hereafter in effect in any State, Territory, or the District of Columbia, which in substance provides that willfully and knowingly advertising, offering for sale, or selling any commodity at less than the price or prices prescribed in such contracts or agreements whether the person so advertising, offering for sale, or selling is or is not a party to such a contract or agreement, is unfair competition and is actionable at the suit of any person damaged thereby.

(4) Neither the making of contracts or agreements as described in paragraph (2) of this subsection, nor the exercise or enforcement of any right or right of action as described in paragraph (3) of this subsection shall constitute an unlawful burden or restraint upon, or interference with, commerce.

(5) Nothing contained in paragraph (2) of this subsection shall make lawful contracts or agreements providing for the establishment or maintenance of minimum or stipulated resale prices on any commodity referred to in paragraph (2) of this subsection, between manufacturers, or between producers, or between wholesalers, or between brokers, or between factors, or between retailers, or between persons, firms, or corporations in competition with each other.

(6) The Commission is hereby empowered and directed to prevent persons, partnerships, or corporations, except banks, common carriers subject to the Acts to regulate commerce, air carriers and foreign air carriers subject to the Civil Aeronautics Act of 1938, and persons, partnerships, or corporations subject to the Packers and Stockyards Act, 1921, except as provided in section 406(b) of said Act, from using unfair methods of competition in commerce and unfair or deceptive acts or practices in commerce.

Approved July 14, 1952.

40. [In effect, the McGuire Act adds to Section 5(a) the provisions designated as 5(a)(2)–5(a)(5). Before this Act, Section 5(a) contained the provisions now designated as 5(a)(1) and 5(a)(6)—Ed.]

Sec. 6   DEVELOPMENT OF CURRENT DOCTRINE   431

Inter alia, why does this enactment amend the Federal Trade Commission Act rather than the Miller-Tydings Amendment? For interesting insights into the tactics of high-pressure lobbying, see the legislative history of the McGuire Act, including especially the material inserted by Senator Morse at 98 Cong.Rec. 8835 et seq. (1952). Note, however, that the McGuire Act was subsequently repealed by the Consumer Goods Pricing Act of 1975. Act of Dec. 12, 1975, Pub.L. No. 94–145, 89 Stat. 801.

2. Mr. Justice Jackson's anti-legislative history position had been stated before the Schwegmann case in a vigorous address published as The Meaning of Statutes: What Congress Says or What the Court Says, 34 A. B.A.J. 535 (1948). In appraising Mr. Justice Jackson's arguments, as set out in the Schwegmann case, reread the Introductory Note at the beginning of Section 4, and consider the following:

> "The argument that the words of a statute express the final legislative intention and should therefore be regarded as the sole authoritative source in ascertaining that intention is essentially fallacious. For it rests on the erroneous assumption that words have a fixed meaning. Words are symbols used for communication —means, not ends, in the legislative process. To employ every available method of accurately determining the intended referents of the statutory language is not necessarily to vary or distort the symbols. The argument that the President approves the statutory words standing alone seems equally invalid. As leader of a major political party and an active participant in the legislative process, the chief executive does not read the words as of first impression; he is usually familiar with the kind of situation at which a statute is aimed. The use of legislative history, therefore, may be as important in determining the President's understanding of the statutory language as it is in ascertaining the intention of Congress." Note, A Re-evaluation of the Use of Legislative History in the Federal Courts, 52 Colum.L.Rev. 125, 134 (1952).

See Jones, The Plain Meaning Rule and Extrinsic Aids in the Interpretation of Federal Statutes, 25 Wash.U.L.Q. 2, 22 (1939).

Consider also the comments of Professor Kenneth C. Davis in his article, Legislative History and the Wheat Board Case, 31 Can.B.Rev. 1 (1953). Regarding Mr. Justice Jackson's arguments based on the House and Senate rules and on the role of the President, Professor Davis remarks (pp. 11–12):

> "This is a neat bundle of specious reasoning. The first three sentences are an argument that statutory clarity is preferable to judicial resort to legislative history. Of course it is. But the court that is confronted with an unclear statute cannot choose between statutory clarity and use of legislative history; the choice having to do with legislative history is to use it or to guess about legislative intent. If the President in approving a bill does not endorse the whole Congressional Record, neither does he endorse the whole set of ill-informed judicial guesses about legislative intent that would quickly fill the U.S. Reports if legislative history could not be considered. Furthermore, both the President in approving or vetoing a bill and congressmen in voting on a bill may get more

guidance from explanations and debates about the bill than from the text of the bill.

He then continues (p. 12):

"Another argument against use of legislative history is that in many cases a thorough search of the legislative history will yield nothing but conflicting leads on the question at issue. That this is true as a matter of fact is undeniable. But is it harmful? The argument is a little like saying that we should not drill for oil because much of the drilling ends with dry holes. The important fact is that some of the drilling yields oil.

"Even if the time and energy of counsel and of judges is in some cases expended on legislative history that fails to throw useful light on specific issues, the pursuit is not wholly wasted. Throughout the English-speaking world during the present century, dissatisfaction has often been expressed about inadequate understanding by judges of social purposes behind major enactments. Can it be that the judges of the federal courts of the United States, by reason of frequent resort to legislative histories, have benefited in some measure, even when the particular legislative history has been found unhelpful on the immediate problem? Does extensive use of legislative history force the judges to keep in closer touch with democratic desires? Is legislative intent usually so elusive that what the judges find often depends to some extent upon their own social philosophies and if so, are those social philosophies likely to be in better tune with the attitudes of parliamentary majorities if the judges are more familiar with legislative programmes and processes?"

In a footnote (n. 31, p. 11), Professor Davis adds:

* * *

"It is hard to understand how Mr. Justice Jackson can oppose use of legislative history on grounds of inaccessibility, as he does, and then propose use of the committee reports, which are not included in the Congressional Record, and refusal to use the proceedings on the floor of each house, which are included in the Congressional Record. Unquestionably, the Congressional Record is more accessible than committee reports."

3. In United States v. Public Utilities Comm. of California, 345 U.S. 295, 73 S.Ct. 706, 97 L.Ed. 1020 (1953), the Supreme Court again gave expression to divergent views regarding resort to legislative history sources. Mr. Justice Reed, delivering the opinion of the Court, referred extensively to such sources, including committee hearings and reports and the Congressional Record as well as other material. The following statements appear in his opinion (id. at 315, 73 S.Ct. at 717–718):

"Where the language and purpose of the questioned statute is clear, courts, of course, follow the legislative direction in interpretation. Where the words are ambiguous, the judiciary may properly use the legislative history to reach a conclusion. And that method of determining congressional purpose is likewise applicable when the literal words would bring about an end completely at variance with the purpose of the statute."

Compare this with Mr. Justice Reed's expressions in the *American Trucking* case. In addition to a separate opinion (345 U.S. 295, at 318, 73 S.Ct. 706, at 719) by Mr. Justice Black, concurring in the result and relying on the reasoning of the Court of Appeals for the Ninth Circuit, the *Public Utilities* case evoked a separate concurring opinion (id. at 319, 73 S.Ct. at 719) by Mr. Justice Jackson, quoted in full herewith, which is of particular interest:

> "I should concur in this result more readily if the Court could reach it by analysis of the statute instead of by psychoanalysis of Congress. When we decide from legislative history, including statements of witnesses at hearings, what Congress probably had in mind, we must put ourselves in the place of a majority of Congressmen and act according to the impression we think this history should have made on them. Never having been a Congressman, I am handicapped in that weird endeavor. That process seems to me not interpretation of a statute but creation of a statute.
>
> "I will forego repeating what I have said about this practice in Schwegmann Bros. v. Calvert Distillers Corp., 341 U.S. 384, 395, 71 S.Ct. 745, 95 L.Ed. 1035. But I do point out that this case is a dramatic demonstration of the evil of it. Neither counsel who argued the case for the State Commission nor the Supreme Court of California had access to the material used by the Court today. Counsel for the Public Utilities Commission of that State stated at the bar, and confirmed by letter, that he had tried without success over a period of four months to obtain the legislative history of § 20 of Part I of the Federal Power Act. He obtained it only four days before argument, in Washington at the Library of this Court. He stated that the City and County Library of San Francisco, the Library of the University of California, and the library of the largest law office in San Francisco were unable to supply it. The City and County Library tried to obtain the material by interlibrary loan from the Library of Congress, but the request was refused. Counsel then attempted to obtain the material from the Harvard Law School Library, but it advised that 'our rules do not permit this kind of material to be sent out on loan.'
>
> "The practice of the Federal Government relying on inaccessible law has heretofore been condemned. Some of us remember vividly the argument in Panama Refining Co. v. Ryan, 293 U.S. 388, 55 S.Ct. 241, 79 L.Ed. 446, in which the Government was obliged to admit that the Executive Orders upon which it had proceeded below had been repealed by another Executive Order deposited with the State Department. No regularized system for their publication had been established. Copies could be obtained at nominal cost by writing to the Department. Having discovered the error, the Government brought it to the attention of the Court. At the argument, however, the Court, led by Mr. Justice Brandeis, subjected government counsel to a raking fire of criticism because of the failure of the Government to make Executive Orders available in

official form. The Court refused to pass on some aspects of the case, and the result was the establishment of a Federal Register.[41]

"Today's decison marks a regression from this modern tendency. It pulls federal law, not only out of the dark where it has been hidden, but into a fog in which little can be seen if found. Legislative history here as usual is more vague than the statute we are called upon to interpret.

"If this were an action to enforce a civil liability or to punish for a crime, I should protest this decision strenuously. However, the decision seems to have operation in the future only. If Congress does not like our legislation, it can repeal it—as it has done a number of times in the past. I therefore concur in the interpretation unanimously approved by the members of the Court who have had legislative experience."

Mr. Justice Frankfurter added the following remarks (id. at 321, 73 S.Ct. at 720–721):

"The light shed by Mr. Justice JACKSON on the underpinning of the Court's opinion makes me unwilling to share responsibility for a decision resting on such underpinning. It is one thing to construe a section of a comprehensive statute in the context of its general scheme, as that scheme is indicated by its terms and by the gloss of those authorized to speak for Congress, either through reports or statements on the floor. It is a very different thing to extrapolate meaning from surmises and speculation and free-wheeling utterances, especially to do so in disregard of the terms in which Congress has chosen to express its purpose.

"Were I confined to the mere text of the legislation we have to construe, with such authoritative elucidation as obviously relevant legislative materials furnish, I would be compelled to find the considerations for fusing, as the Court does, the amended Federal Water Power Act of 1920, 41 Stat. 1063, with Part II of the Federal Power Act of 1935, 49 Stat. 838, 847, too tenuous. In saying this I am wholly mindful of the significance of the decision in Public Utilities Comm. v. Attleboro Steam and Electric Co., 273 U. S. 83, 47 S.Ct. 294, 71 L.Ed. 549 (1927). Preoccupation with other matters pending before the Court precludes an independent pursuit by me of all the tributaries in search of legislative purpose that the Court has followed. I am therefore constrained to leave the decision of this case to those who have no doubts about the matter."

For Mr. Justice Frankfurter's views on interpretation and interpretive methods, see his well-known article Some Reflections on the Reading of Statutes, 47 Colum.L.Rev. 527 (1947).

4. Mr. Justice Jackson's complaints about the unavailability of the legislative materials cited by Mr. Justice Reed in the *Public Utilities* case are reviewed in Finley, Crystal Gazing: The Problem of Legislative History,

---

41. This history is set out in more detail in Jackson, Struggle for Judicial Supremacy, pp. 89–91.

45 A.B.A.J. 1281 (1959). The author, an experienced law librarian, states (pp. 1282–3):

> " * * * The Federal Water Power Act was passed in 1920, long before legislative histories were being cited extensively. It is undoubtedly true that there was no *compiled* history of the Act, and of the 1935 amendments. But it seemed inconceivable that only "in Washington" could counsel find the hearings, reports and debates on that act. After a survey of libraries in the San Francisco area, it turns out that everything cited by the Court, except the bills, *was* available. All of the reports and debates were in several San Francisco libraries. The Court cited a hearing on water power, held in 1918, which was available in the California State Library in Sacramento. All other hearings cited by the Court were in the University of California Library in Berkeley, just across the bay.
>
> "Justice Jackson continued that a California library 'tried to obtain the material by interlibrary loan from the Library of Congress, but the request was refused'. The Library of Congress, according to Mr. Legare Obear, who is chief of the loan section, has several sets of congressional hearings and reports for the past fifty years and will lend them to any qualified library. True, they will not lend bills. In this case it could have been that the Government attorneys had already borrowed all copies of the material. But if the request was for the 'legislative history of the Federal Water Power Act of 1920 as amended,' the Library of Congress might be justified in 'refusing.' Such a request amounts to passing the research chore from the borrower to the lender."

On the availability of legislative history material in general, she notes (p. 1283):

> " * * * [N]o library, however large or however prosperous, has a *compiled* history of every federal law. Actually the practice of compiling histories is a fairly recent development; only in rare cases will you discover a compiled history of any federal law more than twenty-five years old. That does not mean that the legislative history of every law is not available. It is not in a book that you can take from the shelf, or borrow from a library, perhaps, but the material is nonetheless available. There are over five hundred depository libraries scattered through the country; usually there are several in a large city. Although these libraries have the privilege of selecting the classes of publications they wish to receive, it is most unlikely that any sizeable city is without a set of the Congressional Record and the Congressional Serial set, which collects the committee reports. Hearings may be only in the state library or the library of a large university. It is true that the bills may not be readily available, but they are usually reprinted in the debates, reports or hearings."

5. The Law Commission and the Scottish Law Commission issued a report and a proposal for legislation in 1969 on The Interpretation of Statutes in Great Britain. Prominent among the provisions of the draft bill

(not as yet enacted by Parliament) embodying the Commission recommendations is one (Sec. 2(a)) stating that in the process of interpretation "a construction which would promote the general legislative purpose underlying the provision in question is to be preferred to a construction which would not." [See the recent case of James Buchanan & Co. Ltd. v. Babco Forwarding & Shipping (U.K.) Ltd., [1977] 1 Q.B. 208, indicating possible liberalization of British interpretative practices in respect of the weight accorded purpose or policy.—Ed.] As to materials which may be considered by British courts as aids to interpretation, the Commission's draft bill (Sec. 1(1)(a)–(e)) provides as follows:

> 1.—(1) In ascertaining the meaning of any provision of an Act, the matters which may be considered shall, in addition to those which may be considered for that purpose apart from this section, include the following, that is to say—
>
> (a) all indications provided by the Act as printed by authority, including punctuation and side-notes, and the short title of the Act;
>
> (b) any relevant report of a Royal Commission, Committee or other body which had been presented or made to or laid before Parliament or either House before the time when the Act was passed;
>
> (c) any relevant treaty or other international agreement which is referred to in the Act or of which copies had been presented to Parliament by command of Her Majesty before that time, whether or not the United Kingdom were bound by it at that time;
>
> (d) any other document bearing upon the subject-matter of the legislation which had been presented to Parliament by command of Her Majesty before that time;
>
> (e) any document (whether falling within the foregoing paragraphs or not) which is declared by the Act to be a relevant document for the purposes of this section.

Most interesting was the Commissions' refusal to endorse judicial resort to legislative debates. On that subject, the Commission report had this to say (par. 61, page 36):

> "[W]e have reached the conclusion that at present reports of Parliamentary proceedings should not be used by the courts for the interpretation of statutes. We recognise that in principle there is much to be said in favour of relaxing the rule as to the exclusion of such reports. In supporting the existing law on this subject we are much influenced by three considerations: (a) the difficulty arising from the nature of our Parliamentary process of isolating information which will assist the courts in interpreting statutes; (b) the consequent difficulty of providing such information as could be given in a reasonably convenient and readily accessible form; and (c) the possibility that in some cases the function of legislative material in the interpretative process could be better performed by specially prepared explanatory material [see Sec. 1(1)(e), supra—Ed.] available to Parliament when a Bill is intro-

duced and modified, if necessary, to take account of amendments during its passage through Parliament."

6. A relatively recent expression of anti-legislative history views is contained in The Interpretation and Application of Statutes (1975) by Professor Reed Dickerson. Professor Dickerson, while opposing resort to the Plain Meaning approach, argues that the internal legislative history of a statute should not be deemed a part of its context for interpretative purposes because of problems as to (1) reliability, (2) relevance, and (3) availability and as to (4) whether such materials are "adequately taken account of" in the statutory text. As to (1) and (2), do the cases indicate that courts can satisfactorily weigh—and should make the effort to weigh—this kind of evidence? or that it would be better for them to abandon such efforts? In deciding how these questions should be answered, consider—as a minimum—not only the cases read so far but also the remaining cases and materials in this section (Section 6). As to (3), see Note 4, supra. As to (4), ponder in particular the implications of Commissioner v. Acker, the last case in this section. Professor Dickerson also contends, inter alia, that the benefits gained from consulting internal legislative history do not justify the cost and inconvenience that result from so multiplying the materials to be researched for purposes of counseling, advocacy and adjudication. This argument can be better appraised as one gains actual experience in research on statutory questions. Professor Dickerson acknowledges that at least some of the internal legislative history sources may properly be consulted in relation to "judicial law making" in connection with statutes, even though they should not be utilized in statutory interpretation. Is the distinction thus suggested viable as a practical matter?

UNITED STATES v. McKESSON & ROBBINS, INC.

Supreme Court of the United States, 1956.
351 U.S. 305, 76 S.Ct. 937, 100 L.Ed. 1209.

Mr. Chief Justice WARREN delivered the opinion of the Court.

This is a direct appeal by the Government under the Expediting Act, 32 Stat. 823, as amended by 62 Stat. 869, 15 U.S.C.A. § 29, from a decision of the District Court for the Southern District of New York, interpreting the scope of the exemption from the antitrust laws provided by "fair trade" legislation.

Appellee, a Maryland corporation with its home office in New York, is the largest drug wholesaler in the United States. Operating through 74 wholesale divisions located in 35 states, it sells drugstore merchandise of various brands to retailers, principally drugstores, substantially throughout the nation. For the fiscal year ended March 31, 1954, its sales of all drug products amounted to $338,000,000.

Appellee is also a manufacturer of its own line of drug products, the total sales of which amounted to $11,000,000 for the year ended March 31, 1954. Its manufacturing operation is conducted through a single manufacturing division, McKesson Laboratories, located at Bridgeport, Connecticut. This division, like each of appellee's wholesale divisions, has a separate headquarters and a separate staff of employees, but none of the 75 divisions is separately incorporated. All are component parts of the same corporation and are responsible to the corporation's president and board of directors.

Appellee distributes its own brand products to retailers through two channels: (1) directly to retailers, and (2) through independent wholesalers. The major portion of its brand products is distributed to retailers through its own wholesale divisions. Appellee also makes direct sales to important retailers through its manufacturing division. Most of appellee's sales to independent wholesalers are made by its manufacturing division, but its wholesale divisions sold approximately $200,000 of McKesson brand products to other wholesalers during the fiscal year ended June 30, 1952.

To the extent possible under state law, appellee requires all retailers of its brand products to sell them at "fair trade" retail prices fixed by appellee. These prices are set forth in published schedules of wholesale and retail prices.

Appellee also has "fair trade" agreements with 21 independent wholesalers who buy from its manufacturing division. Sixteen of these independents compete with appellee's wholesale divisions. The other 5 compete with the manufacturing division for sales to chain drugstores located in their trading areas. On June 6, 1951, in accordance with appellee's "fair trade" policy, a vice president in charge of merchandising notified appellee's wholesale divisions that—

> "None of our wholesale divisions will sell any McKesson labeled products to any wholesaler who has not entered into a fair trade contract with McKesson Laboratories."

As a result, 73 of the independent wholesalers who had been dealing with McKesson wholesale divisions entered into "fair trade" agreements with McKesson by which they bound themselves in reselling its brand products to adhere to the wholesale prices fixed by it. Each of these independent wholesalers is in direct competition with the McKesson wholesale division from which it buys.

The Government, under Section 4 of the Sherman Act, brought this civil action for injunctive relief against appellee in the District Court. The complaint charged that appellee's "fair trade" agreements with independent wholesalers with whom it was in competition constituted illegal price fixing in violation of Section 1 of the Act. Appellee admitted the contracts, but claimed that they were exempted from the Sherman Act by the Miller-Tydings Act and the McGuire Act.[42]

The Government moved for summary judgment on the ground that these Acts do not immunize McKesson's agreements with other

---

42. [The McGuire Act appears in full, supra at p. 429—Ed.]

Sec. 6   DEVELOPMENT OF CURRENT DOCTRINE   439

wholesalers, since they expressly exclude from their exemption from the antitrust laws contracts "between wholesalers" or "between persons, firms, or corporations in competition with each other." The district judge denied the motion. He recognized that price fixing is illegal *per se* under the Sherman Act, but announced that in "fair trade" cases "No inflexible standard should be laid down to govern in advance." He was "unwilling, at this stage of case law development of legislatively sanctioned resale price fixing" to apply the *per se* rule "in fair trade situations absent a factual showing of illegality." Such a showing, he said, could not be made "simply by pointing to *some* restraint of competition." The " 'true test of legality' " of "fair trade" agreements between a producer-wholesaler and independent wholesalers, the court held, "is whether some additional restraint destructive of competition is occasioned." [43]

The case then proceeded to trial before another district judge, who concurred in the "ruling that fair trade price fixing by a producer-wholesaler was not per se illegal under the Sherman Act," and held that the Government's evidence did not establish an "additional restraint" within the meaning of the test previously enunciated in the case. He ordered the complaint dismissed, and the Government took a direct appeal under the Expediting Act. We noted probable jurisdiction.

The issue presented is a narrow one of statutory interpretation. The Government does not question the so-called vertical "fair trade" agreements between McKesson and retailers of McKesson brand products. It challenges only appellee's price-fixing agreements with independent wholesalers with whom it is in competition.

Section 1 of the Sherman Act provides:

"Every contract, combination in the form of trust or otherwise, or conspiracy, in restraint of trade or commerce among the several States, or with foreign nations, is hereby declared to be illegal *   *   *."

It has been held too often to require elaboration now that price fixing is contrary to the policy of competition underlying the Sherman Act and that its illegality does not depend on a showing of its unreasonableness, since it is conclusively presumed to be unreasonable. It makes no difference whether the motives of the participants are good or evil; whether the price fixing is accomplished by express contract or by some more subtle means; whether the participants

---

43. 122 F.Supp., at pages 337–339. The district judge provided an illustration of the kind of conduct which might satisfy his test:
 "If, for example, it could be established that a producer became a wholesaler, though not in competition with an independent wholesaler, and stipulated prices for his own and the independent wholesaler as a first step toward and with intent to gouge consumers, that might suffice *prima facie* as violation of the Sherman Act outside the privilege of the fair trade statutes."

possess market control; whether the amount of interstate commerce affected is large or small; or whether the effect of the agreement is to raise or to decrease prices.

In United States v. Socony-Vacuum Oil Co., 310 U.S. 150, 60 S. Ct. 811, 84 L.Ed. 1129, in holding price-fixing agreements to be illegal *per se*, this Court said:

> "Congress has not left with us the determination of whether or not particular price-fixing schemes are wise or unwise, healthy or destructive. * * * the Sherman Act, so far as price-fixing agreements are concerned, establishes one uniform rule applicable to all industries alike."

And it has been said by this Court:

> "A distributor of a trade-marked article may not lawfully limit by agreement, express or implied, the price at which or the persons to whom its purchaser may resell, except as the seller moves along the route which is marked by the Miller-Tydings Act."

The question before us is whether the price-fixing agreements challenged herein move along that route. If they do not, they are illegal *per se*. There is no basis for supposing that Congress, in enacting the Miller-Tydings and McGuire Acts, intended any change in the traditional *per se* doctrine. The District Court was plainly in error in attempting to create a category of agreements which are outside the exemption of those Acts but which should nevertheless be spared from application of the *per se* rule.

In the Miller-Tydings Act, passed as a rider to a District of Columbia revenue bill, Congress was careful to state that its exemption of certain resale price maintenance contracts from the prohibitions of the antitrust laws "shall not make lawful any contract or agreement, providing for the establishment or maintenance of minimum resale prices on any commodity herein involved, between manufacturers, or between producers, or *between wholesalers*, or between brokers, or between factors, or between retailers, or *between persons, firms, or corporations in competition with each other.*" [44] (Emphasis supplied.)

Fifteen years later, Congress attached an almost identical proviso to the McGuire Act.[45] We are to take the words of these statutes

---

44. 50 Stat. 693. This proviso qualified the proviso immediately preceding it, which amended § 1 of the Sherman Act so as to make lawful resale price maintenance contracts entered into by manufacturers of branded or trademarked goods if such contracts are authorized by state law as to intrastate transactions and if the commodity affected is in "free and open competition with commodities of the same general class produced or distributed by others. * * *"

45. 66 Stat. 632. The McGuire Act amended § 5(a) of the Federal Trade Commission Act by adding, *inter alia* § 5(a)(2). This specifically exempts from the antitrust laws price fixing

"in their normal and customary meaning." Schwegmann Bros. v. Calvert Corp., 341 U.S. 384, 388, 71 S.Ct. 745, 747, 95 L.Ed. 1035.

Appellee is admittedly a wholesaler with resale price maintenance contracts with 94 other wholesalers who are in competition with it. Thus, even if we read the proviso so that the words "in competition with each other" modify "between wholesalers," the agreements in question would seem clearly to be outside the statutory exemption. Appellee concedes that the proviso does not exempt a contract between two competing independent wholesalers fixing the price of a brand product produced by neither of them.[46] Yet it urges that what would be illegal if done between competing independent wholesalers becomes legal if done between an independent wholesaler and a competing wholesaler who is also the manufacturer of the brand product. This is so, appellee maintains, because in contracting with independent wholesalers it acted solely as a manufacturer selling to buyers rather than as a competitor of these buyers. But the statutes provide no basis for sanctioning the fiction of McKesson, the country's largest drug wholesaler, acting only as a manufacturer when it concludes "fair trade" agreements with competing wholesalers. These were agreements "between wholesalers."

Any doubts which might otherwise be raised as to the propriety of considering a manufacturer-wholesaler as a "wholesaler" are dispelled by the last phrase of the proviso in question, which continues the proscription against price-fixing agreements "between persons, firms, or corporations in competition with each other." Congress thus made as plain as words can make it that, without regard to categories or labels, the crucial inquiry is whether the contracting parties compete with each other. If they do, the Miller-Tydings and McGuire Acts do not permit them to fix resale prices. The Court stated in Schwegmann Bros. v. Calvert Corp., 341 U.S. 384, 389, 71 S.Ct. 745, 748, that this proviso "expressly continues the prohibitions of the Sherman Act against 'horizontal' price fixing by those in competi-

---

under "fair trade" agreements which bind not only retailers who are parties to the agreement but also retailers who refuse to sign the agreement. [Accord, Hudson Distributors, Inc. v. Eli Lilly & Co., 377 U.S. 386, 84 S.Ct. 1273, 12 L.Ed.2d 394 (1964)—Ed.] As in the Miller-Tydings Act, the statutory exemption was qualified by an important proviso. This stated:

"(5) Nothing contained in paragraph (2) of this subsection shall make lawful contracts or agreements providing for the establishment or maintenance of minimum or stipulated resale prices on any commodity referred to in paragraph (2) of this subsection, between manufacturers, or between producers, or *between wholesalers*, or between brokers, or between factors, or between retailers, or *between persons, firms, or corporations in competition with each other*." (Emphasis supplied.)

46. Appellee's brief, p. 6. In the District Court and in its motion to affirm filed in this Court, however, appellee claimed that the proviso applies only to agreements "between manufacturers of competing products, or between wholesalers of competing products, or retailers of such products, fixing the prices at which *two or more* competitive products are to be sold." (Appellee's emphasis.) Motion to affirm, pp. 5–6.

tion with each other at the same functional level." [47] Since appellee competes "at the same functional level" with each of the 94 wholesalers with whom it has price-fixing agreements, the proviso prevents these agreements from falling within the statutory exemption.

Appellee argues that a brief colloquy on the Senate floor between a supporter of the McGuire Act and an inquiring Senator shortly before the Act was passed should dictate a meaning contrary to that revealed by the Act's plain language. But, at best, the statement was inconclusive.[48] And the Senator whose statement is relied on was not

[47]. Previous phrases of the proviso appear in state "fair trade" laws, upon which the proviso seems to have been modeled. FTC Report on "Resale Price Maintenance," pp. 80–81 (1945). The last phrase, however, has apparently never been included in any state statute. Thus, meticulous inclusion of this phrase in the federal acts is not without significance.

[48]. 98 Cong.Rec. 8870. Senator Humphrey, in answer to an inquiry by Senator Sparkman, said:

"* * * If, for example, when a producer, who sells to distributors, wholesalers, retailers, and consumers, makes a resale price-maintenance agreement relative to a commodity made by him and bearing a trade-mark or brand, with a distributor, wholesaler, or retailer who resells such commodity at either the wholesale, or retail level, there exists a vertical resale price-maintenance contract which would be lawful under the bill if the requirements of paragraph (2) are met.

"On the other hand, *if one wholesaler enters into a resale price-maintenance agreement with another wholesaler prescribing the price at which they both sell a trade-marked or branded commodity which they both buy from the producer, that agreement would be horizontal and would not be made lawful.*

"In other words, wholesalers getting together on a price are acting illegally. For a manufacturer to get together with other manufacturers to maintain prices is illegal, but for a manufacturer to say that a certain product will sell at a certain price from the manufacturer down to the retailer is legal under the limitations prescribed in paragraph (2) of section 5(a) of the Federal Trade Commission Act.

"In general, the test of whether a resale price-maintenance contract is vertical is if the contract is between a seller and buyers who resell the original seller's product; whereas, the test of whether a resale price-maintenance contract is horizontal is if it is between competing sellers between whom the relation of buyer and seller or reseller does not exist as to the product involved.

"It is important to keep this distinction in mind, because *many producers of trade-marked items sell them to consumers, retailers, and wholesalers alike.*

"*Under the bill, such firms may make resale price-maintenance contracts with both wholesalers and retailers because such contracts are vertical, that is, between sellers and buyers.* While in one sense firms in this position function not only as producers but also as wholesalers and retailers, they may still lawfully make contracts with other wholesalers and retailers, when in making such contracts they act as producers of a trade-marked or branded commodity, rather than as wholesalers and retailers entering into forbidden horizontal resale price-maintenance contracts with other wholesalers or other retailers." (Emphasis added.)

It should be noted that these remarks appear to be confined to the "between wholesalers" and "between retailers" phrases and do not deal with the "corporations in competition" phrase. And, even as to the former, it is not at all clear that Senator Humphrey was discussing the situation where actual competition exists between the manufacturer-wholesaler and independent wholesalers. As in-

in charge of the bill, nor was he a member of any committee that had considered it. Moreover, the McGuire Act was not a Senate bill, having been passed by the House of Representatives prior to this Senate discussion. There is nothing in the proceedings of the House to indicate that the meaning for which appellee contends should be given to the Act. Similarly, except to show congressional concern that the prohibition against "horizontal" price fixing be continued, the Senate and House debates on the proviso in the Miller-Tydings Act are of little assistance with respect to the problem before us.

The court below did not rely on the legislative history, finding it to be "unedifying and unilluminating." We agree with this appraisal, but are not troubled by it since the language of the proviso in question is unambiguous. It excludes from the exemption from the *per se* rule of illegality resale price maintenance contracts between firms competing on the same functional level.

Both the Government and appellee press upon us economic arguments which could reasonably have caused Congress to support their respective positions.[49] We need not concern ourselves with such speculation. Congress has marked the limitations beyond which price fixing cannot go. We are not only bound by those limitations but we

dicated in note [46], supra, until we noted probable jurisdiction, appellee flatly disagreed with an important part of this statement.

49. The Government maintains that a resale price maintenance agreement between a manufacturer-wholesaler and competing independent wholesalers, in addition to eliminating competition between the parties, enables the former, because of its leverage as a manufacturer of branded products, to dictate the latter's prices on these products. Such an agreement, the Government claims, also leaves the manufacturer-wholesaler free to undersell the independent wholesalers when dealing with large retailers directly through its manufacturing division. And if the manufacturer's own wholesale outlets are inefficient, resale price maintenance permits it to insulate those outlets from the inroads of more efficient operators by setting its "fair trade" price higher than otherwise. According to the Government, none of these effects is present where price fixing exists between independent wholesalers and a nonintegrated manufacturer.

Appellee contends that the economic effects of "fair trading" are the same whether or not the manufacturer has its own wholesale outlets, since the protection which resale price maintenance provides to the manufacturer's good will "necessarily involves elimination of price competition among different outlets for the manufacturer's own branded merchandise." In both situations, appellee claims, the manufacturer makes "at the source, as a manufacturer, * * * downstream price fixing arrangements with its outlets."

The court below indicated an awareness of the economic arguments on both sides but refused to follow "either of alternate horns * * * in the dilemma of fair trade agreements with independent wholesalers by a manufacturer who is also a wholesaler * * *." 122 F.Supp. at page 337. Instead, the district judge advocated a case-by-case examination of the economic setting in which the question arises, with the burden on the Government to show "some *additional* restraint destructive of competition." 122 F.Supp. at page 339.

For discussion of these economic contentions and the conclusions which they are designed to support, see Weston, Resale Price Maintenance and Market Integration: Fair Trade or Foul Play? 22 Geo.Wash.L.Rev. 658; Note, 64 Yale L.J. 426; 54 Col. L.Rev. 282.

are bound to construe them strictly, since resale price maintenance is a privilege restrictive of a free economy. Cf. United States v. Masonite Corp., 316 U.S. 265, 280, 62 S.Ct. 1070, 1078, 86 L.Ed. 1461.

The judgment of the District Court dismissing the complaint must, therefore, be reversed and the case remanded for further proceedings not inconsistent with this opinion.

Reversed and remanded.

Mr. Justice HARLAN, whom Mr. Justice FRANKFURTER and Mr. Justice BURTON join, dissenting.

Lack of sympathy with an Act of Congress does not justify giving to it a construction that cannot be rationalized in terms of any policy reasonably attributable to Congress. Rather our duty, as always, is to seek out the policy underlying the Act and, if possible, give effect to it. In this instance, I think the Court has departed from that rule by giving the Miller-Tydings and McGuire Acts an artificial construction which produces results that could hardly have been intended by Congress.

The purpose of the state fair-trade laws is to allow the manufacturer of a brand-named product to protect the goodwill his name enjoys by controlling the prices at which his branded products are resold. Old Dearborn Distributing Co. v. Seagram-Distillers Corp., 299 U.S. 183, 193–194, 57 S.Ct. 139, 144, 81 L.Ed. 109. The necessary result—indeed, the very object—is to permit the elimination of price competition in the branded product among those who sell it. Congress has sanctioned those laws in the Miller-Tydings and McGuire Acts, considering them not to be offensive to federal antitrust policy.[50] Sufficient protection to the public interest was deemed to be afforded by the competition among different brands, a safeguard made express by the provision of the Miller-Tydings and McGuire Acts denying fair-trade contracts exemption from the antitrust laws unless the fair-traded product is "in free and open competition with commodities of the same general class." In short, the very purpose of the Acts is to permit a manufacturer to set the resale price for his own products while preserving competition between brands—that is, between the fair-traded item and similar items produced by other manufacturers.

If we accept the legislative judgment implicit in the Acts that resale price maintenance is necessary and desirable to protect the goodwill attached to a brand name, there is no meaningful distinction be-

50. The Court refers to the Miller-Tydings Act as having been "passed as a rider to a District of Columbia revenue bill." It is pertinent to note that, in passing the later McGuire Act, Congress not only reaffirmed the policy of the Miller-Tydings Act but also eliminated the restrictive effect of this Court's decision in Schwegmann Bros. v. Calvert Distillers Corp., 341 U.S. 384, 71 S.Ct. 745, 95 L.Ed. 1035, as regards "non-signers" of fair-trade contracts.

Sec. 6   *DEVELOPMENT OF CURRENT DOCTRINE*   445

tween the fair-trade contracts of integrated and non-integrated manufacturers. Certainly the integrated manufacturer has as strong a claim to protection of his goodwill as a non-integrated manufacturer, and the economic effect of the contracts is the same. In both cases price competition in the resale of the branded product is eliminated, and in neither case does the price fixing extend beyond the manufacturer's own product. While the Government concedes the right of a non-integrated manufacturer to eliminate price competition in his products between wholesalers, it finds a vice not contemplated by the Acts when one of the "wholesalers" is also the manufacturer, for then the contracts eliminate competition between the very parties to the contracts. But, in either case, all price competition is eliminated, and I am unable to see what difference it makes between whom the eliminated competition would have existed had it not been eliminated. The other bases of distinction suggested by the Government are equally tenuous and reflect a subtlety of analysis for which there is no support in either the Acts or their history.

So unsatisfactory, indeed, are the Government's attempts to rationalize the result contended for, that the Court chooses not to rely upon them, finding the language of the provisos so clear as to make it unnecessary even to hypothesize a consistent rationale attributable to Congress that might justify the discrimination against integrated producers. Indeed, not even the fact that the only legislative history directly in point is squarely opposed to the Court's reading of the statute (see note [48] of the Court's opinion, 76 S.Ct. 942), prompts enough doubt in the Court to require an inquiry into the purpose of the Acts. The Court's reasoning is this: the provisos except from the Acts contracts "between wholesalers" or "between persons, firms, or corporations in competition with each other"; McKesson is a "wholesaler" as well as a manufacturer and is also "in competition with" independent wholesalers; its contracts with independent wholesalers are therefore forbidden contracts "between wholesalers" and between "corporations in competition with each other." This verbalistic argument can be answered by the equally verbalistic one that the fair-trade contracts, being made in connection with the sale of its own branded products, were made by McKesson in its capacity as a "manufacturer" rather than as a competing "wholesaler." Neither argument being more conclusive than the other, the answer to the problem can be found only by looking to the purpose of the provisos and its relation to the basic policy of permitting resale price maintenance of branded goods.

As noted above, the Acts necessarily contemplate the elimination of price competition in the resale of a particular branded product and rely for protection of the public interest upon competition between brands. Viewed in the light of this purpose, the provisos become readily understandable. The vice of price-fixing agreements between those in competition with each other, whether at the manufacturing, wholesaling, or retailing level, is that they can be utilized to eliminate competition *between brands*. Thus manufacturers might agree to fix the resale prices of their competing brands in relation to each other; the same result, on an even broader scale, could be achieved by agreements between wholesalers or retailers. Further, agreements initiated by anyone other than the owner of the brand name are unnecessary to the protection of goodwill, the very justification for permitting fair-trade contracts. Thus an agreement between wholesalers to fix the price of a product bearing the trade name of neither would serve no purpose other than the elimination of competition. Interpreting the provisos in the light of these considerations, I conclude that an integrated manufacturer selling its products under fair-trade contracts to independent wholesalers should be deemed to be acting as a "manufacturer" rather than as a "wholesaler." This interpretation of the provisos fits with their terms and produces, rather than an arbitrary discrimination hardly intended by Congress, a result fully in harmony with the policy of the Acts to permit manufacturers to maintain the resale prices of their branded products while preserving competition between brands.[51]

For these reasons, therefore, I would hold McKesson's contracts to be within the Miller-Tydings and McGuire Acts and would affirm the judgment below.

NOTES

1. State Fair Trade Laws were subjected to increasing challenge as the years went by. A number of states repealed their Fair Trade Laws; in others, they were invalidated by the courts as unconstitutional. The Consumer Goods Pricing Act of 1975, which became effective on March 11, 1976, repealed both the Miller-Tydings Amendment and the McGuire Act. Act of December 12, 1975, Pub.L. No. 94–145, 89 Stat. 801, 15 U.S.C.A. §§ 1, 45(a). Resale price maintenance has thus clearly come once again under the ban of the anti-trust laws, except in the case of alcoholic beverages. As to the special status of alcoholic beverages, see, e. g., Rice v. Alcoholic Beverages Control Appeals Bd. of California, 67 Cal.App.3d 985, 137 Cal.Rptr. 213 (Ct.App.1977).

2. Consider in connection with United States v. McKesson & Robbins Inc., supra, the following comment by Mr. Justice Frankfurter dissenting in Massachusetts Bonding & Ins. Co. v. United States, 352 U.S. 128, 138, 77 S. Ct. 186, 191, 1 L.Ed.2d 189, 196 (1956):

> "Underlying the Court's reasoning is the belief that the language of the 1947 amendment is so clear that it would require creative reconstruction of the amendment to limit the amount of the judgment to the maximum recoverable under the Massachusetts Death Act. On more than one occasion, but evidently not frequently

---

51. The Federal Trade Commission, the administrative agency specially charged with administering the McGuire Act, has reached like conclusions. See Eastman Kodak Co., 3 CCH Trade Reg.Rep. (10th ed.), par. 25,291.

enough, Judge Learned Hand has warned against restricting the meaning of a statute to the meaning of its 'plain' words. 'There is no surer way to misread any document than to read it literally. * * *' Guiseppi v. Walling, 144 F.2d 608, 624 (D.C.Cir. 1944) (concurring opinion). Of course one begins with the words of a statute to ascertain its meaning, but one does not end with them. The notion that the plain meaning of the words of a statute defines the meaning of the statute reminds one of T. H. Huxley's gay observation that at times 'a theory survives long after its brains are knocked out.' One would suppose that this particular theory of statutory construction had had its brains knocked out in Boston Sand & Gravel Co. v. United States, 278 U.S. 41, 48, 49 S.Ct. 52, 53–54, 73 L.Ed. 170 (1928)."

3. In Zuber v. Allen, 396 U.S. 168, 90 S.Ct. 314, 24 L.Ed.2d 345 (1970), the Supreme Court stated, per Mr. Justice Harlan: "We consider our conclusions in no way undermined by the colloquy on the floor between Senator Copeland and Senator Murphy upon which the dissent places such emphasis. A committee report represents the considered and collective understanding of those Congressmen involved in drafting and studying proposed legislation. Floor debates reflect at best the understanding of individual Congressmen. It would take extensive and thoughtful debate to detract from the plain thrust of a committee report in this instance." (p. 186) In a dissenting opinion, Mr. Justice Black took issue with the majority's treatment of the floor debates, observing that "anyone acquainted with the realities of the United States Senate knows that the remarks of the floor manager [Senator Murphy] are taken by other Senators as reflecting the views of the committee itself." Mr. Justice Rehnquist, dissenting in the recent case of Simpson v. United States, 435 U.S. 6, 17–18, 98 S.Ct. 909, 915, 55 L.Ed.2d 70, 80 (1978), made the following statements:

"* * * the decisions of this Court have established that some types of legislative history are substantially more reliable than others. The report of a joint conference committee of both Houses of Congress, for example, or the report of a Senate or a House committee, is accorded a good deal more weight than the remarks even of the sponsor of a particular portion of a bill on the floor of the chamber. (Citations omitted.) It is a matter of common knowledge that at any given time during the debate, particularly a prolonged debate, of a bill the members of either House in attendance on the Floor may not be great, and it is only these members, or those who later read the remarks in the Congressional Record, who will have the benefit of the Floor remarks. In the last analysis, it is the statutory language embodied in the enrolled bill which Congress enacts, and that must be our first reference point in interpreting its meaning."

In Chrysler Corp. v. Brown, 441 U.S. 281, 311, 99 S.Ct. 1705, 1722, 60 L.Ed.2d 208, 231 (1979), Rehnquist, J.'s opinion for a virtually unanimous Court went still further, arguing that "[t]he remarks of a single legislator, even the sponsor, are not controlling in analyzing legislative history * * * [such remarks] must be considered with the Reports of both Houses and the statements of other Congressmen" as well as with the statute in question. Compare Chicago, Milwaukee, St. Paul & Pacific Railroad Co. v. Acme Fast Freight, Inc., 336 U.S. 465, 69 S.Ct. 692, 93 L.Ed. 817 (1948) where statements made in debate on the House floor by Representative Wolverton, ranking minority member of the standing committee, were given greater weight in interpretation than contrary statements contained in the committee's own formal report on the bill concerned. It appeared from the Representative's statements that, due to limitations of time, the formal report had not been submitted to committee or subcommittee members for their approval before issuance. The Supreme Court (per Vinson, C. J.) commented as follows (pp. 472–476):

> "In weighing the relative importance of [the Congressman's] statement and the committee report, a number of additional facts assume importance. The bill under consideration was reported unanimously by the House Committee on Interstate and Foreign Commerce. Congressman Wolverton, who was the ranking minority member of the committee, spoke in behalf of the bill and presented the only extended exposition of its provisions. His explanation of its meaning was not challenged or contradicted by any member of the committee. On the contrary, his part in its drafting was recognized by the chairman of the committee, and his remarks have been quoted as authority by the Interstate Commerce Commission.
>
> "In this posture of events, the committee report can be given little weight. A report not previously submitted to members of the committee and expressly contradicted without challenge on the floor of the House by a ranking member of the committee can hardly be considered authoritative. The Committee of Conference, of which Representative Wolverton was a member, adopted § 1013 exactly as it appeared in the House amendment. It bore, at that time, the gloss placed upon it on the floor of the House. [In the Congressional Record's report of debate on the bill as it emerged from conference, Representative Wolverton had indicated that his earlier floor remarks on the provisions in question remained applicable to the conference bill—Ed.] Under those circumstances we cannot construe the statute [in the manner called for by the committee report]."

4. In Federal Trade Comm. v. Anheuser-Busch, Inc., 363 U.S. 536, 80 S.Ct. 1267, 4 L.Ed.2d 1385 (1960), involving construction of a section of the Robinson-Patman Act, respondent relied heavily on a statement made during Congress' consideration of that Act by Representative Utterback, a manager of the conference bill, which included the disputed provision in its final form. Conceding that this statement might be read as affirming the interpretation urged by respondent, the Court unanimously refused to follow it, observing (363 U.S. at 553, 80 S.Ct. at 1276): "[T]he primary function of statutory construction is to effectuate the intent of Congress, and that function cannot properly be discharged by reliance upon a statement of a single Congressman, in the face of the weighty countervailing considerations which are present in this case." The conclusion reached was found by the court to be supported, *inter alia*, by assumptions made in prior cases, which assumptions were "firmly rooted in the structure of the statute." Only by adopting this conclusion, the Court declared, could the dis-

Sec. 6 **DEVELOPMENT OF CURRENT DOCTRINE** 449

puted provision "be administered as Congress intended," and a contrary result "would derange this integrated statutory scheme." Compare City of Los Angeles Department of Water and Power v. Manhart, 435 U.S. 702, 98 S.Ct. 1370, 55 L.Ed.2d 657 (1978).

5. With respect to the use of Congressional debates in *McKesson* and other cases, some points deserving of notice were made by the late Senator Richard L. Neuburger in a provocative article entitled The Congressional Record Is Not a Record appearing in the New York Times Magazine, April 20, 1958, at p. 14, reprinted in 104 Cong.Rec. 6816–6818 (1958). Senator Neuburger remarked, *inter alia:*

> " * * * the Congressional Record which, since 1873, has been the daily account of proceedings in our Senate and House of Representatives when they are in session * * * is one of the most important publications in the land, for it is supposed to report faithfully the debates and discussions which shape the laws governing 171 million Americans and their role in world affairs.
>
> "I use the word 'supposed' advisedly, because the official transcript of debates in the Senate and House is frequently revised, amended, subtracted from, and even embellished with lengthy additions. These changes occur before the transcript ever reaches the printed pages of the Congressional Record. Senators and Representatives are permitted to doctor and edit their speeches, virtually at will. It is for this reason that I have introduced a resolution to write into the rules of the Senate that no changes of a substantive nature can henceforth be made in the text of what is taken down by the Senate's staff of skilled shorthand reporters.
>
> * * *
>
> "Let me emphasize that no personal opprobrium attaches to this practice, nor should it. The practice has become part of Congressional custom. It is now virtually second nature for a Senator or Representative to revise remarks which he uttered on the floor. Every Member does it—frequently out of self-protection, because his antagonist in debate is quite likely to do so. The author of this article has done it, although he trusts he has done it with circumspection. The only way to end the habit is by a rule which cuts off the privilege of all legislators simultaneously.
>
> * * *
>
> "The House of Representatives allows far greater latitude even than the Senate in tolerating distortion of the Congressional Record. A Member of the House can speak perfunctorily for 2 minutes on the floor and then receive unanimous consent to 'revise and extend' his remarks. He later can transform such sweeping permission into an address of 60-minute proportions which is published in the Congressional Record as though spoken in its entirety on the floor. * * *"

See also, Mantel, The Congressional Record: Fact or Fiction of the Legislative Process, 12 W.Pol.Q. 981 (1959). And see also The Record: Stirring Speeches in Absentia, 33 Cong.Q.Weekly Rep. 527–529 (Mar. 15, 1975), discussing instances of speeches inserted into published floor debates by absent legislators.

Under new rules promulgated by the Joint Committee on Printing effective March 1, 1978, it is now required in the House and Senate that speeches or other material not actually uttered on the floor be marked in the Record at the beginning and end by a black dot or "bullet." 124 Cong. Rec. H 1605 (daily ed. Mar. 1, 1978). Henceforth, it will be clear, if the rule is observed, that matter so marked was never spoken in debate. Unfortunately, however, it will still not be possible to rely on the absence of dots or "bullets" as a guarantee that particular material was so spoken. This is because the new rules also provide that as long as the beginning of the speech, etc.—say, the first sentence—is recited on the floor, the whole text, including the unrecited balance, can be printed without dots or "bullets" as though it had all been delivered in debate. Efforts to persuade Congress to identify *all* unspoken material are continuing. Representative Steiger (R. Wis.), a leader in the movement to reform the Record in this respect, introduced resolutions—e. g., H. Res. 479, 95th Cong., 1st Sess. (1977) (supported by 145 co-sponsors)—to accomplish this purpose. Identical measures were introduced in the Senate by Senator Packwood (R. Ore.). See, e. g., S.Res. 70, 95th Cong., 1st Sess. (1977) (supported by 14 co-sponsors). Representative Steiger reported an estimate by the Government Printing Office that some 70% of the material in the Record was never uttered in either chamber. It is apparently feared, inter alia, that a stricter rule would extend unduly the hours devoted to floor debate. See, generally, 36 Cong.Q. Weekly Rep. 348 (Feb. 11, 1978).

What are the implications of all this for courts and lawyers in statutory interpretation?

6. An article by a Member of Congress has called attention to the emergence of the "planned colloquy" as an element of the legislative process in Congress. See Moorehead, A Congressman Looks at the Planned Colloquy and Its Effect in the Interpretation of Statutes, 45 A.B.A.J. 1314 (1959). The "planned colloquy" is described as "a friendly exchange of questions and answers about the pending legislation between members, one of whom is usually a member of the committee from which the legislation emanated * * * [the exchange having been] carefully planned by the parties for the express purpose of providing a legislative interpretation of a statutory provision which might otherwise be differently interpreted." Such a colloquy may be designed on the one hand simply to explain the impact of particular provisions. Or it may be aimed, on the other hand, at circumventing parliamentary rules barring amendment or, perhaps, at establishing a policy which it is feared would raise serious political opposition if stated explicitly in the bill concerned. What is the significance of this development for the appraisal and use of floor debate materials as aids to construction?

7. Foti v. Immigration and Naturalization Service, 375 U.S. 217, 84 S.Ct. 306, 11 L.Ed.2d 281 (1963) involved interpretation of "§ 106(a) of the Immigration and Nationality Act, 8 U.S.C.A. § 1105a(a) * * * as added by § 5(a) of Public Law 87–301, approved September 26, 1961, 75 Stat. 651, 8 U.S.C.A. (Supp. IV, 1962) § 1105a." The Supreme Court based its reading on the "historical background of the Immigration and Nationality Act, the manifest purpose of Congress in enacting § 106(a), and the context of the statutory language when viewed against the prevailing administrative practices and procedures, and pertinent legislative history of § 106(a)."

After discussing the development of administrative practice on the subject at hand, the Court stated (pp. 223–24):

> "It must be concluded that Congress knew of this familiar administrative practice and had it in mind when it enacted § 106(a). These usages and procedures, which were actually followed when the provision was enacted, must reasonably be regarded as composing the context of the legislation. A colloquy between Congressmen Walter, Lindsay and Moore, all knowledgeable in deportation matters, is definitely corroborative of this view. This colloquy occurred during the House debates on the predecessor to the bill which was enacted in 1961 and contained § 106(a). * * * With the dissenters below, we feel that the court's speculation that few congressmen were present at the time of this exchange was unwarranted and probably immaterial."

In an accompanying footnote, the Court observed that

> "Representative Walter was the chairman of a subcommittee of the House Judiciary Committee responsible for immigration and nationality matters, author and chief sponsor of the measure under consideration, and a respected congressional leader in the whole area of immigration law. Representative Lindsay was thoroughly familiar with the problems in this area and the role of discretionary determinations denying suspension in the deportation process, as a result of having represented the Government, three years earlier, in Jay v. Boyd, 351 U.S. 345, 76 S.Ct. 919, 100 L.Ed. 1242 (1956). Representative Moore was a co-sponsor of the bill under discussion and a member of the House Judiciary Committee from which the bill containing § 106(a) was reported out."

Post Adoption Material: Some Queries

Although not without its critics (see e. g. R. Dickerson, The Interpretation and Application of Statutes 195 (1975)), the practice of using legislative history in interpreting statutes seems firmly established in American courts today. To what extent should courts use similar material which comes into existence *after* the statute is adopted?

1. Nashville Milk Co. v. Carnation Co., 355 U.S. 373, 78 S.Ct. 352, 2 L.Ed.2d 340 (1958), illustrates the possibility that, when a statutory question arises, there may be at hand *post-adoption* extrinsic aid material stemming from legislative sources and dealing with the provisions in issue. In the Nashville case, which involved interpretation of the Robinson-Patman Act of 1936, Mr. Justice Harlan's majority opinion, concurred in by four other justices, included a review of legislative history sources documenting various phases of the enactment of the statute by Congress. At the close of this review (p. 382), Mr. Justice Harlan quoted, "by way of epitomizing the conclusions to be drawn from the legislative history," a statement—strongly supporting the majority interpretation—which had been made in 1950 by Representative Patman (a co-author of the

Robinson-Patman Act) in testimony before a subcommittee of the House Committee on the Judiciary (Hearings on H.R. 7905, 81st Cong., 2d Sess., p. 48 (1950)). Mr. Justice Douglas, joined in dissent by three other members of the Court, commented (footnote 2, p. 387) in regard to use of this testimony: "In determining the legislative intent, reliance can hardly be placed on statements of Representative Patman, made in 1950, *some 14 years after the passage of the Robinson-Patman Act * * *.*" Compare Ramspeck v. Federal Trial Examiners Conference, 345 U.S. 128, 73 S.Ct. 570, 97 L.Ed. 872 (1953), in which Mr. Justice Minton stated for the Court (footnote 9, p. 143):

> "Respondents' brief and the dissenting opinion filed herein quote a sentence from a letter of September 6, 1951, from Senator McCarran, Chairman of the Senate Judiciary Committee, to Chairman Ramspeck of the Civil Service Commission, as follows: 'It was intended that [examiners] be very nearly the equivalent of judges even though operating within the Federal system of administrative justice.' S.Doc. No. 82, 82d Cong., 1st Sess., p. 9. We do not feel justified in regarding this sentence, taken out of context and written over five years after the Administrative Procedure Act was enacted, as illustrative of the intent of Congress at the time it passed the Act."

Compare also, for example, the following—among a number of pertinent cases: American Newspaper Publishers Ass'n v. National Labor Relations Bd., footnote 8, 345 U.S. 100, 108, 73 S.Ct. 552, 556, 97 L. Ed. 852, 859 (1953), National Labor Relations Bd. v. Lion Oil Co., 352 U.S. 282, 77 S.Ct. 330, 1 L.Ed.2d 331 (1957), United States v. Wise, 370 U.S. 405, 411, 82 S.Ct. 1354, 1358–1359, 8 L.Ed.2d 590, 594–595 (1962), Federal Trade Comm. v. Sun Oil Co., footnote 11, 371 U.S. 505, 521, 83 S.Ct. 358, 368, 9 L.Ed.2d 466, 480 (1963), United States v. Philadelphia Nat. Bank, 374 U.S. 321, 348–9, 83 S.Ct. 1715, 1733–1734, 10 L.Ed.2d 915, 936 (1963), United States v. Southwestern Cable Co., 392 U.S. 157, 170, 88 S.Ct. 1994, 2001, 20 L.Ed.2d 1001, 1012 (1968) and Blanchette v. Connecticut General Ins. Corps., 419 U.S. 102, 132, 95 S.Ct. 335, 353, 42 L.Ed.2d 320, 347 (1974). In the Lion Oil case, the majority (per Warren, C.J.) observed (p. 291):

> "Although a 1948 committee report is no part of the legislative history of a statute [i. e., the Taft-Hartley Act] enacted in 1947, we note that the Joint Committee on Labor-Management Relations, made up of members of the Congress which passed the Taft-Hartley Act, in its final report reached the same conclusion we do * * *."

Mr. Justice FRANKFURTER, concurring in part and dissenting in part, and joined on the point by Mr. Justice HARLAN, averred (p. 299) that this "subsequent legislative history affords persuasive evidence" that the Court's conclusion is "a reasonable interpretation of what the Taft-Hartley Congress legislated." A controversy over the use of post-adoption material arose in the Supreme Court in New York State Dept. of Social Services v. Dublino, 413 U.S. 405, 93 S.Ct. 2507, 37 L.Ed.2d 688 (1973). At issue was the question whether the Work Incentive (WIN) Program in the Social Security Act was intended by Congress to debar the states from adopting additional rules —such as the New York Work Rules—in the same area. After considering a pre-enactment standing committee report which it judged ambiguous on the issue of Congressional preemption, the majority added in footnote 19 of its opinion: "Perhaps the most revealing legislative expressions confirm, subsequent to enactment, a congressional desire to preserve supplementary work programs, not to supersede them." The footnote went on to relate that after invalidation of the New York Work Rules by a three-judge District Court, members of the New York congressional delegation became concerned that the court had misconstrued the intent of Congress. It then quoted brief colloquies subsequently held, on the Senate floor, between Senator Buckley and the chairman of the Senate committee that had reported the WIN program and, on the House floor, between Congressman Carey and the chairman of the committee which had been responsible for the legislation in the House. In both colloquies, the Chairmen disclaimed a preemptive intent. The dissenting opinion of Mr. Justice Marshall, joined by Mr. Justice Brennan, responded (in footnote 17) as follows:

> " * * * I cannot let pass without comment the extraordinary use the Court makes of legislative 'history', in relying on exchanges on the floor of the House and Senate that occurred *after* the decision by the District Court in this case. * * * Although reliance on floor exchanges has been criticized in this Court, Schwegmann Bros. v. Calvert Distillers Corp., 341 U.S. 384, 71 S.Ct. 745, 95 L.Ed. 1035 (1951) (Jackson J., concurring), there is some force to the more generally accepted proposition that such exchanges, particularly when sponsors of a bill or committee chairmen are involved, are relevant to a determination of the purpose Congress sought to achieve in enacting the bill. United States v. St. Paul, M. & M. R. Co., 247 U.S. 310, 38 S.Ct. 525, 62 L.Ed. 1130 (1918). For legislators know how legislative history is made, and they ought to be aware of the importance of floor exchanges. If they disagree with the interpretation placed on the bill in such exchanges, they may offer amendments or vote against it. Thus, Congress, in enacting a statute, may fairly be taken to have endorsed the interpretations offered in such exchanges. None of this is true of post-enactment floor exchanges, which have no bearing on pending legislation and to which a disinterested legis-

lator might well pay scant attention. If Senator Buckley or Representative Carey wished to have a congressional expression of intent on the issue of pre-emption, they were not barred from introducing legislation."

Based on consideration of the foregoing cases and comments and of the nature of the problem involved, what weight, if any, should be accorded to such post-adoption materials in statutory interpretation? Why?

2. Note the following extract from the opinion of the court in State Wholesale Grocers v. Great Atlantic and Pacific Tea Co., 154 F.Supp. 471 (N.D.Ill.1957), at 484–485:

"In this case, all parties have cited excerpts from Congressman Patman's book, The Robinson-Patman Act, which was written after the Robinson-Patman Act was adopted by Congress. It should be observed that while resort to the legislative history of an act that appears to be ambiguously drawn is a practice that has long been accepted in American Jurisprudence, I cannot accept the practice of citing, as authority, books or other publications subsequently written by legislators concerning what was or was not intended to be covered by a particular act previously adopted by Congress while the author was a member thereof. In Congressman Patman's book, several questions were put to the author concerning whether, under certain facts, a particular practice would constitute a violation of the Act. The author then stated his opinion whether, on the facts so given, the Robinson-Patman Act would have been violated. The parties in this case have attempted to draw an analogy between the facts of this case and the facts of the particular example-case which best suits their purposes. They conclude this line of persuasion by urging a ruling consistent with the particular advisory opinion rendered by Congressman Patman. While resort by the courts to such a novel procedure of resolving an issue might be a convenient way of disposing of these Robinson-Patman Act cases, it is a practice which would amount to an abandonment by the courts of their judicial function and, as such, cannot be condoned. Although legislative histories may be considered by the courts, a book subsequently written by a legislator, even though he be a co-author of the Act, and with all respect to his good intentions in writing such a book, should be given no consideration by a court in determining whether there has or has not been a violation of a particular act. Such a book might be helpful to a businessman as a guide in conducting his business practices but courts of law should resort to more competent authority."

Compare American Newspaper Publishers Ass'n v. National Labor Relations Bd., footnote 8, cited supra note 1, and compare Iowa State Univ. Research Foundation, Inc. v. Sperry Rand Corp., 444 F.2d 406 (1971). The Iowa State Case involved a question of interpretation of the Patent Act of 1952. To resolve this question the court referred, *inter alia*, to statements contained in lectures, published after passage of the Act, by the Examiner-in-Chief of the Patent Office, a draftsman of the Act. To the objection that the Examiner-in-Chief had not included these statements in his testimony at the pre-enactment legislative hearings, and that they could not be deemed a part of the legislative history, the court responded: "We agree, but nonetheless [the lectures are] entitled to the weight ordinarily accorded an acknowledged authority in his field." Id. at 409. After analysis and reflection, do you agree with the quoted judicial views as to the propriety of resort to the Patman book and as to the propriety of resort to the Examiner-in-Chief's lectures? Should these materials be accorded differing treatment? In this connection, consider whether the judicial treatment of these materials should differ from that accorded the materials referred to in note 1, supra. If not, why not? If so, how and why?

3. How should a court treat proffered affidavits or testimony by legislators as to the proper interpretation of a statute in whose enactment they have participated? Why? See, e. g., Cartwright v. Sharpe, 40 Wis.2d 494, 162 N.W.2d 5 (1968), and see 97 U. of Pa.L. Rev. 293 (1948), discussing United States v. Howell Electric Motors Co., 78 F.Supp. 627 (E.D.Mich.1948). Compare Ballard v. Anderson, 4 Cal.3d 873, 95 Cal.Rptr. 1, 6–7, 484 P.2d 1345, 1350–51 (1971).

4. Section 70c of the Bankruptcy Act was the subject of a controversial interpretation by the U.S. Court of Appeals for the Second Circuit in Constance v. Harvey, 215 F.2d 571 (1954). In Lewis v. Manufacturers Nat. Bank of Detroit, 364 U.S. 603, 81 S.Ct. 347, 5 L. Ed.2d 323 (1961), the Supreme Court considered the same provision. After reviewing the underlying theory of § 70c as legislatively developed, the scheme of the Bankruptcy Act, and the consequences of competing interpretations, the Supreme Court refused to follow the line indicated by Constance v. Harvey. In a footnote to the Lewis opinion (364 U.S. 603, 607, 81 S.Ct. 347, 349 at footnote 6) the Court called attention to the fact that following the decision in Constance v. Harvey, Congress had passed a bill to change its holding, which bill suffered a Presidential "pocket veto." The Court set out the text of a Presidential message to Congress regarding the veto. 106 Cong.Rec. A7013 (Sept. 16, 1960). This statement objected to the bill on the ground that the provisions dealing with priority of liens—one of the two main concerns of the bill—would, as drawn, unnecessarily prejudice the administration of federal tax laws, though the need for legislation on priority of liens was acknowledged. No objection was made to the provision amending § 70c to deal with

Constance v. Harvey, the other main concern of the bill. The President's statement, in conclusion, expressed a belief that the defects of the bill could be corrected "without compromising its primary and commendable purpose." Ibid. The Court then went on to quote from the House standing committee report on the bill a paragraph pointing to inequities that might result from construing § 70c in accord with Constance v. Harvey. How should the judicial treatment of the Congressional action, the committee report and the veto message involved here differ, if at all, from that accorded the extrinsic aid materials referred to in notes 1 and 2, supra? Why? Similar questions should be weighed in relation to Waterman Steamship Corp. v. United States, 381 U.S. 252, 85 S.Ct. 1389, 14 L.Ed.2d 370 (1965), which is to be compared with the Lewis case. Mr. Justice Goldberg's majority opinion in *Waterman* reads in pertinent part as follows (pp. 268–9):

> "Finally, petitioner argues that the congressional history subsequent to the enactment of the 1946 statute supports its interpretation of the Act. In 1950, Congress passed an amendment to the 1946 Act, designed to provide precisely the tax result here contended for by petitioner. This amendment, however, was vetoed by President Truman. While both House and Senate Committee Reports contain statements that this amendment was deemed simply a clarifying one which expressed the intent of the original Act, see H.R.Rep.No.1342, 81st Cong., 1st Sess., 1; S.Rep.No.1915, 81st Cong., 2d Sess., 1, it was vetoed by President Truman on the ground that, on the contrary, he considered it to vitiate the intent of Congress in enacting the 1946 Act. * * * [Quoted text of veto message omitted.] Thus, it is apparent that the President and Congress disagreed over the meaning of a law passed by a prior Congress, and that the President, deeming the amendment to depart from the purpose of the original statute, refused to approve it so that the amendment was not enacted into law. This Court has pointed out on previous occasions that 'the views of a subsequent Congress form a hazardous basis for inferring the intent of an earlier one.' United States v. Price, 361 U.S. 304, 313, 80 S.Ct. 326, 331–32, 4 L.Ed.2d 334 (1960); United States v. Philadelphia Nat. Bank, 374 U.S. 321, 348–349, 83 S.Ct. 1715, 1733–34, 10 L.Ed.2d 915 (1963). This is particularly true where a President (the same President who signed the original Act) vetoes a 'clarifying' amendment on the grounds that, in his view, it does not clarify but rather vitiates the intent of the Congress that passed the original Act. As this Court held in Fogarty v. United States, 340 U.S. 8, 71 S.Ct. 5, 95 L.Ed. 10 (1950), in considering a similar situation, the abortive action of the subsequent Congress

'would not supplant the contemporaneous intent of the Congress which enacted the * * * Act.' Id., at 14. See also United States v. Wise, 370 U.S. 405, 411, 82 S.Ct. 1354, 1358–59, 8 L.Ed.2d 590 (1962)."

Compare the problems raised by the materials in this and the preceding notes to those raised by Federal Housing Administration v. The Darlington, Inc., and the accompanying notes and cases, infra p. 528.

5. In reflecting on the problems of post-adoption materials, consider the bearing and merits of the views quoted herewith from Curtis, A Better Theory of Legal Interpretation, 3 Vand.L.Rev. 407, 414–16 (1950):

"If our courts are going to decide our cases on what they think our legislatures would have done, would they not be better occupied with what the present legislature or the next legislature will do than turn themselves into a historical society reading papers on what some past legislature might then have done?

"This doctrine of guessing at what the legislature would have done is no better than asking what the legislature intended. It too puts the court back to the time when the statute was passed, shoving the whole process of interpretation as far back into the past as possible. It has the same archaic, regressive ring as the orthodox doctrine.

"As soon as a statute is enacted, it joins the rest of the law, and together with all the rest it speaks to the judge at the moment he decides a case. When it was enacted, to be sure, it was a command, uttered at a certain time in certain circumstances, but it became more than that. It became a part of the law which is now telling the judge, with the case before him and a decision confronting him, what he should now do. And isn't this just what the legislature wanted? The legislature had fashioned the statute, not for any immediate occasion, but for an indefinite number of occasions to arise in an indefinite future, until it was repealed or amended. It was to be used or applied to any such occasion, not only to the variety which might arise out of the particular situation out of which the statute itself had arisen and which had stimulated the legislature to pass it. If that were all the legislature had wanted, or if you please, intended, to do, it could have and should have used more specific terms.

"The legislature which passed the statute has adjourned and its members gone home to their constituents or to a long rest from all lawmaking. So why bother about what they intended or what they would have done? Better be prophetic than archeological, better deal with the future than the past, better pay a decent respect for a future legislature than stand in awe of one that has folded up its papers and joined its friends at the country club or in the cemetery. Better that the courts should set their decisions up against the possibility of correction than make them under the shadow of a fiction which amounts to a denial of any responsibility for the result.

"There are lawyers who will call this a crude alternative, my suggestion that the courts would do better to try to anticipate the wishes of their present and future masters than divine their past intentions. It seems crude, partly because lawyers prefer the past to the future, partly because it is candid, and candor is more formidable than any let's pretend. What the courts do, or at any rate say now they do, is not crude. It's rococo. Let the courts deliberate on what the present or a future legislature would do after it had read the court's opinion, after the situation has been explained, after the court has exhibited the whole fabric of the law into which this particular bit of legislation has had to be adjusted. The legislature would then be acting, if it did act, in the light of the tradition of the whole of law, which is what the courts expound and still stand for."

The immediate occasion for the foregoing comments was Vermilya-Brown Co. v. Connell, 335 U.S. 377, 69 S.Ct. 140, 93 L.Ed. 76 (1948). Apart from their relevance, already suggested, to the problem of post-adoption material, are they pertinent to appraisal of the interpretive methods employed in any of the cases earlier considered? If so, which cases, and why? More broadly, what account should be taken of Mr. Curtis's points and views in developing a sound general theory and approach in regard to statutory interpretation? Compare Bishin, The Law-Finders: An Essay in Statutory Interpretation, 38 So.Cal.L.Rev. 1 (1965).

COMMISSIONER v. ACKER

Supreme Court of the United States, 1959.
361 U.S. 87, 80 S.Ct. 144, 4 L.Ed. 127.

Mr. Justice WHITTAKER delivered the opinion of the Court.

This case presents the question whether, under the Internal Revenue Code of 1939, the failure of a taxpayer to file a declaration of estimated income tax, as required by § 58,[52] not only subjects him to

---

52. Section 58, as amended, provides, in pertinent part, that:
"Every individual * * * shall, at the time prescribed in subsection (d), make a declaration of his estimated tax for the taxable year if [his gross income from wages or other sources can reasonably be expected to exceed stated sums, showing] the amount which he estimates as the amount of tax under this chapter for the taxable year,

Sec. 6   *DEVELOPMENT OF CURRENT DOCTRINE*   459

the addition to the tax prescribed by § 294(d)(1)(A) for failure to file the declaration, but also subjects him to the further addition to the tax prescribed by § 294(d)(2) for the filing of a "substantial underestimate" of his tax.

Section 294(d)(1)(A) provides, in substance, that if a taxpayer fails to make and file "a declaration of estimated tax," within the time prescribed, there shall be added to the tax an amount equal to 5% of each installment due and unpaid, plus 1% of such unpaid installments for each month except the first, not exceeding an aggregate of 10% of such unpaid installments.[53]

Section 294(d)(2), in pertinent part, provides:

"(2) Substantial underestimate of estimated tax.

"If 80 per centum of the tax (determined without regard to the credits under sections 32 and 35) * * * exceeds the estimated tax (increased by such credits), there shall be added to the tax an amount equal to such excess, or equal to 6 per centum of the amount by which such tax so determined exceeds the estimated tax so increased, whichever is the lesser * * *." 26 U.S.C.A. § 294(d)(2).

Section 29.294–1(b)(3)(A) of Treasury Regulation 111, promulgated under the Internal Revenue Code of 1939, contains the statement that:

"In the event of a failure to file the required declaration, the amount of the estimated tax for the purposes of [§ 294(d)(2)] is zero."

Respondent, without reasonable cause, failed to file a declaration of his estimated income tax for any of the years 1947 through 1950. The Commissioner imposed an addition to the tax for each of those

---

53. Section 294(d)(1)(A), as amended, provides, in pertinent part, that:

"(A) Failure to file declaration.
"In the case of a failure to make and file a declaration of estimated tax within the time prescribed * * * there shall be added to the tax 5 per centum of each installment due but unpaid, and in addition, with respect to each such installment due but unpaid, 1 per centum of the unpaid amount thereof for each month (except the first) or fraction thereof during which such amount remains unpaid. In no event shall the aggregate addition to the tax under this subparagraph with respect to any installment due but unpaid, exceed 10 per centum of the unpaid portion of such installment. For the purposes of this subparagraph the amount and due date of each installment shall be the same as if a declaration had been filed within the time prescribed showing an estimated tax equal to the correct tax reduced by the credits under sections 32 and 35." 26 U.S.C.A. (1952 ed.) § 294(d)(1)(A).

without regard to any credits under Sections 32 and 35 for taxes withheld at source * * *; the amount which he estimates as [such] credits * * *; and [that] the excess of the [estimated tax] over the [estimated credits] shall be considered the estimated tax for the taxable year." 26 U.S.C.A. (1952 ed.) § 58.

years under § 294(d)(1)(A) for failure to file the declaration, and also imposed a further addition to the tax for each of those years under § 294(d)(2) for a "substantial underestimate" of the tax. The Tax Court sustained the Commissioner's imposition of both additions. The Court of Appeals affirmed with respect to the addition imposed for failure to file the declaration, but reversed with respect to the addition imposed for substantial underestimation of the tax, holding that § 294(d)(2) does not authorize the treatment of a taxpayer's failure to file a declaration of estimated tax as the equivalent of a declaration estimating no tax, and that the regulation, which purports to do so, is not supported by the statute and is invalid. 258 F.2d 568. Because of a conflict among the circuits [54] we granted the Commissioner's petition for certiorari. 358 U.S. 940, 79 S.Ct. 346, 3 L.Ed.2d 348.

The first and primary question that we must decide is whether there is any expressed or necessarily implied provision or language in § 294(d)(2) which authorizes the treatment of a taxpayer's failure to

---

54. After the Sixth Circuit had delivered its opinion in this case but before it had decided the Commissioner's petition for rehearing, the Third Circuit, in Abbott v. Commissioner, 258 F.2d 537, and the Fifth Circuit, in Patchen v. Commissioner, 258 F.2d 544, held that the failure of a taxpayer to file a declaration of estimated tax subjected him not only to the "addition to the tax" imposed by § 294(d)(1)(A) for failure to file a declaration, but also to the "addition to the tax" imposed by § 294(d)(2) for a "substantial underestimate" of his tax. Less than two months earlier, the Ninth Circuit, too, had so held in Hansen v. Commissioner, 258 F.2d 585.

From the beginning of litigation involving the question here presented, a large majority of the published opinions of the District Courts have held that § 294(d)(2) does not authorize the treatment of a taxpayer's failure to file any declaration at all as the equivalent of a declaration estimating his tax to be zero, and that the regulation attempts to amend and extend the statute and is therefore invalid. See, e. g., United States v. Ridley, D.C., 120 F.Supp. 530, 538; United States v. Ridley, D.C., 127 F.Supp. 3, 11; Owen v. United States, D.C., 134 F.Supp. 31, 39, modified on another point sub nom. Knop v. United States, 8 Cir., 234 F.2d 760; Powell v. Granquist, D.C., 146 F.Supp. 308, 312, affirmed 9 Cir., 252 F.2d 56; Hodgkinson v. United States, 57–1 U.S.T.C. ¶ 9294; Jones v. Wood, D.C., 151 F.Supp. 678; Glass v. Dunn, 56–2 U.S.T.C. ¶ 9840; Stenzel v. United States, D.C., 150 F.Supp. 364; Todd v. United States, 57–2 U.S.T.C. ¶ 9768; Erwin v. Granquist, 57–2 U.S.T.C. ¶ 9732, aff'd 9 Cir., 253 F.2d 26; Barnwell v. United States, D.C., 164 F.Supp. 430. Three District Court opinions have held the other way, Palmisano v. United States, 159 F.Supp. 98; Farrow v. United States, 150 F.Supp. 581; and Peterson v. United States, 141 F.Supp. 382; and the Tax Court has consistently so held. See, e. g., Buckley v. Commissioner, 29 T.C. 455; Garsaud v. Commissioner, 28 T.C. 1086, 1090.

The 1954 Internal Revenue Code has eliminated the question here presented as respects taxable years beginning after January 1, 1955, by providing for a single addition to the tax of 6% of the amount of underpayment, whether for failure to file a declaration of estimated tax or timely to pay the quarterly installments or for a substantial underestimation of the tax. 26 U.S.C.A. § 6654. But the question is still a live one because of the pendency of a substantial number of cases which arose under and are governed by the 1939 Code.

Sec. 6   DEVELOPMENT OF CURRENT DOCTRINE   461

file a declaration of estimated tax as, or the equivalent of, a declaration estimating his tax to be zero.

We are here concerned with a taxing Act which imposes a penalty.[55] The law is settled that "penal statutes are to be construed strictly," Federal Communications Commission v. American Broadcasting Co., 347 U.S. 284, 296, 74 S.Ct. 593, 601, 98 L.Ed. 699, and that one "is not to be subjected to a penalty unless the words of the statute plainly impose it," Keppel v. Tiffin Savings Bank, 197 U.S. 356, 362, 25 S.Ct. 443, 445, 49 L.Ed. 790. See, e. g., Tiffany v. National Bank of Missouri, 18 Wall. 409, 410, 21 L.Ed. 862; Elliott v. Railroad Co., 99 U.S. 573, 576, 25 L.Ed. 292.

Viewing § 294(d)(2) in the light of this rule, we fail to find any expressed or necessarily implied provision or language that purports to authorize the treatment of a taxpayer's failure to file a declaration of estimated tax as, or the equivalent of, a declaration estimating his tax to be zero. This section contains no words or language to that effect, and its implications look the other way. By twice mentioning, and predicating its application upon, "the estimated tax" the section seems necessarily to contemplate, and to apply only to, cases in which a declaration of "the estimated tax" has been made and filed. The fact that the section contains no basis or means for the computation of any addition to the tax in a case where no declaration has been filed would seem to settle the point beyond all controversy. If the section had in any appropriate words conveyed the thought expressed by the regulation it would thereby have clearly authorized the Commissioner to treat the taxpayer's failure to file a declaration as the equivalent of a declaration estimating his tax at zero and, hence, as constituting a "substantial underestimate" of his tax. But the section contains nothing to that effect, and, therefore, to uphold this addition to the tax would be to hold that it may be imposed by regulation, which, of course, the law does not permit. United States v. Calamaro, 354 U.S. 351, 359, 77 S.Ct. 1138, 1143, 1 L.Ed.2d 1394; Koshland v. Helvering, 298 U.S. 441, 446–447, 56 S.Ct. 767, 769–770, 80

---

55. Although the Commissioner concedes that the addition to the tax imposed by § 294(d)(1)(A) for failure to file a declaration of estimated tax is a penalty, he contends that the addition to the tax imposed by § 294(d)(2) for substantial underestimation of the tax may not be so regarded. He attempts to support a distinction upon the ground that the amount of the addition imposed by § 294(d)(1)(A) of 5%, plus 1% per month of unpaid installments, not exceeding an aggregate of 10% of such unpaid installments, does not represent a normal interest rate, whereas, he argues, the addition of the maximum of 6% that may be imposed under § 294(d)(2) is a normal interest rate and should not be regarded as a penalty but as interest to compensate the Government for delayed payment.

We think this argument is unsound, for both of the additions are imposed for the breach of statutory duty, and both are characterized by the same language. Each is stated in the respective sections to be an "addition to the tax" itself; and, being such, it cannot be interest. Moreover, being "addition[s] to the tax," both additions are themselves as subject to statutory interest as the remainder of the tax. 26 U.S.C.A. § 292(a).

L.Ed. 1268; Manhattan General Equipment Co. v. Commissioner, 297 U.S. 129, 134, 56 S.Ct. 397, 399, 80 L.Ed. 528.

The Commissioner points to the fact that both the Senate Report [56] which accompanied the bill that became the Current Tax Payment Act of 1943,[57] and the Conference Report [58] relating to that bill, contained the statement which was later embodied in the regulation. He then argues that by reading § 294(d)(2) in connection with that statement in those reports it becomes evident that Congress intended by § 294(d)(2) to treat the failure to file a declaration as the equivalent of a declaration estimating no tax. He urges us to give effect to the congressional intention which he thinks is thus disclosed. However, these reports pertained to the forerunner of the section with which we are now confronted, and not to that section itself. Bearing in mind that we are here concerned with an attempt to justify the imposition of a second penalty for the same omission for which Congress has specifically provided a separate and very substantial penalty, we cannot say that the legislative history of the initial enactment is so persuasive as to overcome the language of § 294(d)(2) which seems clearly to contemplate the filing of an estimate before there can be an underestimate.

The Commissioner next argues that the fact that Congress, with knowledge of the regulation, several times amended the 1939 Code but left § 294(d)(2) unchanged, shows that Congress approved the regulation, and that we should accordingly hold it to be valid. This argument is not persuasive, for it must be presumed that Congress also knew that the courts, except the Tax Court, had almost uniformly held that § 294(d)(2) does not authorize an addition to the tax in a case where no declaration has been filed, and that the regulation is invalid. But the point is immaterial, for Congress could not add to or expand this statute by impliedly approving the regulation.

These considerations compel us to conclude that § 294(d)(2) does not authorize the treatment of a taxpayer's failure to file a declaration of estimated tax as the equivalent of a declaration estimating his tax to be zero. The questioned regulation must therefore be regarded "as no more than an attempted addition to the statute of something which is not there." United States v. Calamaro, supra, 354 U.S. at page 359, 77 S.Ct. at page 1143.

Affirmed.

56. S.Rep. No. 221, 78th Cong., 1st Sess., p. 42; 1943 Cum.Bull. 1314, 1345.

57. Section 5(b) of the Current Tax Payment Act of 1943, c. 120, 57 Stat. 126, introduced into the 1939 Code what, as amended, is now § 294(d)(2) of that Code.

58. H.R.Conf.Rep. No. 510, 78th Cong., 1st Sess., p. 56; 1943 Cum.Bull. 1351, 1372.

Mr. Justice FRANKFURTER, whom Mr. Justice CLARK and Mr. Justice HARLAN join, dissenting.

English courts would decide the case as it is being decided here. They would do so because English courts do not recognize the relevance of legislative explanations of the meaning of a statute made in the course of its enactment. If Parliament desires to put a gloss on the meaning of ordinary language, it must incorporate it in the text of legislation. See Plucknett, A Concise History of the Common Law (5th ed.), 330–336; Amos, The Interpretation of Statutes, 5 Camb.L. J. 163; Davies, The Interpretation of Statutes, 35 Col.L.Rev. 519; Lord Haldane in Viscountess Rhondda's Claim, [1922] 2 A.C. 339, 383–384. Quite otherwise has been the process of statutory construction practiced by this Court over the decades in scores and scores of cases. Congress can be the glossator of the words it legislatively uses either by writing its desired meaning, however odd, into the text of its enactment, or by a contemporaneously authoritative explanation accompanying a statute. The most authoritative form of such explanation is a congressional report defining the scope and meaning of proposed legislation. The most authoritative report is a Conference Report acted upon by both Houses and therefore unequivocally representing the will of both Houses as the joint legislative body.

No doubt to find failure to file a declaration of estimated income to be a "substantial underestimate" would be to attribute to Congress a most unlikely meaning for that phrase in § 294(d)(2) *simpliciter*. But if Congress chooses by appropriate means for expressing its purpose to use language with an unlikely and even odd meaning, it is not for this Court to frustrate its purpose. The Court's task is to construe not English but congressional English. Our problem is not what do ordinary English words mean, but what did Congress mean them to mean. "It is said that when the meaning of language is plain we are not to resort to evidence in order to raise doubts. That is rather an axiom of experience than a rule of law and does not preclude consideration of persuasive evidence if it exists." Boston Sand & Gravel Co. v. United States, 278 U.S. 41, 48, 49 S.Ct. 52, 54, 73 L. Ed. 170.

Here we have the most persuasive kind of evidence that Congress did not mean the language in controversy, however plain it may be to the ordinary user of English, to have the ordinary meaning. These provisions were first enacted in the Current Tax Payment Act of 1943, c. 120, 57 Stat. 126, as additions to § 294(a) of the Internal Revenue Code of 1939. The Conference Report, H.R.Conf.Rep. No. 510, p. 56, and the Senate Report, S.Rep.No. 221, p. 42, both gave the provision dealing with substantial underestimation of taxes the following gloss:

> "In the event of a failure to file any declaration where one is due, the amount of the estimated tax for the purposes of this provision will be zero."

The revision of the section eight months later by the Revenue Act of 1943, c. 63, 58 Stat. 21, did not affect its substance, and this provision, therefore, continued to carry the original gloss. While the Court adverts to this congressional definition, it disregards its controlling significance.[59]

I agree with the construction placed upon the provision by the Third, Fifth, and Ninth Circuits. Abbott v. Commissioner, 3 Cir., 1958, 258 F.2d 537; Patchen v. Commissioner, 5 Cir., 1958, 258 F.2d 544; Hansen v. Commissioner, 9 Cir., 1958, 258 F.2d 585.

Current Status of the Plain Meaning Rule

In Cass v. United States, 417 U.S. 72, 94 S.Ct. 2167, 40 L.Ed.2d 668 (1974), the petitioners argued in the Supreme Court of the United States that the statute in question was plain and that resort to legislative history was thus unnecessary and improper. The Supreme Court indicated in response that the Congressional intent as expressed in the statute was "sufficiently doubtful to warrant our resort to extrinsic aids," but it took the occasion to reiterate in terms the statement made in the *American Trucking* case that "[W]hen aid to construction of the meaning of words, as used in the statute, is available, there certainly can be no 'rule of law' which forbids its use, however clear the words may appear on 'superficial examination.'" The Court's position thus still seemed in 1974—albeit in dicta—to be definitely in favor of resort to extrinsic aids regardless of the clarity of the statute.

In a 1975 article—See Murphy, Old Maxims Never Die: The Plain Meaning Rule and Statutory Interpretation in the Modern Federal Courts, 75 Colum.L.Rev. 1299—the current status of the plain meaning rule in the federal courts was reviewed. Despite occasional use of "plain meaning" terminology, as in U. S. v. Oregon, 366 U.S. 643, 648, 81 S.Ct. 1278, 1280, 6 L.Ed.2d 575 (1975), the author reported at 1303–1305:

"With the possible exception of Packard Motor Co. v. NLRB, 330 U.S. 485, 67 S.Ct. 789, 91 L.Ed. 1040 [(1947)], in no case since American Trucking has the Supreme Court actually refused to look at legislative history. And only re-

---

59. The essential reliance of the Court is on its characterization of § 294(d)(2) as a penalty. No adequate justification for this exists. Section 294(d)(2) on its face indicates that it is in the nature of an interest charge, designed to compensate the Treasury for delay in receipt of funds which a reasonably accurate estimate would have disclosed to be due and owing. Significantly, this charge is imposed regardless of fault, while § 294(d)(1)(A), a true penalty provision, authorizes no addition to tax when the failure to file is shown "to be due to reasonable cause and not to willful neglect." Had taxpayer here had reasonable cause for failure to file, the 10% addition under § 294(d)(1)(A) could not have been imposed. Yet taxes would have been withheld by him pending the filing of a final return for the year. Section 294(d)(2) provides the Government a definite means for ascertaining the compensation for this loss of funds.

Sec. 6   DEVELOPMENT OF CURRENT DOCTRINE   465

cently the court reaffirmed [citing Cass] its receptivity to legislative history in all cases. * * *

"The approach of the lower federal courts is less easy to characterize. In a number of cases the courts use language similar to that of United States v. Oregon, that is, where the language of the statute is clear, there is 'no need' to resort to legislative history. As with the Supreme Court this incantation has not prevented the courts from looking at the history. * * *

"There are, however, a number of cases which seem to be true throwbacks to the Caminetti era. Some of those in which the courts do seem to reject relevant legislative history on the basis of the rule are: Easson v. C. I. R. [294 F.2d 653], a 1961 decision of the Court of Appeals for the Ninth Circuit, and Gilbert v. C. I. R. [241 F.2d 491], a 1957 decision by the same court; Globe Seaways, Inc. v. Panama Canal Co. [509 F.2d 969], a 1975 decision of the Court of Appeals for the Fifth Circuit; Mandel Brothers v. FTC [254 F.2d 18], American Community Builders, Inc. v. C. I. R. [301 F.2d 7], and United States v. Zions Savings and Loan Association [313 F.2d 331], decisions by the Court of Appeals for the Seventh Circuit in 1958, 1962 and 1963, respectively; and Heilman v. Levi [391 F.Supp. 1106 (E.D.Wisc.1975)] * * *.

"Finally, there are the cases which in terms hark back to the pure plain meaning rule, but which nevertheless permit the use of legislative history."

The same article at p. 1305 describes as "the most fully articulated avowal of the plain meaning rule in thirty years" a filed dissenting opinion by Judge Mansfield of the Court of Appeals for the Second Circuit in United States v. Reid, 517 F.2d 953, 967 (1975), which contends that, despite earlier suggestions in the same court that the plain meaning doctrine has become outmoded, "it remains very much alive and viable." To support this contention, Judge Mansfield quotes *inter alia* the *American Trucking* case—a reference the majority of the court characterizes as "rather strange"!

Such behavior in the lower federal courts would seem clearly out of bounds following the Supreme Court's action in Train v. Colorado Public Interest Research Group, Inc., 426 U.S. 1, 96 S.Ct. 1938, 48 L. Ed.2d 434 (1976). In that case, the Court had occasion to review a decision by the Court of Appeals for the Tenth Circuit presenting the view that since the statute before it was plain and unambiguous, it "need not resort to legislative history." The Supreme Court reversed. Writing for a unanimous court, Mr. Justice Marshall expressly declared that "[t]o the extent that the Court of Appeals excluded reference to the legislative history of the FWPCA in discerning its meaning, the Court was in error." The *American Trucking* and *Cass* cases and Professor Murphy's article were cited in support and the Court's opinion went on to rely extensively on pertinent floor debates and other legislative history material.

Notwithstanding all this, the Murphy suggestion that "old maxims never die" later received some apparent support when, in Tennessee Valley Authority v. Hill, 437 U.S. 153, 98 S.Ct. 2279, 57 L.Ed.2d 117 (1978) (the well-known "snail darter" case), the following language appeared in footnote 29 of Chief Justice Burger's opinion for the majority:

> "When confronted with a statute which is plain and unambiguous on its face, we ordinarily do not look to legislative history as a guide to its meaning. Ex Parte Collett, 337 U.S. 55, 61, 69 S.Ct. 944, 93 L.Ed. 1207, 10 A.L.R.2d 921 (1949), and cases cited therein. Here it is not *necessary* to look beyond the words of the statute. We have undertaken such an analysis only to meet Mr. Justice Powell's suggestion that the 'absurd' result reached in this case * * * is not in accord with congressional intent."

These remarks accompanied a detailed review of the legislative history of the statute in question.

State cases continue to refer to and rely upon the plain meaning rule from time to time. See, e. g., American Metal Climax, Inc. v. Claimant of Butler, 188 Colo. 116, 532 P.2d 951 (1975); State v. Park, 55 Hawaii 610, 525 P.2d 586 (1974); Slate v. Zitomer, 275 Md. 534, 341 A.2d 789 (1975); State v. Camp, 286 N.C. 148, 209 S.E.2d 754 (1974); Rabon v. South Carolina State Highway Dept., 258 S.C. 154, 187 S.E.2d 652 (1972); and State v. Racine, 133 Vt. 111, 329 A.2d 651 (1974).

NOTE

At this point, drawing on the preceding materials of this Chapter, try to define for yourself the elements of a sound working approach to statutory interpretation for use in tackling statutory problems in your courses and elsewhere. An effort of this kind will be found in Kernochan, Statutory Interpretation: An Outline of Method, 3 Dalhousie L.J. 333 (1976).

SOME EXERCISES IN FINDING, STATING AND RESOLVING ISSUES UNDER THE PRESIDENT'S EXECUTIVE ORDER OF AUGUST 15, 1971

Following is an extract from the text of the President's Executive Order of August 15, 1971 regarding stabilization of prices, rents, wages and salaries:

> Whereas, in order to stabilize the economy, reduce inflation, and minimize unemployment, it is necessary to stabilize prices, rents, **wages and salaries; and**

Whereas, the present balance-of-payments situation makes it especially urgent to stabilize prices, rents, wages and salaries in order to improve our competitive position in world trade and to protect the purchasing power of the dollar:

Now, therefore, by virtue of the authority vested in me by the Constitution and statutes of the United States, including the Economic Stabilization Act of 1970 (P.L. 91–379, 84 Stat. 799), as amended, it is hereby ordered as follows:

SECTION 1. (A) Prices, rents, wages and salaries shall be stabilized for a period of 90 days from the date hereof at levels not greater than the highest of those pertaining to a substantial volume of actual transactions by each individual, business, firm or other entity of any kind during the 30-day period ending Aug. 14, 1971, for like or similar commodities or services. If no transactions occurred in that period, the ceiling will be the highest price, rent, salary or wage in the nearest preceding 30-day period in which transactions did occur. No person shall charge, assess or receive, directly or indirectly in any transaction, prices or rents in any form higher than those permitted hereunder, and no person shall, directly or indirectly, pay or agree to pay in any transaction wages or salaries in any form, or to use any means to obtain payment of wages and salaries in any form, higher than those permitted hereunder, whether by retroactive increase or otherwise.

(B) Each person engaged in the business of selling or providing commodities or services shall maintain available for public inspection a record of the highest prices or rents charged for such or similar commodities or services during the 30-day period ending Aug. 14, 1971.

(C) The provisions of Sections 1 and 2 hereof shall not apply to the prices charged for raw agricultural products.

SECTION 2. (A) There is hereby established the Cost-of-Living Council, which shall act as an agency of the United States and which is hereinafter referred to as the council.

* * *

SECTION 3. (A) Except as otherwise provided herein, there are hereby delegated to the council all of the powers conferred on the President by the Economic Stabilization Act of 1970.

* * *

SECTION 4. (A) The council, in carrying out the provisions of this order, may (I) prescribe definitions for any terms used herein, (II) make exceptions or grant exemptions, (III) issue regulations and orders and (IV) take such other actions as it determines to be necessary and appropriate to carry out the purposes of this order.

* * *

SECTION 5. The council may require the maintenance of appropriate records or other evidence, which are necessary in carrying out the provisions of the order, and may require any person to maintain and produce for examination such records or other evidence, in such form as it shall require, concerning prices, rents, wages and salaries and all related matters. The council may make such exemptions from any requirement otherwise imposed as are consistent with the purposes of this order. Any type of record or evidence required under regulations issued under this order shall be retained for such period as the council may prescribe.

* * *

SECTION 7. (A) Whoever willfully violates this order or any order or regulation issued under authority of this order shall be fined not more than $5,000 for each such violation.

(B) The council shall in its discretion request the Department of Justice to bring actions for injunctions authorized under Section 205 of the Economic Stabilization Act of 1970 whenever it appears to the council that any person has engaged, is engaged or is about to engage in any acts or practices constituting a violation of any regulation or order issued pursuant to this order.

* * *

1. You are counsel to National Motors, a major U.S. automobile manufacturer. Company executives, trying to appraise the business impact of the Executive Order, supra, would like to know whether the Order requires postponement of

> (a) general price increases for passenger cars decided upon by National in July and bulletined to its dealers on August 9 to take effect for purchases made on or after August 23, 1971;

> (b) general price increases on the third of three types of trucks manufactured by National, bulletined to take effect August 23, 1971, prices on the first two types having been raised to dealers effective August 10 (must the latter prices be rolled back?);

> (c) general post-August 15 price increases scheduled for the Company's imported Japanese-made sport cars, even in the event that the affiliated Japanese manufacturer during the 90-day period mentioned in the Order raises the price (exclusive of any U.S. import surcharge) at which National must import from him;

> (d) general employee wage increases agreed upon by the Company in June collective bargaining sessions with the unions and scheduled and announced for implementation beginning September first;

> (e) wage increases to selected individuals based on merit and scheduled to take effect September first;

Sec. 7 *WEIGHT OF PRIOR INTERPRETATIONS* 469

(f) general increases in employee pension allowances and health and welfare benefits also agreed upon in June bargaining to take effect in September.

Finally, can you as attorney charge National higher fees for your August efforts than you charged for comparable legal work performed in July?

2. You are counsel to Pinnacle Peach Farms, Inc., a large grower of peaches. The corporation's officers need your advice as to whether the President's Executive Order prevents

(a) Pinnacle from charging the customary seasonal prices for fresh peaches in October, which prices are normally higher in the trade than those charged for fresh peaches in July and August;

(b) the Deadeye Frozen Foods Company from charging higher prices to its frozen-peach customers in the event that Pinnacle institutes a general price increase on the fresh peaches it sells to Deadeye for freezing;

(c) the Botulinus Canners Cooperative from charging higher prices to its canned-peach customers in the event that Pinnacle institutes a general price increase on the fresh peaches it sells to Botulinus for canning.

3. As counsel to the Sitzmark Christmas Card company which regularly sells its Christmas cards to dealers at half price at seasons other than Christmas, advise the Company as to whether under the Executive Order it can, as usual, sell its Christmas cards at the full Christmas price beginning November 1, 1971?

SECTION 7. THE WEIGHT OF PRIOR INTERPRETATIONS

WOOLLCOTT v. SHUBERT

Court of Appeals of New York, 1916.
217 N.Y. 212, 111 N.E. 829.

[Reread opinion, supra p. 368, with special reference to the nature and treatment of prior interpretations in that case.]

Donahue v. Warner Bros., 2 Utah 2d 256, 272 P.2d 177 (1954), arose out of the exhibition in Utah, for profit, of the movie "Look for the Silver Lining," a musical show, which incidentally portrayed the life of the late Jack Donahue, a famous singer, dancer and comedian. Plaintiffs in the case, the widow and daughters of Donahue, sued for compensation and exemplary damages and an injunction, relying on the following Utah statutory provisions, adopted in 1909, which were modeled, with minor modifications, on an earlier New York statute:

> U.C.A.1953, Sec. 76–4–8. Any person who uses for advertising purposes or for purposes of trade, or upon any postal card, the name, portrait or picture of any person, if such person is living, without first having obtained the written consent of such person, or if a minor, of his parent or guardian, or, if such person is dead, without the written consent of his heirs or personal representatives, is guilty of a misdemeanor.
>
> Sec. 9. Any living person, or the heirs or personal representatives of any deceased person, whose name, portrait or picture is used within this state for advertising purposes or for purposes of trade, without the written consent first obtained as provided in the next preceding section may maintain an action against such person so using his name, picture or portrait to prevent and restrain the use thereof; and may in the same action recover damages for any injuries sustained by reason of such use, and, if the defendant shall have knowingly used such person's name, portrait or picture in such manner as is declared to be unlawful, the jury or court, if tried without a jury, in its discretion, may award exemplary damages.

Plaintiffs contended that the use of a person's name or picture in any manner involving the profit motive was a use "for purposes of trade" forbidden by these provisions. Defendants argued that the provisions were meant to apply only to actual advertising or to promotion of sales of a collateral commodity. The Supreme Court of Utah decided in favor of the defendants, concluding that the showing was not for "purposes of trade" under the Act. *Inter alia,* various New York cases under the original New York statute were urged upon the Utah court. One such case was Rhodes v. Sperry & Hutchinson & Co., 193 N.Y. 223, 85 N.E. 1097, 34 L.R.A.N.S. 1143 (1908), affirmed 220 U. S. 502, 31 S.Ct. 490, 55 L.Ed. 561 (1911), which was said to have interpreted the New York statute as addressed to advertising and sales promotion. Other New York cases urged on the court, decided in 1913 and later years, extended the New York act to other situations. In regard to the New York cases the Utah court observed:

> "It is well settled that 'when the legislature of a state has used a statute of another state or country as a guide for the preparation and enactment of a statute, the courts of the adopting state will usually adopt the construction placed on the statute in the jurisdiction of its inception.' Thus the enactment of the Utah statute at a time when the language of the Rhodes case above * * * [cited] was the declared law of New York seems to indicate that the intent of the

Utah Legislature was to give a right of action only when the name was used in advertising or sales promotion schemes. It is here pertinent to observe, however, in view of later New York decisions, that although our Legislature may be assumed to have been aware of the construction of the statute by the courts of the state of its origin at the time of our enactment, that principle does not apply to decisions of the state of origin handed down after the time the legislation was adopted, as it would not have been known to, and could not have been in the contemplation of our Legislature. While such later cases may be helpful and in some instances persuasive, we are of course not obliged to follow the subsequent New York decisions, which have given a broader scope to the operation of their statute than we believe was intended for our enactment * * *."

On examination, the court refused to follow the later New York cases in extending the statute as sought by the plaintiff. It grounded this refusal on the "difficulties and uncertainties" found to ensue from extension, posing substantial problems for the courts and for the practical operations of publishers and other purveyors of public information, as well as raising serious constitutional questions. In this area the public interest in free expression in the channels of public information was to be preferred to the right of privacy. Besides such considerations, the text of the statute itself (particularly the narrowing effect of the "any postcard" phrase) and its title (referring only to advertising) were found by the court to demand a restrictive reading. And the same result was said to be called for by legislative history, the court noting that "[n]ear the beginning of the 1909 legislative session Governor Spry, in his message, recommended legislation 'to prevent the use of the name of any public institution of the state, or the official title of any of its officers, *for the purpose of advertising or promoting the sale of any article of merchandise* or stock in any corporation' (emphasis added)."

In Iacone v. Cardillo, 208 F.2d 696 (2d Cir. 1953), the opinion of the court, per Medina, Circuit Judge, reads in pertinent part as follows:

"The question whether claimant is entitled to a scheduled award for the loss of an eye industrially blind as the result of a previous, non-industrial accident, is a novel one under the federal Longshoremen's and Harbor Workers' Compensation Act, 33 U.S.C.A. § 901 et seq. Decisions on this problem under the various state workmen's compensation laws are in hopeless conflict. * * *

"The New York cases merit particular attention in interpreting the Longshoremen's and Harbor Workers' Compensation Act, since the federal statute is based upon the

New York Workmen's Compensation Law, McK.Consol. Laws, c. 67. See Lawson v. Suwanee Fruit & Steamship Co., 1949, 336 U.S. 198 at page 205, 69 S.Ct. 503, at page 506, 93 L.Ed. 611. The rulings by the New York Courts, however, complicate the situation further, as the law at the time of the enactment of the federal statute had been interpreted to deny recovery in such situations, Ladd v. Foster Brothers Mfg. Co., 3d Dept. 1923, 205 A.D. 794, 200 N.Y.S. 258, and it was later held in a case dealing with the loss by enucleation of an already defective eye that the injured employee was entitled to a scheduled award. Riegle v. Fordon, 1948, 273 A.D. 213, 76 N.Y.S.2d 523, affirmed 298 N.Y. 560, 81 N.E.2d 101.

* * *

"This Court would be following established principles of statutory construction were we simply to adopt the New York decisions as they existed at the time of the enactment of the federal law. * * *

"This would hold true notwithstanding the fact that the New York courts have since altered their interpretation of the New York Workmen's Compensation Law on this point. Interpretations subsequent to adoption, while perhaps entitled to 'respectful consideration,' * * * are persuasive only, not binding, * * * and indeed are often held to be of little or no weight. * * * Consequently, even a complete about-face by the courts of the jurisdiction from which the statute has been adopted in no way requires the adopting jurisdiction to follow the new interpretation. * * *

"Such a rule seems clearly desirable. For 'legislative intent,' vague as the concept often is, nevertheless forms a fundamental canon of statutory interpretation. There is a good deal of substance in the view that a legislature, in adopting a statute from another jurisdiction, is aware of, and by its acquiescence generally approves, the existing judicial construction of that statute. But this reasoning fails if applied to decisions subsequent to adoption, and, while the desire for uniformity and the respect for the ability of other tribunals in handling the same problem would seem to compel at least a respectful consideration of these later decisions, they are in no way more than persuasive, and indeed, by force of logic, may in their conflict with legislative intent as represented by "adoption" of the earlier decisions, be far from helpful.

"But, like all such mechanical rules of statutory interpretation, so too the principle that the legislature adopts existing decisions when it adopts legislation is limited in its application. It would not, for example, bind this court where the fundamental purpose of the statute itself is subverted by an otherwise applicable decision of the other jurisdiction. See 82 C.J.S., Statutes, § 373(a), and cases there cited. Accordingly, while not without power to reach our own conclusion in any event, the state of the authorities in the various jurisdictions, and especially in New York, would seem to make it our duty in the case before us to lay aside what may be deemed at most a convenient guide to the ascertainment of legislative intent, and examine the precise problem on its own merits, in terms of the basic purposes of compensation law."

* * *

[Upon consideration of the claim in light of the purposes and provisions of the statute, the court affirmed the district court's order denying an award.]

NOTES

1. "It is a doctrine of the American courts, very generally accepted, that when a state enacts a British statute which has received, in the mother country, a fixed and established judicial interpretation, the legislature will be supposed to adopt that statute with the interpretation put upon it. The principle has been several times recognized in this court, with respect to statutes borrowed from other states.

"If an old statute incorporated into our jurisprudence, having frequent and important bearing and application to the business and prosperity of the community, has received a uniform exposition in the country or state from which it was borrowed, it is reasonable to assume that the legislature intended to introduce into our law the statute, with the judicial exposition of it." Marqueze v. Caldwell, 48 Miss. 23, 31 (1873). See Sutherland, Statutes and Statutory Construction § 52.02 (4th ed. Sands 1973).

2. The rule of presumed adoption is not a conclusive test. It is rather another aid in the task of statutory construction, and should be weighed with all other extraneous factors. Furthermore, the rule is not without exceptions. "The rule will be followed by this court except when the decision of the parent state does not appeal to us as founded on right reasoning, or conflicts with prior holdings of this court, or is not in harmony with the spirit of our institutions, or when to follow it would lead to the denial of a constitutional right." Esterly v. Broadway Garage Co., 87 Mont. 64, 71, 285 P. 172 (1930). See Note, Construction of a Statute Borrowed from Another Jurisdiction, 43 Harv.L.Rev. 623 (1930).

3. The rule of presumed adoption is particularly in point in the construction of a uniform statute. "If, therefore, the section of the Uniform Sales Act here in question has been construed by the court of last resort of any state in which the Uniform Sales Act is in force, then I conceive it to be the duty of this court to follow such construction in order to comply with the spirit and purpose * * * and to maintain the uniformity of the provisions of the Uniform Sales Act. It would be utterly futile for the Legislatures of the several states to adopt uniform laws upon any subject if

each court of the several states followed the notion of its members with regard to how a particular provision should be construed and applied." Stewart v. Hansen, 62 Utah 281, 284, 218 P. 959, 44 A.L.R. 340 (1923).

ALASKA STEAMSHIP CO. v. UNITED STATES

Supreme Court of the United States, 1933.
290 U.S. 256, 54 S.Ct. 159, 78 L.Ed. 302.

Certiorari to review the affirmance of a judgment dismissing a suit against the United States under the Tucker Act.

Mr. Justice STONE delivered the opinion of the Court.

In this suit, brought under the Tucker Act, 24 Stat. 505, in the District Court for Western Washington, petitioner sought compensation at an agreed rate for the transportation of certain destitute seamen from Ketchikan, Alaska, to Seattle, under the provisions of § 4578 R.S., as amended, 46 U.S.C.A. § 679. That section imposes on masters of United States vessels homeward bound the duty, upon request of consular officers, to receive and carry destitute seamen to the port of destination at such compensation not exceeding a specified amount as may be agreed upon by the master with a consular officer, and authorizes the consular officer to issue certificates for such transportation, "which shall be assignable for collection." By § 4526 R.S., 17 Stat. 269, as amended December 21, 1898, 30 Stat. 755, 46 U.S.C.A. § 593, seamen, whose term of service is terminated by loss or wreck of their vessel, are "destitute seamen," and are required to be transported as provided in § 4578.

The demand in the present case was for compensation for the transportation of the crew of the S. S. Depere, owned by petitioner, which had been wrecked on the Alaska coast and for that reason had been unable to complete her voyage. The crew was received and carried to Seattle on petitioner's S. S. Yukon, on certificate of the deputy customs collector of Alaska that he had agreed with the master for their transportation at a specified rate. The Comptroller General refused payment upon the certificate on the sole ground that it was the duty of petitioner to transport to the United States the crew of its own wrecked vessel, and that the Congressional appropriation for the relief of American seamen was not available to compensate the owner for performing that duty. Judgment of the district court dismissing the complaint, 60 F.2d 135, was affirmed by the Court of Appeals for the Ninth Circuit, on the ground that the certificate of the deputy collector authorizing the transportation did not satisfy the requirement of the statute that the certificate should be that of a consular officer. 63 F.2d 398. This court granted certiorari.

The government, conceding that the statute by long administrative practice has been construed as authorizing payment for transportation of seamen from Alaska on the certificate of deputy customs collectors, insists that it does not authorize payment to the owner for the transportation of the crew of his own wrecked vessel and that such has been its administrative construction.

1. If the statutory language is to be taken literally, the certificate, which by R.S. § 4578 is authority for the transportation and evidence of the right of the vessel to compensation, must be that of a consular officer. Deputy collectors of customs are not consular officers and there are no consular officers in Alaska. If the right to compensation is dependent upon certification by a consular officer the statutes providing for transportation of destitute seamen can be given no effect in Alaska. But the meaning of this provision must be ascertained by reading it with related statutes and in the light of a long and consistent administrative practice.

Since 1792 the statutes of the United States have made provision for the return of destitute seamen to this country upon suitable action taken by consular officers of the United States. And since 1803 the government has undertaken to compensate for their transportation. Beginning in 1896, Congress has made provision for the relief of American seamen shipwrecked in Alaska in annual appropriation bills for the maintenance of the diplomatic and consular service. The appropriation bill for that year, 29 Stat. 186, and every later one has extended the benefits of the appropriation for the relief of American seamen in foreign countries to "American seamen shipwrecked in Alaska." The appropriation for 1922 and 1923, c. 204, 42 Stat. 599, 603; c. 21, 42 Stat. 1068, 1072, contained the proviso, not appearing in previous acts, that no part of the appropriation should be available for payment for transportation in excess of a specified rate agreed upon by a consular officer and the master of the vessel. The proviso did not appear in subsequent appropriation acts, but by Act of January 3, 1923, 43 Stat. 1072, it was transferred to its proper place in the shipping laws, where it now appears in § 680 of Title 46 of the United States Code. The Act of 1929, 45 Stat. 1098, applicable when the seamen in the present case were transported, appropriated $70,000 "for relief, protection and burial of American seamen in foreign countries, in the Panama Canal Zone, and in the Philippine Islands, and shipwrecked American seamen in the Territory of Alaska, in the Hawaiian Islands, in Porto Rico and in the Virgin Islands." By the amendment of R.S. § 5226 of December 21, 1898, 30 Stat. 755, 46 U.S.C.A., § 593, it was provided that where the service of a seaman terminates by reason of the loss or wreck of the vessel, "he shall not be entitled to wages for any period beyond such termination of the service and shall be considered as a destitute seaman, and shall be treated and transported to port of shipment," as provided in R.S. § 4578. No exception is made in the case of transportation of seamen from Alaska or other dependencies of the United States.

Thus, from 1896 to the present time, there has been a definite obligation on the part of the government to provide transportation for shipwrecked seamen without reference to the place where shipwrecked, and funds have been annually appropriated for the purpose of carrying out that obligation in the case of seamen shipwrecked in Alaska. As appears from the findings of the trial court, not challenged here, the appropriations have been expended for the transportation of shipwrecked seamen from Alaska, in conformity to a practice established and consistently followed at least since 1900. Certificates for the transportation of shipwrecked seamen have been regularly signed and issued by the collector of customs or the deputy collector in Alaska upon forms provided by the Bureau of Navigation of the Department of Commerce. That Bureau, which has a general superintendence over merchant seamen of the United States, 46 U.S. C.A., §§ 1 and 2, has regularly supplied its customs officials and its agents in Alaska with these forms, with instructions that they were to be used in arranging transportation of shipwrecked seamen to the United States, as provided by the sections of the statute to which reference has been made. The stipulated amounts due for the transportation, as certified, have been regularly paid without objection upon presentation of the certificate to the disbursing officer of the United States.

Courts are slow to disturb the settled administrative construction of a statute long and consistently adhered to. Brown v. United States, 113 U.S. 568, 571, 5 S.Ct. 648, 28 L.Ed. 1079; United States v. Philbrick, 120 U.S. 52, 59, 7 S.Ct. 413, 30 L.Ed. 559; United States v. G. Falk & Bro., 204 U.S. 143, 151, 27 S.Ct. 191, 51 L.Ed. 411. This is especially the case where, as here, the declared will of the legislative body could not be carried out without the construction adopted. That construction must be accepted and applied by the courts when, as in the present case, it has received Congressional approval, implicit in the annual appropriations over a period of thirty-five years, the expenditure of which was effected by resort to the administrative practice, and in amendments by Congress to the statutes relating to transportation of destitute seamen without modification of that practice. United States v. G. Falk & Bro., supra; compare United States v. Missouri Pacific R. Co., 278 U.S. 269, 49 S.Ct. 133, 73 L.Ed. 322.

2. The rejection of petitioner's claim by the Comptroller General rests upon the supposed duty of the owner to transport to the home port the seamen of its own wrecked vessel. Diligent search by counsel of the ancient learning of the admiralty has failed to disclose the existence of any such duty.

* * *

The Department of Commerce, not the Comptroller General, is charged with the administration of the statute, 4 Comptroller General Rep., 252, 253, and its administrative practice should be followed if thought to be controlling. But in any case, there is no ambiguity or uncertainty in the statute with respect to the point urged by the government, and, in carrying it out as written, there is no administrative difficulty which would call for construction. The rulings of the Comptroller General rest upon a proposition so plainly contrary to law and so plainly in conflict with the statute as to leave them without weight as administrative constructions of it. United States v. Missouri Pacific R. Co., supra.

Reversed.

NOTE

In Bingler v. Johnson, 394 U.S. 741, 749–50, 89 S.Ct. 1439, 1444–45, 22 L.Ed.2d 695, 703–4 (1969), the Supreme Court commented with respect to a contemporaneous administrative construction in these terms: "[I]t is fundamental, of course, that as 'contemporaneous constructions by those charged with the administration of' the Code, the Regulations 'must be sustained unless unreasonable and plainly inconsistent with the revenue statutes' and 'should not be overruled except for weighty reasons.'" Compare Houghton v. Payne, 194 U.S. 88, 24 S.Ct. 590, 48 L.Ed. 888 (1904) where a contemporaneous construction of an Act of Congress of 1879 by the Postmaster General was followed until 1902 when it was reversed by the then Postmaster General. The administrative construction of 1902 was upheld by a divided Court. Compare also Zuber v. Allen, 396 U.S. 168, 90 S.Ct. 314, 24 L.Ed.2d 345 (1969) where the Supreme Court disapproved the construction put upon a statute by the Department of Agriculture, stating (at pp. 192–3):

> "While this Court has announced that it will accord great weight to a departmental construction of its own enabling legislation, especially a contemporaneous construction, see Udall v. Tallman, 380 U.S. 1, 16, 85 S.Ct. 792, 801, 13 L.Ed.2d 616 (1965); Power Reactor Dev. Co. v. International Union of Electrical, Radio and Machine Workers, 367 U.S. 396, 408, 81 S.Ct. 1529, 1535, 6 L.Ed.2d 294 (1961); it is only one input in the interpretational equation. Its impact carries most weight when the administrators participated in drafting and directly made known their views to Congress in committee hearings. * * * In such circumstances, absent any indication that Congress differed with the responsible department, a court should resolve any ambiguity in favor of the administrative construction, if such construction enhances the general purposes and policies underlying the legislation. * * * The Court may not, however, abdicate its ultimate responsibility to construe the language employed by Congress."

UNITED STATES v. AMERICAN TRUCKING ASS'NS

Supreme Court of the United States, 1940.
310 U.S. 534, 60 S.Ct. 1059, 84 L.Ed. 1345.

[Review this case, supra p. 402, with special reference to the Supreme Court's treatment of the rulings of the Interstate Commerce Commission and the Wage and Hour Division of the Department of Labor.]

CAMMARANO v. UNITED STATES

Supreme Court of the United States, 1959.
358 U.S. 498, 79 S.Ct. 524, 3 L.Ed.2d 462.

Mr. Justice HARLAN delivered the opinion of the Court.

These cases, coming to us from two different Circuits, present identical issues, and may appropriately be dealt with together in one opinion. The issues involve the interpretation and validity of Treas. Reg. 111, § 29.23(o)–1 and § 29.23(q)–1 as applied by the courts below to deny deduction as "ordinary and necessary" business expenses under § 23(a)(1)(A) of the Internal Revenue Code of 1939 [60] to sums expended by the respective taxpayer petitioners in furtherance of publicity programs designed to help secure the defeat of initiative measures then pending before the voters of the States of Washington and Arkansas.

The Treasury Regulations in question each provides in pertinent part that no deduction shall be allowed to "sums of money expended for lobbying purposes, the promotion or defeat of legislation, the exploitation of propaganda, including advertising other than trade advertising * * *." [61] Both Courts of Appeals held that these provisions render nondeductible sums paid by petitioners to organizations which expended them in extensive publicity programs designed to persuade the voters to cast their ballots against state initiative measures, even though the passage of those measures would have seriously affected, or indeed wholly destroyed, the taxpayers' businesses—and that so interpreted the Regulations are a valid exercise of the Commissioner's rule-making power. We granted certiorari because of the recurring nature of the question, and because of its importance to the proper administration of the Internal Revenue laws. 355 U.S. 952, 78 S.Ct. 541, 2 L.Ed.2d 529; 356 U.S. 966, 78 S.Ct. 1007, 2 L.Ed.2d 1073.

A brief review of the facts in the two cases is necessary to an understanding of the issues.

No. 29: In 1948 petitioners William and Louise Cammarano, husband and wife, jointly owned a one-fourth interest in a partner-

---

60. That section (26 U.S.C.A. § 23(a)(1)(A)) provides in pertinent part:

"§ 23. Deductions from gross income. In computing net income there shall be allowed as deductions:

"(a) Expenses.

"(1) Trade or Business Expenses.

"(A) In General. All the ordinary and necessary expenses paid or incurred during the taxable year in carrying on any trade or business * * *."

61. Only § 29.23(o)–1, which reads on individuals, is involved as to petitioners Cammarano, and only § 29.23(q)–1, reading on corporations, as to petitioner F. Strauss & Son, Inc. Because the language and effect of the two Regulations are in all relevant respects identical they will be discussed throughout this opinion as if they were one.

Sec. 7   WEIGHT OF PRIOR INTERPRETATIONS   479

ship engaged in the distribution of beer at wholesale in the State of Washington. The partnership was a member of the Washington Beer Wholesalers Association. In December 1947 the Association had established a trust fund as a repository for assessments collected from its members to help finance a statewide publicity program urging the defeat of "Initiative to the Legislature No. 13," a measure to be submitted to the electorate at the general election of November 2, 1948, which would have placed the retail sale of wine and beer in Washington exclusively in the hands of the State. During 1948 petitioners' partnership paid to the trust fund $3,545.15, of which petitioners' pro rata share was $886.29. The trust fund collected a total of $53,500, which was turned over to an Industry Advisory Committee organized by wholesale and retail wine and beer dealers, which in turn expended it as part of contributions totaling $231,257.10 for various kinds of advertising directed to the public, none of which referred to petitioners' wares as such and all of which urged defeat of Initiative No. 13.[62] The initiative was defeated.

In preparing their joint income tax return for 1948, petitioners deducted as a business expense the $886.29 paid to the Association's trust fund as their share of the partnership assessment. The deduction was disallowed by the Commissioner, and petitioners paid under protest the additional sum thus due and sued in the District Court for refund. That court ruled that the payments made to the trust fund were "expended for * * * the * * * defeat of legislation" within the meaning of Treas.Reg. 111, § 29.23(o)–1 and were therefore not deductible as ordinary and necessary business expenses under § 23(a)(1)(A) of the Internal Revenue Code of 1939. The Court of Appeals affirmed, holding the Regulation applicable and valid as applied. 9 Cir., 246 F.2d 751.

No. 50: Petitioner F. Strauss & Son, Inc., is a corporation engaged in the wholesale liquor business in Arkansas. In 1950 an initiative calling for an election on statewide prohibition was placed on the ballot to be voted on in the state general election on November 7, 1950. In May of that year Strauss, together with eight other Arkansas liquor wholesalers, organized Arkansas Legal Control Associates, Inc., as a means of coordinating their efforts to persuade the voters of Arkansas to vote against the proposed prohibition measure. Between May 30 and November 30, 1950, Arkansas Legal Control Associates collected a total of $126,265.84, which was disbursed for various forms of publicity concerning the proposed Act.[63] Strauss' contribution amounted to $9,252.67.

---

62. A typical advertisement paid for by the Industry Advisory Committee, signed by "Men & Women Against Prohibition," begins "We intend to Vote Against Initiative 13—because it would mean a return to the speakeasy, the bootlegger, the gangster—and, finally, state-wide Prohibition! We urge our friends and neighbors to do likewise."

63. A typical advertisement, which ran in all Arkansas daily and weekly newspapers, and which shows as its

The initiative measure was defeated in the November election. On its 1950 income tax return Strauss deducted the $9,252.67 as a business expense. The Commissioner disallowed the deduction and Strauss filed a timely petition in the Tax Court seeking a redetermination of the deficiency asserted. That court upheld the action of the Commissioner in disallowing the claimed deduction, and the Court of Appeals unanimously affirmed. 8 Cir., 251 F.2d 724.

Since 1918 regulations promulgated by the Commissioner under the Internal Revenue Code have continuously provided that expenditures for the "promotion or defeat of legislation * * *," or for any of the other purposes specified in the "corporate" Regulation now before us, are not deductible from gross corporate income; and since 1938 regulations containing identical language have forbidden such deductions from individual income.[64] During this period of more than 40 years these regulatory provisions have been before this Court on only one occasion. In Textile Mills Security Corporation v. Commissioner of Internal Revenue, 314 U.S. 326, 62 S.Ct. 272, 86 L. Ed. 249, it was held that the Commissioner properly disallowed the deduction of sums paid by a corporation to a publicist and two legal experts employed to help secure the passage of legislation designed to secure the return of certain properties in this country seized during World War I under the provisions of the Trading With the Enemy Act, 50 U.S.C.A. Appendix, § 1 et seq. This holding was squarely based on the regulatory provisions now embodied in Treas.Reg. 111, § 29.23(q)–1, which were found valid and applicable to the facts involved in that case, although the very business of the taxpayer seek-

---

sponsor "Arkansas Against Prohibition," begins:

"What Does 'One Quart' Prohibition Really Mean? There's nothing like it anywhere * * * it's novel * * * it's unique. But it's sinister * * * it's a plan to destroy the strictly-regulated alcohol beverage business and to turn that business over to the bootlegger."

64. Article 143 of Treas.Reg. 33 (1918 ed.) denied deductibility as ordinary and necessary business expenses to corporate expenditures for "lobbying purposes, the promotion or defeat of legislation, the exploitation of propaganda * * *." The prohibition against corporate deduction of such expenditures first appears in its present form in Art. 562 of Treas. Reg. 45 (1919 ed.), promulgated under the Revenue Act of 1918. Thereafter it so appears continuously without change. See Art. 562 of Treas.Reg. 45 (1920 ed.), 62, 65, and 69, promulgated under the Revenue Acts of 1918, 1921, 1924, and 1926, Art. 262 of Treas.Reg. 74 and 77, promulgated under the Revenue Acts of 1928 and 1932, Art. 23(o)–2 of Treas.Reg. 86, promulgated under the Revenue Act of 1934, Art. 23(q)–1 of Treas.Reg. 94 and 101, promulgated under the Revenue Acts of 1936 and 1938, §§ 19.-23(q)–1, 29.23(q)–1, and 39.23(q)–1 of Treas.Reg. 103, 111, and 118, respectively, promulgated under the Internal Revenue Code of 1939.

The prohibition against individual deductibility of such expenditures first appears in Art. 23(o)–1 of Treas.Reg. 101, promulgated under the Revenue Act of 1938, and thereafter in §§ 19.-23(o)–1, 29.23(o)–1, and 39.23(o)–1 of Treas.Reg. 103, 111, and 118, respectively, promulgated under the Internal Revenue Code of 1939.

In the proposed Income Tax Regulations under the 1954 Code the prohibitions are consolidated in § 1.162–15.

Sec. 7 *WEIGHT OF PRIOR INTERPRETATIONS* 481

ing the deduction was the direction of the publicity program in the course of which the expenditures were made.

Petitioners suggest that Textile Mills is not dispositive of the present cases, either as to the applicability of the Regulations upon the facts disclosed by these records or as to the validity of those Regulations under the statute if they are found to be applicable. Essentially, petitioners' contentions are (1) that the Regulations cannot properly be construed as applicable to expenditures made in connection with efforts to promote or defeat the passage of legislation by persuasion of the general public as opposed to direct influence on legislative bodies, that is "lobbying"; (2) that in any case the Regulations are inapplicable to expenditures made in connection with initiative measures; and (3) that if construed as applicable to the facts here presented the Regulations are invalid as contrary to the plain terms of § 23(a)(1)(A) of the 1939 Code and possibly as unconstitutional under the First Amendment.

We need not be long detained by the question of the applicability of the Regulations to petitioners' expenditures. First, we see no justification for reading into these regulatory provisions the implied exceptions which petitioners would have us there find. We cannot accept petitioners' argument that Textile Mills should be read as limiting such provisions to direct dealings with legislators, insidious or otherwise. The deductions whose propriety was before the Court in that case were for expenditures, characterized by the Court of Appeals as being for "matters of publicity, 'including the making of arrangements for speeches, contacting the press, in respect of editorial comments, and news items,'" and for the preparation of "brochures" involving "a comprehensive study of the history of the treatment of persons and property in war," 3 Cir., 117 F.2d 62, 65, 63, all designed to influence the opinions of the general public. Apart from Textile Mills, the Courts of Appeals have uniformly applied these Regulations to expenditures for publicity directed to the general public on legislative matters. See e. g., Revere Racing Ass'n v. Scanlon, 1 Cir., 232 F.2d 816; American Hardware & Equipment Co. v. Commissioner of Internal Revenue, 4 Cir., 202 F.2d 126; Roberts Dairy Co. v. Commissioner of Internal Revenue, 8 Cir., 195 F.2d 948; Sunset Scavenger Co. v. Commissioner of Internal Revenue, 9 Cir., 84 F.2d 453. Petitioners' reading of these Regulations would make all but the reference to "lobbying" pure surplusage. We think that the Regulations must be construed to mean what they say—that not only lobbying expenses, but also sums spent for "the promotion or defeat of legislation, the exploitation of propaganda, including advertising other than trade advertising" are nondeductible.

Likewise unpersuasive is petitioners' suggested distinction between expenses incurred in attempting to promote or defeat legislation pending before legislatures and those incurred in furthering or combatting an initiative measure. We think that initiatives are plainly "legislation" within the meaning of these Regulations. Had the measures involved in these cases been passed by the people of Washington and Arkansas they would have had the effect and status of ordinary laws in every respect. The Constitutions of the States of Washington and Arkansas both explicitly recognize that in providing for initiatives they are vesting legislative power in the people.[65] Every court which has considered the question has found these provisions to be fully as applicable to initiatives and referendums as to any other kind of legislation. * * *

A contrary reading of the Regulations would, indeed, be anomalous, for it would mean that expenses of publicity campaigns directed to the public to influence it in turn to persuade its legislative representatives to vote for or against pending bills would be encompassed by the Regulations and denied deductibility, whereas a less-diluted form of persuasion and influence, directed to the voters as legislators, would be left at large so far as the Regulations are concerned. We see no reason to give so artificial and strained a construction to the pertinent language.[66]

The cornerstone of petitioners' argument is that Treas.Reg. 111, § 29.23(*o*)–1 and § 29.23(q)–1 are invalid if interpreted to apply to the expenditures here at issue. It is contended that sums expended by a taxpayer to preserve his business from destruction are deductible as ordinary and necessary business expenses under the Code as a

---

65. Amendment 7 of the Constitution of the State of Washington provides in pertinent part:

"Art. 2, Sec. 1. *Legislative Powers, Where Vested*—The legislative authority of the state of Washington shall be vested in the legislature, consisting of a senate and house of representatives, which shall be called the legislature of the State of Washington, but the people reserve to themselves the power to propose bills, laws, and to enact or reject the same at the polls, independent of the legislature * * *."

Amendment 7 of the Arkansas Constitution contains a virtually identical provision.

66. Petitioners place heavy reliance on the Commissioner's acquiescence until 1958 in a 1944 decision of the Tax Court allowing deduction to expenditures—found otherwise to qualify under § 23(a)(1), (A) of the 1939 Code —incurred by a taxpayer in connection with a self-operative amendment to the Missouri Constitution, on the ground that "no legislation was needed or involved." Smith v. Commissioner, 3 T.C. 696. Whether or not under the Regulations here at issue a distinction can rationally be drawn between a popularly enacted constitutional amendment and an initiative, we do not see how the fact that the Tax Court and the Commissioner for a period made such a distinction, compare Smith v. Commissioner, supra, with McClintock-Trunkey Co. v. Commissioner, 19 T.C. 297, reversed on other issues, 9 Cir., 217 F.2d 329, helps petitioners' case, as the Commissioner and the Tax Court have been entirely consistent in their position that expenditures connected with initiatives—as in the present cases— are not deductible.

The Tax Court appears to have modified its view since the Smith case even as to expenditures made in connection with constitutional amendments. See Mosby Hotel Co. v. Commissioner, decided October 22, 1954, P-H 1954 TC Mem.Dec. ¶ 54,288. And the Commissioner has recently withdrawn his acquiescence in the Smith decision. See Rev.Rul. 58–255, 1958–1 Cum.Bull. 91.

matter of law, and that therefore a regulation purporting to deny deductibility to such expenditures is plainly contrary to the statute and *ipso facto* invalid. Petitioners rely upon Commissioner of Internal Revenue v. Heininger, 320 U.S. 467, 64 S.Ct. 249, 88 L.Ed. 171, where this Court held that attorney's fees incurred by a mail-order dentist in resisting a postal fraud charge which would have ended his business were deductible as an ordinary and necessary business expense.

We do not think that Heininger governs the present cases, nor that it establishes as broad a rule of law as petitioners suggest. In Heininger this Court held no more than that expenditures without which a business enterprise would inevitably suffer adverse effects, and the granting of deductibility to which would frustrate no "sharply defined national or state policies," 320 U.S., at page 473, 64 S.Ct. at page 253 (see also Commissioner of Internal Revenue v. Sullivan, 356 U.S. 27, 78 S.Ct. 512, 2 L.Ed.2d 559), were deductible as ordinary and necessary business expenses under the statute. Here the deductions sought are prohibited by Regulations which themselves constitute an expression of a sharply defined national policy, further demonstration of which may be found in other sections of the Internal Revenue Code.

As was said in Textile Mills, "the words 'ordinary and necessary' are not so clear and unambiguous in their meaning and application as to leave no room for an interpretative regulation. The numerous cases which have come to this Court on that issue bear witness to that." 314 U.S., at page 338, 62 S.Ct. at page 279. In the present cases there is before us regulatory language of more than 40 years' continuous duration expressly providing that sums expended for the activities here involved shall not be considered an ordinary and necessary business expense under the statute. The provisions of the Internal Revenue Code which underlie the Regulations have been repeatedly re-enacted by the Congress without the slightest suggestion that the policy expressed in these regulatory measures does other than precisely conform to its intent.

In 1934 the Court of Appeals for the Ninth Circuit denied deduction to expenses incurred in connection with a referendum which would, if passed, have increased the taxpayer's business. Old Mission Portland Cement Co. v. Commissioner of Internal Revenue, * * * [69 F.2d 676]. And in 1936 the same court in Sunset Scavenger Co. v. Commissioner of Internal Revenue, * * * [84 F.2d 453], reversed the Board of Tax Appeals to hold that the regulatory language now before us, through repeated re-enactment by Congress of the underlying legislation, already had acquired the force of law, and applied it to deny deductibility to expenditures made by an incorporated association of garbage collectors for a publicity program directed to the general public urging the defeat of legislation which would have injured the business of the Association's membership. The court recognized that the Board of Tax Appeals had twice previously held similar expenditures deductible so long as not made for an illegal purpose,[67] but pointed out that in both of those cases the effect of the Regulation had been entirely disregarded, and that they were therefore not sound authority. Three years later the Congress, in the face of these decisions, again re-enacted without change in the 1939 Code the "ordinary and necessary" business expense section.

It is also noteworthy that Congress, in its 1954 re-enactment of the Internal Revenue Code, again adopted the "ordinary and necessary" provision without substantive change, following consistent rulings by the courts subsequent to the 1939 re-enactment holding these Regulations applicable to sums spent in efforts to persuade the general public of the desirability or undesirability of proposed legislation affecting the taxpayer's business. [Citations omitted.] Although the tax years involved in the cases before us are 1948 and 1950, and a 1954 re-enactment of course cannot conclusively demonstrate the propriety of an administrative and judicial interpretation and application as made to transactions occurring before the re-enactment, the 1954 action of Congress is significant as indicating satisfaction with the interpretation consistently given the statute by the Regulations here at issue and in demonstrating its prior intent. Cf. United States v. Stafoff, 260 U.S. 477, 480, 43 S.Ct. 197, 199, 67 L.Ed. 358.

Under these circumstances we think that the Regulations have acquired the force of law. This is not a case where the Government seeks to cloak an interpretative regulation with immunity from judicial examination as to conformity with the statute on which it is based simply because Congress has for some period failed affirmatively to act to change the interpretation which the regulation gives to an otherwise unambiguous statute. Cf. Jones v. Liberty Glass Co., 332 U.S. 524, 68 S.Ct. 229, 92 L.Ed. 142. Nor is it a case where no reliable inference as to Congress' intent can be drawn from re-enactment of a statute because of a conflict between administrative and judicial interpretation of the statute at the time of its re-enactment. Cf. Commissioner of Internal Revenue v. Glenshaw Glass Co., 348 U. S. 426, 431, 75 S.Ct. 473, 476, 99 L.Ed. 483. Here we have unambiguous regulatory language, adopted by the Commissioner in the early days of federal income tax legislation, in continuous existence since

---

67. G. T. Wofford v. Commissioner of Internal Revenue, 15 B.T.A. 1225; Los Angeles & Salt Lake R. Co. v. Commissioner of Internal Revenue, 18 B.T.A. 168. Cf. Lucas v. Wofford, 5 Cir., 49 F.2d 1027, where a petition by the Commissioner for review of the decision in G. T. Wofford, supra, was denied upon a finding that the expenditures involved were not made "to secure the passage or defeat of any legislation." 49 F.2d at page 1028.

After this Court's decision in Textile Mills the Board of Tax Appeals recognized that the Regulation was applicable to expenditures incurred in a "proper and legal attempt to prevent [business] injury" by endeavoring to secure the defeat of legislation. Bellingrath v. Commissioner of Internal Revenue, 46 B.T.A. 89, 92.

that time, and consistently construed and applied by the courts on many occasions to deny deduction of sums expended in efforts to persuade the electorate, even when a clear business motive for the expenditure has been demonstrated.

In these circumstances we consider that what was said in Massachusetts Mutual Life Ins. Co. v. United States, 288 U.S. 269, 273, 53 S.Ct. 337, 339, 77 L.Ed. 739, applies here:

> "This action [of Congress in re-enacting a statute] was taken with knowledge of the construction placed upon the section by the official charged with its administration. If the legislative body had considered the Treasury interpretation erroneous, it would have amended the section. Its failure so to do requires the conclusion that the regulation was not inconsistent with the intent of the statute [citations] unless, perhaps, the language of the act is unambiguous and the regulation clearly inconsistent with it. [citation]."

This Court has heretofore recognized that the "ordinary and necessary" language of the Code is hardly unambiguous, see Textile Mills Securities Corporation v. Commissioner of Internal Revenue, supra, and we cannot say that these Regulations are clearly, or even apparently, inconsistent with it. Cf. Trust of Bingham v. Commissioner of Internal Revenue, 325 U.S. 365, 65 S.Ct. 1232, 89 L.Ed. 1670.

The statutory policy is further evidenced by the treatment given by Congress to the tax status of organizations, otherwise qualified for exemption as organized exclusively for "religious, charitable, scientific, literary or educational purposes," which engage in activities designed to promote or defeat legislation. As early as 1934 Congress amended the Code expressly to provide that no tax exemption should be given to organizations, otherwise qualifying, a substantial part of the activities of which "is carrying on propaganda, or otherwise attempting, to influence legislation," and that deductibility should be denied to contributions by individuals to such organizations. Revenue Act of 1934, §§ 101(6), 23(o)(2), 48 Stat. 700, 690. And a year thereafter, when the Code was for the first time amended to permit corporations to deduct certain contributions not qualifying as "ordinary and necessary" business expenses, an identical limitation was imposed. Revenue Act of 1935, § 102(c), 49 Stat. 1016. These limitations, carried over into the 1939 and 1954 Codes, made explicit the conclusion derived by Judge Learned Hand in 1930 that "political agitation as such is outside the statute, however innocent the aim * * *. Controversies of that sort must be conducted without public subvention; the Treasury stands aside from them." Slee v. Commissioner of Internal Revenue, 2 Cir., 42 F.2d 184, 185, 72 A.L.R. 400. The Regulations here contested appear to us to be but a further expression of the same sharply defined policy.

[Omitted here are the Court's consideration and rejection of a claim that the Regulation if read to deny deduction raises First Amendment issues.]

Affirmed.

[The concurring opinion of Mr. Justice DOUGLAS is omitted.]

NOTES

1. In Helvering v. R. J. Reynolds Tobacco Co., 306 U.S. 110, 59 S.Ct. 423, 83 L.Ed. 536 (1939), the question was whether gains accruing to a corporation in 1929 from purchase and resale of its own shares were "gross income" under Section 22(a) of the Revenue Act of 1928, and thus taxable. A Treasury Regulation in effect when the shares were resold provided that such gains were not "gross income." This administrative interpretation had been long established and uniform. Successive revenue acts following its establishment had reenacted without material change the statutory definition of gross income. In 1934 a Treasury Decision amended the Regulations to provide that corporate gains of the type concerned were included in gross income. The Commissioner of Internal Revenue contended in the Reynolds case that this amendment applied retroactively to require treatment of the 1929 corporate gains as gross income and urged that since § 22(a) had also been reenacted without change in 1936 and 1938 the amendment had been approved by Congress. The Supreme Court, deciding in favor of the corporate taxpayer, stated (p. 116):

> Since the legislative approval of existing regulations by reenactment of the statutory provision to which they appertain gives such regulations the force of law, we think Congress did not intend to authorize the Treasury to repeal the rule of law that existed during the period for which the tax is imposed. We need not now determine whether, as has been suggested, the alteration of the existing rule, even for the future, requires a legislative declaration or may be shown by reenactment of the statutory provision unaltered after a change in the applicable regulation. As the petitioner points out, Congress has, in the Revenue Acts of 1936 and 1938, retained § 22(a) of the 1928 Act *in haec verba*. From this it is argued that Congress has approved the amended regulation. It may be that by the passage of the Revenue Act of 1936 the Treasury was authorized thereafter to apply the regulation in its amended form. But we have no occasion to decide this question since we are of opinion that the reenactment of the section, without more, does not amount to sanction of retroactive enforcement of the amendment, in the teeth of the former regulation which received Congressional approval, by the passage of successive Revenue Acts including that of 1928."

Compare the Court's statements shortly thereafter in Helvering v. Wilshire Oil Co., 308 U.S. 90, 60 S.Ct. 18, 84 L.Ed. 101 (1939) that reenactment "does not mean that a regulation interpreting a provision of one act becomes frozen into another act merely by reenactment of that provision, so that that administrative interpretation cannot be changed prospectively through exercise of appropriate rule-making powers," (p. 100) and that the "dilution of administrative powers" resulting from a contrary conclusion "would deprive the administrative process of some of its most valuable qualities—ease of adjustment to change, flexibility in light of experience, swiftness in meeting new or emergency situations." (p. 101.) In Helvering v. Reynolds, 313 U.S. 428, 61 S.Ct. 971, 85 L.Ed. 1438 (1941), the Court said that the "[reenactment] rule is no more than an aid in statutory construction. While it is useful at times in resolving statutory ambiguities, it does not mean that the prior construction has become so embedded in the law that only Congress can effect a change." (p. 432.) See also American Chicle Co. v. U. S., 316 U.S. 450, 62 Sup.Ct. 1144, 86 L.Ed. 1591 (1942). For a more recent case on the subject, see National Muffler Dealers Ass'n, Inc. v. United States, 440 U.S. 472, 99 S.Ct. 1304, 59 L.Ed.2d 519 (1979).

2. Section 3290 of subchapter B of Chapter 27A (Wagering Taxes) of the Internal Revenue Code of 1939 imposed an annual $50 special occupational tax on, *inter alia*, those "engaged in receiving wagers for or on behalf of any person" who, as specified in another section of the Code, is "engaged in the business of accepting wagers." Persons liable to this § 3290 tax, first enacted in 1951, were required to register with the collector of the district; and for failure to pay the tax prescribed a fine of not less than $1000 and not more than $5000 was provided. United States v. Calamaro, 354 U.S. 351, 77 S.Ct. 1138, 1 L.Ed.2d 1394 (1957) considered the applicability of § 3290 to one of the participants in a type of lottery called the "numbers game" which was expressly included among the wagering transactions covered by the statute. "A numbers game," the Court explained, "involves three principal functional types of individuals: (1) the 'banker,' who deals in the numbers and against whom the player bets; (2) the 'writer,' who, for the banker, does the actual selling of the numbers to the public, and who records on triplicate slips the numbers sold to each player and the amount of his wager; and (3) the 'pick-up man,' who collects wagering slips from the writer and delivers them to the banker. If there are winnings to be distributed, the banker delivers the required amount to the writer, who in turn pays off the successful players." (p. 353.) The specific question in Calamaro was whether the respondent, "a pick-up man for a Philadelphia banker, receiving for his services a salary of $40 a week, but having no proprietary interest in this numbers enterprise," was subject to the special occupational tax provided in § 3290. The Supreme Court (per Mr. Justice Harlan) determined, one justice dissenting, that Calamaro was not subject to the tax, declaring, "We do not think that either the language or purpose of this statute, as revealed by its legislative history, supports the position of the Government." (p. 355.) In the Court's view, the "pick-up man," in contrast to the "writer," is not "engaged in receiving wagers" under § 3290. " * * * Congress did not choose to subject all employees of gambling enterprises to the tax and reporting requirements but was content to impose them on persons actually 'engaged in receiving wagers.' Neither we nor the Commissioner may rewrite the statute simply because we may feel that the scheme it created could be improved upon." (p. 357.) Of particular interest here is the Court's treatment of the prior administrative construction, embodied in Treasury Regulation 132, § 325.41, Example 2 (26 CFR 1957 Cum. Pocket Supp.) issued shortly after the enactment of § 3290 and reading as follows:

> "Example (2). B operates a numbers game. He has an arrangement with ten persons, who are employed in various capacities, such as bootblacks, elevator operators, news dealers, etc., to

receive wagers from the public on his behalf. B also employs a person to collect from his agents the wagers received on his behalf.

"B, his ten agents, and the employee who collects the wagers received on his behalf are each liable for the special tax."

Apart from finding some inconsistency between this and another part of the same Regulation, the Court disposed of this construction in these terms:

"Finally, the Government points to the fact that the Treasury Regulations relating to the statute purport to include the pick-up man among those subject to the § 3290 tax, and argues (a) that this constitutes an administrative interpretation to which we should give weight in construing the statute, particularly because (b) section 3290 was carried over *in haec verba* into § 4411 of the Internal Revenue Code of 1954. We find neither argument persuasive. In light of the above discussion, we cannot but regard this Treasury Regulation as no more than an attempted addition to the statute of something which is not there. As such the regulation can furnish no sustenance to the statute. Nor is the Government helped by its argument as to the 1954 Code. The regulation had been in effect for only three years, and there is nothing to indicate that it was ever called to the attention of Congress. The re-enactment of § 3290 in the 1954 Code was not accompanied by any congressional discussion which throws light on its intended scope. In such circumstances we consider the 1954 re-enactment to be without significance. * * *"

Is this treatment of a prior administrative construction followed by reenactment consistent or inconsistent with that in the *Cammarano* case, supra? How and why? Compare United States v. Correll, 389 U.S. 299, 88 S.Ct. 445, 19 L.Ed.2d 537 (1967), upholding a ruling (dating from 1940) by the Commissioner of Internal Revenue under § 162(a)(2) of the Internal Revenue Code of 1954. Citing references to the rule in Senate and House Committee reports on the '54 Code, the Supreme Court concluded "Congress was well aware of the Commissioner's rule when it retained in § 162(a)(2) the precise terminology * * * used in 1921." The case thus fell "within the settled principle that 'Treasury regulations and interpretations long continued without substantial change, applying to unamended or substantially reenacted statutes, are deemed to have received Congressional approval and have the effect of law.'"

FISHGOLD v. SULLIVAN DRYDOCK & REPAIR CORPORATION

Circuit Court of Appeals of the United States, Second Circuit, 1946.
154 F.2d 785, affirmed 328 U.S. 275, 66 S.Ct. 1105, 90 L.Ed. 1230 (1946).

Appeal from District Court of the United States for the Eastern District of New York.

Before L. HAND, CHASE, and FRANK, Circuit Judges.

L. HAND, Circuit Judge. Local 13 of the Industrial Union of Marine and Shipbuilding Workers of America appeals from a judg-

Sec. 7   WEIGHT OF PRIOR INTERPRETATIONS   489

ment awarding damages to the plaintiff for his loss of wages because of two lay-offs by his employer, the Sullivan Drydock and Repair Corporation, against which alone the action was brought. The union intervened, and charged itself with the defence; the United States, the Railway Labor Executives Association and the Congress of Industrial Organizations have filed briefs, as amici. The appeal raises only the proper interpretation of subdivision (b) and (c) of § 8 of the Selective Training and Service Act of 1940, as amended in 1944 (§ 308(b) and § 308(c), 50 U.S.C.A. Appendix, which we quote in the margin).[68] The facts as found by the judge were as follows.

The plaintiff entered the employ of the Sullivan Drydock and Repair Corporation as a welder, on December 21, 1942, and was steadily employed as such until May 22, 1943, when he was inducted into the Army. He served until July 12, 1944, and was then honorably discharged, and received a certificate of the kind described in § 8(a), 50 U.S.C.A. Appendix § 308(a). At that time he concededly was, and he has since been, qualified as a first-class welder; and the company restored him to this former position on August 21, 1944, and has never dismissed him. The controversy here at bar arises because on three occasions: Viz., on April 9, April 11, and from May 17 to May 24, inclusive, it refused to give him any work, because there was not enough on those days to occupy all hands. In so refusing it preferred other welders, not veterans, who had a higher shop seniority than the plaintiff: this in accordance with the agreement between the company and the union. The plaintiff's position is that, as a veteran, § 8(b) and (c) gave him priority over all his fellows except other veterans; the union's position is that those sections merely restored him to the same place in the shop hierarchy which he would

---

68. "8(b) In the case of any such person who, in order to perform such training and service, has left or leaves a position, other than a temporary position, in the employ of any employer and who (1) receives such certificate, (2) is still qualified to perform the duties of such position, and (3) makes application for reemployment within ninety days after he is relieved from such training and service or from hospitalization continuing after discharge for a period of not more than one year—
"(A) if such position was in the employ of the United States Government, its Territories or possessions, or the District of Columbia, such person shall be restored to such position or to a position of like seniority, status, and pay;
"(B) if such position was in the employ of a private employer, such employer shall restore such person to such position or to a position of like seniority, status, and pay unless the employer's circumstances have so changed as to make it impossible or unreasonable to do so."
"8(c) Any person who is restored to a position in accordance with the provisions of paragraph (A) or (B) of subsection (b) shall be considered as having been on furlough or leave of absence during his period of training and service in the land or naval forces, shall be so restored without loss of seniority, shall be entitled to participate in insurance or other benefits offered by the employer pursuant to established rules and practices relating to employees on furlough or leave of absence in effect with the employer at the time such person was inducted into such forces, and shall not be discharged from such position without cause within one year after such restoration."

have had, if he had been on leave of absence during the period of his service. The judge held with the plaintiff and the union appealed.

Subsection B of § 8(b) is the operative source of the privilege on which the plaintiff relies; it reads as follows: "Such employer shall restore such person to such position or to a position of like seniority, status and pay unless the employer's circumstances have so changed as to make it impossible or unreasonable to do so." "Such position" is nowhere defined except as "a position other than a temporary position, in the employ of any employer." Taking this clause by itself, it seems to us beyond debate that it was not intended that the veteran should gain in seniority. It will be observed that the grant is in the alternative: he is to be "restored" to his original position, or to one of "like seniority, status and pay," whenever possible. The phrase, "like seniority" means the "same seniority" as before; and it necessarily precludes any gain in seniority. It follows that, if the original position is no longer open, the substitute shall be a position of no greater, though no less, seniority than the lost position. But if that be true, there can be no implication that, if the original position be not lost, but be still available, the veteran shall be restored to it with a gain in priority; for that would pre-suppose that Congress did not intend the substitute to be as nearly a complete substitute for the lost original as it was possible to make it, a hypothesis absurd on its face. Hence we must start with the proposition that subsection B of § 8(b) not only did not grant any step up in seniority, but positively denied any.

Subdivision (c) confirms the intention so disclosed. As subsection B reads, it would probably be understood to restore the veteran only to that same position which he held when he was inducted. That was, however, thought to be unfair; for while he was in the service, there were likely to be such changes in the personnel that when he came back, he might find himself junior to those over whom he had had priority when he left. To remedy this, by an amendment made while the bill was in Congress, he was given the same status that he would have had, if he had been "on furlough or leave of absence" while he was in the service. How far that differed from his position, had he remained actively at work, does not appear; but clearly the amendment presupposed that a difference there might be. Having in this way declared how the veteran's interim position "shall be considered," Congress added that he should be "restored without loss of seniority." Had the purpose been, not only to insure the veteran that he should not lose any more steps upon the ladder than if he had been on leave, but also that he should go to the top, we cannot conceive that Congress would have expressed itself in the words, "without loss of seniority." They have no such express meaning, and their implications are directly the opposite; for they disclose a concern against his possible demotion inconsistent with any implied belief in his promotion. For these reasons we are satisfied that, except for the concluding phrase of subdivision (c) there can be no doubt that textually the union's construction is the right one. It remains to consider that phrase which, as we understand it, is the chief reliance of those who take the opposite view.

It declares that the veteran "shall not be discharged from such position within one year after such restoration"; and we should, so far as possible, interpret it so as not to conflict with the rest of the section; in particular, so as to leave untouched the privilege of seniority, as it is earlier defined. There is no difficulty in doing so, if "discharge" means a permanent end to the relation of employment, a separation, a dismissal; and that is indeed its ordinary meaning. For example, the Oxford Dictionary (Vol. II, p. 412, subtitle "Discharge" I, 3), reads: "To relieve of a charge or office; (more usually) to dismiss from office, service or employment; to cashier": this in distinction with "Layoff," (Supplement, p. 8): "A period during which a workman is temporarily dismissed or allowed to leave his work; that part or season of the year during which activity in a particular business or game is partly or completely suspended; an off-season." It seems to us that Congress used "discharge" in this sense: i. e., that the veteran was to be assured of his job for the same period —a year—for which he was to be drafted; but that the job to which he was "restored"—as that very word implies—was to be subject to the same conditions to which the old job had been subject, with only the exception that it should be better in so far as a leave of absence for the year might improve it. The value of that assurance would indeed vary. In a closed shop it would presumably add little, for the union would not allow a member to be discharged without cause anyway. In an open shop the same would be true, if it were partly unionized, and the veteran were in the union; but, whenever for any reason he had not that protection it prevented his being turned out, so long as he behaved himself, and that was an advantage of no mean importance. We do not know what proportion of those in industry are not in unions; but their number is certainly very large, and, even though the clause was of value only to them, they are numerous enough to give it a purpose; to say nothing of the possibility that statutory protection may be an important supplement to union protection.

When we consider the situation at the time that the Act was passed—September, 1940—it is extremely improbable that Congress should have meant to grant any broader privilege than as we are measuring it. It is true that the nation had become deeply disturbed at its defenseless position, and had begun to make ready; but it was not at war, and the issue still hung in the balance whether it ever would be at war. If we carry ourselves back to that summer and autumn, we shall recall that the presidential campaigns of both parties avoided commitment upon that question, and that each candidate particularly insisted that no troops should be sent overseas. The original act limited service to one year, and it was most improbable that within that time we should be called upon to fight upon our own soil; as indeed the event proved, for we were still at peace in September, 1941. Congress was calling young men to the colors to give them an adequate preparation for our defence, but with no forecast of the appalling experiences which they were later to undergo. Against that background it is not likely that a proposal would then have been accepted which gave industrial priority, regardless of their length of employment, to unmarried men—for the most part under thirty—over men in the thirties, forties or fifties, who had wives and children dependent upon them. Today, in the light of what has happened, the privilege then granted may appear an altogether inadequate equivalent for their services; but we have not to decide what is now proper; we are to reconstruct, as best we may, what was the purpose of Congress when it used the words in which § 8(b) and § 8(c) were cast.

The plaintiff argues, however, that, regardless of their original scope, these sections have in any event by administrative interpretation and by later legislation, taken on the meaning which he claims. We shall consider first the administrative interpretations. Section 8(g) directs the Director of Selective Service to establish a "Personnel Division" which shall "render aid in the replacement in their former positions of, or in securing positions for * * * persons who have satisfactorily completed any period of their training and service under this Act," and on March 5, 1944, the Director issued a memorandum (No. 190–A, Part IV, § 4(b)), which read: "A veteran who has been reinstated to his former position cannot be displaced by another on the ground that the latter has greater seniority rights." Section 8(e) directs the proper district attorney, "if reasonably satisfied" that a veteran "is entitled" to the benefits of the Act, to "appear and act as attorney" for him to enforce his rights; and the Attorney General, as appears from his intervention as amicus in this action, has read the law like the Director of Selective Service. On the other hand, the National War Labor Board adopted the opposite view in Re Scovill Manufacturing Co., 21 W.L.R. 200; as have several of its arbitrators; and the Solicitor of the Department of Labor did the same in an instruction for the guidance of federal conciliators in dealing with war veterans (16 L.R.R. 481).

So far as we can find, these are the only interpretative rulings that have as yet appeared by officials who can be said to have been charged with any duty in administering the Act; and it can hardly be said that they have had that consistency to which we should yield our judgment. We do not forget that the canon which the plaintiff invokes is not confined to decisions inter partes, like those of the Federal Trade Commission, the Interstate Commerce Commission, the

Labor Board, or the Tax Court; it extends also to the interpretations of officials, charged with the duty of enforcing statutes. Skidmore v. Swift & Co., 323 U.S. 134, 65 S.Ct. 161; Great Northern R. Co. v. United States, 315 U.S. 262, 62 S.Ct. 529, 86 L.Ed. 836. Whether the weight to be given to such rulings is less than to regulations for the conduct of, or decisions in, contested cases, has never been expressly decided, though was intimated in Skidmore v. Swift, supra, 323 U.S. at page 139, 65 S.Ct. at page 164; and see Judge Frank's dissent in Duquesne Warehouse v. Railroad Retirement Board, 2 Cir., 148 F.2d 473, 485–487. There is indeed a basis for making such a distinction because the position of a public officer, charged with the enforcement of a law, is different from one who must decide a dispute. If there is a fair doubt, his duty is to present the case for the side which he represents, and leave decision to the court, or the administrative tribunal, upon which lies the responsibility of decision. If he surrenders a plausible construction, it will, at least it may, be surrendered forever; and yet it may be right. Since such rulings need not have the detachment of a judicial, or semi-judicial decision, and may properly carry a bias, it would seem that they should not be as authoritative; and of this sort were the rulings of the Director and the Attorney General in the case at bar, unlike the decisions of the War Labor Board and the direction of the Solicitor of the Labor Department. Be that as it may, concededly all such considerations are only cautionary, and not authoritative; for in the end, after whatever reserve, upon the courts rests the ultimate responsibility of declaring what a statute means: as the Supreme Court recognized in its last word upon the subject. Jewell Ridge Coal Corp. v. Local, 325 U.S. 161, 65 S.Ct. 1063. We should have to be in much greater doubt than we are, if we were to yield, even to a more uniform administrative interpretation than exists here.

There remains the question whether the amendment of § 8 in December, 1944, 50 U.S.C.A. Appendix § 308, and the extension of the whole act until May 15, 1946, is to be taken as embodying the Director's position. The amendment, taken alone, only extended the time within which a veteran might apply for reinstatement from forty days to ninety days, and made that period begin from the termination of "hospitalization continuing after discharge for a period of not more than one year," if he was in a hospital. Of itself this indicated no other change in intent; but the Director's ruling had been made for over six months in December, 1944. Moreover, Colonel Keesling, of the Director's office, in one part of his testimony before the subcommittee of the Committee on Military Affairs, stated the Director's position. His later remarks were, perhaps, somewhat ambiguous, and we are left in doubt as to the final impression which his testimony as a whole may have left on the subcommittee. After he had first mentioned the subject, the presiding chairman, Mr. Costello, wished to revert to it, and the Colonel thereupon read the Act as it stood, and a colloquy ensued which we quote in the margin.[69] He was then speaking of the fact that the veteran's absence from the shop should be counted as though he were on leave, or on furlough; and whether his hearers assumed that this was consistent with what he had said before, or supplanted it, is not entirely certain.

However, we cannot in any event assimilate the situation to that to which courts so frequently resort in aid of the interpretation of ambiguous language; i. e., reenactment without change after administrative interpretation. McCaughn v. Hershey Chocolate Co., 283 U.S. 488, 492, 51 S.Ct. 510, 75 L.Ed. 1183; National Lead Co. v. United States, 252 U.S. 140, 146, 40 S.Ct. 237, 64 L.Ed. 496; Massachusetts Mutual Life Insurance Co. v. United States, 288 U.S. 269, 273, 53 S.Ct. 337, 77 L.Ed. 739. The rationale of that canon must be, either that those in charge of the amendment are familiar with existing rulings, or that they mean to incorporate them, whatever they may be. The second would hardly be tenable; we should hesitate to say that Congress might enact as law regulatory provisions with which it concededly had no acquaintance. On the other hand, if we are to suppose, in the absence of evidence to the contrary, that Congress is familiar with all existing administrative interpretations, and is content to accept them when it makes no change, it would seem that the force of that assumption should vary with the circumstances. For example, successive recensions of the Internal Revenue Act are the result of detailed conferences between the Treasury and the committees of Congress; and there is good reason to assume that, in so far as the statute is not changed, existing regulations and even less formal interpretations are expressly affirmed. That may well be a proper inference in the case of all general recensions, accompanied as these ordinarily are by continuous and intimate consultation with administrative officers. But it would seem hazardous to carry such a conclusion to the situation here at bar. So far as concerns any actual

---

69. "Mr. Johnson: And the time he serves in the armed forces does not affect his seniority?
"Colonel Keesling: That is right. He shall be restored without loss of seniority.
"Mr. Harness: Does that mean he does not lose any of the seniority he has acquired up to the time of his induction, or that he gets that seniority that has accrued to him while he was working, plus the time he served in the Army?
"Colonel Keesling: The latter is right.
"Mr. Harness: Whose construction is that?
"Colonel Keesling: Ours. The language is clear. It says that a person so restored shall be restored without loss of seniority.

"Mr. Johnson: It is not clear that that means his former seniority.
"Colonel Keesling: Would it not be loss of seniority if a nonveteran increased his seniority by 2 years without crediting an employee with 2 years' seniority for the 2 years he spent in the armed forces?
"Mr. Johnson: It might mean without loss of what he had before.
"Colonel Keesling: That is not the way we have construed it.
"There has not been any difference of opinion on that as far as the labor groups are concerned. The act says any person who is restored shall be restored without loss of seniority."

information conveyed to Congress, it was at most confined to the occasion which we have discussed, for it would be gratuitous to suppose that the same information ever reached the Senate Committee of Military Affairs. That aside, the same ambiguity arises here, if we were to impute to Congress a knowledge of all administrative rulings, as arises from the rulings themselves, for the decisions of the National Labor Relations Board and of the Solicitor of the Labor Department both preceded the amendment of § 8(c). To suppose that Congress was familiar with one set of rulings and not with the other would be baseless in fact, and involve the canon in greater uncertainty than already attaches to its use, which—be it said with all deference—is by no means negligible. We should be clutching at straws and relying on phantoms, if we were to suppose that the re-enactment of this section with its very specific amendment was intended to effect so vital a change in industrial relations. Certainly we should be unwarranted in believing that Congress would have made so far reaching a change without notice to those who had an interest equal with the veterans themselves—the unions. Finally, as in the case of the effect of such rulings unaccompanied by any amendment of the statute, when all is said, the canon is only a help when the intent is otherwise in doubt; and, after every allowance for the differences which have actually arisen, we cannot bring ourselves to abandon the construction we have adopted. As for judicial interpretation, this is the first appeal; and the only decisions in the district courts are apparently equally divided. Whirls v. The Trailmobile Co., D.C.S.D. Ohio, 64 F.Supp. 713, is against the view we take; Olin Industries Inc. v. Barnett, D.C.S.D.Ill., 64 F.Supp. 722 is in accord. The fact that we are ourselves not agreed cautions us that we should not be too sure of our conclusion; and obviously the really important matter is that the question should reach the Supreme Court as soon as possible.

We cannot conclude without expressing the hope, though it may not be realized, that our decision may not be taken as indicating any indifference to the claims of those who stood by the nation in the hour of its need at the hazard, and so often with the loss, of all that life holds dear.

Judgment reversed; complaint dismissed.

[The dissenting opinion of CHASE, J. is omitted.]

GIROUARD v. UNITED STATES

Supreme Court of the United States, 1946.
328 U.S. 61, 66 S.Ct. 826, 90 L.Ed. 1084.

Certiorari to the United States Circuit Court of Appeals for the First Circuit.

Mr. Justice DOUGLAS delivered the opinion of the Court.

In 1943 petitioner, a native of Canada, filed his petition for naturalization in the District Court of Massachusetts. He stated in his application that he understood the principles of the government of the United States, believed in its form of government, and was willing to take the oath of allegiance (54 Stat. 1157, 8 U.S.C.A. § 735(b)), which reads as follows:

"I hereby declare, on oath, that I absolutely and entirely renounce and abjure all allegiance and fidelity to any foreign prince, potentate, state, or sovereignty of whom or which I have heretofore been a subject or citizen; that I will support and defend the Constitution and laws of the United States of America against all enemies, foreign and domestic; that I will bear true faith and allegiance to the same; and that I take this obligation freely without any mental reservation or purpose of evasion: So help me God."

To the question in the application "If necessary, are you willing to take up arms in defense of this country?" he replied, "No (Noncombatant) Seventh Day Adventist." He explained that answer before the examiner by saying "it is a purely religious matter with me, I have no political or personal reasons other than that." He did not claim before his Selective Service board exemption from all military service, but only from combatant military duty. At the hearing in the District Court petitioner testified that he was a member of the Seventh Day Adventist denomination, of whom approximately 10,000 were then serving in the armed forces of the United States as noncombatants, especially in the medical corps; and that he was willing to serve in the army but would not bear arms. The District Court admitted him to citizenship. The Circuit Court of Appeals reversed, one judge dissenting. 1 Cir., 149 F.2d 760. It took that action on the authority of United States v. Schwimmer, 279 U.S. 644, 49 S.Ct. 448, 73 L.Ed. 889; United States v. Macintosh, 283 U.S. 605, 51 S.Ct. 570, 75 L.Ed. 1302, and United States v. Bland, 283 U.S. 636, 51 S.Ct. 569, 75 L.Ed. 1319, saying that the facts of the present case brought it squarely within the principles of those cases. The case is here on a petition for a writ of certiorari which we granted so that those authorities might be re-examined.

The Schwimmer, Macintosh and Bland cases involved, as does the present one, a question of statutory construction. At the time of those cases, Congress required an alien, before admission to citizenship, to declare on oath in open court that "he will support and defend the Constitution and laws of the United States against all enemies, foreign and domestic, and bear true faith and allegiance to the same." It also required the court to be satisfied that the alien had during the five year period immediately preceding the date of his application "behaved as a man of good moral character, attached to the principles of the Constitution of the United States, and well disposed to the good order and happiness of the same." Those provisions were reenacted into the present law in substantially the same form.

While there are some factual distinctions between this case and the Schwimmer and Macintosh cases, the Bland case on its facts is indistinguishable. But the principle emerging from the three cases obliterates any factual distinction among them. As we recognized in Re Summers, 325 U.S. 561, 572, 577, 65 S.Ct. 1307, 1313, 1316, they stand for the same general rule—that an alien who refuses to bear arms will not be admitted to citizenship. As an original proposition, we could not agree with that rule. The fallacies underlying it were, we think, demonstrated in the dissents of Mr. Justice Holmes in the Schwimmer case and of Mr. Chief Justice Hughes in the Macintosh case.

The oath required of aliens does not in terms require that they promise to bear arms. Nor has Congress expressly made any such finding a prerequisite to citizenship. To hold that it is required is to read it into the Act by implication. But we could not assume that Congress intended to make such an abrupt and radical departure from our traditions unless it spoke in unequivocal terms.

The bearing of arms, important as it is, is not the only way in which our institutions may be supported and defended, even in times of great peril. Total war in its modern form dramatizes as never before the great cooperative effort necessary for victory. The nuclear physicists who developed the atomic bomb, the worker at his lathe, the seaman on cargo vessels, construction battalions, nurses, engineers, litter bearers, doctors, chaplains—these, too, made essential contributions. And many of them made the supreme sacrifice. Mr. Justice Holmes stated in the Schwimmer case, 279 U.S. at page 655, 49 S.Ct. at page 451, 73 L.Ed. 889, that "the Quakers have done their share to make the country what it is." And the annals of the recent war show that many whose religious scruples prevented them from bearing arms, nevertheless were unselfish participants in the war effort. Refusal to bear arms is not necessarily a sign of disloyalty or a lack of attachment to our institutions. One may serve his country faithfully and devotedly though his religious scruples make it impossible for him to shoulder a rifle. Devotion to one's country can be as real and as enduring among non-combatants as among combatants. One may adhere to what he deems to be his obligation to God and yet assume all military risks to secure victory. The effort of war is indivisible; and those whose religious scruples prevent them from killing are no less patriots than those whose special traits or handicaps result in their assignment to duties far behind the fighting front. Each is making the utmost contribution according to his capacity. The fact that his role may be limited by religious convictions rather than by physical characteristics has no necessary bearing on his attachment to his country or on his willingness to support and defend it to his utmost.

Petitioner's religious scruples would not disqualify him from becoming a member of Congress or holding other public offices. While Article VI, Clause 3 of the Constitution provides that such officials, both of the United States and the several States, "shall be bound by Oath or Affirmation, to support this Constitution," it significantly adds that "no religious Test shall ever be required as a Qualification to any Office or public Trust under the United States." The oath required is in no material respect different from that prescribed for aliens under the Naturalization Act. It has long contained the provision "that I will support and defend the Constitution of the United States against all enemies, foreign and domestic; that I will bear true faith and allegiance to the same; that I take this obligation freely, without any mental reservation or purpose of evasion." R.S. § 1757, 5 U.S.C.A. § 16. As Mr. Chief Justice Hughes stated in his dissent in the Macintosh case, 283 U.S. at page 631, 51 S.Ct. at page 577, 75 L. Ed. 1302, "the history of the struggle for religious liberty, the large number of citizens of our country from the very beginning who have been unwilling to sacrifice their religious convictions, and in particular, those who have been conscientiously opposed to war and who would not yield what they sincerely believed to be their allegiance to the will of God"—these considerations make it impossible to conclude "that such persons are to be deemed disqualified for public office in this country because of the requirement of the oath which must be taken before they enter upon their duties."

There is not the slightest suggestion that Congress set a stricter standard for aliens seeking admission to citizenship than it did for officials who make and enforce the laws of the nation and administer its affairs. It is hard to believe that one need forsake his religious scruples to become a citizen but not to sit in the high councils of state.

As Mr. Chief Justice Hughes pointed out (United States v. Macintosh, supra, 283 U.S. at page 633, 51 S.Ct. at page 578, 75 L.Ed. 1302), religious scruples against bearing arms have been recognized by Congress in the various draft laws. This is true of the Selective Training and Service Act of 1940, 54 Stat. 889, 50 U.S.C.A. Appendix, § 305(g), as it was of earlier acts. He who is inducted into the armed services takes an oath which includes the provision "that I will bear true faith and allegiance to the United States of America; that I will serve them honestly and faithfully against all their enemies whomsoever." 41 Stat. 809, 10 U.S.C.A. § 1581. Congress has thus recognized that one may adequately discharge his obligations as a cit-

Sec. 7   *WEIGHT OF PRIOR INTERPRETATIONS*   499

izen by rendering non-combatant as well as combatant services. This respect by Congress over the years for the conscience of those having religious scruples against bearing arms is cogent evidence of the meaning of the oath. It is recognition by Congress that even in time of war one may truly support and defend our institutions though he stops short of using weapons of war.

That construction of the naturalization oath received new support in 1942. In the Second War Powers Act, 56 Stat. 176, 182, 8 U.S.C.A. § 1001, Congress relaxed certain of the requirements for aliens who served honorably in the armed forces of the United States during World War II and provided machinery to expedite their naturalization. Residence requirements were relaxed, educational tests were eliminated, and no fees were required. But no change in the oath was made; nor was any change made in the requirement that the alien be attached to the principles of the Constitution. Yet it is clear that these new provisions cover non-combatants as well as combatants. If petitioner had served as a non-combatant (as he was willing to do), he could have been admitted to citizenship by taking the identical oath which he is willing to take. Can it be that the oath means one thing to one who has served to the extent permitted by his religious scruples and another thing to one equally willing to serve but who has not had the opportunity? It is not enough to say that petitioner is not entitled to the benefits of the new Act since he did not serve in the armed forces. He is not seeking the benefits of the expedited procedure and the relaxed requirements. The oath which he must take is identical with the oath which both non-combatants and combatants must take. It would, indeed, be a strange construction to say that "support and defend the Constitution and laws of the United States of America against all enemies, foreign and domestic" demands something more from some than it does from others. That oath can hardly be adequate for one who is unwilling to bear arms because of religious scruples and yet exact from another a promise to bear arms despite religious scruples.

Mr. Justice Holmes stated in the Schwimmer case, 279 U.S. at pages 654, 655, 49 S.Ct. at page 451, 73 L.Ed. 889: "if there is any principle of the Constitution that more imperatively calls for attachment than any other it is the principle of free thought—not free thought for those who agree with us but freedom for the thought that we hate. I think that we should adhere to that principle with regard to admission into, as well as to life within this country." The struggle for religious liberty has through the centuries been an effort to accommodate the demands of the State to the conscience of the individual. The victory for freedom of thought recorded in our Bill of Rights recognizes that in the domain of conscience there is a moral power higher than the State. Throughout the ages men have suffered death rather than subordinate their allegiance to God to the authority of the State. Freedom of religion guaranteed by the First Amendment is the product of that struggle. As we recently stated in United States v. Ballard, 322 U.S. 78, 86, 64 S.Ct. 882, 886, 88 L.Ed. 1148, "Freedom of thought, which includes freedom of religious belief, is basic in a society of free men. West Virginia State Board of Education v. Barnette, 319 U.S. 624, 63 S.Ct. 1178, 87 L.Ed. 1628, 147 A.L.R. 674." The test oath is abhorrent to our tradition. Over the years Congress has meticulously respected that tradition and even in time of war has sought to accommodate the military requirements to the religious scruples of the individual. We do not believe that Congress intended to reverse that policy when it came to draft the naturalization oath. Such an abrupt and radical departure from our traditions should not be implied. See Schneiderman v. United States, 320 U.S. 118, 132, 63 S.Ct. 1333, 1340, 87 L.Ed. 1796. Cogent evidence would be necessary to convince us that Congress took that course.

We conclude that the Schwimmer, Macintosh and Bland cases do not state the correct rule of law.

We are met, however, with the argument that even though those cases were wrongly decided, Congress has adopted the rule which they announced. The argument runs as follows: Many efforts were made to amend the law so as to change the rule announced by those cases; but in every instance the bill died in committee. Moreover, in 1940 when the new Naturalization Act was passed, Congress reenacted the oath in its pre-existing form, though at the same time it made extensive changes in the requirements and procedure for naturalization. From this it is argued that Congress adopted and reenacted the rule of the Schwimmer, Macintosh, and Bland cases. Cf. Apex Hosiery Co. v. Leader, 310 U.S. 469, 488, 489, 60 S.Ct. 982, 989, 990, 84 L.Ed. 1311, 128 A.L.R. 1044.

We stated in Helvering v. Hallock, 309 U.S. 106, 119, 60 S.Ct. 444, 451, 84 L.Ed. 604, 125 A.L.R. 1368, that "It would require very persuasive circumstances enveloping Congressional silence to debar this Court from re-examining its own doctrines." It is at best treacherous to find in Congressional silence alone the adoption of a controlling rule of law. We do not think under the circumstances of this legislative history that we can properly place on the shoulders of Congress the burden of the Court's own error. The history of the 1940 Act is at most equivocal. It contains no affirmative recognition of the rule of the Schwimmer, Macintosh and Bland cases. The silence of Congress and its inaction are as consistent with a desire to leave the problem fluid as they are with an adoption by silence of the rule of those cases. But for us, it is enough to say that since the date of those cases Congress never acted affirmatively on this question but once and that was in 1942. At that time, as we have noted, Congress specifically granted naturalization privileges to noncombatants who like petitioner were prevented from bearing arms by their religious scruples. That was affirmative recognition that one could be attached to the principles of our government and could support and de-

Sec. 7   WEIGHT OF PRIOR INTERPRETATIONS   501

fend it even though his religious convictions prevented him from bearing arms. And, as we have said, we cannot believe that the oath was designed to exact something more from one person than from another. Thus the affirmative action taken by Congress in 1942 negatives any inference that otherwise might be drawn from its silence when it re-enacted the oath in 1940.

Reversed.

Mr. Justice JACKSON took no part in the consideration or decision of this case.

Mr. Chief Justice STONE dissenting.

I think the judgment should be affirmed, for the reason that the court below, in applying the controlling provisions of the naturalization statutes, correctly applied them as earlier construed by this Court, whose construction Congress has adopted and confirmed.

In three cases decided more than fifteen years ago, this Court denied citizenship to applicants for naturalization who had announced that they proposed to take the prescribed oath of allegiance with the reservation or qualification that they would not, as naturalized citizens, assist in the defense of this country by force of arms or give their moral support to the government in any war which they did not believe to be morally justified or in the best interests of the country. See United States v. Schwimmer, 279 U.S. 644, 49 S.Ct. 448, 73 L.Ed. 889; United States v. Macintosh, 283 U.S. 605, 51 S.Ct. 570, 75 L.Ed. 1302; United States v. Bland, 283 U.S. 636, 51 S.Ct. 569, 75 L.Ed. 1319.

In each of these cases this Court held that the applicant had failed to meet the conditions which Congress had made prerequisite to naturalization by § 4 of the Naturalization Act of June 29, 1906, c. 3592, 34 Stat. 596, the provisions of which, here relevant, were enacted in the Nationality Act of October 14, 1940. See c. 876, 54 Stat. 1137, as amended by the Act of March 27, 1942, c. 199, 56 Stat. 176, 182, 183, and by the Act of December 7, 1942, c. 690, 56 Stat. 1041, 8 U.S. C.A. §§ 707, 723a, 735, 1001 et seq., Section 4 of the Naturalization Act of 1906, paragraph "Third", provided that before the admission to citizenship the applicant should declare on oath in open court that "he will support and defend the Constitution and laws of the United States against all enemies, foreign and domestic, and bear true faith and allegiance to the same." And paragraph "Fourth" required that before admission it be made to appear "to the satisfaction of the court admitting any alien to citizenship" that at least for a period of five years immediately preceding his application the applicant "has behaved as a man of good moral character, attached to the principles of the Constitution of the United States, and well disposed to the good order and happiness of the same." In applying these provisions in the cases mentioned, this Court held only that an applicant who is unable to take the oath of allegiance without the reservations or qualifications insisted upon by the applicants in those cases manifests his want of attachment to the principles of the Constitution and his unwillingness to meet the requirements of the oath, that he will support and defend the Constitution of the United States and bear true faith and allegiance to the same, and so does not comply with the statutory conditions of his naturalization. No question of the constitutional power of Congress to withhold citizenship on these grounds was involved. That power was not doubted. See Selective Draft Law Cases (Arver v. United States), 245 U.S. 366, 38 S.Ct. 159, 62 L.Ed. 349, L.R.A.1918C, 361, Ann.Cas.1918B, 856; Hamilton v. Regents, 293 U. S. 245, 55 S.Ct. 197, 79 L.Ed. 343. The only question was of construction of the statute which Congress at all times has been free to amend if dissatisfied with the construction adopted by the Court.

With three other Justices of the Court I dissented in the Macintosh and Bland cases, for reasons which the Court now adopts as ground for overruling them. Since this Court in three considered earlier opinions has rejected the construction of the statute for which the dissenting Justices contended, the question, which for me is decisive of the present case, is whether Congress has likewise rejected that construction by its subsequent legislative action, and has adopted and confirmed the Court's earlier construction of the statutes in question. A study of Congressional action taken with respect to proposals for amendment of the naturalization laws since the decision in the Schwimmer case, leads me to conclude that Congress has adopted and confirmed this Court's earlier construction of the naturalization laws. For that reason alone I think that the judgment should be affirmed.

The construction of the naturalization statutes, adopted by this Court in the three cases mentioned, immediately became the target of an active, publicized legislative attack in Congress which persisted for a period of eleven years, until the adoption of the Nationality Act in 1940. Two days after the Schwimmer case was decided, a bill was introduced in the House, H.R. 3547, 71st Cong., 1st Sess., to give the Naturalization Act a construction contrary to that which had been given to it by this Court and which, if adopted, would have made the applicants rejected by this Court in the Schwimmer, Macintosh and Bland cases eligible for citizenship. This effort to establish by Congressional action that the construction which this Court had placed on the Naturalization Act was not one which Congress had adopted or intended, was renewed without success after the decision in the Macintosh and Bland cases, and was continued for a period of about ten years. All of these measures were of substantially the same pattern as H.R. 297, 72d Cong., 1st Sess., introduced December 8, 1931, at the first session of Congress, after the decision in the Macintosh case. It provided that no person otherwise qualified "shall be debarred from citizenship by reason of his or her religious views or philosophical opinions with respect to the lawfulness of war as a means of settling international disputes, but every alien admitted to citizenship shall be subject to the same obligation as the native-born citizen." H.R. 3547, 71st Cong., 1st Sess., introduced immediately after the decision in the Schwimmer case, had contained a like provision, but with the omission of the last clause beginning "but every alien." Hearings were had before the House Committee on Immigration and Naturalization on both bills at which their proponents had stated clearly their purpose to set aside the interpretation placed on the oath of allegiance by the Schwimmer and Macintosh cases. There was opposition on each occasion. Bills identical with H.R. 297 were introduced in three later Congresses. None of these bills were reported out of Committee. The other proposals, all of which failed of passage * * *, had the same purpose and differed only in phraseology.

Thus, for six successive Congresses, over a period of more than a decade, there were continuously pending before Congress in one form or another proposals to overturn the rulings in the three Supreme Court decisions in question. Congress declined to adopt these proposals after full hearings and after speeches on the floor advocating the change. 72 Cong.Rec. 6966–7; 75th Cong.Rec. 15354–7. In the meantime the decisions of this Court had been followed in Clarke's Case, 301 Pa. 321, 152 A. 92; Beale v. United States, 8 Cir., 71 F.2d 737; In re Warkentin, 7 Cir., 93 F.2d 42. In Beale v. United States, supra, [71 F.2d 739] the court pointed out that the proposed amendments affecting the provisions of the statutes relating to admission to citizenship had failed saying: "We must conclude, therefore, that these statutory requirements as construed by the Supreme Court have Congressional sanction and approval."

Any doubts that such were the purpose and will of Congress would seem to have been dissipated by the reenactment by Congress in 1940 of Paragraphs "Third" and "Fourth" of § 4 of the Naturalization Act of 1906, and by the incorporation in the Act of 1940 of the very form of oath which had been administratively prescribed for the applicants in the Schwimmer, Macintosh and Bland cases. See Rule 8(c), Naturalization Regulations of July 1, 1929.

The Nationality Act of 1940 was a comprehensive, slowly matured and carefully considered revision of the naturalization laws. The preparation of this measure was not only delegated to a Congressional Committee, but was considered by a committee of Cabinet members, one of whom was the Attorney General. Both were aware of our decisions in the Schwimmer and related cases and that no other question pertinent to the naturalization laws had been as persistently and continuously before Congress in the ten years following the decision in the Schwimmer case. The modifications in the provisions of Paragraphs "Third" and "Fourth" of § 4 of the 1906 Act show conclusively the careful attention which was given to them.

In the face of this legislative history the "failure of Congress to alter the Act after it had been judicially construed, and the enactment by Congress of legislation which implicitly recognizes the judicial construction as effective, is persuasive of legislative recognition that the judicial construction is the correct one. This is the more so where, as here, the application of the statute * * * has brought forth sharply conflicting views both on the Court and in Congress, and where after the matter has been fully brought to the attention of the public and the Congress, the latter has not seen fit to change the statute." Apex Hosiery Co. v. Leader, 310 U.S. 469, 488, 489, 60 S. Ct. 982, 989, 84 L.Ed. 1311, 128 A.L.R. 1044. And see to like effect United States v. Ryan, 284 U.S. 167–175, 52 S.Ct. 65–68, 76 L.Ed. 224; United States v. Elgin, J. & E. R. Co., 298 U.S. 492, 500, 56 S. Ct. 841, 843, 80 L.Ed. 1300; State of Missouri v. Ross, 299 U.S. 72, 75, 57 S.Ct. 60, 62, 81 L.Ed. 46; cf. Helvering v. Winmill, 305 U.S. 79, 82, 83, 59 S.Ct. 45, 46, 47, 83 L.Ed. 52. It is the responsibility of Congress, in reenacting a statute, to make known its purpose in a controversial matter of interpretation of its former language, at least when the matter has, for over a decade, been persistently brought to its attention. In the light of this legislative history, it is abundantly clear that Congress has performed that duty. In any case it is not lightly to be implied that Congress has failed to perform it and has delegated to this Court the responsibility of giving new content to language deliberately readopted after this Court has construed it. For us to make such an assumption is to discourage, if not to deny, legislative responsibility. By thus adopting and confirming this Court's construction of what Congress had enacted in the Naturalization Act of 1906 Congress gave that construction the same legal significance as though it had written the very words into the Act of 1940.

The only remaining question is whether Congress repealed this construction by enactment of the 1942 amendments of the Nationality Act. That Act extended special privileges to applicants for naturalization who were aliens and who have served in the armed forces of the United States in time of war, by dispensing with or modifying existing requirements, relating to declarations of intention, period of residence, education, and fees. It left unchanged the requirements that the applicant's behavior show his attachment to the principles of the Constitution and that he take the oath of allegiance. In adopting the 1942 amendments Congress did not have before it any question of the oath of allegiance with which it had been concerned when it adopted the 1940 Act. In 1942 it was concerned with the grant of special favors to those seeking naturalization who had worn the uniform and rendered military service in time of war and who could satisfy such naturalization requirements as had not been dispensed with by the amendments. In the case of those entitled to avail themselves of these privileges, Congress left it to the naturalization authorities, as in other cases, to determine whether, by their applications and their conduct in the military service they satisfy the requirements for naturalization which had not been waived.

It is pointed out that one of the 1942 amendments, 8 U.S.C.A. § 1004, provided that the provisions of the amendment should not apply to "any conscientious objector who performed no military duty whatever or refused to wear the uniform." It is said that the implication of this provision is that conscientious objectors who rendered noncombatant service and wore the uniform were, under the 1942 amendments, to be admitted to citizenship. From this it is argued that since the 1942 amendments apply to those who have been in noncombatant, as well as combatant, military service, the amendment must be taken to include some who have rendered noncombatant service who are also conscientious objectors and who would be admitted to citizenship under the 1942 amendments, even though they made the same reservations as to the oath of allegiance as did the applicants in the Schwimmer, Macintosh and Bland cases. And it is said that although the 1942 amendments are not applicable to petitioner, who has not been in military service, the oath cannot mean one thing as to him and another as to those who have been in the noncombatant service.

To these suggestions there are two answers. One is that if the 1942 amendment be construed as including noncombatants who are also conscientious objectors, who are unwilling to take the oath without the reservations made by the applicants in the Schwimmer, Macintosh and Bland cases, the only effect would be to exempt noncombatant conscientious objectors from the requirements of the oath, which had clearly been made applicable to all objectors, including petitioner, by the Nationality Act of 1940, and from which petitioner was not exempted by the 1942 amendments. If such is the construction of the 1942 Act, there is no constitutional or statutory obstacle to Congress' taking such action. Congress if it saw fit could have admitted to citizenship those who had rendered noncombatant service, with a modified oath or without any oath at all. Petitioner has not been so exempted.

Since petitioner was never in the military or naval forces of the United States, we need not decide whether the 1942 amendments authorized any different oath for those who had been in noncombatant service than for others. The amendments have been construed as requiring the same oath, without reservations, from conscientious objectors, as from others. In re Nielsen, D.C., 60 F.Supp. 240. Not all of those who rendered noncombatant service were conscientious objectors. Few were. There were others in the noncombatant service who had announced their conscientious objections to combatant service, who may have waived or abandoned their objections. Such was the experience in the First World War. See "Statement Concerning the Treatment of Conscientious Objectors in the Army", prepared and published by direction of the Secretary of War, June 18, 1919. All such could have taken the oath without the reservations made by the applicants in the Schwimmer, Macintosh and Bland cases and would have been entitled to the benefits of the 1942 amendments provided they had performed military duty and had not refused to wear the uniform. The fact that Congress recognized by indirection, in 8 U.S.C.A. § 1004, that those who had appeared in the role of conscientious objectors, might become citizens by taking the oath of allegiance and establishing their attachment to the principles of the Constitution, does not show that Congress dispensed with the requirements of the oath as construed by this Court and plainly confirmed by Congress in the Nationality Act of 1940. There is no necessary inconsistency in this respect between the 1940 Act and the 1942 amendments. Without it repeal by implication is not favored. United States v. Borden Co., 308 U.S. 188, 198, 199, 203–206, 60 S.Ct. 182, 188, 189, 190–192, 84 L.Ed. 181; State of Georgia v. Pennsylvania R. Co., 324 U.S. 439, 457, 65 S.Ct. 716, 726; United States Alkali Export Ass'n v. United States, 325 U.S. 196, 209, 65 S.Ct. 1120, 1128. The amendments and their legislative history give no hint of any purpose of Congress to relax, at least for persons who had rendered no military service, the requirements of the oath of allegiance and proof of attachment to the Constitution as this Court had interpreted them and as the Nationality Act of 1940 plainly required them to be interpreted. It is not the function of this Court to disregard the will of Congress in the exercise of its constitutional power.

Mr. Justice REED and Mr. Justice FRANKFURTER join in this opinion.

NOTE

In his biography of Chief Justice Stone, Harlan Fiske Stone: Pillar of the Law (1956), Professor Alpheus Thomas Mason relates at pp. 804–806 the disagreement between Stone and his law clerks over his stance in the *Girouard* case. Shortly after he announced his dissent, he was taken ill and died later that day (April 22, 1946).

CLEVELAND v. UNITED STATES

Supreme Court of the United States, 1946.
329 U.S. 14, 67 S.Ct. 13, 91 L.Ed. 12.

Certiorari to the United States Circuit Court of Appeals for the Tenth Circuit.

Mr. Justice DOUGLAS delivered the opinion of the Court.

Petitioners are members of a Mormon sect, known as Fundamentalists. They not only believe in polygamy; unlike other Mormons,[70]

---

[70]. The Church of Jesus Christ of Latter-Day Saints has forbidden plural marriages since 1890. See Toncray v. Budge, 14 Idaho 621, 654, 655, 95 P. 26.

Sec. 7 WEIGHT OF PRIOR INTERPRETATIONS 507

they practice it. Each of petitioners, except Stubbs, has, in addition to his lawful wife, one or more plural wives. Each transported at least one plural wife across state lines [71] either for the purpose of cohabiting with her, or for the purpose of aiding another member of the cult in such a project. They were convicted of violating the Mann Act, 36 Stat. 825, 18 U.S.C.A. § 398, on a trial to the court, a jury having been waived. D.C., 56 F.Supp. 890. The judgments of conviction were affirmed on appeal. 10 Cir., 146 F.2d 730. The cases are here on petitions for certiorari which we granted in view of the asserted conflict between the decision below and Mortensen v. United States, 322 U.S. 369, 64 S.Ct. 1037, 88 L.Ed. 1331.

The Act makes an offense the transportation in interstate commerce of "any woman or girl for the purpose of prostitution or debauchery, or for any other immoral purpose". The decision turns on the meaning of the latter phrase, "for any other immoral purpose".

United States v. Bitty, 208 U.S. 393, 28 S.Ct. 396, 52 L.Ed. 543, involved a prosecution under a federal statute making it a crime to import an alien woman "for the purpose of prostitution, or for any other immoral purpose." 34 Stat. 898, 899, § 3. The act was construed to cover a case where a man imported an alien woman so that she should live with him as his concubine. Two years later the Mann Act was passed. Because of the similarity of the language used in the two acts the Bitty case became a forceful precedent for the construction of the Mann Act. Thus one who transported a woman in interstate commerce so that she should become his mistress or concubine was held to have transported her for an "immoral purpose" within the meaning of the Mann Act. Caminetti v. United States, 242 U.S. 470, 37 S.Ct. 192, 61 L.Ed. 442, L.R.A.1917F, 502, Ann.Cas. 1917B, 1168.

It is argued that the Caminetti decision gave too wide a sweep to the Act; that the Act was designed to cover only the white slave business and related vices; that it was not designed to cover voluntary actions bereft of sex commercialism; and that in any event it should not be construed to embrace polygamy which is a form of marriage and, unlike prostitution or debauchery or the concubinage involved in the Caminetti case, has as its object parenthood and the creation and maintenance of family life. In support of that interpretation an exhaustive legislative history is submitted which, it is said, gives no indication that the Act was aimed at polygamous practices.

While Mortensen v. United States, supra, 322 U.S. at page 377, 64 S.Ct. at page 1041, 88 L.Ed. 1331, rightly indicated that the Act was aimed "primarily" at the use of interstate commerce for the conduct of the white slave business we find no indication that a profit

---

71. Petitioners' activities extended into Arizona, California, Colorado, Idaho, Utah and Wyoming.

motive is a *sine qua non* to its application. Prostitution, to be sure, normally suggests sexual relations for hire.[72] But debauchery has no such implied limitation. In common understanding the indulgence which that term suggests may be motivated solely by lust.[73] And so we start with words which by their natural import embrace more than commercialized sex. What follows is "any other immoral purpose". Under the *ejusdem generis* rule of construction the general words are confined to the class and may not be used to enlarge it. But we could not give the words a faithful interpretation if we confined them more narrowly than the class of which they are a part.

That was the view taken by the Court in the Bitty and Caminetti cases. We do not stop to re-examine the Caminetti case to determine whether the Act was properly applied to the facts there presented. But we adhere to its holding which has been in force for almost 30 years, that the Act, while primarily aimed at the use of interstate commerce for the purposes of commercialized sex, is not restricted to that end.

We conclude, moreover, that polygamous practices are not excluded from the Act. They have long been outlawed in our society. As stated in Reynolds v. United States, 98 U.S. 145, 164, 25 L.Ed. 244: "Polygamy has always been odious among the northern and western nations of Europe, and, until the establishment of the Mormon Church, was almost exclusively a feature of the life of Asiatic and of African people. At common law, the second marriage was always void (2 Kent, Com. 79), and from the earliest history of England polygamy has been treated as an offense against society."

As subsequently stated in Mormon Church v. United States, 136 U.S. 1, 49, 10 S.Ct 792, 805, 34 L.Ed. 481, "The organization of a community for the spread and practice of polygamy is, in a measure, a return to barbarism. It is contrary to the spirit of Christianity and of the civilization which Christianity has produced in the western world." And see Davis v. Beason, 133 U.S. 333, 10 S.Ct. 299, 33 L.Ed. 637. Polygamy is a practice with far more pervasive influences in society than the casual, isolated transgressions involved in the Caminetti case. The establishment or maintenance of polygamous households is a notorious example of promiscuity. The permanent advertisement of their existence is an example of the sharp repercussions which they have in the community. We could conclude that Congress excluded these practices from the Act only if it were clear that the Act is confined to commercialized sexual vice. Since we cannot say it is, we see no way by which the present transgressions can

---

72. "Of women: The offering of the body to indiscriminate lewdness for hire (esp. as a practice or institution); whoredom, harlotry." 8 Oxford English Dictionary 1497.

73. "Vicious indulgence in sensual pleasures." 3 Oxford English Dictionary, 79; "Excessive indulgence in sensual pleasures of any kind; gluttony; intemperance; sexual immorality; unlawful indulgence of lust." 3 Century Dict.Rev.Ed. 1477.

be excluded. These polygamous practices have long been branded as immoral in the law. Though they have different ramifications, they are in the same genus as the other immoral practices covered by the Act.

The fact that the regulation of marriage is a state matter does not, of course, make the Mann Act an unconstitutional interference by Congress with the police powers of the States. The power of Congress over the instrumentalities of interstate commerce is plenary; it may be used to defeat what are deemed to be immoral practices; and the fact that the means used may have "the quality of police regulations" is not consequential. Hoke v. United States, 227 U.S. 308, 323, 33 S.Ct. 281, 284, 57 L.Ed. 523, 43 L.R.A.,N.S., 906, Ann.Cas.1913E, 905; see Athanasaw v. United States, 227 U.S. 326, 33 S.Ct. 285, 57 L.Ed. 528, Ann.Cas.1913E, 911; Wilson v. United States, 232 U.S. 563, 34 S.Ct. 347, 58 L.Ed. 728.

Petitioners' second line of defense is that the requisite purpose was lacking. It is said that those petitioners who already had plural wives did not transport them in interstate commerce for an immoral purpose. The test laid down in the Mortensen case was whether the transportation was in fact "the use of interstate commerce as a calculated means for effectuating sexual immorality." 322 U.S. page 375, 64 S.Ct. page 1041, 88 L.Ed. 1331. There was evidence that this group of petitioners in order to cohabit with their plural wives found it necessary or convenient to transport them in interstate commerce and that the unlawful purpose was the dominant motive. In one case the woman was transported for the purpose of entering into a plural marriage. After a night with this petitioner she refused to continue the plural marriage relationship. But guilt under the Mann Act turns on the purpose which motivates the transportation, not on its accomplishment. Wilson v. United States, supra, 232 U.S. at pages 570, 571, 34 S.Ct. 349, 350, 58 L.Ed. 728.

It is also urged that the requisite criminal intent was lacking since petitioners were motivated by a religious belief. That defense claims too much. If upheld, it would place beyond the law any act done under claim of religious sanction. But it has long been held that the fact that polygamy is supported by a religious creed affords no defense in a prosecution for bigamy. Reynolds v. United States, supra. Whether an act is immoral within the meaning of the statute is not to be determined by the accused's concepts of morality. Congress has provided the standard. The offense is complete if the accused intended to perform, and did in fact perform, the act which the statute condemns, viz., the transportation of a woman for the purpose of making her his plural wife or cohabiting with her as such.

We have considered the remaining objections raised and find them without merit.

Affirmed.

Mr. Justice BLACK and Mr. Justice JACKSON think that the cases should be reversed. They are of opinion that affirmance requires extension of the rule announced in the Caminetti case and that the correctness of that rule is so dubious that it should at least be restricted to its particular facts.

Mr. Justice RUTLEDGE, concurring.

I concur in the result. Differences have been urged in petitioners' behalf between these cases and Caminetti v. United States, 242 U.S. 470, 37 S.Ct. 192, 61 L.Ed. 442, L.R.A.1917F, 502, Ann.Cas. 1917B, 1168. Notwithstanding them, in my opinion it would be impossible rationally to reverse the convictions, at the same time adhering to Caminetti and later decisions perpetuating its ruling.

It is also suggested, though not strongly urged, that Caminetti was wrongly decided and should be overruled. Much may be said for this view. In my opinion that case and subsequent ones following it extended the Mann Act's coverage beyond the congressional intent and purpose, as the dissenting opinion of Mr. Justice McKenna convincingly demonstrated. 242 U.S. at page 496, 37 S.Ct. at page 198. Moreover as I also think, this legislation and the problems presented by the cases arising under it are of such a character as does not allow this Court properly to shift to Congress the responsibility for perpetuating the Court's error.

Notwithstanding recent tendency, the idea cannot always be accepted that Congress, by remaining silent and taking no affirmative action in repudiation, gives approval to judicial misconstruction of its enactments. See Girouard v. United States, 328 U.S. 61, 66 S.Ct. 826. It is perhaps too late now to deny that, legislatively speaking as in ordinary life, silence in some instances may give consent.[74] But it would be going even farther beyond reason and common experience to maintain, as there are signs we may be by way of doing, that in legislation any more than in other affairs silence or nonaction always is acquiescence equivalent to action.

There are vast differences between legislating by doing nothing and legislating by positive enactment, both in the processes by which the will of Congress is derived and stated[75] and in the clarity and certainty of the expression of its will. And there are many reasons, other than to indicate approval of what the courts have done, why Con-

---

74. As an original matter, in view of the specific and constitutional procedures required for the enactment of legislation, it would seem hardly justifiable to treat as having legislative effect any action or nonaction not taken in accordance with the prescribed procedures.

75. Legislative intent derived from nonaction or "silence" lacks all the supporting evidences of legislation enacted pursuant to prescribed procedures, including reduction of bills to writing, committee reports, debates, and reduction to final written form, as well as voting records and executive approval. Necessarily also the intent must be derived by a form of negative inference, a process lending itself to much guesswork.

gress may fail to take affirmative action to repudiate their misconstruction of its duly adopted laws. Among them may be the sheer pressure of other and more important business. See Moore v. Cleveland R. Co., 6 Cir., 108 F.2d 656, 660. At times political considerations may work to forbid taking corrective action. And in such cases, as well as others, there may be a strong and proper tendency to trust to the courts to correct their own errors, see Girouard v. United States, supra, 328 U.S. 69, 66 S.Ct. at page 830, as they ought to do when experience has confirmed or demonstrated the errors' existence.

The danger of imputing to Congress, as a result of its failure to take positive or affirmative action through normal legislative processes, ideas entertained by the Court concerning Congress' will, is illustrated most dramatically perhaps by the vacillating and contradictory courses pursued in the long line of decisions imputing to "the silence of Congress" varied effects in commerce clause cases. That danger may be and often is equally present in others. More often than not the only safe assumption to make from Congress' inaction is simply that Congress does not intend to act at all. Cf. United States v. American Trucking Ass'ns, 310 U.S. 534, 550, 60 S.Ct. 1059, 1067, 84 L.Ed. 1345. At best the contrary view can be only an inference, altogether lacking in the normal evidences of legislative intent and often subject to varying views of that intent. In short, although recognizing that by silence Congress at times may be taken to acquiesce and thus approve, we should be very sure that, under all the circumstances of a given situation, it has done so before we so rule and thus at once relieve ourselves from and shift to it the burden of correcting what we have done wrongly. The matter is particular, not general, notwithstanding earlier exceptional treatment and more recent tendency. Just as dubious legislative history is at times much overridden, so also is silence or inaction often mistaken for legislation.

I doubt very much that the silence of Congress in respect to these cases, notwithstanding their multiplication and the length of time during which the silence has endured, can be taken to be the equivalent of bills approving them introduced in both houses, referred to and considered by committees, discussed in debates, enacted by majorities in both places, and approved by the executive. I doubt, in other words, that, in view of all the relevant circumstances including the unanticipated consequences of the legislation, such majorities could have been mustered in approval of the Caminetti decision at any time since it was rendered. Nor is the contrary conclusion demonstrated by Congress' refusal to take corrective action.[76]

---

76. Since the Caminetti decision two bills have been introduced to limit the effect of that case. S. 2438, 73d Cong., 2d Sess.; S. 101, 75th Cong., 1st Sess. Neither was reported out of committee. In such circumstances the failure of Congress to amend the Act raises no presumption as to its intent. Order of Railway Conductors of America v. Swan, 7 Cir., 152 F.2d 325, 329.

The Caminetti case, however, has not been overruled and has the force of law until a majority of this Court may concur in the view that this should be done and take action to that effect. This not having been done, I acquiesce in the Court's decision.

Mr. Justice MURPHY, dissenting.

Today another unfortunate chapter is added to the troubled history of the White Slave Traffic Act. It is a chapter written in terms that misapply the statutory language and that disregard the intention of the legislative framers. It results in the imprisonment of individuals whose actions have none of the earmarks of white slavery, whatever else may be said of their conduct. I am accordingly forced to dissent.

* * *

The result here reached is but another consequence of this Court's long-continued failure to recognize that the White Slave Traffic Act, as its title indicates, is aimed solely at the diabolical interstate and international trade in white slaves, "the business of securing white women and girls and of selling them outright, or of exploiting them for immoral purposes." H.Rep.No.47, 61st Cong., 2d Sess., p. 11; S.Rep.No.886, 61st Cong., 2d Sess., p. 11. The Act was suggested and proposed to meet conditions which had arisen in the years preceding 1910 and which had revealed themselves in their ugly details through extensive investigations. The framers of the Act specifically stated that it is not directed at immorality in general; it does not even attempt to regulate the practice of voluntary prostitution, leaving that problem to the various states. Its exclusive concern is with those girls and women who are "unwillingly forced to practice prostitution" and to engage in other similar immoralities and "whose lives are lives of involuntary servitude." Ibid. A reading of the legislative reports and debates makes this narrow purpose so clear as to remove all doubts on the matter. And it is a purpose that has absolutely no relation to the practice of polygamy, however much that practice may have been considered immoral in 1910.

Yet this Court in Caminetti v. United States, 242 U.S. 470, 37 S.Ct. 192, 61 L.Ed. 442, L.R.A.1917F, 502, Ann.Cas.1917B, 1168, over the vigorous dissent of Justice McKenna in which Chief Justice White and Justice Clarke joined, closed its eyes to the obvious and interpreted the broad words of the statute without regard to the express wishes of Congress. I think the Caminetti case can be factually distinguished from the situation at hand since it did not deal with polygamy. But the principle of the Caminetti case is still with us today, the principle of interpreting and applying the White Slave Traffic Act in disregard of the specific problem with which Congress was concerned. I believe the issue should be met squarely and the Caminetti case overruled. It has been on the books for nearly 30 years and its age does not justify its continued existence. Stare decisis certainly does not require a court to perpetuate a wrong for which it was responsible, especially when no rights have accrued in reliance on the error. Cf. Helvering v. Hallock, 309 U.S. 106, 121, 122, 60 S.Ct. 444, 452, 453, 84 L.Ed. 604, 125 A.L.R. 1368. Otherwise the error is accentuated; and individuals, whatever may be said of their morality, are fined and imprisoned contrary to the wishes of Congress. I shall not be a party to that process.

The consequence of prolonging the Caminetti principle is to make the federal courts the arbiters of the morality of those who cross state lines in the company of women and girls. They must decide what is meant by [242 U.S. 470, 37 S.Ct. 195] "any other immoral purpose" without regard to the standards plainly set forth by Congress. I do not believe that this falls within the legitimate scope of the judicial function. Nor does it accord the respect to which Congressional pronouncements are entitled.

Hence I would reverse the judgments of conviction in these cases.

NOTE

The *Cleveland* case, the *Mortensen* case, and other Supreme Court decisions concerning the scope of application of the Mann Act are discussed at length in Levi, An Introduction to Legal Reasoning 13–40 (1949).

WINDUST v. DEPARTMENT OF LABOR AND INDUSTRIES

Supreme Court of Washington, 1958.
52 Wash.2d 33, 323 P.2d 241.

MALLERY, Justice.

Aubra H. Windust died on March 29, 1954, at the age of sixty-one years, while working for the Glacier Sand and Gravel Company as an operator of a ready-mix concrete truck.

On April 28, 1954, his widow filed a claim for a pension with the department of labor and industries, which the supervisor rejected upon the ground that there was no injury within the contemplation of the worken's compensation act. The board of industrial insurance appeals sustained the supervisor's order, and claimant appealed to the superior court. From its judgment of dismissal, she appeals to this court.

As a driver of the ready-mix concrete truck, one of the workman's customary duties was to walk out on the catwalk on the side of the truck, step up about two feet and look into the drum to see how much concrete was in it. He fell dead, on the day in question, just as he was stepping up to look into the drum. Appellant contends this act incident to his employment constituted an *injury* under the workmen's compensation act. It is not denied that the workman had been looking into the drum to ascertain the amount of remaining concrete, whenever his duties required it, for approximately ten years.

The workman's death was due to a myocardial infarction involving the interventricular septum caused by fatty deposits on the inside of the heart arteries, known as arteriosclerosis, which so narrowed them that not enough blood could pass through to supply the heart muscle. Dr. Sloan's testimony followed the customary pattern that, if the workman had not engaged in his work but had been receiving proper medical treatment at the time he looked into the drum, he would not have died.

This satisfied the rule of McCormick Lumber Co. v. Department of Labor and Industries, 7 Wash.2d 40, 108 P.2d 807, 815, which is:

> " * * * An accident arises out of the employment when the required exertion producing the accident is too great for the man undertaking the work, *whatever the degree of exertion or the condition of the workman's health.*"

This formula justifies holding that the recurring duties of a job and acts incident thereto constitute *injuries*, whenever a workman's heart ailment has progressed to the point where a restriction of activities is essential to his survival.

The rule of the McCormick case has represented for many years the decisional weight of authority in this state. If the doctrine of *stare decisis* is applicable to cases which interpret a statute, we are not now free to depart from that rule, notwithstanding its obvious conflict with the statute.

The statute in question is RCW 51.08.100 [cf. Rem.Rev.Stat. (Sup.), § 7675; Rem.Supp.1941, § 7679–1]. It provides:

> "'Injury' means a sudden and tangible happening, of a traumatic nature, producing an immediate or prompt result, and occurring from without; an occupational disease; and such physical condition as results from either."

This situation, in which the statute is amended or repealed by a court-made rule, warrants an examination of the doctrine of *stare decisis* and the proper occasion for its application. This is its definition in Webster's New International Dictionary (2d Ed.):

> "Literally, to stand by decided matters; * * * as implying the doctrine or policy of following rules or principles laid down in previous judicial decisions unless they contravene the ordinary principles of justice. This principle had an important part in the development of the English common law."

Indeed, the common law is comprised of that body of court decisions in the nonstatutory field to which the doctrine of *stare decisis* applies. The rule of law of those cases was promulgated by the courts for the inescapable reason that pending litigation had to be disposed of, even though there was no legislative enactment that governed the issue therein. Uniform and equal justice naturally required subsequent adherence to such decisions in the absence of pertinent legislation. In the sense that the promulgation of a rule of law is legislation, the courts can and do properly legislate in nonstatutory fields. Every case governed by *stare decisis,* rather than statute law, is a proper occasion for judicial legislation. However, the courts may only so legislate in fields left vacant by the legislature. A legislative enactment, intended to be comprehensive upon a subject, preempts that field, with the result that the court's constitutional function with regard to it is thereafter limited to an interpretation of what the legislature meant by the language used in the statute.

The application of the doctrine of *stare decisis* is, of course, not the same thing as the interpretation of a statute. The distinction was made clear in Petersen v. Department of Labor and Industries, 40 Wash.2d 635, 245 P.2d 1161, 1162, wherein we said:

> "Cases involving statutory interpretation require that we restrict ourselves to a determination of the meaning of the statutory language in question. In this they differ from cases concerned with rules of the common law wherein wisdom and practicality, in the light of human experience, inhere in the judicial process.
>
> "Statutory cases have a fixed base from which we always start. Thus, they are unlike common-law cases wherein the later cases supersede the earlier ones to the extent of any differences between them."

The cumulative effect of many slight deviations is demonstrated by the rule of Ashford v. Reese, 132 Wash. 649, 233 P. 29, which, in 1925, held that a vendee under an executory contract to purchase real property, acquired no title or interest, legal or equitable, in it. It has never been overruled, yet, in a series of subsequent cases, it has been whittled away until nothing remains. 32 Wash.L.Rev. 130. Each case revamped the law a little in order to do justice on its particular facts. It is the cumulative effect of these little deviations that produced the final result.

The application of the doctrine of *stare decisis* to the interpretation of a statute will, more often than not, lead to the eventual repeal or amendment of the statute, just as it has in the instant case.

When Chief Justice Hughes said the law is what the supreme court says it is, he meant, with regard to statute law, that the function of *interpreting* a statute belongs to the supreme court. Interpretation of the meaning of a statute ends where the amendment or repeal of it begins.

The court repeal of a statute by the application of the doctrine of *stare decisis*, makes it pertinent to look at the *function* of the court. Under our constitution there is a limit to the application of the doctrine of *stare decisis*. That limitation inheres in our checks and balance form of constitutional democracy, which vests the legislative power in the legislature and the people, subject only to certain constitutional prohibitions and limitations.

Of course, it is the duty of the court to invalidate a statute if it contravenes the constitution. Such a holding has as its purpose the implementation of the supremacy of the constitution. For the court to repeal a statute for no other reason than that it conflicts with the doctrine of *stare decisis*, is an obvious encroachment upon the legislative branch of the government. Unfortunately, the checks and balance system of our constitution is implemented, as to the manner in which the courts shall function, only by our discriminative self-restraint. Its exercise alone will avoid arbitrary judicial invasion of the other departments of government.

The gravity of substantial judicial encroachment upon the legislature, under the guise of following the doctrine of *stare decisis*, warrants a reference to the admonition in Petersen v. Department of Labor and Industries, supra, that "Statutory cases have a fixed base from which we always start." It may be added that only the *statute* contains the authoritative language in which the law is couched. A constant paraphrasing of the statutes by the court, such as is done in the McCormick case, initiates the process exemplified in Ashford v. Reese, supra, by which an accumulation of small changes overrules the law. By that process, more and more weight is inevitably given to opinions and less and less to the statute until, as in the McCormick case, the law is all opinion and no statute.

Since the doctrine of *stare decisis* is not applicable to a case of statutory interpretation, we advert directly to the language of the statute to ascertain if there has been an *injury* in the instant case.

> " 'Injury' means a *sudden and tangible happening,* of a traumatic nature, producing an immediate or prompt result, and occurring from without; * * *" (Italics ours.) RCW 51.08.100, supra.

We are constrained to hold that the routine act of ten years' standing is not an injury as a matter of law. Interpreting this particular and exact language of the statute in Mork v. Department of Labor and Industries, 48 Wash.2d 74, 291 P.2d 650, 652, we said:

> "The act of the deceased in returning to his station is not an industrial accident. As we said in Higgins v. Department of Labor and Industries, 27 Wash.2d 816, 180 P.2d 559, 564:
>
> > " 'There is no sudden and tangible happening in the present case, no matter of notoriety, nor an event which can

be fixed in time, but rather an incapacity due to the relatively slow and insidious inroads of a progressive and apparently incurable disease.'"

In Haerling v. Department of Labor and Industries, 49 Wash.2d 403, 301 P.2d 1078, 1080, we also interpreted a "sudden and tangible happening," as used in the statutory definition of an injury. In that case, the workman was a deputy sheriff who died of a coronary occlusion while at home in bed. His claim was predicated upon the fact that "From May 4, 1953, until early June, 1953, he was doing the work of three men, and working thirteen to eighteen hours a day." He was denied recovery on the ground that

"* * * there is no sudden and tangible happening of a traumatic nature, upon which the workman relies as the cause of his *injury*. * * *

"The cumulative effect of long continued routine and customary duties upon a workman, regardless of the hours devoted thereto, is not a sudden and tangible happening. The statute contemplates a *happening*, of a traumatic nature, producing an immediate and prompt result in order for the *injury* resulting therefrom to be compensable under the act. A cumulative effect, however injurious, is noncompensable unless it constitutes an industrial disease, not here in issue."

These interpretations of *injury* accord well with the statute, and, indeed, no other interpretation is possible, without doing violence to the English language.

Let it be understood that we now follow the language of the statute, which is the only authoritative statement of the law, and we do not reach the instant result by following the Mork and Haerling cases as *stare decisis*. They are consulted only because of the proper judicial objective in maintaining the symmetry of the law. The furtherance of this objective, and the recurring citation of the McCormick case in the briefs of claimant appellants generally, convince us of the need to overrule it, which we specifically do.

All of the heart cases which follow the McCormick rule are hereby overruled. [Citations omitted.]

The judgment is affirmed.

HILL, C. J., and DONWORTH, WEAVER and OTT, JJ., concur.

DONWORTH, Justice (concurring).

I concur in the majority opinion but wish to state my views on *stare decisis* in addition to what is said on the subject therein.

The original workmen's compensation act, adopted in 1911, defined "injury" as follows:

> "The words injury or injured, as used in this act, refer only to an injury resulting from some fortuitous event as distinguished from the contraction of disease." Laws of 1911, chapter 74, § 3, p. 349.

In Frandila v. Department of Labor and Industries, 1926, 137 Wash. 530, 243 P. 5, this court had occasion to construe the above quoted statute. There the workman, while engaged in digging a ditch and chopping a root at the bottom of the ditch, suddenly collapsed and died. The testimony established that the workman was suffering from hardening of the arteries and that he died from either a rupture of a blood vessel or from embolism. This court, in allowing recovery to the widow, * * * said:

> " * * * an accident exists when a man undertaking work is unable to withstand the exertion required to do it, whatever may be the degree of exertion used or the condition of the workman's health."

In the next session of the legislature, in 1927, the definition of the word "injury" (which definition still exists at the present time) was materially changed * * *. [See text p. 514, supra.]

In Metcalf v. Department of Labor and Industries, 1932, 168 Wash. 305, 11 P.2d 821, the workman was working rapidly sawing a tree that had fallen across the road in order to get the road reopened for travel with the least possible delay. The task required more than ordinary exertion. When the log was almost sawed through, the workman fell over and died of a cerebral hemorrhage.

The appellant (department of labor and industries) strenuously contended that such a strain was not an injury under the 1927 definition of injury quoted above.

* * *

In upholding the claim for compensation, the court * * * said:

> "The fact that his arteries had so hardened that death was likely to result 'from a sudden and tangible happening of a traumatic nature' does not deprive Mr. Metcalf's widow and minor child of their right to statutory benefits. It was not the Legislature's purpose to limit the provisions of the Workmen's Compensation Act to only such persons as approximate physical perfection."

The cases interpreting the 1927 definition of the injury are extensively reviewed in McCormick Lumber Co. v. Department of Labor and Industries, 1941, 7 Wash.2d 40, 108 P.2d 807, 815, which was heard *en banc*, two judges dissenting. In that case, the workman (a logger) collapsed and died while sawing a tree. A post-mortem examination of the body revealed that the deceased had been suffering from chronic conditions of endocarditis, myocarditis, and gastritis. There was expert testimony that the exertion required in sawing the tree was a contributing factor in his death. This court held that the death was the result of an injury, stating that:

> "* * * An accident arises out of the employment when the required exertion producing the accident is too great for the man undertaking the work, *whatever the degree of exertion or the condition of the workman's health.*"

However, Judge Simpson, in his dissenting opinion (in which Judge Robinson concurred), pointed out that the judicial interpretation of the 1927 definition of injury went far beyond the ordinary meaning of the words used by the legislature, saying:

> "The mere fact that the man happened to be engaged in performing the functions of his employment at the moment his progressive disease reached its climax, at which point any exertion, any movement, any effort would cause the diseased heart to cease its function, should not be considered as creating a situation in which compensation becomes proper. In such a case industry is not the *cause* of the injury, but simply provides the setting for it. To impose upon industry the risk created by progressive diseases, such as heart trouble, apoplexy, embolism, and the like, reaching their climaxes at a time while the workmen are *engaged in performing their everyday functions* is to greatly outdistance the legislature's intention, and throws a far greater burden on industry than the act itself was intended to impose, *if its language is to be regarded as expressive of its intent.* In effect * * * the interpretation of the majority serves to make of our act an insurance system, rather than a compensation system, and to do so certainly violates the purpose of those who passed the act.

> "It may be that every workman injured or suffering in any manner while he is working should receive compensation or insurance therefor. However, such matters are within the province of the legislative body. * * *"

(Italics ours.)

[Citations to nine cases said to follow the rule of the *McCormick* case are omitted.]

In some of our later cases, which are best exemplified by Mork v. Department of Labor and Industries, 1955, 48 Wash.2d 74, 291 P.2d 650, 652, we have refused to follow the McCormick rule.

[Discussion of the *Mork*, *Higgins*, *Petersen*, and *Haerling* cases, which disregarded the *McCormick* rule, is omitted.]

Thus we have two irreconcilable lines of decisions of this court in which we have reached inconsistent conclusions as to the application of RCW 51.08.100 (enacted in 1927 and re-enacted in 1939) to persons suffering heart attacks while in the performance of extrahazardous work.

I am of the opinion that the decision of Department One in Metcalf v. Department of Labor and Industries, supra (the first such case arising under the workmen's compensation act to reach this court after the legislature changed the definition of the word "injury" in 1927), was wrong in failing to give effect to the fundamental change in the statute.

* * *

In my opinion, the doctrine of *stare decisi*s does not require us to perpetuate the error of the Metcalf and McCormick cases. As we said in In re Yand's Estate, 23 Wash.2d 831, 162 P.2d 434, 437, quoting, with approval, from a decision of the New York court of appeals:

> " 'But the doctrine of *stare decisis*, like almost every other legal rule, is not without its exceptions. It does not apply to a case where it can be shown that the law has been misunderstood or misapplied, or where the former determination is evidently contrary to reason. The authorities are abundant to show that in such cases it is the duty of courts to re-examine the question. Chancellor Kent, commenting upon the rule of *stare decisis*, said that more than a thousand cases could then be pointed out, in the English and American reports, which had been overruled, doubted or limited in their application. He added that "it is probable that the records of many of the courts of this country are replete with hasty and crude decisions; and in such cases ought to be examined without fear, and revised without reluctance, rather than to have the character of our law impaired, and the beauty and harmony of the system destroyed, by the perpetuity of error." ' Rumsey v. New York & N. E. R. Co., 133 N.Y. 79, 30 N.E. 654, 655, 15 L.R.A. 618, 28 Am.St.Rep. 600."

See, also, Hutton v. Martin, 41 Wash.2d 780, 252 P.2d 581.

It is argued that the legislature, in re-enacting portions of the industrial insurance act in 1939, including the definition of injury originally enacted in 1927, must be deemed to have thereby adopted this court's interpretation of that definition, as stated in Metcalf v. Department of Labor and Industries, supra, and subsequent cases. The answer to this contention is that, if the legislature desired to change the basic plan from a workmen's compensation act to a health and accident plan effective during working hours, it should not do so obliquely or indirectly, but should be required to *expressly* declare its intention to do so.

Such a change in policy is too catastrophic to be inferred from the legislature's failure to correct the effect of our erroneous decision in the Metcalf case, which should be expressly overruled.

I think that, in determining whether or not there has been an injury compensable under the workmen's compensation act, we are limited by the statutory definition of the word injury. In my opinion, the legislature, in enacting the 1927 amendment, only intended to provide compensation for accidental injuries occurring in extrahazardous employment, and not to compensate workmen or their families for every heart attack which might come on during working hours.

* * *

OTT, J., concurs.

FOSTER, Justice (dissenting).

The court's decision announced today should have been made twenty-five years ago when Metcalf v. Department of Labor and Industries, 168 Wash. 305, 11 P.2d 821, was filed. It would have been as right then as it is wrong now. The ancient aphorism, "Better late than never," is not always true and if there be justification for the comment by the cynical wag that "Consistency is the hobgoblin of little minds," certainly this court is not so contaminated.

[Justice Foster's review, at this point, of the development of the Washington statute and cases is omitted in view of the discussion thereof in the preceding opinions.]

The writer of this dissent was assistant attorney general and counsel for the appellant department of labor and industries in the Metcalf case, which was appealed upon the single proposition that the 1927 amended definition of "injury" changed the law and abrogated the rule announced in Frandila v. Department of Labor and Industries, supra. * * *

* * *

* * * The conclusion was that * * * [Metcalf's] death was the result of * * * injury within the statutory definition * * *.

The Metcalf case was followed almost immediately by McArthur v. Department of Labor and Industries, 168 Wash. 405, 12 P.2d 418, which allowed compensation for the rupture of a duodenal ulcer by overexertion.

In McCormick Lumber Co. v. Department of Labor and Industries, 1941, 7 Wash.2d 40, 108 P.2d 807, for the first time the attorney general took the position that the 1927 amendment of the definition of the word "injury" did not change the rule announced in the earlier cases and that the question was no longer open because of the intervening decisions.

The case was heard *en banc*, and again the court reviewed the entire judicial history of the problem but refused to recede from the position announced in the prior cases. Any vestige of doubt should have been removed by Merritt v. Department of Labor and Industries, 41 Wash.2d 633, 251 P.2d 158, in which the court again reviewed all of the cases and declared the rule had been uniformly followed, and again declined to recede.

By repeated decisions covering a period of more than forty years, the decisional law of the state is that "An accident arises out of the employment when the required exertion producing the accident is too great for the man undertaking the work, *whatever the degree of exertion or the condition of the workman's health.*" [77]

We are told that *stare decisis* does not apply to statutory construction, and it is said that Petersen v. Department of Labor and Industries, 40 Wash.2d 635, 245 P.2d 1161, sustains this view. The court was not there concerned with *stare decisis* nor its application in the field of statutory construction, and indeed, no decision was made upon that point nor could have been.

On the contrary, *stare decisis* applies most vigorously in the field of statutory construction. The summary of 21 C.J.S. Courts, § 214, P. 388, is as follows:

> "The doctrine of stare decisis applies with full force to decisions construing statutes or ordinances, especially where the construction has been long acquiesced in, and decisions construing other statutes are authoritative if such statutes are nearly identical with the one under review."

and it is said in 14 Am.Jur. 287, § 66:

> " * * * It has been said that the court of last resort of a state will not overrule one of its prior decisions construing a statute where the legislature has held several sessions since such decision without modifying or amending the statute, because it may be claimed justly that the legislature has acquiesced in the decision, and therefore a fair case is presented for the application of the doctrine of stare decisis. * * *"

I am very greatly indebted to Mr. Fred W. Catlett for his painstaking study [78] in which he points out that stability in the law is its most desirable attribute, and, if this were not so, we should have a government of men and not of law.[79] Legal scholars agree with the

---

77. McCormick Lumber Co. v. Department of Labor and Industries, supra [7 Wash.2d 40, 108 P.2d 815].

78. "The Development of the Doctrine of Stare Decisis and the Extent to Which it Should be Applied" 21 Wash.L.Rev. 158.

79. "The majority of this court changes on the average once every nine years, without counting the changes of death and resignation. If each new set of judges shall consider themselves at liberty to overthrow the doctrine of their predecessors, our system of jurisprudence (if sys-

Sec. 7   *WEIGHT OF PRIOR INTERPRETATIONS*   523

statement of Mr. Justice Brandeis: "It is more important that the applicable rule of law be settled than that it be settled right." [80] Stability in the decisional law construing statutes is as important as stability in decisions affecting real property, for the meaning of the statutes should not change with the personnel of the court.

Harmonizing with the prevailing current of judicial opinions in the United States, the decisional law of this state is that the construction placed upon a statute by this court becomes a part of the statute itself. Indeed, this court said so in Yakima Valley Bank & Trust Co. v. Yakima County, 149 Wash. 552, 271 P. 820, 821:

> "It is a familiar rule of statutory construction that when a statute has once been construed by the highest court of the state that construction is as much a part of the statute as if it were originally written into it. * * *"

[References to other Washington cases on the same point are omitted.]

Moreover, we have here the re-enactment in 1939 *in haec verba* of the 1927 definition of the word "injury," during which interval there were ten more uniform decisions by this court. Under such circumstances, the legislature is conclusively presumed to be familiar with the decisions construing the statute and to have adopted the statute as so construed. This court said as much in In re Lindholm's Estate, 6 Wash.2d 366, 107 P.2d 562, 564:

> "* * * It may therefore be assumed that, by reenacting the proviso, the legislature adopted the construction placed thereon by this court in the Sherwood case [In re Sherwood's Estate, 122 Wash. 648, 211 P. 734]."

Such is the plain statement in 2 Lewis' Sutherland Statutory Construction (2d Ed.) 929, 930, § 499 (333).[81]

Specifically, this court recently held itself bound by the prior construction of the word "employer" in the industrial insurance act, because the legislature had not changed the definition in the intervening nine years. Such was the decision in Nyland v. Department of Labor and Industries, 41 Wash.2d 511, 513, 250 P.2d 551. Here, however, the body of decisional law construing the statute is not only extensive, but the interval of time is three times as great.

---

tem it can be called) would be the most fickle, uncertain and vicious that the civilized world ever saw. * * *" Hole v. Rittenhouse, 25 Pa. 491, 2 Phila. 411, 417–418.

80. Burnet v. Coronado Oil & Gas Co., 285 U.S. 393, 406, 52 S.Ct. 443, 447, 76 L.Ed. 815.

81. "* * * The re-enactment of a statute after a judicial construction of its meaning is to be regarded as a legislative adoption of the statute as thus construed. * * *" 2 Lewis' Sutherland Statutory Construction (2d Ed.) 929, 930, § 499 (333).

See, also, 82 C.J.S. Statutes § 370 b, p. 848; 50 Am.Jur. 461, § 442, note 18.

A change in the statute as interpreted by this court over a quarter of a century, may not be made by a change in judicial interpretation without encroaching on the function of the legislature. It is now beyond the sphere of judicial action and exclusively within the domain of the legislative branch of the government. Such was the rule announced by the supreme court of Kansas in the following six unequivocal sentences:

"* * * Courts do not write legislation. That is the function of the legislature. Our duty is to declare and apply legislative acts and to construe statutes and constitutions in accordance with the will of the lawmaking power where its construction becomes necessary. When such construction has been given to a law and finally established as a part thereof, it is as much a part of it as if embodied therein in plain and unmistakable language. When that situation exists, it is the province of the legislature alone to change the law if it deems advisable. The courts should not attempt it. * * *" State v. One Bally Coney Island No. 21011 Gaming Table, 174 Kan. 757, 258 P.2d 225, 228.

The question has arisen in at least ten other states and in each instance similar conclusions were reached. * * *

* * *

The powerful argument of Chief Justice Harlan Fiske Stone in his dissent in Girouard v. United States, 328 U.S. 61, 76, 66 S.Ct. 826, 833, 90 L.Ed. 1084, is most apropos:

"It is the responsibility of Congress, in reenacting a statute, to make known its purpose in a controversial matter of interpretation of its former language, at least when the matter has, for over a decade, been persistently brought to its attention. In the light of this legislative history, it is abundantly clear that Congress has performed that duty. In any case it is not lightly to be implied that Congress has failed to perform it and has delegated to this Court the responsibility of giving new content to language deliberately readopted after this Court has construed it. For us to make such an assumption is to discourage, if not to deny, legislative responsibility. By thus adopting and confirming this Court's construction of what Congress had enacted in the Naturalization Act of 1906 Congress gave that construction the same legal significance as though it had written the very words into the Act of 1940."

But we are told that the legislature adopted the construction of the statute in the Mork case (Mork v. Department of Labor and Industries, 48 Wash.2d 74, 291 P.2d 650) by the re-enactment of the definition of "injury" in Laws of 1957, chapter 70, § 11, after the decision in the Mork case.

The answer to this is twofold: (1) The court in the Mork opinion, which was a departmental one, did not undertake to overrule the earlier cases on the subject, many of which were *en banc* decisions; and (2) by a line of cases recently reaffirmed, the law in force at the time of the injury controls throughout the life of the claim. [Citations omitted.]

The one hope of salvation and stability from this judicial morass is that the legislative branch of the government will come to the rescue.

Such are the reasons for my dissent.

ROSELLINI, J., concurs.

FINLEY, Justice (dissenting).

I agree substantially with the well documented dissent of FOSTER, J., but wish to express my views on this matter, separately.

The majority change the public policy of this state regarding the so-called heart cases arising under the workmen's compensation act. The change is an abrupt one. It is a reversal of a public policy which has stood for approximately twenty-five years (since the Metcalf case, 1932, 168 Wash. 305, 11 P.2d 821) without revision by the legislative branch of state government. The change is accomplished by judicial action in a field which, I think, is primarily the concern of the legislature. Furthermore, I believe that the legislature, through interim committee studies, public hearings, and otherwise, is much better equipped than the court to gather facts and statistics relative to the problem involved. It follows that the legislature should be in a better position to make a more scientific, or at least a more knowledgeable, decision or disposition of this problem of state public policy.

By way of justification of the end result reached, the majority opinion suggests (a) that the court erred approximately twenty-five years ago in the Metcalf case, supra, and improperly indulged in judicial legislation, substituting its judgment for that of the legislature; (b) that the court today perceives the true legislative purpose of the statute as enacted by the legislative branch more than twenty-five years ago; (c) that the doctrine of *stare decisis* is inapplicable as to judicial decisions involving interpretation of statutes, and that the doctrine is in no way a restriction upon the majority in effecting a reversal of public policy in the instant case; (d) that it is the responsibility of the court, although somewhat belatedly, to effect the indicated change in public policy as to the heart cases.

If it can be said that the court in the Metcalf case indulged in *judicial legislation*, the action of the majority *under the circumstances in the instant case* clearly falls in the same category.

Employers and workmen under the act are the two groups directly concerned as to the public policy question involved. Each group has been effectively and intelligently represented in every session of the legislature for the last twenty-five years. Thus, the problem involved is not one that might go for many years without any attention from the legislature for lack of interest, activity, or legislative representation on the part of persons most concerned. For the above reason alone, it seems to me that the court should do nothing to change the existing state policy in the heart cases, and that, under the circumstances, any change should be left most appropriately to the legislature.

As is well known, the doctrine of *stare decisis* is not an absolute bar to judicial reconsideration of previously decided cases. However, if there ever was an instance where circumstances justified an application of the doctrine of *stare decisis*, the present case, at least in my best judgment, seems to be such an instance. The majority opinion suggests that the result might be different if the doctrine of *stare decisis* was applicable, but it states categorically that *stare decisis* is not applicable to cases involving the interpretation of statutes. The only authority cited in support of his novel proposition is Petersen v. Department of Labor and Industries, 40 Wash.2d 635, 245 P.2d 1161. The language of that decision does support the view of the majority. However, the Petersen case cites no authority to support the thesis which limits the applicability of the doctrine of *stare decisis*. In fact, the Petersen case seems to stand in a field by itself; otherwise, the great and overwhelming weight of authority is to the contrary. The majority decide that the administration of the workmen's compensation act as to the so-called "heart cases" is to be changed. To reach that result it is unnecessary to discard the stability provided through the doctrine of *stare decisis* by stating it does not apply to judicial decisions involving the interpretation of statutes.

It seems to me that the real problem at hand is whether it is the responsibility of this court to effectuate a significant change in the public policy of this state as to the heart cases under the workmen's compensation act. No facade of resounding legal rhetoric should obscure this fact or the fact that the decision of the majority does make an abrupt change in the public policy of this state in the so-called heart cases.

I believe that the action of the majority in the instant case is untimely, undesirable and unnecessary for the very practical reasons indicated hereinabove. It is my best judgment that discretion is the better part of valor, and that, in the instant case, the court should defer to the prerogatives and the judgment of the legislature, as well as to the possibility of action by that branch of state government.

ROSELLINI, J., concurs.

Sec. 7 WEIGHT OF PRIOR INTERPRETATIONS 527

NOTES

1. Consider, in relation to the three preceding cases and to materials studied earlier, the statement in Mr. Justice White's opinion for the majority in Illinois Brick Co. v. Illinois, 431 U.S. 720, 736, 97 S.Ct. 2061, 2070, 52 L.Ed.2d 707, 719 (1977) that "we must bear in mind that considerations of *stare decisis* weigh heavily in the area of statutory construction, where Congress is free to change this Court's interpretation of its legislation."

2. United Gas Improvement Co. v. Continental Oil Co., 381 U.S. 392, 85 S.Ct. 1517, 14 L.Ed.2d 466 (1965) involved the interpretation of Section 1(b) of the Natural Gas Act providing that "the provisions of this Act shall apply * * * to the sale in interstate commerce of natural gas for resale * * * but shall not apply * * * to the production or gathering of natural gas." Having earlier read the term "sale" in this provision to include so-called "well-head" gas sales to interstate pipeline companies for resale in interstate commerce, the Supreme Court, per Mr. Justice Harlan, determined in this case that "sale" also included the sale to an interstate pipeline company of leases covering proven and developed gas reserves to be sold in interstate commerce. A further question was raised as to whether these lease-sales were nonetheless outside the Act as falling under the exemption for "production or gathering." In dealing with this issue, the Court first ruled that even though a sale occurred, as here, before production or gathering were ended, the sale was still covered by the Act. But the principal argument for exemption was based on precedent—in particular, FPC v. Panhandle Eastern Pipeline Co., 337 U.S. 498 [69 S.Ct. 1251, 93 L. Ed. 1499] (1949) in which the Court had earlier found that the disposition of undeveloped leases fell within "production or gathering." The Court met this argument by distinguishing *Panhandle* and ruled against exemption. *Panhandle* was distinguished by virtue of the facts (a) that the leases in that case were undeveloped and (b) that *Panhandle* involved a transfer to a production company for sale in intrastate commerce. The Court observed in this connection:

> "The language of *Panhandle* is unquestionably broad. But flat statements such as '[o]f course leases are an essential part of production,' 337 U.S., at 505, should not be taken to cover more than the particular kind of leases that were before the Court; it should not be considered as embracing each and every transfer that can be put in lease form. Concepts of *stare decisis* in statutory interpretation apply to the *holdings* with which the case-by-case method of decision surrounds a statute. To recognize no differences between the *Panhandle* transfers and those in issue here, and in the name of *stare decisis* to hold that Commission jurisdiction depends on the form rather than the substance of the transaction, would turn the case-by-case process against itself."

Of special interest is the brief dissenting opinion of Mr. Justice Douglas here quoted in full:

> "While I dissented in Federal Power Comm'n v. Panhandle Eastern Pipeline Co., 337 U.S. 498 [69 S.Ct. 1251, 93 L.Ed. 1499 (1949)], it is not conceivable to me that the majority that made up the Court in that case would adhere to what is done today. That would be

irrelevant if we dealt with a constitutional matter, as issues of that magnitude are always open for reexamination. But since we deal with the vagaries of a statute with no constitutional overtones, I think the matter should be left where *Panhandle Eastern Pipeline* left it, saving for the Congress, of course, the power to expand the regime of the federal bureaucracy if it desires. It is sometimes customary for a court to distinguish precedents to the vanishing point, creating an illusion of certainty in the law while leaving only a shadow of an ancient landmark. That is within the judicial competence and has been done before. But where the issue has been so hotly contested as it was in the *Panhandle Eastern Pipeline Co.* and when the Court has been so explicit in bringing traffic in gas leases under the 'production or gathering of natural gas' which Congress left to the States, I would adhere to that result until Congress changes it."

3. Mr. Justice Black, dissenting in Boys Markets, Inc. v. Retail Clerks' Union, 398 U.S. 235, 90 S.Ct. 1583, 26 L.Ed.2d 199 (1970), discussed *stare decisis* at some length in challenging the majority's overruling of Sinclair Refining Co. v. Atkinson, a case interpreting the Norris LaGuardia Act in relation to § 301(a) of the Labor Management Relations Act. He argued that in such cases an additional factor—beyond ordinary *stare decisis* policies of continuity and predictability—must be weighed, to wit, the deference courts owe the legislature as primary lawmaker. While initial interpretation of a statute by the courts is "proper and unavoidable, in any system in which courts have the task of applying general statutes in a multitude of situations," any subsequent "reinterpretation" is "gratuitous" and amounts to an amendment invading the legislative province. "Having given our view on the meaning of a statute, our task is concluded, absent extraordinary circumstances." Mr. Justice Black added, however, that *stare decisis* does not foreclose all reconsideration. Reconsideration is always proper in the area of constitutional law, for example, and even on statutory questions "new facts or changes in circumstances might warrant reexamination of past decisions in exceptional cases under exceptional circumstances." In his view, such circumstances did not exist in the case at bar.

4. Each of the cases just read has been presented primarily for the light it sheds on the treatment accorded by a court to prior judicial rulings on a statute it is called on to interpret. What light, if any, do these same cases, or other statutory cases studied in Legal Method (beginning with the opinions in Johnson v. Southern Pacific Co., supra p. 327), shed on the precedential value of a judicial ruling under one statute in a case arising under another? On the subject of this last question, consider, e. g., United States v. Demko, 385 U.S. 149, 87 S.Ct. 382, 17 L.Ed.2d 258 (1966).

FEDERAL HOUSING ADMINISTRATION v. THE DARLINGTON, INC.

Supreme Court of the United States, 1958.
358 U.S. 84, 79 S.Ct. 141, 3 L.Ed.2d 132.

Mr. Justice DOUGLAS delivered the opinion of the Court.

This case involves a construction of § 608 of the National Housing Act, 56 Stat. 303, 12 U.S.C.A. § 1743, as amended by § 10 of the

Veterans' Emergency Housing Act of 1946, 60 Stat. 207, 214, and the Regulations issued thereunder. The aim of the Act as stated in § 608(b)(2) is to provide housing for veterans of World War II and their immediate families. That end is to be achieved by authorizing the Federal Housing Administration to insure mortgages covering those projects. § 608(a). Mortgagors, eligible for insurance, are to be approved by the agency, which is empowered to require them "to be regulated or restricted as to rents or sales, charges, capital structure, rate of return, and methods of operation." § 608(b)(1).

Appellee is a South Carolina corporation formed in 1949 to obtain FHA mortgage insurance for an apartment house to be constructed in Charleston. The insurance issued and the apartment was completed. The Regulations, promulgated under the Act (24 CFR § 280 et seq.), provide that the mortgaged property shall be "designed principally for residential use, conforming to standards satisfactory to the Commissioner, and consisting of not less than eight (8) rentable dwelling units on one site * * *." § 280.34. The Regulations further provide:

> "No charge shall be made by the mortgagor for the accommodations offered by the project in excess of a rental schedule to be filed with the Commissioner and approved by him or his duly constituted representative prior to the opening of the project for rental, which schedule shall be based upon a maximum average rental fixed prior to the insurance of the mortgage, and shall not thereafter be changed except upon application of the mortgagor to, and the written approval of the change by, the Commissioner." § 280.30(a).

Veterans and their families are given preference in the rentals; and discrimination against families with children is prohibited. § 280.24.

Appellee submitted to FHA its schedule of monthly rates for its different types of apartments. No schedule of rates for transients was supplied. Indeed there was no representation to FHA that any of the apartments would be furnished. But an affiliate of appellee without FHA knowledge furnished a number of apartments; and some were leased to transients on a daily basis at rentals never submitted to nor approved by FHA, part of the rental going to the affiliate as "furniture rental." Though appellee, as required by the Regulations (§ 280.30(f)), made reports to FHA, it made no disclosure to the agency that it had either furnished some apartments or rented them to transients. But it continued to rent furnished apartments to transients both before and after 1954 when § 513 was added to the Act. 68 Stat. 610, 12 U.S.C.A. § 1731b. The new section contained in subsection (a) the following declaration of congressional purpose:

> "The Congress hereby declares that it has been its intent since the enactment of the National Housing Act that

housing built with the aid of mortgages insured under that Act is to be used principally for residential use; and that this intent excludes the use of such housing for transient or hotel purposes while such insurance on the mortgage remains outstanding." And see H. R. Rep. No. 1429, 83d Cong., 2d Sess., p. 17; S.Rep. No. 1472, 83d Cong., 2d Sess., p. 31.[82]

Appellee persisted in its rental of space to transients. Appellant FHA persisted in maintaining that the practice was not authorized. In 1955 appellee brought this suit for a declaratory judgment that so long as it operates its property "principally" for residential use, keeps apartments available for extended tenancies, and complies with the terms of the Act in existence at the time it obtained the insurance, it is entitled to rent to transients. The District Court gave appellee substantially the relief which it demanded. 142 F.Supp. 341. On appeal, we remanded the cause for consideration by a three-judge court pursuant to 28 U.S.C.A. § 2282. 352 U.S. 977, 77 S.Ct. 381, 1 L.Ed.2d 363. On the remand a three-judge court adopted the earlier findings and conclusions of the single judge, 154 F.Supp. 411, attaching however certain conditions to the decree unnecessary to discuss here. It held that rental to transients was not barred by § 608 and that § 513(a) as applied to respondent was unconstitutional. The case is here on direct appeal. 28 U.S.C.A. § 1253.

We take a different view. We do not think the Act gave mortgagors the right to rent to transients. There is no express provision one way or the other; but the limitation seems fairly implied. We deal with legislation passed to aid veterans and their families,[83] not with a law to promote the hotel or motel business. To be sure, the Regulations speak of property "designed principally for residential use" (§ 280.34)—words that by themselves would not preclude transient rentals. But those words as the Senate Report on the 1954 Amendment indicates,[84] were evidently used so as not to preclude

---

82. The Act provides that, except for certain exceptions not relevant here, no new or existing multifamily housing with respect to which a mortgage is insured by the FHA shall be operated for transient purposes. § 513(b). The Commissioner is authorized to define "rental for transient or hotel purposes" but in any event rental for any period less than 30 days constitutes rental for such purposes. § 513(e).

83. S.Rep. No. 1130, 79th Cong., 2d Sess.; H.R.Rep. No. 1580, 79th Cong., 2d Sess.

84. S.Rep. No. 1472, 83d Cong., 2d Sess., p. 31, states:

"Your committee does not believe the spirit of this intent is violated by the operation of a commercial establishment included to serve the needs of families residing in rental projects operated as permanent residential housing projects (as distinguished from those operated to provide transient accommodations) but it firmly believes that the operation of such establishments should not be conducted in such a manner as to convert the use of all or any portion of the housing units in the project from permanent residential use to a project furnishing transient accommodations * * *."

some commercial rentals. Moreover, the Regulation goes on to describe the property that is insured as "dwelling units." Id. The word "dwelling" in common parlance means a permanent residence. A person can of course take up permanent residence even in a motel or hotel. But those who come for a night or so have not chosen it as a settled abode. Yet the idea of permanency pervades the concept of "dwelling." That was the construction given to § 608 by FHA in 1947 when it issued its book Planning Rental Housing Projects. "Housing" was there interpreted to mean "dwelling quarters for families—quarters which offer complete facilities for family life." There again the quality of permanency is implicit.[85] And if the provisions of appellee's charter are deemed relevant, it is not without interest to note the requirement that "Dwelling accommodations of the corporation shall be rented at a maximum average rental per room per month * * *." Again the focus is on permanency.

In 1946 FHA made provisions in its application forms for estimates of annual operating expenses of the project. None of the expenses incident to transient accommodations—such as linen supply and cleaning expenses—were listed. Once more we may infer that the insurance program was not designed in aid of transients.

In a letter to field offices in 1951 explaining the criteria to be considered in passing on rent schedules and methods of operation, the FHA instructed them to: " * * * bear in mind that the objective of this Administration is the production of housing designed for occupancy of a relatively permanent nature and that transient occupancy is contrary to policy. No approval will be granted with respect to a proposal anticipating transient occupancy." That interpretation of the Act is clear and unambiguous, and, taken with the Regulations, indicates that the authority charged with administration of the statute construed it to bar rental to transients.

Moreover, as already mentioned, prior approval by FHA of all rental schedules was always required by § 280.30 of the Regulations

---

85. The same tone is exhibited in the Committee Reports on the various amendments to § 608. For instance, in reporting the Veterans' Emergency Housing Act of 1946 the Senate Committee on Banking and Currency stated:

"Since a main purpose of these provisions [authorizations of additional insurance] is to reduce the risks assumed by builders in order to encourage a large volume of *housing*, the committee calls special attention to the fact that this portion of the bill places emphasis upon *rental housing*. It is the specific intent of the committee that those in charge of the program shall make every reasonable effort to obtain a substantial volume of *rental housing*—or in any event *housing* held for rental during the emergency—through the operation of title VI, both with respect to multifamily units and individual units. While home ownership is to be encouraged, a large percentage of veterans do not yet possess the certainty of income or of location, or the financial means, to purchase homes at this time. The bill as approved by the House of Representatives included this attention to *rental housing*." S.Rep. No. 1130, 79th Cong., 2d Sess., p. 8. (Italics added.)

and appellee never obtained nor sought approval of a schedule of rents for transients.

It is true that FHA felt it had the authority to approve rental schedules for transients. It gave such approval in a dozen or more instances where it felt the public interest required it. We need not stop to inquire whether FHA had that authority.[86] We have said enough to indicate that no right or privilege to rent to transients is expressly included in the Act nor fairly implied. The contemporaneous construction of the Act by the agency entrusted with its administration is squarely to the contrary. In circumstances no more ambiguous than the present we have allowed contemporaneous administrative construction to carry the day against doubts that might exist from a reading of the bare words of a statute. See United States v. American Trucking Ass'ns, 310 U.S. 534, 549, 60 S.Ct. 1059, 1067, 84 L.Ed. 1345; Norwegian Nitrogen Products Co. v. United States, 288 U.S. 294, 315, 53 S.Ct. 350, 77 L.Ed. 796. When Congress passed the 1954 Amendment, it accepted the construction of the prior Act which bars rentals to transients. Subsequent legislation which declares the intent of an earlier law is not, of course, conclusive in determining what the previous Congress meant. But the later law is entitled to weight when it comes to the problem of construction. See United States v. Stafoff, 260 U.S. 477, 480, 43 S.Ct. 197, 67 L.Ed. 358; Sioux Tribe v. United States, 316 U.S. 317, 329–330, 62 S.Ct. 1095, 1100–1101, 86 L.Ed. 1501. The purpose of the Act, its administrative construction, and the meaning which a later Congress ascribed to it all point to the conclusion that the housing business to be benefited by FHA insurance did not include rental to transients.

If the question be less clear and free from doubt than we think, it is still one that lies in the periphery where vested rights do not attach. If we take as our starting point what the Court said in the Sinking-Fund Cases, 99 U.S. 700, 718, 25 L.Ed. 496—"Every possible presumption is in favor of the validity of a statute, and this continues until the contrary is shown beyond a rational doubt"—we do not see how it can be said that the 1954 Act is unconstitutional as applied. Appellee is not penalized for anything it did in the past. The new Act applies prospectively only. So there is no possible due process issue on that score. As stated in Fleming v. Rhodes, 331 U.S. 100, 107, 67 S.Ct. 1140, 1144, 91 L.Ed. 1368, "Federal regulation of future action based upon rights previously acquired by the person regulated is not prohibited by the Constitution. So long as the Constitution authorizes the subsequently enacted legislation, the fact that its provisions limit or interfere with previously acquired rights does not condemn it. Immunity from federal regulation is not gained through forehanded contracts." [87]

---

86. The 1954 Amendment expressly gave FHA that power in certain limited situations. See § 513(b).

87. In Fleming a landlord had obtained a judgment of eviction in a state court prior to the enactment of the

Moreover, one has to look long and hard to find even a semblance of a contractual right rising to the dignity of the one involved in Lynch v. United States, 292 U.S. 571, 54 S.Ct. 840, 78 L.Ed. 1434. The Constitution is concerned with practical, substantial rights, not with those that are unclear and gain hold by subtle and involved reasoning. Congress by the 1954 Act was doing no more than protecting the regulatory system which it had designed. Those who do business in the regulated field cannot object if the legislative scheme is buttressed by subsequent amendments to achieve the legislative end. Cf. Veix v. Sixth Ward Ass'n, 310 U.S. 32, 60 S.Ct. 792, 84 L.Ed. 1061; Keefe v. Clark, 322 U.S. 393, 64 S.Ct. 1072, 88 L.Ed. 1346. Invocation of the Due Process Clause to protect the rights asserted here would make the ghost of Lochner v. New York, 198 U.S. 45, 25 S.Ct. 539, 49 L.Ed. 937, walk again.

Reversed.

Mr. Justice STEWART took no part in the consideration or decision of this case.

Mr. Justice FRANKFURTER, dissenting.

Here we have not the application of some broad, generalized legal conception, either of a statutory nature, like "restraint of trade" in the Sherman Law, 15 U.S.C.A. §§ 1–7, 15 note, or a constitutional provision, like "due process of law" or "the equal protection of the laws." Such conceptions do not carry contemporaneous fixity. By their very nature they imply a process of unfolding content.

Our immediate problem is quite different. The pre-1954 Housing Act does not leave us at large for judicial application of a generalized legislative policy in light of developing circumstances. The pre-1954 statute deals with a particularized problem in a particularized way. It presents the usual question of statutory construction where language is not clear enough to preclude human ingenuity from creating ambiguity. It is outside the judicial function to add to the scope of legislation. The task is imaginatively to extrapolate the contemporaneous answer that the Legislature would have given to an unconsidered question; here, whether rentals to transients were totally prohibited. It was not until 1954 that the Congress did deal with the question of the right of apartment-house owners to rent even a small number of apartments to transients without even remotely seeking to evade or to disadvantage the interests of veterans in whose behalf the Government, through the Federal Housing Administration,

Price Control Extension Act, under which the Administrator had promulgated rules prohibiting removal of the tenants from the leased premises on the grounds asserted by the landlord. It was held that the landlord could be enjoined from evicting the tenants under the state judgment, as any "vested" rights by reason of the state judgment were acquired subject to the possibility of their dilution through Congress' exercise of its paramount regulatory power.

insured the mortgages of private owners. The opinions of the District Court and my brother HARLAN seem to me compelling on the construction of the pre-1954 legislation.

This brings me to the validity of the 1954 enactment which presents for me a much more difficult question than that of the problem of statutory construction just considered. This is so because of the very weighty presumption of constitutionality that I deem it essential to attribute to any Act of Congress. This case falls between such cases sustaining the retroactive validity of legislation adversely affecting an existing interest as Paramino Co. v. Marshall, 309 U.S. 370, 60 S.Ct. 600, 84 L.Ed. 814, and Fleming v. Rhodes, 331 U.S. 100, 67 S.Ct. 1140, 91 L.Ed. 1368, on the one hand, and Lynch v. United States, 292 U.S. 571, 54 S.Ct. 840, 78 L.Ed. 1434, on the other. While, to be sure, differentiation between "remedy" and "right" takes us into treacherous territory, the difference is not meaningless. The two earlier cases cited may fairly be deemed to sustain retroactive remedial modifications even though they affect existing "rights," while the Lynch case is a clear instance of the complete wiping out of what Mr. Justice Brandeis, in his opinion for the Court, called "vested rights." 292 U.S. at page 577, 54 S.Ct. at page 842. Insofar as the 1954 Act applied to the earlier Darlington mortgage, it did not completely wipe out "vested rights." But on the proper construction of § 608, in the circumstances found by the District Court and not here challenged, the unavoidable application of the 1954 Act to the Darlington mortgage did substantially impair the "vested rights" of respondent. I would be less than respecting the full import of the Lynch case did I not apply it to the present situation.

Accordingly, I join Mr. Justice HARLAN'S opinion.

Mr. Justice HARLAN, whom Mr. Justice FRANKFURTER and Mr. Justice WHITTAKER join, dissenting.

The question in this case is whether appellee Darlington is entitled to rent to transients (that is, so far as this case is concerned, for periods of less than 30 days) a small number of apartments in its building, which is covered by a mortgage insured by the FHA. Darlington's FHA mortgage was consummated and insured in December 1949. At that time neither the controlling statute, § 608 of the National Housing Act, 56 Stat. 303, as amended, 12 U.S.C.A. § 1743, nor the regulations issued thereunder, 24 CFR § 280 et seq., contained any provision prohibiting rentals to transients. Such provisions are found for the first time in § 513 of the Housing Act of 1954, 68 Stat. 610, 12 U.S.C.A. § 1731b, passed some five years after this mortgage was made.

A three-judge District Court, largely adopting the findings and conclusions of the single district judge before whom this case was originally heard, held that as the law stood in 1949, when the mortgage here involved was issued, Darlington was not forbidden to make *occasional* transient rentals, and that the Federal Housing Administrator may not now prohibit such rentals since that would involve an unconstitutional retroactive application of the relevant provisions of the Housing Act of 1954.[88] This Court now holds that under the statute and regulations as they stood in 1949 Darlington was never entitled to make *any* transient rentals, and that in any event the prohibitory provisions of the 1954 Act may be applied to prevent such rentals. From these holdings I must dissent.

In construing the earlier statute the Court, in my opinion, has proceeded on an erroneous premise. The Court holds that "no right or privilege to rent to transients is expressly included in the [pre-1954] Act nor fairly implied." In my view, however, the true issue is not whether the statute under which Darlington's mortgage was insured *gave* the right to an FHA–insured mortgagor to make such rentals, but rather whether it *prohibited* such a mortgagor from making them. Given this as the issue, it seems to me that the record is compelling against the Court's conclusion as to § 608, that the provisions of the 1954 Act cannot be applied to one in Darlington's position, and that the decision below was clearly right.

1. As already noted, § 608 and the regulations implementing it were barren of any provision excluding rentals to transients at the time Darlington's mortgage was insured by the FHA.

2. The District Court found that (1) Darlington's rentals to transients even at the height of Charleston's transient season constituted no more than ten percent of the building's total available occupancy; (2) "no person entitled to priority has ever been rejected, and no one desiring so-called 'permanent' occupancy of an apartment has been required to wait any time to obtain same"; and (3) Darlington "does not advertise as a hotel, has no license as such, and no signs appear indicating its willingness to accept transients." 142 F.Supp. at page 349. According the utmost effect to the conceded purpose of § 608 to provide housing for World War II veterans and their families, and to the recitals in the regulations to the effect that property subject to FHA mortgages shall be "designed *principally* for residential use" (italics supplied), I am unable to understand why Darlington's practices, as found by the lower court, should be regarded as violative of either the letter or spirit of these statutory or regulatory provisions. Not until the passage of the 1954 Act do we find any suggestion that the words "designed principally for residential use" were, in the language of the Court, "evidently used so as not to preclude some commercial [as distinguished from transient] rentals."

---

88. The opinion of the district judge who first heard this case is reported at 142 F.Supp. 341. Subsequent references to the decision below are to that opinion.

* * *

3. As the FHA conceded and the District Court found, nothing in Darlington's charter, bylaws, mortgage or mortgage note, all of which were subject to the FHA's advance approval, expressly restricted its right "to lease apartments in its project for periods of less than thirty (30) days." The only period of rental limitation appearing in any of these instruments was the following, contained in Darlington's charter: "Dwelling accommodations of the [appellee] shall not be rented for a period in excess of three years * * *." 142 F.Supp. at page 346. It is too much to attribute to the word "dwelling," as the Court now in effect does, an implied prohibition of less-than-30-days rentals.

4. The FHA had in a number of instances before 1954 actually given specific approval to less-than-30-days rentals by insured mortgagors where veteran demand for housing had fallen off, and when in 1955 Darlington inquired of the FHA the basis of its position that less-than-30-days rentals by such mortgagors were not permissible the agency simply referred appellee to the provisions of the Housing Act of 1954. These events conclusively show that the Housing Administration did not construe the statute or regulations before 1954 to prohibit transient rentals altogether.

5. There is nothing in this record to indicate that Darlington was engaged in any kind of a scheme to subvert the purposes of this federal housing legislation. Its occasional transient rentals seem to have been nothing more than an effort to plug the gap in its revenues left by a falling off of the demand for long-term apartment space, and do not depict a *sub rosa* hotel operation.

Upon these undisputed facts, which are reinforced by other factors detailed in the two opinions below, I can find no basis for impugning the soundness of the District Court's holding that under the law as it existed at the time Darlington embarked upon this project nothing prohibited it from making the occasional transient rentals shown by this record. The 1954 Act was new, and not merely confirmatory, legislation.

Hence I consider that the FHA's position in this case must stand or fall on whether the less-than-30-days rental provision of the 1954 Act, which in terms applies to mortgagors insured before as well as after the Act's effective date (see 12 U.S.C.A. § 1731b(b)), can be given application to Darlington to increase the obligations assumed by it under its 1949 contract with the United States. I do not think it can. As the District Court correctly put it: "When the United States enters into contractual relations, its rights and duties therein are governed generally by the law applicable to contracts between private individuals." 142 F.Supp. at page 351. See Lynch v. United States, 292 U.S. 571, 54 S.Ct. 840, 78 L.Ed. 1434; Sinking-Fund Cases, 99 U.S. 700, 718, 25 L.Ed. 496. What was said in the Lynch case as to contracts of war-risk insurance applies here: "As Congress had the power * * * to issue them, the due process clause prohibits the United States from annulling them, unless, indeed, the action taken falls within the federal police power or some other paramount power." 292 U.S. at page 579, 54 S.Ct. at page 843. I do not understand the Housing Administration to contend that the United States possesses general regulatory power over appellee outside the contractual relationship, and the Court has pointed to no such "paramount power" by which the imposition of the 1954 Act's prohibitions might be justified in this case. Under these circumstances I see no reason for disregarding the principles set forth in the cases cited, particularly when the District Court with ample justification found that "the 1954 Act is designed to afford relief for private interests, as distinguished from public purposes * * *." 142 F.Supp. at page 353.[89] Indeed the Court's treatment of this case seems to reinforce my view about the 1954 Act; else why all this straining to bring the matter under the pre-1954 statute?

I would affirm.

NOTES

1. Consider, in connection with problems posed by the 1954 act in the *Darlington* case, the implications of including this clause in a statute:

> *Liberal Interpretation.* This act shall be liberally construed to carry out its purposes.

or either of the following clauses:

> *Saving Clause.* Nothing in this act shall be construed to impair or affect the obligation of any contract lawfully made prior to the effective date of this act.

> *Severability.* It is the intent of the legislature, in enacting this act, that if any part or application of the act is held invalid, the remainder of the act or its application to other situations or persons shall not be affected thereby.

Does inclusion of a definition section in a statute—see, e. g., Problem Case No. 3, supra p. 321—raise related questions? Are the same or different problems raised by the general construction statutes which are to be found in the U.S. Code and on the statute books of New York and a number of other states? Consult several of these acts, cited herewith, to familiarize yourself with the kind of material they normally contain. See, e. g., 1 U.S.C.A. §§ 1–6 (1977); Ala.Code, tit. 1, §§ 1–1–1 – 1–1–16 (1975 and Supp.1978); Ariz.Rev.Stat.Ann. §§ 1–211 – 1–218 (1974 and Supp.1979); Conn.Gen.Stat. Ann., tit. 1, §§ 1–1 – 1–3b (1969 and Supp.1979); Del.Code Ann., tit. 1, §§ 301–308 (1974 and Supp.1978); Ill.Ann.Stat., ch. 131, §§ 1–4.3 (1953 and Supp.1979); Mass.Ann. Laws, ch. 4, §§ 6–7 (1973 and Supp.1979); Mich. Comp.Laws Ann. §§ 8.3–8.5 (1967 and Supp.1979); N.Y.Gen.Constr. Law

---

89. This fact is demonstrated by the rather unusual provision of the 1954 Act which gives hotel operators and owners the right to seek federal court injunctions against violations of the transient rental prohibition of the statute. 68 Stat. 611. 12 U.S.C.A. § 1731b(i). * * *

(McKinney 1951 and Supp.1979); Ohio Rev.Code Ann. §§ 1.01–1.59 (1971 and Supp.1978); and Wis.Stat.Ann. §§ 990.001–990.07 (1958 and Supp. 1979). Among various provisions dealing with interpretation, the general construction laws are likely to include, for example, a set of definitions broadly applicable to legislative enactments. Section 1 of 1 U.S.C.A. is illustrative:

> Section 1. Words denoting number, gender, and so forth
>
> In determining the meaning of any Act of Congress, unless the context indicates otherwise—
>
> words importing the singular include and apply to several persons, parties, or things;
>
> words importing the plural include the singular;
>
> words importing the masculine gender include the feminine as well;
>
> words used in the present tense include the future as well as the present;
>
> the words "insane" and "insane person" and "lunatic" shall include every idiot, lunatic, insane person, and person non compos mentis;
>
> the words "person" and "whoever" include corporations, companies, associations, firms, partnerships, societies, and joint stock companies, as well as individuals;
>
> "officer" includes any person authorized by law to perform the duties of the office;
>
> "signature" or "subscription" includes a mark when the person making the same intended it as such;
>
> "oath" includes affirmation, and "sworn" includes affirmed;
>
> "writing" includes printing and typewriting and reproductions of visual symbols by photographing, multigraphing, mimeographing, manifolding, or otherwise.

Whether or not there is a general construction law in a given jurisdiction, there may be construction provisions addressed to particular divisions of the statute law. See, e. g., New York Penal Law § 5.00, quoted in the Note on p. 555, infra.

2. Section 22 of the Internal Security Act of 1950 requires deportation of any alien "who was at the time of entering the United States, or has been at any time thereafter * * * a member of any one of the classes of aliens enumerated in section 1(2)"; and subparagraph C of § 1(2) lists, as one such class, "[a]liens who are members of or affiliated with * * * the Communist Party of the United States." In Galvan v. Press, 347 U.S. 522, 74 S.Ct. 737, 98 L.Ed. 911 (1954), it was contended *inter alia*, that these provisions called for deportation only of such aliens as were members of the Communist Party with full awareness of, and commitment to, its advocacy of violence. The Supreme Court (per Mr. Justice Frankfurter) rejected this contention, with two justices dissenting. In view of the fact that subparagraph E of § 1(2) regarding alien members of certain other organizations, provided—unlike C—a specific exception for "innocent dupes,"

the Court declared that "it seems clear that Congress did not exempt 'innocent' members of the Communist Party." In further support of its interpretation, the Court added:

> "While the legislative history of the 1950 Act is not illuminating on the scope of 'member,' considerable light was shed by authoritative comment in the debates on the statute which Congress enacted in 1951 to correct what it regarded as the unduly expanded interpretation by the Attorney General of 'member' under the 1950 Act. 65 Stat. 28. The amendatory statute dealt with certain specific situations which had been brought to the attention of Congress and provided that where aliens had joined a proscribed organization (1) when they were children, (2) by operation of law, or (3) to obtain the necessities of life, they were not to be deemed to have been 'members.' In explaining the measure, its sponsor, Senator McCarran, stated repeatedly and emphatically that 'member' was intended to have the same meaning in the 1950 Act as had been given it by the courts and administrative agencies since 1918. * * *
>
> "[These] repeated statements that 'member' was to have the same meaning under the 1950 Act as previously, preclude an interpretation limited to those who were fully cognizant of the Party's advocacy of violence. For the judicial and administrative decisions prior to 1950 do not exempt aliens who joined an organization unaware of its program and purposes. * * *"

For additional cases in which it appears that the statute being construed has undergone amendment and that the amendatory legislation or its legislative history involves an interpretation of the statute pertinent to the case at hand, see e. g., Rainwater v. United States, 356 U.S. 590, 78 S.Ct. 946, 2 L.Ed.2d 996 (1958); United States v. Price, 361 U.S. 304, 80 S.Ct. 326, 4 L.Ed.2d 334 (1960); S.E.C. v. Capital Gains Research Bureau, Inc., 375 U.S. 180, 84 S.Ct. 275, 11 L.Ed.2d 237 (1963); Haynes v. U. S., 390 U.S. 85, 88 S.Ct. 722, 19 L.Ed.2d 923 (1968); Red Lion Broadcasting Co. v. F.C.C., 395 U.S. 367, 89 S.Ct. 1794, 23 L.Ed.2d 371 (1969).

3. With the *Darlington* and *Galvan* cases, supra, compare, Flora v. United States, infra. Compare also, for example, Sioux Tribe v. United States, 316 U.S. 317, 62 S.Ct. 1095, 86 L.Ed. 1501 (1942); United States v. United Mine Workers, 330 U.S. 258, 67 S.Ct. 677, 91 L.Ed. 884 (1947); Paragon Jewel Coal Co. v. Commissioner of Internal Revenue, 380 U.S. 624, 85 S.Ct. 1207, 14 L.Ed.2d 116 (1965); Seymour v. Superintendent of Washington State Penitentiary, 368 U.S. 351, 82 S.Ct. 424, 7 L.Ed.2d 346 (1962); and Mattz v. Arnett, 412 U.S. 481, 93 S.Ct. 2245, 37 L.Ed.2d 92 (1973).

FLORA v. UNITED STATES

Supreme Court of the United States, 1960.
362 U.S. 145, 80 S.Ct. 630, 4 L.Ed.2d 623.

Mr. Chief Justice WARREN delivered the opinion of the Court.

The question presented is whether a Federal District Court has jurisdiction under 28 U.S.C.A. § 1346(a)(1), of a suit by a taxpayer for the refund of income tax payments which did not discharge the entire amount of his assessment.

This is our second consideration of the case. In the 1957 Term, we decided that full payment of the assessment is a jurisdictional prerequisite to suit, 357 U.S. 63, 78 S.Ct. 1079, 2 L.Ed.2d 1165. Subsequently the Court granted a petition for rehearing. 360 U.S. 922, 79 S.Ct. 1430, 3 L.Ed.2d 1538. The case has been exhaustively briefed and ably argued. After giving the problem our most careful attention, we have concluded that our original disposition of the case was correct.

* * *

The Statute

The question raised in this case has not only raised a conflict in the federal decisions, but has also in recent years provoked controversy among legal commentators. In view of this divergence of expert opinion, it would be surprising if the words of the statute inexorably dictated but a single reasonable conclusion. Nevertheless, one of the arguments which has been most strenuously urged is that the plain language of the statute precludes, or at the very least strongly militates against, a decision that full payment of the income tax assessment is a jurisdictional condition precedent to maintenance of a refund suit in a District Court. If this were true, presumably we could but recite the statute and enter judgment for petitioner—though we might be pardoned some perplexity as to how such a simple matter could have caused so much confusion. Regrettably, this facile an approach will not serve.

* * *

We conclude [following consideration of the face of the statute— Ed.] that the language of § 1346(a)(1) can be more readily construed to require payment of the full tax before suit than to permit suit for recovery of a part payment. But, as we recognized in the prior opinion, the statutory language is not absolutely controlling, and consequently resort must be had to whatever other materials might be relevant.

Legislative History and Historical Background

Although frequently the legislative history of a statute is the most fruitful source of instruction as to its proper interpretation, in this case that history is barren of any clue to congressional intent.

* * *

Thus there is presented a vexing situation—statutory language which is inconclusive and legislative history which is irrelevant. This, of course, does not necessarily mean that § 1346(a)(1) expresses no congressional intent with respect to the issue before the Court; but it does make that intent uncommonly difficult to divine.

Sec. 7   WEIGHT OF PRIOR INTERPRETATIONS   541

It is argued, however, that the puzzle may be solved through consideration of the historical basis of a suit to recover a tax illegally assessed. * * *

* * *

If this [i. e., the historical background referred to, the face of the statute, and the legislative history—Ed.] were all the material relevant to a construction of § 1346(a)(1), determination of the issue at bar would be inordinately difficult. * * * There are, however, additional factors which are dispositive.

We are not here concerned with a single sentence in an isolated statute, but rather with a jurisdictional provision which is a keystone in a carefully articulated and quite complicated structure of tax laws. From these related statutes, all of which were passed after 1921, it is apparent that Congress has several times acted upon the assumption that § 1346(a)(1) requires full payment before suit. Of course, if the clear purpose of Congress at any time had been to permit suit to recover a part payment, this subsequent legislation would have to be disregarded. But, as we have stated, the evidence pertaining to this intent is extremely weak, and we are convinced that it is entirely too insubstantial to justify destroying the existing harmony of the tax statutes.[90] The laws which we consider especially pertinent are the statute establishing the Board of Tax Appeals (now the Tax Court), the Declaratory Judgment Act, 28 U.S.C.A. § 2201 et seq., and § 7422(e) of the Internal Revenue Code of 1954.

The Board of Tax Appeals

The Board of Tax Appeals was established by Congress in 1924 to permit taxpayers to secure a determination of tax liability before payment of the deficiency. The Government argues that the Congress which passed this 1924 legislation thought full payment of the tax assessed was a condition for bringing suit in a District Court; that Congress believed this sometimes caused hardship; and that Congress set up the Board to alleviate that hardship. Petitioner denies this, and contends that Congress' sole purpose was to enable taxpayers to prevent the Government from collecting taxes by exercise of its power of distraint.

We believe that the legislative history surrounding both the creation of the Board and the subsequent revisions of the basic statute supports the Government. [The Court here cites the House Committee Report on the 1924 legislation.—Ed.] * * *

Moreover, throughout the congressional debates are to be found frequent expressions of the principle that payment of the full tax was a precondition to suit * * *.

* * *

---

90. [Compare expressions of Warren, C.J., in United States v. Wise, 370 U.S. 405, 411–414, 82 S.Ct. 1354, 1360, 8 L.Ed.2d 590, 595–596 (1962) and United States v. Muniz, footnote 14, 374 U.S. 150, 158, 83 S.Ct. 1850, 1855–1856, 10 L.Ed.2d 805, 812–813 (1963)—Ed.]

In sum, even assuming that one purpose of Congress in establishing the Board was to permit taxpayers to avoid distraint, it seems evident that another purpose was to furnish a forum where full payment of the assessment would not be a condition precedent to suit. The result is a system in which there is one tribunal for prepayment litigation and another for post-payment litigation, with no room contemplated for a hybrid of the type proposed by petitioner.

The Declaratory Judgment Act

The Federal Declaratory Judgment Act of 1934 was amended by § 405 of the Revenue Act of 1935 expressly to except disputes "with respect to Federal taxes." * * *

It is clear enough that one "radical departure" which was averted by the amendment was the potential circumvention of the "pay first and litigate later" rule by way of suits for declaratory judgments in tax cases. Petitioner would have us give this Court's imprimatur to precisely the same type of "radical departure," since a suit for recovery of but a part of an assessment would determine the legality of the balance by operation of the principle of collateral estoppel. With respect to this unpaid portion, the taxpayer would be securing what is in effect—even though not technically—a declaratory judgment. The frustration of congressional intent which petitioner asks us to endorse could hardly be more glaring, for he has conceded that his argument leads logically to the conclusion that payment of even $1 on a large assessment entitles the taxpayer to sue—a concession amply warranted by the obvious impracticality of any judicially created jurisdictional standard midway between *full* payment and *any* payment.

Section 7422(e) of the 1954 Code

One distinct possibility which would emerge from a decision in favor of petitioner would be that a taxpayer might be able to split his cause of action, bringing suit for refund of part of the tax in a Federal District Court and litigating in the Tax Court with respect to the remainder. In such a situation the first decision would, of course, control. Thus if for any reason a litigant would prefer a District Court adjudication, he might sue for a small portion of the tax in that tribunal while at the same time protecting the balance from distraint by invoking the protection of the Tax Court procedure. On the other hand, different questions would arise if this device were not employed. For example, would the Government be required to file a compulsory counterclaim for the unpaid balance in District Court under Rule 13 of the Federal Rules of Civil Procedure, 28 U.S.C.A.? If so, which party would have the burden of proof?

Section 7422(e) of the 1954 Internal Revenue Code makes it apparent that Congress has assumed these problems are nonexistent except in the rare case where the taxpayer brings suit in a District

Court and the Commissioner then notifies him of an additional deficiency. Under § 7422(e) such a claimant is given the option of pursuing his suit in the District Court or in the Tax Court, *but he cannot litigate in both.* Moreover, if he decides to remain in the District Court, the Government may—but seemingly is not required to—bring a counterclaim; and if it does, the taxpayer has the burden of proof. If we were to overturn the assumption upon which Congress has acted, we would generate upon a broad scale the very problems Congress believed it had solved.

These, then, are the basic reasons for our decision, and our views would be unaffected by the constancy or inconstancy of administrative practice. However, because the petition for rehearing in this case focused almost exclusively upon a single clause in the prior opinion—"there does not appear to be a single case before 1940 in which a taxpayer attempted a suit for refund of income taxes without paying the full amount the Government alleged to be due," 357 U.S. at page 69, 78 S.Ct. at page 1083—we feel obliged to comment upon the material introduced upon reargument. The reargument has, if anything, strengthened, rather than weakened, the substance of this statement, which was directed to the question whether there has been a consistent understanding of the "pay first and litigate later" principle by the interested government agencies and by the bar.

[After reviewing the cases brought to its attention on rehearing and after disposing of the claim that a decision for the government will work great hardship on taxpayer, the Court concludes:]

In sum, if we were to accept petitioner's argument, we would sacrifice the harmony of our carefully structured twentieth century system of tax litigation, and all that would be achieved would be a supposed harmony of § 1346(a)(1) with what might have been the nineteenth century law had the issue ever been raised. Reargument has but fortified our view that § 1346(a)(1), correctly construed, requires full payment of the assessment before an income tax refund suit can be maintained in a Federal District Court.

Affirmed.

[The dissenting opinion of Mr. Justice WHITTAKER, joined by Mr. Justice FRANKFURTER, Mr. Justice HARLAN, and Mr. Justice STEWART, and the dissenting opinion of Mr. Justice FRANKFURTER are omitted.]

SECTION 8. MAXIMS

INTRODUCTORY NOTE

By the time you have reached this point in the present Chapter, you should have built up, as a by-product of your study of the cases in the three preceding Sections, a substantial catalog of the judicial presumptions and rules of thumb known as "maxims" or "canons" of statutory construction. Before you begin preparing the cases in this Section, it is suggested that you check through the past cases and make a list of all the maxims relied on or mentioned in the preceding statutory interpretation opinions. This Section is designed to acquaint you with a few important samples of the almost countless maxims that courts have formulated or thrown off at one time or another and to give you the basis for an appraisal of the role of maxims in contemporary statutory litigation.

One of the difficulties inherent in the use of maxims is suggested by Karl N. Llewellyn in his article "Remarks on the Theory of Appellate Decision and the Rules or Canons About How Statutes Are to be Construed," 3 Vand.L.Rev. 395 (1950). Professor Llewellyn described the use of maxims as a "thrust and parry maneuver," pointing to the fact that one or more maxims can often be found to support either side of an issue of interpretation. In spite of their frequent mutual inconsistency and their generality, maxims may nonetheless play a role in the decision of interpretative questions and thus are still of some practical importance in the presentation of statutory cases. An awareness of their virtues and failings is a necessary part of the lawyer's equipment. In analyzing the cases that follow, keep in mind some questions that need answering in relation to maxims. Are the maxims encountered all of the same kind or are there significant differences of character among them which affect their use? What ultimate value have maxims as rules for decision? How are they used, and how should they be used, and what weight is or should be assigned them, in counseling, advocacy and decision-making? What relation do the maxims bear to the general interpretive approaches—legislative intent and "plain meaning"—earlier discussed?

WEILER v. DRY DOCK SAVINGS INSTITUTION

Supreme Court of New York, Appellate Division, First Department, 1940.
258 App.Div. 581, 17 N.Y.S.2d 192.

Appeal by the defendant from a determination of the Appellate Term of the Supreme Court, First Department, entered in the office of the clerk of the county of New York on the 7th day of July, 1939, affirming a judgment of the Municipal Court of the City of New York, Borough of Manhattan, First District.

COHN, J. The question presented by this appeal is whether section 234 of the Real Property Law, which declares void as against public policy and wholly unenforcible agreements exempting lessors from liability for their own negligence, embraces contracts made prior to the enactment of the statute as well as contracts made subsequent thereto.

Plaintiff, on March 23, 1937, leased from defendant for a period of two years a store and basement located in the borough of Manhat-

Sec. 8   MAXIMS   545

tan, New York City, the term to commence May 1, 1937. Paragraph 9 of the lease exonerated the landlord from any liability for water damage to property caused by its own negligence. So far as pertinent it reads: "Landlord shall not be liable for any damage to property * * * resulting from * * * water * * * which may leak from any part of said building or from the pipes * * * or any other cause of whatsoever nature, whether caused by or due to the negligence of landlord, landlord's agents, servants, employees," etc.

On June 5, 1937, section 234 of the Real Property Law became effective. It provides as follows:

"§ 234. Agreements exempting lessors from liability for negligence void and unenforceable. Every covenant, agreement or understanding in or in connection with or collateral to any lease of real property exempting the lessor from liability for damages for injuries to person or property caused by or resulting from the negligence of the lessor, his agents, servants or employees, in the operation or maintenance of the demised premises or the real property containing the demised premises shall be deemed to be void as against public policy and wholly unenforceable."

Fifty-two days after this law had been placed upon the statute books, and on July 27, 1937, plaintiff's merchandise was damaged by water by reason of defendant's alleged negligence. Thereupon plaintiff commenced an action for the recovery of the property damage thus sustained. At the trial plaintiff proved negligence and damage. Defendant rested without offering any evidence, but moved to dismiss upon the ground stated in an affirmative defense that paragraph 9 of the lease exculpated it from liability. Plaintiff relied upon section 234 of the Real Property Law to sustain his claim. The trial court granted judgment for plaintiff in the sum of $150 and from the determination of the Appellate Term which affirmed that judgment this appeal has been taken by permission of the Appellate Term.

The language of the statute does not indicate a legislative attempt to have the act include agreements executed before the statute took effect. The words used relating to agreements exempting lessors from liability for negligence declared that "Every covenant * * * *shall be deemed* to be void as against public policy and wholly unenforceable." (Italics ours.) A statute using words importing futurity, such as "shall be," is regarded as prospective only. Dalziel v. Rosenfeld, 265 N.Y. 76, 79, 191 N.E. 841; Book 1 McKinney's Consolidated Laws of New York, § 18. The general rule is that statutes are to be construed as prospective only and that it takes a clear expression of the legislative purpose to justify a retroactive application. Jacobus v. Colgate, 217 N.Y. 235, 240, 111 N.E. 837,

Ann.Cas.1917E, 369; Isola v. Weber, 147 N.Y. 329, 41 N.E. 704; Union Pacific R. R. v. Laramie Stock Yards, 231 U.S. 190, 34 S.Ct. 101, 58 L.Ed. 179; Endlich on the Interpretation of Statutes, §§ 271, 273. In Endlich on the Interpretation of Statutes the rule is stated in the following language (at p. 367): "It is chiefly where the enactment would prejudicially affect vested rights, or the legal character of past transactions, that the rule in question prevails. Every statute, it has been said, which takes away or impairs vested rights acquired under existing laws, or creates a new obligation, or imposes a new duty, or attaches a new disability in respect of transactions or considerations already past, must be presumed, out of respect to the Legislature, to be intended not to have a retrospective operation."

"To know the obligation of a contract we look to the laws in force at its making." W. B. Worthen Co. v. Kavanaugh, 295 U.S. 56, 60, 55 S.Ct. 555, 79 L.Ed. 1298, 97 A.L.R. 905. At the time the lease between the parties was executed in March, 1937, it was the established law of this State that landlord and tenant could enter into a contract exempting the landlord from liability for his own negligence and that such an agreement was not contrary to the public policy of the State. The rule which furnished a guide to all as to whether a contract between lessor and lessee might contain an exculpatory clause such as we have here was enunciated by the Court of Appeals in Kirshenbaum v. General Outdoor Adv. Co., 258 N.Y. 489, 180 N.E. 245, 84 A.L.R. 645, decided on March 3, 1932. In that case the court, in an opinion written by Kellogg, J., said (at p. 495): "Stipulations between a landlord and tenant, determining which shall bear a loss arising from non-repair or mis-repair of the tenement, and which shall be immune, are not matters of public concern. Moreover, the two stand upon equal terms; neither the one nor the other is under any form of compulsion to make the stipulations; either may equally well accept or refuse entry into the relationship of landlord and tenant. We think it clear that public policy does not condemn the immunity clause voluntarily agreed upon by these parties."

It is entirely reasonable to assume that in reliance upon the ruling in the Kirshenbaum case, this defendant entered into the lease containing an immunity clause similar to the one in that case and that it depended upon that ruling in efforts to protect itself against liability for damages sustained in the demised premises. It is fair also to assume that had this defendant believed that it would be liable in damages as claimed here, the cost of insuring itself against such liability would have been a consideration in the amount of rent fixed by the lease. A retroactive application of the statute would operate as a distinct hardship upon those, including this defendant, who rested upon the law as it had been set forth in the Kirshenbaum case and as it had existed up to June 5, 1937, when the new act became effective.

[The court here discusses briefly the constitutionality of sec. 234, if it were given retroactive effect.]

* * * We think that a retroactive construction of this statute might well result in its being declared unconstitutional. Where a statute is susceptible of two interpretations, one of which would render it unconstitutional and the other constitutional, the court should adopt that construction which saves its constitutionality. Matthews v. Matthews, 240 N.Y. 28, 35, 147 N.E. 237, 38 A.L.R. 1079.

For all of the foregoing reasons we conclude that section 234 of the Real Property Law is not retroactive and that it does not embrace agreements made prior to June 5, 1937, but that it applies only to contracts made on that date or thereafter. The determination of the Appellate Term and the judgment of the Municipal Court should accordingly be reversed and judgment directed for the defendant, with costs to the defendant in all courts.

MARTIN, P. J., GLENNON, DORE and CALLAHAN, JJ., concur.

Determination appealed from and judgment of the Municipal Court unanimously reversed and judgment directed for the defendant, with costs to the defendant in all courts.

NOTES

1. The decision of the main case was affirmed on appeal to the New York Court of Appeals, 284 N.Y. 630, 29 N.E.2d 938 (1940).

2. Did the court in the main case give the statute merely a literal interpretation? To what do the words, "shall be deemed", refer? "Deemed" by whom, and when? If "deemed" includes the decision of this court, did this court obey literally the direction of sec. 234 that such a covenant "shall be deemed void"?

3. In Addiss v. Selig, 264 N.Y. 274, 190 N.E. 490 (1934), the court, in construing a statute not to operate retroactively, said:

> "Statutes dealing with matters other than those of procedure will not be interpreted as retroactive unless such intent of the Legislature clearly appears from its terms."

Why should statutes dealing with procedural matters be treated differently?

4. The rule of construction that a statute is presumed, in the absence of clear expression to the contrary, to operate prospectively, is generally accepted. See, for example, Hassett v. Welch, 303 U.S. 303, 58 S.Ct. 559, 82 L. Ed. 858 (1938).

McBOYLE v. UNITED STATES

Supreme Court of the United States, 1931.
283 U.S. 25, 51 S.Ct. 340, 75 L.Ed. 816.

Certiorari to the Circuit Court of Appeals for the Tenth Circuit to review a judgment affirming a conviction under the Motor Vehicle Theft Act.

Mr. Justice HOLMES delivered the opinion of the Court.

The petitioner was convicted of transporting from Ottawa, Illinois, to Guymon, Oklahoma, an airplane that he knew to have been stolen, and was sentenced to serve three years' imprisonment and to pay a fine of $2,000. The judgment was affirmed by the Circuit Court of Appeals for the Tenth Circuit. 43 F.2d 273. A writ of certiorari was granted by this Court on the question whether the National Motor Vehicle Theft Act applies to aircraft. Act of October 29, 1919, c. 89, 41 Stat. 324; U.S.Code, Title 18, § 408. That Act provides: "Sec. 2. That when used in this Act: (a) The term 'motor vehicle' shall include an automobile, automobile truck, automobile wagon, motor cycle, or any other self-propelled vehicle not designed for running on rails; * * * Sec. 3. That whoever shall transport or cause to be transported in interstate or foreign commerce a motor vehicle, knowing the same to have been stolen, shall be punished by a fine of not more than $5,000, or by imprisonment of not more than five years, or both."

Section 2 defines the motor vehicles of which the transportation in interstate commerce is punished in § 3. The question is the meaning of the word "vehicle" in the phrase "any other self-propelled vehicle not designed for running on rails." No doubt etymologically it is possible to use the word to signify a conveyance working on land, water or air, and sometimes legislation extends the use in that direction, e. g., land and air, water being separately provided for, in the Tariff Act, September 22, 1922, c. 356, § 401(b), 42 Stat. 858, 948. But in everyday speech "vehicle" calls up the picture of a thing moving on land. Thus in Rev.Stats. § 4, intended, the Government suggests, rather to enlarge than to restrict the definition, vehicle includes every contrivance capable of being used "as a means of transportation on land." And this is repeated, expressly excluding aircraft, in the Tariff Act, June 17, 1930, c. 997, § 401(b); 46 Stat. 590, 708. So here, the phrase under discussion calls up the popular picture. For after including automobile truck, automobile wagon and motor cycle, the words "any other self-propelled vehicle not designed for running on rails" still indicate that a vehicle in the popular sense, that is a vehicle running on land, is the theme. It is a vehicle that runs, not something, not commonly called a vehicle, that flies. Airplanes were well known in 1919, when this statute was passed; but it is admitted that they were not mentioned in the reports or in the debates in Congress. It is impossible to read words that so carefully enumerate the different forms of motor vehicles and have no reference of any kind to aircraft, as including airplanes under a term that usage more and more precisely confines to a different class. The counsel for the petitioner have shown that the phraseology of the statute as to motor vehicles follows that of earlier statutes of Connecticut, Delaware, Ohio, Michigan and Missouri, not to mention the late Regulations of Traffic for the District of Columbia, Title 6, c. 9, § 242, none of which can be supposed to leave the earth.

Although it is not likely that a criminal will carefully consider the text of the law before he murders or steals, it is reasonable that a fair warning should be given to the world in language that the common world will understand, of what the law intends to do if a certain line is passed. To make the warning fair, so far as possible the line should be clear. When a rule of conduct is laid down in words that evoke in the common mind only the picture of vehicles moving on land, the statute should not be extended to aircraft, simply because it may seem to us that a similar policy applies, or upon the speculation that, if the legislature had thought of it, very likely broader words would have been used. United States v. Thind, 261 U.S. 204, 209, 43 S.Ct. 338, 67 L.Ed. 616.

Judgment reversed.

NOTES

1. "The rule that penal laws are to be construed strictly is perhaps not much less old than construction itself. It is founded on the tenderness of the law for the rights of individuals; and on the plain principle that the power of punishment is vested in the legislature, not in the judicial department. It is the legislature, not the court, which is to define a crime, and ordain its punishment.

"It is said that, notwithstanding this rule, the intention of the law maker must govern in the construction of penal, as well as other statutes. This is true. But this is not a new independent rule which subverts the old. It is a modification of the ancient maxim, and amounts to this, that though penal laws are to be construed strictly, they are not to be construed so strictly as to defeat the obvious intention of the legislature." Marshall, C. J., in United States v. Wiltberger, 5 Wheat. 76, 5 L.Ed. 37 (1820).

It has been suggested that, with the exception of cases involving honest attempts at compliance and statutes which are inapplicable to changed social or economic conditions or which prescribe a disproportionate penalty "there is no sound reason for a general doctrine of strict construction of penal statutes, and *prima facie* all such should have as liberal a construction as statutes generally." Hall, Strict or Liberal Construction of Penal Statutes, 48 Harv.L.Rev. 748, esp. 756 et seq. (1935).

2. On the requirement of definiteness in statutes, Connally v. General Construction Company, 269 U.S. 385, 46 S.Ct. 126, 70 L.Ed. 322 (1926), states the doctrine as follows:

"That the terms of a penal statute creating a new offense must be sufficiently explicit to inform those who are subject to it what conduct on their part will render them liable to its penalties, is a well-recognized requirement, consonant alike with ordinary notions of fair play and the settled rules of law. And a statute which either forbids or requires the doing of an act in terms so vague that men of common intelligence must necessarily guess at its meaning and differ as to its application, violates the first essential of due process of law. International Harvester Co. v. Kentucky, 234 U.S. 216, 221, 34 S.Ct. 853, 854, 58 L.Ed. 1284; Collins v. Kentucky, 234 U.S. 634, 638, 34 S.Ct. 924, 925, 58 L.Ed. 1510.

"The question whether given legislative enactments have been thus wanting in certainty has frequently been before this court. In some of the cases the statutes involved were upheld; in others, declared invalid. The precise point of differentiation in some instances is not easy of statement. But it will be enough for present purposes to say generally that the decisions of the court upholding statutes as sufficiently certain, rested upon the conclusion that they employed words or phrases having a technical or other special meaning, well enough known to enable those within their reach to correctly apply them, Hygrade Provision Co. v. Sherman, 266 U.S. 497, 502, 45 S.Ct. 141, 142, 69 L.Ed. 402; Omaechevarria v. Idaho, 246 U.S. 343, 348, 38 S.Ct. 323, 325, 62 L.Ed. 763, or a well-settled common law meaning, notwithstanding an element of degree in the definition as to which estimates might differ, Nash v. United States, 229 U.S. 373, 376, 33 S.Ct. 780, 781, 57 L.Ed. 1232; International Harvester Co. v. Kentucky, supra, p. 223 of 234 U.S., p. 855 of 34 S.Ct., or, as broadly stated by Mr. Chief Justice White in United States v. Cohen Grocery Co., 255 U.S. 81, 92, 41 S.Ct. 298, 301, 65 L.Ed. 516, 14 A.L.R. 1045, 'that, for reasons found to result either from the text of the statutes involved or the subjects with which they dealt, a standard of some sort was afforded.' See, also, Waters Pierce Oil Co. v. Texas (No. 1), 212 U.S. 86, 108, 29 S.Ct. 220, 226, 53 L.Ed. 417. Illustrative cases on the other hand are International Harvester Co. v. Kentucky, supra, Collins v. Kentucky, supra, and United States v. Cohen Grocery Co., supra, and cases there cited. The Cohen Grocery Case involved the validity of § 4 of the Food Control Act of 1917, which imposed a penalty upon any person who should make 'any unjust or unreasonable rate or charge in handling or dealing in or with any necessaries.' It was held that these words fixed no ascertainable standard of guilt, in that they forbade no specific or definite act."

While a number of the earlier cases discussing the requirement of definiteness focused—like the Cohen Grocery case cited supra—on statutes involving economic regulation, the requirement in recent years has figured more prominently as an instrument for the protection of First Amendment freedoms. See, e. g., Coates v. Cincinnati, 402 U.S. 611, 91 S.Ct. 1686, 29 L.Ed. 2d 214 (1971) where a city ordinance making it a criminal offense for "three or more persons to assemble * * * on any of the sidewalks * * * and there conduct themselves in a manner annoying to persons passing by * * *" was held unconstitutionally vague because it subjected the exercise of the right of assembly to an unascertainable standard. As observed in Cramp v. Board of Public Instruction, 368 U.S. 278, 287, 82 S.

Ct. 275, 280, 7 L.Ed.2d 285, 292 (1961): "The vice of unconstitutional vagueness is further aggravated where * * * the statute in question operates to inhibit the exercise of individual freedoms affirmatively protected by the Constitution."

A summary of the various aspects of the definiteness requirement is contained in Grayned v. Rockford, 408 U.S. 104, 92 S.Ct. 2294, 33 L.Ed.2d 222 (1972), upholding an anti-noise ordinance and cautioning wisely (p. 110) that "we can never expect mathematical certainty from our language."

For an illuminating and full discussion of definiteness in statutes, see Note, The Void-For-Vagueness Doctrine in the Supreme Court, 109 U. of Pa.L.Rev. 67 (1960).

UNITED STATES v. ALPERS

Supreme Court of the United States, 1950.
338 U.S. 680, 70 S.Ct. 352, 94 L.Ed. 457.

Mr. Justice MINTON delivered the opinion of the Court.

The question in this case is whether the shipment of obscene phonograph records in interstate commerce is prohibited by § 245 of the Criminal Code, which makes illegal the interstate shipment of any "obscene * * * book, pamphlet, picture, motion-picture film, paper, letter, writing, print, or other matter of indecent character."

Respondent was charged by an information in three counts with knowingly depositing with an express company for carriage in interstate commerce packages "containing certain matter of an indecent character, to-wit: phonograph records impressed with recordings of obscene, lewd, lascivious and filthy language and obscene, lewd, lascivious and filthy stories." Respondent, having waived jury trial, was found guilty by the District Court on two counts and was assessed a fine on each. The Court of Appeals reversed, 9 Cir., 175 F. 2d 137. We granted certiorari to examine the applicability of § 245 of the Criminal Code to the facts of this case. 338 U.S. 813, 70 S.Ct. 75.

The pertinent provisions of the statute are as follows: "Whoever shall * * * knowingly deposit or cause to be deposited with any express company or other common carrier [for carriage in interstate commerce] any obscene, lewd, or lascivious, or any filthy book, pamphlet, picture, motion-picture film, paper, letter, writing, print, or other matter of indecent character * * * shall be fined not more than $5,000 or imprisoned not more than five years, or both." 41 Stat. 1060, 18 U.S.C.A. § 1462.

It is conceded that the phonograph records were obscene and indecent. The only question is whether they come within the prohibition of the statute.

We are aware that this is a criminal statute and must be strictly construed. This means that no offense may be created except by the words of Congress used in their usual and ordinary sense. There are no constructive offenses. United States v. Resnick, 299 U.S. 207, 210, 57 S.Ct. 126, 127, 81 L.Ed. 127. The most important thing to be determined is the intent of Congress. The language of the statute may not be distorted under the guise of construction, or so limited by construction as to defeat the manifest intent of Congress. United States v. Raynor, 302 U.S. 540, 552, 58 S.Ct. 353, 358, 82 L.Ed. 413.

In interpreting the statute as applied to this case the Court of Appeals invoked the rule of *ejusdem generis*. Since the words "book, pamphlet, picture, motion-picture film, paper, letter, writing, print" appearing in the statute refer to objects comprehensible by sight only, the court construed the general words, "other matter of indecent character" to be limited to matter of the same genus. The Court of Appeals held phonograph records without the statute, so interpreted, since phonograph records are comprehended by the sense of hearing.

When properly applied, the rule of *ejusdem generis* is a useful canon of construction. But it is to be resorted to not to obscure and defeat the intent and purpose of Congress, but to elucidate its words and effectuate its intent. It cannot be employed to render general words meaningless. Mason v. United States, 260 U.S. 545, 554, 43 S.Ct. 200, 202, 67 L.Ed. 396. * * *

We think that to apply the rule of *ejusdem generis* to the present case would be "to defeat the obvious purpose of legislation." The obvious purpose of the legislation under consideration was to prevent the channels of interstate commerce from being used to disseminate any matter that, in its essential nature, communicates obscene, lewd, lascivious or filthy ideas. The statute is more fully set out in the margin.[91] It will be noted that Congress legislated with respect to a number of evils in addition to those proscribed by the portion of the statute under which respondent was charged. Statutes are construed in their entire context. This is a comprehensive statute, which should not be constricted by a mechanical rule of construction.

---

91. "Whoever shall bring or cause to be brought into the United States, or any place subject to the jurisdiction thereof, from any foreign country, or shall therein knowingly deposit or cause to be deposited with any express company or other common carrier [for carriage in interstate or foreign commerce] any obscene, lewd, or lascivious, or any filthy book, pamphlet, picture, motion-picture film, paper, letter, writing, print, or other matter of indecent character, or any drug, medicine, article, or thing designed, adapted, or intended for preventing conception, or producing abortion, or for any indecent or immoral use; or any written or printed card, letter, circular, book, pamphlet, advertisement, or notice of any kind giving information, directly or indirectly, where, how, or of whom, or by what means any of the hereinbefore mentioned articles, matters, or things may be obtained or made; or whoever shall knowingly take or cause to be taken from such express company or other common carrier any matter or thing the depositing of which for carriage is herein made unlawful, shall be fined not more than $5,000 or imprisoned not more than five years, or both." 18 U.S.C.A. § 1462.

We find nothing in the statute or its history to indicate that Congress intended to limit the applicable portion of the statute to such indecent matter as is comprehended through the sense of sight. True, this statute was amended in 1920 to include "motion-picture film." We are not persuaded that Congress, by adding motion-picture film to the specific provisions of the statute, evidenced an intent that obscene matter not specifically added was without the prohibition of the statute; nor do we think that Congress intended that only visual obscene matter was within the prohibition of the statute. The First World War gave considerable impetus to the making and distribution of motion-picture films. And in 1920 the public was considerably alarmed at the indecency of many of the films. It thus appears that with respect to this amendment, Congress was preoccupied with making doubly sure that motion-picture film was within the Act, and was concerned with nothing more or less.

Upon this record we could not hold, nor do we wish to be understood to hold, that the applicable portion of the statute is all-inclusive. As we have pointed out, the same statute contains other provisions relating to objects intended for an indecent or immoral use. But the portion of the statute here in issue does proscribe the dissemination of matter which, in its essential nature, communicates obscene ideas. We are clear therefore that obscene phonograph records are within the meaning of the Act. The judgment of the Court of Appeals is reversed, and the judgment of the District Court is affirmed.

Reversed.

Mr. Justice DOUGLAS took no part in the consideration or decision of this case.

Mr. Justice BLACK, with whom Mr. Justice FRANKFURTER and Mr. Justice JACKSON concur, dissenting.

I am unable to agree that the conduct of this respondent was made an offense by the language of the statutory provision on which his conviction rests. That provision forbids deposit with an express company, for interstate carriage, of "any obscene, lewd, or lascivious, or any filthy book, pamphlet, picture, motion-picture film, paper, letter, writing, print, or other matter of indecent character * * *." 18 U.S.C.A. § 1462. The crime with which respondent was charged involved phonograph records, which do not come under any specific category listed in the statute. Consequently the information against respondent could only charge violation of the provision's general language barring shipment of "other matter of indecent character." The Court sustains the conviction here by reasoning that a phonograph record is "matter" within the meaning of this congressional prohibition.

Our system of justice is based on the principle that criminal statutes shall be couched in language sufficiently clear to apprise people of the precise conduct that is prohibited. Judicial interpretation deviates from this salutory principle when statutory language is expanded to include conduct that Congress might have barred, but did not, by the language it used. Compare United States v. Weitzel, 246 U.S. 533, 543, 38 S.Ct. 381, 382, 62 L.Ed. 872, with United States v. Sullivan, 332 U.S. 689, 693–694, 68 S.Ct. 331, 334, 92 L.Ed. 297.

The reluctance of courts to expand the coverage of criminal statutes is particularly important where, as here, the statute results in censorship. According to dictionary definitions, "matter" undeniably includes phonograph records and the substances of which they are made. Indeed, dictionaries tell us that "matter" encompasses all tangibles and many intangibles, including material treated or to be treated in a book, speech, legal action or the like; matter for discussion, argument, exposition, etc.; and material treated in the medieval metrical romances. The many meanings of "matter" are warning signals against giving the word the broad construction adopted by the Court.

History is not lacking in proof that statutes like this may readily be converted into instruments for dangerous abridgments of freedom of expression. People of varied temperaments and beliefs have always differed among themselves concerning what is "indecent." Sculpture, paintings and literature, ranked among the classics by some, deeply offend the religious and moral sensibilities of others. And those which offend, however priceless or irreplaceable, have often been destroyed by honest zealots convinced that such destruction was necessary to preserve morality as they saw it.

Of course there is a tremendous difference between cultural treasures and the phonograph records here involved. But our decision cannot be based on that difference. Involved in this case is the vital question of whether courts should give the most expansive construction to general terms in legislation providing for censorship of publications or pictures found to be "indecent," "obscene," etc. Censorship in any field may so readily encroach on constitutionally protected liberties that courts should not add to the list of items banned by Congress.

In the provision relied on, as well as elsewhere in the Act, Congress used language carefully describing a number of "indecent" articles and forbade their shipment in interstate commerce. This specific list applied censorship only to articles that people could read or see; the Court now adds to it articles capable of use to produce sounds that people can hear. The judicial addition here may itself be small. But it is accomplished by a technique of broad interpretation which too often may be successfully invoked by the many people who want the law to proscribe what other people may say, write, hear, see, or read. I cannot agree to any departure from the sound practice of narrowly construing statutes which by censorship restrict liberty of communication.

Since Congress did not specifically ban the shipment of phonograph records, this Court should not do so.

NOTES

1. New York Penal Law, § 5.00 provides:
The rule that a penal statute is to be strictly construed does not apply to this chapter or any of the provisions thereof, but all such provisions must be construed according to the fair import of their terms, to promote justice and effect the objects of the law.

2. Compare, with respect to operation of the *ejusdem generis* rule, King v. United States, 379 U.S. 329, 85 S.Ct. 427, 13 L.Ed.2d 315 (1964).

3. 18 U.S.C.A. § 1715 provides criminal penalties for mailing "pistols, revolvers, and other firearms capable of being concealed on the person." If a defendant has put into the mails a sawed-off shotgun with a barrel length of 10 inches and an overall length of 22½ inches has he violated this Act? Does the rule of *ejusdem generis* help to resolve this issue? In U. S. v. Powell, 423 U.S. 87, 96 S.Ct. 316, 46 L.Ed.2d 228 (1975), the Supreme Court declined to apply the *ejusdem generis* rule to narrow the coverage of the general terms to embrace "only those weapons which could be concealed as readily as pistols or revolvers" and approved a conviction for mailing a sawed-off shotgun as described. The Court relied on evidence of a broad Congressional purpose in the statute's legislative history. The firearm statute was also upheld against the challenge that, as thus construed, it failed to meet constitutional standards of definiteness. Compare with Powell, the Gooch case, infra p. 562 (cited and quoted in the Court's opinion in Powell) and the Alpers case, supra (also referred to).

Noscitur A Sociis

Noscitur a sociis, a commonly used maxim of statutory interpretation, is illustrated by the following two cases.

1. In May and June, 1949, a strike occurred in the Michigan plants of the Ford Motor Company. As a result, necessary parts were not delivered to Ford's New Jersey assembly plants and these plants were partially shut down. The New Jersey local unions to which the New Jersey plant employees belonged did not authorize or approve or participate in the Michigan strike, and certain of the New Jersey employees sought unemployment compensation for the shutdown period. Award of benefits to these employees was contested by the Ford Motor Company but finally allowed in Ford Motor Co. v. New Jersey Dept. of Labor and Industry, 5 N.J. 494, 76 A.2d 256 (1950). At issue in this case was a statutory provision disqualifying any individual from such benefits "[f]or any week with respect to which it is found that his unemployment is due to a stoppage of work which exists because of a labor dispute at the factory, establishment, or other premises at which he is or was last employed." Ford urged, among other things, that the New Jersey and Michigan Ford plants were parts of a single Ford "establishment" within the meaning of the statute and that the stoppage was thus a disqualifying labor dis-

pute thereunder. This contention was answered by the Supreme Court of New Jersey in part as follows:

> "The force of the term [establishment] is on well-settled principles restrained by the accompanying words and the declared policy of the statute and the means employed for its execution. Ordinarily, the coupling of words denotes an intention that they shall be understood in the same general sense. The natural, ordinary and general meaning of terms and expressions may be limited, qualified and specialized by those in immediate association. Words of general and specific import take color from each other when associated together, and thus the word of general significance is modified by its associates of restricted sense. The general word is qualified by the particular word. * * * The principle is expressed in the doctrine of *noscitur a sociis* and the variant rule of *ejusdem generis*. A word is known from its associates. * * * If 'establishment' be given the broad significance urged by Ford, then the words 'factory' and 'other premises' would have no meaning whatever. * * * The phrase ' "factory, establishment or other premises" takes color, not from "establishment" as the plaintiff would have it, but rather from the word "factory." In common parlance * * * [factory] ordinarily means a single industrial plant. No one, for instance, would speak of the many units of General Motors Corporation, scattered as they are throughout several states, as a factory. * * * By embodying in the phrase the word "establishment," the legislative intent was to broaden the field of operation and extend the beneficence of the act to those employed in places other than factories,' such as banks, theaters, hotels, mercantile houses and other places not of the factorial class. [Citation omitted.]"

In deciding the statutory issue in favor of the employee-claimants, the court also considered the purpose of the act in question and the effect of other provisions thereof, as well as various case precedents.

2. Another federal case, Polaroid Corp. v. Commissioner, 278 F.2d 148 (1st Cir. 1960), affirmed sub nom. Jarecki v. G.D. Searle & Co., 367 U.S. 303, 81 S.Ct. 1579, 6 L.Ed.2d 859 (1961), construed a statutory provision prescribing special tax treatment for "income resulting from exploration, discovery, or prospecting * * *." The income in question came principally from the manufacture and sale of the Polaroid Land Camera, and the court refused to accept the taxpayer's contention that the term "discovery" must be taken to com-

prehend inventions of various kinds. In support of a narrower reading of this term, the court observed:

> "* * * [T]he word ['discovery'] is not isolated, but is sandwiched between the words 'exploration' and 'prospecting.' The government, accordingly, invokes the doctrine of *noscitur a sociis*. In case of ambiguity this is an 'appropriate and reasonable,' though not always determinative test. Russell Motor Car Co. v. United States, 261 U.S. 514, 519, 43 S.Ct. 428, 430, 67 L.Ed. 778 (1923). On a proper occasion 'such association justifies, if it does not imperatively require,' the application of a restricted meaning. Neal v. Clark, 95 U.S. 704, 709, 24 L.Ed. 586 (1877). It is particularly appropriate where one meaning of each of the grouped words has a readily apparent common denominator. Thus the words 'barrel,' 'lock' and 'stock' have each, individually, a number of different meanings. But if used in the phrase, 'lock, stock and barrel' there could be little difficulty in determining which particular one of the several meanings was intended. The word 'discovery' is clearly identified with the mining industry. * * * So also are 'exploration' and 'prospecting.' Accordingly we find a consistent, integrated unit, each portion of which casts light upon the other."

The court's interpretation was also supported by reference to other provisions, and to the general pattern, of the statute concerned, to legislative history, and to "difficult administrative problems" said to attend the construction urged by the taxpayer.

See, also, National Muffler Dealers Ass'n, Inc. v. United States, 440 U.S. 472, 99 S.Ct. 1304, 59 L.Ed.2d 519 (1979).

Last Antecedent

F.T.C. v. Mandel Brothers, Inc., 359 U.S. 385, 79 S.Ct. 818, 3 L.Ed.2d 893 (1959) considered, *inter alia*, the question whether defendant Mandel Brothers' retail sales slips, which failed to contain certain information, violated the provisions of Section 3 of the Fur Products Labeling Act forbidding false "invoicing." It was argued that a retail sales slip issued to a consumer was not an "invoice," which was defined in Section 2(f) of the Act as "a written account, memorandum or catalog, which is issued in connection with any commercial dealing in fur products or furs, and describes the particulars of any fur products or furs, transported or delivered to a purchaser, consignee, factor, bailee, correspondent, or agent, or any other person who is engaged in dealing commercially in fur products or furs." While the Court of Appeals had held that the limiting final clause "who is engaged in dealing commercially in fur products or furs" modified not only "any other person" but also all the preceding terms including "purchaser," thus excluding consumers, the Supreme Court ruled that this limiting clause was applicable only to the last antecedent, "any other person." It cited in support the maxim that referential and qualifying words and phrases refer solely to the last antecedent unless a contrary intention appears. Also advanced in support of this ruling was the purpose of the Act (characterized as a remedial statute) to protect consumers, a purpose confirmed by the legislative history text and title of the Act. It was further urged that the result thus reached was important for the effective administration of the Act and consonant with a consistent, contemporaneous administrative construction said to be "entitled to great weight."

TAYLOR v. MICHIGAN PUBLIC UTILITIES COMMISSION

Supreme Court of Michigan, 1922.
217 Mich. 400, 186 N.W. 485.

Original petition by Claude O. Taylor for a writ of mandamus directed to the Michigan Public Utilities Commission.

WIEST, J. Plaintiff, in behalf of himself and others like situated, by petition invoked the Michigan Public Utilities Commission to fix the rate to be paid for gas by consumers in the city of Grand Rapids, on the ground that the franchise contract between the city and the gas company had expired, and without right the company was exacting an excessive rate. The Commission declined to act on the ground that, the franchise having expired, the statute provides that the jurisdiction of the Commission can only be invoked by the municipality and not by consumers, residents of the city.

We are asked to issue the writ of mandamus compelling the commission to assume jurisdiction and to act upon the petition. The sole question presented is:

"Whether the Michigan Public Utilities Commission possesses the authority and power, under Act No. 419, P.A. Mich.1919, to receive said petition, entertain jurisdiction of the subject-matter, proceed with a hearing, and make an effective order or decree, both temporary and permanent, with respect to the gas rate in the city of Grand Rapids."

The statutes provides:

"Sec. 4. In addition to the rights, powers and duties vested in and imposed on said Commission by the preceding section, its jurisdiction shall be deemed to extend to and include the control and regulation, including the fixing of rates and charges, of all public utilities within this state producing, transmitting, delivering or furnishing gas for heating or lighting purposes for the public use. Subject to the provisions of this act the said Commission shall have the same measure of authority with reference to such utilities as is granted and conferred with respect to railroads and railroad companies under the various provisions of the statutes creating the Michigan Railroad Commission and defining its powers and duties. The power and authority granted by this act shall not extend to, or include, any power of regulation or control of any municipally owned utility; and it shall be the duty of said Commission on the request of any city or village to give advice and render such assistance as may be reasonable and expedient with respect to the operation of any utility owned and operated by such city or village. In no case shall the Commission have power to change or alter the rates or charges fixed in, or regulated by, any franchise or agreement heretofore or hereafter granted or made by any city, village or township. It shall be competent for any municipality and any public utility operating within the limits of said municipality, whether such utility is operating under the terms of a franchise or otherwise, to join in submitting to the Commission any question involving the fixing or determination of rates or charges, or the making of rules or conditions of service, and the Commission shall thereupon be empowered, and it shall be its duty to make full investigation as to all matters so submitted and to fix and establish such reasonable maximum rates and charges, and prescribe such rules and conditions of service and make such determination and order relative thereto as shall be just and reasonable. Such order when so made shall have like force and effect as other orders made under the provisions of this act. In any case where a franchise under which a utility is, or has been, operated, including street railways shall have heretofore expired or shall hereafter expire, the municipality shall have the right to petition the Commission to fix the rates and charges of said utility in accordance with the provisions of this act, or to make complaint as herein provided with reference to any practice, service or regulation of such utility, and thereupon said Commission shall have full jurisdiction in the premises.

* * *

"Sec. 8. Upon complaint in writing that any rate, classification, regulation or practice charged, made or observed by any public utility is unjust, inaccurate, or improper, to the prejudice of the complainant, the Commission shall proceed to investigate the matter," etc.

The Michigan Public Utilities Commission is a creature of the statute, has no inherent or common-law power, and its jurisdiction in any instance must affirmatively appear in the statute before it can be invoked or exercised.

"Expressio unius est exclusio alterius" has been a long time legal maxim and a safe guide in the construction of statutes marking powers not in accordance with the common law.

"No maxim of the law is of more general or uniform application, and it is never more applicable than in the construction and interpretation of statutes." Broom's Legal Maxims, p. 663, cited in Whitehead v. Cape Henry Syndicate, 105 Va. 463, 54 S.E. 306.

When what is expressed in a statute is creative, and not in a proceeding according to the course of the common law, it is exclusive, and the power exists only to the extent plainly granted. Where a statute creates and regulates and prescribes the mode and names the parties granted right to invoke its provisions, that mode must be followed, and none other, and such parties only may act. Lewis' Sutherland, Statutory Construction, §§ 491–493. The provisions of this statute cannot be enlarged by implication, as they expressly exclude any such intendment. The maxim "Expressum facit cessare tacitum" is also of applicability here. This law designates the actors, and when a law designates the actors none others can come upon the stage. The words of the statute are restrictive, and the designation therein of the municipality as the party to give the Commission jurisdiction operates to the exclusion of plaintiff. The matter falls squarely within the provision of the statute granting the exclusive privilege to the municipality to petition the Commission to fix the rates and charges in case the franchise of the company has expired.

We held in Home Telephone Co. v. Michigan Railroad Commission, 174 Mich. 219, 140 N.W. 496, that—

> "Grievances which afflict the community must be redressed by those to whom the law has intrusted the duty of interference."

We are of the opinion that, the franchise of the utility company having expired, the Commission could act only upon petition by the municipality.

The writ is denied, but, the question presented being of public interest, no costs are awarded.

STONE, BIRD, and STEERE, JJ., concurred with WIEST, J.

FELLOWS, C. J. I agree that the writ should be denied. I do not agree that the Michigan Public Utilities Commission is so limited in power as my Brother WIEST concludes it is. I recognize that the Commission is created by statute, and, to the statute creating it, it must look for its power. Its power must be specifically conferred, or must be necessarily incident to the specific grant.

I am not persuaded that the statute is ambiguous, but if it is open to construction I am not impressed that we should limit ourselves in seeking the legislative intent to the use of two legal maxims, however valuable aids they may be in the construction of a statute. If the statute is open to construction, we must seek to discover the legislative intent, and all aids available in such search should be called to our assistance. In Williams v. Mayor, etc., of Detroit, 2 Mich. 560, it was said:

> "It was strongly urged by the counsel for the complainant, on the argument of this cause, that the special enumeration of powers in article 14 of the Constitution, entitled 'Finance and Taxation,' exclude all others that might be implied, and that the maxims of the law, Expressio unius est exclusio alterius, and Expressum facit cessare tacitum, are strictly applicable in the construction of the Constitution with regard to the powers of the Legislature over the subject of taxation. That certain legal maxims or rules of construction, which have been found generally applicable, afford important aid in arriving at the intention of those who framed the law, every lawyer will admit, but that there are some instruments or laws to which such maxims cannot be strictly applied, without doing manifest violence to the plain intent of the framers of the law, is also a matter of common experience."

I shall not review the legislation creating the Interstate Commerce Commission and the various state commissions. Primarily this legislation was brought about by the discriminatory rates, services, and practices of the carriers advantageous to favored shippers. But the powers of these commissions have gradually been broadened to include general regulation of public utilities. The history of this legislation shows, not a contraction of the powers of the commissions, but an extension of them. The present Michigan Public Utilities Commission, created by Act 419, Public Acts 1919, took over all the powers of the former Michigan Railroad Commission, except as otherwise provided in the act creating it. It extended the jurisdiction of the Commission to bring within its regulatory power gas heating and lighting companies. The former Michigan Railroad Commission, as to the utilities it regulated, was not limited in its action exclusively to cases brought before it on complaint, but could act of its own motion. Sections 8130(e), 8133(f), 6699, C.L.1915.

Taking into consideration the fact that there has been a continued broadening of the powers of the commissions, including our own, it is difficult for me to conceive that it was the legislative intent to so circumscribe the power of the Commission as to prohibit it from acting under the facts disclosed by this record except on the application of the municipality. In permitting the municipality to institute proceedings, I do not conclude that it was the legislative intent to exclude all other proceedings. Such a construction would permit a gas heating and lighting company whose franchise had expired to operate at will without regulation as to rates, service, or discrimination, unless the municipality petitioned the Commission to take jurisdiction. I cannot feel that the language used in this act should be so construed, or that such was the legislative will.

While I am persuaded that the Commission had the power to accept and act upon the petition filed with it by the plaintiff and others, I do not think this court should, upon the facts appearing in this record, compel such action by mandamus, a discretionary writ. It appears from this record that the city of Grand Rapids and the gas company were negotiating at the time this application was filed with a view of arbitrating the rate, preliminary to the granting of a new franchise. These negotiations were being conducted in good faith, and I think the Commission might, in its discretion, withhold action until the city and the gas company had an opportunity to conclude their negotiations.

I therefore concur in the result reached by Justice WIEST that the writ should be denied.

MOORE, SHARPE and CLARK, JJ., concurred with FELLOWS, C. J.

GOOCH v. UNITED STATES

Supreme Court of the United States, 1936.
297 U.S. 124, 56 S.Ct. 395, 80 L.Ed. 522.

On Certificate from the United States Circuit Court of Appeals for the Tenth Circuit.

Arthur Gooch was convicted under the Federal Kidnapping Act, and he appealed to the Circuit Court of Appeals, which certified certain questions.

Mr. Justice McREYNOLDS delivered the opinion of the Court.

By permission of section 346, 28 U.S.C.A., the Circuit Court of Appeals, 10th Circuit, has certified two questions and asked instruction.

1. Is holding an officer to avoid arrest within the meaning of the phrase, "held for ransom or reward or otherwise," in the act of June 22, 1932, as amended May 18, 1934 (48 Stat. 781), 18 U.S.C.A. § 408a?

2. Is it an offense under section 408a, supra, to kidnap and transport a person in interstate commerce for the purpose of preventing the arrest of the kidnaper?

The statement revealing the facts and circumstances out of which the questions arise follows—

"Gooch was convicted and sentenced to be hanged under an indictment charging that he, with one Nix, kidnaped two officers at Paris, Texas, 'for the purpose of preventing his (Gooch's) arrest by the said peace officers in the State of Texas', and transported them in interstate commerce from Paris, Texas to Pushmataha County, Oklahoma, and at the time of the kidnaping did bodily harm and injury to one of the officers from which bodily harm the officer was suffering at the time of his liberation by Gooch and Nix in Oklahoma.

"The proof supports the charge. It established these facts: Gooch and Nix, while heavily armed, were accosted by the officers at Paris, Texas. To avoid arrest, Gooch and Nix resisted and disarmed the officers, unlawfully seized and kidnaped them and transported them by automobile from Texas to Oklahoma, and liberated them in the latter State. During the time Gooch and Nix were kidnaping the officers they inflicted serious bodily injury upon one of the officers, from which injury he was suffering at the time of such liberation in the State of Oklahoma."

The Act of June 22, 1932, c. 271, 47 Stat. 326, provided:

"That whoever shall knowingly transport or cause to be transported, or aid or abet in transporting, in interstate or foreign commerce, any person who shall have been unlawfully seized, confined, inveigled, decoyed, kidnaped, abducted, or carried away by any means whatsoever and held for ransom or reward shall, upon conviction, be punished by imprisonment in the penitentiary for such term of years as the court, in its discretion, shall determine."

The amending Act of May 18, 1934, c. 301, 48 Stat. 781, 18 U.S.C.A. § 408a, declares:

"Whoever shall knowingly transport or cause to be transported, or aid or abet in transporting, in interstate or foreign commerce, any person who shall have been unlawfully seized, confined, inveigled, decoyed, kidnaped, abducted, or carried away by any means whatsoever and held for ransom or reward *or otherwise, except, in the case of a minor, by a parent thereof,* shall, upon conviction, be punished (1) by death if the verdict of the jury shall so recommend, provided that the sentence of death shall not be imposed by the court if, prior to its imposition, the kidnaped person has been liberated unharmed, or (2) if the death penalty shall not apply nor be imposed the convicted person shall be punished by imprisonment in the penitentiary for such term of years as the court in its discretion shall determine."

Counsel for Gooch submit that the words "ransom or reward" import "some pecuniary consideration or payment of something of value"; that as the statute is criminal the familiar rule of ejusdem generis must be strictly applied; and finally, it cannot properly be said that a purpose to prevent arrest and one to obtain money or something of pecuniary value are similar in nature.

The original act (1932) required that the transported person should be held "for ransom or reward." It did not undertake to define the words and nothing indicates an intent to limit their meaning to benefits of pecuniary value. Generally, reward implies something given in return for good or evil done or received.

Informed by experience during two years, and for reasons satisfactory to itself, Congress undertook by the 1934 act to enlarge the earlier one and to clarify its purpose by inserting "or otherwise, except, in the case of a minor, by a parent thereof," immediately after "held for ransom or reward." The history of the enactment emphasized this view.

The Senate Judiciary Committee made a report, copied in the margin,[92] recommending passage of the amending bill and pointing out the broad purpose intended to be accomplished.

The House Judiciary Committee made a like recommendation and said:

> "This bill, as amended, proposes three changes in the act known as the 'Federal Kidnaping Act.' First, it is proposed to add the words 'or otherwise, except, in the case of a minor, by a parent thereof.' This will extend Federal jurisdiction under the act to persons who have been kidnaped

---

92. "The Committee on the Judiciary, having had under consideration the bill (S. 2252) to amend the act forbidding the transportation of kidnaped persons in interstate commerce, reports the same favorably to the Senate and recommends that the bill do pass.

"The purpose and need of this legislation are set out in the following memorandum from the Department of Justice:

"S. 2252; H.R. 6918: This is a bill to amend the act forbidding the transportation of kidnaped persons in interstate commerce—act of June 22, 1932 (U.S.C.A., ch. 271, title 18, sec. 408a), commonly known as the 'Lindbergh Act.' This amendment adds thereto the word 'otherwise' so that the act as amended reads: 'Whoever shall knowingly transport * * * any person who shall have been unlawfully seized * * * and held for ransom or reward or otherwise shall, upon conviction, be punished. * * *' The object of the addition of the word 'otherwise' is to extend the jurisdiction of this act to persons who have been kidnaped and held, not only for reward, but for any other reason.

"In addition, this bill adds a proviso to the Lindbergh Act to the effect that in the absence of the return of the person kidnaped and in the absence of the apprehension of the kidnaper during a period of 3 days, the presumption arises that such person has been transported in interstate or foreign commerce, but such presumption is not conclusive.

"I believe that this is a sound amendment which will clear up border-line cases, justifying Federal investigation in most of such cases and assuring the validity of Federal prosecution in numerous instances in which such prosecution would be questionable under the present form of this act. S.Rep. 534, 73d Cong., 2d Sess., March 22, 1934."

and held, not only for reward, but for any other reason, except that a kidnaping by a parent of his child is specifically exempted. * * * H.Rep.1457, 73d Cong., 2d Sess., May 3, 1934."

Evidently, Congress intended to prevent transportation in interstate or foreign commerce of persons who were being unlawfully restrained in order that the captor might secure some benefit to himself. And this is adequately expressed by the words of the enactment.

The rule of ejusdem generis, while firmly established, is only an instrumentality for ascertaining the correct meaning of words when there is uncertainty. Ordinarily, it limits general terms which follow specific ones to matters similar to those specified; but it may not be used to defeat the obvious purpose of legislation. And, while penal statutes are narrowly construed, this does not require rejection of that sense of the words which best harmonizes with the context and the end in view. United States v. Hartwell, 6 Wall. 385, 395, 18 L.Ed. 830; Johnson v. Southern Pacific Co., 196 U.S. 1–17, 18, 25 S.Ct. 158, 49 L.Ed. 363; United States v. Bitty, 208 U.S. 393, 402, 28 S.Ct. 396, 52 L.Ed. 543; United States v. Mescall, 215 U.S. 26–31, 32, 30 S.Ct. 19, 54 L.Ed. 77.

Holding an officer to prevent the captor's arrest is something done with the expectation of benefit to the transgressor. So also is kidnaping with purpose to secure money. These benefits, while not the same, are similar in their general nature and the desire to secure either of them may lead to kidnaping. If the word "reward," as commonly understood, is not itself broad enough to include benefits expected to follow the prevention of an arrest, they fall within the broad term, "otherwise."

The words "except, in the case of a minor, by a parent thereof" emphasize the intended result of the enactment. They indicate legislative understanding that in their absence a parent, who carried his child away because of affection, might subject himself to condemnation of the statute. Brown v. Maryland, 12 Wheat. 419, 438, 6 L.Ed. 678.

Both questions must be answered in the affirmative.

NOTE

United States v. Healy, 376 U.S. 75, 84 S.Ct. 553, 11 L.Ed.2d 527 (1964) considered a federal grand jury indictment alleging that defendants had kidnaped at gunpoint the pilot of a private airplane and compelled him to transport them from Florida to Cuba. Count 1 of the indictment charged defendants with having thereby violated 18 U.S.C.A. § 1201, the Federal Kidnaping Act. The District Court for the Southern District of Florida, before trial, dismissed the indictment on several grounds, indicating in regard to Count 1 that a kidnaping is not "for ransom or reward or otherwise" as required by § 1201(a), unless committed for the pecuniary benefit of the defendant. Reversing the judgment of dismissal, the Supreme Court made the following observations on this aspect of the case (pp. 81–82):

> "By interpreting 18 U.S.C.A. § 1201 to require a motive of pecuniary profit, the District Court disregarded the plain holding of Gooch v. United States * * *. The Court's conclusion [in the Gooch case] that the amended statute covered the facts before it was clearly in accord with the congressional purpose.
>
> "The Courts of Appeals have consistently followed *Gooch* * * * and appellees do not challenge the authority of that case. While recognizing that the statute is not limited to kidnapings for pecuniary gain, they assert that it is restricted to kidnapings for an otherwise *illegal* purpose. This contention is without support in the language of the provision, its legislative history, judicial decisions, or reason. The wording certainly suggests no distinction based on the ultimate purpose of a kidnaping; were one intended, the exclusion of parent-child kidnapings would have been largely superfluous, since such conduct is rarely the result of an intrinsically illegal purpose. Nothing in the reports or debates supports appellees' position. In two cases, Wheatley v. United States, 159 F.2d 599, 600 [(4th Cir. 1946)]; Bearden v. United States, 304 F.2d 532 (5th Cir. 1962) (judgment vacated on another ground 372 U.S. 252, 83 S.Ct. 875, 9 L.Ed.2d 732 (1963)), Courts of Appeals have assumed that the applicability of the statute does not turn on the illegality of the ultimate purpose of the kidnaper. No policy considerations support appellees' strained reading of 18 U.S.C.A. § 1201. A murder committed to accelerate the accrual of one's rightful inheritance is hardly less heinous than one committed to facilitate a theft; by the same token, we find no compelling correlation between the propriety of the ultimate purpose sought to be furthered by a kidnaping and the undesirability of the act of kidnaping itself. Appellees rely on the principle of strict construction of penal statutes, but that maxim is hardly a directive to this Court to invent distinctions neither reflective of the policy behind congressional enactments nor intimated by the words used to implement the legislative goal."

SECTION 9. SOME STATUTORY PROBLEMS

A. A PROBLEM ON THE USE OF MAXIMS

The Rivers and Harbors Act of 1899, 30 Stat. 1121, was adopted by the 55th Congress of the United States on March 3, 1899. The provisions of that Act, which are pertinent to this problem and some subsequent problems in this book, are as follows:

Chap. 425.—An Act making appropriations for the construction, repair, and preservation of certain public works on rivers and harbors, and for other purposes.

Be it enacted by the Senate and House of Representatives of the United States of America in Congress assembled, That the following sums of money be, and are hereby, appropriated, to be paid out of any money in the Treasury not otherwise appropriated, to be immediately available, and to be expended under the direction of the Secretary of War [93] and the supervision of the Chief of Engineers, for the construction, completion, repair, and preservation of the public works hereinafter named:

Improving Moosabec Bar, Maine: Completing improvement, eleven thousand dollars.

For construction of breakwater from Mount Desert to Porcupine Island, Maine: Continuing improvement, twenty thousand dollars.

Improving harbor at Sullivan Falls, Maine, in accordance with the approved project, five thousand dollars.

Improving Carvers Harbor, at Vinalhaven, Maine: Continuing improvement, fifteen thousand dollars. * * *

[The remainder of Section 1, consisting of almost twenty-nine pages of appropriations similar to those quoted immediately above, is omitted; as are also Section 2, making an appropriation for surveys, examinations and incidental repairs for which there are no special appropriations, Sections 3–6, providing for investigations of the advisability of building a canal across Panama, and Sections 7 and 8, requiring certain reports and information from the Secretary of War and the Chief of Engineers regarding river and harbor works.]

SEC. 9. That it shall not be lawful to construct or commence the construction of any bridge, dam, dike, or causeway over or in any port, roadstead, haven, harbor, canal, navigable river, or other navigable water of the United States until the consent of Congress to the building of such structures shall have been obtained and until the plans for the same shall have been submitted to and approved by the Chief of Engineers and by the Secretary of War: *Provided,* That such structures may be built under authority of the legislature of a State across rivers and other waterways the navigable portions of which lie wholly within the limits of a single State, provided the location and plans thereof are submitted to and approved by the Chief of Engineers and by the Secretary of War before construction is commenced: *And provided further,* That when plans for any bridge or other structure have been approved by the Chief of Engineers and by the Secretary of War, it shall not be lawful to deviate from such plans either before or after completion of the structure unless the modification of said plans has previously been submitted to and received the approval of the Chief of Engineers and of the Secretary of War.

---

93. [The title of the Secretary of War was changed to "Secretary of the Army" by § 205(a) of the Act of July 26, 1947, 61 Stat. 501.—Ed.]

SEC. 10. That the creation of any obstruction not affirmatively authorized by Congress, to the navigable capacity of any of the waters of the United States is hereby prohibited; and it shall not be lawful to build or commence the building of any wharf, pier, dolphin, boom, weir, breakwater, bulkhead, jetty, or other structures in any port, roadstead, haven, harbor, canal, navigable river, or other water of the United States, outside established harbor lines, or where no harbor lines have been established, except on plans recommended by the Chief of Engineers and authorized by the Secretary of War; and it shall not be lawful to excavate or fill, or in any manner to alter or modify the course, location, condition, or capacity of, any port, roadstead, haven, harbor, canal, lake, harbor of refuge, or inclosure within the limits of any breakwater, or of the channel of any navigable water of the United States, unless the work has been recommended by the Chief of Engineers and authorized by the Secretary of War prior to beginning the same.

SEC. 11. That where it is made manifest to the Secretary of War that the establishment of harbor lines is essential to the preservation and protection of harbors he may, and is hereby authorized to cause such lines to be established, beyond which no piers, wharves, bulkheads, or other works shall be extended or deposits made, except under such regulations as may be prescribed from time to time by him: *Provided,* That whenever the Secretary of War grants to any person or persons permission to extend piers, wharves, bulkheads, or other works, or to make deposits in any tidal harbor or river of the United States beyond any harbor lines established under authority of the United States, he shall cause to be ascertained the amount of tide water displaced by any such structure or by any such deposits, and he shall, if he deem it necessary, require the parties to whom the permission is given to make compensation for such displacement either by excavating in some part of the harbor, including tidewater channels between high and low water mark, to such an extent as to create a basin for as much tide water as may be displaced by such structure or by such deposits, or in any other mode that may be satisfactory to him.

SEC. 12. That every person and every corporation that shall violate any of the provisions of sections nine, ten, and eleven of this Act, or any rule or regulation made by the Secretary of War in pursuance of the provisions of the said section fourteen,[94] shall be deemed guilty of a misdemeanor, and on conviction thereof shall be punished by a fine not exceeding twenty-five hundred dollars nor less than five hundred dollars, or by imprisonment (in the case of a natural person) not exceeding one year, or by both such punishments, in the discretion of the court. And further, the removal of any struc-

---

94. [The Act of Feb. 20, 1900, 31 Stat. 31, amended this section by striking out the word "fourteen" and inserting in lieu thereof the word "eleven." —Ed.]

tures or parts of structures erected in violation of the provisions of the said sections may be enforced by the injunction of any circuit court [95] exercising jurisdiction in any district in which such structures may exist, and proper proceedings to this end may be instituted under the direction of the Attorney-General of the United States.

SEC. 13. That it shall not be lawful to throw, discharge, or deposit, or cause, suffer, or procure to be thrown, discharged, or deposited either from or out of any ship, barge, or other floating craft of any kind, or from the shore, wharf, manufacturing establishment, or mill of any kind, any refuse matter of any kind or description whatever other than that flowing from streets and sewers and passing therefrom in a liquid state, into any navigable water of the United States, or into any tributary of any navigable water from which the same shall float or be washed into such navigable water; and it shall not be lawful to deposit, or cause, suffer, or procure to be deposited material of any kind in any place on the bank of any navigable water, or on the bank of any tributary of any navigable water, where the same shall be liable to be washed into such navigable water, either by ordinary or high tides, or by storms or floods, or otherwise, whereby navigation shall or may be impeded or obstructed: *Provided,* That nothing herein contained shall extend to, apply to, or prohibit the operations in connection with the improvement of navigable waters or construction of public works, considered necessary and proper by the United States officers supervising such improvement or public work: *And provided further,* That the Secretary of War, whenever in the judgment of the Chief of Engineers anchorage and navigation will not be injured thereby, may permit the deposit of any material above mentioned in navigable waters, within limits to be defined and under conditions to be prescribed by him, provided application is made to him prior to depositing such material; and whenever any permit is so granted the conditions thereof shall be strictly complied with, and any violation thereof shall be unlawful.

SEC. 14. That it shall not be lawful for any person or persons to take possession of or make use of for any purpose, or build upon, alter, deface, destroy, move, injure, obstruct by fastening vessels thereto or otherwise, or in any manner whatever impair the usefulness of any sea wall, bulkhead, jetty, dike, levee, wharf, pier, or other work built by the United States, or any piece of plant, floating or otherwise, used in the construction of such work under the control of the United States, in whole or in part, for the preservation and improvement of any of its navigable waters or to prevent floods, or as boundary marks, tide gauges, surveying stations, buoys, or other established marks, nor remove for ballast or other purposes any stone or other material composing such works: *Provided,* That the Secre-

---

95. [The powers and duties of circuit courts were transferred to district courts by § 291 of the Act of March 3, 1911, 36 Stat. 1167.—Ed.]

tary of War may, on the recommendation of the Chief of Engineers, grant permission for the temporary occupation or use of any of the aforementioned public works when in his judgment such occupation or use will not be injurious to the public interest.

SEC. 15. That it shall not be lawful to tie up or anchor vessels or other craft in navigable channels in such a manner as to prevent or obstruct the passage of other vessels or craft; or to voluntarily or carelessly sink or permit or cause to be sunk, vessels or other craft in navigable channels; or to float loose timber and logs, or to float what is known as sack rafts of timber and logs in streams or channels actually navigated by steamboats in such manner as to obstruct, impede, or endanger navigation.[96] And whenever a vessel, raft, or other craft is wrecked and sunk in a navigable channel, accidentally or otherwise, it shall be the duty of the owner of such sunken craft to immediately mark it with a buoy or beacon during the day and a lighted lantern at night, and to maintain such marks until the sunken craft is removed or abandoned, and the neglect or failure of the said owner so to do shall be unlawful; and it shall be the duty of the owner of such sunken craft to commence the immediate removal of the same, and prosecute such removal diligently, and failure to do so shall be considered as an abandonment of such craft, and subject the same to removal by the United States as hereinafter provided for.

SEC. 16. That every person and every corporation that shall violate, or that shall knowingly aid, abet, authorize, or instigate a violation of the provisions of sections thirteen, fourteen, and fifteen of this Act shall be guilty of a misdemeanor, and on conviction thereof shall be punished by a fine not exceeding twenty-five hundred dollars nor less than five hundred dollars, or by imprisonment (in the case of a natural person) for not less than thirty days nor more than one year, or by both such fine and imprisonment, in the discretion of the court, one-half of said fine to be paid to the person or persons giving information which shall lead to conviction. And any and every master, pilot, and engineer, or person or persons acting in such capacity, respectively, on board of any boat or vessel who shall knowingly engage in towing any scow, boat, or vessel loaded with any material specified in section thirteen of this Act to any point or place of deposit or discharge in any harbor or navigable water, elsewhere than within the limits defined and permitted by the Secretary of War, or who shall wilfully injure or destroy any work of the United States contemplated in section fourteen of this Act, or who shall wilfully obstruct the channel of any waterway in the manner contemplated in section fifteen of this Act, shall be deemed guilty of a violation of this Act, and shall upon conviction be punished as hereinbefore provided in this section, and shall also have his license revoked or sus-

---

96. [The Act of May 9, 1900, 31 Stat. 172, amended this section by authorizing the Secretary of War to make regulations governing the running of loose logs, steamboats, and rafts on certain streams.—Ed.]

pended for a term to be fixed by the judge before whom tried and convicted. And any boat, vessel, scow, raft, or other craft used or employed in violating any of the provisions of sections thirteen, fourteen, and fifteen of this Act shall be liable for the pecuniary penalties specified in this section, and in addition thereto for the amount of the damages done by said boat, vessel, scow, raft, or other craft, which latter sum shall be placed to the credit of the appropriation for the improvement of the harbor or waterway in which the damage occurred, and said boat, vessel, scow, raft, or other craft may be proceeded against summarily by way of libel in any district court of the United States having jurisdiction thereof.

SEC. 17. That the Department of Justice shall conduct the legal proceedings necessary to enforce the foregoing provisions of sections nine to sixteen, inclusive, of this Act; and it shall be the duty of district attorneys of the United States to vigorously prosecute all offenders against the same whenever requested to do so by the Secretary of War or by any of the officials hereinafter designated, and it shall furthermore be the duty of said district attorneys to report to the Attorney-General of the United States the action taken by him against offenders so reported, and a transcript of such reports shall be transmitted to the Secretary of War by the Attorney-General;
* * *.

* * *

SEC. 19. That whenever the navigation of any river, lake, harbor, sound, bay, canal, or other navigable waters of the United States shall be obstructed or endangered by any sunken vessel, boat, water craft, raft, or other similar obstruction, and such obstruction has existed for a longer period than thirty days, or whenever the abandonment of such obstruction can be legally established in a less space of time, the sunken vessel, boat, water craft, raft, or other obstruction shall be subject to be broken up, removed, sold, or otherwise disposed of by the Secretary of War at his discretion, without liability for any damage to the owners of the same: *Provided,* That in his discretion, the Secretary of War may cause reasonable notice of such obstruction of not less than thirty days, unless the legal abandonment of the obstruction can be established in a less time, to be given by publication, addressed "To whom it may concern," in a newspaper published nearest to the locality of the obstruction, requiring the removal thereof: *And provided also,* That the Secretary of War may, in his discretion, at or after the time of giving such notice, cause sealed proposals to be solicited by public advertisement, giving reasonable notice of not less than ten days, for the removal of such obstruction as soon as possible after the expiration of the above specified thirty days' notice, in case it has not in the meantime been so removed, these proposals and contracts, at his discretion, to be conditioned that such vessel, boat, water craft, raft, or other obstruction, and all cargo and property contained therein, shall become the property of the contractor, and the contract shall be awarded to the bidder making the proposition most advantageous to the United States: *Provided,* That such bidder shall give satisfactory security to execute the work: *Provided further,* That any money received from the sale of any such wreck, or from any contractor for the removal of wrecks, under this paragraph shall be covered into the Treasury of the United States.

SEC. 20. That under emergency, in the case of any vessel, boat, water craft, or raft, or other similar obstruction, sinking or grounding, or being unnecessarily delayed in any Government canal or lock, or in any navigable waters mentioned in section nineteen, in such manner as to stop, seriously interfere with, or specially endanger navigation, in the opinion of the Secretary of War, or any agent of the United States to whom the Secretary may delegate proper authority, the Secretary of War or any such agent shall have the right to take immediate possession of such boat, vessel, or other water craft, or raft, so far as to remove or to destroy it and to clear immediately the canal, lock, or navigable waters aforesaid of the obstruction thereby caused, using his best judgment to prevent any unnecessary injury; and no one shall interfere with or prevent such removal or destruction: *Provided,* That the officer or agent charged with the removal or destruction of an obstruction under this section may in his discretion give notice in writing to the owners of any such obstruction requiring them to remove it: *And provided further,* That the expense of removing any such obstruction as aforesaid shall be a charge against such craft and cargo; and if the owners thereof fail or refuse to reimburse the United States for such expense within thirty days after notification, then the officer or agent aforesaid may sell the craft or cargo, or any part thereof that may not have been destroyed in removal, and the proceeds of such sale shall be covered into the Treasury of the United States.

Such sum of money as may be necessary to execute this section and the preceding section of this Act is hereby appropriated out of any money in the Treasury not otherwise appropriated, to be paid out on the requisition of the Secretary of War.

That all laws or parts of laws inconsistent with the foregoing sections ten [97] to twenty, inclusive, of this Act are hereby repealed: *Provided,* That no action begun, or right of action accrued, prior to the passage of this Act shall be affected by this repeal.

* * *

[Omitted are: Section 18, giving the Secretary of War powers in regard to bridges obstructing navigation, Section 21, dealing with bids on the completion of certain rivers and harbors projects, and Section 22, directing the Secretary of War to make preliminary surveys concerning the advisability of improving certain named rivers and harbors.]

---

97. [The Act of Feb. 20, 1900, 31 Stat. 31, amended this section by striking out the word "ten" and inserting in lieu thereof the word "nine."—Ed.]

Sec. 9   *SOME STATUTORY PROBLEMS*   573

Wesley Winge, a retired airline pilot, owns an air taxi and aerial sightseeing service that flies customers up and down the Hudson Valley and along the shorelines of New York, New Jersey and Connecticut. Two seaplanes used by the service are based at a facility located on the Hudson River some distance north of New York City. In addition to a small headquarters building and a pier, to which the planes are moored, the facility includes an old stone breakwater on which there is a storage tank of moderate size used to store aviation gasoline.

Not far from Winge's facility is the local branch headquarters of another organization, the Hudson Valley Preservation League (HVPL), a volunteer group whose members maintain an "anti-pollution watch" along the River in an effort to restore it to something like its former unpolluted state. Winge's facility has been under close observation for some time as a suspected pollution source.

Recently two events occurred which brought Winge into confrontation with HVPL and the law enforcement authorities.

First, owing to a defective valve, a substantial quantity of commercially valuable 100-octane aviation gasoline leaked into the River one night from the gas tank of one of the seaplanes. The defect was unknown to Winge and had not been turned up in the course of reasonably thorough inspections by his mechanic. On discovering the leak in the morning, Winge acted promptly to repair it. The results of the night's leakage were observed by HVPL watchers and reported to the authorities.

Second, a short while thereafter, Winge deemed it necessary to empty and did empty his storage tank (one-sixth full at the time) of its remaining fuel, causing this fuel to be discharged into the River. The discharged fuel had been found to contain some impurities, stemming either from the condition of the tank or of the gas itself which had been purchased at cut rates. These impurities might have posed some flight dangers. Winge emptied the tank in order to clean it and refill it with fresh higher quality gasoline. The discharge was observed by HVPL watchers and was again reported to authorities.

Winge is charged with twice violating Section 13 of the Rivers and Harbors Act of 1899, supra.

What are the statutory issues?

What maxim arguments might be used in arguing each of the principal issues on behalf of (a) Wesley Winge and (b) the United States?

N.B. Be sure to read the whole Act (as presented in the preceding pages), and not Section 13 alone, in working out answers to the preceding questions.

B. A PROBLEM UNDER THE RIVERS AND HARBORS ACT

The Kent Power and Light Co. (KPL), a privately owned utility, has since 1969 operated a nuclear power facility at Columbia Point on the shores of King's River, a navigable waterway, in the State of Kent. KPL's Columbia Point facility draws water at normal temperatures from King's River to cool the nuclear reactor and then returns this same water to the River. The used water is discharged into the River in the same state in which it was originally received, except that the temperature of the water as discharged is substantially in excess of normal river-water temperatures.

In 1979, KPL was indicted for violation of the Rivers and Harbors Act of 1899 on the ground that KPL's discharge of heated water violated Section 13 of that Act. It was averred that KPL's discharge of heated water had a devastating effect on the marine life of King's River, which at the place of discharge had previously supported a rare combination of terrestrial, marine and amphibious life. KPL did not seek to deny or disprove that its plant discharged heated water in the fashion, and with the effect, described.

After trial without a jury (the jury had been waived by KPL) in the United States District Court for Kent, KPL was convicted of violating Section 13 and substantial fines were assessed against it pursuant to Section 16. KPL appealed, the sole question presented for review on this appeal being whether or not KPL's admitted activities violated Section 13.

Assume you are a law clerk to one of the judges participating in the decision on KPL's appeal. The judge asks you to recommend how he should vote on the question presented, and to do all the appropriate research and prepare a draft opinion for him on the matter. You are to presume that all procedural requirements have been complied with and that the question indicated is properly before the court for decision.

As to your research, the text of the Rivers and Harbors Act insofar as pertinent to this problem is set out in the preceding problem on the use of maxims, supra, and should be carefully studied as a basis for identifying and dealing with the issues. Your thorough research reveals, for the purposes of this problem, only the following additional pertinent material:

    1. Section 13 of the Rivers and Harbors Act of 1899 was based on, and repealed and replaced, two pre-existing federal statutes:

        a. an 1890 statutory provision which made it unlawful to discharge, or suffer to be discharged, in navigable waters "any ballast, stone, slate, gravel, earth, rubbish, wreck, filth, slabs, sawdust, slag, cinders, ashes, refuse, or other waste of any kind * * * which shall tend to impede or obstruct navigation."

b. an 1894 statutory provision which made it unlawful to discharge, or suffer to be discharged, in harbors or navigable rivers for which Congress had appropriated money for improvement, "any ballast, refuse, dirt, ashes, cinders, mud, sand, dredgings, sludge, acid, or any other matter of any kind other than that flowing from streets and sewers and passing therefrom in a liquid state."

These two pre-existing federal statutes in turn drew upon two earlier federal statutes, still in effect, relating to New York Harbor:

c. an 1886 Act making it unlawful to discharge, or permit discharge of, "any ballast, stone, slate, gravel, earth, rubbish, wreck, filth, slabs, sawdust, slag, cinders, or other refuse or mill waste of any kind" into New York Harbor.

d. an 1888 Act (whose title describes it as "an Act to prevent obstructive or injurious deposits") whereby it is forbidden to discharge, or permit discharge, within New York Harbor, of "refuse, dirt, ashes, cinders, mud, sand, dredgings, sludge, acid, or any other matter of any kind other than that flowing from streets and sewers and passing therefrom in a liquid state."

2. During Senate debate on the bill which became the Rivers and Harbors Act of 1899, the Chairman of the Senate standing committee recommending adoption of the bill commented on the menace to navigation posed by waste disposal from factories, ships, etc. and stated that the bill (drafted by the Chief of Engineers) "seeks to consolidate prior Acts, i. e., those of 1890 and 1894, into one Act, and it is generally in accord with these Acts except that slight changes have been made to remove ambiguities." Several other members of the Senate standing committee that recommended the bill noted in debate that the 1899 Act was "intended to codify earlier Acts without effecting any major substantive change." An opponent of the bill remarked in debate that it "appears to narrow prior coverage in various respects."

3. In 1966, the United States Supreme Court ruled in United States v. Standard Oil Co., 384 U.S. 224, 86 S.Ct. 1427, 16 L.Ed.2d 492, that the defendant oil company was subject to criminal penalties for violation of Section 13 of

the Rivers and Harbors Act of 1899 as a result of having accidentally discharged a quantity of commercially valuable and highly flammable 100-octane aviation gasoline into navigable waters. A majority of the Court (per Douglas, J.), commenting on the legislative history (including the predecessor statutes) of the 1899 Act, stated that the "serious injury sought to be remedied was caused in part by obstacles that impeded navigation and in part by pollution." It concluded that the key words of Section 13 included "all foreign substances and pollutants apart from those 'flowing from streets and sewers and passing therefrom in a liquid state' into the watercourse."

4. Until December 1970, the Corps of Engineers' published interpretation of Section 13 had for a number of years construed that section's prohibitions as limited to discharges that threatened to impede navigation. In December 1970, the Corps—joined by the Department of Justice—published revised views construing Section 13 as applying to pollutant discharges not interfering with navigation.

5. a. Federal Water Pollution Control legislation, originating as far back as 1948, made provision during the 1960's and early 1970's for standards (to be determined in large part by the states) of water quality to govern discharge of pollutants into navigable waters. This water quality legislation, substantially amended in April 1970, was widely criticized as ineffective. Neither this legislation (tolerating pollutant discharges subject to the standards referred to) nor its legislative history dealt in terms with the interrelations between such legislation and Section 13 of the Rivers and Harbors Act, except that Section 13 was expressly recognized in a savings clause as continuing in effect.

b. The Federal Water Pollution Control Act Amendments of 1972 (FWPCA '72) drastically revised the law and provided a wide-ranging federal system of control in relation to pollutant discharges into navigable waters. Federal not state standards were henceforth to govern water quality and all pollutant discharges were forbidden except under pollution permits granted by the Environmental Protection Agency in compliance with federal standards. 1985 was set as a target date for the general elimination of all pollutant discharges. Section 511 of FWPCA '72 stated that the new legislation:

> " * * * shall not be construed as limiting the authority of any officer or agency of the United States under any other law not inconsistent with this Act."

Although it was provided that pollutant discharges subject to certain other named statutes were henceforth to be regulated under the FWPCA '72, Section 13 of the Rivers and Harbors Act was nowhere mentioned.

Draft a compact, well-organized opinion for the judge for whom you are clerk

(A) setting out the statutory issue or issues raised;

(B) giving your recommended decision on the applicability of Section 13; and

(C) justifying your decision on the issue or issues raised and dealing with each item of the research materials referred to above and with the probable arguments of counsel for the U. S. and counsel for KPL.

C. PROBLEMS UNDER THE COMPREHENSIVE DRUG ABUSE PREVENTION AND CONTROL ACT OF 1970

Following are pertinent provisions of Subchapter I (Control and Enforcement) of the Comprehensive Drug Abuse Prevention and Control Act of 1970, 84 Stat. 1242:

PART A. INTRODUCTORY PROVISIONS

§ 801. *Congressional findings and declarations*

The Congress makes the following findings and declarations:

(1) Many of the drugs included within this subchapter have a useful and legitimate medical purpose and are necessary to maintain the health and general welfare of the American people.

(2) The illegal importation, manufacture, distribution, and possession and improper use of controlled substances have a substantial and detrimental effect on the health and general welfare of the American people.

(3) A major portion of the traffic in controlled substances flows through interstate and foreign commerce. Incidents of the traffic which are not an integral part of the interstate or foreign flow, such as manufacture, local distribution, and possession, nonetheless have a substantial and direct effect upon interstate commerce. * * *

* * *

(6) Federal control of the intrastate incidents of the traffic in controlled substances is essential to the effective control of the interstate incidents of such traffic.

* * *

§ 802. *Definitions*

As used in this subchapter:

* * *

(6) The term "controlled substance" means a drug or other substance, or immediate precursor, included in schedule I, II, III, IV, or V of part B of this subchapter. The term does not include distilled spirits, wine, malt beverages, or tobacco, as those terms are defined or used in subtitle E of the Internal Revenue Code of 1954.

* * *

(8) The terms "deliver" or "delivery" mean the actual, constructive, or attempted transfer of a controlled substance, whether or not there exists an agency relationship.

* * *

(10) The term "dispense" means to deliver a controlled substance to an ultimate user or research subject by, or pursuant to the lawful order of, a practitioner, including the prescribing and administering of a controlled substance and the packaging, labeling, or compounding necessary to prepare the substance for such delivery. The term "dispenser" means a practitioner who so delivers a controlled substance to an ultimate user or research subject.

(11) The term "distribute" means to deliver (other than by administering or dispensing) a controlled substance. The term "distributor" means a person who so delivers a controlled substance.

* * *

(14) The term "manufacture" means the production, preparation, propagation, compounding, or processing of a drug or other substance, either directly or indirectly or by extraction from substances of natural origin, or independently by means of chemical synthesis or by a combination of extraction and chemical synthesis, and includes any packaging or repackaging of such substance or labeling or relabeling of its container; except that such term does not include the preparation, compounding, packaging, or labeling of a drug or other substance in conformity with applicable State or local law by a practitioner as an incident to his administration or dispensing of such drug or substance in the course of his professional practice. The term "manufacturer" means a person who manufactures a drug or other substance.

* * *

(16) The term "narcotic drug" means any of the following, whether produced directly or indirectly by extraction from substances of vegetable origin, or independently by means of chemical synthesis, or by a combination of extraction and chemical synthesis:

(A) Opium, coca leaves, and opiates.

(B) A compound, manufacture, salt, derivative, or preparation of opium, coca leaves, or opiates.

(C) A substance (and any compound, manufacture, salt derivative, or preparation thereof) which is chemically identical with any of the substances referred to in clause (A) or (B).

Such term does not include decocainized coca leaves or extracts of coca leaves, which extracts do not contain cocaine or ecgonine.

(17) The term "opiate" means any drug or other substance having an addiction-forming or addiction-sustaining liability similar to morphine or being capable of conversion into a drug having such addiction-forming or addiction-sustaining liability.

* * *

(20) The term "practitioner" means a physician, dentist, veterinarian, scientific investigator, pharmacy, hospital, or other person licensed, registered, or otherwise permitted, by the United States or the jurisdiction in which he practices or does research, to distribute, dispense, conduct research with respect to, administer, or use in teaching or chemical analysis, a controlled substance in the course of professional practice or research.

* * *

(25) The term "ultimate user" means a person who has lawfully obtained, and who possesses, a controlled substance for his own use or for the use of a member of his household or for an animal owned by him or by a member of his household.

* * *

PART B. AUTHORITY TO CONTROL; STANDARDS AND SCHEDULES

§ 811. *Authority and criteria for classification of substances—Rules and regulations of Attorney General; hearing*

(a) The Attorney General shall apply the provisions of this subchapter to the controlled substances listed in the schedules established by section 812 of this title and to any other drug or other substance added to such schedules under this subchapter. Except as provided in subsections (d) and (e) of this section, the Attorney General may by rule—

(1) add to such a schedule or transfer between such schedules any drug or other substance if he—

(A) finds that such drug or other substance has a potential for abuse, and

(B) makes with respect to such drug or other substance the findings prescribed by subsection (b) of section 812 of this title for the schedule in which such drug is to be placed; or

(2) remove any drug or other substance from the schedules if he finds that the drug or other substance does not meet the requirements for inclusion in any schedule.

* * *

§ 812. *Schedules of controlled substances—Establishment*

* * *

(c) [The schedules] shall, unless and until amended pursuant to section 811 of this title, consist of the following drugs or other substances by whatever official name, common or usual name, chemical name, or brand name designated:

Schedule I

* * *

(b) Unless specifically excepted or unless listed in another schedule, any of the following opium derivatives, their salts, isomers, and salts of isomers whenever the existence of such salts, isomers, and salts of isomers is possible within the specific chemical designation:

* * *

(10) Heroin

* * *

(c) Unless specifically excepted or unless listed in another schedule, any material, compound, mixture or preparation, which contains any quantity of the following hallucinogenic substances, or which contains any of their salts, isomers and salts of isomers whenever the existence of such salts, isomers, and salts of isomers is possible within the specific chemical designation:

(9) Lysergic acid diethylamide.

(10) Marihuana.

* * *

Schedule IV

* * *

(11) Phenobarbital

* * *

PART C. REGISTRATION OF MANUFACTURERS, DISTRIBUTORS, AND DISPENSERS OF CONTROLLED SUBSTANCES

§ 821. *Rules and regulations*

The Attorney General is authorized to promulgate rules and regulations and to charge reasonable fees relating to the registration and control of the manufacture, distribution, and dispensing of controlled substances.

§ 822. *Persons required to register—Annual registration*

(a) Every person who manufactures, distributes, or dispenses any controlled substance or who proposes to engage in the manufacture, distribution, or dispensing of any controlled substance, shall obtain annually a registration issued by the Attorney General in accordance with the rules and regulations promulgated by him.

(b) Persons registered by the Attorney General under this subchapter to manufacture, distribute, or dispense controlled substances are authorized to possess, manufacture, distribute, or dispense such substances (including any such activity in the conduct of research) to the extent authorized by their registration and in conformity with the other provisions of this subchapter.

(c) The following persons shall not be required to register and may lawfully possess any controlled substance under this subchapter:

(1) An agent or employee of any registered manufacturer, distributor, or dispenser of any controlled substance if such agent or employee is acting in the usual course of his business or employment.

(2) A common or contract carrier or warehouseman, or an employee thereof, whose possession of the controlled substance is in the usual course of his business or employment.

(3) An ultimate user who possesses such substance for a purpose specified in section 802(25) of this title.

* * *

§ 825. *Labeling and packaging—Symbol*

(a) It shall be unlawful to distribute a controlled substance in a commercial container unless such container, when and as required by regulations of the Attorney General, bears a label * * * containing an identifying symbol for such substance in accordance with such regulations. A different symbol shall be required for each schedule of controlled substances.

* * *

(c) The Secretary [of Health, Education and Welfare] shall prescribe regulations * * * which shall provide that the label of a drug listed in schedule II, III, or IV shall, when dispensed to or for a patient, contain a clear, concise warning that it is a crime to transfer the drug to any person other than the patient.

(d) It shall be unlawful to distribute controlled substances in schedule I or II, and narcotic drugs in schedule III or IV, unless the bottle or other container, stopper, covering, or wrapper thereof is securely sealed as required by regulations of the Attorney General.

* * *

§ 828. Order forms—Unlawful distribution of controlled substances

(a) It shall be unlawful for any person to distribute a controlled substance in schedule I or II to another except in pursuance of a written order of the person to whom such substance is distributed, made on a form to be issued by the Attorney General in blank in accordance with subsection (d) of this section and regulations prescribed by him pursuant to this section.

* * *

(c)(1) Every person who in pursuance of an order required under subsection (a) of this section distributes a controlled substance shall preserve such order for a period of two years, and shall make such order available for inspection and copying by officers and employees of the United States duly authorized for that purpose by the Attorney General, and by officers or employees of States or their political subdivisions who are charged with the enforcement of State or local laws regulating the production, or regulating the distribution or dispensing of controlled substances and who are authorized under such laws to inspect such orders.

(2) Every person who gives an order required under subsection (a) of this section shall, at or before the time of giving such order, make or cause to be made a duplicate thereof on a form to be issued by the Attorney General in blank in accordance with subsection (d) of this section and regulations prescribed by him pursuant to this section, and shall, if such order is accepted, preserve such duplicate for a period of two years and make it available for inspection and copying by the officers and employees mentioned in paragraph (1) of this subsection.

* * *

§ 829. Prescriptions—Schedule II substances

(a) Except when dispensed directly by a practitioner, other than a pharmacist, to an ultimate user, no controlled substance in schedule II, which is a prescription drug as determined under the Federal Food, Drug, and Cosmetic Act, may be dispensed without the written prescription of a practitioner, except that in emergency situations, as prescribed by the Secretary by regulation after consultation with the Attorney General, such drug may be dispensed upon oral prescription * * *. No prescription for a controlled substance in schedule II may be refilled.

(b) Except when dispensed directly by a practitioner, other than a pharmacist, to an ultimate user, no controlled substance in schedule III or IV, which is a prescription drug as determined under the Federal Food, Drug, and Cosmetic Act, may be dispensed without a written or oral prescription * * *. Such prescriptions may not be filled or refilled more than six months after the date thereof or be re-

Sec. 9 SOME STATUTORY PROBLEMS 583

filled more than five times after the date of the prescription unless renewed by the practitioner.

* * *

PART D. OFFENSES AND PENALTIES

§ 841. *Prohibited acts A—Unlawful acts*

(a) Except as authorized by this subchapter, it shall be unlawful for any person knowingly or intentionally—

(1) to manufacture, distribute, or dispense, or possess with intent to manufacture, distribute, or dispense, a controlled substance

* * *

(b) Except as otherwise provided in section 845 of this title, any person who violates subsection (a) of this section shall be sentenced as follows:

(1)(A) In the case of a controlled substance in schedule I or II which is a narcotic drug, such person shall be sentenced to a term of imprisonment of not more than 15 years, a fine of not more than $25,000, or both. If any person commits such a violation after one or more prior convictions of him for an offense punishable under this paragraph, or for a felony [98] under any other provision of this subchapter or subchapter II of this chapter or other law of the United States relating to narcotic drugs, marihuana, or depressant or stimulant substances, have become final, such person shall be sentenced to a term of imprisonment of not more than 30 years, a fine of not more than $50,000, or both. Any sentence imposing a term of imprisonment under this paragraph shall, in the absence of such a prior conviction, impose a special parole term of at least 3 years in addition to such term of imprisonment and shall, if there was such a prior conviction, impose a special parole term of at least 6 years in addition to such term of imprisonment.

(B) In the case of a controlled substance in schedule I or II which is not a narcotic drug or in the case of any controlled substance in schedule III, such person shall be sentenced to a term of imprisonment of not more than 5 years, a fine of not more than $15,000 or both. If any person commits such a violation after one or more prior convictions of him for an offense punishable under this paragraph, or for a felony under any other provision of this subchapter or subchapter II of this chapter or other law of the United States relating to narcotic drugs, marihuana, or depressant or stimulant substances, have become final, such person shall be sentenced to a term of imprisonment of not more than 10 years, a fine of not more than $30,000, or both. Any sentence imposing a term of imprisonment un-

---

98. [A felony is defined as "any offense punishable by death or imprisonment for a term exceeding one year." 18 U.S.C.A. § 1(1) (1969).—Ed.]

der this paragraph, shall, in the absence of such a prior conviction, impose a special parole term of at least 2 years in addition to such term of imprisonment and shall, if there was such a prior conviction, impose a special parole term of at least 4 years in addition to such term of imprisonment.

(2) In the case of a controlled substance in schedule IV, such person shall be sentenced to a term of imprisonment of not more than 3 years, a fine of not more than $10,000, or both. If any person commits such a violation after one or more prior convictions of him for an offense punishable under this paragraph, or for a felony under any other provision of this subchapter or subchapter II of this chapter or other law of the United States relating to narcotic drugs, marihuana, or depressant or stimulant substances, have become final, such person shall be sentenced to a term of imprisonment of not more than 6 years, a fine of not more than $20,000, or both. Any sentence imposing a term of imprisonment under this paragraph shall, in the absence of such a prior conviction, impose a special parole term of at least one year in addition to such term of imprisonment and shall, if there was such a prior conviction, impose a special parole term of at least 2 years in addition to such term of imprisonment.

* * *

(4) Notwithstanding paragraph (1)(B) of this subsection, any person who violates subsection (a) of this section by distributing a small amount of marihuana for no remuneration shall be treated as provided in subsections (a) and (b) of section 844 of this title.

* * *

§ 843. *Prohibited acts C—Unlawful acts*

* * *

(b) It shall be unlawful for any person knowingly or intentionally to use any communication facility in committing or in causing or facilitating the commission of any act or acts constituting a felony under any provision of this subchapter or subchapter II of this chapter. Each separate use of a communication facility shall be a separate offense under this subsection. For purposes of this subsection, the term "communication facility" means any and all public and private instrumentalities used or useful in the transmission of writing, signs, signals, pictures, or sounds of all kinds and includes mail, telephone, wire, radio, and all other means of communication.

(c) Any person who violates this section shall be sentenced to a term of imprisonment of not more than 4 years, a fine of not more than $30,000, or both; except that if any person commits such a violation after one or more prior convictions of him for violation of this section, or for a felony under any other provision of this subchapter or subchapter II of this chapter or other law of the United States relating to narcotic drugs, marihuana, or depressant or stimulant substances, have become final, such person shall be sentenced to a term of imprisonment of not more than 8 years, a fine of not more than $60,000, or both.

§ 844. *Penalty for simple possession; conditional discharge and expunging of records for first offense*

(a) It shall be unlawful for any person knowingly or intentionally to possess a controlled substance unless such substance was obtained directly, or pursuant to a valid prescription or order, from a practitioner, while acting in the course of his professional practice, or except as otherwise authorized by this subchapter or subchapter II of this chapter. Any person who violates this subsection shall be sentenced to a term of imprisonment of not more than one year, a fine of not more than $5,000, or both, except that if he commits such offense after a prior conviction or convictions under this subsection have become final, he shall be sentenced to a term of imprisonment of not more than 2 years, a fine of not more than $10,000, or both.

[For first offenders, § 844(b) makes available to the court a discretionary sanction alternative to those in § 844(a) and involving: possible deferring of the judgment of guilty; probation; dismissal of proceedings and discharge; and in the case of offenders under twenty-one, the expunging of records of proceedings against them.]

* * *

§ 845. *Distribution to persons under age twenty-one*

(a) Any person at least eighteen years of age who violates section 841(a)(1) of this title by distributing a controlled substance to a person under twenty-one years of age is (except as provided in subsection (b) of this section) punishable by (1) a term of imprisonment, or a fine, or both, up to twice that authorized by section 841(b) of this title, and (2) at least twice any special parole term authorized by section 841(b) of this title, for a first offense involving the same controlled substances and schedule.

[For a second and subsequent offenses, § 845(b) authorizes penalties up to three times as severe as those in (a) supra.]

§ 846. *Attempt and conspiracy*

Any person who attempts or conspires to commit any offense defined in this subchapter is punishable by imprisonment or fine or both which may not exceed the maximum punishment prescribed for the offense, the commission of which was the object of the attempt or conspiracy.

* * *

SUBCHAPTER II. IMPORT AND EXPORT

§ 951. *Definitions*

(a) For purposes of this subchapter—

(1) The term "import" means, with respect to any article, any bringing in or introduction of such article into any area (whether or

not such bringing in or introduction constitutes an importation within the meaning of the tariff laws of the United States).

* * *

(b) Each term defined in section 802 of this title shall have the same meaning for purposes of this subchapter as such term has for purposes of subchapter I of this chapter.

§ 952. *Importation of controlled substances—Controlled substances in schedules I or II and narcotic drugs in schedules III, IV, or V; exceptions*

(a) It shall be unlawful to import into the customs territory of the United States from any place outside thereof (but within the United States), or to import into the United States from any place outside thereof, any controlled substance in schedule I or II of subchapter I of this chapter [subject to exceptions for medical and scientific purposes, etc., administered by the Attorney General] * * *.

* * *

§ 960. *Prohibited acts A—Unlawful acts*

(a) Any person who—

(1) contrary to section 952, 953, or 957 of this title, knowingly or intentionally imports or exports a controlled substance, * * * shall be punished as provided in subsection (b) of this section.

(b)(1) In the case of a violation under subsection (a) of this section with respect to a narcotic drug in schedule I or II, the person committing such violation shall be imprisoned not more than fifteen years, or fined not more than $25,000, or both. If a sentence under this paragraph provides for imprisonment, the sentence shall include a special parole term of not less than three years in addition to such term of imprisonment.

(2) In the case of a violation under subsection (a) of this section with respect to a controlled substance other than a narcotic drug in schedule I or II, the person committing such violation shall be imprisoned not more than five years, or be fined not more than $15,000, or both. If a sentence under this paragraph provides for imprisonment, the sentence shall, in addition to such term of imprisonment, include (A) a special parole term of not less than two years if such controlled substance is in schedule I, II, III, or (B) a special parole term of not less than one year if such controlled substance is in schedule IV.

* * *

Problem 1

Narcotics agents observed suspicious activity in an abandoned tenement. Surveillance disclosed that three or four men were frequenting the building, sometimes carrying large packages in, and emerging several times a day with smaller packages and returning empty-handed some hours later. One of the men—Smith—was followed and arrested in the act of selling a small bag of heroin to an elderly addict. Two additional such bags were found in the lining of his hat. From Smith it was learned that the building was being used for the storage and "cutting" of heroin. Pursuant to a valid warrant, agents entered the tenement and apprehended Gray in one of the rooms in the act of "cutting" and packaging a supply of heroin. While they were arresting Gray in one of the rooms, a third person, a boy of 17 named Moore, appeared at the door of the room. Unaware of what was going on, Moore called to Gray—"I took the bag of horse like you said and gave it to the man and here's the $50 he gave me." When searched he had nothing untoward in his pockets, or otherwise on his person, except the $50 referred to. Moore was arrested along with Gray. Also arrested was a fourth man, Wilkes, who was found asleep in an adjacent room of the tenement. Wilkes had no drugs or drug paraphernalia on his person but when arrested was under the influence of heroin and bore physical indicia—i. e., fresh needlemarks —in plain view attesting to a current addiction. It was not possible to establish any operating connection between Wilkes and the other three arrestees. Moore and Wilkes were first offenders; Smith had a previous conviction for stealing a large quantity of phenobarbital from a drug-supply house; Gray had two prior convictions for selling heroin. What violations, if any, of the Act of 1970 would it be appropriate to charge each one with? What penalties apply?

Problem 2

A post-football-game party took place at the quarters of Iota Omicron Upsilon, a freewheeling fraternity on the campus of Riverbank College. Following an anonymous tip, the party was infiltrated by agents of the local constabulary dressed in the fashion of college students. As the proceedings approached a peak, the agents identified themselves and made a number of arrests. Those arrested included, among others, one Dirk Stover, a 20-year-old senior whom the agents had observed handing out packets of marijuana cigarettes to three other party guests, one of whom was a girl sixteen years of age (known as such to Stover), the other two being over twenty-one. Stover, who had never previously committed any criminal offense, was then indicted for violating the Act of 1970 (hereafter referred to as the Drug Control Act) as set out before problem 1 supra. After validly waiving his right to a jury trial, he was tried without a jury. The trial established the facts already described and, in addition, it was proved (a) that Stover had handed out, in all, a total of three packets of marijuana cigarettes (each packet containing ten cigarettes) at the party, one to the 16-year-old guest referred to and (b) that each of the three guests to whom Stover gave a packet paid him two dollars therefor, which was the same amount Stover had earlier paid to obtain each packet.

Assume you are law clerk to the trial judge sitting in the Stover case. You are assigned to prepare a draft opinion for the judge. Assume that all jurisdictional and other procedural requirements have been properly met and that the application of the Drug Control Act to the facts of this case is properly before the court for decision.

Prepare a detailed outline of the requested draft opinion (1) indicating how, if at all, the Drug Control Act's prohibitions and penalties apply to Stover's case, (2) stating any statutory issues raised as to violations or penalties, (3) ruling on the issues and (4) justifying the rulings. The opinion should deal with the probable arguments of the prosecution and of defense counsel.

Your most careful researches yield only the following pertinent material (in addition to the text of the Drug Control Act and the facts recited earlier) to be considered in preparing your outline of the requested opinion:

1. The House standing committee report accompanying H.R. 18583, the bill that was enacted as the Drug Control Act, contained in substance these general remarks:

> This bill undertakes to improve upon existing law by making more discriminating distinctions between drugs, and between the penalties associated with them, and to this end it takes into account each drug's potential for abuse and harm and its social implications. The bill also modifies the existing pattern of penalties because it has become apparent that severity of penalty is not the final answer to drug abuse. Provisions for mandatory minimum sentences—which hamper rehabilitation and interfere with judicial discretion—have been eliminated except as to a special class of professional criminals. The idea is to create more flexibility in handling first offenders and those who might actually be salvaged, while bearing down with great intensity upon the pusher and the peddler.

2. An earlier version of Sec. 841(b)(4), reading as follows, appeared in a bill, S. 3246, which was a forerunner of the Drug Control Act as finally adopted:

> (4) Notwithstanding paragraph (1)(B) of this subsection, any person who violates subsection (a) of this section by distributing a small amount of marijuana for no remuneration or insignificant remuneration not involving a profit shall be treated as provided in subsections (a) and (b) of section 844 of this title.

The Senate standing committee report on S. 3246 stated:

> The language of 841(b)(4) is intended to cover the type of situation where a college student makes a quasi-dona-

tive transfer of one or two marijuana cigarettes and receives 50 cents or a dollar in exchange to cover the cost of the marijuana. Transfers of larger quantities in exchange for larger amounts of money, or transfers for profit, are not intended to be covered by this section
* * *

S. 3246 was passed by the Senate in January, 1970 but was then reworked by the House of Representatives and combined with other provisions into a new House bill, H.R. 18583, which was adopted by the House in September 1970 and then presented for floor consideration in the Senate in October. H.R. 18583, as thus presented, omitted Sec. 841(b)(4) entirely.

3. Following is a verbatim extract from the Congressional Record of October 7, 1970 reporting Senate debate on H.R. 18583 which was finally enacted as the Drug Control Act on October 27, 1970. As will be seen, this extract records the adoption, as an amendment, of the provision which is the present Sec. 841(b)(4).

AMENDMENT NO. 1028

Mr. HUGHES. Mr. President, I call up my amendment No. 1028 and ask that it be stated.

The PRESIDING OFFICER. The amendment will be stated.

The assistant legislative clerk proceeded to read the amendment.

Mr. HUGHES. Mr. President, I ask unanimous consent that further reading of the amendment be dispensed with, and that the amendment be printed in the Record.

The PRESIDING OFFICER. Without objection, it is so ordered; and, without objection, the amendment will be printed in the Record.

The amendment, ordered to be printed in the Record, is as follows:

[After section 841(b)(3) insert the following:

(4) Notwithstanding paragraph (1)(B) of this subsection, any person who violates subsection (a) of this section by distributing a small amount of marijuana for no remuneration shall be treated as provided in subsection (a) and (b) of section 844 of this title.]

Mr. HUGHES. Mr. President, I ask unanimous consent that the names of the Senator from New York (Mr. Javits), the Senator from Colorado (Mr. Dominick), and the Senator from Massachusetts (Mr. Kennedy) be added as cosponsors of this amendment.

The PRESIDING OFFICER. Without objection, it is so ordered.

Mr. HUGHES. Mr. President, I ask unanimous consent to have printed in the Record a statement that would have been made by the Senator from Massachusetts (Mr. Kennedy) had he been able to be present this evening.

There being no objection, the statement of Senator Kennedy was ordered to be printed in the Record, as follows:

PENALTIES FOR DISTRIBUTION OF A SMALL QUANTITY OF MARIHUANA WITHOUT REMUNERATION

Mr. KENNEDY. Mr. President, this amendment would provide that persons who distribute a small quantity of marihuana, without sale or remuneration, would be subject to the penalties for possession, rather than the heavier penalties for manufacture and heavy trafficking. Passage of the amendment would make the bill more equitable and more responsive to the situation of our nation's young people.

Many youngsters may be in a situation where they are with friends, where they give a marihuana cigarette or a small quantity of marihuana to one or two others—not as professional pushers, not to make a profit, but in a casual and informal way.

It would be an unrealistic over-reaction to treat persons convicted of such activity in the same way as large-scale pushers of heroin are treated. Yet that is the effect of the bill at the present time.

Persons so convicted would be subject to five years in jail and a fine of up to $15,000 for the first offense. They would not be eligible for the provision in the possession section whereby the court may put an offender on probation for one year and then, in its discretion, strike the guilty finding from his record so that he is not restricted for life as a result of his marihuana offense as a youth.

An estimated 12–20 million Americans have tried marihuana. In hearings which I chaired last spring at a Massachusetts high school, the president of the senior class testified that an estimated 50–60% of the students have tried marihuana.

This is a widespread phenomenon. We must respond with compassion and understanding and try to correct it in a reasonable fashion.

I am opposed to the legalization of marihuana. I do not believe that society should have another legal intoxicant, besides alcohol. I believe, however, that we must pursue vigorously the studies called for in this bill and presently underway on the likely effects if marihuana were legalized.

But in the meantime, we also should not penalize a whole generation of young persons who are growing up fully exposed, fully tempted by the mysteries of the drug culture. We should not brand them for life for the lesser marihuana violations.

Therefore, I urge my colleagues to vote for this amendment.

Mr. HUGHES. Mr. President, this amendment has been accepted by the managers of the bill.

Mr. BYRD of West Virginia. Mr. President, may we have order?

The PRESIDING OFFICER. The Senate will be in order.

Mr. HUGHES. Mr. President, this amendment is an amendment that was passed by the Senate last January in the original Senate-passed bill. It would make those persons who are guilty of distributing marihuana for no remuneration subject to the same penalties as those persons who are charged with possession, rather than subject to penalties for trafficking and distribution.

The penalty for first offense possession is up to 1 year, up to $5,000 or both; second and subsequent offenses are double this.

The penalty for first offense trafficking or distribution is up to 5 years, up to $15,000 or both, and a special parole term of 2 years; second and subsequent offenses are double this.

Also, if a person at least 18 years old distributes to a person under 21, any penalty for distribution is doubled.

Trafficking provisions should apply to the large distributor, rather than to the person who is only using the drug with his friends. The latter individual falls within the intention of the possession provisions.

A provision very similar to this was adopted by the Senate as section 501(c)(4) of S. 3246, the Controlled Dangerous Substances Act of 1969, when it passed the Senate earlier this year.

Mr. President, this amendment would place those persons who are guilty of distributing marihuana for no remuneration in the same category as those persons who are charged with possession. The amendment refers to those persons who have small amounts of marihuana or smoke it with friends. They would be subject to the same penalties as those persons charged with possession rather than subject to penalties for trafficking and distribution.

Mr. DODD. Mr. President, I believe we should accept the amendment. This is a compassionate amendment, and it is in keeping with the bill we passed in January. I commend the Senator for offering the amendment. I believe it should be agreed to.

Mr. HRUSKA. Mr. President, will the Senator yield?

Mr. HUGHES. I yield.

Mr. HRUSKA. Mr. President, I concur with the Senator from Connecticut. The objective of the amendment is good. It had been discussed in committee and was considered. Legalistically it may present some difficulty because of the definition of the word "small." But it is an amendment to which I have no objection, and I join the Senator from Connecticut in accepting it.

Mr. DOMINICK. Mr. President, will the Senator yield?

The PRESIDING OFFICER (Mr. Hansen). The time of the Senator has expired.

Mr. HRUSKA. Mr. President, I yield the Senator from Colorado 1 minute.

Mr. DOMINICK. Mr. President, there are a great number of young people who have been experimenting with marihuana. It has not proven to be something to which they are addictive or that would ruin their health. Unless we do something about decreasing the penalties, as suggested by the Senator from Iowa, I think we are further increasing the problems of credibility of the Government as far as young people are concerned.

I support the amendment.

* * *

The PRESIDING OFFICER. Do Senators yield back their time?

Mr. HUGHES. Mr. President, I yield back the remainder of my time.

Mr. DODD. I yield back the remainder of my time.

THE PRESIDING OFFICER. All time having been yielded back, the question is on agreeing to the amendment of the Senator from Iowa.

The amendment was agreed to.

[Note that Senator Hruska was the ranking minority member, and Senators Dodd and Kennedy were members, of the Senate Committee on the Judiciary which was in charge of the Senate debate on H.R. 18583; Senators Hughes, Kennedy and Dominick were members of the Senate Committee on Labor and Public Welfare which, though not in charge of S. 3246, had been active with the Judiciary Committee in shaping its provisions.]

Problem 3

Martin Webley and his family returned by air on August 15 of this year from a holiday in Mexico. All the family luggage was cleared through customs upon their return to New York, save one duffle bag. This duffle bag contained apparel belonging to various family members but was mainly devoted to the clothing and other belongings of Webley's 19-year-old son, Orestes, a young man who, notwithstanding paternal grumblings, affected a "liberated" life style. Due to airline mishandlings, the duffle bag somehow became separated from the rest of the Webley luggage at the Mexican terminal. When after inquiry the error and the bag were discovered, the airline forwarded the bag to New York on a later flight which arrived August 17. Orestes having returned to college, Webley père went himself to the airport customs shed with the appropriate claim check in order to retrieve the missing duffle bag. When customs officers searched the bag, they found, to Webley's horror and surprise, a plastic container full of marijuana, wrapped in a pair of Orestes's dungarees. Mr. Webley was placed under arrest and charged with violation of the Act of 1970. After his arrest, Webley consented to be searched by arresting officers who found in his pocket a large drugstore prescription bottle, properly labeled, bearing the name M. Murgatroyd, and containing phenobarbital (a depressant substance classified as a "prescription drug" under the Federal Food, Drugs and Cosmetics Act.) As a result of this, Webley was charged with a further violation of the Act—even after he had truthfully protested that these capsules had been validly and legally prescribed by the family doctor for Webley's aunt, Martha Murgatroyd, currently visiting the Webleys, and that he had just picked them up at the drugstore on her behalf and was taking them home to her. When Mr. Webley was at length able to contact his son Orestes, the latter admitted originally placing the marijuana in the duffle bag early during the Mexican holiday. He insisted, however, that he had meant to remove the marijuana from the bag and leave it in Mexico before their departure but had forgotten to do so.

What, if any, provisions of the Act have been violated by Mr. **Webley? by Orestes?**

Problem 4

Miller was suspected by narcotics agents of being an unregistered drug "pusher" or vendor. An old friend of Miller's, one Kruller, who—unknown to Miller—was a government special agent, was detailed to try to make a purchase of heroin from Miller so that Miller could be apprehended. Miller, at first, firmly refused Kruller's request, saying he was "no longer into drugs" himself and was not selling them. Kruller pleaded with Miller for several hours unsuccessfully. Finally, Miller yielded to Kruller's desperate pleading after Kruller told him—untruthfully—that he (Kruller) and his wife Irma (whom Miller also knew very well) were both seriously ill, that they could not get drugs in any other way and were in the direst and most extreme need. Miller disappeared for an hour and then upon his return, handed Kruller a small quantity of heroin saying "Here, don't ask me to do this again. I only did it for you and Irma. Just pay me the $40 it cost me." Kruller paid Miller $40 and Miller was arrested for violating the 1970 Act.

How if at all did Miller violate the Act and to what penalty, if any, is he liable?

Chapter VI

COORDINATION OF JUDGE–MADE AND STATUTE LAW

INTRODUCTORY NOTE

The text extracts and cases in this chapter all concern a basic problem of legal method and judicial craftsmanship, the problem of adjustment of statutory directions to the body of existing law. At this stage of your Legal Method course, you have some understanding of the case law judicial process and a general awareness of the problems and techniques of statutory interpretation. This chapter provides a kind of meeting place for the case law and statutory interpretation parts of the course. What is, and what should be, a court's general approach in adjusting statutory directions to the body of existing law? Is it today accurate to say, as Sir Frederick Pollock said of the English courts in 1882, that the methods employed by common law judges in resolving possible overlappings between statutory directions and case law principles

> " * * * cannot well be accounted for except upon the theory that Parliament generally changes the law for the worse, and that the business of the judge is to keep the mischief of its interference within the narrowest possible bounds"? [1]

Which of the cases in the present chapter might be cited to support Pollock's critical thesis, and which of the cases in the chapter exemplify a more hospitable judicial attitude towards statutory innovations? Where does each case stand with relation to the fourfold scale proposed in the extract from Dean Pound's essay immediately following?

The title and general problem of this chapter are suggested by the last paragraph quoted from the article by Harlan F. Stone, infra. The Johnson cases revisited at the outset raise questions, *inter alia*, about the operation and status of the old canon that statutes in derogation of the common law are to be strictly construed. How, if at all, do the statutory problems in the succeeding cases differ from the problem in the Johnson cases?

1. Essays in Jurisprudence and Ethics 85 (1882).

ROSCOE POUND, COMMON LAW AND LEGISLATION

21 Harv.L.Rev. 383 (1908).

Four ways may be conceived of in which courts in such a legal system as ours might deal with a legislative innovation. (1) They might receive it fully into the body of the law as affording not only a rule to be applied but a principle from which to reason, and hold it, as a later and more direct expression of the general will, of superior authority to judge-made rules on the same general subject; and so reason from it by analogy in preference to them. (2) They might receive it fully into the body of the law to be reasoned from by analogy the same as any other rule of law, regarding it, however, as of equal or coordinate authority in this respect with judge-made rules upon the same general subject. (3) They might refuse to receive it fully into the body of the law and give effect to it directly only; refusing to reason from it by analogy but giving it, nevertheless, a liberal interpretation to cover the whole field it was intended to cover. (4) They might not only refuse to reason from it by analogy and apply it directly only, but also give to it a strict and narrow interpretation, holding it down rigidly to those cases which it covers expressly. The fourth hypothesis represents the orthodox common law attitude towards legislative innovations. Probably the third hypothesis, however, represents more nearly the attitude toward which we are tending. The second and first hypotheses doubtless appeal to the common law lawyer as absurd. He can hardly conceive that a rule of statutory origin may be treated as a permanent part of the general body of the law, but it is submitted that the course of legal development upon which we have entered already must lead us to adopt the method of the second and eventually the method of the first hypothesis.

JAMES M. LANDIS, STATUTES AND THE SOURCES OF LAW

Harvard Legal Essays 213 (1934).

Beyond the accepted boundaries that can be accorded to statutory interpretation, however, lies a more neglected but more significant field. This concerns the place that statutes are to occupy in the ultimate processes of law-making by judges. Certainly statutes can never embrace within their sweep all human activity that law is called upon to order. Even the latitudinarian methods of statutory interpretation evolved by civilian theorists—sometimes gossamer-like in their fineness and subtlety and so scarcely able to withstand the rough and ready tumble of actual legal administration—have failed to net the interstices so tightly as to confine the judicial process merely to textual construction. However, to admit the existence of wide areas for legal administration beyond the direct governance of statutes is not to assume that statutes have no part in the solution of problems impossible to bring within the reach of their terms.

I.

Historically statutes have never played such a confined role in the development of English law. Instead, much of what is ordinarily regarded as "common law" finds its source in legislative enactment. The flexible instrument of conspiracy, both in its criminal and civil aspects, has a definite statutory origin. Doctrines that surround the enforcement of the labor contract in its manifold aspects have grown out of a statute-born policy. One needs only recall such legislation as the Statute of Frauds or the Statute of Limitations to conjure up a vast body of law springing from parliamentary enactment and yet independent of its terms, even interpretatively applied. English and American land law responds to the same tests and reveals upon analysis that many of its germinating ideas have a statutory origin. The American doctrine of common-law statutes is in itself testimony to this concept of the statute as a nursing mother of the law. It is small wonder, therefore, the common-law courts at an early stage developed the doctrine of the equity of the statute. To ascribe its origin, as latter-day judges and commentators have done, to the poor draftsmanship of the early statutes which naturally excused judges in extending them beyond their terms, is to ignore the nature of the tasks that then confronted the judiciary. It assumes a refined conception of the separation of powers alien to English political life until the time of Anne. But more than this, it fails to recognize that law had then to be made in some fashion, and that as sure sources for its making lay in the policies outlined by a parliament as in the customs of a people.

The doctrine of the equity of the statute was a double-edged device. As Plowden so sagely observed, merely knowing the letter of the statute does not mean that you know its sense, "for sometimes the Sense is more confined and contracted than the Letter, and sometimes it is more large and extensive." Under its authority exceptions dictated by sound policy were written by judges into loose statutory generalizations, and, on the other hand, situations were brought within the reach of the statute that admittedly lay without its express terms. No apology other than the need for a decent administration of justice was indulged in by judges who invoked its aid. Definite principles, therefore, as to the circumstances which would justify extending statutes to cover cases beyond the scope of their language seem never to have been evolved. Rather there was simply the urge to do equity and so mould the law to conform more closely to its recognized aims.

The cases in which judges resorted to the equity of the statute do, however, reveal several recurring factors. Legislation of an early date is often special in character, applying, like the judgment of a court, to a particular situation brought to the attention of Parliament. The modern concept of wide and generalized legislative powers was of slow growth. Statutes would thus be restricted in their application to designated individuals or be limited in their incidence to a named locality. But the same mischief, to use Coke's favorite phrase, would call for like treatment in like situations, and the recognition of this fact led judges to extend the remedies or restrictions of the special act to other persons and other localities similarly circumstanced. Behind this treatment of special legislation lay the revolutionizing idea that "when the Words of a Statute enact one Thing, they enact all other Things which are in a like Degree." Such a concept obviously carried the principle of the equity of the statute beyond that of merely transmuting special into general legislation. Enabling judges to distill from a statute its basic purpose, they could then employ it to slough off the archaisms in their own legal structure. Even general legislation could thus be made to yield a meaning for law beyond its expressed operative effect. The class of situations to which the statutory remedy was expressly made applicable were but illustrative of other analogous cases that deserved to be governed by the same principle. The extension of one remedy beyond its recognized common-law area by the statute justified judges in giving another remedy the same expansive effect. The imposition of liability in a defined series of circumstances was not exhaustive, but offered a reason for fastening liability upon similar conduct.

The leavening influence of this principle in the development of early common law has still to be adequately explored. Its significance, though clearly appreciated by the early writers even up to the time of Coke, has been largely obscured by later commentators like Blackstone, who, like the social contract theorists, held to the faith of a full-fledged system of common law. The rise of equity, permeating law with ideas originating within a coordinate judicial system, has undoubtedly served to obscure the significance of this early attitude toward legislation as one of the major dynamic forces in the law's development. But the present-day importance of ancient statutes is ample evidence of the weight that should be accorded to the method of their treatment in the early law. The essence of that method lay in the recognition by judges that behind the formal fiat of the statute lay an aim that challenged their sympathetic attention, and that the appropriate exercise of judicial power permitted courts to advance ends so emphatically asserted.

HARLAN FISKE STONE, THE COMMON LAW IN THE UNITED STATES

50 Harv.L.Rev. 4 (1936).

It is the fashion in our profession to lament both the quantity and quality of our statute-making, not, it is true, without some justification. But our role has been almost exclusively that of destructive critics, usually after the event, of the inadequacies of legislatures. There has been little disposition to look to our own shortcomings in failing, through adaptation of old skills and the development of new ones, to realize more nearly than we have the ideal of a unified system of judge-made and statute law woven into a seamless whole by the processes of adjudication.

The reception which the courts have accorded to statutes presents a curiously illogical chapter in the history of the common law. Notwithstanding their genius for the generation of new law from that already established, the common-law courts have given little recognition to statutes as starting points for judicial law-making comparable to judicial decisions. They have long recognized the supremacy of statutes over judge-made law, but it has been the supremacy of a command to be obeyed according to its letter, to be treated as otherwise of little consequence. The fact that the command involves recognition of a policy by the supreme lawmaking body has seldom been regarded by courts as significant, either as a social datum or as a point of departure for the process of judicial reasoning by which the common law has expanded.

The attitude of our courts toward statute law presents a contrast to that of the civilians who have been more ready to regard statutes in the light of the thesis of the civil law that its precepts are statements of general principles, to be used as guides to decision. Under that system a new statute may be viewed as an exemplification of a general principle which is to take its place beside other precepts, whether found in codes or accepted expositions of the jurists, as an integral part of the system, there to be extended to analogous situations not within its precise terms. With the modern practice of drawing a statute as a statement of a general rule, I can perceive no obstacle which need have precluded our adoption of a similar attitude except our unfamiliarity with the civilian habit of thought. The Scottish law, with its Roman law foundation, took this position, and the House of Lords, common-law learning and background notwithstanding, found no difficulty in approving it as applied to local statutes, in passing on appeals from the Scottish courts.

But quite apart from such a possibility, I can find in the history and principles of the common law no adequate reason for our failure to treat a statute much more as we treat a judicial precedent, as both a declaration and a source of law, and as a premise for legal reasoning. We have done practically that with our ancient statutes, such as the statutes of limitations, frauds and wills, readily molding them to fit new conditions within their spirit, though not their letter, possibly because their antiquity tends to make us forget or minimize their legislative origin. Professor Landis of this Law School has recently pointed out in a valuable discussion of "Statutes and the Sources of Law" numerous examples in the Year Books of the application of the doctrine of the "equity of the statute" by which statutes were treated, in effect, as sources of law which by judicial decision could be extended to apply to situations analogous to those embraced within their terms. Apart from its command, the social policy and judgment, expressed in legislation by the lawmaking agency which is supreme, would seem to merit that judicial recognition which is freely accorded to the like expression in judicial precedent. But only to a limited extent do modern courts feel free, by resort to standards of conduct set up by legislation, to impose liability or attach consequences for the failure to maintain those or similar standards in similar but not identical situations, or to make the statutory recognition of a new type of right the basis for the judicial creation of rights in circumstances not dissimilar. Professor Landis and others have developed the subject with a detail unnecessary to consider now. It is enough for my purpose that they show that the legislative function has been reduced to mere rule making by the process of narrow judicial interpretation of statutes, and in consequence of the renunciation by the courts, where statutes are concerned, of some of their own lawmaking powers.

That such has been the course of the common law in the United States seems to be attributable to the fact that, long before its important legislative expansion, the theories of Coke and Blackstone of the self-sufficiency and ideal perfection of the common law, and the notion of the separation of powers and of judicial independence, had come to dominate our juristic thinking. The statute was looked upon as in the law but not of it, a formal rule to be obeyed, it is true, since it is the command of the sovereign, but to be obeyed grudgingly, by construing it narrowly and treating it as though it did not exist for any purpose other than that embraced within the strict construction of its words. It is difficult to appraise the consequences of the perpetuation of incongruities and injustices in the law by this habit of narrow construction of statutes and by the failure to recognize that, as recognitions of social policy, they are as significant and rightly as much a part of the law, as the rules declared by judges. A generation ago no feature of our law administration tended quite so much to discredit law and lawyers in the lay mind. A narrow literalism too often defeated the purpose of remedial legislation, while a seeming contest went on with the apparent purpose of ascertaining whether the legislatures would ultimately secure a desired reform or the courts would succeed in resisting it.

Happily the abrasive effect of the never-ending judicial labor of making a workable system of our law, so largely composed of statutes, is bringing about a more liberal attitude on the part of the courts. Fortunately, too, law schools have begun to study and investigate the problem involved in an adequate union of judge-made with statute law. They are developing the underlying principles for its solution, which rest basically on a more adequate recognition that a statute is not an alien intruder in the house of the common law, but a guest to be welcomed and made at home there as a new and powerful aid in the accomplishment of its appointed task of accommodating the law to social needs. But there still remains much to be done. The better organization of judge-made and statute law into a coordinated system is one of the major problems of the common law in the United States.

At least two other distinguished judges have expressed views in favor of increased use of statutes as analogies or as premises for reasoning in judicial decision-making. See Schaefer, Precedent and Policy, 34 U.Chi.L.Rev. 3, 18–22 (1966) and Traynor, Statutes Revolving in Common Law Orbits, 17 Catholic U.L.Rev. 401 (1968).

JOHNSON v. SOUTHERN PACIFIC CO.

Circuit Court of Appeals, Eighth Circuit, 1902.
117 F. 462.

JOHNSON v. SOUTHERN PACIFIC CO.

Supreme Court of the United States, 1904.
196 U.S. 1, 25 S.Ct. 158, 49 L.Ed. 363.

[Review these cases, supra, p. 327 et seq., with special reference to each court's treatment of the relation between the statute in issue and the preexisting common law.]

KING v. CITY OF OWENSBORO

Court of Appeals of Kentucky, 1920.
187 Ky. 21, 218 S.W. 297.

Opinion of the Court by WILLIAM ROGERS CLAY, Commissioner—

Edith King, a married woman, was fined $30.00 by the police court of Owensboro for selling intoxicating liquor without a license. On appeal to the Daviess circuit court she was again found guilty and her punishment fixed at a fine of $100.00 and costs. She appeals.

It is first insisted that the court erred in permitting the city to prove the license ordinance by filing a certified copy of only parts thereof. The copy introduced in evidence was certified by the city clerk as a true and correct copy. The record before us shows only those parts of the ordinance relating to liquor license. If, as a matter of fact, the certified copy of the ordinance was not complete, the defendant should have objected to its introduction on that ground, but not having done so, she cannot avail herself of the error of the trial court, if any, in permitting only a partial copy of the ordinance to be introduced in evidence.

It is next insisted that the court erred in authorizing the jury to find the defendant guilty if they believed from the evidence, to the exclusion of a reasonable doubt, that she, without license so to do, "either by herself, or by or through any person connected with her, sold any beer to the witness, John Walt." It appears that defendant and her husband lived at 112 Madison street, and that the defendant conducted a disorderly house at 120 Madison street, the adjoining residence. The beer was stored in an outhouse. The husband carried the key. He directed the negro to deliver the beer to 120 Madison street. There was evidence to the effect that the defendant herself sold beer to John Walt, and this evidence is uncontradicted. There was also certain evidence that the inmates of the house sold intoxicating liquors and turned over the proceeds to the defendant. While the use of the words, "or by or through any person connected with her," was not technically correct, we are not disposed to hold that the error was prejudicial, in view of the fact that the evidence that defendant herself sold beer to the witness, Walt, was uncontradicted.

Another ground urged for reversal is that the court erred in not giving the jury the whole law of the case, it being insisted that the jury should have been told in substance that if they believed from the evidence that the defendant acted jointly with her husband in selling the liquor, or sold the liquor in his presence, the law presumed that, she acted in obedience to his command and under his coercion, and they should find her not guilty, unless they believed from the evidence that she acted of her free will and volition. It may be conceded that, even at the time of Blackstone, it had been the rule of the common law for a thousand years that where a crime, with some exceptions, was committed by a married woman, conjointly with, or in the presence of, her husband, *prima facie* she was not criminally liable, as it was presumed that she acted in obedience to his commands or under his coercion. 13 R.C.L. p. 1238. It may also be conceded that the rule has been applied to all classes of misdemeanors, and even within recent years to the illegal sale of intoxicating liquors. Mulvey v. State, 43 Ala. 316, 94 Am.Dec. 684; State v. Cleaves, 59 Me. 298, 8 Am.Rep. 422, 4 Bl.Com. 28. While it is said that the reason for the rule is not quite clear, it is evident that it must have had its foundation in the peculiar relation which existed between husband and wife in the earlier days. At common law the husband had almost absolute control over the person of his wife; she was in a condition of complete dependence; could not contract in her own name; was bound to obey; she had no will and her legal existence was merged into that of her husband so that they were termed and regarded as one in law, "the husband being that one." 13 R.C.L. p. 983; Elliot v. Waring, 5 T.B.Mon. 338, 17 Am.Dec. 69; MacKinley v. McGregor, 3 Whart., Pa., 369, 31 Am.Dec. 522. But these conditions have changed. Even at an early day courts of equity disregarded the fiction that husband and wife were one, and treated them as separate and distinct persons where it was necessary to protect the rights of the wife. Elliot v. Waring, supra; Winebrinner v. Weisiger, 3 T.B.Mon. 32. Indeed, the early rule that the husband might chastise his wife in moderation was never recognized or enforced in this state. Richardson v. Lawhon, 4 Ky.Law Rep. 998. By the act of March 15, 1894, now sections 2127, and 2128, Kentucky Statutes, the rights and liabilities of husband and wife are materially changed. Under that act, the husband has no estate or interest in his wife's property, but the wife holds and owns all of her estate to her separate and exclusive use, and free from the debts, liabilities or control of her husband. By virtue of that act the wife may make contracts, sue and be sued, collect her rents, and may sell and dispose of her personal property. In the case of Lane v. Bryant, 100 Ky. 138, 37 S.W. 584, 18 Ky.Law Rep. 658, 36 L.R.A. 709, this court declined to follow the common law rule that a husband was liable for slanderous words spoken by his wife, on the ground that the rule had been changed by the above statute, the court saying: "The rule is a harsh one at best, and, with the progress of civilization and the changes by a wise modern legislature of the relations between husband and wife as to the right of property and personal control by the husband, it would seem absurd, in this enlightened age, to regard the wife as a mere machine, made to labor and to talk as the husband directs, and to make him liable on that ground for her torts, when not committed by his direction or procurement." After calling attention to the provisions of the act of March 15, 1894, the court added: "While it may be and is the marital duty of both to aid each other in the support and maintenance of each and of their children, the control and use of the wife's property by her is independent of the husband, nor subject to his control, and the familiar doctrine that the legal existence of the wife is merged in that of the husband no longer exists; and as on this rule is based the common law liability of the husband for the wife's torts, and even for her debts contracted before her marriage, the reason for enforcing this doctrine is gone, and past adjudications on the subject will not be followed. The unity of person has been destroyed, and to say that it still exists with the constant legislation of this state endeavoring to secure the wife in her person and property, and at last by the act of March, 1894, making the wife equal of the husband in the control and use of property, would be opposed to the plain legislative intent, and result in enforcing a doctrine that has neither wisdom nor justice in it." In the more recent case of Turner v. Heavrin, 182 Ky. 65, 206 S. W. 23, 4 A.L.R. 562, the court, while recognizing the common law rule that a wife could not sue for criminal conversation with her husband, held that the rule had been changed by the act of 1894, and that a wife now had the right to bring such an action.

It will thus be seen that the one person idea of the marriage relation, as expounded by the common law authorities, can no longer be made the touchstone of a married woman's rights or capacities. Nagle v. Tieperman, 74 Kan. 32, 85 P. 941, 9 L.R.A.,N.S., 674, affirmed 74 Kan. 32, 88 P. 969, 9 L.R.A.,N.S., 674, 10 Ann.Cas. 977. Being secure in her person and property, and her separate identity having been established, it is clear that the means, through which a husband exercised control and dominion over the person and property of his wife, no longer exist. Having sought and obtained these new rights and privileges, which have placed her upon a plane of equality with her husband, she must accept the corresponding obligations and responsibilities which those rights and privileges entail, and can no longer take shelter under the supposed dominion of her husband. This is the view taken by the Supreme Court of Tennessee in the case of Morton v. State, 141 Tenn. 357, 209 S.W. 644, 4 A.L.R. 264, where it was held that the supposed duress of a woman by reason of marriage, which relieves her of liability for crimes committed in the presence of her husband, depends upon her disability by virtue of the marriage, and is destroyed by statutes emancipating her from such disability. We therefore conclude that there is no longer a presumption that a married woman, who commits a crime conjointly with, or in the presence of, her husband, acts under his coercion. It follows that the court's failure to instruct the jury to that effect was not error.

Judgment affirmed.

NOTES

1. Did any statute of Kentucky abolish the rule which was contended for in the principal case, namely, that action by a wife in the presence of her husband is presumed to be in obedience to his command and under his coercion? Did the court find that the statute of any other State had done so? What was the subject matter dealt with in the Kentucky statutes cited by the court?

2. On what basis does the court conclude that the "one-person idea of the marriage relation, as expounded by the common law authorities" is no longer the "touchstone" of a married woman's rights? Does the principal case illustrate Mr. Justice Stone's suggestion about treating a statute as "both a declaration and a source of law and as a premise for legal reasoning"?

3. The classic comment on the common law rule unsuccessfully urged by the defendant in this case is found not in the treatises or law reviews but in Dickens' Oliver Twist:

> "'It was all Mrs. Bumble. She *would* do it,' urged Mr. Bumble; first looking round to ascertain that his partner had left the room.
>
> "'That is no excuse,' replied Mr. Brownlow. 'You were present on the occasion of the destruction of these trinkets, and indeed are the more guilty of the two, in the eye of the law; for the law supposes that your wife acts under your direction.'
>
> "'If the law supposes that,' said Mr. Bumble, squeezing his hat emphatically in both hands, 'the law is a ass—a idiot. If

that's the eye of the law, the law is a bachelor; and the worst I wish the law is, that his eye may be opened by experience—by experience.'

"Laying great stress on the repetition of these two words, Mr. Bumble fixed his hat on very tight, and putting his hands in his pockets, followed his helpmate downstairs." Dodd, Mead Ill.Ed. 519 (1943).

PANAMA RAILROAD CO. v. ROCK

Supreme Court of the United States, 1924.
266 U.S. 209, 45 S.Ct. 58, 69 L.Ed. 250.

Error to a judgment of the Circuit Court of Appeals, which affirmed a judgment recovered by Rock in the District Court for the Canal Zone for damages resulting from the death of his wife, due, as it was alleged, to negligence of the Railroad Company.

Mr. Justice SUTHERLAND delivered the opinion of the Court.

This is an action brought in the District Court for the Canal Zone by James Rock to recover damages for the death of his wife, alleged to have resulted in 1918 from the negligence of the railroad company, while she was being transported as a passenger. Upon the verdict of a jury, final judgment was rendered for plaintiff, which was affirmed by the Circuit Court of Appeals. 272 F. 649. The sole question presented for our determination is whether, under the law of the Canal Zone then in force, there was a right of action.

It is settled that at common law no private cause of action arises from the death of a human being. Insurance Co. v. Brame, 95 U.S. 754, 756, 24 L.Ed. 580. The right of action, both in this country and in England, depends wholly upon statutory authority. Dennick v. Railroad Co., 103 U.S. 11, 21, 26 L.Ed. 439; Seward v. The "Vera Cruz", L.R., 10 App.Cases 59, 70. This Court, also, after elaborate consideration, held that no such action could be maintained in the courts of the United States under the general maritime law. The Harrisburg, 119 U.S. 199, 7 S.Ct. 140, 30 L.Ed. 358. And the general rule of the Roman civil law seems to have been the same as that of the common law. Such was the conclusion of the Supreme Court of Louisiana in a case which was discussed with great fullness and learning at the bar and well considered by that court upon its original presentation and upon rehearing. Hubgh v. New Orleans & C. R. R. Co., 6 La.Ann. 495, 509–511.

But it is contended that the action is maintainable under Art. 2341 of the Civil Code of Panama, which became operative in the Canal Zone by Executive Order of May 9, 1904. That article reads:

"He who shall have been guilty of an offense or fault, which has caused another damage, is obliged to repair it, without prejudice to the principal penalty which the law imposes for the fault or offense committed."

The applicable passage of the Executive Order is, "The laws of the land, with which the inhabitants are familiar, and which were in force on February 26, 1904, will continue in force in the Canal Zone * * * until altered or annulled by the said Commission. * * *"

The Act of Congress of August 24, 1912, c. 390, § 2, 37 Stat. 560, 561, had the effect of confirming this article as valid and binding within the Canal Zone.

The provision under consideration apparently was adopted from the Code of Chile by the several States of Colombia, the adoption by Panama being in 1860. The contention is that the provision in the Chilean Code, in substance, was taken from the Code Napoleon and is to be found, also, in the Civil Code of Spain; that both the French and the Spanish courts had interpreted it as justifying an action such as we are here reviewing; and the familiar rule is invoked that a provision adopted by one country from the laws of another country is presumed to carry with it the meaning which it had acquired by the known and settled construction of the latter. Undoubtedly the decisions of the French courts were to the effect stated. La Bourgogne, 210 U.S. 95, 138, 28 S.Ct. 664, 52 L.Ed. 973. It must be borne in mind, however, that the South American countries named were predominantly Spanish in race and language, and, therefore, it may scarcely be doubted that the statute was taken directly from the Spanish and not the French Code. It follows that the presumption that the French construction was adopted with the adoption of the statute cannot be indulged. Texas & Pacific Ry. Co. v. Humble, 181 U.S. 57, 65, 21 S.Ct. 526, 45 L.Ed. 747. Moreover, there is nothing in any of the circumstances called to our attention to support an inference that the statute was adopted with knowledge of the French construction. See Hunter v. Truckee Lodge, 14 Nev. 24, 38–40. The earliest decision of the Spanish courts of which we are informed was in 1894, Borrero v. Compania Anonyma de la Luz Electrica, 1 Porto Rico Fed. 144, 147, long after the adoption of the statute by either Chile, Colombia or Panama. The presumption in respect of the adoption of the Spanish construction, therefore, has no foundation upon which to rest and must, likewise, be rejected. Stutsman County v. Wallace, 142 U.S. 293, 312, 12 S.Ct. 227, 35 L.Ed. 1018. We are not advised that the courts of Chile had construed the provision prior to its adoption by Panama; and it is asserted and not denied, that prior to its adoption by the Executive Order and congressional act, there had been no decision on the question by the courts of either Colombia or Panama.

It remains, then, only to inquire whether the asserted right of action exists in virtue of the language of the statute independently construed. Upon that question decisions of the various Spanish-speaking countries are of persuasive force only; and even that is overcome or greatly diminished when it is shown that the cognate statute in Porto Rico, and, for aught that appears to the contrary, in the other Spanish-speaking countries, is supported by procedural or other provisions lending aid to its construction as a death statute. In the Borrero Case (p. 146) it is said:

> "Under the practice formerly existing in Porto Rico, in a proper case the law provided for, not only criminal proceedings, but for indemnification on account of the unlawful act to those entitled to it, all in the same proceeding; but those entitled to the civil indemnity could decline to proceed with the criminal action, and yet sue for civil liability. Article 16 of the Penal Code provided that one liable for a misdemeanor was also liable civilly. Both the penal and civil liability could be determined in the same proceeding; and article 123 provided: 'The action to demand restitution, reparation, or indemnification is also transmitted to the heirs of the person injured.'"

The Supreme Court of Louisiana in the Hubgh Case, supra, considering the similar provision in the Louisiana Code, held that it did not include a civil action for death. This conclusion was reached after submitting the language to the test of civil law as well as common law principles.

The Executive Order continued in force in the Canal Zone the laws of the land "with which the inhabitants are familiar;" and this, in effect, was ratified by the Act of Congress of 1912. Immediately following, the native population disappeared and the inhabitants of the Canal Zone since, largely American, have been only employees of the Canal and of those doing business in the Zone, who, it is to be presumed, were familiar with the rule of the common law rather than the construction said to have been put upon the statute by the various Spanish-speaking countries. As early as 1910, the Supreme Court of the Canal Zone declared that the courts of the Zone were "in duty bound to follow the rules of statutory construction of the courts of common law and ascertain by them the meaning and the spirit of the codes." Kung Ching Chong v. Wing Chong, 2 Canal Zone Supreme Court, 25, 30. In the later case of Fitzpatrick v. The Panama Railroad Co., Id. 111, decided in 1913, the same court said (p. 121): " * * * if there is doubt or uncertainty as to the construction and interpretation of the laws here existing prior to February 26, 1904, the courts of the Canal Zone should accept and adopt that construction which more clearly harmonizes with the recognized principles of jurisprudence prevailing in the United States."

Under all the circumstances, we conclude that the reach of the statute is to be determined by the application of common law principles, Panama R. R. Co. v. Bosse, 249 U.S. 41, 45, 39 S.Ct. 211, 63 L. Ed. 466; and, applying these principles, it is clear that the general language of Art. 2341 does not include the right of action here asserted. It would not be difficult to find generalizations of the common law quite as comprehensive in terms as the provision now under review—as, for example, "There is no wrong without a remedy"; but, nevertheless, under the principles of the common law, it has required specific statutes to fix civil liability for death by wrongful act; and it is this requirement, rather than the construction put upon the statute in civil law countries, that the inhabitants of the Canal Zone are presumed to be familiar with, and which affords the rule by which the meaning and scope of the statute in question are to be determined.

Judgment reversed.

Mr. Justice HOLMES, dissenting.

There is no dispute that the language of the Civil Code of Panama, Art. 2341, which has been quoted, is broad enough on its face to give an action for negligently causing the death of the plaintiff's wife. Taken literally it gives such an action in terms. The article of the Code Napoleon from which it is said to have been copied is construed by the French Courts in accord with its literal meaning. La Bourgogne, 210 U.S. 95, 138, 139, 28 S.Ct. 664, 52 L.Ed. 973. It would seem natural and proper to accept the interpretation given to the article at its source, and by the more authoritative jurists who have had occasion to deal with it, irrespective of whether that local interpretation was before or after its adoption by Spanish States, so long as nothing seriously to the contrary is shown. The only thing that I know of to the contrary is the tradition of the later common law. The common law view of the responsibility of a master for his servant was allowed to help in the interpretation of an ambiguous statute in Panama R. R. Co. v. Bosse, 249 U.S. 41, 45, 39 S.Ct. 211, 63 L.Ed. 466, for reasons there stated. But those reasons have far less application here, even if we refer to the common law apart from statute, and in any case are not enough to override the plain meaning of statutory words.

The common law as to master and servant, whatever may be thought of it, embodied a policy that has not disappeared from life. But it seems to me that courts in dealing with statutes sometimes have been too slow to recognize that statutes even when in terms covering only particular cases may imply a policy different from that of the common law, and therefore may exclude a reference to the common law for the purpose of limiting their scope. Johnson v. United States, 163 F. 30, 32, 18 L.R.A.,N.S., 1194. Without going into the reasons for the notion that an action (other than an appeal) does not lie for causing the death of a human being, it is enough to say that they have disappeared. The policy that forbade such an action, if it was more profound than the absence of a remedy when a man's body was hanged and his goods confiscated for the felony, has been shown not to be the policy of present law by statutes of the United States and of most if not all of the States. In such circumstances it seems to me that we should not be astute to deprive the words of the Panama Code of their natural effect.

The decision in the Hubgh Case, 6 La.Ann. 495, stands on nothing better than the classic tradition that the life of a free human being (it was otherwise with regard to slaves), did not admit of valuation, which no longer is true sentimentally, as is shown by the statutes, and which economically is false.

I think that the judgment should be affirmed.

THE CHIEF JUSTICE, Mr. Justice McKENNA and Mr. Justice BRANDEIS concur in this opinion.

NOTE

"The adoption of Lord Campbell's Act in 1846 (9 & 10 Vict. c. 93), giving an action to the executor for the use of wife, husband, parent or child, marks the dawn of a new era. In this country, statutes substantially the same in tenor followed in quick succession in one state after another, till today there is not a state of the Union in which a remedy is lacking. Congress joined in the procession, first with the Employers' Liability Act for railway employees (45 U.S.C.A. §§ 51, 59), next with the Merchant Marine Act of 1920 for seamen and their survivors (46 U.S.C.A. § 688), and again with an act of the same year (March 30, 1920, c. 111, §§ 1, 2, 41 Stat. 537; 46 U.S.C.A. §§ 761, 762), not limited to seamen, which states the legal consequences of death upon the high seas.

"Death statutes have their roots in dissatisfaction with the archaisms of the law which have been traced to their origin in the course of this opinion. It would be a misfortune if a narrow or grudging process of construction were to exemplify and perpetuate the very evils to be remedied. There are times when uncertain words are to be wrought into consistency and unity with a legislative policy which is itself a source of law, a new generative impulse transmitted to the legal system." Cardozo, J., in Van Beeck v. Sabine Towing Co., 300 U.S. 342, 57 S.Ct. 452, 81 L.Ed. 685 (1937).

FUNK v. UNITED STATES

Supreme Court of the United States, 1933.
290 U.S. 371, 54 S.Ct. 212, 78 L.Ed. 369.

Certiorari to review the affirmance of a conviction upon an indictment for conspiracy to violate the National Prohibition Law.

Mr. Justice SUTHERLAND delivered the opinion of the Court.

The sole inquiry to be made in this case is whether in a federal court the wife of the defendant on trial for a criminal offense is a competent witness in his behalf. Her competency to testify against him is not involved.

The petitioner was twice tried and convicted in a federal court upon an indictment for conspiracy to violate the prohibition law. His conviction on the first trial was reversed by the circuit court of appeals upon a ground not material here. 46 F.2d 417. Upon the second trial, as upon the first, defendant called his wife to testify in his behalf. At both trials she was excluded upon the ground of incompetency. The circuit court of appeals sustained this ruling upon the first appeal, and also upon the appeal which followed the second trial. 66 F.2d 70. We granted certiorari, limited to the question as to what law is applicable to the determination of the competency of the wife of the petitioner as a witness.

Both the petitioner and the government, in presenting the case here, put their chief reliance on prior decisions of this court. The government relies on United States v. Reid, 12 How. 361, 13 L.Ed. 1023; Logan v. United States, 144 U.S. 263, 12 S.Ct. 617, 36 L.Ed. 429; Hendrix v. United States, 219 U.S. 79, 31 S.Ct. 193, 55 L.Ed. 102, and Jin Fuey Moy v. United States, 254 U.S. 189, 41 S.Ct. 98, 65 L.Ed. 214. Petitioner contends that these cases, if not directly contrary to the decisions in Benson v. United States, 146 U.S. 325, 13 S. Ct. 60, 36 L.Ed. 991, and Rosen v. United States, 245 U.S. 467, 38 S. Ct. 148, 62 L.Ed. 406, are so in principle. We shall first briefly review these cases, with the exception of the Hendrix case and the Jin Fuey Moy case, which we leave for consideration until a later point in this opinion.

* * *

It is well to pause at this point to state a little more concisely what was held in these cases. It will be noted, in the first place, that the decision in the Reid case was not based upon any express statutory provision. The court found from what the congressional legislation omitted to say, as well as from what it actually said, that in establishing the federal courts in 1789 some definite rule in respect of the testimony to be taken in criminal cases must have been in the mind of Congress; and the rule which the court thought was in the mind of that body was that of the common law as it existed in the thirteen original states in 1789. The Logan case in part rejected that view and held that the controlling rule was that of the common law in force at the time of the admission of the state in which the particular trial was had. Taking the two cases together, it is plain enough that the ultimate doctrine announced is that in the taking of testimony in criminal cases, the federal courts are bound by the rules of the common law as they existed at a definitely specified time in the respective states, unless Congress has otherwise provided.

With the conclusion that the controlling rule is that of the common law, the Benson case and the Rosen case do not conflict; but both cases reject the notion, which the two earlier ones seem to accept, that the courts, in the face of greatly changed conditions are still chained to the ancient formulae and are powerless to declare and enforce modifications deemed to have been wrought in the common law itself by force of these changed conditions. Thus, as we have seen, the court in the Benson case pointed to the tendency during the preceding years to enlarge the domain of competency, significantly saying that the changes had been wrought not only by legislation but also "partially by judicial construction"; and that it was the *spirit* (not the *letter*, be it observed) of this legislation which had controlled the decisions of the courts and steadily removed the merely technical barriers in respect of incompetency, until generally no one was excluded from giving testimony, except under certain peculiar conditions which are set forth. It seems difficult to escape the conclusion that the specific ground upon which the court there rested its determination as to the competency of a codefendant was that, since the defendant had been rendered competent, the competency of the codefendant followed as a natural consequence.

This view of the matter is made more positive by the decision in the Rosen case. The question of the testimonial competency of a person jointly indicted with the defendant was disposed of, as the question had been in the Benson case, "in the light of general authority and sound reason." The conclusion which the court reached was based not upon any definite act of legislation, but upon the trend of congressional opinion and of legislation (that is to say of legislation generally), and upon the great weight of judicial authority which, since the earlier decisions, had developed in support of a more modern rule. In both cases the court necessarily proceeded upon the theory that the resultant modification which these important considerations had wrought in the rules of the old common law was within the power of the courts to declare and make operative.

That the present case falls within the principles of the Benson and Rosen cases, and especially of the latter, we think does not reasonably admit of doubt.

The rules of the common law which disqualified as witnesses persons having an interest, long since, in the main, have been abolished both in England and in this country; and what was once regarded as a sufficient ground for excluding the testimony of such persons altogether has come to be uniformly and more sensibly regarded as affecting the credit of the witness only. Whatever was the danger that an interested witness would not speak the truth—and the danger never was as great as claimed—its effect has been minimized almost to the vanishing point by the test of cross-examination, the increased intelligence of jurors, and perhaps other circumstances. The modern rule which has removed the disqualification from persons accused of crime gradually came into force after the middle of the last century, and is today universally accepted. The exclusion of the husband or wife is said by this court to be based upon his or her interest in the event. Jin Fuey Moy v. United States, supra. And whether by this is meant a practical interest in the result of the prosecution or merely a sentimental interest because of the marital relationship, makes little difference. In either case, a refusal to permit the wife upon the ground of interest to testify in behalf of her husband, while permitting him, who has the greater interest, to testify for himself, presents a manifest incongruity.

Nor can the exclusion of the wife's testimony, in the face of the broad and liberal extension of the rules in respect of the competency of witnesses generally, be any longer justified, if it ever was justified, on any ground of public policy. It has been said that to admit such testimony is against public policy because it would endanger the harmony and confidence of marital relations, and, moreover, would subject the witness to the temptation to commit perjury. Modern legislation, in making either spouse competent to testify in behalf of the other in criminal cases, has definitely rejected these notions, and in the light of such legislation and of modern thought they seem to be altogether fanciful. The public policy of one generation may not, under changed conditions, be the public policy of another. Patton v. United States, 281 U.S. 276, 306, 50 S.Ct. 253, 74 L.Ed. 854, 70 A.L.R. 263.

The fundamental basis upon which all rules of evidence must rest—if they are to rest upon reason—is their adaptation to the successful development of the truth. And since experience is of all teachers the most dependable, and since experience also is a continuous process, it follows that a rule of evidence at one time thought necessary to the ascertainment of truth should yield to the experience of a succeeding generation whenever that experience has clearly demonstrated the fallacy or unwisdom of the old rule.

It may be said that the court should continue to enforce the old rule, however contrary to modern experience and thought, and however opposed, in principle, to the general current of legislation and of judicial opinion, it may have become, leaving to Congress the responsibility of changing it. Of course, Congress has that power; but if Congress fail to act, as it has failed in respect of the matter now under review, and the court be called upon to decide the question, is it not the duty of the court, if it possess the power, to decide it in accordance with present day standards of wisdom and justice rather than in accordance with some outworn and antiquated rule of the past? That this court has the power to do so is necessarily implicit in the opinions delivered in deciding the Benson and Rosen cases. And that implication, we think, rests upon substantial ground. The rule of the common law which denies the competency of one spouse to testify in behalf of the other in a criminal prosecution has not been modified by congressional legislation; nor has Congress directed the federal courts to follow state law upon that subject, as it has in respect of some other subjects. That this court and the other federal courts, in this situation and by right of their own powers, may decline to enforce the ancient rule of the common law under conditions as they now exist we think is not fairly open to doubt.

In Hurtado v. California, 110 U.S. 516, 530, 4 S.Ct. 111, 292, 28 L.Ed. 232, this court, after suggesting that it was better not to go too far back into antiquity for the best securities of our liberties, said:

> "It is more consonant to the true philosophy of our historical legal institutions to say that the spirit of personal liberty and individual right, which they embodied, was preserved and developed by a progressive growth and wise adaptation to new circumstances and situations of the forms and processes found fit to give, from time to time, new expression and greater effect to modern ideas of self-government.
>
> "This flexibility and capacity for growth and adaptation is the peculiar boast and excellence of the common law."
>
> * * *

To concede this capacity for growth and change in the common law by drawing "its inspiration from every fountain of justice," and at the same time to say that the courts of this country are forever bound to perpetuate such of its rules as, by every reasonable test, are found to be neither wise nor just, because we have once adopted them as suited to our situation and institutions at a particular time, is to deny to the common law in the place of its adoption a "flexibility and capacity for growth and adaptation" which was "the peculiar boast and excellence" of the system in the place of its origin.

The final question to which we are thus brought is not that of the power of the federal courts to amend or repeal any given rule or principle of the common law, for they neither have nor claim that power, but it is the question of the power of these courts, in the complete absence of congressional legislation on the subject, to declare and effectuate, upon common law principles, what is the present rule upon a given subject in the light of fundamentally altered conditions, without regard to what has previously been declared and practiced. It has been said so often as to have become axiomatic that the common law is not immutable but flexible, and by its own principles adapts itself to varying conditions. In Ketelsen v. Stilz, 184 Ind. 702, 111 N.E. 423, Ann.Cas.1918A, 965, the supreme court of that state, after pointing out that the common law of England was based upon usages, customs and institutions of the English people as declared from time to time by the courts, said (p. 707):

> "The rules so deduced from this system, however, were continually changing and expanding with the progress of society in the application of this system to more diversified circumstances and under more advanced periods. The common law by its own principles adapted itself to varying con-

ditions and modified its own rules so as to serve the ends of justice as prompted by a course of reasoning which was guided by these generally accepted truths. One of its oldest maxims was that where the reason of a rule ceased, the rule also ceased, and it logically followed that when it occurred to the courts that a particular rule had never been founded upon reason, and that no reason existed in support thereof, that rule likewise ceased, and perhaps another sprang up in its place which was based upon reason and justice as then conceived. No rule of the common law could survive the reason on which it was founded. It needed no statute to change it but abrogated itself."

That court then refers to the settled doctrine that an adoption of the common law in general terms does not require, without regard to local circumstances, an unqualified application of all its rules; that the rules, as declared by the English courts at one period or another, have been controlling in this country only so far as they were suited to and in harmony with the genius, spirit and objects of American institutions; and that the rules of the common law considered proper in the eighteenth century are not necessarily so considered in the twentieth. "Since courts have had an existence in America," that court said (p. 708), "they have never hesitated to take upon themselves the responsibility of saying what are the proper rules of the common law."

* * *

It results from the foregoing that the decision of the court below, in holding the wife incompetent, is erroneous. But that decision was based primarily upon Hendrix v. United States and Jin Fuey Moy v. United States, supra, and in fairness to the lower court it should be said that its decision was fully supported by those cases.

* * * Both the Hendrix and Jin Fuey Moy cases are out of harmony with the Rosen and Benson cases and with the views which we have expressed. In respect of the question here under review, both are now overruled.

Judgment reversed.

Mr. Justice CARDOZO concurs in the result.

Mr. Justice McREYNOLDS and Mr. Justice BUTLER are of opinion that the judgment of the court below is right and should be affirmed.

NOTE

Under a Workmen's Compensation Act the appellant employer had been ordered to pay compensation to the mother of an employee who was an illegitimate son. The statute provided for compensation to, among others, "Parent or parents" of the employee. *Held*: the mother of an illegitimate child is a "parent" within the meaning of the statute. "While by common acceptation the word 'parent,' without limiting, defining or qualifying language, is ordinarily used to designate a legitimate relationship between a mother or father and their issue, yet the trend of modern legislation and court decisions has been toward a more liberal use of the term as regards the mother of an illegitimate child." Marshall v. Industrial Comm., 342 Ill. 400, 174 N.E. 534 (1931). Does this case—or do others previously studied—suggest that you may have to search other statutes as well as common law decisions in order to find the meaning of the statutory term in question?

HAWKINS v. UNITED STATES *

Supreme Court of the United States, 1958.
358 U.S. 74, 79 S.Ct. 136, 3 L.Ed.2d 125.

Mr. Justice BLACK delivered the opinion of the Court.

Petitioner was convicted and sentenced to five years imprisonment by a United States District Court in Oklahoma on a charge that he violated the Mann Act, 18 U.S.C.A. § 2421, by transporting a girl from Arkansas to Oklahoma for immoral purposes. Over petitioner's objection the District Court permitted the Government to use his wife as a witness against him.[2] Relying on Yoder v. United States, 80 F.2d 665, the Court of Appeals for the Tenth Circuit held that this was not error. 249 F.2d 735. As other Courts of Appeals have followed a long-standing rule of evidence which bars a husband or wife from testifying against his or her spouse,[3] we granted certiorari. 355 U.S. 925, 78 S.Ct. 383, 2 L.Ed.2d 356.

The common-law rule, accepted at an early date as controlling in this country, was that husband and wife were incompetent as witnesses for or against each other. The rule rested mainly on a desire to foster peace in the family and on a general unwillingness to use testimony of witnesses tempted by strong self-interest to testify falsely. Since a defendant was barred as a witness in his own behalf because of interest, it was quite natural to bar his spouse in view of the prevailing legal fiction that husband and wife were one person. See 1 Coke, Commentary upon Littleton (19th ed. 1832), 6. b. The rule yielded to exceptions in certain types of cases, however. Thus, this Court in Stein v. Bowman, 13 Pet. 209, 10 L.Ed. 129, while recognizing the "general rule that neither a husband nor wife can be a witness for or against the other," noted that the rule does not apply "where the husband commits an offence against the person of his wife." 13 Pet. at page 221. But the Court emphasized that no ex-

---

* Modified by Trammel v. United States, infra Appendix, which was decided on February 27, 1980.

2. While the wife had been placed under bond to appear in District Court, she offered no objection in court to testifying against her husband.

3. See, e. g., Paul v. United States, 3 Cir., 79 F.2d 561; Brunner v. United States, 6 Cir., 168 F.2d 281; United States v. Walker, 2 Cir., 176 F.2d 564.

ception left spouses free to testify for or against each other merely because they so desired. 13 Pet. at page 223.[4]

Aside from slight variations in application, and despite many critical comments, the rule stated in Stein v. Bowman was followed by this and other federal courts until 1933 when this Court decided Funk v. United States, 290 U.S. 371, 54 S.Ct. 212, 78 L.Ed. 369.[5] That case rejected the phase of the common-law rule which excluded testimony by spouses *for* each other. The Court recognized that the basic reason underlying this exclusion of the evidence had been the practice of disqualifying witnesses with a personal interest in the outcome of a case. Widespread disqualifications because of interest, however, had long since been abolished both in this country and in England in accordance with the modern trend which permitted interested witnesses to testify and left it for the jury to assess their credibility. Certainly, since defendants were uniformly allowed to testify in their own behalf, there was no longer a good reason to prevent them from using their spouses as witnesses. With the original reason for barring favorable testimony of spouses gone the Court concluded that this aspect of the old rule should go too.

The Funk case, however, did not criticize the phase of the common-law rule which allowed either spouse to exclude adverse testimony by the other, but left this question open to further scrutiny. 290 U.S. at page 373, 54 S.Ct. at page 212; Griffin v. United States, 336 U.S. 704, 714–715, 69 S.Ct. 814, 818–819, 93 L.Ed. 993. More recently, Congress has confirmed the authority asserted by this Court in Funk to determine admissibility of evidence under the "principles of the common law as they may be interpreted * * * in the light of reason and experience." Fed.Rules Crim.Proc., 26, 18 U.S.C.A. The Government does not here suggest that authority, reason or experience requires us wholly to reject the old rule forbidding one spouse to testify against the other. It does ask that we modify the rule so that while a husband or wife will not be compelled to testify against the other, either will be free to do so voluntarily. Nothing in this Court's cases supports such a distinction between compelled and voluntary testimony, and it was emphatically rejected in Stein v. Bowman, supra, a leading American statement of the basic principles on which the rule rests. 13 Pet. at page 223. Consequently, if we are to modify

---

4. Stein v. Bowman was a civil action involving testimony of a wife about conversations she had with her husband. The opinion shows, however, that the Court was concerned with the broader question here involved.

5. See, e. g., Miles v. United States, 103 U.S. 304, 305, 26 L.Ed. 481; Graves v. United States, 150 U.S. 118, 14 S.Ct. 40, 37 L.Ed. 1021; Jin Fuey Moy v. United States, 254 U.S. 189, 41 S.Ct. 98, 65 L.Ed. 214. Compare Benson v. United States, 146 U.S. 325, 331–333, 13 S.Ct. 60, 61–62, 36 L.Ed. 991. For criticism of the rule, see 7 Bentham, Rationale of Judicial Evidence (Bowring ed. 1843), 480–486; 2 Wigmore, Evidence (3d ed. 1940), §§ 600–620; 8 id., §§ 2227–2245; Hutchins and Slesinger, Some Observations on the Law of Evidence: Family Relations, 13 Minn.L. Rev. 675.

the rule as the Government urges, we must look to experience and reason, not to authority.

While the rule forbidding testimony of one spouse *for* the other was supported by reasons which time and changing legal practices had undermined, we are not prepared to say the same about the rule barring testimony of one spouse *against* the other. The basic reason the law has refused to pit wife against husband or husband against wife in a trial where life or liberty is at stake was a belief that such a policy was necessary to foster family peace, not only for the benefit of husband, wife and children, but for the benefit of the public as well. Such a belief has never been unreasonable and is not now. Moreover, it is difficult to see how family harmony is less disturbed by a wife's voluntary testimony against her husband than by her compelled testimony. In truth, it seems probable that much more bitterness would be engendered by voluntary testimony than by that which is compelled. But the Government argues that the fact a husband or wife testifies against the other voluntarily is strong indication that the marriage is already gone. Doubtless this if often true. But not all marital flare-ups in which one spouse wants to hurt the other are permanent. The widespread success achieved by courts throughout the country in conciliating family differences is a real indication that some apparently broken homes can be saved provided no unforgivable act is done by either party. Adverse testimony given in criminal proceedings would, we think, be likely to destroy almost any marriage.

Of course, cases can be pointed out in which this exclusionary rule has worked apparent injustice. But Congress or this Court, by decision or under its rule-making power, 18 U.S.C.A. § 3771, can change or modify the rule where circumstances or further experience dictates. In fact, specific changes have been made from time to time. Over the years the rule has evolved from the common-law absolute disqualification to a rule which bars the testimony of one spouse against the other unless both consent. See Stein v. Bowman, supra; Funk v. United States, supra; Benson v. United States, 146 U.S. 325, 331–333; United States v. Mitchell, 2 Cir., 137 F.2d 1006, 1008. In 1887 Congress enabled either spouse to testify in prosecutions against the other for bigamy, polygamy or unlawful cohabitation. 24 Stat. 635. See Miles v. United States, 103 U.S. 304, 315–316, 26 L.Ed. 481. Similarly, in 1917, and again in 1952, Congress made wives and husbands competent to testify against each other in prosecutions for importing aliens for immoral purposes. 39 Stat. 878 (1917), re-enacted as 66 Stat. 230, 8 U.S.C.A. § 1328.

Other jurisdictions have been reluctant to do more than modify the rule. English statutes permit spouses to testify against each other in prosecutions for only certain types of crimes. See Evidence of Spouses in Criminal Cases, 99 Sol.J. 551. And most American States retain the rule, though many provide exceptions in some classes of cases.[6] The limited nature of these exceptions shows there is still a widespread belief, grounded on present conditions, that the law should not force or encourage testimony which might alienate husband and wife, or further inflame existing domestic differences. Under these circumstances we are unable to subscribe to the idea that an exclusionary rule based on the persistent instincts of several centuries should now be abandoned. As we have already indicated, however, this decision does not foreclose whatever changes in the rule may eventually be dictated by "reason and experience."

Notwithstanding the error in admitting the wife's testimony, we are urged to affirm the conviction upon the alternative holding of the Court of Appeals that her evidence was harmless to petitioner. See Fed.Rules Crim.Proc., 52(a). But after examining the record we cannot say that her testimony did not have substantial influence on the jury. See Kotteakos v. United States, 328 U.S. 750, 764–765, 66 S.Ct. 1239, 1247–1248, 90 L.Ed. 1557. Interstate transportation of the prosecutrix between Arkansas and Oklahoma was conceded, and the only factual issue in the case was whether petitioner's dominant purpose in making the trip was to facilitate her practice of prostitution in Tulsa, Oklahoma.[7] The prosecutrix testified that petitioner agreed to take her to Tulsa where she could earn money by working as a prostitute with a woman called "Jane Wilson." Petitioner denied any intention on his part that the prosecutrix engage in such activity and testified, in effect, that her transportation was only an accommodation incidental to a business trip he was making to Oklahoma City, Oklahoma. Petitioner's dominant purpose for the trip was thus a sharply contested issue of fact which, on the evidence in the record, the jury could have resolved either way depending largely on whether

---

6. See 2 Wigmore, Evidence (3d ed. 1940), § 488; 8 id., § 2240; Note, 38 Va.L.Rev. 359, 362–367.

7. The Mann Act, 18 U.S.C.A. § 2421, provides: "Whoever knowingly transports in interstate or foreign commerce * * * any woman or girl for the purpose of prostitution or debauchery, or for any other immoral purpose * * *

* * *

"Shall be fined not more than $5,000 or imprisoned not more than five years, or both."

In construing this Act, we have held: "The statute thus aims to penalize only those who use interstate commerce with a view toward accomplishing the unlawful purposes. * * * An intention that the women or girls shall engage in the conduct outlawed by Section 2 must be found to exist before the conclusion of the interstate journey and must be the dominant motive of such interstate movement. And the transportation must be designed to bring about such result. Without that necessary intention and motivation, immoral conduct during or following the journey is insufficient to subject the transporter to the penalties of the Act.

* * *

"* * * What Congress has outlawed by the Mann Act * * * is the use of interstate commerce as a calculated means for effectuating sexual immorality." Mortensen v. United States, 322 U.S. 369, 374–375, 64 S.Ct. 1037, 1040–1041, 88 L.Ed. 1331. See Cleveland v. United States, 329 U.S. 14, 19–20, 67 S.Ct. 13, 15–16, 91 L.Ed. 12. Cf. Hansen v. Haff, 291 U.S. 559, 563, 54 S.Ct. 494, 495, 78 L.Ed. 968.

it believed the prosecutrix or the petitioner. The Government placed "Jane Wilson" on the stand. In response to questions by the Assistant United States Attorney she swore that she was petitioner's wife and that she was a prostitute at the time petitioner took the prosecutrix to Tulsa. Not wholly satisfied with this testimony the prosecutor brought out for the first time on redirect examination that "Jane Wilson" had been a prostitute before she married petitioner. The mere presence of a wife as a witness against her husband in a case of this kind would most likely impress jurors adversely. When to this there is added her sworn testimony that she was a prostitute both before and after marriage we cannot be sure that her evidence, though in part cumulative, did not tip the scales against petitioner on the close and vital issue of whether his prime motivation in making the interstate trip was immoral. See Krulewitch v. United States, 336 U.S. 440, 444–445, 69 S.Ct. 716, 718–719, 93 L.Ed. 790. At least, use of the wife's testimony was a strong suggestion to the jury that petitioner was probably the kind of man to whom such a purpose would have been perfectly natural.

Reversed.

Mr. Justice STEWART, concurring.

The rule of evidence we are here asked to re-examine has been called a "sentimental relic." [8] It was born of two concepts long since rejected: that a criminal defendant was incompetent to testify in his own case, and that in law husband and wife were one. What thus began as a disqualification of either spouse from testifying at all yielded gradually to the policy of admitting all relevant evidence, until it has now become simply a privilege of the criminal defendant to prevent his spouse from testifying against him. Compare Stein v. Bowman, 13 Pet. 209, 10 L.Ed. 129; Wolfle v. United States, 291 U.S. 7, 14, 54 S.Ct. 279, 280, 78 L.Ed. 617; Funk v. United States, 290 U.S. 371, 54 S.Ct. 212, 78 L.Ed. 369.[9]

Any rule that impedes the discovery of truth in a court of law impedes as well the doing of justice. When such a rule is the product of a conceptualism long ago discarded, is universally criticized by scholars, and has been qualified or abandoned in many jurisdictions, it should receive the most careful scrutiny.[10] Surely "reason and ex-

---

8. See Comment, Rule 23(2) of the Uniform Rules of Evidence.

9. We are not dealing here with the quite different aspect of the marital privilege covering confidential communications between husband and wife. See Wolfle v. United States, 291 U.S. 7, 54 S.Ct. 279, 78 L.Ed. 617.

10. Apparently some nineteen States have either abolished or substantially modified this privilege. See Note, 38 Va.L.Rev. 359, 365. In England the process has been a selective one, accomplished by legislation. See Evidence of Spouses in Criminal Cases, 99 Sol.J. 551. In 1938, the American Bar Association's Committee on Improvements in the Law of Evidence favored the abolition of the privilege on the part of the accused, 63 A.B.A. Rep. 595.

perience" require that we do more than indulge in mere assumptions, perhaps naive assumptions, as to the importance of this ancient rule to the interests of domestic tranquility.[11]

In the present case, however, the Government does not argue that this testimonial privilege should be wholly withdrawn. We are asked only to hold that the privilege is that of the witness and not the accused. Under such a rule the defendant in a criminal case could not prevent his wife from testifying against him, but she could not be compelled to do so.

A primary difficulty with the Government's contention is that this is hardly the case in which to advance it. A supplemental record filed subsequent to the oral argument shows that before "Jane Wilson" testified, she had been imprisoned as a material witness and released under $3,000 bond conditioned upon her appearance in court as a witness for the United States. These circumstances are hardly consistent with the theory that her testimony was voluntary. Moreover, they serve to emphasize that the rule advanced by the Government would not, as it argues, create "a standard which has the great advantage of simplicity." On the contrary, such a rule would be difficult to administer and easy to abuse. Seldom would it be a simple matter to determine whether the spouse's testimony were really voluntary, since there would often be ways to compel such testimony more subtle than the simple issuance of a subpoena, but just as cogent. Upon the present record, and as the issues have been presented to us, I therefore concur in the Court's decision.

NOTES

1. Compare Wyatt v. United States, 362 U.S. 525, 80 S.Ct. 901, 4 L. Ed.2d 931 (1960), Lewis v. Benedict Coal Corp., 361 U.S. 459, 80 S.Ct. 489,

---

11. The facts in the present case illustrate how unrealistic the Court's basic assumption may be. At the time of the acts complained of the petitioner's wife was living apart from him under an assumed name. At the time she testified they were also living apart. In his testimony the petitioner referred to her as his "ex-wife," explaining when his counsel corrected him that he and his wife had never lived together very much.

Before assuming that a change in the present rule would work such a wholesale disruption of domestic felicity as the Court's opinion implies, it would be helpful to know the experience in those jurisdictions where the rule has been abandoned or modified. It would be helpful also to have the benefit of the views of those in the federal system most qualified by actual experience with the operation of the present rule—the district judges and members of the practicing bar. The Judicial Conferences of the several Circuits would provide appropriate forums for imparting that kind of experience. 28 U.S.C.A. § 333.

It is obvious, however, that all the data necessary for an intelligent formulation "in the light of reason and experience" could never be provided in a single litigated case. This points to the wisdom of establishing a continuing body to study and recommend uniform rules of evidence for the federal courts, as proposed by at least two of the Circuit Judicial Conferences. See Annual Report of the Proceedings of the Judicial Conference of the United States, September 18–20, 1957, p. 43. See Joiner, Uniform Rules of Evidence for the Federal Courts. 20 F.R.D. 429.

4 L.Ed.2d 442 (1960), and United States v. Dege, described infra p. 711. In the *Wyatt* case the defendant had been tried and convicted of knowingly transporting a woman in interstate commerce for purposes of prostitution in violation of the Mann Act. At the trial, the woman so transported, who had married defendant after the offense and before the trial, was ordered, despite her objection and that of defendant, to testify and did testify for the prosecution. On certiorari, following a court of appeals decision upholding the district court's rulings and result, the Supreme Court affirmed. Mr. Justice Harlan's majority opinion reads in pertinent part, as follows:

* * *

"*First*. Our decision in Hawkins established, for the federal courts, the continued validity of the common-law rule of evidence ordinarily permitting a party to exclude the adverse testimony of his or her spouse. However, as that case expressly acknowledged, the common law has long recognized an exception in the case of certain kinds of offenses committed by the party against his spouse. Exploration of the precise breadth of this exception, a matter of some uncertainty, * * * can await a case where it is necessary. For present purposes it is enough to note that every Court of Appeals which has considered the specific question now holds that the exception, and not the rule, applies to a Mann Act prosecution, where the defendant's wife was the victim of the offense. * * *

" * * * [W]e now unhesitatingly approve the rule followed in five different Circuits. * * *

"*Second*. * * *

"The United States argues that, once having held, as we do, that in such a case as this the petitioner's wife could not be prevented from testifying voluntarily, Hawkins establishes that she may be compelled to testify. * * * This argument fails to take account of the setting of our decision in Hawkins. * * * In declining to hold that the party had no privilege, we manifestly did not thereby repudiate the privilege of the witness.

"While the question has not often arisen, it has apparently been generally assumed that the privilege resided in the witness as well as in the party. * * * [W]e decline to accept the view that the privilege is that of the party alone.

"*Third*. Neither can we hold that, whenever the privilege is unavailable to the party, it is *ipso facto* lost to the witness as well. It is a question in each case, or in each category of cases, whether, in light of the reason which has led to a refusal to recognize the party's privilege, the witness should be held compellable. Certainly, we would not be justified in laying down a general rule that both privileges stand or fall together. We turn instead to the particular situation at bar.

"Where a man has prostituted his own wife, he has committed an offense against both her and the marital relation, and we have today affirmed the exception disabling him from excluding her testimony against him. It is suggested, however, that this exception has no application to the witness-wife when she chooses to remain silent. The exception to the party's privilege, it is said, rests on the necessity of preventing the defendant from sealing his wife's lips by his own unlawful act, * * * and it is argued that where the wife has chosen not to 'become the instrument' of her husband's downfall, it is her own privilege which is in question, and the reasons for according it to her in the first place are fully applicable.

"We must view this position in light of the congressional judgment and policy embodied in the Mann Act. 'A primary purpose of the Mann Act was to protect women who were weak from men who were bad.' Denning v. United States, 5 Cir., 247 F. 463, 465 (5th Cir. 1918). It was in response to shocking revelations of subjugation of women too weak to resist that Congress acted. See H.R.Rep.No.47, 61st Cong., 2d Sess., pp. 10–11. As the legislative history discloses, the Act reflects the supposition that the women with whom it sought to deal often had no independent will of their own, and embodies, in effect, the view that they must be protected against themselves. Compare 18 U.S.C.A. § 2422 (consent of women immaterial in prosecution under that section). It is not for us to re-examine the basis of that supposition.

"Applying the legislative judgment underlying the Act, we are led to hold it not an allowable choice for a prostituted witness-wife 'voluntarily' to decide to protect her husband by declining to testify against him. For if a defendant can induce a woman, against her 'will,' to enter a life of prostitution for his benefit—and the Act rests on the view that he can—by the same token it should be considered that he can, at least as easily, persuade one who has already fallen victim to his influence that she must also protect him. To make matters turn upon *ad hoc* inquiries into the actual state of mind of particular women, thereby encumbering Mann Act trials with a collateral issue of the greatest subtlety, is hardly an acceptable solution.

"*Fourth.* What we have already said likewise governs the disposition of the petitioner's reliance on the fact that his marriage took place after the commission of the offense. Again, we deal here only with a Mann Act prosecution, and intimate no view on the applicability of the privilege of either a party or a witness similarly circumstanced in other situations. The legislative assumption of lack of independent will applies as fully here. As the petitioner by his power over the witness could, as we have considered should be assumed, have secured her promise not to testify, so, it should be assumed, could he have induced her to go through a marriage ceremony with him, perhaps 'in contemplation of evading justice by reason of the very rule which is now sought to be invoked.' * * *"

* * *

The dissenting opinion (Warren, C. J., joined by Mr. Justice Black and Mr. Justice Douglas) states: "The only relevant difference [between Hawkins and Wyatt] is that here the wife herself was the person allegedly transported by the husband for purposes of prostitution. * * * [T]his does not warrant the radical departure from the *Hawkins* rule which the Court now sanctions." Chief Justice Warren also noted that "The Court does not and could not rely upon the record to prove that petitioner's wife was somehow mesmerized by him when she was on the witness stand. The evidence, in point of fact, strongly suggests that the wife played a managerial role in the sordid enterprise which formed the basis for the prosecution." The Chief Justice then objected to the Court's application of Mann Act policy, arguing, "This equation of the legislative judgment involved in fashioning a criminal statute with the judgment involved in the Court's restriction of the husband-wife privilege * * * overlooks the critically different nature of these problems." While the social interests involved not surprisingly led Congress to make consent immaterial in the former situation, he contended, "The testimonial privilege * * * presents questions of quite a different order, since there is a significant interest traditionally regarded as supporting the privilege, as we recognized in *Hawkins*—the preservation of the conjugal relationship. And where the wife refuses to testify, there is strong evidence that there is still a marital relationship to be protected." He declared that "this decision is uniquely legislative and not judicial" and found this "demonstrated by the fact that, both in England and in this country, changes in the common-law privilege have been wrought primarily by legislatures." It was also remarked that while "[e]very state has a statute governing the matter * * * [t]he many differences among these statutes * * * [show] the divergent views which may be held with respect to the relative importance of the factors involved. * * * [A]pparently only a small minority of States have passed statutes which make the wife competent to testify in a prosecution against her husband for pandering or white slavery when she is the female involved, and only some of these make her compellable as well as competent." The Chief Justice referred in particular to the past action and attitude of Congress regarding the privilege, stating, "As the Court pointed out in *Hawkins*, in 1887 Congress passed a statute which permitted either spouse to testify in prosecutions of the other for the crimes of bigamy, polygamy, or unlawful cohabitation, but *stipulated that neither should be compelled to testify.* 24 Stat. 635. Apparently Congress believed that this provision gave sufficient protection to the spouse-witness, and that the interest of the State in securing convictions was outweighed by the considerations supporting the right of the spouse-witness not to testify against her will. Even more in point is the 1917 legislation by which Congress made spouses competent to testify against each other in prosecutions for the importation of aliens for immoral purposes. 39 Stat. 878–879, re-enacted as 66 Stat. 230, 8 U.S.C. § 1328, 8 U.S.C.A. § 1328. Thus Congress has acted with respect to the scope of the privilege in prosecutions under a statute kindred to § 2421, but has remained silent so far as § 2421 itself is concerned. The negative implication does not require elaboration. Moreover, it should be noted that even under § 1328 the testimony of the spouse is made only 'admissible and competent,' not compellable." In a footnote the dissenting opinion dealt specifically with the *Funk* case as follows: "The nature of relevant action by Congress and by the state legislatures * * * distinguishes this case from Funk v. United States * * *. The contrast between this case and *Funk*, where the Court was able to rely upon 'the general current of legislation and of judicial opinion,' * * * is striking. * * *"

2. See Note, 74 Dick.L.Rev. 499 (1969).

MORAGNE v. STATES MARINE LINES, INC.

Supreme Court of the United States, 1970.
398 U.S. 375, 90 S.Ct. 1772, 26 L.Ed.2d 339.

Mr. Justice HARLAN delivered the opinion of the Court.

We brought this case here to consider whether The Harrisburg, 119 U.S. 199, 7 S.Ct. 140, 30 L.Ed. 358, in which this Court held in 1886 that maritime law does not afford a cause of action for wrongful death, should any longer be regarded as acceptable law.

The complaint sets forth that Edward Moragne, a longshoreman, was killed while working aboard the vessel *Palmetto State* on navigable waters within the State of Florida. Petitioner, as his widow and representative of his estate, brought this suit in a state court against respondent States Marine Lines, Inc., the owner of the vessel, to recover damages for wrongful death and for the pain and suffering experienced by the decedent prior to his death. The claims were predicated upon both negligence and the unseaworthiness of the vessel.

States Marine removed the case to Federal District Court for the Middle District of Florida on the basis of diversity of citizenship, see 28 U.S.C.A. §§ 1332, 1441, and there filed a third-party complaint against respondent Gulf Florida Terminal Company, the decedent's employer, asserting that Gulf had contracted to perform stevedoring services on the vessel in a workmanlike manner and that any negligence or unseaworthiness causing the accident resulted from Gulf's operations.

Both States Marine and Gulf sought dismissal of the portion of petitioner's complaint that requested damages for wrongful death on the basis of unseaworthiness. They contended that maritime law provided no recovery for wrongful death within a State's territorial waters, and that the statutory right of action for death under Florida law, Florida Statutes § 768.01 (1965), F.S.A., did not encompass unseaworthiness as a basis of liability. The District Court dismissed the challenged portion of the complaint on this ground, citing this Court's decision in The Tungus v. Skovgaard, 358 U.S. 588, 79 S.Ct. 503, 3 L.Ed.2d 524 (1959), and cases construing the state statute, but made the certification necessary under 28 U.S.C.A. § 1292(b) to allow petitioner an interlocutory appeal to the Court of Appeals for the Fifth Circuit.

The Court of Appeals took advantage of a procedure furnished by state law, Florida Statutes § 25.031 (1965), F.S.A., to certify to the Florida Supreme Court the question whether the state wrongful death statute allowed recovery for unseaworthiness as that concept is understood in maritime law. After reviewing the history of the Florida Act, the state court answered this question in the negative. 211 So.2d 161 (Fla.1968). On return of the case to the Court of Appeals, that court affirmed the District Court's order, rejecting petitioner's argument that she was entitled to reversal under federal maritime law without regard to the scope of the state statute. 409 F.2d 32 (1969). The court stated that its disposition was compelled by our decision in *The Tungus.* We granted certiorari, 396 U.S. 900, 90 S. Ct. 212, 24 L.Ed.2d 176 (1969), and invited the United States to participate as *amicus curiae,* id., at 952, 90 S.Ct., at 423, 24 L.Ed.2d 418, to reconsider the important question of remedies under federal maritime law for tortious deaths on state territorial waters.

In *The Tungus* this Court divided on the consequences that should flow from the rule of maritime law that "in the absence of a statute there is no action for wrongful death," first announced in *The Harrisburg.* All members of the Court agreed that where a death on state territorial waters is left remediless by the general maritime law and by federal statutes, a remedy may be provided under any applicable state law giving a right of action for death by wrongful act. However, four Justices dissented from the Court's further holding that "when admiralty adopts a State's right of action for wrongful death, it must enforce the right as an integrated whole, with whatever conditions and limitations the creating State has attached." 358 U.S., at 592, 79 S.Ct., at 506. The dissenters would have held that federal maritime law could utilize the state law to "supply a remedy" for breaches of federally imposed duties, without regard to any substantive limitations contained in the state law. Id., at 597, 599, 79 S.Ct., at 509, 510.

The extent of the role to be played by state law under *The Tungus* has been the subject of substantial debate and uncertainty in this Court, see Hess v. United States, 361 U.S. 314, 80 S.Ct. 341, 4 L.Ed.2d 305 (1960); Goett v. Union Carbide Corp., 361 U.S. 340, 80 S.Ct. 357, 4 L.Ed.2d 341 (1960), with opinions on both sides of the question acknowledging the shortcomings in the present law. See 361 U.S., at 314–315, 338–339, 80 S.Ct., at 343, 356. On fresh consideration of the entire subject, we have concluded that the primary source of the confusion is not to be found in *The Tungus,* but in *The Harrisburg,* and that the latter decision, somewhat dubious even when rendered, is such an unjustifiable anomaly in the present maritime law that it should no longer be followed. We therefore reverse the judgment of the Court of Appeals.[12]

---

12. Respondents argue that petitioner is foreclosed from seeking a remedy for wrongful death under general maritime law by her failure to invoke that law at the proper time in the courts below. In the state trial court, which was bound to apply federal maritime law in a case within federal admiralty jurisdiction, e. g., Hess v. United States, 361 U.S., at 318, 80 S.Ct., at 345; McAllister v. Magnolia Petroleum Co., 357 U.S. 221, 78 S.Ct. 1201, 2 L.Ed.2d 1272 (1958), petitioner supported her unseaworthiness claim solely by arguing that the Florida death statute encompassed recovery for unseaworthiness. Under federal law as declared by *The Tungus,* this was the only theory on which she could proceed, short of a challenge—which she did not make —to the validity of *The Tungus* itself.

I

The Court's opinion in *The Harrisburg* acknowledged that the result reached had little justification except in primitive English legal history—a history far removed from the American law of remedies for maritime deaths. That case, like this, was a suit on behalf of

After the District Court on removal rejected her claim, petitioner presented to the Court of Appeals only the question of the interpretation of the state statute, until that question was definitively settled against her by the State Supreme Court on referral.

At that point, petitioner moved the Court of Appeals to uphold her claim as a matter of federal law, despite the state court's ruling. In her brief in support of this motion, petitioner urged that the rule of *The Tungus* was unsound; that the Florida Supreme Court's decision in this case was the first since *The Tungus* in which a state court had read its wrongful death act to exclude unseaworthiness; and that the lack of uniformity thus produced dictated a reexamination of *The Tungus* and adoption of the views of the dissenters in that case. The Court of Appeals heard oral argument on the motion and granted petitioner leave to file a further brief after argument. Respondents opposed the motion and moved to affirm on the basis of *The Tungus*, respondent Gulf arguing that "Appellant [petitioner] has no Federal or maritime action for wrongful death," and that "the issues discussed in Appellant's Brief have been thoroughly argued in Briefs heretofore filed." Neither respondent opposed consideration of the motion on the ground that the issue had not been properly raised.

The Court of Appeals affirmed, stating: "No useful purpose will be served by additional review of pertinent authority upon the issue of law presented in this appeal. It is sufficient to say that in The Tungus v. Skovgaard, * * * the United States Supreme Court held that the question whether a State Wrongful Death Act encompasses a cause of action for unseaworthiness is a question to be decided by the courts of that state."

While this language is not in itself wholly clear, we think it evident in the circumstances that the Court of Appeals considered and rejected petitioner's attack on *The Tungus*. After granting petitioner an opportunity to present that attack at length, and without receiving any objections from respondents to its consideration, the Court of Appeals cannot be presumed to have refused to entertain it. Rather, we read the opinion as stating that the court deemed itself bound by *The Tungus* despite petitioner's challenge to that decision. The Court of Appeals had earlier voiced strong criticism of the prevailing law in this area, but had concluded that it was bound to follow *The Harrisburg* and *The Tungus*. Kenney v. Trinidad Corp., 349 F.2d 832, 840–841 (C.A.5th Cir. 1965).

Since the Court of Appeals, without objection, treated the merits of petitioner's attack on *The Tungus*, we need not consider whether she might otherwise be precluded from pressing that attack here because of her default in failing to urge the same theory in the trial courts. See Neely v. Martin K. Eby Constr. Co., 386 U.S. 317, 330, 87 S.Ct. 1072, 1081, 18 L. Ed.2d 75 (1967); Giordenello v. United States, 357 U.S. 480, 78 S.Ct. 1245, 2 L.Ed.2d 1503 (1958); California v. Taylor, 353 U.S. 553, 557, n. 2, 77 S. Ct. 1037, 1039, 1 L.Ed.2d 1034 (1957); Husty v. United States, 282 U.S. 694, 701–702, 51 S.Ct. 240, 242, 75 L.Ed. 629 (1931); Tyrrell v. District of Columbia, 243 U.S. 1, 37 S.Ct. 361, 61 L. Ed. 557 (1917); cf. Curtis Publishing Co. v. Butts, 388 U.S. 130, 145, 87 S. Ct. 1975, 1986, 18 L.Ed.2d 1094 (1917) (opinion of Harlan, J.). Her challenge to *The Tungus* is properly before us on certiorari, and, of course, it subsumes the question of the continuing validity of *The Harrisburg*, upon which *The Tungus* rests. At this Court's suggestion, 396 U.S. 952, 90 S.Ct. 423, 24 L.Ed.2d 418 (1969), the parties and *amici* have fully addressed themselves to both decisions.

the family of a maritime worker for his death on the navigable waters of a State. Following several precedents in the lower federal courts, the trial court awarded damages against the ship causing the death, and the circuit court affirmed, ruling that death by maritime tort "may be complained of as an injury, and the wrong redressed under the general maritime law." 15 F. 610, 614 (1885). This Court, in reversing, relied primarily on its then recent decision in Insurance Co. v. Brame, 95 U.S. 754, 24 L.Ed. 580 (1878), in which it had held that in American common law, as in English, "no civil action lies for an injury which results in death." Id., at 756.[13] In *The Harrisburg*, as in *Brame*, the Court did not examine the justifications for this common-law rule; rather, it simply noted that "we know of no country that has adopted a different rule on this subject for the sea from that which it maintains on the land," and concluded, despite contrary decisions of the lower federal courts both before and after *Brame*, that the rule of *Brame* should apply equally to maritime deaths. 119 U.S., at 213, 7 S.Ct., at 146.[14]

Our analysis of the history of the common-law rule indicates that it was based on a particular set of factors that had, when *The Harrisburg* was decided, long since been thrown into discard even in England, and that had never existed in this country at all. Further, regardless of the viability of the rule in 1886 as applied to American land-based affairs, it is difficult to discern an adequate reason for its extension to admiralty, a system of law then already differentiated in many respects from the common law.

One would expect, upon an inquiry into the sources of the common-law rule, to find a clear and compelling justification for what seems a striking departure from the result dictated by elementary principles in the law of remedies. Where existing law imposes a primary duty, violations of which are compensable if they cause injury, nothing in ordinary notions of justice suggests that a violation should be nonactionable simply because it was serious enough to cause death. On the contrary, that rule has been criticized ever since its inception,

13. *Brame* was decided, of course, at a time when the federal courts under Swift v. Tyson, 41 U.S. 1, 10 L.Ed. 865 (1842), expounded a general federal common law.

14. The Court stated:
"The argument everywhere in support of such suits in admiralty has been, not that the maritime law, as actually administered in common law countries, is different from the common law in this particular, but that the common law is not founded on good reason, and is contrary to 'natural equity and the general principles of law.' Since, however, it is now established that in the courts of the United States no action at law can be maintained for such a wrong in the absence of a statute giving the right, and it has not been shown that the maritime law, as accepted and received by maritime nations generally, has established a different rule for the government of the courts of admiralty from those which govern courts of law in matters of this kind, we are forced to the conclusion that no such action will lie in the courts of the United States under the general maritime law." Ibid.

and described in such terms as "barbarous." E. g., Osborn v. Gillett, 8 L.R.Exch. 88, 94 (1873) (Lord Bramwell, dissenting); Pollock, The Law of Torts 55 (Landon ed. 1951); 3 Holdsworth, History of English Law, 676–677 (3d ed. 1927). Because the primary duty already exists, the decision whether to allow recovery for violations causing death is entirely a remedial matter. It is true that the harms to be assuaged are not identical in the two cases: in the case of mere injury, the person physically harmed is made whole for his harm, while in the case of death, those closest to him—usually spouse and children—seek to recover for their total loss of one on whom they depended. This difference, however, even when coupled with the practical difficulties of defining the class of beneficiaries who may recover for death, does not seem to account for the law's refusal to recognize a wrongful killing as an actionable tort. One expects, therefore, to find a persuasive, independent justification for this apparent legal anomaly.

Legal historians have concluded that the sole substantial basis for the rule at common law is a feature of the early English law that did not survive into this century—the felony-merger doctrine. See Pollock, supra, at 52–57; Holdsworth, The Origin of the Rule in Baker v. Bolton, 32 L.Q.Rev. 431 (1916). According to this doctrine, the common law did not allow civil recovery for an act that constituted both a tort and a felony. The tort was treated as less important than the offense against the Crown, and was merged into, or pre-empted by, the felony. Smith v. Sykes, 1 Freem. 224, 89 Eng.Rep 160 (K.B. 1677); Higgins v. Butcher, Yelv. 89, 80 Eng.Rep. 61 (K.B. 1607). The doctrine found practical justification in the fact that the punishment for the felony was the death of the felon and the forfeiture of his property to the Crown; thus, after the crime had been punished, nothing remained of the felon or his property on which to base a civil action. Since all intentional or negligent homicide was felonious, there could be no civil suit for wrongful death.

The first explicit statement of the common-law rule against recovery for wrongful death came in the opinion of Lord Ellenborough, sitting at *nisi prius*, in Baker v. Bolton, 1 Camp. 493, 170 Eng.Rep. 1033 (1808). That opinion did not cite authority, nor give supporting reasoning, nor refer to the felony-merger doctrine in announcing that "[i]n a civil court, the death of a human being could not be complained of as an injury." Ibid. Nor had the felony-merger doctrine seemingly been cited as the basis for the denial of recovery in any of the other reported wrongful-death cases since the earliest ones, in the 17th century. E. g., Smith v. Sykes, supra; Higgins v. Butcher, supra. However, it seems clear from those first cases that the rule of Baker v. Bolton did derive from the felony-merger doctrine, and that there was no other ground on which it might be supported even at the time of its inception. The House of Lords in 1916 confirmed this historical derivation, and held that although the felony-merger doctrine was no longer part of the law, the rule against recovery for wrongful death should continue except as modified by statute. Admiralty Commissioners v. S. S. Amerika [1917] A.C. 38. Lord Parker's opinion acknowledged that the rule was "anomalous * * * to the scientific jurist," but concluded that because it had once found justification in the doctrine that "the trespass was drowned in the felony," it should continue as a rule "explicable on historical grounds" even after the disappearance of that justification. Id., at 44, 50; see 3 Holdsworth, History of English Law 676–677 (3d ed. 1927). Lord Sumner agreed, relying in part on the fact that this Court had adopted the English rule in *Brame*. Although conceding the force of Lord Bramwell's dissent in Osborn v. Gillett, 8 L.R.Exch. 88 (1873), against the rule, Lord Parker stated that it was not "any part of the functions of this House to consider what rules ought to prevail in a logical or scientific system of jurisprudence," and thus that he was bound simply to follow the past decisions. (1917) A.C., at 42–43.[15]

The historical justification marshaled for the rule in England never existed in this country. In limited instances American law did adopt a vestige of the felony-merger doctrine, to the effect that a civil action was delayed until after the criminal trial. However, in this country the felony punishment did not include forfeiture of property; therefore, there was nothing, even in those limited instances, to bar a subsequent civil suit. E. g., Grosso v. Delaware, Lackawanna & West. R. Co., 50 N.J.L. 317, 319–320, 13 A. 233 (1888); Hyatt v. Adams, 16 Mich. 180, 185–188 (1867); see Prosser, Torts 8, 920–924 (3d ed. 1964). Nevertheless, despite some early cases in which the rule was rejected as "incapable of vindication," e. g., Sullivan v. Union Pac. R. Co., 23 Fed.Cas. pp. 368, 371 (No. 13,599) (C.C.D.Neb. 1874); Shields v. Yonge, 15 Ga. 349 (1854); cf. Cross v. Guthery, 2 Root 90, 92 (Conn.1794), American courts generally adopted the English rule as the common law of this country as well. Throughout the period of this adoption, culminating in this Court's decision in *Brame*, the courts failed to produce any satisfactory justification for applying the rule in this country.

Some courts explained that their holdings were prompted by an asserted difficulty in computation of damages for wrongful death or

---

15. The decision in *S. S. Amerika* was placed also on an alternative ground, which is independently sufficient. In that case, which arose from a collision between a Royal Navy submarine and a private vessel, the Crown sought to recover from the owners of the private vessel the pensions payable to the families of navy sailors who died in the collision. The first ground given for rejecting the claim was that the damages sought were too remote to be protected by tort law, because the pensions were voluntary payments and because they were not a measure of "the future services of which the Admiralty had been deprived." Id., at 42, 50–51. Similar alternative reasoning was given in *Brame*, which involved a similar situation. 95 U. S., at 758–759, 24 L.Ed. 580. Thus, in neither case was the enunciation of the rule against recovery for wrongful death necessary to the result.

by a "repugnance * * * to setting a price upon human life." E. g., Connecticut Mut. Life Ins. Co. v. New York & N. H. R. Co., 25 Conn. 265, 272–273 (1856); Hyatt v. Adams, supra, 16 Mich. at 191. However, other courts have recognized that calculation of the loss sustained by dependents or by the estate of the deceased, which is required under most present wrongful-death statutes, see Smith, Wrongful-Death Damages in North Carolina, 44 N.C.L.Rev. 402, 405, nn. 17, 18 (1966), does not present difficulties more insurmountable than assessment of damages for many nonfatal personal injuries. See Hollyday v. The David Reeves, 12 Fed.Cas. pp. 386, 388 (No. 6,625 (D.C.D.Md.1879); Green v. Hudson River R. Co., 28 Barb. 9, 17–18 (N.Y.1858).

It was suggested by some courts and commentators that the prohibition of nonstatutory wrongful-death actions derived support from the ancient common-law rule that a personal cause of action in tort did not survive the death of its possessor, e. g., Eden v. Lexington & Frankfurt R. Co., 53 Ky. 204, 206 (1853); and the decision in Baker v. Bolton itself may have been influenced by this principle. Holdsworth, The Origins of the Rule in Baker v. Bolton, 32 L.Q.Rev. 431, 435 (1916). However, it is now universally recognized that because this principle pertains only to the victim's own personal claims, such as for pain and suffering, it has no bearing on the question whether a dependent should be permitted to recover for the injury he suffers from the victim's death. See id.; Pollock supra, at 53; Winfield, Death as Affecting Liability in Tort, 29 Col.L.Rev. 239–250, 253 (1929).

The most likely reason that the English rule was adopted in this country without much question is simply that it had the blessing of age. That was the thrust of this Court's opinion in *Brame*, as well as many of the lower court opinions. E. g., Grosso v. Delaware, Lackawanna & West. R. Co., supra. Such nearly automatic adoption seems at odds with the general principle, widely accepted during the early years of our Nation, that while "our ancestors brought with them * * * [the] general principles [of the common law] and claimed it as their birthright; * * * they brought with them and adopted only that portion which was applicable to their situation." Van Ness v. Pacard, 27 U.S. 137, 144, 7 L.Ed. 374 (1829) (Story, J.); The Lottawanna, 88 U.S. 558, 571–574, 22 L.Ed. 654 (1875); see R. Pound, The Formative Era of American Law 93–97 (1938); H. Hart & A. Sacks, The Legal Process 450 (tent. ed. 1958). The American courts never made the inquiry whether this particular English rule, bitterly criticized in England, "was applicable to their situation," and it is difficult to imagine on what basis they might have concluded that it was.

Further, even after the decision in *Brame*, it is not apparent why the Court in *The Harrisburg* concluded that there should not be a different rule for admiralty from that applied at common law. Maritime law had always, in this country as in England, been a thing apart from the common law. It was, to a large extent, administered by different courts; it owed a much greater debt to the civil law;[16] and, from its focus on a particular subject matter, it developed general principles unknown to the common law. These principles included a special solicitude for the welfare of those men who undertook to venture upon hazardous and unpredictable sea voyages. See generally G. Gilmore & C. Black, The Law of Admiralty 1–11, 253 (1957); Edelman, Maritime Injury and Death 1 (1960). These factors suggest that there might have been no anomaly in adoption of a different rule to govern maritime relations, and that the common-law rule, criticized as unjust in its own domain, might wisely have been rejected as incompatible with the law of the sea. This was the conclusion reached by Chief Justice Chase, prior to *The Harrisburg*, sitting on circuit in The Sea Gull, 21 Fed.Cas. p. 909 (No. 12,578) (C.C.D.Md. 1867). He there remarked that

> "there are cases, indeed, in which it has been held that in a suit at law no redress can be had by the surviving representative for injuries occasioned by the death of one through the wrong of another; but these are all common-law cases, and the common law has its peculiar rules in relation to this subject, traceable to the feudal system and its forfeitures, * * * and certainly it better becomes the humane and liberal character of proceedings in admiralty to give than to withhold the remedy, when not required to withhold it by established and inflexible rules." Id., at 910.

Numerous other federal maritime cases, on similar reasoning, had reached the same result. E. g., The Columbia, 27 F. 704 (D.C.S.D.N.Y.1886); The Manhasset, 18 F. 918 (D.C.E.D.Va.1884); The E. B. Ward, Jr., 17 F. 456 (D.C.C.C.E.D.La.1883); The Garland, 5 F. 924 (D.C.E.D.Mich.1881); Holmes v. Oregon & C. Ry., 5 F. 75 (D.C.D.Or.1880); The Towanda, 24 Fed.Cas. p. 74 (No. 14,109) (C.C.E.D.Pa.1877); Plummer v. Webb, 19 Fed.Cas. p. 894 (No. 11,234) (D. Maine 1825); Hollyday v. The David Reeves, 12 Fed.Cas. p. 386 (No. 6,625) (D.Md.1879). Despite the tenor of these cases, some decided after *Brame*, the Court in *The Harrisburg* concluded that "the admiralty judges in the United States did not rely for their jurisdiction on any rule of the maritime law different from that of the common law, but [only] on their opinion that the rule of the English common law

---

16. The Court in *The Harrisburg* acknowledged that, at least according to the courts of France, the civil law did allow recovery for the injury suffered by dependents of a person killed. It noted, however, that the Louisiana courts took a different view of the civil law, and that English maritime law did not seem to differ in this regard from English common law. 119 U.S., at 205, 212–213, 7 S.Ct., at 142, 146. See generally Grigsby v. Coast Marine Service, 412 F.2d 1011, 1023–1029 (C.A. 5th Cir. 1969) (Brown, J.); 1 Benedict, Admiralty 2 (6th ed. Knauth 1940); 4 id., at 358.

was not founded in reason, and has not become firmly established in the jurisprudence of this country." 119 U.S., at 208, 7 S.Ct. at 144. Without discussing any considerations that might support a different rule for admiralty, the Court held that maritime law must be identical in this respect to the common law.

II

We need not, however, pronounce a verdict on whether *The Harrisburg*, when decided, was a correct extrapolation of the principles of decisional law then in existence. A development of major significance has intervened, making clear that the rule against recovery for wrongful death is sharply out of keeping with the policies of modern American maritime law. This development is the wholesale abandonment of the rule in most of the areas where it once held sway, quite evidently prompted by the same sense of the rule's injustice that generated so much criticism of its original promulgation.

To some extent this rejection has been judicial. The English House of Lords in 1937 emasculated the rule without expressly overruling it. Rose v. Ford (1937) A.C. 826. Lord Atkin remarked about the decision in *S. S. Amerika* that "[t]he reasons given, whether historical or otherwise, may seem unsatisfactory," and that "if the rule is really based on the relevant death being due to felony, it should long ago have been relegated to a museum." At any rate, he saw "no reason for extending the illogical doctrine * * * to any case where it does not clearly apply." (1937) A.C., at 833, 834. Lord Atkin concluded that, while the doctrine barred recognition of a claim in the dependents for the wrongful death of a person, it did not bar recognition of a common-law claim in the decedent himself for "loss of expectation of life"—a claim that vested in the person in the interval between the injury and death, and thereupon passed, with the aid of a survival statute, to the representative of his estate. He expressed no doubt that the claim was "capable of being estimated in terms of money: and that the calculation should be made." Id., at 834.[17] Thus, except that the measure of damages might differ, the representative was allowed to recover on behalf of the heirs what they could not recover in their own names.

Much earlier, however, the legislatures both here and in England began to evidence unanimous disapproval of the rule against recovery for wrongful death. The first statute partially abrogating the rule was Lord Campbell's Act, 9 and 10 Vict. c. 93 (1846), which granted recovery to the families of persons killed by tortious conduct, "al-

17. Lord Wright, concurring, stated: "In one sense it is true that no money can be compensation for life or the enjoyment of life, and in that sense it is impossible to fix compensation for the shortening of life. But it is the best the law can do. It would be paradoxical if the law refused to give any compensation at all because none could be adequate." Id., at 848.

though the Death shall have been caused under such circumstances as amount in Law to Felony." [18]

In the United States, every State today has enacted a wrongful-death statute. See Smith, supra. The Congress has created actions for wrongful deaths of railroad employees, Federal Employers' Liability Act, 45 U.S.C.A. §§ 51, 59; of merchant seamen, Jones Act, 46 U.S.C.A. § 688; and of persons on the high seas, Death on the High Seas Act, 46 U.S.C.A. §§ 761, 762.[19] Congress has also, in the Federal Tort Claims Act, 28 U.S.C.A. § 1346(b), made the United States subject to liability in certain circumstances for negligently caused wrongful death to the same extent as a private person. See, e. g., Richards v. United States, 369 U.S. 1, 82 S.Ct. 585, 7 L.Ed.2d 492 (1962).

These numerous and broadly applicable statutes, taken as a whole, make it clear that there is no present public policy against allowing recovery for wrongful death. The statutes evidence a wide rejection by the legislatures of whatever justifications may once have existed for a general refusal to allow such recovery. This legislative establishment of policy carries significance beyond the particular scope of each of the statutes involved. The policy thus established has become itself a part of our law, to be given its appropriate weight not only in matters of statutory construction but also in those of decisional law. See Landis, Statutes and the Sources of Law, in Harvard Legal Essays 213, 226–227 (1934). Mr. Justice Holmes, speaking also for Chief Justice Taft and Justices Brandeis and McKenna, stated on the very topic of remedies for wrongful death:

> "[I]t seems to me that courts in dealing with statutes sometimes have been too slow to recognize that statutes even when in terms covering only particular cases may imply a policy different from that of the common law, and therefore may exclude a reference to the common law for the purpose of limiting their scope. Johnson v. United States, 163 F. 30, 32. Without going into the reasons for the notion that an

---

18. It has been suggested that one reason the common-law rule was tolerated in England as long as it was may have been that the relatives of persons killed by wrongful acts often were able to exact compensation from the wrongdoer by threatening to bring a "criminal appeal." The criminal appeal was a criminal proceeding brought by a private person, and was for many years more common than indictment as a means of punishing homicide. Though a successful appeal would not produce a monetary recovery, the threat of one served as an informal substitute for a civil suit for damages. Over the years, indictment became more common, and the criminal appeal was abolished by statute in 1819. 59 Geo. 3, c. 46. See Holdsworth, The Origin of the Rule in Baker v. Bolton, 32 L. Q.Rev. 431, 435 (1916); Admiralty Commissioners v. S. S. Amerika (1917) A.C., at 58–59.

19. See also Conservation Act, 16 U.S.C.A. § 457; Outer Continental Shelves Lands Act, 43 U.S.C.A. §§ 1331–1343 (making state wrongful-death statutes applicable to particular areas within federal jurisdiction). Cf. n. [27], infra.

action (other than an appeal) does not lie for causing the death of a human being, it is enough to say that they have disappeared. The policy that forbade such an action, if it was more profound than the absence of a remedy when a man's body was hanged and his goods confiscated for the felony, has been shown not to be the policy of present law by statutes of the United States and of most if not all of the States." Panama R. Co. v. Rock, 266 U.S. 209, 216, 45 S.Ct. 58, 60, 69 L.Ed. 250 (1924) (dissenting opinion.) [20]

Dean Pound subsequently echoed this observation, concluding that "today we should be thinking of the death statutes as part of the general law." Pound, Comment on State Death Statutes—Application to Death in Admiralty, 13 NACCA L.J. 188, 189 (1954); see Cox v. Roth, 348 U.S. 207, 210, 75 S.Ct. 242, 244, 99 L.Ed. 260 (1955).

This appreciation of the broader role played by legislation in the development of the law reflects the practices of common-law courts from the most ancient times. As Professor Landis has said, "much of what is ordinarily regarded as 'common law' finds its source in legislative enactment." Landis, supra, at 214. It has always been the duty of the common-law court to perceive the impact of major legislative innovations and to interweave the new legislative policies with the inherited body of common-law principles—many of them deriving from earlier legislative exertions.

The legislature does not, of course, merely enact general policies. By the terms of a statute, it also indicates its conception of the sphere within which the policy is to have effect. In many cases the scope of a statute may reflect nothing more than the dimensions of the particular problem that came to the attention of the legislature, inviting the conclusion that the legislative policy is equally applicable to other situations in which the mischief is identical. This conclusion is reinforced where there exists not one enactment but a course of legislation dealing with a series of situations, and where the generality of the underlying principle is attested by the legislation of other jurisdictions. Id., at 215–216, 220–222. On the other hand the legislature may, in order to promote other, conflicting interests, prescribe with particularity the compass of the legislative aim, erecting a strong inference that territories beyond the boundaries so drawn are not to feel the impact of the new legislative dispensation. We must, therefore, analyze with care the congressional enactments that have abrogated the common-law rule in the maritime field to determine the

---

20. The *Rock* case involved the question whether an action for wrongful death was maintainable in the Panama Canal Zone, under a general statute that simply embodied the civil-law principle of liability for damage caused by fault. The majority's decision, engrafting onto this statute the common-law rule forbidding such recovery despite the fact that the rule had then been rejected by every relevant jurisdiction, was immediately repudiated by congressional action. Act of Dec. 29, 1926, § 7, 44 Stat. 927; see Landis, supra, at 227.

impact of the fact that none applies in terms to the situation of this case. See Part III, infra. However, it is sufficient at this point to conclude, as Mr. Justice Holmes did 45 years ago, that the work of the legislatures has made the allowance of recovery for wrongful death the general rule of American law, and its denial the exception. Where death is caused by the breach of a duty imposed by federal maritime law, Congress has established a policy favoring recovery in the absence of a legislative direction to except a particular class of cases.

III

Our undertaking, therefore, is to determine whether Congress has given such a direction in its legislation granting remedies for wrongful deaths in portions of the maritime domain. We find that Congress has given no affirmative indication of an intent to preclude the judicial allowance of a remedy for wrongful death to persons in the situation of this petitioner.

From the date of *The Harrisburg* until 1920, there was no remedy for death on the high seas caused by breach of one of the duties imposed by federal maritime law. For deaths within state territorial waters, the federal law accommodated the humane policies of state wrongful-death statutes by allowing recovery whenever an applicable state statute favored such recovery.[21] Congress acted in 1920 to furnish the remedy denied by the courts for deaths beyond the jurisdiction of any State, by passing two landmark statutes. The first of these was the Death on the High Seas Act, 46 U.S.C.A. § 761 et seq. Section 1 of that Act provides that:

> "Whenever the death of a person shall be caused by wrongful act, neglect, or default occurring on the high seas beyond a marine league from the shore of any State, * * * the personal representative of the decedent may maintain a suit for damages in the district courts of the United States, in admiralty, for the exclusive benefit of the decedent's wife, husband, parent, child or dependent relative against the vessel, person, or corporation which would have been liable if death had not ensued."

Section 7 of the Act further provides:

> "The provisions of any State statute giving or regulating rights of action or remedies for death shall not be affected

---

21. The general understanding was that the statutes of the coastal States, which provided remedies within territorial waters, did not apply beyond state boundaries. This Court had suggested, in an early case where the plaintiff and defendant were of the same State, that the law of that State could be applied to a death on the high seas, if the State intended its law to have such scope. The Hamilton, 207 U.S. 398, 28 S.Ct. 133, 52 L.Ed. 264 (1907). However, probably because most state death statutes were not meant to have application to the high seas, this possibility did little to fill the vacuum.

by this [Act]. Nor shall this [Act] apply to the Great Lakes or to any waters within the territorial limits of any State * * *."

The second statute was the Jones Act, 46 U.S.C.A. § 688, which, by extending to seamen the protections of the Federal Employers' Liability Act, provided a right of recovery against their employers for negligence resulting in injury or death. This right follows from the seaman's employment status and is not limited to injury or death occurring on the high seas.[22]

The United States, participating as *amicus curiae*, contended at oral argument that these statutes, if construed to forbid recognition of a general maritime remedy for wrongful death within territorial waters, would perpetuate three anomalies of present law. The first of these is simply the discrepancy produced whenever the rule of *The Harrisburg* holds sway: Within territorial waters, identical conduct violating federal law (here the furnishing of an unseaworthy vessel) produces liability if the victim is merely injured, but frequently not if he is killed. As we have concluded, such a distinction is not compatible with the general policies of federal maritime law.

The second incongruity is that identical breaches of the duty to provide a seaworthy ship, resulting in death, produce liability outside the three-mile limit—since a claim under the Death on the High Seas Act may be founded on unseaworthiness, see Kernan v. American Dredging Co., 355 U.S. 426, 430, n. 4, 78 S.Ct. 394, 397, 2 L.Ed.2d 382 (1958)—but not within the territorial waters of a State whose local statute excludes unseaworthiness claims. The United States argues that since the substantive duty is federal, and federal maritime jurisdiction covers navigable waters within and without the three-mile limit, no rational policy supports this distinction in the availability of a remedy.

The third, and assertedly the "strangest" anomaly is that a true seaman—that is, a member of a ship's company, covered by the Jones Act—is provided no remedy for death caused by unseaworthiness within territorial waters, while a longshoreman, to whom the duty of seaworthiness was extended only because he performs work tradition-

---

22. In 1927 Congress passed the Longshoremen's and Harbor Workers' Compensation Act, 33 U.S.C.A. §§ 901–950, granting to longshoremen the right to receive workmen's compensation benefits from their employers for accidental injury or death arising out of their employment. These benefits are made exclusive of any other liability for employers who comply with the Act. The Act does not, however, affect the longshoreman's remedies against persons other than his employer, such as a shipowner, and therefore does not bear on the problem before us except perhaps to serve as yet another example of congressional action to allow recovery for death in circumstances where recovery is allowed for nonfatal injuries.

ally done by seamen, does have such a remedy when allowed by a state statute.[23]

There is much force to the United States' argument that these distinctions are so lacking in any apparent justification that we should not, in the absence of compelling evidence, presume that Congress affirmatively intended to freeze them into maritime law. There should be no presumption that Congress has removed this Court's traditional responsibility to vindicate the policies of maritime law by ceding that function exclusively to the States. However, respondents argue that an intent to do just that is manifested by the portions of the Death on the High Seas Act quoted above.

The legislative history of the Act suggests that respondents misconceive the thrust of the congressional concern. Both the Senate and House Reports consist primarily of quoted remarks by supporters of the proposed Act. Those supporters stated that the rule of *The Harrisburg*, which had been rejected by "[e]very country of western Europe," was a "disgrace to a civilized people." "There is no reason why the admiralty law of the United States should longer depend on the statute laws of the States. * * * Congress can now bring our maritime law into line with the laws of those enlightened nations which confer a right of action for death at sea." The Act would accomplish that result "for deaths on the high seas, leaving unimpaired the rights under state statutes as to deaths on waters within the territorial jurisdiction of the States. * * * This is for the pur-

---

23. A joint contributor to this last situation, in conjunction with the rule of *The Harrisburg*, is the decision in Gillespie v. United States Steel Corp., 379 U.S. 148, 85 S.Ct. 308, 13 L.Ed.2d 199 (1964), where the Court held that the Jones Act, by providing a claim for wrongful death based on negligence, precludes any state remedy for wrongful death of a seaman in territorial waters—whether based on negligence or unseaworthiness. The Court's ruling in *Gillespie* was only that the Jones Act, which was "intended to bring about the uniformity in the exercise of admiralty jurisdiction required by the Constitution, * * * necessarily supersedes the application of the death statutes of the several States." Id., at 155, 85 S.Ct., at 155. The ruling thus does not disturb the seaman's rights under general maritime law, existing alongside his Jones Act claim, to sue his employer for injuries caused by unseaworthiness, see McAllister v. Magnolia Petroleum Co., 357 U.S. 221, 78 S.Ct. 1201, 2 L.Ed.2d 1272 (1958), or for death on the high seas caused by unseaworthiness, see Kernan v. American Dredging Co., 355 U.S. 426, 430, n. 4, 78 S.Ct. 394, 397, 2 L.Ed.2d 382 (1958); Doyle v. Albatross Tanker Corp., 367 F.2d 465 (C.A.2d Cir. 1966); cf. Pope & Talbot, Inc. v. Hawn, 346 U.S. 406, 74 S.Ct. 202, 98 L.Ed. 143 (1953). Likewise, the remedy under general maritime law that will be made available by our overruling today of *The Harrisburg* seems to be beyond the preclusive effect of the Jones Act as interpreted in *Gillespie*. The existence of a maritime remedy for deaths of seamen in territorial waters will further, rather than hinder, "uniformity in the exercise of admiralty jurisdiction"; and, of course, no question of preclusion of a *federal* remedy was before the Court in *Gillespie* or its predecessor, Lindgren v. United States, 281 U.S. 38, 50 S.Ct. 207, 74 L.Ed. 686 (1930), since no such remedy was thought to exist at the time those cases were decided. See G. Gilmore & C. Black, supra, at 304; but cf. Kernan v. American Dredging Co., 355 U.S., at 429–430, 78 S.Ct., at 397.

pose of uniformity, as the States cannot properly legislate for the high seas." S.Rep.No.216, 66th Cong., 1st Sess.; H.R.Rep.No.674, 66th Cong., 2d Sess. The discussion of the bill on the floor of the House evidenced the same concern that a cause of action be provided "in cases where there is now no remedy," 59 Cong.Rec. 4486, and at the same time that "the power of the States to create actions for wrongful death in no way be affected by enactment of the federal law." The Tungus v. Skovgaard, 358 U.S., at 593, 79 S.Ct., at 507.

Read in light of the state of maritime law in 1920, we believe this legislative history indicates that Congress intended to ensure the continued availability of a remedy, historically provided by the States, for deaths in territorial waters; its failure to extend the Act to cover such deaths primarily reflected the lack of necessity for coverage by a federal statute, rather than an affirmative desire to insulate such deaths from the benefits of any federal remedy that might be available independently of the Act. The void that existed in maritime law up until 1920 was the absence of any remedy for wrongful death on the high seas. Congress, in acting to fill that void, legislated only to the three-mile limit because that was the extent of the problem.[24] The express provision that state remedies in territorial waters were not disturbed by the Act ensured that Congress' solution of one problem would not create another by inviting the courts to find that the Act pre-empted the entire field, destroying the state remedies that had previously existed.

The beneficiaries of persons meeting death on territorial waters did not suffer at that time from being excluded from the coverage of the Act. To the contrary, the state remedies that were left undisturbed not only were familiar but also may actually have been more generous than the remedy provided by the new Act. On the one hand, the primary basis of recovery under state wrongful-death statutes was negligence. On the other hand, the substantive duties imposed at that time by general maritime law were vastly different from those that presently exist. "[T]he seaman's right to recover damages for injuries caused by the unseaworthiness of the ship was an obscure and relatively little used remedy," perhaps largely because prior to this Court's decision in Mahnich v. Southern S. S. Co., 321 U.S. 96, 64 S.Ct. 455, 88 L.Ed. 561 (1944), the shipowner's duty was only to use due diligence to provide a seaworthy ship. G. Gilmore & C. Black, supra, at 315, 361; Tetreault, Seamen, Seaworthiness, and

24. Similarly, when Parliament abrogated the English common-law rule by passing Lord Campbell's Act, it provided that "nothing therein contained shall apply to that part of the United Kingdom called Scotland." 9 and 10 Vict. c. 93, § 6 (1846). The decisional law of Scotland had long recognized a right to recover for wrongful death; thus the mischief at which the statute aimed could be cured without disturbing Scottish law. The Act "excluded Scotland from its operation because a sufficient remedy already existed there when in England none existed at all." Admiralty Commissioners v. S. S. Amerika (1917) A.C., at 51–52.

the Rights of Harbor Workers, 39 Cornell L.Q. 381, 392–393, 396 (1954). Nonseamen on the high seas could generally recover for ordinary negligence, but even this was virtually denied to seamen under the peculiar maritime doctrine of The Osceola, 189 U.S. 158, 175, 23 S.Ct. 483, 487, 47 L.Ed. 760 (1903). Congress in 1920 thus legislated against a backdrop of state laws that imposed a standard of behavior generally the same as—and in some respects perhaps more favorable than—that imposed by federal maritime law.

Since that time the equation has changed drastically, through this Court's transformation of the shipowner's duty to provide a seaworthy ship into an absolute duty not satisfied by due diligence. See, e. g., Mahnich v. Southern S. S. Co., supra; Mitchell v. Trawler Racer, Inc., 362 U.S. 539, 80 S.Ct. 926, 4 L.Ed.2d 941 (1960). The unseaworthiness doctrine has become the principal vehicle for recovery by seamen for injury or death, overshadowing the negligence action made available by the Jones Act, see G. Gilmore & C. Black, supra, at 315–332; and it has achieved equal importance for longshoremen and other harbor workers to whom the duty of seaworthiness was extended because they perform work on the vessel traditionally done by seamen. Seas Shipping Co. v. Sieracki, 328 U.S. 85, 66 S.Ct. 872, 90 L. Ed. 1099 (1946). The resulting discrepancy between the remedies for deaths covered by the Death on the High Seas Act and for deaths that happen to fall within a state wrongful death statute not encompassing unseaworthiness could not have been foreseen by Congress. Congress merely declined to disturb state remedies at a time when they appeared adequate to effectuate the substantive duties imposed by general maritime law. That action cannot be read as an instruction to the federal courts that deaths in territorial waters, caused by breaches of the evolving duty of seaworthiness, must be *damnum absque injuria* unless the States expand their remedies to match the scope of the federal duty.

To put it another way, the message of the Act is that it does not by its own force abrogate available state remedies; no intention appears that the Act have the effect of foreclosing any nonstatutory federal remedies that might be found appropriate to effectuate the policies of general maritime law.[25]

25. We note that § 1 of the Act, which authorizes "a suit for damages in the district courts of the United States, in admiralty," has been construed to place exclusive jurisdiction on the admiralty side of the federal courts for suits under the Act, e. g., Devlin v. Flying Tiger Lines, Inc., 220 F.Supp. 924 (D.C.S.D.N.Y.1963), although there was earlier authority to the contrary. Bugden v. Trawler Cambridge, 319 Mass. 315, 65 N.E.2d 533 (1946). If we found from the legislative history that Congress imposed exclusive jurisdiction because of a desire to avoid the presentation of wrongful-death claims to juries, that might support an inference that Congress meant to forbid nonstatutory maritime actions for wrongful death, which might come before state or federal juries. Cf. Fitzgerald v. United States Lines, 374 U.S. 16, 83 S.Ct. 1646, 10 L.Ed.2d 720 (1963). However, that is not the case. The only discussion of exclusive jurisdiction in the legislative history is found in the House floor debates, during

Ch. 6　　　　　　　　　COORDINATION　　　　　　　　　639

That our conclusion is wholly consistent with the congressional purpose is confirmed by the passage of the Jones Act almost simultaneously with the Death on the High Seas Act. As we observed in Gillespie v. United States Steel Corp., 379 U.S. 148, 155, 85 S.Ct. 308, 312, 13 L.Ed.2d 199 (1964), the Jones Act was intended to achieve "uniformity in the exercise of admiralty jurisdiction" by giving seamen a federal right to recover from their employers for negligence regardless of the location of the injury or death. That strong concern for uniformity is scarcely consistent with a conclusion that Congress intended to *require* the present nonuniformity in the effectuation of the duty to provide a seaworthy ship. Our recognition of a right to recover for wrongful death under general maritime law will assure uniform vindication of federal policies, removing the tensions and discrepancies that have resulted from the necessity to accommodate state remedial statutes to exclusively maritime substantive concepts. E. g., Hess v. United States, 361 U.S. 314, 80 S.Ct. 341, 4 L.Ed.2d 305 (1960); Goett v. Union Carbide Corp., 361 U.S. 340, 80 S.Ct. 357, 4 L.Ed.2d 341 (1960).[26] Such uniformity not only will further the concerns of both of the 1920 Acts but also will give effect to the constitutionally based principle that federal admiralty law should

the course of which Representative Volstead, floor manager of the bill and chairman of the Judiciary Committee, told the members that exclusive jurisdiction would follow necessarily from the fact that the Act would be part of the federal maritime law. 59 Cong.Rec. 4485. This erroneous view disregards the "saving clause" in 28 U.S.C.A. § 1333, and the fact that federal maritime law is applicable to suits brought in state courts under the permission of that clause. See n. [12], supra. When asked whether it was true that jury trials would never be available in suits under the Act, Representative Volstead replied: "I do not think so. Perhaps, for certain purposes, under the practice that prevails, they might have a jury, but ordinarily a jury is not allowed. However, I do not know much about admiralty practice." 59 Cong.Rec. 4485. From this we can derive no expression of policy bearing on the matter under discussion.

26. The incongruity of forcing the States to provide the sole remedy to effectuate duties that have no basis in state policy is highlighted in this case. The Florida Supreme Court ruled that the state wrongful-death act was concerned only with "traditional common-law concepts," and not with "concepts peculiar to maritime law such as 'unseaworthiness' and the comparative negligence rule." It found no reason to believe that the Florida Legislature intended to cover, or even considered, the "completely foreign" maritime duty of seaworthiness. 211 So.2d, at 164, 166. Federal law, rather than state, is the more appropriate source of a remedy for violation of the federally imposed duties of maritime law. Cf. Hill, The Law-Making Power of the Federal Courts: Constitutional Preemption, 67 Col.L.Rev. 1024 (1967); Note, The Federal Common Law, 82 Harv.L.Rev. 1512, 1523–1525 (1969).

It is worth noting that this problem of lack of congruence between maritime duties and state remedies was not presented in *The Harrisburg*. The problem there was that the relevant state statutes of limitations had run, and petitioner sought a federal remedy to which they would not be applicable. The Cout did not discuss the standards of behavior comprehended by the state law or by maritime law, and nothing indicates that the state law was not wholly adequate to vindicate substantive maritime policies in a suit brought within the state-prescribed period. Cf. McAllister v. Magnolia Petroleum Co., 357 U.S. 221, 78 S.Ct. 1201, 2 L.Ed.2d 1272 (1958).

be "a system of law coextensive with, and operating uniformly in, the whole country." The Lottawanna, 88 U.S. 558, 575, 22 L.Ed. 654 (1875).

We conclude that the Death on the High Seas Act was not intended to preclude the availability of a remedy for wrongful death under general maritime law in situations not covered by the Act.[27] Because the refusal of maritime law to provide such a remedy appears to be jurisprudentially unsound and to have produced serious confusion and hardship, that refusal should cease unless there are substantial countervailing factors that dictate adherence to *The Harrisburg* simply as a matter of *stare decisis*. We now turn to a consideration of those factors.

IV

Very weighty considerations underlie the principle that courts should not lightly overrule past decisions. Among these are the desirability that the law furnish a clear guide for the conduct of individuals, to enable them to plan their affairs with assurance against untoward surprise; the importance of furthering fair and expeditious adjudication by eliminating the need to relitigate every relevant proposition in every case; and the necessity of maintaining public faith in the judiciary as a source of impersonal and reasoned judg-

---

27. Respondents purport to find such a preclusive intent in two other federal statutes in related areas, the Conservation Act, 16 U.S.C.A. § 457, and the Outer Continental Shelves Lands Act, 43 U.S.C.A. §§ 1331–1343. The former provides: "In the case of the death of any person by the neglect or wrongful act of another within a national park or other place subject to the exclusive jurisdiction of the United States, within the exterior boundaries of any State, such right of action shall exist as though the place were under the jurisdiction of the State within whose exterior boundaries such place may be * * *." Although Judge Learned Hand once suggested that this statute applied to admiralty, Puleo v. H. F. Moss & Co., 159 F.2d 842, 845 (1947), he quickly reconsidered, Guerrini v. United States, 167 F.2d 352, 355 (1948), and it now seems clear that it does not. See The Tungus v. Skovgaard, 358 U.S. 588, at 609, n. 9, 79 S.Ct. 503, at 515 (Brennan, J.); cf. Rodrigue v. Aetna Cas. & Sur. Co., 395 U.S. 352, 89 S.Ct. 1835, 23 L.Ed. 2d 360 (1969). The congressional decision to place under state laws such areas as national parks, which are carved from existing state territories and are subject to no other general body of law, carries no implication of a similar intent in the vastly different realm of the admiralty.

The latter statute was before this Court in Rodrigue v. Aetna Cas. & Sur. Co., 395 U.S. 352, 89 S.Ct. 1835, 23 L.Ed. 2d 360 (1969). We there determined that the Act was intended to treat artificial islands, located beyond the three-mile limit, not as vessels upon the high seas but "as though they were federal enclaves in an upland State." Because the Act "deliberately eschewed the application of admiralty principles to these novel structures," id., at 355, 89 S.Ct. at 1837, they were held subject to the substantive standards of state law except when an inconsistent federal law applied. This special dispensation for a modern problem to which maritime law was thought "inapposite," id., at 363, 89 S.Ct. at 1841, has no analogue in this case. It is undisputed that the duties owed by respondents to petitioner's husband were determined by maritime law, and were the same within as without the three-mile limit.

ments. The reasons for rejecting any established rule must always be weighed against these factors.

The first factor, often considered the mainstay of *stare decisis*, is singularly absent in this case. The confidence of people in their ability to predict the legal consequences of their actions is vitally necessary to facilitate the planning of primary activity and to encourage the settlement of disputes without resort to the courts. However, that confidence is threatened least by the announcement of a new remedial rule to effectuate well-established primary rules of behavior. There is no question in this case of any change in the duties owed by shipowners to those who work aboard their vessels. Shipowners well understand that breach of the duty to provide a seaworthy ship may subject them to liability for injury regardless of where it occurs, and for death occurring on the high seas or in the territorial waters of most States. It can hardly be said that shipowners have molded their conduct around the possibility that in a few special circumstances they may escape liability for such a breach. Rather, the established expectations of both those who own ships and those who work on them are that there is a duty to make the ship seaworthy and that a breach of that federally imposed duty will generally provide a basis for recovery. It is the exceptional denial of recovery that disturbs these expectations. "If the new remedial doctrine serves simply to reenforce and make more effectual well-understood primary obligations, the net result of innovation may be to strengthen rather than to disturb the general sense of security." H. Hart & A. Sacks, supra, at 485, 574–577, 585–595, 606–607; Pound, Some Thoughts About Stare Decisis, 13 NACCA L.J. 19 (1954).

Nor do either of the other relevant strands of *stare decisis* counsel persuasively against the overruling of *The Harrisburg*. Certainly the courts could not provide expeditious resolution of disputes if every rule were fair game for *de novo* reconsideration in every case. However, the situation we face is far removed from any such consequence as that. We do not regard the rule of *The Harrisburg* as a closely arguable proposition—it rested on a most dubious foundation when announced, has become an increasingly unjustifiable anomaly as the law over the years has left it behind, and, in conjunction with its corollary, *The Tungus*, has produced litigation spawning confusion in an area that should be easily susceptible to more workable solutions. The rule has had a long opportunity to prove its acceptability, and instead has suffered universal criticism and wide repudiation. To supplant the present disarray in this area with a rule both more simple and more just will further, not impede, efficiency in adjudication. Finally, a judicious reconsideration of precedent cannot be as threatening to public faith in the judiciary as continued adherence to a rule unjustified in reason, which produces different results for breaches of duty in situations that cannot be differentiated in policy.

Respect for the process of adjudication should be enhanced, not diminished, by our ruling today.[28]

V

Respondents argue that overruling *The Harrisburg* will necessitate a long course of decisions to spell out the elements of the new "cause of action." We believe these fears are exaggerated, because our decision does not require the fashioning of a whole new body of federal law, but merely removes a bar to access to the existing general maritime law. In most respects the law applied in personal-injury cases will answer all questions that arise in death cases.

Respondents argue, for example, that a statute of limitations must be devised or "borrowed" for the new wrongful-death claim. However, petitioner and the United States respond that since we have simply removed the barrier to general maritime actions for fatal injuries, there is no reason—in federal admiralty suits at least[29] that such actions should not share the doctrine of laches immemorially applied to admiralty claims. In applying that doctrine, the argument runs, the courts should give consideration to the two-year statute of limitations in the Death on the High Seas Act, just as they have always looked for analogy to appropriate state or foreign statutes of limitations. See Kenney v. Trinidad Corp., 349 F.2d 832, 840 (C.A. 5th Cir. 1965); G. Gilmore & C. Black, supra, at 296, n. 149, 628. We need not decide this question now, because the present case was brought within a few months of the accident and no question of timeliness has been raised. The argument demonstrates, however, that the difficulties should be slight in applying accepted maritime law to actions for wrongful death.

The one aspect of a claim for wrongful death that has no precise counterpart in the established law governing nonfatal injuries is the

28. Respondents point out that a bill has been introduced in the United States Senate, by request, which would, among other things, extend the Death on the High Seas Act to include deaths in state territorial waters. S. 3143, 91st Cong., 1st Sess. To date no hearings have been scheduled or other action taken on the bill. The mere possibility of future legislation in this field does not, of course, affect the legal merits of petitioner's claim that the rule of *The Harrisburg* is no longer a valid part of maritime law. See United States v. W. M. Webb, Inc., 397 U.S. 179, 194, n. 21, 90 S.Ct. 850, 857, 25 L.Ed. 2d 207 (1970).

Nor do we think that Congress' failure to take action on the pending bill, or to pass a similar measure over the years as the law of deaths on territorial waters became more incongruous, provides guidance for the course we should take in this case. To conclude that Congress, by not legislating on this subject, has in effect foreclosed, by negative legislation as it were, reconsideration of prior judicial doctrine would be to disregard the fact that "Congress has largely left to this Court the responsibility for fashioning the controlling rules of admiralty law." Fitzgerald v. United States Lines Co., 374 U.S. 16, 20, 83 S.Ct. 1646, 1650, 10 L.Ed.2d 720 (1963).

29. See McAllister v. Magnolia Petroleum Co., 357 U.S. 221, 224, 78 S.Ct. 1201, 1204, 2 L.Ed.2d 1272 (1958).

such neglect. In support of this we need only cite our own decision in Bott v. Pratt, 33 Minn. 323, 23 N.W. 237, 53 Am.Rep. 47.

Defendant contends that this is only true where a right of action for the alleged negligent act existed at common law; that no liability existed at common law for selling poison without labelling it, and therefore none exists under this statute, no right of civil action being given by it. Without stopping to consider the correctness of the assumption that selling poison without labelling it might not be actionable negligence at common law, it is sufficient to say that, in our opinion, defendant's contention proceeds upon an entire misapprehension of the nature and gist of a cause of action of this kind. The common law gives a right of action to every one sustaining injuries caused proximately by the negligence of another. The present is a common-law action, the gist of which is defendant's negligence, resulting in the death of plaintiff's intestate. Negligence is the breach of legal duty. It is immaterial whether the duty is one imposed by the rule of common law requiring the exercise of ordinary care not to injure another, or is imposed by a statute designed for the protection of others. In either case the failure to perform the duty constitutes negligence and renders the party liable for injuries resulting from it. The only difference is that in the one case the measure of legal duty is to be determined upon common-law principles, while in the other the statute fixes it, so that the violation of the statute constitutes conclusive evidence of negligence, or, in other words, negligence *per se.* The action in the latter case is not a statutory one, nor does the statute give the right of action in any other sense except that it makes an act negligent which otherwise might not be such, or at least only evidence of negligence. All that the statute does is to establish a fixed standard by which the fact of negligence may be determined. The gist of the action is still negligence, or the non-performance of a legal duty to the person injured.

What has been already said suggests the answer to the further contention that if any civil liability exists it is only against the clerk who sold the poison, and who alone is criminally liable. Whether the act constituting the actionable negligence was such on common-law principles, or is made such by statute, the doctrine of agency applies, to wit, that the master is civilly liable for the negligence of his servant committed in the course of his employment, and resulting in injuries to third persons.

Judgment affirmed.

MARTIN v. HERZOG

Court of Appeals of New York, 1920.
228 N.Y. 164, 126 N.E. 814.

Appeal from an order of the Appellate Division of the Supreme Court in the second judicial department, entered February 2, 1917, reversing a judgment in favor of plaintiff entered upon a verdict and granting a new trial.

The nature of the action and the facts, so far as material, are stated in the opinion.

CARDOZO, J. The action is one to recover damages for injuries resulting in death.

Plaintiff and her husband, while driving toward Tarrytown in a buggy on the night of August 21, 1915, were struck by the defendant's automobile coming in the opposite direction. They were thrown to the ground, and the man was killed. At the point of the collision the highway makes a curve. The car was rounding the curve when suddenly it came upon the buggy, emerging, the defendant tells us, from the gloom. Negligence is charged against the defendant, the driver of the car, in that he did not keep to the right of the center of the highway (Highway Law, sec. 286, subd. 3; sec. 332; Consol. Laws, ch. 25). Negligence is charged against the plaintiff's intestate, the driver of the wagon, in that he was traveling without lights (Highway Law, sec. 329a, as amended by L.1915, ch. 367). There is no evidence that the defendant was moving at an excessive speed. There is none of any defect in the equipment of his car. The beam of light from his lamps pointed to the right as the wheels of his car turned along the curve toward the left; and looking in the direction of the plaintiff's approach, he was peering into the shadow. The case against him must stand, therefore, if at all, upon the divergence of his course from the center of the highway. The jury found him delinquent and his victim blameless. The Appellate Division reversed, and ordered a new trial.

We agree with the Appellate Division that the charge to the jury was erroneous and misleading. The case was tried on the assumption that the hour had arrived when lights were due. It was argued on the same assumption in this court. In such circumstances, it is not important whether the hour might have been made a question for the jury. Todd v. Nelson, 109 N.Y. 316, 325, 16 N.E. 360. A controversy put out of the case by the parties is not to be put into it by us. We say this by way of preface to our review of the contested rulings. In the body of the charge the trial judge said that the jury could consider the absence of light "in determining whether the plaintiff's intestate was guilty of contributory negligence in failing to have a light upon the buggy as provided by law. I do not mean to say that the absence of light necessarily makes him negligent, but it is a fact for your consideration." The defendant requested a ruling that the absence of a light on the plaintiff's vehicle was "*prima facie* evidence of contributory negligence." This request was refused, and the jury were again instructed that they might consider the absence of lights as some evidence of negligence, but that it was not conclusive evidence. The plaintiff then requested a charge that "the fact that the plaintiff's intestate was driving without a light is not negligence in itself," and to this the court acceded. The defendant saved his rights by appropriate exceptions.

We think the unexcused omission of the statutory signals is more than some evidence of negligence. It is negligence in itself. Lights are intended for the guidance and protection of other travelers on the highway. Highway Law, sec. 329a. By the very terms of the hypothesis, to omit, willfully or heedlessly, the safeguards prescribed by law for the benefit of another that he may be preserved in life or limb, is to fall short of the standard of diligence to which those who live in organized society are under a duty to conform. That, we think, is now the established rule in this state. Amberg v. Kinley, 214 N.Y. 531, 108 N.E. 830, L.R.A.1915E, 519; Karpeles v. Heine, 227 N.Y. 74, 124 N.E. 101; Jetter v. N. Y. & H. R. R. Co., 41 N.Y. 154, 2 Abb.Ct.App.Dec. 458; Cordell v. N. Y. C. & H. R. R. Co., 64 N.Y. 535, 538; Marino v. Lehmaier, 173 N.Y. 530, 536, 66 N.E. 572, 61 L.R.A. 811; cf. Texas & Pacific Ry. Co. v. Rigsby, 241 U.S. 33, 39, 40, 36 S.Ct. 482, 60 L.Ed. 874; Prest-O-Lite Co. v. Skeel, 182 Ind. 583, 600, 601, 106 N.E. 365, Ann.Cas.1917A, 474; Newcomb v. Boston Protective Dept., 146 Mass. 596, 16 N.E. 555, 4 Am.St.Rep. 354; Bourne v. Whitman, 209 Mass. 155, 163, 95 N.E. 404, 35 L.R.A.,N.S., 701. Whether the omission of an absolute duty, not willfully or heedlessly, but through unavoidable accident, is also to be characterized as negligence, is a question of nomenclature into which we need not enter, for it does not touch the case before us. There may be times, when if jural niceties are to be preserved, the two wrongs, negligence and breach of statutory duty, must be kept distinct in speech and thought, Pollock Torts (10th ed.), p. 458; Clark & Linseil Torts (6th ed.), p. 493; Salmond Jurisprudence (5th ed.), pp. 351, 363; Texas & Pac. Ry. Co. v. Rigsby, supra, p. 43; Chicago, B. & Q. Ry. Co. v. U. S., 220 U.S. 559, 31 S.Ct. 612, 55 L.Ed. 582. In the conditions here present they come together and coalesce. A rule less rigid has been applied where the one who complains of the omission is not a member of the class for whose protection the safeguard is designed. Amberg v. Kinley, supra; Union Pac. Ry. Co. v. McDonald, 152 U.S. 262, 283, 14 S.Ct. 619, 38 L.Ed. 434; Kelley v. N. Y. State Rys., 207 N.Y. 342, 100 N.E. 1115; Ward v. Hobbs, 4 App.Cas. 13. Some relaxation there has also been where the safeguard is prescribed by local ordinance, and not by statute. Massoth v. D. & H. C. Co., 64 N.Y. 524, 532; Knupfle v. Knickerbocker Ice Co., 84 N.Y. 488. Courts have been reluctant to hold that the police regulations of boards and councils and other subordinate officials create rights of action beyond the specific penalties imposed. This has led them to say that the violation of a statute is negligence, and the violation of a like ordinance is only evidence of negligence. An ordinance, however, like a statute, is a law within its sphere of operation, and so the distinction has not escaped criticism. Jetter v. N. Y. & H. R. R. Co., supra; Knupfle v.

Knickerbocker Ice Co., supra; Newcomb v. Boston Protective Dept., supra; Prest-O-Lite Co. v. Skeel, supra. Whether it has become too deeply rooted to be abandoned, even if it be thought illogical, is a question not now before us. What concerns us at this time is that even in the ordinance cases, the omission of a safeguard prescribed by statute is put upon a different plane, and is held not merely some evidence of negligence, but negligence in itself. Massoth v. D. & H. R. R. Co., supra; and cf. Cordell v. N. Y. C. & H. R. R. Co., supra. In the case at hand, we have an instance of the admitted violation of a statute intended for the protection of travelers on the highway, of whom the defendant at the time was one. Yet the jurors were instructed in effect that they were at liberty in their discretion to treat the omission of lights either as innocent or culpable. They were allowed to "consider the default as lightly or gravely" as they would (Thomas, J., in the court below). They might as well have been told that they could use a like discretion in holding a master at fault for the omission of a safety appliance prescribed by positive law for the protection of a workman. Scott v. International Paper Co., 204 N.Y. 49, 97 N.E. 413; Fitzwater v. Warren, 206 N.Y. 355, 99 N.E. 1042, 42 L.R.A.,N.S., 1229; Texas & Pac. Ry. Co. v. Rigsby, 241 U.S. 33, 36 S.Ct. 482, 60 L.Ed. 874. Jurors have no dispensing power by which they may relax the duty that one traveler on the highway owes under the statute to another. It is error to tell them that they have. The omission of these lights was a wrong, and being wholly unexcused was also a negligent wrong. No license should have been conceded to the triers of the facts to find it anything else.

We must be on our guard, however, against confusing the question of negligence with that of the causal connection between the negligence and the injury. A defendant who travels without lights is not to pay damages for his fault unless the absence of lights is the cause of the disaster. A plaintiff who travels without them is not to forfeit the right to damages unless the absence of lights is at least a contributing cause of the disaster. To say that conduct is negligence is not to say that it is always contributory negligence. "Proof of negligence in the air, so to speak, will not do" Pollock Torts (10th ed.), p. 472. We think, however, that evidence of a collision occurring more than an hour after sundown between a car and an unseen buggy, proceeding without lights, is evidence from which a causal connection may be inferred between the collision and the lack of signals. Lambert v. Staten Island R. R. Co., 70 N.Y. 104, 109, 110; Walsh v. Boston & Maine Railroad, 171 Mass. 52, 58, 50 N.E. 43; The Pennsylvania, 19 Wall. 125, 136, 137, 22 L.Ed. 148; Fisher v. Village of Cambridge, 133 N.Y. 527, 532, 30 N.E. 663. If nothing else is shown to break the connection, we have a case *prima facie* sufficient, of negligence contributing to the result. There may indeed be times when the lights on a highway are so many and so bright that lights on a wagon are superfluous. If that is so, it is for the offender to go forward with the evidence, and prove the illumination as a kind of substituted performance. She says that the scene of the accident was illumined by moonlight, by an electric lamp, and by the lights of the approaching car. Her position is that if the defendant did not see the buggy thus illumined, a jury might reasonably infer that he would not have seen it anyhow. We may doubt whether there is any evidence of illumination sufficient to sustain the jury in drawing such an inference, but the decision of the case does not make it necessary to resolve the doubt, and so we leave it open. It is certain that they were not required to find that lights on the wagon were superfluous. They might reasonably have found the contrary. They ought, therefore, to have been informed what effect they were free to give, in that event, to the violation of the statute. They should have been told not only that the omission of the lights was negligence, but that it was *"prima facie* evidence of contributory negligence," i. e., that it was sufficient in itself unless its probative force was overcome (Thomas, J., in court below) to sustain a verdict that the decedent was at fault. Kelly v. Jackson, 6 Pet. 622, 632, 8 L.Ed. 523. Here, on the undisputed facts, lack of vision, whether excusable or not, was the cause of the disaster. The defendant may have been negligent in swerving from the center of the road, but he did not run into the buggy purposely, nor was he driving while intoxicated, nor was he going at such a reckless speed that warning would of necessity have been futile. Nothing of the kind is shown. The collision was due to his failure to see at a time when sight should have been aroused and guided by the statutory warnings. Some explanation of the effect to be given to the absence of those warnings, if the plaintiff failed to prove that other lights on the car or the highway took their place as equivalents, should have been put before the jury. The explanation was asked for, and refused.

We are persuaded that the tendency of the charge and of all the rulings following it, was to minimize unduly, in the minds of the triers of the facts, the gravity of the decedent's fault. Errors may not be ignored as unsubstantial when they tend to such an outcome. A statute designed for the protection of human life is not to be brushed aside as a form of words, its commands reduced to the level of cautions, and the duty to obey attenuated into an option to conform.

The order of the Appellate Division should be affirmed, and judgment absolute directed on the stipulation in favor of the defendant, with costs in all courts.

[The dissenting opinion of HOGAN, J., is omitted.]

PROBLEMS

In connection with the preceding two cases, consider these problems:

1. You are practicing law in the mythical State of Columbia, which has a statute making it a criminal offense, punishable by a

$500 fine for each violation, for any mining company to use any form of illumination in its mines except electric torches and lamps. The statute says nothing about civil liability to persons injured by forbidden types of lighting equipment. Your client, a medical social worker, was in a Black Coal Co. mine investigating the causes of silicosis when an explosion occurred and injured her. She had noticed before the explosion that the mine was being lighted by oil flares.

If you believe there may be a cause of action: (1) What facts must you be able to prove? (2) What legal arguments would you plan to make and expect to confront in opposition to your client's claim?

2. Jones, who has just stolen some property, is being pursued by Smith, a policeman. Jones runs through an open door of the factory building of Space Toys, Inc., sprints to the fourth floor and, en route to another exit, falls down an unguarded elevator shaft. Smith, in hot pursuit, falls down the same shaft. Both are injured. A statute of the State makes it a misdemeanor for the owner of a building to maintain an unfenced or otherwise unprotected elevator shaft.

In suits by Jones and Smith against Space Toys, Inc., what issues are presented? What result or results seem proper?

NOTE

On the general subject of judicial development of tort actions for damages for violation of legislative provisions, see 4 Restatement, Second, Torts, § 874A and appended Comment (1979).

SIRKIN v. FOURTEENTH ST. STORE

Supreme Court of New York, Appellate Division, 1908.
124 App.Div. 384, 108 N.Y.S. 830.

Action by Samuel Sirkin against the Fourteenth Street Store. From a determination of the Appellate Term (55 Misc. 288, 105 N.Y. S. 179), affirming a judgment of the City Court for plaintiff (54 Misc. 135, 105 N.Y.S. 638), defendant, by leave of the Appellate Term, appeals.

LAUGHLIN, J. The action is brought to recover $1,555.81, being the purchase price of certain hosiery and wrappers sold and delivered by the plaintiff to the defendant. The defendant is a corporation conducting a department store in the city of New York, and the plaintiff is a manufacturer of or dealer in goods of the character described. The defendant, for a separate answer and defense, alleged, in substance, that the plaintiff, without its knowledge or consent, and pursuant to an unlawful, fraudulent, and criminal design, and for the purpose of influencing the purchase of the goods by the defendant's purchasing agent, agreed to pay him a sum of money equal to 5 per cent. of the purchase price of the goods to be ordered by him; that the orders for these goods were obtained pursuant to such unlawful, fraudulent, and criminal design and agreement; that, after the goods were ordered and delivered, the plaintiff, pursuant to his agreement with the defendant's purchasing agent, paid the latter the sum of $75 without other consideration than placing the orders for the goods with the plaintiff; and that the ordering and delivery of the goods and the agreement and the arrangement to pay and the payment were part of an entire transaction which was against public policy, illegal, void, and contrary to the statutory law of the state of New York. Upon the trial the plaintiff proved that the orders for the goods were given by the defendant's purchasing agent, and the delivery of the goods to the defendant and nonpayment. The plaintiff then moved for judgment upon the evidence and on the pleadings, upon the ground that the affirmative defense was insufficient in law. Counsel for the defendant objected to the motion, and asked leave to prove the facts alleged in the separate defense. The court thereupon directed a verdict in favor of the plaintiff for the purchase price of the goods, together with interest thereon. The learned judge who presided in the City Court wrote an elaborate and instructive opinion in support of his decision, upon the theory that, while the agreement on the part of the plaintiff to pay the agent of the defendant was void as against public policy, yet, inasmuch as the goods had been delivered, the defendant would not be permitted to retain the goods and decline to pay therefor. The learned Appellate Term supplemented this opinion with their views at length to the same effect.

I am of opinion that the judgment is wrong, and should be reversed. It must be assumed that the defendant might have proved, upon the separate defense set up in its answer, that the corrupt offer and agreement on the part of the plaintiff to pay the defendant's agent 5 per cent. on the orders received was the inducing cause for placing the orders with the plaintiff, and that the agreement on the part of the latter so to place the orders constituted one transaction. If so, the court should not be astute to discover a theory upon which they may be separated, and they should be deemed inseparable. In any view, it would seem that the defendant might have shown that the offer of an agreement to pay the bribe was made and accepted as a consideration for the giving by the defendant's purchasing agent, then or subsequently, the orders for the goods. That the bribe was conditioned upon plaintiff's giving the contract is demonstrated by his agreement to pay a percentage of the selling price of the goods, according to the orders received. It should be regarded, therefore, practically as if the agreement had expressly provided that the purchasing agent of the defendant should receive a specified percentage of the moneys actually received by the plaintiff on orders so placed with him; thus, in effect, forming but one contract with these parties, and a different consideration running to the agent from that running to his principal. It must be assumed, therefore, that each order for goods given by the agent was given pursuant to one general corrupt agreement, embracing all orders to be given, or pursuant to separate corrupt agreements with respect to each. The corrupt practice of secretly offering bribes to servants, agents, and employés to induce them to place contracts for their masters or employers had spread to such an alarming extent in this state that its viciousness and dishonesty and demoralizing tendencies attracted the attention of the Legislature at its session in 1905 (Laws 1905, p. 225, c. 136), and led it to declare it to be a misdemeanor to give or receive such a bribe by enacting section 384r of the Penal Code, which provides as follows:

> "Corrupt Influencing of Agents, Employés or Servants. Whoever gives, offers or promises to an agent, employé or servant, any gift or gratuity whatever, without the knowledge and consent of the principal, employer or master of such agent, employé or servant, with intent to influence his action in relation to his principal's, employer's or master's business; or an agent, employé or servant, who, without the knowledge and consent of his principal, employer or master, requests or accepts a gift or gratuity or a promise to make a gift or to do an act beneficial to himself, under an agreement or with an understanding that he shall act in any particular manner to his principal's, employer's or master's business, or an agent, employé or servant, who, being authorized to procure materials, supplies or other articles either by purchase or contract for his principal, employer or master, or to employ service or labor for his principal, employer or master, receives directly or indirectly for himself or for another, a commission, discount or bonus from the person who makes such sale or contract, or furnishes such materials, supplies or other articles, or from a person who renders such service or labor; and any person who gives or offers such an agent, employé or servant such commission, discount or bonus shall be guilty of a misdemeanor and shall be punished by a fine of not less than five hundred dollars, or by such fine and by imprisonment for not more than one year."

There can be no doubt that the act of the plaintiff in bribing the purchasing agent of the defendant was a violation of this section of the Penal Code. The plaintiff, therefore, in obtaining the contract upon which he bases this action, committed a crime, and, as already observed, whether the purchasing agent of the defendant agreed to place the orders at the same time the plaintiff agreed to give him the bribe, or whether the orders were given subsequently, but based upon the plaintiff's unlawful contract to bribe the agent, is immaterial. The Legislature has not expressly declared either that the contract to pay the bribe or the contract induced by the bribe is void or unenforceable. A contract, however, made in violation of a penal statute, although not expressly prohibited or declared to be void, is prohibited, void, and unenforceable, whether executory or executed (Griffith v. Wells, 3 Denio, 226; Barton v. Port Jackson & N. T. P. R. Co., 17 Barb. 397). A contract to do an illegal act or to aid another in violating the law is likewise void and unenforceable, whether executory or executed. Goodrich v. Houghton, 134 N.Y. 115, 31 N.E. 516; Materne v. Horwitz, 101 N.Y. 469, 5 N.E. 331; Brinkman v. Eisler (City Ct.N.Y.) 7 N.Y.S. 193, affirmed (City Ct.N.Y.) 16 N.Y.S. 154; Hull v. Ruggles, 56 N.Y. 484. Upon the same principle one who is required by law to procure a license to conduct any trade, calling, or profession may not recover for services rendered or property sold, without first obtaining such license, regardless of whether or not it was known by the person for whom the services were rendered or to whom the property was sold that the license had not been obtained. Johnson v. Dahlgren, 166 N.Y. 354, 59 N.E. 987; Schnaier v. Hotel Co., 82 App.Div. 25, 81 N.Y.S. 633; Accetta v. Zupa, 54 App.Div. 33, 66 N.Y.S. 303; Griffith v. Wells, supra. It is therefore quite clear that the purchasing agent could not enforce the contract to recover the consideration agreed to be paid to him; and it may be here observed that this would have been so under the common law, if the statute had not been enacted, for the contract contravened public policy. Harrington v. Victoria Graving Dock Co., L.R. 3 Q.B.D. 549. The question appears to be presented now for the first time as to whether this is the limitation of the disability for violating the penal statute, or whether the court may refuse its aid to the party obtaining the contract for the purchase or sale of property, or for work, in violation of the statute, upon the same ground that it leaves a party to a contract which is void as against public policy, or offends against good morals, where it finds him. It is manifest that the Legislature in enacting this penal statute intended to emphasize and extend the public policy of the common law, which rendered such contracts by agents for their own benefit void. It being the province of the Legislature to declare the public policy of the state, it is the duty of the court to be guided thereby in administering the law. The acts of the plaintiff, not only offended against good morals and public policy at common law, but constituted a crime under the statutory law of this state; and he is here seeking the aid of the court to enforce a contract which he procured by violating our penal statute. Nothing could be more corrupting, nor have a greater tendency to lead to disloyalty and dishonesty on the part of servants, agents, and employés, and to a betrayal of the confidence and trust reposed in them, than these practices which the Legislature has endeavored to stamp out; and I think nothing will be more effective in stopping the growth and spread of this corrupting and now criminal custom than a decision that the courts will refuse their aid to a guilty vendor or vendee, or to any one who has obtained a contract by secretly bribing the servant, agent, or employé of another to purchase or sell property, or to place the contract with him. * * *

The learned counsel for the plaintiff contends that it does not appear that the contract price is more than the fair market value of the property. It would seem on the facts that it is 5 per cent. more than the plaintiff desired for his property; and, if these practices are allowed, the tendency will be not only to keep prices up, but to raise them, and the nominal price, if the custom should become general, would not represent the selling price of property. Public policy requires that an agent, servant, or employé shall perform the duties of his employment involving discretion and trust, with a single purpose of serving his master or employer; and the master or employer, for the salary or compensation which he has agreed to pay, has a right to expect honest, faithful, loyal service, rendered with a sole regard to his interests. The tendency of this practice is to make the servant disloyal, and to have his action not only influenced, but controlled, by his personal interests, rather than by the duties of his employment. The temptation will be either to agree for his master or employer to pay more than the fair market price of property purchased, or fair market value of work to be performed, or to accept property or work of an inferior quality or grade, in order that he may receive for himself a larger percentage. The servant would be accountable to his master or employer for any moneys thus received, but that affords no adequate remedy, for the reason that such contracts are made secretly, and it would be difficult to discover or prove the facts. The vice lies in making the agreement without the knowledge of the master. Of course, it is perfectly competent for a master to employ a servant as a purchasing or selling agent, and to give him a commission upon the purchase price or allow a commission to be paid by the vendee upon the selling price, and it may well be, as was recently held in Ballin v. Fourteenth Street Store, 54 Misc. 359, 105 N.Y.S. 1028, affirmed (Sup.) 108 N.Y.S. 26, that, where the bribe is received with the knowledge of the master, the statute does not apply, and the contract of sale will be enforced. It is perfectly plain that, if the contract had not been performed by the plaintiff, the defendant, upon discovering the fact that its agent had been bribed to place the contract, would have had the right to rescind. Smith v. Seattle L. S. & E. Ry. Co., 72 Hun, 202, 25 N.Y.S. 368. It is contended that its only remedies upon discovering the facts were to rescind the contract, or, if that were impracticable, to counterclaim for any damages it has sustained by reason of the plaintiff's fraud in inducing the contract, and that by a failure to rescind or thus counterclaim it is deemed to have ratified and affirmed the contract. I am of opinion that this is not a case in which the rule of ratification, applicable to ordinary contracts induced by fraud, should be applied. The public policy of our state forbids the ratification, as well as the making, of such a contract. Usually private contracts concern only the parties thereto, and it is optional with a person who has discovered that he has been defrauded whether to ratify the contract or to rescind it. There is ordinarily, at least, no general public policy involved in such cases.

* * *

There is no force in the contention that this contract does not contravene public policy, because it may be proved without proving the illegal contract between the plaintiff and the purchasing agent of the defendant, pursuant to which it was made. The rule is stated in Chitty on Contracts, 654, that the test as to "whether a demand connected with a transaction is capable of being enforced at law is whether the plaintiff requires any aid from the illegal transaction to establish his case." This rule is quoted approvingly in Gray v. Hook, 4 N.Y. 449, and Woodworth v. Bennett, 43 N.Y. 273, 3 Am.Rep. 706. It is technically accurate if confined to the plaintiff's case; but the rule has since been extended, and it is now well settled that, if the illegality appears by the evidence developed by the plaintiff or by the evidence presented by the defendant, there can be no recovery, and that, even though the contract may be in writing and apparently valid, the illegality may be shown by surrounding facts and circumstances, as is conclusively established by the case of Ernst v. Crosby, 140 N.Y. 364, 35 N.E. 603, where a recovery for rent on a lease in writing apparently valid, for it showed that the house was to be used for the purposes of a residence only, was defeated upon proof that the house was to the knowledge of the landlord to be used for immoral purposes. In this particular case the defendant is an innocent party. It is argued, however, that he should not be permitted to retain the goods without paying for them. The rule of public policy under which courts refuse their aid to enforce contracts was not established to protect the parties, and the court suspends action when the foundation is properly laid by the evidence presented by either party.
* * *

* * *

If the orders were not given at the time the bribe was offered, so that the agreement to bribe and the agreement to place the orders constituted one transaction which would vitiate the whole, they were at least based upon and placed pursuant to the agreement of the plaintiff to bribe the purchasing agent of the defendant, which brings the case fairly within the rule that every agreement, although founded in part on a new legal consideration, founded upon, auxiliary to, or made to carry into effect any of the unexecuted provisions of a previous illegal contract, is void even though completely executed by one party, and will not be enforced at the instance of the party who has executed it. [Citations omitted.] In Armstrong v. Toler, supra, Chief Justice Marshall, writing for the court, sustained an instruction to the jury that:

> "Where the contract grows immediately out of, and is connected with, an illegal or immoral act, a court of justice

will not lend its aid to enforce it. And if the contract be, in fact, one connected with the illegal transaction, and growing immediately out of it, though it be, in fact, a new contract, it is equally tainted by it."

I am therefore of opinion that the defendant should have been permitted to prove the facts pleaded as a separate defense, and that, if they be established, the plaintiff will then be shown to have committed a crime in obtaining the very contracts which he asks the aid of the court to enforce, and should be denied assistance.

The learned counsel for the appellant in his brief in reply reiterates and quotes at great length an argument from his first brief. This practice is condemned as improper, useless, and unnecessarily increasing the labor of the court.

It follows that the determination and judgment should be reversed and a new trial granted, with costs to the appellant, excepting the disbursements for printing the brief in reply, to abide the event.

McLAUGHLIN and CLARKE, JJ., concur.

SCOTT, J. (dissenting). The defendant under a contract of purchase has received plaintiff's goods to the value of $1,555.81, and either now has them, or has sold them and retained the proceeds. It now objects to paying for them, but neither tenders back the goods nor offers to return the proceeds, nor asserts that he suffered any loss or damage by reason of the purchase. Its defense is in effect a plea in bar. It says that the purchase was negotiated by one McGuiness, its purchasing agent; and, for the purpose of inducing the purchase, plaintiff agreed to pay and did pay, McGuiness a commission upon the purchase price, in violation of section 387r of the Penal Code (chapter 136, p. 225, Laws 1905); that this agreement to pay and payment to McGuiness, being a criminal act, so taints with illegality the purchase thereby induced, that the court should refuse to enforce the contract of purchase, and permit defendant to retain plaintiff's goods without paying for them. It is proposed to uphold the defendant in this position because it is believed that such a decision will be most effective in stopping the growth and spread of the corrupting and now criminal custom of paying secret commissions to purchasing agents. It is not contended that the Legislature decreed that contracts, otherwise valid, and wholly executed, should be unenforceable if induced by giving a secret commission to the purchaser's agent; and, while it might lie within the power of the Legislature to add this consequence to the penalties already prescribed for a violation of the statute, that is a matter for legislative, and not judicial, action. The unlawful agreement between plaintiff and McGuiness was no part of the contract between plaintiff and defendant, and, in order to prove the latter, it was not necessary to prove the existence of the former. It needs neither argument nor the citation of authorities to establish the proposition that McGuiness could not have recovered from plaintiff the agreed percentage because the contract to pay it was in itself a criminal act. The contract between plaintiff and defendant was not criminal, and was fully executed. Undoubtedly the secret agreement to pay a commission to plaintiff was a fraud on defendant, and rendered the contract voidable at its option. Smith v. Seattle L. S. & E. Ry. Co., 72 Hun, 202, 25 N.Y.S. 368. It might, if it had discovered the fraud in time, have refused to receive the goods, or, having received them, might have tendered them back, or might even now counterclaim for the damages it suffered from the fraud, if, in fact and law, it could show that it had suffered damage. The statute which has made that a crime, which heretofore was merely immoral, has affixed to that crime an appropriate penalty. It is no part of our duty to assume legislative power and prescribe an additional punishment, nor are we to assume, in the absence of allegations to that effect, that the defendant did, in fact, suffer damage as a result of plaintiff's unlawful agreement with McGuiness.

The determination of the Appellate Term should be affirmed, with costs.

PATTERSON, P. J., concurs.

MARX v. JAFFE

Superior Court of New Jersey, Appellate Division, 1966.
92 N.J.Super. 143, 222 A.2d 519.

Before Judges GAULKIN, LABRECQUE and BROWN.

PER CURIAM.

Plaintiff instituted this action to recover on an alleged loan to defendant represented by checks totaling $13,000. Defendant contends that the money received by him did not constitute a loan, but was, instead, an advance rebate to the U-Neek Super Market (U-Neek), a now bankrupt corporation of which defendant was principal stockholder, under an agreement whereby U-Neek would purchase its milk requirements from Clinton Milk Company (Clinton), a dairy controlled by plaintiff. He urges that this was in contravention of N.J.S.A. 4:12A–30 which precluded agreements whereby the price of milk was reduced below that fixed by the Director of the Office of Milk Industry.

The trial court, sitting without a jury, determined that plaintiff was entitled to recover the amount of the checks issued to defendant, less $1,000 in credits earned by U-Neek under the rebate agreement.

We remanded the matter for further factual findings on questions which we deemed essential to our determination of the appeal. In response to our specific inquiry, the trial court found: (1) checks totaling $13,000 were made payable to defendant personally and he agreed to make repayment; (2) defendant deposited the full amounts in the account of U-Neek; (3) plaintiff and defendant agreed that the latter's indebtedness would be reduced by an amount equal to 10% of all sales of milk or milk products by Clinton Milk Company to U-Neek Super Market; (4) plaintiff's intention in advancing the monies was to circumvent N.J.S.A. 4:12A–30; (5) defendant acted on behalf of U-Neek and plaintiff knew he was so acting. The judge concluded that the parties' agreement was contrary to N.J.S.A. 4:12A–30, but that the penalty provisions of the statute were intended by the Legislature to be exclusive; consequently, the agreement was enforceable.

We are in accord with the conclusion of the trial judge that the agreement between the parties was violative of the statute. The device of couching the rebate agreement between U-Neek, represented by defendant, and Clinton, controlled by plaintiff, in the guise of a personal loan between the individuals does not alter the true nature of the transaction. We also recognize that by instituting this action against defendant personally, plaintiff hopes not only to avoid the impact of N.J.S.A. 4:12A–30, but also to avoid being a mere general creditor of the insolvent corporation, which would be his status had the "loan" been made directly to U-Neek.

Our accord with the trial judge that the agreement violates the statute does not extend to his conclusion that it is nonetheless enforceable because the Legislature had prescribed the exclusive penalties for violations thereof. Violators of the act subject themselves to a penalty of not more than $50 for the first offense and not more than $200 for the second offense, N.J.S.A. 4:12A–39, and the possible suspension or revocation of their licenses. N.J.S.A. 4:12A–35; In re E. J. McGovern Dairy Products, Inc., 60 N.J.Super. 163, 158 A.2d 689 (App.Div.1959).

The fact that the alleged loan transaction contravenes the statute clearly renders the agreement illegal. Brooks v. Cooper, 50 N.J.Eq. 761, 771, 26 A. 978, 21 L.R.A. 617 (E. & A. 1893); Restatement, Contracts, § 580 (1932). However, merely to call a contract illegal is not to state the effects of such illegality. In each case the legislative intent must be sought. John J. Carlin, Inc. v. O'Connor, 126 N.J.L. 243, 245–246, 17 A.2d 584 (E. & A. 1941).

In N.J.S.A. 4:12A–30 the Legislature provided that any rebate "contract, arrangement, agreement or understanding is hereby prohibited and declared to be contrary to the public interest * * *." This express prohibition of any bargain which reduces milk prices below the fixed minimum, coupled with the declaration that such bargains are contrary to the public interest, manifests the legislative intention that such bargains are unenforceable and that the statutory penalties are cumulative.

It is said to be an established rule that "the law will not assist either party to an illegal contract. The parties being *in pari delicto*, it will leave them where it finds them. If the contract be still executory, it will not enforce it, and if already executed, it will not restore the *status quo ante*." Cameron v. International Alliance of Theatrical Stage Employees, Local 384, 118 N.J.Eq. 11, 20, 176 A. 692, 697, 97 A.L.R. 594 (E. & A.1935). The rule finds particular application in this case for two reasons. First, the explicit prohibition of any rebate agreement makes it manifest that such an agreement could not be enforced by one of the parties thereto were it wholly executory. Enforcement would promote the private interest at the expense of the public interest. Second, neither the partial execution in the instant case, nor any other factors, bring this matter within any of the exceptions to the general rule of nonenforceability. See generally, Restatement, op. cit., §§ 598–609.

This is not an instance where refusal to enforce or rescind an illegal bargain would produce a harmful effect on the parties for whose protection the law making the bargain illegal exists. In such cases enforcement or rescission, whichever is appropriate, is allowed. Id., § 601; Cameron v. International Alliance of Theatrical Stage Employees, supra, at pp. 20–21, 176 A. 692. Here, on the contrary, the Legislature has expressly determined that the public interest in a constant flow of wholesome milk to consumers requires price regulation. Abbotts Dairies, Inc. v. Armstrong, 14 N.J. 319, 330, 102 A.2d 372 (1954). The public interest does not require that the court give either efficacy or consolation to the efforts of a party to an agreement to subvert the administratively determined price structure.

Further, this is not an instance where enforcement commends itself, despite illegality, in order to avoid an unjust forfeiture. See 6A Corbin, Contracts, § 1522, pp. 761–2 (1962). That consideration is inapplicable where the result accomplished by enforcement is expressly prohibited by statute. Restatement, op. cit., §§ 600, 603. More importantly, however, there is no unjust forfeiture in the present case. Plaintiff delivered the advance rebate to defendant with knowledge that the monies were to be a fund for U-Neek. Defendant was a mere conduit, despite the efforts of the parties to cloak him otherwise. It would be incongruous to reward plaintiff with a position superior to that of the creditors of the now insolvent U-Neek because of his efforts to circumvent N.J.S.A. 4:12A–30.

In summary, we hold that the statutory prohibition of rebate agreements requires that no phase of this agreement may be enforced.

Reversed and remanded for the entry of judgment for defendant. No costs.

NOTE

The phrase "in pari delicto" appearing in the court's opinion is a short way of referring to the maxim: in pari delicto potior est conditio defendentis (when the parties are equally in the wrong, the position of the defendant is the stronger). The maxim is quite frequently invoked in cases on illegal bargains.

MODERN INDUSTRIAL BANK v. TAUB

Court of Errors and Appeals of New Jersey, 1946.
134 N.J.L. 260, 47 A.2d 348.

Action on a note by the Modern Industrial Bank against William L. Taub and Isidor Ostroff, severally and jointly. Judgment for plaintiff. The Supreme Court, 133 N.J.L. 285, 44 A.2d 176, affirmed the judgment against Ostroff but reversed as to Taub and directed the issuance of a venire de novo, and the defendants appeal and the plaintiff cross-appeals.

HEHER, Justice. The action is upon a promissory note made by defendant Taub to the order of Riker & Company, Inc., and indorsed by Taub and the defendant Ostroff. The answer introduced by Taub and Ostroff was struck out as either sham or frivolous; and there was summary judgment for plaintiff. The Supreme Court affirmed the judgment against Ostroff, but reversed as to Taub and directed the issuance of a venire de novo. While the appeal was taken in the names of both defendants, they attack only the judgment against Ostroff. Plaintiff's cross appeal challenges the Supreme Court's reversal of the judgment against Taub.

The note in suit evidences the maker's promise to pay the payee, a real estate broker not licensed as such under R.S. 45:15–1 et seq., N.J.S.A., a commission for negotiating a sale of the Strand Hotel property in Atlantic City; and the primary question at issue is whether the note is void and therefore unenforceable against either the maker or the indorsers, even in the hands of a holder in due course. The contention is also made that both indorsements were affixed after the delivery of the instrument to the payee broker, and without a new, independent consideration, and no contractual liability could thereby arise.

If the note has the qualities of a negotiable instrument, there can be no doubt that plaintiff is a holder in due course, and there is no issue of fact in that regard. The contention contra is sham. There is no competent testimony tending to overcome plaintiff's specific proof in that behalf.

Turning to the basic question, the insistence is that the note is void ab initio, in that it stems from "a transaction prohibited by statute and contrary to public policy," and by the same token, is a non-negotiable instrument, and plaintiff is not a holder in due course entitled to the protection accorded such by the Negotiable Instruments Act, R.S. 7:2–1 et seq., N.J.S.A. The cases of Kenney v. Paterson Milk & Cream Co., 110 N.J.L. 141, 164 A. 274, 88 A.L.R. 1416, and

Fisher v. Brehm, 100 N.J.L. 341, 126 A. 444, 37 A.L.R. 695, are cited in support of these propositions.

But the subject matter of Fisher v. Brehm was a check given in payment of a gambling debt; and it was held void, and therefore unenforceable by a holder in due course, under the express provision of Section 3 of the Gaming Act of 1877, Comp.Stat.1910, p. 2624, now R.S. 2:57–3, N.J.S.A., that all such contracts "shall be utterly void and of no effect." The real estate brokers licensing act, supra, is not so framed. It prohibits engagement in such brokerage business without the license therein provided; and its sanctions consist solely of pecuniary penalties recoverable by the commission therein created in the several district courts and courts of common pleas, with imprisonment for a period not exceeding thirty days as the alternative if there be default in payment of a judgment therefor.

The question is one of legislative intention. The particular statute is to be construed in the light of the provisions of sections 55, 57 and 59 of the Negotiable Instruments Act, R.S. 7:2–55, 7:2–57, 7:2–59, N.J.S.A., that the "title" of a person who "negotiates an instrument is defective" within the intendment of the act "when he obtained the instrument, or any signature thereto, by fraud, duress, or force and fear, or other unlawful means, or for an *illegal consideration*, or when he negotiates it in breach of faith, or under such circumstances as amount to a fraud," but that a holder in due course holds the instrument "free from *any defect of title of prior parties*, and free from defenses available to prior parties among themselves, and many enforce payment of the instrument for the full amount thereof against all parties liable thereon"; and that every holder is deemed prima facie to be a holder in due course, but when it is shown that the title of any person who has negotiated the instrument was defective, the burden is on the holder to prove that he or some person under whom he claims acquired the title as a holder in due course, except as to a party who became bound on the instrument prior to the acquisition of such defective title. This policy of protection of the holder in due course is outstanding and fundamental in a statute designed to make for substantial uniformity in the laws governing commercial paper; and we are of the view that a purpose to modify that policy as regards an instrument of this class given to an unlicensed real estate broker for services rendered in violation of the licensing statute should be expressed in clear and explicit terms. Negotiable bills and notes are contrived to circulate as substitutes for money, as a medium of exchange, without the burden of inquiry; and the statutory rights of a holder in due course are of the very essence of this policy. The integrity of commercial paper should not be left to implication and the attendant uncertainty.

A statute must be construed with reference to the entire system of which it forms a part. Statutes in pari materia are construed as one act, and the whole harmonized, if possible; and statutes upon cognate subjects may be considered in arriving at the legislative intention, though not strictly in pari materia. This principle is essential to give unity to the laws, and to connect them in a symmetrical system. Implied repealers are not favored in the law. When there is no express repeal, none is presumed to have been intended; and the effect of a new statute upon a long established statutory policy is always in view. If the expression is susceptible of two meanings, that will be adopted which comports with the general public policy of the State, as manifested by its legislation, rather than that which runs counter to such policy. It is to be presumed that the lawmaking body did not intend to disregard or modify a long settled statutory policy, unless the purpose so to do is declared in certain and unequivocal terms. Lewis' Sutherland Statutory Construction, 2d Ed., sections 267, 443, 447, 448, 487, 516, 581.

We come now to the application of these principles.

Under the cited sections of the Negotiable Instruments Act, the inquiry is whether the particular instrument is utterly void ab initio or the consideration is illegal or contrary to public policy or the note is the fruit of an illegal transaction. If void, it is nonnegotiable, and the Negotiable Instruments Act has no application; if the instrument is grounded in an illegal transaction, or the consideration is illegal or against public policy, the title of the holder in due course is unimpeachable, and he is not subject to the defenses open to prior parties inter se. It is the general rule that mere illegality or contravention of public policy does not void a negotiable instrument unless the statute so ordains in unambiguous language. If the statute does not, in terms, declare the instrument void, or render it unenforceable in the hands of a holder in due course, the rule of the Negotiable Instruments Act applies in all its vigor. Statutes will not be read as rendering such instruments void and unenforceable by a holder in due course unless that intention indubitably appears. Such is the general course of authority; and, if the Uniform Negotiable Instruments Act is to serve its purpose, the harmonious current of interpretation and application elsewhere cannot be disregarded here. These are the typical cases in other jurisdictions: [citations omitted].

Here, the particular licensing statute, unlike the Gaming Act, merely subjects the unlicensed practitioner to a prescribed pecuniary penalty. It does not render void and unenforceable as to a holder in due course negotiable commercial paper growing out of such engagements; and the marked difference in treatment is significant of the legislative intention. For the distinction between a "void" and an "illegal" contract, see John J. Carlin, Inc. v. O'Connor, 126 N.J.L. 243, 17 A.2d 584.

The case of Kenney v. Paterson Milk & Cream Co., supra, is not in point. That was a suit between the immediate parties to an illegal contract for the services of an unlicensed broker. And the case of Gionti v. Crown Motor Freight Co., 128 N.J.L. 407, 26 A.2d 282, is in the same category.

* * *

The judgment against Ostroff is affirmed, and the judgment of the Supreme Court reversing the judgment against Taub is reversed and the judgment of the Common Pleas is affirmed.

PROBLEMS

In connection with the preceding three cases, consider these problems:

1. A statute in the State of Columbia says:

> "Any person who shall work, or employ another to work, in excess of 8 hours per day as driver of an omnibus or other vehicle carrying passengers for hire shall be guilty of a misdemeanor punishable by a fine of not more than $500 or imprisonment for 30 days, or both such fine and imprisonment."

Plaintiff driver was required by defendant bus company to work 10 hours daily for a rush period of a week. The employer promised to pay plaintiff double time for the hours over 8 on each day. Now, having been denied the extra pay, plaintiff sues for it.

What arguments might be made for the parties? What should the decision be and why?

2. Another bus company employee, this time in the State of New York, was injured on the job and has been awarded workmen's compensation. The employer sues, claiming the award is contrary to law and should be set aside. As basis for the claim, the employer proves that the employee hired some six months before the injury, falsified his employment application. The application asked whether the applicant had ever been employed before as a bus driver and this employee wrote that he had not. Actually, he had been so employed and had been fired for dropping fares into his pocket rather than the authorized receptacle. The present employer would not have hired him had it known this. The employer cites a New York statute providing that "a person who obtains employment by any false statement in writing as to his name, residence, previous employment or qualifications is guilty of a misdemeanor." It is argued that the employer-employee relationship required for the award of workmen's compensation is founded in this case on an illegal contract. Therefore, the employer urges, the award is invalid.

What are the arguments on both sides? Would you sustain or set aside the award of workmen's compensation? Why?

UNITED STATES v. ACME PROCESS EQUIPMENT CO.

Supreme Court of the United States, 1966.
385 U.S. 138, 87 S.Ct. 350, 17 L.Ed.2d 249.

Mr. Justice BLACK delivered the opinion of the Court.

The respondent, Acme Process Equipment Company, brought this action against the United States in the Court of Claims to recover damages for breach of a contract under which Acme undertook through itself and subcontractors to manufacture 2,751 75-mm. recoilless rifles for about $337 per rifle. Among other defenses, the United States alleged that it had rightfully canceled its contract with Acme because three of Acme's principal employees had accepted compensation for awarding subcontracts in violation of the Anti-Kickback Act set out in part below.[30] The Court of Claims found, as facts, that the kickbacks had been paid as alleged and that this was the ground on which the United States had canceled the prime contract with Acme, but construed the Act as not authorizing the cancellation. 347 F.2d 509, 171 Ct.Cl. 324. We hold that it does.

I.

In October 1952, Acme hired Harry Tucker, Jr., and his associate, James Norris, for the purpose of establishing and managing a new division of the company to handle government contracts. Norris was made general manager of production with authority to submit bids, sign government contracts, and award subcontracts. Tucker was placed in charge of sales, government contracts, and expediting subcontract operations. Prior to this time Tucker had entered into a contract with All Metals Industries, Inc., under which he was to re-

---

[30]. Section 1 of the Anti-Kickback Act, 60 Stat. 37, as amended, 74 Stat. 740, 41 U.S.C.A. § 51, provides in pertinent part:

"That the payment of any fee, commission, or compensation of any kind or the granting of any gift or gratuity of any kind, either directly or indirectly, by or on behalf of a subcontractor, * * * (1) to any officer, partner, employee, or agent of a prime contractor holding a negotiated contract entered into by any department, agency, or establishment of the United States for the furnishing of supplies, materials, equipment or services of any kind whatsoever * * * as an inducement for the award of a subcontract or order from the prime contractor * * * is hereby prohibited. The amount of any such fee, commission, or compensation or the cost or expense of any such gratuity or gift, whether heretofore or hereafter paid or incurred by the subcontractor, shall not be charged, either directly or indirectly, as a part of the contract price charged by the subcontractor to the prime contractor * * *. The amount of any such fee, cost, or expense shall be recoverable on behalf of the United States from the subcontractor or the recipient thereof by setoff * * * or by an action in an appropriate court of the United States. * * *"

Section 4 of the Act, 41 U.S.C.A. § 54, provides:

"Any person who shall knowingly, directly or indirectly, make or receive any such prohibited payment shall be fined not more than $10,000 or be imprisoned for not more than two years, or both."

ceive a commission for all sales to customers, including Acme, procured by him. Tucker's employment contract with Acme specifically stated that he represented and would continue to represent firms in other lines of business, but Acme did not consult with any of his other clients at the time Tucker was hired.

Late in October, Tucker advised his superiors at Acme of the proposed Army contract for rifles, and at Tucker's suggestion, Acme submitted a bid of $337 per rifle. Since Acme's bid was the lowest, the Army began negotiations with Acme culminating in the award of the contract in January 1953. The negotiations were handled by Tucker and Norris for Acme. Since it was contemplated that the project would be largely subcontracted, leaving to Acme only the final finishing and assembly of components, the Army expressed a keen interest in Acme's proposed subcontractors. Not only did it review Acme's subcontracting plans and require Acme to notify it of changes in those plans during the final stages of negotiation, but the contract eventually awarded required government approval of all subcontracts in excess of $25,000. All Metals, because its proposed subcontract amounted to one-third of the amount of the prime contract, actually participated in the negotiations between Acme and the Army.

During this period of negotiation two other developments took place. Tucker obtained agreements from two other potential subcontractors to pay him commissions on any orders he could procure from Acme. Army contracting officers warned Acme's president, Joshua Epstein, that Tucker was suspected of having engaged in contingent-fee arrangements with other government contractors.

Finally, Acme was awarded the prime contract. Although the price was fixed at $337 per rifle, the contract contained a price redetermination clause under which, after 30% of the rifles were delivered, the parties could negotiate the price on past and future shipments upward or downward, with an upper limit of $385 per rifle. Within a few weeks after the prime contract was awarded, All Metals and the other two companies with which Tucker had prior kickback arrangements obtained subcontracts from Acme.[31] Tucker was paid his kickbacks, but, apparently unsatisfied with the amount of his payoff, he got Jack Epstein, the superintendent of the chief Acme plant and the son of Acme's president and principal stockholder, to join the kickback conspiracy. Together Epstein and Tucker threatened to cancel All Metals' subcontract unless it paid $25,000 to a dummy corporation owned by Tucker, Norris, and Epstein for fictitious consulting services. All Metals reluctantly acceded to the shakedown. The amount paid to Tucker, Norris, and Epstein was charged to Acme through an increase in the subcontract price.

31. Shortly after the prime contract was awarded, two other companies paid Tucker's father and Norris' assistant kickbacks for obtaining subcontracts from Acme. This made a total of five subcontracts obtained through kickbacks.

Although they knew that Tucker was representing other companies and had been notified of the Army's suspicions of Tucker's involvement in contingent-fee arrangements, other officials of Acme were not aware of the kickback activities of Tucker, Norris, and Epstein until late in 1953. At that time, Acme's president caused the resignation of the three suspected officials.

In 1956 Tucker, Norris, and Epstein were indicted for violation of the then Anti-Kickback Act, 60 Stat. 37.[32] After presentation of the Government's case, the District Court granted the defendants' motion for acquittal on the ground that the Act—which at that time embraced only "cost-plus-a-fixed-fee or other cost reimbursable" government contracts—did not apply to Acme's contract, a fixed-price contract with a provision for limited price redetermination. The court found the defendants' actions "despicable and morally reprehensible, but unfortunately within the narrow letter of the law." The court recommended that Congress amend the Anti-Kickback Act "to include as a crime the vicious and immoral type of conduct that has been exhibited in this case." United States v. Norris, Crim. No. 18535 (D.C.E.D.Pa.), April 14, 1956.

The District Court's opinion did indeed spur the Comptroller General to recommend amendatory legislation and in 1960 the Anti-Kickback Act was amended to apply to all "negotiated contracts."[33] The civil provision of the amended Act was made retroactive to allow government recovery of kickbacks "whether heretofore or hereafter paid or incurred by the subcontractor."

II.

The Anti-Kickback Act, as originally passed in 1946 and as amended in 1960, provides two express sanctions for its violation: (1) fine or imprisonment for one who makes or receives a kickback, and (2) recovery of the kickback by the United States. The Court of Claims held, and it is argued here, that had Congress wanted "to provide the additional remedy of contract annulment, it could have done so" by express language, 347 F.2d, at 521, 171 Ct.Cl. 343, and of course it could have. But the fact that it did not see fit to provide for such a remedy by express language does not end the matter. The Anti-Kickback Act not only "prohibited" such payments, but clearly expressed a policy decidedly hostile to them. They were recognized as devices hurtful to the Government's procurement practices. Extra expenditures to get subcontracts necessarily add to government costs in cost-plus-a-fixed-fee and other cost reimbursable contracts. And

---

32. This was the original Anti-Kickback Act passed by Congress in 1946. It expressly prohibited kickbacks only to employees of "a prime contractor holding a contract * * * on a cost-plus-a-fixed-fee or other cost reimbursable basis * * *."

33. See generally H.R.Rep.No.1880, S. Rep.No.1585, 86th Cong., 2d Sess., U.S.Code Cong. & Admin.News 1960, p. 3292. The Act, as amended, is set out in part in note [30], supra.

this is also true where the prime contract is a negotiated fixed-price contract with a price redetermination clause, such as the prime contract is here. The kickbacks here are passed on to the Government in two stages. The prime contractor rarely submits his bid until after he has tentatively lined up his subcontractors. Indeed, as here, the subcontractors frequently participate in negotiation of the price contract. The subcontractor's tentative bid will, of course, reflect the amount he contemplates paying as a kickback, and then his inflated bid will be reflected in the prime contractor's bid to the Government. At the renegotiation stage, where the prime contractor's actual cost experience is the basis for price redetermination, any kickbacks, paid by subcontractors and passed on to the prime contractor after the prime contract is awarded, will be passed on to the Government in the form of price redetermination upward.[34]

Acme argues, however, that the express provision for recovery of kickbacks is enough to protect the Government from increased costs attributable to them. But this argument rests on two false assumptions. The first is that kickbacks can easily be detected and recovered. This is hardly the case. Kickbacks being made criminal means that they must be made—if at all—in secrecy. Though they necessarily inflate the price to the Government, this inflation is rarely detectable. This is particularly true as regards defense contracts where the products involved are not usually found on the commercial market and where there may not be effective competition. Such contracts are generally negotiated and awarded without formal advertising and competitive bidding, and there is often no opportunity to compare going prices with the price negotiated by the Government.[35] Kickbacks will usually not be discovered, if at all, until after the prime contract is let. The second false assumption underlying Acme's argument is that the increased cost to the Government is necessarily equal to the amount of the kickback which is recoverable. Of course, a subcontractor who must pay a kickback is likely to include the amount of the kickback in his contract price. But this is not all. A subcontractor who anticipates obtaining a subcontract by virtue of a kickback has little incentive to stint on his cost estimates. Since he plans to obtain the subcontract without regard to the economic merits of his proposal, he will be tempted to inflate that proposal by more than the amount of the kickback. And even if the Government could isolate

---

34. This is precisely what happened here before the Government canceled Acme's contract. Acme in 1953 submitted cost data for price redetermination purposes that included the charges of the five subcontractors which had paid kickbacks to Acme's employees. These subcontracting charges in turn included the amounts paid as kickbacks. Had the kickbacks not been discovered and the contract not been canceled, Acme would have been able to use these costs to renegotiate the price per rifle from $337 to $385. Such price redetermination could have cost the Government about $132,000 more on the entire contract.

35. See S.Rep.No.1585, supra, n. [33], at 3.

and recover the inflation attributable to the kickback, it would still be saddled with a subcontractor who, having obtained the job other than on merit, is perhaps entirely unreliable in other ways. This unreliability in turn undermines the security of the prime contractor's performance—a result which the public cannot tolerate, especially where, as here, important defense contracts are involved.

III.

In United States v. Mississippi Valley Co., 364 U.S. 520, 563, 81 S.Ct. 294, 316, 5 L.Ed.2d 268, the Court recognized that "a statute frequently implies that a contract is not to be enforced when it arises out of circumstances that would lead enforcement to offend the essential purpose of the enactment." The Court there approved the cancellation of a government contract for violation of the conflict-of-interest statute on the ground that "the sanction of nonenforcement is consistent with and essential to effectuating the public policy embodied in" the statute. Ibid. We think the same thing can be said about cancellation here.

The Court of Claims, in holding that the Anti-Kickback Act does not authorize government cancellation because of its violation, distinguished *Mississippi Valley Co.* on the ground that the Anti-Kickback Act, unlike the conflict-of-interest statute, provides a civil as well as a criminal remedy. But we do not deem the provision of a civil remedy in the Anti-Kickback Act decisive. Where there is a mere conflict of interest, no concrete monetary rewards may have been received or paid which the Government can recover in a civil action. But where there is commercial bribery in the form of a kickback, there is something specific which the Government can recover, and hence it was quite natural for Congress to provide this express remedy. There is absolutely no indication in the legislative history of the Anti-Kickback Act that Congress, in providing a civil remedy for a more tangible evil, intended to preclude other civil sanctions necessary to effectuate the purpose of the Act.

There is likewise no merit to the Court of Claims' distinction of the *Mississippi Valley Co.* case on the ground that there the criminal provision of the conflict-of-interest statute was violated whereas here the kickback conspirators were acquitted of violating the Anti-Kickback Act as it existed when the kickbacks occurred, prior to 1960. As we have seen, Acme's employees were acquitted on the technical ground that Acme's prime contract was not a "cost reimbursable" contract to which the Act then expressly applied. It is unnecessary for us to decide whether this holding was correct.[36] For whether the kickbacks here contravened the narrow letter of the criminal law,

---

[36]. See United States v. Barnard, 255 F.2d 583, cert. denied, 358 U.S. 919, 79 S.Ct. 287, 3 L.Ed.2d 238, holding that a fixed-price contract with provision for unlimited price redetermination is a "cost reimbursable" contract.

strictly construed, they clearly were violative of the public policy against kickbacks first expressed by Congress in 1946. If Congress then limited the reach of the Act to cost reimbursable contracts, it was only because other types of negotiated contracts were rarely in use then. Though the recent extensive use of other forms of negotiated contracts led Congress in 1960 to amend the Act to cover clearly these types of contracts and to close the technical loophole opened by the acquittal of Acme's employees, the congressional policy against *all* kickbacks was not changed. Congress merely reiterated its recognition of the evil and sought to correct the letter of the law to effectuate its longstanding policy. In making the civil remedy of the 1960 Act retroactive, Congress clearly indicated that there had been no basic change in the public policy against kickbacks.

This public policy requires that the United States be able to rid itself of a prime contract tainted by kickbacks. Though the kickbacks did not take place until after the prime contract was awarded to Acme, the kickback arrangements existed either at the time the prime contract was awarded or shortly thereafter, and at least one of the kickbacking subcontractors actually participated in the negotiation of the prime contract. These circumstances, as well as the price redetermination feature of the prime contract, produced a great likelihood that the cost of the prime contract to the Government and the reliability of Acme's performance under it would be directly affected by the fact that the prime contract was to be performed largely through subcontracts obtained by kickbacks.

The Court of Claims, in holding that the Act does not authorize government cancellation because of kickbacks, relied heavily on its finding that none of the officers of Acme were aware of the kickbacks. But as previously stated those of Acme's employees and agents who did know were in the upper echelon of its managers. One of the guilty employees was the general manager of one of the company's chief plants and the son of Acme's president, and the two other kickback receivers were in charge of operations, sales, and government contracts. They were the kind of company personnel for whose conduct a corporation is generally held responsible. Cf. Gleason v. Seaboard Air Line R. Co., 278 U.S. 349, 49 S.Ct. 161, 73 L.Ed. 415. Since Acme selected those agents to carry on its business in obtaining and performing government contracts, there is no obvious reason why their conduct in that field should not be considered as Acme's conduct, particularly where it touches the all-important subject of kickbacks. And here, as this Court said about the conflict-of-interest statute in United States v. Mississippi Valley Co., supra, at 565, 81 S.Ct., at 317, it is appropriate to say that it is the "inherent difficulty in detecting corruption which requires that contracts made in violation of * * * [the Anti-Kickback Act] be held unenforceable, even though the party seeking enforcement ostensibly appears entirely innocent."

The judgment of the Court of Claims is reversed with directions to sustain the United States' right to cancel the prime contract.

It is so ordered.

NOTE ON IMPLYING PRIVATE CIVIL REMEDIES IN RELATION TO FEDERAL STATUTES

In Texas & Pacific Railway Co. v. Rigsby, 241 U.S. 33, 36 S.Ct. 482, 60 L.Ed. 874 (1916), the plaintiff, a switchman, sought damages from the defendant railroad, his employer, for injuries arising from the latter's violation of a federal statute (the Act of 1893, see Problem 4, supra p. 324, as amended in 1910) requiring that railroad "cars * * * be equipped with secure * * * grab irons." Defendant argued, inter alia, that the federal statute in question, while providing for penalties in suits on behalf of the United States, did not give injured employees a right to bring a civil action for damages for violations (could such an argument have been made in Johnson v. Southern Pacific Co., supra p. 327?), at least where the employee is not engaged in interstate commerce. The Supreme Court ruled that the statute could apply whether or not plaintiff was engaged in commerce, and that it was constitutional when so applied. As to the private right of action, the court noted that such a right had "never been doubted" (citing, e. g., Johnson v. Southern Pacific Co.), despite the absence of express statutory language conferring such a right. It added (241 U.S. at 39, 36 S.Ct. at 484): "A disregard of the command of the statute is a wrongful act, and when it results in damage to one of the class for whose especial benefit the statute was enacted, the right to recover damages from the party in default is implied, according to a doctrine of the common law * * * [that] 'in every case, where a statute enacts or prohibits a thing for the benefit of a person, he shall have a remedy upon the same statute for the thing enacted for his advantage, or for the recompense of a wrong done to him contrary to the said law.'" Compare Osborne v. McMasters, supra p. 644. The Supreme Court's recognition of the private right of action in *Rigsby* was supported by reference to the title of the statute, to a 1910 proviso therein containing a reservation as to "liability in any remedial action for the death or injury of an employee" and to § 8 of the original Act of 1893. To the extent that the Supreme Court in the *Rigsby* case, and in *Acme*, supra, allowed remedies beyond those established by the applicable Congressional legislation, was its action within the judicial power granted to the federal courts, which is limited by the U.S. Constitution (Art. III, Sec. 2) and federal statutes to civil actions "arising under the Constitution, laws, or treaties of the United States"? Why? Consider in particular the meaning of "laws" in the quoted phrase. Does the rule announced in Erie Railroad v. Tompkins, supra p. 241, affect your answer—and, if so, why and how—as to either the *Rigsby* case or the *Acme* case? *Rigsby* and the later developments of the federal law on implying civil remedies (including the well-known fourfold test announced in Cort v. Ash, 422 U.S. 66, 95 S.Ct. 2080, 45 L.Ed.2d 26, in 1975) were reexamined by the Supreme Court during its 1978 and 1979 terms, especially in the following case, in Touche Ross & Co. v. Redington, infra p. 693, and in Transamerica Mortgage Advisers, Inc. v. Lewis, infra p. 695.

CANNON v. UNIVERSITY OF CHICAGO

Supreme Court of the United States, 1979.
441 U.S. 677, 99 S.Ct. 1946, 60 L.Ed.2d 560.

Mr. Justice STEVENS delivered the opinion of the Court.

Petitioner's complaints allege that her applications for admission to medical school were denied by the respondents because she is a woman. Accepting the truth of those allegations for the purpose of its decision, the Court of Appeals held that petitioner has no right of action against respondents that may be asserted in a federal court. 559 F.2d 1063. We granted certiorari to review that holding. 438 U.S. 914, 98 S.Ct. 3142, 57 L.Ed.2d 1159.

Only two facts alleged in the complaints are relevant to our decision. First, petitioner was excluded from participation in the respondents' medical education programs because of her sex. Second, these education programs were receiving federal financial assistance at the time of her exclusion. These facts, admitted *arguendo* by respondents' motion to dismiss the complaints, establish a violation of § 901(a) of Title IX of the Education Amendments of 1972 (hereinafter "Title IX").

That section, in relevant part, provides:

"No person in the United States shall, on the basis of sex, be excluded from participation in, be denied the benefits of, or be subjected to discrimination under any education program or activity receiving Federal financial assistance * * *."

The statute does not, however, expressly authorize a private right of action by a person injured by a violation of § 901. For that reason, and because it concluded that no private remedy should be inferred, the District Court granted the respondents' motions to dismiss. 406 F.Supp. 1257, 1259.

The Court of Appeals agreed that the statute did not contain an implied private remedy. Noting that § 902 of the Act establishes a procedure for the termination of federal financial support for institutions violating § 901, the Court of Appeals concluded that Congress intended that remedy to be the exclusive means of enforcement. It recognized that the statute was patterned after Title VI of the Civil Rights Act of 1964 (hereinafter "Title VI"), but rejected petitioners' argument that Title VI included an implied private cause of action. 559 F.2d, at 1071–1075.

After the Court of Appeals' decision was announced, Congress enacted the Civil Rights Attorneys Fee Awards Act of 1976, which authorizes an award of fees to prevailing private parties in actions to enforce Title IX. The court therefore granted a petition for rehearing to consider whether, in the light of that statute, its original interpretation of Title IX had been correct. After receiving additional briefs and arguments, the court concluded that the 1976 Act was not intended to create a remedy that did not previously exist. The court also noted that the Department of Health, Education, and Welfare had taken the position that a private cause of action under Title IX should be implied, but the court disagreed with that agency's interpretation of the Act. In sum, it adhered to its original view, 559 F.2d, at 1077–1080.

The Court of Appeals quite properly devoted careful attention to this question of statutory construction. As our recent cases—particularly Cort v. Ash, 422 U.S. 66, 95 S.Ct. 2080, 45 L.Ed.2d 26—demonstrate, the fact that a federal statute has been violated and some person harmed does not automatically give rise to a private cause of action in favor of that person. Instead, before concluding that Congress intended to make a remedy available to a special class of litigants, a court must carefully analyze the four factors that *Cort* identifies as indicative of such an intent. Our review of those factors persuades us, however, that the Court of Appeals reached the wrong conclusion and that petitioner does have a statutory right to pursue her claim that respondents rejected her application on the basis of her sex. After commenting on each of the four factors, we shall explain why they are not overcome by respondents' countervailing arguments.

I

First, the threshold question under *Cort* is whether the statute was enacted for the benefit of a special class of which the plaintiff is a member. That question is answered by looking to the language of the statute itself. Thus, the statutory reference to "any employee of any such common carrier" in the 1893 legislation requiring railroads to equip their cars with secure "grab irons or handholds," see 27 Stat. 531, 532, made "irresistible" the Court's earliest "inference of a private right of action,"—in that case in favor of a railway employee who was injured when a grab iron gave way. Texas & Pacific R. Co. v. Rigsby, 241 U.S. 33, 40, 36 S.Ct. 482, 484, 60 L.Ed. 874.

Similarly, it was statutory language describing the special class to be benefited by § 5 of the Voting Rights Act of 1965 that persuaded the Court that private parties within that class were implicitly authorized to seek a declaratory judgment against a covered State. Allen v. State Board of Elections, 393 U.S. 544, 554–555, 89 S.Ct. 817, 825–826, 22 L.Ed.2d 1. The dispositive language in that statute—"No person shall be denied the right to vote for failure to comply with [a new state enactment covered by, but not approved under, § 5],"—is remarkably similar to the language used by Congress in Title IX. * * *

The language in these statutes—which expressly identifies the class Congress intended to benefit—contrasts sharply with statutory language customarily found in criminal statutes, such as that construed in *Cort*, supra, and other laws enacted for the protection of the general public.[37] There would be far less reason to infer a pri-

---

[37]. Not surprisingly, the right- or duty-creating language of the statute has generally been the most accurate indicator of the propriety of implication of a cause of action. With the exception of one case, in which the relevant statute reflected a special policy against judicial interference, this Court has never refused to imply a cause of action where the language of the statute explicitly conferred a right directly on a class of persons that included the plaintiff in the case. See Sullivan v. Little Hunting Park, 396 U.S. 229, 238, 90 S.Ct. 400, 405, 24 L.Ed.2d 386 (42 U.S.C.A. § 1982: "All citizens of the United States shall have the same right * * * as is enjoyed by white citizens thereof. * * *"); Allen v. State Board of Elections, supra (42 U.S.C.A. § 1973c: "No person shall be denied the right to vote * * *."); Jones v. Alfred H. Mayer Co., 392 U.S. 409, 414–415, and n. 13, 88 S.Ct. 2186, 2189–2190, 20 L.Ed.2d 1189 (same as in *Sullivan* supra); Tunstall v. Brotherhood of Locomotive Engineers, 323 U.S. 210, 213, 65 S.Ct. 235, 237, 89 L.Ed. 187 (§ 2, Fourth of the Railway Labor Act: "Employees shall have the right to organize and bargain collectively through representatives * * *."); Steele v. Louisville & N. R. Co., 323 U.S. 192, 207, 65 S.Ct. 226, 234, 89 L.Ed. 173 (same); Virginian Ry. Co. v. Federation, 300 U.S. 515, 545, 57 S.Ct. 592, 598, 81 L.Ed. 789 (§ 2, Ninth of the Railway Labor Act: "the carrier shall treat with the *representative* so certified" (emphasis added)); Texas & N. O. R. Co. v. Railway Clerks, 281 U.S. 548, 568–570, 50 S.Ct. 427, 433, 74 L.Ed. 1034 (§ 2, Third of the Railway Labor Act: "Representatives * * * shall be designated by the respective *parties* * * * without interference, influence, or coercion exercised by either party * * *." (emphasis added); Texas & Pacific R. Co. v. Rigsby, supra (27 Stat. 532: "any employee of any such common carrier * * *.") Analogously, the Court has implied causes of action in favor of the United States in cases where the statute creates a duty in favor of the public at large. See Wyandotte Transportation Co. v. United States, 389 U.S. 191, 200–202, 88 S.Ct. 379, 385–386, 19 L.Ed.2d 407 (33 U.S.C.A. § 409: "It shall not be lawful [to obstruct navigable waterways]"); United States v. Republic Steel Corp., 362 U.S. 482, 80 S.Ct. 884, 4 L.Ed.2d 903 (same).

The only case that deviates from this pattern is Santa Clara Pueblo v. Martinez, 436 U.S. 49, 98 S.Ct. 1670, 56 L.Ed.2d 106 which involved Title I of the Indian Civil Rights Act of 1968, 25 U.S.C.A. § 1302(8): "No Indian tribe * * * shall deny to any person within its jurisdiction the equal protection of the laws." *Martinez*, however, involved an attempt to imply a cause of action in a virtually unique situation—i. e., against an Indian tribe, protected by a strong presumption of autonomy and self-government, as well as by a special duty on the part of the Federal Government to deal fairly and openly, and by a legislative history indicative of an intent to limit severely judicial interference in tribal affairs. 436 U.S., at 55, 58–59, 63–64, 67–70, and n. 30, 98 S.Ct., at 1675, 1677, 1680, 1681–1683. In this situation, the fourth

vate remedy in favor of individual persons if Congress, instead of drafting Title IX with an unmistakable focus on the benefited class, had written it simply as a ban on discriminatory conduct by recipients of federal funds or as a prohibition against the disbursement of

Cort factor was brought into special play. The *Martinez* Court determined that the strong presumption against implication of federal remedies where they might interfere with matters "traditionally relegated to state law," *Cort,* supra, 422 U.S., at 78, 95 S.Ct., at 2088, was equally applicable in circumstances where the federal remedies would interfere with matters traditionally relegated to the control of semisovereign Indian tribes.

Even *Martinez,* however, "recognized the propriety of inferring a federal cause of action for the enforcement of civil rights, even when Congress has spoken in declarative terms." Id., 436 U.S., at 61, 98 S.Ct., at 1678; see Sullivan v. Little Hunting Park, supra, 396 U.S., at 238, 90 S.Ct., at 405; Allen v. State Board of Elections, supra; Jones v. Alfred H. Mayer Co., supra, 392 U.S. at 414 n. 13, 88 S.Ct., at 2189. This principle, which is directly applicable in the present Title IX context, is but a manifestation of the pattern noted above because a statute declarative of a civil right will almost have to be stated in terms of the benefited class. Put somewhat differently, because the right to be free of discrimination is a "personal" one, see, e. g., Teamsters v. United States, 431 U.S. 324, 361–372, 97 S.Ct. 1843, 1867–1873, 52 L.Ed.2d 396; Franks v. Bowman Transportation Co., 424 U.S. 747, 772, 96 S.Ct. 1251, 1267, 47 L.Ed.2d 444, a statute conferring such a right will almost have to be phrased in terms of the persons benefited.

Conversely, the Court has been especially reluctant to imply causes of actions under statutes that create duties on the part of persons for the benefit of the public at large. See Piper v. Chris-Craft Industries, 430 U.S. 1, 97 S.Ct. 926, 51 L.Ed.2d 124 ("unlawful" conduct); Cort v. Ash, supra ("unlawful" conduct); Securities Investor Protection Corp. v. Barbour, 421 U.S. 412, 95 S.Ct. 1733, 44 L.Ed. 2d 263 (duty of SIPC to "discharge obligations"); National Railroad Passenger Corp. v. National Assn. of Railroad Passengers, 414 U.S. 453, 94 S.Ct. 690, 38 L.Ed.2d 646 (forbidding "action, practice, or policy inconsistent" with the Act); Wheedlin v. Wheeler, 373 U.S. 647, 83 S.Ct. 1441, 10 L.Ed.2d 605 (setting procedure for procuring congressional subpoena); T. I. M. E., Inc. v. United States, 359 U.S. 464, 79 S.Ct. 904, 3 L.Ed.2d 952 ("duty of every common carrier * * * to establish * * * just and reasonable rates * * *."); Montana-Dakota Utilities Co. v. Northwestern Public Service Co., 341 U.S. 246, 71 S.Ct. 692, 95 L.Ed. 912 (similar duty of gas pipeline companies). The Court has deviated from this pattern on occasion. See J. I. Case Co. v. Borak, 377 U.S. 426, 84 S.Ct. 1555, 12 L.Ed.2d 423 (implying a cause of action under a securities provision describing "unlawful conduct"); Superintendent of Insurance v. Bankers Life & Casualty Co., 404 U.S. 6, 13 n. 9, 92 S.Ct. 165, 169, 30 L.Ed.2d 128 (implying a cause of action under Rule 10b–5, which describes certain unlawful manipulative conduct in the securities area); Machinists v. Central Airlines, 372 U.S. 682, 83 S.Ct. 956, 10 L.Ed.2d 67 (implied cause of action under section of the Railway Labor Act creating "a duty" on the part of common carriers to establish boards of adjustment). At least the latter two cases can be explained historically, however. In *Superintendent of Insurance,* the Court explicitly acquiesced in the 25-year-old acceptance by the lower federal courts of a 10b–5 causes of action. See also Ernst & Ernst v. Hochfelder, 425 U.S. 185, 196, 96 S.Ct. 1375, 1382, 47 L.Ed.2d 668; Blue Chips Stamps v. Manor Drug, 421 U. S. 723, 730, 95 S.Ct. 1917, 1922, 44 L.Ed.2d 539. In *Machinists,* the Court explicitly followed the lead of various earlier cases in which it had implied cause of actions under various sections of the Railway Labor Act, albeit where the statutory provisions more explicitly identified a class of benefited persons. See *Tunstall,* supra; *Steele,* supra; *Virginian Railway,* supra; *Texas & N. O. R. Co.,* supra.

public funds to educational institutions engaged in discriminatory practices.

Unquestionably, therefore, the first of the four factors identified in *Cort* favors the implication of a private cause of action. Title IX explicitly confers a benefit on persons discriminated against on the basis of sex, and petitioner is clearly a member of that class for whose special benefit the statute was enacted.

Second, the *Cort* analysis requires consideration of legislative history. We must recognize, however, that the legislative history of a statute that does not expressly create or deny a private remedy will typically be equally silent or ambiguous on the question. Therefore, in situations such as the present one "in which it is clear that federal law has granted a class of persons certain rights, it is not necessary to show an intention to *create* a private cause of action, although an explicit purpose to *deny* such cause of action would be controlling." *Cort*, supra, 422 U.S., at 82, 95 S.Ct., at 2090 (emphasis in original). But this is not the typical case. Far from evidencing any purpose to *deny* a private cause of action, the history of Title IX rather plainly indicates that Congress intended to create such a remedy.

Title IX was patterned after Title VI of the Civil Rights Act of 1964. Except for the substitution of the word "sex" in Title IX to replace the words "race, color, or national origin" in Title VI, the two statutes use identical language to describe the benefited class. Both statutes provide the same administrative mechanism for terminating federal financial support for institutions engaged in prohibited discrimination. Neither statute expressly mentions a private remedy for the person excluded from participation in a federally funded program. The drafters of Title IX explicitly assumed that it would be interpreted and applied as Title VI had been during the preceding eight years.

In 1972 when Title IX was enacted, the critical language in Title VI had already been construed as creating a private remedy. Most particularly, in 1967, a distinguished panel of the Court of Appeals for the Fifth Circuit squarely decided this issue in an opinion that was repeatedly cited with approval and never questioned during the ensuing five years. In addition, at least a dozen other federal courts reached similar conclusions in the same or related contexts during those years. It is always appropriate to assume that our elected representatives, like other citizens, know the law; in this case, because of their repeated references to Title VI and its modes of enforcement, we are especially justified in presuming both that those representatives were aware of the prior interpretation of Title VI and that that interpretation reflects their intent with respect to Title IX.

Moreover, in 1969, in *Allen*, supra, this Court had interpreted the comparable language in § 5 of the Voting Rights Act as sufficient to authorize a private remedy. Indeed, during the period between the enactment of Title VI in 1964 and the enactment of Title IX in 1972, this Court had consistently found implied remedies—often in cases much less clear than this.[38] It was *after* 1972 that this Court decided Cort v. Ash and the other cases cited by the Court of Appeals in support of its strict construction of the remedial aspect of the statute.[39] We, of course, adhere to the strict approach followed in our recent cases, but our evaluation of congressional action in 1972 must take into account its contemporary legal context. In sum, it is not only appropriate but also realistic to presume that Congress was thoroughly familiar with these unusually important precedents from this and other federal courts and that it expected its enactment to be interpreted in conformity with them.

It is not, however, necessary to rely on these presumptions. The package of statutes of which Title IX is one part also contains a provision whose language and history demonstrate that Congress itself understood Title VI, and thus its companion, Title IX, as creating a private remedy. Section 718 of the Education Amendments authorizes federal courts to award fees to the prevailing parties, other than the United States, in private actions brought against local educational agencies, States, state agencies, and the United States to enforce Title VI in the context of elementary and secondary education. The language of this provision explicitly presumes the availability of private suits to enforce Title VI in the education context. For many such suits, no express cause of action was then available; hence Congress must have assumed that one could be implied under Title VI itself. That assumption was made explicit during the debates on § 718. It was also aired during the debates on other provisions in the Education Amendments of 1972 and on Title IX itself, and is consistent with the Executive Branch's apparent understanding of Title VI at the time.

Finally, the very persistence—before 1972 and since, among judges and executive officials, as well as among litigants and their counsel, and even implicit in decisions of this court—of the assumption that both Title VI and Title IX created a private right of action

---

38. In the decade preceding the enactment of Title IX, the Court decided six implied-cause-of-action cases. In all of them a cause of action was found. Superintendent of Insurance v. Bankers Life & Casualty Co., supra; Sullivan v. Little Hunting Park, supra; *Allen*, supra; Jones v. Alfred H. Mayer Co., supra; Wyandotte Transportation Co. v. United States, supra; J. I. Case Co. v. Borak, supra. See generally n. [37], supra.

39. The Court of Appeals relied on National Railroad Passenger Corp. v. National Assn. of Railroad Passengers, supra; Securities Investor Protection Corp. v. Barber, supra, and Cort v. Ash, supra. In subsequent cases the Court has continued to give careful attention to claims that a private remedy should be implied in statutes which omit any express remedy. See Santa Clara Pueblo v. Martinez, supra; Piper v. Chris-Craft Industries, supra. The Court's decidedly different approach since 1972 to cause of action by implication has not gone without scholarly notice. E. g., Pitt, Standing to Sue Under the Williams Act After *Chris-Craft*: A Leaky Ship on Troubled Waters, 34 Bus.Law. 117, 120, 162 (1978).

for the victims of illegal discrimination and the absence of legislative action to change that assumption provide further evidence that Congress at least acquiesces in, and apparently affirms, that assumption. * * * We have no doubt that Congress intended to create Title IX remedies comparable to those available under Title VI and that it understood Title VI as authorizing an implied private cause of action for victims of the prohibited discrimination.

Third, under *Cort*, a private remedy should not be implied if it would frustrate the underlying purpose of the legislative scheme. On the other hand, when that remedy is necessary or at least helpful to the accomplishment of the statutory purpose, the Court is decidedly receptive to its implication under the statute.[40]

Title IX, like its model Title VI, sought to accomplish two related, but nevertheless somewhat different, objectives. First, Congress wanted to avoid the use of federal resources to support discriminatory practices; second, it wanted to provide individual citizens effective protection against those practices. Both of these purposes were repeatedly identified in the debates on the two statutes.

The first purpose is generally served by the statutory procedure for the termination of federal financial support for institutions engaged in discriminatory practices. That remedy is, however, severe and often may not provide an appropriate means of accomplishing the second purpose if merely an isolated violation has occurred. In that situation, the violation might be remedied more efficiently by an order requiring an institution to accept an applicant who had been improperly excluded. Moreover, in that kind of situation it makes little sense to impose on an individual, whose only interest is in obtaining a benefit for herself, or on HEW, the burden of demonstrating that an institution's practices are so pervasively discriminatory that a complete cut-off of federal funding is appropriate. The award of individual relief to a private litigant who has prosecuted her own suit is not only sensible but is fully consistent with—and in some cases even necessary to—the orderly enforcement of the statute.

The Department of Health, Education, and Welfare, which is charged with the responsibility for administering Title IX, perceives no inconsistency between the private remedy and the public remedy.[41]

---

40. See Allen v. State Board of Elections, supra, 393 U.S., at 556, 89 S.Ct., at 826; Wyandotte Transportation Co. v. United States, supra, 389 U.S., at 202, 88 S.Ct., at 386; J. I. Case Co. v. Borak, supra, 377 U.S., at 432, 84 S.Ct., at 1559; Machinists v. Central Airlines, supra, 372 U.S., at 690, 83 S.Ct., at 961.

41. It has been suggested that, at least in the absence of an exhaustion requirement, private litigation will interfere with HEW's enforcement procedures under § 902 of Title IX. The simple answer to this suggestion is that the Government itself perceives no such interference under the circumstances of this case, and argues that if the possibility of interference arises in another case, appropriate action can be taken by the relevant court at that time. * * *

In addition, Congress itself was apparently not worried about such interfer-

On the contrary, the agency takes the unequivocal position that the individual remedy will provide effective assistance to achieving the statutory purposes. * * * The agency's position is unquestionably correct.[42]

Fourth, the final inquiry suggested by *Cort* is whether implying a federal remedy is inappropriate because the subject matter involves an area basically of concern to the States. No such problem is raised by a prohibition against invidious discrimination of any sort, including that on the basis of sex. Since the Civil War, the Federal Government and the federal courts have been the " '*primary* and powerful reliances' " in protecting citizens against such discrimination. Steffel v. Thompson, 415 U.S. 452, 464, 94 S.Ct. 1209, 1218, 39 L.Ed. 2d 505 (emphasis in original), quoting F. Frankfurter & J. Landis, The Business of the Supreme Court 65 (1928). Moreover, it is the expenditure of federal funds that provides the justification for this particular statutory prohibition. There can be no question but that this aspect of the *Cort* analysis supports the implication of a private federal remedy.

In sum, there is no need in this case to weigh the four *Cort* factors; all of them support the same result. Not only the words and history of Title IX, but also its subject matter and underlying pur-

---

ence when it passed Title IX. As discussed, supra, * * *, the statute of which Title IX is a part also contains a provision, § 718, allowing attorney's fees under Title VI. No matter how narrowly that provision is read, it certainly envisions private enforcement suits apart from the administrative procedures that Title VI, like Title IX, expressly creates. If such suits would not hamper administrative enforcement of Title VI against local and state school officials, it is hard to see how they would do so with respect to other recipients of federal funds.

True, this Court has sometimes refused to imply private rights of action where administrative or like remedies are expressly available. E. g., National Railroad Passenger Corp. v. National Assn. of Railroad Passengers, supra; T. I. M. E., Inc. v. United States, supra. But see Cort v. Ash, supra, 422 U.S. at 79, 95 S.Ct., at 2088; Superintendent of Insurance v. Banker's Life & Casualty Co., supra; Wyandotte Transportation Co. v. United States, supra; J. I. Case Co. v. Borak, supra. But it has never withheld a private remedy where the statute explicitly confers a benefit on a class of persons and where it does not assure those persons the ability to activate and participate in the administrative process contemplated by the statute. See Rosado v. Wyman, 397 U.S. 397, 406 n. 8, 90 S.Ct. 1207, 1214, 25 L.Ed.2d 442; cf. Cort v. Ash, supra, 422 U.S., at 74–75, 95 S.Ct., at 2086; Calhoon v. Harvey, supra. * * *

42. In its submissions to this Court, as well as in other public statements, HEW has candidly admitted that it does not have the resources necessary to enforce Title IX in a substantial number of circumstances:

"As a practical matter, HEW cannot hope to police all federally funded education programs, and even if administrative enforcement were always feasible, it often might not redress individual injuries. An implied private right of action is necessary to ensure that the fundamental purpose of Title IX, the elimination of sex discrimination in federally funded education programs, is achieved." Reply Brief for the Federal Respondents, at 6.

See also 40 Fed.Reg. 24148–24159.

* * *

poses, counsel implication of a cause of action in favor of private victims of discrimination.

II

Respondents' principal argument against implying a cause of action under Title IX is that it is unwise to subject admissions decisions of universities to judicial scrutiny at the behest of disappointed applicants on a case-by-case basis. They argue that this kind of litigation is burdensome and inevitably will have an adverse effect on the independence of members of university committees.

This argument is not original to this litigation. It was forcefully advanced in both 1964 and 1972 by the congressional opponents of Title VI and Title IX, and squarely rejected by the congressional majorities that passed the two statutes. In short, respondents' principal contention is not a legal argument at all; it addresses a policy issue that Congress has already resolved.

History has borne out the judgment of Congress. Although victims of discrimination on the basis of race, religion, or national origin have had private Title VI remedies available at least since 1965, * * *, respondents have not come forward with any demonstration that Title VI litigation has been so costly or voluminous that either the academic community or the courts have been unduly burdened. Nothing but speculation supports the argument that university administrators will be so concerned about the risk of litigation that they will fail to discharge their important responsibilities in an independent and professional manner.[43]

III

Respondents advance two other arguments that deserve brief mention. Starting from the premise that Title IX and Title VI should receive the same construction, respondents argue (1) that a comparison of Title VI with other titles of the Civil Rights Act of 1964 demonstrates that Congress created express private remedies whenever it found them desirable; and (2) that certain excerpts from the legislative history of Title VI foreclose the implication of a private remedy.

Even if these arguments were persuasive with respect to Congress' understanding in 1964 when it passed Title VI, they would not overcome the fact that in 1972 when it passed Title IX, Congress was under the impression that Title VI could be enforced by a private action and that Title IX would be similarly enforceable. * * * "For

---

43. Furthermore, unless respondents are arguing that Title IX (and, by implication, Title VI) is itself unconstitutional, this argument is entirely misconceived. Whatever disruption of the academic community may accompany an occasional individual suit seeking admission is dwarfed by the relief expressly contemplated by the statute—a cut off of all federal funds. * * *

the relevant inquiry is not whether Congress correctly perceived the then state of the law, but rather what its perception of the state of the law was." Brown v. GSA, 425 U.S. 820, 828, 96 S.Ct. 1961, 1966, 48 L.Ed.2d 402. But each of respondents' arguments is, in any event, unpersuasive.

The fact that other provisions of a complex statutory scheme create express remedies has not been accepted as a sufficient reason for refusing to imply an otherwise appropriate remedy under a separate section. See, e. g., J. I. Case Co. v. Borak, supra; Wyandotte Transportation Co. v. United States, supra. Rather, the Court has generally avoided this type of "excursion into extrapolation of legislative intent," Cort v. Ash, supra, 422 U.S., at 82 n. 14, 95 S.Ct., at 2090, unless there is other, more convincing, evidence that Congress meant to exclude the remedy. See National Railroad Passenger Corp. v. National Assn. of Railroad Passengers, supra, 414 U.S., at 458–461, 94 S.Ct., at 693–694.

With one set of exceptions, the excerpts from the legislative history cited by respondents as contrary to implication of a private remedy under Title VI, were all concerned with a procedure for terminating federal funding. None of them evidences any hostility toward an implied private remedy to terminate the offending discrimination. They are consistent with the assumption expressed frequently during the debates that such a judicial remedy—either through the kind of broad construction of state action under § 1983 adopted by the Court of Appeals for the Fourth Circuit in Simkins v. Moses H. Cone Memorial Hospital, 323 F.2d 959 (1963), or through an implied remedy —would be available to private litigants regardless of how the fund cutoff issue was resolved.

The only excerpt relied upon by respondent that deals precisely with the question whether the victim of discrimination has a private remedy under Title VI was a comment by Senator Keating. In it, he expressed disappointment at the administration's failure to include his suggestion for an express remedy in its final proposed bill. Our analysis of the legislative history convinces us, however, that neither the administration's decision not to incorporate that suggestion expressly in its bill, nor Senator Keating's response to that decision, is indicative of a rejection of a private right of action against recipients of federal funds. Instead, the former appears to have been a compromise aimed at protecting individual rights without subjecting the Government to suits, while the latter is merely one Senator's isolated expression of a preference for an express private remedy. In short, neither is inconsistent with the implication of such a remedy. Nor is there any other indication in the legislative history that any Member of Congress voted in favor of the statute in reliance on an understanding that Title VI did not include a private remedy.

IV

When Congress intends private litigants to have a cause of action to support their statutory rights, the far better course is for it to specify as much when it creates those rights. But the Court has long recognized that under certain limited circumstances the failure of Congress to do so is not inconsistent with an intent on its part to have such a remedy available to the persons benefited by its legislation. Title IX presents the atypical situation in which *all* of the circumstances that the Court has previously identified as supportive of an implied remedy are present. We therefore conclude that petitioner may maintain her lawsuit, despite the absence of any express authorization for it in the statute.

The judgment of the Court of Appeals is reversed and the case is remanded for further proceedings consistent with this opinion.

Mr. Chief Justice BURGER concurs in the judgment.

Mr. Justice REHNQUIST, with whom Mr. Justice STEWART joins, concurring.

Having joined the Court's opinion in this case my only purpose in writing separately is to make explicit what seems to me already implicit in that opinion. I think the approach of the Court, reflected in its analysis of the problem in this case and cases such as Santa Clara Pueblo v. Martinez, 436 U.S. 49, 98 S.Ct. 1670, 56 L.Ed.2d 106 (1978), Cort v. Ash, 422 U.S. 66, 95 S.Ct. 2080, 45 L.Ed.2d 26 (1975), and National Railroad Passenger Corp. v. National Association of Railroad Passengers, 414 U.S. 453, 94 S.Ct. 690, 38 L.Ed.2d 646 (1974), is quite different from the analysis in earlier cases such as J. I. Case Co. v. Borak, 377 U.S. 426, 84 S.Ct. 1555, 12 L.Ed.2d 423 (1964). The question of the existence of a private right of action is basically one of statutory construction. * * * And while state courts of general jurisdiction still enforcing the common law as well as statutory law may be less constrained than are federal courts enforcing laws enacted by Congress, the latter must surely look to those laws to determine whether there was an intent to create a private right of action under them.

We do not write on an entirely clean slate, however, and the Court's opinion demonstrates that Congress at least during the period of the enactment of the several titles of the Civil Rights Act tended to rely to a large extent on the courts to *decide* whether there should be a private right of action, rather than determining this question for itself. Cases such as J. I. Case v. Borak, supra, and numerous cases from other federal courts, gave Congress good reason to think that the federal judiciary would undertake this task.

I fully agree with the Court's statement that "[w]hen Congress intends private litigants to have a cause of action to support their statutory rights, the far better course is for it to specify as much when it creates those rights." * * * It seems to me that the factors to which I have here briefly adverted apprise the lawmaking branch of the Federal Government that the ball, so to speak, may well now be in its court. Not only is it "far better" for Congress to so specify when it intends private litigants to have a cause of action, but for this very reason this Court in the future should be extremely reluctant to imply a cause of action absent such specificity on the part of the Legislative Branch.

Mr. Justice WHITE, with whom Mr. Justice BLACKMUN joins, dissenting.

[Mr. Justice White's opinion (omitted here) argued that the terms, legislative history and scheme of Title VI (on which Title IX was explicitly modeled) showed that Congress—rather than intending to provide a new private cause of action—contemplated that agency action would be the principal mechanism in Title VI for enforcing the federal policy of nondiscrimination. Termination of funding was not intended as the only, or even primary, agency weapon. Private Title VI suits were envisaged under 42 U.S.C.A. § 1983 against public agencies engaged in discrimination but not against private recipients of federal funds not acting under color of state law. § 718 of the Act did no more in respect of suits against private interests than provide for fees in § 1983 suits to end private discrimination under color of state law. Lower federal court cases preceding enactment of Title IX should not be read as going farther than this. In recent Supreme Court cases (see *Sullivan, Jones* and *Allen* cases, cited by the majority, supra) implying private rights of action to enforce civil rights, the private right was either compatible (*Sullivan, Jones*) with the statutory purpose or merely triggered (*Allen*) the statutory enforcement scheme rather than, as here, displacing it.]

Mr. Justice POWELL, dissenting.

I agree with Mr. Justice WHITE that even under the standards articulated in our prior decisions, it is clear that no private action should be implied here. It is evident from the legislative history reviewed in his dissenting opinion that Congress did not intend to create a private action through Title IX of the Education Amendments of 1972. It also is clear that Congress deemed the administrative enforcement mechanism it did create fully adequate to protect Title IX rights. But as mounting evidence from the courts below suggests, and the decision of the Court today demonstrates, the mode of analysis we have applied in the recent past cannot be squared with the doctrine of the separation of powers. The time has come to reappraise our standards for the judicial implication of private causes of action.[44]

44. The phrase "private cause of action" may not have a completely clear meaning. As the term is used herein, I refer to the right of a pri-

Under Art. III, Congress alone has the responsibility for determining the jurisdiction of the lower federal courts. As the Legislative Branch, Congress also should determine when private parties are to be given causes of action under legislation it adopts. As countless statutes demonstrate, including titles of the Civil Rights Act of 1964, Congress recognizes that the creation of private actions is a legislative function and frequently exercises it. When Congress chooses not to provide a private civil remedy, federal courts should not assume the legislative role of creating such a remedy and thereby enlarge their jurisdiction.

The facts of this case illustrate the undesirability of this assumption by the Judicial Branch of the legislative function. Whether every disappointed applicant for admission to a college or university receiving federal funds has the right to a civil court remedy under Title IX is likely to be a matter of interest to many of the thousands of rejected applicants. It certainly is a question of vast importance to the entire higher educational community of this country. But quite apart from the interests of the persons and institutions affected, respect for our constitutional system dictates that the issue should have been resolved by the elected representatives in Congress after public hearings, debate, and legislative decision. It is not a question properly to be decided by relatively uninformed federal judges who are isolated from the political process.

In recent history, the Court has tended to stray from the Art. III and separation of powers principle of limited jurisdiction. This, I believe, is evident from a review of the more or less haphazard line of cases that led to our decision in Cort v. Ash, 422 U.S. 66, 95 S.Ct. 2080, 45 L.Ed.2d 26 (1975). The "four factor" analysis of that case is an open invitation to federal courts to legislate causes of action not authorized by Congress. It is an analysis not faithful to constitutional principles and should be rejected. Absent the most compelling evidence of affirmative congressional intent, a federal court should not infer a private cause of action.

I

The implying of a private action from a federal regulatory statute has been an exceptional occurrence in the past history of this Court. A review of those few decisions where such a step has been taken reveals in almost every case special historical circumstances that explain the result, if not the Court's analysis. These decisions suggest that the doctrine of implication applied by the Court today not only represents judicial assumption of the legislative function, but also lacks a principled precedential basis.

vate party to seek judicial relief from injuries caused by another's violation of a legal requirement. In the context of legislation enacted by Congress, the legal requirement involved is a statutory duty.

A

The origin of implied private causes of actions in the federal courts is said to date back to Texas & Pacific R. Co. v. Rigsby, 241 U.S. 33, 36 S.Ct. 482, 60 L.Ed. 874 (1916). A close look at the facts of that case and the contemporary state of the law indicates however, that *Rigsby's* reference to the "inference of a private right of action," id., at 40, 36 S.Ct. at 484, carried a far different connotation than the isolated passage quoted by the Court, * * *, might suggest. The narrow question presented for decision was whether the standards of care defined by the Federal Safety Appliance Act's penal provisions applied to a tort action brought against an interstate railroad by an employee not engaged in interstate commerce at the time of his injury. The jurisdiction of the federal courts was not in dispute, the action having been removed from state court on the ground that the defendant was a federal corporation. See Moore v. Chesapeake & O. R. Co., 291 U.S. 205, 215 n. 6, 54 S.Ct. 402, 406, 78 L.Ed. 755 (1934). Under the regime of Swift v. Tyson, 16 Pet. 1, 41 U.S. 1, 10 L.Ed. 865 (1842), then in force, the Court was free to create the substantive standards of liability applicable to a common-law negligence claim brought in federal court. The practice of judicial reference to legislatively determined standards of care was a common expedient to establish the existence of negligence. See Thayer, Public Wrong and Private Action, 27 Harv.L.Rev. 317 (1914). *Rigsby* did nothing more than follow this practice, and cannot be taken as authority for the judicial creation of a cause of action not legislated by Congress. * * *

For almost 50 years after *Rigsby* this Court recognized an implied private cause of action in only one other statutory context.[45] Four decisions held that various provisions of the Railway Labor Act

---

45. During this period the Court did uphold the implication of civil remedies in favor of the Government, see Wyandotte Transportation Co. v. United States, 389 U.S. 191, 88 S.Ct. 379, 19 L.Ed.2d 407 (1967); United States v. Republic Steel Corp., 362 U.S. 482, 80 S.Ct. 884, 4 L.Ed.2d 903 (1960), and strongly suggested that private actions could be implied directly from particular provisions of the Constitution, Bell v. Hood, 327 U.S. 678, 684, 66 S.Ct. 773, 776, 90 L.Ed. 939 (1946). See also Jacobs v. United States, 290 U.S. 13, 54 S.Ct. 26, 78 L.Ed. 142 (1933). Both of these issues are significantly different from the implication of a private remedy from a federal statute. In *Wyandotte* and *Republic Steel*, the Government already had a "cause of action" in the form of its power to bring criminal proceedings under the pertinent statutes. Thus the Court was confronted only with the question whether the Government could exact less drastic civil penalties as an alternative means of enforcing the same obligations. And this Court's traditional responsibility to safeguard constitutionally protected rights, as well as the freer hand we necessarily have in the interpretation of the Constitution, permits greater judicial creativity with respect to implied constitutional causes of action. Moreover, the implication of remedies to enforce constitutional provisions does not interfere with the legislative process in the way that the implication of remedies from statutes can. See Part III, infra.

of 1926 could be enforced in a federal court. The case for implication of judicial remedies was especially strong with respect to this Act, as Congress had repealed its predecessor, Title III of the Transportation Act of 1920, after Pennsylvania R. Co. v. Railroad Labor Board, 261 U.S. 72, 43 S.Ct. 278, 67 L.Ed. 536 (1923), and Pennsylvania Federation v. Pennsylvania R. Co., 267 U.S. 203, 45 S.Ct. 307, 69 L.Ed. 574 (1925), had held that judicial enforcement of its terms was not available. Convinced that Congress had meant to accomplish more through the 1926 Act, and faced with the absence of an express administrative or judicial enforcement mechanism, the Court in Texas & N. O. R. Co. v. Railway Clerks, 281 U.S. 548, 50 S.Ct. 427, 74 L.Ed. 1034 (1930), upheld an injunction enforcing the Act's prohibition of employer interference in employees' organizational activities. Buttressed by 1934 amendments to the Act that indicated congressional approval of this step, the Court in Virginia Railway Co. v. System Federation, 300 U.S. 515, 57 S.Ct. 592, 81 L.Ed. 789 (1937), extended judicial enforcement to the Act's requirement that an employer bargain with its employees' authorized representative. Finally, in Steele v. Louisville & N. R. Co., 323 U.S. 192, 65 S.Ct. 226, 89 L.Ed. 173 (1944), and Tunstall v. Brotherhood of Locomotive Engineers, 323 U.S. 210, 65 S.Ct. 235, 89 L.Ed. 187 (1944), the Court further held that the duty of a union not to discriminate among its members also could be enforced through the federal courts. In each of these cases enforcement of the Act's various requirements could have been restricted to actions brought by the Board of Mediation (later the Mediation Board), rather than by private parties. But whatever the scope of the judicial remedy, the implication of some kind of remedial mechanism was necessary to provide the enforcement authority Congress clearly intended.[46]

During this same period, the Court frequently turned back private plaintiffs seeking to imply causes of action from federal statutes. See, e. g., Wheeldin v. Wheeler, 373 U.S. 647, 83 S.Ct. 1441, 10 L.Ed.2d 605 (1963); T. I. M. E. v. United States, 359 U.S. 464, 79 S.

---

46. The Court states that a private cause of action also was implied in Machinists v. Central Airlines, 372 U.S. 682, 83 S.Ct. 956, 10 L.Ed.2d 67 (1963), a case involving an amendment of the Railway Labor Act applicable to airlines. Ante, at [n. 37]. A careful reading of that case suggests that it presented a somewhat different question. Under § 204 of the 1936 amendments to the Act, boards of adjustment were established to resolve labor grievances. The Court held that a claim based on a collective-bargaining agreement that had been interpreted by such a board presented a federal question under 28 U.S.C.A. § 1331. The cause of action came directly from the agreement, not from any provision of the Act, and the only issue was whether this already existing private cause of action could be brought in a federal court. See Mishkin, The Federal "Question" in the District Courts, 53 Colum.L.Rev. 157, 166 (1953). Cf. Smith v. Kansas City Title & Trust Co., 255 U.S. 180, 41 S.Ct. 243, 65 L.Ed. 577 (1921). Although as a practical matter this result entails many of the same problems involved in the implication of a private cause of action, * * *, at least analytically the problems are quite different.

Ct. 904, 3 L.Ed.2d 952 (1959); General Committee v. Southern Pacific Co., 320 U.S. 338, 64 S.Ct. 142, 88 L.Ed. 85 (1943); General Committee v. M.-K.-T. R. Co., 320 U.S. 323, 64 S.Ct. 146, 88 L.Ed. 76 (1943); Switchmen's Union v. National Mediation Board, 320 U.S. 297, 64 S.Ct. 95, 88 L.Ed. 61 (1943). Throughout these cases, the focus of the Court's inquiry generally was on the availability of means other than a private action to enforce the statutory duty at issue. Even in cases where the statute might be said to have been enacted for the benefit of a special class comprising the plaintiff, the factor to which the Court today attaches so much importance, * * *, the Court refused to create a private action if Congress had provided some other means of enforcing such duties. See, e. g., Switchmen's Union v. National Mediation Board, supra, at 300–301, 64 S.Ct. at 96–97.

A break in this pattern occurred in J. I. Case Co. v. Borak, 377 U.S. 426, 84 S.Ct. 1555, 12 L.Ed.2d 423 (1964). There the Court held that a private party could maintain a cause of action under § 14(a) of the Securities Exchange Act of 1934, in spite of Congress' express creation of an administrative mechanism for enforcing that statute. I find this decision both unprecedented and incomprehensible as a matter of public policy. The decision's rationale, which lies ultimately in the judgment that "[p]rivate enforcement of the proxy rules provides a necessary supplement to Commission action," id., at 432, 84 S.Ct., at 1560, ignores the fact that Congress, in determining the degree of regulation to be imposed on companies covered by the Securities Exchange Act, already had decided that private enforcement was unnecessary. More significant for present purposes, however, is the fact that *Borak*, rather than signaling the start of a trend in this Court, constitutes a singular and, I believe, aberrant interpretation of a federal regulatory statute.

Since *Borak*, this Court has upheld the implication of private causes of actions derived from federal statutes in only three extremely limited sets of circumstances. First, the Court in Jones v. Alfred H. Mayer Co., 392 U.S. 409, 88 S.Ct. 2186, 20 L.Ed.2d 1189 (1968); Sullivan v. Little Hunting Park, Inc., 396 U.S. 229, 90 S.Ct. 400, 24 L.Ed.2d 386 (1969); and Johnson v. Railway Express Agency, Inc., 421 U.S. 454, 95 S.Ct. 1716, 44 L.Ed.2d 295 (1975), recognized the right of private parties to seek relief for violations of 42 U.S.C.A. §§ 1981 and 1982. But to say these cases "implied" rights of action is somewhat misleading, as Congress at the time these statutes were enacted expressly referred to private enforcement actions.[47] Further-

---

47. Both §§ 1981 and 1982 are derived from § 1 of the Civil Rights Act of 1866, which was re-enacted in pertinent part in §§ 16 and 18 of the Civil Rights Act of 1870. Section 3 of the 1866 Act provided that:

"[T]he district courts of the United States * * * shall have * * * cognizance * * *, of all causes, civil and criminal, affecting persons who are denied * * * any of the rights secured

more, as in the Railway Labor Act cases, Congress had provided no alternative means of asserting these rights. Thus the Court was presented with the choice between regarding these statutes as precatory or recognizing some kind of judicial proceeding.

Second, the Court in Allen v. State Board of Elections, 393 U.S. 544, 89 S.Ct. 817, 22 L.Ed.2d 1 (1969), permitted private litigants to sue to enforce the preclearance provisions of § 5 of the Voting Rights Act of 1965. As the Court seems to concede, this decision was reached without substantial analysis, * * *, and in my view can be explained only in terms of this Court's special and traditional concern for safeguarding the electoral process. In addition, as Mr. Justice WHITE notes, the remedy implied was very limited, thereby reducing the chances that States would be exposed to frivolous or harassing suits.

Finally, the Court in Superintendent of Insurance v. Bankers Life & Cas. Co., 404 U.S. 6, 92 S.Ct. 165, 30 L.Ed. 128 (1971), ratified 25 years of lower court precedent that had held a private cause of action available under the Securities Exchange Commission's Rule 10b–5. As the Court concedes, ante, at [n. 37], this decision reflects the unique history of Rule 10b–5, and did not articulate any standards of general applicability.

These few cases applying *Borak* must be contrasted with the subsequent decisions where the Court refused to imply private actions. In Calhoon v. Harvey, 379 U.S. 134, 85 S.Ct. 292, 13 L.Ed.2d 190 (1964), the Court refused to permit private suits in derogation of administrative remedies to enforce Title IV of the Labor-Management

to them by the first section of this act; * * *. The jurisdiction in civil and criminal matters hereby conferred on the district and circuit courts of the United States shall be exercised and enforced in conformity with the laws of the United States, so far as such laws are suitable to carry the same into effect; but in all cases where such laws are not adapted to the object, or are deficient in the provisions necessary to furnish suitable remedies and punish offences against law, the common law, as modified and changed by the constitution and statutes of the State wherein the court having jurisdiction of the cause * * * is held, so far as the same is not inconsistent with the Constitution and laws of the United States, shall be extended to and govern said courts in the trial and disposition of such cause * * *." 14 Stat. 27.

Section 18 of the 1870 Act made this section applicable to § 16 of the later Act. Subsequently Congress, through § 1 of the Civil Rights Act of 1871, indicated in even more explicit terms that private actions would be available to prevent official interference with the rights guaranteed by § 1 of the 1866 Act. See Chapman v. Houston, Welfare Rights Organization, 441 U.S., at 627–628, 99 S.Ct., at 1921 (1979) (Powell, J., concurring). Although one might conclude, in light of the 1871 Act, that the 1866 and 1870 Acts did not provide for private actions but merely permitted federal courts to entertain state-law actions affecting the denial of civil rights, an equally plausible reading of those statutes is that Congress created a federal cause of action to enforce § 1 of the 1866 Act.

Reporting and Disclosure Act of 1959, in spite of that statute's command, *inter alia*, that "every member in good standing * * * shall have the right to vote for or otherwise support the candidates or candidates of his choice * * *." 29 U.S.C.A. § 481(e). In National Railroad Passenger Corp. v. National Assn. of Railroad Passengers, 414 U.S. 453, 94 S.Ct. 690, 38 L.Ed.2d 646 (1974), the Court reversed a lower court's implication of a private action to challenge violations of the Rail Passenger Service Act of 1970, in light of the Attorney General's express enforcement authority. And in Securities Investor Protection Corp. v. Barbour, 421 U.S. 412, 95 S.Ct. 1733, 44 L.Ed.2d 263 (1975), we refused to allow private actions under the Securities Investor Protection Act of 1970, which also was enforceable by administrative proceedings and government suits.[48]

B

It was against this background of almost invariable refusal to imply private actions, absent a complete failure of alternative enforcement mechanisms and a clear expression of legislative intent to create such a remedy, that Cort v. Ash, 422 U.S. 66, 95 S.Ct. 2080, 45 L.Ed.2d 26 (1975), was decided. In holding that no private action could be brought to enforce 18 U.S.C.A. § 610, a criminal statute, the Court referred to four factors said to be relevant to determining generally whether private actions could be implied. Id., at 78, 95 S.Ct., at 2087. As Mr. Justice WHITE suggests, * * *, these factors were meant only as guideposts for answering a single question, namely whether Congress intended to provide a private cause of action. The conclusion in that particular case was obvious. But as the opinion of the Court today demonstrates, the *Cort* analysis too easily may be used to deflect inquiry away from the intent of Congress, and to permit a court instead to substitute its own views as to the desirability of private enforcement.

Of the four factors mentioned in *Cort*, only one refers expressly to legislative intent. The other three invite independent judicial lawmaking. Asking whether a statute creates a right in favor of a private party, for example, begs the question at issue. What is involved is not the mere existence of a legal right, but a particular person's

---

48. Since *Borak* the Court also has entertained several cases involving challenges to various state welfare programs based in part on the Social Security Act. See, e. g., Rosado v. Wyman, 397 U.S. 397, 90 S.Ct. 1207, 25 L.Ed.2d 442 (1970); King v. Smith, 392 U.S. 309, 88 S.Ct. 2128, 20 L.Ed. 2d 1118 (1968). Most of these decisions did not confront the cause-of-action issue at all; none of them addressed the question whether a private cause-of-action could be implied. In some instances there were conclusory, and in my view incorrect, statements to the effect that 42 U.S.C.A. § 1983 might provide a basis for asserting these claims. See Chapman v. Houston Welfare Rights Organization, supra, 441 U.S., at 644–646, 99 S.Ct., at 1929–1930. (Powell, J., concurring). The silence of these decisions with respect to inferring a private cause of action cannot be taken as authority for the implication of one.

right to invoke the power of the courts to enforce that right.[49] See n. [44], supra. Determining whether a private action would be consistent with the "underlying purposes" of a legislative scheme permits a court to decide for itself what the goals of a scheme should be, and how those goals should be advanced. See Note, 43 Ford.L.Rev. 441, 454–455, 458 (1974). Finally, looking to state law for parallels to the federal right simply focuses inquiry on a particular policy consideration that Congress already may have weighed in deciding not to create a private action.

That the *Cort* analysis too readily permits courts to override the decision of Congress not to create a private action is demonstrated conclusively by the flood of lower court decisions applying it. Although from the time *Cort* was decided until today this Court consistently has turned back attempts to create private actions, see Chrysler Corp. v. Brown, 441 U.S. 281, 99 S.Ct. 1705, 60 L.Ed.2d 208 (1979); Santa Clara Pueblo v. Martinez, 436 U.S. 49, 98 S.Ct. 1670, 56 L.Ed. 2d 30 (1978); Piper v. Chris-Craft Industries, 430 U.S. 1, 97 S.Ct. 926, 51 L.Ed.2d 124 (1977), other federal courts have tended to proceed in exactly the opposite direction. In the four years since we decided *Cort*, no less than 20 decisions by the courts of appeals have implied private actions from federal statutes. * * * It defies reason to believe that in each of these statutes Congress absentmindedly forgot to mention an intended private action. Indeed, the accelerating trend evidenced by these decisions attests to the need to re-examine the *Cort* analysis.

II

In my view, the implication doctrine articulated in *Cort* and applied by the Court today engenders incomparably greater problems than the possibility of occasionally failing to divine an unexpressed congressional intent. If only a matter of statutory construction were involved, our obligation might be to develop more refined criteria which more accurately reflect congressional intent. "But the unconstitutionality of the course pursued has now been made clear" and compels us to abandon the implication doctrine of *Cort*. Erie R. Co. v. Tompkins, 304 U.S. 64, 77–78, 58 S.Ct. 817, 822, 82 L.Ed. 1188 (1938).

As the above-cited 20 decisions of the courts of appeals illustrate, *Cort* allows the Judicial Branch to assume policymaking authority vested by the Constitution in the Legislative Branch. It also invites

---

49. The Court attempts to avoid the question-begging nature of this inquiry by emphasizing the precise phrasing of the statute at issue. * * * Aside from its failure to contend with relevant decisions that do not conform to the perceived pattern, see, e. g., Calhoon v. Harvey, 379 U.S. 134, 85 S.Ct. 292, 13 L.Ed.2d 190 (1964); Switchmen's Union v. National Mediation Board, 320 U.S. 297, 64 S.Ct. 95, 88 L.Ed.2d 61 (1943), the Court's approach gives undue significance to essentially stylistic differences in legislative draftsmanship.

Congress to avoid resolution of the often controversial question whether a new regulatory statute should be enforced through private litigation. Rather than confronting the hard political choices involved, Congress is encouraged to shirk its constitutional obligation and leave the issue to the courts to decide.[50] When this happens, the legislative process with its public scrutiny and participation has been bypassed, with attendant prejudice to everyone concerned. Because the courts are free to reach a result different from that the normal play of political forces would have produced, the intended beneficiaries of the legislation are unable to ensure the full measure of protection their needs may warrant. For the same reason, those subject to the legislative constraints are denied the opportunity to forestall through the political process potentially unnecessary and disruptive litigation. Moreover, the public generally is denied the benefits that are derived from the making of important societal choices through the open debate of the democratic process.

The Court's implication doctrine encourages, as a corollary to the political default by Congress, an increase in the governmental power exercised by the federal judiciary. The dangers posed by judicial arrogation of the right to resolve general societal conflicts have been manifest to this Court throughout its history. * * * As the Court observed only last Term:

> "Our system of government is, after all, a tripartite one, with each branch having certain defined functions delegated to it by the Constitution. While '[i]t is emphatically the province and duty of the judicial department to say what the law is,' Marbury v. Madison, 1 Cranch 137, 177, 2 L.Ed. 60 (1803), it is equally—and emphatically—the exclusive province of Congress not only to formulate legislative policies and mandate programs and projects, but also to establish their relative priority for the Nation. Once Congress, exercising its delegated powers, has decided the order of priorities in a given area, it is for the Executive to administer the laws and for the courts to enforce them when enforcement is sought.

* * *

50. Mr. Justice Rehnquist, perhaps considering himself temporarily bound by his position in Regents of the University of California v. Bakke, 438 U.S. 265, 418–421, 98 S.Ct. 2733, 2814–2815, 57 L.Ed.2d 750 (1978) (opinion of Stevens, J.), concurs in the Court's decision today. But writing briefly, he correctly observes "that Congress at least during the period of the enactment of the several titles of the Civil Rights Act tended to rely to a large extent on the **courts to *decide* whether there should** be a private right of action, rather than determining this question for itself," concurring op., ante * * *. It does not follow, however, that this Court is obliged to indulge Congress in its refusal to confront these hard questions. In my view, the very reasons advanced by Mr. Justice Rehnquist why "this Court in the future should be extremely reluctant to imply a cause of action" absent specific direction by Congress * * * apply to this case with special force.

"Our individual appraisals of the wisdom or unwisdom of a particular course consciously selected by the Congress is to be put aside in the process of interpreting a statute. Once the meaning of an enactment is discerned and its constitutionality determined, the judicial process comes to an end. We do not sit as a committee of review, nor are we vested with the power of veto." TVA v. Hill, 437 U.S. 153, 194–195, 98 S.Ct. 2279, 2301–2302, 57 L.Ed.2d 117 (1978).

See also United States v. New York Telephone Co., 434 U.S. 159, 179, 98 S.Ct. 364, 375, 54 L.Ed.2d 376 (1977), (Stevens, J., dissenting) ("The principle of limited federal jurisdiction is fundamental * * *").[51]

It is true that the federal judiciary necessarily exercises substantial powers to construe legislation, including, when appropriate, the power to prescribe substantive standards of conduct that supplement federal legislation. But this power normally is exercised with respect to disputes over which a court already has jurisdiction, and in which the existence of the asserted cause of action is established.[52] Implication of a private cause of action, in contrast, involves a significant additional step. By creating a private action, a court of limited jurisdiction necessarily extends its authority to embrace a dispute Con-

---

51. Mr. Justice Frankfurter described these dangers with characteristic eloquence:

"Disregard of inherent limits in the effective exercise of the Court's 'judicial Power' * * * may well impair the Court's position as the ultimate organ of 'the supreme Law of the Land' in the vast range of legal problems, often strongly entangled in popular feeling, on which this Court must pronounce. The Court's authority—possessed of neither the purse nor the sword—ultimately rests on sustained public confidence in its moral sanction. Such feeling must be nourished by the Court's complete detachment, in fact and in appearance, from political entanglements and by abstention from injecting itself into the clash of political forces in political settlements." Baker v. Carr, 369 U.S. 186, 267, 82 S.Ct. 691, 737–738, 7 L.Ed.2d 663 (1962) (dissenting opinion).

Alexander Bickel identified the practical difficulties in judicial exercise of governmental power:

"The judicial process is too principle-prone and principle-bound—it has to be, there is no other justification or explanation for the role it plays. It is also too remote from conditions, and deals, case by case, with too narrow a slice of reality. It is not accessible to all the varied interests that are in play in any decision of great consequence. It is, very properly, independent. It is passive. It has difficulty controlling the stages by which it approaches a problem. It rushes forward too fast, or it lags; its pace hardly ever seems just right. For all these reasons, it is, in a vast, complex, changeable society, a most unsuitable instrument for the formation of policy." A. Bickel, The Supreme Court and the Idea of Progress 175 (1970).

52. See, e. g., United States v. Kimbell Foods, Inc., 440 U.S. 715, 99 S.Ct. 1448, 59 L.Ed.2d 711 (1979); Textile Workers Union v. Lincoln Mills, 353 U.S. 448, 77 S.Ct. 912, 1 L.Ed.2d 972 (1957); Clearfield Trust Co. v. United States, 318 U.S. 363, 63 S.Ct. 573, 87 L.Ed. 838 (1943); P. Bator, P. Mishkin, D. Shapiro, & H. Wechsler, Hart and Wechsler's The Federal Courts and the Federal System 756–832 (1973); Friendly, In Praise of Erie—And of the New Federal Common Law, 39 N.Y.U.L.Rev. 383 (1964).

gress has not assigned it to resolve. Cf. Jacobson v. New York, N. H. & H. R. Co., 206 F.2d 153 (CA1 1953) (Magruder, C. J.), aff'd *per curiam*, 347 U.S. 909, 74 S.Ct. 474, 98 L.Ed. 1067 (1954); Note Implying Civil Remedies From Federal Regulatory Statutes, 77 Harv.L.Rev. 285, 286–287 (1963).[53] This runs contrary to the established principle that "[t]he jurisdiction of the federal courts is carefully guarded against expansion by judicial interpretation * * *." American Fire & Cas. Co. v. Finn, 341 U.S. 6, 17, 71 S.Ct. 534, 542, 95 L.Ed. 702 (1951), and conflicts with the authority of Congress under Art. III to set the limits of federal jurisdiction. * * *

The facts of this case illustrate how the implication of a right of action not authorized by Congress denigrates the democratic process. Title IX embodies a national commitment to the elimination of discrimination based on sex, a goal the importance of which has been recognized repeatedly by our decisions. * * * But because Title IX applies to most of our Nation's institutions of higher learning, it also trenches on the authority of the academic community to govern itself, an authority the free exercise of which is critical to the vitality of our society. * * * Arming frustrated applicants with the power to challenge in court his or her rejection inevitably will have a constraining effect on admissions programs. The burden of expensive, vexatious litigation upon institutions whose resources often are severely limited may well compel an emphasis on objectively measured academic qualifications at the expense of more flexible admissions criteria that bring richness and diversity to academic life.[54] If such a significant incursion into the arena of academic polity is to be made, it is the constitutional function of the Legislative Branch, subject as it is to the checks of the political process, to make this judgment.[55]

---

53. Because a private action implied from a federal statute has as an element the violation of that statute, * * *, the action universally has been considered to present a federal question over which a federal court has jurisdiction under 28 U.S.C.A. § 1331. Thus when a federal court implies a private action from a statute, it necessarily expands the scope of its federal-question jurisdiction.

* * *

54. Although the burdens of administrative regulation applied to colleges and universities through Title IX are not insubstantial, that process is at least under the control of government officials whose personal interests are not directly implicated and whose actions are subject to congressional oversight. Private litigation, by contrast, is subject to no such checks.

55. We have recognized in other contexts that implication of a private cause of action can frustrate those alternative processes that exist to resolve such disputes and, given the costs of federal litigation today, may dramatically revise the balance of interests struck by the legislation. See Santa Fe Industries v. Green, 430 U. S. 462, 478–479, 97 S.Ct. 1292, 1303–1304, 51 L.Ed.2d 480 (1977); Blue Chip Stamps v. Manor Drug Stores, 421 U.S. 723, 739–744, 95 S.Ct. 1917, 1927–1929, 44 L.Ed.2d 539 (1975). That this concern applies fully to litigation under Title IX is borne out by the facts of this case. Petitioner's undergraduate grade point average in basic sciences was 3.17, far below the 3.70 overall average of the University of Chicago's entering class, and her medical college admission test scores were in the bottom half of the appli-

Congress already has created a mechanism for enforcing the mandate found in Title IX against gender-based discrimination. At least in the view of Congress, the fund termination power conferred on HEW is adequate to ensure that discrimination in federally funded colleges and universities will not be countenanced. The current position of the Government notwithstanding, overlapping judicial and administrative enforcement of these policies inevitably will lead to conflicts and confusion; our national goal of equal opportunity for men and women, as well as the academic community, may suffer. A federal court should resolve all doubts against this kind of self-aggrandizement, regardless of the temptation to lend its assistance to the furtherance of some remedial end deemed attractive.

III

In sum, I believe the need both to restrain courts that too readily have created private causes of action, and to encourage Congress to confront its obligation to resolve crucial policy questions created by the legislation it enacts, has become compelling. Because the analysis suggested by *Cort* has proven inadequate to meet these problems, I would start afresh. Henceforth, we should not condone the implication of any private action from a federal statute absent the most compelling evidence that Congress in fact intended such an action to exist. Where a statutory scheme expressly provides for an alternative mechanism for enforcing the rights and duties created, I would be especially reluctant ever to permit a federal court to volunteer its services for enforcement purposes. Because the Court today is enlisting the federal judiciary in just such an enterprise, I dissent.

In Touche Ross & Co. v. Redington, 442 U.S. 560, 99 S.Ct. 2479, 61 L.Ed.2d 82 (1979), decided shortly after the *Cannon* case the question before the Supreme Court was "whether customers of securities brokerage firms that are required to file certain financial reports with regulatory authorities by § 17(a) of the Securities Exchange Act of 1934 * * * have an implied cause of action for damages

---

cant group. More than 2,000 applicants for the 104 positions at Chicago had better academic qualifications than petitioner. Furthermore, petitioner's age exceeded restrictions at both Chicago and Northwestern. If Title IX prohibits only purposeful discrimination such as would violate the Constitution were state action involved, a conclusion that seems foregone in light of our holding with respect to Title VI of the Civil Rights Act of 1964 in Regents of the University of California v. Bakke, supra, 438 U.S. at 284–287, 98 S.Ct. at 2745– 2747 (opinion of Powell, J.); id., at 328–350, 98 S.Ct. at 2768–2779 (opinion of Brennan, White, Marshall, and Blackmun, JJ.), then the chances of petitioner's proving that the neutral age requirements used by Chicago and Northwestern are unlawful seem infinitesimal. Yet these schools have been forced to use their scarce resources to defend against this suit at three levels of our federal judicial system, and in light of the Court's holding today they must contend with at least one more round of proceedings.

under § 17(a) against accountants who audit such reports based on misstatements contained in the reports." § 17(a) provided in pertinent part as follows:

> "Every national securities exchange, every member thereof * * * and every broker or dealer registered pursuant to * * * this title, shall make, keep and preserve for such periods, such accounts, correspondence * * * and other records, and make such reports, as the Commission by its rules and regulations may prescribe as necessary or appropriate in the public interest or for the protection of investors."

Plaintiffs contended, inter alia, that *Touche Ross* by its improper audit and certification and filing of answers to questionnaires had prevented the regulatory authorities from learning the true financial condition of the broker in question until it was too late for such authorities to take remedial action to forestall liquidation or lessen its adverse financial consequences for the customers.

A majority of the Supreme Court justices (per Mr. Justice Rehnquist), noting that in the current term the Court had been asked no less than five times to decide whether a private remedy was implicit in a statute not expressly providing one, decided that no such remedy should be implied in the instant case. It was said that the "question of the existence of a statutory cause of action is, of course, one of statutory construction" and that arguments for implying a private action based on tort principles were misplaced. Citing *Cannon*, the Court observed that the fact that a federal statute is violated and some person is harmed does not automatically give rise to a private cause of action. Our task, it stated, is "limited solely to determining whether Congress intended to create the private right of action * * *. And as with any case involving the interpretation of a statute, our analysis must begin with the language of the statute itself." In past cases implying private remedies, the court argued, the statute involved at least prohibited certain conduct or created federal rights in favor of private parties, but § 17(a) did neither and provided no basis for inferring a civil cause of action for damages. The legislative history was found to be silent on the question of a private right of action. And "where, as here, the plain language of the provision weighs against implication," the absence of any suggestion in the legislative history that § 17(a) might give rise to such an action reinforced the Court's decision. Further justification was found in "the statutory scheme": first, § 17(a) was flanked by provisions explicitly granting private causes of action, showing that Congress provided one expressly when it wanted one; second, § 18(a), the principal express civil remedy for misstatements in reports, was limited to purchasers and sellers of securities making the Court reluctant to provide a significantly broader remedy under § 17(a). As to the argument (based on the *Cort* factors) that an implied private remedy was necessary to "effectuate the purposes of the Act," the Court refused to weigh the merits of this claim, remarking that *Cort* did not decide that each of the four factors therein was entitled to equal weight. "The central inquiry remains whether Congress intended to create, either expressly or by implication, a private cause of action. Indeed, the first three factors discussed in *Cort* * * * are ones traditionally relied upon in determining legislative intent * * *. At least in such a case as this, [where the statute grants no private rights to any identifiable class and proscribes no conduct and the legislative history simply does not speak to the issue], the inquiry ends there." Plaintiff's reliance (based on the *Borak* case) on § 27 and on the Act's claimed remedial purpose to protect customers was misplaced. § 27 was said to grant jurisdiction to the federal courts and provide for venue and service of process; it created no cause of action. The *Borak* case was to be read as implying a cause of action from § 14(a) rather than § 27. And § 17(a)'s remedial purpose did not by itself require implication of a private damage action. "[S]ince Borak, we have adhered to a stricter standard * * * [for implying such a remedy] and we follow that stricter standard today * * *. The ultimate question is one of congressional intent, not one of whether this Court thinks it can improve upon the statutory scheme * * *."

Mr. Justice Powell took no part in the decision of the *Touche Ross* case. Mr. Justice Brennan, who had written the majority opinion in Cort v. Ash, supra, and articulated its fourfold test, joined in Rehnquist, J.'s majority opinion. In a brief concurring comment, he stated that "[u]nder the tests established in our prior cases, no cause of action should be implied," and added: "I agree that when as here a statute clearly does not 'create a federal right in favor of the plaintiff' * * * and there is * * * in the legislative history no 'indication of legislative intent * * * to create such a remedy' * * * the remaining two *Cort* factors cannot by themselves be a basis for implying a right of action." The sole dissenter in *Touche Ross* was Mr. Justice Marshall who concluded that application of the four *Cort* factors in this case required the Supreme Court to imply a civil remedy in favor of the plaintiffs.

In Transamerica Mortgage Advisers, Inc. v. Lewis, 444 U.S. 11, 100 S.Ct. 242, 62 L.Ed.2d 146 (1979), by a narrow margin (5–4), the Supreme Court rejected—at least in part—the contentions of a shareholder of a real estate investment trust (Mortgage Trust of America) that the Investment Advisers Act of 1940 should be read as authorizing certain civil remedies—not explicitly provided for by the terms of the Act—against the defendant trustees, investment advisers, et al., based on various alleged frauds and breaches of fiduciary duty. In essence, the Act (§ 206) forbade investment advisers "to employ any device, scheme, or artifice to defraud any client * * * or to engage in any transaction, practice, or course of business which operates as a fraud or deceit upon any client * * *." It empowered the SEC (§ 209) to sue to enjoin violations and provided (§ 215) that contracts whose formation or performance would violate the Act "shall be void * * * as regards the rights of" the violator. The Supreme Court majority (per Mr. Justice Stewart) stressed, as in *Touche Ross*, that the problem in such cases is "basically a matter of statutory construction", i. e., "whether Congress intended to create the private remedy asserted." It examined the language and legislative history of the Act. These were said to show an intent to benefit clients of investment advisers and impose enforceable fiduciary obligations, and the majority noted that Congress's failure expressly to consider a private remedy was "not inevitably inconsistent with an intent * * * to make [it] * * * available" and that "[s]uch an intent may appear implicitly in the language or structure of the statute, or in the circumstances of its enactment". Looking to § 215, the majority concluded that its language fairly implied a specific and limited right to private relief, and that the "customary legal incidents of voidness" would flow from § 215, "including the availability of a suit for rescission or for an injunction against continued operation of the contract, and for restitution". But, relying on Congressional intent, the majority then refused to read § 206 as implying the availability of private actions against violators for damages or other monetary relief. It adduced in support of this ruling (a) that Congress expressly provided elsewhere in the Act for criminal penalties and for resort by the SEC to civil suits and administrative sanctions; (b) that in previous securities acts, and in investment company legislation accompanying the 1940 Act, Congress expressly authorized private suits for damages in prescribed circumstances; (c) that references to "actions at law" and "liability" in the jurisdictional section (§ 214) had been deleted in the course of enactment; and (d) that Congress in 1970 added limited private damage relief to the Investment Company Act but, in 1975, failed to act on a proposal to incorporate "actions at law" in § 214 of the Investment Advisers Act. Finally, the majority rejected plaintiff's arguments based on the advantages of a private damage remedy and its relation to state law and quoted *Touche Ross* to the effect that the four *Cort* factors were not all entitled to equal weight and that Congressional intent (here judged negative) was determinative. Mr. Justice Powell, concurred in the majority opinion, viewing it as compatible with his dissent in *Cannon*. Mr. Justice White, joined by Justices Brennan, Marshall and Stevens, dissented. The dissenters argued that the majority's position could not be reconciled with earlier Supreme Court decisions implying private damage remedies under substantially similar language in other securities laws and that it produced an anomalous result by distinguishing between legal and equitable relief. Invoking legislative intent in their turn, the dissenters relied on the four *Cort* factors as "the criteria through which this intent could be discerned". Application of the four factors was found to justify not only the private relief approved by the majority under § 215 but private suits for damages as well. The Act was enacted for the benefit of clients of investment advisers. § 215 showed that Congress contemplated a private remedy and merely specified in § 215 one consequence of violation of § 206. Where private rights of action exist, it was urged, the court may award complete relief including damages. The majority's reliance on expressio unis (rejected in *Cort*) in relation to the omission of "actions at law" from § 214, (a jurisdictional, not a substantive, provision), and in relation to later Congressional action and inaction, was repudiated. Their refusal to apply the third and fourth *Cort* tests was deplored where, as here (in contrast to *Touche Ross*), the first test was admittedly satisfied. Private damage actions were found by the dissent to be consistent with and even essential to effective enforcement of the Act, given the size of the task and SEC's limited resources. And the state laws applicable to investment advisers were not, in their view, such as to make it inappropriate to infer a private federal damage remedy.

NOTE

Based on perusal of the foregoing federal cases, what is your synthesis of the law applicable to future cases where it is argued that civil remedies should be implied by federal courts in relation to federal statutes that do not expressly provide them? Consider, in this connection, the following questions—among others: What is the current vitality, if any, of the fourfold *Cort* test? Have Mr. Justice Powell's views now prevailed? Should they? Why? Is it accurate, or wise, to characterize the implication question as solely one of legislative intent? What are the consequences of so doing? Was the majority in *Touche Ross* right to reject exploration of the third *Cort* test? Compare *Transamerica*. After *Touche Ross* and *Transamerica*, would *Rigsby* be decided the same way? *Acme*? Would the cases cited in footnote [52] of Mr. Justice Powell's opinion be affected by *Touche Ross* and *Transamerica*? or Moragne v. States Marine Line, Inc.? What is now the status of arguments based on the *expressio unius* maxim in this context?

SCHUSTER v. CITY OF NEW YORK

Court of Appeals of New York, 1958.
5 N.Y.2d 75, 180 N.Y.S.2d 265, 154 N.E.2d 534.

VAN VOORHIS, Judge.

Plaintiff's intestate supplied information to the Police Department of the City of New York leading to the arrest of a dangerous fugitive from justice known as Willie Sutton, a criminal of national reputation. Schuster's part in Sutton's capture was widely publicized. Schuster immediately received communications threatening his life, of which he notified the police. Three weeks later Schuster was shot and killed while approaching his home in the evening. There is no suggestion that Schuster was an underworld character. On the contrary, he appears to have been a public spirited young man who had studied Sutton's picture on an FBI flyer that had been posted in his father's dry-goods store, asking for Sutton's whereabouts.

The complaint is drawn upon the theory that Schuster was shot in consequence of the information about Sutton supplied by Schuster to the police, and that the City of New York owes a special duty under the circumstances alleged to protect persons who have thus co-operated in law enforcement. It is alleged that the city failed to exercise reasonable care in supplying Schuster with police protection upon demand, that Schuster's death was due to negligence of the city in recklessly exposing him to danger, in advising him that the threats upon his life were not seriously made, in failing to supply him with a bodyguard and in heedlessly imparting to him a false impression of safety and lack of danger. The action is not based on any absolute liability claimed to exist on the part of the city but upon its alleged failure to use ordinary or reasonable care for his security.

This being a motion addressed to the sufficiency in law of the complaint, the objection taken by the city may be dismissed at once that plaintiff will be unable to prove that Schuster's death was the result of his having informed upon Sutton. It is a sufficient answer to that objection that the complaint alleges that Schuster's death did result from the negligence of the city previously stated. No more needs to be alleged in a pleading (Sandy v. Wicks, 256 App.Div. 1007, 11 N.Y.S.2d 110). It would be premature to hold now that plaintiff will be unable to prove this allegation at the trial for the reason that no individual has been indicted thus far for Schuster's murder. Plaintiff is entitled to a day in court upon this issue, which should not be prejudged in advance of trial. Perhaps by the time of the trial the identity of Schuster's murderer will have become known and the cause of his act be further clarified. It might even be held, without identification of Schuster's assailant, that the probability is so great of his having been shot by reason of his disclosures resulting in Sutton's capture, that a question of fact would be created on this issue. Questions such as that should be reserved for a trial, and cannot be disposed of by a motion to test the legal sufficiency of the complaint on which all of the allegations of fact must be assumed to be true.

The single issue now presented is whether a municipality is under any duty to exercise reasonable care for the protection of a person in Schuster's situation. Predictions of dire financial consequences to municipalities are waved in our faces if Schuster's estate is allowed to recover for his death. An array of authorities is cited on the proposition that there is no liability to the general public from failure of police or fire protection. (Murrain v. Wilson Line, 270 App.Div. 372, 59 N.Y.S.2d 750, affirmed 296 N.Y. 845, 72 N.E.2d 29; Steitz v. City of Beacon, 295 N.Y. 51, 64 N.E.2d 704, 163 A.L.R. 342; Moch Co. v. Rensselaer Water Co., 247 N.Y. 160, 159 N.E. 896, 62 A. L.R. 1199; Rocco v. City of New York, 282 App.Div. 1012, 126 N.Y. S.2d 198). One might think that the floodgates of liability have been opened in negligence and compensation cases against municipalities and other defendants where the liability is less clear than it is under the allegations of this complaint (cf. 31 Texas L.Rev. 630). In our view the public (acting in this instance through the City of New York) owes a special duty to use reasonable care for the protection of persons who have collaborated with it in the arrest or prosecution of criminals, once it reasonably appears that they are in danger due to their collaboration. If it were otherwise, it might well become difficult to convince the citizen to aid and co-operate with the law enforcement officers (see Note, 58 W.Va.L.Rev. 308). To uphold such a liability does not mean that municipalities are called upon to answer in damages for every loss caused by outlaws or by fire. Such a duty to Schuster bespeaks no obligation enforcible in the courts to exercise the police powers of government for the protection of every member of the general public. Nevertheless, where persons actually have aided in the apprehension or prosecution of enemies of society under the criminal law, a reciprocal duty arises on the part of society to use reasonable care for their police protection, at least where reasonably demanded or sought. Such a duty would be performed by the regular organs of government, in this instance, by the City of New York. The duty of everyone to aid in the enforcement of the law, which is as old as history, begets an answering duty on the part of government, under the circumstances of contemporary life, reasonably to protect those who have come to its assistance in this manner.

Municipalities have been held liable to a bystander negligently shot by a policeman engaged in an altercation with another (Wilkes v. City of New York, 308 N.Y. 726, 124 N.E.2d 338); to a taxicab driver shot by a passenger negligently placed in his cab by policemen (Lubelfeld v. City of New York, 4 N.Y.2d 455, 176 N.Y.S.2d 302, 151 N.E.2d 862); to the estate of an arrested man who died from pneumonia caused by exposure in the jail and failure to treat a fractured hip and elbow (Dunham v. Village of Canisteo, 303 N.Y. 498, 104 N. E.2d 872); to the estate of a man negligently shot by a policeman for making a disturbance while intoxicated (Flamer v. City of Yonkers, 309 N.Y. 114, 127 N.E.2d 838); to the estate of a man arrested for public intoxication who died from cerebral hemorrhage in consequence of failure of the police to procure medical aid (O'Grady v. City of Fulton, 4 N.Y.2d 717, 171 N.Y.S.2d 108, 148 N.E.2d 317); to a wife shot by her husband to whom the police had negligently returned a pistol (Benway v. City of Watertown, 1 A.D.2d 465, 151 N.Y.S.2d 485); and to a bystander injured while directing traffic at the instance of a police officer (Adamo v. P. G. Motor Freight, 4 A. D.2d 758, 164 N.Y.S.2d 874). In McCrink v. City of New York, 296 N.Y. 99, 71 N.E.2d 419 a city was held liable for negligently having omitted to discharge a police officer by whom plaintiff's intestate was shot. In Meistinsky v. City of New York, 309 N.Y. 998, 132 N. E.2d 900, the estate of a hold-up victim recovered who had been killed by an untrained officer's bullets. Negligence of the city was found in its omission to use reasonable care in training the police officer so that he could shoot straight and hit the criminal instead of his victim. None of these actions could have been brought until after the waiver of governmental immunity by section 12–a (now § 8) of the Court of Claims Act (Bernardine v. City of New York, 294 N.Y. 361, 62 N.E. 2d 604, 161 A.L.R. 364), but in each of them liability arose from negligence of a city in the exercise of the police power, and in at least two of them the negligence consisted in nonfeasance rather than in misfeasance (McCrink v. City of New York, supra; Meistinsky v. City of New York, supra).

That distinction at best furnishes an incomplete formula, as the opinion of the court by Chief Judge Cardozo says in Moch Co. v. Rensselaer Water Co. (supra, 247 N.Y. at page 167, 159 N.E. at page 898). The opinion in the *Moch* case states: "If conduct has gone forward to such a stage that inaction would commonly result, not negatively merely in withholding a benefit, but positively or actively in working an injury, there exists a relation out of which arises a duty to go forward. Bohlen, Studies in the Law of Torts, p. 87."

In a situation like the present, government is not merely passive; it is active in calling upon persons "in possession of any information regarding the whereabouts of" Sutton, quoting from the FBI flyer, to communicate such information in aid of law enforcement. Where that has happened, as here, or where the public authorities have made active use of a private citizen in some other capacity in the arrest or prosecution of a criminal, it would be a misuse of language to say that the law enforcement authorities are merely passive. They are active in calling upon the citizen for help, and in utilizing his help when it is rendered. They have gone forward to such a stage, paraphrasing the opinion in the *Moch* case (supra), that inaction in furnishing police protection to such persons would commonly result, not negatively merely in withholding a benefit, but positively or actively in working an injury. Under such circumstances, we there said "there exists a relation out of which arises a duty to go forward". Such a relationship existed here. The duty of Schuster to aid in law enforcement by informing the police of the whereabouts of Sutton is implied by the decision in Babington v. Yellow Taxi Corp., 250 N.Y. 14, 164 N.E. 726, 61 A.L.R. 1354. For present purposes it matters little whether this duty be described as legal or moral (People ex rel. Central Trust Co. v. Prendergast, 202 N.Y. 188, 197, 199–200, 95 N. E. 715, 718–719).

The reciprocal governmental duty to take reasonable measures to assure protection, to be sure, did not develop into enforcible legal liability until government waived its immunity from suit by the adoption of section 12–a (now § 8) of the Court of Claims Act in 1929, nor was the effect of such waiver fully understood until the decision in 1945 of Bernardine v. City of New York (supra). This waiver of governmental immunity removed the bar that previously prevented actions based on negligence of the police and made possible recoveries in the cases which have been cited. In one sense all of those causes of action grew out of the waiver of governmental immunity. But they were not created by waiver of governmental immunity, but by the common law, which

> "is the legal embodiment of practical sense. It is a comprehensive enumeration of principles sufficiently elastic to meet the social development of the people. Its guiding star has always been the rule of right and wrong, and in this country its principles demonstrate that there is in fact, as well as in theory, a remedy for all wrongs. The capacity of common law for growth and adaptation to new conditions is one of its most admirable features." 11 Am.Jur., Common Law, § 2, pp. 154–155.

While governmental immunity remained in effect, this type of court action remained in abeyance. It remained in abeyance not on account of absence of duty on the part of a municipality to the injured or deceased person, but for the reason that where the factual basis of the claim was involved in the performance of a governmental function (such as police duty), the State had not permitted itself or its political subdivisions or municipal corporations to be sued. Where the immunity was removed, this bar no longer stood against the enforcement of civil liability arising from breach of a duty that existed before, but which could not be enforced until the immunity was waived.

Even before the removal of governmental immunity, the Supreme Court of the United States had occasion to declare the duty of government toward a private citizen who reports a violation of law to the law enforcement authorities. The case of In re Quarles, 158 U.S. 532, 15 S.Ct. 959, 39 L.Ed. 1080 concerned the prosecution of persons who by concerted action conspired to prevent a private citizen from informing against a criminal. Quoting from its opinion in Ex parte Yarbrough, 110 U.S. 651, 4 S.Ct. 152, 157, 28 L.Ed. 274, the United States Supreme Court said in the Quarles case that it is the duty of government to see that a private citizen may exercise freely the right to notify the enforcement authorities of law violations,

> "and to protect him from violence while so doing, or on account of so doing. This duty does not arise solely from the interest of the party concerned, but from the necessity of

the government itself that its service shall be free from the adverse influence of force and fraud practiced on its agents".

The Quarles case (supra) envisages a civic duty as well as a right to inform, and contemplates that the informant shall be protected on account of doing so. Although not employed as a sleuth, such a person comes into the relationship of the government's "agent".

Such a duty on the part of government to persons aiding in law enforcement is recognized by section 1848 [See Note 1, infra—Ed.] of the Penal Law, Consol.Laws, c. 40. That section creates an absolute liability against municipal corporations for damages arising from the personal injury or death of persons injured or killed while aiding policemen at their direction in making arrests. The existence of some duty on the part of the private citizen to assist in law enforcement is so plain that this statute makes it a misdemeanor to refuse to aid a police officer upon his command. This statute goes farther in some respects than the cause of action alleged in the instant complaint, in that it does not rest the liability of the municipality upon its negligence but imposes liability whenever such a person is injured or killed while aiding an officer in making an arrest. It is true that Schuster's case does not fall within the coverage of this statute, inasmuch as he was not shot while Sutton was being arrested but three weeks later. He was commanded in a certain sense to assist in Sutton's apprehension, in view of the widely published notices calling upon all private citizens to report Sutton's whereabouts to the public authorities. If the case fell within this statute, negligence would not have to be established against the City of New York in failing to supply police protection to Schuster, or in advising him that such protection was not necessary; the city would have had to pay to his estate upon merely showing that he had been called upon to aid in Sutton's arrest and had been killed while doing so. This statute does not measure the entire length and breadth of the city's liability for negligence of the police, as the cases cited earlier in this opinion show. The existence of section 1848 of the Penal Law does not defeat plaintiff's common-law cause of action. On the contrary, it reflects a public policy that municipalities shall respond in damages to private citizens or their estates who have been injured and killed as a result of aiding in law enforcement. This statute contains no language barring plaintiff's common-law remedy. The rule is that "A statute in the affirmative, without any negative expressed or implied, takes away no preexisting rights or remedies; as a general rule, it operates merely to furnish an additional remedy for the enforcement of a right" (McKinney's Cons.Laws of N. Y., Book 1, Statutes, § 34). This commentary continues: "The affirmative statute is merely declaratory and does not repeal the common law relating to the subject; on the contrary, the two rules coexist. In other words, where a remedy existed at common law for the wrong or injury against which a remedial statute is directed, if such statute provides a more enlarged or a summary or more efficient remedy for the party aggrieved, but does not in terms or by necessary implication deprive him of the remedy which existed at common law, the statutory remedy is considered as merely cumulative, and the party injured may resort to either at his election" (citing Tremain v. Richardson, 68 N.Y. 617, and other cases).

Section 1848 of the Penal Law, while it recognizes a duty on the part of municipal corporations to persons who are killed or injured from aiding in the apprehension of criminals, neither expressly nor by implication repeals the common-law remedy. It does not purport to cover the same ground as the cause of action alleged in the complaint, and thereby to preclude the maintenance of a common-law action. The statute goes farther in some respects, by making liability absolute to those who come within its terms. The instant action is based on negligence. It is grounded on negligence of the police in the failure to exercise reasonable care for the protection of Schuster after he had received threatening letters as a result of its becoming publicly known that he had been instrumental in the arrest of Sutton. In contrast, the statutory cause of action lies in cases to which it applies even if the police and other public authorities have taken the utmost care. This in itself indicates that no implied exclusion of a common-law remedy for negligence could have been intended, inasmuch as the statute has nothing to do with negligence. The statute and the common-law right of action are different in scope. What is important is that the governmental policy behind the statute indicates care and solicitude for the private citizen who co-operates with the public authorities in the arrest and prosecution of criminals. That is the bearing which section 1848 of the Penal Law has on this case. Statutes have played their part in the formation of the common law, and, like court decisions that are not strictly analogous, sometimes point the way into other territory when the animating principle is used as a guide. Michalowski v. Ey, 4 N.Y.2d 277, 282, 174 N.Y.S. 2d 6, 10, 150 N.E.2d 399, 402, citing Pound, Common Law and Legislation, 21 Harv.L.Rev. 383, 385–386; Stone, The Common Law in the United States, 50 Harv.L.Rev. 4, 13. Here Schuster's case is within the spirit if not the coverage of section 1848 of the Penal Law. The remedy supplied by that section is not available to plaintiff, but the care and solicitude which it manifests toward those who aid in law enforcement dispels any inference that the public policy of the State is the other way. This section contains nothing which implies that the Legislature intended to nullify plaintiff's common-law remedy for negligence under the circumstances described.

The judgment appealed from should be reversed, and defendant's motion to dismiss the complaint should be denied, with costs in all courts.

[A separate concurring opinion, by Judge McNALLY, is omitted here. It argues that the assumption by the police department of the partial protection of Schuster carried with it the obligation not to terminate such protection if in the exercise of reasonable care it was apparent that its acceptance of Schuster's services and information and its public acknowledgment of his role either enlarged or prolonged the risk to him of bodily harm.]

Chief Judge CONWAY (dissenting).

[Judge Conway argues, *inter alia*, that the broad duty imposed on the police by the New York City Charter is a duty to protect the general public from crime—neglect of this duty does not create liability to individuals. He continues:]

The majority opinion is premised on the idea that "the public (acting in this instance through the City of New York) owes a special duty to use reasonable care for the protection of persons who have collaborated with it in the arrest or prosecution of criminals, once it reasonably appears that they are in danger due to their collaboration." Apparently the majority proposes to leave it to a jury to determine (1) when it reasonably appears that the "collaborator" is in danger and (2) whether the public has exercised reasonable care for the protection of such person. We cannot agree that the public is under any such special duty.

Certainly, no statute imposes such a special duty on the public and we are unable to find any warrant in common law for the imposition of such a special duty. The majority holds that such duty is owed to the individual since there is imposed upon the individual a duty to aid in the enforcement of the law. We disagree with this sweeping premise and so, reject the proposition as unsound. Our State does not put its residents under any duty to take steps either to prevent the commission of crime or to bring the offender to justice, after its commission. * * * The offer of a reward, rather than the imposition of a legal duty, has been the modern means employed to induce private citizens to aid the police in the enforcement of the law. * * * [T]he reward is the *quid pro quo* not only for the information disclosed but for the assumption of the risks of disclosure as well. The public is not put under an additional special duty of protecting the recipient of the reward.

We recognize, of course, that countless numbers of persons willingly identify those accused of crime, without thought of monetary reward. Such persons are undoubtedly aware of the fact that they, themselves, are the beneficiaries of their own acts, for every resident of a community is benefited by the apprehension, conviction and incarceration of lawless persons at large in the community. One thing is certain—whether the citizen or resident who co-operates with the police in identifying a criminal does so out of a selfish motive or out of an altruistic motive, in so doing he is not discharging a duty imposed upon him by law. Thus falls the premise of the majority to the effect that the duty of everyone to aid in the enforcement of the law begets an answering duty on the part of government reasonably to protect those who come to its assistance. It is true that under certain circumstances a person is placed under a legal duty to aid the law enforcement authorities, i. e., where *commanded* by an officer to aid him in arresting any person, or in retaking any person who has escaped from legal custody, or in executing any legal process (Penal Law, § 1848). Having imposed such a duty on individuals, the Legislature has imposed upon the State a reciprocal duty to pay damages to any individual injured as a consequence of obeying the command or, if death results, to pay damages to the personal representative of the deceased. Section 1848 of the Penal Law is not applicable here for the reasons that (1) the intestate's acts in connection with the arrest of Sutton were not performed pursuant to the command of an officer but were voluntary in nature and (2) the intestate's death did not arise out of and within the course of the arrest within the meaning of section 1848 of the Penal Law—his death occurred several weeks after the arrest had been made.

* * *

Duties have their genesis in concepts of reasonableness. It would be unreasonable, if not impossible, for a community to support a police force of the dimensions required to discharge such a duty. At least three policemen working around the clock would be required for *each* witness in *each* such case. Reasonableness demands that the need for *special* police protection be left to the absolute discretion of the Police Department. It is a well-known fact that few witnesses or informers are murdered or assaulted by reason of their having assisted in the enforcement of the law. This is some evidence of the fact that, by and large, the Police Department exercises sound discretion in these matters. Now, it may be argued that since there are few deaths or assaults the city can well afford to pay damages to the one assaulted or to the estate of the one killed. That, however, is not the question. The question is whether the duty of furnishing *special* police protection is to be imposed upon the public. If such duty exists special protection can properly be demanded by every witness who identifies a criminal, for there is a likelihood that every criminal will have associates of a violent bent. If such special duty exists the police cannot refuse to give it. Such a situation should not be brought into existence. The need for special protection must be left to the absolute discretion of the police force. A mere mistake in judgment by the department should not be the basis for the imposition of liability upon the municipality else, as we have noted, to discharge its duty and at the same time to avoid liability, the police department will find itself faced with the impossible task of supplying *all* witnesses and *all* informers with special protection until that point of time is reached when it becomes a virtual certainty that no harm will befall the particular witness or informer. To withdraw the protection at any point short of this will, under the rule now being announced by the majority, subject the municipality to possible liability at the hands of a jury. The truth of this becomes evident when it is realized that in the present case the majority is content to let a jury determine whether to return a judgment against the city even though (a) there is no proof available as to who shot and killed Schuster and (b) there is no proof available as to whether the threats made to Schuster were made by his assassin or simply by a crank.

It is further suggested that the city may properly be held liable for having prematurely withdrawn partial protection of Schuster. Support for this holding is said to be found in the rule that "one who assumes to act, even though gratuitously, may thereby become subject to the duty of acting carefully, if he acts at all * * * (Glanzer v. Shepard, 233 N.Y. 236, 239, 135 N.E. 275, 23 A.L.R. 1425)." We believe that the quoted rule cannot reasonably be said to have application to a situation such as that presented here. Under that rule one who assumes to act, where he is not legally bound to act, is required to act with such care that *he* not injure, or aggravate an existing injury, assuming that there be one, of the one to whom he offers aid. Assistance given which in no way harms the recipient thereof is not actionable. In affording Schuster partial special protection the police did not bring about his death. Likewise in withdrawing the partial special protection the police did not bring about Schuster's death. In withdrawing the special protection gratuitously given, the police left Schuster in precisely the same position as he was in before the partial special protection was given. The withdrawal did not aggravate or alter the situation in the slightest. Schuster's death was caused solely by the act of an unknown assailant. The public at no time owed him *special* protection against such assailant. They gratuitously gave him partial special protection but it cannot fairly be said that such partial special protection, or the withdrawal thereof, increased the danger of injury to Schuster or in any way contributed to his death.

Nor may the city be cast in damages upon the ground that statements and assurances given by certain members of the police force lulled plaintiff's intestate into a relaxation of vigilance and a false sense of security. Briefly, the allegations are that the police falsely represented that the intestate was not endangered by reason of "threatening and menacing telephone calls, anonymous letters, missives, notes and messages" and that the police falsely represented that the telephone calls, etc., were the work of "crackpots" and "cranks" and were "child's stuff". It is clear that the statements made by the police were expressions of opinion, not expressions of fact upon which the intestate had a right to rely. They could hardly have been more than expressions of opinion in view of the fact that the identity of those who threatened the intestate was unknown. No fraud action may be grounded on a mere expression of opinion.

In sum, the police force of the City of New York is under a broad duty to protect the *general* public from every form of crime. However, this duty does not inure to the benefit of individual members of the public.

The judgment should be affirmed, with costs.

[In a brief opinion, omitted here, DESMOND, J. urges as a separate ground of dissent that the suit is "based on a mere guess" that Schuster was killed for informing on Sutton.]

FROESSEL, Judge (dissenting).

I concur with Chief Judge CONWAY and Judge DESMOND for affirmance. Without the support of a statute or a single applicable judicial precedent, the majority is about to announce a new rule of law, namely, that every city, town and village of this State may now be held in heavy damages if their police departments fail to give such protection to an informer as a jury may later determine was adequate. And this, notwithstanding the fact that the Legislature of this State, which created these governmental agencies, has already manifested, by its enactment of section 1848 of the Penal Law, how far it has been willing to go in allowing compensation to persons aiding the police.

[In paragraphs omitted here, FROESSEL, J. argues the inadequacy of the allegations of the complaint dealing with the publicizing of Schuster's role by the police; with the scope of protection actually undertaken by the police; with the relation between Schuster's informing and his death. He calls attention to the absence of a factual allegation that the breach of the asserted police duty was a cause of Schuster's death. Agreeing with CONWAY, C. J., that the police had no legal duty to guard Schuster, he reviews New York cases and concludes that it is "settled in this State that a municipality is not liable for inadequate police or fire protection." *Matter of Quarles and Butler* is distinguished as are the *McCrink* and *Meistinsky* cases which are characterized as based on misfeasance. On Section 1848, Judge Froessel has this to say:

> Section 1848 of the Penal Law is clearly inapplicable. That section sets the limit to which the Legislature has been willing to go in establishing liability against municipal corporations to compensate individuals who aid the police. One can only conclude therefrom that the Legislature, as a matter of public policy, does not wish to extend liability to situations not embraced within the statute, for, as we said in the *Steitz* case * * * [295 N.Y. 51],

"An intention to impose upon the city the crushing burden of such an obligation [liability to individual citizens for inadequate fire protection] should not be imputed to the Legislature in the absence of language clearly designed to have that effect."

Nevertheless, the majority would now rewrite the statute and extend its operation to informers.

Like Judge Conway, Judge Froessel denies that the according and withdrawal of partial protection by the police gave rise to any duty. He too stresses that existing legislation contemplates a system of rewards for informers, apart from Section 1848 which is here inapplicable. He echoes Judge Conway's concern for the practical burden placed on the police by the majority's ruling.]

DYE and FULD, JJ., concur with VAN VOORHIS, J.

McNALLY[56] concurring in a separate opinion in which DYE, FULD and VAN VOORHIS, JJ., also concur.

CONWAY, C. J., and DESMOND and FROESSEL, JJ., dissent and vote to affirm, each in a separate opinion in which the others concur.

BURKE, J., taking no part.

Judgment reversed, motion to dismiss complaint denied and matter remitted to Special Term for the entry of the essential order, with costs in all courts.

NOTES

1. New York Penal Law § 1848 referred to in all the opinions in the *Schuster* case provided in pertinent part as follows:

§ 1848. *Refusing to aid officer in making an arrest*

A person, who, after having been lawfully commanded to aid an officer in arresting any person, or in re-taking any person who has escaped from legal custody, or in executing any legal process, wilfully neglects or refuses to aid such officer is guilty of a misdemeanor. Where such a command is obeyed and the person obeying it is killed or injured or his property or that of his employer is damaged and such death, injury or damage arises out of and in the course of aiding an officer in arresting or endeavoring to arrest a person or re-taking or endeavoring to re-take a person who has escaped from legal custody or executing or endeavoring to execute any legal process, the person or employer so injured or whose property is so damaged or the personal representatives of the person so killed shall have a cause of action to recover the amount of such

---

[56]. Designated pursuant to section 5 of article VI of the State Constitution in place of Burke, J., disqualified.

damage or injury against the municipal corporation by which such officer is employed at the time such command is obeyed. * * *

2. The following general comment was made by Justice Walter V. Schaefer of the Illinois Supreme Court on the use of statutes as premises for reasoning:

"The new way with a statute which Dean Pound predicted is not yet here. But it is clear, I think, that the common law's insulation from statutes is thinner than it was. The shift has not been pronounced; the instances are still sporadic. But such a shift in attitude can be measured accurately only from a perspective more remote than ours. I should guess that the pace will accelerate as advocates become alert to the possibility that decisions in common law cases can be influenced by principles drawn from the statutes." Schaefer, Precedent and Policy, 34 U.Chi.L.Rev. 3, 22 (1966).

Compare the remarks of Chief Justice Roger J. Traynor of the Supreme Court of California in Traynor, Statutes Revolving in Common Law Orbits, 17 Catholic U.L.Rev. 401, 426–7 (1968):

" * * * Across the centuries many a judge has seen fit to speak the speech of an exemplary statute in a new rule to protect or bring to justice the litigants whose problems were not covered by the statute. The real problem is not whether judges should make use of statutes, but how they can make optimum use of them.

"One might better ask how they can make optimum use of the statutes that are inherently serviceable as sources of judicial lawmaking. There are of course countless statutes that will govern indefinitely without becoming relevant to a particular case. As to those that could be relevant, there are two problems. How do relevant statutes come to the attention of a judge? If they do come to his attention, how does he make a discriminating choice of a statute as a basis for a judicial rule?

"There is no orderly research of statutes comparable to the orderly research of cases. The problem at the outset is that they are not systematically catalogued as cases are. There are no comparable cross-references to make their interrelations clear or to identify their antecedents. How can a judge be sure that between counsel's efforts and his own all pertinent materials have been rounded up? Suppose there lies undiscovered some pertinent statute still at large? Cases may arise in which no statute is even in issue, and yet a statute may exist that would be of the greatest relevance as a basis for judicial analogy, and that a judge should study as closely as any judicial precedent if he is to make a rational decision.

"There is great need not only for a systematic cataloguing and research of statutes but also for systematic criticism. Although some of the mounting statutes engage the attention of scholarly critics there is no steady evaluation of the work product of legislators comparable with the continuous criticism of judicial decisions.

Moreover, there are few internal controls or external controls on the mass production of bad or indifferent statutes. * * *

* * *

"We are still far from betterment measured by the goal of rational processes of lawmaking in all the lanes of law. We might well concentrate on a preliminary goal, better use in the judicial process of the good laws that often emerge amid the variegated products of the legislative process. There must be teamwork to that end. If the librarians and researchers will systematize the study of statutes, if the watchbirds will sharpen their watch on legislatures in action, if commentators will set forth salient qualities or defects of legislative products, the judges will surely make better use than they have of the statutes revolving in common-law orbits. * * *"

PROBLEM

In the State of Columbia, Peter Jones took from his wife's handbag, which she was carrying at the time, a watch which she had just inherited from her father. He took this watch with the intention, openly stated, of keeping it for his own purposes. He declared he was not going to return it then or any other time. Moreover, he promptly sold the watch and used the proceeds to buy himself a new suit. By way of reply to his wife's heated and continuing remonstrances and her requests for return of the watch, Jones advised her to "go jump in the lake." Instead, she visited the district attorney. Thereafter, on the basis of the foregoing facts, Jones was arrested and indicted for larceny under section 1000 of the State of Columbia's Penal Law.

The facts as related above and incorporated in the indictment were at no time disputed by Jones; but he demurred to the indictment on the ground that the facts stated did not constitute a crime. The demurrer was overruled. At the trial following, the facts stated in the indictment were proved and he was convicted of larceny. Jones appealed. The sole question on his appeal is whether the facts stated in the indictment and proved on the trial constitute larceny under section 1000. It is to be assumed that all procedural requirements were properly complied with in Jones's case and that the question just stated was properly before the appellate court for decision.

A thorough search of the pertinent legal sources turns up the information hereinafter set out for consideration in connection with Jones v. State of Columbia.

Section 1000 of the Columbia Penal Law reads:

"A person who with the intent to deprive or defraud another of the use and benefit of property belonging to such other or with the intent to appropriate the same to the use of the taker wrongfully takes by any means whatever from the possession of the true owner any money, personal property or article of value of any kind, steals such property and is guilty of the crime of larceny and upon conviction thereof shall be punishable as provided in section 1234 of this Article."

This quoted provision, first adopted in 1830, has not been changed since that time, though the whole Penal Law, of which section 1000 is a part, was revised in matters of form and reenacted in 1940.

Twenty years after the adoption in 1830 of the provision now designated as section 1000 of the Penal Law, the first Married Women's Act was adopted in the State of Columbia. Prior to 1850, under the common law rules then governing in Columbia: married women were disabled from holding property in their own right; moreover, husband and wife were legally deemed one person, with "the husband being the one." By virtue of the Married Women's Act of 1850 and a later Act of 1870, wives were given the right to take by inheritance or otherwise and to own property separately, and to sue and be sued with respect to their separate property. Following adoption of these Acts, civil suits at common law were permitted by the courts to be brought by wives against their husbands based on the latter's wrongful interference with the wife's separate property. In 1935, the State of Columbia adopted a third act concerning married women, giving them the right to sue others, including their own husbands, in tort cases involving injury to person or character. The 1935 Act expressly abolished the old presumption of the husband's coercion or instigation.

Assume that you are counsel for the State of Columbia on appeal. Prepare a compact outline (a) stating the issue or issues raised by this case and (b) indicating the arguments you would make on behalf of the State. The arguments should not be mere abstract statements of legal rules but should be related to the facts and law of this case. You should indicate, and include answers to, the arguments defendant Jones is likely to make.

After the outline has been completed it will be instructive to compare your work with Judge Desmond's opinion for the New York Court of Appeals in People v. Morton, 308 N.Y. 96, 123 N.E.2d 790 (1954).

In United States v. Dege, 364 U.S. 51, 80 S.Ct. 1589, 4 L.Ed.2d 1563 (1960), the Supreme Court reviewed a District Court's dismissal of an indictment under the federal conspiracy statute, 18 U.S.C.A.

§ 371. This statute, originally enacted in 1867 and reenacted without material change in 1948, reads as follows:

§ 371. *Conspiracy to commit offense or to defraud United States*

If two or more persons conspire either to commit any offense against the United States, or to defraud the United States, or any agency thereof in any manner or for any purpose, and one or more of such persons do any act to effect the object of the conspiracy, each shall be fined not more than $10,000 or imprisoned not more than five years, or both.

If, however, the offense, the commission of which is the object of the conspiracy, is a misdemeanor only, the punishment for such conspiracy shall not exceed the maximum punishment provided for such misdemeanor. June 25, 1948, c. 645, 62 Stat. 701.

The ground for the District Court's dismissal was that the indictment did not state an offense since a husband and wife are legally incapable of conspiring within the meaning of § 371. In reversing the decision, a majority of six Justices of the Supreme Court, per Frankfurter, J., commented in part as follows:

* * *

"The question raised * * * is clear-cut and uncomplicated. The claim that husband and wife are outside the scope of an enactment of Congress in 1948, making it an offense for two persons to conspire, must be given short shrift once we heed the admonition of this Court that 'we free our minds from the notion that criminal statutes must be construed by some artificial and conventional rule,' United States v. Union Supply Co., 215 U.S. 50, 55, 30 S.Ct. 15, 16, 54 L.Ed. 87 [(1909)], and therefore do not allow ourselves to be obfuscated by medieval views regarding the legal status of woman and the common law's reflection of them. Considering that legitimate business enterprises between husband and wife have long been commonplace in our time, it would enthrone an unreality into a rule of law to suggest that man and wife are legally incapable of engaging in illicit enterprises and therefore, forsooth, do not engage in them.

"None of the considerations of policy touching the law's encouragement or discouragement of domestic felicities on the basis of which this Court determined appropriate rules for testimonial compulsion as between spouses, Hawkins v. United States, 358 U.S. 74, 79 S.Ct. 136, 3 L.Ed.2d 125 (1958), supra, and Wyatt v. United States, 362 U.S. 525, 80 S.Ct. 901, 4 L.Ed.2d 931 (1960), supra, [and see Trammel v. United States, infra Appendix—Ed.] are relevant to yielding to the claim that an unqualified interdiction by

Congress against a conspiracy between two persons precludes a husband and wife from being two persons. Such an immunity to husband and wife as a pair of conspirators would have to attribute to Congress one of two assumptions: either that responsibility of husband and wife for joint participation in a criminal enterprise would make for marital disharmony or that a wife must be presumed to act under the coercive influence of her husband and, therefore, cannot be a willing participant. The former assumption is unnourished by sense; the latter implies a view of American womanhood offensive to the ethos of our society.

"The fact of the matter is that we are asked to write into law a doctrine that parrot-like has been repeated in decisions and texts from what was given its authoritative expression by Hawkins early in the eighteenth century. * * *

* * *

"For this court now to act on Hawkins's formulation of the medieval view that husband and wife 'are esteemed but as one Person in Law, and are presumed to have but one Will' would indeed be 'blind imitation of the past.' It would require us to disregard the vast changes in the status of women—the extension of her rights and correlative duties—whereby a wife's legal submission to her husband has been wholly wiped out, not only in the English-speaking world generally but emphatically so in this country.

"* * * It would be an idle parade of learning to document the statement that these common-law disabilities were extensively swept away in our different state of society, both by legislation and adjudication, long before the originating conspiracy Act of 1867 was passed. Suffice it to say that we cannot infuse into the conspiracy statute a fictitious attribution to Congress of regard for the medieval notion of woman's submissiveness to the benevolent coercive powers of a husband in order to relieve her of her obligation of obedience to an unqualifiedly expressed Act of Congress by regarding her as a person whose legal personality is merged in that of her husband making the two one."

WARREN, C. J., dissenting, joined by Mr. Justice BLACK and Mr. Justice WHITTAKER, observed, *inter alia:*

"If the Court's opinion reflects all that there is to this case, it is astonishing that it has taken so many years for the federal judiciary to loose itself from the medieval chains of the husband-wife conspiracy doctrine. * * * I submit that this simplistic an approach will not do.

* * *

"* * * [H]owever rapidly nineteenth century jurisprudence moved toward a recognition of the individuality of women in other areas, it is wholly inaccurate to imply that the law of conspiracy changed apace. In fact, the earliest case repudiating the husband-wife doctrine which the Government has been able to cite is Dalton v. People, 68 Colo. 44, 189 P. 37 [(1920)], which was decided, as the Government puts it, '[a]s early as 1920.' And if the doctrine is an anachronism today, as the Court says, its unusual hardiness is demonstrated by the fact that the decision of the Court represents a departure from the general rule which prevails today in the English-speaking world. As recently as 1957, the Privy Council approved the husband-wife doctrine, and other Commonwealth courts are in accord. For American decisions, see Annotations 4 A.L.R. 266; 71 A.L.R. 1116; 46 A.L.R.2d 1275.

"Thus it seems clear that if the 1867 statute is to be construed to reflect Congress' intent as it was in 1867, the Court's decision is erroneous. And I believe that we must focus upon that intent, inasmuch as there is no indication that Congress meant to change the law by the 1948 legislation which re-enacted without material variation the old conspiracy statute. Surely when a rule of law is well-established in the common law and is part of the legislative purpose when a relevant statute is passed, that rule should not be rejected by this Court in the absence of an explicit subsequent repudiation of it by Congress. Consequently, I would be compelled to dissent whether or not I believed the rule to be supported by reason.

"But more, I cannot agree that the rule is without justification. * * *

"It is not necessary to be wedded to fictions to approve the husband-wife conspiracy doctrine, for one of the dangers which that doctrine averts is the prosecution and conviction of persons for 'conspiracies' which Congress never meant to be included within the statute. A wife, simply by virtue of the intimate life she shares with her husband, might easily perform acts that would technically be sufficient to involve her in a criminal conspiracy with him, but which might be far removed from the arms-length agreement typical of that crime. It is not a medieval mental quirk or an attitude 'unnourished by sense' to believe that husbands and wives should not be subjected to such a risk, or that such a possibility should not be permitted to endanger the confidentiality of the marriage relationship. While it is easy enough to ridicule Hawkins' pronouncement in Pleas of the Crown from a metaphysical point of view, the concept of the 'oneness' of a married couple may reflect an abiding belief that the communion between husband and wife is such that their actions are not always to be regarded by the criminal law as if there were no marriage.

"By making inroads in the name of law enforcement into the protection which Congress has afforded to the marriage relationship, the Court today continues in the path charted by the recent decision in Wyatt v. United States."

MORTON v. MANCARI

Supreme Court of the United States, 1974.
417 U.S. 535, 94 S.Ct. 2474, 41 L.Ed.2d 290.

Mr. Justice BLACKMUN delivered the opinion of the Court.

The Indian Reorganization Act of 1934 accords an employment preference for qualified Indians in the Bureau of Indian Affairs [BIA]. Appellees, non-Indian BAI employees, challenged this preference as contrary to the anti-discrimination provisions of the Equal Employment Opportunity Act of 1972, and as violative of the Due Process Clause of the Fifth Amendment. A three-judge federal district court concluded that the Indian preference under the 1934 Act was impliedly repealed by the 1972 Act. Mancari v. Morton, 359 F. Supp. 585 (D.C.N.M.1973). We noted probable jurisdiction in order to examine the statutory and constitutional validity of this longstanding Indian preference. 414 U.S. 1142, 94 S.Ct. 893, 39 L.Ed.2d 99 (1974).

I

Section 12 of the Indian Reorganization Act, also known as the Wheeler-Howard Act, 48 Stat. 986 (1934), 25 U.S.C.A. § 472, provides:

"The Secretary of the Interior is directed to establish standards of health, age, character, experience, knowledge, and ability for Indians who may be appointed, without regard to civil-service laws, to the various positions maintained, now or hereafter, by the Indian Office,[57] in the administration of functions or services affecting any Indian tribe. Such qualified Indians shall hereafter have the preference to appointment to vacancies in any such positions."[58]

57. The Indian Health Service was transferred in 1954 from the Department of the Interior to the Department of Health, Education and Welfare. Act of August 5, 1954, § 1, 68 Stat. 674, 42 U.S.C.A. § 2001. Presumably, despite this transfer, the reference in § 12 to the "Indian Office" has continuing application to the Indian Health Service. See 5 CFR § 213.3116(b)(8) (1974).

58. There are earlier and more narrowly drawn Indian preference statutes. 25 U.S.C.A. §§ 44, 45, 46, 47, and 274. For all practical purposes,

In June 1972, pursuant to this provision, the Commissioner of Indian Affairs, with the approval of the Secretary of the Interior, issued a directive (Personnel Management Letter No. 72–12) stating that the BIA's policy would be to grant a preference to qualified Indians not only, as before, in the initial hiring stage, but also in the situation where an Indian and a non-Indian, both already employed by the BIA, were competing for a promotion within the Bureau.[59] The record indicates that this policy was implemented immediately.

Shortly thereafter, appellees, who are non-Indian employees of the BIA at Albuquerque,[60] instituted this class action, on behalf of themselves and other non-Indian employees similarly situated, in the United States District Court for the District of New Mexico, claiming that the "so-called 'Indian Preference Statutes'" were repealed by the 1972 Equal Employment Opportunity Act and deprived them of rights to property without due process of law, in violation of the Fifth Amendment.[61] Named as defendants were the Secretary of the Interior, the Commissioner of Indian Affairs, and the BIA Directors for the Albuquerque and Navajo Area Offices. Appellees claimed that implementation and enforcement of the new preference policy "placed and will continue to place [appellees] at a distinct disadvantage in competing for promotion and training programs with Indian employees, all of which has and will continue to subject the [appel-

these were replaced by the broader preference of § 12. Although not directly challenged in this litigation, these statutes, under the District Court's decision, clearly would be invalidated.

59. The directive stated:
"The Secretary of the Interior announced today [June 23, 1972] he has approved the Bureau's policy to extend Indian preference to training and to filling vacancies by original appointment, reinstatement, and promotion. The new policy was discussed with the national president of the National Federation of Federal Employees under national consultation rights NFFE has with the Department. Secretary Morton and I jointly stress that careful attention must be given to protecting the rights of non-Indian employees. The new policy provides as follows: Where two or more candidates who meet the established qualification requirements are available for filling a vacancy, if one of them is an Indian, he shall be given preference in filling the vacancy. This new policy is effective immediately and is incorporated into all existing programs such as the promotion program. Revised manual releases will be issued promptly for review and comment. You should take immediate steps to notify all employees and recognized unions of this policy."

60. The appellees state that none of them is employed on or near an Indian reservation. Brief for Appellees 8. The District Court described the appellees as "teachers * * * or programmers, or in computer work." Mancari v. Morton, 359 F.Supp. 585, 587 (N.M.1973).

61. The specific question whether § 12 of the 1934 Act authorizes a preference in promotion as well as in initial hiring was not decided by the District Court and is not now before us. We express no opinion on this issue. See Freeman v. Morton, D.C. Cir., 499 F.2d 494 (1974). See also Mescalero Apache Tribe v. Hickel, 432 F.2d 956 (CA10 1970), cert. denied, 401 U.S. 981, 91 S.Ct. 1195, 28 L.Ed.2d 333 (1971) (preference held inapplicable to reduction in force).

lees] to discrimination and deny them equal employment opportunity."

A three-judge court was convened pursuant to 28 U.S.C.A. § 2282 because the complaint sought to enjoin, as unconstitutional, the enforcement of a federal statute. Appellant Amerind, a nonprofit organization representing Indian employees of the BIA, moved to intervene in support of the preference; this motion was granted by the District Court and Amerind thereafter participated at all stages of the litigation.

After a short trial focusing primarily on how the new policy, in fact, has been implemented, the District Court concluded that the Indian preference was implicitly repealed by § 11 of the Equal Employment Opportunity Act of 1972, Pub.L. 92–261, 86 Stat. 111, 42 U.S. C.A. (Supp. II 1973) § 2000e–16(a), proscribing discrimination in most federal employment on the basis of race.[62] Having found that Congress repealed the preference, it was unnecessary for the District Court to pass on its constitutionality. The court permanently enjoined appellants "from implementing any policy in the Bureau of Indian Affairs which would hire, promote, or reassign any person in preference to another solely for the reason that such person is an Indian." The execution and enforcement of the judgment of the District Court was stayed by Mr. Justice Marshall on August 16, 1973, pending the disposition of this appeal.

II

The federal policy of according some hiring preference to Indians in the Indian service dates at least as far back as 1834.[63] Since that time, Congress repeatedly has enacted various preferences of the general type here at issue.[64] The purpose of these preferences, as

62. Section 2000e–16(a) reads:
"All personnel actions affecting employees or applicants for employment (except with regard to aliens employed outside the limits of the United States) in military departments as defined in section 102 of Title 5, in executive agencies (other than the General Accounting Office) as defined in section 105 of Title 5 (including employees and applicants for employment who are paid from nonappropriated funds), in the United States Postal Service and the Postal Rate Commissioner, in those units of the Government of the District of Columbia having positions in the competitive service, and in those units of the legislative and judicial branches of the Federal Government having positions in the competitive service, and in the Library of Congress shall be made free from any discrimination based on race, color, religion, sex, or national origin."

63. Act of June 30, 1834, § 9, 4 Stat. 737, 25 U.S.C.A. § 45:
"In all cases of the appointments of interpreters or other persons employed for the benefit of the Indians, a preference shall be given to persons of Indian descent, if such can be found, who are properly qualified for the execution of the duties."

64. Act of May 17, 1882, § 6, 22 Stat. 88, and Act of July 4, 1884, § 6, 23 Stat. 97, 25 U.S.C.A. § 46 (employment of clerical, mechanical, and other help on reservations and about agencies); Act of August 15, 1894, § 10, 28 Stat. 313, 25 U.S.C.A. § 44 (employment of herders, teamsters,

variously expressed in the legislative history, has been to give Indians a greater participation in their own self-government;[65] to further the Government's trust obligation toward the Indian tribes;[66] and to reduce the negative effect of having non-Indians administer matters that affect Indian tribal life.[67]

The preference directly at issue here was enacted as an important part of the sweeping Indian Reorganization Act of 1934. The overriding purpose of that particular Act was to establish machinery whereby Indian tribes would be able to assume a greater degree of self-government, both politically and economically.[68] Congress was seeking to modify the then-existing situation whereby the primarily non-Indian-staffed BIA had plenary control, for all practical purposes, over the lives and destinies of the federally recognized Indian tribes. Initial congressional proposals would have diminished substantially the role of the BIA by turning over to federally chartered self-governing Indian communities many of the functions normally performed by the Bureau.[69] Committee sentiment, however, ran

---

and laborers, "and where practicable in all other employments" in the Indian service); Act of June 7, 1897, § 1, 30 Stat. 83, 25 U.S.C.A. § 274 (employment as matrons, farmers, and industrial teachers in Indian schools); Act of June 25, 1910, § 23, 36 Stat. 861, 25 U.S.C.A. § 47 (general preference as to Indian labor and products of Indian industry).

65. Senator Wheeler, co-sponsor of the 1934 Act, explained the need for a preference as follows:

"We are setting up in the United States a civil service rule which prevents Indians from managing their own property. It is an entirely different service from anything else in the United States because these Indians own this property. It belongs to them. What this policy of this Government is and what it should be is to teach these Indians to manage their own business and control their own funds and to administer their own property, and the civil service has worked very poorly so far as the Indian Service is concerned. * * *" Hearings before the Senate Committee on Indian Affairs on S. 2755 and S. 3645 (Part 2), 73d Cong., 2d Sess., 256 (1934).

66. A letter, contained in the House Report to the 1934 Act, from President F. D. Roosevelt to Congressman Howard states:

"We can and should, without further delay, extend to the Indian the fundamental rights of political liberty and local self-government and the opportunities of education and economic assistance that they require in order to attain a wholesome American life. This is but the obligation of honor of a powerful nation toward a people living among us and dependent upon our protection." H.R.Rep. No. 1804, 73d Cong., 2d Sess., 8 (1934).

67. "If the Indians are exposed to any danger, there is none greater than the residence among them of unprincipled white men." H.R.Rep. No. 474, 23d Cong., 1st Sess., 98 (1834) (letter dated February 10, 1834, from Indian Commissioners to the Secretary of War).

68. As explained by John Collier, Commissioner of Indian Affairs:

"[T]his bill is designed not to prevent the absorption of Indians in white communities, but rather to provide for those Indians unwilling or unable to compete in the white world some measures of self-government in their own affairs." Hearings on S. 2755 before the Senate Committee on Indian Affairs (Part 1), 73d Cong., 2d Sess., 26 (1934).

69. Hearings before the House Committee on Indian Affairs on H.R.

against such a radical change in the role of the BIA.[70] The solution ultimately adopted was to strengthen tribal government while continuing the active role of the BIA, with the understanding that the Bureau would be more responsive to the interests of the people it was created to serve.

One of the primary means by which self-government would be fostered and the Bureau made more responsive was to increase the participation of tribal Indians in the BIA operations.[71] In order to achieve this end, it was recognized that some kind of preference and exemption from otherwise prevailing civil service requirements was necessary.[72] Congressman Howard, the House sponsor, expressed the need for the preference:

> "The Indians have not only been thus deprived of civic rights and powers, but they have been largely deprived of the opportunity to enter the more important positions in the service of the very bureau which manages their affairs. Theoretically, the Indians have the right to qualify for the Federal civil service. In actual practice there has been no adequate program of training to qualify Indians to compete in these examinations, especially for technical and higher positions; and even if there were such training, the Indians would have to compete under existing law, on equal terms with multitudes of white applicants * * *. The various services on the Indian reservations are actually local rather than Federal services and are comparable to local municipal and county services, since they are dealing with purely local Indian problems. It should be possible for Indians with the requisite vocational and professional training to enter the service of their own people without the necessity of competing with white applicants for these positions. This bill permits them to do so." 78 Cong.Rec. 11729 (1934).

7902, Readjustment of Indian Affairs, 73d Cong., 2d Sess., 1–7 1934 [House Hearings]. See also Mescalaro Apache Tribe v. Jones, 411 U.S. 145, 152–153, fn. 9, 93 S.Ct. 1267, 1272–1273, 36 L.Ed.2d 114 (1973).

70. House Hearings 491–497.

71. "[Section 12] was intended to integrate the Indian into the government service connected with the administration of his affairs. Congress was anxious to promote economic and political self-determination for the Indian" (footnote omitted). Mescalero Apache Tribe v. Hickel, 432 F.2d, at 960.

72. The bill admits qualified Indians to the position [sic] in their own service.

"Thirty-four years ago, in 1900, the number of Indians holding regular positions in the Indian Service, in proportion to the total of positions, was greater than it is today.

"The reason primarily is found in the application of the generalized civil service to the Indian Service, and the consequent exclusion of Indians from their own jobs." House Hearings 19 (Memorandum dated February 19, 1934, submitted by Commissioner Collier to the Senate and House Committees on Indian Affairs).

Congress was well aware that the proposed preference would result in employment disadvantages within the BIA for non-Indians.[73] Not only was this displacement unavoidable if room were to be made for Indians, but it was explicitly determined that gradual replacement of non-Indians with Indians within the Bureau was a desirable feature of the entire program for self-government.[74] Since 1934, the BIA has implemented the preference with a fair degree of success. The percentage of Indians employed in the Bureau rose from 34% in 1934 to 57% in 1972. This reversed the former downward trend, see n. [72], supra, and was due, clearly, to the presence of the 1934 Act. The Commissioner's extension of the preference in 1972 to promotions within the BIA was designed to bring more Indians into positions of responsibility and, in that regard, appears to be a logical extension of the congressional intent. See Freeman v. Morton, supra, and n. [61], supra.

III

It is against this background that we encounter the first issue in the present case: whether the Indian preference was repealed by the Equal Employment Opportunity Act of 1972. Title VII of the Civil Rights Act of 1964, 78 Stat. 253, was the first major piece of federal legislation prohibiting discrimination in *private* employment on the basis of "race, color, religion, sex, or national origin." 42 U.S.C.A. § 2000e-2(a). Significantly, §§ 701(b) and 703(i) of that Act explicitly exempted from its coverage the preferential employment of Indians by Indian tribes or by industries located on or near Indian reservations. 42 U.S.C.A. §§ 2000e(b) and 2000e-2(i).[75] This exemption reveals a clear congressional recognition, within the framework of Title VII, of the unique legal status of tribal and reservation-based ac-

---

73. Rep. Carter, an opponent of the bill, placed in the Congressional Record the following observation by Commissioner Collier at the Committee Hearings:
"[W]e must not blind ourselves to the fact that the effect of this bill if worked out would unquestionably be to replace white employees by Indian employees. I do not know how fast, but ultimately it ought to go very far indeed." 78 Cong.Rec. 11737 (1934).

74. "It should be possible for Indians to enter the service of their own people without running the gauntlet of competition with whites for these positions. Indian progress and ambition will be enormously strengthened as soon as we adopt the principle that the Indian Service shall gradually become, in fact as well as in name, an Indian service predominantly in the hands of educated and competent Indians." 78 Cong.Rec. 11731 (1934) (remarks of Rep. Howard).

75. Section 2000e(b) excludes "an Indian Tribe" from the Act's definition of "employer." Section 2000e–2(i) states:
"Nothing contained in this subchapter shall apply to any business or enterprise on or near an Indian reservation with respect to any publicly announced employment practice of such business or enterprise under which a preferential treatment is given to any individual because he is an Indian living on or near a reservation."

tivities. The Senate sponsor, Senator Humphrey, stated on the floor by way of explanation:

> "This exemption is consistent with the Federal Government's policy of encouraging Indian employment and with the special legal position of Indians." 110 Cong.Rec. 12723 (1964).[76]

The 1964 Act did not specifically outlaw employment discrimination by the federal government.[77] Yet the mechanism for enforcing long-outstanding Executive Orders forbidding government discrimination has proved ineffective for the most part.[78] In order to remedy this, Congress, by the 1972 Act, amended the 1964 Act and proscribed discrimination in most areas of federal government. See n. [62], supra. In general, it may be said that the substantive anti-discrimination law embraced in Title VII was carried over and applied to the Federal Government. As stated in the House Report,

> "To correct this entrenched discrimination in the Federal service, it is necessary to insure the effective application of uniform, fair and strongly enforced policies. The present law and the proposed statute do not permit industry and labor organizations to be the judges of their own conduct in the area of employment discrimination. There is no reason why government agencies should not be treated similarly." H.R.Rep. No. 92–238, on H.R. 1746, 92d Cong., 1st Sess. 24–25 (1971).

Nowhere in the legislative history of the 1972 Act, however, is there any mention of Indian preference.

Appellees assert, and the District Court held, that since the 1972 Act proscribed racial discrimination in government employment, the Act necessarily, albeit *sub silentio*, repealed the provision of the 1934

---

76. Senator Mundt supported these exemptions on the Senate floor by claiming that they would allow Indians "to benefit from Indian preference programs now in operation or later to be instituted." 110 Cong. Rec. 13702 (1964).

77. The 1964 Act, however, did contain a proviso, expressed in somewhat precatory language:
"That it shall be the policy of the United States to insure equal employment opportunities for Federal employees without discrimination because of race, color, religion, sex or national origin." 78 Stat. 254.

This statement of policy was reenacted as 5 U.S.C.A. § 7151, 80 Stat. 523 (1966), and the 1964 Act's proviso was repealed, id., at 662.

78. "This disproportionatte [sic] distribution of minorities and women throughout the Federal bureaucracy and their exclusion from higher level policy-making and supervisory positions indicates the government's failure to pursue its policy of equal opportunity.

"A critical defect of the Federal equal employment program has been the failure of the complaint process. That process has impeded rather than advanced the goal of the elimination of discrimination in Federal employment." H.R.Rep. No. 92–238, on H.R. 1746, 92d Cong., 1st Sess., 23–24 (1971).

Act, that called for the preference in the BIA of one racial group, Indians, over non-Indians:

> "When a conflict such as in this case, is present, the most recent law or Act should apply and the conflicting Preferences passed some 39 years earlier should be impliedly repealed." Brief for Appellees 7.

We disagree. For several reasons we conclude that Congress did not intend to repeal the Indian preference and that the District Court erred in holding that it was repealed.

First: There are the above-mentioned affirmative provisions in the 1964 Act excluding coverage of tribal employment and of preferential treatment by a business or enterprise on or near a reservation. 42 U.S.C.A. §§ 2000e(b) and 2000e–2(i). See n. [75], supra. These 1964 exemptions as to private employment indicate Congress' recognition of the longstanding federal policy of providing a unique legal status to Indians in matters concerning tribal or "on or near" reservation employment. The exemptions reveal a clear congressional sentiment that an Indian preference in the narrow context of tribal or reservation-related employment did not constitute racial discrimination of the type otherwise proscribed. In extending the general antidiscrimination machinery to federal employment in 1972, Congress in no way modified these private employment preferences built into the 1964 Act, and they are still in effect. It would be anomalous to conclude that Congress intended to eliminate the longstanding statutory preferences in BIA employment, as being racially discriminatory, at the very same time it was reaffirming the right of tribal and reservation-related private employers to provide Indian preference. Appellees' assertion that Congress implicitly repealed the preference as racially discriminatory, while retaining the 1964 preferences, attributes to Congress irrationality and arbitrariness, an attribution we do not share.

Second: Three months after Congress passed the 1972 amendments, it enacted two *new* Indian preference laws. These were part of the Education Amendments of 1972, 86 Stat. 235, 20 U.S.C.A. §§ 887c(a) and (d), and § 1119a. The new laws explicitly require that Indians be given preference in government programs for training teachers of Indian children. It is improbable, to say the least, that the same Congress which affirmatively approved and enacted these additional and similar Indian preferences was, at the same time, condemning the BIA preference as racially discriminatory. In the total absence of any manifestation of supportive intent, we are loathe to imply this improbable result.

Third: Indian preferences, for many years, have been treated as exceptions to Executive Orders forbidding government employment discrimination.[79] The 1972 extension of the Civil Rights Act to government employment is in large part merely a codification of prior anti-discrimination Executive Orders that had proved ineffective because of inadequate enforcement machinery. There certainly was no indication that the substantive proscription against discrimination was intended to be any broader than that which previously existed. By codifying the existing anti-discrimination provisions, and by providing enforcement machinery for them, there is no reason to presume that Congress affirmatively intended to erase the preferences that previously had co-existed with broad anti-discrimination provisions in Executive Orders.

Fourth: Appellees encounter head-on the "cardinal rule * * * that repeals by implication are not favored." Posadas v. National City Bank, 296 U.S. 497, 503, 56 S.Ct. 349, 352, 80 L.Ed. 351 (1963); Wood v. United States, 16 Pet. 342–343, 363, 10 L.Ed. 987 (1842); Universal Interpretative Shuttle Corp. v. Washington Metropolitan Area Transit Comm'n, 393 U.S. 186, 193, 89 S.Ct. 354, 358, 21 L.Ed.2d 334 (1968). They and the District Court read the congressional silence as effectuating a repeal by implication. There is nothing in the legislative history, however, that indicates affirmatively any congressional intent to repeal the 1934 preference. Indeed, as explained above, there is ample independent evidence that the legislative intent was to the contrary.

This is a prototypical case where an adjudication of repeal by implication is not appropriate. The preference is a longstanding, important component of the Government's Indian program. The anti-discrimination provision, aimed at alleviating minority discrimination in employment, obviously is designed to deal with an entirely different and, indeed, opposite problem. Any perceived conflict is thus more apparent than real.

In the absence of some affirmative showing of an intention to repeal, the only permissible justification for a repeal by implication is when the earlier and later statutes are irreconcilable. Georgia v. Pennsylvania R. Co., 324 U.S. 439, 456–457, 65 S.Ct. 716, 725–726, 89 L.Ed. 1051 (1945). Clearly, this is not the case here. A provision aimed at furthering Indian self-government by according an employment preference within the BIA for qualified members of the gov-

---

79. See, e. g., Ex. Order 7423, July 26, 1936, 1 Fed.Reg. 885–886. When President Eisenhower issued an Order prohibiting discrimination on the basis of race in the civil service, Exec. Order 10577, No. 22, 1954, 19 Fed. Reg. 7521, § 4.2, he left standing earlier Executive Orders containing exceptions for the Indian service. Id., § 301. See also 5 CFR § 213.-3112(a)(7)(1974), which provides a civil service exemption for:

"All positions in the Bureau of Indian Affairs and other positions in the Department of the Interior directly and primarily related to the providing of services to Indians when filled by the appointment of Indians who are one-fourth or more Indian blood."

See also 5 CFR § 213.3116(b)(8) (1974) (Indian Health Services).

erned group can readily co-exist with a general rule prohibiting employment discrimination on the basis of race. Any other conclusion can be reached only by formalistic reasoning that ignores both the history and purposes of the preference and the unique legal relationship between the Federal Government and tribal Indians.

Furthermore, the Indian preference statute is a specific provision applying to a very specific situation. The 1972 Act, on the other hand, is of general application. Where there is no clear intention otherwise, a specific statute will not be controlled or nullified by a general one, regardless of the priority of enactment. See, e. g., Bulova Watch Co. v. United States, 365 U.S. 753, 758, 81 S.Ct. 864, 6 L. Ed.2d 72 (1961); Rodgers v. United States, 185 U.S. 83, 87–89, 22 S. Ct. 582, 583–584, 46 L.Ed. 816 (1902).

The courts are not at liberty to pick and choose among congressional enactments, and when two statutes are capable of co-existence, it is the duty of the courts, absent a clearly expressed congressional intention to the contrary, to regard each as effective. "When there are two acts upon the same subject, the rule is to give effect to both if possible * * *. The intention of the legislature to repeal 'must be clear and manifest.'" United States v. Borden Co., 308 U.S. 188, 198, 60 S.Ct. 182, 188, 84 L.Ed. 181 (1939). In light of the factors indicating no repeal, we simply cannot conclude that Congress consciously abandoned its policy of furthering Indian self-government when it passed the 1972 amendments.

We therefore hold that the District Court erred in ruling that the Indian preference was repealed by the 1972 Act.

[In the final section (IV) of its opinion, omitted here, the court finds that the preference in question does not violate the Due Process Clause of the Fifth Amendment.]

The judgment of the District Court is reversed and the case is remanded for further proceedings consistent with this opinion.

It is so ordered.

Judgment reversed and case remanded.

NOTE

1. How would you characterize the coordination problem in the principal case? Where in these materials have you encountered a similar problem?

2. The presumption against repeals by implication appears more often in the cases than any other maxim of statutory construction except, perhaps, the doctrine of strict construction of penal statutes. On the rules applicable to repeals by implication, see 1A Sutherland, Statutes and Statutory Construction § 23.09 et seq. (4th ed. Sands, 1973).

The implied repeals problem is made less difficult for the courts to the extent that the draftsman of the new statute does a respectable job of background research and so is able to include a comprehensive express repealer clause (table of past acts expressly repealed) in the new statute. The "tailoring" of a bill to the existing case and statute law on the subject is the constant concern of the skilled legislative draftsman. As to the essential research requirements for a professional job of legislative bill-drafting, see Source and Development of Legislative Proposals in Section 1, The Legislative Process, Chapter V, supra, and see Department of Legislation, Notes for a Legislative Research Check List, 36 A.B.A.J. 685 (1950).

SOME FINAL PROBLEMS
Problem 1

(a) In March, 1967, a supertanker bound up the Mississippi River for Baton Rouge, Louisiana, collided with a barge owned by the Lowe Co. The barge sank in such a position as to create an impediment to navigation. The Government was notified at once and markers were set out as required by law. A few days later, Lowe Co. notified the Government that the barge was being abandoned. The United States refused, however, to accept abandonment or to assume responsibility for removing the wreck, and in December 1967, brought an action—conducted by the Department of Justice—against Lowe Co. The Government charged, and Lowe Co. did not deny, that negligence in the equipping, manning, and mooring of the barge had caused the sinking; it sought an order directing Lowe Co. to remove the sunken vessel.

(b) A barge owned by Redd Inc. and loaded with 2,200,000 pounds of liquid chlorine sank in September 1966 while being towed by a tug (also owned by Redd Inc.) in the Mississippi River. Redd Inc. immediately set out markers as required by law and at first made some attempts to locate and raise the wreck, which was impeding navigation. But then, in November 1966, it informed the Army Corps of Engineers that it believed further efforts to raise the barge would be unsuccessful and stated it was abandoning the vessel. The Government, after a study of the situation, concluded that there was serious danger of leakage and, further, that if any chlorine escaped, it would probably be in the form of lethal chlorine gas, which might cause a large number of casualties. The Government demanded that Redd Inc. remove the barge. Redd Inc. refused to do so.

The United States then moved to avert a catastrophe by raising the barge and its deadly cargo. This operation, carried out at a reasonable cost of some $3,081,000 to the United States, proved successful in early 1968. The barge and its cargo were then sold by the United States for some $85,000. Redd Inc. does not dispute the Government's right to retain the proceeds of this sale.

The United States demanded that the owners and operators of the barge reimburse the Government for its expenses. This demand was rejected. In March 1968, the Government, through the Department of Justice, brought a suit against Redd Inc., charging negligence in the design, towing, manning, mooring, and equipping of the barge. The Government sought to recover the costs it incurred in removing the wreck less the proceeds of sale of barge and cargo.

Assuming the truth of the facts as set out above and alleged by the United States government, was the government—relying on Sections 15 and 16 of the Rivers and Harbors Act, supra p. 570, and in the light of other provisions of the Act—entitled to

(a) an order requiring Lowe Co. to remove its sunken barge from the Mississippi River, and

(b) reimbursement by Redd Inc. for the costs incurred by the Government (less proceeds of sale) in removing the chlorine-laden barge from the Mississippi River?

Identify the issues and, using only the text of the Act, supra, work out your recommended answers and supporting arguments.

Problem 2

A year ago Ira Welsh, a citizen and resident of the State of Kent, was an employee in good standing of the Truegrit Insurance Co. Truegrit was and is a large insurer incorporated and doing business in Kent. In mid-January 1980, 20% of the weekly wages payable by Truegrit to Welsh were subjected to garnishment (see the statutory definition of garnishment, infra), at the instance of Kingsway Supermarket, Inc., a Kent firm to which Welsh had an unpaid debt of long standing. Pursuant to this garnishment, 20% of Welsh's weekly wages were required to be withheld for payment of the debt. Truegrit discharged Welsh from its employ at the end of January following the garnishment.

Upset by the discharge, Welsh complained to the Secretary of Labor (via the Wage and Hour Division of the Labor Department) that his discharge violated the Consumer Credit Protection Act of 1968, a statute discussed hereafter. When the Secretary of Labor refused to act (no reason was disclosed for the refusal), Welsh filed a complaint against Truegrit in the federal district court for the State of Kent alleging that he had been discharged due to the garnishment and that his discharge violated Subchapter II of the Consumer Credit Protection Act of 1968 and asking for reinstatement and for back pay, exemplary damages and attorney fees in amounts totaling over $20,000. Truegrit moved to dismiss the complaint. The district court upheld Truegrit's motion, on the ground that the Act provided no basis for Welsh's action, and entered judgment accordingly. Welsh appealed to the Court of Appeals for the 12th Circuit (which embraces the State of Kent).

Assume you are a law clerk to one of the three judges of the Court of Appeals to whom the case of Welsh vs. Truegrit Insurance

Co. has been assigned for decision. The judge has asked you to prepare a memorandum—in effect a draft opinion—covering the case. You are to assume that the sole question before the court is whether Welsh's claim for relief is supported by federal law. Assume further that all requirements for presenting this question to the Court of Appeals for decision have been properly met.

The only federal statute in point in this case is the above-mentioned Consumer Credit Protection Act of 1968 (hereinafter referred to as CCPA). This important enactment is divided into three subchapters.

Subchapter II of the CCPA, of central concern here, is entitled "Restrictions on Garnishment." Insofar as pertinent to this problem, Subchapter II provides as follows:

§ 1671. *Congressional findings and declaration of purpose*

(a) The Congress finds:

(1) The unrestricted garnishment of compensation due for personal services encourages the making of predatory extensions of credit. Such extensions of credit divert money into excessive credit payments and thereby hinder the production and flow of goods in interstate commerce.

(2) The application of garnishment as a creditors' remedy frequently results in loss of employment by the debtor, and the resulting disruption of employment, production, and consumption constitutes a substantial burden on interstate commerce.

* * *

§ 1672. *Definitions*

For purposes of this subchapter:

* * *

(c) The term "garnishment" means any legal or equitable procedure through which the earnings of any individual are required to be withheld for payment of any debt.

§ 1673. *Restriction on garnishment—maximum allowable garnishment*

[Insofar as relevant here, this section limits to 25% the amount of weekly wages subject to garnishment.]

§ 1674. *Restriction on discharge from employment by reason of garnishment*

(a) No employer may discharge any employee by reason of the fact that his earnings have been subjected to garnishment for any one indebtedness.

(b) Whoever willfully violates subsection (a) of this section shall be fined not more than $1,000, or imprisoned not more than one year, or both.

* * *

§ 1676. *Enforcement by Secretary of Labor*

The Secretary of Labor, acting through the Wage and Hour Division of the Department of Labor, shall enforce the provisions of this subchapter.

§ 1677. *Effect on State laws*

This subchapter does not annul, alter, or affect, or exempt any person from complying with, the laws of any State

(1) prohibiting garnishments or providing for more limited garnishments than are allowed under this subchapter, or

(2) prohibiting the discharge of any employee by reason of the fact that his earnings have been subjected to garnishment for more than one indebtedness.

Subchapter I (known as the "Truth in Lending" Act) of the CCPA contains elaborate requirements for the disclosure of information by creditors in consumer credit transactions and it is stipulated that the Federal Trade Commission "shall enforce such requirements." Criminal penalties are prescribed for willful and knowing violations. § 1640 of Subchapter I provides that creditors failing to make required disclosures to other persons are liable to such persons for damages within stated limits and for the costs of suit and reasonable attorney's fees. At the end of Subchapter I are several provisions regulating credit advertising followed by a section (§ 1665) stating that "There is no liability [under such provisions] on the part of any owner or personnel, as such, of any medium in which [credit advertising] appears."

Subchapter III of the CCPA, which is devoted to "Credit Reporting Agencies," lays down detailed requirements governing the activities of such agencies and provides that any consumer reporting agency or user of credit information is liable to affected consumers: (1) under § 1681n, in case of willful violations, for actual damages, for such punitive damages as the court may allow and for the costs of suit and reasonable attorney's fees, and (2) under § 1681o in the case of negligent violations, for actual damages, and for costs of the action and reasonable attorney's fees. There are criminal penalties for designated violations of Subchapter III (§§ 1671q and r). And it is declared (§ 1681s) that compliance with Subchapter III requirements "shall be enforced by the Federal Trade Commission."

Your careful and thorough researches disclose only the following additional material that may be pertinent to the present case:

1. During the debate on the floor of the House of Representatives on the bill which (with minor amendments not relevant here)

became the present CCPA, an amendment was offered to delete the criminal penalty in § 1674(b) as confusing, unjust and inappropriate in its impact on corporate employers. The standing committee chairman in charge of the bill spoke briefly in opposition to the amendment saying:

> "The only penalty provided is the criminal penalty which is modest by federal standards. Without it there is nothing to stop employers from firing an employee on the basis of one garnishment, even though garnishment may have been unjustly invoked."

The amendment was also opposed by a Representative from New York, who was a member of the responsible standing committee concerned and was the principal architect, in committee, of the garnishment provisions as reported by the committee and later enacted into law. This Representative stated:

> "This amendment would completely destroy the garnishment provisions which were unanimously adopted in committee. It would take the teeth out of § 1674."

The Chairman of the Subcommittee on Consumer Affairs (which, within the responsible standing committee, had originally developed the proposed CCPA) commented:

> "Let's not jeopardize § 1674. We are concerned here to reduce the hardships and disruptions from discharges based on one garnishment, recognizing the frequently unfair use of garnishment by unscrupulous creditors. We know from our studies that the debt in question is often fraudulent, saddled on a poor ignorant person who is trapped in an easy credit scheme, is charged double for something he couldn't pay for even at a proper price and then hounded into giving up his pound of flesh and being fired besides."

Apart from these remarks there was no further debate on this amendment which was then rejected by a voice vote. The Senate accepted without comment the House's version of Subchapter II.

2. The House Standing Committee Report accompanying the CCPA to the House floor where it was adopted without substantial change reads in pertinent part as follows:

> "Subchapter I
>
> "Your committee believes administrative enforcement of the credit disclosure provisions is crucial to the legislative purpose. Administrative enforcement brings expertise to the problem and can give broad, effective implementation to the disclosure principle. Consumers may have neither the means or knowledge to file their own suits or to instigate criminal proceedings. Further provision is made, however,

for liability within stated limits to an aggrieved consumer to supplement administrative enforcement against offending creditors. To avoid burdensome suits, there is a specific prohibition of such liability in connection with credit advertising.

"Subchapter II

"Your committee believes it is necessary to impose some restrictions on garnishment as part of its overall regulation of consumer credit. Garnishment is frequently an essential element in predatory credit-extension activities and creates serious disruption. There is a causal connection between harsh garnishment procedures and high levels of personal bankruptcy. We have limited the amounts subject to garnishment and restricted post-garnishment discharges. Enforcement is vested in the Secretary of Labor."

The Senate Standing Committee Report on this legislation contained the same language as above.

3. Attached to the foregoing House Committee Report is a separate Statement of Supplemental Views by the Representative from New York mentioned above, containing this passage:

"Originally our committee had provided for prohibition of all garnishments, but it became clear that a more delicate balance of competing interests was needed. Using the New York garnishment law (which has had excellent results) as a basis, I offered an amendment [i. e., the present provisions of subchapter II—Ed.] which was approved by the committee. It limits garnishment amounts and restricts garnishment discharges, thus benefiting employee-consumers, while recognizing that creditors do need some instrument of last resort for collecting legitimate debts when the debtor is gainfully employed. We know that employers intensely dislike garnishments because they often impose substantial extra costs for bookkeeping and administration and can be very vexatious indeed, for example where garnishments multiply or the employer becomes involved in litigation between competing creditors. Employers are apt to judge very unfavorably the character of employees who lay themselves open to such procedures. Under our bill the employer can discharge an employee whose wages are subjected to garnishment for more than one indebtedness."

4. Under the New York Statute extant in 1968 (referred to in the Supplemental Views just quoted) which was used as a model for Subchapter II of the CCPA, an employee whose employer was served with not more than one garnishment on the employee's behalf in a

twelve-month period was protected from any dismissal based on such a garnishment. (N.B. that in 1969, this provision was changed to a general prohibition against dismissals based on garnishment.) This New York Statute in 1968 and at all times thereafter contained a section stating that an employee dismissed in violation of the provisions restricting dismissals for garnishment could thereafter sue for damages for lost wages (not to exceed 6 weeks' wages) and that the court was empowered though not required to order reinstatement of the employee. The pattern of garnishment legislation prevailing in other states is varied. Some, including Kent, do not restrict garnishment or discharges based thereon. A few have turned to the outright prohibition of garnishment. Some have developed limits on the amount of wages subject to garnishment. Others, with or without such limits, restrict discharges based on garnishment as New York originally did. The State of Kent's legislature is now considering proposals along the lines of New York's 1969 law.

5. The precise question raised by Welsh v. Truegrit has been presented in three district courts in other circuits. Two of these district courts, in the 9th and 7th Circuits respectively, decided in favor of defendant; the third, in the 5th Circuit, decided for the plaintiff. All wrote terse opinions purporting to rely, without elaboration, on "legislative intent." The court deciding for the plaintiff referred in addition to the rule about "remedial statutes." In Secretary of Labor v. O'Toole, decided by the Court of Appeals for the 8th Circuit in 1976 under Subchapter II of the CCPA, the Secretary of Labor was granted an injunction against an employer who had wrongfully discharged several employees because of wage garnishments. The court noted in passing that the Supreme Court had ruled that administrative enforcement action was discretionary, not mandatory, in character, under Subchapters I and III. It surmised that the same result would hold under II.

Prepare a compact well-organized memorandum (draft opinion) for the judge for whom you are a clerk

(a) indicating the issue or issues raised,

(b) giving your recommended decision on such issue or issues, and

(c) justifying your decision and dealing with the various materials presented above and with the probable arguments of counsel for Welsh and counsel for Truegrit.

If there are cases in this casebook that bear on the resolution of the present case, identify them and indicate what they contribute.

Problem 3

Ms. Suzy Cue, a beautiful and petite photographer's model residing in the State of Kent, gave a party on January 1, 1980 at her Kent country home for some twenty close friends. One of these friends, Ms. Linda Hopp, arrrived in a car driven by a boyfriend who had not been invited to the party. The boyfriend was the thirty-year-old Mr. Buck Wing, a former pro-football player of notable size and strength, with a reputation as a heavy drinker and "cut-up." Unwilling to offend Linda, Suzy acquiesced—albeit with some reluctance and misgiving—in the addition of Buck to her party.

Suzy had set out for her guests a self-service bar containing a large and varied array of alcoholic beverages. During the evening Buck helped himself generously to Suzy's whiskey, becoming progressively more loud, obnoxious and unsteady. Some time before midnight, as the annoyance of the other guests became more pronounced, Buck lurched to the bar one last time. Despite Suzy's ineffectual protests, he shouted belligerently that he was having "one for the road," downed a half tumbler of whiskey, and then, gathering up Linda, installed her in his car and drove away at a furious speed. Careening out of Suzy's driveway and on to the highway, Buck lost control of his car at the first curve. The car thereupon slammed into an empty, properly parked vehicle—a fabulously expensive custom-built Rolls Royce—totally demolishing it. Neither Buck nor Linda was hurt.

Mr. Sam Barr, the owner of the demolished car, finding that Buck was "judgment-proof" (i.e., uninsured and virtually penniless), brought a suit for damages for negligence against Suzy Cue in the appropriate trial court of general jurisdiction (the Superior Court) of the State of Kent. Mr. Barr's complaint recited the facts already set out, supra. Ms. Cue in response filed a motion to dismiss for failure to state a claim on which relief could be granted.

Assume you are the judge of the Superior Court to whom the case of Barr v. Cue is assigned. Assume further that all procedural prerequisites have been met and that the sole question to be decided by you is whether or not the motion to dismiss should be granted or denied.

Assume finally that the combined researches of your law clerk and yourself, conducted with great care and thoroughness in preparation for your decision of the case and for the writing of your opinion, reveal only the material set out hereafter regarding the pertinent law and other considerations.

A. *Statutes, Decisions, etc., of States Other than Kent*

(1) Common Law

In most states there is no legislation bearing directly or indirectly on the Barr v. Cue problem. The common law in such states is generally to the effect that one who sells or gives intoxicating liquor to another person (even one already visibly intoxicated) is not liable in negligence or otherwise to third parties for injury or damage they suffer as a result of such other person's drunken behaviour. It is said that it is the voluntary consumption not the supplying of the liquor which is the proximate cause of the injury or damage.

In about a dozen states, cases have departed from this general rule and have allowed recovery by complainants suing commercial dispensers of liquor in negligence, based on the latters' sale of liquor to obviously intoxicated persons who thereafter caused serious injuries to the complainants. In at least one such decision the court looked for support to the state's Alcoholic Beverage Control Act forbidding liquor licensees to "permit any visibly intoxicated person to enter or remain on the licensed premises."

There is, however, a significant case from New Jersey—see Linn v. Rand, 140 N.J.Super. 212, 356 A.2d 15 (1976)—which goes farther. In this case, the plaintiff who had been injured when hit by a car driven by an intoxicated minor, brought suit against a social host who had served liquor to the minor before the accident. The New Jersey Superior Court vacated the trial court's grant of summary judgment for defendant, and sent the case back for trial, stating that upon adequate proof it would be allowable for a jury

> "to determine that a social host who serves excessive amounts of alcoholic beverages to a visibly intoxicated minor, knowing the minor was about to drive a car on the public highways, could reasonably foresee or anticipate an accident or injury as a reasonably foreseeable consequence of his negligence in serving the minor."

An earlier decision by the Supreme Court of New Jersey had found that a tavern owner (the holder of a liquor license) was liable to the representatives of an innocent third party killed by the drunken driving of a minor to whom the defendant had supplied alcoholic beverages shortly before the accident. In the Linn case, the court saw no reason to limit this earlier holding to licensees; it described its goal as the doing of "substantial justice in light of the mores and needs of our modern day life" and cited the "ever-increasing incidence of serious automobile accidents resulting from drunken driving."

(2) Legislation, etc.

A small number of states have so-called "Dram Shop Acts." The Connecticut "Dram Shop" statute, Conn.Gen.Stat.Ann. § 30–102, provides as follows:

> "If any person, by himself or his agent, sells any alcoholic liquor to an intoxicated person, and such purchaser, in consequence of such intoxication, thereafter injures the person or property of another, such seller shall pay just damages to the person injured, up to the amount of twenty thousand dollars, or to persons injured in consequence of such intoxication up to an aggregate amount of fifty thousand dollars, to be recovered in an action under this section, pro-

vided the aggrieved person or persons shall give written notice to such seller within sixty days of the occurence of such injury to person or property of his or their intention to bring an action under this section. * * *"

Some other state statutes of this kind, which contain broader language than the Connecticut statute as to persons liable, have nonetheless been construed to provide a civil cause of action only against commercial sellers of liquor.

Most recently, the Supreme Court of California has decided the pertinent case of Coulter v. Superior Court of San Mateo County, 21 Cal.3d 144, 145 Cal.Rptr. 534, 577 P.2d 669 (1978). The plaintiff Coulter in this case suffered personal injuries as a passenger in a vehicle being driven by an intoxicated person, one Ms. Williams, when the vehicle collided with roadway abutments. Coulter sought to recover damages for such injuries from the owner and the manager of an apartment complex who, he alleged in the first count of his complaint, had negligently served excessively large quantities of alcohol to Ms. Williams in the recreation room of the complex, even though they knew, or should have known, that she was excessively intoxicated and was especially susceptible to alcohol, and though they knew she intended to drive thereafter and knew or should have foreseen that their actions would create serious risks of harm to plaintiffs and others. A demurrer to the claim thus presented was overruled by the Court on two grounds. First, it found that liability on these facts could be based on § 25602 of the California Business and Professional Code providing that

> "Every person who sells, furnishes, gives or causes to be sold, furnished or given away, any alcoholic beverage to * * * any obviously intoxicated person is guilty of a misdemeanor."

It pointed to an earlier case which, referring to this statute, found a licensed purveyor of alcohol civilly liable.

Second, it found that imposing liability on the social host in this case was "fully compatible with general negligence principles." It said

> "we think it evident that the service of alcoholic beverages to an obviously intoxicated person by one who knows that such intoxicated person intends to drive a motor vehicle creates a *reasonably foreseeable* risk of injury to those on the highway. * * * [O]ne who serves alcoholic beverages under such circumstances fails to exercise reasonable care."

The court concluded, however, that a demurrer should be sustained to a second count of the plaintiff's complaint which failed to allege that defendants affirmatively "furnished" alcohol and only alleged that they "permitted" Ms. Williams to drink on the premises and, in some unspecified manner, "aided, abetted, participated" in and "encouraged" her excessive drinking.

B. *Statutes, Decisions, etc. of the State of Kent*

(1) Common Law

There is no Kent case law directly on point on the question raised in Barr v. Cue. No Kent state court has ruled on the liability of commercial dispensers of liquor to third persons for their injuries or damage resulting from the acts of intoxicated persons to whom such dispensers have provided liquor; but in Conger v. Strutt (1967) the federal district court in Kent decided in a diversity case that a commercial dispenser was liable in such circumstances.

(2) Legislation, etc.

Kent has had since 1920, the following provision as a part of its Alcoholic Beverage Control Law:

> § 101. Any purveyor of alcoholic beverages licensed by the Kent Liquor Control Commission who dispenses such beverages to any visibly intoxicated person shall be guilty of a misdemeanor punishable by a fine of not more than $1,000 or by imprisonment for not more than one year or by both such fine and such imprisonment. The license of any purveyor found to have dispensed liquor in violation of this section shall be revoked if in the judgment of the Commission, after notice and hearing, the public interest shall so require.

In 1976, the Kent Legislature (both houses) voted overwhelmingly against the adoption of a proposed "Dram Shop" statute identical to the Connecticut Dram Shop Act quoted supra. One major element in the defeat of this proposed statute was a massive lobbying effort mounted by the Kent Retail Liquor Dealers Association in combination with other organizations representing restaurateurs, tavern owners, bar operators, etc.

Bills paralleling the California statute quoted earlier (see the text of § 25602 at p. 734 supra) were introduced in 1968, 1974 and 1977 in the Kent legislature but were never reported out of committee.

The Kent Motor Vehicle Department has compiled apparently reliable statistics showing that there were 257,846 adult misdemeanor arrests for drunken driving in the State of Kent during 1977. For the year 1977, alcohol was designated by the Department as the "primary collision factor" in 28.3 percent of all fatal motor vehicle accidents and in 11 percent of all injury accidents. Federal administrative agencies have reliably reported that "alcohol has been associated with over half the deaths and major injuries suffered in automobile accidents each year for many years." FBI statistics show that more than 17,000 young people under 18 were arrested for driving under the influence of alcohol in 1977, representing an increase of over 160% in five years.

Write a judicial opinion in the case of Barr v. Cue described supra. In writing your opinion you are of course expected to draw on the insights and materials of this casebook, citing them where appropriate. Apart from this, you are to assume that the foregoing discussion of the applicable law is complete.

Your judicial opinion should (1) give your decision whether to grant or deny Ms. Cue's motion to dismiss; (2) indicate the issue or issues raised in Barr v. Cue and your resolution of them; and (3) justify your resolution of such issue or issues, taking account of the appropriate legal method considerations and dealing with the principal arguments that would probably have been made by each party.

Chapter VII

HISTORICAL AND JURISPRUDENTIAL PERSPECTIVES ON LAW AND ITS STUDY

INTRODUCTORY NOTE

This is the final chapter of the casebook, and a little stock-taking seems in order. In their study of Legal Method, students have seen law in the making in legislatures, courts and agencies and have developed something resembling a professional's understanding of case law and legislation, and of the techniques involved in the use of these authoritative legal sources for practical professional purposes. Whatever his or her notion of "the law" may have been at the start of the semester, the first-year student knows now that law is at least as much an art as a science and that excellence in what has been called the "art of lawyering" (or, in another professional context, the "art of judging") requires that legal materials be approached not as inert data but with imaginative and disciplined awareness of the possibilities and limits of their use.

The main emphasis of the casebook and the course has been on method, skills, technique—and properly so. In a lawyer's life, as in the life of a surgeon, high-mindedness and generous social impulses are no substitute for professional insight and skill. No one can be genuinely creative as a lawyer, or serve responsibly as advocate or counselor for people, institutions and causes, without first mastering the lawyer's craft. But to say that law's authoritative materials and ingrained methods of reasoning have to be understood before the student can move on to more advanced inquiry is not to suggest for a moment that law is only a technology or that university legal education is chiefly a training course for legal technicians. Law is not just something lawyers work with; it is, among other things, a behavioral norm, a social process, and a cultural form reflecting the conditions, needs, and aspirations of the larger society from which it springs. These further dimensions of law's nature and functioning will be explored in depth throughout the student's three law school years. The text materials in this last chapter are included in the casebook to indicate the intellectual range of the law student's future inquiries and to suggest broader perspectives for the understanding and appraisal of the materials and modes of thought to which the first-year student has been introduced in Legal Method.

The first section of this chapter considers the purposes law serves in society and asks the question, central in the evaluation of any legal rule or institution, of what law is *for*. Section 2 brings the perspective of history to bear, specifically on our own legal institutions, and deals with the origins and the nature of the "common law" and the historical process by which common law ideas were transplanted from England to the United States. Section 3 is addressed to the greatest and perhaps most elusive of law's perennial questions, the problem of justice, considered not as a philosophical abstraction but in the context of practical dispute-settlement. The text materials in Section 1 and Section 3 are largely drawn from the 1973 John Dewey Lectures in Legal Philosophy at Columbia University, which that year were "offered by way of jurisprudential commentary on the vitally important things our first year students have just been learning about law's ways and means in their first semester courses, most explicitly in the course here called Legal Method." The Dewey Lectures were published in full as H. W. Jones, "An Invitation to Jurisprudence," 74 Columbia Law Review 1023 (1974), and the extracts in this chapter, condensed and revised and with the original footnotes omitted, are published with the permission of the Columbia Law Review.

SECTION 1. THE SOCIAL ENDS TO WHICH LAW IS MEANS

The tasks of law are in the here and now, not in some postulated community of saints but in the social world as it is and can reasonably be expected to become, given the aspirations, interests and varying inclinations of the human ingredients of which society is composed. A discussion of law's social ends-in-view is thus concerned not with perfect societies or ultimate ends of man but with certain minimum conditions which, in the light of historical experience and the testimony of wise men and women, seem indispensable to human contentment, creativity and happiness in society.

Some of these conditions—not all of them by any means, but some very important ones—are or can be brought about and maintained by law, and by no other force or instrument of society. Two of these minimum conditions come to mind at once: the existence of effective institutions for the preservation of the public peace and safety and the availability of trustworthy procedures for the authoritative settlement of disputes between individuals or between individual citizens and the state. These are high, perhaps most imperative of all, among law's ends-in-view; their social necessity is manifest and would only be disserved by elaboration. Ways of peace-keeping and dispute-settlement can be discerned in the most "primitive" of human societies; no people would wittingly assume a social condition in which every person is at the prey of everyone else and individual disputes are always resolved to the advantage of the stronger in arms.

A social environment would be intolerable without the existence of efficacious institutions for peace-keeping and dispute-settlement, but genuine "social tranquility" has further requirements and overtones. By almost anybody's definition, a good society is, among other things, a society in which creativity is unhobbled by constant apprehensions, diversity flourishes without group or class hostility, and inevitable social change is accepted not as something terrifying but as something to be planned for. We are brought, then, to three other of law's social ends-in-view: (1) the maintenance of a reasonable security of individual expectations, (2) the resolution of conflicting social interests, and (3) the channeling of social change. This is far from a complete tally of law's tasks in society. No such catalogue could be attempted in a section ten times as long as this one. Nonetheless, the three tasks just listed do go, as Contracts scholars used to say "to the essence" of law in society and are items that must be taken into account in any serious attempt at evaluation of a questioned legal rule or institution.

Security of Expectations

Life in society is limited and unimaginative if men and women cannot plan their future conduct with reasonable assurance that the rules will not be changed after a commitment or investment, of effort or money, is made. Crusty old Jeremy Bentham, whose ideas on man and society retain a surprising freshness for those who will read him without textbook preconceptions, put "security," in the sense of security of individual expectations, at the first place in his hierarchy of law's social values. In Bentham's view, even constitutional liberty is an "expectation"—that one's freedom will not be interfered with arbitrarily by public power-holders—and property, contract and reparation for injury are founded not in natural right or human will, as earlier legal philosophers had it, but on expectation, and the securing of this expectation can only be the work of law. "Without law," wrote Bentham, "there is no security, and therefore no abundance, not even a certainty of subsistence; and, in such a state of things, the only equality which could obtain would be equality of poverty."

The maintenance of reasonable security of expectations has seemed so compelling as one of law's ends-in-view that there is a whole armory of legal ideas and legal institutions designed to provide it: constitutional provisions like the guarantee against *ex post facto* criminal laws, judicial policies like that embodied in the emerging doctrine of prospective operation of overruling decisions, and, indeed, the principle of *stare decisis* with its special force, as you will have observed, in the "reliance areas" of the law where it is realistic to assume that action was taken on the strength of known judicial precedents.

In our society, and particularly as concerns larger commercial, industrial and property interests, lawyers—legal counselors—are the principal agents for the engineering of expectations. The counselor in his law office is the retailer of the legal system for those who know when to turn to him, and can afford to consult him, to make it as sure as such things can be that the expectations arising from contracts, settlements, wills, negotiations and transactions will, in the course of time, be realized in fact. The vast programs of the 1960's to provide legal services for poor people and for people of modest means might well be examined in the same perspective. Are not these programs, when extended from courtroom advocacy to office counseling, an effort to give the expectations of the less fortunately placed members of our society a security comparable to that heretofore enjoyed only by the well-to-do? Office counseling for the poor lacks the drama of a criminal defense or a consumers' class action, but the need is great and the opportunities for service hardly yet tapped. Who knows, perhaps there will not be too many lawyers after all.

For, make no mistake about it, security of expectations is not just a rich man's value. It can be even more important to a poor person or to a person of moderate means. If you have twenty substantial property or contractual interests, and one goes sour, you may be angered or inconvenienced, but are not impoverished. But if you have only one or two more humble expectations—a pension, seniority in a job, the promise of a small legacy, an assurance of child support payments, or a low-rent long-term lease on your apartment—disappointment of that expectation can be disastrous. One can quarrel with Bentham's stubborn insistence that "the cultivation of 'security'" is "the main object of law"—that is, with his placement of security above even equality and subsistence as values to be served by law-government. But is any assessment of a judicial decision or legislative enactment a complete assessment if it fails to ask Bentham's question: will this decision or statute promote or undermine security of individual expectations?

The Resolution of Conflicting Social Interests

Card-carrying jurisprudents are fond of seeking out the areas of agreement, the shared values and communities of interest, that supposedly underlie every legal and political system. This high-minded endeavor is subject to a certain limitation: the need for law arises not when people agree on what should be done for the good of all but when their interests, demands and aspirations come into collision. A great truth of political philosophy is condensed in Judge Learned Hand's description of democracy as "a political contrivance by which the group conflicts inevitable in all society find a relatively harmless outlet in the give and take of legislative compromise." How then are we to characterize law? Hand's answer is again no-nonsense and unsentimental: "the law is no more than the formal expression of that tolerable compromise that we call justice, without which the rule of the tooth and claw must prevail."

The theme that law's central task is the containment and management of inevitable group conflicts runs through the writings of the late Roscoe Pound, whom we think of as the founder of at least the American version of what has become known as "sociological jurisprudence." Contemporary law students are sometimes put off by Pound's style, which can be heavy and unduly taxonomic, but the best of his work—as in his long and classic study, A Survey of Social Interests—stands like a rock against the efforts of jurisprudential revisionists to belittle it. In Pound's theory of social interests, legal institutions—legislatures, administrative commissions and courts—are interpreted as, above all, agencies for the balancing and weighing of the competing group demands that arise in any society:

> "Looked at functionally, the law is an attempt to satisfy, to reconcile, to harmonize, to adjust these overlapping and often conflicting claims and demands * * * so as to give effect to the greatest total of interests or to the interests that weigh most in our civilization, with the least sacrifice of the scheme of interests as a whole."

Manifestly, it is in the legislatures, national and state, that the great conflicts of group interest are typically fought out or bargained out and, at least provisionally, resolved. But in the universe of Pound's "sociological jurisprudence," even constitutional adjudication is thought of as far less the formal application of constitutional principles than the responsible weighing of the competing group interests —debtors and creditors, employers and employees, majorities and minorities—that can come to courts as well as legislatures. When one asked Pound whether a recent Supreme Court decision was a "good" decision or a "bad" one, he had a way of answering not in terms of the correctness or incorrectness of the Court's application of constitutional precedents or doctrine but in terms of how thoughtfully and disinterestedly the Court had weighed the conflicting social interests involved in the case and how fair and durable its adjustment of the interest-conflicts promised to be. Try this approach to legal evaluation on the next ten cases you read, in Constitutional Law or any other course. You may become conscious of analytical dimensions beyond any you had originally seen in the controversy.

The existence of law in a vast and pluralistic society will not and cannot bring about a perfect harmony of competing demands, convictions and aspirations. We ask too much of law—and something we would not want anyway—if we look to law to prevent the occurrence of social controversy and the airing of social grievances. "Trouble" cases will continue to arise; indeed, experience in every country demonstrates that there are many more open and expressed conflicts of interest in a society in which law prevails than in a feudal or otherwise closed system in which appeal to law can be made only by the stronger or better placed. The rule of law has as its practical and achievable end-in-view the maintenance of a balance—sometimes a delicate balance—in which competing interest-group claims are voiced, listened to and weighed through peaceful political or judicial procedures and decided authoritatively and with the consent, however grudging, of the disappointed parties.

So, whether we are entirely happy about it or not, compromise —the reasoned accommodation of opposed interests—is a central and indispensable technique in the legislative and judicial resolution of competing social interests. All-or-nothing people are at times useful catalysts, but they are never effective legal reformers. If sociological jurisprudence has a message for today and tomorrow, it may be that those who have the power and responsibility for the resolution of competing social interests reach the soundest decisions when they listen—really listen, which is the hardest thing in the world for a law-trained person to do—to the inevitably extreme demands of all the contending social factions and then strive for the way of "tolerable" adjustment and ultimate social reconciliation. A compromise, to be durable, must be fair. To resolve deeply felt conflicting social interests on a winner-take-all basis, as has been done so often in legal history, is to forget that winners and losers are going to have to live in the same society for a long, long time.

The Channeling of Social Change

Lawyers have no particular credentials as social prophets, but there is one thing every law student can be quite sure about: tomorrow's society will be different from today's in its material conditions and moral attitudes, just as today's society is far different from that of fifty or even twenty-five years ago. "Nothing steadfastly *is*," said Heraclitus, "Everything is becoming," and these words express a truth that lawyers, no less than philosophers and theologians, must understand and learn to live with. This is not to say that change is always and necessarily progress; history records about as many social changes for the worse as for the better. Change is simply predictable, inevitable and ceaseless as the basic social fact. In the words of the old song, "We don't know where we're going, but we're on our way."

This sets one of law's most important ends-in-view. Law, thought of merely as a body of doctrine and aggregate of institutions, is neither for social change nor against it. What law does—or can do when its legislators, judges and practicing lawyers are socially aware and professionally resourceful—is to provide institutions and procedures for the channeling of inevitable social change in ways that make sought reforms effective with the minimum possible impairment of law's other ends-in-view: the public peace, just dispute-settlement, reasonable security of expectations and tolerable adjustment of conflicting social interests. Law's principles, institutions and procedures are there to be drawn on for the social task at hand, but they have to be used. The channeling of social change can be accomplished only through continuing acts of creative and informed intuition by men and women who combine genuine mastery of legal techniques with equally profound understanding of social forces.

It has become a truism that law must be kept up to date, responsive to the continuing processes of social change. Present-day judges are very much aware that concepts and categories received from law's past—privity of contract, sovereign immunity, "fault" in divorce actions and many more—may not order contemporary phenomena effectively and justly. It is not that these concepts were necessarily wrong when they were handed down; we are too quick to assume that. It is simply that, whatever their original justification, they offer the wrong answers for today's problems. One hates, in a way, to see old friends like negligence, consideration and "state action" withering away in vitality and influence, but, to borrow a phrase from Justice Roger Traynor, "the number they have called is no longer in service."

To say that law must be kept responsive to changing social conditions and social attitudes is, however, to state only half of the equation. The relation between law and social change is reciprocal, for law, in its turn, can have a molding effect on social development. The imperatives of the legal order carry at least prima facie rightness for most members of society. More often than not, a legal principle, if soundly conceived and resolutely enforced, becomes a kind of self-fulfilling prophecy and creates the social climate necessary for its acceptance. When wisely and imaginatively employed, law is far more than an instrument of command; it is organized society's principal resource for the engineering of that widespread and supportive public assent—the true consent of the governed—without which great social initiatives never really get off the ground. Perhaps this is the most important way in which law operates—or can be drawn on—for the sound and effective channeling of social change.

This note has now touched base with five of our law's most visible ends-in-view: preservation of the public peace and safety, the settlement of individual disputes, the maintenance of security of expectations, the resolution of conflicting social interests, and the channeling of social change. This is no complete inventory of law's tasks, nor is it a neat set of mutually exclusive teleological pigeonholes. There are manifest overlappings—for example, the resolution of conflicting social interests is one of the ways in which law helps to channel the forces of social change—and some of law's ends-in-view can come into collision with others, as when law's adjustment to social change involves some unavoidable impairment of the security of individual expectations. In law as in ethics, the hardest task is often not the identification of values but the assignment of priorities when, in a specific problem context, one value cannot be fully served without some sacrifice of another. But even and particularly when values cut across one another, disinterested and informed judgment on legal and social problems requires that each of the competing ends-in-view be understood in its full claim as an aspect or dimension of what law is *for*: the creation and preservation of a social environment in which, to the degree manageable in a complex and imperfect world, the quality of human life can be spirited, improving and unimpaired.

SECTION 2. THE COMMON LAW AND ITS RECEPTION IN THE UNITED STATES

The Rise of the Common Law

Pre-Conquest England had no centralized judicial system and practically no law of nationwide application. A few great controversies between personages might be brought to the attention of the King and his council, but most claims and disputes were decided in local tribunals and in accordance with local customary law, which often varied very substantially from locality to locality. The first and indispensable step in the rise of the common law was the centralization of the English judicial system that was brought about in the centuries following the Norman Conquest, and particularly from the reign of Henry II. By about 1300, the administration of civil and criminal justice in England had come to be largely dominated by royal courts, staffed by professional judges appointed by the King and holding office during his pleasure. (The principle of judicial independence, that is, of judicial tenure during good behavior, emerges much later, not until the 17th century.)

The older local courts did not disappear, and would not for centuries, but their importance was diminished by steady widening of the authority of the royal courts and by an economic phenomenon strangely reminiscent of our own time, a continuing decline in the value of money. An old dividing line, customary in origin but affirmed by the Statute of Gloucester in the late 13th century, had set 40 shillings as the minimum jurisdictional amount for proceedings in the royal courts, leaving claims that involved less than 40 shillings for authoritative disposition by the local courts. 40 shillings was at first a substantial jurisdictional limitation; a craftsman of the Middle Ages was unlikely to earn that much as a year's pay. But as inflation came on, 40-shilling transactions became run of the mill, the function of the local courts began to resemble that of present-day small claims courts, and the business of the royal judiciary vastly increased.

The English common law was created and fashioned by three great royal courts: the Court of Common Pleas, the Court of King's Bench, and the Court of Exchequer. The first of these, the Court of Common Pleas, was the great forge of common law doctrine throughout the 13th, 14th, 15th and 16th centuries, because it was for that

Sec. 2   THE COMMON LAW   745

very long time the nearest thing to a court of general jurisdiction in the royal judicial system. A claimant could not proceed in the Court of Common Pleas without first securing a "writ" from the Chancery authorizing the Court to hear and decide the case, but the categories of claims ("forms of action") for which writs were available were reasonably numerous and various and covered, or could be stretched by ingenious common law pleaders to cover, most of the civil controversies that were likely to arise in medieval England. The Court of Common Pleas is the court referred to in Magna Carta (1215), in which King John makes the concession that "the common pleas shall not follow [us in our journeys] but shall be held in some certain place," soon fixed as Westminster Hall in London, and the court's name reflects an early classification of legal proceedings into "pleas of the Crown," meaning proceedings in which the state is the moving party, and "common pleas," meaning the claims of private persons against each other.

Because of its largely exclusive jurisdiction in the generality of civil cases, the Court of Common Pleas was incomparably the most important court in the early history of the common law; the cases on the Common Pleas docket in the 14th and 15th centuries were far more numerous than those on the dockets of King's Bench and Exchequer combined. But over the years, and by the manipulation of "legal fictions" and other jurisdiction-expanding devices too complex to be gone into in this brief note, the judges of the Court of King's Bench and the Court of Exchequer kept broadening their originally limited jurisdiction in ordinary civil cases and so accomplished a whittling away of the longtime exclusive jurisdiction of the Court of Common Pleas. By the time this process was completed, surely before 1600, the Court of King's Bench and the Court of Exchequer were hearing and deciding private disputes of many kinds and so exercising, with a few important exceptions, virtually concurrent jurisdiction with the Court of Common Pleas.

How did the judges of the King's courts reach and justify their decisions in particular controversies? Roman law had not been "received" in England as it had been in most of the regions of continental Europe where remnants of the Roman Empire had held on longer. The very first common law judges, who would, of course, have been justices of the Court of Common Pleas, thus had the task of hunching-out decisions in what we have called (supra, pages 75–112) "New Questions" cases, and without the help of much even "persuasive" authority. With experience and reasonably steady royal support, these early judges and those who succeeded them developed competence in dispute-settlement and soon sought, as judges do, to make their decisions more evenhanded and rational. *Cases* can make *law*, as we saw early on, and this is how the common law came into being; an accumulation of remembered *ad hoc* judgments became, in time, a body of more or less consistent case law doctrine, the "common law of England."

Although judicial decisions were not officially or regularly published during the early centuries of the common law, the justices of the King's courts, few in number and well acquainted with each other, had a reasonably good idea of what they, their colleagues of the King's judiciary, and their predecessors in office had ruled in past controversies. When the recollections of the judges failed, their professional brethren of the practicing bar were ready with a reminder of what the past rulings had been. A recognizable legal profession, attendant on the royal courts, had come into existence in England even before the decisional practice of the King's justices was regularized into what we think of as the common law. This professional community consisted of the royal justices and the advocates who practiced regularly before them, most notably the members of the Order of Serjeants, who enjoyed a monopoly of the right to appear in the Court of Common Pleas and from whose close-knit ranks most of the King's justices were appointed. Reliable reporting of judicial decisions did not begin until the 16th century, but the practice of arguing from past cases and justifying decisions by reference to the past rulings of the same or another common law court came to characterize adjudication in the courts of Common Pleas, King's Bench and Exchequer long before there were trustworthy court reports to be drawn on and cited.

As the reporting of decisions improved, arguments based on past judicial authority became the advocate's chief and almost sole reliance in the three common law courts. By the time of Sir Edward Coke, who was Chief Justice of Common Pleas (and later, briefly, of the Court of King's Bench) in the reign of James I, the doctrine of precedent existed in England in much the form, and with most of the refinements, it has today. By the time of the American Revolution, a century and a half later, the principle of *stare decisis* was firmly established as a basic policy of English law, and the common law was a comprehensive, sophisticated and endlessly intricate body of authoritative case law.

HARRY W. JONES, THE RECEPTION OF THE COMMON LAW IN THE UNITED STATES [1]

How did the common law of England get over here, and to stay? In an opinion written a little more than fifty years after the Declara-

1. The following pages are part of a much longer study, "The Common Law in the United States: English Themes and American Variations," commissioned for the Bicentennial Observance of the American Bar Association and published in full in Political Separation and Legal Continuity (Jones ed., 1976). This extract is reprinted here with the permission of the American Bar Association.

tion of Independence, Justice Story said of the common law that "our ancestors brought with them its general principles and claimed it as their birthright." [2] This is at best a figure of speech, and I greatly doubt that Story meant it as more than that. If there had been lawyers among those who sailed to Virginia in 1607 and to Plymouth in 1620, they would undoubtedly have brought the principles of the common law along with them as their most precious baggage, but the time for lawyers in America had not yet come. The historian-jurist Daniel J. Boorstin gives us a better picture of colonial law as it was in the beginning:

> "Legal proceedings of the early years give us the impression of a people without much legal training and with few lawbooks who were trying to reproduce substantially what they knew 'back home.' Far from being a crude and novel system of popular law, or an attempt to create institutions from pure Scripture, what they produced was instead a layman's version of English legal institutions." [3]

The history of law in the several colonies of British North America during the century and a half between the first successful settlements and the commencement of the Revolution is a complicated story, one that has to be studied colony by colony.[4] The thirteen colonies that became the original states of the United States had very different histories. More than a century lies between the original patent to the Virginia Company in 1606 and George II's charter of 1732 to Oglethorpe and his Georgia associates. Eight of the colonial charters were granted between 1625 and 1689, a time of profound English constitutional crisis in which the United Kingdom experienced, within less than seven decades, the Civil War, the execution of Charles I, the Commonwealth, the Stuart Revolution, the Glorious Revolution that ousted James II, and the Act of Settlement that followed the accession of William and Mary. Manifestly English statesmen of the seventeenth century had other things on their mind than colonial management, and most of the time the colonies of British North America were left to go their separate ways, in legal matters as in others.

The inhabitants of the several colonies were by no means all of a piece. Quite different motivations had brought people to one colony or another, and they had emigrated from the United Kingdom at sig-

2. VanNess v. Pacard, 27 U.S. (2 Pet.) 137, 143–44, 7 L.Ed. 374 (1829).

3. The Americans: The Colonial Experience 27 (1958).

4. Particularly intensive study has been given to the colonial law of Massachusetts. Haskins, Law and Authority in Early Massachusetts (1960); Nelson, The Impact of Legal Change on Massachusetts Society, 1760–1830 (1975); Smith, Colonial Justice in Western Massachusetts (1961). Valuable essays on the law in other colonies are contained in Law and Authority in Colonial America (Billias ed. 1965).

nificantly different times. Royalists, fearful of the Commonwealth or distrustful of its "levelling" tendencies, made their way to Virginia and the Carolinas; by contrast, at least one of the Regicides escaped the process of the Restoration and lived out his days peacefully in New England. Many early settlers had come from towns far distant from London and knew little about the common law as administered by the royal courts at Westminster. When the people of a particular colony set up simple legal institutions along the general lines of what they remembered from "back home," their model was not necessarily the Court of Common Pleas; it might have been some local tribunal in the English county or neighborhood from which that group of settlers had come.[5]

So law and legal institutions were very different from colony to colony in the seventeenth century, reflecting differences in historical experience, in soil and climate and in the religious and social views of the people. Thus, for example, Holy Scripture, as interpreted by Puritan divines, was an important source of authority, particularly for criminal law, in seventeenth century Massachusetts and Connecticut. The founders of Pennsylvania, even before they established their settlements, had forsworn the lawyerish and contentious common law and fully codified precepts they thought better designed for the society they hoped to create in the New World. Projects to simplify and codify the law, although never as fully achieved as in Pennsylvania, were undertaken in several colonies, and we can assume from this widespread drive towards law-simplification that the methods of the common law were thought of as too technical, too full of professional subtleties, for the simpler and more egalitarian conditions of colonial social life. The early colonial legal orders were not, in short, full-fledged members of the common law family. And how could they have been? How could the common law system of Coke and Hale have been made to work in a society where there were few law books, practically no lawyers—and these often distrusted as tricksters and stirrers up of strife—and no professionally trained judges? Even in a commercially active colony like New York, no professionally trained judge occupied the bench until 1700; none served in Delaware before the Revolution.

Colonial law and judicial administration became increasingly professionalized in the first half of the eighteenth century. The evolution towards regularity and formal rationality in the operation of legal institutions was not as rapid in some colonies as in others, but it is discernible to a substantial degree everywhere. This is always true in developing countries, as America then was. Every colony had its substantial property holders who looked to law for the security of their expectations. Commerce was on the rise, not only local business

5. Goebel, "King's Law and Local Custom in Seventeenth Century New England," 31 Colum.L.Rev. 416 (1931).

but also intercolonial bargains and overseas trade with England, and commercial undertakings, then as now, required reasonably certain law—and competent lawyers to structure transactions in sensible and effective form. The stage is now set in the colonies for the historically demonstrable cycle: (1) the security of interests and transactions requires some regularization of the law; (2) but the regularization of law creates an urgent need for lawyers; and (3) lawyers, when they come, bring about law's further regularization.

American lawyers of the eighteenth century varied greatly in their origins and education. A number of them were native-born Englishmen, some of whom had been imported to assist Royal Governors in the legal aspects of colonial administration. Most were native Americans. In New England and the middle colonies, apprenticeship was the usual route to the profession. In other colonies, particularly in South Carolina and Virginia, it was common for aspiring lawyers to attend the Inns of Court in London, which were not then at their educational best but were probably better than anything in the colonies. More than one hundred Americans were admitted to one or another of the Inns of Court before 1775, including John Dickinson, the principal draftsman of the Articles of Confederation, and several signers of the Declaration of Independence.

The one thing these varied American law professionals had in common was that they were all schooled—to the extent that they were schooled at all—in the English common law, whether they had puzzled over it as clerk-apprentices or heard it expounded on its home grounds in London. Whether their common law knowledge was rudimentary, as was true of most of them, or genuinely professional, as was true of a fair number, it was all the law they knew. So, to most members of the eighteenth century legal profession in America, the regularization of the law meant, above all, more knowledgeable and sophisticated use in litigation and counseling of the principles and precedents of the common law of England.

There were no American court reports or law treatises, so colonial lawyers, without worrying too much about a precise theory of reception, customarily invoked the authority of such English abridgments, textbooks and precedents as were accessible in colonial law libraries. Colonial judges were not always persuaded by English authority, but professionally trained judges were coming to the bench now in most of the colonies, and some of the lay judges were developing an amateur's familiarity with common law concepts and a certain practical skill in the reading of cases and statutes. One of the most interesting aspects of colonial law is that, although professionally trained practicing lawyers were few in the colonies, a certain modest knowledge of law was widely dispersed in the population generally. A prosperous and reasonably well educated Southern planter or Pennsylvania physician of the years 1750–1776 was likely to know far more about law and legal institutions than his opposite number would know today. We must not be too ready to assume that the farmers, businessmen and surgeons who were appointed to colonial and state courts in the years before and immediately after the Revolution were much less sophisticated in legal matters than the professionally educated judges with whom they served. By the time the Revolution began, legal processes were less refined and far less technical in the colonies than at Westminster, but a British barrister would not have found the lawways of Boston, Philadelphia, Baltimore or New York too remote from his own experience.

The common law thus came to the colonies of British North America not in the ideological baggage of the first settlers but a century or so later, with the emergence of an accredited and active legal profession, the development of reasonable competence in the judiciary and the regularization of adversary procedures and precedent-based methods of legal reasoning. The principles of the English common law are now to be drawn on as sources of guidance for colonial decision-making. But not all of them find acceptance. When I quoted Justice Story to the effect that "our ancestors" brought the principles of the common law of England along with them, I neglected to quote the rest of his sentence: "but they brought with them and adopted only that portion which was applicable to their condition." Here the great Justice is on sure ground. Nowhere in British North America was the English common law received lock, stock and barrel. The selective nature of the reception is evident in any examination of the state of law in the colonies in the years immediately preceding the Revolution.

In some of the colonies, particularly where the judges and the leaders of the practicing bar were English-trained or had studied law more or less systematically, as Jefferson had with George Wythe at William and Mary, English precedents were more compelling than in other colonies, but no colony's case-law was a precise copy of the decisional law of England. And, since historical circumstances, physical conditions and prevailing social attitudes differed markedly from colony to colony, the law of South Carolina, say, in an important area of litigation might be quite different from the case-law of New York or Pennsylvania—just as such differences exist today to vex federal judges in Erie v. Tompkins situations. Differences in colonial legislation added further to the regional variety of colonial law. By the time independence arrives, the thirteen members of the emerging American union are all well on the way towards being "common law" jurisdictions in the full sense, but common law doctrine exists in America not in a single authorized version but in thirteen.

The process of reception continued with little change in tempo or direction during and after the Revolution. But independence made it necessary to formulate a theory of reception. English case-law was presumably applicable, within limits, so long as what were now American states had been colonies of the British Crown. But why and by what mandate should English law be any more authoritative in the now independent states than the law of any other foreign country? In state after state, efforts were made to state the theory and the limits of the reception in explicit terms. This proved to be a difficult drafting assignment, largely because the enacting state conventions and legislatures were by no means sure how much of the English law they wanted to receive and how much to reject.

It was manifest, of course, that such English law as was received in a state would remain in force only at sufferance, that is, would be subject to future change by action of the state legislature. This provided only a point of departure. Other problems remained, technical problems an outsider might say but important ones for practical adjudication. Was the reception to be only of the "common law" in a strict sense, that is, the English case-law, or were any Acts of Parliament to be received, too? Should English judicial precedents be accepted as authoritative only if handed down in England before a stated time, and, if so, should the cut-off date be set at July 4, 1776, or at the date of the state's first settlement as a colony, or at some time in between? The draftsmen of the various state reception statutes struggled manfully with problems like these. We should not be too hard on them if they failed to anticipate every possible issue and so left difficult questions of construction for nineteenth century courts. After all, the great draftsmen of the Constitution of the United States did not settle everything either and left at least a few issues of interpretation for subsequent Supreme Court determination.

The most influential of the state reception statutes was the one enacted by the Virginia Convention of May, 1776. Most but not all of the other states followed suit during or immediately after the Revolutionary War, as did most of the new states admitted to the Union during the nineteenth century. A few models are of particular interest. By the Virginia reception ordinance of 1776, the common law of England, except where superseded by local statute, was declared to be "the rule of decision" in the state's courts, a form of words that will reappear in section 34 of the Judiciary Act of 1789.[6] In the New York Constitution of 1777, the phraseology is different: "such parts of the common law of England," as, together with British and colonial legislation, formed the law of the colony of New York on April 17, 1775, "shall be and continue the law of the state." The common law reached the Northwest Territory, and so ultimately the states of Ohio, Indiana, Illinois, Michigan, Wisconsin and Minnesota, by expansive judicial interpretation of the equivocal provisions in the Ordinance of 1787 that the judges of the Territory "shall have a common law jurisdiction" and the Territory's inhabitants "shall always be en-

6. "The laws of the several states, except where the constitution, treaties or statutes of the United States shall otherwise require or provide, shall be regarded as *rules of decision* in trials at common law in the courts of the United States." (Italics added.)

titled to the benefit of judicial proceedings according to the course of the common law."

Whatever the words of the specific statutory or constitutional text, the result brought about by judicial interpretation was substantially the same: reception of such doctrines of the English case-law as the state's judges deem suitable to the conditions and needs of their place and time. May we surmise that the course of reception in the states of the United States would have been about the same if the reception statutes had never been enacted? Would not the state courts have accomplished the reception on their own? Consider Fitch v. Brainerd,[7] an 1805 decision from Connecticut.

Connecticut Yankees were always frugal in the exercise of lawmaking power. Connecticut did not enact a new state constitution as almost every other state did in 1776 or 1777, remaining content with its colonial charter as supplemented by its Fundamental Orders, and Connecticut legislators seem to have seen no reason to enact a reception statute. Was it proper, then, to draw on common law authority in deciding the question, presented to the court in Fitch v. Brainerd, whether a married woman could dispose of her real estate by will? In the absence of legislative authorization, this seemed highly questionable for, in the court's own words, "the common law of England hath not, as such, nor ever had, any force here." Was the common law then to be banished from Connecticut, as Connecticut's neighbor, Massachusetts, had banished Roger Williams almost two hundred years earlier? Our apprehensions were premature, because the court's next word is "yet"—and what a "yet":

> Yet, in the progress of our affairs, whatever was imagined at the beginning, it long since became necessary, in order to avoid arbitrary decisions, and for the sake of rules, which habit had rendered familiar, as well as the wisdom of ages matured, to make that law our own, by practical adoption—with such exceptions as a diversity of circumstances, and the incipient customs of our own country, require. The same may be said of ancient English statutes, not penal, whose corrective and equitable principles had become so interwoven with the common law, as to be scarcely distinguishable therefrom.

One senses in this paragraph, written not long after the Revolution and before the War of 1812, a kind of dialogue of early American reception. "The common law of England hath not any force here" says the Revolutionary spirit. "Yet," and now speaks the workaday judge, it is necessary for practical reasons "to make that law our own."

It was cases like this that I had most in mind when I said, in my opening paragraph, that American continuity with the English past

---

7. 2 Conn. 163 (1805).

was "only a necessity." Early American judges were, as we have seen, schooled exclusively in the common law, and they thought in terms of its structural concepts. The legal philosophy to which they all subscribed committed them to a ceaseless quest for certainty, even if that certainty be, as they must have known it to be, often more formal than real. The declaratory theory of the judicial process dominated eighteenth and nineteenth century legal philosophy and demanded that every decision be justified somehow by reference to pre-existing law. In conventional legal thought, and particularly in the pre-realist Blackstonian jurisprudence of the time, law was something always to be found by judges and never made by them. Alexander Hamilton seems to us a legal realist in comparison with other statesmen of his time, but even he had hewed to the declaratory line in Number 78 of the Federalist Papers:

> "To avoid an arbitrary discretion in the courts, it is indispensable that they should be bound down by strict rules and precedents, which serve to define and point out their duty in every particular case that comes before them."

If strict rules and precedents had to be found for "every particular case," where were the American courts to look to find them, other than in the corpus of English common law doctrine? The only other conceivable source was the civil law, the principles of the classical Roman law as it had been received by then in France and other European countries. But few American lawyers and judges read foreign languages, even French, and how, in any event, would an ordinary American lawyer or judge have had access to the great civil law treatises? The common law, by contracts, was familiar, accessible, if only in Blackstone's compendium, and not particularly alien if one was careful to prune away its inconvenient shoots, as a court could always do by invoking the precept that reception of the common law did not extend to those of its principles that were unsuitable to American conditions. It was fore-ordained, we can see now, that American courts would go the way of reception untroubled by the awkwardness or incompleteness of the state reception statutes and, wanting any reception statute at all, receive the common law by practical adoption.

"One of the chief difficulties confronting a student of our legal history," wrote Cardozo, "is that the whole subject of the reception of English law, both common and statutory, was not thought out in any consistent way, but was left unsettled and in the air." Throughout the nineteenth century and even into the twentieth, state courts of last resort were faced on occasion with elusive questions as to precisely what case-law rules and what English statutes had or had not been received as law in a particular state. Was Henry VIII's Statute of Uses to be taken as an ingredient of the received "common law of England," and were the provisions of the Statute of Frauds to be regarded as in force in an American state, even though the state's legislature had never enacted Sir Heneage Finch's 1677 statutory text?

There was no single true answer to complex questions like those just mentioned, so the reception of the common law was never precisely the same in any two states. To undertake a meticulous state-by-state comparison of these differences in detail would, however, be to lose the forest for the trees. There was, in any event, no great disagreement from state to state on three general propositions concerning the scope and limits of the reception: *First*, that "the common law of England," in this reception context, includes the principles and precedents of the Court of Chancery as well as the principles and precedents of the Courts of Common Pleas, King's Bench and Exchequer, and also includes, as received sources of the law, such Acts of Parliament as had become woven into the fabric of common law thought; *Second*, that the reception of English law is subject to a cut-off date, usually 1776 or some date prior to the outbreak of the Revolution, so that decisions handed down by English courts after that date are not "received" but are, at best, only "persuasive authority;" and *Third*, that English law, decisional or statutory, is to be given controlling effect in American decision-making only to the extent that it is suitable to local institutions and conditions. This third general proposition of reception is incomparably the most important of the three. We have touched on it a few times before in this discussion, and now it is time to address ourselves to it more directly.

Roscoe Pound and others have written at length about the ways in which the judges of the formative period of American law at once "received" the principles of the English common law and transformed them for American use. Because of the prevailing distrust of judicial discretion, American judges of the early nineteenth century were reluctant policy-makers. But they had a kind of "activism" thrust upon them. How could common law decision-making be a slot machine affair when it was always appropriate, even obligatory, for counsel to argue and the court to consider whether cited English precedents were "suitable to the conditions" of a particular state and time? To understand the realities of selective reception, let us consider an example or two, of many that might be chosen. It was a rule of the English common law, established well before the eighteenth century, that the owner of cattle, sheep or other barnyard stock was strictly liable for damages done when his animals trespassed on another's land. Was this common law doctrine to be "received" in states of the middle and far west, where materials for fencing were limited, and cattle customarily grazed on the open lands? The courts held not, on the ground that the old English rule was not suitable for local American conditions. The common law doctrine of strict liability for animal trespasses was appropriate for the English countryside. It could find no home on the range.

Sec. 2 THE COMMON LAW 755

Our other example, earlier and from the eastern part of the United States is an ancient lights case, Parker & Edgarton v. Foote,[8] decided by the Supreme Court of Judicature of New York in 1838. The plaintiff and the defendant were neighbors, and the defendant, by erecting a store occupying the entire space between the two houses, had practically blocked out the windows on one side of the plaintiff's house. By the developed rule of the English common law, a landowner in the plaintiff's position was entitled to damages for the stopping of his lights. Did New York's reception of the common law give the plaintiff the same remedy in New York? The court's answer, one typical of selective reception at work, is a brisk rejection of the English doctrine (at page 318):

> "It may do well enough in England; and I see that it has recently been sanctioned with some qualification, by an act of parliament. Stat. 2 & 3, Will. IV, c. 71, Sec. 3. But it cannot be applied in the growing cities and villages of this country, without working the most mischievous consequences. * * * It cannot be necessary to cite cases to prove that those portions of the common law of England which are hostile to the spirit of our institutions, or which are not adapted to the existing state of things in this country, form no part of our law."

This was enough to dispose of the case, but the court, as courts so often do, went on to justify its rejection of the English doctrine on a second ground, that the English precedents were handed down in England after the cut-off date on New York's reception (at page 318):

> "And besides, it would be difficult to prove that the rule in question was known to the common law previous to the 19th of April, 1775. There were two *nisi prius* decisions at an earlier day, but the doctrine was not sanctioned in Westminster Hall until 1786, when the case of Darwin v. Upton was decided by the K.B."

So we have in one case a reminder of both of the theoretical limits on American reception of the common law: the English doctrine must be suitable for local American conditions, and it must have been established by decisions handed down in England before 1776 or whatever other date the particular state has fixed as the cut-off on its reception.

Most of the state reception statutes specify or necessarily imply a cut-off date, but there is considerable variety in the dates selected. In New York, as we have just seen, it was April 19, 1775. In Virginia and the states which followed Virginia's "rule of decision" reception model, the date is fixed earlier, at least insofar as English statutes are concerned, at "the fourth year of the reign of James I," that

---

8. 19 Wend. 309 (1838).

is, 1607, the year of the first Virginia settlement. In states where the reception statute prescribes no cut-off date and in those in which the courts themselves decreed the reception of English law by "practical adoption," the virtually uniform judicial construction is that what was received is the common law of England as it stood no later than July 4, 1776.

These varying cut-off dates are of antiquarian interest, but we have to be careful not to take them too literally. As a matter of pure theory, American reception may have been limited to the English law as it existed on some set date—1775, 1776 or whatever—but as a matter of demonstrable fact, English judicial decisions handed down long after 1776 exerted a profound influence on nineteenth century American adjudication. The reception of the common law in the United States remained unfinished business long after American independence was established. Whatever cut-off date may have been recited in this or that state reception statute, American courts did not regard the spring of English common law doctrine as one that went dry for them on the day American independence was proclaimed. Throughout the formative period of American law and well into the later years of the nineteenth century, what was received here was not the closed book of English law as of 1776 but the open book of developing English common law doctrine.

Is this a hazardous thesis, one that goes too far beyond the conventional theory of reception? Let me answer, as law professors always do, with another question, addressed to the lawyers in the house. If you were asked for a list of leading cases, apart from great constitutional causes like Marbury v. Madison, would Hadley v. Baxendale be one of the decisions you could recall by name? Or Rylands v. Fletcher? What of Tulk v. Moxhay, Lumley v. Gye, and Priestly v. Fowler? (I mention Priestly v. Fowler as a reminder that not all American borrowings from England were happy ones.) We would all recall these cases by name and would know that they were all of English origin, although later naturalized here. But has it ever occurred to you—as it had not to me before I began to write this essay —that these cases, all of which had great influence on American law, were decided long after 1776, the earliest of the five in 1837 and the latest, Rylands v. Fletcher, in 1868?

Consider two other illustrations, somewhat different in legal character but fully as influential in their respective ways: Lord Campbell's Act, which was borrowed and with full billing to its English sponsor in virtually every American jurisdiction, and the *M'Naghten Rules* on criminal responsibility. But Parliament did not enact Lord Campbell's Fatal Accidents Act until 1846, and the *M'Naghten Rules* were not given in the House of Lords until 1843. If we think of reception narrowly, as something limited to pre-Revolutionary English law, all the precedents and other sources just mentioned seem out of bounds and were perhaps never entitled to American entry permits.

Why did the English law, even the decisions and other legal developments after 1776, continue to exert influence on the growth of the law in America, probably even a greater influence than before independence? It is not that there was any great affection for Englishmen or English institutions in the decades that followed the Revolutionary War. Continuing estrangement of Americans from what Jefferson had called "the ties of our common kindred" brought the common law itself into disfavor for a time, at least in its original English version. New Jersey in 1799 enacted a statute, not repealed until 1818, providing that no British decision handed down after July 4, 1776 and no exposition of common law principles published in England after that date was to be "received or read in any court of law or equity in this state as law or evidence of the law." By a Kentucky statute of 1807, reports of post-1776 English cases were "not to be read or considered as authority * * * in the courts of this Commonwealth," and the legal historian, Lawrence Friedman, furnishes us with a telling anecdote of how Henry Clay, arguing a case in the Court of Appeals of Kentucky, was stopped when he tried to read from one of Lord Ellenborough's judgments and told that "the book must not be used at all in court."[9]

Measures taken to bar the use of post-1776 English authority were unavailing; to enact them was to buck an irresistible tide. American lawyers and judges persisted in drawing on continuing English judicial experience because they needed legal authority and had nowhere else to turn. Professor Friedman tells us that when the Kentucky court stopped Clay's reading from the Ellenborough judgment, Clay's co-counsel protested that the Kentucky legislature had no more power to pass the no-citation statute of 1807 than to "prohibit a judge the use of his spectacles." This was a wonderfully apt way of putting it; reference to English precedents, including precedents later than 1776, had become second nature to American law professionals.

American judges and lawyers of the nineteenth century had greater access to English court reports than they had had in the eighteenth. Eager to locate authority somewhere, and so to avoid the charge of "arbitrary" law-making, American courts were happy to find English decisions in point and cited them as supporting authority without worrying too much about when the English courts had handed them down. These citations of post-1776 English decisions were usually made without explicit explanation or apology, but if counsel for the other side raised the point that the cited case was not authoritative because decided after the cut-off date, a justifying theo-

---

9. L. Friedman, A History of American Law, 97–98 (1973).

ry was always at hand: that the decision, though formally announced in England after 1776, was merely declaratory of the common law as it had always been.

Throughout the nineteenth century, post-1776 English judicial decisions vastly influenced the course of common law development in America. They were highly "persuasive" sources, even if not formally and fully authoritative. To fail to see this is to underestimate the scope of the American reception of English law. To be sure, the post-1776 English decisions were not absolutely "binding" on American courts—as if any precedents ever were—and an American court that disagreed sharply with the English result or reasoning could always disregard it, just as it could always put aside English decisions of any date as unsuitable to American conditions. But, by and large, nineteenth century American judges were interested in knowing what English courts were doing in comparable cases of the time and were inclined to give great weight to the English example. The American Revolution was receding into the past, and Blackstone, the Dr. Spock of early American law, had exerted his incomparable influence on American legal thought. To a lawyer brought up on Blackstone's Commentaries, as practically all lawyers were in the frontier states, English law was almost the immutable law of nature, certainly nothing for a self-taught country lawyer to quarrel with.[10]

Nothing I have said should be taken to underestimate the great discretion American judges had in the acceptance or rejection of English common law doctrines. They could, and on occasion did, flatly reject English case authority on one theory or the other, as they do today in the acceptance or rejection of the "persuasive authority" of decisions from other states of the United States. But, more often than not, they chose to make the English case-law their own. Was this simple follow-the-leader, an unwillingness to face up to the creative responsibilities of the judicial function? Or was it, as I am inclined to think, a certain feeling that the common law could never be expounded quite as truly as in its old home?

The citation and appraisal of English case precedents has become something of a rarity in present-day American judicial opinions, although by no means as rare as English citation of American authority. Local precedents have multiplied almost to the point of embarrassment in most states, and, even when there is no full-fledged state precedent at hand, a state court is more likely to turn to the persuasive authority of decisions from other American jurisdictions as presumably reflecting conditions more like its own than English condi-

---

10. "In the first century of American independence, the Commentaries [of Blackstone] were not merely an approach to the study of law; for most lawyers they constituted all there was of the law. In view of the scarcity of lawbooks during the earliest years of the Republic, and the limitations of life on the frontier, it is not surprising that Blackstone's convenient work became the bible of American lawyers." D. Boorstin, The Mysterious Science of the Law 3–4 (1941).

tions are. And contemporary American appellate courts are far less desperate in their quest for pre-existing legal authority than their predecessors were. The typical American appellate court judge of our day is more comfortable with the responsibilities of interstitial law-making that are inherent in the judicial function and not unduly embarrassed when he and his colleagues have to justify a difficult decision on frankly stated policy grounds. The American reception of English case-law is over, in a sense, and has been for perhaps a hundred years. But the common law has developed in the United States as in England in its characteristic one-step-at-a-time way, this ill-fated precedent restricted to its special facts by later decisions, the next happier precedent given increased scope and extension by analogy. Case-law principles, like old families, have long and researchable pedigrees. When one traces the case-by-case history of even the best established American case-law rule, the odds are considerably better than even money that he will find at least one "received" English ancestor in its line of descent.

The reception of law is a complex cultural and intellectual phenomenon, and one not to be oversimplified. When a scholar speaks of the reception of the Roman law in the countries of Western Europe, he does not mean that French or German or Dutch courts try or ever tried to apply the law that would have been applied in Constantinople or Alexandria by an imperial judge of the classical period of Roman law. Reception is never antiquarian—or passive. The judges to whom the process is entrusted have greater discretion and responsibility than is commonly supposed. We have seen the judicial process at work here, broadening the reach of the American reception by extending it to post-1776 English decisions and, at the same time, making reception more selective by putting aside English precedents deemed unsuitable for American conditions.

On balance, and when the process of reception is completed, the continuity of English and American legal ideas is unmistakable. In law, as in religion, the New Dispensation is never identical with the Old, but the New Dispensation is never quite understood by one who does not see how deeply it is rooted in the older tradition.

SECTION 3. DISPUTE–SETTLEMENT AND THE PROBLEM OF JUSTICE

The preamble to the Constitution of the United States declares that one of the Constitution's great purposes is "to establish Justice." No one disagrees with this as an abstract formulation. But what does justice mean in the real world and specifically in the context of practical dispute-settlement?

Justice is not a cleanly defined term in common speech or even in philosophical and jurisprudential usage. The ordinary language philosopher is dismayed by the number and variety of the meanings the word bears. In some contexts, as when used in the phrase "the administration of justice," "justice" means essentially and little more than the efficient operation of legal institutions. In other contexts, an appeal to "justice" signifies a reference to some moral norm higher than the imperative of the positive law, to conscience, for example, or to some asserted precept of the "natural" law. Or consider the quite different, even contradictory, things that may be signified in legal discourse by the familiar charge that some statutory policy is being administered "unjustly" by a court or administrative agency. At times, this charge expresses the speaker's conviction that a general policy is being applied unequally, that is, in a way that differs unfairly from person to person or from case to case. But at other times, and probably more often, the charge that a statutory policy is being administered "unjustly" signifies the speaker's belief that the statute is being applied—shall we say?—too equally, that is, in a mechanical and undiscriminating way and to concrete cases within its letter but not within its spirit.

Many sources—religious, philosophical, historical—have contributed to our ideas of the "just." In Greek moral philosophy, "justice," at first, had the connotation of universal virtue, moral perfection in general. From this not too helpful Platonic starting point, Aristotle proceeded to his analysis of justice as a matter of right proportion in interpersonal relations and in the relations of the individual and the state. Thus, there were "distributive justice," the award of state honors and benefits to citizens in proportion to the contribution of each to the *polis* or community; "equalizing justice," the mean between loss and gain in interpersonal transactions; and "corrective (or legal) justice," reparation ordered by the judge in proportion to the harm inflicted by the offender on another person or on the community.

From these Aristotelian categories of particular justice, chiefly from the idea of distributive justice, Roman jurisprudence constructed its theory of justice as a form of dueness, the *suum cuique*, that is, the rendering to each man of that which is his due. The Roman jurist Ulpian's familiar definition, "Justice is the law's constant and perpetual resolve to give every man his due," served, in turn, as a literary source for Thomas Aquinas's definition of justice as a habit of mind pursuant to which the just man gives every other man his due. Ultimately, the idea of *dueness*, the appropriateness of the judgment to the merit or demerit of the claimant, becomes firmly established in Western legal theory.

What clues to better understanding of the problem of justice in dispute-settlement can be found in the vast literature of philosophy, theology and law on "justice" and "the just"? The literature of "justice" is marked by certain recurrent themes, five of which seem particularly relevant to our present inquiry: (1) The concept of the *suum cuique,* that is, of an award or judgment related, or proportionate in some way, to the "due" of the persons before the court; (2) The concept of *equality,* which, it would seem, is the transformation of the *suum cuique* idea wrought by our democratic theory that all men and women have the same "due" insofar as the operations of the political and legal order are concerned; (3) The concept of *regularity and consistency* in the administration of standing law, which is central in the analysis of procedural justice in John Rawls's distinguished book, A Theory of Justice,[11] which many law students will have read in college courses in philosophy or political theory; (4) The concept, supplementing and qualifying justice as regularity, that positive law and day-to-day law administration must conform to at least some *norms of higher moral obligation,* whether these higher norms be set by divine revelation, by the individual human conscience, by the natural law, or by a written or unwritten political constitution; and (5) The concept of *"equity"* in its Aristotelian sense, that is of discriminating individualization, on the occasions when there is need for it, in the application of general legal precepts to concrete social situations.

To be sure, one of these five constituent ideas of "justice" may come into collision with another from time to time—as in criminal law administration when the concept of equality seems to point towards identical sentences for two participants in the same crime and the concept of discriminating individualization towards a less severe or different punishment for one of them than for the other—but this phenomenon is certainly not unique to discussions of "justice" and exists, as we have seen, across the board of legal evaluation.

Where, if anywhere, does the above inventory of five recurring notions or themes of justice take us for the purposes of the present casebook section? We are addressing ourselves, as the student-reader will remember, not to justice as a quality of personal moral character and not to "social" or "distributive" justice as an ideal end of organized society but to justice in the context of practical dispute-settlement. Is it possible to discern all or any of the five stated "justice" ideas at work in this adjudicative context? If so, what tasks are thereby set for one who wants to clarify his or her ideas about the realities of law in action?

The Justice Beyond Regularity

The going gets heavy as soon as one begins to think of justice not as an abstraction to be argued about but as a problem for analysis. Part of the difficulty is that once we have chosen any one of the

---

11. A Theory of Justice (1971) deals, in the main, with "social" or "distributive" justice and touches only incidentally on the problem of justice in the settlement of disputes. But there are illuminating passages on procedural justice and the "rule of law," e. g., at 54–60, 235–43. "Justice as regularity" is Rawls's shorthand term for the concept of regularity and consistency in the administration of law. Id. at 235.

five "justice" themes, even provisionally, as our clue for understanding and interpretation of the realities of dispute-settlement, one of the other "justice" ideas suddenly surfaces and disrupts the enterprise. To explore this, consider the posture of a righteous and properly hard-boiled judge. He is, we assume, a rigorous legal positivist, so let us call him Judge John Austin.[12]

Judge Austin's choice, a bullet vote, is for "justice as regularity." What of the *suum cuique*, the idea of dueness as justice. Judge Austin's answer is brusque: "A claimant's *due* is whatever he is entitled to get under the established rules of law." The dialogue continues. Question: "What of equality as an aspect of justice?" Answer: "Equality is, and can be secured only by, the even-handed and precise application of law's general rules." What of discriminating individualization as a mode of justice? "Widow and orphan cases you mean?" our judicial friend will rejoin. "Mushheadedness. Hard cases make bad law, but only if you yield to their temptation." Press Judge Austin further, and he will ultimately counter with something like this: "Justice in adjudication is the consistent and impartial application of the law as it is."

Pretty easy sailing for Judge Austin so far. But then, if he is still amenable to theoretical discussion, ask him if his concept of "justice as regularity" would extend to the Nuremberg Laws of Nazi Germany. If they had been applied by the Nazi courts with regularity and consistency—as, God help us, they largely were—would we apply the characterization "just" to the decisions so reached? Coming closer home, was "justice" accomplished when state courts in the American South regularly and consistently applied the laws of slavery that existed, before the Civil War, in their precedents and statute books? Or, to raise the question in painful but less dramatically tragic terms, what of one hundred years of fairly regular and consistent application of the then existing defenses of assumption of risk, fellow servant negligence and contributory fault in employer's liability litigation, which left the inevitable casualties of the Industrial Revolution remediless and destitute? This was regularity, to be sure, but was it justice? And so Judge Austin, being an honorable man and not a word-chopper, will add another indispensable ingredient to his justice formula: "Justice, I meant, is the consistent and impartial application of *just* general law." And now—to use the technical language of philosophy—we have a whole new ball game.

---

12. John Austin (1790–1859) began the analytical tradition that has been maintained in English jurisprudence since his day. His most influential work, The Province of Jurisprudence Determined (1832), was based on lectures given at the University of London. In Austin's perspective, law is essentially imperative, the commands of the sovereign, and jurisprudence "is concerned with law as it necessarily *is*, rather than law as it *ought* to be; with law as it must be, *be it good or bad*, rather than law as it must be, if it be good." See 1 J. Austin, Lectures on Jurisprudence 33 (4th ed. 1873).

How Justice Ideas Can Influence the Outcome of Cases

In the imaginary dialogue just conducted, why was a judge used as the other party, rather than one of the many legal philosophers who, in their time, began with adjudicative "justice as regularity" and then were moved, by further reflection or experience, to the view that meaningful "justice" has to involve more than the fidelity of officials to the existing positive law? It was not for the purpose of poking fun at Judge Austin. He is quite right to honor "justice as regularity," and he is inauthentic in his social role if he thinks of himself as Solomon or as Louis IX under that Vincennes oak tree. The point is rather that Judge Austin, as a trial judge or as one member of a collegial appellate court, does more than make theoretical justice evaluations. He is—more often than you or even he may think—in a position to decide cases according to his justice evaluations. When he does that, if he does, no one is going to put up a sign telling you exactly what is going on in Judge Austin's court. But to miss it is to miss a vital, even if wayward, impulse in the life of the law.

It is here that the observer, whether he be a law student, a social scientist or a legal philosopher, has to look beneath the surface of things to see the influence of higher law notions and other justice ideas on decisions that may be formally justified, in the published opinions, on less subjective—more legally respectable—grounds. Except for a few aberrations like Lord Coke's usually over-estimated opinion in *Dr. Bonham's Case,* Anglo-American legal theory has rejected the natural law idea that "an unjust law is no law at all" and hence without obligation or force in practical adjudication. Judge Austin, for one, would be horrified by this distinctive natural law claim. But think of the strategies that Judge Austin or an appellate bench of five, seven or nine Judge Austins might use—not will inevitably use, just might conceivably use—to avoid the application, in actual disputes, of a general legal rule which strikes him or them as profoundly "unjust" because it violates some deeply held higher law conviction of theirs, or it seems to them unequal or unfair in formulation, or they are convinced that it gives certain worthy claimants less than their due.

First possibility: the repugnant general law, it now appears—although no one had ever quite thought of this before—is in clear violation of the due process of law guaranteed by the fifth and fourteenth amendments to the Constitution. Or, to push the strategy a little farther, as in the Supreme Court's 1965 decision in the birth control case, Griswold v. Connecticut,[13] the offensive law, it now appears, contravenes one of the "penumbral" guarantees "formed by emana-

---

13. 381 U.S. 479, 85 S.Ct. 1678, 14 L. Ed.2d 510 (1965).

tions from" the specific guarantees of the Bill of Rights. Fancy footwork that and, as so often, in a very good cause. Constitutional law, one begins to see, is in one aspect—or can be used as—a kind of institutionalized natural law system through which justice evaluations are brought into play, and with controlling force, in practical adjudication.

Consider another strategy, one more familiar to you from the legislation half of Legal Method. In this version, the judges will not hold the unjust—as they deem it—law unconstitutional; they may simply give it so restrictive an interpretation that it never seems to apply in an actual case. In England, where there is no written constitution and no doctrine of judicial review, the courts for centuries have used restrictive interpretation as the strategy for effectuation of their deeply held "justice" evaluations.

There are other ways in which justice ideas can influence the outcome of litigation. A judge, let us say, is faced with a case in which one side relies on a general law the judge finds morally or socially deplorable. Will you be astonished or outraged if the judge—with or without the aid of a jury—so "finds" the facts that the controversy is taken out of the reach of the disprized rule? This is a strategy perhaps familiar to you from *Bushell's Case* in which a sturdy English jury, with the ultimate support of the High Court of England, paid formal deference to the oppressive religious censorship laws—in English constitutional theory no court and certainly no jury could strike them down—but avoided applying them to William Penn and William Mead by finding, as a fact, that Penn and Mead were not guilty of doing what they most indisputably had done.

The Procedural Dimension of Substantive Justice

Mention of *Bushell's Case* takes us into another aspect of the problem of justice in the settlement of disputes. Let us, again, take "justice as regularity" as our take-off point. Regularity in law administration requires consistency, logical cohesion in the exposition and application of general rules to the specific instances falling properly within them. This, for the moment, we designate as the *law* side of adjudicative regularity. But "justice as regularity" has its *facts* side, too. If Nicola Sacco and Bartolomeo Vanzetti did not, in fact, commit the Braintree murders with which they were charged, their conviction was "unjust" even in the minimum regularity sense of the concept of justice. And the convictions would have been unjust, on this assumption of the two men's factual innocence, even if their trial had been conducted not by the choleric and biased Judge Thayer but by one of the ablest and best qualified of the country's fine trial judges.

Justice, even "justice as regularity," postulates the application of law's general rules not simply to the facts as reconstructed and characterized in the course of the judicial process but to the facts as they occurred in the real world. It is as important to justice that the facts of a dispute be accurately "found"—in our odd legal way of putting it—as that the rules brought to bear on the facts so "found" be logically and coherently applied. Here are some of the most intractable difficulties for the problem of justice in the settlement of disputes. The late Judge Jerome Frank hammered away for many years at the thesis that far more injustice is done in the courts by unscientific and inaccurate fact-finding than by misinterpretation of statutes or distortion of case-law doctrines. Fair and reliable procedure is not only an element and historic symbol of "justice as regularity;" it is an indispensable condition without which no aspect of justice is attainable.

Difficult as it is to develop and expound legal doctrine soundly and imaginatively, it is even more difficult to "find" the true facts of a case, that is, to reconstruct in a courtroom, through fallible witnesses and probably long after the event, the full and precise details of an occurrence or transaction. To make a complex task even harder going, legal procedures embody, and must inevitably embody, social values beyond and quite other than the immediate end of accurate fact-finding. It would be wonderfully convenient if we could use a single standard of evaluation to appraise every existing rule of civil and criminal procedure, that is, simply ask, in each instance, how well the questioned rule is calculated to serve the end of accuracy in the ultimate reconstruction of disputed facts. But other values keep cutting across that.

An example or two should be sufficient to make the point. One cannot think of any occasion when a man or woman is likely to speak quite as truthfully as to his or her religious confessor or physician. If the sole end of procedural law were the reconstruction of factual truth, these statements would rank high as evidence. Yet, and for reasons that are quite remote from fact determination, these statements are privileged communications that cannot be compelled at a trial. Another example. There is not much doubt about the probative value and reliability of evidence secured by wiretapping. But evidence secured by this means, as by other "unreasonable searches and seizures," is excluded in court, not because it is without probative value—it is likely to have almost too much probative value—but because the free admission of such evidence might provide incentives for police practices that would make us all "less secure in our persons, houses, papers and effects." These are only a few of the procedural dimensions of the problem of justice. No theory of justice in adjudication is even remotely complete if its reckoning does not take full account of them.

Justice as Individualization

There is a very old lawyer story about the advocate who won the jury verdict in a major case and sent his client a triumphant telegram reading "JUSTICE HAS TRIUMPHED"—only to receive a return wire, "APPEAL AT ONCE." So we return to the fifth of our recurring themes in the literature of justice, the concept of discriminating individualization, on the occasions when there is need for it, in the application of general legal precepts to concrete human situations.

This requires some shift in our point of perception. The problems we have considered thus far were, by and large, problems related, in one way or another, to "justice as regularity" in the day-to-day operations of our dispute-settling institutions. Regularity, we have seen, is harder to attain in practical adjudication than it is commonly supposed to be—and will on occasion yield to the competing pressure of other "justice" ideas—but it is a pervasive, though sometimes vulnerable, value of the legal order and so not to be discounted. We are not too troubled when we discover that the "obedience to system" exhibited in the actual operation of our adjudicative institutions is rather less than perfect obedience. We would have cause for concern, however, if these institutions were not "obedient to system" in most contexts and most of the time. To put it another way, regularity is not the whole story of "justice," but it is a basic and very significant part of it.

"Justice as regularity" requires, manifestly, that law's precepts be general in statement. Without generality in law, there could be no equality in the legal order, no impersonality or formal rationality in judicial decision making. The idea of the legal precept as a measure, a norm, a general rule, is deeply ingrained in our legal philosophy.

But generality, in Edwin Patterson's words, "is not an unmixed blessing":

> The generality of law can lead to "good" or "bad" consequences, and is thus not an "ideal" attribute of law. It is one which law has, for better or for worse.

Anyone who has worked seriously through a line of appellate decisions will agree with Patterson that the blessings of legal generality are "not unmixed." To be general, a precept must be abstract, and the inclusiveness of any abstract formulation is achieved only by sacrificing something of concrete reality. "All men are mortal" enables us to deduce that Socrates, too, is mortal, but that does not catch the uniqueness of Socrates. In Whitehead's words: "No code of verbal statement can ever exhaust the shifting background of presupposed fact."

The classic statement of this dimension of the problem of justice comes, rather surprisingly, from Aristotle, a philosopher far more inclined in his general world view to universals than to singulars:

> [L]aw is always a general statement, yet there are cases which it is not possible to cover in a general statement. In matters therefore where, while it is necessary to speak in

general terms, it is not possible to do so correctly, the law takes into consideration the majority of cases, although it is not unaware of the error this involves. And this does not make it a wrong law; for the error is not in the law nor in the lawgiver, but in the nature of the case: the material of conduct is essentially irregular * * *. This is the essential nature of the equitable: it is a rectification of law where law is defective because of its generality." [14]

You will note that Aristotle, too, saw law's generality as a "not unmixed" blessing; the "equitable" is "rectification of law where law is defective *because of* its generality."

Aristotle's idea of the "equitable" is, you will remember, one of the five recurring themes of justice, "justice as individualization." And, as was true of our other justice ideas, it can be seen at work in the dispute-settling operations of the courts. There is no need to go far afield for examples; a tendency towards "justice as individualization" is exhibited almost everywhere in the common law judicial process. Even in our law's central working policy, the doctrine of precedent, we can discern a basic inclination that runs more to concrete cases than to abstract and general rules. The doctrine of precedent is grossly misunderstood when thought of as no more than a way to achieve regularity and predictability in the application of case-law principles. Of course it has that function; like cases are to be decided alike. But common law method—and this includes judicial method in the application of statutes—is intractably case-minded, fully as sensitive to the factual differences in cases as to their factual similarities. What we like to call the "legal mind" is a problem-oriented habit of thought that begins with close and sustained study of the facts of the case at hand and uses legal generalizations as tools for the analysis and characterization of the fact situation of that case.

Judges fully share this common law fact-mindedness. They, too, by training and tradition, are more at home with concrete problems than with formal generalizations. The judge sitting in any case does his best, of course, to follow the general law. But he also wants to reach what strikes him as the fair result in the particular case before him. More often than not, if the judge gets proper assistance from counsel in the case, he can attain both his sought objectives. There is no paradox in this; it is a consequence of our legal system's built-in responsiveness to the appeal of justice in concrete situations. In the method of the common law, "regularity" permits, even requires, far more case-by-case "individualization" than conventional legal philosophy has ever been aware of.

14. Aristotle, 5 Nicomachean Ethics (Rackham transl.), in Morris, The Great Legal Philosophers 25 (1959).

The idea of "justice as individualization" finds expression not only in our received techniques for the use of legal sources but also, and more obviously, in the form of the sources themselves. Outside observers, even some philosophers who should know better, tend to think and write about the law as if it were a body of very specific rules, an aggregate of precise and narrowly worded propositions like "A will is invalid unless witnessed by two persons." There are cut-and-dried propositions like these, many of them, but in most areas of the law the most important precepts are likely to be stated in terms of far wider connotation. As Cardozo wrote as long ago as 1921: "We are tending more and more towards an appreciation of the truth that, after all, there are few rules; there are chiefly standards and degrees."

Examples abound, if one looks for them. In the law of contracts, an unbargained-for promise that has induced action by the promisee is binding on the promisor "if injustice can be avoided only by enforcement of the promise." There is no tension here between the demand of general legal policy and the claim of justice in the concrete case; the legal principle itself incorporates individual justice as the governing standard. It is much the same in the law of torts, with its standard of the "reasonably prudent man," and in the law of trusts, where a free-wheeling standard of "fiduciary obligation" is dominant and omnipresent. And what of constitutional "due process of law," which not only is a "standard" in Cardozo's sense but employs the word "due," the most durable justice word of them all? Statutes and case-law principles expressed in standards like these do more than authorize case-by-case individualization in the decisional process; they invite and command it. "Justice as individualization" is no longer an appeal *from* the law in these contexts; it has been made the legal norm.

It is simplistic and misleading to think of adjudication as a process in which rules are primary and cases mere generalization fodder. But the notion that law lives by rules alone is a notion that dies hard, perhaps because we academic lawyers, professors and students alike, are unduly preoccupied with the appellate courts—where the distinctive task is that of clarifying and developing the general law—and give insufficient attention to the trial courts, where the task of "just" individual decision is central and, to the judge and jury, compelling. "Justice as individualization" is a fact of law's life. One who fails to see the constant interplay, in practical adjudication, of general rule and concrete case is missing an important part of the action.

By Way of Conclusion

This exploration of the problem of justice in the settlement of disputes has been intended as a descriptive not a normative discussion. The foregoing pages have not dealt with the question whether justice ideas *should or should not*, as an ideal matter, be influential in the decision of cases, but with the question whether, in fact, they *are* so influential in practical day-to-day adjudication. The first-year law student will find, as his or her study of law progresses, that the themes or ideas associated with what we call "justice" are not just external standards to be brought to bear for the evaluation of case law and legislative precepts. They are also ideas that can be seen at work—not always by any means, but quite often enough—in practical adjudication.

There is no denying that intellectual and political hazards come into view when we take our analysis beyond "justice as regularity." Grave hazards they are: the inevitable element of subjectivity in "justice" evaluations, the likelihood that "justice" ideas will differ from court to court and judge to judge and that judicial evaluations of "the just" may be at odds with—even out of touch with—the moral attitudes that prevail in an executive office, an elected legislature, or the community at large. But these risks are part and parcel of the problem of justice in dispute-settlement; we shall not make them go away by ignoring them. Recognition that the hazards are there, and are inseparable from the opportunities and occasions of what we think of as "justice," serves rather to emphasize again how vitally important it is that our judges be chosen from the best the profession can offer, that they be mature, intellectually sophisticated and self-examining men and women. Decisions proceeding from "justice" evaluations are not necessarily irrational, as is commonly supposed. With a good judge, and with the full factual merits before the court, "justice" evaluations, too, can be "reasoned," that is, in John Dewey's words, "the outcome of inquiry, comparison of alternatives, weighing of facts." The realm of "the just," one likes to think, is not impenetrable to rational inquiry and reflection.

It is essential to a sound social environment that disputes be settled authoritatively and finally. It is almost as essential that they be settled "justly." "Important as it is that people should get justice," Lord Chancellor Hershell once said, "it is even more important that they be made to feel and see that they are getting it." If the old Chancellor was right, as many scholars of society think he was, perhaps it is just as well that the several justice ideas with which we have been concerned in this section are at work, as they so often are, in judicial dispute-settlement. For these ideas of justice—vague and contradictory as they sometimes seem to be—are widely entertained in society by people for whom legal rules and principles are as unintelligible as classical Greek. Justice ideas may, on occasion, play hob with law's consistency and regularity but perhaps—just arguably—they serve to bring the results of adjudication a bit closer into line with prevailing social attitudes and so help, a little, to make people "feel and see that they are getting justice." Is anything in the world of law more urgent and important than that?

*

APPENDIX

TRAMMEL v. UNITED STATES

Supreme Court of the United States, 1980.
— U.S. —, 100 S.Ct. 906, 63 L.Ed.2d 186

Mr. Chief Justice BURGER delivered the opinion of the Court.

We granted certiorari to consider whether an accused may invoke the privilege against adverse spousal testimony so as to exclude the voluntary testimony of his wife. 440 U.S. 934, 99 S.Ct. 1277, 59 L.Ed.2d 492 (1979). This calls for a re-examination of Hawkins v. United States, 358 U.S. 74, 79 S.Ct. 136, 3 L.Ed.2d 125 (1958).

I

On March 10, 1976, petitioner Otis Trammel was indicted with two others, Edwin Lee Roberts and Joseph Freeman, for importing heroin into the United States from Thailand and the Philippine Islands and for conspiracy to import heroin in violation of 21 U.S.C.A. §§ 952 (a), 962(a), and 963. The indictment also named six unindicted co-conspirators, including petitioner's wife Elizabeth Ann Trammel.

According to the indictment, petitioner and his wife flew from the Philippines to California in August 1975, carrying with them a quantity of heroin. Freeman and Roberts assisted them in its distribution. Elizabeth Trammel then travelled to Thailand where she purchased another supply of the drug. On November 3, 1975, with four ounces of heroin on her person, she boarded a plane for the United States. During a routine customs search in Hawaii, she was searched, the heroin was discovered, and she was arrested. After discussions with Drug Enforcement Administration agents, she agreed to cooperate with the Government.

Prior to trial on this indictment, petitioner moved to sever his case from that of Roberts and Freeman. He advised the court that the Government intended to call his wife as an adverse witness and asserted his claim to a privilege to prevent her from testifying against him. At a hearing on the motion, Mrs. Trammel was called as a Government witness under a grant of use immunity. She testified that she and petitioner were married in May 1975 and that they remained married.[1] She explained that her cooperation with the Government was based on assurances that she would be given lenient treatment.[2]

1. In response to the question whether divorce was contemplated, Mrs. Trammel testified that her husband had said that "I would go my way and he would go his." (App., at 27).

2. The Government represents to the Court that Elizabeth Trammel has not been prosecuted for her role in the conspiracy.

She then described, in considerable detail, her role and that of her husband in the heroin distribution conspiracy.

After hearing this testimony, the District Court ruled that Mrs. Trammel could testify in support of the Government's case to any act she observed during the marriage and to any communication "made in the presence of a third person"; however, confidential communications between petitioner and his wife were held to be privileged and inadmissible. The motion to sever was denied.

At trial, Elizabeth Trammel testified within the limits of the court's pretrial ruling; her testimony, as the Government concedes, constituted virtually its entire case against petitioner. He was found guilty on both the substantive and conspiracy charges and sentenced to an indeterminate term of years pursuant to the Federal Youth Corrections Act, 18 U.S.C.A. § 5010(b).[3]

In the Court of Appeals petitioner's only claim of error was that the admission of the adverse testimony of his wife, over his objection, contravened this Court's teaching in Hawkins v. United States, 358 U.S. 74, 79 S.Ct. 136, 3 L.Ed.2d 125 (1958), and therefore constituted reversible error. The Court of Appeals rejected this contention. It concluded that *Hawkins* did not prohibit "the voluntary testimony of a spouse who appears as an unindicted co-conspirator under grant of immunity from the Government in return for her testimony." 583 F.2d 1166, 1168 (CA10 1978).

II

The privilege claimed by petitioner has ancient roots. Writing in 1628, Lord Coke observed that "it hath been resolved by the Justices that a wife cannot be produced either against or for her husband." 1 Coke, A Commentarie upon Littleton 6b (1628). See, generally, 8 J. Wigmore, Evidence § 2227 (McNaughton rev. 1961). This spousal disqualification sprang from two canons of medieval jurisprudence: first, the rule that an accused was not permitted to testify in his own behalf because of his interest in the proceeding; second, the concept that husband and wife were one, and that since the woman had no recognized separate legal existence, the husband was that one. From those two now long-abandoned doctrines, it followed that what was inadmissible from the lips of the defendant-husband was also inadmissible from his wife.

Despite its medieval origins, this rule of spousal disqualification remained intact in most common-law jurisdictions well into the 19th century. See 8 Wigmore, § 2333. It was applied by this Court in Stein v. Bowman, 13 Pet. 209, 220–223, 10 L.Ed. 129 (1839), in Graves v. United States, 150 U.S. 118, 14 S.Ct. 40, 37 L.Ed. 1021 (1893), and

---

3. Roberts and Freeman were also convicted. Roberts was sentenced to two years imprisonment. Freeman received an indeterminate sentence under the Youth Corrections Act.

again in Jin Fuey Moy v. United States, 254 U.S. 189, 195, 41 S.Ct. 98, 101, 65 L.Ed. 214 (1920), where it was deemed so well established a proposition as to "hardly requir[e] mention." Indeed, it was not until 1933, in Funk v. United States, 290 U.S. 371, 54 S.Ct. 212, 78 L.Ed. 369, that this Court abolished the testimonial disqualification in the federal courts, so as to permit the spouse of a defendant to testify in the defendant's behalf. *Funk*, however, left undisturbed the rule that either spouse could prevent the other from giving adverse testimony. Id., at 373, 54 S.Ct., at 212. The rule thus evolved into one of privilege rather than one of absolute disqualification. See J. Maguire, Evidence, Common Sense and Common Law, at 78–92 (1947).

The modern justification for this privilege against adverse spousal testimony is its perceived role in fostering the harmony and sanctity of the marriage relationship. Notwithstanding this benign purpose, the rule was sharply criticized.[4] Professor Wigmore termed it "the merest anachronism in legal theory and an indefensible obstruction to truth in practice." 8 Wigmore, § 2228, at 221. The Committee on the Improvement of the Law of Evidence of the American Bar Association called for its abolition. 63 American Bar Association Reports, at 594–595 (1938). In its place, Wigmore and others suggested a privilege protecting only private marital communications, modeled on the privilege between priest and penitent, attorney and client, and physician and patient. See 8 Wigmore, § 2332 et seq.[5]

These criticisms influenced the American Law Institute, which, in its 1942 Model Code of Evidence, advocated a privilege for marital confidences, but expressly rejected a rule vesting in the defendant the right to exclude all adverse testimony of his spouse. See American Law Institute, Model Code of Evidence, Rule 215 (1942). In 1953 the Uniform Rules of Evidence, drafted by the National Conference of Commissioners on Uniform State Laws, followed a similar course; it limited the privilege to confidential communications and "abolishe[d] the rule, still existing in some states, and largely a sentimental relic, of not requiring one spouse to testify against the other in a criminal ac-

---

4. See Brosman, Edward Livingston and Spousal Testimony in Louisiana, 11 Tulane L.Rev. 243 (1937); Hutchins and Slesinger, Some Observations on the Law of Evidence: Family Relations, 13 Minn.L.Rev. 675 (1929); Note, 24 Calif.L.Rev. 472 (1936); Note, 35 Mich.L.Rev. 329 (1936); Note, 10 So.Cal.L.Rev. 94 (1935); Note, 20 Minn.L.Rev. 693 (1935).

5. This Court recognized just such a confidential marital communications privilege in Wolfle v. United States, 291 U.S. 7, 54 S.Ct. 279, 78 L.Ed. 617 (1934), and in Blau v. United States, 340 U.S. 332, 71 S.Ct. 301, 95 L.Ed. 306 (1951). In neither case, however, did the Court adopt the Wigmore view that the communications privilege be substituted *in place of* the privilege against adverse spousal testimony. The privilege as to confidential marital communications is not at issue in the instant case; accordingly, our holding today does not disturb *Wolfle* and *Blau*.

tion." See Rule 23(2) and comments. Several state legislatures enacted similarly patterned provisions into law.[6]

In Hawkins v. United States, 358 U.S. 74, 79 S.Ct. 136, 3 L.Ed.2d 125 (1958), this Court considered the continued vitality of the privilege against adverse spousal testimony in the federal courts. There the District Court had permitted petitioner's wife, over his objection, to testify against him. With one questioning concurring opinion, the Court held the wife's testimony inadmissible; it took note of the critical comments that the common-law rule had engendered, id., at 76, and n. 4, 79 S.Ct., at 137, but chose not to abandon it. Also rejected was the Government's suggestion that the Court modify the privilege by vesting it in the witness spouse, with freedom to testify or not independent of the defendant's control. The Court viewed this proposed modification as antithetical to the widespread belief, evidenced in the rules then in effect in a majority of the States and in England, "that the law should not force or encourage testimony which might alienate husband and wife, or further inflame existing domestic differences." Id., at 79, 79 S.Ct., at 139.

Hawkins, then, left the federal privilege for adverse spousal testimony where it found it, continuing "a rule which bars the testimony of one spouse against the other unless both consent." Id., at 78, 79 S.Ct., at 138. Accord, Wyatt v. United States, 362 U.S. 525, 528, 80 S.Ct. 901, 903, 4 L.Ed.2d 931 (1960).[7] However, in so doing, the Court made clear that its decision was not meant to "foreclose whatever changes in the rule may eventually be dictated by 'reason and experience.' " 358 U.S., at 79, 79 S.Ct., at 139.

III

A

The Federal Rules of Evidence acknowledge the authority of the federal courts to continue the evolutionary development of testimonial privileges in federal criminal trials "governed by the principles of the common law as they may be interpreted * * * in the light of reason and experience." Fed.Rule Evid. 501. Cf. Wolfle v. United States, supra, at 12, 54 S.Ct., at 279 (1934). The general mandate of

---

6. See Note, Competency of One Spouse to Testify Against the Other in Criminal Cases Where the Testimony Does Not Relate to Confidential Communications: Modern Trend, 38 Va.L.Rev. 359 (1952).

7. The decision in *Wyatt* recognized an exception to *Hawkins* for cases in which one spouse commits a crime against the other. 362 U.S., at 526, 80 S.Ct., at 902. This exception, placed on the ground of necessity, was a longstanding one at common law. See Lord Audley's Case, 123 Eng.Rep. 1140 (1931); 8 Wigmore § 2239. It has been expanded since then to include crimes against the spouse's property, see Herman v. United States, 220 F.2d 219, 226 (CA 4 1955), and in recent years crimes against children of either spouse, United States v. Allery, 526 F.2d 1362 (CA8 1975). Similar exceptions have been found to the confidential marital communications privilege. See 8 Wigmore, § 2338.

Rule 501 was substituted by the Congress for a set of privilege rules drafted by the Judicial Conference Advisory Committee on Rules of Evidence and approved by the Judicial Conference of the United States and by this Court. That proposal defined nine specific privileges, including a husband-wife privilege which would have codified the *Hawkins* rule and eliminated the privilege for confidential marital communications. See Fed.Rule of Evid., Proposed Rule 505. In rejecting the proposed rules and enacting Rule 501, Congress manifested an affirmative intention not to freeze the law of privilege. Its purpose rather was to "provide the courts with the flexibility to develop rules of privilege on a case-by-case basis," 120 Cong.Rec. 40891 (1974) (statement of Rep. Hungate), and to leave the door open to change. See also S.Rep. No. 93–1277, 93d Cong., 2d Sess., 11 (1974); H.R.Rep. No. 93–650, 93d Cong., 1st Sess., 8 (1973).[8]

Although Rule 501 confirms the authority of the federal courts to reconsider the continued validity of the *Hawkins* rule, the long history of the privilege suggests that it ought not to be casually cast aside. That the privilege is one affecting marriage, home, and family relationships—already subject to much erosion in our day—also counsels caution. At the same time we cannot escape the reality that the law on occasion adheres to doctrinal concepts long after the reasons which gave them birth have disappeared and after experience suggests the need for change. This was recognized in *Funk* where the Court "decline[d] to enforce * * * ancient rule[s] of the common law under conditions as they now exist." 290 U.S., at 382, 54 S.Ct., at 215. For, as Mr. Justice Black admonished in another setting, "[w]hen precedent and precedent alone is all the argument that can be made to support a court-fashioned rule, it is time for the rule's creator to destroy it." Francis v. Southern Pacific Co., 333 U.S. 445, 471, 68 S.Ct. 611, 623, 92 L.Ed. 798 (1948) (Black, J., dissenting).

B

Since 1958, when *Hawkins* was decided, support for the privilege against adverse spousal testimony has been eroded further. Thirty-one jurisdictions, including Alaska and Hawaii, then allowed an accused a privilege to prevent adverse spousal testimony. 358 U.S., at 81, n. 3, 79 S.Ct., at 140 (Stewart, J., concurring). The number has

8. Petitioner's reliance on 28 U.S.C.A. § 2076 for the proposition that this Court is without power to reconsider *Hawkins* is ill founded. That provision limits this Court's *statutory* rulemaking authority by providing that rules "creating, abolishing, or modifying a privilege shall have no force or effect unless * * * approved by act of Congress." It was enacted principally to insure that state rules of privilege would apply in diversity jurisdiction cases unless Congress authorized otherwise. In Rule 501 Congress makes clear that § 2076 was not intended to prevent the federal courts from developing testimonial privilege law in federal criminal cases on a case-by-case basis "in light of reason and experience"; indeed Congress encouraged such development.

now declined to 24.[9] In 1974, the National Conference on Uniform States Laws revised its Uniform Rules of Evidence, but again rejected the *Hawkins* rule in favor of a limited privilege for confidential communications. See Uniform Rules of Evidence, Rule 504. That proposed rule has been enacted in Arkansas, North Dakota, and Oklahoma—each of which in 1958 permitted an accused to exclude adverse spousal testimony.[10] The trend in state law toward divesting the ac-

9. Eight states provide that one spouse is incompetent to testify against the other in a criminal proceeding: see Haw.Rev.Stat. § 621–18 (1968); Iowa Code § 622.7 (1979); Miss.Code Ann. § 13–1–5 (Cum.Supp. 1978); N.C.Gen.Stat. § 8–57 (Cum. Supp.1977); Ohio Rev.Code Ann. § 2945.42; Pa.Stat.Ann., Tit. 42, §§ 5913, 5915 (Purdon Supp.1979); Tex. Crim.Proc.Code Ann. Art. 38.11 (Vernon 1979); Wyo.Stat. § 1–12–104 (1977).

Sixteen states provide a privilege against adverse spousal testimony and vest the privilege in both spouses or in the defendant-spouse alone: see Alaska Crim.Proc. Rules 26(b)(2) (Supp.Sept.1968); Colo.Rev.Stat. § 13–90–107 (1974); Idaho Code § 9–203 (Cum.Supp.1978); Mich.Comp.Laws § 600.2162 (Mich.Stat.Ann. § 27A.2162 (Callaghan 1976)); Minn.Stat.Ann. § 595.02 (West Cum.Supp.1978); Mo. Ann.Stat. § 546.260 (Vernon 1953); Mont.Rev.Code Ann. § 95–3011 (Cum. Supp.1975); Neb.Rev.Stat. § 27–505 (1975); Nev.Rev.Stat. § 49.295 (1977); N.J.Stat.Ann. § 2A:84A–17 (West 1976); N.M.Stat.Ann. § 20–4–505 (Cum.Supp.1975); Ore.Rev.Stat. § 44.040 (1977); Utah Code Ann. § 78–24–8 (1977); Va.Code § 19.2–271.2 (Cum.Supp.1978); Wash.Rev. Code Ann. § 5.60.060 (Supp.1979); W.Va.Code § 57–3–3 (1966).

Nine states entitle the witness-spouse alone to assert a privilege against adverse spousal testimony: see Ala. Code, Tit. 12, § 21–227 (1977); Cal. Evid.Code §§ 970–973 (West 1966); Conn.Gen.Stat.Ann. § 54–84 (West Cum.Supp.1979); Ga.Code Ann. § 38–1604 (1974); Ky.Rev.Stat. § 421.210 (Cum.Supp.1978); La.Rev.Stat.Ann. § 15:461 (West 1967); Md.Cts. and Jud.Proc.Code Ann. §§ 9–101, 9–106 (1974); Mass.Ann.Laws ch. 233, § 20 (Law Co-op 1974); R.I.Gen.Laws § 12–17–10 (1970).

The remaining 17 states have abolished the privilege in criminal cases: see Ariz.Rev.Stat.Ann. § 12–2231 (Supp. 1978); Ark.Stat.Ann. § 28–1001, Rules 501 and 504 (Cum.Supp.1977); Del. Code Ann., Tit. 11, § 3502 (1975); Fla.Stat.Ann. §§ 90.501, 90.504 (West Supp.1979); Ill.Ann.Stat. ch. 38, § 155–1 (Smith-Hurd Cum.Supp.1979); Ind.Code Ann. §§ 34–1–14–4, 34–1–14–5 (Burns 1973); Kan.Stat.Ann. §§ 60–407, 60–428 (1976); Me.Rev.Stat. Ann., Maine Rules of Evidence, Rules 501, 504 (West Supp.1978); N.H.Rev. Stat.Ann. § 516.27 (1974); N.Y.Crim. Proc.Law § 60.10 (McKinney 1971); N.Y.Civ.Proc.Law §§ 4502, 4512 (McKinney 1963); N.D.Cent.Code, N.D. Rules of Evidence, Rules 501, 504 (Supp.1977); Okla.Stat.Ann., Tit. 12, §§ 2103, 2501, 2504 (West Cum.Supp. 1978–1979); S.C.Code § 19–11–30 (1977); S.D. Compiled Laws Ann. §§ 19–13–1, 19–13–12 thru 19–13–15 (Supp.1978); Tenn.Code Ann. § 40–2404 (1975); Vt.Stat.Ann., Tit. 12, § 1605 (1973); Wis.Stat.Ann. §§ 905.01, 905.05 (West 1975).

In 1901, Congress enacted a rule of evidence for the District of Columbia that made husband and wife "competent but not compellable to testify for or against each other," except as to confidential communications. This provision, which vests the privilege against adverse spousal testimony in the witness spouse, remains in effect. See 31 Stat. 1358 §§ 1068, 1069, recodified as D.C.Code § 14–306 (1973).

10. In 1965, California took the privilege from the defendant-spouse and vested it in the witness-spouse, accepting a study commission recommendation that the "latter [was] more likely than the former to determine whether or not to claim the privilege on the basis of the probable effect on the marital relationship." See Cal.Evid. Code §§ 970–973 and 1 California Law Revision Commission, Recommenation and Study relating to The Marital "For or Against" Testimonial Privilege at F–5 (1956). See also

cused of the privilege to bar adverse spousal testimony has special relevance because the law of marriage and domestic relations are concerns traditionally reserved to the states. See Sosna v. Iowa, 419 U.S. 393, 404, 95 S.Ct. 553, 559, 42 L.Ed.2d 532 (1975). Scholarly criticism of the *Hawkins* rule has also continued unabated.[11]

C

Testimonial exclusionary rules and privileges contravene the fundamental principle that "the public . . . has a right to every man's evidence." United States v. Bryan, 339 U.S. 323, 331, 70 S.Ct. 724, 730, 94 L.Ed. 884 (1950). As such, they must be strictly construed and accepted "only to the very limited extent that permitting a refusal to testify or excluding relevant evidence has a public good transcending the normally predominant principle of utilizing all rational means for ascertaining truth." Elkins v. United States, 364 U.S. 206, 234, 80 S.Ct. 1437, 1454, 4 L.Ed.2d 1669 (1960) (Frankfurter, J., dissenting). Accord, United States v. Nixon, 418 U.S. 683, 709–710, 94 S.Ct. 3090, 3108–3109, 41 L.Ed.2d 1039 (1974). Here we must decide whether the privilege against adverse spousal testimony promotes sufficiently important interests to outweigh the need for probative evidence in the administration of criminal justice.

It is essential to remember that the *Hawkins* privilege is not needed to protect information privately disclosed between husband and wife in the confidence of the marital relationship—once described by this Court as "the best solace of human existence." Stein v. Bowman, 13 Pet., at 223. Those confidences are privileged under the independent rule protecting confidential marital communications. Blau v. United States, 340 U.S. 332, 71 S.Ct. 301, 95 L.Ed. 306 (1951); see n. 5, supra. The *Hawkins* privilege is invoked, not to exclude private marital communications, but rather to exclude evidence of criminal acts and of communications made in the presence of third persons.

No other testimonial privilege sweeps so broadly. The privileges between priest and penitent, attorney and client, and physician and

6 California Law Revision Commission, Tentative Privileges Recommendations—Rule 27.5, at 243–244 (1964).

Support for the common-law rule has also diminished in England. In 1972 a study group there proposed giving the privilege to the witness-spouse, on the ground that "if [the wife] is willing to give evidence * * * the law would be showing excessive concern for the preservation of marital harmony if it were to say she must not do so." Criminal Law Revision Committee, Eleventh Report Evidence (General), at 93.

11. See Reutlinger, Policy, Privacy and Prerogatives: A Critical Examination of the Proposed Federal Rules of Evidence as They Affect Marital Privilege, 61 Calif.L.Rev. 1353, 1384–1385 (1973); Orfield, The Husband-Wife Privileges in Federal Criminal Procedure, 24 Ohio St.L.J. 144 (1963); Rothstein, 12 Int. and Comp.L.Qt. 1189 (1963); Note, 1977 Ariz.St.L.J. 411; Note, 17 St. Louis L.Rev. 107 (1972); Note, 15 Wayne L.Rev. 1287, 1334–1337 (1969); 52 J. Crim.L. 74 (1961); Note, 56 Nw.U.L. Rev. 208 (1961); Note, 32 Temp.L. Qt. 351 (1959); Note, 33 Tul.L.Rev. 884 (1959).

patient limit protection to private communications. These privileges are rooted in the imperative need for confidence and trust. The priest-penitent privilege recognizes the human need to disclose to a spiritual counselor, in total and absolute confidence, what are believed to be flawed acts or thoughts and to receive priestly consolation and guidance in return. The lawyer-client privilege rests on the need for the advocate and counselor to know all that relates to the client's reasons for seeking representation if the professional mission is to be carried out. Similarly, the physician must know all that a patient can articulate in order to identify and to treat disease; barriers to full disclosure would impair diagnosis and treatment.

The *Hawkins* rule stands in marked contrast to these three privileges. Its protection is not limited to confidential communications; rather it permits an accused to exclude all adverse spousal testimony. As Jeremy Bentham observed more than a century and a half ago, such a privilege goes far beyond making "every man's house his castle," and permits a person to convert his house into "a den of thieves." 5 Rationale of Judicial Evidence 340 (1827). It "secures, to every man, one safe and unquestionable and ever ready accomplice for every imaginable crime." Id., at 338.

The ancient foundations for so sweeping a privilege have long since disappeared. Nowhere in the common-law world—indeed in any modern society—is a woman regarded as chattel or demeaned by denial of a separate legal identity and the dignity associated with recognition as a whole human being. Chip by chip, over the years those archaic notions have been cast aside so that "[n]o longer is the female destined solely for the home and the rearing of the family, and only the male for the marketplace and the world of ideas." Stanton v. Stanton, 421 U.S. 7, 14, 15, 95 S.Ct. 1373, 1377, 1378, 43 L.Ed.2d 688 (1975).

The contemporary justification for affording an accused such a privilege is also unpersuasive. When one spouse is willing to testify against the other in a criminal proceeding—whatever the motivation—their relationship is almost certainly in disrepair; there is probably little in the way of marital harmony for the privilege to preserve. In these circumstances, a rule of evidence that permits an accused to prevent adverse spousal testimony seems far more likely to frustrate justice than to foster family peace.[12] Indeed, there is reason to believe that vesting the privilege in the accused could actually undermine the marital relationship. For example, in a case such as this, the Government is unlikely to offer a wife immunity and lenient treatment if

---

12. It is argued that abolishing the privilege will permit the Government to come between husband and wife, pitting one against the other. That, too, misses the mark. Neither *Hawkins*, nor any other privilege, prevents the Government from enlisting one spouse to give information concerning the other or to aid in the other's apprehension. It is only the spouse's testimony in the courtroom that is prohibited.

it knows that her husband can prevent her from giving adverse testimony. If the Government is dissuaded from making such an offer, the privilege can have the untoward effect of permitting one spouse to escape justice at the expense of the other. It hardly seems conducive to the preservation of the marital relation to place a wife in jeopardy solely by virtue of her husband's control over her testimony.

IV

Our consideration of the foundations for the privilege and its history satisfy us that "reason and experience" no longer justify so sweeping a rule as that found acceptable by the Court in *Hawkins*. Accordingly, we conclude that the existing rule should be modified so that the witness spouse alone has a privilege to refuse to testify adversely; the witness may be neither compelled to testify nor foreclosed from testifying. This modification—vesting the privilege in the witness spouse—furthers the important public interest in marital harmony without unduly burdening legitimate law enforcement needs.

Here, petitioner's spouse chose to testify against him. That she did so after a grant of immunity and assurances of lenient treatment does not render her testimony involuntary. Cf. Bordenkircher v. Hayes, 434 U.S. 357, 98 S.Ct. 663, 54 L.Ed.2d 604 (1978). Accordingly, the District Court and the Court of Appeals were correct in rejecting petitioner's claim of privilege, and the judgment of the Court of Appeals is affirmed.

Affirmed.

Mr. Justice STEWART, concurring in the judgment.

Although agreeing with much of what the Court has to say, I cannot join an opinion that implies that "reason and experience" have worked a vast change since the *Hawkins* case was decided in 1958. In that case the Court upheld the privilege of a defendant in a criminal case to prevent adverse spousal testimony, in an all-but-unanimous opinion by Mr. Justice Black. Today the Court, in another all-but-unanimous opinion, obliterates that privilege because of the purported change in perception that "reason and experience" have wrought.

The fact of the matter is that the Court in this case simply accepts the very same arguments that the Court rejected when the Government first made them in the *Hawkins* case in 1958. I thought those arguments were valid then,[1] and I think so now.

---

1. "The rule of evidence we are here asked to re-examine has been called a 'sentimental relic.' It was born of two concepts long since rejected: that a criminal defendant was incompetent to testify in his own case, and that in law husband and wife were one. What thus began as a disqualification of either spouse from testifying at all yielded gradually to the policy of admitting all relevant evidence, until it has now become

The Court is correct when it says that "[t]he ancient foundations for so sweeping a privilege have long since disappeared." Ante, at 913. But those foundations had disappeared well before 1958; their disappearance certainly did not occur in the few years that have elapsed between the *Hawkins* decision and this one. To paraphrase what Mr. Justice Jackson once said in another context, there is reason to believe that today's opinion of the Court will be of greater interest to students of human psychology than to students of law.[2]

simply a privilege of the criminal defendant to prevent his spouse from testifying against him.

"Any rule that impedes the discovery of truth in a court of law impedes as well the doing of justice. When such a rule is the product of a conceptualism long ago discarded, is universally criticized by scholars, and has been qualified or abandoned in many jurisdictions, it should receive the most careful scrutiny. Surely 'reason and experience' require that we do more than indulge in mere assumptions, perhaps naive assumptions, as to the importance of this ancient rule to the interests of domestic tranquility." Hawkins v. United States, 358 U.S. 74, 81–82, 79 S.Ct. 136, 140, 3 L.Ed.2d 125 (concurring opinion) (citations and footnotes omitted).

2. See Zorach v. Clauson, 343 U.S. 306, 325, 72 S.Ct. 679, 689, 96 L.Ed. 954 (dissenting opinion).

INDEX

References are to Pages

ADMINISTRATIVE AGENCIES
Adjudication by, 10–12
Administrative Procedure Act of 1946, subject to, 11, 17
Interpretations by, see Administrative Interpretation of statutes,
Reasons for creation, 50–53
Rule-making by, 16–17, 18–19
Volume of business of, 10–12, 50, 53

ADMINISTRATIVE INTERPRETATION OF STATUTES
Legislative adoption of, 462, 474–495
Repeal of, after reenactment of statute, 486–488
Weight of, 402–413, 474–495

BORROWED STATUTES
See Legislative Adoption of Prior Administrative and Judicial Interpretation

BREACH OF WARRANTY
See Product Liability

CASE LAW
See also Common Law; Dictum; Holding of a Case; Judicial Decisions; New Questions; Procedure; Stare Decisis
Form of law, as, 2–3
How cases make law, 3–4
Legislation, compared with, 12
Origins and nature of, 3–12

CASE METHOD OF LAW STUDY
Essential devices of, 31–35
History of, 25–26
Presuppositions of, 26–31

COMMITTEES, LEGISLATIVE
See Legislative Process, National; Legislative Process, State

COMMON LAW
English origins of, 744–746
Precedent, doctrine of, as basic principle of, 5–7
Reception in the United States,
  Generally, 746–759
  Colonial law, 747–750
  Selective scope of, 750–755
  State reception statutes, 751–752, 755–756

CONSTITUTION OF THE UNITED STATES
Legislation, as, 14–15
Supreme law of the land, 14

COORDINATION OF JUDGE–MADE AND STATUTE LAW
See Statutes as Analogies or Premises for Judicial Reasoning

COURTS
See also Case Law; Diversity Jurisdiction of Federal Courts; Judicial Decisions
English, early, 744–746
Federal courts,
  Appeals, courts of, 45–46
  Described in general, 41–48
  District courts, 42–44
  Jurisdiction of, 43–44
  Rules of procedure in, 21, 44
  State decisions in, status of, 241–254
  Supreme Court of the United States, 41, 42, 47–48
State courts,
  Appellate courts, 39–41
  Described in general, 37–41
  New York courts, chart of, 49
  Trial courts, 37–39

DECLARATORY ACTS
See Statutes, Interpretation of

DICTUM
See also Holding of a Case; Stare Decisis
Defined, 113–114
Followed in later cases, 131
Holding, distinguished from, 112–132

DIVERSITY JURISDICTION OF FEDERAL COURTS
Authority for, 43–44
Federal courts in diversity cases, role of, 241–253

EQUITY OF THE STATUTE
See Statutes as Analogies or Premises for Judicial Reasoning

EXTRINSIC AIDS TO STATUTORY INTERPRETATION
See also Administrative Interpretation of Statutes; Legislative Adoption of Prior Administrative and Judi-

INDEX

EXTRINSIC AIDS TO STATUTORY INTERPRETATION—Cont'd
cial Interpretation; Legislative Process, National; Legislative Process, State
Amendments made or proposed during passage, 342, 358–359
Antecedent legislation, 357–358, 369–371, 404, 440–441, 478–488
Changes in bills in course of legislative process, 364–367, 407–408
Conference committee report, 363, 463
Congressional Record, 449–451
Dictionary, 392
Executive materials, 341–342, 373, 471
Floor debates, 358–360, 372–373, 413–451
General construction laws, 537–538
Hearings, 365–367, 375, 410
Post-adoption materials, 451–458
Standing committee reports, 353–354, 363, 397–398, 407–408
Statutes in pari materia, 392–393, 403–404, 548–549

HOLDING OF A CASE
See also Dictum; Stare Decisis
Defined, 113–114
Dictum, distinguished from, 112–132
Distinguishing cases, 121–123
Method for determining, 112–132

IMPLYING CIVIL REMEDIES IN FEDERAL STATUTES
See Statutes as Analogies or Premises for Judicial Reasoning

INTENTION OF THE LEGISLATURE
See Legislative Intent

INTERPRETATION OF STATUTES
See Statutes, Interpretation of

INTRINSIC AIDS TO STATUTORY INTERPRETATION
Declarations of legislative purpose and preambles, 322, 339
Definitions in statutes, 322–323, 360–361, 513–526, 537–538, 548
Standard statutory clauses (liberal interpretation, savings, severability, for example), 537
Titles, short titles, 320, 322, 324, 330, 352, 397

JUDICIAL DECISIONS
Concurring opinions in, 24, 64
Dictum, see Dictum
Dissenting opinions in, 24
Holding, see Holding of a Case
New questions, on, see New Questions
Opinion of the court, significance of, 24
Overruling of precedent, see Stare Decisis
Retroactive effect of, see Retroactive Effect of Judicial Decisions

JUDICIAL DECISIONS—Cont'd
Reversal of,
Defined, 8
Distinguished from overruling, 8
Synthesis of, see Synthesis of Judicial Decisions

JUDICIAL LAW, SOURCES OF
See also New Questions
Community understanding as, 106–107
Custom as, 105–106
Decisions from other jurisdictions as, 7, 80–87, 97
Statutes as, 100–105, 594–736
Treaties as, 69–71

JUSTICE
Dispute-settlement, in context of,
Generally, 759–769
Affecting outcome of litigation, 763–764
Generality of law, inequities in, 766–767
Individualization, as, 767–768
Procedural dimension of, 764–765
Regularity, as element of, 761–769
Meanings of, varying by context, 759–760
Recurrent themes of, in literature, 760–761

LAW
Purposes and social ends of,
Dispute-settlement, 738
Expectations, security of, 739–740
Peace-keeping and safety, 738
Social change, channeling of, 739, 742–743
Social interests, conflicting, resolution of, 739, 740–742

LAWYERS
Advocate, as, 22
Agents for engineering of expectation, as, 739–740
Colonial times, in, 749
Counselor, as, 22–23
Generalist, as, 21
Judge, as, 23–24
Tasks of, 21–24

LEGISLATION
See also Legislative History; Statutes, Interpretation of
Case law, compared with, 12, 318
Constitution of the United States as, 14–15
Definiteness, requirement of, 549–555
Drafting of, difficulties encountered in, 346–349
Federal administrative regulations as, 14, 16–17
Federal statutes as, 14, 15
Form of law, as, 2–3
Method of stating issues in, 318–327

INDEX

LEGISLATION—Cont'd
Municipal ordinance as, 14, 19–20
Prospective operation of, favored, 544–547
Retroactive operation of, presumption against, 544–547
Rules of court as, 20–21
State administrative regulations as, 14, 18–19
State constitutions as, 14, 17–18
State statutes as, 14, 18
Status of different types of, as authority, 14–21
Textual rigidity of, 12, 318
Treaties with foreign states as, 15–16
Types of, 13–21

LEGISLATIVE ADOPTION OF PRIOR ADMINISTRATIVE AND JUDICIAL INTERPRETATION
Action or inaction of legislature, by inference from, 474–543
Borrowed statutes, presumed adoption of, 368–373, 469–474

LEGISLATIVE HISTORY
See also Extrinsic Aids to Statutory Interpretation; Intrinsic Aids to Statutory Interpretation; Plain Meaning Rule
Statutory interpretation, use of, in, 333–446

LEGISLATIVE INTENT
See also Extrinsic Aids to Statutory Interpretation; Intrinsic Aids to Statutory Interpretation; Legislative History; Plain Meaning Rule; Statutes, Interpretation of
Ascertainment of, difficulties in, 344–345
Committee's intent as equivalent to, 364–367
Courts, duty of, to discover and apply, 344–345
Definable as purpose or specific intent, 345
Exceptions to statutory commands, used to create, 349–355
Interpretation according to, 327–388
Plain meaning rule forecloses inquiry into, 389
Primary rule of construction, 344
Purpose, as, 345, 367–387
Specific intent, as, 345, 349–367

LEGISLATIVE PROCESS, NATIONAL
See also Extrinsic Aids to Statutory Interpretation; Legislature, National
Generally, 255–309
Conference committees, 301–304
Executive participation in, 262–265, 279, 286, 304–307

LEGISLATIVE PROCESS, NATIONAL—Cont'd
Filibusters, 297–299
Fiscal and budget procedures of, 281–285
Floor consideration, securing of, 285, 287–293
Floor debates, 293–301, 304, 306–307
Hearings, 279
Introduction and reference of bills, 267–269
Legislative documents, 270–272, 280, 303
Legislative drafting and research services, 266–267
Legislative leadership, 286–287
Rules Committee, 288, 290–293
Source of legislative proposals, 261–267
Standing committees, 273–280

LEGISLATIVE PROCESS, STATE
See also Extrinsic Aids to Statutory Interpretation; Legislature, State
Generally, 309–317
Conference committees, 314–315
Executive participation in, 315–317
Floor consideration, securing of, 313
Floor debates, 313–314
Interim committees, 312, 315
Legislative councils, 312, 315
Legislative documents, 311, 314–315
Legislative drafting and research services, 312–313
Legislative leadership, 309, 313–314
Source of legislative proposals, 315–316
Standing committees, 309–312

LEGISLATURE, NATIONAL
See also Legislative Process, National
Functions, powers and structure of, 257–261

LEGISLATURE, STATE
See also Legislative Process, State
Functions, powers and structure of, 257–259, 261, 309–311

LIABILITY OF MANUFACTURERS OR SELLERS OF GOODS
See Product Liability

MAXIMS OF STATUTORY CONSTRUCTION
See also Statutes, Interpretation of
Common law, statutes in derogation of, to be strictly construed, 330, 340, 594–600
Consistency, rule of, 329–330, 352, 364–366
See Statutes in Pari Materia
Ejusdem generis rule, 548–549, 551–555, 564–565
Expressio unius est exclusio alterius, 329–330, 558–561
Function and status of, 543–544

INDEX

References are to Pages

MAXIMS OF STATUTORY CONSTRUCTION—Cont'd
Last antecedent, doctrine of, 368–373, 557–558
Legislative history, effect when in conflict with, 562–565
Noscitur a Sociis, 555–557
Penal statutes, strict construction of, 330–333, 341, 461, 548–549, 551–552, 565–566
Plain meaning rule, see Plain Meaning Rule
Prospective construction, rule of, 220–239, 528–547
Remedial statutes, liberal construction of, 328
Repeals by implication, presumption against, 357–359, 723–725
Retroactive application of statutes, not favored, 545–547
Use of, in general, 543–566
Words to be given technical meaning according to usage in the trade regulated, 376–377

NEW QUESTIONS
See also Judicial Law, Sources of
Judicial decisions on, 75–112

OVERRULING OF PRECEDENT
See Stare Decisis

PLAIN MEANING RULE
See also Legislative Intent; Statutes, Interpretation of
Current status of, 464–466
Defined, 388–389
Interpretation according to the, 327–335, 388–401, 405, 419–420
Interpretation precluded under, 329, 388–401

POST-ADOPTION MATERIALS
See Extrinsic Aids to Statutory Interpretation; Statutes, Interpretation of

PRECEDENT
See Case Law; Common Law; Holding of a Case; Stare Decisis

PRIVITY OF CONTRACT
See Product Liability

PROBLEM CASES
Act of 1885 on Foreign Contract Labor, under, 383–387
Comprehensive Drug Abuse Prevention and Control Act of 1970, under, 577–593
Coordination of judge-made and statute law, on, 725–736
Holding-dictum distinction, on, 124–125
Illegal contract, on, 663
Implication of civil remedies for violation of statute, on, 710–711

PROBLEM CASES—Cont'd
Negligence per se, on, 649–650
President's Executive Order of August 15, 1971, under, 466–469
Rivers and Harbors Act, under, 574–577
Statutory issues, on stating of, 319–326
Synthesis of judicial decisions, on, 217–219
Use of maxims, on, 566–573

PROCEDURE
Appeal, on, 63–64
Charge to jury as source of substantive law questions, 60–61, 71–73
Demurrer, 57–59, 66–71
Execution of the judgment, 63
Importance of, in determining holding of case, 54–55, 64–73
Motion to dismiss for failure to state cause of action, 57–58, 66–71
Motions after verdict, 61–63
Pleading stage, 55–59
Substantive law, compared with, 54, 247
Trial stage, 59–61

PRODUCT LIABILITY
Bases for,
  Deceit, 134–136, 155, 159
  Express warranty, 134–136, 188–191, 194–201
  Implied warranty, 154–157, 175–209
  Negligence, 136–175, 184
  Negligence per se, 185–187
  Strict liability, 201–219
Caveat Emptor, doctrine of, in, 135–136
Negligence distinguished from breach of warranty, 175–180
Privity of contract, need for, in, 138–209
Property damage, liability for, in, 180–182
Uniform Commercial Code, 185, 192, 217
Uniform Sales Act, as basis of warranty, 175–178, 185–186

PROSPECTIVE OVERRULING
See Retroactive Effect of Judicial Decisions

PURPOSE INTERPRETATION
See Statutes, Interpretation of

RATIO DECIDENDI
See Holding of a Case; Stare Decisis

REPEALS OF STATUTES BY IMPLICATION
See Statutes as Analogies or Premises for Judicial Reasoning

RES JUDICATA
Defined, 7
Stare decisis, distinguished from, 7–8

INDEX

References are to Pages

RETROACTIVE EFFECT OF JUDICIAL DECISIONS
Generally, 220–239
Prospective overruling, 221–239

SOCIOLOGICAL JURISPRUDENCE
Described, 741–742

STARE DECISIS
See also Case Law; Dictum; Holding of a Case
Generally, 111–132
Administrative adjudication, applicability of, in, 11–12
Authority,
  Hierarchy of, within jurisdiction, 6, 240
  Weight of, from another jurisdiction, 5, 8–10, 241
Interpretation of statutes, applicability of, in, 513–528
Like cases, prior decision binding only in, 6, 122–124
Meaning of, 5
Overruling of precedents, 8, 24, 125–131, 241–247
Res judicata, distinguished from, 7–8

STATUTE LAW
See Legislation

STATUTES, INTERPRETATION OF
See also Administrative Interpretation of Statutes; Extrinsic Aids to Statutory Interpretation; Intrinsic Aids to Statutory Interpretation; Legislation; Legislative Adoption of Prior Administrative and Judicial Interpretation; Legislative History; Legislative Intent; Maxims of Statutory Construction; Plain Meaning Rule
Changed circumstances, in light of, 378–383, 548–549
Conditions at time of enactment, in light of, 378–381, 491–492
"Equity of the statute," according to, 354

STATUTES, INTERPRETATION OF—Cont'd
Evil to be remedied, in light of, 352–354
Intention of the legislature, interpretation according to, 327–383
Judicial function in, 344–346
Legislative declarations of intent, 527–543
Method of stating issues in, 318–327
Specific intent, 345, 349–367
Words, ambiguity of, 346–349, 355–357

STATUTES AS ANALOGIES OR PREMISES FOR JUDICIAL REASONING
See also Common Law; Product Liability; Statutes, Interpretation of
Case law, in development of, 68–71, 100–105, 594–736
Equity of statute, 353, 596–597
Implying of civil remedies from federal statutes, 670–697
Interpretation of statutes, in, 378–383, 537–543, 604–608
Negligence per se, violation of statutes as, 185–187, 644–649
Prohibitory statutes, effect on contracts, 650–670
Repeal of statutes by implication, not favored, 660–663, 715–725
Statutes, reception of, by common law courts, 594–600

STATUTES IN PARI MATERIA
See Extrinsic Aids to Statutory Interpretation

STRICT PRODUCT LIABILITY
See Product Liability

SYNTHESIS OF JUDICIAL DECISIONS
Defined, 132
Necessity for, 132–133
Product liability cases as example of, 134–219
Purposes of, 132–133
Technique of, 133–134